HARRAP'S

English

POCKET
DICTIONARY

HARRAP'S

English

POCKET
DICTIONARY

edited by
P. H. Collin

HARRAP
LONDON

First published in Great Britain 1983
by HARRAP BOOKS Ltd
Chelsea House, 26 Market Square,
Bromley, Kent BR1 1NA

Reprinted 1984, 1987
Second Edition revised and reset 1991

ISBN 0-245-60141-4

Typeset in Times and Univers by
Kynoch Dataset Limited, Birmingham
and printed in Great Britain by
Richard Clay, Bungay, Suffolk

About This Dictionary

This entirely revised dictionary lists the words most commonly used in English, giving definitions and in many cases examples of use. Grammar notes are given in many entries – irregular plurals for nouns, comparatives and superlatives for adjectives, past forms for verbs. Where a word is commonly used with a preposition, that preposition is given in bold letters.

To make the dictionary as compact as possible, many derived words are listed under the main headwords and do not appear separately: so *package* is to be found under *pack*, *secrecy* under *secret*, etc.

Abbreviations used in the Dictionary

adj.	adjective	*inter.*	interjection
adv.	adverb	*n.*	noun
Am.	American	*pl.*	plural
approx.	approximately	*prep.*	preposition
def.	definite	*sl.*	slang
e.g.	for example	*sth.*	something
esp.	especially	*usu.*	usually
indef.	indefinite	*v.*	verb
inf.	informal		

Pronunciation

The following signs are used to show the pronunciation of words in the dictionary.

Where there are several pronunciations which are current only the most common are indicated, **-r** is never pronounced at the end of words, but when a word ending in **-r** is followed by a vowel the **-r** can be pronounced.

Words are also marked with a sign (') to show where the strong beat should be placed, but this is only a guide; the pronunciation of a word can change depending on the position of the word in a sentence.

æ	back	ə	afraid	ð	then	p	penny
ɑ:	farm	əu	boat	dʒ	just	r	round
ɒ	top	əuə	lower	f	fog	s	some
aɪ	pipe	ɜ:	word	g	go	ʃ	short
au	how	i:	heap	h	hand	t	too
aɪə	fire	ɪ	hit	j	yes	tʃ	chop
auə	flower	ɪə	hear	k	catch	θ	thing
ɔ:	bought	u:	school	χ	loch	v	voice
ɔɪ	toy	ʊ	book	l	last	w	was
e	fed	ʌ	but	m	mix	z	zoo
eə	hair	b	back	n	nut	ʒ	treasure
eɪ	take	d	dog	ŋ	sing		

Alphabet

These are the letters of the English alphabet, showing their pronunciation.

Aa	eɪ	**Hh**	eɪtʃ	**Oo**	əʊ	**Vv**	vi:
Bb	bi:	**Ii**	aɪ	**Pp**	pi:	**Ww**	dʌblju:
Cc	si:	**Jj**	dʒeɪ	**Qq**	kju:	**Xx**	eks
Dd	di:	**Kk**	keɪ	**Rr**	ɑ:	**Yy**	waɪ
Ee	i:	**Ll**	el	**Ss**	es	**Zz**	zed
Ff	ef	**Mm**	em	**Tt**	ti:		
Gg	dʒi:	**Nn**	en	**Uu**	ju:		

Aa

a, an [*stressed* eɪ, æn; *unstressed* ə, ən] (a *before words beginning with a consonant, and before words beginning with* u *pronounced* juː; **an** *before* a, e, i, o *or* u *and before* h *where it is not pronounced*) *indefinite article* (*a*) one; **give me a stamp and an envelope.** (*b*) not a particular one; **he has a big nose.** (*c*) for each one/in each one; **thirty kilometres an hour.** (*d*) a certain; **I know a Dr Smith.**

A1 [eɪˈwʌn] in very good condition.

aardvark [ˈɑːdvɑːk] *n.* ant-eating animal of South America.

AB [ˈeɪˈbiː] *n.* ordinary seaman.

aback [əˈbæk] *adv.* **taken aback** = surprised, usu. unpleasantly.

abacus [ˈæbəkəs] *n.* (*pl.* **-ses**) device for counting, made of small beads which slide along rods in a frame.

abaft [əˈbɑːft] *adv.* (*of ships*) behind the other.

abalone [æbəˈləʊnɪ] *n.* type of Pacific shellfish.

abandon [əˈbændən] *v.* (*a*) to leave. (*b*) to give up. **abandonment,** *n.* giving up.

abase [əˈbeɪs] *v.* (*a*) (*formal*) to make s.o. low; **to a. oneself** = to grovel/to apologise. (*b*) to humiliate.

abashed [əˈbæʃt] *adj.* ashamed.

abate [əˈbeɪt] *v.* to become less strong. **abatement,** *n.* reduction (in tax).

abattoir [ˈæbətwɑː] *n.* slaughterhouse/ place where animals are killed for meat.

abbess [ˈæbes] *n.* (*pl.* **-es**) woman in charge of nuns in a convent.

abbey [ˈæbɪ] *n.* Christian religious establishment with living quarters, etc., grouped round a church.

abbot [ˈæbət] *n.* man in charge of monks in an abbey.

abbreviate [əˈbriːvɪeɪt] *v.* to shorten (words, names). **abbreviation** [əbriːvɪˈeɪʃn] *n.* group of letters representing a larger word.

ABC [eɪbiːˈsiː] *n.* the letters of the alphabet.

abdicate [ˈæbdɪkeɪt] *v.* to give up the throne. **abdication** [æbdɪˈkeɪʃn] *n.* giving up (of a throne).

abdomen [ˈæbdəmen] *n.* lower part of the body, containing the stomach, bowels, etc. **abdominal** [æbˈdɒmɪnl] *adj.* referring to the abdomen.

abduct [æbˈdʌkt] *v.* to remove (s.o.) by force. **abduction,** *n.* removal (of s.o.) by force. **abductor,** *n.* person who abducts s.o.

abeam [əˈbiːm] *adv.* (*of ships*) side by side.

aberration [æbəˈreɪʃn] *n.* (*a*) change from what is usual. (*b*) sudden attack of forgetfulness; **mental a.** = slight confusion. **aberrant** [əˈberənt] *adj.* abnormal/not usual.

abet [əˈbet] *v.* (**abetted**) to aid and a. s.o. = to be s.o.'s accomplice in a crime. **abettor,** *n.* person who abets s.o.

abeyance [əˈbeɪəns] *n.* suspension (of a law, etc.); **in a.** = not being applied.

abhor [əbˈhɔː] *v.* to feel hatred/horror for (sth). **abhorrent** [əbˈhɒrənt] *adj.* disgusting/which makes you shudder. **abhorrence,** *n.* horror/great dislike.

abide [əˈbaɪd] *v.* (*a*) to stick to/to follow; **to a. by a promise** = to stand by what you have promised. (*b*) (*only with negative*) to like; **I can't a. the smell of garlic. abiding,** *adj.* which stays/remains.

ability [əˈbɪlɪtɪ] *n.* power to do sth; capability; **to the best of my a.** = as best I can.

ab initio [æbɪˈnɪʃɪəʊ] *adj.* (course) which starts from the beginning.

abject [ˈæbdʒekt] *adj.* (*a*) very miserable. (*b*) cowardly/extremely humble. **abjectly,** *adv.* in a miserable/humble way.

abjure [æbˈdʒʊə] *v.* to swear not to do sth.

ablation [æˈbleɪʃn] *n.* operation to remove an organ.

ablaze [əˈbleɪz] *adv.* in flames.

able [ˈeɪbl] *adj.* having the ability (**to do** sth); **a. seaman** = first class seaman in the Royal Navy. **ably** [ˈeɪblɪ] *adv.* very efficiently.

ablutions [əˈbluːʃənz] *n. pl.* (*formal*) washing (face/hands, etc.).

abnormal [æbˈnɔːml] *adj.* not normal. **abnormally,** *adv.* not normally/unusually. **abnormality** [æbnɔː'mælɪtɪ] n. (pl. **abnormalities**) being abnormal; unusualness/peculiarity.

ABO [eɪbiː'əʊ] n. system of classifying blood by the letters A, B and O.

aboard [ə'bɔːd] adv. & prep. on/in (a ship/aircraft/train/bus).

abode [ə'bəʊd] n. (formal) home; **of no fixed a.** = with no permanent address; **right of a.** = the right to live in a country.

abolish [ə'bɒlɪʃ] v. to cancel/to remove. **abolition** [æbə'lɪʃn] n. act of abolishing. **abolitionist,** n. person who is in favour of abolition (esp. of slavery/ capital punishment).

abominable [ə'bɒmɪnəbl] adj. horrible/ disgusting; **the a. snowman** = yeti. **abominably,** adv. in a horrible way. **abominate** [ə'bɒmɪneɪt] v. to dislike intensely. **abomination** [əbɒmɪ'neɪʃn] n. unpleasant/nasty thing.

aborigine [æbə'rɪdʒɪnɪ] n. member of a race which was living in a country before the country was colonized: original inhabitant. **aboriginal. 1.** adj. referring to aborigines. **2.** n. aborigine.

abortion [ə'bɔːʃn] n. (deliberate) miscarriage of an unborn child. **abort,** v. (a) to cause an abortion to (s.o.). (b) to stop (a project) taking place. **abortionist,** n. person who carries out an illegal abortion. **abortive,** adj. (plan) which fails.

abound [ə'baʊnd] v. (in) to be full of.

about [ə'baʊt] adv. & prep. (a) in various places; **cups lying a. on the floor; there's a lot of flu a.** (b) concerning; **tell me a. your book; what do you want to speak to me a.? how a. a cup of tea?** = would you like a cup of tea? (c) (in the army) round; **a. turn** = facing the opposite direction. (d) approximately; **a. three metres square; at a. four o'clock.** (e) on the point (of doing sth); **just a. to go out.** (f) in the process of doing sth; **while you're a. it, can you post this letter?**

above [ə'bʌv] adv. & prep. (a) higher than; **a. the clouds; the temperature was a. 40°.** (b) louder than; **I can't hear you a. the noise.** (c) **they're living a. their means** = more extravagantly than they can afford. (d) earlier on (in a book); higher up (on a page). **aboveboard,** adj. open/honest; not corrupt.

abracadabra [æbrəkə'dæbrə] n. traditional magic spell.

abrade [æ'breɪd] v. to scrape off (a surface).

abrasion [ə'breɪʒn] n. scraping off (of the skin). **abrasive** [ə'breɪzɪv] **1.** adj. (a) grinding (substance). (b) sharp/rude (manner, comment). **2.** n. rough substance for smoothing a surface.

abreast [ə'brest] adv. in a row; level (with sth); **cycling three a.** = three bicycles side by side; **to keep a. of/ with sth** = to keep up with the latest developments.

abridged [ə'brɪdʒd] adj. shortened. **abridgement,** n. shortened version (of a long book).

abroad [ə'brɔːd] adv. in or to another country.

abrogate ['æbrəgeɪt] v. (formal) to end (a law, a treaty). **abrogation** [æbrə-'geɪʃn] n. ending (of a treaty).

abrupt [ə'brʌpt] adj. sudden (departure); brusque (way of speaking). **abruptly,** adv. suddenly; brusquely. **abruptness,** n. suddenness; brusqueness.

abscess ['æbses] n. (pl. **-es**) collection of pus in the body.

abscond [əb'skɒnd] v. to run away.

abseil ['æbseɪl] v. to come down a cliff or wall by means of a fixed rope coiled around one's body.

absence ['æbsəns] n. (a) not being there; **she was sentenced in her a.** (b) lack; **in the a. of a map we had to ask our way. absent 1.** adj. ['æbsənt] not present. **2.** v. [əb'sent] **to a. oneself** = to stay away (from class/a meeting) deliberately. **absentee** [æbsən'tiː] n. person who is absent; **a. landlord** = landowner who does not live near his land and takes no interest in it. **absenteeism,** n. deliberately staying away from work. **absent-minded,** adj. forgetful. **absent-mindedly,** adv. forgetfully. **absent-mindedness,** n. being often forgetful.

absolute ['æbsəluːt] adj. complete; **the president assumed a. power** = became a dictator; **the government has an a. majority of ten** = has a majority of ten over all the other parties in Parliament. **absolutely,** adv. totally. **absolutism,**

n. political theory that governments should have absolute power.

absolution [æbsə'luːʃn] *n.* blessing by a priest to forgive sin.

absolve [əb'zɒlv] *v.* to remove blame for a sin from (s.o.); to release (s.o.) from a promise.

absorb [əb'zɔːb] *v.* (*a*) to soak up (liquid); to deaden (a shock); to accept (a stranger/outside body) into a group. (*b*) **absorbed in** = completely busy with; **it's an absorbing story** = it holds your attention. **absorbent,** *adj.* which absorbs; **a. cotton** = cotton wool. **absorber,** *n.* **shock a.** = part of a car which softens the shock of a bump to the passengers. **absorption** [əb'zɔːpʃn] *n.* act of absorbing.

abstain [əb'steɪn] *v.* (**from**) not to do sth deliberately; **Mr Smith abstained** = refused to vote. **abstainer,** *n.* person who does not drink alcohol.

abstemious [əb'stiːmɪəs] *adj.* not drinking (or eating) too much. **abstemiousness,** *n.* not drinking (or eating) too much.

abstention [əb'stenʃn] *n.* refusal to do sth; **several abstentions** = several people did not vote.

abstinence ['æbstɪnəns] *n.* not drinking/eating to excess; **total a.** = not drinking any alcohol.

abstract 1. *adj* ['æbstrækt] not concrete; (painting) which does not reproduce sth recognizable. 2. *n.* ['æbstrækt] (*a*) quality of not being concrete; **in the a.** = without mentioning specific cases. (*b*) abstract picture. (*c*) summary. 3. *v.* [əb'strækt] (*a*) to remove; to steal. (*b*) to summarize. **abstracted,** *adj* vague/dreamy; thoughtful. **abstraction,** *n.* (*a*) removing; stealing. (*b*) vague idea.

abstruse [əb'struːs] *adj.* very difficult to understand.

absurd [əb'sɜːd] *adj.* very odd; ridiculous. **absurdity,** *n.* fact of being absurd. **absurdly,** *adv.* ridiculously.

abundant [ə'bʌndənt] *adj.* in large quantities. **abundance,** *n.* large quantity. **abundantly,** *adv.* copiously; very much.

abuse 1. *n.* [ə'bjuːs] (*a*) wrong use/bad use. (*b*) evil. (*c*) rude words/insults;

term of a. = rude/insulting word. (*d*) very bad treatment (often sexual, of a person, such as a child. 2. *v.* [ə'bjuːz] (*a*) to put to wrong use; **he abused my confidence** = he took advantage of my confidence. (*b*) to insult. (*c*) to ill-treat; to make bad use of. **abusive** [ə'bjuːsɪv] *adj.* insulting.

abut [ə'bʌt] *v.* (**abutted**) (*formal*) **to a. on a property** = to be next to a property.

abysmal [ə'bɪzml] *adj.* extremely large; **the weather was a.** = very bad. **abysmally,** *adv.* extremely badly.

abyss [ə'bɪs] *n.* (*pl.* **-es**) very deep hole; very deep part of the sea.

Ac symbol for actinium.

AC *abbrev. for* alternating current.

A/C = account.

acacia [ə'keɪʃə] *n.* common tropical tree which produces gum.

academic [ækə'demɪk] 1. *adj.* (*a*) abstract (idea, question). (*b*) relating to study, esp. at a university; **a. staff** = teaching staff at university. 2. *n.* university teacher. **academically,** *adv.* referring to academic matters/to teaching at university. **academician** [ækædə'mɪʃn] *n.* member of an academy. **academy** [ə'kædəmɪ] *n.* (*a*) specialized teaching establishment; (*in Scotland*) selective secondary school; **military a.** = training school for army officers; **a. of music** = school for musicians. (*b*) society for the promotion of art/science.

ACAS ['eɪkæs] *n.* the Advisory Conciliation and Arbitration Service.

accede [ək'siːd] *v.* (*a*) **to a. to the throne** = to become king or queen. (*b*) (*formal*) to agree (**to**).

accelerate [æk'seləreɪt] *v.* (to cause to) go faster. **acceleration** [æksela'reɪʃn] *n.* going faster. **accelerator** [æk'seləreɪtə] *n.* pedal (in a car) which allows more petrol into the engine, and increases speed.

accent ['æksənt] *n.* (*a*) way of pronouncing; **an Irish a.** (*b*) small sign over a letter to show that it is pronounced differently. (*c*) stress. **accentor,** *n.* small brown singing bird. **accentuate** [ək'sentjʊeɪt] *v.* to stress/to make more obvious. **accentuation** [əksentjʊ'eɪʃn] *n.* stressing.

accept [ək'sept] v. (a) to take (thing which is offered). (b) to agree (to do sth). (c) **accepted custom** = sth which is usually done. **acceptability**, n. being acceptable. **acceptable**, adj. which you can easily accept. **acceptance**, n. (a) receiving (of thing offered). (b) agreement (to do sth).

access ['ækses] 1. n. way of getting to person/place; **a. road** = road leading off a main road to buildings; **to have easy a. to** = to be able to get sth easily. 2. v. to call up information which is stored in a computer. **accessible** [ək'sesɪbl] adj. able to be reached easily. **accessibility** [əksesɪ'bɪlɪtɪ] n. being accessible.

accession [ək'seʃn] n. **a. (to the throne)** = becoming king or queen; **the treaty of A.** = the treaty by which the UK became a member of the EC. **accessions**, n. pl. new books added to a library.

accessory [ək'sesərɪ] 1. n. (a) piece of minor equipment which is added to main items; **a. bag** = bag for carrying extra items to attach to a camera. (b) non-essential items of clothing (handbag, gloves, hat, etc.). (c) **charged with being an a. to the crime** = with helping to commit the crime. 2. adj. non-essential.

accident ['æksɪdənt] n. thing which happens by chance, often with unfortunate results; **I discovered the documents by a.; fatal a.** = accident where s.o. is killed. **accidental** [æksɪ'dentl] 1. adj. by accident; not on purpose. 2. n. (in music) additional sharp, flat or natural. **accidentally**, adv. by accident; not on purpose. **accident-prone**, adj. (person) who is likely to have a lot of accidents.

acclaim [ə'kleɪm] 1. n. great shout of praise. 2. v. to greet with a shout of praise. **acclamation** [æklə'meɪʃn] n. act of acclaiming.

acclimatize, Am. **acclimate** [ə'klaɪmətaɪz, ə'klaɪmət] v. to make (sth/s.o.) used to a new climate or a new way of living. **acclimatization,** Am. **acclimation** [əklaɪmətaɪ'zeɪʃn, əklaɪ'meɪʃn] n. becoming acclimatized.

accolade ['ækɒleɪd] n. sign of praise; giving of a knighthood to s.o.

accommodate [ə'kɒmədeɪt] v. (a) to adapt; to supply (s.o.) with sth. (b) to provide lodging for (s.o.). **accommodating**, adj. helpful; giving satisfaction; always ready to help. **accommodation** [əkɒmə'deɪʃn] n. (a) place to live/to sleep; **all the a. in the town has been booked.** (b) agreement/compromise. (c) adjustment.

accompany [ə'kʌmpnɪ] v. (a) to go with; **sauce to a. the fish** = to be served with the fish. (b) to play (usu. the piano) while s.o. sings or plays another instrument. **accompaniment**, n. (a) thing which accompanies. (b) music played to accompany a soloist. **accompanist**, n. person who accompanies a soloist.

accomplice [ə'kʌmplɪs] n. person who helps another person commit a crime.

accomplish [ə'kʌmplɪʃ] v. to finish/to carry out (a plan, etc.). **accomplished**, adj. gifted/talented; skilled. **accomplishment**, n. (a) finishing (of a task). (b) **accomplishments** = talents.

accord [ə'kɔːd] n. (a) agreement; **with one a.** = all together/in agreement. (b) **of your own a.** = spontaneously/with no prompting. **accordance**, n. agreement; **in a. with your instructions** = following your instructions. **accordingly**, adv. in consequence. **according to**, adv. (a) as s.o. says or writes; as stated by s.o. (b) by/in relation to; **separate the children into groups a. to their ages.**

accordion [ə'kɔːdɪən] n. **(piano) a.** = musical instrument with a bellows and a keyboard. **accordionist**, n. person who plays an accordion.

accost [ə'kɒst] v. to go/to come up to (s.o.) and speak to them.

account [ə'kaunt] 1. n. (a) story/description; **by all accounts** = according to what everyone said. (b) statement of money; **bank a.** = money deposited in a bank; **current a.** = account from which you can draw money without giving notice; **savings a.** = account where you put money regularly; **deposit a.** = account where you leave money for some time and on which interest is paid; **to pay money on a.** = to pay part of the total bill in advance; **expense a.** = money which a businessman is allowed to spend on entertainment and personal expenses which are paid for by his firm. (c) **accounts (of a firm)** = statement showing the financial position of a firm; **accounts department** = department in a company dealing with money. (d) **he turned the accident to a.** = he was able to profit from the accident. (e) **he was called to a.** = he was asked to explain; **she gave a good a. of herself** = she came out of the game/examination, etc., very well. (f) **to take sth into a.** = to make allowances for sth. (g) **on a. of** = because of; **I was worried on her a.** = I was afraid sth might happen to her; **on no a.** = not under any circumstances. **2.** v. **to a. for sth** = to explain. **accountability** [əkaʊntə'bɪlɪtɪ] n. being accountable **(for** sth). **accountable,** adj. responsible. **accountancy,** n. theory/profession of being an accountant. **accountant,** n. person who deals with the accounts (of a company); **chartered a.** = person who has passed high-level examinations in accountancy. **accounting,** n. accountancy.

accoutrements [ə'ku:trəmənts] n. pl. (usu. bulky or complicated) equipment which is carried.

accredit [ə'kredɪt] v. to authorize.

accretion [ə'kri:ʃn] n. increase in size by gradual additions.

accrue [ə'kru:] v. to increase by addition. **accrual,** n. increase made by addition.

acct. abbrev. for account.

accumulate [ə'kju:mjʊleɪt] v. to pile up. **accumulation** [əkju:mjʊ'leɪʃn] n. act of accumulating; pile/heap. **accumulator** [ə'kju:mjʊleɪtə] n. electric battery which can be recharged.

accurate ['ækjʊrət] adj. completely correct. **accuracy,** n. being accurate; complete correctness. **accurately,** adv. completely correctly.

accuse [ə'kju:z] v. to say that s.o. has done sth wrong; **the police accused him of stealing the car. accusation** [ækjʊ'zeɪʃn] n. saying that s.o. has done sth wrong. **accusative** [ə'kju:zətɪv] adj. & n. (in grammar) (case) which shows the object of a verb. **accused,** n. person who has been accused of a crime. **accuser,** n. person who accuses

s.o. **accusing,** adj. **in an a. tone** = as if accusing. **accusingly,** adv. as if accusing.

accustom [ə'kʌstəm] v. to make (s.o.) used **(to** sth).

ace [eɪs] n. (a) playing card which shows only one spot; **the a. of diamonds.** (b) person who is very brilliant at doing sth; **an a. pilot.** (c) (in tennis) shot which your opponent cannot return.

acerbate ['æsəbeɪt] v. to make worse.

acerbity [ə'sɜ:bɪtɪ] n. (formal) sharpness (of flavour/character).

acetate ['æsɪteɪt] n. type of man-made fibre.

acetic [ə'si:tɪk] adj. referring to vinegar.

acetone ['æsɪtəʊn] n. colourless liquid, used to dissolve solids.

acetylene [ə'setɪli:n] n. gas which burns with a very bright light.

ache [eɪk] **1.** n. pain; (see **toothache, headache,** etc.). **2.** v. to hurt. **aching,** adj. which hurts.

achieve [ə'tʃi:v] v. to succeed in doing (sth); to reach (a goal). **achievement,** n. what you achieve; successful undertaking/exploit.

Achilles' heel [ə'kɪli:z'hi:l] n. weak spot. **Achilles' tendon,** n. tendon at the back of the ankle.

achromatic [ækrəʊ'mætɪk] adj. without colour.

acid ['æsɪd] **1.** n. usually liquid chemical substance which contains hydrogen, corrodes some metals, and turns litmus paper red; **a. drops** = boiled sweets with a sharp taste; **the a. test** = test which will show the true value of sth. **2.** adj. bitter/unpleasant. **acidify,** v. to make substances acid. **acidity** [ə'sɪdɪtɪ] n. (a) acid contents. (b) bitterness. **acid rain,** n. rain with a high level of acidity, caused by pollution.

acknowledge [ək'nɒlɪdʒ] v. (a) to admit (that sth is true). (b) to reply to say you have received (a letter). **acknowledgement,** n. admission (that sth is true); reply stating that you have received sth; **my letter has not had any a.** = no one has replied to it; (in a book) **acknowledgements** = the list of people the author wants to thank for help.

acme ['ækmɪ] n. highest point.

acne ['æknɪ] n. skin disease, with spots on the face/neck, etc.

acolyte ['ækəlaɪt] *n.* person who helps a priest during religious ceremonies.

aconite ['ækənaɪt] *n.* small spring flower which is poisonous.

acorn ['eɪkɔːn] *n.* fruit of an oak tree.

acoustic [ə'kuːstɪk] **1.** *adj.* referring to sound; **a. coupler** = device for linking a computer to a telephone handset, allowing data to be transmitted; **a. guitar** = ordinary guitar (as opposed to an electric guitar). **2.** *n.* **acoustics** = (i) study of sound; (ii) ability to carry sound without distortion.

acquaint [ə'kweɪnt] *v.* (*a*) to inform. (*b*) **to be acquainted with** = to know. **acquaintance,** *n.* (*a*) knowing; **to make the a. of** = to get to know. (*b*) person you know (slightly).

acquiesce [ækwɪ'es] *v.* (*formal*) to agree. **acquiescence,** *n.* agreement. **acquiescent,** *adj.* in agreement.

acquire [ə'kwaɪə] *v.* to get into your possession; **acquired immunodeficiency syndrome (AIDS)** = condition, caused by a virus, where the body's immune system breaks down, making the patient susceptible to any infection. **acquisition** [ækwɪ'zɪʃn] *n.* (*a*) act of acquiring. (*b*) thing you have acquired. **acquisitive** [ə'kwɪzɪtɪv] *adj.* always ready to acquire things. **acquisitiveness,** *n.* love of acquiring things.

acquit [ə'kwɪt] *v.* (**acquitted**) (*a*) to decide that someone is innocent. (*b*) **he acquitted himself well** = he did well. **acquittal,** *n.* decision that a person is innocent.

acre ['eɪkə] *n.* unit for measuring the area of land (4840 square yards or 0.45 hectares). **acreage** ['eɪkrɪdʒ] *n.* area in acres.

acrid ['ækrɪd] *adj.* bitter/pungent (smell).

acrimonious [ækrɪ'məʊnɪəs] *adj.* bitter (argument). **acrimony** ['ækrɪmənɪ] *n.* bitterness (of argument).

acrobat ['ækrəbæt] *n.* person who does spectacular physical exercises. **acrobatic** [ækrə'bætɪk] *adj.* referring to spectacular exercises. **acrobatics,** *n. pl.* spectacular physical exercises.

acronym ['ækrənɪm] *n.* word (like NATO) formed from the initials of other words.

acropolis [ə'krɒpəlɪs] *n.* castle, protecting a town in ancient Greece.

across [ə'krɒs] *adv. & prep.* (*a*) from one side to the other; **it is 500 metres a.** (*b*) on the other side; **a. the street.** (*c*) **I came/ran a. this** = I found it. **across-the-board,** *adj.* which applies to everything or everyone.

acrostic [ə'krɒstɪk] *n.* poem/puzzle in which the first letters of each line form a word.

acrylic [ə'krɪlɪk] *adj. & n.* (material/paint) made from acid.

act [ækt] **1.** *n.* (*a*) thing which is done; **we caught him in the a.** = as he was doing it; **a. of God** = natural disaster which cannot be prevented. (*b*) **A. (of Parliament)** = law voted by Parliament. (*c*) large section of a play. **2.** *v.* (*a*) to play (a part in a play). (*b*) to do sth; **to a. on behalf of** = represent; **to a. as** = do the work of. (*c*) to behave. (*d*) to take effect/to work. **acting. 1.** *adj.* **a. chairman** = person who is taking the place of the chairman. **2.** *n.* profession of an actor.

action ['ækʃn] *n.* (*a*) doing; **out of a.** = not working. (*b*) thing done. (*c*) **the a. of the play** = what happens in it. (*d*) mechanism (of a watch). (*e*) lawsuit; **an a. for libel.** (*f*) warfare; **killed in a.** = on the battlefield. **actionable,** *adj.* (sth) for which s.o. could bring a lawsuit against you. **activate** ['æktɪveɪt] *v.* to put into action. **active** ['æktɪv] *adj.* vigorous/agile; (volcano) which still erupts; **on a. service** = on the battlefront. **actively,** *adv.* in an active way. **activist,** *n.* person who actively supports a political policy. **activity** [æk'tɪvɪtɪ] *n.* (*a*) movement/being active. (*b*) occupation. **actor, actress** ['æktə, 'æktrəs] *n.* (*pl.* **-es**) person who acts in the theatre/films/on television.

actinium [æk'tɪnɪəm] *n.* (*element:* Ac) radioactive metal.

actual ['æktjʊəl] *adj.* real; **in a. fact** = really. **actuality** [æktjʊ'ælɪtɪ] *n.* reality. **actually,** *adv.* really.

actuary ['æktjʊərɪ] *n.* person who calculates insurance rates. **actuarial** [æktjʊ-'eərɪəl] *adj.* referring to insurance rates.

actuate ['æktjʊeɪt] *v.* to set in motion/to start off.

acuity [ə'kjuːɪtɪ] *n.* sharpness (of sight).

acumen ['ækjuːmən] *n.* ability to make shrewd decisions.

acupuncture ['ækjʊpʌŋktʃə] n. way of healing and curing by placing the tips of needles in the skin. **acupuncturist,** n. doctor who practises acupuncture.

acute [ə'kju:t] adj. (a) very sharp (angle). (b) sudden serious (illness/pain). (c) perceptive. **acutely,** adv. very sharply (aware). **acuteness,** n. sharpness (of pain); seriousness (of illness); clearness (of hearing).

ad [æd] n. inf. advertisement; **small ads** = small advertisements for staff/articles for sale, etc.

AD ['eɪ'di:] abbreviation for Anno Domini (Latin for in the year of our Lord) (used to show dates after the birth of Christ) **923 AD.**

adage ['ædɪdʒ] n. old wise saying.

adagio [ə'dɑ:dʒɪəʊ] n. slow piece of music.

Adam ['ædəm] n. inf. **I don't know him from A.** = I have no idea who he is; **A.'s apple** = lump in the front of a man's neck.

adamant ['ædəmənt] adj. fixed in your opinion/intentions.

adapt [ə'dæpt] v. to change (sth) so that it fits; to make (sth) more suitable. **adaptability** [ədæptə'bɪlɪtɪ] n. ease of adapting yourself to new circumstances. **adaptable,** adj. able to (be) adapt(ed) easily. **adaptation** [ædæp-'teɪʃn] n. written work which is adapted from another. **adapter, adaptor,** n. electric plug which allows several plugs to be fitted to the same socket; small disc which allows a record with a large central hole to be fitted on a turntable.

add [æd] v. (a) to join (sth to sth else). (b) to say/to write sth more. (c) to make a total. **addendum** [ə'dendəm] n. (pl. addenda) piece added, as at the end of a book. **add up,** v. to make a total of (figures); **these figures don't add up** = the total given is incorrect.

adder ['ædə] n. viper.

addict ['ædɪkt] n. person who cannot stop himself from doing sth (usu. which is harmful to himself); **drug a.** = person who cannot stop taking a drug; **TV a.** = person who is always watching television. **addicted** [ə'dɪktɪd] adj. (to) (person) who cannot stop (taking a drug). **addiction** [ə'dɪkʃn] n. **drug**

a. = inability to stop taking a drug. **addictive,** adj. which causes addiction.

addition [ə'dɪʃn] n. (a) act of adding; **in a.** = added to this; also. (b) thing added. **additional,** adj. further. **additive** ['ædɪtɪv] n. substance, usu. chemical, which is added.

addled ['ædld] adj. rotten (egg).

address [ə'dres] 1. n. (pl. -es) (a) number of house, name of street, town, county, etc., where a person lives/where an office is situated; **a. book** = book containing a list of addresses. (b) formal speech. 2. v. (a) to write the name and address of the person/the firm to whom sth is being sent. (b) to speak to (s.o.). (c) (in golf) to aim at the ball. **addressee** [ædre'si:] n. person to whom a letter is addressed.

adduce [ə'dju:s] v. (formal) to bring added proof (of sth).

adenoids ['ædənɔɪdz] n. pl. small growths in the back of the throat. **adenoidal** [ædɪ'nɔɪdl] adj. referring to the adenoids.

adept ['ædept] adj. & n. (person who is) clever (at doing sth).

adequate ['ædɪkwət] adj. (large) enough. **adequately,** adv. enough.

adhere [əd'hɪə] v. to stick (to). **adherence,** n. sticking/attachment. **adherent,** n. person who belongs to (a society, etc.).

adhesion [əd'hi:ʒn] n. attachment/sticking; ability to stick. **adhesive** [əd'hi:zɪv] 1. adj. which sticks; **a. tape** = plastic tape which sticks; **a. plaster** = material used to stick bandages over wounds. 2. n. glue.

ad hoc [æd'hɒk] adj. which applies to a particular case.

adieu [ə'dju:] n. (poetic) goodbye.

ad infinitum [ædɪnfɪ'naɪtəm] adv. for ever.

adipose ['ædɪpəʊs] adj. fatty (tissue).

adjacent [ə'dʒeɪsənt] adj. (to) next to/touching/side by side.

adjective ['ædʒəktɪv] n. word used to describe a noun. **adjectival** [ædʒek-'taɪvl] adj. used like an adjective. **adjectivally,** adv. like an adjective.

adjoin [ə'dʒɔɪn] v. to be next to sth/to touch sth.

adjourn [ə'dʒɜ:n] v. to put off (a meet-

ing) to a later date; **let's a. to the bar** =
let's stop talking here and continue in
the bar. **adjournment,** *n.* putting off (a
meeting) to a later date.

adjudicate [ə'dʒu:dɪkeɪt] *v.* to give a
decision (in a dispute); to be the
judge (in a competition). **adjudication**
[ədʒu:dɪ'keɪʃn] *n.* decision (in a dispute); judging (of a competition).
adjudicator [ə'dʒu:dɪkeɪtə] *n.* judge.

adjunct ['ædʒʌŋkt] *n.* thing additional
(to sth).

adjust [ə'dʒʌst] *v.* to put right by making
a slight change. **adjustable,** *adj.* which
can be changed slightly. **adjuster,**
adjustor *n.* person who calculates the
extent of losses in an insurance claim.
adjustment, *n.* slight change made (**to**
a mechanism).

adjutant ['ædʒətənt] *n.* army officer
who assists in administration.

ad-lib ['æd'lɪb] *v.* (**ad-libbed**) *inf.* to
speak without a script.

administer [əd'mɪnɪstə] *v.* to govern/
to rule (a country/an office); to run
(a company/an estate); **to a. an oath
to s.o.** = to make s.o. swear an
oath. **admin,** *n. informal* administrative work. **administrate** *v.* to see
that justice is done. **administration**
[ədmɪnɪ'streɪʃn] *n.* ruling (of a country);
the government. **administrative,** *adj.*
which administers; referring to administration. **administrator,** *n.* person who
rules/governs.

admirable ['ædmərəbl] *adj. see* **admire.**

admiral ['ædmərəl] *n.* highest-ranking
officer in the navy; **red a.** = type of red
and black butterfly. **the Admiralty,** *n.*
British government department dealing
with the navy.

admire [əd'maɪə] *v.* to look at (sth) with
pleasure. **admirable** ['ædmərəbl] *adj.*
remarkable; excellent. **admirably,** *adv.*
remarkably; excellently. **admiration**
[ædmə'reɪʃn] *n.* feeling of pride/pleas-
ure. **admirer** [əd'maɪərə] *n.* person who
admires. **admiring,** *adj.* (look) showing admiration. **admiringly,** *adv.* in an
admiring way.

admission [əd'mɪʃn] *n.* (*a*) being allowed to enter; **no a.** = no one can
enter. (*b*) saying that sth is true.
admissible [əd'mɪsɪbl] *adj.* (evidence)
that can be admitted.

admit [əd'mɪt] *v.* (**admitted**) (*a*) to
allow to enter. (*b*) to say that sth is
true. (*c*) to accept (evidence/idea, etc.).
admittance, *n.* entrance. **admittedly,**
adv. according to general opinion.

admixture [æd'mɪkstʃə] *n.* thing which
is added to make a mixture.

admonish [əd'mɒnɪʃ] *v.* to scold s.o./to
tell s.o. off. **admonition** [ædmə'nɪʃn]
n. scolding.

ad nauseam [æd'nɔ:zɪəm] *adv.* until
one is sick of it.

ado [ə'du:] *n.* **without any more a.** =
without any more fuss.

adobe [ə'dəubɪ] *n.* bricks made from clay
dried in the sun.

adolescence [ædə'lesns] *n.* period between childhood and being an adult.
adolescent, *adj. & n.* (referring to) a
young person between child and adult.

adopt [ə'dɒpt] *v.* (*a*) to take (s.o.) legally
as your son or daughter. (*b*) to follow/
to take up (a line of argument); to put
on (an air). (*c*) to prescribe (a book) for
use in class. **adoption** [ə'dɒpʃn] *n.* (*a*)
legal taking of a child as your own. (*b*)
prescribing (of a book) for use in class.
adoptive, *adj.* who has (been) adopted.

adore [ə'dɔ:] *v.* to love very
strongly. **adorable,** *adj.* pretty/lovely.
adoration [ædə'reɪʃn] *n.* strong love/
worship. **adorer,** *n.* person who adores.

adorn [ə'dɔ:n] *v.* to cover with or-
naments/to decorate. **adornment,** *n.*
adorning; ornament.

adrenal [ə'dri:nəl] *adj.* referring to the
kidneys. **adrenalin(e)** [ə'drenəlɪn] *n.*
secretion which is produced by a gland
when s.o. is excited/afraid.

adrift [ə'drɪft] *adv.* **to cast a boat a.** =
to let a boat float without control; **to cut
yourself a.** = to separate yourself.

adroit [ə'drɔɪt] *adj.* skilful/clever (with
your hands). **adroitly,** *adv.* smartly.

adsorb [æd'zɔ:b] *v.* to form a thin film
on the surface of sth.

adulation [ædju'leɪʃn] *n.* wild praise/ex-
cessive flattery.

adult ['ædʌlt, ə'dʌlt] *adj. & n.* grown-up
(person); fully grown (animal).

adulterate [ə'dʌltəreɪt] *v.* to water
down; to add sth of inferior quality to
(a substance).

adulterer, adulteress [ə'dʌltərə, ə-

'dʌltərəs] n. person who commits adultery. **adulterous**, adj. referring to adultery. **adultery**, n. (of married person) having sexual intercourse with s.o. to whom he/she is not married.

ad valorem [ædvə'lɔːrəm] adj. (tax) calculated on the value of the thing being taxed.

advance [əd'vɑːns] **1.** n. (a) forward movement: **a. guard** = troops sent ahead of the main force. (b) **in a.** = early; beforehand. (c) **to make advances to** = to try to attract. (d) payment made early. **2.** v. (a) to go forward. (b) to put forward; **he advanced me £10** = he gave me £10 as an early payment. **advanced**, adj. (a) (subject) which is studied after several years' initial study; **a. student** = student who has studied for several years. (b) **the season is well a.** = the season is coming to an end; **in an a. state of decay** = very decayed. **advancement**, n. progress (of science, etc.).

advantage [əd'vɑːntɪdʒ] n. useful thing which will help you to be successful; **to take a. of** = to profit from; **to take a. of s.o.** = to cheat for your own benefit; **her dress shows off her figure to a.** = makes her figure look perfect. **advantageous** [ædvən'teɪdʒəs] adj. profitable/useful.

advent ['ædvent] n. (a) coming; arrival. (b) **Advent** = church season before Christmas.

adventitious [ædven'tɪʃəs] adj. (root) which develops from a plant's stem and not from another root.

adventure [əd'ventʃə] n. new, exciting and dangerous experience. **adventurer**, n. person who aims to make a fortune by taking risks. **adventurous**, adj. bold (person); exciting (life). **adventurously**, adv. boldly. **adventurousness**, n. being adventurous.

adverb ['ædvɜːb] n. word used to describe a verb/an adjective/another adverb. **adverbial** [əd'vɜːbɪəl] adj. used as an adverb. **adverbially**, adv. like an adverb.

adversary ['ædvəsrɪ] n. person you are fighting against.

adverse ['ædvɜːs] adj. (a) contrary (winds). (b) bad; unfavourable (conditions). **adversely**, adv. badly. **adversity** [əd'vɜːsɪtɪ] n. difficulty.

advert 1. ['ædvɜːt] n. inf. advertisement. **2.** [æd'vɜːt] v. (formal) to refer to.

advertise ['ædvətaɪz] v. to show that sth is for sale/to publicize sth; **he advertised for a new secretary** = put an advertisement in the paper asking people to apply for the job; **there's no need to a. the fact** = there's no need to tell everyone the secret. **advertisement** [əd'vɜːtɪsmənt] n. announcement that sth is for sale/is wanted. **advertiser**, n. person who advertises. **advertising**, n. action of announcing the sale of sth; business of describing goods for sale; **a. agency** = firm which designs and places advertisements.

advice [əd'vaɪs] n. (a) suggestion as to what should be done; **a piece of a.** (b) **a. note** = paper which tells you that goods have been shipped.

advise [əd'vaɪz] v. to suggest what should be done. **advisability**, n. being recommended. **advisable**, adj. which you would recommend. **advisedly**, adv. after a lot of thought. **adviser, advisor**, n. person who gives advice. **advisory**, adj. **in an a. capacity** = as an adviser.

advocacy ['ædvəkəsɪ] n. pleading for; support for.

advocate 1. n. ['ædvəkət] (a) person who pleads for a cause. (b) (in Scotland) lawyer who pleads in court. **2.** ['ædvəkeɪt] v. to recommend/to plead.

adze [ædz] n. axe with the blade at right angles to the handle.

aegis ['iːdʒɪs] n. (formal) **under the a. of** = supported/patronized by.

aeolian [iː'əʊlɪən] adj. caused by the wind.

aeon ['iːɒn] n. very long time.

aerate [eə'reɪt] v. to fill sth with air or gas.

aerial ['eərɪəl] **1.** adj. referring to the air. **2.** n. device for sending or receiving radio or TV signals.

aerie ['iːrɪ] n. Am. see **eyrie**.

aerobatics [eərə'bætɪks] n. pl. trick flying (as a display).

aerobic [eə'rəʊbɪk] adj. needing oxygen to take place or to exist. **aerobics**, n. pl. exercises to improve the body's use of oxygen.

aerodrome ['eərədrəʊm] *n.* small airfield.

aerodynamics [eərədaɪ'næmɪks] *n.* science of movement of flying bodies in the air.

aerofoil ['eərəfɔɪl] *n.* wing surface of a plane.

aeronautical [eərə'nɔ:tɪkl] *adj.* referring to aircraft flying. **aeronautics,** *n.* science of flying aircraft.

aerophagia [eərəʊ'feɪdʒɪə] *n.* habit of swallowing air.

aeroplane ['eərəpleɪn] *n.* machine that flies.

aerosol ['eərəsɒl] *n.* canister filled under pressure, which sends out a spray when the button is pushed.

aerospace ['eərəʊspeɪs] *n.* the space around the earth, including the atmosphere.

aesthete ['i:sθi:t] *n.* person who appreciates beauty in art. **aesthetic** [i:s'θetɪk] *adj.* pleasing from an artistic point of view. **aesthetically,** *adv.* from an artistic point of view.

afar [ə'fɑ:] *adv.* **from a.** = from a long way away.

affable ['æfəbl] *adj.* pleasant/courteous. **affability** [æfə'bɪlɪtɪ] *n.* pleasantness/ courtesy. **affably,** *adv.* in a pleasant/ friendly way.

affair [ə'feə] *n.* (*a*) business; **that's my a.** = it's my business and not yours; **his affairs** = his business. (*b*) **he's having an a. with her** = he's her lover. (*c*) **the present state of affairs** = how things are at present.

affect [ə'fekt] *v.* (*a*) to pretend/to put on. (*b*) to touch/to change sth. **affectation** [æfek'teɪʃn] *n.* pretence. **affected,** *adj.* pretended/put on. **affecting,** *adj.* touching/which makes you feel emotion. **affection** [ə'fekʃn] *n.* liking/love. **affectionate,** *adj.* showing love or fondness for s.o. **affectionately,** *adv.* in a loving way.

affidavit [æfɪ'deɪvɪt] *n.* written sworn statement.

affiliate [ə'fɪlɪeɪt] *v.* to link (a small group to a larger one). **affiliation** [əfɪlɪ-'eɪʃn] *n.* **political a.** = political link.

affinity [ə'fɪnɪtɪ] *n.* (*pl.* **affinities**) closeness/similarity of character; strong attraction.

affirm [ə'fɜ:m] *v.* (*a*) to state. (*b*) to make a statement (in court, instead of taking the oath). **affirmation** [æfə'meɪʃn] *n.* statement. **affirmative** [ə'fɜ:mətɪv] **1.** *adj.* agreeing. **2.** *n.* **the answer is in the a.** = the answer is yes. **affirmatively,** *adv.* **he answered a.** = he answered yes.

affix [ə'fɪks] *v.* (*formal*) to attach.

afflict [ə'flɪkt] *v.* to torture/to torment. **affliction** [ə'flɪkʃn] *n.* torment; cause of distress.

affluence ['æfluəns] *n.* wealth. **affluent,** *adj.* rich; **a. society** = society where most people have enough money.

afford [ə'fɔ:d] *v.* to have enough money to pay for (sth).

afforestation [æfɒrɪ'steɪʃn] *n.* planting trees to make a forest.

affray [ə'freɪ] *n.* (*formal*) fight between several people in public.

affront [ə'frʌnt] **1.** *n.* offence. **2.** *v.* to insult.

afield [ə'fi:ld] *adv.* **to go far a.** = to go a long way.

afire [ə'faɪə] *adj.* on fire.

aflame [ə'fleɪm] *adj.* (*formal*) on fire.

aflatoxin [æflə'tɒksɪn] *n.* poisonous substance which forms on seeds and nuts.

afloat [ə'fləʊt] *adv.* floating.

afoot [ə'fʊt] *adv.* **there's a plan a.** = a plan is being prepared; **there's sth a.** = sth is being plotted.

aforesaid [ə'fɔ:sed] *adj.* (*formal*) which has been mentioned before.

aforethought [ə'fɔ:θɔ:t] *adj.* (*formal*) **with malice a.** = having planned the crime beforehand.

afraid [ə'freɪd] *adj.* (*a*) frightened (by); **she's a. of the dark.** (*b*) sorry to have to say; **I'm a. she's ill.**

afresh [ə'freʃ] *adv.* (all over) again.

African ['æfrɪkən] *adj. & n.* (person) from Africa; **A. violet** = small houseplant with blue or pink flowers.

Afro- ['æfrəʊ] *prefix meaning* African/between Africa and another country.

Afro ['æfrəʊ] *adj. & n.* **A.** (**hairstyle**) = type of bouffant hairstyle.

aft [ɑ:ft] *adv.* at/towards the back of a ship.

after ['ɑ:ftə] **1.** *adv.* next/later. **2.** *prep.* next to/following; **the police are a. you** = the police are looking for you; **what's he a.?** = what does he want?

a. you = please go first. **3.** *conj.* following the time when. **afterbirth,** *n.* placenta which comes out of the womb after the birth of young. **aftercare,** *n.* care for people after an operation, etc. **aftereffects,** *n. pl.* effects that follow on sth. **afterglow,** *n.* glow in the sky after the sun has set. **afterhours,** *adj.* (trading) after a stock exchange has closed. **aftermath,** *n.* what takes place after a catastrophe. **afternoon,** *n.* part of the day between 12 noon and evening. **afters,** *n. pl.* (*in a meal*) *inf.* sweet pudding/dessert. **aftersales service,** *n.* maintenance (of a car/a machine, etc.) by the manufacturer/the agent after it has been sold. **aftershave,** *n.* **a.** (**lotion**) = lotion for soothing the face after shaving. **aftershock,** *n.* lighter earth tremor felt after a major earthquake. **afterthought,** *n.* thing which you think of later. **afterwards,** *adv.* after that; next/later.

Ag *symbol for* silver.

again [əˈgeɪn, əˈgen] *adv.* once more; **once a.** = another time; **a. and a.** = several times; **now and a.** = sometimes; *inf.* **come a.?** = could you repeat that?

against [əˈgenst] *prep.* (*a*) touching. (*b*) contrary to (rules, etc.); **he's a. lending her any more money** = he's opposed to lending her money.

agaric [əˈgærɪk] *n.* type of fungus.

agate [ˈægət] *n.* semi-precious stone, usu. with bands of different colours.

age [eɪdʒ] **1.** *n.* (*a*) number of years you have lived; **under a.** = below the legal age (to do sth). (*b*) period; **the Stone A.** (*c*) **for ages** = for a very long time. **2.** *v.* to become old. **aged 1.** *adj.* [eɪdʒd] **a. 74** = 74 years old. **2.** [ˈeɪdʒɪd] (*a*) *adj.* very old. (*b*) *n.* **the a.** = old people. **ageless,** *adj.* which does not grow old or look old.

agency [ˈeɪdʒənsɪ] *n.* (*a*) office which represents a larger firm/which works on behalf of another firm; **we have the a. for Ford cars** = we are the distributors for Ford cars. (*b*) means.

agenda [əˈdʒendə] *n.* list of things to be discussed at a meeting.

agent [ˈeɪdʒənt] *n.* (*a*) person who represents s.o. else; **secret a.** = spy. (*b*) substance which has an effect on another;

a. provocateur = person who provokes people to commit crimes, esp. crimes against the state.

agglomeration [əglɒməˈreɪʃn] *n.* large urban area.

aggrandizement [əˈgrændɪzmənt] *n.* making larger/more powerful.

aggravate [ˈægrəveɪt] *v.* to make worse. **aggravating,** *adj. inf.* annoying. **aggravation** [ægrəˈveɪʃn] *n.* worsening (of a quarrel); *inf.* annoyance.

aggregate [ˈægrɪgət] *n.* (*a*) total; **in the a.** = as a total. (*b*) mixture of sand, gravel, etc., with cement.

aggression [əˈgreʃn] *n.* hostility; attacking; **act of a.** = attack. **aggressive** [əˈgresɪv] *adj.* hostile; attacking. **aggressively,** *adv.* violently. **aggressiveness,** *n.* being aggressive. **aggressor,** *n.* attacker.

aggrieved [əˈgriːvd] *adj.* upset; hurt.

aggro [ˈægrəʊ] *n.* (*no pl.*) *Sl.* violent quarrelling/disagreement.

aghast [əˈgɑːst] *adj.* horrified.

agile [ˈædʒaɪl] *adj.* lightfooted; (animal/person) who can climb/swing/run, etc., very easily. **agility** [əˈdʒɪlɪtɪ] *n.* being agile.

agio [ˈædʒɪəʊ] *n.* charge made for converting money to another currency.

agitate [ˈædʒɪteɪt] *v.* to stir up public opinion (**for/against** sth). **agitation** [ædʒɪˈteɪʃn] *n.* (*a*) worry. (*b*) **political a.** = political unrest. **agitator** [ˈædʒɪteɪtə] *n.* person who stirs up political unrest.

AGM [eɪdʒiːˈem] Annual General Meeting.

agnostic [ægˈnɒstɪk] *adj. & n.* (person) who believes that nothing can be known about God. **agnosticism,** *n.* belief that nothing can be known about God.

ago [əˈgəʊ] *adv.* in the past; **three years a.**

agog [əˈgɒg] *adj.* **all a.** = very eager.

agonize [ˈægənaɪz] *v.* to worry (**over** a decision). **agonized,** *adj.* as if in pain/in agony. **agonizing,** *adj.* (*a*) sharp (pain). (*b*) upsetting, painful (decision).

agony [ˈægənɪ] *n.* extreme pain/extreme discomfort; **a. column** = letters and advice about personal problems in a newspaper.

agoraphobia [ægərəˈfəʊbɪə] *n.* irrational fear of public places or open spaces.

agrarian [ə'greəriən] *adj.* dealing with the land.

agree [ə'gri:] *v.* (*a*) (**with**) to say that you think the same way as (s.o.). (*b*) (**to**) to say yes to (a suggestion). (*c*) **eggs don't a. with me** = make me feel ill. **agreeable**, *adj.* (*a*) pleasant. (*b*) in agreement; **are you a. to this?** = do you agree? **agreeably**, *adv.* pleasantly. **agreement**, *n.* act of saying yes; **to be in a. with** = to agree with.

agriculture ['ægrikʌltʃə] *n.* use of the land for growing crops/raising animals, etc. **agricultural** [ægrɪ'kʌltʃərəl] *adj.* referring to agriculture. **agribusiness**, *n.* farming and making products for farmers, seen as a business.

agronomy [ə'grɒnəmi] *n.* study of agriculture.

aground [ə'graund] *adv.* no longer afloat; **the ship went a.**

ahead [ə'hed] *adv.* in front; in advance (of a time); **full speed a.** = go forward as fast as possible.

ahoy [ə'hɔɪ] *inter.* used by sailors to call a ship.

AI = artificial insemination.

aid [eɪd] **1.** *n.* (*a*) help; **first a.** = help to injured/sick people; **first-a. kit** = box with bandages/medicines, etc.; **in a. of the Red Cross** = to help the Red Cross. (*b*) instrument to help; **a hearing a. 2.** *v.* to help.

AID = artificial insemination by donor.

aide [eɪd] *n.* assistant (of a president, etc.).

aide-de-camp [eɪddə'kɒŋ] *n.* (*pl.* **aides-**) officer who assists a senior officer.

AIDS = acquired immunodeficiency syndrome.

ail [eɪl] *v.* (*old*) to be ill. **ailing** ['eɪlɪŋ] *adj.* sick. **ailment** ['eɪlmənt] *n.* minor illness.

aileron ['eɪlərɒn] *n.* flap on the edge of an aircraft's wing.

aim [eɪm] **1.** *n.* target; what you are trying to do; **he took a.** = he pointed his gun at the target. **2.** *v.* (*a*) to plan/to intend to do. (*b*) to point (**at**). **aimless**, *adj.*, **aimlessly**, *adv.* with no particular plan.

air ['eə] **1.** *n.* (*a*) mixture of gases which we breathe, and which surrounds the earth; **travel by a.** = in an aircraft; **in the a.** = not yet decided; **on the a.**

= speaking live on TV/on radio. (*b*) little tune. (*c*) appearance/feeling. **2.** *v.* to freshen (a room, clothes, etc.) by giving more air. **airbase**, *n.* military airfield. **airbed**, *n.* inflatable plastic/rubber mattress. **airborne**, *adj.* carried in the air. **airbrake**, *n.* (*a*) movable part on an aircraft to slow it down. (*b*) brake (on trucks) which works by compressed air. **air-conditioned**, *adj.* cooled by an air-conditioner. **air-conditioner**, *n.* machine which keeps a room at the right temperature. **air-conditioning**, *n.* cooling of the air by an air-conditioner. **aircooled**, *adj.* (engine) cooled by air, not by water. **aircraft**, *n.* (*pl.* **aircraft**) machine which flies. **aircraft carrier**, *n.* large warship which carries aircraft and has a long deck for landing and taking off. **aircraftman, aircraftwoman**, *n.* (*pl.* **-men, -women**) lowest rank in the Royal Air Force. **aircrew**, *n.* the crew of an aircraft. **airfield**, *n.* small private or military aerodrome. **air force**, *n.* military air defence organization. **airfreight. 1.** *n.* shipping goods by air. **2.** *v.* to ship goods by air. **airgun**, *n.* gun which shoots pellets using compressed air. **air hostess**, *n.* woman who works on a passenger aircraft, serving meals and looking after the passengers. **airily**, *adv.* in an airy way. **airless**, *adj.* with no air or wind; stuffy. **air letter**, *n.* very light piece of writing paper which, when folded and stuck down, becomes its own envelope. **airlift. 1.** *n.* transport of emergency supplies/people by air. **2.** *v.* to transport emergency supplies/people by air. **airline**, *n.* company which runs passenger or cargo air services. **airlock**, *n.* blockage in the flow of a liquid in a pipe (caused by air). **airmail**, *n.* & *adv.* (mail) sent by air. **airman**, *n.* (*pl.* **-men**) man serving in an air force. **air mattress**, *n.* mattress which can be inflated. **airplane**, *n. Am.* aeroplane. **air pocket**, *n.* sudden turbulence in air. **airport**, *n.* commercial installation where passenger and cargo planes land and take off. **air raid**, *n.* attack by military aircraft. **airship**, *n.* large inflated balloon driven by an engine. **airsick**, *adj.* sick because of travelling by air. **airsickness,** *n.* feeling of being airsick. **airspeed,** *n.* speed of an aircraft in the air. **airstrip,** *n.* small runway where planes can land and take off. **air terminal,** *n.* station in a town where air passengers can take buses to an airport. **airtight,** *adj.* not letting in any air. **air traffic control,** *n.* control of the movement of aircraft by people on the ground. **airway,** *n.* passage (such as the throat) through which air passes in the body. **airworthiness,** *n.* safety of an aircraft for use. **airy,** *adj.* **(-ier, -iest)** (*a*) full of air. (*b*) vague (promise). **airy-fairy,** *adj.* impractical (plan).

aisle [aɪl] *n.* gangway; side part in a church parallel to the nave.

ajar [əˈdʒɑː] *adj.* (*of door/window*) slightly open.

aka [eɪkeɪˈeɪ] = also known as.

akimbo [əˈkɪmbəʊ] *adv.* **with her arms a.** = with her hands on her hips.

akin [əˈkɪn] *adj.* similar (**to**).

Al *symbol for* aluminium.

alabaster [ˈæləbɑːstə] *n.* smooth white stone.

à la carte [ælæˈkɑːt] *adv.* & *adj.* (meal) made of several dishes ordered separately from a menu.

alacrity [əˈlækrɪtɪ] *n.* speed.

à la mode [ælæˈmɒd] *adv. Am.* served with ice cream.

alarm [əˈlɑːm] **1.** *n.* thing which gives a loud warning; **false a.** = warning signal which is false; **fire a.** = bell which rings when a fire breaks out; **a. (clock)** = clock which rings at a certain time. **2.** *v.* to warn (s.o.); to frighten (s.o.). **alarmist,** *adj.* & *n.* (person) who is unnecessarily worried by sth.

alas [əˈlæs] *inter. showing sadness.*

albatross [ˈælbətrɒs] *n.* (*pl.* **-es**) very large white sea bird.

albedo [ælˈbiːdəʊ] *n.* ability to reflect light.

albeit [ɔːlˈbiːɪt] *conj.* (*formal*) although.

albino [ælˈbiːnəʊ] *n.* animal or person born with pale skin, white hair, and pink eyes.

album [ˈælbəm] *n.* (*a*) large book for sticking things in. (*b*) long-playing record.

albumen, albumin [ˈælbjʊmən] *n.* white part of an egg.

alchemy [ˈælkəmɪ] *n.* medieval chemistry, aimed at converting metals. to gold. **alchemist,** *n.* person who studied alchemy.

alcohol [ˈælkəhɒl] *n.* intoxicating liquid distilled from a fermented mixture. **alcoholic** [ælkəˈhɒlɪk] **1.** *adj.* referring to alcohol. **2.** *n.* person who is addicted to drinking alcohol. **alcoholism,** *n.* addiction to drinking alcohol.

alcove [ˈælkəʊv] *n.* small recess in a wall.

alder [ˈɔːldə] *n.* tree which often grows near water.

ale [eɪl] *n.* type of beer.

alert [əˈlɜːt] **1.** *adj.* watchful; lively. **2.** *n.* **to be on the a.** = to be watchful/ to watch out for sth; **he gave the a.** = he gave a warning signal. **3.** *v.* **to a. s.o. to** = to warn s.o. of. **alertness,** *n.* watchfulness; promptness (in doing sth).

alfalfa [ælˈfælfə] *n.* lucerne.

alfresco [ælˈfreskəʊ] *adj.* & *adv.* in the open air; **an a. meal.**

algae [ˈældʒiː] *n. pl.* tiny water plants with no stems or leaves.

algebra [ˈældʒɪbrə] *n.* branch of mathematics where numbers are replaced by letters. **algebraic** [ældʒɪˈbreɪk] *adj.* referring to algebra.

algorithm [ˈælgərɪðm] *n.* plan for working out a complicated calculation.

alias [ˈeɪlɪəs] **1.** *adv.* otherwise known as. **2.** *n.* (*pl.* **-es**) assumed name.

alibi [ˈælɪbaɪ] *n.* proof that you were somewhere else when a crime was committed.

alien [ˈeɪlɪən] **1.** *adj.* foreign (**to**). **2.** *n.* foreigner.

alienate [ˈeɪlɪəneɪt] *v.* to turn away/to repel. **alienation** [eɪlɪəˈneɪʃn] *n.* turning away/repelling.

alight [əˈlaɪt] **1.** *v.* (*formal*) **to a. from** = to get off (a train/bus, etc.). **2.** *adj.* on fire.

align [əˈlaɪn] *v.* to put (yourself/sth) in line; to put (yourself) on the same side as. **alignment,** *n.* row (of objects); putting (countries) on the same side.

alike [əˈlaɪk] *adv.* almost the same.

alimentary [ælɪˈmentərɪ] *adj.* which feeds; **a. canal** = tube by which food goes into the stomach, and passes through the body.

alimony ['ælɪmənɪ] *n.* money paid regularly by a husband to his divorced wife.

alive [ə'laɪv] *adj.* (*a*) living/not dead. (*b*) **a. to** = aware of. (*c*) lively.

alkali ['ælkəlaɪ] *n.* substance which will neutralize an acid, and which turns litmus paper blue. **alkaline,** *adj.* not acid.

all [ɔ:l] **1.** *adj. & pron.* (*a*) everything; everyone; **a. the children; a. of us prefer beer.** (*b*) (*in tennis*) **fifteen a.** = fifteen points each. (*c*) **once (and) for a.** = for the last time; **not at a.** = certainly not; **a. but** = nearly. **2.** *adv.* completely; **dressed a. in blue; a. at once/a. of a sudden** = suddenly; *inf.* **not a. there** = mad. **all in,** *adj.* (*a*) *inf.* worn out. (*b*) **a.-in** = including everything; **a.-in price. all-night,** *adj.* which goes on for the whole night. **all-out,** *adj.* complete (strike); **we must make an a.-out effort** = we must do everything. **all right** [ɔ:l'raɪt] *adj.* (*a*) fine; well. (*b*) yes, I will. **all-round,** *adj.* general; **a.-round athlete** = person who is good at all sorts of sports. **all-rounder,** *n.* person who can do anything, esp. cricketer who can play in any position. **all-star,** *adj.* with many stars appearing. **all-time,** *adj.* (greatest level, etc.) ever.

Allah ['ælæ] *n.* Muslim name for God.

allay [ə'leɪ] *v.* to calm (fear/anger).

allegation [ælɪ'geɪʃn] *n.* suggestion as if it were fact. **allege** [ə'ledʒ] *v.* to suggest (as a fact that). **alleged,** *adj.* suggested. **allegedly** [ə'ledʒɪdlɪ] *adv.* as is alleged.

allegiance [ə'li:dʒəns] *n.* faithfulness; **they swore a. to the President** = they swore to obey him.

allegory ['ælɪgərɪ] *n.* piece of writing where the characters represent abstract qualities or defects. **allegorical** [ælɪ'gɒrɪkl] *adj.* referring to allegory.

allegro [ə'legrəʊ] *adv. & adj.* (*in music*) played quite fast.

allergy ['ælədʒɪ] *n.* illness caused by a reaction to irritant substances. **allergen,** *n.* substance (such as pollen) which produces an allergic reaction. **allergic** [ə'lɜ:dʒɪk] *adj.* reacting badly against; **I am a. to grass pollen; she is a. to jazz** = dislikes it intensely.

alleviate [ə'li:vɪeɪt] *v.* to lessen/to soften. **alleviation** [əli:vɪ'eɪʃn] *n.* lessening.

alley ['ælɪ] *n.* (*a*) very narrow street. (*b*) **skittle a./bowling a.** = long narrow area for playing skittles.

alliance [ə'laɪəns] *n.* link between two groups or countries.

allied ['ælaɪd] *adj.* (*a*) linked by an alliance; **the a. powers** = western countries linked against communist states. (*b*) linked.

alligator ['ælɪgeɪtə] *n.* large flesh-eating reptile living in tropical rivers.

alliteration [əlɪtə'reɪʃn] *n.* use of repeated consonants at the beginning of words in poetry.

allocate ['æləkeɪt] *v.* to give (sth) as a share (for a particular purpose. **allocation** [ælə'keɪʃn] *n.* division/giving as a share; amount allocated.

allot [ə'lɒt] *v.* (**allotted**) to share out between several people. **allotment,** *n.* (*a*) sharing out. (*b*) small plot of land leased by a town to a citizen (esp. for growing vegetables).

allow [ə'laʊ] *v.* (*a*) **to a. s.o. to do sth** = to let (s.o. do sth). (*b*) to give; **we will a. you six weeks to pay. allowable,** *adj.* which is permitted; **a. expenses** = expenses which are allowed against tax. **allowance,** *n.* (*a*) money paid regularly; **family a.** = money paid each week by the State to families with children. (*b*) **to make allowances for** = take into account.

alloy ['ælɔɪ] **1.** *n.* mixture of two or more metals. **2.** *v.* to mix (metals).

allspice ['ɔ:lspaɪs] *n.* small round tropical seed used as a spice.

allude [ə'lu:d] *v.* **to a. to sth** = to refer to sth indirectly or briefly.

allure [ə'ljʊə] *v.* to attract. **alluring,** *adj.* attractive.

allusion [ə'lu:ʒn] *n.* slight reference. **allusive,** *adj.* which makes reference to sth.

alluvial [ə'lu:vɪəl] *adj.* (soil/land) which has been deposited by rivers. **alluvium,** *n.* soil which has been deposited by a river.

ally 1. *n.* ['ælaɪ] person/country who is on the same side as you in a quarrel or war. **2.** *v.* [ə'laɪ] **to a. oneself to** = to join forces with/to support.

alma mater [ælmə'meɪtə] *n.* school or college which s.o. has attended.

almanac ['ɔːlmənæk] *n.* calendar which also contains advice or information.

almighty [ɔːl'maɪtɪ] **1.** *adj. inf.* very powerful; **an a. row** = a very loud noise. **2.** *n.* the **A.** = God.

almond ['ɑːmənd] *n.* nut from a tree of the peach family.

almoner ['ɑːmənə] *n.* (*old*) person in a hospital who sees that the patients are happy and well fed.

almost ['ɔːlməʊst] *adv.* nearly; not quite.

alms [ɑːmz] *n. pl.* (*old*) gift to old/ sick/poor people. **almshouses,** *n. pl.* houses formerly built as homes for the poor.

aloe ['æləʊ] *n.* desert plant with thick leaves and bitter juice.

aloft [ə'lɒft] *adv.* (*formal*) high up (in the air).

alone [ə'ləʊn] *adj. & adv.* with no one else.

along [ə'lɒŋ] **1.** *prep.* **a. the road** = from one end of the road to the other; for some distance down the road. **2.** *adv.* **come a. with me** = come with me; **all a.** = from the beginning; **they don't get a. very well together** = they do not agree. **alongside,** *adv. & prep.* beside.

aloof [ə'luːf] *adv. & adj.* coldly/un-friendly; **they kept a.** = they did not mix with others. **aloofness,** *n.* cold superciliousness.

alopecia [æləʊ'piːsɪə] *n.* baldness.

aloud [ə'laʊd] *adv.* loud enough to be heard; in a loud voice.

alp [ælp] *n.* mountain or mountain meadow in Switzerland.

alpaca [æl'pækə] *n.* wool from a llama.

alpha ['ælfə] *n.* first letter of the Greek alphabet.

alphabet ['ælfəbet] *n.* letters used to write words, laid out in a set order (A, B, C, etc.). **alphabetical** [ælfə-'betɪkl] *adj.* **in a. order** = in order based on the first letter of each word. **alphabetically,** *adv.* in alphabetical order.

alpine ['ælpaɪn] *adj. & n.* referring to high mountains; (plant) which grows on high mountains. **alpinist** *n.* person who climbs mountains.

already [ɔːl'redɪ] *adv.* by now.

alright [ɔːl'raɪt] *adj. & inter. inf.* = **all right.**

alsatian [æl'seɪʃn] *n.* large dog (of German origin) often used as a guard dog.

also ['ɔːlsəʊ] *adv.* as well/at the same time.

altar ['ɒltə] *n.* table in church/temple for religious ceremonies.

alter ['ɒltə] *v.* to change. **alteration** [ɒltə'reɪʃn] *n.* change.

altercation [ɔːltə'keɪʃn] *n.* (*formal*) argument.

alternate 1. *adj.* [ɔːl'tɜːnət] every other/ missing one each time. **2.** *v.* ['ɔːltəneɪt] to put (sth) in place of sth else, and then switch them round. **alternately** [ɔːl'tɜːnətlɪ] *adv.* in turns; one first and then the other. **alternating,** *adj.* (electric current) which flows one way and then the other. **alternative** [ɔːl'tɜːnətɪv] *n. & adj.* thing in place of sth else. **alternatively,** *adv.* on the other hand. **alternator** ['ɔːltəneɪtə] *n.* device which produces alternating current.

although [ɔːl'ðəʊ] *conj.* in spite of the fact that.

altimeter ['æltɪmɪːtə] *n.* instrument for measuring altitude.

altitude ['æltɪtjuːd] *n.* height (measured above the level of the sea).

alto ['æltəʊ] *n.* (*pl.* **-os**) (man with a) high-pitched voice; (woman with a) low-pitched voice.

altogether [ɔːltə'geðə] *adv.* considering everything together.

altruism ['æltruɪzəm] *n.* being unselfish. **altruistic,** *adj.* unselfish.

alum ['æləm] *n.* natural mineral salt.

aluminium [ælju'mɪnjəm], *Am.* **aluminum** [ə'luːmɪnəm] *n.* (*element:* Al) light white metal.

alumnus [ə'lʌmnəs] *n.* (*pl.* **alumni** [ə'lʌmnaɪ]) *Am.* graduate (of a college/ university).

always ['ɔːlweɪz] *adv.* every time/all the time.

alyssum ['ælɪsəm] *n.* low garden plant with small white flowers.

Alzheimer's disease ['æltseɪməz dɪ-'ziːz] *n.* condition where a patient becomes prematurely senile.

am [æm] *v. see* **be.**

a.m. ['eɪ'em] *adv.* in the morning.

amalgam [ə'mælgəm] *n.* (*formal*) mixture of substances. **amalgamate** [ə'mælgəmeɪt] *v.* to mix together/to link up. **amalgamation** [əmælgə'meɪʃn] *n.* amalgamating; things amalgamated.

amanuensis [æmænju:'ensɪs] *n.* person who writes for s.o. else.

amaryllis [æmə'rɪlɪs] *n.* lily.

amass [ə'mæs] *v.* to pile up (a fortune).

amateur ['æmətɜ:] *n. & adj.* (person) who is not paid to do sth; (person) who does sth because he likes doing it. **amateurish**, *adj.* not very well done.

amatory ['æmətəri] *adj.* referring to love.

amaze [ə'meɪz] *v.* to surprise. **amazed**, *adj.* surprised. **amazement**, *n.* surprise. **amazing**, *adj.* very surprising.

ambassador, **ambassadress** [æm'bæsədə, -dres] *n.* person who represents a country in another country.

amber ['æmbə] *n.* (*a*) yellow or orange translucent stone made of fossilized resin. (*b*) orange traffic light between green and red.

ambergris ['æmbəgrɪ] *n.* substance from sperm whales, used in making perfume.

ambidextrous [æmbɪ'dekstrəs] *adj.* (person) who can use either right or left hand equally well.

ambience ['æmbɪəns] *n.* surroundings. **ambient**, *adj.* which surrounds; **a. temperature** = temperature of the air around sth.

ambiguous [æm'bɪgjʊəs] *adj.* which has two possible meanings. **ambiguity** [æmbɪ'gju:ɪtɪ] *n.* state of having two possible meanings; vagueness.

ambit ['æmbɪt] *n.* general area covered by sth.

ambition [æm'bɪʃn] *n.* desire to improve your status in the world. **ambitious**, *adj.* wanting to get on in the world; (project) which aims very high.

ambivalent [æm'bɪvələnt] *adj.* undecided/with two points of view.

amble ['æmbl] *v.* **he was ambling along** = walking slowly along.

ambrosia [æm'brəʊzɪə] *n.* delectable food.

ambulance ['æmbjʊləns] *n.* van for taking sick people to hospital. **ambulanceman**, *n.* man who drives, or helps in, an ambulance.

ambush ['æmbʊʃ] **1.** *n.* (*pl.* -es) surprise attack. **2.** *v.* to attack by surprise.

ameliorate [ə'mi:ljəreɪt] *v.* (*formal*) to make better. **amelioration** [əmi:ljə-'reɪʃn] *n.* becoming better.

amen [ɑ:'men, eɪ'men] *inter.* word (*meaning* let this be so) which is used at the end of Christian prayers; **I say a. to that** = I agree entirely.

amenable [ə'mi:nəbl] *adj.* docile/easygoing; **a. to new ideas** = willing to accept new ideas.

amend [ə'mend] *v.* to change (for the better). **amendment**, *n.* change, esp. suggested change to a proposal. **amends** *n.* **to make a. for something** = to compensate for an injury, etc.

amenity [ə'mi:nɪtɪ] *n.* (*a*) pleasantness (of a place); **a. bed** = bed in a separate room in a public hospital. (*b*) sport and entertainment facility; **a. centre** = building housing (for example) a cinema, auditorium, gymnasium, swimming pool.

American [ə'merɪkən] **1.** *adj.* referring to America; **A. plan** = full board (in a hotel). **2.** *n.* person from the United States.

amethyst ['æməθɪst] *n.* purple precious stone.

amiable ['eɪmɪəbl] *adj.* pleasant. **amiability** [eɪmɪə'bɪlɪtɪ] *n.* being amiable. **amiably**, *adv.* pleasantly.

amicable ['æmɪkəbl] *adj.* friendly. **amicably**, *adv.* in a friendly way.

amid(st) [ə'mɪd(st)] *prep.* in the middle of. **amidships**, *adv. & prep.* in the middle of a ship.

amino acid [ə'mi:nəʊ 'æsɪd] *n.* acid found in protein, necessary for growth.

amiss [ə'mɪs] *adv. & adj.* **don't take it a.** = don't be annoyed; **something is a.** = has gone wrong.

amity ['æmɪtɪ] *n.* friendship.

ammeter ['æmɪtə] *n.* device for measuring electricity in amperes.

ammonia [ə'məʊnɪə] *n.* gas made of hydrogen and nitrogen, which has a strong smell.

ammonite ['æmənaɪt] *n.* fossil shell like that of a large snail.

ammunition [æmju'nɪʃn] *n.* (*no pl.*) bullets/shells, etc., for using in warfare/hunting.

amnesia [æm'ni:zɪə] *n.* medical state when you forget everything.

amnesty ['æmnəstɪ] **1.** *n.* pardon (to criminals). **2.** *v.* to offer (criminals) a pardon.

amniotic fluid ['æmnɪɒtɪk 'fluɪd] *n.* liquid surrounding a baby in the womb.

amoeba [ə'miːbə] *n.* (*pl.* **amoebas, amoebae** [ə'miːbiː]) tiny organism consisting of a single cell.

amok [ə'mɒk] *adv.* **to run a.** = to run wild killing people.

among(st) [ə'mʌŋ(st)] *prep.* (*a*) in the middle of. (*b*) out of.

amoral [eɪ'mɒrəl] *adj.* with no sense of values/of morality.

amorous ['æmərəs] *adj.* tending to fall in love; showing (sexual) love.

amorphous [ə'mɔːfəs] *adj.* having no particular shape.

amortize ['æmɔːtaɪz] *v.* to write off (a debt).

amount [ə'maʊnt] **1.** *n.* (*a*) quantity. (*b*) sum (of money). **2.** *v.* to add up (**to**); **it amounts to the same thing** = it means the same.

amour propre [æmuːə 'prɒpr] *n.* respect for oneself.

amp, ampere [æmp, 'æmpeə] *n.* quantity of electricity flowing in a current.

ampersand ['æmpəsænd] *n.* printing sign (&) meaning 'and'.

amphetamine [æm'fetəmiːn] *n.* drug which stimulates.

amphibian [æm'fɪbɪən] *n.* (*a*) animal which lives both in water and on land. (*b*) (military) vehicle that moves in water and on land. **amphibious,** *adj.* which lives/travels in water and on land.

amphitheatre ['æmfɪθɪətə] *n.* (*a*) Greek or Roman circular theatre. (*b*) lecture hall with rows of seats rising in tiers.

amphora ['æmfərə] *n.* Greek or Roman wine jar.

ample ['æmpl] *adj.* (*a*) large. (*b*) enough/sufficient. **amply,** *adv.* in large enough quantity.

amplify ['æmplɪfaɪ] *v.* (*a*) to make (a sound, etc.) louder. (*b*) to develop (sth) in more detail. **amplification** [æmplɪfɪ'keɪʃn] *n.* development; making louder. **amplifier,** *n.* machine which amplifies a sound.

ampoule ['æmpuːl] *n.* small container containing liquid for injections.

amputate ['æmpjʊteɪt] *v.* to cut off (a limb). **amputation** [æmpjʊ'teɪʃn] *n.* cutting off.

amuck = amok

amulet ['æmjʊlet] *n.* lucky charm.

amuse [ə'mjuːz] *v.* to give (s.o.) pleasure; **to a. yourself** = to spend time happily. **amusement,** *n.* pleasure; **a. arcade** = hall with slot machines for playing games, etc. **amusing,** *adj.* which makes you laugh.

an [æn, ən] *see* **a.**

anabolic steroids ['ænə'bɒlɪk 'sterɔɪdz] *n.* chemical substances which make the body create more tissue.

anachronism [ə'nækrənɪzəm] *n.* thing which is out of keeping with the period. **anachronistic** [ənækrə'nɪstɪk] *adj.* which is not in keeping with the period.

anaconda [ænə'kɒndə] *n.* very large snake.

anaemia, *Am.* **anemia** [ə'niːmɪə] *n.* illness caused by lack of red cells in the blood. **anaemic** [ə'niːmɪk] *adj.* looking pale; suffering from anaemia.

anaerobic [æneə'rəʊbɪk] *adj.* not needing oxygen to take place.

anaesthetic, *Am.* **anesthetic** [ænəs-'θetɪk] *n.* substance which makes you lose consciousness; **local a.** = substance which numbs part of the body. **anaesthesia** [ænɪs'θiːzɪə] *n.* loss of consciousness from being given an anaesthetic. **anaesthetist** [ə'niːsθətɪst] *n.* doctor who gives anaesthetics. **anaesthetize** [ə'niːsθətaɪz] *v.* to give (s.o.) an anaesthetic.

anaglypta [ænə'glɪptə] *n.* wallpaper with an embossed pattern.

anagram ['ænəgræm] *n.* word or phrase containing the letters of another word or phrase jumbled up (e.g. *Cathy* and *yacht*).

anal ['eɪnl] *adj.* referring to the anus.

analgesic [ænəl'dʒiːzɪk] *adj. & n.* (drug) which relieves pain. **analgesia,** *n.* absence of pain.

analogous [ə'næləgəs] *adj.* similar/parallel. **analog** ['ænəlɒg] *adj.* (computer) working on a more or less continuous signal. **analogy** [ə'nælədʒɪ] *n.* similarity/parallel.

analyse ['ænəlaɪz] *v.* to examine (sth)

closely to see how it is formed. **analysis** [ə'nælɪsɪs] n. (pl. **analyses** [ə'nælɪsiːz]) close examination. **analyst** ['ænəlɪst] n. (a) person who carries out analyses. (b) psychoanalyst. **analytical** [ænə'lɪtɪkl] adj. which examines closely in detail.

anarchy ['ænəkɪ] n. total lack of order or government. **anarchic** [ə'nɑːkɪk] adj. lacking in order. **anarchist,** n. person who believes in anarchy.

anathema [ə'næθəmə] n. curse; **it's a. to him** = he dislikes it intensely.

anatomy [ə'nætəmɪ] n. structure (esp. of a body). **anatomical** [ænə'tɒmɪkl] adj. relating to the structure of the body.

ancestor ['ænsestə] n. member of your family many generations ago. **ancestral** [æn'sestrəl] adj. **a. home** = home of a family for many generations. **ancestry** ['ænsestrɪ] n. origin (of a family).

anchor ['æŋkə] 1. n. (a) heavy metal hook dropped to the bottom of the sea to hold a ship in one place; **they dropped a. in the bay; the ship was at a.** (b) thing which holds secure/which gives security. 2. v. to drop anchor; hold (a ship) with an anchor. **anchorage,** n. place where ships can anchor safely. **anchorman,** n. main presenter on a TV news show.

anchovy ['æntʃəvɪ, æn'tʃəʊvɪ] n. small fish with a strong taste.

ancient ['eɪnʃənt] adj. very old.

ancillary [æn'sɪlərɪ] adj. secondary; **a. workers** = cleaners/porters, etc., in hospitals.

and [ænd, ənd] conj. showing connection between two things; **try a. sing** = try to sing.

andante [æn'dæntɪ] adv. & adj. (in music) played quite slowly.

andiron ['ændaɪən] n. metal stand to hold logs in a hearth.

android ['ændrɔɪd] adj. shaped like a man.

anecdote ['ænɪkdəʊt] n. short humorous story told by s.o.

anemia [ə'niːmɪə] n. Am. see **anaemia.**

anemometer [æni'mɒmɪtə] n. instrument for measuring wind. **anemograph,** n. instrument which records wind force on paper.

anemone [ə'nemənɪ] n. small flower;

sea a. = animal living in the sea which looks like a flower.

aneroid ['ænərɔɪd] adj. **a. barometer** = barometer which measures atmospheric pressure by the movement of a vacuum box.

anesthetic [ænɪs'θetɪk] n. Am. see **anaesthetic.**

aneurism ['ænjʊrɪzəm] n. swelling of an artery.

anew [ə'njuː] adv. (formal) again.

angel ['eɪndʒl] n. heavenly being with wings; inf. kind person. **angelic** [æn'dʒelɪk] adj. looking innocent/like an angel.

angelica [æn'dʒelɪkə] n. sweet-smelling plant of which the green stalks are preserved in sugar and used in desserts.

angelus ['ændʒeləs] n. service said in Roman Catholic churches, esp. at sunset.

anger ['æŋgə] 1. n. great annoyance. 2. v. to make (s.o.) annoyed.

angina [æn'dʒaɪnə] n. pains in the chest.

angle ['æŋgl] 1. n. (a) corner; **right a.** = angle of 90°; **acute a.** = angle of less than 90°; **obtuse a.** = angle of more than 90°. (b) point of view. 2. v. (a) to kick a ball/to shoot at an angle and not straight. (b) **to a. for a rise** = to try to get an increase in salary by dropping hints. **angler,** n. person who fishes with a rod. **angling,** n. fishing with a rod.

Anglican ['æŋglɪkən] adj. & n. (person) belonging to the Church of England.

anglicism ['æŋglɪsɪzəm] n. way of saying sth which is English or influenced by English.

Anglo- ['æŋgləʊ] prefix meaning English/between England and another country. **anglophile,** n. person who likes England. **anglophobe,** n. person who hates England.

angora [æŋ'gɔːrə] n. & adj. (animal) with thick very soft wool; **a. cat; a. rabbit; a. jumper.**

angostura [æŋgə'stuːrə] n. bitter substance used to flavour drinks.

angry ['æŋgrɪ] adj. (-ier, -iest) very annoyed. **angrily,** adv. in an angry way.

angstrom ['æŋstrɒm] n. unit of measurement of wavelengths.

anguish ['æŋgwɪʃ] n. great suffering. **anguished,** adj. showing great suffering.

angular ['æŋgjʊlə] *adj.* (*of rock*) sharp/ with sharp angles; (*of person*) with prominent bones.

aniline ['ænɪliːn] *n.* liquid produced from coal, used to make paint and plastics.

animal ['ænɪml] *n.* living creature which is not a plant.

animate ['ænɪmeɪt] *v.* (*a*) to make lively. (*b*) to draw on a film a series of cartoon figures, each with slightly different poses, so that when the film is projected the figures appear to move; **animated cartoon**. **animation** [ænɪ'meɪʃn] *n.* (*a*) liveliness/vivacity. (*b*) act of making an animated cartoon.

animosity, animus [ænɪ'mɒsɪtɪ, 'ænɪməs] *n.* unfriendly attitude/hostility (**towards**).

anion [æ'naɪən] *n.* negative ion.

aniseed ['ænɪsiːd] *n.* plant whose seeds are used to flavour sweets and drinks.

ankle ['æŋkl] *n.* part of your body joining the foot to the leg; **a. socks** = short socks which stop just above the ankles; **a.-deep** = up to one's ankles.

annals ['ænlz] *n. pl.* written yearly account of events/discoveries, etc., which have taken place.

anneal [ə'niːl] *v.* to strengthen (sth) by heating and cooling.

annex [ə'neks] *v.* to join (one country to another). **annexation** [ænek'seɪʃn] *n.* joining of one country to another. **annexe** ['æneks] *n.* (*a*) building attached to another building. (*b*) document attached to another document.

annihilate [ə'naɪəleɪt] *v.* to destroy completely. **annihilation** [ənaɪə'leɪʃn] *n.* complete destruction.

anniversary [ænɪ'vɜːsərɪ] *n.* day which falls on the same date as an important event in the past.

annotate ['ænəteɪt] *v.* to make notes on (sth); to add notes to (a book). **annotation**, *n.* adding of (notes); note added.

announce [ə'naʊns] *v.* to tell publicly. **announcement**, *n.* public statement. **announcer**, *n.* person on radio or TV who announces programmes, reads the news, etc.

annoy [ə'nɔɪ] *v.* to make (s.o.) angry. **annoyance**, *n.* state of being annoyed. **annoyed**, *adj.* angry; irritated.

annual ['ænjʊəl] **1.** *adj.* which happens once a year. **2.** *n.* plant that lives for one year only; book which comes out in a new edition each year. **annualized**, *adj.* shown on an annual basis. **annually**, *adv.* every year.

annuity [ə'njuːɪtɪ] *n.* sum of money which is paid annually.

annul [ə'nʌl] *v.* (**annulled**) to end/to cancel. **annulment**, *n.* cancellation.

annular ['ænjuːlə] *adj.* shaped like a ring.

anode ['ænəʊd] *n.* positive electric terminal. **anodize**, *v.* to cover (metal) with a film by using it in electrolysis.

anodyne ['ænədaɪn] *adj. & n.* (medicine) which makes pain less strong; (thing) which stops you worrying.

anoint [ə'nɔɪnt] *v.* to put oil on (a person) as part of a religious ceremony.

anomaly [ə'nɒməlɪ] *n.* thing which is unusual/which does not fit into the normal pattern. **anomalous**, *adj.* abnormal/strange.

anon [ə'nɒn] **1.** *adv.* soon. **2.** = anonymous.

anonymous [ə'nɒnɪməs] *adj.* (person) who does not give his name; **a. letter** = a letter with no signature. **anonymity** [ænə'nɪmɪtɪ] *n.* hiding of your name. **anonymously**, *adv.* without giving your name.

anopheles [æ'nɒfeliːz] *n.* mosquito which transmits malaria.

anorak ['ænəræk] *n.* waterproof jacket with a hood.

anorexia nervosa [ænə'reksɪə nɜː-'vəʊsə] *n.* condition where you refuse to eat because of worry that you may become fat.

another [ə'nʌðə] *adj. & pron.* (*a*) (one) more. (*b*) a different one. (*c*) **one a.** = each other.

answer ['ɑːnsə] **1.** *n.* reply. **2.** *v.* to reply; **to a. back** = reply rudely. **answerable**, *adj.* responsible (**for** something **to** a person). **answering**, *adj.* in answer; **a. service** = recorded message on the telephone which answers automatically for s.o. who is out.

ant [ænt] *n.* small insect living in large communities. **anteater**, *n.* animal which eats ants. **anthill**, *n.* mound of earth containing an ants' nest.

antagonize [æn'tægənaɪz] v. to arouse s.o.'s hostility. **antagonism**, n. hostility/opposition. **antagonist**, n. opponent. **antagonistic** [æntægə'nɪstɪk] adj. hostile.

antarctic [æn'tɑːktɪk] adj. & n. (referring to) the area around the South Pole. **Antarctica**, n. region around the South Pole.

ante ['æntɪ] n. money gambled by a player at the beginning of a game of poker.

ante- ['æntɪ] prefix meaning before.

antecedent [æntɪ'siːdənt] n. earlier form of sth; thing which comes before.

antedate ['æntɪdeɪt] v. to put an earlier date on (a cheque); to happen earlier.

antediluvian [æntɪdɪ'luːvɪən] adj. very ancient.

antelope ['æntɪləʊp] n. type of deer found in Africa.

antenatal [æntɪ'neɪtl] adj. before birth; **a. clinic** = clinic for pregnant women.

antenna [æn'tenə] n. (a) (pl. -ae [æn'teniː]) feeler/sensitive apparatus for sensing. (b) (pl. -as) Am. aerial.

anterior [æn'tɪərɪə] adj. which comes earlier.

anteroom ['æntɪruːm] n. small room leading to a larger room.

anthelmintic [ænθel'mɪntɪk] adj. & n. (substance) to remove worms.

anthem ['ænθəm] n. choral music (for a special occasion); **national a.** = official music of a country, played to honour the state.

anther ['ænθə] n. tip of a stamen which carries pollen.

anthology [æn'θɒlədʒɪ] n. collection of poems/stories, etc., by various people in one book. **anthologize**, v. to put (a poem) into an anthology.

anthracite ['ænθrəsaɪt] n. hard coal which gives off a lot of heat but not much smoke or flame.

anthrax ['ænθræks] n. serious disease of cattle, which can be caught by people.

anthropoid ['ænθrəpɔɪd] adj. & n. (ape) which is like a man.

anthropology [ænθrə'pɒlədʒɪ] n. study of man. **anthropological** [ænθrəpə-'lɒdʒɪkl] adj. referring to the study of man. **anthropologist** [ænθrə-'pɒlədʒɪst] n. scientist who studies man.

anthropomorphic [ænθrəpə'mɔːfɪk] adj. (religion, etc.) which gives gods, animals, etc., the form of human beings.

anti- ['æntɪ] prefix meaning against; **anti-tank gun; anti-malaria tablet; anti-inflationary measures. anti-semitic**, adj. against Jews.

antibiotic [æntɪbaɪ'ɒtɪk] adj. & n. (drug) which kills bacteria.

antibody ['æntɪbɒdɪ] n. chemical substance built up in the body to fight a particular disease.

anticipate [æn'tɪsɪpeɪt] v. (a) to act because you see sth is about to happen. (b) to expect sth to happen. **anticipation** [æntɪsɪ'peɪʃn] n. expectation that sth will happen. **anticipatory**, adj. which anticipates.

anticlimax [æntɪ'klaɪmæks] n. (pl. -es) feeling of being let down when sth exciting does not happen.

anticlockwise [æntɪ'klɒkwaɪz] adj. & adv. in the opposite direction to the hands of a clock.

antics ['æntɪks] n. pl. playing around; fooling.

anticyclone [æntɪ'saɪkləʊn] n. area of high atmospheric pressure.

antidote ['æntɪdəʊt] n. (to) thing which counteracts the effects of a poison.

antifreeze ['æntɪfriːz] n. liquid put in the radiator of a car to prevent its freezing in cold weather.

antigen ['æntɪdʒən] n. substance which produces antibodies.

antihistamine [æntɪ'hɪstəmiːn] n. medicine which prevents allergies.

antimony ['æntɪmənɪ] n. (element: Sb) white metal used to make alloys.

antipathy [æn'tɪpəθɪ] n. (to) feeling of not liking s.o./sth.

antiperspirant [æntɪ'pɜːspɪrənt] n. spray which stops you perspiring.

antiphon ['æntɪfɒn] n. (religious) chant for two sets of singers, each singing in turn. **antiphonal**, adj. (sung) like an antiphon.

antipodes [æn'tɪpədiːz] n. pl. opposite side of the earth, esp. Australia and New Zealand. **antipodean** [æntɪpə-'diːən] adj. from the antipodes.

antipyretic [æntɪpaɪə'retɪk] adj. & n. (substance) which reduces fever.

antiquary ['ænti'kwəri] *n.* person who collects, studies, or sells antiques. **antiquarian** [ænti'kweəriən] *adj.* a. **bookseller** = bookseller who sells old books.

antiquated ['æntikweitid] *adj.* old (and decrepit).

antique [æn'ti:k] **1.** *adj.* very old (and valuable). **2.** *n.* old and valuable object; **a. shop** = shop which sells old objects.

antiquity [æn'tikwiti] *n.* ancient times.

antirrhinum [ænti'rainəm] *n.* summer flower, the snapdragon.

antiseptic [ænti'septik] *adj. & n.* (substance) which prevents a wound becoming septic.

antisocial [ænti'səuʃl] *adj.* disliking society; bad for society; **a. hours** = hours of work outside the normal period.

antistatic [ænti'stætik] *adj.* which stops the effect of static electricity.

antithesis [æn'tiθəsis] *n.* (*pl.* **-theses**) [-θəsi:z] opposite.

antitoxin [ænti'toksin] *n.* substance which counteracts the effects of a toxin. **antitoxic,** *adj.* which counteracts a toxin.

antivenene [ænti'veni:n] *n.* substance which counteracts snake bites.

antivivisectionist [æntivivi'sekʃənist] *n.* person who is opposed to using live animals for experiments.

antler ['æntlə] *n.* horn (on deer).

antonym ['æntənim] *n.* word which means the opposite of another word.

anus ['einəs] *n.* (*pl.* **-es**) hole through which animals produce waste matter from the bowels.

anvil ['ænvil] *n.* (*a*) block on which a blacksmith beats hot metal. (*b*) one of the ossicles in the ear.

anxiety [æŋ'zaiəti] *n.* (*a*) great worry (about). (*b*) eagerness (to). **anxious** ['æŋkʃəs] *adj.* (*a*) very worried. (*b*) eager (to). **anxiously,** *adv.* worriedly.

any ['eni] **1.** *adj. & pron.* (*a*) it does not matter which. (*b*) some; **have you a. sugar? I haven't got a.; he hasn't a. money. 2.** *adv.* **I can't go a. further =** I can go no further.

anybody ['enibodi] *pron.* (*a*) it does not matter who. (*b*) some person; **hardly a.** = very few.

anyhow ['enihau] **1.** *adv.* carelessly. **2.** *conj.* = **anyway.**

anyone ['eniwʌn] *pron.* = **anybody.**

anything ['eniθiŋ] *pron.* (*a*) it does not matter what; **hardly a.** = almost nothing. (*c*) **like a.** = very strongly; **raining like a.** = pouring down.

anyway ['eniwei] *adv. & conj.* in any case.

anywhere ['eniweə] *prep.* (*a*) it does not matter where. (*b*) somewhere; **can you see it a.?**

AOB [eiəu'bi:] = any other business.

aorta [ei'ɔ:tə] *n.* main artery taking blood from the heart.

apace [ə'peis] *adv.* (*formal*) fast.

apart [ə'pɑ:t] *adv.* (*a*) separated. (*b*) separate; **the watch came a.** = fell to pieces; **can you tell them a.?** = can you say which is which? (*c*) **a. from** = except.

apartheid [ə'pɑ:tait] *n.* policy in South Africa of segregating the black people from the white.

apartment [ə'pɑ:tmənt] *n.* (*a*) set of rooms in a large building, as a separate living unit. (*b*) *Am.* flat; **a. block** = block of flats.

apathy ['æpəθi] *n.* lack of interest. **apathetic** [æpə'θetik] *adj.* uninterested.

ape [eip] **1.** *n.* large man-like monkey with no tail. **2.** *v.* to imitate (s.o.).

aperient [ə'piəriənt] *adj. & n.* substance which makes the bowels work.

aperitif [ə'periti:f] *n.* drink taken before a meal to give you an appetite.

aperture ['æpətʃə] *n.* hole; opening.

apex ['eipeks] *n.* (*pl.* **-es**) top (of a triangle).

aphasia [ə'feizjə] *n.* being unable to speak, caused by brain damage.

aphid, aphis ['eifid, 'eifis, 'æfis] *n.* (*pl.* **aphides**) small insect which sucks the sap from plants.

aphorism ['æfərizəm] *n.* short wise saying.

aphrodisiac [æfrə'diziæk] *n. & adj.* (substance) which increases sexual desire.

apiary ['eipiəri] *n.* place where bees are kept. **apiarist,** *n.* (*formal*) beekeeper.

apiculture ['æpikʌltʃə] *n.* keeping of bees (for honey).

apiece [ə'pi:s] *adv.* each.

aplomb [ə'plom] *n.* calmness/self-confidence.

apocalyptic [əpɒkə'lɪptɪk] *adj.* which prophesies doom. **Apocalypse,** *n.* last book of the New Testament, prophesying doom.

apocryphal [ə'pɒkrɪfl] *adj.* probably untrue. **Apocrypha,** *npl.* collection of texts of the Old Testament which are not accepted as genuine.

apogee ['æpədʒiː] *n.* highest point (in the orbit of a planet/in the career of a statesman, etc.).

apologetic [əpɒlə'dʒetɪk] *adj.* making excuses; saying you are sorry. **apologetically,** *adv.* in an apologetic way. **apologist,** *n.* person who writes or speaks on behalf of a cause. **apologize** [ə'pɒlədʒaɪz] *v.* to say you are sorry. **apology,** *n.* saying you are sorry; **my apologies for being late** = I'm sorry I'm late.

apoplexy ['æpəpleksɪ] *n.* sudden inability to move caused by a stroke. **apoplectic** [æpə'plektɪk] *adj.* (*a*) referring to apoplexy. (*b*) red-faced.

apostasy [æ'pɒstəsɪ] *n.* abandoning a religious belief.

apostle [ə'pɒsl] *n.* one of the twelve men who were the original disciples of Jesus; **a. spoon** = small spoon with the figure of an apostle on the end of the handle. **apostate** [ə'pɒsteɪt] *n.* person who has given up his beliefs. **apostolic** [æpəs-'tɒlɪk] *adj.* of the apostles.

a posteriori [eɪpɒsteri'ɔːrɪ] *adj.* based on observed facts.

apostrophe [ə'pɒstrəfɪ] *n.* printing sign (') which shows either that a letter has been left out (**weren't**) or with s to show possession (**a boy's coat, the girls' team**).

apotheosis [əpɒθɪ'əʊsɪs] *n.* making s.o. into a god.

appal [ə'pɔːl] *v.* to frighten/to make horrified. **appalling,** *adj.* horrible/frightening. **appallingly,** *adv.* frighteningly.

apparatus [æpə'reɪtəs] *n.* (*no pl.*) equipment (for doing scientific tests, etc.

apparel [ə'pærəl] *n.* (*formal*) clothes.

apparent [ə'pærənt] *adj.* which seems. **apparently,** *adv.* as it seems.

apparition [æpə'rɪʃn] *n.* ghost; thing which seems strange.

appeal [ə'piːl] **1.** *n.* (*a*) asking for (help, etc.). (*b*) request to the law courts to reconsider a verdict. (*c*) attraction; **sex a.** = physical attraction. **2.** *v.* (*a*) to ask **for.** (*b*) **to a. to** = (i) to ask (s.o.) to judge; (ii) to attract. **appealing,** *adj.* attractive; as if asking for help. **appellant,** *n.* person who appeals.

appear [ə'pɪə] *v.* (*a*) to come into sight. (*b*) to be present (**at**). (*c*) to act (**in** a play). (*d*) to seem. **appearance,** *n.* (*a*) how a thing or person looks. (*b*) being present; **to put in an a.** = to be present.

appease [ə'piːz] *v.* to try to avoid/to soothe. **appeasement,** *n.* policy of avoiding conflict.

appellation [æpə'leɪʃn] *n.* (*formal*) name.

append [ə'pend] *v.* to attach/to join. **appendage,** *n.* thing attached.

appendix [ə'pendɪks] *n.* (*a*) (*pl.* **appendixes**) small tube attached to main intestine. (*b*) (*pl.* **appendices** [ə'pendɪsiːz]) section at the back of a book giving information which is additional to the text. **appendectomy** [æpen'dektəmɪ] *n.* operation to remove an appendix. **appendicitis** [əpendɪ-'saɪtɪs] *n.* illness caused by inflammation of the appendix.

appertain [æpə'teɪn] *v.* (*formal*) to be relevant.

appetite ['æpɪtaɪt] *n.* desire to eat, etc. **appetizer,** *n.* snack taken with drinks before the main meal. **appetizing,** *adj.* which makes you want to eat.

applaud [ə'plɔːd] *v.* to clap or cheer to show you appreciate sth. **applause,** *n.* clapping and cheering.

apple ['æpl] *n.* common hard fruit, growing on a tree; tree which bears this fruit.

appliance [ə'plaɪəns] *n.* (*a*) machine/device. (*b*) fire engine.

appliqué [ə'pliːkeɪ] *n.* decoration made by sewing shaped pieces of cloth on to a larger piece.

apply [ə'plaɪ] *v.* (*a*) to put (sth) on sth. (*b*) to be relevant. (*c*) to ask s.o. **for** sth (esp. a job). (*d*) **to a. yourself** = to work hard. **applicable** [ə'plɪkəbl] *adj.* which refers to. **applicant** ['æplɪkənt] *n.* person who applies for a job; candidate. **application** [æplɪ'keɪʃn] *n.* (*a*) action of putting something on something; **for external a. only** = only to be used on the skin. (b) asking for (a job, etc.); **a. form** = form to be filled in when applying. **applied,** adj. (science) which is put to practical use.

appoint [əˈpɔɪnt] v. to give (s.o.) a job (as). **appointed,** adj. (a) arranged/stated. (b) equipped/furnished. **appointment,** n. (a) being given a job. (b) meeting time which has been agreed. (c) **appointments** = furniture and equipment.

apportion [əˈpɔːʃn] v. (formal) to divide up/to share out.

apposite [ˈæpəzɪt] adj. fitting/appropriate (remark). **apposition,** n. putting a word next to another; **noun in a.** = noun used as an adjective to describe another noun.

appraise [əˈpreɪz] v. to judge the value of (sth). **appraisal,** n. evaluation.

appreciate [əˈpriːʃɪeɪt] v. (a) to feel the value of (sth). (b) to increase in value. **appreciable,** adj. which can be felt. **appreciably,** adv. in a way which could be felt. **appreciation** [əpriːʃɪˈeɪʃn] n. (a) estimation (of the value of sth). (b) increase in value. **appreciative** [əˈpriːʃjətɪv] adj. praising.

apprehend [æprɪˈhend] v. to arrest (a criminal). **apprehension** [æprɪˈhenʃn] n. fear. **apprehensive,** adj. afraid/nervous. **apprehensively,** adv. nervously.

apprentice [əˈprentɪs] n. youth who works with a skilled man to learn from him. **apprenticeship,** n. time you spend as an apprentice.

apprise [əˈpraɪz] v. (formal) to inform (s.o. of sth).

appro [ˈæprəʊ] n. inf. **on a.** = on approval.

approach [əˈprəʊtʃ] 1. n. (pl. -es) (a) way of dealing (with a problem). (b) **he made approaches to her to join his firm** = he contacted her to ask her to join his firm. (c) way into; **a. road** = road leading to a main road. 2. v. (a) to go near. (b) to deal with (a question). **approachable,** adj. easy to talk to. **approaching,** adj. which is coming closer.

approbation [æprəˈbeɪʃn] n. (formal) approval.

appropriate 1. adj. [əˈprəʊprɪət] suitable/which fits. 2. v. [əˈprəʊprɪeɪt] to seize (sth which belongs to s.o. else). **appropriation** [əprəʊprɪˈeɪʃn] n. (a) seizure. (b) money voted to a budget.

approve [əˈpruːv] v. to express agreement with (sth); to allow; **to a. of sth** = to be in agreement with sth. **approval,** n. allowing (sth); **on a.** = on trial. **approving,** adj. which shows agreement. **approvingly,** adv. showing agreement.

approximate 1. adj. [əˈprɒksɪmət] rough (calculation). 2. v. [əˈprɒksɪmeɪt] to be nearly correct. **approximately,** adv. roughly. **approximation** [əprɒksɪˈmeɪʃn] n. rough estimate.

appurtenance [əˈpɜːtənəns] n. (formal) thing which is connected to or belongs to sth else.

APR = Annual(ized) Percentage Rate.

après-ski [æpreɪˈskiː] n. (parties) which take place in the evening after a day's skiing.

apricot [ˈeɪprɪkɒt] n. yellow fruit with large stone grown in warm countries; tree which bears apricots.

April [ˈeɪprəl] n. 4th month of the year. **April Fool,** n. person who is tricked on April 1st. **April Fool's Day,** n. April 1st/day when people are tricked.

a priori [eɪpraɪˈɔːrɪ] adj. based on theory or assumptions.

apron [ˈeɪprən] n. (a) piece of cloth, worn over clothes to protect them when working. (b) area in an airport where aircraft are parked.

apropos [æprəˈpəʊ] adv. referring to.

apse [æps] n. rounded end of a church.

apt [æpt] adj. (a) expression which fits well. (b) likely (to). **aptitude,** n. ability; **a. test** = test to see if you are fitted for a job. **aptly,** adv. fittingly. **aptness,** n. fitness (of an expression).

aqualung [ˈækwəlʌŋ] n. skindiver's portable oxygen apparatus.

aquamarine [ækwəməˈriːn] 1. adj. dark blue-green. 2. n. semi-precious blue stone.

aquaplane [ˈækwəpleɪn] v. (of car) to slide along the wet surface of a road.

aquarium [əˈkweərɪəm] n. (a) tank for keeping fish. (b) exhibition where fish are displayed.

Aquarius [ə'kweərɪəs] *n.* one of the signs of the Zodiac, shaped like a man carrying water.

aquatic [æ'kwætɪk] *adj.* which lives in water; **a. plants.**

aquatint ['ækwətɪnt] *n.* print which has been shaded to look like a drawing.

aqueduct ['ækwɪdʌkt] *n.* channel which takes water over land.

aqueous ['ækwɪəs] *adj.* containing water.

aquifer ['ækwɪfə] *n.* layer of porous rock in which water gathers.

aquiline ['ækwɪlaɪn] *adj.* hooked (nose).

Ar *symbol for* argon.

Arab ['ærəb] **1.** *adj.* referring to Arabia. **2.** *n.* Muslim person living in Arabia or some other Near Eastern countries. **Arabian** [ə'reɪbɪən] *adj.* referring to Arabia. **Arabic** ['ærəbɪk] **1.** *n.* language spoken by Arabs. **2.** *adj.* **arabic numerals** = signs for numbers written 1, 2, 3, 4, etc. **arabis,** *n.* small garden plant, with little white flowers.

arabesque [ærə'besk] *n.* complicated design of leaves/flowers.

arable ['ærəbl] *adj. & n.* (land) which is good for growing crops.

arachnid [ə'ræknɪd] *n.* type of animal with eight legs, such as a spider.

arbitrage ['ɑːbɪtreɪdʒ] *n.* buying shares in a company which is likely to be taken over, so as to sell them later at a profit. **arbitrageur,** *n.* person whose business is arbitrage.

arbitrate ['ɑːbɪtreɪt] *v.* to judge between two parties in a quarrel. **arbiter,** *n.* person who decides (usu. on questions of fashion). **arbitrarily,** *adv.* at random. **arbitrary,** *adj.* (decision) taken at random. **arbitration** [ɑːbɪ'treɪʃn] *n.* judgement in a dispute. **arbitrator** ['ɑːbɪtreɪtə] *n.* person who judges a dispute.

arboreal [ɑː'bɔːrɪəl] *adj.* living in trees.

arboretum [ɑːbə'riːtəm] *n.* collection of trees grown for study.

arbour ['ɑːbə] *n.* shady place where trees are trained to form a shelter.

arc [ɑːk] *n.* (*a*) part of a circle. (*b*) electric spark jumping between two points. **arc-lamp, arc-light,** *n.* very bright light. **arc-welding,** *n.* welding by an electric arc.

arcade [ɑː'keɪd] *n.* covered area with an arched roof; **shopping a.** = row of shops covered by a roof.

arcane [ɑː'keɪn] *adj.* mysterious/secret.

arch [ɑːtʃ] **1.** *n.* (*pl.* **-es**) (*a*) vault/rounded structure forming a roof, or top of a door. (*b*) **triumphal a.** = large construction with a rounded vault over a carriageway, usu. built to celebrate a victory. (*c*) rounded part under the foot. **2.** *v.* to make (sth) round. **3.** *adj.* wicked and playful. **arched,** *adj.* made with an arch. **archway,** *n.* passage/entrance with an arch.

arch- [ɑːtʃ] *prefix meaning* greatest; **arch-enemy.**

archaeology [ɑːkɪ'ɒlədʒɪ] *n.* study of ancient civilization; **industrial a.** = study of old machinery/factories/mines, etc. **archaeological** [ɑːkɪə'lɒdʒɪkl] *adj.* referring to archaeology. **archaeologist** [ɑːkɪ'ɒlədʒɪst] *n.* person who studies archaeology.

archaic [ɑː'keɪɪk] *adj.* very ancient.

archangel ['ɑːkeɪndʒl] *n.* highest rank of angel.

archbishop [ɑːtʃ'bɪʃəp] *n.* very important bishop/leader of bishops.

archer ['ɑːtʃə] *n.* person who shoots with a bow and arrow. **archery,** *n.* sport of shooting arrows at a target.

archetype ['ɑːkɪtaɪp] *n.* original version from which other versions can be copied. **archetypal,** *adj.* original; perfect (example).

archipelago [ɑːkɪ'peləgəʊ] *n.* (*pl.* **-os**) group of islands.

architect ['ɑːkɪtekt] *n.* person who designs buildings. **architecture,** *n.* design of buildings. **architectural,** *adj.* referring to architecture.

architrave ['ɑːkɪtreɪv] *n.* moulding around a door or window.

archives ['ɑːkaɪvz] *n. pl.* collection of documents, esp. public or historical records. **archivist** ['ɑːkɪvɪst] *n.* librarian who looks after archives.

arctic ['ɑːktɪk] *adj. & n.* (referring to) the area around the North Pole; extremely cold (weather).

ardent ['ɑːdənt] *adj.* very strenuous; keen. **ardently,** *adv.* strenuously/fiercely.

ardour, *Am.* **ardor** ['ɑːdə] *n.* violence (of emotions).

arduous ['ɑːdjʊəs] *adj.* very difficult/ hard (task). **arduously,** *adv.* with great difficulty.

are [ɑː] *v. see* **be.**

area ['eərɪə] *n.* (*a*) space; measure of the surface of sth. (*b*) region; **the sterling a.** = the countries where the £ sterling is the main exchange currency. (*c*) general subject.

areca [ə'riːkə] *n.* type of tropical nut.

arena [ə'riːnə] *n.* space where sports and fights take place.

Argentine, **Argentinian** ['ɑːdʒəntaɪn, ɑːdʒən'tɪnjən] **1.** *adj.* referring to Argentina. **2.** *n.* person from Argentina.

argon ['ɑːgɒn] *n.* (*element:* Ar) inert gas.

argue ['ɑːgjuː] *v.* to discuss without agreeing; to quarrel. **arguable,** *adj.* which is open to discussion. **argument,** *n.* (*a*) quarrel/discussion without agreement. (*b*) reasoning. **argumentative** [ɑːgjʊ'mentətɪv] *adj.* (person) who likes to quarrel.

aria ['ɑːrɪə] *n.* long solo song in opera.

arid ['ærɪd] *adj.* very dry. **aridity** [ə'rɪdɪtɪ] *n.* extreme dryness.

Aries ['eəriːz] *n.* one of the signs of the Zodiac, shaped like a ram.

arise [ə'raɪz] *v.* (**arose; arisen**) (*a*) to appear; to start. (*b*) to result **from.**

aristocrat ['ærɪstəkræt] *n.* person who is born into the aristocracy. **aristocracy** [ærɪ'stɒkrəsɪ] *n.* top rank (by birth) of society. **aristocratic** [ærɪstə'krætɪk] *adj.* referring to the aristocracy; superior (attitude).

arithmetic [ə'rɪθmetɪk] *n.* calculations with figures. **arithmetical** [ærɪθ'metɪkl] *adj.* referring to arithmetic.

arm [ɑːm] **1.** *n.* (*a*) part of the body between hand and shoulder; **a. in a.** = with their arms linked. (*b*) thing shaped like an arm; piece at the side of a chair to rest your arms on. (*c*) narrow stretch of sea running inland. (*d*) **arms** = weapons; **up in arms about** = very angry/furious. **2.** *v.* to equip with weapons. **armaments,** *n. pl.* heavy weapons/war equipment. **armband,** *n.* piece of cloth worn round your arm. **armchair,** *n.* chair with arms. **armed,** *adj.* equipped with weapons;

the a. forces = the army, navy and air force. **armful,** *n.* load carried in your arms. **armhole,** *n.* hole in a piece of clothing through which you put your arms. **armour,** *Am.* **armor,** *n.* (*a*) metal protective clothes for medieval soldiers. (*b*) thick protecting material covering ships or tanks. **armoured,** *adj.* protected by metal; **a. car** = military car made of thick metal which carries a small gun. **armour-plated,** *adj.* protected by thick metal plates. **armoury,** *n.* place where weapons are kept; all arms (belonging to a country). **armpit,** *n.* part of your body under where your arm joins the shoulder. **armrest,** *n.* thing which you rest your arm on. **army,** *n.* all the soldiers of a country.

armada [ɑː'mɑːdə] *n.* fleet of warships.

armadillo [ɑːmə'dɪləʊ] *n.* small South American animal covered with a flexible shell.

armageddon [ɑːmə'gedən] *n.* great final battle.

armature ['ɑːmətjə] *n.* moving part of an electric motor; coil in a dynamo.

armistice ['ɑːmɪstɪs] *n.* decision to stop fighting temporarily.

aroma [ə'rəʊmə] *n.* (pleasant) smell (of coffee/wine, etc.). **aromatic** [ærə'mætɪk] *adj.* (herb) with a strong pleasant smell.

arose [ə'rəʊz] *v. see* **arise.**

around [ə'raʊnd] **1.** *adv.* (*a*) surrounding a place. (*b*) in an indefinite place. **2.** *prep.* (*a*) surrounding. (*b*) approximately.

arouse [ə'raʊz] *v.* (*a*) to wake. (*b*) to excite (emotion).

arpeggio [ɑː'pedʒɪəʊ] *n.* (*pl.* -os) chord with the notes played one after the other and not all together.

arrange [ə'reɪndʒ] *v.* (*a*) to put in order. (*b*) to adapt (a piece of music). (*c*) to organize. **arrangement,** *n.* (*a*) way in which something is laid out. (*b*) organizing. (*c*) agreement.

arrant ['ærənt] *adj.* (old) complete.

array [ə'reɪ] **1.** *n.* display. **2.** *v.* (*a*) to set out in order. (*b*) (*formal*) to dress (in fine costume).

arrears [ə'rɪəz] *n.* **to be in a.** = to be late (in doing sth).

arrest [əˈrest] **1.** *n.* being held (by the police) on a charge; **he's under a.; cardiac a.** = stoppage of the heart. **2.** *v.* to hold (s.o.) for breaking the law. **arresting,** *adj.* which attracts the attention.

arris [ˈærɪs] *n.* **a. rail** = horizontal triangular plank which holds the upright planks of a fence.

arrive [əˈraɪv] *v.* to reach a place; (*of baby*) to be born. **arrival,** *n.* (*a*) reaching a place. (*b*) person who has arrived.

arrogant [ˈærəgənt] *adj.* very proud. **arrogance,** *n.* being very proud; thinking that you are superior. **arrogantly,** *adv.* proudly.

arrow [ˈærəʊ] *n.* (*a*) long stick with a sharp point which is shot by a bow. (*b*) sign showing the way to a place. **arrowroot,** *n.* flour made from the root of an American plant.

arse [ɑːs] *n.* (*vulgar*) buttocks.

arsenal [ˈɑːsənl] *n.* store of weapons.

arsenic [ˈɑːsnɪk] *n.* (*element:* As) powerful poison.

arson [ˈɑːsn] *n.* criminal act of setting fire to a property. **arsonist,** *n.* person who sets fire to property.

art [ɑːt] *n.* painting, drawing, sculpture and music; **a. gallery** = museum of paintings, sculptures, etc.; **arts subjects** = subjects (such as languages, history, etc.) which are not sciences. **artful,** *adj.* clever; up to the latest tricks. **artfully,** *adv.* cleverly. **artless,** *adj.* natural/not forced; naive.

artefact [ˈɑːtɪfækt] *n.* object (usu. a tool) made by man.

arteriosclerosis [ɑːtɪərɪəʊskləˈrəʊsɪs] *n.* hardening of the arteries (esp. in old age).

artery [ˈɑːtərɪ] *n.* (*a*) tube that blood flows through from the heart to other parts of the body. (*b*) important road. **arterial** [ɑːˈtɪərɪəl] *adj.* referring to an artery.

artesian [ɑːˈtiːʒn] *adj.* **a. well** = well drilled in the ground which does not require a pump to make the water rise.

arthritis [ɑːˈθraɪtɪs] *n.* illness where joints become swollen and stiff. **arthritic** [ɑːˈθrɪtɪk] *adj.* stiff from arthritis.

arthrodesis [ɑːθrəʊˈdiːsɪs] *n.* operation to fix a hip joint so that it does not move. **arthroplasty** [ˈɑːθrəʊplæstɪ] *n.* operation to replace a hip joint with an artificial one. **arthropod,** *n.* animal with a body formed of joined sections, such as a spider.

artichoke [ˈɑːtɪtʃəʊk] *n.* (*a*) **(globe) a.** = green vegetable like the flower of a thistle. (*b*) **(Jerusalem) a.** = root vegetable like a bumpy potato.

article [ˈɑːtɪkl] *n.* (*a*) clause (in agreement). (*b*) piece of writing in a newspaper, etc. (*c*) thing/object. (*d*) part of speech; **'the' is a definite a.; 'a' is an indefinite a.**

articulate 1. *v.* [ɑːˈtɪkjʊleɪt] (*a*) to speak (a word). (*b*) to join; **articulated lorry** = lorry with a trailer. **2.** *adj.* [ɑːˈtɪkjʊlət] clear-speaking. **articulation** [ɑːtɪkjʊˈleɪʃn] *n.* joint.

artifice [ˈɑːtɪfɪs] *n.* trick. **artificer,** *n.* skilled craftsman (esp. on a ship). **artificial** [ɑːtɪˈfɪʃl] *adj.* which is an imitation/not the real thing; **a. respiration** = reviving s.o. who is nearly dead. **artificiality,** *n.* falseness/not being sincere. **artificially,** *adv.* unnaturally.

artillery [ɑːˈtɪlərɪ] *n.* section of the army concerned with guns; **the a.** = the guns. **artilleryman,** *n.* (*pl.* **-men**) soldier working on guns.

artisan [ɑːtɪˈzæn] *n.* skilled workman/craftsman.

artist [ˈɑːtɪst] *n.* person who draws, paints, or plays music. **artistic** [ɑːˈtɪstɪk] *adj.* (person) who has a feeling or skill for art; (thing) which looks good because it is made by an artistic person. **artistically,** *adv.* with art. **artistry** [ˈɑːtɪstrɪ] *n.* skill in art.

artiste [ɑːˈtiːst] *n.* performer in a theatre (esp. dancer/acrobat).

arty [ˈɑːtɪ] *adj. inf.* pretending to be artistic.

arum [ˈeərəm] *n.* lily with a tall white flower.

as [æz, əz] *conj.* (*a*) like. (*b*) because. (*c*) at the same time that. (*d*) doing the job of; acting the part of. (*e*) in a certain way. (*f*) **as for** = referring to/concerning. (*g*) **as from** = starting from. (*h*) **if/as though** = like/seeming. (*i*) **as long as** = on condition that. (*j*) **as soon as** =

immediately. (*k*) **as to** = referring to. (*l*) **as well as** = in addition to.

As *symbol for* arsenic.

asap [eɪeseɪ'piː] = as soon as possible.

asbestos [æs'bestəs] *n.* mineral substance which is fireproof. **asbestosis** [æsbesˈtəʊsɪs] *n.* lung disease caused by breathing in particles of asbestos.

ascend [ə'send] *v.* (*formal*) to go up. **ascendancy,** *n.* influence. **ascendant,** *n.* rising; **in the a.** = becoming powerful/popular. **ascension** [ə'senʃn], **ascent** [ə'sent] *n.* going up.

ascertain [æsə'teɪn] *v.* (*formal*) to check/to find out (the facts). **ascertainable,** *adj.* which can be checked.

ascetic [ə'setɪk] **1.** *adj.* (way of life) where you do not allow yourself any comfort or pleasure. **2.** *n.* religious person who does not allow himself any pleasures. **asceticism,** *n.* belief in an ascetic way of life.

ASCII [ˈæski] American Standard Code for Information Interchange.

ascorbic [æ'skɔːbɪk] *adj.* **a. acid** = vitamin C occurring in oranges, vegetables, etc.

ascot [ˈæskət] *n. Am.* cravat.

ascribe [æ'skraɪb] *v.* (*formal*) to attribute (sth to s.o.). **ascribable,** *adj.* which can be ascribed.

aseptic [ə'septɪk] *adj.* sterilized/with no infection.

asexual [eɪseksjuəl] *adj.* not involving sex.

ash [æʃ] *n.* (*pl.* **ashes**) (*a*) common tree in northern countries; wood of this tree. (*b*) dust left after something has burnt. (*c*) **ashes** = remains of a person's body after cremation. (*d*) **the Ashes** = cricket trophy, played for by teams from England and Australia. **ashcan,** *n. Am.* container for putting rubbish in. **ashen** [ˈæʃən] *adj.* very pale. **ashpan,** *n.* (*in a stove*) box for collecting ash. **ashtray,** *n.* ∗small bowl for putting ash from cigarettes, etc.

ashamed [ə'ʃeɪmd] *adj.* sorry because of sth wrong.

ashlar [ˈæʃlə] *n.* (*no pl.*) building stones cut square.

ashore [ə'ʃɔː] *adv.* on land.

Asian [ˈeɪʒn] *adj. & n.* (person) from Asia. **Asiatic** [eɪsɪ'ætɪk] *adj.* referring to Asia.

aside [ə'saɪd] **1.** *adv.* to one side; *Am.* **a. from** = apart from. **2.** *n.* words spoken in a play which the other characters are not supposed to hear.

asinine [ˈæsɪnaɪn] *adj.* stupid.

ask [ɑːsk] *v.* (*a*) to put a question (**about**); **to a. after s.o.** = to inquire about s.o.'s health. (*b*) **to a. for** = to request/to want (sth) to be given to you. (*c*) to invite (s.o. **to** a party, etc.). **asking,** *n.* **it's yours for the a.** = you only have to ask for it and you will get it.

askance [ə'skɑːns] *adv.* **to look at sth/ s.o. a.** = to be suspicious of.

askew [ə'skjuː] *adv.* not straight.

aslant [ə'slɑːnt] *adv.* sloping.

asleep [ə'sliːp] *adj.* sleeping.

asp [æsp] *n.* small poisonous snake.

asparagus [ə'spærəgəs] *n.* cultivated plant of which you eat the new shoots as a vegetable.

aspect [ˈæspekt] *n.* (*a*) direction which a house faces. (*b*) side; way of looking at sth.

aspen [ˈæspən] *n.* small tree with leaves which tremble in the wind.

asperity [æ'sperɪtɪ] *n.* sharpness.

aspersions [ə'spɜːʃnz] *n. pl.* bad comments (**on** s.o.).

asphalt [ˈæsfælt] **1.** *n.* mixture of tar and sand which is used for surfacing roads. **2.** *v.* to cover with asphalt.

asphyxiate [əs'fɪksɪeɪt] *v.* to stifle/to kill (s.o.) by preventing them from breathing. **asphyxia, asphyxiation** [əsfɪksɪ'eɪʃn] *n.* being unable to breathe.

aspic [ˈæspɪk] *n.* meat jelly.

aspidistra [æspɪ'dɪstrə] *n.* type of indoor plant.

aspirate [ˈæspɪrət] *adj. & n.* (sound) which has to be breathed (as 'h' in 'horse').

aspire [ə'spaɪə] *v.* (**to**) to have the ambition to do sth. **aspirant** [ˈæspərənt] *n.* person who aspires to do sth. **aspiration** [æspɪ'reɪʃn] *n.* ambition. **aspiring,** *adj.* ambitious/hopeful.

aspirin [ˈæsprɪn] *n.* (tablet of) common drug taken to stop headaches/colds, etc.

ass [æs] *n.* (*pl.* **-es**) (*a*) donkey. (*b*) stupid person. (*c*) *Am. Sl.* buttocks.

assailant [ə'seɪlənt] *n.* person who attacks (s.o.).

assassinate [ə'sæsɪneɪt] v. to kill (s.o.) for political reasons. **assassin,** n. person who kills for political reasons. **assassination** [əsæsɪ'neɪʃn] n. political murder.

assault [ə'sɔːlt] **1.** n. attack; **a. course** = ground where soldiers practise attacks. **2.** v. to attack.

assay [ə'seɪ] **1.** n. test to see how pure metal is. **2.** v. to test (metal) to see how pure it is.

assegai ['æsəgaɪ] n. native spear from Southern Africa.

assemble [ə'sembl] v. to get together; to put together. **assembly,** n. (a) meeting. (b) putting together; **a. line** = continuous moving line in a factory, where machines, etc., are put together.

assent [ə'sent] **1.** n. agreement; **Royal A.** = formality by which a Bill approved by Parliament becomes an Act. **2.** v. to agree (**to**).

assert [ə'sɜːt] v. to state firmly; **to a. yourself** = take a firm position. **assertion** [ə'sɜːʃn] n. statement (of rights). **assertive,** adj. forceful.

assess [ə'ses] v. (a) to calculate the amount of damages/of tax which should be paid. (b) to value. (c) to estimate. **assessment,** n. (a) calculation of damages/of tax. (b) calculation of value. (c) estimate. **assessor,** n. person who assesses.

asset ['æset] n. (a) valuable thing which belongs to you. (b) pl. **assets** = anything owned which can be sold to pay debts. **asset-stripper,** n. person who buys a company and sells its assets.

assiduous [ə'sɪdjʊəs] adj. regular and very careful. **assiduity** [æsɪ'djuːɪtɪ] n. regularity of work. **assiduously,** adv. regularly and very carefully; without fail.

assign [ə'saɪn] v. (a) to appoint (s.o. **to** do sth). (b) to transfer sth **to** s.o. **assignation** [æsɪg'neɪʃn] n. (a) transfer (of property). (b) lovers' meeting. **assignment,** n. (a) delegation (of a task to s.o.). (b) work which you have been told to do.

assimilate [ə'sɪmɪleɪt] v. to digest (food); to learn and understand (facts). **assimilation** [əsɪmɪ'leɪʃn] n. act of assimilating food or information.

assist [ə'sɪst] v. to help (s.o.). **assistance,** n. help. **assistant. 1.** n. person who helps. **2.** adj. deputy.

assizes [ə'saɪzɪz] n. pl. (old) local courts held in various parts of England and Wales at regular intervals (now the Crown Courts).

associate 1. v. [ə'səʊsɪeɪt] (**with**) to link (with s.o.)/to be linked (to s.o./sth). **2.** n. [ə'səʊsɪət] person who is linked to s.o. **association** [əsəʊsɪ'eɪʃn] n. group/ society; **a. football** = soccer.

assonance ['æsənəns] n. rhyme using vowels only.

assorted [ə'sɔːtɪd] adj. (a) matched. (b) mixed. **assortment,** n. collection/mixture.

assuage [ə'sweɪdʒ] v. (formal) to calm/ to soothe.

assume [ə'sjuːm] v. (a) to take (power, responsibility) upon yourself. (b) to suppose. **assumed,** adj. false. **assumption** [ə'sʌmpʃn] n. (a) taking up (of office). (b) belief that sth is true, even if it has not been proved.

assure [ə'ʃʊə] v. (a) to make safe/certain. (b) to state/to affirm. **assurance,** n. (a) promise. (b) **life a.** = insurance against death. (c) calm; feeling of certainty. **assured** adj. certain. **assuredly** [ə'ʃʊərədlɪ] adv. certainly.

aster ['æstə] n. garden plant with star-shaped flowers.

asterisk ['æstərɪsk] n. sign (*) to indicate some special mention.

astern [ə'stɜːn] adv. behind a ship; (of ship) **to go a.** = to go backwards.

asteroid ['æstərɔɪd] n. very small planet.

asthma ['æsmə] n. wheezing, usu. caused by allergy. **asthmatic** [æs'mætɪk] adj. & n. (person) who suffers from asthma.

astigmatism [ə'stɪgmətɪzəm] n. condition of the eyes where the image focuses correctly at one angle but not at another. **astigmatic** [æstɪg'mætɪk] adj. referring to astigmatism.

astonish [ə'stɒnɪʃ] v. to surprise. **astonishing,** adj. surprising. **astonishingly,** adv. surprisingly. **astonishment,** n. surprise.

astound [ə'staʊnd] v. to surprise completely. **astounding,** adj. very surprising.

astrakhan [æstrə'kæn] *n*. dark fur from the skin of black lambs.

astral ['æstrəl] *adj*. referring to stars.

astray [ə'streɪ] *adv*. lost; **to go a.** = get lost; **to lead a.** = to lead into bad habits.

astride [ə'straɪd] *adv. & prep*. with your legs on either side (of).

astringent [ə'strɪndʒənt] **1.** *adj*. harsh/ severe (comments, etc.). **2.** *n*. medicine/cosmetic for closing pores, etc. **astringency,** *n*. being astringent.

astrology [ə'strɒlədʒɪ] *n*. art of foretelling events from the stars and planets. **astrologer,** *n*. person who gives advice based on reading the position of the stars. **astrological** [æstrə'lɒdʒɪkl] *adj*. referring to astrology.

astronaut ['æstrənɔ:t] *n*. person who travels in a spacecraft.

astronomy [ə'strɒnəmɪ] *n*. science of studying the stars, the sun and the universe. **astronomer,** *n*. person who studies astronomy. **astronomical** [æstrə'nɒmɪkl] *adj*. (*a*) referring to astronomy. (*b*) *inf*. very large. **astronomically,** *adv*. (*a*) using astronomy. (*b*) *inf*. enormously.

astrophysics [æstrəʊ'fɪzɪks] *n*. study of the physics of the universe.

astute [ə'stju:t] *adj*. clever/wise. **astutely,** *adv*. cleverly. **astuteness,** *n*. being astute.

asunder [ə'sʌndə] *adv*. (*old*) apart.

asylum [ə'saɪləm] *n*. (*a*) place of refuge; **political a.** = permission to stay in a country when one is politically undesirable in one's own. (*b*) (*old*) mental hospital.

asymmetry [æ'sɪmətrɪ] *n*. lack of symmetry. **asymmetrical** [æsɪ'metrɪkl] *adj*. not symmetrical.

at [æt, ət] *prep*. (*a*) (*showing time or place*) **at the office; at night.** (*b*) (*showing speed or rate*) **at 100 miles an hour; at 20p a pound.** (*c*) (*showing cause*) **she laughed at my old coat.** (*d*) busy; **at work.** (*e*) **at first** = at the beginning; **at once** = immediately.

ataraxia [ætə'ræksɪə] *n*. excessive calmness.

atavistic [ætə'vɪstɪk] *adj*. reverting to the characteristics of one's ancestors.

ataxia [æ'tæksɪə] *n*. being unable to coordinate the use of muscles.

ate [et] *v. see* eat.

atheism ['eɪθɪɪzəm] *n*. believing there is no god. **atheist,** *n*. person who believes there is no god. **atheistic** [eɪθɪ'ɪstɪk] *adj*. referring to atheism.

athlete ['æθli:t] *n*. person who takes part in sport, in particular, running, jumping, throwing; **athlete's foot** = skin infection on the feet. **athletic** [æθ'letɪk] *adj*. referring to sport. **athletics,** *n*. organized sports where you run, jump or throw.

Atlantic [ət'læntɪk] *n*. **the A. (Ocean)** = ocean separating Europe and Africa from North and South America.

atlas ['ætləs] *n*. (*pl.* -es) book of maps.

atmosphere ['ætməsfɪə] *n*. (*a*) air which surrounds the earth. (*b*) general feeling (at a party, etc.). **atmospheric** [ætməs'ferɪk] *adj*. referring to the atmosphere. **atmospherics,** *n. pl*. electric disturbances which interfere with radio or TV signals.

atoll ['ætɒl] *n*. tropical coral island.

atom ['ætəm] *n*. (*a*) basic particle of matter. (*b*) very small thing. **atomic** [ə'tɒmɪk] *adj*. referring to physical atoms; **a. bomb** = bomb which uses nuclear energy; **a. number** = number of protons in one atom of a chemical element; **a. weight** = ratio of the mass of an atom of an element to the mass of carbon 12. **atomize** ['ætəmaɪz] *v*. to reduce to very fine particles. **atomizer,** *n*. device for atomizing, esp. a spray for scent.

atonal [eɪ'təʊnəl] *adj*. without any tones.

atone [ə'təʊn] *v*. to make amends (**for**). **atonement,** *n*. making amends (**for** a sin).

atrium ['ætrɪəm] *n*. (*a*) central court of a large building, usu. with a glass roof. (*b*) one of the chambers of the heart.

atrocious [ə'trəʊʃəs] *adj*. (*a*) very wicked. (*b*) very bad. **atrociously,** *adv*. very badly. **atrocity** [ə'trɒsɪtɪ] *n*. very wicked deed.

atrophy ['ætrəfɪ] **1.** *n*. wasting away (of a limb). **2.** *v*. to waste away.

attach [ə'tætʃ] *v*. to fasten. **attaché** [ə'tæʃeɪ] *n*. specialized member of the staff on an embassy; **a commercial a. attaché case,** *n*. small case for carrying papers. **attachment,** *n*. (*a*) device which is attached to something else. (*b*) affection.

attack [əˈtæk] **1.** *n.* (*a*) starting to fight. (*b*) sudden start of a disease. **2.** *v.* to start fighting (s.o.). **attacker,** *n.* person who attacks.

attain [əˈteɪn] *v.* to reach (an age, an ambition). **attainable,** *adj.* which can be reached. **attainment,** *n.* (*a*) reaching. (*b*) **attainments** = talents/ intellectual capacities.

attainder [æˈteɪndə] *n.* former method of punishing a state criminal, by passing an Act of Parliament.

attempt [əˈtempt] **1.** *n.* try. **2.** *v.* to try.

attend [əˈtend] *v.* (*a*) **to a. to s.o.** = to look after s.o. (*b*) to be present at. **attendance,** *n.* being present. **attendant,** *n.* person (in a museum) who guards the exhibits; person who is on duty (in a public lavatory, etc.).

attention [əˈtenʃn] *n.* (*a*) careful thought about sth. (*b*) (*of soldiers*) **to stand to a.** = to stand straight with heels together. **attentive** [əˈtentɪv] *adj.* (*a*) paying attention; careful. (*b*) taking care of (s.o.). **attentively,** *adv.* with attention.

attenuate [əˈtenjʊeɪt] *v.* (*formal*) to make thinner/weaker; **attenuating circumstances** = circumstances which reduce the blame attached to a crime. **attenuation,** *n.* becoming weaker.

attest [əˈtest] *v.* (*formal*) (**to**) to say that sth is true.

attic [ˈætɪk] *n.* room under the roof of a house.

attire [əˈtaɪə] *n.* (*no pl.*) (*formal*) clothing. **attired,** *adj.* (**in**) wearing.

attitude [ˈætɪtjuːd] *n.* (*a*) way of standing/sitting, etc. (*b*) way of thinking.

attorney [əˈtɜːnɪ] *n.* (*a*) *esp. Am.* lawyer. (*b*) **power of a.** = power to act on behalf of s.o. else.

attract [əˈtrækt] *v.* to make (sth) come towards you. **attraction** [əˈtrækʃn] *n.* (*a*) pull. (*b*) ability to attract (s.o.)/to make (s.o.) interested. (*c*) thing which attracts people. **attractive,** *adj.* pleasant-looking. **attractively,** *adv.* in an attractive way.

attribute 1. *n.* [ˈætrɪbjuːt] (*a*) quality. (*b*) symbol. **2.** *v.* [əˈtrɪbjuːt] **to a. sth to s.o.** = to say that sth belongs to s.o.

attributable [əˈtrɪbjʊtəbl] *adj.* which can be attributed to s.o.

attrition [əˈtrɪʃn] *n.* wearing down; **war of a.** = war to be won by wearing down your enemy's forces.

attuned to [əˈtjuːnd tʊ] *adj.* aware of (latest fashions, etc.).

Au *symbol for* gold.

aubergine [ˈəʊbəʒiːn] *n.* eggplant.

aubrietia [ɔːˈbriːʃə] *n.* low growing plant with bright purple flowers.

auburn [ˈɔːbən] *adj.* reddish chestnut-coloured (hair).

auction [ˈɔːkʃn] **1.** *n.* sale where the item is sold to the highest bidder. **2.** *v.* to sell (sth) to the highest bidder. **auctioneer** [ɔːkʃəˈnɪə] *n.* person who is in charge of an auction. **auction off,** *v.* to sell (sth) by auction to get rid of it. **auction rooms,** *n. pl.* place where auctions are carried out.

audacious [ɔːˈdeɪʃəs] *adj.* very daring. **audaciously,** *adv.* daringly. **audacity** [ɔːˈdæsɪtɪ] *n.* daring.

audible [ˈɔːdɪbl] *adj.* which can be heard. **audibility** [ɔːdɪˈbɪlɪtɪ] *n.* capacity for being heard. **audibly** [ˈɔːdɪblɪ] *adv.* in an audible way.

audience [ˈɔːdɪəns] *n.* (*a*) people listening to a concert/watching a film or play, etc. (*b*) (*formal*) hearing.

audio-typist [ˈɔːdɪəʊˈtaɪpɪst] *n.* typist who types from a recorded tape.

audio-visual [ɔːdɪəʊˈvɪzjʊəl] *adj.* referring to a method of teaching using tapes, records, films, etc.

audit [ˈɔːdɪt] **1.** *n.* official checking of accounts. **2.** *v.* to check (the accounts of a company). **auditor,** *n.* expert accountant who checks the accounts of a company, etc.

audition [ɔːˈdɪʃn] **1.** *n.* testing of the suitability of actors/dancers, etc., for a job. **2.** *v.* (*a*) to test the suitability of (an actor/dancer, etc., for a job). (*b*) (*of actor*) **to a. for a part** = to go to a test for a part.

auditorium [ɔːdɪˈtɔːrɪəm] *n.* huge hall for meetings/concerts, etc.

au fait [əʊˈfeɪ] *adj.* familiar (**with**).

auf Wiedersehen [aʊfˈviːdəzeɪn] (*German*) goodbye.

auger [ˈɔːgə] *n.* tool for boring holes.

augment [ɔːgˈment] *v.* to increase.

augmentation [ɔːgmen'teɪʃn] *n.* increase.

augur ['ɔːgə] *v.* to be a sign for the future.

august [ɔː'gʌst] *adj.* solemn and dignified.

August ['ɔːgəst] *n.* 8th month of the year.

auk [ɔːk] *n.* large black and white sea bird.

aunt [aːnt] *n.* sister of your mother or father; wife of an uncle. **auntie, aunty,** *n.* familiar name for an aunt.

au pair [əʊ'peə] *adj. & n. (pl.* **au pairs**) **she is going to France as an au pair (girl)** = she is going to live with a French family to do light housework (and learn French).

aura ['ɔːrə] *n.* general feeling surrounding a person/a place.

aural ['ɔːrəl] *adj.* using the ear. **aurally,** *adv.* by listening.

au revoir [əʊrə'vwaːr] *(French)* goodbye.

auricle ['ɔrɪkl] *n. (a)* outside part of the ear. *(b)* space in the heart which fills with blood and then pumps it into the ventricles.

aurora [ə'rɔːrə] *n.* **a. borealis** = the Northern lights/bright lights seen in the sky in the far North.

auscultation [ɔːskəl'teɪʃn] *n.* listening to the chest of a patient, using a stethoscope.

auspices ['ɔːspɪsɪz] *n. pl. (a)* forecast/ signs of the future. *(b)* patronage; **under the a. of** = subsidized/organized by. **auspicious** [ɔː'spɪʃəs] *adj.* favourable/ lucky. **auspiciously,** *adv.* favourably.

Aussie ['ɒzi] *n. & adj. inf.* Australian.

austere [ɔː'stɪə] *adj.* cold/severe; without luxury. **austerity** [ɔː'sterɪti] *n.* absence of luxury.

Australian [ɒs'treɪlɪən] **1.** *adj.* referring to Australia. **2.** *n.* person from Australia. **Australasian,** *adj.* referring to Australasia (the part of the Southern Hemisphere including Australia, New Zealand, and the Pacific Islands).

Austrian ['ɒstrɪən] **1.** *adj.* referring to Austria. **2.** *n.* person from Austria.

autarchy ['ɔːtaːki] *n.* self rule, situation where a state rules itself.

autarky ['ɔːtaːki] *n.* self-sufficiency.

authentic [ɔː'θentɪk] *adj.* real; genuine. **authenticate** [ɔː'θentɪkeɪt] *v.* to swear that sth is true. **authenticity** [ɔːθen-'tɪsɪti] *n.* being authentic.

author ['ɔːθə] *n.* person who writes books, etc. **authorship,** *n.* identity of the author.

authority [ɔː'θɒrɪti] *n. (a)* power. *(b)* permission. *(c)* source. *(d)* ruling committee or group. *(e)* expert. **authoritarian** [ɔːθɒrɪ'teərɪən] *adj.* exercising strict control. **authoritative** [ɔː'θɒrɪtətɪv] *adj. (a)* commanding. *(b)* which sounds as if it is correct. **authoritatively,** *adv.* in an authoritative way.

authorize ['ɔːθəraɪz] *v.* to give (s.o.) permission. **authorization** [ɔːθəraɪ-'zeɪʃn] *n.* permission.

autistic [ɔː'tɪstɪk] *adj.* suffering from autism. **autism,** *n.* mental illness which makes you withdrawn and unable to communicate.

auto- ['ɔːtəʊ] *prefix meaning* self; **automatic; automobile.**

autobiography [ɔːtəbaɪ'ɒgrəfi] *n.* life story of a person written by himself. **autobiographical** [ɔːtəbaɪə-'græfɪkl] *adj.* referring to the life of the writer.

autocracy [ɔː'tɒkrəsi] *n.* system of government by one man. **autocrat** ['ɔːtəkræt] *n.* dictator/person who does not allow anyone else to rule him. **autocratic** [ɔːtə'krætɪk] *adj.* ruled by one man. **autocratically,** *adv.* like a dictator.

autocue ['ɔːtəʊkjuː] *n.* trademark for a screen with the text printed on it to help television announcers to speak while looking into the camera.

autogamy [ɔː'tɒgəmi] *n.* self-fertilization.

autograph ['ɔːtəgraːf] **1.** *n.* signature (of a famous person). **2.** *v.* **to a. a book for s.o.** = to write your signature in it.

automat ['ɔːtəmæt] *n.* automatic vending machine. **automated,** *adj.* controlled by automation. **automatic** [ɔːtə'mætɪk] *adj. & n.* (device) which works by itself. **automatically,** *adv.* working by itself. **automation** [ɔːtə-'meɪʃn] *n.* installation of machinery to make a process more automatic. **automaton** [ɔː'tɒmətən] *n. (pl.* **-ta)**

doll which moves with a motor inside it; person who acts like a robot.

automobile ['ɔːtəməbiːl] *n. esp. Am.* car. **automotive** [ɔːtə'məʊtɪv] *adj.* referring to cars.

autonomy [ɔː'tɒnəmɪ] *n.* self-government. **autonomous,** *adj.* (region) which governs itself.

autopsy ['ɔːtɒpsɪ] *n.* cutting up of a dead body to discover the cause of death.

autosuggestion [ɔːtəʊsə'dʒestʃən] *n.* state where a person makes himself believe sth. about himself.

autumn ['ɔːtəm] *n.* season of the year when the leaves fall off the trees. **autumnal** [ɔː'tʌmnl] *adj.* referring to autumn.

auxiliary [ɔːg'zɪlɪərɪ] **1.** *n.* (*a*) helper. (*b*) verb which is used to form part of another verb. **2.** *adj.* (person/machine) which helps.

avail [ə'veɪl] **1.** *v.* **to a. oneself of** = to use. **2.** *n.* **of no a.** = no use. **availability** [əveɪlə'bɪlɪtɪ] *n.* being available. **available,** *adj.* ready to be used; which can be obtained.

avalanche ['ævəlɑːnʃ] *n.* fall of snow down a mountainside.

avant-garde [ævɒŋ'gɑːd] *adj.* experimental (music/drama).

avarice ['ævərɪs] *n.* state of not wanting to spend money. **avaricious** [ævə'rɪʃəs] *adj.* wanting to hoard money and not spend it.

avenge [ə'vendʒ] *v.* to pay s.o. back for (a crime). **avenger,** *n.* person who pays back a crime.

avenue ['ævənjuː] *n.* (*a*) wide, tree-lined, road in a city. (*b*) two parallel rows of trees. (*c*) way of approaching a problem.

aver [ə'vɜː] *v.* (*formal*) to state.

average ['ævərɪdʒ] **1.** *n.* (*a*) figure arrived at when a total is divided by the number of figures added. (*b*) **on a.** = as a general rule. (*c*) sharing of costs of an insurance. **a. adjuster** = person who calculates how much insurance should be paid. **2.** *adj.* general; ordinary. **3.** *v.* to work out as an average.

averse [ə'vɜːs] *adj.* **he is a. to hard work** = he dislikes it. **aversion** [ə'vɜːʃn] *n.* (*a*) (**to**) to dislike. (*b*) **my pet a.** = thing I dislike most.

avert [ə'vɜːt] *v.* (*a*) to turn away (one's eyes). (*b*) to prevent (a disaster).

aviary ['eɪvɪərɪ] *n.* building for keeping birds in.

aviation [eɪvɪ'eɪʃn] *n.* art/technology of flying (aircraft). **aviator** ['eɪvɪeɪtə] *n.* aeroplane pilot.

avid ['ævɪd] *adj.* eager/enthusiastic. **avidly,** *adv.* eagerly.

avocado (pear) [ævə'kɑːdəʊ ('peə)] *n.* (*pl.* **-os**) green tropical fruit with a large stone in the middle, eaten as a vegetable.

avocet ['ævəset] *n.* white wader with a long bill which is curved upwards.

avoid [ə'vɔɪd] *v.* (*a*) to try not to do (sth). (*b*) to keep away from. **avoidable,** *adj.* which you could have avoided. **avoidance,** *n.* act of avoiding.

avoirdupois [ævədə'pɔɪz] *n.* system of weights based on ounces, pounds, etc.

avowal [ə'vaʊəl] *n.* (*formal*) admission. **avowed** [ə'vaʊd] *adj.* stated; admitted.

avuncular [ə'vʌŋkjʊlə] *adj.* like an uncle.

await [ə'weɪt] *v.* to wait for.

awake [ə'weɪk] **1.** *v.* (**awoke; awoken**) (*a*) to wake (s.o.) up. (*b*) to become aware of. **2.** *adj.* not sleeping.

awaken [ə'weɪkn] *v.* to wake/to arouse. **awakening,** *n.* **a rude a.** = a sharp shock.

award [ə'wɔːd] **1.** *n.* (*a*) prize. (*b*) decision which settles a dispute. **2.** *v.* to give (a prize, etc.).

aware [ə'weə] *adj.* knowing. **awareness,** *n.* state of being aware.

awash [ə'wɒʃ] *adj.* covered with a liquid.

away [ə'weɪ] *adv.* (*a*) not here/far; **a. match** = at another team's ground. (*b*) **the birds were singing a.** = they were going on singing; **right a.** = immediately.

awe [ɔː] *n.* fear/terror. **awe-inspiring, awesome,** *adj.* frightening. **awe-struck,** *adj.* frightened/full of terror.

awful ['ɔːfl] *adj.* (*a*) (*old*) very frightening. (*b*) very bad/very strong; unpleasant. **awfully,** *adv. inf.* very.

awhile [ə'waɪl] *adv.* for a short time.

awkward ['ɔːkwəd] *adj.* (*a*) difficult. (*b*) embarrassing. (*c*) clumsy. **awkwardly,** *adv.* with difficulty; inconveniently. **awkwardness,** *n.* (*a*) embarrassment. (*b*) difficulty.

awl [ɔːl] *n.* tool used for making small holes.

awning ['ɔːnɪŋ] *n.* canvas roof stretched out to protect from the sun or rain.

awoke, awoken [ə'wəuk, ə'wəukn] *v.* see **awake**.

AWOL ['eɪwɒl] = absent without leave.

awry [ə'raɪ] *adv.* not straight.

axe, *Am.* **ax** [æks] **1.** *n.* instrument with a sharp metal head for chopping wood; **to have an a. to grind** = a particular point of view to put across. **2.** *v.* to reduce (expenditure); to sack (staff).

axil ['æksɪl] *n.* place where a leaf joins a stem.

axiom ['æksɪəm] *n.* well-known saying/ obviously true statement. **axiomatic** [æksɪə'mætɪk] *adj.* obvious; well-known.

axis ['æksɪs] *n.* (*pl.* **axes** ['æksiːz]) imaginary line through centre of a sphere.

axle ['æksl] *n.* rod going through the middle of a wheel.

ayatollah [aɪə'tɒlə] *n.* Muslim leader.

aye [aɪ] *n.* yes; **the ayes have it** = more people have voted yes than no.

azalea [ə'zeɪlɪə] *n.* small shrub with showy scented flowers.

azo ['eɪzəu] *n.* **a. dyes** = dyes added to food to give it a better colour.

azure ['eɪʒə] *adj.* blue like the sky.

Bb

Ba *symbol for* barium.

BA [biː'eɪ] Bachelor of Arts.

babble ['bæbl] **1.** *n.* (*a*) trickling sound (of water). (*b*) chatter. **2.** *v.* (*a*) to make a trickling sound. (*b*) to chatter.

babe [beɪb] *n.* (*formal*) baby.

babel ['beɪbl] *n.* loud noise of talking.

baboon [bə'buːn] *n.* large African monkey.

baby ['beɪbɪ] *n.* (*a*) very young child; **to have a b.** = to give birth to a baby; **the b. of the family** = the youngest of the children; **he was left holding the b.** = he had to sort out all the problems left to him by others. (*b*) small animal. (*c*) small object; **b. grand (piano). baby - carriage,** *n. Am.* pram. **baby carrier,** *n.* canvas cot with handles for carrying a baby. **babyish,** *adj.* like a baby.

baby-sit, *v.* (**baby-sat**) to look after children while their parents are out.

baby-sitter, *n.* person who baby-sits.

bachelor ['bætʃələ] *n.* (*a*) unmarried man; **b. pad** = small flat for a single person; **b. girl** = unmarried woman. (*b*) holder of a first degree from a university.

bacillus [bə'sɪləs] *n.* (*pl.* **bacilli** [bæ'sɪlaɪ]) type of bacterium.

back [bæk] **1.** (*a*) part of body down the spine between neck and buttocks; **he did it behind my b.** = without my knowing; **I was glad to see the b. of him** = I was glad to see him go; **to put s.o.'s b. up** = to annoy s.o.; **we've broken the b. of the work** = we have done most of the work. (*b*) opposite part/side to the front; **he knows London like the b. of his hand** = very well indeed; **I have an idea at the b. of my mind** = I have the beginnings of an idea; **in the b. of beyond** = away out of a town/in an inaccessible place; **b. to front** = the wrong way round. (*c*) sportsman who plays in a defensive position in football/ hockey, etc. **2.** *adj.* (*a*) referring to the rear; **he's had to take a b. seat** = he's had to take a less prominent position; **b. seat driver** = passenger in a car who offers the driver unwanted advice. (*b*) in arrears; **b. pay** = pay which is owed to s.o. **3.** *adv.* (*a*) to the rear; **stand b.** = move backwards; **please sit b., I can't see** = please lean backwards in your chair. (*b*) in return; **I'll call you b.** = I'll phone you again; **as soon as I get b. to the office** = as soon as I return to the office. (*c*) ago; **a few years b. 4.** *v.* (*a*) to (make sth) go backwards; **can you b. the car into the garage? he backed away from the madman.** (*b*) to support (with money). (*c*) to gamble on (a horse). (*d*) (*of wind*) to blow in another direction. **backache,** *n.* pain in the back. **back bencher,** *n.* ordinary member of parliament. **backbiting,** *n.* sharp criticism. **backbone,** *n.* spine/column of bones forming the main support of the back. **backbreaking,** *adj.* very hard (work). **backchat,** *n.* replying rudely. **backcloth,** *n.* (*in theatre*) painted sheet at the back of the stage. **backdate,** *v.* to put an earlier date than true on (a cheque). **back down,** *v.* to retreat from your former position. **backdrop,** *n.* (*in theatre*) painted sheet at the back of the stage. **backer,** *n.* person who supports sth with money; person who gambles money on horse racing. **backfire,** *v.* (*of a car*) to make a small bang, due to misfiring of the ignition; (*of a plan*) to go wrong with unfortunate consequences for the planner. **backgammon,** *n.* game like draughts played on a special board. **background,** *n.* the back part of a painting against which the foreground stands out; **he comes from a working class b.** = his family is working class; **b. music** = music played quietly in a film or in a restaurant. **backhand,** *adj. & n.* (tennis/table tennis shot) played with the back of the racket/bat. **backhanded,** *adj.* (compliment) that could be taken also as an insult. **backhander,** *n.* (*a*) blow/shot with the back of the hand. (*b*) *Sl.* bribe. **backing,** *n.* (*a*) material used on the back of sth to strengthen it. (*b*) musical accompaniment to a singer or instrument. (*c*) (financial) support. (*d*) reversing (of a car). **backlash,** *n.* reverse effect (of a political or social move); **white b.** = reaction among white people against measures taken to protect black people. **backless,** *adj.* (dress, etc.) with no back. **backlog,** *n.* work not done/bills not paid. **back number,** *n.* old copy of a magazine or newspaper. **back out,** *v.* (*a*) to reverse out. (*b*) to decide not to continue (with a project). **backpack,** *n.* bag carried on a walker's back. **backpacker,** *n.* person who goes backpacking. **backpacking,** *n.* going for a long walk, carrying your clothes, food, tent, etc., in a backpack. **backpedal,** *v.* (-pedalled) (*a*) to pedal backwards. (*b*) to reverse your opinions. **backside,** *n. inf.* buttocks. **backsliding,** *n.* going back to a bad habit after having reformed. **backspace,** *n.* moving a cursor back one space on a computer monitor. **backstage,** *adv. & adj.* in the parts of a theatre where the audience can't go; behind the scenes/hidden from view. **backstairs,** *n.* stairs (for servants) in the back part of a large house.

backstroke, *n.* style of swimming on your back. **backtrack,** *v.* to change your opinion. **back up,** *v.* (*a*) to support (s.o.). (*b*) to make a copy of a computer file, for security reasons. (*c*) *Am.* to reverse a car. **backup (copy)** *n.* copy of a computer file or disk. **backward,** *adj.* (*a*) slow/retarded (child); (country) which is not industrially advanced. (*b*) **b. in paying bills** = slow in paying. **backwardness,** *n.* being backward. **backwards,** *adv.* in reverse/towards the rear; **he knows the song b.** = extremely well. **backwater,** *n.* (*a*) small slow-moving branch of a river. (*b*) quiet/old-fashioned place. **backwoods,** *n. pl.* forest; **they live in the b.** = they live far from other houses. **backwoodsman,** *n.* (*pl.* -men) person who lives in the forest; *inf.* old reactionary peer. **backyard,** *n.* small paved area behind a house.

bacon ['beɪkn] *n.* pork which has been salted or smoked; *inf.* **it saved his b.** = it got him out of the difficult situation.

bacterium [bæk'tɪərɪəm] *n.* (*pl.* **bacteria**) microscopic organism which produces germs or decay. **bacterial, bacteriological** [bæktɪərɪə'lɒdʒɪkl] *adj.* referring to bacteria. **b. warfare** = method of conducting war by using bacteria to kill the enemy. **bacteriologist** [bæktɪərɪ'ɒlədʒɪst] *n.* scientist who specializes in bacteriology. **bacteriology,** *n.* study of bacteria.

bad [bæd] **1.** *adj.* (**worse, worst**) (*a*) not good; **b. meat; b. driver.** (*b*) wicked. (*c*) unpleasant; **b. news; she's in a b. temper.** (*d*) serious; **b. accident.** (*e*) diseased; injured; **b. leg. 2.** *n.* (*a*) **there's a lot of b. in these potatoes** = a lot of rotten bits. (*b*) **I'm £10 to the b.** = I have lost/wasted £10. **baddy,** *n. inf.* villain. **badlands,** *n. Am.* land which cannot be cultivated. **badly,** *adv.* (**worse, worst**) (*a*) not well (done). (*b*) seriously (wounded). (*c*) very much; **he b. needs a shave.**

bade [bæd] *v. see* **bid.**

badge [bædʒ] *n.* small sign worn to show that you belong to a group, or simply as a decoration.

badger ['bædʒə] **1.** *n.* wild animal with striped black and white head which lives

underground and comes out at night. **2.**
v. to bother (s.o.); **he badgered me into
giving him £5.**

badinage [ˈbædɪˈnɑːʒ] *n.* light teasing
talk.

badminton [ˈbædmɪntən] *n.* game for
two or four people, played with rackets
and a shuttlecock.

baffle [ˈbæfl] **1.** *n.* shield (to cut out
noise). **2.** *v.* (*a*) to puzzle. (*b*) to
frustrate. **bafflement,** *n.* being baffled.

bag [bæg] **1.** *n.* (*a*) thing made of paper/
cloth/plastic which you can carry things
in; **carrier b.** = bag made of stiff
paper with two handles for shopping;
shopping b. = large bag for carrying
shopping; *inf.* **bags of money** = lots of
money. (*b*) **bags under the eyes** = puffy
layer of skin beneath the eyes showing
that you are ill or tired. (*c*) *inf.* **it's in
the b.** = the deal is agreed. (*d*) animals
killed while hunting. (*e*) *inf.* **old b.** =
dirty old woman. **2.** *v.* (**bagged**) to catch
(an animal when hunting); *inf.* **bags I
go first** = I claim the right to go first.
baggy, *adj.* (**-ier, -iest**) (*of clothes*) too
big/hanging in folds.

bagasse [bæˈgæs] *n.* residue left after
crushing sugar cane.

bagatelle [bægəˈtel] *n.* (*a*) game where
small metal balls are sent round a
board. (*b*) unimportant thing.

baggage [ˈbægɪdʒ] *n.* (*no pl.*) luggage.

bagpipes [ˈbægpaɪps] *n. pl.* musical instrument made of an air sack attached
to pipes.

bail [beɪl] *n.* (*a*) small piece of wood
resting on the top of stumps in cricket.
(*b*) money paid to a court as surety for
a prisoner's temporary release; **he was
released on b. of £500. bailer,** *n.* scoop
for removing water from a boat. **bail
out,** *v.* (*a*) to scoop water out of (a
boat); to help (s.o.) who is in financial
difficulties. (*b*) to bale out. (*c*) to pay
money to let a prisoner out temporarily
between hearings.

Bailey bridge [ˈbeɪlɪˈbrɪdʒ] *n.* prefabricated bridge which is supported by
boats.

bailiff [ˈbeɪlɪf] *n.* court official who can
seize property in payment of debts. (*b*)
landowner's agent on an estate.

bairn [beən] *n.* (*in Scotland*) child.

bait [beɪt] **1.** *n.* fly, worm, etc., used to
attract fish or animals. **2.** *v.* to attach
bait to (a hook or trap).

baize [beɪz] *n.* green cloth made of wool.

bake [beɪk] *v.* to cook (in an oven).
bakehouse, *n.* building with ovens
for baking. **baker,** *n.* person who
makes bread and cakes; **baker's dozen**
= thirteen. **baker's,** *n.* shop selling
bread and cakes. **bakery,** *n.* shop
and workshop of a baker. **baking. 1.**
n. cooking (in an oven); **b. dish** =
fireproof dish which can be put in the
oven; **b. tray** = flat sheet of metal for
baking biscuits, etc. on. **2.** *adv.* **b. hot**
= extremely hot. **baking powder,** *n.*
powder which when added to a cake mix
helps it to rise.

balaclava [bæləˈklɑːvə] *n.* **b. (helmet)**
= knitted woollen helmet covering the
whole head and neck, with a round
opening for the face.

balalaika [bæləˈlaɪkə] *n.* Russian
stringed instrument like a small guitar.

balance [ˈbæləns] **1.** *n.* (*a*) machine
which weighs; **the result hangs in the
b.** = you cannot tell which way the result will turn out. (*b*) staying steady; **to
keep/to lose one's b.; the b. of power**
= the division of power between countries. (*c*) what remains after all payments have been made; **we have a b. of
£25 in the bank; b. of payments** = difference between money obtained from
exports and money paid for imports by
a country; **b. sheet** = statement drawn
up at the end of a year showing the
financial situation of a company. **2.** *v.*
(*a*) to remain in one position without
falling. (*b*) to make (sth) stand without
falling. (*c*) to counteract the effect of
(sth). (*d*) **to make the accounts b.** =
to make the total of income and expenditure cancel each other out. **balanced,**
adj. level; sensible.

balcony [ˈbælkənɪ] *n.* (*a*) small terrace
jutting out from an upper floor. (*b*)
upper terrace of seats in a ˈtheatre/
cinema.

bald [bɔːld] *adj.* (*a*) with no hair. (*b*)
not elaborate; **a b. statement of fact.
balding,** *adj.* becoming bald. **baldly,**
adv. drily. **baldness,** *n.* lack of hair.

balderdash [ˈbɔːldədæʃ] *n.* nonsense.

bale [beɪl] **1.** *n.* large bundle. **2.** *v.* **to b. out** = to jump out of a crashing aircraft with the help of a parachute.

baleful ['beɪlfʊl] *adj.* threatening/unpleasant; **a b. look. balefully,** *adv.* in a baleful way.

balk [bɔːlk] *v.* (*a*) to prevent s.o. from doing sth. (*b*) **to b. at sth** = to refuse to do sth.

ball [bɔːl] *n.* (*a*) round object for playing games; **keep the b. rolling** = keep everything moving; **I'll start the b. rolling** = I'll start things off; **he's on the b.** = he knows his job very well/he is up to date; **they won't play b.** = they won't cooperate with us. (*b*) thing with a round shape; **a b. of wool.** (*c*) formal dance. (*d*) *Am.* baseball; **b. park** = area set aside for playing baseball. **ball-and-socket,** *adj.* (joint) where a ball at the end of one rod/bone fits a socket at the end of another. **ball bearing,** *n.* bearing using a ring of little steel balls; one of these steel balls. **ballboy, ballgirl,** *n.* boy or girl who picks up the balls during a tennis match. **ballcock,** *n.* mechanism with a valve operated by a floating ball (for filling cisterns). **ballpoint,** *adj.* **b. pen** = pen with a tiny ball which is automatically coated with ink from a tube. **ballroom,** *n.* large room for formal dances; **b. dancing** = formal dancing.

ballad ['bæləd] *n.* romantic popular song or poem telling a story. **ballade,** *n.* form of poetry, with a repeated refrain.

ballast ['bæləst] *n.* (*a*) material carried in ship/balloon to give extra weight. (*b*) stones used to bed down railway sleepers.

ballet ['bæleɪ] *n.* (*a*) dancing as a spectacle for public performance; **b. dancer.** (*b*) piece danced for performance; **the ballet 'Swan Lake'.** (*c*) company which performs ballets. **ballerina** [bælə'riːnə] *n.* woman ballet dancer.

ballistics [bə'lɪstɪks] *n.* science of shooting bullets or shells.

balloon [bə'luːn] *n.* large round object which is inflated; **hot-air b.** = large passenger-carrying balloon inflated with hot air. **ballooning,** *n.* sport of racing large passenger-carrying balloons.

ballot ['bælət] **1.** *n.* voting by pieces of paper; **a secret b.** = election where the votes of individual voters are not disclosed; **postal b.** = election where voters can send their votes by post; **b. paper** = paper with names of candidates against which the voter makes a cross; **b. box** = sealed box for putting ballot papers in. **2.** *v.* to vote by pieces of paper. **ballot-rigging,** *n.* illegal arrangement of votes in a ballot, so that one side wins.

ballyhoo [bælɪ'huː] *n. Am.* energetic publicizing (during an election campaign, etc.).

balmy ['bɑːmɪ] *adj.* fragrant/soft (air/breeze).

balsa ['bɔːlsə] *n.* very light wood (used for making models).

balsam ['bɔːlsəm] *n.* fragrant flowering plant.

balustrade [bælə'streɪd] *n.* stone fence made of small carved pillars along the edge of a terrace/balcony, etc. **baluster** ['bæləstə] *n.* small pillar.

bamboo [bæm'buː] *n.* tropical plant which provides tall, strong, jointed canes; **b. shoots** = young shoots of bamboo which can be eaten.

bamboozle [bæm'buːzl] *v.* to trick/to puzzle (s.o.).

ban [bæn] **1.** *n.* law/instruction which forbids sth; **a b. on smoking in cinemas. 2.** *v.* (**banned**) to forbid (sth).

banal [bə'nɑːl] *adj.* ordinary/trivial. **banality** [bə'nælɪtɪ] *n.* ordinariness.

banana [bə'nɑːnə] *n.* long yellow tropical fruit; **b. republic** = corrupt central American state.

band [bænd] **1.** *n.* (*a*) thin loop of material for tying things together. (*b*) **bands** = strips of white cloth worn round the neck by lawyers/clergymen. (*c*) group of frequencies in radio transmission. (*d*) group of people. (*e*) group of musicians, esp. playing brass and percussion instruments. **2.** *v.* to form a group. **bandmaster,** *n.* leader of a brass band. **bandsman,** *n.* (*pl.* **bandsmen**) musician playing in a band. **bandstand,** *n.* small stage (in public gardens) for outdoor concerts. **bandwagon,** *n.* **to jump on the b.** = to join a popular movement/to start to do sth which is already proving popular.

bandage ['bændɪdʒ] **1.** *n.* piece of cloth to tie round a wound/round a twisted ankle, etc. **2.** *v.* to tie a cloth round a wound.

bandanna [bæn'dænə] *n.* large silk handkerchief.

bandeau ['bændəʊ] *n.* ribbon to tie back the hair.

bandit ['bændɪt] *n.* robber/brigand.

bandy ['bændɪ] **1.** *adj.* **he has b. legs** = when he stands with feet together, his knees do not touch. **2.** *v.* **(bandied) to b. about** = to shout/write (words to several people).

bane [beɪn] *n.* **it's the b. of my life** = it's what annoys me most.

bang [bæŋ] **1.** *n.* (*a*) loud noise; **supersonic b.** = loud noise made when an aircraft goes faster than the speed of sound. (*b*) sharp blow. (*c*) hair cut straight across the forehead. **2.** *v.* to make a bang (by hitting sth). **3.** *inter. showing noise of an explosion;* **the gun suddenly went b.; b. in the middle** = right in the middle. **banger,** *n.* (*a*) firework that goes bang. (*b*) *Sl.* old car. (*c*) *inf.* sausage. **banging,** *n.* noise of repeated bangs.

bangle ['bæŋgl] *n.* bracelet made of metal or rigid material.

banish ['bænɪʃ] *v.* to send (s.o.) away/to exile (s.o.); to get rid of (sth).

banisters ['bænɪstəz] *n. pl.* set of vertical rods with a handrail along the side of stairs.

banjo ['bændʒəʊ] *n.* stringed instrument with a round body.

bank [bæŋk] **1.** *n.* (*a*) long mound of earth/sand/snow, etc. (*b*) edge of a river or canal. (*c*) row (of lights). (*d*) institution for keeping or lending money; **merchant b.** = bank which deals with lending large sums of money to businesses; **clearing banks** = banks which issue cheques; **b. charges** = charges made by a bank for its services; **b. holiday** = public holiday when the banks are closed. **2.** *v.* (*a*) to pile up in a long mound; **they banked up the side of the canal** = they reinforced the canal banks; **the snow banked up along the road** = the wind blew the snow into banks. (*b*) (*of plane*) to roll to one side. (*c*) to put money into a

bank; to use a bank; **where do you b.?** = which bank do you use? (*d*) **I'm banking on taking two weeks off next month** = I'm counting on/relying on taking two weeks off. **banker,** *n.* person who directs a bank. **banking,** *n.* the profession of being a banker. **banknote,** *n.* paper money issued by a bank. **bankroll,** *v. inf.* to pay for (a project). **bankrupt,** *adj. & n.* (person) whose debts exceed his assets and who has been declared incapable of meeting his debts; **he has been declared b. bankruptcy,** *n.* state of being bankrupt.

banksia ['bæŋksɪə] *n.* Australian shrub with yellow flowers.

banner ['bænə] *n.* (*a*) long flag; **b. headlines** = very large headlines in a newspaper. (*b*) large piece of material with a slogan written on it, carried in a procession or protest march.

banns [bænz] *n. pl.* official statement in church of intention to marry.

banquet ['bæŋkwɪt] *n.* large formal dinner. **banqueting hall,** *n.* large room where banquets are held.

bantam ['bæntəm] *n.* breed of very small chickens.

bantamweight, *n.* light weight in boxing between flyweight and featherweight.

banter ['bæntə] *n.* sarcastic teasing comments. **bantering,** *adj.* (tone of voice) used when making light sarcastic comments.

banyan ['bænjæn] *n.* tropical tree with roots which come down from the branches.

baobab ['bæəʊbæb] *n.* very large tropical tree, found in Africa.

bap [bæp] *n.* soft flat white bread roll.

baptize [bæp'taɪz] *v.* to admit s.o. to the church and give them a Christian name. **baptism** ['bæptɪzəm] *n.* church ceremony where s.o. is given a Christian name. **baptismal** [bæp'tɪzml] *adj.* referring to baptism.

bar [bɑː] **1.** *n.* (*a*) long piece (of metal/chocolate, etc.). (*b*) obstacle; **harbour b.** = ridge of sand at the entrance to a harbour; **colour b.** = objection to persons because of the colour of their skin. (*c*) place where drinks are served;

saloon b. = room in a pub with carpets and comfortable chairs; **public b.** = room in a pub which is less comfortable than the saloon bar; **milk b./snack b./sandwich b.** = counter/shop where milk/snacks/sandwiches are served. (*d*) place where a prisoner stands in court; **b. of the house** = place where people who are not MPs are asked to appear before the House of Commons. (*e*) officially recognized lawyers; **he was called to the b.** = he became a barrister. (*f*) division (in music). (*g*) unit of atmospheric pressure. 2. *v.* (**barred**) to block (a road); to stop (s.o. **from** doing sth). 3. *prep.* **b. none** = with no exceptions. **bar code**, *n.* system of lines printed on a product which can be read by a computer. **barring**, *prep.* excepting.

barb [bɑːb] *n.* small tooth (on a fishhook or arrow). **barbed**, *adj.* with sharp points; **b. comment** = sharp critical comment; **b. wire** = wire (for fences) with sharp spikes.

barbarian [bɑːˈbeərɪən] *n.* wild/uncivilized person. **barbaric** [bɑːˈbærɪk] *adj.* cruel/uncivilized. **barbarity** [bɑːˈbærɪtɪ] *n.* cruelty. **barbarous** [ˈbɑːbərəs] *adj.* cruel/uncivilized.

barbecue [ˈbɑːbɪkjuː] 1. *n.* (*a*) charcoal fire/grill for cooking food outdoors. (*b*) meal cooked on a barbecue. 2. *v.* to cook on a barbecue.

barber [ˈbɑːbə] *n.* man who cuts men's hair.

barbiturate [bɑːˈbɪtjʊrət] *n.* drug which sends you to sleep.

bard [bɑːd] *n.* (*formal*) poet.

bare [ˈbeə] 1. *adj.* (*a*) naked/not covered with clothes or leaves. (*b*) just enough; **a b. living** = just enough to live on; **b. necessities** = absolutely essential items for existence; **elected with a b. majority** = with a very small majority. 2. *v.* to strip naked; **he bared his soul** = he told all his innermost thoughts. **bareback**, *adj. & adv.* riding a horse with no saddle. **barefaced**, *adj.* crude/cynical (lie). **barefoot**, *adv.* with no shoes on. **barefooted**, *adj.* with no shoes on. **bareheaded**, *adv. & adj.* with no hat on. **barely**, *adv.* hardly/scarcely; **I b. had enough money to pay the bill. bareness**, *n.* nakedness.

bargain [ˈbɑːgɪn] 1. *n.* (*a*) thing bought; sale agreed; **to strike a b.** = to agree on a sale; **he drives a hard b.** = he is a tough negotiator. (*b*) thing bought more cheaply than it usually is; **into the b.** = as well as everything else; **b. basement** = part of a shop where cheap items are sold; **b. offer** = special offer of goods at low prices. 2. *v.* (*a*) to negotiate a sale; **I got more than I bargained for** = more than I expected. (*b*) to haggle. **bargaining**, *n.* discussion about prices/wages, etc.: **collective b.** = discussion between management and unions to fix new salaries for union members.

barge [bɑːdʒ] 1. *n.* large flat-bottomed cargo boat on inland waters. 2. *v.* to bump heavily (**into**). **bargee** [bɑːˈdʒiː] *n.* man in charge of a barge. **barge pole**, *n.* long pole for moving a barge along; *inf.* **I wouldn't touch it with a b. p.** = I don't recommend getting involved with it in any way.

baritone [ˈbærɪtəʊn] *adj. & n.* (singer with a) voice between tenor and bass.

barium [ˈbeərɪəm] *n.* (*element:* Ba) white soft metal; **b. meal** = liquid which you drink before having your stomach X-rayed, which will show up clearly on the X-ray.

bark [bɑːk] 1. *n.* (*a*) outer part of a tree. (*b*) loud noise made by dog; **his b. is worse than his bite** = he is not as terrifying as he sounds. 2. *v.* (*a*) **he barked his shin on the rock** = he scraped the skin off his shin. (*b*) to make a loud call like a dog; **to b. up the wrong tree** = to get the wrong idea. **barker**, *n.* person who calls out to advertise sth in the street. **barking**, *n.* continuous calls of dogs.

barley [ˈbɑːlɪ] *n.* cereal crop; **pearl b.** = grains of barley used in cooking; **b. sugar** = sweet made of boiled sugar; **b. wine** = very strong beer.

barmaid [ˈbɑːmeɪd] *n.* woman who serves drinks in a bar. **barman** [ˈbɑːmən] *n.* (*pl.* **-men**) man who serves drinks in a bar.

barmy [ˈbɑːmɪ] *adj.* (**-ier, -iest**) *inf.* mad.

barn [bɑːn] *n.* large farm building for storing grain or hay. **barnyard**, *n.* yard in a farm.

barnacle ['bɑːnəkl] n. (a) small shellfish which clings to the bottoms of ships/ to submerged wooden posts, etc. (b) **b. goose** = common northern goose.

barney ['bɑːnɪ] n. Sl. argument.

barometer [bəˈrɒmɪtə] n. instrument for measuring atmospheric pressure, and therefore for forecasting the weather. **barometric** [bærəˈmetrɪk] adj. referring to a barometer; **b. pressure.**

baron ['bærən] n. lowest rank of hereditary peers, now also title of life peers. **baroness**, n. wife of a baron; title of a life peeress. **baronet**, n. hereditary knight. **baronial** [bəˈrəʊnɪəl] adj. large/ sumptuous (castle).

baroque [bəˈrɒk] adj. in the ornate style of architecture of the late 17th and 18th centuries.

barrack ['bærək] 1. n. **barracks** = buildings where soldiers, sailors, or airmen are housed; **b. room** = dormitory for soldiers, etc.; **b. room lawyer** = person who organizes protests against authority without knowing the true facts. 2. v. to shout to show displeasure; **they barracked our football team.**

barracuda [bærəˈkjuːdə] n. large tropical fish.

barrage ['bærɑːʒ] n. (a) dam across a river, etc. (b) rapid fire (of guns/questions).

barrel ['bærəl] n. (a) large wooden container (for wine/oil/fish/oysters, etc.); **he's got me over a b.** = in a very awkward situation. (b) firing tube (on a gun). (c) **b. organ** = machine for making music when a handle is turned.

barren ['bærən] adj. unproductive (land); (woman/animal) who cannot have young; (tree) which does not produce fruit. **barrenness**, n. being barren.

barricade [bærɪˈkeɪd] 1. n. makeshift heap of cars/rubbish, etc., made to block a street. 2. v. to block (a street/ a door).

barrier ['bærɪə] n. thing which stops you moving forward.

barrister ['bærɪstə] n. lawyer who is allowed to speak in court.

barrow ['bærəʊ] n. (a) small wheeled truck which is pushed by hand. (b) mound of earth piled over a prehistoric tomb. **barrow boy**, n. man who sells things from a barrow in the street.

bartender ['bɑːtendə] n. barman.

barter ['bɑːtə] 1. n. exchange (of one product for another). 2. v. to exchange (one product for another).

basalt ['bæsɔːlt] n. black volcanic rock.

base [beɪs] 1. n. (a) bottom part. (b) military camp; **air force b.** (c) substance which is the main part of a mixture. (d) chemical compound which reacts with an acid to form a salt. 2. v. **to b. sth on** = to use sth as a base. 3. adj. low/cheap; **b. metal** = not a precious metal.

baseball ['beɪsbɔːl] n. American team game played with a bat and ball. **baseboard**, n. Am. decorative board running along the bottom edge of a wall in a room. **baseless**, adj. (accusation) without any basis in fact. **basement**, n. floor beneath the ground floor.

bash [bæʃ] 1. n. (pl. -es) (a) your car has had a b. = something has bumped into your car. (b) inf. **go on, have a b.** = go on, try to do it. 2. v. to hit (sth) hard.

bashful ['bæʃful] adj. shy/modest. **bashfully**, adv. shyly. **bashfulness**, n. being bashful.

basic ['beɪsɪk] adj. elementary; **b. vocabulary** = most commonly used words. **basically**, adv. at bottom. **basics** pl. n. simple and important facts; **to get back to b.** = to consider the basic points again.

BASIC ['beɪsɪk] Beginners All-purpose Symbolic Instruction Code.

basil ['bæzl] n. type of scented herb.

basilica [bəˈzɪlɪkə] n. (a) large rectangular church. (b) large catholic church.

basin ['beɪsn] n. large bowl; **wash b.** = bowl in a bathroom with taps giving running water for washing the hands.

basis ['beɪsɪs] n. (pl. **bases**) (scientific) reason.

bask [bɑːsk] v. to lie (in the sun/in glory).

basket ['bɑːskɪt] n. container made of woven straw/cane, etc.; **b. chair** = chair made of woven cane. **basketball** ['bɑːskɪtbɔːl] n. team game where you try to throw a ball into a small net high up. **basketwork**, n. making of baskets; objects made of woven straw/cane, etc.

bas-relief ['bæsrɪliːf] *n.* type of carving in stone where the figures stand out against (but are joined to) the background.

bass 1. [bæs] *n.* type of edible freshwater fish. **2.** [beɪs] *adj. & n. (pl. -es)* low/ deep voice or music; **double b.** = instrument like a very large cello; **b. guitar/trombone** = large guitar/ trombone tuned to play low notes; **b. clef** = sign in music showing that the notes are lower.

basset ['bæsɪt] *n.* **b. (hound)** = breed of dog with short legs and long ears.

bassoon [bə'suːn] *n.* low-pitched wind instrument. **bassoonist,** *n.* person who plays a bassoon.

bastard ['baːstəd] *adj. & n.* (person) not born of married parents; (thing) which is not pure; *inf.* nasty person/thing.

baste [beɪst] *v.* (*a*) to sew (material) loosely. (*b*) to spread juices over (meat which is cooking).

bastion ['bæstɪən] *n.* fortified part/ stronghold.

bat [bæt] **1.** *n.* (*a*) small mammal which flies by night and hangs upside down to rest. (*b*) instrument for hitting a ball (in some games); **he did it off his own b.** = he did it on his own initiative. **2.** *v.* (**batted**) (*a*) to be one of the two batsmen (in cricket); (*of a cricket team*) to have the turn to strike. (*b*) **she never batted an eyelid** = she did not show any surprise. **batsman,** *n. (pl. -men)* cricketer who is at the wicket.

batch [bætʃ] *n. (pl. -es)* quantity of bread/cakes baked at one time; group of letters/goods taken together.

bated ['beɪtɪd] *adj.* **with b. breath** = holding your breath.

bath [baːθ] **1.** *n.* (*a*) large container for washing all the body. (*b*) container for a liquid; container full of a liquid; (*c*) act of washing all the body; **to have a b.** (*d*) bath full of water; **will you run my b. for me?** = will you fill the bath with water for me? (*e*) **public baths** = large (public) building with a swimming pool. **2.** *v.* to wash (s.o./yourself) all over; **he is bathing the baby. bathmat,** *n.* small mat to step on as you get out of the bath. **bath oil,** *n.* scented oil to put in a bath. **bathrobe,** *n.* (*a*) loose coat of towelling worn before or after a bath. (*b*) *Am.* man's dressing-gown. **bathroom,** *n.* room with a bath, wash basin and sometimes a toilet. **bath salts,** *n. pl.* scented crystals to put in a bath. **bathtowel,** *n.* very large towel for drying yourself after a bath. **bathtub,** *n. esp. Am.* bath/container for washing all the body.

bathe [beɪð] **1.** *n.* swim. **2.** *v.* (*a*) to swim. (*b*) to wash (a wound) carefully. (*c*) *Am.* to have a bath. **bather,** *n.* person who is swimming. **bathing,** *n.* swimming (in the sea, river or a pool); **b. costume** = piece of clothing worn when swimming.

bathos ['beɪθɒs] *n.* sudden drop from a serious subject to a trivial one.

bathysphere ['bæθɪsfɪə] *n.* round pres-surized cabin for exploring deep parts of the sea. **bathyscaph,** *n.* type of small submarine, used for underwater research.

batik [bæ'tiːk] *n.* type of cloth, coloured in patterns by dyeing it with wax designs on it.

batman ['bætmən] *n. (pl. -men)* officer's servant.

baton ['bætn] *n.* stick (of orchestra conductor or policeman).

batrachian [bə'treɪkɪən] *n.* amphibian, such as a toad.

battalion [bə'tælɪən] *n.* part of the army often commanded by a lieutenant-colonel.

batten ['bætn] **1.** *n.* thin strip of wood. **2.** *v.* (*on ship*) **to b. down the hatches** = to close down the hatch covers before a storm.

batter ['bætə] **1.** *n.* thin liquid mixture of flour/eggs/milk, for making pancakes, etc. **2.** *v.* to hit hard and continuously. **battered,** *adj.* which has been hit hard; **b. babies/wives** = babies/wives who have been constantly ill-treated. **battering ram,** *n.* long beam used to break down castle gates.

battery ['bætərɪ] *n.* (*a*) group of artillery guns. (*b*) container with a cell or several cells charged with electricity. (*c*) hut with cages for raising large numbers of chickens. (*d*) **assault and b.** = criminal charge of attacking s.o. with violence. **battery-powered** *adj.* worked by an electric battery.

battle ['bætl] 1. *n.* important fight between large enemy forces; **the B. of Trafalgar; a b. royal** = a great struggle. 2. *v.* to fight (**against**). **battleaxe,** *n. inf.* large fierce woman. **battlefield,** *n.* site of a battle. **battlefront,** *n.* line along which fighting is taking place. **battlements,** *n. pl.* top part of a castle wall, with a walk for soldiers. **battleship,** *n.* very large warship.

batty ['bætɪ] *adj. inf.* mad.

bauble ['bɔːbl] *n.* (*formal*) cheap piece of jewellery.

baud rate ['bɔːdreɪt] *n.* number of signal changes transmitted per second.

baulk [bɔːlk] *v. see* **balk.**

bauxite ['bɔːksaɪt] *n.* mineral from which aluminium is produced.

bawdy ['bɔːdɪ] *adj.* rude/coarse.

bawl [bɔːl] *v.* to shout loudly. **bawl out,** *v. Am.* to criticize (s.o.).

bay [beɪ] 1. *n.* (*a*) fragrant shrub whose leaves are used in cooking. (*b*) large rounded inlet in a coast; **the B. of Biscay.** (*c*) arch of a bridge; section of a church between pillars; **b. window** = window which projects from an outside wall. (*d*) special section set back from the road; **parking b.** = place marked for parking; **loading b.** = place where lorries can be parked with a high platform for loading. (*e*) light brown horse. (*f*) **to keep attackers at b.** = to keep them away. 2. *v.* (*of hunting dog*) to bark.

bayonet ['beɪənət] *n.* sharp blade attached to the end of a rifle.

bazaar [bə'zɑː] *n.* (*a*) oriental market. (*b*) market selling goods for charity.

bazooka [bə'zuːkə] *n.* small anti-tank gun.

b. & b. = bed and breakfast.

BBC [biːbiː'siː] British Broadcasting Corporation.

BC ['biː'siː] *abbrev. for* before Christ; **Julius Caesar died in 44 BC.**

be [biː] *v.* (**I am, you are, he is, we/they are; I/he was, we/you/they were; he has been**) 1. (*a*) (*describing a person or thing*) **the house is big.** (*b*) to add up to; **two and three are five.** (*c*) to exist/to live; **where are we? there he is; how are you today? tomorrow is Friday.** (*d*) to feel; **I am cold; they are**

hungry. (*e*) to go; **have you ever been to New York? the police had been into every room.** (*f*) (*showing time*) **it is four o'clock.** (*g*) (*showing future*) **he is to see the doctor tomorrow.** 2. (*used to make part of verbs*) **I am coming; he has been waiting for hours;** (*passive use*) **he was killed by a train. being.** 1. *adj.* **for the time b.** = temporarily/for now. 2. *n.* (*a*) existence; **the association came into b. in 1946.** (*b*) **human b.** = person.

beach [biːtʃ] 1. *n.* (*pl.* **-es**) stretch of sand/pebbles by the side of the sea. 2. *v.* to bring (a boat) on to the beach. **beachcomber,** *n.* person who collects things thrown up on the beach by the sea. **beachhead,** *n.* small area occupied by troops at the beginning of an invasion from the sea. **beachwear,** *n.* (*no pl.*) clothes to wear on the beach.

beacon ['biːkən] *n.* light (used as a signal); **radio b.** = radio transmitter which guides aircraft into an airport; **Belisha b.** = orange globe light which marks a zebra crossing.

bead [biːd] *n.* (*a*) small ornament with a hole so that it can be threaded. (*b*) small drop of liquid. **beading,** *n.* thin strip of wood (usu. carved in a pattern) used to decorate. **beady,** *adj.* **b. eyed** = with eyes small and bright like beads.

beagle ['biːgl] *n.* breed of dog used for hunting.

beak [biːk] *n.* hard covering of a bird's mouth.

beaker ['biːkə] *n.* metal/plastic cup, usu. with no handle; glass container used in scientific experiments.

beam [biːm] 1. (*a*) large block of wood used in building. (*b*) ray (of light/sound); **radio b.** = wavelength for radio transmission. (*c*) width of a ship; *inf.* **he's broad in the b.** = rather fat. 2. *v.* (*a*) to send out rays. (*b*) to smile. **beaming,** *adj.* radiant (sunshine/smile/face). **beam in on,** *v.* to take (sth) as a target.

bean [biːn] *n.* (*a*) vegetable with edible seeds (and pods); *inf.* **full of beans** = full of vigour. (*b*) **coffee beans** = fruit of the coffee plant which, when roasted and ground, are used to make coffee.

bear ['beə] 1. *n.* (*a*) large furry wild animal; **polar b.** = large white bear living in Arctic regions; **teddy b.** = toy bear. (b) person who believes the stock market prices will fall. **2.** v. (**bore; has borne**) (a) to carry; **this tree has borne fruit every year; the deposit bears interest at 5%.** (b) to stand/to put up with; **I can't b. noise.** (c) to support; **will this branch b. my weight?** (d) to turn; **b. right at the crossroads.** (e) to aim; **the enemy brought their guns to b. on our ship. bearable,** adj. which you can put up with. **bear down on,** v. to advance heavily towards (s.o.). **bearer,** n. person who carries sth. **beargarden,** n. **don't turn the place into a b.** = don't make a row and mess everywhere. **bearing,** n. (a) **ball bearings** = set of small balls around an axle to spread the weight evenly and make the wheel turn smoothly. (b) **to get your bearings** = to find out where you are; **to lose your bearings** = to lose all idea of where you are. (c) **stately b.** = stately way of standing/walking. **bear out,** v. to confirm. **bearskin,** n. tall fur hat worn by a soldier. **bear up,** v. to survive cheerfully. **bear with,** v. to endure patiently.

beard ['bɪəd] n. hair on the lower part of a man's face; whiskers on a mussel/oyster, etc. **bearded,** adj. with a beard. **beardless,** adj. with no beard.

beast [biːst] n. (a) wild animal; **b. of burden** = donkey/horse, etc., trained to carry loads. (b) nasty person. **beastliness,** n. nastiness (of person). **beastly,** adj. nasty.

beat [biːt] **1.** n. (a) regular sound; **heart b.** (b) regular measure in music. (c) area regularly patrolled by a policeman. **2.** v. (**beat; has beaten**) (a) to hit hard several times. (b) to chase (birds); **we b. a hasty retreat** = we went away very quickly; **don't b. about the bush** = get to the point quickly; Sl. **b. it!** = go away! (c) to defeat. (d) to do better than (a record). (e) to stir (eggs, etc.) vigorously. **beat back,** v. to push back. **beat down,** v. (a) to flatten (corn). (b) **I beat down his price** = I reduced the price he was asking by haggling; **he beat me down** = he made me reduce my price. (c) (of the sun) to strike hard on. **beaten,** adj. **off the b. track** = away

from other houses. **beater,** n. (a) person who drives birds towards the people who will shoot them. (b) machine for beating eggs. **beating,** n. act of hitting. **beat up,** v. (a) to whip (cream). (b) to attack (s.o.).

beatify [biː'ætɪfaɪ] v. to declare (s.o.) blessed (as the first step to declaring s.o. a saint). **beatification** [biːætɪfɪ'keɪʃn] n. declaring s.o. blessed.

Beaufort scale ['bəʊfət'skeɪl] n. scale for measuring wind strengths.

beautiful ['bjuːtɪful] adj. very pleasing to look at. **beaut,** n. inf. (esp. Australian) a beautiful thing/person. **beautician,** n. person who makes people beautiful (by applying makeup, etc.). **beautifully,** adv. in a very pleasing way. **beautify,** v. to make sth beautiful. **beauty,** n. state of being beautiful; **b. salon** = clinic specializing in women's appearance; **b. spot** = (i) famous beautiful place; (ii) dark spot, usu. on the face.

beaver ['biːvə] **1.** n. small American mammal which lives in water and makes dams with trees which it gnaws down. **2.** v. **to b. away at sth** = to work hard at sth.

becalmed [bɪ'kɑːmd] adj. (of a sailing ship) not able to move because there is no wind.

became [bɪ'keɪm] v. see **become**.

because [bɪ'kɒz] conj. for the reason that; owing to the fact that. **because of,** prep. on account of.

beck [bek] n. (a) (in North of England) mountain stream. (b) **he is always at her b. and call** = he always does exactly what she wants him to do.

beckon ['bekən] v. to make a sign (to s.o.) to come.

become [bɪ'kʌm] v. (**became; has become**) to change into sth different; **what became of him?** = what happened to him? **becoming,** adj. **her dress is very b.** = her dress suits her very well.

becquerel ['bekərel] n. SI unit of radiation.

bed [bed] **1.** n. (a) piece of furniture for sleeping on; **double b.** = bed for two people; **single b.** = bed for one person; **to go to b.** = to lie down in bed to sleep for the night; **he took to his b.** = he was ill and had to stay in bed; **to make the b.** = to straighten the bedclothes after getting out of bed. (b) bottom (of a river/lake); **oyster b.** = collection of oysters at the bottom of the sea; **watercress b.** = mass of watercress growing in a river. (c) area of garden kept for plants. 2. v. (**bedded**) (a) **to b. down** = to give (horses) fresh straw; **to b. down railway sleepers** = to lay them on ballast. (b) **to b. out plants** = to put out plants in a flower bed. **bedclothes,** n. pl. sheets/blankets, etc., on a bed. **bedcover,** n. cloth which covers a bed during the daytime. **bedding,** n. (a) bedclothes (mattress/pillows, etc.); straw (for horses). (b) **bedding out** = putting out (of plants) into flower beds; **bedding plants** = plants suitable for putting in flower beds. **bedfellow,** n. person who sleeps in the same bed; person who is associated with s.o. **bedjacket,** n. warm jacket worn in bed. **bedpan,** n. bowl for passing waste water into when lying in bed. **bedridden,** adj. forced to stay in bed because of illness. **bedrock,** n. bottom rock beneath various mineral seams. **bedroom,** n. room for sleeping in. **bedside,** n. side of a bed; **b. manner** = attitude of a doctor to his sick patient. **bed-sitting room** [bed'sɪtɪŋ ruːm] inf. **bed-sitter, bedsit,** n. bedroom and living room combined. **bedsore,** n. sore which is caused by lying in bed for long periods. **bedspread,** n. decorative cloth to put over a bed. **bedstead,** n. solid frame of a bed. **bedtime,** n. time to go to bed; **it's past your b.** = it's later than the time you usually go to bed.

bedevilled [bɪ'devld] adj. surrounded (with difficulties).

bedlam ['bedləm] n. loud noise; chaos.

bedraggled [bɪ'drægld] adj. wet and dirty.

bee [biː] n. small insect which makes honey. **bee-eater,** n. small tropical bird, which eats insects such as bees. **beehive,** n. box in which a colony of bees lives. **beekeeper,** n. person who keeps bees. **beekeeping,** n. keeping of bees (for honey). **beeline,** n. straight line; **he made a b. for the drinks** = he went straight to the drinks. **beeswax,** n. wax produced by bees, used as a polish.

beech [biːtʃ] n. (pl. **-es**) large northern tree; wood of this tree.

beef [biːf] 1. n. (a) meat from a bull or cow; **corned b.** = beef which has been salted. (b) inf. grumble. 2. v. inf. to grumble (**about**). **beefburger** ['biːfbɜːgə] n. round flat cake of minced beef. **beefy,** adj. (**-ier, -iest**) muscular.

beep [biːp] 1. n. short high sound made by an electronic device, such as a computer. 2. v. to make a short high-pitched sound.

beer ['bɪə] n. alcoholic drink made from malt, flavoured with hops; a glass of this drink. **beery,** adj. referring to beer.

beet [biːt] n. (a) **sugar b.** root vegetable grown for processing into sugar. (b) beetroot. **beetroot,** n. dark red root vegetable.

beetle ['biːtl] n. small winged insect with a hard cover over its wings.

beetling ['biːtlɪŋ] adj. (cliff) which is high and looks threatening.

befall [bɪ'fɔːl] v. (**befell; has befallen**) (formal) to happen (to).

befit [bɪ'fɪt] v. (formal) (**befitted**) to suit.

before [bɪ'fɔː] adv., prep. & conj. (a) in front (of). (b) earlier (than). **beforehand,** adv. in advance.

befriend [bɪ'frend] v. to be friendly to and help (s.o.).

beg [beg] v. (**begged**) (a) to ask for money. (b) to ask; **to b. a favour of s.o.** = to ask s.o. a favour; **I b. your pardon** = excuse me. **beggar,** n. person who asks for money; inf. **lucky beggar!** = what a lucky person! **beggarly,** adj. small/poor (wage). **begging,** n. asking for money; **it's going b.** = no one wants it.

beget [bɪ'get] v. (**beget; begot; has begotten**) (old) to give birth to; to produce.

begin [bɪ'gɪn] v. (**began; has begun**) to start; **b. again** = start from the beginning. **beginner,** n. person who is starting to do sth. **beginning,** n. first part/start; **at the b.** = to start with.

begonia [bɪ'gəʊnɪə] n. pot plant with large bright flowers.

begrudge [bɪ'grʌdʒ] v. to feel resentment because of sth s.o. has or does; **I don't b. him his money.**

beguile [bɪ'gaɪl] v. to make (time) pass quickly and pleasantly.

behalf [bɪ'hɑːf] n. (a) **I am speaking on b. of the association** = I am speaking to get support for the association. (b) **acting on my b.** = acting for me. (c) **don't worry on my b.** = do not worry about me.

behave [bɪ'heɪv] v. to act; **b. yourself** = be good. **behaved**, adj. **well-behaved child** = polite/quiet child; **badly-behaved child** = child who is rude/dirty/noisy. **behaviour**, Am. **behavior**, n. conduct/way of acting. **behavioural**, adj. concerning the behaviour of human beings.

behead [bɪ'hed] v. to cut off a head.

behind [bɪ'haɪnd] 1. adv. (a) after; **he stayed b.** = he stayed at the place everyone started from. (b) late; **I am b. with my work.** 2. prep. (a) at the back of; **what is really b. it all?** = what is the real cause of it all? **I'm b. you completely** = I'm in full support. (b) late/retarded (by comparison with s.o. else); less advanced than (s.o.). 3. n. inf. buttocks. **behindhand**, adv. late.

behold [bɪ'hʊld] v. (**beheld**) (formal) to see. **beholder**, n. person who sees.

beholden [bɪ'hʊldən] adj. (formal) grateful (**to** s.o. **for** sth).

behove [bɪ'hʊv] v. to be fitting.

beige [beɪʒ] adj. pale fawn colour.

belated [bɪ'leɪtɪd] adj. late. **belatedly**, adv. late.

belay [bɪ'leɪ] v. to attach a rope.

belch [beltʃ] 1. n. (pl. -es) noise made when bringing up gas from the stomach. 2. v. (a) to make a noise by bringing up gas from the stomach through the mouth. (b) to pour **out** (smoke, flames).

beleaguered [bɪ'liːgəd] adj. in a difficult position; surrounded by enemies.

belfry ['belfrɪ] n. tower for bells.

Belgian ['beldʒən] 1. adj. referring to Belgium. 2. n. person from Belgium.

belie [bɪ'laɪ] v. (formal) to hide/to show (sth) wrongly.

believe [bɪ'liːv] v. to feel sure of (sth), without any proof; **I b. so** = I think that is correct; **to b. in sth** = to believe that sth exists. **belief**, n. feeling sure of sth. **believable**, adj. which one can believe. **believer**, n. person who believes in sth, esp. God.

belittle [bɪ'lɪtl] v. to make (sth) seem small or unimportant.

bell [bel] n. metal cup-shaped object which makes a ringing sound when hit; mechanism to make a ringing sound; **that rings a b.** = that reminds me of something. **bellboy**, Am. **bellhop**, n. messenger boy employed in a hotel. **bellpush**, n. button which rings a bell when pushed. **bell tower**, n. tower for bells.

belladonna ['belə'dɒnə] n. deadly nightshade, a poisonous plant.

belle [bel] n. beautiful woman.

bellicose ['belɪkəʊs] adj. (formal) warlike.

belligerent [bə'lɪdʒərənt] 1. adj. warlike. 2. n. country fighting a war. **belligerency**, n. being belligerent.

bellow ['beləʊ] 1. n. loud cry (of bull/angry person). 2. v. to make a loud cry.

bellows ['beləʊz] n. pl. apparatus for blowing air into a fire to make it burn brightly.

belly ['belɪ] n. (pl. -ies) inf. abdomen. **bellyache**. 1. n. pain in the stomach. 2. v. inf. to complain bitterly (**about** sth). **bellyflop**, n. inf. **to do a b.** = to fall flat on to the water instead of diving into it. **bellyful**, n. inf. **I've had a b. of his complaints** = I've had as many of his complaints as I can stand.

belong [bɪ'lɒŋ] v. (a) **to b. to s.o.** = to be s.o.'s property. (b) **to be to a club** = be a member (of a club). **belongings**, n. pl. personal property.

beloved [bɪ'lʌvd] 1. adj. whom s.o. loves. 2. n. person who is loved by s.o.

below [bɪ'ləʊ] 1. adv. lower down. 2. prep. lower than; **the temperature never goes b. 25°.**

belt [belt] 1. n. (a) strap which goes round your waist; **seat b.** = belt in a car or aircraft which holds you safely in place. (b) zone; **green b.** = area round a town where building is not permitted. 2. v. (a) Sl. **to b. along** = to go very fast. (b) Sl. **b. up!** = keep quiet! (c) inf. **they were belting out a song** = singing a song very loudly.

bemoan [bɪ'məʊn] v. (formal) to complain about (sth).

bemused [bɪ'mjuːzd] adj. bewildered/puzzled.

bench [bentʃ] n. (pl. -es) (a) long hard seat (for several people). (b) the

b. = group of magistrates who try cases in court. (c) table (for working). **benchmark,** n. standard against which something can be tested.

bend [bend] **1.** n. (a) curve; **S-bend** = double curve in a pipe; inf. **round the b.** = quite mad. (b) **the bends** = illness in divers caused by coming up from a deep dive too quickly. **2.** v. (**bent**) to make (a straight object) curved; to curve. **bend down,** v. to stoop.

beneath [bɪ'ni:θ] **1.** adv. underneath/ below. **2.** prep. under; **he thinks it is b. him** = he thinks it is too unimportant for him to deal with.

benediction [benɪ'dɪkʃn] n. blessing (in church).

benefactor, benefactress ['benɪfæktə, 'benɪfæktrəs] n. person who gives s.o./a society money.

beneficent [bɪ'nefɪsənt] adj. (formal) (person) who does good.

beneficial [benɪ'fɪʃl] adj. which does good; useful.

beneficiary [benɪ'fɪʃərɪ] n. (pl. -ies) person who inherits sth from a person who has died.

benefit ['benɪfɪt] **1.** n. (a) profit/advantage. (b) payment; **unemployment b.** = payment (by the state) to unemployed people; **maternity b.** = payment to a woman who has had a baby. **2.** v. to be of profit.

benevolence [bə'nevələns] n. goodness/charity. **benevolent,** adj. good/ charitable; **b. dictatorship** = dictatorship which provides for the wellbeing of the people. **benevolently,** adv. in a benevolent way.

benighted [bɪ'naɪtəd] adj. uneducated.

benign [bɪ'naɪn] adj. (a) pleasant (person). (b) non-malignant (growth).

bent [bent] **1.** adj. (a) curved. (b) **he is b. on becoming a sailor** = he is very keen to become a sailor. (c) Sl. dishonest. **2.** n. **she has a natural b. to be a nurse** = she has an instinct to become a nurse. **3.** v. see also **bend**.

benzene ['benzi:n] n. liquid obtained from coal, which is used as a fuel and causes cancer. **benzine** ['benzi:n] n. liquid mixture obtained from petroleum, and used for cleaning.

bequeath [bɪ'kwi:ð] v. to leave (property/money) **to** s.o. when you die. **bequest** [bɪ'kwest] n. property left to s.o.

berberis ['bɜ:bərɪs] n. plant with small red berries, grown for decoration.

bereaved [bɪ'ri:vd] n. **the b.** = (i) widow/widower; (ii) family of a person who has died. **bereavement,** n. loss of member of the family through death.

beret ['berɪ] n. round cloth or felt cap with no peak.

beriberi [berɪ'berɪ] n. tropical disease of the nervous system.

berry ['berɪ] n. (pl. -ies) fruit of a shrub.

berserk [bə'zɜ:k] adj. **to go b.** = to go wild/mad.

berth [bɜ:θ] **1.** n. (a) place where a ship ties up to a quay; **to give a wide b.** = to avoid sth at all costs. (b) bed (in a ship/train). **2.** v. to tie up (a ship).

beryl ['berɪl] n. type of precious stone.

beseech [bɪ'si:tʃ] v. (**beseeched/ besought** [bɪ'sɔ:t]) (formal) to ask (s.o. **to do** sth).

beset [bɪ'set] v. (**beset**) to surround, causing problems. **besetting sin,** n. defect which is always present.

beside [bɪ'saɪd] prep. at the side of; **b. the point** = nothing to do with the subject. **besides** [bɪ'saɪdz] **1.** prep. other than. **2.** adv. also/in any case.

besiege [bɪ'si:dʒ] v. (of troops/newspaper reporters) to surround.

besought [bɪ'sɔ:t] v. see **beseech**.

bespoke [bɪ'spəʊk] adj. **b. tailor** = tailor who makes clothes to measure.

best [best] (superlative of good and well) **1.** adj. & n. very good; better than anyone/anything else; **b. man** = friend of the bridegroom who helps him at a wedding; **the b. of it is that** = the most interesting/funniest part of the story is that; **do your b.** = do as well as you can; **for the b. part of an hour** = for almost a whole hour; **to the b. of my knowledge** = as far as I know. **2.** adv. in a way which is better than anyone else; **best-dressed** = wearing the most fashionable clothes. **bestseller,** n. book/article that sells in very large numbers.

bestial ['bestjəl] adj. like a beast. **bestiality** [bestɪ'ælɪtɪ] n. being bestial.

bestir [bɪ'stɜ:] v. (formal) **to b. yourself** = to get the energy to do sth.

bestow [bɪ'stəʊ] v. (formal) to give.

bet [bet] **1.** *n.* money put down as a pledge when you try to forecast the result of a race, etc., and which you lose if you guess wrongly. **2.** *v.* (**bet**) to offer to pay money if what you think will happen does not happen; **he b. me £10 the Prime Minister would lose the election; I b. you he's going to be late** = I am quite sure. **better**, *n.* person who bets. **betting**, *n.* placing of bets; **b. shop** = office where you can bet money on horse races.

beta ['bi:tə] *n.* second letter of the Greek alphabet. **beta blocker** *n.* drug which reduces the heart's activity.

betake [bɪ'teɪk] *v.* (**betook**) (*formal*) to take.

betel ['bi:tl] *n.* type of tropical nut.

bête noire [bet'nwɑ:] *n.* thing which you dislike particularly.

betide [bɪ'taɪd] *v.* (*formal*) to happen to (s.o.).

betray [bɪ'treɪ] *v.* to reveal a secret about s.o. to his enemies. **betrayal**, *n.* giving s.o. up to his enemies.

betroth [bɪ'trəʊð] *v.* (*formal*) to engage s.o. to marry. **betrothal**, *n.* act of betrothing s.o.

better ['betə] (*comp. of* **good** *and* **well**) **1.** *adj.* superior; of higher quality; less ill; finer (weather). **2.** *adv.* **I'm feeling b.** = I'm feeling less ill; **he thought b. of it** = he decided not to do what he had planned; **you'd b. be going** = it's time you went; **he's b. off where he is** = he's in a better position where he is. **3.** *v.* to **b. oneself/one's position** = to improve one's position.

between [bɪ'twi:n] *prep.* with things on both sides; **b. you and me** = privately; **in b.** = in the middle of.

betwixt [bɪ'twɪkst] *prep* (*old*) between.

bevel ['bevl] **1.** *n.* angled edge of a flat surface. **2.** *v.* (**bevelled**) to give a flat surface an angled edge.

beverage ['bevərɪdʒ] *n.* drink.

bevy ['bevɪ] *n.* (*pl.* **-ies**) group (esp. of girls).

bewail [bɪ'weɪl] *v.* (*formal*) to complain about (sth).

beware [bɪ'weə] *v.* to **b. of** = to watch out for.

bewilder [bɪ'wɪldə] *v.* to puzzle. **bewilderment**, *n.* puzzle/surprise.

bewitch [bɪ'wɪtʃ] *v.* to charm/to cast a spell on. **bewitching**, *adj.* charming (girl).

beyond [bɪ'jɒnd] **1.** *adv.* further than; on the other side of; **it's b. a joke** = it's no longer funny.

biannual [baɪ'ænjʊəl] *adj.* which happens twice a year. **biannually**, *adv.* twice a year.

bias ['baɪəs] *n.* (*a*) **to cut material on the b.** = slantwise/diagonally; **b. binding** = narrow strip of material cut on the bias, used for hemming. (*b*) slant/strong opinion in one direction. (*c*) tendency to turn in one direction (of a bowl in a game of bowls). **biased**, *adj.* showing strong opinion in one direction/prejudiced.

bib [bɪb] *n.* small cloth tied under a baby's chin.

bible ['baɪbl] *n.* (*a*) book of Christian or Jewish scriptures. (*b*) important book of reference. **biblical** ['bɪblɪkl] *adj.* referring to the bible.

bibliography [bɪblɪ'ɒgrəfɪ] *n.* list of books/articles referring to a special subject. **bibliographer**, *n.* person who writes a bibliography. **bibliographical** [bɪblɪə'græfɪkl] *adj.* (details) referring to a particular subject. **bibliophile** ['bɪblɪəʊfaɪl] *n.* person who loves books.

bibulous ['bɪbjʊləs] *adj.* fond of drinking.

bicameralism [baɪ'kæmərəlɪzm] *n.* system of government where there are two parts of parliament, such as a national assembly and a senate.

bicarbonate [baɪ'kɑ:bənət] *n.* **b. of soda** = chemical used as a medicine for stomach pains or as an ingredient in cooking.

bicentenary [baɪsen'ti:nərɪ] *n.* anniversary of 200 years. **bicentennial** [baɪsen'tenɪəl] *adj.* referring to a bicentenary.

biceps ['baɪseps] *n.* large muscle in the top part of the arm.

bicker ['bɪkə] *v.* to quarrel.

bicycle ['baɪsɪkl] **1.** *n.* two-wheeled vehicle driven by pedals. **2.** *v.* to ride on a bicycle.

bid [bɪd] **1.** *n.* offer/attempt; **he made a b. for power** = he tried to seize power; **takeover b.** = attempt to take over a company. **2.** *v.* (*a*) (**bid/bade** [bæd]; **has bidden**) to wish; **he bade me farewell.** (*b*) (**bid; has bid**) to make an offer at an auction. **bidder**, *n.* person who makes an offer at an auction. **bidding**, *n.* (*a*) command; **I did it at his b.** = I did it because he told me to do it. (*b*) offers made at an auction.

bide [baɪd] *v.* **to b. your time** = to wait for the right moment.

bidet ['biːdeɪ] *n.* low washbasin for washing the genitals.

biennial [baɪ'enjəl] *adj. & n.* (plant) which flowers in its second year; (event) which occurs every two years. **biennially**, *adv.* every two years.

bier ['bɪə] *n.* table/hearse for carrying a coffin.

biff [bɪf] **1.** *n. inf.* hit. **2.** *v. inf.* to hit.

bifocal [baɪ'fəʊkl] *adj. & n.* **b. spectacles/ bifocals** = spectacles with two types of lens in each frame, one for reading and one for long distance.

bifurcate ['baɪfəkeɪt] *v.* to split. **bifurcation** [baɪfə'keɪʃn] *n.* splitting (of a road).

big [bɪg] **1.** *adj.* (**bigger, biggest**) large; **b. game** = large animals (lions, etc.) which are hunted for sport. **2.** *adv.* **to talk b.** = to pretend to be important. **bighead**, *n. inf.* person who is proud of himself and shows off. **bigwig**, *n.* important person in an official position.

bigamy ['bɪgəmɪ] *n.* action of illegally marrying a second wife/husband, when the first is still alive and has not been divorced. **bigamist**, *n.* person who is illegally married to two people at the same time. **bigamous**, *adj.* **b. marriage** = illegal marriage when you are already married to s.o. else.

bight [baɪt] *n.* (*a*) loop of a rope. (*b*) wide curved bay.

bigot ['bɪgət] *n.* person with a narrow-minded attitude to religion/politics; fanatic. **bigoted**, *adj.* with very unbending ideas about religion/politics, etc. **bigotry**, *n.* narrow-minded attitude to religion/politics, etc.

bike [baɪk] *n. inf.* bicycle.

bikini [bɪ'kiːnɪ] *n.* brief two-piece bathing costume for women.

bilateral [baɪ'lætərəl] *adj.* on two sides; **b. agreement** = agreement between two sides.

bilberry ['bɪlbərɪ] *n.* small edible blue berry growing in northern mountains; plant which bears these berries.

bile [baɪl] *n.* bitter fluid produced by the liver to digest fat.

bilge [bɪldʒ] *n.* dirty water (in a ship's hull); *inf.* nonsense.

bilingual [baɪ'lɪŋgwəl] *adj.* using two languages; (person) who can speak two languages equally fluently.

bilious ['bɪlɪəs] *adj.* sick; **he had a b. attack** = he was sick. **biliousness**, *n.* feeling sick.

bilk [bɪlk] *v.* to cheat (s.o.) **of** sth.

bill [bɪl] *n.* (*a*) hard covering of a bird's mouth. (*b*) note showing the amount of money you have to pay. (*c*) proposed act of parliament. (*d*) *Am.* banknote. (*e*) poster (showing what is on at a theatre); **to top the b.** = to be mentioned at the top of a list as the most important item; **that will fill the b.** = will be very suitable. (*f*) **b. of fare** = menu. **billboard**, *n. Am.* large wooden panel for posters. **billfold**, *n. Am.* wallet for banknotes. **billhook**, *n.* large hooked knife, used for cutting small branches.

billabong ['bɪləbɒŋ] *n.* (*in Australia*) loop in a river where there is no current.

billet ['bɪlɪt] **1.** *n.* lodgings (for soldiers). **2.** *v.* to lodge (soldiers) **on** s.o.

billiards ['bɪljədz] *n.* game involving hitting balls with a long rod on a smooth green-covered table. **billiard ball, billiard table**, *n.* ball/table used in the game of billiards.

billion ['bɪljən] *n.* one million millions; *Am.* one thousand millions; **billions of letters** = a great many letters.

billow ['bɪləʊ] **1.** *n.* large wave. **2.** *v.* to move in large waves.

billy can ['bɪlɪkæn] *n.* small can used (esp. by hikers) for cooking.

billy goat ['bɪlɪgəʊt] *n.* male goat.

biltong ['bɪltɒŋ] *n.* dried beef, eaten in Southern Africa.

bimbo ['bɪmbəʊ] *n. Sl.* attractive young girl.

bimonthly [baɪ'mʌnθlɪ] **1.** *adj.* every two months; twice a month. **2.** *n.* magazine appearing every fortnight.

bin [bɪn] *n.* storage box; **pedal b.** = rubbish container which opens with a pedal; **bread b.** = box for keeping bread fresh.

binary ['baınərı] *adj.* in twos; **b. system** = where numbers are shown by the figures 1 and 0 only.

bind [baınd] **1.** *n. Sl.* nuisance. **2.** *v.* (**bound** [baʊnd]) (*a*) to tie. (*b*) to cover (a book). (*c*) to oblige (s.o.) to do sth.; **to b.** (**s.o.**) **over** = to make s.o. promise to obey the law for a period of time. **binder,** *n.* (*a*) bookbinder. (*b*) stiff cover for holding and protecting loose sheets of paper/magazines. **bindery,** *n.* factory which binds books. **binding, 1.** *adj.* **this contract is b. on both parties** = both parties have to do what it says. **2.** *n.* outside cover of a book. **bindweed,** *n.* type of climbing weed.

binge [bındʒ] *n. inf.* wild drunken party.

bingo ['bıŋgəʊ] *n.* game (played in public) where the aim is to cover up all the numbers on a card as they are called out.

binnacle ['bınəkl] *n.* box containing the compass on a ship.

binocular [bı'nɒkjʊlə] **1.** *adj.* **b. vision** = ability to see the same object with two eyes, and therefore to judge distance. **2.** *n. pl.* **binoculars** = double glasses for seeing long distances.

binomial [baı'nəʊmıəl] *adj.* (theory) based on two figures; **b. classification** = way of classifying plants and animals, using two Latin names.

biochemistry [baıəʊ'kemıstrı] *n.* science of the chemical constituents of animals or plants. **biochemical,** *adj.* referring to biochemistry. **biochemist,** *n.* person who studies the chemical composition of animals or plants.

biodegradable [baıəʊdı'greıdəbl] *adj.* which decomposes naturally to form harmless material.

biography [baı'ɒgrəfı] *n.* story of the life of s.o. **biographer,** *n.* person who writes a biography. **biographical** [baıə'græfıkl] *adj.* referring to a biography.

biology [baı'ɒlədʒı] *n.* study of living things. **biological** [baıə'lɒdʒıkl] *adj.* referring to living things; **b. warfare** = war in which germs are used. **biologist,** *n.* person who studies biology.

biomass ['baıəʊmæs] *n.* all living organisms in a certain place.

bionic [baı'ɒnık] *adj.* with powers reinforced by electronic devices.

biophysics [baıəʊ'fızıks] *n.* science of the physics of living things.

biopsy ['baıɒpsı] *n.* operation to remove a growth/a piece of tissue.

biorhythms ['baıəʊrıðmz] *n. pl.* cycles of activity which are said to recur regularly in each person's life.

bipartite [baı'pɑːtaıt] *adj.* with two sides taking part.

biped ['baıped] *n.* animal with two legs.

biplane ['baıpleın] *n.* aircraft with two sets of wings, one above the other.

birch [bɜːtʃ] **1.** *n.* (*pl.* -es) **silver b.** = common northern tree with white bark. **2.** *v.* to beat with a bundle of twigs.

bird [bɜːd] *n.* (*a*) animal with wings and feathers. (*b*) *inf.* person. (*c*) *inf.* girl. **bird's-eye view,** *n.* view from high up looking down. **bird watcher,** *n.* person who studies birds. **bird watching,** *n.* study of birds.

biretta [bı'retə] *n.* small cap worn by a Catholic priest.

biro ['baıərəʊ] *n.* (*pl.* -os) trademark for a ballpoint pen.

birth [bɜːθ] *n.* being born; **he is French by b.** = he has French nationality because his parents are French; **b. certificate** = official document showing date and place of s.o.'s birth; **b. control** = method of preventing pregnancy; **b. rate** = average number of children born per thousand population; **to give b. to** = to have (a child)/to produce (young). **birthday,** *n.* date on which you were born; **in his b. suit** = naked/ with no clothes on. **birthmark,** *n.* mark on the skin which is there from birth. **birthplace,** *n.* place where s.o. was born/sth was invented. **birthright,** *n.* right which you inherit at birth.

biscuit ['bıskıt] *n.* small hard cake, usu. sweet; **cheese and biscuits** = cheese with dry unsweetened biscuts; **water biscuits** = biscuits made of flour and water.

bisect [baı'sekt] *v.* to cut into two equal parts.

bisexual [baı'seksjʊəl] *adj.* who is attracted to both sexes.

bishop ['bıʃəp] *n.* (*a*) church leader in charge of a diocese. (*b*) piece in chess shaped like a bishop's hat. **bishopric,** *n.* post of bishop.

bismuth ['bızməθ] *n.* (*element:* Bi) white metal used in medicine.

bison ['baɪsn] *n.* (*pl.* **bison**) large wild ox or cow.

bistro ['bi:strəʊ] *n.* (*pl.* **-os**) small restaurant serving continental food.

bit [bɪt] *n.* (*a*) small piece; **a b. longer** = a little while longer; **the chair has come to bits** = has fallen apart; **she's thrilled to bits** = very pleased; **he is a b. of a nuisance** = he is rather a nuisance; **b. by b.** = in stages; **not a b. of use** = of no use at all; **he's every b. as ugly as you said** = just as ugly; **b. part** = small part (in a play). (*b*) piece of metal for making holes which is placed in a drill. (*c*) piece of metal going through a horse's mouth to which the reins are attached. (*d*) small piece of information (in a computer). (*e*) *v. see also* **bite**. **bitty,** *adj. inf.* disconnected; made of many little bits.

bitch [bɪtʃ] **1.** *n.* (*pl.* **-es**) (*a*) female dog. (*b*) *inf.* unpleasant woman. **2.** *v. inf.* to complain.

bite [baɪt] **1.** *v.* (**bit; has bitten**) (*a*) to cut with teeth; **he bit my head off** = he spoke angrily to me. (*b*) to work/to have effect. **2.** *n.* (*a*) mouthful. (*b*) place where you have been bitten. **biting,** *adj.* sharp (wind); piercing (cold); sharp (remark).

bitten ['bɪtn] *v. see* **bite**.

bitter ['bɪtə] **1.** *adj.* (*a*) not sweet; sour. (*b*) resentful/cruel; **to the b. end** = right to the very end. (*c*) very cold. **2.** *n.* light-coloured beer which is not sweet. **bitterly,** *adv.* sharply/resentfully. **bitterness,** *n.* resentment.

bittern ['bɪtən] *n.* marsh bird which makes a booming call.

bitumen ['bɪtjʊmən] *n.* black substance, like tar. **bituminous** [bɪ'tju:mɪnəs] *adj.* referring to bitumen.

bivalve ['baɪvælv] *n.* shellfish with two shells hinged together.

bivouac ['bɪvʊæk] *v.* (**bivouacked**) to camp out in the open without a tent.

bizarre [bɪ'zɑ:] *adj.* very strange.

blab [blæb] *v.* (**blabbed**) *inf.* to talk too much/to gossip.

black [blæk] **1.** *adj.* (**-er, -est**) (*a*) of a very dark colour, the opposite of white; **b. coffee** = coffee without milk or cream; **b. economy** = section of the economy where earnings are not declared for tax; **b. ice** = dangerous layer of thin ice on a road; **I'm in his b. books** = he's angry with me; **b. box** = device which stores information about an aircraft's flight; **b. market** = selling illegally, at high prices, products which are not normally available. (*b*) bad; **b. spot** = place where traffic accidents often happen. **2.** *n.* (*a*) very dark colour, opposite to white; **to be in the b.** = to have money in a bank account. (*b*) person whose skin is very dark-coloured. **3.** *v.* to refuse to handle (goods) in support of a strike. **blackball,** *v.* to vote against (s.o.) joining a club. **blackberry,** *n.* common wild fruit, growing on long prickly stems. **blackbird,** *n.* common northern bird, the male of which has black feathers and yellow beak. **blackboard,** *n.* board on the wall which can be written on. **blackcurrant,** *n.* common black soft fruit grown in the garden. **blacken,** *v.* to make black. **blackfellow,** *n.* (*in Australia*) aborigine. **blackfly,** *n.* small black aphis. **blackguard** ['blægɑ:d] *n.* scoundrel/wicked person. **blackhead,** *n.* blocked pore which shows up as a black dot on the skin. **blackish,** *adj.* rather black. **blackleg,** *n.* person who goes to work in spite of order to go on strike. **blacklist. 1.** *n.* list of undesirable things or people. **2.** *v.* to put (s.o.'s name) on a list of undesirable people. **blackmail. 1.** *v.* to make s.o. pay money by threatening to reveal some unpleasant or shameful detail about them. **2.** *n.* act of blackmailing. **blackmailer,** *n.* person who blackmails. **Black Maria,** *n. Sl.* police van used to transport prisoners. **blackness,** *n.* total darkness. **black out,** *v.* (*a*) to wipe off/to cover up (a name). (*b*) to faint/to lose consciousness. (*c*) to cut off the electricity. **blackout,** *n.* (*a*) loss of consciousness. (*b*) sudden stoppage of electricity supply. **blacksmith,** *n.* man who makes horseshoes, gates, etc., out of metal. **blackthorn,** *n.* wild prickly bush, with white flowers.

bladder ['blædə] *n.* (*a*) bag in the body where urine is stored. (*b*) bag inside a ball which is inflated.

blade [bleɪd] *n.* (*a*) cutting part of knife,

etc. (b) thin leaf of grass. (c) one arm of a propeller. (d) flat part at the end of an oar.

blame [bleɪm] **1.** n. criticism of s.o. for having done sth; **to get the b. for** = to be said to be responsible for. **2.** v. **to b. s.o. for sth** = to say that sth was caused by s.o.; **he is to b. for the accident** = he is responsible for the accident; **I don't b. you** = I think you were quite right. **blameless,** adj. pure/innocent. **blameworthy,** adj. (person) who can rightly be blamed.

blanch [blɑːntʃ] v. (a) to put quickly into boiling water. (b) to turn white.

blancmange [blə'mɒnʒ] n. dessert like a cream jelly flavoured with chocolate/strawberry, etc.

bland [blænd] adj. smooth/not striking; (food) without much flavour. **blandly,** adv. in a smooth casual way. **blandness,** n. smoothness; lack of any striking features.

blandishments ['blændɪʃmənts] n. pl. attractive flattery.

blank [blæŋk] **1.** adj. (-er, -est) (a) (paper, etc.) with nothing on it; **b. cheque** = cheque where the figures are not written in; **b. verse** = poetry which does not rhyme; **he looked b.** = he looked lost/surprised. (b) **b. cartridge** = with no bullet in it. **2.** n. (a) white space (with nothing printed on it); **my mind is a b.** = I cannot remember anything; **he drew a b.** = he failed to make any progress. (b) cartridge with no bullet in it. **blankly,** adv. with vacant expression.

blanket ['blæŋkɪt] **1.** n. woollen bed covering; **electric b.** = electrically heated pad to warm a bed; **b. order** = order which covers many items. **2.** v. to cover (with fog, etc.).

blare ['bleə] **1.** n. loud noise. **2.** v. to make a loud noise.

blarney ['blɑːnɪ] n. talk which is intended to trick.

blasé ['blɑːzeɪ] adj. with a couldn't-careless attitude.

blaspheme [blæs'fiːm] v. to swear; to talk without respect for God. **blasphemer,** n. person who swears. **blasphemous** ['blæsfəməs] adj. showing no respect for religion; anti-reli-

gious (talk). **blasphemy,** n. disrespect for religion; swearing.

blast [blɑːst] **1.** n. (a) sharp blowing of wind. (b) short whistle. (c) **going full b.** = working at full power. (d) explosion; shock wave from an explosion. **2.** v. (a) to blow up. (b) to ruin. **blast furnace,** n. furnace used to make steel. **blast off,** v. (of rocket) to take off. **blast-off,** n. departure of a rocket.

blatant ['bleɪtənt] adj. obvious/unmistakable. **blatantly,** adv. obviously/unmistakably.

blaze [bleɪz] **1.** n. (a) fierce fire; **she worked like blazes** = she worked extremely hard. (b) white mark made by cutting away the bark of a tree; white mark on the forehead of an animal. **2.** v. (a) to burn fiercely. (b) **to b. a trail** = to mark a path by cutting the bark on trees/to be the first to do something. **blazing,** adj. fiery; **a b. row** = a violent quarrel.

blazer ['bleɪzə] n. jacket worn with a badge to show membership of a club/school.

blazon ['bleɪzn] **1.** n. coat of arms. **2.** v. to proclaim (sth).

bleach [bliːtʃ] **1.** n. substance which takes the colour out of something. **2.** v. to take the colour out of sth. **bleachers,** n. pl. Am. raised tiers of seats at a sports stadium.

bleak [bliːk] adj. (-er, -est) cold/inhospitable. **bleakly,** adv. in a cold/inhospitable way.

bleary ['blɪərɪ] adj. watery/dim (eyes). **bleary-eyed,** adj. with watery eyes.

bleat [bliːt] **1.** n. noise made by a sheep or goat. **2.** v. to make a noise like a goat/sheep; **what is he bleating on about?** = what does he keep on complaining about?

bleed [bliːd] **1.** n. **a nose b.** = loss of blood from the nose. **2.** v. (bled) to lose blood; **my heart bleeds for you** = I am very sorry for you.

bleep [bliːp] **1.** n. small noise made by a radio/a radar screen. **2.** v. (of a radio) to make a small noise. **bleeper,** n. machine which makes a bleep.

blemish ['blemɪʃ] **1.** n. (pl. -es) imperfection/mark. **2.** v. to spoil.

blench [blenʃ] v. to tremble with fear.

blend [blend] **1.** n. mixture (of coffee/

tea/tobacco). **2.** *v.* to mix. **blender,** *n.* machine for mixing food.

bless [bles] *v.* to make sacred; to bring happiness/wealth to (s.o.); **well I'm blessed!** = I am surprised; *inf.* **b. you!** = *phrase said when someone sneezes.* **blessed** ['blesɪd] *adj.* (*a*) protected by God. (*b*) *inf.* cursed/annoying. **blessing,** *n.* (*a*) thing which is useful/which brings happiness; **it's a b. in disguise** = it doesn't look like it, but it is very useful. (*b*) short prayer, esp. before or after a meal.

blether ['bleðə] *n.* silly talk.

blew [blu:] *v. see* **blow.**

blight [blaɪt] **1.** *n.* fungoid disease (attacking vegetables/leaves, etc.). **2.** *v.* to spoil/to ruin. **blighter,** *n. inf.* fellow/man.

blimp [blɪmp] *n.* small airship.

blind [blaɪnd] **1.** *n.* (*a*) covering (over a window); **Venetian b.** = blind made of many horizontal flat strips of wood or plastic. (*b*) **the b.** = people who cannot see. **2.** *adj.* not able to see; **to turn a b. eye to sth** = pretend not to notice; **b. alley** = (i) alley with no way out; (ii) position with no prospect of progress; **b. spot** = (i) part of the road which a motorist cannot see; (ii) thing which s.o. is incapable of understanding. **3.** *v.* to prevent s.o. from seeing; to make s.o. blind. **4.** *adv.* **flying b.** = flying an aircraft, using the instruments only. **blindfold. 1.** *n.* bandage put over s.o.'s eyes to prevent him from seeing. **2.** *v.* to put a bandage over s.o.'s eyes. **blindly,** *adv.* without being able to see. **blindness,** *n.* not being able to see.

blink [blɪŋk] **1.** *n. inf.* **on the b.** = not working properly. **2.** *v.* to close your eyelids very quickly. **blinkers,** *n.* shades put on a horse's eyes to prevent it from looking sideways.

blip [blɪp] *n.* small dot of light on a radar screen.

bliss [blɪs] *n.* great happiness. **blissful,** *adj.* extremely happy. **blissfully,** *adv.* happily.

blister ['blɪstə] **1.** *n.* bump on the skin (with water underneath) made by rubbing; **b. pack** = type of container, where the product is covered by a stiff plastic bubble. **2.** *v.* to make bumps on the surface (of sth).

blithely ['blaɪðlɪ] *adv.* in a happy carefree way.

blithering ['blɪðərɪŋ] *adj. inf.* awful.

blitz [blɪts] **1.** *n.* (*pl.* **-es**) (*a*) bombing (of a town). (*b*) *inf.* **b. on sth** = sudden campaign to clear sth up. **2.** *v.* to bomb.

blizzard ['blɪzəd] *n.* heavy snowstorm with strong winds.

bloated ['bləʊtɪd] *adj.* full; too fat.

bloater ['bləʊtə] *n.* dried salt herring.

blob [blɒb] *n.* large spot.

bloc [blɒk] *n.* (*political*) group.

block [blɒk] **1.** *n.* (*a*) piece/lump of stone or wood). (*b*) large building; *Am.* **he lives two blocks away** = there are two crossroads between here and his house. (*c*) group; **b. vote** = vote by a group voting together. (*d*) **b. capitals/letters** = capital letters. (*e*) **b. and tackle** = arrangement of pulleys and ropes for lifting heavy objects. **2.** *v.* to prevent sth going past; **the lorry blocked the road for hours. blockade** [blɒ'keɪd] **1.** *n.* preventing supplies being brought into a place. **2.** *v.* to prevent supplies being brought into a place. **blockage,** *n.* blocking. **block up,** *v.* to stop (a hole), to fill (a pipe).

bloke [bləʊk] *n. inf.* man.

blond, blonde [blɒnd] *adj. & n.* (man/woman) with fair hair.

blood [blʌd] *n.* red liquid in the body; **b. group** = type of blood a person has; **b. donor** = person who gives blood to be used in operations; **b. pressure** = pressure at which the heart pumps blood; **b. transfusion** = giving blood to a sick person. **it makes my b. boil** = it makes me very angry; **his b. ran cold** = he was scared. **blood bank,** *n.* place where blood is stored until it is needed for transfusions. **bloodbath,** *n.* massacre. **bloodcurdling,** *adj.* very frightening. **bloodhound,** *n.* dog trained to follow tracks. **bloodless,** *adj.* with no blood; **b. revolution** = revolution where no one was killed. **bloodshed,** *n.* killing. **bloodshot,** *adj.* red (eyes). **bloodsports,** *n. pl.* sports which involve killing animals. **bloodstain,** *n.* stain caused by blood. **bloodstained,** *adj.* stained with blood. **bloodstock,** *n.* race horses. **bloodstream,** *n.* flow of blood round the body. **bloodsucker,** *n.* animal which sucks your blood. **blood test,** *n.* test to show the condition of the blood. **bloodthirsty,** *adj.* cruel/liking gory details. **blood vessel,** *n.* vein/artery which carries blood. **bloody,** *adj.* (**-ier, -iest**) (*a*) covered with blood; where much blood has been shed; (*b*) *Sl.* awful. **bloody-minded,** *adj. inf.* awkward/uncooperative.

bloom [blu:m] **1.** *n.* (*a*) flower; **the apple trees are in full b.** = all the apple flowers are out. (*b*) velvety skin (of a peach); dust (on skin of a grape). (*c*) **b. of youth** = healthy glow of a young person. (*d*) layer of algae on the surface of the water. **2.** *v.* to flower/to flourish. **bloomer,** *n.* (*a*) *inf.* mistake. (*b*) *inf.* **bloomers** = wide knickers.

blossom ['blɒsəm] **1.** *n.* flower (on trees). **2.** *v.* to flower.

blot [blɒt] **1.** *n.* dirty spot; drop (of ink on paper). **2.** *v.* (**blotted**) to drop a spot (of ink) on sth; to dry the ink on a letter. **blotter,** *n.* pad of blotting paper. **blotting paper,** *n.* thick absorbent paper for drying ink. **blotto** ['blɒtəʊ] *adj. inf.* drunk.

blotch [blɒtʃ] *n.* large patch of colour. **blotchy,** *adj.* (face) with patches of red.

blouse [blaʊz] *n.* (woman's) shirt.

blow [bləʊ] **1.** *n.* knock/punch. **2.** *v.* (**blew** [blu:]; **has blown**) to make air move; (*of air*) to move; **it's blowing hard** = there is a strong wind; **he blew his nose** = he cleared his nose by blowing down it into a handkerchief; **to b. a fuse** = to burn out a fuse by overloading it. **blow away,** *v.* to move (sth) away by blowing. **blow down,** *v.* to fall down/to make (sth) fall down by blowing. **blow dry,** *v.* (**blow drying**) to dry (s.o.'s hair) with a blower. **blow-dry,** *n.* act of drying hair with a blower. **blower,** *n.* (*a*) device which blows. (*b*) *Sl.* telephone. **blowfly,** *n.* large blue-green fly that is attracted to meat. **blowlamp,** *n.* lamp with strong gas jet for stripping old paint. **blow off,** *v.* to go off/to make (sth) go off by blowing. **blow out,** *v.* to go out/to make (sth) go out by blowing. **blowout,** *n.* (*a*) *inf.* huge meal. (*b*) bursting (of a tyre). **blow over,** *v.* (*of*

storm) to end; to knock (sth) down by blowing. **blowpipe,** *n.* pipe through which poison arrows can be blown. **blowtorch,** *n.* blow lamp. **blow up,** *v.* (*a*) to explode. (*b*) to destroy by explosives. (*c*) to fill (sth) with air. (*d*) to enlarge (a photograph). **blowy,** *adj.* windy.

blowsy ['blaʊzɪ] *adj.* common, redfaced (woman).

blubber ['blʌbə] **1.** *n.* fat (of a whale/seal). **2.** *v.* to cry noisily.

bludgeon ['blʌdʒən] **1.** *n.* large stick for hitting people. **2.** *v.* to beat (s.o.) with a stick.

blue [blu:] **1.** *adj.* (**-er, -est**) (*a*) coloured like the sky; **b. baby** = baby with blue skin caused by heart disease; **once in a b. moon** = very seldom. (*b*) pornographic; **b. movies.** (*c*) sad. **2.** *n.* (*a*) colour like that of the sky; **out of the b.** = as a complete surprise. (*b*) **blues** = Black American folk music, the basis of jazz. **bluebell,** *n.* common blue wild flower/wild hyacinth. **blueberry,** *n. Am.* small blue berry; plant which bears this berry. **bluebottle,** *n.* large blue-green fly that is attracted to meat. **blue chip (share),** *n.* share in a safe company. **blue collar worker,** *n.* manual worker. **blue-eyed,** *adj.* with blue eyes; **blue-eyed boy** = favourite. **Blue laws,** *n. Am.* laws which regulate what can be done on a Sunday. **blue-pencil,** *v.* (**-pencilled**) to censure. **blueprint,** *n.* detailed plan. **bluish,** *adj.* rather blue.

bluff [blʌf] **1.** *n.* (*a*) steep rocky hill. (*b*) trick; **to call s.o.'s b.** = to claim (successfully) that s.o. is tricking/is lying. **2.** *adj.* down-to-earth/straightforward (person). **3.** *v.* to trick/to pretend. **bluffly,** *adv.* in a straightforward way. **bluffness,** *n.* being blunt/straightforward.

blunder ['blʌndə] **1.** *n.* mistake. **2.** *v.* (*a*) to make a mistake. (*b*) **to b. into** = to bump into. **blundering,** *adj.* clumsy.

blunt [blʌnt] **1.** *adj.* (*a*) not sharp. (*b*) straightforward/almost rude. **2.** *v.* to make blunt. **bluntly,** *adv.* frankly/almost rudely. **bluntness,** *n.* being blunt.

blur [blɜː] **1.** *n.* indistinct picture. **2.** *v.* (**blurred**) to make indistinct.

blurb [blɜːb] *n.* piece of publicity describing a book.

blurt [blɜːt] *v.* to let out (a secret).

blush [blʌʃ] **1.** *n.* (*pl.* **-es**) red shade (on skin). **2.** *v.* to go red (with embarrassment).

bluster [blʌstə] **1.** *n.* swaggering talk; air of defiance. **2.** *v.* to swagger/to show off. **blustery**, *adj.* strong (wind/gale).

BMA [biːemˈeɪ] British Medical Association.

boa [ˈbəʊə] *n.* **b. constrictor** = large tropical snake which kills animals by wrapping itself round them and squeezing them; **feather b.** = type of scarf made of feathery material.

boar [bɔː] *n.* male pig, usu. wild.

board [bɔːd] **1.** *n.* (*a*) large flat piece of wood, etc.; **ironing b.** = narrow table for ironing. (*b*) food; **b. and lodging** = food and housing; **full b.** = bed and all meals (in a hotel). (*c*) group of people in charge of a business. (*d*) **to go on b.** = to go on to a ship/into an aircraft. **2.** *v.* (*a*) to go on to a (ship/bus), into (an aircraft). **boarder,** *n.* child who lives at school. **boarding,** *adj.* (*a*) **b. card** = card which allows you to go into an aircraft. (*b*) **b. house** = house where you pay to lodge; **b. school** = school where the children live during term. **boardroom,** *n.* room where a board of directors meets. **board up,** *v.* to cover (windows/doors) with boards to prevent burglars getting into an empty house.

boast [bəʊst] **1.** *n.* act of boasting. **2.** *v.* (*a*) (**of/about**) to talk about how clever/strong/handsome, etc., you are. (*b*) to possess (sth), and be proud. **boaster,** *n.* person who is always boasting. **boastful,** *adj.* very proud; always boasting.

boat [bəʊt] *n.* (small) ship; **b. train** = train which connects with a boat; **we're all in the same b.** = we're all in equal circumstances. **boater,** *n.* flat straw hat. **boathouse,** *n.* shed for rowing boats. **boating,** *n.* rowing (for pleasure). **boatman,** *n.* (*pl.* **-men**) man in charge of boats. **boatswain** [ˈbəʊsn] *n.* (*at sea*) man in charge of the boats and sails.

bob [bɒb] **1.** *n.* (*a*) little curtsy. (*b*) hair tied in a knot. **2.** *v.* (**bobbed**) to move quickly up and down.

bobbin [ˈbɒbɪn] *n.* small reel for holding thread (for a sewing machine/a spinning machine).

bobble [bɒbl] *n.* little fluffy ball; **b. hat** = woolly hat with a fluffy ball.

bobby [ˈbɒbɪ] *n.* policeman. **bobby-pin,** *n. Am.* flat hairpin. **bobby-socks,** *n. pl. Am.* girls' ankle socks.

bobsleigh [ˈbɒbsleɪ] *n.* sledge with two runners, used for racing.

bode [bəʊd] *v.* **it bodes ill** = it promises to bring ruin.

bodgie [ˈbɒdʒɪ] *n.* (*in Australia*) hooligan.

bodice [ˈbɒdɪs] *n.* top part (of a dress).

bodkin [ˈbɒdkɪn] *n.* large thick needle used for threading tape or elastic.

body [ˈbɒdɪ] *n.* (*pl.* **-ies**) (*a*) main structure of an animal or person; main part of an animal or person not including the head and limbs; **dead b.** = corpse. (*b*) group of people. (*c*) main part (of a building/a car, etc.). (*d*) strength (of wine). **bodily. 1.** *adj.* of the body; **to cause s.o. grievous b. harm** = to attack s.o. and beat him up. **2.** *adv.* **they carried him out b.** = they lifted him up and carried him. **bodyguard,** *n.* person or group of people who guards s.o. **bodywork,** *n.* outer covering of a car.

boffin [ˈbɒfɪn] *n. inf.* scientist/inventor.

bog [bɒg] **1.** *n.* (*a*) area of marshland. (*b*) *Sl.* toilet. **2.** *v.* (**bogged**) **to get bogged down** = to get stuck (in mud); **the discussion got bogged down in details** = they got stuck in details. **boggy,** *adj.* marshy.

bogey [ˈbəʊgɪ] *n.* (*a*) (*also* **bogeyman**) thing which frightens children. (*b*) (*in golf*) normal number of strokes which a player should take to play a hole.

boggle [ˈbɒgl] *v.* to be reluctant (**at** = to do sth); **the mind boggles** = it is impossible to imagine.

bogie [ˈbəʊgɪ] *n.* pivoted set of wheels on a railway carriage.

bogus [ˈbəʊgəs] *adj.* false.

bohemian [bəʊˈhiːmɪən] *adj. & n.* (person) living a wild/unconventional life.

boil [bɔɪl] **1.** *n.* (*a*) swelling in the body full of infected matter. (*b*) **the kettle is on the b.** = the water is boiling; **bring the water to the b.** = make the water boil. **2.** *v.* (*a*) to heat (a liquid) until it bubbles. (*b*) to cook in boiling water; **hard-boiled egg** = egg which has been cooked until it is solid (usu. eaten cold). **boil away**, *v.* to evaporate (through boiling). **boil down**, *v.* (*a*) to evaporate (through boiling); to reduce (a piece of writing). (*b*) to be reduced to; **it all boils down to whether he will resign willingly or not** = the main question is, will he resign willingly or not. **boiler**, *n.* large metal receptacle for boiling water; main heater for central heating; **b. suit** = blue overalls. **boiling.** 1. *n.* action of heating a liquid until it bubbles; **100°C is the b. point of water.** 2. *adj.* (liquid) which is boiling or very hot; **it is b. in this room** = it is very hot. 3. *adv.* **b. hot** = very hot. **boil over**, *v.* to rise in a pan when boiling, and run over the sides.

boisterous ['bɔɪstrəs] *adj.* noisy/violent (crowd/wind/sea, etc.). **boisterously**, *adv.* in a boisterous way. **boisterousness**, *n.* noise/violence.

bold [bəʊld] *adj.* (**-er, -est**) (*a*) strongly marked (colour/outline). (*b*) daring/brave. **boldly**, *adv.* bravely/defiantly. **boldness**, *n.* daring/bravery.

bole [bəʊl] *n.* tree trunk.

bolero *n.* (*a*) [bə'leərəʊ] type of Spanish dance. (*b*) ['bɒlərəʊ] short sleeveless jacket worn by women.

boll [bɒl] *n.* seed head of the cotton plant.

bollard ['bɒlɑːd] *n.* low post on a quay for a ship's rope, or in the road to indicate where traffic should go.

bolshie ['bɒlʃi] *adj. inf.* difficult/uncooperative (person).

bolster ['bəʊlstə] 1. *n.* long pillow going right across a bed. 2. *v.* (*also* **to bolster up**) to support (s.o. who is falling).

bolt [bəʊlt] 1. *n.* (*a*) flash of lightning with thunder; **it came as a b. from the blue** = it came as a complete surprise. (*b*) metal rod which slides into a hole to secure a door. (*c*) metal rod with a screw which fastens with a nut. (*d*) **to make a b. for** = to rush towards. 2. *v.* (*a*) to run fast/to escape; **the horse bolted** = the horse got out of control. (*b*) to eat quickly and with big mouthfuls. (*c*) to fasten (a door) with a bolt. (*d*) to fasten with a bolt and nut. 3. *adv.* **sitting b. upright** = sitting straight upright.

bomb [bɒm] 1. *n.* (*a*) large explosive weapon, often dropped from an aircraft; **b. disposal** = removing the fuse from an unexploded bomb. **it went like a b.** = it went very well indeed. (*b*) (*in Australia*) old car. (*c*) *inf.* lot of money. 2. *v.* to drop bombs on. **bombard** [bɒm'bɑːd] *v.* to attack (repeatedly). **bombardment**, *n.* attack (with bombs/shells/questions). **bomber**, *n.* special aircraft for dropping bombs. **bombshell**, *n.* great (unpleasant) surprise.

bombastic [bɒm'bæstɪk] *adj.* flowery/boasting (way of speaking).

bona fide ['bəʊnə'faɪd] 1. *adj.* made in good faith; **a bona fide offer.** 2. *n.* **the police are checking on his bona fides** = they are checking that he is speaking the truth.

bonanza [bə'nænzə] *n.* great wealth (discovered suddenly).

bond [bɒnd] 1. *n.* (*a*) link; joining together. (*b*) paper showing that money has been lent to the government; **premium bonds** = bonds which are eligible to win a lottery. (*c*) contract. (*d*) **in b.** = in a customs warehouse. 2. *v.* to link/to join (with glue). **bondage**, *n.* slavery. **bonded warehouse**, *n.* warehouse containing goods in bond.

bone [bəʊn] 1. *n.* one of the solid white pieces which make up the framework of the body; **b. dry** = completely dry; **b. idle** = completely lazy; **I've got a b. to pick with you** = I want to complain about sth which you've done. 2. *v.* to take the bones out of (meat, fish). **boneless**, *adj.* with no bones. **bony**, *adj.* with big bones; with many bones.

bonfire ['bɒnfaɪə] *n.* outdoor fire for burning rubbish or as a celebration.

bongo ['bɒŋgəʊ] *n.* small drum, tapped with the hand.

bonkers ['bɒŋkəz] *adj. Sl.* mad.

bonnet ['bɒnɪt] *n.* (*a*) child's/woman's hat, with a brim framing the face. (*b*) hinged cover for the front part of a car.

bonny ['bɒnɪ] *adj.* (**-ier, -iest**) good-looking and healthy.

bonsai ['bɒnsaɪ] *n.* (art of growing) trees in small pots, pruned so that they remain small.

bonus ['bəʊnəs] *n.* (*pl.* **-es**) extra money; **cost-of-living b.** = extra pay to compensate for the increased cost of living; (*on motor insurance*) **no claim b.** = reduced payment if you have never made a claim.

boo [bu:] **1.** *inter.* call to show disapproval or to surprise. **2.** *v.* to show disapproval by saying 'boo'.

boob [bu:b] *n. Sl.* (*a*) mistake. (*b*) breast.

booby ['bu:bɪ] *n.* silly person. **booby prize,** *n.* (silly) prize given to the last person in a competition. **boobytrap. 1.** *n.* trap to catch s.o. unawares. **2.** *v.* (**boobytrapped**) to set a trap (in a place).

book [bʊk] **1.** *n.* (*a*) printed pages attached together with a cover. (*b*) **exercise b.** = book of blank pages with lines for writing on; **cheque b.** = book of blank cheques; **I'm in his bad books** = he disapproves of me. (*c*) script (of musical). (*d*) **b. of tickets** = several tickets fastened together and sold as a unit; **b. of matches** = cardboard matches fastened together in a card holder. **2.** *v.* (*a*) to reserve (a place/seat/table) on plane/in theatre/in restaurant. (*b*) **he was booked for speeding** = the police have made a charge against him for speeding. **bookable,** *adj.* which can be reserved in advance. **bookbinder,** *n.* person who puts covers on printed sheets to make a book. **bookbinding,** *n.* art of binding books. **bookcase,** *n.* cabinet/set of shelves for keeping books. **bookie,** *n. inf.* person who collects bets before a race. **book in,** *v.* to register (at a hotel). **booking,** *n.* (*a*) reservation (of seats/places); **b. office** = office (at theatre) where you can book seats in advance. (*b*) arrangement (for actor, etc.) to appear at a theatre. **bookish,** *adj.* learned/studious. **book-keeper,** *n.* person who works in the accounts department (in a firm). **book-keeping,** *n.* keeping of accounts. **booklet,** *n.* small book with only a few pages. **booklover,** *n.* person who loves (and collects) books. **bookmaker,** *n.* person who collects bets before a race. **bookmark(er),** *n.* long, narrow, piece of card/cloth/leather used to keep your place in a book. **bookmobile** ['bʊkməbi:l] *n.* travelling library. **bookseller,** *n.* person who sells books. **bookshelf,** *n.* shelf for keeping books. **bookshop,** *n.* shop selling books. **bookstall, bookstand,** *n.* kiosk (in railway station, etc.) selling books and magazines. **bookstore,** *n. Am.* bookshop. **book trade,** *n.* the book producing and selling industry. **book up,** *v.* to reserve. **bookworm,** *n.* person who reads many books.

boom [bu:m] **1.** *n.* (*a*) floating barrier across a harbour. (*b*) long rod attached to the lower edge of a sail; long rod (for holding a microphone over speakers' heads). (*c*) low muffled sound. (*d*) sudden increase (in value/sales/general prosperity). **2.** *v.* (*a*) to make a low muffled sound. (*b*) to increase suddenly/to become more prosperous.

boomerang ['bu:məræŋ] **1.** *n.* curved piece of wood which, when thrown, comes back to the thrower. **2.** *v.* to backfire/to rebound.

boon [bu:n] **1.** *n.* advantage/blessing. **2.** *adj.* **b. companion** = great friend.

boor [bɔ:, 'bʊə] *n.* rough/uncouth man. **boorish,** *adj.* rude/uncouth.

boost [bu:st] **1.** *n.* help/publicity. **2.** *v.* (*a*) to help/to promote. (*b*) to increase (voltage in electricity cable). **booster,** *n.* (*a*) apparatus for increasing voltage. (*b*) **b. rocket** = rocket which helps keep up the speed of the main rocket; **b. shot** = injection which keeps up the protection given by a former injection.

boot [bu:t] **1.** *n.* (*a*) footwear which goes above the ankle; **the b. is on the other foot** = the situation is just the opposite. (*b*) back part of a car (where the luggage can be put). **2.** *v.* (*a*) to kick. (*b*) (*computers*) to carry out a set of instructions automatically. **bootee,** *n.* small knitted boot for babies. **bootlaces,** *n. pl.* very long laces for boots. **bootleg,** *adj.* illegal (whisky, etc.). **bootlegger,** *n.* person who makes/transports illegal spirits.

booth [bu:ð] *n.* (*a*) (covered) stall at a market/fair. (*b*) small enclosed space for one person.

booty ['bu:tɪ] *n.* treasure captured in a war.

booze [bu:z] **1.** *n. inf.* alcoholic drink. **2.** *inf.* to drink (alcohol!). **boozer,** *n. inf.*

(a) person who drinks a lot. (b) bar/ public house.

boracic [bə'ræsɪk] adj. chemical substance used in ointments.

borax ['bɔːræks] n. white powder used in making glass and as an antiseptic.

Bordeaux mixture ['bɔːdəʊ'mɪkstʃə] n. sulphur spray, used on plants.

border ['bɔːdə] 1. n. frontier/edge; **flower b.** = edging of flowers along a flower bed. 2. v. **France borders on Germany** = France touches Germany; **it is a film which borders on the indecent** = which is almost indecent. **bordering,** adj. close to. **borderline,** n. line between two surfaces; **b. case** = case which is on the dividing line (between two types).

bore [bɔː] 1. n. (a) width of a tube. (b) person/thing which makes you fed up; **what a b.** = what a nuisance. (c) wave in a river caused by the tide. 2. v. (a) to make (a hole). (b) to make (s.o.) fed up (with you); **I'm bored stiff** = very bored. (c) see also **bear. boredom,** n. being bored. **borehole,** n. exploratory hole made to see if there are any mineral/oil deposits in the ground. **boring,** adj. which makes you lose interest completely.

born [bɔːn] adj. **he was b. in 1962** = his birth took place in 1962; **she's a b. actress** = she has always had a gift for acting; **I wasn't b. yesterday** = I'm not as stupid as you think.

borne [bɔːn] v. see **bear.**

boron ['bɔːrɒn] n. (element: B) brown powder which resists high temperatures and is used to make borax.

borough ['bʌrə] n. large town (with a governing council).

borrow ['bɒrəʊ] v. to take (sth) for a short time with the owner's permission; to take (money) from a bank, etc., for a time, usu. paying interest on it. **borrower,** n. person who borrows (money, etc.). **borrowing,** n. (a) act of borrowing money. (b) money borrowed.

borzoi [bɔː'zɔɪ] n. breed of long-haired hound.

bosom ['buzəm] n. breast; **b. companion** = close friend.

boss [bɒs] 1. n. (pl. -es) inf. (a) person who is in charge. (b) round knob. 2. v. inf. to command/to give orders; **she bosses him around** = she is always telling him what to do. **boss-eyed,** adj. Sl. squinting. **bossiness,** n. being bossy. **bossy,** adj. (-ier, -iest) (person) always giving orders.

bosun ['bəʊsn] n. (at sea) man in charge of the boats and sails.

botany ['bɒtənɪ] n. study of plants. **botanical** [bə'tænɪkl] adj. relating to plants; **b. gardens** = gardens scientifically arranged to show different species of plants. **botanist** ['bɒtənɪst] n. person who studies plants.

botch [bɒtʃ] v. to ruin/to make a mess of (a job).

both [bəʊθ] 1. adj. & pron. two persons/ objects together. 2. adv. at the same time.

bother ['bɒðə] 1. n. worry/annoyance. 2. v. (a) to annoy (s.o.). (b) to take trouble (to do sth). **bothered,** adj. worried/ embarrassed.

bottle ['bɒtl] 1. n. (a) tall glass/plastic container for liquids; **hot water b.** = container for hot water which is used for warming beds. (b) (slang) courage. 2. v. to put into a bottle; **bottled fruit** = fruit preserved in sealed jars. **bottle bank,** n. public container for old bottles. **bottle-feeding,** n. feeding of babies by a bottle, not at the breast. **bottleneck,** n. (a) narrow part of a bottle. (b) narrow road (where traffic often gets jammed). **bottle up,** v. (a) to hold back (one's feelings). (b) to jam (traffic). **bottling,** n. putting into bottles, esp. preserving fruit in sealed jars.

bottom ['bɒtəm] 1. n. (a) lowest part; base; **prices have touched rock b.** = they are at their lowest; **he came b. of the class** = he had the worst marks. (b) buttocks. 2. adj. lowest. **bottomless,** adj. with no bottom. **bottomry,** n. mortgage of a ship.

botulism ['bɒtjʊlɪzəm] n. illness caused by bacteria in food.

bouclé ['buːkleɪ] n. wool with many loops in it.

boudoir ['buːdwɑː] n. small private room for a woman.

bouffant ['buːfɒŋ] adj. fluffy (hairstyle).

bougainvillea [buːgən'vɪlɪə] *n.* tropical climbing plant with purple or pink flowers.

bough [baʊ] *n.* large branch.

bought [bɔːt] *v. see* **buy.**

boulder ['bəʊldə] *n.* large rock.

boulevard ['buːləvɑːd] *n.* wide road.

bounce [baʊns] **1.** *n.* (*a*) springiness; **the bed has a lot of b. in it.** (*b*) **he's got a lot of b.** = he is full of energy. **2.** *v.* (*a*) to spring up and down; to make (sth) spring up and down; **the ball bounced down the stairs.** (*b*) *inf.* **his cheque bounced** = there was not enough money in the account to pay the sum on the cheque. **bouncer,** *n.* (*a*) (*in cricket*) ball which bounces very high. (*b*) person who throws undesirable customers out of a restaurant/club, etc. **bouncing,** *adj.* (ball) which bounces; **b. baby** = healthy-looking baby. **bouncy,** *adj.* (*a*) which bounces well. (*b*) (person) who is full of energy.

bound [baʊnd] **1.** *n.* leap. **2.** *adj.* (*a*) **b. for South America** = leaving for/on the way to South America; **homeward b.** = on the way home. (*b*) tied up. (*c*) obliged. (*d*) very likely; **they are b. to be late.** (*e*) *see also* **bind. 3.** *v.* to leap. **bounden,** *adj.* **b. duty** = obligation. **boundless,** *adj.* without any limits. **bounds,** *n.* limits/edges; **out of b.** = (place) where people are not allowed to go.

boundary ['baʊndrɪ] *n.* frontier/outer limit of sth; (*in cricket*) **to hit a b.** = to hit the ball beyond the edge of the field.

bounty ['baʊntɪ] *n.* (*a*) giving of (money). (*b*) money given as a reward or in excess of usual wages. **bountiful,** *adj.* generous.

bouquet [bʊ'keɪ] *n.* artistically arranged bunch of flowers.

bourbon ['bɜːbən] *n. Am.* corn whisky.

bourgeois ['bʊəʒwɑː] *adj. & n.* middle-class (person). **bourgeoisie** [bʊəʒwɑ-'ziː] *n.* the middle class.

bout [baʊt] *n.* (*a*) sports contest. (*b*) attack (of illness).

boutique [buː'tiːk] *n.* small shop selling fashionable clothes/perfume, etc.; small clothing department in a large store.

bovine ['bəʊvaɪn] *adj.* referring to cows and bulls; **b. spongiform en-cephalopathy** = disease of cattle, which affects the brain, and is possibly connected to scrapie.

bow[1] ['bəʊ] *n.* (*a*) long piece of wood with taut string joining both ends, used for shooting arrows. (*b*) wooden rod with hair stretched taut between its ends, used for playing a violin or other stringed instrument. (*c*) ribbon/tie knotted to look like a butterfly. **bow-legged,** *adj.* with legs which curve apart at the knee. **bow tie,** *n.* short necktie tied in a bow. **bow window,** *n.* window projecting out from the wall in a curve.

bow[2] [baʊ] **1.** *n.* (*a*) salute made by bending the body forward. (*b*) (*usu.* **bows**) front part of a ship. (*c*) rower who sits nearest the bow of a rowing boat. **2.** *v.* to bend forward. **bowsprit,** *n.* horizontal mast going forward from the bows of a ship.

bowdlerize ['baʊdləraɪz] *v.* to cut indecent parts from (a book).

bowels (*sometimes* **bowel**) ['baʊəlz] *n.* intestines; **in the b. of the earth** = deep underground.

bower ['baʊə] *n.* shelter covered by trees or plants.

bowl [bəʊl] **1.** *n.* (*a*) wide container (of china/plastic, etc.). (*b*) wooden ball for playing game of bowls. (*c*) **bowls** = game where wooden balls are rolled to try to get nearest to small target ball. **2.** *v.* (*a*) to throw a ball, esp. in cricket. (*b*) to roll a bowl (in a game of bowls). **bowler,** *n.* (*a*) person who plays bowls. (*b*) (*in cricket*) person who throws the ball to the opposing batsman. (*c*) **b. (hat)** = black round-topped man's hat. **bowling,** *n.* (*a*) game of bowls; **b. green** = grass pitch for playing bowls. (*b*) game of knocking down skittles with a large ball; **b. alley** = hall for bowling. **bowl over,** *v.* to knock down/to surprise.

box [bɒks] **1.** *n.* (*pl.* **-es**) (*a*) container with a lid; **letter b./pillar b.** = box in the street for posting leters; **letter b.** = slit in a door for delivering letters or newspapers; **b. number** = number of a box in the post office/newspaper office where letters will be kept for you and delivered in bulk. (*b*) evergreen tree, with very small leaves; hard wood from this tree. (c) small balcony room in a theatre; cubicle for a horse; place where a witness gives evidence in court. (d) smack (on the ear). **2.** v. (a) **to b. s.o.'s ears** = to smack s.o. on the ears. (b) to fight an opponent in the boxing ring. **boxer**, n. (a) man who practises the sport of boxing. (b) breed of large dog with short hair. **boxing**, n. sport of fighting with gloves in a ring; **B. Day** = day after Christmas Day, 26th December. **box office**, n. office in a theatre where you buy tickets. **boxroom**, n. small room for keeping boxes, cases, unused objects. **box spanner**, n. spanner with a ring-shaped end which fits over nuts.

boy [bɔɪ] n. male child; **old b.** = old friend/old man/former pupil of a school. **boyfriend**, n. young male friend. **boyhood**, n. youth/time of life when you are a boy. **boyish**, adj. like a boy. **Boy Scouts**, n. social/educational organization for boys.

boycott ['bɔɪkɒt] **1.** n. act of boycotting. **2.** v. to refuse to have anything to do with s.o./sth.

BP ['bi:'pi:] British Pharmacopœia; British Petroleum.

BR [bi:'ɑ:] British Rail.

bra [brɑ:] n. inf. brassière/woman's undergarment for supporting the breasts.

brace [breɪs] **1.** n. (a) support; (on teeth) metal clamp to make teeth grow straight. (b) **braces** = elastic straps over the shoulders to hold up trousers. (c) pair; **a b. of grouse** = two grouse. (d) tool for holding a bit to drill holes. **2.** v. to support/to strengthen; **he braced himself for the ordeal** = he stiffened his muscles to prepare himself for the ordeal. **bracing**, adj. invigorating/healthy (climate).

bracelet ['breɪslət] n. ornamental chain/band worn round the wrist.

bracken ['brækən] n. wild fern growing often in open country.

bracket ['brækɪt] **1.** n. (a) support (for shelf, etc., against a wall). (b) printing symbol showing that sth is separated from the rest of the text. (c) (administrative) group; **the middle-income b. 2.** v. (a) to put (words) into brackets. (b) to link; **his name was bracketed with that of the mayor.**

brackish ['brækɪʃ] adj. salty/undrinkable water.

bract [brækt] n. part of a plant which is shaped like a leaf but can be coloured like a flower.

brad [bræd] n. small nail with a flat head.

bradawl ['brædɔ:l] n. boring tool for making holes (esp. in leather).

brag [bræg] v. (**bragged**) to boast.

Brahmin ['brɑ:mɪn] n. highest-ranking Hindu; Am: very important person (esp. in the civil service).

braid [breɪd] **1.** n. plaited decoration. **2.** v. to plait (hair) with ribbon.

braille [breɪl] n. system of raised dots on paper for the blind to read by touch.

brain [breɪn] **1.** n. nervous centre of the head which thinks and directs the body; **use your b.** = think hard; **she's got brains** = she's intelligent; inf. **b. drain** = departure of highly intelligent people to other countries in order to work for higher salaries. **2.** v. to knock s.o. out by hitting him on the head. **brainchild**, n. original idea/plan thought up by s.o. **braininess**, n. intelligence. **brainless**, adj. idiotic/stupid. **brainpower**, n. intelligence/ability to think or reason. **brainstorm**, n. sudden mad idea. **brainwash**, v. to indoctrinate (s.o.)/to make s.o. think in a totally different manner from before. **brainwave**, n. brilliant idea. **brainy**, adj. (**-ier, -iest**) inf. intelligent.

braise [breɪz] v. to cook (meat/vegetables) in a covered pot with very little liquid.

brake [breɪk] **1.** n. mechanism for stopping a car/bicycle, etc.; **hand b.** = brake operated by a hand lever. **2.** v. to stop/to slow down by applying the brakes. **braking**, n. putting on the brakes; **b. distance** = distance a car travels after the brakes are applied before it comes to a halt.

bramble ['bræmbl] n. wild blackberry.

bran [bræn] n. skins of wheat seeds which are separated from the flour.

branch [brɑ:ntʃ] **1.** n. (pl. **-es**) (a) limb of a tree. (b) offshoot; **b. of a river**; **b. line** = minor railway line. (c) office (of a bank, etc.); store (of a chain of stores). **2.** v. **to b. out** = to spread out/to diversify.

brand [brænd] 1. *n.* (*a*) identification mark made (on cattle) by a hot iron. (*b*) named product made by one manufacturer. 2. *v.* (*a*) to mark (cattle) with a hot iron. (*b*) **he was branded as a thief** = he was called a thief. **branded,** *adj.* (*a*) marked (cattle, etc.). (*b*) (goods) with a brand name. **brand name,** *n.* name applied to one product. **brand-new,** *adj.* completely new.

brandish ['brændıʃ] *v.* to wave (sth) about.

brandy ['brændı] *n.* strong alcohol distilled from wine; glass of this alcohol; **b. snap** = thin rolled biscuit flavoured with ginger.

brash [bræʃ] *adj.* vulgar, pushing.

brass [brɑːs] *n.* (*a*) yellow metal made from copper and zinc; **top b.** = directors/high-ranking officers; **to get down to b. tacks** = to discuss the basic problem. (*b*) musical instruments made of brass; **a b. band.** (*c*) *inf.* money. (*d*) (*in church*) memorial plate made of brass. **brass rubbing,** *n.* reproduction of a brass plate by covering it with paper and rubbing with wax. **brassy,** *adj.* (*a*) (noise) like that of brass instruments. (*b*) rude, loud-mouthed (person).

brassicas ['bræsıkəz] *n. pl.* plants of the cabbage family.

brassière ['bræzıə] *n.* woman's undergarment for supporting the breasts.

brat [bræt] *n.* rude child.

bravado [brə'vɑːdəʊ] *n.* reckless bravery.

brave [breɪv] 1. *adj.* (-er, -est) not afraid; courageous. 2. *v.* to defy. 3. *n.* male American Indian fighter. **bravely,** *adv.* with courage. **bravery,** *n.* courage.

bravo [brɑː'vəʊ] *inter. showing* approval.

brawl [brɔːl] 1. *n.* wild fight. 2. *v.* to fight wildly. **brawler,** *n.* person who is fighting wildly.

brawn [brɔːn] *n.* (*a*) chopped meat mixed with jelly to form a loaf. (*b*) muscle power. **brawny,** *adj,* muscular/strong.

bray [breɪ] *v.* to make a loud call like a donkey.

brazen ['breɪzn] 1. *adj.* (*a*) like brass/made of brass. (*b*) shameless. 2. *v.* **he brazened it out** = he impudently got through the awkward situation.

brazier ['breɪzɪə] *n.* metal basket for burning coal.

Brazilian [brə'zılıən] 1. *adj.* referring to Brazil. 2. *n.* person from Brazil.

breach [briːtʃ] 1. *n.* (*pl.* **-es**) (*a*) crack (in a defence/dam). (*b*) breaking (of a law/promise); **b. of the peace** = rowdy action; **b. of faith** = going back on what has been promised; **b. of promise** = refusing to marry s.o. after having promised to do so. 2. *v.* to split; to make a crack in (a wall).

bread [bred] *n.* (*no pl.*) food made from flour, water and yeast baked in an oven; **wholemeal b.** = bread made from flour which contains the whole grain; **bread-and-butter letter** = letter written to say thank you for hospitality; **b. bin** = metal/plastic container for keeping bread fresh. **breadcrumbs,** *n. pl.* bread broken up into very small pieces. **breadline,** *n.* **he's on the b.** = he has hardly enough money to live on. **breadwinner,** *n.* person who earns money to feed the family.

breadth [bredθ] *n.* (*a*) measurement of how broad or wide sth is. (*b*) wideness (of views).

break [breɪk] 1. *n.* (*a*) split/crack (where two parts have broken). (*b*) quarrel. (*c*) **b. in the weather** = change in the weather. (*d*) rest period; **coffee b.** = period where you stop work for a cup of coffee; **morning b.** = short period of play during the morning at school. (*e*) **he had a lucky b.** = his bad luck changed. (*f*) **at b. of day** = at dawn. (*g*) series of shots in snooker. 2. *v.* (**broke; has broken**) (*a*) to fall to pieces/to smash (sth) into pieces; **we'll b. our journey at Edinburgh** = we'll stop for a while at Edinburgh; **my watch is broken** = my watch has stopped working; **it broke her heart** = she was extremely upset; **he broke the record for the high jump** = did better than anyone had ever done before. (*b*) **we are breaking even** = we are not making a loss or a profit. (*c*) not to keep (a promise/a rule). (*d*) **the storm broke** = storm suddenly started; **the day was breaking** = daylight was coming. (*e*) (*of boy's voice*) to become deeper as the boy grows older. (*f*) to cushion (a fall). (*g*) (*of wave*) to grow tall and crash down. **breakable,** *adj.* which can easily be broken. **breakables,** *n. pl.* fragile objects (glasses/cups, etc.). **breakages,** *n. pl.* breaking (of glass, etc.); things which have been broken. **break away,** *v.* to escape/to be detached (**from**). **breakaway,** *adj.* which has become detached; **the b. nationalist party** = the nationalist party which has split off from a larger party. **break down,** *v.* (*a*) to smash (sth). (*b*) to collapse; to go wrong. (*c*) to list (items). **breakdown,** *n.* (*a*) collapse; **nervous b.** = state where you become severely depressed. (*b*) list under various headings. (*c*) **we had a b. on the motorway** = our car stopped working; **b. truck** = truck which tows away cars which do not work. **breaker,** *n.* (*a*) big wave which is breaking. (*b*) person who buys old cars, etc., to take them to bits and sell the parts. **breakfast** ['brekfəst] **1.** *n.* first meal of the day; **b. cup** = large cup; **wedding b.** = meal (often lunch) after a wedding; **continental b.** = breakfast of bread and coffee; **English b.** = breakfast with cereals, bacon and eggs, toast and coffee or tea. **2.** *v.* to eat the first meal of the day; **break in,** *v.* (*a*) to smash in. (*b*) to interrupt. (*c*) to train (a horse). **break-in,** *n.* burglary. **breaking,** *n.* (*a*) action of smashing/falling to pieces. (*b*) **b. and entering** = crime of breaking into s.o.'s property. **break into,** *v.* to smash in order to enter. **break loose,** *v.* to escape. **breakneck,** *adj.* **at b. speed** = extremely fast. **break off,** *v.* (*a*) to split away/to crack; to remove (sth) by breaking. (*b*) to stop; **they have broken off negotiations. break open,** *v.* to smash (in order to open). **break out,** *v.* (*a*) to start; **war has broken out.** (*b*) to escape; **three prisoners broke out from prison. breakout,** *n.* escape. **break through,** *v.* to smash in order to go through. **breakthrough,** *n.* sudden success (in science). **break up,** *v.* (*a*) to smash to pieces. **break it up!** = stop fighting; **they had a quarrel and broke up** = did not work/live together any more. (*b*) to go on holiday; **school breaks up on Tuesday.** (*c*) (*of weather*) to get worse. **breakup,** *n.* coming to pieces/falling apart. **breakwater,** *n.*

wall/fence going into the sea to prevent waves from battering the coast.

bream [bri:m] *n.* (*pl.* **bream**) type of fat edible fish.

breast [brest] *n.* (*a*) one of two milk-giving organs in a woman's body; **b. feeding** = feeding a child with milk from the breast. (*b*) chest/front part of the top of the body; **b. pocket** = pocket on the front of a jacket; **b. stroke** = swimming stroke where both arms stretch out together and are brought back to the chest.

breath [breθ] *n.* air which goes into and out of the body; **out of b./gasping for b.** = having difficulty in breathing; **don't waste your b. on them** = don't waste time talking to them; **it took my b. away** = I was completely astonished; **he muttered under his b.** = quietly; **a b. of wind** = a slight breeze. **breathalyse** ['breθəlaɪz] *v.* to test (a driver) to see if he is drunk. **breathalyser,** *n.* instrument for testing if a driver has drunk too much alcohol. **breathless,** *adj.* out of breath/panting. **breathlessly,** *adv.* in a rush/without taking time to breathe. **breathtaking,** *adj.* so exciting/beautiful that it takes your breath away.

breathe [bri:ð] *v.* to suck air in or out through the nose or mouth; **b. deeply** = take in lots of air; **don't b. a word about it!** = don't say anything about it. **breather,** *n.* rest period; **I'm going out for a b.** = I'm going out to get some fresh air. **breathing,** *n.* act of taking air in and out of the body; **b. apparatus** = mask, etc., which allows you to breathe when in gas/smoke, etc.; **b. space** = rest period.

bred [bred] *v. see* **breed.**

breech [bri:tʃ] *n.* (*pl.* **-es**) (*a*) back part of a gun where the ammunition is loaded. (*b*) **b. birth** = birth in which the baby's buttocks appear first. (*c*) **breeches** = trousers which come down to below the knees; **breeches buoy** = device, like a canvas seat, used to rescue people at sea.

breed [bri:d] **1.** *n.* particular race of animal. **2.** *v.* (**bred**) to produce young animals/plants; **I was born and bred in the country** = I was born and grew up in the country; **well-bred person** =

s.o. who is polite/who has been well educated. **breeder,** n. (a) person who breeds (animals). (b) **(fast) b. reactor** = nuclear machine which makes a surplus of nuclear material. **breeding,** n. (a) production of animals. (b) training in good manners.

breeze [bri:z] **1.** n. slight wind; **a stiff breeze** = quite a strong wind. **2.** v. **he breezed into the restaurant** = he rushed in looking very pleased with himself. **breeze-block,** n. light building block used for building inside walls. **breezily,** adv. in a happy-go-lucky way. **breezy,** adj. (a) windy. (b) happy-go-lucky.

brethren ['breðrən] n. pl. (religious) brothers.

breve [bri:v] n. long note in music.

breviary ['bri:vjəri] n. book of Roman Catholic prayers.

brevity ['breviti] n. conciseness/ shortness.

brew [bru:] **1.** n. liquid which has been brewed. **2.** v. (a) to make (beer/tea). (b) **there's trouble brewing** = there is trouble coming. **brewer,** n. person who makes beer; **brewer's yeast** = yeast used in brewing beer, and taken in tablet form as a source of vitamin B. **brewery,** n. place where beer is made.

briar ['braiə] n. prickly wild bush (esp. rose). **briar pipe,** n. pipe made from briar wood.

bribe [braib] **1.** n. money given illegally to s.o. to get sth done. **2.** v. to give (s.o.) money illegally to get sth done. **bribery,** n. act of bribing.

bric-à-brac ['brikəbræk] n. (no pl.) ornaments or furniture of little value.

brick [brik] n. block of baked clay, used for building; **he dropped a b.** = he made an unfortunate remark by mistake. **brick-built,** adj. built of bricks. **bricklayer,** n. person who builds with bricks. **brick up,** v. to fill in (window/ doorway) with bricks. **brickwork,** n. bricks built up into a wall. **brickworks,** n. factory where bricks are made.

bride [braid] n. woman who is about to get married or who has just got married. **bridal,** adj. referring to a wedding. **bridegroom,** n. man who is about to get married or who has just got married. **bridesmaid,** n. unmarried woman who is the bride's attendant at a wedding.

bridge [bridʒ] **1.** n. (a) construction to take a road/railway across a river/road/ railway line. (b) top part of a ship where a captain stands. (c) top of the nose. (d) (in a violin) support for the strings. (e) type of card game for four people. **2.** v. to put a bridge across (a river, etc.). **bridgehead,** n. preliminary position held by attackers who have attacked across water. **bridge roll,** n. small long soft roll of white bread. **bridging loan,** n. short-term loan, esp. one to help s.o. buy a house before he has sold his old one.

bridle ['braidl] **1.** n. headstraps (for a horse). **2.** v. (a) to hold back (a horse). (b) to take offence. **bridlepath, bridleway,** n. path for horseriders.

brief [bri:f] **1.** adj. short. **2.** n. (a) papers concerning a legal case. (b) instructions. (c) **briefs** = short knickers/ underpants. **3.** v. to give a case to (a lawyer); to give (s.o.) information/ instructions. **briefcase,** n. small case for carrying papers. **briefing,** n. conference where information is given. **briefly,** adv. shortly/speaking for a short time.

brigade [bri'geid] n. (a) army group, smaller than a division. (b) **fire b.** = group of people whose job is to fight fires. **brigadier** [brigə'diə] n. army officer in charge of a brigade; rank in the army above colonel.

brigand ['brigənd] n. robber.

bright [brait] adj. (-er, -est) (a) shining very strongly/having a very vivid colour; **to look on the b. side of things** = to be optimistic. (b) intelligent. **brighten,** v. (a) to make bright. (b) **she brightened up when she saw him** = she became more cheerful; **the weather is brightening up** = it is getting finer. **brightly,** adv. (a) with a strong light. (b) in an intelligent/cheerful tone of voice. **brightness,** n. strength (of light); intelligence (of person).

brill [bril] n. (pl. brill) type of flat white edible sea fish.

brilliant ['briljənt] **1.** adj. (a) very shiny. (b) very clever. **2.** n. diamond. **brilliance,** n. brightness; intelligence.

brim [brim] **1.** n. edge. **2.** v. (brimmed) **the glass was brimming over with wine**

= the glass was overflowing. **brimful,** *adj.* very full/full to overflowing.

brindled ['brɪndld] *adj.* (*of animals*) brown with streaks of another colour.

brine [braɪn] *n.* salt water.

bring [brɪŋ] *v.* (**brought** [brɔːt]; **has brought**) to take (sth/s.o.) to this place. **bring about,** *v.* to cause/to make (sth) happen. **bring along,** *v.* to bring with you. **bring-and-buy,** *n.* type of market where people bring or buy homemade or secondhand goods. **bring back,** *v.* to return (here); **that picture brings it all back to me** = makes me remember it all. **bring down,** *v.* to make (sth/s.o.) fall down; to lower (sth). **bring forward,** *v.* **to bring forward the date of the meeting** = to arrange an earlier date for it. **bring in,** *v.* to make (sth/s.o.) come in. **bring off,** *v.* to succeed in; **he brought it off** = he did it successfully. **bring on,** *v.* to produce/to make grow; **you've brought it on yourself** = it's your own fault. **bring out,** *v.* to make (sth/s.o.) come out; **to b. out a new book** = to publish a new book; **to b. out the colour** = to make the colour more noticeable/ more effective. **bring round,** *v.* (*a*) to carry (sth) to s.o.'s house. (*b*) to revive (s.o.) who is unconscious. **bring up,** *v.* (*a*) to raise (a subject). (*b*) to vomit. (*c*) to educate in manners.

brink [brɪŋk] *n.* edge (of cliff); **on the b. of a nervous breakdown** = very close to having a nervous breakdown.

briny ['braɪnɪ] *adj.* salty; *inf.* **the b.** = the sea.

brisk [brɪsk] *adj.* (**-er, -est**) rapid. **briskly,** *adv.* rapidly.

brisket ['brɪskɪt] *n.* beef from the breast of an animal.

brisling ['brɪzlɪŋ] *n.* small sea fish, like a sardine.

bristle ['brɪsl] **1.** *n.* short stiff hair (on animal/brush). **2.** *v.* (*a*) to take offence. (*b*) **to b. with** = to be full of/covered with. **bristly,** *adj.* covered with short stiff hair.

British ['brɪtɪʃ] *adj. & n.* referring to Great Britain; **the B.** = the people of Great Britain. **the B. Isles** = group of islands off the north coast of Europe, including England, Wales, Scotland, Ireland, and many smaller islands. **Brit,** *n. Sl.* a Briton. **Briton** ['brɪtn] *n.* person from Great Britain.

brittle ['brɪtl] *adj.* which breaks easily. **brittleness,** *n.* fragility.

broach [brəʊtʃ] *v.* (*a*) to open (a cask of wine, etc.). (*b*) to start talking about (a problem).

broad [brɔːd] *adj.* (**-er, -est**) very wide; **in b. daylight** = in full daylight; **a b. Scottish accent** = a strong accent; **b. beans** = type of beans with large flat seeds. **broadcast. 1.** *n.* radio/television programme; **outside b.** = radio/television programme recorded in the open air, not in a studio. **2.** *v.* (**broadcast**) (*a*) to sow (by throwing seed by hand). (*b*) to send out by radio/television; **they b. an appeal to the people.** (*c*) to tell everyone (the news); **don't b. the fact** = keep it a secret. **3.** *adv.* (sowing) by throwing the seed by hand. **4.** *adj.* sent by radio/television. **broadcaster,** *n.* person who speaks on the radio/television. **broaden,** *v.* to make wider; **travel broadens the mind** = travel makes your knowledge/interest more extensive. **broadloom,** *adj.* (carpet) woven in a very wide strip. **broadly,** *adv.* **b. speaking** = in a general way. **broadminded,** *adj.* tolerant; not easily taking offence. **broad-shouldered,** *adj.* with wide shoulders. **broadside,** *n.* (*a*) firing of all the guns on one side of a ship. (*b*) sharp written or spoken criticism. (*c*) **b. on** = with the side moving forwards.

brocade [brə'keɪd] *n.* thick cloth with a raised pattern.

broccoli ['brɒkəlɪ] *n.* (*pl.* **broccoli**) cabbage-like vegetable of which the flower-heads are eaten.

brochure ['brəʊʃə] *n.* small book; small publicity pamphlet.

brogue [brəʊg] *n.* (*a*) heavy shoe with patterned leather top. (*b*) accent (usu. Irish).

broil [brɔɪl] *v.* to grill. **broiler,** *n.* chicken specially bred for roasting.

broke [brəʊk] *adj. inf.* **to be flat b.** = to have no money; *see also* **break.**

broken ['brəʊkən] *adj.* (*a*) in pieces; **a b. home** = home where the parents have separated. (*b*) spoken with a foreign accent and with many mistakes. (*c*) *see also* **break. broken-down,** *adj.* not working. **broken-hearted,** *adj.* very upset/sad.

broker ['brəʊkə] *n.* person who deals in shares/insurance; **honest b.** = person who tries to mediate. **brokerage,** *n.* fee charged by a broker for his work.

brolly ['brɒlɪ] *n. inf.* umbrella.

bromide ['brəʊmaɪd] *n.* (*a*) chemical used to make a calming medicine. (*b*) photographic paper.

bronchial ['brɒŋkɪəl] *adj.* referring to the respiratory tubes; **b. asthma** = asthma in the lungs. **bronchi,** *n. pl.* air passages leading into the lungs. **bronchitis** [brɒŋ'kaɪtɪs] *n.* disease of the respiratory tubes.

bronze [brɒnz] *n.* metal made from copper and tin; **B. Age** = prehistoric period when men used weapons of bronze. **bronzed,** *adj.* tanned/sunburnt.

brooch [brəʊtʃ] *n.* ornament to pin on to clothing.

brood [bruːd] **1.** *n.* group of chicks/small children. **2.** *v.* to have gloomy thoughts; **she's brooding over a plan** = she is pondering a plan. **broody,** *adj.* (*a*) (hen) preparing to sit on a clutch of eggs; (woman) who wants to have a baby. (*b*) (person) who has gloomy thoughts.

brook [brʊk] **1.** *n.* small stream. **2.** *v.* to allow/to accept.

broom [bruːm] *n.* (*a*) shrub with yellow flowers. (*b*) brush with long handle for sweeping the floor. **broomstick,** *n.* long handle of a broom.

bros [brɒs] = brothers.

broth [brɒθ] *n.* light soup; **Scotch b.** = thick soup from drinking infected milk.

brothel ['brɒθl] *n.* house of prostitutes.

brother ['brʌðə] *n.* (*a*) male child of the same parents as another child. (*b*) man belonging to a monastic order. **brotherhood,** *n.* fraternity; companionship (between men). **brother-in-law,** *n.* (*pl.* **brothers-in-law**) brother of your husband or wife; husband of your sister; husband of the sister of your husband or wife. **brotherly,** *adj.* as of brothers.

brought [brɔːt] *v. see* **bring.**

brow [braʊ] *n.* (*a*) forehead/top part of the face above the eyes. (*b*) line of hair above each eye. (*c*) rounded top of a hill. **browbeat,** *v.* (**browbeat; has browbeaten**) to intimidate (s.o.).

brown [braʊn] **1.** *adj.* (**-er, -est**) coloured like the colour of wood or soil. **2.** *n.* colour of wood or soil. **3.** *v.* to go brown; to make brown. **browned off,** *adj. inf.* fed up. **brownie,** *n.* (*a*) girl in the younger section of the Girl Guides. (*b*) *Am.* small chocolate cake. **brownish,** *adj.* rather brown.

browse [braʊz] *v.* (*a*) (*of animal*) to wander about eating grass. (*b*) (*of person*) to wander round a shop looking at goods for sale. **browser,** *n.* person who is browsing in a shop.

brucellosis [brəsel'əʊsɪs] *n.* disease caught from drinking infected milk.

bruise [bruːz] **1.** *n.* mark made on the skin by a blow. **2.** *v.* to get/to make marks on the skin from a blow. **bruiser,** *n.* fighter.

brunch [brʌntʃ] *n.* large meal (as a combination of breakfast and lunch) taken in the middle of the morning.

brunette [bruː'net] *adj. & n.* (woman) with brown hair.

brunt [brʌnt] *n.* **to bear the b. of** = to suffer most from.

brush [brʌʃ] **1.** *n.* (*pl.* **-es**) (*a*) instrument with a handle and hair/wire/nylon bristles for painting or cleaning. (*b*) scrub land. (*c*) cleaning with a brush. (*d*) short argument/fight with an opponent. (*e*) piece of carbon which makes an electric contact. (*f*) tail (of a fox). **2.** *v.* (*a*) to clean with a brush. (*b*) to go past sth touching it gently. **brush aside,** *v.* to reject. **brush away,** *v.* to clear away with a brush. **brush down,** *v.* to brush (sth) vigorously. **brush off,** *v.* to clean (sth) off with a brush. **brush-off,** *n. inf.* **to give s.o. the b.-off** = to send s.o. away without agreeing to what they want. **brush up,** *v.* (*a*) to make (yourself) smart. (*b*) to improve (your knowledge of). **brushwood,** *n.* low undergrowth.

brusque [bruːsk] *adj.* abrupt/impolite. **brusquely,** *adv.* rudely.

Brussels sprouts ['brʌslz'spraʊts] *n. pl.* vegetable like tiny cabbages.

brute [bruːt] *n.* (*a*) animal. (*b*) rude/

violent person; **to use b. force** = to use rough methods. **brutal,** *adj.* violent.
brutality [bru:ˈtælɪtɪ] *n.* violent action. **brutalize,** *v.* to beat (s.o.). **brutally,** *adv.* in a brutal way. **brutish,** *adj.* rude/violent.

bryony [ˈbraɪənɪ] *n.* type of climbing plant with poisonous berries.

BSc [bi:es'si:] Bachelor of Science.

BSE [bi:es'i:] = bovine spongiform encephalopathy.

bubble [ˈbʌbl] **1.** *n.* small amount of air trapped in liquid. **2.** *v.* to make bubbles. **bubbly. 1.** *adj.* with bubbles. **2.** *n. inf.* champagne.

bubonic plague [bju:ˈbɒnɪk ˈpleɪg] *n.* fatal disease, transmitted by rats.

buck [bʌk] **1.** *n.* (a) male deer/rabbit. (b) *Am. inf.* dollar. (c) *inf.* **to pass the b.** = to hand responsibility on to s.o. else. **2.** *v.* (*of horse*) to jump in the air (with rounded back). **bucked,** *adj.* very pleased and encouraged. **buckteeth,** *n. pl.* teeth which stick out in front. **buck up,** *v.* (a) *inf.* to make (s.o.) feel more lively. (b) *inf.* **buck up!** = hurry up!/cheer up!

bucket [ˈbʌkɪt] **1.** *n.* round container with an open top and a handle. **2.** *v. inf.* (*of rain*) **to b. down** = to pour down. **bucketful,** *n.* quantity contained in a bucket. **bucket seat,** *n.* rounded seat (in a car). **bucket shop,** *n.* cheap travel agent.

buckle [ˈbʌkl] **1.** *n.* metal fastener for attaching a belt/strap/shoe. **2.** *v.* (a) to attach (sth) with a metal clasp. (b) to bend/to collapse.

buckram [ˈbʌkrəm] *n.* thick cloth for covering books.

buckshee [bʌk'shi:] *adv. inf.* free.

buckwheat [ˈbʌkwi:t] *n.* dark grain, giving a brown flour.

bucolic [bju:ˈkɒlɪk] *adj.* referring to the countryside.

bud [bʌd] **1.** *n.* (a) point on a plant where a new shoot is appearing; flower not yet opened; **the roses are in b.** = the flowers are ready to open. (b) *Am. inf.* friend. **2.** *v.* (**budded**) (a) to make buds. (b) to graft a bud. **budding,** *adj.* (flower) not yet open; **b. concert pianist** = person who hopes to be a concert pianist.

Buddhism [ˈbʊdɪzəm] *n.* religion following the teaching of Buddha.

Buddhist, *adj. & n.* (person) who follows the teaching of Buddha.

buddleia [ˈbʌdlɪə] *n.* garden shrub with long purple flowers.

buddy [ˈbʌdɪ] *n. Am. inf.* friend.

budge [bʌdʒ] *v.* to move.

budgerigar [ˈbʌdʒərɪgɑ:] *n.* blue or green tropical bird like a small parrot.

budget [ˈbʌdʒɪt] **1.** *n.* list of proposed expenditure; **the B.** = the government's declaration of proposals for tax and expenditure. **2.** *v.* **to b. for** = to plan how to spend money on sth.

budgie [ˈbʌdʒɪ] *n. inf.* budgerigar.

buff [bʌf] **1.** (a) *adj. & n.* (of a) pale yellowy-brown colour. (b) *n. inf.* enthusiast. **2.** *v.* to polish/to shine.

buffalo [ˈbʌfələʊ] *n.* (*pl.* **-oes/-o**) large wild ox or cow (in America and tropical countries).

buffer [ˈbʌfə] *n.* (a) shock-absorbing pad, esp. at end of railway line; **b. state** = small country between two larger states, which may be antagonistic to each other; **b. zone** = area between two areas of fighting. (b) *Sl.* **old b.** = old man.

buffet[1] [ˈbʊfeɪ] *n.* (a) self-service snack bar (in railway station, etc.); **b. car** = railway coach containing a buffet. (b) self-service meal. (c) sideboard.

buffet[2] [ˈbʌfɪt] *v.* to bang/to jolt.

buffoon [bəˈfu:n] *n.* fool/clown. **buffoonery,** *n.* foolish action.

bug [bʌg] **1.** *n.* (a) small insect which sucks. (b) *Am.* any small insect. (c) *inf.* germ. (d) hidden microphone. (e) defect in a computer program. **2.** *v.* (**bugged**) (a) to install a hidden microphone in (a room). (b) *inf.* **what's bugging you?** = what's bothering you? **bugbear,** *n.* thing which you hate.

bugle [ˈbju:gl] *n.* military trumpet. **bugler,** *n.* person who blows a bugle.

build [bɪld] **1.** *n.* size/shape (of person). **2.** *v.* (**built** [bɪlt]; **has built**) to construct; to make by putting pieces together. **builder,** *n.* person who constructs houses, etc. **building,** *n.* (a) constructing; **b. land** = land for construction of houses. (b) construction; house/office block; **b. society** = society which lends money to people to buy houses. **build up,** *v.* to construct/to create/to increase. **built-in,** *adj.* (cupboards, etc.) which are constructed as part of a building. **built-up**, *adj.* built-up area = area of a town where there are many buildings.

bulb [bʌlb] *n.* (*a*) fleshy underground stem of a plant, which produces leaves and flowers in spring. (*b*) glass globe full of gas which produces light when an electric current passes through it. **bulbous**, *adj.* fat and rounded.

bulge [bʌldʒ] 1. *n.* swelling. 2. *v.* to swell out (**with**).

bulimia [buˈlimiə] *n.* disease where you have a craving to eat and force yourself to vomit.

bulk [bʌlk] *n.* large quantity; size; **in b.** = in large quantities; **b. purchase** = purchase in large quantities; **the b. of our sales** = most of our sales. 2. *v.* **to b. large** = to be important; to take up a lot of room. **bulkhead**, *n.* dividing wall in a ship or aircraft. **bulkiness**, *n.* being bulky. **bulky**, *adj.* (**-ier, -iest**) very large/taking up an inconvenient amount of room.

bull [bul] *n.* (*a*) male ox. (*b*) male of certain species. (*c*) person who believes the stock market prices will rise. (*d*) official pronouncement by the pope. (*e*) *Sl.* rubbish/nonsense. **bulldog**, *n.* breed of squat, flatfaced dogs. **bulldoze**, *v.* (*a*) to knock down/to clear using a bulldozer. (*b*) to force; **he bulldozed his proposal through the committee** = forced them to agree to it. **bulldozer**, *n.* large tractor with a shovel in front for moving earth. **bullfight**, *n.* entertainment in Spain, where a man fights a bull. **bullfighter**, *n.* man who fights bulls. **bullfinch**, *n.* small finch with red breast. **bullfrog**, *n.* large frog. **bullock**, *n.* castrated bull. **bullring**, *n.* arena where bullfights take place. **bull's-eye**, *n.* centre point of a target.

bullet [ˈbulit] *n.* piece of metal fired from a revolver or small gun. **bullet-proof**, *adj.* (waistcoat/window) specially made so that bullets cannot pierce it.

bulletin [ˈbulitin] *n.* piece of information; report on a situation.

bullion [ˈbuljən] *n.* gold or silver bars.

bully [ˈbuli] 1. *n.* person who frightens people who are weaker than he is; **b. boys** = thugs. 2. *v.* to intimidate (s.o.). **bully beef**, *n. inf.* corned beef. **bully off**, *v.* (*in hockey*) to start the game.

bulrush [ˈbulrʌʃ] *n.* (*pl.* **-es**) tall reed with a brown furry head.

bulwark [ˈbulwək] *n.* side of a ship which rises higher than the deck.

bum [bʌm] 1. *n. inf.* (*a*) buttocks. (*b*) *Am.* tramp; person who loafs about doing nothing. 2. *v.* (**bummed**) *inf.* **to b. off s.o.** = to live at s.o.'s expense.

bumble [ˈbʌmbl] *v.* to move/do things in a clumsy way. **bumblebee**, *n.* large furry bee.

bumf [bʌmf] *n. Sl.* paper (usu. useless documents); toilet paper.

bump [bʌmp] 1. *n.* (*a*) slight shock from hitting sth lightly. (*b*) small bulge on the body (from being hit). 2. *v.* to hit sth (lightly); **I bumped into him at the station** = I met him by chance. **bump off**, *v. inf.* to murder. **bumpy**, *adj.* (**-ier, -iest**) uneven (path/flight).

bumper [ˈbʌmpə] *n.* (*a*) something very large; **a b. crop.** (*b*) metal or rubber strip at front and rear of a car to protect it when it is hit.

bumptious [ˈbʌmpʃəs] *adj.* (person) full of his own importance.

bun [bʌn] *n.* (*a*) small cake; (*b*) hair wound round in a knot at the back of the head.

bunch [bʌntʃ] 1. *n.* (*pl.* **-es**) (*a*) cluster (of things) tied together; **the pick of the b.** = the best out of the group. (*b*) group (of racing cyclists). 2. *v.* (*in sport*) to form a group.

bundle [ˈbʌndl] 1. *n.* parcel (of papers, etc.); group of nerves. 2. *v.* to tie (several things) together.

bung [bʌŋ] 1. *n.* stopper; thing which stops up a hole (in a cask). 2. *v.* (*a*) to block/to stop up a hole. (*b*) *inf.* **b. it in the wastepaper basket** = throw it in the wastepaper basket.

bungalow [ˈbʌŋgələu] *n.* house with only a ground floor.

bungle [ˈbʌŋgl] *v.* to do (sth) badly. **bungler**, *n.* person who has done a job badly.

bunion [ˈbʌnjən] *n.* painful swelling at the base of the big toe.

bunk [bʌŋk] *n.* (*a*) bed attached to a wall; **b. beds** = two beds, one on top of the other. (*b*) *inf.* **to do a b.** = to run away. (*c*) *inf.* nonsense.

bunker [ˈbʌŋkə] *n.* (*a*) coalhole. (*b*)

sandy pit on a golf course. (c) fortified gun emplacement.

bunny ['bʌnɪ] n. pet name for a rabbit.

bunting ['bʌntɪŋ] n. (a) type of small singing bird. (b) (no pl.) strings of small flags.

buoy [bɔɪ] **1.** n. floating marker showing a channel (in a river/at the entrance to a harbour). **2.** v. **to b. s.o. up** = to cheer s.o. up. **buoyancy,** n. ability to float; **b. aid** = type of life jacket made of blocks of light substance, worn by yachtsmen. **buoyant,** adj. (a) which can float easily. (b) full of vigour.

burble ['bɜːbl] **1.** n. low murmur. **2.** v. to murmur softly.

burden ['bɜːdn] **1.** n. (a) heavy load; sth which is hard to do/to bear; **beast of b.** = animal (like a donkey) used to carry loads; **to make s.o.'s life a b.** = to make things difficult for s.o. (b) theme music of a song. **2.** v. to load.

bureau ['bjʊərəʊ] n. (pl. **bureaux** ['bjʊərəʊz]) (a) office; **information b.** = office which collects and hands out information. (b) (antique) desk; Am. chest of drawers.

bureaucracy [bjʊə'rɒkrəsɪ] n. rule by civil servants. **bureaucrat** ['bjʊərəkræt] n. civil servant. **bureaucratic** [bjʊərə-'krætɪk] adj. referring to the civil service.

burgeon ['bɜːdʒn] v. to begin to grow.

burgh ['bʌrə] n. (Scotland) borough.

burglar ['bɜːglə] n. person who enters a house to steal; **b. alarm** = electric alarm which rings if a burglar attempts to enter the house. **burglary,** n. robbery committed by a burglar. **burgle,** v. to steal from (a house).

burgundy ['bɜːgəndɪ] n. type of French red wine.

burial ['berɪəl] n. act of burying (a dead body); **b. ground** = cemetery.

burlap ['bɜːlæp] n. thick canvas.

burlesque [bɜː'lesk] **1.** adj. & n. light satirical (play). **2.** v. to satirize.

burly ['bɜːlɪ] adj. (-ier, -iest) strong/solid (man).

Burmese [bɜː'miːz] **1.** adj. coming from Burma. **2.** n. (a) person from Burma. (b) language spoken in Burma.

burn [bɜːn] **1.** n. (a) place (on the body) which has been burnt. (b) (in Scotland) stream. **2.** v. (**burnt/burned; has burnt/**burned) (a) to destroy by fire; **he burnt his fingers** = he suffered a loss/he did not do at all as well as he expected; **he's burnt his boats/his bridges** = he can't go back now. (b) to use as a fuel. **burn down,** v. to destroy by fire. **burner,** n. apparatus for burning. **burn out,** v. **the fire has burnt itself out** = the fire has gone out because there was nothing left to burn. **burnt,** adj. which has gone black with fire.

burnish ['bɜːnɪʃ] v. to make (sth) shine by rubbing.

burp [bɜːp] **1.** n. noise made when bringing up gas from the stomach through the mouth. **2.** v. to make a burp.

burr [bɜː] n. (a) prickly part of a plant, containing seeds, which clings to clothes, etc. (b) country accent with a strongly pronounced 'r'. (c) rough edge to a piece of cut metal.

burrow ['bʌrəʊ] **1.** n. hole in the ground where rabbits live. **2.** v. to make a long hole underground.

bursar ['bɜːsə] n. person in charge of the finances of a school/college. **bursary,** n. scholarship/money given to a student to help him pay for his studies.

burst [bɜːst] **1.** n. (a) sudden explosion; **b. of gunfire; b. of laughter.** (b) sudden attack; **b. of speed. 2.** v. (**burst; has burst**) to explode/to break open; **she b. into the room** = she rushed into the room; **the boy b. into tears** = he started to cry; **he was bursting to tell everyone the secret** = he was eagerly waiting to tell the secret. **burst open,** v. to (make sth) come open with a bang. **burst out,** v. to shout out; **he burst out laughing.**

bury ['berɪ] v. to put (sth) into a hole in the ground.

bus [bʌs] **1.** n. (pl. **-es**) motor vehicle for carrying passengers; **school b.** = bus which takes children to school. **2.** v. (**bussed**) to take (children) to school in a different part of the town in order to mix racial groups. **busman,** n. (pl. **-men**) person who works on a bus; **a busman's holiday** = spending your spare time doing sth similar to your normal job. **bussing,** n. action of sending children to school in a different part of the town in order to mix racial groups. **bus stop,** *n.* place where a bus stops regularly to let people on or off.

busby ['bʌzbɪ] *n.* tall fur hat worn by some soldiers.

bush [buʃ] *n.* (*pl.* **-es**) (*a*) plant which is smaller than a tree. (*b*) **the b.** = wild uncultivated land (in Africa/Australia); **b. fire** = fire in wild uncultivated land; **b. pilot** = pilot of a plane flying in the bush. **bushed,** *adj. inf.* tired out. **bushman,** *n.* (*pl.* **-men**) native of the African bush. **bushy,** *adj.* growing thickly.

bushel ['buʃl] *n.* measure for grain (= 8 gallons).

business ['bɪznəs] *n.* (*pl.* **-es**) (*a*) affair; **it's none of your b.** = it has nothing to do with you. (*b*) commercial work; **to do b. with s.o.** = to trade with s.o.; **do you think he means b.?** = do you think he is serious? (*c*) commercial firm. **businesslike,** *adj.* practical/serious. **businessman, businesswoman,** *n.* (*pl.* **-men/-women**) person who works in a commercial company.

busker ['bʌskə] *n.* person who sings/plays a musical instrument, to entertain people in the street.

bust [bʌst] **1.** *n.* (*a*) sculpture of head and shoulders. (*b*) measurement round a woman's breasts. **2.** *adj. inf.* broken. **3.** *v.* (**busted/bust**) *inf.* to break.

bustard ['bʌstəd] *n.* large brown bird, which runs fast.

bustle ['bʌsl] **1.** *n.* (*a*) pad at the back of a dress (in Victorian times). (*b*) rushing around. **2.** *v.* to rush around.

busy ['bɪzɪ] *adj.* (**-ier, -iest**) occupied with doing sth; **he is b. mending the car; b. street** = street with lots of pedestrians and traffic. **busily,** *adv.* in a busy way. **busybody,** *n.* person who interferes in other people's affairs.

but [bʌt] *conj., adv. & prep.* (*suggesting the opposite/a reservation*) **he is tall b. his sister is short; nothing b.** = only; **b. for his letter, we would not have known he was here** = if it had not been for his letter.

butane ['bjuːteɪn] *n.* gas (often used for cooking or heating).

butch [butʃ] *adj. Sl.* (*of woman*) very masculine.

butcher ['butʃə] **1.** *n.* (*a*) person who prepares and sells meat. (*b*) *Sl.* **but-**cher's** = look; **let's have a butcher's at it. 2.** *v.* (*a*) to kill in cold blood. (*b*) to chop (sth) about. **butcher's,** *n.* shop which sells meat. **butchery,** *n.* massacre/brutal killing.

butler ['bʌtlə] *n.* main male servant in a large house.

butt [bʌt] **1.** *n.* (*a*) large barrel for keeping water. (*b*) end of a cigarette. (*c*) shoulder end of a rifle. (*d*) place where you practise shooting. (*e*) person who is often teased. (*f*) push (with the head). (*g*) *Am. inf.* buttocks. **2.** *v.* (*a*) to push (s.o.) with your head. (*b*) **to b. in** = to interrupt a conversation.

butter ['bʌtə] **1.** *n.* solid yellow fat made from cream. **2.** *v.* to spread butter on (sth); **to b. s.o. up** = to flatter s.o. **buttercup,** *n.* common bright yellow wild flower. **butterfingers,** *n.* person who can't catch/who drops things. **butterfly,** *n.* insect with brightly coloured wings. **buttermilk,** *n.* thin milk left after butter has been churned. **butterscotch,** *n.* sweet made from butter and sugar.

buttock(s) ['bʌtək(s)] *n.* fleshy part of the body which you sit on.

button ['bʌtn] **1.** *n.* small object stitched to clothes for attaching one part of clothing to another; small round object which you press to make a machine work; **b. mushroom** = small round mushroom which is not fully grown. **2.** *v.* to attach with buttons. **buttonhole. 1.** *n.* (*a*) hole for putting a button through. (*b*) flower stuck in the hole in a lapel. **2.** *v.* **to b. s.o.** = to trap s.o. and talk to him at length.

buttress ['bʌtrəs] **1.** *n.* (*pl.* **-es**) supporting pillar (reinforcing a wall). **2.** *v.* to support.

butty ['bʌtɪ] *n. Sl.* sandwich.

buxom ['bʌksəm] *adj.* plump and attractive (woman).

buy [baɪ] **1.** *v.* (**bought** [bɔːt] **has bought**) to get by paying money. **2.** *n.* thing which you have bought/which you might buy; **a good b.** = a bargain. **buyer,** *n.* person who buys, esp. person who buys stock for a large store. **buy out,** *v.* to buy a partner's share in a business.

buzz [bʌz] **1.** *n.* (*a*) (*pl.* **-es**) noise like a bee. (*b*) *inf.* telephone call; **give me a**

b. **tomorrow. 2.** *v.* (*a*) to make a noise like a bee. (*b*) (*of aircraft*) to fly close to (another aircraft) to force it to go away. **buzzer,** *n.* device which makes a buzzing noise. **buzz off,** *v. inf.* to go away. **buzz word,** *n.* word which is frequently used.

buzzard ['bʌzəd] *n.* kind of bird of prey.

by [baɪ] **1.** *prep.* (*a*) near. (*b*) before; **by ten o'clock.** (*c*) using; **by airmail; by car.** (*d*) **painting by Rembrandt** = which Rembrandt painted; **play by Shakespeare** = which Shakespeare wrote. (*e*) **by yourself** = alone. (*f*) **by the dozen** = a dozen at a time. **2.** *adv.* (*a*) near; **put some money by for a rainy day** = put money to one side/save money. (*b*) past; **he drove by without stopping. by-election,** *n.* election to fill a place left vacant by the death/resignation of a representative. **bygone. 1.** *adj.* past/former. **2.** *n.* thing which comes from the past; **let bygones be bygones** = forget past insults. **by-law,** *n.* law which is passed by a municipal council. **bypass. 1.** *n.* (*a*) road which goes round a town. (*b*) **heart b.** = operation to insert a tube to go round a diseased part of an artery. **2.** *v.* to go round (a town), avoiding the centre; to avoid (sth) by going round it. **by-product,** *n.* secondary product made as a result of manufacturing something else. **by-road,** *n.* small local road. **bystander,** *n.* person standing near the scene of action. **byway,** *n.* small path/road. **byword,** *n.* (for) famous example.

bye [baɪ] *n.* (*in cricket*) run scored without the batsman having hit the ball; **to have a b.** = to pass to the next round of a sporting tournament without having to play.

bye(-bye) [baɪ(baɪ)] *inter.* used when leaving someone.

byre ['baɪə] *n.* cowshed.

byte [baɪt] *n.* series of bits processed by a computer as one piece.

Cc

C *symbol for* carbon.
Ca *symbol for* calcium.
cab [kæb] *n.* taxi. **cab-driver,** *n.* person who drives a taxi.

cabal [kæˈbɑːl] *n.* small group of politicians who plot in secret.

cabaret ['kæbəreɪ] *n.* entertainment given in a restaurant or club.

cabbage ['kæbɪdʒ] *n.* green leafy vegetable; **c. white** = common type of white butterfly.

caber ['keɪbə] *n.* log of wood thrown in Scottish games.

cabin ['kæbɪn] *n.* (*a*) small room on a ship. (*b*) small hut. (*c*) interior of an aircraft; **c. crew** = air hostesses and stewards.

cabinet ['kæbɪnət] *n.* (*a*) piece of furniture with shelves. (*b*) central committee of ministers in a government; **shadow c.** = committee formed by the main opposition party to parallel the actual cabinet. **cabinetmaker,** *n.* woodworker who makes furniture.

cable ['keɪbl] **1.** *n.* (*a*) thick rope/wire; **c. railway** = railway where wagons are pulled up a steep hill by a cable. (*b*) telegraph wire for sending messages under the sea. (*c*) message sent by telegraph. (*d*) **c. TV** = television sent by cable. **2.** *v.* to send a message to (s.o.) by telegraph. **cablecar,** *n.* cabin on a cable railway. **cablegram,** *n.* telegram sent by cable.

caboodle [kəˈbuːdl] *n. inf.* **the whole c.** = everything.

cacao [kəˈkɑːəʊ] *n.* tropical tree, of which the seeds provide cocoa and chocolate.

cache [kæʃ] *n.* hidden store.

cachet ['kæʃeɪ] *n.* special mark.

cackle ['kækl] **1.** *n.* noise made by hens; *Sl.* **cut the c.** = stop chattering. **2.** *v.* to chatter.

cacophony [kəˈkɒfənɪ] *n.* loud unpleasant mixture of sounds. **cacophonous,** *adj.* unpleasantly noisy.

cactus ['kæktəs] *n.* (*pl.* **cacti** ['kæktaɪ]) prickly plant which grows in the desert.

cad [kæd] *n.* (*old*) unpleasant/dishonest person. **caddish,** *adj.* like a cad.

cadaver [kəˈdɑːvə] *n.* corpse. **cadaverous,** *adj.* looking like a corpse.

CAD/CAM = computer-assisted design/computer-assisted manufacture.

caddie ['kædɪ] **1.** *n.* person who carries the clubs for a golfer. **2.** *v.* to act as a caddie (**for** s.o.).

caddis fly ['kædɪsflaɪ] *n.* insect living near water.

caddy ['kædɪ] *n.* (*pl.* **caddies**) box for keeping tea in.

cadence ['keɪdəns] *n.* rhythm (of music/poetry).

cadenza [kə'denzə] *n.* flowery piece for a solo instrument in the middle of concerto/symphony, etc.

cadet [kə'det] *n.* young person training for the armed services.

cadge [kædʒ] *v.* to scrounge/to try to get (sth) without having to pay for it. **cadger,** *n.* person who cadges.

cadmium ['kædmɪəm] *n.* (*element:* Cd) grey metal which can be poisonous to human beings.

cadre ['kɑːdə] *n.* (*a*) small group of expert people in a political party or the army. (*b*) active specialist working in a political party.

caecum ['siːkəm] *n.* wide part of the large intestine.

caesarean [sɪ'zeərɪən] *n.* **c.** **(section)** = operation on a pregnant woman to deliver her baby through the wall of the womb.

café ['kæfeɪ] *n.* small restaurant selling snacks or light meals, but not alcoholic drinks.

cafeteria [kæfɪ'tɪərɪə] *n.* self-service restaurant.

caffeine ['kæfiːn] *n.* stimulating substance in coffee and tea.

cage [keɪdʒ] **1.** *n.* enclosure of wire or with metal bars for keeping birds or animals. **2.** *v.* to put in a cage.

cagey ['keɪdʒɪ] *adj.* (**cagier, cagiest**) secretive/unwilling to reveal sth. **cagily,** *adv.* in a cagey way. **caginess,** *n.* being cagey.

cahoots [kə'huːts] *n. inf.* **to be in c. with s.o.** = to work with s.o., against another person.

cairn [keən] *n.* heap of stones to mark an important spot. **cairngorm,** *n.* type of semi-precious stone found in Scotland.

caisson [kə'suːn] *n.* watertight enclosure, as in a dry dock.

cajole [kə'dʒəʊl] *v.* to persuade by flattering. **cajolery,** *n.* act of flattering.

cake [keɪk] **1.** *n.* (*a*) cooked food made of eggs, flour and sugar, usu. eaten cold; *Sl.* **it's a piece of c.** = it is very easy;

you can't have your c. and eat it = you can't benefit from two quite opposite things. (*b*) block of soap. **2.** *v.* to form a dry crust.

calamine ['kæləmaɪn] *n.* **c. lotion** = pink liquid put on skin to soothe and stop itching.

calamity [kə'læmɪtɪ] *n.* disaster. **calamitous,** *adj.* very unfortunate/disastrous.

calcareous [kæl'keərɪəs] *adj.* (soil) containing chalk.

calceolaria [kælsɪəʊ'leərɪə] *n.* house plant, with coloured boat-shaped flowers.

calcinate ['kælsɪneɪt] *v.* to burn to ashes.

calcium ['kælsɪəm] *n.* (*a*) (*element:* Ca) grey metal which forms bones. (*b*) white substance found in water, lime, etc. **calcify,** *v.* to turn (sth) into calcium.

calculate ['kælkjʊleɪt] *v.* to work out (a sum); to estimate (quite accurately); **calculated insult** = deliberate insult. **calculable,** *adj.* which can be calculated. **calculating,** *adj.* (person) who plans clever schemes. **calculation** [kælkjʊ'leɪʃn] *n.* act of calculating; sum which has been calculated. **calculator,** *n.* electronic machine for doing sums. **calculus,** *n.* (*a*) mathematical way of calculating. (*b*) stone formed inside the body.

caldron ['kɔːldrən] *n. Am. see* **cauldron.**

calendar ['kælendə] *n.* sheet showing the days and months of a year; **c. month, c. year** = month/year as shown on a calendar.

calendula [kə'lendjuːlə] *n.* yellow flower, the marigold.

calf [kɑːf] *n.* (*pl.* **calves** [kɑːvz]) (*a*) young cow/bull; young (of elephant, etc.). (*b*) leather (from cow's skin). (*c*) fleshy back part of the leg between the ankle and the knee.

calibre, *Am.* **caliber** ['kælɪbə] *n.* (*a*) interior diameter of a gun. (*b*) standing/intellectual ability. **calibrate,** *v.* to mark/to correct degrees on (a thermometer)/to mark units on (a scale). **calibration,** *n.* marking of degrees; degree marked.

calico ['kælɪkəʊ] *n.* thick cotton cloth.

calipers ['kælɪpəz] *see* callipers.

call [kɔːl] *n.* (*a*) shout/cry; song of a bird; **I want a c. at 7 o'clock** = I want to be woken at 7 o'clock; **on c.** = available for duty. (*b*) conversation on the telephone. (*c*) visit. (*d*) need; **there's no c. for alarm. 2.** *v.* (*a*) to shout; **c. me at 7 o'clock** = wake me at 7 o'clock. (*b*) to telephone. (*c*) to give (s.o.) a name. (*d*) to visit. **call back,** *v.* (*a*) to telephone in reply; to telephone again. (*b*) to come back to visit again. **callbox,** *n.* street telephone box. **callboy,** *n.* (*a*) young man in a theatre who tells performers when it is time for them to go on stage. (*b*) young man in a hotel who runs messages. **caller,** *n.* (*a*) person who comes to visit. (*b*) person who telephones. **call for,** *v.* (*a*) **he called for help** = he shouted to ask for help. (*b*) **to c. for s.o.** = to go to s.o.'s house to collect them. (*c*) to need/to require. **call-girl,** *n.* prostitute who can be called by telephone. **call in,** *v.* to call to (s.o.) to make them come in. **calling,** *n.* vocation; job. **call off,** *v.* to cancel. **call on,** *v.* (*a*) to visit. (*b*) to appeal to (s.o.). **call out,** *v.* (*a*) to shout. (*b*) to ask (police/soldiers) to come to help. **call sign,** *n.* letters/words which identify a radio station. **call up,** *v.* (*a*) to telephone. (*b*) to order (s.o.) to join the army. **call-up,** *n.* order to join the army.

calligraphy [kə'lɪgrəfɪ] *n.* art of fine handwriting. **calligraphic** [kælɪ'græfɪk] *adj.* referring to calligraphy.

callipers, calipers ['kælɪpəz] *n. pl.* (*a*) instrument for measuring the diameter of sth round (like a pipe). (*b*) metal frame to support the leg of a disabled person.

callisthenics [kælɪs'θenɪks] *n.* exercises which are supposed to make the body strong and beautiful.

callous ['kæləs] *adj.* hard/unfeeling. **callously,** *adv.* cruelly. **callousness,** *n.* cruelty.

callow ['kæləʊ] *adj.* young and inexperienced.

callus ['kæləs] *n.* (*pl.* -es) hard patch on the skin.

calm [kɑːm] **1.** *adj.* (-er, -est) quiet/not rough. **2.** *n.* period of quiet. **3.** *v.* to become/to make quiet. **calmly,** *adv.* quietly. **calmness,** *n.* period of quiet.

calorie ['kælərɪ] *n.* measure of heat/of energy-giving value of food. **calorific** [kælə'rɪfɪk] *adj.* referring to heat.

calumny ['kæləmnɪ] *n.* lie/false statement. **calumniate** [kə'lʌmnɪeɪt] *v.* to tell lies about (s.o.).

calve [kɑːv] **1.** *v.* to give birth to a calf. **2.** *n. pl. see* **calf.**

calypso [kə'lɪpsəʊ] *n.* type of topical song sung in the West Indies.

calyx ['kælɪks] *n.* (*pl.* -es) outer covering of a flower bud.

cam [kæm] *n.* ring on a camshaft, which makes pistons move up and down.

camaraderie [kæmə'rædərɪ] *n.* friendship among comrades, esp. in the armed forces.

camber ['kæmbə] *n.* bend/curve (in a surface); way in which the road slopes. **cambered,** *adj.* sloping/rounded (surface).

cambric ['kæmbrɪk] *n.* thin cotton cloth.

camcorder ['kæmkɔːdə] *n.* portable cinecamera which records pictures for video.

came [keɪm] *v. see* **come.**

camel ['kæml] *n.* desert animal with one or two humps, used for riding. **camelhair,** *n.* thick pale brown wool, used for making coats, etc.

camellia [kə'miːlɪə] *n.* evergreen bush with pink or white flowers.

cameo ['kæmɪəʊ] *n.* (*a*) small stone with a design of a head which stands out against a darker background. (*b*) small but sharply defined part in a play/film.

camera ['kæmərə] *n.* (*a*) machine for taking photographs. (*b*) **in c.** = in closed session/in secret. **cameraman,** *n.* (*pl.* -men) man who operates a cine-camera.

camomile ['kæməmaɪl] *n.* fragrant plant, of which the dried leaves are used for making hot drinks.

camouflage ['kæməflɑːʒ] **1.** *n.* hiding (sth) by means of colouring, so that it is difficult to see it against the background. **2.** *v.* to hide (sth) so that it is difficult to see it against the background.

camp [kæmp] **1.** *n.* place where people live in tents or cabins in the open; **c. bed** = folding bed; **c. fire** = fire round which campers sit at night; **holiday c.** = place where people spend holidays in cabins and enjoy organized entertainment. **2.**

v. (*a*) to live (on holiday) in a tent. (*b*) **to c. it up** = to put on an affected style. **3.** *adj.* in an affected (often humorously homosexual) style. **camper,** *n.* (*a*) person who lives in a tent or caravan. (*b*) *Am.* small van equipped with beds, tables, cooking facilities, etc. **camping,** *n.* going on holiday with a tent or caravan. **campsite,** *n.* area specially laid out for tents and caravans.

campaign [kæm'peɪn] **1.** *n.* (*a*) organized military movement. (*b*) organized method of working; **a sales c. 2.** *v.* (*a*) to take part in a war. (*b*) (**for**) to work in an organized fashion to achieve an end. **campaigner,** *n.* person who campaigns.

campanology [kæmpə'nɒlədʒɪ] *n.* study of ringing church bells.

campanula [kæm'pænjuːlə] *n.* the bell flower, with blue bell-shaped flowers.

camphor ['kæmfə] *n.* strong-smelling substance which comes from certain trees; **c. balls** = small white balls impregnated with camphor which prevent moths from attacking clothes. **camphorated,** *adj.* impregnated with camphor.

campion ['kæmpjən] *n.* wild plant with small pink flowers.

campus ['kæmpəs] *n.* (*pl.* **-es**) land on which a university/polytechnic is built.

camshaft ['kæmʃɑːft] *n.* shaft with projecting rings which open and close pistons in turn.

can [kæn] **1.** *n.* (*a*) metal box for liquids, esp. for preserving food or drink. (*b*) **watering c.** = bucket with a long spout for watering plants. **2.** *v.* (*a*) (**I/he can;** *neg.* **cannot;** *short form* **can't;** *past* **I/ he could;** *neg.* **could not;** *short form* **couldn't**) able to do sth/knowing how to do sth. (*b*) (**canned**) to put (fruit/ vegetables, etc.) into cans to preserve them. **canned,** *adj.* in a metal box; **c. music** = recorded music. **cannery,** *n.* canning factory.

Canada goose [kænədə'guːs] *n.* large wild goose, with black neck and white chin, originally native of N. America.

Canadian [kə'neɪdjən] **1.** *adj.* referring to Canada. **2.** *n.* person from Canada.

canal [kə'næl] *n.* (*a*) artificial waterway. (*b*) passage in the body.

canapé ['kænəpeɪ] *n.* small cocktail snack.

canary [kə'neərɪ] *n.* small yellow singing bird.

cancan ['kænkæn] *n.* French cabaret dance, where the dancers kick their legs in the air.

cancel ['kænsl] *v.* (**cancelled**) (*a*) to stop (sth which had been planned). (*b*) to mark a postage stamp with a rubber stamp. **cancellation** [kænsə'leɪʃn] *n.* act of cancelling; seat/ticket which is on sale because a purchaser cannot use it. **cancel out,** *v.* to balance (sth) and so remove its force.

cancer ['kænsə] *n.* (*a*) disease of the blood or tissue. (*b*) **Cancer** = one of the signs of the Zodiac, shaped like a crab; **Tropic of C.** = imaginary line 23° 28′ north of the equator. **cancerous,** *adj.* referring to cancer.

candelabra [kændɪ'lɑːbrə] *n.* *pl.* branched candlesticks; chandeliers.

candid ['kændɪd] *adj.* frank/open. **candidly,** *adv.* in a candid way.

candidate ['kændɪdət] *n.* person standing for election; person who has entered for a competition/an examination. **candidacy, candidature,** *n.* act of standing as a candidate.

candied ['kændɪd] *adj.* dried and sugared; **c. peel** = dried orange/lemon peel.

candle ['kændl] *n.* stick of wax with a wick in the centre; **to burn the c. at both ends** = to work hard during the day and enjoy yourself late into the night. **candlelight,** *n.* light from a candle. **candlelit,** *adj.* lit by candles. **candlestick,** *n.* holder for a candle. **candlewick,** *n.* cotton material for bedcovers, with patterns of tufts.

candour, *Am.* **candor** ['kændə] *n.* frankness/openness.

candy ['kændɪ] *n.* *Am.* sweet. **candy-floss,** *n.* molten sugar spun to make a fluffy mass. **candy-striped,** *adj.* with stripes of colour on a white background like certain sweets. **candytuft,** *n.* plant with pink or blue flowers.

cane [keɪn] **1.** *n.* (*a*) stem (esp. of jointed plants like bamboo). (*b*) walking stick (cut from such plants). **2.** *v.* to hit with a cane. **caning,** *n.* beating with a cane.

canine ['keɪnaɪn] **1.** *adj.* referring to dogs. **2.** *n.* **c. (tooth)** = round pointed tooth.

canister ['kænɪstə] *n.* round metal box.

canker ['kæŋkə] *n.* disease/sore which eats into flesh/into wood of trees.

canna ['kænə] *n.* tropical plant, with large leaves and red or orange flowers.

cannabis ['kænəbɪs] *n.* plant, parts of which can be smoked to give a pleasant feeling of relaxation.

canneloni [kænə'ləʊnɪ] *n.* type of pasta, like small pancakes with a meat or spinach filling.

cannibal ['kænɪbl] *n.* person who eats people. **cannibalism,** *n.* custom of eating people. **cannibalize,** *v.* to take pieces of old machinery to repair another machine.

cannon ['kænən] **1.** *n.* (*a*) large gun; gun in an aircraft. (*b*) (*in billiards*) hitting of one ball off the other two. **2.** *v.* to bounce off (another ball/the cushion); to bump (**into** sth). **cannonball,** *n.* large metal ball fired by a cannon.

cannot ['kænət] *v. see* **can.**

canny ['kænɪ] *adj.* (**-ier, -iest**) wise/clever. **cannily,** *adv.* cleverly.

canoe [kə'nuː] **1.** *n.* boat propelled by one or more people with paddles. **2.** *v.* (**canoed**) to travel in a canoe. **canoeing,** *n.* sport of going in a canoe. **canoeist,** *n.* person who paddles a canoe.

canon ['kænən] *n.* (*a*) religious rule or instructions; **c. law** = the church's laws. (*b*) clergyman attached to a cathedral. **canonical,** *adj.* referring to a canon. **canonization,** *n.* declaring s.o. a saint. **canonize,** *v.* to declare (s.o.) a saint.

canopy ['kænəpɪ] *n.* small roof over a platform/balcony, etc.

cant [kænt] *n.* (*a*) hypocrisy/insincere language. (*b*) jargon/language of a certain group of people.

can't [kɑːnt] *v. see* **can.**

cantaloupe ['kæntəluːp] *n.* type of melon with pink flesh.

cantankerous [kæn'tæŋkrəs] *adj.* bad-tempered. **cantankerousness,** *n.* continual bad temper.

cantata [kæn'tɑːtə] *n.* musical piece for several voices and orchestra (usu. on a religious theme).

canteen [kæn'tiːn] *n.* (*a*) private self-service restaurant. (*b*) box containing knives, forks and spoons. (*c*) portable flask for water.

canter ['kæntə] **1.** *n.* gentle gallop. **2.** *v.* to go at a canter; **he cantered home** = he won easily.

canticle ['kæntɪkl] *n.* religious song.

cantilever ['kæntɪliːvə] *n.* projecting support which holds up a balcony/a bridge. **cantilevered,** *adj.* held up by a cantilever.

canto ['kæntəʊ] *n.* (*pl.* **-os**) long section of an epic poem.

canton ['kæntɒn] *n.* administrative division of Switzerland.

canvas ['kænvəs] *n.* (*pl.* **-es**) thick cloth (for making tents/sails, or for painting on); a painting on canvas; **holiday under c.** = camping holiday.

canvass ['kænvəs] *v.* to try to persuade people to vote for s.o./to buy sth. **canvasser,** *n.* person who canvasses. **canvassing,** *n.* going from door to door to persuade people to vote.

canyon ['kænjən] *n.* (*in America*) large valley with perpendicular sides.

cap [kæp] **1.** *n.* (*a*) hat with a peak; **c. and gown** = hat and robes worn by graduates of a university. (*b*) top/cover (of a bottle, pen, etc.). (*c*) small piece of paper with gunpowder. **2.** *v.* (**capped**) (*a*) to top with a cap; to fix a cover on (a pipe) to stop it leaking. (*b*) to name (s.o.) to a national side (in football/rugby/cricket). (*c*) to surpass/to do better than.

CAP = Common Agricultural Policy.

capable ['keɪpəbl] *adj.* competent/able. **capability** [keɪpə'bɪlɪtɪ] *n.* ability. **capably** ['keɪpəblɪ] *adv.* competently/efficiently.

capacity [kə'pæsɪtɪ] *n.* (*a*) amount which a container can hold; **seating c.** = number of seats (in a bus/cinema, etc.). (*b*) **engine c.** = power of an engine. (*c*) ability to do something. (*d*) position; **in his c. as manager. capacitor,** *n.* device for storing an electric charge. **capacious** [kə'peɪʃəs] *n.* very large/which contains a lot.

cape [keɪp] *n.* (*a*) long cloak. (*b*) headland jutting into the sea.

caper ['keɪpə] **1.** *n.* (*a*) jumping/leaping. (*b*) small bitter seed used in cooking.

(c) *inf.* trick. **2.** *v.* **to c. about** = to jump/
to leap.

capillary [kə'pɪlərɪ] *adj.* & *n.* very
thin (tube); very thin blood vessel;
c. attraction = physical phenomenon
where water is drawn up in a thin tube.

capital ['kæpɪtl] **1.** *n.* (a) decorated stone
on the top of a column. (b) large letter.
(c) main city of a country/a state, etc.
(d) money which is invested. (e) **c.
punishment** = execution/legal killing
of a criminal. **2.** *adj.* (a) very important. (b) *inf.* very good. **capitalism,**
n. economic system based on ownership
of resources by individuals or companies and not by the state. **capitalist,**
adj. & *n.* (person) who supports the
theory of capitalism; businessman. **cap-
italization** [kæpɪtəlaɪ'zeɪʃn] *n.* amount
of capital invested in a company.
capitalize ['kæpɪtəlaɪz] *v.* (a) to invest
capital in a company. (b) **to c. on** = to
take advantage of (sth).

capitation [kæpɪ'teɪʃn] *n.* amount of
money allowed to a school for spending
on books and equipment for each pupil.

Capitol ['kæpɪtəl] *n.* building where the
US Congress meets; **on C. Hill** = in the
US Congress.

capitulate [kə'pɪtjuleɪt] *v.* to give in/to
surrender. **capitulation** [kəpɪtjʊ'leɪʃn]
n. surrendering.

capon ['keɪpɒn] *n.* fat castrated chicken.

cappucino [kæpu:'tʃi:nəʊ] *n.* frothy
Italian coffee, with milk and chocolate.

caprice [kə'pri:s] *n.* whim/sudden fancy.
capricious [kə'prɪʃəs] *adj.* whimsical/
prone to change your mind. **capri-
ciousness,** *n.* tendency to change your
mind suddenly.

Capricorn ['kæprɪkɔːn] *n.* one of the
signs of the Zodiac, shaped like a goat;
Tropic of C. = imaginary line 23° 28'
south of the equator.

capsicum ['kæpsɪkəm] *n.* green pepper
(plant).

capsize [kæp'saɪz] *v.* (of boats) to turn
over.

capstan ['kæpstən] *n.* machine which
turns to haul in a rope or anchor.

capsule ['kæpsju:l] *n.* enclosed case;
small case for a dose of medicine which
melts when swallowed; **space c.** = living
compartment in a space rocket.

captain ['kæptɪn] **1.** *n.* (a) officer in
charge of a ship or aircraft. (b) rank in
the army above lieutenant; rank in the
navy above commander. (c) leader of
sports team. **2.** *v.* to lead (an expedition/
a team). **captaincy,** *n.* (a) rank of
captain (in army/navy). (b) post of
leader of a sports team.

caption ['kæpʃn] *n.* phrase printed
beneath a picture.

captious ['kæpʃəs] *adj.* continually finding fault.

captivate ['kæptɪveɪt] *v.* to charm/to
seduce.

captive ['kæptɪv] **1.** *n.* prisoner. **2.** *adj.*
held c. = held as a prisoner. **captivity**
[kæp'tɪvɪtɪ] *n.* imprisonment. **captor,**
n. person who captures s.o. **capture**
['kæptʃə] **1.** *n.* taking of s.o./sth captive.
2. *v.* (a) to take (s.o./sth) captive. (b)
they have captured 10% of the market =
they have taken 10% of the possible sales.

capybara [kæpɪ'bɑːrə] *n.* very large
rodent, native of S. America.

car [kɑ:] *n.* (a) private motor vehicle; **c.
park** = special parking place for cars.
(b) railway wagon. **car pool,** *n.* group
of people who each take turns in driving
all their children to school, etc. **carport,**
n. shelter for a car. **carsick,** *adj.* feeling
ill when travelling by motor vehicle. **car
wash,** *n.* place where cars are washed
automatically.

carafe [kə'ræf] *n.* glass jug for serving
wine.

caramel ['kærəmel] *n.* (a) sweet made
with sugar and butter. (b) burnt
sugar; **c. custard** = pudding of egg
custard topped with browned sugar.
caramelize, *v.* to heat sugar until it
becomes brown.

carapace ['kærəpeɪs] *n.* outside shell (of
an animal).

carat ['kærət] *n.* (a) measure of purity
of gold; **18-c. gold.** (b) weight of a
diamond.

caravan ['kærəvæn] *n.* (a) van with beds,
table, washing facilities, etc., which can
be towed by a car. (b) group of vehicles/
animals travelling together (esp. across
a desert). **caravanning,** *n.* going on
holiday in a caravan.

caraway ['kærəweɪ] *n.* spicy seed used
to flavour cakes and biscuits.

carbamate ['kɑːbəmeɪt] *n.* type of pesticide.

carbine ['kɑːbaɪn] *n.* type of light rifle.

carbohydrate [kɑːbəʊ'haɪdreɪt] *n.* chemical substance containing carbon, hydrogen and oxygen, and derived from sugar; **she eats too many carbohydrates** = too much fattening food.

carbolic [kɑː'bɒlɪk] *adj.* referring to an acid used to disinfect; **c. soap.**

carbon ['kɑːbən] *n.* (*element: C*) substance found in charcoal, soot, diamonds; **c. dioxide** = colourless gas (CO_2) forming a small part of the atmosphere; **c. monoxide** = colourless poisonous gas (CO) present in car exhaust fumes; **c. paper** = paper with black substance on one side, used to make copies in typing; **c. copy** = identical copy. **carbonate,** *n.* salt of carbonic acid. **carbonic** [kɑː'bɒnɪk] *adj.* referring to carbon; **c. acid** = acid formed when carbon dioxide is dissolved in water. **carboniferous** [kɑːbə'nɪfərəs] *adj.* coal-bearing. **carbonize** ['kɑːbənaɪz] *v.* to make into carbon by burning. **carboxyhaemoglobin,** *n.* compound of carbon monoxide and haemoglobin formed when a person inhales car exhaust fumes.

carborundum [kɑːbə'rʌndəm] *n.* hard substance used for polishing or sharpening.

carboy ['kɑːbɔɪ] *n.* very large glass bottle for containing liquids.

carbuncle ['kɑːbʌŋkl] *n.* (*a*) red precious stone. (*b*) large inflamed spot on the skin.

carburettor [kɑːbə'retə] *n.* device in a car for changing liquid petrol into vapour.

carcase/carcass ['kɑːkəs] *n.* (*a*) body of a dead animal ready for the butcher; bones left after you have eaten a cooked bird. (*b*) body (of a person).

carcinogen [kɑː'sɪnədʒən] *n.* substance which causes cancer.

carcinoma [kɑːsɪ'nəʊmə] *n.* cancer.

card [kɑːd] **1.** *n.* (*a*) small rectangle of stiff paper for writing on. (*b*) rectangle of stiff paper with a design on it, used for playing games; **playing cards** = ordinary cards, marked in four designs (diamonds, hearts, clubs, spades); **c. games** = games using packs of special cards; **they were playing cards** = they were playing games of cards (for money). (*c*) (**visiting**) **c.** = small piece of stiff paper with your name and address printed on it; **banker's c./cheque c.** = plastic card given by a bank which guarantees payment of a cheque; **credit c.** = plastic card which allows you to buy goods without paying for them immediately; **smart c.** = plastic card with a built-in microprocessor. (*d*) **cards** = official record of an employee; **he got his cards** = he was told to leave. **2.** *v.* to comb (raw wool). **cardboard,** *n.* thick card, used for packing. **card-index. 1.** *n.* series of small cards classified into alphabetical or numerical order. **2.** *v.* to classify (sth) on to small filing cards. **card-sharper,** *n.* person who cheats at cards to win money.

cardiac ['kɑːdɪæk] *adj.* referring to the heart; **c. arrest** = heart attack.

cardigan ['kɑːdɪgən] *n.* woollen jacket which buttons at the front.

cardinal ['kɑːdɪnl] **1.** *adj.* (*a*) very important (rule, etc.). (*b*) **c. numbers** = numbers which show quantity (1, 2, 3, etc.). **2.** *n.* (*a*) high dignitary of the Catholic church. (*b*) bright red North American bird.

cardiogram ['kɑːdɪəgræm] *n.* chart showing heart beats. **cardiograph,** *n.* machine for recording heart beats in the form of cardiograms. **cardiology** [kɑːdɪ'ɒlədʒɪ] *n.* study of the heart and its diseases. **cardiologist,** *n.* doctor specializing in cardiology. **cardiovascular,** *adj.* referring to the heart and the blood circulation system.

care ['keə] **1.** *n.* (*a*) worry. (*b*) looking after s.o./sth; **to take c.** = to watch out/to be careful; **in the c. of** = being looked after by; (*on a letter*) **Mr White, c. of Mrs Green** = Mr White, at Mrs Green's house. **2.** *v.* (*a*) to worry; **I don't c. if I never see you again.** (*b*) to like; **would you c. for a cake?** (*c*) **to c. for** = to look after. **carefree,** *adj.* without any worries. **careful,** *adj.* cautious/taking care. **carefully,** *adv.* with care. **careless,** *adj.* not paying attention/not taking care. **carelessly,** *adv.* in a careless way. **carelessness**, *n*. being careless. **carer**, *n*. person who looks after another person. **caretaker**, *n*. person who looks after a building; (government) which runs a country temporarily (until a permanent one is elected). **careworn**, *adj* tired because of worries.

careen [kə'riːn] *v*. (*a*) to tilt (a boat) over, so as to clean the bottom. (*b*) *inf*. to go along very fast.

career [kə'rɪə] **1**. *n*. (*a*) life of professional work. (*b*) forward rush. **2**. *v*. to rush forward out of control. **careerist**, *adj. & n.* (person) only aiming at advancing his career.

caress [kə'res] **1**. *n*. (*pl*. **-es**) gentle touch. **2**. *v*. to stroke gently.

caret ['kærɪt] *n*. c. (**sign**) = sign used to show that sth is missing.

cargo ['kɑːgəʊ] *n*. (*pl*. **-oes**) goods carried (esp. on a ship); **c. boat** = ship which carries only goods and no passengers.

caribou ['kærɪbuː] *n*. (*pl*. **caribou**) reindeer of North America.

caricature ['kærɪkətjʊə] **1**. *n*. amusing drawing which satirizes by emphasizing s.o.'s particular features. **2**. *v*. to satirize by emphasizing s.o.'s bad features.

caries ['keəriːz] *n*. (*pl*. **caries**) decayed place in a tooth.

carillon ['kærɪlɒn] *n*. set of bells, usu. in a tower, on which tunes can be played.

carminative ['kɑːmɪnətɪv] *n*. medicine which relieves indigestion.

carmine ['kɑːmɪn] *adj. & n.* bright red (colour).

carnage ['kɑːnɪdʒ] *n*. bloodshed/massacre/killing.

carnal ['kɑːnl] *adj*. referring to the body; sensual.

carnation [kɑː'neɪʃn] *n*. strongly scented flower often worn as a buttonhole.

carnet ['kɑːneɪ] *n*. permit to take goods from one country to another.

carnival ['kɑːnɪvl] *n*. festival often with dancing and eating in the open air.

carnivore ['kɑːnɪvɔː] *n*. animal which eats flesh. **carnivorous** [kɑː'nɪvərəs] *adj*. flesh-eating.

carol ['kærəl] **1**. *n*. special song sung at a particular time of the year; **Christmas c. 2**. *v*. (**carolled**) to sing Christmas carols. **carol-singer**, *n*. person singing Christmas carols (to collect money for charity).

carotid [kæ'rɒtɪd] *n*. artery in the neck.

carouse [kə'raʊz] *v*. to drink alcohol and enjoy yourself. **carousal**, *n*. (*formal*) drunken party.

carousel [kæruː'sel] *n*. (*a*) circular conveyor belt which distributes luggage. (*b*) *Am* merry-go-round.

carp [kɑːp] **1**. *n*. (*pl*. **carp**) fat edible fish often bred in captivity for eating. **2**. *v*. to keep on finding fault with things.

carpel ['kɑːpəl] *n*. female part of a flower.

carpenter ['kɑːpəntə] *n*. person who works with wood, esp. in building. **carpentry**, *n*. art of working with wood.

carpet ['kɑːpɪt] **1**. *n*. woven or knotted covering for the floor; *inf*. **to have s.o. on the c.** = to criticize s.o. **2**. *v*. (*a*) to cover (as) with a carpet. (*b*) *inf*. to criticize (s.o.). **carpetbagger**, *n*. politician who tries to make his fortune in a part of the country which is not his home. **carpeting**, *n*. covering with a carpet; wide piece of carpet. **carpet sweeper**, *n*. device which cleans carpets by means of rotating brushes.

carriage ['kærɪdʒ] *n*. (*a*) action of carrying goods; **c. paid** = the price includes transport. (*b*) open vehicle pulled by a horse; **railway c.** = passenger wagon on a train. (*c*) way of walking. (*d*) movable part on a typewriter which goes from side to side. **carriageway**, *n*. surface of the road on which traffic moves.

carrier ['kærɪə] *n*. (*a*) thing/person who carries; company which transports goods; **luggage c.** = grid on the back of a bicycle for carrying parcels; **c. pigeon** = pigeon specially trained for carrying messages; **c. bag** = large paper or plastic bag with handles. (*b*) person who carries the germ of a disease without suffering and can infect others with it. (*c*) **aircraft c.** = ship which carries aircraft.

carrion ['kærɪən] *n*. (*no pl.*) rotting meat. **carrion crow**, *n*. type of large black crow.

carrot ['kærət] *n*. bright orange root vegetable.

carry ['kærɪ] v. (a) to lift (sth) up and move it from one place to another. (b) to win (a vote). (c) (of sound) to be heard at a distance. (d) to keep (in a shop). **carry along,** v. to carry (sth) which cannot prevent it. **carry away,** v. (a) to take away/to demolish. (b) **to get carried away** = to get overcome with emotion/excitement. **carrycot,** n. rectangular box with handles for carrying a baby. **carry forward,** v. (in book-keeping) to take (a sum) on to the next page or column. **carry off,** v. (a) to win/to take away. (b) **he carried it off very well** = he got through a potentially embarrassing situation very well. **carry on,** v. (a) to continue/to go on. (b) inf. to be very angry. **carry out,** v. to do (sth) successfully. **carry through,** v. to bring (sth) to a finish.

cart [kɑ:t] 1. n. vehicle pulled by a horse; **to put the c. before the horse** = not to put first things first. 2. v. to carry (sth heavy). **carter,** n. person who drives a cart; company which transports goods by road. **carthorse,** n. large strong horse. **cartload,** n. quantity carried in a cart. **cartwheel,** n. (a) wheel of a cart. (b) **to turn cartwheels** = to turn over and over sideways on your outstretched hands and feet.

carte blanche [kɑ:t'blɒnʃ] n. **to have c. b. to do sth** = to be able to do whatever you want.

cartel [kɑ:'tel] n. group of companies which try to fix the price of sth.

cartilage ['kɑ:tɪlɪdʒ] n. strong flexible material which acts as a cushion in joints in the body. **cartilaginous** [kɑ:tɪ'lædʒɪnəs] adj. made of cartilage.

cartographer [kɑ:'tɒgrəfə] n. person who draws maps. **cartographic,** adj. referring to maps. **cartography,** n. science of drawing maps.

carton ['kɑ:tən] n. cardboard box.

cartoon [kɑ:'tu:n] n. (a) funny (often political) drawing. (b) film made of moving drawings. (c) sketch for a painting. **cartoonist,** n. person who draws (political) cartoons.

cartridge ['kɑ:trɪdʒ] n. (a) tube packed with gunpowder and a bullet for firing from a gun. (b) film/recording tape enclosed in a plastic case which fits directly into the camera/tape recorder; tube of ink which fits into a pen. (c) part of a record player which holds the stylus. (d) **c. paper** = kind of thick rough paper.

carve [kɑ:v] v. (a) to cut (meat) up at table. (b) to cut (stone/wood) to make a shape. **carver,** n. (a) person who carves. (b) carving knife. (c) dining chair with arms. **carving,** n. (a) cutting up cooked meat; **c. knife** = large sharp knife for cutting meat. (b) art of cutting stone/wood into shapes. (c) an object which has been made by carving.

caryatid [kær'jætɪd] n. statue of a female figure, which acts as a column holding up a roof.

cascade [kæs'keɪd] 1. n. (artificial) waterfall. 2. v. to fall in large quantities.

case [keɪs] 1. n. (a) box (of goods). (b) protective box or covering. (c) suitcase. (d) way in which sth happens; example; **in any c.** = anyway; **in c. of fire** = if fire breaks out; **just in c.** = to guard against a possible emergency. (e) sick person; **c. history** = details of a patient's past history, progress, etc. (f) legal affair. 2. v. to put (sth) in a case.

casein ['keɪsɪɪn] n. protein found in milk.

casement ['keɪsmənt] n. window that opens on hinges; frame around such a window.

cash [kæʃ] 1. n. money (in coins and notes); **c. crop** = crop grown for sale; **c. desk** = place in a shop where you pay; **c. register** = machine which shows the amount to be paid and has a drawer for keeping money. 2. v. to change (a cheque) into cash; **to c. in on** = to make a lot of money by profiting from sth. **cash and carry,** n. discount warehouse, selling items to the general public. **cash flow,** n. rate at which money comes into and is paid out of a business.

cashew [kə'ʃu:] n. small sweetish nut, often eaten salted.

cashier [kə'ʃi:ə] 1. n. person who deals with money. 2. v. to expel (an officer) from the armed forces.

cashmere ['kæʃmɪə] adj. & n. (made of) fine soft goat's wool.

casing ['keɪsɪŋ] n. hard covering which protects something.

casino [kə'si:nəu] *n.* (*pl.* **-os**) building where you can gamble.

cask [kɑ:sk] *n.* large barrel.

casket ['kɑ:skɪt] *n.* (*a*) ornamental box (for jewels). (*b*) *Am.* coffin.

cassata [kə'sɑ:tə] *n.* Italian ice cream with dried fruit in it.

casserole ['kæsərəʊl] *n.* (*a*) oven-proof covered dish. (*b*) food cooked in a covered dish in the oven.

cassette [kə'set] *n.* (*a*) magnetic tape in a plastic case which can fit directly into a playing or recording machine; **c. player** = machine for playing cassettes; **c. recorder** = machine for recording and playing back cassettes. (*b*) film in a plastic case which fits directly into a camera.

cassock ['kæsək] *n.* long, usu. black, gown worn by priests, choirboys, etc.

cast [kɑ:st] **1.** *n.* (*a*) throwing (of a fishing line). (*b*) plaster shape made from a mould. (*c*) **worm c.** = small pile of earth thrown up by a worm. (*d*) list of actors in a play/film; all the actors in a play/film. (*e*) **c. of mind** = way of thinking. (*f*) squint (in an eye). **2.** *v.* (**cast**) (*a*) to throw. (*b*) to mould metal/plaster. (*c*) to choose actors for a play/film. **3.** *adj.* which has been cast in a mould; **a cast-iron excuse** = a perfect excuse. **cast about for,** *v.* to look for. **cast adrift,** *v.* to abandon (a boat/a family). **cast aside,** *v.* to throw away. **cast away,** *v.* to throw away; **cast away on a desert island** = shipwrecked on a desert island. **castaway,** *n.* person who has been shipwrecked. **cast down,** *v.* to throw down; **they were cast down** = they were miserable. **casting. 1.** *n.* (*a*) moulding of a shape/thing which has been moulded. (*b*) choosing of actors. **2.** *adj.* **c. vote** = vote which decides when the other votes are equal. **cast off,** *v.* (*a*) to calculate roughly the number of pages in (a book), before it is printed. (*b*) to untie the ropes holding a boat. (*c*) (*in knitting*) to finish stitches. **cast-off clothing,** *n.*, **cast-offs,** *n. pl.* clothes which have been thrown away. **cast on,** *v.* to put (stitches) on to the needles when knitting.

castanets [kæstə'nets] *n. pl.* hollow clappers made of wood which are held in the hand and clicked in time to music by Spanish dancers.

caste [kɑ:st] *n.* hereditary class (in Indian society).

castigate ['kæstɪgeɪt] *v.* (*formal*) to punish/to beat s.o. as a punishment; to criticize s.o. sharply.

castle ['kɑ:sl] *n.* (*a*) large fortified building. (*b*) piece in chess which looks like a castle.

castor/caster ['kɑ:stə] *n.* (*a*) sugar c. = pot with holes in the lid for sprinkling sugar; **c. sugar** = fine sugar. (*b*) wheel screwed on to the leg of a chair. **castor oil,** *n.* oil from a palm which is used as a laxative.

castrate [kæ'streɪt] *v.* to remove the testicles from (a male animal). **castration** [kæ'streɪʃn] *n.* act of castrating.

casual ['kæʒʊəl] *adj.* (*a*) not formal; **c. labour** = workers taken on for very short periods. (*b*) not serious. **casually,** *adv.* by chance; in an informal way. **casualness,** *n.* being casual.

casualty ['kæʒʊəltɪ] *n.* person injured or killed in a battle/an accident; person or thing destroyed or damaged; **c. department** = section of a hospital for accident victims.

casuistry ['kæzjuːɪstrɪ] *n.* debating problems in very fine detail.

cat [kæt] *n.* (*a*) furry domestic pet, which purrs and has a long tail; wild animal of the same family as the domestic cat; *inf.* **he let the c. out of the bag** = he revealed the secret; **c. burglar** = burglar who climbs walls or drainpipes to enter a house. (*b*) *inf.* woman who makes spiteful remarks. **catcall,** *n.* whistle/hoot (to show displeasure). **catfish,** *n.* (*pl.* **catfish**) large ugly freshwater fish with whiskers. **catgut,** *n.* gut used as thread. **catmint,** *n.* plant much liked by cats. **catnap,** *n.* short nap. **cat's eyes,** *n.* small glass reflectors showing the centre or sides of a road. **catwalk,** *n.* open metal gangway running along the outside of a ship/building.

catabolism [kæ'tæbɒlɪzm] *n.* breaking down of complex substances into simple chemicals.

cataclysm ['kætəklɪzəm] *n.* disaster. **cataclysmic** [kætə'klɪzmɪk] *adj.* disastrous.

catacombs ['kætəku:mz] *n. pl.* underground rooms (used in ancient times for burying the dead).

catalepsy ['kætəlepsɪ] *n.* state where s.o. becomes unconscious and stiff. **cataleptic,** *adj.* referring to catalepsy.

catalogue, *Am.* **catalog** ['kætəlɒg] **1.** *n.* list of things for sale/in a library/in a museum. **2.** *v.* to make a list of books in a library/of treasures in a museum/ of things for sale. **cataloguer,** *n.* person who specializes in the making of catalogues.

catalysis [kə'tælɪsɪs] *n.* chemical reaction which is helped by a substance which does not itself change. **catalyst** ['kætəlɪst] *n.* chemical substance which helps to produce a chemical reaction; anything which helps sth to take place. **catalytic,** *adj.* referring to catalysis; **c. converter** = device attached to the exhaust pipe of a car to reduce carbon monoxide.

catamaran [kætəmə'ræn] *n.* boat with two parallel hulls.

catapult ['kætəpʌlt] **1.** *n.* strong elastic band on a forked stick, used for throwing stones; **c. launching gear** = mechanism on an aircraft carrier for sending an aircraft into the air. **2.** *v.* to send (an aircraft, etc.) into the air; to put (s.o.) into a new job quickly.

cataract ['kætərækt] *n.* (*a*) waterfall on a river. (*b*) film which grows over the eye and eventually prevents you from seeing.

catarrh [kə'tɑ:] *n.* type of cold caused by inflammation of the nose and bronchial tubes. **catarrhal** [kə'tɑ:rəl] *adj.* referring to catarrh.

catastrophe [kə'tæstrəfɪ] *n.* disaster. **catastrophic** [kætə'strɒfɪk] *adj.* disastrous.

catatonic [kætə'tɒnɪk] *adj.* (condition) where a patient is either violent or stays without moving at all.

catch [kætʃ] **1.** *n.* (*pl.* **-es**) (*a*) things which have been caught; **we had a good c.** = we caught a lot of fish; **he's a good c.** = he is a good prospective husband/worker. (*b*) action of catching (a ball, etc.). (*c*) awkwardness/hitch; **there must be a c. in it** = there must be something wrong with it/there must

be a trap; **c. 22** = vicious circle which cannot be escaped from. **2.** *v.* (**caught**) (*a*) to grab hold of (sth) which is moving; **I didn't c. what you said** = I was not able to hear. (*b*) to get (a disease). (*c*) to find (s.o.) by surprise. **catching,** *adj.* (disease) which can be caught/which is infectious. **catchment area,** *n.* (*a*) land from which a river gets its water. (*b*) area round a school from which all pupils must come. **catch on,** *v.* (*a*) to understand. (*b*) to become fashionable. **catch out,** *v.* to find that (s.o.) has made a mistake; to ask (s.o.) a question to which he does not know the answer. **catch phrase,** *n.* popular phrase, usu. associated with an entertainer or advertisement. **catch up,** *v.* to move faster than s.o. so as to draw level with him. **catchword,** *n.* popular phrase. **catchy,** *adj.* (tune) which is easy to remember.

catechize ['kætɪkaɪz] *v.* to ask questions. **catechism** ['kætɪkɪzəm] *n.* book of religious instruction; religious classes.

category ['kætɪgərɪ] *n.* classification of things/people. **categoric(al)** [kætɪ'gɒrɪk(l)] *adj.* straightforward/definite. **categorically,** *adv.* definitely.

cater ['keɪtə] *v.* to supply food and drink (at a party, etc.). **caterer,** *n.* person who supplies food. **cater for,** *v.* to provide for. **catering,** *n.* supplying of food.

caterpillar ['kætəpɪlə] *n.* insect larva which turns into a moth or butterfly; **c. track** = endless metal belt running round a pair of wheels (on a tank, etc.); **c. tractor** = tractor which runs on caterpillar tracks.

caterwaul ['kætəwɔ:l] *v.* to howl (like cats at night).

cathedral [kə'θi:drəl] *n.* large church which is the seat of a bishop.

catherine wheel ['kæθrɪnwi:l] *n.* firework which spins round and round.

catheter ['kæθɪtə] *n.* very thin tube which can be inserted into the body to remove fluid.

cathode ['kæθəud] *n.* negative electric pole; **c. ray tube** = tube (as in a television set) where a stream of electrons hits a screen.

catholic ['kæθlɪk] **1.** *adj.* (*a*) wide/general (taste). (*b*) referring to the Roman Catholic Church. **Catholic** = member of the Roman Catholic Church. **catholicism** [kə'θɒlɪsɪzəm] *n.* beliefs of the Roman Catholic church.

catkin ['kætkɪn] *n.* flower of a willow or hazel tree.

catsup ['kætsəp] *n. Am.* ketchup.

cattle ['kætl] *n. pl.* animals of the cow family (such as bulls, calves, oxen, etc.). **cattlegrid,** *n.* rails forming a bridge, which prevent farm animals from getting out on to the road.

catty ['kætɪ] *adj.* (**-ier, -iest**) nasty/sharp-tongued (woman).

caucus ['kɔːkəs] *n.* (*pl.* **-es**) group of party members who plan electoral strategy and choose candidates.

caught [kɔːt] *v. see* **catch.**

cauldron, *Am.* **caldron** ['kɔːldrən] *n.* large deep pan for cooking.

cauliflower ['kɒlɪflaʊə] *n.* cabbage-like vegetable with a large white flower head which is eaten; **c. ear** = permanently swollen ear, found in boxers.

caulk ['kɔːk] *v.* to fill the cracks in a boat's hull to make it watertight.

cause [kɔːz] **1.** *n.* (*a*) thing which makes sth happen; **he died from natural causes** = he died naturally, and was not killed in an accident or murdered. (*b*) reason for doing sth. (*c*) noble aim/charity to which it is good to give money. **2.** *v.* to make (sth) happen. **cause célèbre,** *n.* famous court case. **causal,** *adj.* referring to a cause.

causeway ['kɔːzweɪ] *n.* road/path built up on a bank above marshy ground or water.

caustic ['kɔːstɪk] *adj.* (*a*) burning; **c. soda** = chemical used for cleaning. (*b*) sharp (wit). **caustically,** *adv.* in a sharp/witty way.

cauterize ['kɔːtəraɪz] *v.* to burn (a wound) to stop infection. **cauterization** [kɔːtəraɪ'zeɪʃn] *n.* cauterizing.

caution ['kɔːʃn] **1.** *n.* care/precaution. **2.** *v.* to warn. **cautionary,** *adj.* which warns. **cautious,** *adj.* careful/prudent. **cautiously,** *adv.* in a cautious way. **cautiousness,** *n.* being cautious.

cavalcade ['kævəlkeɪd] *n.* procession (usu. of horseriders).

cavalier [kævə'lɪə] *adj.* high-handed/with no respect for other people or customs.

cavalry ['kævəlrɪ] *n.* soldiers on horseback.

cave [keɪv] **1.** *n.* large underground hole in rock or earth; **c. bears** = prehistoric bears which lived in caves; **c. paintings** = paintings on walls of caves done by cavemen. **2.** *v.* **to c. in** = to collapse. **caveman,** *n.* (*pl.* **-men**) primitive man who lived in caves.

caveat ['kæviæt] *n.* warning (esp. against doing sth); **c. emptor** = let the buyer beware.

cavern ['kævən] *n.* very large cave. **cavernous,** *adj.* like a cavern.

caviar(e) ['kævɪɑː] *n.* very expensive delicacy consisting of the eggs of a sturgeon.

cavil ['kævɪl] *v.* (**cavilled**) **to c. at sth** = to object to sth.

cavity ['kævɪtɪ] *n.* hole; **c. wall** = wall made of two rows of bricks with a gap in between.

cavort [kə'vɔːt] *v.* to rush about in excitement.

caw [kɔː] *v.* to make a croaking sound like a crow.

cayenne ['keɪen] *n.* type of hot red pepper.

cayman ['keɪmən] *n.* alligator.

CB ['siː'biː] *abbrev. for* citizens' band.

cc ['siː'siː] *abbrev. for* cubic centimetre.

Cd *symbol for* cadmium.

CD *abbrev. for* compact disk.

cease [siːs] *v.* to stop. **ceasefire,** *n.* agreement to stop shooting (in a war). **ceaseless,** *adj.* without stopping. **ceaselessly,** *adv.* without stopping.

cedar ['siːdə] *n.* large evergreen tree, with sweet-smelling wood; wood from this tree. **cedarwood,** *n.* wood from a cedar.

cede [siːd] *v.* to pass (property/land) **to** s.o. else.

cedilla [sɪ'dɪlə] *n.* accent placed under the letter 'c', showing that it is pronounced 's'.

ceilidh ['keɪlɪ] *n.* (*in Scotland, Ireland*) party with performances of songs and dances.

ceiling ['siːlɪŋ] *n.* (*a*) inside roof over a room. (*b*) upper limit.

celandine ['seləndaɪn] *n.* small wild plant with yellow flowers.

celebrate ['selɪbreɪt] v. (a) to remember a special day with parties and feasts. (b) to perform (a mass). **celebrant,** n. priest who celebrates mass. **celebrated,** adj. very famous. **celebration** [selɪ'breɪʃn] n. festivity. **celebrity** [sə'lebrɪtɪ] n. (a) famous person. (b) being famous.

celeriac [sɪ'lerɪæk] n. vegetable with a thick root tasting like celery.

celerity [sə'lerɪtɪ] n. speed.

celery ['selərɪ] n. white- or green-stemmed plant, eaten as a vegetable, esp. raw as a salad.

celestial [sə'lestjəl] adj. (formal) heavenly/referring to the sky.

celibate ['selɪbət] adj. not married, esp. because of religious vows. **celibacy,** n. state of being celibate.

cell [sel] n. (a) room in a prison/in a monastery; **condemned c.** = cell for a person who has been condemned to death. (b) basic unit of an organism. (c) basic political group. (d) part of an electric battery. **cellular,** adj. made up of many small cells; (cloth) with open holes in it. **cellulitis,** n. inflammation of tissue under the skin.

cellar ['selə] n. underground room or rooms beneath a house.

cello ['tʃeləʊ] n. large stringed musical instrument, smaller than a double bass. **cellist,** n. person who plays the cello.

cellophane ['seləfeɪn] n. trademark for transparent flexible sheet for wrapping or covering.

cellulose ['seljʊləʊs] n. chemical substance found in plants, used for making paper and paint.

Celsius ['selsɪəs] adj. & n. (scale for) measuring temperature, where the boiling point of water is 100°, and the freezing point 0°.

Celt [kelt] n. descendant of a European people now found in Scotland, Ireland, Wales, Brittany, etc. **Celtic,** adj. referring to ancient or modern Celts.

cement [sɪ'ment] 1. n. (a) powder made from limestone heated with clay, which when mixed with water dries hard. (b) mortar. (c) strong glue. 2. v. (a) to stick together with cement. (b) to strengthen/to make close. **cement mixer,** n. machine for mixing cement.

cemetery ['semətrɪ] n. burial ground.

cenotaph ['senətɑːf] n. war memorial; empty tomb.

censer ['sensə] n. (in church) metal receptacle on a chain for burning incense.

censor ['sensə] 1. n. official who inspects letters/newspaper articles/plays/books, etc., to see if they can be sent or published. 2. v. to forbid the publication of (sth) because it may be obscene or may reveal secrets. **censorious** [sen'sɔːrɪəs] adj. critical/which criticizes. **censorship,** n. office of censor; act of censoring.

censure ['senʃə] 1. n. condemnation/criticism. 2. v. to condemn/to criticize (s.o.)

census ['sensəs] n. (pl. -es) official counting of the population of a country.

cent [sent] n. small coin/one-hundredth part of a dollar.

centaur ['sentɔː] n. mythical animal, half man, half horse.

centenary [sen'tiːnərɪ] n. hundredth anniversary. **centenarian** [sentɪ'neərɪən] n. person who is 100 years old or more. **centennial** [sen'tenjəl] adj. referring to a centenary.

centigrade ['sentɪgreɪd] adj. & n. (scale for) measuring temperature where the boiling point of water is 100° and the freezing point 0°.

centilitre, Am. **centiliter** ['sentɪliːtə] n. liquid measure, one hundredth part of a litre.

centimetre, Am. **centimeter** ['sentɪmiːtə] n. measure of length, one hundredth part of a metre.

centipede ['sentɪpiːd] n. creeping animal with a large number of legs.

centre, Am. **center** ['sentə] 1. n. (a) middle; **c. party** = political party in the centre, neither right nor left. (b) large building containing several different units. (c) player who plays in the middle of the field. 2. v. (a) to place in the centre. (b) to put the main emphasis (on). **central,** adj. in the middle; **c. heating** = heating for a whole building which comes from one heating apparatus. **centralization** [sentrəlaɪ'zeɪʃn] n. act of centralizing. **centralize,** v. to put under the control of a central

system. **centrally,** adv. in the middle.
centre forward, n. (in football) player
in the centre of the forward line.
centrifugal [sentrɪ'fju:gl] adj. which
tends to go away from the centre.
centripetal [sentrɪ'pi:tl] adj. which
tends to go towards the centre.
century ['sentʃərɪ] n. (a) hundred years.
(b) (in games) score of one hundred.
ceramic [sə'ræmɪk] adj. made of
pottery. **ceramics,** n. art of working in
pottery.
cereal ['sɪərɪəl] n. (a) grain crop such
as wheat, barley, maize, etc. (b)
(**breakfast**) **c.** = grain foods eaten with
sugar and milk for breakfast.
cerebellum [serɪ'beləm] n. back part of
the brain, which governs balance.
cerebral ['serɪbrəl] adj. (a) referring to
the brain. (b) intellectual (rather than
emotional). **c. palsy** = disorder of the
brain which affects spastics. **cerebrum,**
n. main part of the brain.
ceremony ['serɪmənɪ] n. official occasion; solemn behaviour on an official
occasion; **don't stand on c.** = be
informal. **ceremonial** [serɪ'məunɪəl] 1.
n. way of conducting a ceremony.
2. adj. referring to a ceremony.
ceremonially, adv. with ceremony.
ceremonious adj. with a lot of ceremony. **ceremoniously,** adv. with a lot
of ceremony.
cerise [sə'ri:z] n. bright cherry pink colour.
cert [sɜ:t] n. inf. (a) certainty; **it's a
dead c.** = it is bound to happen. (b)
certificate.
certain ['sɜ:tn] adj. (a) sure. (b) particular. **certainly,** adv. of course.
certainty, n. (a) being certain. (b) sure/
certain thing.
certificate [sə'tɪfɪkət] n. official document which proves/shows sth. **certi-
fiable** [sɜ:tɪ'faɪəbl] adj. (person) who
should be declared insane; (thing)
which should be certified. **certification**
[sɜ:tɪfɪ'keɪʃn] n. act of certifying. **certify**
['sɜ:tɪfaɪ] v. to write a certificate; to
put in writing an official declaration; to
declare (s.o.) insane.
certitude ['sɜ:tɪtju:d] n. certainty.
cervix ['sɜ:vɪks] n. (pl. -es) neck, esp. the
neck of the womb. **cervical,** adj. referring to the cervix.

cessation [se'seɪʃn] n. stopping.
cession ['seʃn] n. ceding.
cesspit, cesspool ['sespɪt, 'sespu:l]
n. underground tank for collecting
sewage.
cf abbrev for confer, meaning to
compare.
CFC [si:ef'si:] abbrev for
chlorofluorocarbon.
cg abbrev for centigram.
chafe [tʃeɪf] v. (a) to rub/to wear out
by rubbing. (b) to become irritated/
annoyed. **chafing dish,** n. dish which
keeps food hot.
chaff [tʃɑ:f] n. (a) dried corn stalks left
after the grain is extracted. (b) good-
humoured teasing.
chaffinch ['tʃæfɪntʃ] n. common pink-
breasted finch.
chagrin ['ʃægrɪn] n. annoyance/sadness.
chain [tʃeɪn] 1. n. (a) series of rings
joined together; **c. reaction** = events/
chemical reactions which build up
rapidly. (b) row (of mountains). (c)
c. store = group of shops belonging
to the same company. 2. v. to attach
with a chain. **chainsaw,** n. saw where
the teeth are set in a continuous chain
driven by a motor. **chain-smoke,** v. to
smoke (cigarettes) one after the other.
chain-smoker, n. person who chain-
smokes.
chair ['tʃeə] 1. n. (a) piece of furniture
for one person to sit on. (b) position
of chairman at a meeting; position of
professor at a university; **in the c.** = in
charge of a meeting. 2. v. to be in charge
of (a meeting). **chairlift,** n. chairs on
a cable which take skiers up a mountain. **chairman,** n. (pl. -men) person
who is in charge of a meeting; head of
a company. **chairmanship,** n. position of chairman; art of being a chairman. **chairperson,** n. person who is in
charge of a meeting. **chairwoman,** n.
(pl. -women) woman who is in charge
of a meeting.
chaise longue [ʃeɪz'lɒŋg] n. chair with
a long seat.
chalcedony [kæl'sedənɪ] n. whitish
stone, a variety of quartz.
chalet ['ʃæleɪ] n. small (holiday) house,
usu. made of wood.
chalice ['tʃælɪs] n. metal cup in which
wine is offered at a communion service.

chalk [tʃɔ:k] 1. *n.* (*a*) soft white rock. (*b*) stick of white or coloured material for writing on a blackboard. 2. *v.* to mark or write with chalk. **chalk up,** *v.* to mark (a score/a victory). **chalky,** *adj.* white like chalk; gritty like chalk.

challenge ['tʃæləndʒ] 1. *n.* invitation to fight/struggle; **to take up the c.** = accept the invitation to fight. 2. *v.* to ask (s.o.) to fight; to ask (s.o.) to prove that they are right. **challenger,** *n.* person who challenges. **challenging,** *adj.* provocative.

chamber ['tʃeɪmbə] *n.* (*a*) room/hall; **council c.** = room where a town council meets; **c. of commerce** = official group of businessmen in a town; **lawyer's chambers** = offices of a lawyer. (*b*) space in a piece of machinery, esp. one of the spaces for cartridges in a revolver. (*c*) space in an organ, such as the heart. (*d*) **c. music** = music for a few instruments, originally played in a small room. **chambermaid,** *n.* woman who cleans rooms in a hotel. **chamberpot,** *n.* pot in which you can urinate, and which is usu. kept in the bedroom.

chameleon [kə'mi:liən] *n.* lizard which changes its colour according to its natural surroundings.

chamfer ['ʃæmfə] *v.* to bevel the edge of (sth).

chammy leather ['ʃæmɪleðə] *n.* very soft leather used for washing windows, etc.

chamois, *n.* (*a*) ['ʃæmwɑ:] mountain goat. (*b*) ['ʃæmɪ] very soft leather.

champ [tʃæmp] 1. *n. inf.* champion. 2. *v.* to chew hard and noisily; **c. at the bit** = to be impatient to go.

champagne [ʃæm'peɪn] *n.* sparkling French white wine. **champers,** *n. inf.* champagne.

champion ['tʃæmpiən] 1. *n.* best person/animal in a particular competition. 2. *v.* to support (a cause) strenuously. **championship,** *n.* (*a*) support of a cause. (*b*) contest to determine who is the champion.

chance [tʃɑ:ns] 1. *n.* (*a*) luck; **games of c.** = games where you gamble on the possibility of winning; **to take chances** = to take risks. (*b*) possibility/opportunity. 2. *v.* (*a*) to happen unexpectedly. (*b*) to risk. **chancy,** *adj. inf.* risky.

chancel ['tʃɑ:nsl] *n.* part of a church near the altar where a choir sits.

chancellery ['tʃɑ:nsəlrɪ] *n.* office of a chancellor; office attached to an embassy.

chancellor ['tʃɑ:nsələ] *n.* (*a*) government minister; (*in Germany/Austria*) = Prime Minister; **C. of the Exchequer** = British finance minister. (*b*) titular head of a university.

Chancery ['tʃɑ:nsərɪ] *n.* one of the divisions of the British High Court.

chandelier [ʃændə'lɪə] *n.* light-fitting hanging from the ceiling with several branches for holding lights.

chandler ['tʃɑ:ndlə] *n.* person who supplies stores for ships.

change [tʃeɪndʒ] 1. *n.* (*a*) difference from what was before; **c. of clothes** = new set of clothes to wear; **to ring the changes** = (i) to ring peals of bells; (ii) to try several alternatives to see which works best. (*b*) money given back when you pay a larger amount than the price asked; (**small**) **c.** = money in coins. 2. *v.* (*a*) to make (sth) different; to become different. (*b*) to put on different clothes; **changing room** = room where you can change into sports clothes. (*c*) (**for**) to give sth in place of sth else; **to c.** (**trains**) = get off one train to catch another. **changeability** [tʃeɪndʒə'bɪlɪtɪ] *n.* being changeable. **changeable,** *adj.* which changes often/is likely to change. **changeless,** *adj.* which never changes. **changeling,** *n.* baby supposed to have been substituted for another by fairies.

channel ['tʃænl] 1. *n.* (*a*) piece of water connecting two seas. (*b*) bed (of a stream); ditch/gutter along which liquid can flow. (*c*) means/ways; **channels of communication** = ways of communicating. (*d*) frequency band for radio or TV. 2. *v.* (**channelled**) to direct/to persuade to take a certain direction.

chant [tʃɑ:nt] 1. *n.* regular singing of a repeated phrase; monotonous song. 2. *v.* to sing to a regular beat.

chaos ['keɪɒs] *n.* confusion. **chaotic** [keɪ'ɒtɪk] *adj.* confused/disorderly.

chap [tʃæp] 1. *n.* (*a*) *inf.* man. (*b*) cooked cheek (of a pig). 2. *v.* to crack (skin).

chaps, *n. pl.* wide leggings worn by cowboys.

chapel ['tʃæpl] *n.* (*a*) small church; part of a large church with a separate altar; place of worship for nonconformists. (*b*) branch of a trades union (in the printing and publishing industry).

chaperon(e) ['ʃæpərəʊn] **1.** *n.* older woman who goes around with a young girl on social visits. **2.** *v.* to protect (a young girl) who is going to a social occasion.

chaplain ['tʃæplɪn] *n.* priest (attached to a private individual or in the armed services). **chaplaincy,** *n.* position of chaplain.

chapped [tʃæpt] *adj.* (of skin) cracked (with cold).

chapter ['tʃæptə] *n.* (*a*) division of a book; **a c. of accidents** = a series of accidents. (*b*) group of priests who administer a cathedral.

char [tʃɑ:] **1.** *n.* (*a*) small freshwater fish. (*b*) *inf.* charwoman. (*c*) *inf.* tea. **2.** *v.* (**charred**) (*a*) *inf.* to do housework for s.o.. (*b*) to burn black.

character ['kærəktə] *n.* (*a*) central being of a person which makes him an individual who is different from all others. (*b*) person in a play/novel. (*c*) odd person. (*d*) letter/symbol used in writing or printing. **characteristic** [kærəktə'rɪstɪk] **1.** *adj.* special/typical. **2.** *n.* special/typical feature. **characteristically,** *adv.* typically. **characterization** [kærəktəraɪ'zeɪʃn] *n.* indication of character. **characterize** ['kærəktəraɪz] *v.* to be a typical feature of (sth). **characterless,** *adj.* ordinary/with no special features.

charade [ʃə'rɑ:d] *n.* (*a*) game where spectators have to guess a word from a scene acted by others. (*b*) action which has no meaning/which is simply a pretence.

charcoal ['tʃɑ:kəʊl] *n.* black material formed by partly burnt wood; **c. grey** = dark, dull grey colour.

chard [tʃɑ:d] *n.* (*pl.* **chard**) green vegetable like spinach.

charge [tʃɑ:dʒ] **1.** *n.* (*a*) money to be paid; **free of c.** (*b*) care (of s.o./sth). (*c*) accusation (of an offence). (*d*) attack (by soldiers running forward).

(*e*) amount of gunpowder in a cartridge/bomb. (*f*) amount of electric current. **2.** *v.* (*a*) to make (s.o.) pay **for** sth. (*b*) (**with**) to accuse (of an offence). (*c*) to put a cartridge in (a gun); to put electricity into (a battery). (*d*) to attack (by running forward). **chargeable,** *adj.* which can be charged. **chargehand,** *n.* leader of a group of workers, under a foreman. **chargepayer,** *n.* person who pays the community charge. **charger,** *n.* (*a*) battle horse. (*b*) device for putting electricity into a car battery. (*c*) large dish for serving meat.

chargé d'affaires [ʃɑ:ʒeɪdæ'feə] *n.* deputy of an ambassador; an official who takes the place of an ambassador.

chariot ['tʃærɪət] *n.* two-wheeled vehicle pulled by horses. **charioteer** [tʃærɪə'tɪə] *n.* person who drives a chariot.

charisma [kə'rɪzmə] *n.* personal appeal. **charismatic** [kærɪz'mætɪk] *adj.* which appeals to the people.

charity ['tʃærɪtɪ] *n.* (*a*) organization which collects money to help the poor or support some cause; giving of money to the poor. (*b*) kindness (to the poor/the oppressed). **charitable,** *adj.* (*a*) which refers to a charity. (*b*) kind/not critical. **charitably,** *adv.* in a charitable way.

charlady ['tʃɑ:leɪdɪ] *n.* charwoman.

charlatan ['ʃɑ:lətən] *n.* person who says he is an expert, but really is not.

charlie, charley ['tʃɑ:lɪ] *n. Sl.* **a proper c.** = a complete fool.

charlotte ['ʃɑ:lɒt] *n.* pudding with fruit and wafers on the outside.

charm [tʃɑ:m] **1.** *n.* (*a*) supposedly magic object; **c. bracelet** = bracelet hung with little ornaments. (*b*) attractiveness. **2.** *v.* (*a*) to bewitch/to put under a spell; **he has a charmed life** = he is very lucky. (*b*) to attract (s.o.)/to make (s.o.) pleased. **charmer,** *n.* person who charms. **charming,** *adj.* attractive.

chart [tʃɑ:t] **1.** *n.* (*a*) map of the sea, a river or lake. (*b*) diagram showing statistics; **the charts** = the list of most popular records. **2.** *v.* (*a*) to make a map of (the sea, a river or lake). (*b*) to make a diagram of; to show (information) in a diagram.

charter ['tʃɑ:tə] **1.** *n.* (*a*) aircraft hired

for a particular flight. (*b*) legal document giving rights or privileges to (a town/a university). **2.** *v.* to hire (an aircraft or boat). **chartered,** *adj.* (accountant, etc.) who has passed his examinations.

charwoman ['tʃɑːwʊmən] *n.* (*pl.* **-women**) woman who does housework for s.o.

chary ['tʃeərɪ] *adj.* reluctant to do sth; cautious.

chase [tʃeɪs] **1.** *n.* hunt; **wild goose c.** = useless search. **2.** *v.* to run after (s.o.) to try to catch them. **chaser,** *n.* alcoholic drink such as beer, drunk after another, stronger, alcoholic drink.

chasm ['kæzəm] *n.* huge crack in the ground.

chassis ['ʃæsɪ] *n.* (*pl.* **chassis** ['ʃæsɪz]) metal framework of a car; undercarriage of an aircraft.

chaste [tʃeɪst] *adj.* (sexually) pure. **chastity** ['tʃæstɪtɪ] *n.* being chaste.

chasten ['tʃeɪsn] *v.* to reprimand; to make (s.o.) less proud. **chastened,** *adj.* meek/less proud.

chastise [tʃæ'staɪz] *v.* (*formal*) to punish. **chastisement,** *n.* punishing.

chasuble ['tʃæzjʊbl] *n.* long sleeveless coat worn by priests at ceremonies.

chat [tʃæt] **1.** *n.* casual friendly talk. **2.** *v.* (**chatted**) to talk in a casual and friendly way; *inf.* **to c. s.o. up** = to get into conversation/to flirt with. **chat show,** *n.* TV show where famous people talk to the host. **chatty,** *adj.* (person) who likes to chat; (letter) full of unimportant news.

chattel ['tʃætl] *n.* object which you possess.

chatter ['tʃætə] **1.** *n.* quick talking. **2.** *v.* to talk quickly and not seriously; **his teeth were chattering** = were rattling because of cold. **chatterbox,** *n.* person who cannot stop talking.

chauffeur ['ʃəʊfə] *n.* person who is paid to drive a car for s.o. else.

chauvinism ['ʃəʊvɪnɪzəm] *n.* excessive pride in your native country. **chauvinist,** *n.* person who is excessively proud of his native country; **male c.** = man who feels that men are superior to women. **chauvinistic** [ʃəʊvɪ'nɪstɪk] *adj.* nationalistic.

cheap [tʃiːp] *adj.* (**-er, -est**) (*a*) not costing a lot of money; **on the c.** = in the cheapest possible way. (*b*) low/sly (joke, etc.). **cheapen,** *v.* to reduce the value of (sth). **cheaply,** *adv.* not expensively/for a low price. **cheapness,** *n.* low cost.

cheat [tʃiːt] **1.** *n.* person who tricks s.o. so that he loses. **2.** *v.* (*a*) to trick (s.o.) so that he loses. (*b*) to try to win by trickery.

check [tʃek] **1.** *n.* (*a*) making sure; examination/test. (*b*) sudden halt. (*c*) (*in chess*) state where your opponent has to move to protect his king. (*d*) pattern of squares in different colours. (*e*) ticket. (*f*) *Am.* bill (in a restaurant). (*g*) *Am.* = **cheque. 2.** *v.* (*a*) to make sure; to examine. (*b*) to bring (s.o.) to a halt. (*c*) (*in chess*) to put the opponent's king in danger. (*d*) to hold back. (*e*) *Am.* to tick/to mark with a sign to show that sth is correct. **checked,** *adj.* with a squared pattern. **checkers,** *n. Am.* = **draughts. check in,** *v.* (*a*) to register when you arrive at a hotel/at an airport/at work. (*b*) to hand in (luggage) for safe keeping. **checklist,** *n.* list which is used for checking. **checkmate,** (*in chess*) **1.** *n.* position where the king cannot move. **2.** *v.* to put your opponent's king in a position from which he cannot escape. **check out,** *v.* (*a*) to leave a hotel; to take (luggage) out of safe keeping. (*b*) *Am.* to verify/to see if sth is correct. **checkout,** *n.* cash desk in a supermarket. **check over,** *v.* to look over sth to make sure it is all there/all in working order. **checkroom,** *n. Am.* cloakroom. **check up on,** *v.* to verify/to see if sth is correct. **checkup,** *n.* complete medical examination; general examination (of a car).

cheek [tʃiːk] **1.** *n.* (*a*) fat side of the face on either side of the nose and below the eye. (*b*) *inf.* rudeness. (*c*) *Sl.* buttock. **2.** *v. inf.* to be rude to (s.o.). **cheekily,** *adv.* in a cheeky way. **cheekiness,** *n.* being cheeky. **cheeky,** *adj.* (**-ier, -iest**) rude.

cheep [tʃiːp] **1.** *n.* little cry, like that made by a baby bird. **2.** *v.* to make a little cry.

cheer ['tʃɪə] **1.** *n.* (*a*) shout of praise

or encouragement. **cheers!** = (i) (*when drinking*) here's to you; (ii) (*when receiving sth*) thank you. **2.** *v.* (*a*) to shout encouragement. (*b*) to comfort; to make happier; (*c*) **to c. up** = to make or become happier; **c. up!** = don't be miserable. **cheerful,** *adj.* happy. **cheerfully,** *adv.* in a cheerful way. **cheerfulness,** *n.* being cheerful. **cheerily,** *adv.* in a cheery way. **cheering,** *n.* cheers of encouragement. **cheerio,** *inter. inf.* goodbye. **cheerleader,** *n.* person who directs the cheering of a crowd. **cheerless,** *adj.* gloomy/sad. **cheery,** *adj.* happy.

cheese [tʃiːz] *n.* solid food made from milk; **a c.** = a whole round cheese. **cheeseburger,** *n.* hamburger with melted cheese on top. **cheesecake,** *n.* tart of sweet pastry and cream cheese with fruit. **cheesecloth,** *n.* thin cotton cloth such as cheeses are wrapped in (often used for light shirts). **cheesed (off),** *adj. inf.* fed up. **cheeseparing. 1.** *adj.* mean. **2.** *n.* meanness. **cheesy,** *adj. inf.* smelling of cheese.

cheetah ['tʃiːtə] *n.* large animal like a leopard, which can run very fast.

chef [ʃef] *n.* (chief) cook (in a restaurant). **chef d'œuvre,** *n.* masterpiece.

chemical ['kemɪkl] **1.** *adj.* referring to chemistry. **2.** *n.* substance (either natural or man-made) which is formed by reactions between elements. **chemically,** *adj.* by a chemical process. **chemist,** *n.* (*a*) person who specializes in chemistry. (*b*) person who makes or sells medicines. **chemistry,** *n.* science of chemical substances, elements, compounds, and their reactions.

chemotherapy ['kiːməʊˈθerəpɪ] *n.* using chemical drugs to fight disease.

chenille [ʃəˈniːl] *n.* soft cotton cloth, with a tufted surface.

cheque, *Am.* **check** [tʃek] *n.* note to a bank asking them to pay money from one account to another; **c. book** = book of blank cheques; **c. (guarantee) card** = card which guarantees that the bank will pay a cheque; **blank c.** = cheque which has no details filled; **crossed c.** = cheque which has two lines drawn across it and can only be paid into a bank.

chequers ['tʃekəz] *n. pl.* squares in a pattern. **chequered,** *adj.* (*a*) laid out in a pattern of squares; **c. flag** = flag used to show the end of a motor race. (*b*) varied/with good and bad parts.

cherish ['tʃerɪʃ] *v.* to love/to treat kindly; to nourish (a hope).

cheroot [ʃəˈruːt] *n.* long thin cigar with both ends open.

cherry ['tʃerɪ] *n.* small summer fruit, growing on a long stalk; **c. (tree)** = tree which bears cherries.

cherub ['tʃerəb] *n.* small fat child-like angel; child who looks like an angel. **cherubic** [tʃəˈruːbɪk] *adj.* round and innocent (face).

chervil ['tʃɜːvɪl] *n.* herb used to flavour soups.

chess [tʃes] *n.* (*no pl.*) game for two people played on a board with sixteen pieces on each side. **chessboard,** *n.* black and white squared board you play chess on. **chessmen,** *n. pl.* pieces used in chess.

chest [tʃest] *n.* (*a*) piece of furniture, like a large box; **c. of drawers** = piece of furniture with several drawers for keeping clothes in; **c. freezer** = freezer of which the top is a lid. (*b*) top front part of the body, where the heart and lungs are; **to get sth off your c.** = to speak frankly about sth which is worrying you.

chesterfield ['tʃestəfiːld] *n.* sofa with soft back and arms.

chestnut ['tʃesnʌt] *n.* (*a*) bright red-brown nut; large tree which grows these nuts; wood of this tree; **sweet c.** = edible chestnut. (*b*) red-brown colour. (*c*) red-brown horse. (*d*) *inf.* old joke; cliché.

chevron ['ʃevrən] *n.* sign shaped like a V.

chew [tʃuː] *v.* to make (sth) soft with your teeth. **chewing gum,** *n.* sweet gum which you chew but do not swallow. **chewy,** *adj.* which can be chewed for a long time.

chianti [kiˈæntɪ] *n.* Italian red wine.

chic [ʃiːk] *adj.* elegant; **radical c.** = fashionable left-wing opinions or people who hold them.

chicane [ʃɪˈkeɪn] *n.* twisting piece of track on a racecourse for motor cars. **chicanery,** *n.* trickery.

chick [tʃɪk] *n.* baby bird, esp. hen.

chickpea, *n.* type of yellow pea.
chickweed, *n.* common weed with small yellow flowers.
chicken ['tʃɪkɪn] **1.** *n.* young farmyard bird, esp. young hen; meat from a (young) hen. **2.** *v. inf.* **to c. out** = to back out of a fight/argument because you are afraid. **chickenfeed,** *n.* not much money/profit. **chicken-livered,** *adj.* scared/frightened. **chickenpox,** *n.* disease (usu. of children) which gives red itchy spots.
chicory ['tʃɪkərɪ] *n.* vegetable of which the leaves are used for salads, and the roots are dried and ground to mix with coffee to make it bitter.
chide [tʃaɪd] *v.* (**chided/chid; was chided**) (*formal*) to criticize.
chief [tʃiːf] **1.** *adj.* most important; **commander-in-chief** = commander above all other officers. **2.** *n.* leader. **chiefly,** *adv.* mainly. **chieftain** ['tʃiːftən] *n.* leader of a tribe.
chiffchaff ['tʃɪftʃæf] *n.* European warbler.
chiffon ['ʃɪfɒn] *n.* type of very thin material.
chignon ['ʃiːnjɒn] *n.* hair tied together in a knot at the back of the head.
chihuahua [tʃɪ'wɑːwɑː] *n.* breed of very small dog.
chilblain ['tʃɪlbleɪn] *n.* painful swelling on hands, feet, etc., caused by the cold.
child [tʃaɪld] *n.* (*pl.* **children** ['tʃɪldrən]) young boy or girl; **it's child's play** = it's very easy. **childbirth,** *n.* act of giving birth to a child. **childhood,** *n.* state of being a child; time when you are a child. **childish,** *adj.* like a child; silly/foolish. **childishly,** *adv.* in a childish way. **childishness,** *n.* being childish. **childless,** *adj.* with no children. **childlike,** *adj.* innocent like a child.
Chilean ['tʃɪlɪən] **1.** *adj.* referring to Chile. **2.** *n.* person from Chile.
chill [tʃɪl] **1.** *n.* (*a*) coldness in the air. (*b*) illness caused by cold. **2.** *v.* to cool. **chilliness,** *n.* coldness. **chilly,** *adj.* cold; not very welcoming.
chilli, *Am.* **chili** ['tʃɪlɪ] *n.* dried seed pod of the pepper plant, used to make very hot sauces.
chime [tʃaɪm] **1.** *n.* ringing of bells. **2.** *v.*

(*of bells*) to ring. **chime in,** *v. inf.* to enter a conversation.
chimney ['tʃɪmnɪ] *n.* tall tube or brick column for taking smoke away from a fire. **chimney pot,** *n.* round top to a chimney on a house. **chimney stack,** *n.* tall chimney rising above the roof of a factory; group of chimneys on the roof of a house. **chimney sweep,** *n.* person who cleans chimneys.
chimpanzee, *inf.* **chimp** [tʃɪmpæn'ziː, tʃɪmp] *n.* type of intelligent ape from Africa.
chin [tʃɪn] *n.* front part of the bottom jaw.
china ['tʃaɪnə] *n.* (*no pl.*) porcelain; cups, plates, etc. made of fine white clay. **c. clay** = fine white clay, used for making china.
chinchilla [tʃɪn'tʃɪlə] *n.* grey fur from a small American animal.
chine [tʃaɪn] *v.* to cut the rib bones from the backbone of (a joint of meat).
Chinese [tʃaɪ'niːz] **1.** *adj.* referring to China. **C. lantern** = garden plant, whose seed pods form bright red balls. **2.** *n.* (*a*) (*pl.* **Chinese**) person from China. (*b*) language spoken in China.
chink [tʃɪŋk] **1.** *n.* (*a*) little crack. (*b*) noise of chinking. **2.** *v.* to make a noise by knocking glasses/metal objects together.
chintz [tʃɪnts] *n.* thick cotton cloth with bright flower patterns, used for upholstery.
chip [tʃɪp] **1.** *n.* (*a*) little piece of wood/stone, etc.; **to have a c. on your shoulder** = to be permanently indignant about sth where you feel you have been treated unfairly. (*b*) long piece of potato fried in oil. (*c*) *Am.* potato crisp. (*d*) **silicon c.** = small piece of silicon, able to store data, used in computers. **2.** *v.* (**chipped**) to break off a small piece of. **chipboard,** *n.* thick board made of small chips of wood glued together, and used in building. **chip in,** *v.* (*a*) to contribute. (*b*) to interrupt. **chip off,** *v.* to break off. **chipped,** *adj.* **c. potatoes** = long pieces of potato fried in oil. **chippings,** *n. pl.* small bits of stone used to make roads.
chipmunk ['tʃɪpmʌŋk] *n.* small North American animal, like a striped squirrel.

chipolata [tʃɪpə'lɑːtə] *n.* long thin sausage.

chiropodist [kɪ'rɒpədɪst] *n.* person who specializes in chiropody. **chiropody,** *n.* treatment of feet.

chiropractor ['kaɪrəpræktə] *n.* person who heals by massage and manipulation of joints.

chirp [tʃɜːp] **1.** *n.* sharp short call of birds/grasshoppers. **2.** *v.* (*of birds/grasshoppers*) to call. **chirpy,** *adj. inf.* bright and cheerful.

chisel ['tʃɪzl] **1.** *n.* metal tool for cutting small pieces of wood/stone, when hit with a hammer. **2.** *v.* (**chiselled**) (*a*) to cut wood/stone with a chisel. (*b*) *Sl.* to swindle.

chit [tʃɪt] *n.* (*a*) note/small invoice. (*b*) young girl.

chitchat ['tʃɪttʃæt] *n.* gossip/talk.

chitterlings ['tʃɪtəlɪŋz] *n. pl.* fried pig's intestines.

chivalrous ['ʃɪvəlrəs] *adj.* courteous/very polite. **chivalry,** *n.* politeness/courtesy.

chives [tʃaɪvz] *n. pl.* onion-like plant with small green leaves.

chivvy ['tʃɪvɪ] *v. inf.* **to c. s.o. up/along** = to make s.o. hurry.

chlorine ['klɔːriːn] *n.* (*element:* Cl) greenish gas used to disinfect swimming pools, etc. **chloride** ['klɔːraɪd] *n.* compound of chlorine with another substance. **chlorinate** ['klɔːrɪneɪt] *v.* to disinfect with chlorine. **chlorination** [klɒrɪ'neɪʃn] *n.* disinfecting with chlorine.

chlorofluorocarbon [klɒrəʊfluˈɔːrəʊ-ˈkɑːbən] *n.* compound of chlorine and fluorine, used in aerosols, which remains in the upper atmosphere and contributes to the greenhouse effect.

chloroform ['klɒrəfɔːm] **1.** *n.* chemical, whose vapour when breathed makes you unconscious. **2.** *v.* to make unconscious with chloroform.

chlorophyll ['klɒrəfɪl] *n.* substance which makes plants green.

choc [tʃɒk] *n. inf.* chocolate. **choc-ice,** *n.* hard block of ice-cream covered with chocolate.

chock [tʃɒk] *n.* small block of wood which prevents wheels turning. **chock-a-block, chock-full,** *adj.* completely full.

chocolate ['tʃɒklət] *n.* (*a*) food made from cacao tree seeds; **plain c.** = bitter chocolate; **milk c.** = sweet chocolate made with milk; **hot c.** = hot drink made of powdered chocolate. (*b*) small sweet made from chocolate. (*c*) dark brown colour.

choice [tʃɔɪs] *n.* thing which you choose; **I haven't any c.** = I have to do it; **c. peaches** = peaches which have been specially selected.

choir ['kwaɪə] *n.* (*a*) group of people singing together. (*b*) part of the church where the choir sits. **choirboy,** *n.* boy who sings in a church choir. **choirmaster,** *n.* person who conducts and rehearses a choir.

choke [tʃəʊk] **1.** *n.* (*a*) blockage in the throat. (*b*) (*in a car engine*) valve which increases the flow of air to the engine; knob on the dashboard which activates this valve. (*c*) central inedible part of a globe artichoke. **2.** *v.* (*a*) to block (a pipe, etc.). (*b*) to stop breathing because you have swallowed sth. **choke back,** *v.* to hold back (tears). **choker,** *n.* piece of ribbon, etc., worn tightly round the neck. **choking,** *adj.* stifling.

cholera ['kɒlərə] *n.* serious infectious disease causing severe diarrhoea.

cholesterol [kə'lestərɒl] *n.* substance in fats and eggs, also produced by the liver, which deposits fat in the arteries.

chomp [tʃɒmp] *v.* to chew noisily.

chook, chookie [tʃuːk(ɪ)] *n. inf.* (*in Australia*) chicken.

choose [tʃuːz] *v.* (**chose; chosen**) to decide to take (sth)/to do one particular thing. **choosing,** *n.* act of making a choice. **choosy,** *adj.* difficult to please.

chop [tʃɒp] **1.** *n.* (*a*) piece of meat with a rib bone. (*b*) *inf.* dismissal. (*c*) jaw, esp. in animals. **2.** *v.* (**chopped**) (*a*) to cut into small pieces with an axe/a knife. (*b*) **to c. and change** = to do first one thing, then another. **chop down,** *v.* to cut down (a tree) with an axe. **chop off,** *v.* to cut off. **chopper,** *n.* (*a*) axe for cutting meat. (*b*) *inf.* helicopter. **choppy,** *adj.* quite rough (sea). **chop suey,** *n.* Chinese dish of fried meat and bean sprouts. **chop up,** *v.* to cut up into little bits.

chopsticks ['tʃɒpstɪks] *n. pl.* long sticks used by oriental people for eating food.

choral ['kɔːrəl] *adj.* referring to a choir.

chorale [kɒ'rɑːl] *n.* piece of music for a choir, based on a hymn.

chord [kɔːd] *n.* (*a*) several notes played together in harmony. (*b*) line which joins two points on the circumference of a circle.

chore [tʃɔː] *n.* piece of routine work, esp. housework.

choreography [kɒrɪ'ɒgrəfɪ] *n.* art of working out the steps for a ballet. **choreographer,** *n.* person who works out the steps for a ballet.

chorister ['kɒrɪstə] *n.* person who sings in a choir.

chortle ['tʃɔːtl] *v.* to chuckle loudly.

chorus ['kɔːrəs] **1.** *n.* (*a*) group of people who sing or dance together. (*b*) part of a song which is repeated by everyone together. **2.** *v.* to say sth all together. **chorus-girl,** *n.* girl who appears as a member of a chorus in a variety show.

chose [tʃəʊz], **chosen** ['tʃəʊzən] *v. see* **choose.**

chough [tʃʌf] *n.* large black bird with a red bill.

chow [tʃaʊ] *n.* (*a*) type of Chinese dog with thick fur. (*b*) *inf.* food.

chowder ['tʃaʊdə] *n. Am.* fish soup.

christen ['krɪsn] *v.* (*a*) to give a name to (a baby) in church; to give a name to (a ship/a bell, etc.) at a ceremony. (*b*) to use (sth) for the first time. **christening,** *n.* ceremony in church where a baby is given a name.

Christian ['krɪstʃən] **1.** *n.* person who believes in Christianity. **2.** *adj.* referring to Christianity; **C. name** = first name given at a ceremony in church. **Christianity** [krɪstɪ'ænɪtɪ] *n.* religion based on the doctrine preached by Jesus Christ and followed by Christians ever since.

Christmas ['krɪsməs] *n.* Christian festival on December 25th; **C. Day** = December 25th; **Father C.** = man dressed in red robes with a long white beard who is believed to bring gifts to children on Christmas Day. **Christmassy,** *adj.* like Christmas.

chromatic [krə'mætɪk] *adj.* referring to colours or to a musical scale.

chrome [krəʊm] *n.* chromium; **c. yellow** = bright yellow. **chromium** ['krəʊmɪəm] *n.* (*element:* Cr) hard shiny metal which does not rust.

chromosome ['krəʊməsəʊm] *n.* one of several elements which form a biological cell, and which carries the genes.

chronic ['krɒnɪk] *adj.* continual/repeating (illness, etc.); *inf.* very bad. **chronically,** *adv.* very badly.

chronicle ['krɒnɪkl] **1.** *n.* record of things which take place; news story. **2.** *v.* to write the history of (events) in the order in which they took place. **chronicler,** *n.* person who writes a chronicle.

chronology [krə'nɒlədʒɪ] *n.* statement of the order in which things happened. **chronological** [krɒnə'lɒdʒɪkl] *adj.* in order of when the events happened. **chronologically,** *adv.* in chronological order.

chronometer [krə'nɒmɪtə] *n.* very accurate watch (as used for timing races).

chrysalis ['krɪsəlɪs] *n.* (*pl.* **-es**) hardcased stage through which a caterpillar passes before turning into a butterfly or moth.

chrysanthemum [krɪ'sænθəməm] *n.* bright-coloured autumn flower.

chub [tʃʌb] *n.* (*pl.* **chub**) fat river fish.

chubby ['tʃʌbɪ] *adj.* (**-ier, -est**) quite plump.

chuck [tʃʌk] **1.** *n.* (*a*) part of a drill which holds the bit. (*b*) type of beef steak. **2.** *v. inf.* to throw. **chucker-out,** *n. inf.* person whose job is to throw undesirable people out of night-clubs.

chuckle ['tʃʌkl] **1.** *n.* quiet laugh. **2.** *v.* to give a quiet laugh.

chuffed [tʃʌft] *adj. Sl.* (*a*) happy/pleased. (*b*) unhappy/annoyed.

chug [tʃʌg] *v.* (**chugged**) to make a regular puffing noise like a steam engine.

chukka ['tʃʌkə] *n.* period of play in a polo match.

chum [tʃʌm] *n. inf.* friend. **chummy,** *adj.* friendly.

chump [tʃʌmp] *n.* (*a*) silly fool. (*b*) **c. chop** = large lamb chop.

chunk [tʃʌŋk] *n.* large thick piece. **chunky,** *adj.* made of large pieces.

church [tʃɜːtʃ] *n.* (*pl.* **-es**) (*a*) large building for Christian religious ceremonies. (*b*) group of Christians together. **churchgoer,** *n.* person who goes to church (regularly). **churchwarden,** *n.* senior member of a parish. **churchyard,** *n.* cemetery round a church.

churlish ['tʃɜːlɪʃ] *adj.* rude. **churlishly,** *adv.* rudely. **churlishness,** *n.* rudeness.

churn [tʃɜːn] **1.** *n.* large metal container for milk; container in which cream is churned. **2.** *v.* to turn cream to make butter. **churn out,** *v. inf.* to produce in a series. **churn up,** *v.* to mix/stir up.

chute [ʃuːt] *n.* (a) slide into water (in a swimming pool). (b) slide for sending things to a lower level.

chutney ['tʃʌtnɪ] *n.* highly-flavoured sauce usu. made with tomatoes, onions, vinegar and spices.

CIA [siːaɪˈeɪ] *abbreviation for* Central Intelligence Agency.

CID [siːaɪˈdiː] *abbreviation for* Criminal Investigation Department.

cider ['saɪdə] *n.* alcoholic drink made from fermented apple juice.

c.i.f. [siːaɪˈef] *abbrev for* cost, insurance, freight.

cigar [sɪˈgɑː] *n.* tight roll of tobacco leaves which you can light and smoke.

cigarette [sɪgəˈret] *n.* chopped tobacco rolled in very thin paper which you can light and smoke. **cigarette case,** *n.* special case for holding cigarettes. **cigarette end,** *n.* end of a cigarette which has been smoked. **cigarette holder,** *n.* holder for putting cigarettes in to smoke.

cinch [sɪntʃ] *n. inf.* (a) thing which is very easy to do. (b) sth. which is certain to work.

cinders ['sɪndəz] *n. pl.* lumps of coarse ash left after coal has been burnt. **cinder track,** *n.* race track covered with cinders.

cine- [sɪnɪ] *prefix* referring to moving pictures; **cine-film. cine-camera** ['sɪnɪkæmərə] *n.* camera for taking moving pictures. **cinema** ['sɪnəmə] *n.* (a) theatre for showing films. (b) art of making moving pictures. **cinematographic** [sɪnəmætəˈgræfɪk] *adj.* referring to the cinema.

cineraria [sɪnəˈreərɪə] *n.* houseplant with blue, pink, or purple flowers.

cinnamon ['sɪnəmən] *n.* spice made from the bark of a tropical tree.

cipher ['saɪfə] *n.* (a) code/secret message. (b) monogram/initials of a name linked together artistically. (c) zero; person of no importance.

circa ['sɜːkə] *prep.* (used of dates) about.

circle ['sɜːkl] **1.** *n.* (a) line forming a round shape. (b) row of seats above the stalls in a theatre. (c) group of people/ society. **2.** *v.* (a) to go round in a ring. (b) to draw a circle round (sth).

circuit ['sɜːkɪt] *n.* (a) trip around sth. (b) area visited by a judge who travels from court to court. (c) path of electricity; **printed c. board** = flat card with metal tracks printed on it to form an electric circuit; **short c.** = fault (caused by crossed wires, etc.) when electricity follows a shorter path than usual; **closed c. television** = private television operating over a short area by cable. **circuitous** [sɜːˈkjuːɪtəs] *adj.* roundabout (way).

circular ['sɜːkjʊlə] *adj. & n.* (sth) round in shape; publicity leaflet given out to many people. **circularize,** *v.* to send circulars to (people).

circulate ['sɜːkjʊleɪt] *v.* (a) to distribute/ to pass round. (b) to move round. **circulation** [sɜːkjʊˈleɪʃn] *n.* (a) act of circulating; **banknotes in c.** = notes which are in use. (b) movement of blood round the body. (c) number of copies of a newspaper, etc., which are sold. **circulatory,** *adj.* referring to circulation of the blood.

circumcise ['sɜːkəmsaɪz] *v.* to remove the foreskin of (a male person). **circumcision** [sɜːkəmˈsɪʒn] *n.* act of removing the foreskin.

circumference [səˈkʌmfərəns] *n.* (distance round) the edge of a circle.

circumlocution [sɜːkəmləˈkjuːʃn] *n.* roundabout way of saying sth.

circumnavigate [sɜːkəmˈnævɪgeɪt] *v.* (*formal*) to sail round (the world). **circumnavigation** [sɜːkəmnævɪˈgeɪʃn] *n.* sailing round the world.

circumscribe [sɜːkəmˈskraɪb] *v.* (*formal*) to draw a line round sth; to set limits to sth. **circumscription** [sɜːkəmˈskrɪpʃən] *n.* limiting; a limited area.

circumspect ['sɜːkəmspekt] *adj.* very careful.

circumstances ['sɜːkəmstənsɪz] *n. pl.*

(*a*) way in which something took place; **in the c.** = as things have turned out like this/as it happens. (*b*) state of one's finances. **circumstantial** [sɜːkəmˈstænʃl] *adj.* giving details; **c. evidence** = evidence which suggests sth but does not offer firm proof. **circumstantiate**, *v.* to give details to prove (sth).

circumvent [sɜːkəmˈvent] *v.* to avoid. **circumvention**, *n.* avoidance.

circus [ˈsɜːkəs] *n.* (*pl.* **-es**) (*a*) travelling show, often given under a large tent, with animals, clowns, etc. (*b*) busy roundabout in the centre of a large town.

cirrhosis [sɪˈrəʊsɪs] *n.* disease of the liver caused esp. by alcohol.

cirrus [ˈsɪrəs] *n.* small very high fleecy cloud.

cissy [ˈsɪsɪ] *n. inf.* man/boy who acts like a girl.

cistern [ˈsɪstən] *n.* water tank.

citadel [ˈsɪtədəl] *n.* fort guarding a town.

cite [saɪt] *v.* (*a*) to quote (a reference, a person) as proof. (*b*) to call (s.o.) to appear in court. **citation** [saɪˈteɪʃn] *n.* (*a*) official document recognizing an act of bravery. (*b*) quotation of sth as a reference or proof. (*c*) summons to appear in court.

citizen [ˈsɪtɪzn] *n.* (*a*) inhabitant of a town. (*b*) person with full rights as an inhabitant of a country; **citizen's arrest** = arrest of a suspected criminal by an ordinary citizen; **citizens' band** = private radio, mainly used by drivers of road vehicles. **citizenship**, *n.* state of being a citizen.

citric [ˈsɪtrɪk] *adj.* **c. acid** = acid found in citrus fruit. **citrus** [ˈsɪtrəs] *n.* **c. fruit** = fruit such as oranges, lemons or grapefruit.

city [ˈsɪtɪ] *n.* (*a*) very large town. (*b*) town created by charter, often with a cathedral; **the C.** = the old centre of London, now the main financial district.

civet [ˈsɪvɪt] *n.* wild cat, which provides a substance used in making perfume.

civic [ˈsɪvɪk] *adj.* referring to a city; **c. centre** = social/sports centre run by a city; **c. authorities** = leaders of a city. **civics**, *n.* study of municipal affairs.

civil [ˈsɪvl] *adj.* (*a*) belonging to the general public, not to the army; **c. service** = the government bureaucracy; **c. servant** = person who works in a government department. (*b*) referring to the ordinary citizen; **c. rights** = the rights of a citizen; **c. rights movement** = campaign to ensure that all citizens have equal rights; **c. war** = war between groups in the same country; **c. defence** = defence by ordinary citizens, not the army; **c. law** = law referring to the citizen, not to criminals; **c. action** = court action brought by one citizen against another; **c. engineer** = person who designs roads, bridges, etc. (*c*) polite. **civilian** [sɪˈvɪljən] *adj. & n.* (person) not belonging to the armed forces; private citizen. **civility**, *n.* politeness. **civilly**, *adv.* politely.

civilize [ˈsɪvɪlaɪz] *v.* (*a*) to educate (primitive people) to a higher level of society. (*b*) to make (s.o.) less rude/uncouth. **civilization** [sɪvɪlaɪˈzeɪʃn] *n.* regular civilized way of conducting society; making s.o. civilized.

civvy [ˈsɪvɪ] *adj. inf.* civilian. **civvies**, *n. pl. inf.* civilian clothes.

Cl *symbol for* chlorine.

clad [klæd] *adj.* covered. **cladding**, *n.* material used for the outside covering of walls.

claim [kleɪm] **1.** *n.* (*a*) demand. (*b*) statement/assertion. **2.** *v.* (*a*) to demand as one's right. (*b*) to state/to assert (without any proof). (*c*) to say you own (sth) which has been left/lost. **claimant**, *n.* person who claims a right.

clairvoyant [kleəˈvɔɪənt] *n.* person who can see in his mind things which are happening elsewhere/who can foretell the future. **clairvoyance**, *n.* act of communicating with spirits/of foretelling the future.

clam [klæm] *n.* large shellfish with a hinged shell.

clamber [ˈklæmbə] *v.* to climb with difficulty.

clammy [ˈklæmɪ] *adj.* (**-ier**, **-iest**) damp and cold; humid (weather). **clamminess**, *n.* being clammy.

clamour, *Am.* **clamor** [ˈklæmə] **1.** *n.* shouting. **2.** *v.* to shout/to demand loudly. **clamorous**, *adj.* noisy/shouting.

clamp [klæmp] **1.** *n.* (*a*) metal pieces which are screwed tightly to hold sth together. (*b*) pile of vegetables covered with earth for storage. **2.** *v.* (*a*) to hold tight with a clamp. (*b*) **to c. down on** = to stop (petty crime, etc.). **clampdown,** *n.* (**on**) severe action to stop sth.

clan [klæn] *n.* Scottish family tribe. **clannish,** *adj.* loyal to the clan; supporting your own group. **clannishness,** *n.* being clannish. **clansman,** *n.* (*pl.* -**men**) member of a clan.

clandestine [klæn'destɪn] *adj.* secret/undercover.

clang [klæŋ] **1.** *n.* loud noise of metal ringing. **2.** *v.* to make a loud ringing noise. **clanger,** *n. inf.* very bad mistake.

clank [klæŋk] **1.** *n.* noise of metal hitting metal. **2.** *v.* to make a noise of metal hitting other metal.

clap [klæp] **1.** *n.* (*a*) beating of hands against each other to show pleasure. (*b*) friendly tap (with the hand). (*c*) loud noise (of thunder). (*d*) *Sl.* gonorrhoea. **2.** *v.* (**clapped**) (*a*) to beat your hands together to show you are pleased. (*b*) to give (s.o.) a friendly tap with the hand. (*c*) to put (s.o. in jail) suddenly. **clapped out,** *adj. Sl.* worn out/broken-down (car, etc.). **clapper,** *n.* swinging metal piece inside a bell which strikes the bell; *inf.* **like the clappers** = very fast. **clapperboard,** *n.* black board with a striped hinged section at the top, used in film-making to indicate the start of a scene. **clapping,** *n.* applause.

claptrap ['klæptræp] *n. inf.* rubbish.

claret ['klærət] *n.* red Bordeaux wine.

clarify ['klærɪfaɪ] *v.* (*a*) to make clear. (*b*) to heat (butter, etc.) until it becomes transparent. **clarification** [klærɪfɪ'keɪʃn] *n.* making clear/explanation.

clarinet [klærɪ'net] *n.* wind instrument in the woodwind group. **clarinettist,** *n.* person who plays a clarinet.

clarion ['klærɪən] *n.* trumpet; **c. call** = loud clear call.

clarity ['klærɪtɪ] *n.* clearness.

clash [klæʃ] **1.** *n.* (*pl.* -**es**) (*a*) loud noise of things hitting each other. (*b*) battle/conflict; shock of two colours seen side by side. **2.** *v.* (*a*) to bang together mak-ing a loud noise. (*b*) not to agree/to be in conflict. (*c*) to fight.

clasp [klɑːsp] **1.** *n.* (*a*) device for holding sth shut. (*b*) brooch. (*c*) act of holding in your hand. **2.** *v.* to hold (sth) tight. **claspknife,** *n.* (*pl.* -**knives**) pocket knife which folds.

class [klɑːs] **1.** *n.* (*pl.* -**es**) (*a*) group of people with the same position in society; **middle c.** = class of professional people/bourgeoisie; **working c.** = class of people who do mainly manual labour; **upper c.** = the rich/the aristocracy. (*b*) group of people (*usu.* children) who study together. (*c*) category/group into which things are classified; **first c.** = very good; **to travel first c.** = in the most expensive seats; **tourist c./economy c.** = less expensive seats on aircraft and ships. **2.** *v.* to put (sth) in a category. **classifiable,** *adj.* which can be classified. **2.** *v.* to put (sth) in a category. **classification** [klæsɪfɪ'keɪʃn] *n.* way of ordering things into categories. **classify** ['klæsɪfaɪ] *v.* to arrange things into groups; **classified information** = information which is officially secret. **classless,** *adj.* with no division into social classes. **classroom,** *n.* room in which a class is taught. **classy,** *adj.* (-**ier,** -**iest**) *inf.* chic/expensive-looking.

classic ['klæsɪk] **1.** *n.* (*a*) great book/play/piece of music/writer/composer, etc. (*b*) **the classics** = Ancient Greek and Roman literature, culture, etc. **2.** *adj.* (*a*) (style) which is elegant and based on that of Greek or Roman architecture/literature, etc. (*b*) typical. **classical,** *adj.* (*a*) referring to the classics. (*b*) serious (music). **classicist,** *n.* person who studies the classics.

clatter ['klætə] **1.** *n.* noise of things hitting together. **2.** *v.* to make a noise.

clause [klɔːz] *n.* (*a*) paragraph in a treaty or legal document. (*b*) part of a sentence; **main c.** = the central part of a sentence; **subordinate clauses** = clauses which depend on the main clause.

claustrophobia [klɒstrə'fəʊbɪə] *n.* terror of being shut inside a closed place. **claustrophobic,** *adj.* referring to claustrophobia.

clavichord ['klævɪkɔːd] *n.* old musical

instrument like a small piano, with a very quiet sound.

clavicle ['klævɪkl] n. collarbone.

claw [klɔ:] **1.** n. (a) nail (of animal/ bird). (b) pincer/part of a crab or lobster which pinches. **2.** v. to scratch with a claw. **claw back,** v. to take back money which has been allocated. **claw hammer,** n. hammer with the back of the head curved and split for removing nails.

clay [kleɪ] n. stiff soil found in river valleys; stiff earth used for making bricks or china. **clayey,** adj. containing clay. **claymore,** n. sword used in Scotland.

clean [kli:n] **1.** adj. (-er, -est) not dirty; **c. break** = complete break; **to come c.** = to confess (to a crime, etc.). **2.** adv. completely. **3.** v. to remove dirt. **cleaner,** n. person/thing which removes dirt; **vacuum c.** = machine for sucking up dirt; **(dry) cleaner's** = shop where clothes can be taken to be cleaned; **oven c.** = strong substance for cleaning dirty ovens. **cleaning,** n. removing dirt. **cleanliness, cleanness** ['klenlɪnəs, 'kli:nnəs] n. state of being clean. **cleanly,** adv. in a clean way. **cleanshaven,** adj. with no beard or moustache.

cleanse [klenz] v. to make very clean; **cleansing cream** = cream for cleansing the skin. **cleanser,** n. material which removes dirt.

clear ['klɪə] **1.** adj. (-er, -est) (a) pure; transparent. (b) with nothing in the way. (c) easily understood. (d) complete. (e) free (of). **2.** adv. in a clear way. **3.** v. (a) to remove (obstacles); **to c. the table** = to remove dirty china and cutlery; **to c. one's throat** = to cough slightly to get ready for speaking. (b) to make clear/pure; to become clear/ pure. (c) to show that s.o. is innocent. (d) not to hit. **clearance,** n. (a) act of removing obstacles; act of removing plants from land; **c. sale** = sale where all the goods are reduced in price to clear them from the shelves. (b) space for sth to pass through. **clear away,** v. to remove (sth) which is in the way; to remove (dirty dishes) from a table. **clear-cut,** adj. definite/distinct.

clear-headed, adj. clever/with a sharp understanding. **clearing,** n. (a) act of removing obstacles. (b) area in a wood where the trees have been cut down. (c) **c. bank** = bank which issues cheques. **clearly,** adv. (a) in a way which is easily understood or heard. (b) obviously. **clearness,** n. being clear. **clear off,** v. (a) to pay off (one's debts). (b) to run away. **clear out,** v. (a) to throw out rubbish from (a room). (b) to go away. **clear up,** v. (a) to make clear/pure. (b) to become brighter. **clearway,** n. road where no parking is allowed.

cleat [kli:t] n. wooden/metal device for attaching ropes on ships.

cleave [kli:v] v. (clove/cleft; has cloven/ cleft) (old) (a) to split. (b) to cling (to). **cleavage** ['kli:vɪdʒ] n. space between the breasts. **cleaver** ['kli:və] n. large axe used by butchers.

clef [klef] n. sign at the beginning of a piece of music which shows whether it is bass or treble.

cleft [kleft] adj. & n. split; **c. palate** = split roof of the mouth; **in a c. stick** = in an awkward situation.

clematis [klə'meɪtɪs] n. climbing garden plant with large purple or pink flowers.

clement ['klemənt] adj. (formal) kind/ soft (weather). **clemency,** n. mercy (to a criminal).

clementine ['klemənti:n] n. small sweet orange with a skin which is easily removed.

clench [klentʃ] v. to close tightly.

clerestory ['klɪəstɔ:rɪ] n. high row of windows in a medieval church.

clergy ['klɜ:dʒɪ] n. priests. **clergyman,** n. (pl. -men) priest or minister, esp. of the Anglican Church.

cleric ['klerɪk] n. (formal) priest/clergyman. **clerical** ['klerɪkl] adj. (a) referring to a clerk. (b) referring to clergy; **c. dress** = black suit and stiff white collar fastening at the back.

clerihew ['klerɪhju:] n. short four-lined humorous poem.

clerk [klɑ:k, Am. klɜ:k] n. (a) person who works in an office; **town c.** = person who administers a town. (b) Am. salesman in a shop.

clever ['klevə] adj. intelligent/able to learn quickly; **c. with one's hands** =

good at making things. **cleverly,** *adv.* in a clever way. **cleverness,** *n.* being clever.

cliché ['kli:ʃeɪ] *n.* saying/phrase which is frequently used.

click [klɪk] **1.** *n.* short sharp sound. **2.** *v.* (*a*) to make a short sharp sound; **to c. one's heels** = to bring the heels of one's boots together to make a noise. (*b*) to be surprisingly successful; **it suddenly clicked** = it was suddenly understood.

client ['klaɪənt] *n.* person with whom you do business/to whom you give a service. **clientele** [kli:ɒn'tel] *n.* all the customers (of a shop).

cliff [klɪf] *n.* high rock face, usu. by the sea. **cliffhanger,** *n.* suspense story; situation where one does not know what will happen.

climacteric [klaɪ'mæktərɪk] *n.* critical point in life, when changes take place in your body.

climate ['klaɪmət] *n.* general weather conditions. **climatic** [klaɪ'mætɪk] *adj.* referring to climate. **climatology** [klaɪmə'tɒlədʒɪ] *n.* study of climate.

climax ['klaɪmæks] *n.* (*pl.* **-es**) peak/greatest amount/highest point. **climactic** [klaɪ'mæktɪk] *adj.* referring to a climax.

climb [klaɪm] **1.** *n.* act of going up; place where you go up. **2.** *v.* to go up. **climb down,** *v.* (*a*) to come down a mountain/a ladder. (*b*) to give in/not to do what you had previously insisted on doing. **climber,** *n.* person who climbs; plant which climbs. **climbing,** *n.* sport of climbing mountains.

clime [klaɪm] *n.* (*formal*) country.

clinch [klɪntʃ] **1.** *n.* (*pl.* **-es**) (*a*) (*in boxing*) a position where both boxers hold on to each other. (*b*) *inf.* close embrace. **2.** *v.* (*a*) (*in boxing*) to hold tight to the other boxer. (*b*) to settle (a deal).

cling [klɪŋ] *v.* (**clung**) to hold tight **to** (sth).

clinic ['klɪnɪk] *n.* specialized medical office or hospital. **clinical,** *adj.* medical; **c. thermometer** = thermometer for taking a person's temperature; **to take a c. view of something** = to look at it coolly. **clinically,** *adv.* in a clinical way. **clinician,** *n.* doctor who treats patients in hospital, but not a surgeon.

clink [klɪŋk] **1.** *n.* (*a*) noise of glasses/metal objects hitting each other. (*b*) *Sl.* prison. **2.** *v.* (*of glasses/metal objects*) to make a noise (when hitting together).

clinker ['klɪŋkə] *n.* (*a*) hard waste material after coal has been burnt. (*b*) (*of boat*) made with planks which overlap.

clip [klɪp] **1.** *n.* (*a*) piece of bent wire for attaching papers, etc., together. (*b*) *inf.* smack. (*c*) *inf.* **at a good c.** = quite fast. **2.** *v.* (**clipped**) (*a*) to attach (papers) together. (*b*) to cut with scissors or shears; to punch holes in (tickets) to show they have been used. **clipper,** *n.* (*old*) fast sailing vessel, used mainly for carrying tea. **clippers,** *n. pl.* small scissors; instrument with a movable blade for cutting hair. **clipping,** *n.* small piece cut out of a newspaper, cut off a hedge, etc.

clique [kli:k] *n.* small select group of people. **cliquey, cliquish,** *adj.* like a clique.

clitoris ['klɪtərɪs] *n.* small erectile part (in female genitals).

cloak [kləʊk] **1.** *n.* long outer coat with no sleeves. **2.** *v.* to cover/to hide as if with a cloak. **cloakroom,** *n.* (*a*) place where you leave your coat in a restaurant/theatre, etc. (*b*) toilet.

clobber ['klɒbə] **1.** *n.* (*no pl.*) *inf.* belongings. **2.** *v. inf.* to ask for money/to tax.

cloche [klɒʃ] *n.* small glass or polythene tent used in gardening for covering young plants.

clock [klɒk] **1.** *n.* machine for telling the time; **alarm c.** = clock which rings a bell to wake you up; **to work right round the c.** = to work all day long. **2.** *v.* **to c. in/out, on/off** = to record your time of arrival or departure at work. **clock golf,** *n.* game like golf where you hit the ball into a central hole from points round a circle. **clockwise,** *adv.* in the same direction as the hands of a clock. **clockwork,** *n.* (*no pl.*) machine which works on a spring which is wound up with a key; **like c.** = smoothly.

clod [klɒd] *n.* large lump of earth.

clog [klɒg] **1.** *n.* wooden shoe. **2.** *v.* (**clogged**) to block.

cloisonné ['klwæzɒneɪ] *n.* type of enamel decoration, where the sections of enamel are separated by little ridges of metal.

cloister ['klɔɪstə] n. (in a monastery) covered walk round a courtyard. **cloistered**, adj. shut up (as in a monastery).

clone [kləʊn] n. plant/animal which is grown from a piece of another plant/animal, and not from a seed.

close[1] [kləʊs] 1. adj. (-er, -est) (a) very near (to); **to keep a c. watch on someone** = to watch someone attentively; **c. election** = election where the winner is separated from the loser by only a small number of votes. (b) shut; **c. season** = season when hunting is forbidden. (c) stuffy. (d) very friendly. 2. adv. near; **she is c. on forty.** 3. n. gardens and houses round a cathedral; small road with houses. **close-fisted**, adj. miserly. **close-fitting**, adj. tight (dress). **closely**, adv. (a) attentively. (b) tightly. **closeness**, n. (a) nearness. (b) stuffiness. **close-up**, n. photograph taken at very close range.

close[2] [kləʊz] 1. n. end. 2. v. (a) to shut. (b) to end (an argument/a debate). (c) to fight (with s.o.). **closed**, adj. shut; **c. shop** = system whereby a firm can only employ members of a certain trade union. **close down**, v. to shut a shop, etc., (permanently); to stop transmitting radio/TV programmes. **close in**, v. (a) **the days are closing in** = the period of daylight is becoming shorter. (b) **to close in on s.o.** = to run s.o. to earth/to come close to s.o. one is chasing. **closing**, 1. adj. final; **c. bid** = last bid at an auction. 2. n. shutting (of a shop, etc.); **early c. day** = day when a shop is shut in the afternoon; **c. time** = time when a pub, etc., closes. **closure** ['kləʊʒə] n. shutting.

closet ['klɒzɪt] 1. n. (a) small room/private office. (b) Am. cupboard. 2. v. to shut oneself up with s.o.

clot [klɒt] 1. n. (a) lump of solidified blood, etc. (b) inf. fool. 2. v. (clotted) to form lumps; **clotted cream** = cream which has been heated until it solidifies.

cloth [klɒθ] n. (a) piece of woven material. (b) woven material.

clothe [kləʊð] v. to dress. **clothes** [kləʊðz] n. pl. things you wear; **c. brush** = brush for cleaning clothes; **c. line** = long rope for hanging wet clothes to dry; **c. horse** = wooden or metal frame for hanging wet clothes to dry; **c. peg**, Am. & in Scotland **c. pin** = small plastic or wooden clip for attaching wet clothes to a clothes line; **c. rail** = rail where several dresses/coats can be hung. **clothing** ['kləʊðɪŋ] n. (no pl.) clothes.

cloud [klaʊd] 1. n. mass of vapour/smoke (in the air); **under a c.** = (a) gloomy; (b) unpopular with the authorities. 2. v. to hide with a cloud. **cloudburst**, n. sudden downpour of rain. **cloudcapped**, adj. (mountain) topped with clouds. **cloudiness**, n. being cloudy. **cloudless**, adj. (sky) with no clouds. **cloudy**, adj. (-ier, -iest) covered with clouds; not clear/not transparent.

clout [klaʊt] 1. n. (a) blow (with the fist). (b) inf. power/influence. 2. v. to give (s.o.) a blow with the fist.

clove [kləʊv] n. (a) spice formed by small dried flower buds of a tropical tree. (b) piece of garlic. **clove hitch**, n. type of knot.

cloven ['kləʊvn] adj. split.

clover ['kləʊvə] n. common weed, used as fodder for cattle; **to be in c.** = to live very comfortably; **c. leaf intersection** = crossroads formed by two motorways and their linking roads, which when seen from above looks like the leaf of clover.

clown [klaʊn] 1. n. (a) man who makes people laugh in a circus. (b) stupid fool. 2. v. (about, around) to play the fool.

cloy [klɔɪ] v. to be sickly sweet.

club [klʌb] 1. n. (a) large stick; **golf c.** = long stick with which you hit the ball when playing golf. (b) one of the four suits in a pack of cards. (c) group of people who allow others to join them (usu. on payment of a fee); **golf c.**; **drama c.** 2. v. (clubbed) (a) to hit with a club. (b) to put all your money **together**. **clubfoot**, n. deformed foot. **clubhouse**, n. house where members of a club meet.

cluck [klʌk] v. (of hen) to make a low noise in the throat.

clue [kluː] n. information which helps you solve a mystery/puzzle; **I haven't a c.** = I do not know at all. **clued up**, adj. inf. expert/knowing a great deal. **clueless**, adj. inf. stupid.

clump [klʌmp] **1.** *n.* group of shrubs, trees, etc. **2.** *v.* to move making a dull noise.

clumsy ['klʌmzɪ] *adj.* (**-ier, -iest**) not graceful; frequently breaking things. **clumsily,** *adv.* in a clumsy way. **clumsiness,** *n.* being clumsy.

clung [klʌŋ] *v. see* **cling.**

clunk [klʌŋk] *n.* noise of heavy metal objects hitting each other.

cluster ['klʌstə] **1.** *n.* group of small objects together. **2.** *v.* to group (**together**).

clutch [klʌtʃ] **1.** *n.* (*pl.* **-es**) (*a*) several eggs laid together in a nest. (*b*) clasp; **into his clutches** = into his hands. (*c*) mechanism for changing the gears in a car; **c. pedal** = pedal which works the clutch; **to let in the c.** = to make the gears connect; **to let out the c.** = to disengage the engine from the gears. **2.** *v.* to grab.

clutter ['klʌtə] **1.** *n.* mass of things left lying about. **2.** *v.* to fill (a room) with a mass of things.

cm *abbrev. for* centimetre.

co- [kəʊ] *prefix meaning* together.

co. [kəʊ, 'kʌmpənɪ] *abbrev. for* company.

Co *symbol for* cobalt.

CO ['siː'əʊ] commanding officer.

c/o *abbrev. for* care of.

coach [kəʊtʃ] **1.** *n.* (*pl.* **-es**) (*a*) large bus for long distance travelling. (*b*) passenger wagon (on a train). (*c*) person who trains sportsmen, etc. **2.** *v.* (*a*) to train (sportsmen). (*b*) to give private lessons to.

coagulate [kəʊ'ægjʊleɪt] *v.* to form into lumps/to cake. **coagulation** [kəʊægjʊ'leɪʃn] *n.* forming into lumps/caking.

coal [kəʊl] *n.* black mineral used as fuel; **coal-fired boiler** = boiler which is heated by coal. **coalfield,** *n.* area of coal underground. **coalhole,** *n.* space in a cellar for storing coal; hole in the ground, through which coal can be delivered into a cellar. **coalmine,** *n.* mine where coal is dug. **coalminer,** *n.* person who mines coal. **coal scuttle,** *n.* box for keeping coal near a fireplace.

coalesce [kəʊə'les] *v.* to join together. **coalescence,** *n.* joining together.

coalition [kəʊə'lɪʃn] *n.* joining together; combination of political parties forming a government.

coarse [kɔːs] *adj.* (**-er, -est**) (*a*) not fine/rough (laugh, etc.). (*b*) rude. (*c*) **c. fishing** = fishing in a river or lake. **coarsely,** *adv.* in a coarse way. **coarsen,** *v.* to make coarse. **coarseness,** *n.* being coarse.

coast [kəʊst] **1.** *n.* land by the sea; **from c. to c.** = across an area of land from one sea to another. **2.** *v.* (*a*) to ride a vehicle without using the engine or the pedals. (*b*) to sail along the coast. **coastal,** *adj.* referring to the coast. **coaster,** *n.* (*a*) ship which sails from port to port along the coast. (*b*) flat dish or small mat for standing a bottle/glass on. **coastguard,** *n.* person who guards a piece of coast (watching out for wrecks/smugglers, etc.). **coastline,** *n.* line of the coast.

coat [kəʊt] **1.** *n.* (*a*) long piece of outdoor clothing which covers the top part of the body. (*b*) fur of an animal. (*c*) layer (of paint, etc.). (*d*) **c. of arms** = symbolic design on the shield of a family/town, etc. **2.** *v.* to cover (sth) with a layer. **coat-hanger,** *n.* piece of wood/wire/plastic on which you hang clothes. **coat-hook,** *n.* hook (on a wall/door) for hanging a coat. **coating,** *n.* covering (of paint, etc.). **coatrack,** *n.* rail where several coats can be hung.

coax [kəʊks] *v.* to persuade (s.o.) to do sth.

coaxial [kəʊ'æksɪəl] *adj.* **c. cable** = electric cable where several wires are laid parallel to each other.

cob [kɒb] *n.* (*a*) seed head (of corn/maize, etc.); **c. nut** = hazel nut. (*b*) male swan. (*c*) short horse. (*d*) round loaf.

cobalt ['kəʊbɔːlt] *n.* (*element:* Co) white metal; blue colour obtained from the metal.

cobber ['kɒbə] *n.* (*in Australia*) *inf.* friend.

cobble ['kɒbl] *v.* to put things **together** roughly. **cobbled,** *adj.* covered with cobblestones. **cobble(stone),** *n.* rounded stone formerly used for paving streets.

cobbler ['kɒblə] *n.* person who mends shoes.

cobra ['kɒbrə] *n.* large poisonous tropical snake.

cobweb ['kɒbweb] *n.* net of fine thread made by a spider.

cocaine [kə'keɪn] *n.* painkilling drug, also used as a stimulant.

coccus ['kɒkəs] *n.* (*pl.* **cocci**) ball-shaped bacterium.

coccyx ['kɒksɪks] *n.* (*pl.* **-es**) small bone at the end of the spine.

cochineal [kɒtʃɪ'ni:l] *n.* red colouring used in cooking.

cochlea ['kɒtʃlɪə] *n.* spiral tube in the inner ear.

cock [kɒk] **1.** *n.* (*a*) male bird (esp. a domestic chicken). (*b*) tap. (*c*) hammer on a gun which fires the cartridge. **2.** *v.* (*a*) to prick up (your ears). (*b*) to put (your head) to one side. (*c*) to set (a gun) ready for firing. **cock-a-doodle doo!** *inter. showing* the noise made by a cock. **cock-a-hoop,** *adj.* triumphant **at. cock-crow,** *n.* early morning.

cockade [kɒ'keɪd] *n.* rosette of ribbons worn on a hat.

cockatoo [kɒkə'tu:] *n.* type of large parrot.

cockchafer ['kɒktʃeɪfə] *n.* large beetle.

cocker ['kɒkə] *n.* type of spaniel.

cockerel ['kɒkrəl] *n.* young cock.

cock-eyed ['kɒkaɪd] *adj. inf.* stupid/odd (idea).

cockle ['kɒkl] **1.** *n.* small edible shellfish with a double shell. **2.** *v.* (*of paper*) to curl up/wrinkle.

cockney ['kɒknɪ] *adj. & n.* (person) who comes from the east part of London; way of speaking of a person from the east part of London.

cockpit ['kɒkpɪt] *n.* place where the pilot sits in an aircraft or boat.

cockroach ['kɒkrəʊtʃ] *n.* (*pl.* **-es**) large brown or black beetle.

cocksure [kɒk'ʃʊə] *adj.* very sure/self-confident.

cocktail ['kɒkteɪl] *n.* mixed alcoholic drink; **c. lounge** = smart lounge bar in a hotel; **c. snacks** = snacks which are eaten with drinks; **fruit c./prawn c.** = mixture of fruit/prawns in salad; **Molotov c.** = grenade made of a bottle of petrol and a fuse which you light before throwing.

cock-up ['kɒkʌp] *n. Sl.* mistake/badly carried out work.

cocky ['kɒkɪ] *adj.* unpleasantly proud and conceited.

cocoa ['kəʊkəʊ] *n.* (*no pl.*) brown powder ground from the seeds of the cacao tree, used for making a drink; drink made in this way.

coconut ['kəʊkənʌt] *n.* large nut from a palm tree; **c. shy** = stall at a fair where you try to hit coconuts with a ball; **c. matting** = rough matting made from the outer fibres of a coconut.

cocoon [kə'ku:n] **1.** *n.* protective case of thread made by a larva before it turns into a moth or butterfly. **2.** *v.* to wrap (sth) up for protection (**in**).

cod [kɒd] *n.* (*pl.* **cod**) large sea fish; **c. liver oil** = oil from the livers of cod.

c.o.d. [si:əʊ'di:] *abbreviation for* cash on delivery.

coda ['kəʊdə] *n.* last part of a piece of music.

coddle ['kɒdl] *v.* (*a*) to spoil/to pamper (s.o.). (*b*) to cook (eggs) in warm, but not boiling, water.

code [kəʊd] **1.** *n.* (*a*) set of laws/of rules of behaviour; **the Highway C.** = rules for drivers; **c. of practice** = rules drawn up by a group, which all members of the group must follow. (*b*) secret signs agreed in advance for sending messages; **the Morse c.** = series of dots and dashes used for sending telegraphic messages; **c. word** = secret agreed word. **2.** *v.* to write (a message) in code.

codeine ['kəʊdi:n] *n.* drug used to relieve pain and produce sleep.

codex ['kəʊdeks] *n.* very ancient manuscript of the Bible.

codger ['kɒdʒə] *n. inf.* man.

codicil ['kəʊdɪsɪl] *n.* additional clause to a will.

codify ['kəʊdɪfaɪ] *v.* to write (rules of conduct/laws) as a code. **codification** [kəʊdɪfɪ'keɪʃn] *n.* act of codifying.

co-director [kəʊdaɪ'rektə] *n.* one of two or more directors.

codling ['kɒdlɪŋ] *n.* small apple used for cooking; **c. moth,** moth whose larvae feed on apples.

co-educational [kəʊedjʊ'keɪʃənl] *adj.* (school) where boys and girls are taught together. **co-ed. 1.** *adj.* co-educational. **2.** *n.* girl who goes to a co-educational school.

coefficient [kəʊɪ'fɪʃənt] *n.* factor in mathematics.

coelacanth ['si:ləkænθ] *n.* prehistoric type of fish which is not extinct.

coellac ['si:lıæk] *adj.* referring to the abdomen.

coerce [kəʊ'ɜːs] *v.* to force. **coercion** [kəʊ'ɜːʃn] *n.* force. **coercive,** *adj.* using force.

coeval [kəʊ'i:vəl] *adj.* belonging to the same generation.

coexist [kəʊɪg'zɪst] *v.* to exist/to live together. **coexistence,** *n.* living together; **peaceful c.** = where countries with different types of government exist side by side in peace. **coexistent,** *adj.* living at the same time (as sth else).

coffee ['kɒfı] *n.* (*a*) seeds of a tropical plant, roasted and ground to make a drink. (*b*) drink made from these beans; **instant c.** = powdered extract of coffee which makes a drink when hot water is poured on it; **c. table** = low table for putting cups/glasses, etc., on; **c. table book** = large colourful art book. **coffee shop,** *n.* small restaurant (often in a hotel) serving snacks.

coffers ['kɒfəz] *n. pl.* money chests. **coffer dam,** *n.* watertight wall which allows work to be done on the bed of a river or the sea.

coffin ['kɒfɪn] *n.* long wooden box in which a dead person is buried or cremated.

cog [kɒg] *n.* tooth (on a toothed wheel). **cog-wheel,** *n.* wheel with teeth round the edge which fit into the teeth on another wheel and make it turn.

cogent ['kəʊdʒənt] *adj.* valid (argument); powerful (reason). **cogency,** *n.* being cogent.

cogitate ['kɒdʒɪteɪt] *v.* to ponder/to think deeply. **cogitation** [kɒdʒɪ'teɪʃn] *n.* deep thought.

cognac ['kɒnjæk] *n.* French brandy.

cognate ['kɒgneɪt] *adj.* (*formal*) with the same origin.

cognizance ['kɒgnɪzəns] *n.* knowledge (of a fact). **cognizant,** *adj.* (**of**) knowing/being aware.

cognoscenti [kɒnjə'ʃentı] *n. pl.* specialists in the arts.

cohabit [kəʊ'hæbɪt] *v.* to live together as man and wife, esp. when not married.

cohere [kəʊ'hɪə] *v.* to hold together; to form a whole. **coherence,** *n.* being coherent. **coherent,** *adj.* clear/logical (ideas). **coherently,** *adv.* clearly/logically. **cohesion** [kəʊ'hi:ʒn] *n.* sticking together. **cohesive** [kəʊ'hi:sɪv] *adj.* which stick together.

cohort ['kəʊhɔ:t] *n.* division of a Roman army; large group of people.

coiffure [kwɑː'fjʊə] *n.* hairstyle. **coiffeur** [kwɑ'fɜ:] *n.* hairdresser.

coil [kɔɪl] **1.** *n.* (*a*) roll (of rope); one loop (in sth coiled). (*b*) **electric c.** = wire wrapped round a shaft which conducts electricity. (*c*) contraceptive device. **2.** *v.* to roll up; to make loops.

coin [kɔɪn] **1.** *n.* piece of metal money. **2.** *v.* (*a*) to strike/to produce (metal money); *inf.* **to coin it** = to make a lot of money. (*b*) to invent (a new word). **coinage,** *n.* (*a*) system of money (of a country). (*b*) new word.

coincide [kəʊɪn'saɪd] *v.* to happen (by chance) at the same time as sth else. **coincidence** [kəʊ'ɪnsɪdəns] *n.* two things which happen together/chance. **coincidental** [kəʊɪnsɪ'dentl] *adj.* happening by coincidence.

coir ['kɔɪə] *n.* coconut fibre.

coition, coitus [kəʊ'ɪʃn, 'kɔɪtəs] *n.* (*formal*) act of sexual intercourse.

coke [kəʊk] *n.* (*a*) (*no pl.*) fuel processed from coal, which gives a very fierce heat. (*b*) *inf.* Coca-Cola/trademark for a type of soft drink. (*c*) *inf.* cocaine.

col [kɒl] *n.* high pass between mountains.

colander ['kɒləndə] *n.* bowl with holes in it for draining water from vegetables.

cold [kəʊld] **1.** *adj.* (-er, -est) (*a*) not hot; **he got c. feet** = he was not brave enough to continue; **c. chisel** = hard steel chisel; **c. war** = fight for power between countries without actually using weapons. (*b*) unfriendly (reception, manner). **2.** *n.* (*a*) state of being cold; **left out in the c.** = left on one side. (*b*) infectious illness when you sneeze and cough; **to catch a c. cold-blooded,** *adj.* (*a*) (animal such as fish) with blood whose temperature varies with its surroundings. (*b*) with no feelings. **coldly,** *adv.* in an unfriendly way. **coldness,** *n.* state of being cold. **cold-shoulder,** *v.* to be deliberately unfriendly to (s.o.).

coleslaw ['kəʊlslɔ:] *n.* cabbage salad.

coley ['kəʊlı] *n.* type of sea fish.

colic ['kɒlɪk] *n.* severe pain in the abdomen. **colitis** [kə'laɪtɪs] *n.* inflammation of the colon.

collaborate [kə'læbəreɪt] *v.* to work together. **collaboration** [kəlæbə'reɪʃn] *n.* collaborating. **collaborator,** *n.* person who collaborates.

collage [kɒ'lɑːʒ] *n.* picture made from pieces of paper, etc., which are stuck on to a backing.

collagen ['kɒlədʒən] *n.* fibres which form tissue.

collapse [kə'læps] **1.** *n.* falling down/ruin. **2.** *v.* to fall down suddenly. **collapsible,** *adj.* which can be folded up.

collar ['kɒlə] **1.** *n.* part of clothing which goes round the neck. **2.** *v. inf.* to grab/to catch (s.o.). **collarbone,** *n.* bone from the top of the ribs to the shoulder blade.

collate [kə'leɪt] *v.* to compare texts, etc. **collation** [kə'leɪʃn] *n.* (a) (*formal*) light cold lunch. (b) comparison of texts. **collator,** *n.* someone who compares texts.

collateral [kə'lætərəl] *adj. & n.* parallel; (security) which is used as an additional guarantee.

colleague ['kɒliːg] *n.* person who works with you.

collect 1. ['kɒlɪkt] *n.* short prayer used on a particular day. **2.** [kə'lekt] *v.* (a) to fetch and bring together. (b) to gather money for charity. (c) *Am.* **to call c.** = to ask the person you are phoning to pay for the call. **collected,** *adj.* calm/not flustered. **collection,** *n.* (a) group of objects brought together. (b) gathering of money; money which has been gathered; **to take a c. for sth. collective,** *adj.* brought together; **c. farm** = farm where everything belongs to and is run by the workers on behalf of the state; **c. bargaining** = negotiations for new salaries carried out between union and management. **collectively,** *adv.* all together. **collector,** *n.* person who collects; **ticket c.** = person who takes used tickets from railway passengers.

colleen [kɒ'liːn] *n.* (*in Ireland*) girl.

college ['kɒlɪdʒ] *n.* teaching establishment (for adults and adolescents); **c. of further education** = college for study after secondary school; **c.**

of education = college for training teachers. **collegiate** [kə'liːdʒɪət] *adj.* belonging to/referring to a college.

collide [kə'laɪd] *v.* **to c. with** = to bump into.

collie ['kɒlɪ] *n.* type of sheepdog.

collier ['kɒlɪə] *n.* (a) coal miner. (b) ship which carries coal. **colliery** ['kɒljərɪ] *n.* coalmine.

collision [kə'lɪʒən] *n.* bumping into sth.

collocation [kɒlə'keɪʃn] *n.* (*formal*) group.

colloid ['kɒlɔɪd] *n.* viscous liquid.

colloquial [kə'ləʊkwɪəl] *adj.* as is commonly spoken; conversational. **colloquialism,** *n.* colloquial expression. **colloquially,** *adv.* as in conversational speech.

collusion [kə'luːʒn] *n.* secret illegal agreement.

colon ['kəʊlən] *n.* (a) large part of the intestines. (b) punctuation sign (:) to show a break in a sentence.

colonel ['kɜːnl] *n.* officer in charge of a regiment; army rank above lieutenant-colonel.

colonnade [kɒlə'neɪd] *n.* row of columns.

colony ['kɒlənɪ] *n.* (a) territory ruled by another country. (b) group of animals/humans living together. **colonial** [kə'ləʊnɪəl] *adj.* referring to a colony/the colonies. **colonialism,** *n.* exploitation of colonies. **colonialist,** *n.* person who advocates colonialism. **colonist** ['kɒlənɪst] *n.* person sent from the home country to settle in a colony. **colonization** [kɒlənaɪ'zeɪʒn] *n.* act of making a colony out of a territory. **colonize,** *v.* to occupy (land) and make it a colony.

colophon ['kɒlɒfən] *n.* printed device which identifies a publisher or printer.

color ['kʌlə] *n. & v. Am. see* **colour. coloration,** *n.* colouring.

Colorado beetle [kɒlərə'dəʊ'biːtl] *n.* striped beetle which attacks potato plants.

colossal [kə'lɒsl] *adj.* (a) very large/huge. (b) splendid. **colossally,** *adv.* greatly/enormously. **colossus,** *n.* (*pl.* -es) huge statue; huge man.

colostomy [kɒ'lɒstəmɪ] *n.* operation to attach a colon to an artificial hole in the belly.

colour, *Am.* **color** ['kʌlə] **1.** *n.* (*a*) shade/ tint which an object has in light; **c. film/ TV** = not black and white; **c. scheme** = arrangement of colours (as in the furnishing of a room); **off c.** = feeling unwell. (*b*) shade (of a person's skin); **c. bar** = bar to s.o. because of the colour of his skin. (*c*) paint; **water colours** = paints which have to be mixed with water. (*d*) **colour(s)** = flag; **with flying colours** = with great success; **in his true colours** = as he really is. (*e*) **colours** = (i) coloured sports shirt; (ii) badge to show that you belong to the first team. **2.** *v.* to paint with colour; to make (sth) coloured. **colorant,** *n.* colouring material. **colour-blind,** *adj.* unable to distinguish some colours (usu. red and green). **colour-blindness,** *n.* being colour-blind. **coloured,** (*a*) *adj.* (illustration) in colour. (*b*) *adj.* & *n.* (person) whose skin is not white. **colourful,** *adj.* brightly coloured; picturesque/full of local colour. **colouring,** *n.* way in which sth is coloured; substance which gives colour to sth (such as food). **colourless,** *adj.* pale/uninteresting.

colt [kəʊlt] *n.* (*a*) young male horse. (*b*) **the colts** = junior sports team. **coltsfoot,** *n.* wild plant with small yellow flowers.

columbine ['kɒləmbaɪn] *n.* garden plant with delicate pink or blue flowers.

column ['kɒləm] *n.* (*a*) tall pillar. (*b*) thing which is round and long; **spinal c.** = backbone; **control c./steering c.** = shaft with a wheel on top for steering an aircraft/a car. (*c*) line of soldiers; **fifth c.** = subversive elements working behind the enemy lines to weaken the morale of the population. (*d*) long thin block of printing on a page; regular article in a newspaper. **columnist** ['kɒləmɪst] *n.* journalist who writes regularly for a paper.

coma ['kəʊmə] *n.* state of unconsciousness. **comatose** ['kəʊmətəʊs] *adj.* (*a*) in a coma. (*b*) sleepy/half awake.

comb [kəʊm] **1.** *n.* (*a*) long-toothed instrument for disentangling hair. (*b*) red crest on the head of a bird (such as a cock). (*c*) honeycomb. **2.** *v.* (*a*) to disentangle (hair). (*b*) to search (an area).

combat ['kɒmbæt] **1.** *n.* fighting. **2.** *v.* to fight. **combatant** ['kɒmbətənt] *adj.* & *n.* (person) who takes part in a fight. **combative,** *adj.* quarrelsome/argumentative.

combine 1. *n.* ['kɒmbaɪn] (*a*) financial/ commercial group. (*b*) **c. (harvester)** = large machine for cutting and threshing grain. **2.** *v.* [kəm'baɪn] to join together. **combination** [kɒmbɪ'neɪʃn] *n.* (*a*) several things joined together. (*b*) series of numbers which open a lock; **a c. lock.** (*c*) **motor-cycle c.** = motorcycle with sidecar. (*d*) **combinations** = long one-piece winter underwear. **combs** [kɒmz] *n. pl. inf.* combinations.

combustion [kəm'bʌstʃən] *n.* burning. **combustible** [kəm'bʌstɪbl] *adj.* & *n.* (substance) which can easily catch fire and burn.

come [kʌm] *v.* (came; has come) (*a*) to arrive here; **c. and see us; c. up to my room.** (*b*) to happen; **how does the door c. to be open?** *inf.* **how c.?** = why/how did it happen? (*c*) to add up to; **it comes to £5; c. to that** = by the way/while we are talking of that. (*d*) **to c.** = in the future. **come across,** *v.* to find. **come after,** *v.* to follow. **come along,** *v.* to arrive. **come back,** *v.* to return. **comeback,** *n.* (*a*) repercussions. (*b*) return (of a singer/ sportsman) after retirement. **come by,** *v.* to obtain. **come down,** *v.* to descend. **comedown,** *n.* humiliation. **come into,** *v.* (*a*) to enter. (*b*) to inherit (money). **come off,** *v.* (*a*) to fall off. (*b*) to result; **he came off badly** = the result was bad for him. **come on,** *v.* (*a*) to hurry. (*b*) to arrive. **come out,** *v.* (*a*) to move outside. (*b*) (*of photograph, etc.*) to result/to show. (*c*) **to c. out (on strike)** = to strike. **come over,** *v.* (*a*) to cross. (*b*) to start to feel; **what has c. over him?** = what is the matter with him? **comer,** *n.* person who comes; **late comers; all comers. come round,** *v.* (*a*) to visit. (*b*) to recover from unconsciousness. (*c*) to change one's way of thinking; to agree with s.o. else. **come to,** *v.* to recover (from unconsciousness). **comeuppance,** *n. inf.* **he got his c.** = he was punished. **coming, 1.** *adj.* approaching. **2.** *n.* arrival; **comings and goings.**

comedy ['kɒmədɪ] *n.* play or film which makes you laugh; funny aspect (of an event). **comedian** [kə'miːdɪən] *n.* man who tells jokes to make people laugh. **comedienne** [kəmiː'dɪ'en] *n.* woman who tells jokes to make people laugh.

comely ['kʌmlɪ] *adj.* attractive (woman).

comestibles [kʌ'mestɪbəlz] *n. pl.* (*formal*) food.

comet ['kɒmɪt] *n.* body which moves visibly through space with a bright tail.

comfort ['kʌmfət] **1.** *n.* (*a*) thing which helps to relive suffering. (*b*) ease of living; *Am.* **c. station** = public toilet. **2.** *v.* to relieve the suffering of (s.o. who is miserable, etc.). **comfortable,** *adj.* soft/relaxing, giving ease. **comfortably,** *adv.* in a soft/relaxing way; **c. off** = having plenty of money. **comforter,** *n.* (*a*) person who comforts. (*b*) long woolly scarf. (*c*) *Am.* eiderdown. (*d*) baby's dummy. **comforting,** *adj.* consoling. **comfortless,** *adj.* harsh/hard. **comfy,** *adj.* (-ier, -iest) *inf.* comfortable.

comfrey ['kʌmfrɪ] *n.* herb, used both medicinally and also to make compost.

comic ['kɒmɪk] **1.** *adj.* funny, amusing. **2.** *n.* (*a*) person who tells jokes to make people laugh. (*b*) children's paper with cartoon stories. **comical,** *adj.* funny. **comically,** *adv.* in a funny way.

comma ['kɒmə] *n.* (*a*) punctuation mark (,) showing a break in a sentence around a clause; **inverted commas** (" ") = printing signs showing speech. (*b*) small brown butterfly with ragged wings.

command [kə'mɑːnd] **1.** *n.* (*a*) order; **c. performance** = play/film put on at the command of the king/queen; **second-in-c.** = officer/person directly under the main commander/director; **in c. of** = in charge of. (*b*) knowledge (of a language). **2.** *v.* (*a*) to order. (*b*) to be in charge of. (*c*) to demand (a price). **commandant** [kɒmən'dænt] *n.* officer in charge of a military base, etc. **commandeer** [kɒmən'dɪə] *v.* to order that (sth) should be given over to the armed forces. **commander** [kə'mɑːndə] *n.* officer in charge (of a corps/ship); rank in the navy below captain. **commanding,**

adj. in command. **commandment,** *n.* rule; **the Ten Commandments** = rules given by God to Moses. **commando,** *n.* (*pl.* -os) group of specially trained shock troops; member of such a group.

commemorate [kə'memərɪt] *v.* to celebrate (the memory of something/a special occasion, etc.). **commemoration** [kəmemə'reɪʃn] *n.* commemorating. **commemorative** [kə'memərətɪv] *adj.* which commemorates.

commence [kə'mens] *v.* (*formal*) to begin. **commencement,** *n.* (*a*) beginning. (*b*) *Am.* day when degrees are awarded at a university.

commend [kə'mend] *v.* (*formal*) to praise. **commendable,** *adj.* praiseworthy. **commendably,** *adv.* in a praiseworthy way. **commendation** [kɒmen'deɪʃn] *n.* official praise. **commendatory** [kə'mendətrɪ] *adj.* which praises.

commensurate [kə'mensjʊrət] *adj.* **c. with** = in proportion to.

comment ['kɒment] **1.** *n.* remark/what you feel about something; **no c.** = I refuse to discuss the matter. **2.** *v.* to make remarks (**on**). **commentary,** *n.* (*a*) remarks about a book, etc. (*b*) spoken report on a football match/horse race, etc. **commentator,** *n.* person who reports on events on the radio or television.

commerce ['kɒmɜːs] *n.* business transactions; **chamber of c.** = association of businessmen. **commercial** [kə'mɜːʃl] **1.** *adj.* dealing with business; **c. vehicle** = vehicle used for business purposes. **2.** *n.* piece of publicity of television. **commercialization** [kəmɜːʃəlaɪ'zeɪʃn] *n.* making sth into a business proposition. **commercialize,** *v.* to make into a business proposition. **commercially,** *adv.* in a commercial way.

commiserate [kə'mɪzəreɪt] *v.* to sympathize (**with** s.o.). **commiseration** [kəmɪzə'reɪʃn] *n.* sympathizing.

commissar [kɒmɪ'sɑː] *n.* political leader (in a communist state).

commissariat [kɒmɪ'seərɪət] *n.* department (esp. in the army) dealing with the supply of food.

commission [kə'mɪʃn] **1.** *n.* (*a*) group

of people which investigates problems of national importance. (b) document naming someone an officer. (c) order for sth to be made/to be used; **out of c.** = not in working order. (d) percentage of sales value given to the salesman. **2.** v. (a) to authorize (s.o.) to be an officer/to authorize (an artist/architect, etc.) to do a piece of work; to put (a ship) into commission. (b) to authorize (a piece of work) to be done. **commissionaire** [kəmɪʃə'neə] n. doorkeeper (in a hotel/office block). **commissioner** [kə'mɪʃnə] n. (a) representative of authority; **c. of police** = highest ranking police officer; **High C.** = ambassador of a Commonwealth country. (b) **c. for oaths** = solicitor who can take sworn statements. (c) member of a commission.

commit [kə'mɪt] v. (**committed**) (a) to carry out (a crime). (b) **to c. s.o. for trial** = to send s.o. to the courts for trial. (c) **to c. oneself** = to promise to do sth. **committed,** adj. firmly believing in (sth). **commitment,** n. (a) promise. (b) agreement to do sth. (c) promise to pay money. **committal,** n. sending of prisoner to the courts for trial.

committee [kə'mɪtɪ] n. official group of people who organize or discuss on behalf of a larger body; **to be on a c.** = to be a member of it.

commode [kə'məʊd] n. (a) chest of drawers. (b) chair with a chamberpot in the seat.

commodious [kə'məʊdɪəs] adj. spacious/large (room/house, etc.).

commodity [kə'mɒdɪtɪ] n. merchandise; thing sold; **basic commodities** = basic foodstuffs and raw materials.

commodore ['kɒmədɔː] n. (a) rank in the Navy above captain. (b) person who directs a yacht club.

common ['kɒmən] **1.** adj. (-er, -est) (a) belonging to everyone/to the public in general; **it is c. knowledge** = everyone knows it. (b) belonging to two or more people; **we have two things in c.; C. Market** = organization linking several European countries for purposes of trade. (c) ordinary/which happens frequently. (d) vulgar/of the lower class. **2.** n. land which belongs

to a community. **commoner,** n. ordinary citizen/not a noble. **common law,** n. law which is derived from decisions of courts, rather than from statutes; **c.-l. wife** = woman who lives with a man as his wife, without being married to him. **commonly,** adv. frequently. **common-or-garden,** adj. ordinary. **commonplace,** adj. & n. (thing) which happens frequently. **commons,** n. (a) **on short commons** = not having enough food. (b) **the (House of) C.** = the lower (elected) house of the British parliament. **commonsense,** n. ordinary good sense. **commonwealth,** n. republic; group of states; **the (British) C.** = association of countries which were formerly colonies of Britain but which are now independent.

commotion [kə'məʊʃən] n. confusion/trouble.

commune 1. n. ['kɒmjuːn] group of people who work together sharing everything. **2.** v. [kə'mjuːn] to be in touch (**with** s.o./sth) in spirit. **communal** [kə'mjuːnəl] adj. (property) held in common/belonging to several people. **communally,** adv. done by several people together.

communicate [kə'mjuːnɪkeɪt] v. (a) (**with**) to pass information to s.o./to be in touch with s.o. (b) **communicating rooms** = rooms with a connecting door; **communicating door** = door which links two rooms. **communicable,** adj. which can be passed on to s.o. **communicant,** n. person who takes Holy Communion. **communication** [kəmjuːnɪ'keɪʃn] n. act of communicating/passing of information; **c. cord** = alarm signal on a train. **communicative** [kə'mjuːnɪkətɪv] adj. talkative; (person) who is willing to give information. **communion,** n. (a) fellowship with s.o.; (b) **Holy C.** = central Christian religious ceremony, celebrating the Last Supper. **communiqué** [kə'mjuːnɪkeɪ] n. official news item given to the press.

communism ['kɒmjʊnɪzəm] n. political doctrine whereby the state owns all industry and land. **communist. 1.** adj. referring to communism. **2.** n. (a) person who believes in communism. (b) member of the Communist Party.

community [kə'mju:nɪtɪ] n. (a) group of people living in one place; **an urban c.** = a town and its inhabitants; **c. centre** = sports/arts centre belonging to a town; **c. charge** = tax levied on all adults which funds local government expenditure; **the European C.** = the Common Market; **religious c.** = group of monks or nuns. (b) the population as a whole. (c) group of organisms living in an area.

commute [kə'mju:t] v. (a) to reduce (a legal penalty). (b) to travel to work in town every day. (c) to pay money instead of doing a piece of work. **commutable**, adj. which can be commuted. **commutation** [kɒmju-'teɪʃn] n. act of commuting a sentence. **commuter**, n. person who travels to work in town every day; **c. train** = train for commuters; **c. belt** = area round a town where commuters live.

compact 1. n. ['kɒmpækt] (a) agreement. (b) small box for carrying face powder. (c) Am. small car. **2.** adj [kəm'pækt] small; tight/close together. **3.** v. to make (sth) compact. **compact disk**, n. metal recording disk, which can hold a larger amount of music than a plastic record, and which is read by a laser in a special player. **compactly**, adv. tightly/close together.

companion [kəm'pænjən] n. (a) person who travels or lives with s.o. (b) handbook. **companionable**, adj. friendly. **companionship**, n. friendship. **companionway**, n. stairway on a ship.

company ['kʌmpənɪ] n. (a) being together with other people; **he is good c.** = he is an entertaining companion; **to part c.** = to split up; **to get into bad c.** = to get in with bad companions. (b) group of soldiers in a battalion; crew of a ship. (c) **theatrical c.** = group of actors who play together. (d) (usu. written **Co.** in names) commercial firm.

compare [kəm'peə] v. to put two things side by side to see how they differ; **he compared our bread to a lump of concrete** = he said it was like a lump of concrete; **his work doesn't c. very well with his brother's** = is not as good as his brother's. **comparability**

[kɒmpərə'bɪlɪtɪ] n. being comparable. **comparable** ['kɒmprəbl] adj. which can be compared. **comparative** [kəm'pærətɪv] **1.** adj. relative. **2.** n. form of an adjective/adverb showing an increase in level; **'better' and 'more stupidly' are the comparatives of 'good' and 'stupidly'. comparatively**, adv. more or less; relatively. **comparison**, n. act of comparing; **there is no c.** = you cannot compare them, one is so much better than the other.

compartment [kəm'pɑ:tmənt] n. division inside a box; separate section in a railway carriage/in a ship.

compass ['kʌmpəs] n. (pl. -es) (a) device which indicates the north by means of a needle. (b) **a pair of compasses** = instrument for drawing a circle. (c) scope/range.

compassion [kəm'pæʃn] n. pity; **to have c. on s.o.** = to take pity on s.o. **compassionate**, adj. merciful/pitying; **c. leave** = extra holiday given to s.o. to visit a sick relative, etc.

compatible [kəm'pætəbl] adj. able to fit with sth. **compatibility** [kəmpætə-'bɪlɪtɪ] n. ability to fit together.

compatriot [kəm'pætrɪət] n. person who comes from the same country.

compel [kəm'pel] v. (**compelled**) to force. **compelling**, adj. which forces; very exciting (story/film).

compendium [kəm'pendɪəm] n. collection (of paper/notes/games).

compensate ['kɒmpenseɪt] v. to pay (s.o.) **for** damage done; to pay **for** a loss. **compensation** [kɒmpen'seɪʃn] n. payment for damage. **compensatory**, adj. which compensates.

compère ['kɒmpeə] **1.** n. host/person who introduces a show. **2.** v. to act as host in a show/to introduce different acts.

compete [kəm'pi:t] v. to try to beat others in a race/a game/a business.

competent ['kɒmpɪtənt] adj. able (to do sth)/capable (of doing sth); efficient. **competence**, n. (a) capability/efficiency. (b) professional responsibilities; **the case is outside the c. of this court. competently**, adv. in a capable/efficient way.

competition [kɒmpə'tɪʃn] n. (a) game

where several teams or people try to win. (*b*) commercial rivalry/trying to sell more than another firm. **competitive** [kəm'petɪtɪv] *adj.* (person) who likes entering competitions; (sport) which is based on competitions; (prices) which aim to compete with those of rival firms. **competitor**, *n.* person who goes in for a competition; rival firm.

compile [kəm'paɪl] *v.* to draw up (a list); to make a collection (of poetry); to write (a dictionary). **compilation** [kɒmpɪ'leɪʃn] *n.* act of compiling; work which has been compiled. **compiler** [kəm'paɪlə] *n.* (*a*) person who compiles. (*b*) computer program which converts coded data to a machine-readable program.

complacent [kəm'pleɪsnt] *adj.* self-satisfied. **complacency**, *n.* being complacent. **complacently**, *adv.* in a complacent way.

complain [kəm'pleɪn] *v.* to grumble because sth is wrong. **complaint**, *n.* (*a*) grumble/statement that sth is wrong. (*b*) illness.

complaisant [kəm'pleɪznt] *adj.* eager to please.

complement 1. *n.* ['kɒmplɪmənt] (*a*) number of people needed to fill sth. (*b*) thing which adds to or fits in with sth else. 2. *v.* [kɒmplɪ-'ment] to complete/to fit in (with sth). **complementary** [kɒmplɪ'mentəri] *adj.* which fills/completes sth.

complete [kəm'pli:t] 1. *adj.* (*a*) full/whole. (*b*) finished. 2. *v.* (*a*) to finish. (*b*) to fill in (a form). **completely**, *adv.* wholly. **completeness**, *n.* fullness (of success). **completion** [kəm'pli:ʃn] *n.* finishing; finish; **c. of a contract** = signing of a contract.

complex ['kɒmpleks] 1. *adj.* complicated. 2. *n.* (*pl.* -es) (*a*) series of buildings. (*b*) repressed emotions/obsessions; **inferiority c.** = feeling that you are inferior; **Œdipus c.** = feeling of hatred for one's father and love for one's mother. **complexity** [kəm'pleksɪtɪ] *n.* complicated nature.

complexion [kəm'plekʃn] *n.* colour of the skin on your face; general way things are.

complicate ['kɒmplɪkeɪt] *v.* to make things complicated. **complicated**, *adj.* with many small details/difficult to understand. **complication** [kɒmplɪ'keɪʃn] *n.* being complicated; second illness which makes the first illness worse.

complicity [kəm'plɪsɪtɪ] *n.* being an accomplice to a crime.

compliment 1. *n.* ['kɒmplɪmənt] praise; **send him my compliments** = send him my good wishes. 2. *v.* ['kɒmplɪment] to praise. **complimentary** [kɒmplɪ'mentəri] *adj.* which praises; **c. ticket** = free ticket.

compline ['kɒmplɪn] *n.* last service of the day.

comply [kəm'plaɪ] *v.* (**with**) to observe (a rule); to obey (an order). **compliance**, *n.* agreement to do sth. **compliant**, *adj.* (person) who agrees to do sth/who obeys the rules.

component [kəm'pəʊnənt] *adj. & n.* (piece) which forms part of sth.

compose [kəm'pəʊz] *v.* (*a*) to make up (music); to write (a letter/a poem). (*b*) **c. yourself** = be calm. **composed**, *adj.* calm/unflustered. **composer**, *n.* person who writes music. **composite** ['kɒmpəzɪt] *adj.* made of several different parts. **composition** [kɒmpə-'zɪʃn] *n.* (*a*) way in which sth is formed. (*b*) piece of music/poem/long essay. (*c*) artificial substance. **compositor** [kəm'pɒzɪtə] *n.* person who sets type for printing. **composure** [kəm'pəʊʒə] *n.* calmness. **compos mentis** ['kɒmpɒs-'mentɪs] *adj.* sane.

compost ['kɒmpɒst] *n.* rotted vegetable matter used as a fertilizer.

compound 1. *adj.* ['kɒmpaʊnd] made up of several parts; **c. fracture** = fracture where the broken bone pierces the skin; **c. interest** = interest calculated each year on the total sum including the previous year's interest. 2. *n.* ['kɒmpaʊnd] (*a*) chemical made up of two or more elements. (*b*) yard enclosed by a fence. 3. *v.* [kəm'paʊnd] (*a*) to come to an agreement with people to whom you owe money. (*b*) to keep information about (a crime) hidden. (*c*) to increase/to aggravate (a crime/a feeling).

comprehend [kɒmprɪ'hend] *v.* (*a*) to understand. (*b*) to include. **com-**

prehensible, *adj.* which can be understood/understandable. **comprehension,** *n.* understanding. **comprehensive,** *adj.* which includes everything; **c. (school)** = school for children of different abilities; **c. education** = system of education where all children go to the same type of school without any selection. **comprehensiveness,** *n.* wide range of knowledge, etc.).

compress 1. *n.* ['kɒmpres] pad of material put on a bruise/sore. **2.** *v.* [kəm'pres] to squeeze into a small space; **compressed air** = air under pressure. **compressor,** *n.* machine which compresses air/gas, etc.

comprise [kəm'praız] *v.* to be formed of.

compromise ['kɒmprəmaız] **1.** *n.* agreement of two opposing points of view, where each side gives way to some extent. **2.** *v.* (*a*) to come to an agreement by giving way. (*b*) to embarrass/to put in a difficult position. **compromising,** *adj.* embarrassing.

comptroller [kən'trəʊlə] *n.* (old) person who controls the finances in an establishment.

compulsion [kəm'pʌlʃn] *n.* force/urge. **compulsive,** *adj.* (person) who cannot stop himself doing sth; **a c. smoker. compulsory,** *adj.* which you are forced to do.

compunction [kəm'pʌŋkʃn] *n.* remorse/regret.

compute [kəm'pju:t] *v.* to calculate. **computation** [kɒmpjʊ'teıʃn] *n.* calculation. **computer,** *n.* electronic machine which calculates and keeps information automatically; **c. bureau** = office which does work on its computers for other companies; **c. fraud** = fraud committed by using a computer. **computer-assisted,** *adj.* helped by using a computer; **c.-a. design. computerization,** *n.* act of computerizing. **computerize,** *v.* (*a*) to process by computer. (*b*) to equip (a business, etc.) with a computer.

comrade ['kɒmreıd] *n.* friend/companion; fellow member of a socialist or communist party. **comradeship,** *n.* fellowship/friendliness.

con [kɒn] **1.** *n.* (*a*) *inf.* deception; **c. man**

= trickster. (*b*) argument against. **2.** *v.* (**conned**) *inf.* to deceive/to trick (s.o.).

concatenation [kɒnkætı'neıʃən] *n.* chain of events.

concave [kɒn'keıv] *adj.* (surface) which is hollowed in the middle like a spoon.

conceal [kən'si:l] *v.* to hide. **concealed,** *adj.* hidden; **c. entrance** = entrance which is difficult to see. **concealment,** *n.* hiding.

concede [kən'si:d] *v.* (*a*) to admit (that you are wrong). (*b*) to admit that you have lost.

conceit [kən'si:t] *n.* high opinion of oneself. **conceited,** *adj.* (person) who thinks too much of himself.

conceive [kən'si:v] *v.* (*a*) to become pregnant. (*b*) to think up (an idea). **conceivable,** *adj.* which can be imagined. **conceivably,** *adv.* in a conceivable way.

concentrate ['kɒnsəntreıt] **1.** *n.* concentrated substance. **2.** *v.* (*a*) (**on**) to pay great attention to (sth). (*b*) to put (all one's resources) together in one place. **concentrated,** *adj.* very strong (juice where water has been extracted). **concentration** [kɒnsən'treıʃn] *n.* (*a*) attentiveness. (*b*) putting all your resources into one area. (*c*) **c. camp** = camp where many political prisoners are held in captivity.

concentric [kən'sentrık] *adj.* (circles) inside each other, each with the same central point.

concept ['kɒnsept] *n.* idea/philosophical notion. **conception** [kən'sepʃn] *n.* (*a*) becoming pregnant. (*b*) idea. **conceptual,** *adj.* referring to concepts. **conceptualize,** *v.* to form a concept of (sth).

concern [kən'sɜ:n] **1.** *n.* (*a*) worry. (*b*) interest; **it is no c. of yours** = it is none of your business. (*c*) firm/business; **a big industrial c. 2.** *v.* (*a*) to deal with; **this concerns you** = is about you; **that does not c. him** = it has nothing to do with him; **as far as money is concerned** = with reference to money. (*b*) **to be concerned (about)** = to worry (about). **concerning,** *prep.* about/referring to.

concert ['kɒnsət] *n.* programme of music played in public. **concerted** [kən'sɜ:tıd] *adj.* (effort/attack) done or planned jointly. **concert hall,** *n.* large hall for giving concerts.

concertina [kɒnsə'tiːnə] **1.** *n.* portable musical instrument with bellows and a set of keys at either end. **2.** *v.* to become crushed/crumpled.

concerto [kən'tʃeətəʊ] *n.* (*pl.* **-os**) piece of music for a solo instrument and orchestra, or for a small group of instruments.

concession [kən'seʃn] *n.* act of conceding/of admitting sth; **to make a c.** = to change what you planned to fit in with s.o. else's wishes.

conch [kɒntʃ] *n.* (*pl.* **-es**) type of sea shell, like a large snail shell. **conchology** [kɒŋ'kɒlədʒɪ] *n.* study of shells.

conciliate [kən'sɪlɪeɪt] *v.* to win over (s.o.) who was previously unfriendly; to reconcile. **conciliation** [kənsɪlɪ'eɪʃn] *n.* act of conciliating; **c. board** = committee set up to arbitrate in industrial disputes. **conciliator** [kən'sɪlɪeɪtə] *n.* person who tries to reconcile people of opposing views. **conciliatory** [kən'sɪlɪətrɪ] *adj.* which is aimed at conciliating.

concise [kən'saɪs] *adj.* short; meaning a lot, but using few words. **concisely,** *adv.* in a concise way. **conciseness, concision** [kən'sɪʒn] *n.* briefness.

conclave ['kɒŋkleɪv] *n.* religious assembly, esp. meeting of cardinals to elect a pope.

conclude [kən'kluːd] *v.* (*a*) to come to an end. (*b*) to deduce/to come to an opinion. (*c*) to arrange (a treaty). **concluding,** *adj.* final. **conclusion** [kən'kluːʒn] *n.* (*a*) end. (*b*) opinion reached by reasoning. **conclusive,** *adj.* decisive/which offers firm proof. **conclusively,** *adv.* in a decisive way.

concoct [kən'kɒkt] *v.* (*a*) to make (a dish of food). (*b*) to make up/to invent (a story). **concoction,** *n.* curious mixture of food or drink.

concomitant [kən'kɒmɪtənt] *adj.* (*formal*) which accompanies/goes with.

concord ['kɒŋkɔːd] *n.* harmony/peace.

concordance [kən'kɔːdəns] *n.* alphabetical list of words used in a book.

concordat [kɒn'kɔːdæt] *n.* agreement (between church and state).

concourse ['kɒŋkɔːs] *n.* (*a*) crowd/mass of people. (*b*) large open space inside a railway station/concert hall, etc.

concrete ['kɒnkriːt] **1.** *adj.* real/firm. **2.** *adj.* & *n.* (made of) hard stonelike substance made by mixing sand, gravel, cement and water. **concrete mixer,** *n.* machine for mixing concrete. **concretion** [kən'kriːʃn] *n.* mass of things which have solidified together.

concubine ['kɒŋkjʊbaɪn] *n.* woman who lives with a man as his second wife, but who is not married to him.

concur [kən'kɜː] *v.* (**concurred**) to agree. **concurrence** [kən'kʌrəns] *n.* agreement. **concurrent** [kən'kʌrənt] *adj.* which happen at the same time. **concurrently,** *adv.* happening at the same time.

concussion [kən'kʌʃn] *n.* shock to the brain caused by being hit on the head. **concussed,** *adj.* in a state of concussion.

condemn [kən'dem] *v.* to blame; to sentence (a criminal); to declare (houses) to be unfit to live in. **condemnation** [kɒndem'neɪʃn] *n.* blame.

condense [kən'dens] *v.* (*a*) to reduce the size of (sth); **condensed milk** = milk which has been concentrated and sweetened. (*b*) (*of steam*) to form drops of water. **condensation** [kɒnden'seɪʃn] *n.* act of condensing; steam which has formed into a film on a cold surface. **condenser,** *n.* part of a machine which turns gas into liquid.

condescend [kɒndɪ'send] *v.* to speak/to act as if you are superior to s.o. else. **condescending,** *adj.* unpleasantly superior (voice/smile, etc.). **condescension,** *n.* acting with a feeling of superiority.

condiment ['kɒndɪmənt] *n.* seasoning for food, such as salt, pepper, mustard.

condition [kən'dɪʃn] **1.** *n.* (*a*) state. (*b*) term (of a bargain); **on c. that** = provided that. (*c*) bad state; **a heart c.** = a weak heart. **2.** *v.* (*a*) to put into good condition. (*b*) to make (s.o.) used to sth; **conditioned reflex** = reaction to a stimulus which has been repeated many times. **conditional,** *adj.* & *n.* provided that certain things happen; part of a verb which shows this; **'I would**

come' is a conditional form of 'to come'. **conditionally,** *adv.* under certain conditions. **conditioner,** *n.* lotion which puts sth (esp. hair) into good condition.

condole [kən'dəʊl] *v.* **to c. with s.o.** = to express your regrets for some tragedy which has happened. **condolences,** *n. pl.* expressions of regret (at the death of s.o.).

condom ['kɒndəm] *n.* rubber contraceptive sheath.

condominium [kɒndə'mɪnɪəm] *n.* (*a*) joint ownership. (*b*) *Am.* building held in joint ownership.

condone [kən'dəʊn] *v.* to excuse/forgive (a crime, etc.).

condor ['kɒndɔ:] *n.* large South American vulture.

conducive [kən'dju:sɪv] *adj.* favourable (to).

conduct 1. *n.* ['kɒndʌkt] way of behaving. **2.** *v.* [kən'dʌkt] (*a*) to lead/to guide/to control (a business, an orchestra); **conducted tour** = tour led by a guide. (*b*) to allow (electricity/heat) to pass through. (*c*) **to c. yourself** = to behave. **conduction** [kən'dʌkʃn] *n.* passing of heat/electricity. **conductivity** [kɒndʌk-'tɪvɪtɪ] *n.* ability to conduct electricity or heat. **conductor,** *n.* (*a*) substance (such as metal) which conducts heat/electricity; **c. rail** = rail which carries electricity for electric trains. (*b*) person who directs an orchestra. (*c*) **bus c.** = person who collects money from the passengers on a bus. (*d*) *Am.* railway guard. **conductress,** *n.* (*pl.* **-es**) woman who collects money from passengers on a bus.

conduit ['kɒndɪt] *n.* tube along which liquids can be passed.

cone [kəʊn] *n.* geometrical figure, round at the base, rising to a point; **ice cream c.** = cornet; **fir c.** = fruit of a fir tree; **nose c.** = pointed end of a rocket. **cone-shaped,** *adj.* shaped like a cone.

confab ['kɒnfæb] *n. inf.* chat/discussion.

confection [kən'fekʃən] *n.* food made of a mixture of sweet things. **confectionery** [kən'fekʃənrɪ] *n.* sweets and cakes. **confectioner's,** *n.* shop selling sweets and cakes.

confederate [kən'fedərət] *n.* person who has joined with others (usu. to do

a crime). **confederacy,** *n.* joining together. **confederation** [kənfedə'reɪʃn] *n.* group (of states/trade unions, etc.).

confer [kən'fɜ:] *v.* (**conferred**) (*a*) to discuss. (*b*) **to c. an honour on s.o.** = to award s.o. an honour. **conference** ['kɒnfərəns] *n.* discussion; meeting of a group/society.

confess [kən'fes] *v.* to admit that you have done sth wrong. **confession** [kən'feʃn] *n.* admission of fault; **to make your c.** = to admit your sins to a priest. **confessional,** *n.* small private box in a church where a priest hears confessions. **confessor,** *n.* priest who hears confessions.

confetti [kən'fetɪ] *n.* small pieces of coloured paper thrown over the bride and bridegroom after a wedding.

confidant, confidante [kɒnfɪ'dænt] *n.* man/woman you tell secrets to.

confide [kən'faɪd] *v.* **to c. in s.o.** = to tell s.o. a secret. **confidence** ['kɒnfɪdəns] *n.* (*a*) feeling sure. (*b*) secrecy; **in c.** = as a secret. (*c*) **c. trick** = trick whereby a trickster gains s.o.'s confidence to steal money from him. **confident,** *adj.* sure (of yourself). **confidently,** *adv.* in a sure way. **confidential** [kɒnfɪ'denʃl] *adj.* secret/private; (secretary) entrusted with confidential matters. **confidentiality,** *n.* being secret/private. **confidentially,** *adv.* in a confidential way.

configuration [kənfɪgə'reɪʃn] *n.* (*a*) (*formal*) shape. (*b*) way in which computer hardware or software are planned.

confine [kən'faɪn] *v.* to restrict/to shut up; **confined to bed** = forced to stay in bed. **confinement,** *n.* (*a*) imprisonment. (*b*) period when a woman gives birth to a baby.

confirm [kən'fɜ:m] *v.* (*a*) to make definite/to make sure. (*b*) **to be confirmed** = to be made a full member of a church. **confirmation** [kɒnfə-'meɪʃn] *n.* (*a*) making sure. (*b*) ceremony in which s.o. is made a full member of the church. **confirmatory,** *adj.* which confirms. **confirmed,** *adj.* permanent; **he is a c. bachelor** = he will never get married.

confiscate ['kɒnfɪskeɪt] *v.* to take away

s.o.'s possessions as a punishment. **confiscation** [kɒnfɪs'keɪʃn] *n.* act of confiscating.

conflagration [kɒnflə'greɪʃn] *n.* (*formal*) big fire.

conflate [kən'fleɪt] *v.* to put together.

conflict 1. *n.* ['kɒnflɪkt] battle/fight. **2.** *v.* [kən'flɪkt] to clash/to contradict.

confluence ['kɒnfluəns] *n.* (*formal*) place where two rivers join together.

conform [kən'fɔːm] *v.* to fit in (**to** a pattern); to act in the same way as other people. **conformist**, *n.* person who conforms. **conformity**, *n.* conforming.

confound [kən'faʊnd] *v.* to confuse/to bother.

confront [kən'frʌnt] *v.* to face up to (a danger); **to c. s.o. with** = to bring s.o. face to face with. **confrontation** [kɒnfrʌn'teɪʃn] *n.* bringing face to face; meeting between opposing sides.

confuse [kən'fjuːz] *v.* to mix/to muddle. **confused**, *adj.* mixed-up/muddled. **confusedly** [kən'fjuːzɪdlɪ] *adv.* in a muddled way. **confusing**, *adj.* muddling. **confusion** [kən'fjuːʒn] *n.* muddle/disorder.

confute [kən'fjuːt] *v.* (*formal*) to prove (sth) wrong. **confutation** [kɒnfjuː-'teɪʃn] *n.* proving wrong.

congeal [kən'dʒiːl] *v.* to set solid; to become solid (as of dried blood).

congenial [kən'dʒiːnɪəl] *adj.* sympathetic/friendly.

congenital [kən'dʒenɪtl] *adj.* (illness/defect) present in a person since birth. **congenitally**, *adv.* from birth.

conger eel ['kɒŋgə iːl] *n.* very large type of eel.

congested [kən'dʒestɪd] *adj.* blocked/crowded. **congestion** [kən'dʒestʃn] *n.* blocking (of streets); filling (of the lungs) with liquid.

conglomeration [kənglɒmə'reɪʃn] *n.* mass of things heaped together. **conglomerate** [kən'glɒmərət] *n.* (*a*) rock made of small pieces fused together. (*b*) many subsidiary companies linked together.

Congolese [kɒŋgə'liːz] *adj. & n.* (person) from the Congo.

congratulate [kən'grætjʊleɪt] *v.* to give (s.o.) good wishes on a special occasion; to praise (s.o.) for some achievement. **congratulations** [kəngrætjʊ'leɪʃnz] *n.* good wishes. **congratulatory** [kən'grætjʊlətrɪ] *adj.* which gives good wishes.

congregate ['kɒŋgrɪgeɪt] *v.* to gather together. **congregation** [kɒŋgrɪ'geɪʃn] *n.* people gathered together; people meeting together in a church.

congress ['kɒŋgres] *n.* meeting of a group of people; **Congress** = the elected legislative body of the United States. **congressional**, *adj.* referring to the US Congress. **congressman**, *n.* (*pl.* **-men**) member of the Congress of the United States.

congruent ['kɒŋgrʊənt] *adj.* which fit together.

conical ['kɒnɪkl] *adj.* shaped like a cone.

conifer ['kɒnɪfə] *n.* tree which bears cones. **coniferous** [kə'nɪfərəs] *adj.* referring to conifers.

conjecture [kən'dʒektʃə] **1.** *n.* guess. **2.** *v.* to guess. **conjectural**, *adj.* possible/which has been guessed at.

conjugal ['kɒndʒʊgl] *adj.* referring to marriage.

conjugate ['kɒndʒʊgeɪt] *v.* to show the different parts of (a verb). **conjugation** [kɒndʒʊ'geɪʃn] *n.* way in which a verb changes according to tense and person.

conjunction [kən'dʒʌŋkʃn] *n.* word which links different parts of a sentence; **in c. with** = together with.

conjunctivitis [kəndʒʌŋktɪ'vaɪtɪs] *n.* inflammation of the eyes.

conjuncture [kən'dʒʌŋktʃə] *n.* circumstances.

conjure ['kʌndʒə] *v.* (*a*) to do tricks with cards/rabbits, etc. (*b*) to call **up** (a spirit/a picture). **conjurer, conjuror**, *n.* person who does tricks. **conjuring**, *n.* magic tricks.

conk [kɒŋk] *n. Sl.* head. **conk out**, *v. inf.* to stop working.

conker ['kɒŋkə] *n. inf.* horse chestnut.

connect [kə'nekt] *v.* to join/to link; **this train connects with the 13.56** = this train arrives in time for you to get off it and catch the 13.56; **they are connected to the Williams family** = they are related to them. **connected**, *adj.* joined/linked; **well c.** = with influential friends and relations. **connection, connexion**, *n.* join/link; **in c. with your visit** = with reference to/concerning your visit; **there is a connection to London** = there is a train which connects with this one for London; **he has connections in the theatre** = he has friends/relations in the theatre.

conning tower ['kɒnɪŋtauə] *n.* highest part of a submarine.

connive [kə'naɪv] *v.* **to c. at sth** = to allow it to take place. **connivance**, *n.* conniving (**at sth**).

connoisseur [kɒnə'sɜ:] *n.* expert/person who knows a lot (about sth).

connote [kə'nəut] *v.* to imply sth in addition. **connotation**, *n.* additional meaning.

connubial [kə'nju:bɪəl] *adj.* (*formal*) referring to marriage.

conquer ['kɒŋkə] *v.* to defeat by force. **conquering**, *adj.* triumphant/victorious. **conqueror**, *n.* person who leads the invasion of a country; state which captures another country. **conquest** ['kɒŋkwest] *n.* (*a*) capturing. (*b*) thing/country which has been captured.

consanguinity [kɒnsæŋ'gwɪnɪtɪ] *n.* (*formal*) connection by blood.

conscience ['kɒnʃəns] *n.* feeling which tells you if you have done right or wrong. **conscience-stricken**, *adj.* ashamed. **conscientious** [kɒnʃɪ'enʃəs] *adj.* who works carefully and well; **c. objector** = person who refuses to join the services because he feels war is wrong. **conscientiously**, *adv.* in a conscientious way.

conscious ['kɒnʃəs] *adj.* aware of things around you; **a c. decision** = a deliberate decision. **consciously**, *adv.* in a conscious way. **consciousness**, *n.* being conscious; **to lose c.** = to become unconscious.

conscript 1. *n.* ['kɒnskrɪpt] person who has been ordered to join the services. **2.** *v.* [kən'skrɪpt] to order (people) to join the services. **conscription** [kən'skrɪpʃn] *n.* legal obligation to join the services.

consecrate ['kɒnsɪkreɪt] *v.* to bless (a new church/a king); to devote (one's life **to** sth). **consecration** [kɒnsɪ'kreɪʃn] *n.* blessing; devoting (of your life).

consecutive [kən'sekjutɪv] *adj.* following one after the other. **consecutively**, *adv.* in order.

consensus [kən'sensəs] *n.* generally agreed opinion.

consent [kən'sent] **1.** *n.* agreement. **2.** *v.* to agree (**to** sth).

consequence ['kɒnsɪkwəns] *n.* (*a*) result. (*b*) importance; **it is of no c.** = it does not matter. **consequent**, *adj.* **c. on** = resulting from. **consequential** [kɒnsɪ'kwenʃl] *adj.* resulting. **consequently**, *adv.* because of this/for this reason.

conserve [kən'sɜ:v] *v.* to save. **conservancy**, *n.* body which controls a river, etc. **conservation** [kɒnsə'veɪʃn] *n.* preservation/saving (of energy, natural resources, old buildings, etc.). **conservationist**, *n.* person who is interested in conservation. **conservatism**, *n.* (*a*) being conservative. (*b*) (*in politics*) policies of the Conservative party. **conservative** [kən'sɜ:vətɪv] *adj.* (*a*) not wanting to change; **C. party** = political party which does not want to change the existing system of government, and which does not favour state control of industry; **a C.** = member of the Conservative Party. (*b*) **at a c. estimate** = at the lowest/most moderate estimate. **conservatively**, *adv.* moderately. **conservatory**, *n.* (*a*) room with large windows, where you keep tropical flowers and plants. (*b*) *also* **conservatoire** [kən'sɜ:vətwɑ:r] academy of music.

consider [kən'sɪdə] *v.* to think deeply about (sth). **considerable**, *adj.* quite large. **considerably**, *adv.* to a great extent. **considerate**, *adj.* full of feeling/understanding towards s.o. **considerately**, *adv.* thoughtfully. **consideration** [kənsɪdə'reɪʃn] *n.* (*a*) being thought about. (*b*) small sum of money. **considering**, *prep.* when you think of/taking into account.

consign [kən'saɪn] *v.* to give (goods) into s.o.'s care. **consignee**, *n.* (*formal*) person who receives goods from s.o. **consignment**, *n.* (*a*) sending of goods. (*b*) goods which have been sent. **consignor**, *n.* person who consigns goods to s.o.

consist [kən'sɪst] *v.* (*a*) (**in**) to have as a basis. (*b*) (**of**) to be made up of. **consistency**, *n.* (*a*) being the same throughout. (*b*) thickness (of a paste, etc.). **consistent**, *adj.* which does not contradict; always the same/unchanging. **consistently**, *adv.* always/permanently.

consistory [kən'sɪstəri] *n.* meeting of the Pope and cardinals at which a decision is taken.

console 1. *n.* ['kɒnsəʊl] (*a*) flat table with the keyboard (of an organ/telex machine, etc.). (*b*) cabinet for a TV set. 2. *v.* [kən'səʊl] to comfort (s.o.) after a loss. **consolation** [kɒnsə'leɪʃn] *n.* comfort; **c. prize** = prize given to s.o. who did not win, but who tried hard.

consolidate [kən'sɒlɪdeɪt] *v.* to make firm/solid. **consolidation** [kənsɒlɪ'deɪʃn] *n.* (*a*) making firm. (*b*) grouping together of small packets from different sources into one large shipment. **consolidator**, *n.* shipping company which groups shipments together.

consommé [kən'sɒmeɪ] *n.* thin clear soup.

consonant ['kɒnsənənt] 1. *n.* (letter representing) a sound which is not a vowel. 2. *adj.* which agrees **with**.

consort 1. *n.* ['kɒnsɔːt] husband or wife (of a queen or king). 2. *v.* [kən'sɔːt] to go around **with** s.o.

consortium [kən'sɔːtɪəm] *n.* (*pl.* **-tia**) group of companies who work together.

conspicuous [kən'spɪkjʊəs] *adj.* very obvious; **he was c. by his absence** = everyone noticed that he was not there. **conspicuously**, *adv.* very obviously.

conspire [kən'spaɪə] *v.* to plot (**to do** sth). **conspiracy** [kən'spɪrəsɪ] *n.* plot. **conspirator**, *n.* plotter. **conspiratorial** [kənspɪrə'tɔːrɪəl] *adj.* like s.o. who is plotting.

constable ['kʌnstəbl] *n.* policeman. **constabulary** [kən'stæbjʊlərɪ] *n.* police force of a district.

constant ['kɒnstənt] *adj.* (*a*) not changing or stopping. (*b*) faithful. **constancy**, *n.* faithfulness. **constantly**, *adv.* all the time.

constellation [kɒnstə'leɪʃn] *n.* group of stars forming a pattern in the sky.

consternation [kɒnstə'neɪʃn] *n.* shock/surprise.

constipated ['kɒnstɪpeɪtɪd] *adj.* unable to empty the bowels regularly. **consti-**

pation [kɒnstɪ'peɪʃn] *n.* slow working of the bowels.

constituent [kən'stɪtjʊənt] 1. *adj.* (part) which makes up a whole. 2. *n.* (*a*) part which goes to make up a whole. (*b*) person who may vote in an electoral area. **constituency**, *n.* area which elects a member of Parliament.

constitute ['kɒnstɪtjuːt] *v.* to make up; to establish. **constitution** [kɒnstɪ'tjuːʃn] *n.* (*a*) bodily health. (*b*) laws and principles which form the basis of a country's organization. **constitutional.** 1. *adj.* referring to the legal basis of a state; (monarchy) where the power is held by an elected government. 2. *n.* short walk which is supposed to be good for the health. **constitutionally**, *adv.* according to the constitution.

constrain [kən'streɪn] *v.* to force. **constraint**, *n.* force.

constrict [kən'strɪkt] *v.* to squeeze/to strangle. **constriction** [kən'strɪkʃn] *n.* constricting.

construct [kən'strʌkt] *v.* to build. **construction** [kən'strʌkʃn] *n.* (*a*) act of building; way in which sth is made up. (*b*) thing which has been built. **constructive**, *adj.* which aims at improving. **constructively**, *adv.* in a constructive way. **constructor**, *n.* builder/person who constructs.

construe [kən'struː] *v.* to take to mean.

consul ['kɒnsəl] *n.* country's representative abroad, particularly looking after the personal affairs of his fellow-countrymen. **consular** ['kɒnsjʊlə] *adj.* referring to a consul; **c. department (of an embassy)** = department which looks after passports and visas. **consulate**, *n.* house/offices of a consul.

consult [kən'sʌlt] *v.* to ask for advice. **consultant**, *n.* specialist who gives advice, esp. medical specialist attached to a hospital. **consultation** [kɒnsʌl'teɪʃn] *n.* act of consulting. **consultative** [kən'sʌltətɪv] *adj.* which gives advice; **c. assembly** = assembly to advise the government. **consulting**, *n.* asking for advice; **c. room** = doctor's office.

consume [kən'sjuːm] *v.* (*a*) to eat or drink. (*b*) to use up. **consumables**, *n.* (*a*) consumer goods. (*b*) (*computers*) paper, ribbons, etc., which are used in peripherals. **consumer,** *n.* person who uses goods or eats food; **c. goods** = goods which are bought by ordinary members of the public (and not by industry). **consumerism,** *n.* fighting for the rights of the consumer.

consummate 1. *adj.* [kən'sʌmɪt] perfect (artist, etc.). **2.** *v.* ['kɒnsəmeɪt] to complete; **to c. a marriage** = to have sexual intercourse for the first time after marriage. **consummation** [kɒnsə'meɪʃn] *n.* completion; end.

consumption [kən'sʌmpʃn] *n.* (*a*) act of consuming; quantity consumed. (*b*) (*old*) tuberculosis. **consumptive,** *adj.* looking as though one is suffering from tuberculosis.

cont. *abbrev for* continued.

contact ['kɒntækt] **1.** *n.* (*a*) touch; **c. lenses** = tiny lenses worn on the eyeballs, replacing glasses. (*b*) person whom you know/whom you have contacted. **2.** *v.* to get into communication with (s.o.).

contagion [kən'teɪdʒn] *n.* passing on of a disease by touching. **contagious** [kən'teɪdʒəs] *adj.* (disease) which is transmitted by touching.

contain [kən'teɪn] *v.* (*a*) to hold/to have inside. (*b*) to hold back/to restrain (an attack, anger). **container,** *n.* (*a*) box/bottle, etc., which holds sth else. (*b*) large case for easy loading on a ship, lorry, etc. **containerization,** *n.* using containers for shipping goods. **containment,** *n.* holding back (an enemy).

contaminate [kən'tæmɪneɪt] *v.* to make bad/dirty. **contaminant,** *n.* substance which contaminates. **contamination** [kəntæmɪ'neɪʃn] *n.* act of contaminating.

contemplate ['kɒntempleɪt] *v.* (*a*) to look at (sth) intently. (*b*) to plan to do sth. **contemplation** [kɒntem-'pleɪʃn] *n.* meditation/deep thought. **contemplative** [kən'templətɪv] *adj.* which meditates.

contemporary [kən'temprərɪ] *adj. & n.* (*a*) (with) (person) who lives at the same time or is (about) the same age as another; (thing) which dates back to the same period as

another thing. (*b*) modern/up-to-date. **contemporaneous** [kəntempə'reɪnɪəs] *adj.* of the same date/period.

contempt [kən'tempt] *n.* feeling of hatred/disrespect for s.o.; **c. of court** = conduct which a judge rules is offensive to a court. **contemptible,** *adj.* which deserves contempt. **contemptuous,** *adj.* scornful (**of**).

contend [kən'tend] *v.* (*a*) (**with**) to fight. (*b*) to state/to believe. **contender,** *n.* person who challenges s.o. to a fight; person who fights.

content 1. *adj.* [kən'tent] (**with**) satisfied/happy. **2.** *n.* (*a*) [kən'tent] satisfaction; **to your heart's c.** = as much as you like. (*b*) ['kɒntent] thing which is contained/which is in a container; **table of contents** = list of chapters/sections in a book; **the contents of the letter** = what was written in it; **mineral c. of water** = percentage of minerals in water. **3.** *v.* [kən'tent] to satisfy. **contented,** *adj.* satisfied/happy. **contentedly,** *adv.* in a contented way. **contentedness,** **contentment,** *n.* being contented.

contention [kən'tenʃn] *n.* (*a*) dispute; **bone of c.** = source of argument. (*b*) statement/belief. **contentious** [kən'tenʃəs] *adj.* (person) who likes arguments; (problem) which is a frequent source of dispute.

conterminous [kɒn'tɜːmɪnəs] *adj.* which has the same limits as sth. else.

contest 1. *n.* ['kɒntest] fight; competition. **2.** *v.* [kən'test] (*a*) to fight (an election). (*b*) to query; argue that (a will) is invalid. **contestant,** *n.* competitor/person who enters a contest.

context ['kɒntekst] *n.* phrase in which a word occurs, which helps show its meaning; **out of c.** = without the surrounding text. **contextual** [kən'tekstjʊəl] *adj.* referring to a context.

contiguous [kən'tɪgjʊəs] *adj.* (*formal*) next to/touching. **contiguity** [kɒntɪ-'gjuːɪtɪ] *n.* being contiguous.

continent ['kɒntɪnənt] **1.** *n.* large mass of land; **on the C.** = in Europe. **2.** *adj.* able to control the passing of urine or excreta. **continental** [kɒntɪ'nentl] *adj.*

(*a*) referring to a continent. (*b*) referring to Europe (excluding the British Isles); **a Continental** = a European (but not an inhabitant of the British Isles); **c. breakfast** = coffee and rolls or bread; **c. climate** = climate with hot dry summers and very cold winters, found in the central parts of continents; **c. quilt** = a duvet, a bag stuffed with feathers, used as the only covering for a bed.

contingent [kən'tɪndʒənt] 1. *adj.* which depends on sth. 2. *n.* group of soldiers, etc. **contingency**, *n.* emergency.

continue [kən'tɪnjuː] *v.* to go on doing sth. **continual**, *adj.* which goes on all the time without stopping. **continually**, *adv.* very frequently; all the time. **continuation** [kəntɪnjʊ'eɪʃn] *n.* (*a*) (*also* **continuance**) going on without stopping. (*b*) extension/thing which has been continued. **continuity** [kɒntɪ'njuːtɪ] *n.* state of continuing without a break; **c. girl** = girl who ensures that each scene in a film follows on smoothly. **continuous** [kən'tɪnjʊəs] *adj.* with no break; **c. stationery** = computer paper, in one long strip, folded in concertina fashion. **continuously**, *adv.* one after the other with no break in between. **continuum**, *n.* thing which continues.

contort [kən'tɔːt] *v.* to twist unnaturally. **contortion** [kən'tɔːʃn] *n.* twisting unnaturally. **contortionist**, *n.* person in a show who twists his body into odd shapes.

contour ['kɒntʊə] *n.* shape of the outline of sth; **c. (line)** = line on a map drawn through points at the same height above sea level.

contra ['kɒntræ] 1. *prep.* against. 2. *n.* **c. entry** = one entry made on one side of an account to balance an entry on the opposite side. 3. *v.* to make a contra entry.

contraband ['kɒntrəbænd] *n.* (*no pl.*) goods on which customs duty has not been paid.

contraception [kɒntrə'sepʃn] *n.* prevention of pregnancy. **contraceptive**, *adj.* & *n.* (thing) which prevents pregnancy.

contract 1. *n.* ['kɒntrækt] (*a*) legal agreement. (*b*) (*in north of Eng-*land) bus or train season ticket. 2. *v.* [kən'trækt] (*a*) to get smaller; to make smaller; to tighten. (*b*) to sign an agreement to do some work. (*c*) to catch (a disease). **contraction** [kən'trækʃn] *n.* shortening; shrinking. **contractor**, *n.* person who does work according to a signed agreement. **contractual**, *adj.* according to a contract.

contradict [kɒntrə'dɪkt] *v.* to deny what s.o. else says. **contradiction** [kɒntrə'dɪkʃn] *n.* saying the opposite. **contradictory**, *adj.* which says the opposite.

contralto [kən'træltəʊ] *n.* (*pl.* **-os**) (woman with a) low-pitched singing voice.

contraption [kən'træpʃn] *n.* machine/device.

contrapuntal [kɒntrə'pʌntl] *adj.* using counterpoint.

contrary ['kɒntrərɪ] 1. *adj.* (*a*) opposite; **c. winds** = winds blowing in the opposite direction to the one you want. (*b*) [kən'treərɪ] rude; always doing the opposite of what you want. 2. *n.* **the c.** = the opposite; **on the c.** = quite the opposite; **to the c.** = stating sth different/opposite. 3. *adv.* in an opposite way (**to**). **contrarily**, *adv.* in a contrary way. **contrariness** [kən'treərɪnəs] *n.* always doing the opposite of what people want/awkwardness (of a child).

contrast 1. *n.* ['kɒntrɑːst] sharp difference. 2. *v.* [kən'trɑːst] to show up the difference between.

contravene [kɒntrə'viːn] *v.* to break the law/the regulations. **contravention** [kɒntrə'venʃn] *n.* breaking of a law.

contribute [kən'trɪbjuːt] *v.* (*a*) to help towards; **to c. to** = write articles for (a newspaper, etc.). (*b*) to give money (**to** a charity). **contribution** [kɒntrɪ'bjuːʃn] *n.* (*a*) article submitted to a newspaper. (*b*) money, etc., given to help sth. **contributor** [kən'trɪbjʊtə] *n.* a person who contributes. **contributory**, *adj.* which helps; **c. factors** = factors which have helped produce the situation.

contrite ['kɒntraɪt] *adj.* (person) who is sorry. **contrition** [kən'trɪʃn] *n.* regret.

contrive [kən'traɪv] *v.* to manage; to plan. **contrivance**, *n.* machine/device. **contrived**, *adj.* artificial/not natural.

control [kən'trəʊl] **1.** *n.* (*a*) authority/power; keeping in order; **under c.** = in order; **birth c.** = limiting of the number of babies born. (*b*) **the controls** = the gears/levers, etc., for directing a machine. (*c*) standard with which the results of an experiment can be compared. **2.** *v.* (**controlled**) (*a*) to direct. (*b*) to limit/to regulate. **controllable**, *adj.* which can be controlled. **controller**, *n.* person who controls. **control tower**, *n.* high building at an airport, which houses the radio operators who direct planes on landing or takeoff.

controversy [kən'trɒvəsɪ] *n.* violent discussion. **controversial** [kɒntrə'vɜːʃl] *adj.* (subject) which provokes violent discussions. **controvert**, *v.* (*formal*) to deny. **controvertible**, *adj.* which can be denied.

contumacious [kɒntjʊ'meɪʃəs] *adj.* (*formal*) persistently disobedient.

contumely ['kɒntjʊmlɪ] *n.* (*formal*) rudeness/insults.

contusion [kən'tjuːʒn] *n.* (*formal*) bruise.

conundrum [kə'nʌndrəm] *n.* riddle.

conurbation [kɒnə'beɪʃn] *n.* very large spread of a built-up area.

convalesce [kɒnvə'les] *v.* to recover after an illness/an operation. **convalescence**, *n.* period when you are convalescing. **convalescent**, *adj.* & *n.* (person) who is convalescing; **c. home** = rest home for people who are convalescing.

convection [kən'vekʃn] *n.* upward movement of heat in air/liquid. **convector**, *n.* heater which warms the air moving through it.

convene [kən'viːn] *v.* to call together (a meeting). **convenor**, *n.* person who convenes.

convenience [kən'viːnɪəns] *n.* (*a*) suitableness; **at your earliest c.** = as soon as it suits you. (*b*) public toilet. (*c*) **all modern conveniences** = all modern comforts (in a house). (*d*) **c. foods** = dishes which are easy/quick to prepare. **convenient**, *adj.* suitable; practical. **conveniently**, *adv.* handily.

convent ['kɒnvənt] *n.* religious house for women.

convention [kən'venʃn] *n.* (*a*) custom/usual way of doing things. (*b*) contract. (*c*) congress/general meeting of an association/political party. **conventional**, *adj.* ordinary/usual; **c. weapons** = ordinary (not nuclear) weapons. **conventionally**, *adv.* in a conventional/ordinary/usual way.

converge [kən'vɜːdʒ] *v.* to come together at a certain place. **convergence**, *n.* meeting. **convergent**, *adj.* meeting at a certain point.

conversant [kən'vɜːsənt] *adj.* familiar (**with** a subject).

converse 1. *n.* ['kɒnvɜːs] the opposite. **2.** *v.* [kən'vɜːs] to talk. **conversation** [kɒnvə'seɪʃn] *n.* talk. **conversational**, *adj.* in conversation. **conversationalist**, *n.* person who converses well. **conversely**, *adv.* in the opposite way.

conversion [kən'vɜːʃn] *n.* (*a*) changing (of one thing into another). (*b*) turning of a person to another religion. (*c*) (in Rugby) converting a goal.

convert 1. *n.* ['kɒnvɜːt] person who has changed religion. **2.** *v.* [kən'vɜːt] (*a*) to turn (s.o.) from one religion to another. (*b*) to change; (in Rugby) **to c. a goal** = to kick the ball over the crossbar between the goal posts after a try has been scored. **converter**, *n.* machine which converts. **convertibility** [kənvɜːtɪ'bɪlɪtɪ] *n.* easiness of change of one currency to another. **convertible** [kən'vɜːtəbl] **1.** *adj.* which can easily be changed (esp. of a currency). **2.** *n.* car with a roof which folds back.

convex ['kɒnveks] *adj.* (surface) which is rounded outwards like the back of a spoon.

convey [kən'veɪ] *v.* to transport/to carry; to give (greetings, etc.). **conveyance**, *n.* (*a*) transporting. (*b*) means of transport. (*c*) transfer of property from one owner to another. **conveyancing**, *n.* transferring of property. **conveyor**, *n.* person who transports/thing which transports; **c. belt** = long moving surface used in a factory to move products through the production processes.

convict 1. *n.* ['kɒnvɪkt] criminal who has been sentenced to prison. **2.** *v.* [kən'vɪkt] to find (s.o.) guilty; to sentence (a criminal) to prison. **conviction** [kən'vɪkʃn] *n.* (*a*) being found guilty. (*b*) firm belief.

convince [kən'vɪns] *v.* **to c. s.o. of sth** = to persuade/to make (s.o.) believe sth. **convincing,** *adj.* (argument) which convinces. **convincingly,** *adv.* in a convincing way.

convivial [kən'vɪvɪəl] *adj.* lively/jolly. **conviviality** [kənvɪvɪ'ælɪtɪ] *n.* liveliness.

convoke [kən'vəʊk] *v.* to call (a meeting). **convocation** [kɒnvə'keɪʃn] *n.* (*a*) calling of a meeting. (*b*) meeting of a church assembly/university.

convoluted ['kɒnvəluːtɪd] *adj.* (*a*) twisted. (*b*) very complicated (story, etc.). **convolution** [kɒnvə'luːʃn] *n.* twisting; complication.

convolvulus [kən'vɒlvjʊləs] *n.* common climbing weed.

convoy ['kɒnvɔɪ] **1.** *n.* group of ships/ lorries travelling together in line under protection. **2.** *v.* to escort/to protect (esp. a line of merchant ships).

convulse [kən'vʌls] *v.* to make (sth/ s.o.) shake. **convulsions,** *n. pl.* violent shaking of the body; violent spasms which make the body twitch. **convulsive,** *adj.* which causes violent shaking.

coo [kuː] *v.* to make soft noises (like a pigeon). **cooing,** *n.* noise made by a pigeon.

cook [kʊk] **1.** *n.* person who prepares food by heating it. **2.** *v.* (*a*) to prepare (food) by heating. (*b*) (*of food*) to be prepared; **dinner is cooking.** (*c*) *inf.* **to c. the books/the accounts** = to falsify the entries in account books. **cookbook,** *n.* book of recipes. **cooker,** *n.* (*a*) stove for cooking. (*b*) cooking apple. **cookery,** *n.* (*no pl.*) art of cooking; **c. book** = cookbook. **cookie,** *n. Am.* biscuit. **cooking,** *n.* action of preparing food, usu. by heating; **c. apple** = sour green apple for cooking.

cool [kuːl] **1.** *adj.* (**-er, -est**) (*a*) quite cold. (*b*) calm. (*c*) unfriendly (reception). **2.** *n.* (*a*) state of being cool; place where it is cool; **in the c. of the evening.** (*b*) *Sl.* calmness; **she lost her c.** = she lost her temper. **3.** *v.* to make cool; to become cool. **coolant,** *n.* substance (usu. water) used

to keep engines cool. **cool down,** *v.* (*a*) to become cool. (*b*) to become calm. **cooler,** *n.* (*a*) thing/machine which cools. (*b*) *Sl.* prison. **cooling.** **1.** *adj.* refreshing (drink, etc.). **2.** *n.* action of becoming cool. **coolly,** *adv.* in a cool/ calm way. **coolness,** *n.* (*a*) being cool. (*b*) calmness. (*c*) unfriendliness (of a reception, etc.). **cool off,** *v.* to become cooler.

coolie ['kuːlɪ] *n.* workman/porter (in the Far East).

coop [kuːp] **1.** *n.* cage for chickens. **2.** *v.* **to be cooped up** = to be shut up inside.

co-op ['kəʊɒp] *n. inf.* cooperative stores.

cooper ['kuːpə] *n.* person who makes barrels.

cooperate [kəʊ'ɒpəreɪt] *v.* to work **with** s.o. **cooperation** [kəʊɒpə'reɪʃn] *n.* working together. **cooperative** [kəʊ-'ɒprətɪv] **1.** *adj. & n.* (shop, etc.) which works on a profit-sharing basis. **2.** *adj.* willing to work with s.o.

co-opt [kəʊ'ɒpt] *v.* to ask (s.o.) to join a committee without being formally elected to it. **co-option,** *n.* act of co-opting.

co-ordinate 1. *n.* [kəʊ'ɔːdɪnət] (*a*) set of figures which fix a point on a map/ graph. (*b*) **co-ordinates** = matching outer clothes for women. **2.** *v.* [kəʊ-'ɔːdɪneɪt] to make things work together/ fit in with each other. **co-ordination** [kəʊɔː'dɪneɪʃn] *n.* co-ordinating. **co-ordinator,** *n.* person who co-ordinates.

coot [kuːt] *n.* black water bird with a white forehead.

co-ownership [kəʊ'əʊnəʃɪp] *n.* ownership by several people or groups.

cop [kɒp] *n. inf.* policeman.

cope [kəʊp] **1.** *n.* long coloured cloak worn by a priest. **2.** *v.* to deal **with**.

copilot ['kəʊpaɪlət] *n.* pilot who is second in command to the captain of an aircraft.

coping ['kəʊpɪŋ] *n.* **c. stone** = top stone on a wall, which protects the wall from the weather.

copious ['kəʊpɪəs] *adj.* plentiful/in good supply. **copiously,** *adv.* in large quantities.

copper ['kɒpə] *n.* (*a*) (*element:* Cu) reddish metal which turns green when exposed to air. (*b*) large pan for boiling water and washing clothes. (*c*) *inf.* policeman. (*d*) small coin made of copper or other brown metal. **copperplate,** *n.* old-fashioned neat round handwriting.

coppice, copse ['kɒpɪs, kɒps] **1.** *n.* wood of young trees. **2.** *v.* **to coppice** = to cut trees down to the ground regularly, so as to produce strong straight shoots.

copra ['kɒprə] *n.* dried coconut kernel used to make oil.

copulate ['kɒpjʊleɪt] *v.* to have sexual intercourse. **copulation** [kɒpjʊ'leɪʃn] *n.* sexual intercourse.

copy ['kɒpɪ] **1.** *n.* (*a*) an imitation/ reproduction. (*b*) book; newspaper. (*c*) material to be used in a newspaper article/in an advertisement, etc. **2.** *v.* to imitate/to make a reproduction of (sth). **copier,** *n.* machine which makes copies. **copying,** *n.* imitation. **copyright,** *n.* right to publish a book/put on a play, etc., and not to have it copied without permission; **in c.** = protected by the laws of copyright. **copywriter,** *n.* person who writes copy for advertisements.

coquette [kɒ'ket] *n.* woman who flirts. **coquettish,** *adj.* flirtatious. **coquetry** ['kɒketrɪ] *n.* being coquettish.

coracle ['kɒrəkl] *n.* light round boat, made of skin.

coral ['kɒrəl] *n.* rock-like substance formed of the skeletons of tiny animals in the sea.

cor anglais ['kɔ:r'ɒŋgleɪ] *n.* bass oboe.

corbel ['kɔ:bl] *n.* piece of stone or wood which juts out from a wall and supports sth (usu. a roof beam).

cord [kɔ:d] *n.* (*a*) string/thin rope. (*b*) string-like part of the body; **spinal c.** (*c*) *inf.* **cords** = corduroy trousers.

cordial ['kɔ:dɪəl] **1.** *adj.* friendly. **2.** *n.* concentrated juice of a fruit to which water is added. **cordiality** [kɔ:dɪ'ælɪtɪ] *n.* friendliness. **cordially,** *adv.* in a cordial way.

cordite ['kɔ:daɪt] *n.* type of explosive.

cordon ['kɔ:dən] **1.** *n.* (*a*) barrier to prevent s.o. escaping; line of police/ soldiers surrounding a point. (*b*) fruit tree grown as a single stem, with side shoots cut back. **2.** *v.* **to c. off a street** = to put up a cordon across a street. **cordon bleu** [kɔ:dɒŋ'blɜ:] *adj.* top quality (cooking).

corduroy ['kɔ:djʊrɔɪ] *n.* velvet-like cloth with ribs.

core [kɔ:] **1.** *n.* central part; **rotten to the c.** = rotten right through; **to take a c. sample** = to cut a long round sample of rock with a drill. **2.** *v.* to scoop out the core of (an apple, etc.).

co-respondent [kəʊrɪ'spɒndənt] *n.* person cited in a divorce case.

corgi ['kɔ:gɪ] *n.* breed of small dogs, with short hair and pointed faces.

coriander [kɒrɪ'ændə] *n.* small plant, whose seeds and leaves are used for flavouring.

cork [kɔ:k] **1.** *n.* (*a*) (material made from) very light bark of a type of oak tree; **c. oak** = oak tree with very light bark. (*b*) stopper which closes wine bottles. **2.** *v.* to put a cork into (a bottle). **corkage,** *n.* charge made by a restaurant for uncorking a customer's own wine bottle. **corked,** *adj.* (wine) which has an unpleasant taste because of a rotting cork. **corkscrew,** *n.* special screwing device for taking corks out of bottles.

corm [kɔ:m] *n.* fat root which can be planted like a bulb.

cormorant ['kɔ:mərənt] *n.* large dark seabird which eats fish.

corn [kɔ:n] *n.* (*a*) cereal crops. (*b*) maize; **sweet c.** = maize grown for human consumption; **c. cob** = head of maize with many seeds. (*c*) painful hard growth (on a foot). **corncrake,** *n.* small bird which lives in cornfields. **cornfield,** *n.* field in which corn is grown. **cornflakes,** *n. pl.* breakfast cereal of crisp pieces of toasted maize. **cornflour,** *n.* maize powder, used in cooking. **cornflower,** *n.* blue flower growing in corn fields. **cornstarch,** *n. Am.* cornflour. **corny,** *adj.* (**-ier, -iest**) *inf.* old/out-of-date (joke).

cornea ['kɔ:nɪə] *n.* transparent covering of the eyeball. **corneal,** *adj.* referring to the cornea.

corned [kɔ:nd] *adj.* salted/preserved (beef).

corner ['kɔ:nə] **1.** *n.* (*a*) angle made by two flat surfaces joining; **she has turned the c.** = she is beginning to recover from an illness. (*b*) (*in football*) free kick taken from the corner of the pitch. **2.** *v.*

(*a*) to turn a corner. (*b*) to monopolize (a market). (*c*) to drive (s.o.) into a corner. **cornerstone,** *n*. (*a*) stone at the bottom of a corner of a building. (*b*) strong foundation/basis.

cornet ['kɔːnɪt] *n*. (*a*) cone-shaped biscuit for holding ice cream. (*b*) trumpet-like brass musical instrument.

cornice ['kɔːnɪs] *n*. decorated moulding round a ceiling/round the eaves (of a building).

cornucopia [kɔːnjuˈkəupɪə] *n*. (*formal*) horn overflowing with fruit and flowers, the symbol of rich harvest.

corolla [kəˈrɒlə] *n*. petals near the centre of a flower.

corollary [kəˈrɒlərɪ] *n*. natural result/thing which follows naturally.

corona [kəˈrəunə] *n*. ring of light; ring of light visible when the sun is totally eclipsed.

coronary ['kɒrənrɪ] *adj*. referring to the arteries to the heart; **c. thrombosis,** *inf*. **a c.** = heart attack caused by blocking of an artery.

coronation [kɒrəˈneɪʃn] *n*. crowning (of a king/queen/emperor).

coroner ['kɒrənə] *n*. person who directs a court to investigate sudden or accidental deaths.

coronet ['kɒrənət] *n*. small crown.

corporal ['kɔːprəl] **1**. *adj*. referring to the body; **c. punishment** = beating/whipping/caning. **2**. *n*. non-commissioned rank in the army below sergeant.

corporate ['kɔːpərət] *adj*. forming a body; **c. plan** = overall plan for a whole company. **corporation** [kɔːpəˈreɪʃn] *n*. (*a*) town council. (*b*) large firm. (*c*) *inf*. large stomach.

corps [kɔː] *n*. (*pl*. **corps** [kɔːz]) military or organized group.

corpse [kɔːps] *n*. dead body.

corpulent ['kɔːpjulənt] *adj*. fat. **corpulence,** *n*. fatness.

corpus ['kɔːpəs] *n*. all the works (of an author).

corpuscle ['kɔːpʌsl] *n*. red or white cell in blood.

corral [kɒˈrɑːl] *Am*. **1**. *n*. fence to enclose cattle. **2**. *v*. to enclose (cattle).

correct [kəˈrekt] **1**. *adj*. accurate/right/true. **2**. *v*. to show the mistakes in (sth); to remove the mistakes from (sth).

correction [kəˈrekʃn] *n*. making correct. **corrective,** *adj*. & *n*. (thing) which corrects. **correctly,** *adv*. accurately. **correctness,** *n*. accuracy (of answer, etc.); rightness (of clothes).

correlate ['kɒrəleɪt] *v*. to correspond to/to be linked to. **correlation** [kɒrəˈleɪʃn] *n*. correspondence/link.

correspond [kɒrɪˈspɒnd] *v*. (*a*) (**to**) to fit in with; to match. (*b*) to write letters; to exchange letters (**with** s.o.). **correspondence,** *n*. (*a*) matching. (*b*) exchange of letters; letters which have come; **c. course** = course of study taken at home with lessons sent by post. **correspondent,** *n*. person who writes letters; journalist who writes articles for newspapers on particular subjects. **corresponding,** *adj*. which fits/matches. **correspondingly,** *adv*. in a similar way.

corridor ['kɒrɪdɔː] *n*. long, narrow passage.

corrigenda [kɒrɪˈdʒendə] *pl. n*. corrections (in a text).

corroborate [kəˈrɒbəreɪt] *v*. to confirm (a statement). **corroboration** [kərɒbəˈreɪʃn] *n*. confirmation of a statement. **corroboratory,** *adj*. which corroborates.

corrode [kəˈrəud] *v*. to rot (metal); to rust. **corrosion** [kəˈrəuʒn] *n*. rusting/eating away (of metal). **corrosive** [kəˈrəusɪv] *adj*. & *n*. (substance) which eats away metal.

corrugated ['kɒrəgeɪtɪd] *adj*. bent into waves; **c. iron; c. paper.**

corrupt [kəˈrʌpt] **1**. *adj*. not honest; (judge, etc.) who takes bribes. **2**. *v*. to make dishonest/to bribe. **corruptibility** [kərʌptəˈbɪlɪtɪ] *n*. being corruptible. **corruptible,** *adj*. (person) who can be bribed. **corruption** [kəˈrʌpʃn] *n*. dishonesty/bribery.

corsage [kɔːˈsɑːʒ] *n*. flowers worn on the front of a dress.

corset ['kɔːsɪt] *n*. tight underwear worn by women to support their bodies.

cortege [kɔːˈteɪʒ] *n*. (*formal*) procession at a funeral.

cortex ['kɔːteks] *n*. outer covering of part of the body, esp. the brain.

cortisone ['kɔːtɪzəun] *n*. hormone medicine used against skin allergies/arthritis, etc.

corvette [kɔː'vet] *n.* small naval gunboat.

cos [kɒz] *n. short for* **cosine. cos lettuce** ['kɒs'letɪs] *n.* type of tall lettuce.

cosh [kɒʃ] **1.** *n. (pl. -es) inf.* short stick for hitting. **2.** *v. inf.* to hit s.o. on the head.

cosine ['kəʊsaɪn] *n. (in mathematics)* ratio between the length of a side forming an acute angle to that of the hypotenuse in a right-angled triangle.

cosmetic [kɒz'metɪk] *adj. & n.* (substance) used in beautifying the face/in improving the look of sth.; **c. surgery** = surgery to improve someone's appearance.

cosmic ['kɒzmɪk] *adj.* referring to the universe. **cosmonaut,** *n.* Soviet astronaut. **cosmos,** *n. (formal)* the universe.

cosmopolitan [kɒzmə'pɒlɪtən] *adj. (a)* made up of people from different parts of the world. *(b)* at ease in different cities/with people of different nationalities.

cosset ['kɒsɪt] *v.* to spoil (s.o.) with comfort.

cost [kɒst] **1.** *n.* amount which you have to pay for sth; **at all costs** = at no matter what price; **c. of living** = money paid for food, clothing, housing, etc., shown as a monthly index figure. **2.** *v. (a)* **(cost)** to have a price of. *(b)* **(costed)** to calculate the price for (sth). **costing,** *n.* calculation of a selling price. **costliness,** *n.* expensiveness. **costly,** *adj.* **(-ier, -iest)** expensive.

co-star ['kəʊstɑː] **1.** *n.* famous actor/actress starring in a film/play with other famous actors/actresses. **2.** *v.* **(co-starred)** to act in a play/film as a co-star.

costermonger ['kɒstəmʌŋgə] *n.* person who sells things from a barrow in the street.

costume ['kɒstjuːm] *n. (a)* set of clothes; **bathing/swimming c.** = woman's swimsuit; **c. jewellery** = cheap imitation jewellery. *(b)* set of clothes for the theatre.

cosy ['kəʊzɪ] **1.** *adj.* **(-ier, -iest)** warm and comfortable. **2.** *n.* woollen cover (for a teapot, etc.). **cosily,** *adv.* comfortably/warmly. **cosiness,** *n.* being cosy.

cot [kɒt] *n.* child's bed with sides; **c. death** = sudden unexplained death of a sleeping baby, possibly caused by overheating.

cottage ['kɒtɪdʒ] *n.* little house in the country; **c. cheese** = soft white cheese made from curds; **c. pie** = minced meat cooked with mashed potatoes on top; **c. industry** = handicrafts made in people's houses. **cottager,** *n.* person who lives in a cottage.

cotter pin ['kɒtəpɪn] *n.* pin with a split end, used to hold parts of a machine together.

cotton ['kɒtn] **1.** *n. (a)* fibre from the downy seed heads of a tropical plant. *(b)* cloth made of this fibre. *(c)* thread (for sewing). **2.** *v. inf.* **to c. on** = to understand. **cotton candy,** *n. Am.* candyfloss. **cotton wool,** *n.* fluffy cotton stuff, used for wiping wounds, applying ointment, etc.

cotyledon [kɒtɪ'liːdən] *n.* first leaf on a seedling.

couch [kaʊtʃ] *n. (pl. -es)* sofa/low bed. **couch grass** [kuːtʃ] *n.* weedlike grass which spreads from underground roots.

couchette [kuː'ʃet] *n.* folding bed in a train.

cougar ['kuːgə] *n. Am.* large brown American wild cat.

cough [kɒf] **1.** *n.* sending air out of the lungs suddenly because of an irritation in the throat; **c. pastille** = medicated sweet sucked to relieve irritation in the throat. **2.** *v.* to send air out of the lungs suddenly because of irritation; *Sl.* **to c. up** = to pay. **coughing,** *n.* series of coughs.

could, couldn't [kʊd, 'kʊdnt] *v. see* **can.**

coulomb ['kuːlɒm] *n.* unit of the quantity of electricity passed in one second over a given point by a current of one ampere.

coulter ['kuːltə] *n.* blade of a plough.

council ['kaʊnsl] *n.* elected committee; *esp.* **town c.** = elected committee which runs the affairs of a town; **c. house** = house rented out by a town council; **c. estate** = group of council houses or flats; **c. chamber** = room in which a town council meets. **councillor,** *n.* elected member of a town council.

counsel ['kaʊnsl] **1.** *n. (a)* advice. *(b)* lawyer/barrister. **counselling,** *n.* giving advice. **counsellor,** *n.* adviser.

count [kaʊnt] **1.** *n.* (*a*) action of counting/adding figures; **to lose c.** = to have no longer any idea of what the total is. (*b*) accusation. (*c*) lower rank of noble. **2.** *v.* (*a*) to add up a total. (*b*) to say numbers in order. (*c*) to rely (**on**). (*d*) to be important. **count down,** *v.* to count backwards (9, 8, 7, 6, etc.). **countdown,** *n.* counting backwards. **counting,** *n.* action of adding up a total. **countless,** *adj.* which cannot be counted/numerous.

countenance ['kaʊntnəns] **1.** *n.* (*formal*) face. **2.** *v.* (*formal*) to approve of (s.o.'s action).

counter ['kaʊntə] **1.** *n.* (*a*) machine which counts. (*b*) small round disc used in games. (*c*) long flat surface in a shop for displaying goods, or in a bank for placing money. **2.** *adj., adv. & prefix.* opposite (**to**). **3.** *v.* (*a*) to stop/to block. (*b*) to reply with an opposing response. **counteract,** *v.* to neutralize/to stop the effects of (sth). **counter-attack. 1.** *n.* attack in return/attack against s.o. who has just attacked you. **2.** *v.* to attack in return. **counter-attraction,** *n.* attraction aimed at luring customers away from a rival. **counterbalance,** *v.* to compensate for a force in one direction by going in the opposite direction. **counterblast,** *n.* strong written or spoken reply to an attack. **countercharge,** *n.* accusation against s.o. who has just accused you. **counterclaim,** *n.* claim made in response to another claim. **counterclockwise,** *adj. & adv. Am.* anticlockwise. **counter-demonstration,** *n.* rival/opposed demonstration in reply to a demonstration. **counter-espionage,** *n.* secret service working against spies. **counterfeit** ['kaʊntəfɪt] **1.** *adj.* false/forged (money). **2.** *v.* to forge/to make false money. **counterfoil,** *n.* slip of paper which you retain after giving s.o. a cheque/an invoice, etc. **countermand,** *v.* to say that (an order) should not be carried out. **countermeasure,** *n.* way of stopping the effects of sth. **counterpane,** *n.* bedcover. **counterpart,** *n.* person who has a similar job/is in a similar situation; parallel thing. **counterpoint,** *n.* combination of melodies in a piece of music. **counterpoise,** *n.* heavy weight which counterbalances. **counter-productive,** *adj.* which produces a contrary effect to the one intended. **Counter Reformation,** *n.* movement in the Catholic church in the 16th century, a response to the Protestant Reformation. **counter-revolution,** *n.* revolt against a revolution. **counter-revolutionary,** *adj. & n.* (person who is) in revolt against a revolution. **countersign,** *v.* to sign (a document) which s.o. else has signed, in order to authorize it. **countersink,** *v.* (**countersank; countersunk**) to make a hole for the head of (a nail or screw) to fit into so that it is level with the surface.

country ['kʌntrɪ] *n.* (*a*) political or geographical unit of land. (*b*) region. (*c*) not town; **in the c. countrified,** *adj.* like the country. **countryman,** *n.* (*pl.* **-men**) person who comes from the same country as you. **countryside,** *n.* the country/the land (excluding towns and cities).

county ['kaʊntɪ] *n.* (*a*) small administrative district; **c. court** = court in England and Wales which hears minor civil cases; **c. town** = main town of a county. (*b*) *inf.* upper-class landowners.

coup [ku:] *n.* (*pl.* **coups** [ku:z]) (*a*) coup d'état. (*b*) successful move. **coup d'état** [ku:deɪ'ta:] *n.* armed overthrow of a government.

coupé ['ku:peɪ] *n.* car with two doors and a fixed roof.

couple ['kʌpl] **1.** *n.* pair/two things/two people together; two people together, esp. a man and a woman; a husband and wife; **a c. of** = (i) two; (ii) a few. **2.** *v.* to link together. **couplet,** *n.* two lines of poetry which rhyme. **coupling,** *n.* metal links for joining two pieces of machinery/two wagons together.

coupon ['ku:pɒn] *n.* piece of paper which acts in place of money/in place of a ticket; **football c.** = form on which you fill up your forecast for the football pools.

courage ['kʌrɪdʒ] *n.* (*no pl.*) bravery. **courageous** [kə'reɪdʒəs] *adj.* brave. **courageously,** *adv.* bravely.

courgette [kʊə'ʒet] *n.* very small marrow.

courier ['kʊrɪə] *n.* person who carries messages; a guide with a package tour.

course [kɔːs] **1.** *n.* (*a*) passing of time; **in the c. of** =during; **in due c.** = eventually. (*b*) road; direction. (*c*) **of c.** = naturally; **as a matter of c.** = in the usual way. (*d*) series of lessons; book/ series of books for studying. (*e*) series of treatments for an illness. (*f*) dish of food for a meal. (*g*) track (for racing). (*h*) **golf c.** = area of land specially designed for playing golf. (*i*) line of bricks (in a wall). **2.** *v.* to flow fast.

court [kɔːt] **1.** *n.* (*a*) tribunal where a judge (and jury) try criminals. (*b*) group of people living round a king or queen. (*c*) area where a game of tennis/squash, etc., is played. **2.** *v.* (*a*) to try to persuade (a woman) to marry you. (*b*) to look for; to try to win (praise, etc.); to risk (disaster). **courteous** ['kɜːtjəs] *adj.* very polite. **courteously**, *adv.* politely. **courtesy** ['kɜːtəsɪ] *n.* politeness; **by c. of** = with the kind permission of; **c. car** = free car waiting for hotel guests at an airport. **courtier** ['kɔːtjə] *n.* member of a royal court. **court-martial** [kɔːt'mɑːʃl] **1.** *n.* trial of a soldier by other soldiers. **2.** *v.* (**court-martialled**) to try (a soldier). **courtroom**, *n.* room where a trial is held. **courtship**, *n.* courting a woman. **courtyard**, *n.* square yard surrounded by buildings.

cousin ['kʌzn] *n.* son or daughter of an uncle or aunt.

couturier [kuː'tjʊrɪeɪ] *n.* dress-designer.

cove [kəʊv] *n.* (*a*) small bay. (*b*) *inf.* man.

coven ['kʌvn] *n.* group of witches.

covenant ['kʌvənənt] **1.** *n.* contract/ agreement; **deed of c.** = official signed agreement (to pay s.o. a sum each year). **2.** *v.* to agree by contract.

Coventry ['kɒvəntrɪ] *n.* **to send s.o. to C.** = to refuse to speak to s.o.

cover ['kʌvə] **1.** *n.* (*a*) thing which is put over sth to protect it; **under c. of night** = under the protection of the dark. (*b*) lid. (*c*) (cardboard) binding of a book; outer pages of a magazine. (*d*) shelter; **to take c.** (*e*) protection (guaranteed by insurance). **2.** *v.* (*a*) to put sth over (sth) to protect it. (*b*) to travel (a certain

distance). (*c*) to point a gun at. (*d*) to be enough to pay for. (*e*) to deal with. (*f*) to protect with insurance. (*g*) to be a reporter at (an event). **coverage**, *n.* amount of space/time devoted to an event in a newspaper/on TV. **covering**. **1.** *n.* thing which covers. **2.** *adj.* **c. letter** = explanatory letter sent with a form/ with another letter, etc. **cover up**, *v.* to hide completely. **cover-up**, *n.* hiding (of a scandal).

coverlet ['kʌvələt] *n.* cover for a bed.

covert ['kʌvət] *adj.* (*formal*) hidden/ secret.

covet ['kʌvɪt] *v.* to want (sth which belongs to s.o. else). **covetous**, *adj.* wanting sth which belongs to s.o. else.

covey ['kʌvɪ] *n.* group (of partridges).

cow [kaʊ] **1.** *n.* (*a*) female animal of the bull family kept to give milk. (*b*) female of certain animals, e.g. the elephant. (*c*) (*in Australia*) *Sl.* unpleasant thing/person. **2.** *v.* to frighten. **cowboy**, *n.* (*a*) man who drives herds of cattle in America. (*b*) *inf.* bad workman who charges too much. **cowhand**, **cowherd**, **cowman**, *n.* man who looks after cattle. **cow parsley**, *n.* common wild plant with tall white flowers. **cowpat**, *n.* round flat cake of cow dung. **cowshed**, *n.* shed for cows. **cowslip**, *n.* common yellow wild flower.

coward ['kaʊəd] *n.* person who is not brave. **cowardice**, *n.* lack of bravery. **cowardly**, *adj.* not brave.

cower ['kaʊə] *v.* to crouch down because of fear.

cowl [kaʊl] *n.* hood (for a monk's habit); cover for a chimney. **cowling**, *n.* cover for an engine.

cowrie ['kaʊrɪ] *n.* colourful seashell.

cox [kɒks] **1.** *n.* (*pl.* **-es**) person who steers a rowing boat. **2.** *v.* to steer a rowing boat. **coxed**, *adj.* (boat) with a cox. **coxless**, *adj.* (boat) without a cox.

coxswain ['kɒksn] *n.* (*a*) officer in charge of a boat. (*b*) person who steers a rowing boat. **coxwainless**, *adj.* coxless.

coy [kɔɪ] *adj.* timid; shy. **coyly**, *adv.* in a coy way. **coyness**, *n.* being coy.

coyote [kɔɪ'əʊtɪ] *n.* small American wolf.

coypu ['kɔɪpu:] *n*. small animal like a beaver.

CPU [si:pi:'ju:] central processing unit.

crab [kræb] *n*. edible ten-footed crustacean with large pincers, which walks sideways; **to catch a c.** = to miss a stroke when rowing; **c. apple** = bitter wild apple. **crabbed**, *adj*. (*a*) bad-tempered. (*b*) (handwriting) which is difficult to read. **crabby**, *adj. inf.* bad-tempered.

crack [kræk] **1**. *n*. (*a*) sharp dry sound. (*b*) sharp blow. (*c*) thin break; split; **at c. of dawn** = at daybreak. (*d*) *inf.* **to have a c. at sth** = to try to do sth. (*e*) *Sl.* strong form of cocaine. **2**. *adj. inf.* first-class. **3**. *v*. (*a*) to make a sharp sound. (*b*) to make a thin split in (sth). (*c*) **to c. jokes** = to tell jokes. (*d*) *inf.* **get cracking!** = start (working, etc.); **cracking pace** = very fast pace. (*e*) to decipher (a code). **crack down on**, *v. inf.* to campaign against. **cracker**, *n*. (*a*) small firework which makes a bang. (*b*) paper tube which makes a little explosion when it is pulled. (*c*) dry unsweetened biscuit. **crackers**, *adj. inf.* mad. **crackpot**, *adj. & n. inf.* mad (person). **crack up**, *v. inf.* (*a*) to praise (sth) extravagantly. (*b*) to collapse.

crackle ['krækl] **1**. *n*. small explosive sounds. **2**. *v*. to make little explosive sounds. **crackling**, *n*. hard cooked pork skin.

cradle ['kreɪdl] **1**. (*a*) baby's bed which can be rocked. (*b*) support (for a piece of machinery). (*c*) starting point (for civilization, etc.). **2**. *v*. to rock (in your arms).

craft [krɑ:ft] *n*. (*a*) artistry; skill; **crafts** = types of work done by hand. (*b*) ship. (*c*) cunning; slyness. **craftily**, *adv*. cunningly. **craftiness**, *n*. cunning; slyness. **craftsman**, *n*. (*pl*. **-men**) artist; person who is expert in using his hands. **craftsmanship**, *n*. skill of a craftsman. **crafty**, *adj*. (**-ier, -iest**) sly.

crag [kræg] *n*. steep rock cliff. **craggy**, *adj*. rough (rock or person's face).

cram [kræm] *v*. (**crammed**) (*a*) to squeeze (**into**). (*b*) to learn facts hurriedly before an examination. **cram-full**, *adj*. very full; overflowing.

cramp [kræmp] **1**. *n*. sudden pain where the muscles tighten up and cannot be relaxed. **2**. *v*. to hinder; to squeeze tight.

crampon, *n*. metal hook/spike attached to boots for climbing in ice and snow.

cranberry ['krænbərɪ] *n*. wild red edible berry.

crane [kreɪn] **1**. *n*. (*a*) tall metal construction for lifting heavy weights. (*b*) long-legged tropical bird. **2**. *v*. to stretch (one's neck). **cranefly**, *n*. common insect with long legs.

cranium ['kreɪnɪəm] *n*. bones covering the top part of the skull. **cranial**, *adj*. referring to the cranium; **c. nerves** = the nerves which link the brain with the head and neck.

crank [kræŋk] **1**. *n*. (*a*) shaft with a right-angled bend, used for communicating motion. (*b*) very odd person. **2**. *v*. to turn or lift with a crank. **crankshaft**, *n*. rod which is turned by a crank. **cranky**, *adj*. odd/bizarre (person).

cranny ['krænɪ] *n*. small crack/small gap.

crap [kræp] *n. sl.* shit/rubbish. **craps** [kræps] *n. Am.* game played with two dice.

crash [kræʃ] **1**. *n*. (*pl*. **-es**) (*a*) loud noise. (*b*) accident; **c. helmet** = helmet worn by motorcyclists to protect them in case of a crash; **c. barrier** = strong fence by the side of a road to prevent cars from running off the road. (*c*) financial collapse. (*d*) complete breakdown of a computer. **2**. *v*. (*a*) to explode; to make a great noise. (*b*) to be damaged/destroyed in an accident; **to c. into** = to hit in an accident. (*c*) to collapse financially. (*d*) (*of a computer*) to break down completely. **3**. *adj*. urgent; **a c. course** = very rapid course. **crash-land**, *v*. to land heavily, without using the undercarriage, so that the aircraft is damaged. **crash-landing**, *n*. act of landing heavily.

crass [kræs] *adj*. (*a*) rude/coarse. (*b*) complete.

crate [kreɪt] **1**. *n*. large rough wooden box. **2**. *v*. to put into a crate.

crater ['kreɪtə] *n*. hole at the top of a volcano; hole made by a bomb.

cravat [krə'væt] *n*. type of scarf worn by men knotted round the neck in place of a tie.

crave [kreɪv] *v*. to want (sth) very much. **craving**, *n*. strong desire (**for**).

craven ['kreɪvn] *adj.* cowardly.

crawl [krɔ:l] **1.** *n.* (*a*) creeping on hands and knees. (*b*) fast swimming stroke with arms going overarm. (*c*) very slow progress. **2.** *v.* (*a*) to move around on hands and knees. (*b*) to creep along slowly. (*c*) to be covered (**with** creeping things).

crayfish ['kreɪfɪʃ] *n.* (*pl.* **crayfish**) kind of fresh-water crustacean like a small lobster.

crayon ['kreɪɒn] *n.* stick of coloured material for drawing.

craze [kreɪz] *n.* mania (**for** sth). **crazily,** *adv.* madly. **craziness,** *n.* madness. **crazy,** *adj.* (**-ier, -iest**) mad; **c. paving** = different-shaped paving stones fitted together.

creak [kri:k] **1.** *n.* squeaky cracking noise. **2.** *v.* to make a squeaky cracking noise. **creaky,** *adj.* which makes a creaking noise.

cream [kri:m] **1.** *n.* (*a*) rich fatty part of milk; **single c.** = runny cream; **double c.** = thick cream; **c. cheese** = rich soft cheese; **the c. of the undergraduates** = the top few. (*b*) smooth paste; **face c. 2.** *adj.* coloured like cream; very pale fawn. **3.** *v.* (*a*) (**off**) to take away the best. (*b*) to whip into a smooth paste. **creamery,** *n.* dairy. **creamy,** *adj.* (**-ier, -iest**) smooth; full of cream.

crease [kri:s] **1.** *n.* fold made by ironing; fold made accidentally. **2.** *v.* (*a*) to iron a fold into (sth). (*b*) to make folds accidentally in (sth).

create [krɪ'eɪt] *v.* (*a*) to make; to invent. (*b*) *inf.* to make a disturbance/a fuss. **creation** [krɪ'eɪʃn] *n.* thing which has been made. **creative,** *adj.* full of ideas; always making sth. **creativity** [krɪeɪ-'tɪvɪtɪ] *n.* aptitude for creating. **creator,** *n.* person who makes/invents sth.

creature ['kri:tʃə] *n.* animal; person.

crèche [kreʃ] *n.* nursery where babies can be left while their parents are at work, etc.

credence ['kri:dəns] *n.* belief (that sth is correct/true).

credentials [krɪ'denʃəlz] *n. pl.* papers which prove your identity or rank so that people can trust you.

credible ['kredɪbl] *adj.* which can be believed. **credibility** [kredɪ'bɪlɪtɪ] *n.*

ability to be believed; **he suffers from a c. gap** = people do not believe him. **credibly,** *adv.* reliably.

credit ['kredɪt] **1.** *n.* (*a*) merit; recognition of quality; **it does you c.** = you are to be praised for it; **he's a c. to the school** = he has made the school proud of him. (*b*) belief; faith. (*c*) time given to pay; **c. card** = card which allows you to buy goods without having to pay immediately; **on c.** = without paying immediately. (*d*) side of an account showing money in hand or which is owed to you; **c. note** = note showing that money is owed you. (*e*) **credits** = list of actors'/directors' names which appear at the beginning or end of a film/ TV programme. **2.** *v.* (**credited**) (*a*) **to c. s.o. with** = to attribute a quality, etc., to s.o. (*b*) to believe. (*c*) to promise to pay (s.o.); to pay money into (an account). **creditable,** *adj.* honourable (deed). **creditably,** *adv.* honourably. **creditor,** *n.* person who is owed money.

credulous ['kredjʊləs] *adj.* (person) who believes anything easily. **credulity** [krɪ'dju:lɪtɪ], **credulousness,** *n.* belief/ trust. **credulously,** *adv.* in a credulous way.

creed [kri:d] *n.* statement of what you believe; **the Apostles' C.** = the statement of Christian faith.

creek [kri:k] *n.* little inlet of the sea; *Am.* small river.

creel [kri:l] *n.* basket to put fish in.

creep [kri:p] **1.** *n.* (*a*) *inf.* sly, unpleasant person. (*b*) **he gives me the creeps** = he makes me shudder. **2.** *v.* (**crept** [krept]) (*a*) to move around stealthily. (*b*) **creeping plant** = plant which spreads close to the ground/which climbs up a wall. (*c*) **it made my flesh c.** = it made me shudder. **creeper,** *n.* plant which climbs over walls. **creepy,** *adj.* (**-ier, -iest**) *inf.* which makes you shudder. **creepy-crawly** *n. inf.* insect.

cremate [krɪ'meɪt] *v.* to burn (a dead body). **cremation,** *n.* burning of a dead body. **crematorium** [kremə'tɔ:rɪəm] *n.* (*pl.* **-ia**) place where bodies are burnt.

crenellated ['krənəleɪtɪd] *adj.* (castle wall) with openings to shoot through.

creole ['kri:əʊl] *adj. & n.* (person) of mixed West Indian and European descent.

creosote ['krɪəsəʊt] **1.** *n.* dark brown liquid, used for protecting wood from rotting. **2.** *v.* to paint with creosote.

crepe [kreɪp] *n.* (*a*) **c. paper** = slightly crinkly coloured paper; **c. bandage** = bandage made of wrinkled elastic cloth. (*b*) **c. soles** = thick wrinkled rubber soles for shoes.

crept [krept] *v. see* **creep.**

crescendo [krɪ'ʃendəʊ] *n.* (*pl.* **-os**) increasing noise (esp. in music).

crescent ['kresnt] *n.* (*a*) curved shape, like a new moon. (*b*) street which forms a semicircle.

cress [kres] *n.* (*no pl.*) small green salad plant, usu. eaten with seedlings of mustard.

crest [krest] *n.* (*a*) top (of hills/waves). (*b*) plumes/fleshy growth on the head of a bird. (*c*) coat of arms. **crestfallen,** *adj.* discouraged/depressed.

cretin ['kretɪn] *n.* person who is mentally weak; *inf.* very stupid person. **cretinous,** *adj.* very stupid.

crevasse [krɪ'væs] *n.* deep crack in a glacier.

crevice ['krevɪs] *n.* small crack in a rock/wall.

crew [kru:] *n.* (*a*) people who work a boat/aircraft/bus, etc. (*b*) gang. **crewcut,** *n.* very short haircut.

crib [krɪb] **1.** *n.* (*a*) manger/box for food for horses or cows. (*b*) baby's bed. (*c*) model of the scene of the first Christmas displayed in a church at Christmas time. (*d*) word-for-word translation/list of answers to help a bad student with homework. **2.** *v.* (**cribbed**) to copy.

cribbage ['krɪbɪdʒ] *n.* card game where the points are marked by pegs on a special board.

crick [krɪk] **1.** *n.* **c. in the neck** = sprain/pulled muscle in the neck. **2.** *v.* to pull a muscle in (one's neck).

cricket ['krɪkɪt] *n.* (*a*) small jumping insect, like a grasshopper. (*b*) game played between two teams of eleven players using bats, hard balls and wickets as targets; *inf.* **it isn't c.** = it is not fair. **cricketer,** *n.* person who plays cricket.

crime [kraɪm] *n.* illegal act. **criminal** ['krɪmɪnl] **1.** *adj.* referring to an illegal act. **2.** *n.* person who commits a crime.

criminally, *adv.* so bad as to be against the law. **criminology** [krɪmɪ'nɒlədʒɪ] *n.* study of crime.

crimp [krɪmp] *v.* to press into waves or folds.

crimson ['krɪmzn] *adj. & n.* deep red colour.

cringe [krɪndʒ] *v.* (*a*) to bend to avoid a blow. (*b*) to be excessively humble.

crinkle ['krɪŋkl] *v.* to fold making many small creases. **crinkly,** *adj.* (**-ier, -iest**) with many creases/curls.

crinoline ['krɪnəli:n] *n.* (*old*) very wide skirt.

cripple ['krɪpl] **1.** *n.* person who is disabled or lame. **2.** *v.* (*a*) to make (s.o.) disabled. (*b*) to prevent (a machine/a factory) from working.

crisis ['kraɪsɪs] *n.* (*pl.* **crises** ['kraɪsi:z]) critical moment; turning point.

crisp [krɪsp] **1.** *adj.* (**-er, -est**) dry and brittle; sharp/cold (air); crunchy (lettuce). **2.** *n.* (**potato**) **crisps** = thin slices of potato fried until they are crisp. **crispness,** *n.* being crisp. **crispy,** *adj.* very crisp.

criss-cross ['krɪskrɒs] **1.** *adj.* with lines crossing in two directions. **2.** *v.* to go backwards and forwards in different directions.

criterion [kraɪ'tɪərɪən] *n.* (*pl.* **criteria**) standard by which things are judged.

critic ['krɪtɪk] *n.* (*a*) person who examines sth and comments on it, esp. person who writes comments on new plays and films for a newspaper. (*b*) person who comments unfavourably on sth/who finds fault with sth. **critical,** *adj.* (*a*) dangerous (situation); extremely urgent/important (decision); very serious (medical condition). (*b*) unfavourable (comment). **critically,** *adv.* in a critical way. **criticism** ['krɪtɪsɪzəm] *n.* (*a*) comment; **literary c.** = comment on a work of literature. (*b*) unfavourable comment. **criticize,** *v.* to comment unfavourably on (sth). **critique** [krɪ'ti:k] *n.* piece of careful literary criticism.

croak [krəʊk] **1.** *n.* hoarse noise (like that made by frogs). **2.** *v.* to make a hoarse sound. **croaky,** *adj.* (**-ier, -iest**) hoarse (voice).

crochet ['krəʊʃeɪ] **1.** *n.* type of knitting

using one needle with a hook at the end. **2.** *v.* (**crocheted** ['krəʊʃeɪd]; **crocheting** ['krəʊʃeɪŋ]) to make (sth) using a hooked needle. **crochet-hook,** *n.* hooked needle for crocheting.

crock [krɒk] *n.* (*a*) rough earthenware pot. (*b*) *inf.* broken-down car or person. **crockery,** *n.* (*no pl.*) rough pottery tableware.

crocodile ['krɒkədaɪl] *n.* (*a*) large meat-eating reptile living in rivers in Africa; **she wept c. tears** = she pretended to cry when she was not in any way sad. (*b*) long line of schoolchildren walking in pairs.

crocus ['krəʊkəs] *n.* (*pl.* **-es**) purple, yellow or white spring flower.

croft [krɒft] *n.* (*in Scotland*) small farm held by a tenant. **crofter,** *n.* farmer who holds a croft.

croissant ['krwæsɒŋ] *n.* rolled pastry, made in the shape of a crescent.

crone [krəʊn] *n.* ugly old witch.

crony ['krəʊnɪ] *n.* old friend.

crook [krʊk] **1.** *n.* (*a*) bend. (*b*) long stick with a bent top; (*c*) *inf.* criminal. **2.** *adj.* (*in Australia*) *Sl.* ill. **crooked** ['krʊkɪd] *adj.* (*a*) bent. (*b*) dishonest. **crookedly,** *adv.* in a bent way; not straight.

croon [kruːn] *v.* to sing in a low voice. **crooner,** *n.* person who croons.

crop [krɒp] **1.** *n.* (*a*) vegetables/grain, etc., grown for food. (*b*) part of a bird's throat shaped like a bag. (*c*) small whip used by a rider. (*d*) short haircut. **2.** *v.* (**cropped**) (*a*) to cut (a hedge/s.o.'s hair) short. (*b*) (*of sheep*) to eat (grass) so that it is very short. **cropper,** *n.* *inf.* **he came a c.** = (i) he fell badly; (ii) his plans did not succeed. **crop up,** *v.* to occur.

croquet ['krəʊkeɪ] *n.* lawn game played with hoops, balls and mallets.

croquette [krə'ket] *n.* small ball of mashed potato, covered with bread-crumbs and fried.

crosier ['krəʊzɪə] *n.* staff (like a crook) carried by a bishop.

cross [krɒs] **1.** *n.* (*a*) shape with two lines cutting across each other at right angles. (*b*) shape of a vertical line, with another cutting across it at right angles, forming the symbol of the Christian church; wooden construction of this shape; **the Red C.** = international rescue and medical organisation. (*c*) thing which is hard to bear. (*d*) mixture of two breeds; mixture of two different things. **2.** *v.* (*a*) **to c. oneself** = to make a sign of the cross on oneself. (*b*) to put two lines across (a cheque) so that it can only be paid into a bank account. (*c*) to go across; to place across; **crossed line** = telephone connection where you can hear other people talking. (*d*) to breed (two animals/plants) together. **3.** *adj.* (*a*) opposed/contrary; **they are at c. purposes** = they are in disagreement; **to talk at c. purposes** = to misunderstand what each other is saying. (*b*) bad-tempered/angry. **crossbar,** *n.* beam which goes across a space. **crossbill,** *n.* type of bird, with a bill of which the top part crosses over the bottom. **crossbreed,** *n.* animal produced by crossing two animals of different breeds. **crosscheck,** *v.* to check again to make sure. **cross-country,** *adj.* & *n.* (race) across fields and along roads, not on a track. **cross-examination,** *n.* searching questioning by an opposing lawyer. **cross-examine,** *v.* to ask (s.o.) searching questions. **crosseyed,** *adj.* (person) whose eyes do not face forward; (person) with a squint. **cross-fertilize,** *v.* to fertilize (one plant) with another variety. **crossfire,** *n.* gunfire from two directions, so that the fire crosses. **cross-grained,** *adj.* bad-tempered. **crossing,** *n.* (*a*) act of going across. (*b*) place where you cross; **pedestrian c.** = place where pedestrians can cross a street; **level c.** = place where a road crosses a railway line. **crosslegged,** *adj.* & *adv.* with one ankle over the other. **crossly,** *adv.* in an angry way. **cross off, cross out,** *v.* to draw a line through (sth written). **cross-question,** *v.* to cross-examine. **cross-questioning,** *n.* cross-examining. **cross-reference,** *n.* line in a reference book telling you to look in another section for further information. **crossroads,** *n.* *pl.* place where two roads cross. **cross-section,** *n.* (*a*) diagram as if a cut had been made across sth. (*b*) sample. **crosswalk,** *n.* *Am.* pedestrian crossing. **crosswind,**

n. wind blowing across a road, etc. **crosswise,** *adv.* in the shape of a cross. **crossword,** *n.* puzzle where small squares have to be filled with letters forming words to which clues are given.

crosse [krɒs] *n.* stick with a net, used in playing lacrosse.

crotch [krɒtʃ] *n.* (*pl.* **-es**) place where the two legs fork.

crotchet ['krɒtʃɪt] *n.* note in music lasting two quavers or half as long as a minim. **crotchety,** *adj.* (*a*) bad-tempered. (*b*) odd/slightly mad; capricious.

crouch [kraʊtʃ] *v.* to bend down low.

croup [kru:p] *n.* (*a*) infection in the throat, which makes children cough noisily. (*b*) rear part of a horse.

croupier ['kru:pɪə] *n.* person who is in charge of a gaming table.

crow [krəʊ] **1.** *n.* large common black bird; **as the c. flies** = in a straight line. **2.** *v.* (*a*) (*of a cockerel*) to call. (*b*) **to c. over s.o.** = to exclaim happily because you have beaten s.o. **crowbar,** *n.* large metal lever for opening boxes. **crow's-feet,** *n.* little wrinkles at the outer corners of the eyes. **crow's nest,** *n.* platform on top of a mast for a lookout.

crowd [kraʊd] **1.** *n.* mass of people. **2.** *v.* to group together.

crown [kraʊn] **1.** *n.* (*a*) gold and jewelled headdress for a king/queen, etc. (*b*) symbol of monarchy; **counsel for the c.** = lawyer representing the state. (*c*) top (of the head, a tooth, etc.). (*d*) type of coin. **2.** *v.* (*a*) to make (s.o.) king/queen/emperor, etc. by placing a crown on his head. (*b*) to be a splendid end to (sth). (*c*) *inf.* to hit (s.o.) on the head. (*d*) to reward. (*e*) to put a false top on (a tooth). **crown cork,** *n.* metal and cork cap on a bottle. **Crown Court,** *n.* court in various places in England and Wales which tries major criminal cases. **Crown Prince,** *n.* eldest son of a king, who will inherit the throne.

crucial ['kru:ʃl] *adj.* extremely important/critical. **crucially,** *adv.* vitally/critically.

crucible ['kru:sɪbl] *n.* small pot used for heating substances in chemical experiments.

crucifix ['kru:sɪfɪks] *n.* (*pl.* **-es**) statue representing Jesus Christ on the cross. **crucifixion** [kru:sɪ'fɪkʃn] *n.* killing by nailing to a cross. **crucify,** *v.* to kill (s.o.) by nailing to a cross.

crude [kru:d] **1.** *adj.* (**-er, -est**) (*a*) unpurified; unrefined (oil). (*b*) rude/ill-mannered. **2.** *n.* unrefined oil. **crudely,** *adv.* in a crude way. **crudeness, crudity,** *n.* being crude.

cruel ['kru:əl] *adj.* (**crueller, cruellest**) which causes pain/suffering. **cruelly,** *adv.* savagely/unkindly. **cruelty,** *n.* being cruel.

cruet ['kru:ɪt] *n.* set of containers for salt, pepper, mustard, etc.

cruise [kru:z] **1.** *n.* long pleasure voyage in a ship calling at different ports. **2.** *v.* (*a*) to go about steadily (in a boat) visiting places. (*b*) to travel at an even speed. **cruiser,** *n.* large warship, smaller than a battleship; **cabin c.** = motor boat with a cabin for living in.

crumb [krʌm] *n.* small piece (of bread, etc.). **crumble** ['krʌmbl] **1.** *n.* dessert made of fruit covered with a mixture of flour, fat and sugar. **2.** *v.* to break into small pieces. **crumbly,** *adj.* which easily falls to pieces.

crummy ['krʌmɪ] *adj.* (**-ier, -iest**) *inf.* rotten/no good.

crumpet ['krʌmpɪt] *n.* thick round batter cake, served toasted with butter.

crumple ['krʌmpl] *v.* to crush/to screw up into a ball.

crunch [krʌntʃ] **1.** *n.* (*pl.* **-es**) (*a*) sound of sth crisp being crushed. (*b*) *inf.* crisis point; **when it comes to the c. 2.** *v.* to crush (sth crisp); to chew (sth hard). **crunchy,** *adj.* hard and crisp.

crupper ['krʌpə] *n.* piece of leather which fastens round a horse's tail to keep the saddle in place.

crusade [kru:'seɪd] **1.** *n.* (*a*) medieval campaign by Christians against Muslims who occupied the Holy Land. (*b*) campaign. **2.** *v.* to campaign/to fight (**against** or **for**). **crusader,** *n.* person who goes on a crusade.

crush [krʌʃ] **1.** *n.* (*a*) drink made of fruit juice. (*b*) mass of people squeezed together. (*c*) girl's infatuation. **2.** *v.* to squash.

crust [krʌst] *n.* hard exterior (of bread/

cake/the earth, etc.). **crusty,** adj. (**-ier, -iest**) (bread) with a hard crust.

crustacean [krʌ'steɪʃn] n. one of many types of animals with hard shells, mainly living in the sea, such as lobsters, crabs, etc.

crutch [krʌtʃ] n. (pl. **-es**) (a) lame person's long stick which goes under the armpit. (b) crotch.

crux [krʌks] n. central point of a problem; **the c. of the matter.**

cry [kraɪ] 1. (a) act of making tears. (b) shout; exclamation (esp. of pain). (c) call (of a bird/animal). 2. v. (a) to make tears. (b) (also **cry out**) to shout; to exclaim (in pain). **crying,** adj. scandalous/which needs putting right. **cry off,** v. to decide not to do sth which you had promised to do.

cryogenics [kraɪəʊ'dʒenɪks] n. study of very low temperatures.

crypt [krɪpt] n. cellar under a church.

cryptic ['krɪptɪk] adj. secret; mysterious.

crypto- ['krɪptəʊ] prefix hidden.

cryptogam ['krɪptəgæm] n. plant (like moss) which has no flowers.

cryptogram ['krɪptəgræm] n. message written in a secret language; coded message. **cryptography,** n. study of codes.

crystal ['krɪstl] n. (a) chemical formation of regular-shaped solids. (b) very clear bright glass. **crystalline,** adj. shaped like a crystal; clear as a crystal. **crystallization** [krɪstəlaɪ'zeɪʃn] n. formation of crystals. **crystallize** ['krɪstəlaɪz] v. (a) to form crystals. (b) to preserve fruit in sugar. (c) to take shape. **crystallography** [krɪstə'lɒgrəfɪ] n. study of crystals.

Cu symbol for copper.

cub [kʌb] n. (a) young animal (esp. bear/fox). (b) C. **Scout** = boy in the younger section of the Boy Scouts.

Cuban ['kjuːbn] 1. adj. referring to Cuba. 2. n. person from Cuba.

cubby-hole ['kʌbɪhəʊl] n. small dark cupboard/hiding place.

cube [kjuːb] 1. n. (a) geometric solid shape where all six sides are square and join each other at right angles. (b) the result where a number is multiplied by itself twice; **c. root** = number which when multiplied by itself twice produces

a given number. 2. v. (a) to multiply (a number) by itself twice. (b) **cubed sugar** = sugar in square lumps. **cubic,** adj. solid; **c. capacity** = capacity to hold something; **c. centimetre** = (i) cube where each side measures one centimetre; (ii) the volume of this size.

cubicle ['kjuːbɪkl] n. small room (in a dormitory); changing room (in a shop/at swimming baths).

cubism ['kjuːbɪzəm] n. art movement where geometric shapes predominate. **cubist,** adj. & n. (painter) using geometric shapes.

cuckoo ['kʊkuː] 1. n. common summer bird, which lays its eggs in other birds' nests. 2. adj. inf. stupid. **cuckoo clock,** n. clock where a small bird makes a noise like a cuckoo to call the time.

cucumber ['kjuːkʌmbə] n. long vegetable used in salads or for pickling.

cud [kʌd] n. food chewed a second time.

cuddle ['kʌdl] 1. n. a hug. 2. v. to hug and kiss (s.o.). **cuddlesome, cuddly,** adj. warm and soft.

cudgel ['kʌdʒl] 1. n. large stick for hitting people with; **to take up the cudgels on s.o.'s behalf** = to go to defend s.o. 2. v. (**cudgelled**) **to c. one's brains** = to think hard.

cue [kjuː] n. (a) (in a play) the line which indicates that you speak or act next; **to take your c. from s.o.** = to follow s.o. closely/to do as s.o. does. (b) long stick for playing billiards/snooker.

cuff [kʌf] 1. n. (a) end of the sleeve round the wrist; **speaking off the c./ an off the c. speech** = speech made without any notes; impromptu speech. (b) Am. folded part at the bottom of each leg of a pair of trousers. (c) smack (with an open hand). 2. v. to give (s.o.) a smack. **cuff-links,** n. pl. fasteners, usually linked with a chain, for attaching shirt cuffs.

cuirass [kwi'ræs] n. armour for the top part of the body.

cuisine [kwɪ'ziːn] n. style of cooking.

cul-de-sac ['kʌldəsæk] n. small street open at only one end.

culinary ['kʌlɪnərɪ] adj. referring to cooking.

cull [kʌl] v. to kill (some animals in a herd) when there are too many of them.

cullet ['kʌlɪt] *n.* broken glass for recycling.

culminate ['kʌlmɪneɪt] *v.* to reach a climax/to end (**in**). **culmination** [kʌlmɪ-'neɪʃn] *n.* final point/grand ending.

culottes [kju'lɒts] *n. pl.* woman's wide shorts, like a split skirt.

culpable ['kʌlpəbl] *adj.* guilty. **culpability** [kʌlpə'bɪlɪtɪ] *n.* guilt.

culprit ['kʌlprɪt] *n.* person who has done something wrong.

cult [kʌlt] *n.* religious or semi-religious worship; **c. hero** = person worshipped by a group of admirers.

cultivate ['kʌltɪveɪt] *v.* (*a*) to dig and water (the land) to grow plants; to grow (plants). (*b*) to do everything to win (s.o.'s friendship). **cultivated,** *adj.* (person) who has been educated/who is civilized. **cultivation** [kʌltɪ'veɪʃn] *n.* (*a*) act of cultivating. (*b*) education. **cultivator,** *n.* (*a*) farmer/person who cultivates. (*b*) small motor-powered plough.

culture ['kʌltʃə] *n.* (*a*) cultivation of plants/pearls. (*b*) growing (of germs in a laboratory). (*c*) civilization. **cultural,** *adj.* referring to culture. **cultured,** *adj.* (*a*) civilized; well educated (person). (*b*) (pearl) which has been artificially grown.

culvert ['kʌlvət] *n.* drain which goes under a road in a pipe.

cumbersome ['kʌmbəsəm] *adj.* large and heavy.

cumin ['kʌmɪn] *n.* herb whose seeds are used for flavouring.

cummerbund ['kʌməbʌnd] *n.* type of decorative belt worn by men.

cumulative ['kju:mjʊlətɪv] *adj.* which accumulates; which grows by adding new parts.

cumulus ['kju:mjʊləs] *n.* type of large white cloud; rounded masses of clouds.

cuneiform ['kju:nɪfɔ:m] *adj. & n.* type of ancient writing done on wet clay with a stick.

cunning ['kʌnɪŋ] **1.** *n.* (*a*) cleverness. (*b*) trickery. **2.** *adj.* (*a*) clever. (*b*) tricky/sly.

cup [kʌp] **1.** *n.* (*a*) bowl with a handle for drinking tea or coffee, etc. (*b*) silver goblet or vase given as a prize in sporting events/competitions, etc.; **c. final** = final match for a football championship; **c. tie** = preliminary match for a football championship. **2.** *v.* (**cupped**) to put (hands) in the shape of a cup. **cupful,** *n.* quantity held by a cup.

cupboard ['kʌbəd] *n.* large piece of furniture with shelves and doors; alcove in a wall with shelves and doors.

cupidity [kju:'pɪdɪtɪ] *n.* greed; desire for sth.

cupola ['kju:pələ] *n.* small dome.

cuppa ['kʌpə] *n. inf.* cup of tea.

cur [kɜ:] *n.* dirty dog.

curare [kjʊə'rɑ:rɪ] *n.* S. American poison, now used to relax the muscles.

curate ['kjʊərət] *n.* minor priest who helps the parish priest. **curacy,** *n.* post of curate.

curator [kju'reɪtə] *n.* person in charge of a museum.

curb [kɜ:b] **1.** *n.* (*a*) = **kerb.** (*b*) brake/thing which holds you back. **2.** *v.* to brake; to hold back.

curd [kɜ:d] *n.* solid food made from sour milk. **curdle** ['kɜ:dl] *v.* to (cause to) go sour.

cure ['kjʊə] **1.** *n.* (*a*) making better. (*b*) remedy. **2.** *v.* (*a*) to make better. (*b*) to preserve (fish/pork, etc.) by salting/smoking, etc.; to preserve (skins) to make leather. **curable,** *adj.* (disease) which can be cured. **curative,** *adj.* which can cure.

curettage [kjure'ta:ʒ] *n.* scraping of the inside of part of the body. **curette,** *n.* surgical instrument for scraping.

curfew ['kɜ:fju:] *n.* period when no one is allowed on the streets.

curie ['kjʊərɪ] *n.* unit of measurement of radioactivity.

curio ['kjʊərɪəʊ] *n.* (*pl.* **-os**) old/rare object.

curiosity [kjʊərɪ'ɒsɪtɪ] *n.* (*a*) desire for knowledge. (*b*) odd/rare object. **curious** ['kjʊərɪəs] *adj.* (*a*) wanting to know. (*b*) odd/peculiar. **curiously,** *adv.* oddly.

curl [kɜ:l] **1.** *n.* lock of wavy twisted hair. **2.** *v.* (*a*) to make (hair) wave/twist. (*b*) to grow in waves/twists naturally. **curler,** *n.* small tube for wrapping hair round to make it curl. **curling,** *n.* team game where heavy weights are slid across ice towards a target. **curl up,** *v.* to roll up into a ball. **curly,** *adj.* (**-ier, -iest**) with natural waves, twists.

curlew ['kɜ:lju:] *n*. brown wading bird with a long curved beak.

currant ['kʌrənt] *n*. (*a*) small black or red soft fruit; bush of this fruit. (*b*) small dried grape.

currency ['kʌrənsɪ] *n*. (*a*) (system of) money; **hard c.** = money which can be easily exchanged internationally. (*b*) being well known; **to gain c.** = to become more frequently heard.

current ['kʌrənt] **1.** *n*. flow of water/air/electricity. **2.** *adj*. of the present time; frequent; **c. affairs** = things which are happening at the present moment; **c. account** = bank account from which you can draw money without giving notice. **currently,** *adv*. at the present time.

curriculum [kə'rɪkjʊləm] *n*. list of subjects studied in a school, etc. **c. vitae** ['vi:taɪ] = summary of biographical details, esp. details of education and work experience.

curry ['kʌrɪ] **1.** *n*. hot spice; dish made with hot spice; **c. powder. 2.** *v*. (*a*) to cook with hot spices. (*b*) to brush down (a horse). (*c*) **to c. favour with s.o.** = to try to make s.o. favour you. **currycomb,** *n*. stiff brush for brushing a horse.

curse [kɜ:s] **1.** *n*. (*a*) evil magic spell. (*b*) swear word. (*c*) calamity/evil. (*d*) *inf*. **the c.** = woman's menstrual periods. **2.** *v*. (*a*) to cast an evil spell on (s.o.). (*b*) to swear.

cursive ['kɜ:sɪv] *adj*. (writing) with the letters joined together.

cursor ['kɜ:sə] *n*. spot of light which moves round a computer screen, showing where work is being done.

cursory ['kɜ:sərɪ] *adj*. rapid/superficial (inspection/glance). **cursorily,** *adv*. rapidly.

curt [kɜ:t] *adj*. (-er, -est) abrupt. **curtly,** *adv*. abruptly. **curtness,** *n*. being curt.

curtail [kɜ:'teɪl] *v*. to shorten; to reduce. **curtailment,** *n*. act of curtailing.

curtain ['kɜ:tn] **1.** *n*. long piece of material hanging by hooks from a pole, covering a window or cutting off the stage in a theatre. **2.** *v*. (*also* **c. off**) to hide/to cover with a curtain. **curtain-call,** *n*. calling of an actor to take a bow after the end of a performance. **curtain-rod,** *n*. rod on which a curtain is hung.

curtsy ['kɜ:tsɪ] **1.** *n*. respectful movement made by women/girls, by bending the knees and putting one foot forward. **2.** *v*. **to c. to s.o.** = to make a curtsy to s.o.

curve [kɜ:v] **1.** *n*. rounded shape like a semi-circle. **2.** *v*. to make a rounded shape. **curvaceous** [kɜ:'veɪʃəs] *adj*. (girl) with a rounded figure. **curvature** ['kɜ:vətʃə] *n*. bending of something into a curve; **c. of the spine** = abnormal bending of the spine. **curved,** *adj*. rounded.

cushion ['kʊʃn] **1.** *n*. bag filled with feathers, etc., for sitting/leaning on. **2.** *v*. to soften (a blow).

cushy ['kʊʃɪ] *adj*. (-ier, -iest) *inf*. easy (job).

cusp [kʌsp] *n*. point where two curves meet.

cuspidor ['kʌspɪdɔ:] *n*. bowl into which one can spit.

cussed ['kʌsɪd] *adj*. *inf*. awkward and contrary. **cussedness** ['kʌsɪdnəs] *n*. *inf*. being cussed.

custard ['kʌstəd] *n*. cream made with eggs, milk and sugar; also with a special powder and milk. **custard tart,** *n*. pastry case filled with custard and baked.

custody ['kʌstədɪ] *n*. keeping. **custodial sentence,** *n*. sentence which sends a convicted person to prison. **custodian** [kʌ'stəʊdɪən] *n*. person who keeps sth safe; guardian of an ancient monument, etc.

custom ['kʌstəm] *n*. (*a*) habit. (*b*) using of a shop; **custom-built/custom-made** = made to special order. **customarily,** *adv*. usually. **customary,** *adj*. habitual. **customer,** *n*. client/person who buys in a shop. **customize,** *v*. to convert (car) to a customer's special and peculiar requirements. **customs,** *n*. (*a*) tax on goods imported into a country. (*b*) **Customs and Excise** = the government department/office which inspects imports, imposes taxes on alcohol, and deals with VAT.

cut [kʌt] **1.** *n*. (*a*) reduction (in salary); breaking off (electricity supply). (*b*) opening made with a sharp blade; small wound. (*c*) **short c.** = way which is shorter than usual. (*d*) way in which a suit/jacket, etc., is made. (*e*) piece/slice of meat. (*f*) *inf.* share (of profits, etc.). **2.** (**cut**) (*a*) to make an opening (using a sharp blade); to wound (with a knife); to shorten; to reduce. (*b*) to divide (a pack of playing cards) in half. (*c*) not to look at (s.o.) whom you know. (*d*) to miss (a lecture). **3.** *adj.* which has been cut. **cut down,** *v.* to chop down (a tree); to reduce (an amount). **cut in,** *v.* to interrupt a conversation; to move in quickly in front of another car in traffic. **cut off,** *v.* to disconnect (electricity supply); to remove; to stop (s.o.) reaching a place. **cut out,** *v.* (*a*) to stop (eating sth, etc.). (*b*) to remove a small piece by cutting it from a large piece (of paper, etc.); **he is not cut out for the army** = he does not fit in with/is not suitable for the army. **cut-price,** *adj.* cheap. **cutter,** *n.* (*a*) person who cuts. (*b*) machine which cuts. (*c*) small, fast boat. **cut-throat,** *adj.* vicious/intense. **cutting, 1.** *adj.* which cuts; sharply critical (remark). **2.** *n.* (*a*) small piece of paper cut out of a newspaper. (*b*) little piece of a plant which will take root if stuck in the ground. **cut up,** *v.* to make into small pieces by cutting; *inf.* **cut up** = very upset.

cutaneous [kju:'teɪnɪəs] *adj.* referring to the skin.

cute [kju:t] *adj. inf.* nice. **cuteness,** *n.* niceness.

cuticle ['kju:tɪkl] *n.* skin round a fingernail or toenail.

cutlass ['kʌtləs] *n.* short sword, used in the navy and in cavalry.

cutlery ['kʌtlərɪ] *n.* (*no pl.*) knives, forks and spoons.

cutlet ['kʌtlət] *n.* (*a*) thin slice of meat (usu. with the rib bone attached). (*b*) fried patty made with meat, etc.

cuttlefish ['kʌtlfɪʃ] *n.* animal (like a squid) which lives in the sea and squirts ink when attacked.

cv [si:'vi:] *n.* curriculum vitae.

cwt *abbrev for* hundredweight.

cyanide ['saɪənaɪd] *n.* strong poison.

cybernetics [saɪbə'netɪks] *n.* science of the communication of information.

cyclamen ['sɪkləmən] *n.* common indoor plant with pink flowers which grow from a corm.

cycle ['saɪkl] **1.** *n.* (*a*) period during which sth returns. (*b*) series of songs or poems. **2.** *v.* to go on a bicycle. **cyclic, cyclical** ['sɪklɪk(l)] *adj.* occuring in cycles. **cycling,** *n.* riding a bicycle as a sport. **cyclist,** *n.* person who rides a bicycle.

cyclone ['saɪkləun] *n.* tropical storm.

cyclostyled ['saɪkləstaɪld] *adj.* (copy) produced from a stencil.

cyclotron ['saɪkləutron] *n.* machine which accelerates the spiral movement of particles, used in nuclear processes.

cygnet ['sɪgnət] *n.* baby swan.

cylinder ['sɪlɪndə] *n.* shape like a tube; part of an engine, of this shape, in which a piston moves. **cylindrical** [sɪ'lɪndrɪkl] *adj.* tube-shaped.

cymbals ['sɪmbəlz] *n. pl.* pair of round metal plates which are banged together to make a loud noise in music.

cynic ['sɪnɪk] *n.* person who mocks/who doubts that anything is good. **cynical,** *adj.* referring to a cynic. **cynically,** *adv.* in a cynical, mocking way. **cynicism** ['sɪnɪsɪzəm] *n.* being cynical.

cynosure ['saɪnəsjuə] *n.* centre of attraction.

cypress ['saɪprəs] *n.* (*pl.* -es) tall slim evergreen tree.

Cypriot ['sɪprɪət] **1.** *adj.* referring to Cyprus. **2.** *n.* person from Cyprus.

cyst [sɪst] *n.* small growth on or inside the body. **cystitis** [sɪs'taɪtɪs] *n.* inflammation of the bladder. **cystoscopy,** *n.* operation to examine the bladder by means of a very small telescope on the end of a tube.

cytology [saɪ'tɒlədʒɪ] *n.* study of cells.

Czech [tʃek] **1.** *adj.* referring to Czechoslovakia. **2.** *n.* (*a*) person from Czechoslovakia. (*b*) language spoken in Czechoslovakia.

Dd

dab [dæb] **1.** *n.* (*a*) light tap. (*b*) *inf.* **a d. hand at poker** = very good at playing poker. (*c*) small flat fish. (*d*) small quantity. **2.** *v.* (**dabbed**) to give (sth) a light tap; **to d. (sth) on** = to apply (paint, etc.) by pressing lightly.

dabble ['dæbl] *v.* to paddle (in water); **he dabbles in politics** = he does a little political work.

dabchick ['dæbtʃɪk] *n.* common small dark waterbird with a red forehead.

dace [deɪs] *n.* (*pl.* **dace**) small edible freshwater fish.

dachshund ['dækshʊnd] *n.* breed of long low dog (originally from Germany).

dactyl ['dæktɪl] *n.* measure (one long and two short syllables) used in Latin poetry.

dad [dæd], **daddy** ['dædɪ] *n. inf.* father. **daddy-long-legs,** *n.* insect with very long legs.

dado ['deɪdəʊ] *n.* (*pl.* **-os**) lower part of a wall, which is panelled or painted differently from the upper part.

daffodil ['dæfədɪl] *n.* spring flower in shades of yellow, with a trumpet-shaped centre.

daft [dɑːft] *adj. inf.* silly.

dagger ['dægə] *n.* short knife; **at daggers drawn** = bitter enemies.

daguerreotype [də'gerɪəʊtaɪp] *n.* photographic process, where the image is captured on silver-coated plate.

dahlia ['deɪlɪə] *n.* autumn garden flower (produced from a bulbous root).

Dail [dɔɪl] *n.* lower house of the Irish Parliament.

daily ['deɪlɪ] **1.** *adj.* every day. **2.** *adv.* **twice d.** = two times a day. **3.** *n.* (*a*) newspaper published every weekday. (*b*) woman who comes to a house every day to do housework.

dainty ['deɪntɪ] *adj.* (**-ier, -iest**) delicate; small. **daintily,** *adv.* delicately.

dairy ['deərɪ] *n.* place where milk, cream and butter are processed or sold; **d. produce** = milk, butter, cream and cheese. **d. farm** = farm which produces milk. **dairyman,** *n* (*pl.* **-men**) man who looks after dairy cows.

dais ['deɪs] *n.* low platform (in large hall).

daisy ['deɪzɪ] *n.* small pink and white summer flower; **d. wheel printer** = typewriter/computer printer, where the characters are on the ends of spokes of a wheel.

dale [deɪl] *n.* (*in north of England*) valley.

dally ['dælɪ] *v.* to idle; to spend time doing nothing. **dalliance,** *n.* (*old*) idling.

dalmatian [dæl'meɪʃn] *n.* large white dog with black spots.

dam [dæm] **1.** *n.* (*a*) wall (of earth or concrete) blocking a river, etc. (*b*) female mammal which is a mother. **2.** *v.* (**dammed**) to block (a river) by building a wall across it.

damage ['dæmɪdʒ] **1.** *n.* (*a*) harm (done to things, not to people). (*b*) **damages** = payment ordered by a court to a victim. (*c*) *inf.* total of a bill. **2.** *v.* to spoil or harm (sth).

damask ['dæməsk] *n.* kind of patterned material, used esp. for tablecloths, etc. **damascene,** *adj.* (steel) decorated with patterns of silver or gold.

dame [deɪm] *n.* (*a*) (*in a pantomime*) old woman (usu. played by a man). (*b*) *Am. inf.* woman. (*c*) title given to women (*equivalent to* Sir *for men*).

damn [dæm] **1.** *n.* curse. **2.** *v.* to condemn; to curse; to criticize. **3.** *inter. inf.* expressing annoyance. **damnable,** *adj.* cursed. **damnation** [dæm'neɪʃn] *n.* state of being eternally condemned. **damned,** *adj. inf.* very annoying. **damning,** *adj.* which shows that sth is wrong.

damp [dæmp] **1.** *n.* wetness; **rising d.** = humidity which creeps up walls of a house; **d. course** = strip of material inserted in a wall to prevent damp rising. **2.** *adj.* (**-er, -est**) rather wet. **3.** *v.* to wet; to reduce (enthusiasm). **dampen,** *v.* to damp. **damper,** *n.* (*a*) gloom. (*b*) plate at the back of a fireplace which regulates the draught. (*c*) soft pad which touches a piano string to soften the tone. (*d*) (*in Australia*) flat bread made from flour and water, cooked on a fire. **dampness,** *n.* state of being wet. **damp-proof,** *adj.* resistant to wet.

damsel ['dæmzl] *n.* (*old*) girl.

damson ['dæmzən] *n.* small purple plum; tree which bears this fruit.

dance [dɑːns] **1.** *n* (*a*) way of moving to music. (*b*) evening entertainment where people dance. **2.** *v.* (*a*) to move (in time to music). (*b*) to jump up and down (with excitement). **dancer,** *n.* person who dances; **ballet d.** = person who dances in ballet.

dandelion ['dændɪlaɪən] *n.* wild plant with yellow flowers and bitter sap.

dandruff ['dændrʌf] *n.* small pieces of dry skin (in the hair).

dandy ['dændɪ] *n.* man who is too interested in clothes. **dandified**, *adj.* like a dandy.

Dane [deɪn] *n.* person from Denmark; **Great D.** = breed of very large short-haired dog.

danger ['deɪndʒə] *n.* risk; possibility of harm or death; **in d.** = at risk; **out of d./off the d. list** = no longer likely to die; **d. money** = extra payment to a worker in a dangerous job. **dangerous**, *adj.* which can cause injury or death. **dangerously**, *adv.* in a dangerous way.

dangle ['dæŋgl] *v.* to (cause to) hang limply.

Danish ['deɪnɪʃ] **1.** *adj.* referring to Denmark; **D. pastry** = sweet pastry cake with jam or fruit folded in it. **2.** *n.* language spoken in Denmark.

dank [dæŋk] *adj.* cold and damp.

daphne ['dæfnɪ] *n.* small shrub with pink flowers which appear very early in the spring.

dapper ['dæpə] *adj.* smart/elegant.

dappled ['dæpld] *adj.* covered with patches of light and dark colour.

Darby and Joan ['dɑːbɪəndʒəʊn] *n.* happy old couple.

dare ['deə] **1.** *n.* act of daring s.o. to do sth. **2.** *v.* (*a*) to be brave enough (to do sth); **I d. say** = perhaps/probably. (*b*) to challenge (s.o.) to do sth by suggesting it is cowardly not to do it. **daredevil**, *adj. & n.* (person) full of reckless bravery. **daring. 1.** *adj.* brave but foolish. **2.** *n.* foolish bravery.

dark [dɑːk] **1.** *adj.* (**-er, -est**) (*a*) with little or no light. (*b*) not a light colour; **d. horse** = person/thing which succeeds though not expected to do so; **D. Ages** = period between the end of the Roman civilization in Northern Europe and the Middle Ages. (*c*) **keep it d.** = keep it a secret. (*d*) gloomy. **2.** *n.* (*a*) absence of light. (*b*) **to keep s.o. in the d.** = to keep sth a secret from s.o. **darken**, *v.* to become dark. **darkly**, *adv.* in a gloomy way. **darkness**, *n.* absence of light. **darkroom**, *n.* room with a special light, in which you can develop and print films.

darling ['dɑːlɪŋ] *n. & adj.* (person) loved; lovable.

darn [dɑːn] **1.** *v.* to mend (clothes). **2.** *n.* place where clothe been mended. **darning**, *n.* actio mending; clothes which are waitin be mended.

dart [dɑːt] **1.** *n.* (*a*) light arrow with a sharp point. (*b*) small heavy arrow with feathers (for playing a game with); **darts** = games where two teams throw small heavy arrows at a round target. (*c*) small tuck sewn into a garment to make it fit. (*d*) quick rush. **2.** *v.* to run fast. **dartboard**, *n.* round target at which darts are thrown.

dash [dæʃ] **1.** *n.* (*pl.* **-es**) (*a*) small amount. (*b*) little line. (*c*) sudden rush. **2.** *v.* (*a*) to rush. (*b*) to smash (sth). **dashboard**, *n.* instrument panel in a car. **dashing**, *adj.* very smart and energetic (person).

dastardly ['dɑːstədlɪ] *adj.* cowardly and unpleasant.

data ['deɪtə] *n.* statistical information; **d. bank** = store of information in a computer; **d. protection** = keeping information or computer records safely, so that they cannot be copied. *see also* **datum. database**, *n.* data stored in a computer, which can be used to provide information of various kinds. **data processing**, *n.* analysis of statistical information using a computer.

date [deɪt] **1.** *n.* (*a*) number of a day, month or year; **up to d.** = recent; **he is bringing the book up to d.** = he is revising the book to put in the most recent information; **out of d.** = not modern; **the book is three years out of d.** (*b*) agreed meeting time. (*c*) fruit of a date palm. **2.** *v.* (*a*) to write the number of the day on (sth). (*b*) to give the date of (an antique, etc.). (*c*) *Am.* to agree to meet (s.o. of the opposite sex) at a particular time. (*c*) **this house dates from 1600** = this house has existed since 1600. (*d*) to seem old-fashioned. **datable**, *adj.* which can be dated. **dated**, *adj.* old-fashioned. **dateless**, *adj.* with no date. **dateline**, *n.* heading (with date and place) of a report from a foreign correspondent. **date line**, *n.* line of longitude (in the Pacific Ocean) which indicates the change in date from east to west. **date palm,** *n.* palm tree which provides small, very sweet brown fruit.

dative ['deɪtɪv] *adj.* & *n.* (*in grammar*) (case) showing giving.

datum ['deɪtəm] *n.* (*pl.* **data**) piece of information.

daub [dɔ:b] **1.** *n.* (*a*) smear. (*b*) *inf.* bad painting. **2.** *v.* to smear with paint/with mud, etc.

daughter ['dɔ:tə] *n.* female child (of a parent). **daughter-in-law,** *n.* (*pl.* **daughters-in-law**) son's wife.

daunt [dɔ:nt] *v.* to discourage. **nothing daunted** = not frightened. **dauntless,** *adj.* fearless.

davenport ['dævənpɔ:t] *n.* (*a*) *Am.* sofa. (*b*) small writing desk.

davit ['dævɪt] *n.* (*on a ship*) small crane for lowering the lifeboats into the sea.

dawdle ['dɔ:dl] *v.* to walk slowly and aimlessly.

dawn [dɔ:n] **1.** *n.* (*a*) beginning of day, when the sun rises. (*b*) beginning of civilization). **2.** *v.* (*a*) (*of day*) to begin. (*b*) **it dawned on him that** = he began to realize that.

day [deɪ] *n.* (*a*) period of time lasting 24 hours. (*b*) period of time from morning to night. (*c*) light. (*d*) **two apples a d.** = every day. (*e*) **one d./ some d.** = sometime in the future. (*f*) period (in the past). **daybreak,** *n.* early morning when the sun is about to rise. **day centre,** *n.* place where elderly or disabled people can meet and be looked after during the day. **daydream. 1.** *n.* dream which you have during the day when you are not asleep. **2.** *v.* to think about other things; not to concentrate. **daylight,** *n.* light of day; **d. saving time** = system of advancing the clocks in summer to take advantage of the longer daylight period. **day release,** *n.* system where a worker is allowed time from work to attend a course of study. **daytime,** *n.* **in the d.** = during the day.

daze [deɪz] **1.** *n.* state of not being mentally alert. **2.** *v.* to stun (s.o.).

dazzle ['dæzl] *v.* to blind (temporarily). **dazzling,** *adj.* very bright (light).

db, dB *abbrev. for* decibel.

D & C *abbrev. for* dilation and curettage.

DC *abbrev. for* direct current.

DDT [di:di:'ti:] *n.* common insecticide.

deacon ['di:kən] *n.* minor priest. **deaconess,** *n.* woman who can direct services (in some Protestant churches)

dead [ded] **1.** *adj.* (*a*) not alive; (telephone line, etc.) not working. (*b*) complete (silence, etc.). (*c*) no longer used. **2.** *n.* (*a*) **the d.** =dead people. (*b*) **at d. of night** = in the middle of the night. **3.** *adv.* (*a*) completely. (*b*) exactly. **dead beat,** *adj. inf.* tired out. **deaden,** *v.* to make (a sound) quieter; to make (a blow) soft. **dead end,** *n.* (street/way) leading nowhere. **dead heat,** *n.* race where two people come in equal first. **dead letter,** *n.* (*a*) letter which cannot be delivered. (*b*) law which is no longer obeyed. **deadline,** *n.* date by which sth has to be done. **deadliness,** *n.* being deadly. **deadlock. 1.** *n.* state where two sides cannot agree. **2.** *v.* to (cause to) be unable to agree. **deadly,** *adj.* (**-ier, -iest**) so strong as to kill; **d. nightshade** = very poisonous plant. **deadpan,** *adj.* not showing any emotion.

deaf [def] **1.** *adj.* (**-er, -est**) unable to hear; having difficulty in hearing. **2.** *n.* **the d.** = people who cannot hear. **deaf-aid,** *n.* small device which helps a deaf person to hear. **deafen,** *v.* to make deaf (by a loud noise). **deafening,** *adj.* so loud as to make you deaf. **deafness,** *n.* state of being deaf.

deal [di:l] **1.** *n.* (*a*) large quantity; **a good d. better** = much better. (*b*) handing out (playing cards). (*c*) (business) affair. (*d*) wood from a pine tree. **2.** *v.* (**dealt** [delt]) (*a*) to hand out. (*b*) **to d. with** = to organize to solve a problem. (*c*) **to d. in** = to buy and sell. **dealer,** *n.* person who buys and sells. **dealership,** *n.* business of a dealer. **dealings,** *n. pl.* business/affairs.

dean [di:n] *n.* person in charge of lecturers or priests. **deanery,** *n.* position or house of a dean (in a cathedral).

dear ['dɪə] *adj.* (**-er, -est**) (*a*) well liked; loved. (*b*) (*addressing someone at the beginning of a letter*) **D. Mr Smith; D. Sir.** (*c*) expensive. **2.** *inter.* **oh d.!** = how annoying! **dearly,** *adv.* tenderly; very much.

dearth [dɜ:θ] *n.* scarcity.

death [deθ] *n.* act of dying. **d. duty** =

tax paid on money left by dead person; **d. mask** = plaster mask made of s.o.'s face, after death; **d. rate** = number of people who die (as a percentage of the population). **deathbed**, *n.* bed on which s.o. is dying. **deathless**, *adj.* which will live for ever. **deathly**, *adv.* as if dead. **deathtrap**, *n.* dangerous place. **death watch beetle**, *n.* beetle which bores holes in wood and makes a clicking sound.

deb [deb] *n. inf.* debutante.

débâcle [deɪˈbɑːkl] *n.* (a) sudden defeat/collapse. (b) breakup of ice on a river in spring.

debar [dɪˈbɑː] *v.* (**debarred**) **to d. s.o. from sth** = to forbid s.o. to do sth.

debase [dɪˈbeɪs] *v.* to degrade; to reduce the value of (sth, esp. the value of the metal in coinage). **debasement**, *n.* act of debasing.

debate [dɪˈbeɪt] **1.** *n.* formal discussion. **2.** *v.* to discuss. **debatable**, *adj.* not absolutely certain.

debauched [dɪˈbɔːtʃt] *adj.* (person) who spends his time in wild living and enjoys immoral pleasures. **debauchery**, *n.* wild living.

debenture [dɪˈbentʃə] *n.* document showing that a company agrees to repay a debt, and to pay a fixed interest on it, the money being secured on the company's assets.

debilitate [dɪˈbɪlɪteɪt] *v.* to make weak. **debility**, *n.* weakness.

debit [ˈdebɪt] **1.** *n.* (money) which is owed; **on the d. side** = against (a proposal). **2.** *v.* to deduct money from (an account).

debonair [debəˈneə] *adj.* carefree/relaxed (air).

debrief [diːˈbriːf] *v.* to ask (s.o.) questions to obtain information about a mission which he has just completed. **debriefing**, *n.* obtaining information about a mission by questioning the person who carried it out.

debris [ˈdebriː] *n.* pieces (of a demolished building/crashed aircraft, etc.).

debt [det] *n.* money owed to s.o.; **he is in d.** = he owes money. **debtor**, *n.* person who owes money.

debug [diːˈbʌg] *v.* (**debugged**) to remove bugs from (sth); to correct errors in a computer program.

debunk [dɪˈbʌŋk] *v. inf.* to disprove.

debut [ˈdeɪbjuː] *n.* first appearance (of an artist/actor, etc.). **debutante**, *n.* girl who goes into adult society for the first time.

deca- [ˈdekə] *prefix meaning* ten.

decade [ˈdekeɪd] *n.* period of ten years.

decadence [ˈdekədəns] *n.* decline in moral values. **decadent**, *adj.* declining in moral values.

decaffeinated [diːˈkæfɪneɪtɪd] *adj.* (coffee) which has had the caffeine removed.

decal [ˈdiːkæl] *n. Am.* sticker/piece of plastic or paper with a pattern or slogan which you can stick to a surface as a decoration.

decamp [diːˈkæmp] *v. inf.* to go away.

decant [dɪˈkænt] *v.* to pour (liquid, esp. wine) from a bottle into another container. **decanter**, *n.* glass bottle which wine is poured into before serving.

decapitate [dɪˈkæpɪteɪt] *v.* to cut off the head of (s.o.). **decapitation** [dɪkæpɪˈteɪʃn] *n.* act of cutting off a head.

decarbonize [deˈkɑːbənaɪz] *v.* to remove carbon deposits from (a petrol engine).

decathlon [dɪˈkæθlən] *n.* sporting competition where each athlete competes in ten different types of sport.

decay [dɪˈkeɪ] **1.** *n.* falling into ruin; rotting. **2.** *v.* to fall into ruin; to rot.

decease [dɪˈsiːs] *n.* (*formal*) death. **deceased**, *n.* dead person.

deceit [dɪˈsiːt] *n.* trickery. **deceitful**, *adj.* tricking. **deceitfully**, *adv.* in a deceitful way. **deceive** [dɪˈsiːv] *v.* to trick; to make (s.o.) believe sth which is not true.

decelerate [diːˈseləreɪt] *v.* to (make sth) go slower. **deceleration** [diːseləˈreɪʃn] *n.* going slower.

December [dɪˈsembə] *n.* 12th month of the year.

decent [ˈdiːsənt] *adj.* (a) honest. (b) quite good. **decency**, *n.* honour; good morals. **decently**, *adv.* in a decent way.

decentralize [diːˈsentrəlaɪz] *v.* to move (authority/offices) from the centre. **decentralization** [diːsentrəlaɪˈzeɪʃn] *n.* act of decentralizing.

deception [dɪˈsepʃn] *n.* fraud; making s.o. believe sth which is not true.

deceptive, *adj.* not as it looks. **deceptively,** *adv.* in a way which deceives.

decibel ['desɪbel] *n.* unit of measurement of noise.

decide [dɪ'saɪd] *v.* to make up your mind (to do sth). **decided,** *adj.* (*a*) firm (tone, manner). (*b*) certain/obvious (difference, etc.). **decidedly,** *adv.* (*a*) in a firm manner. (*b*) certainly.

deciduous [dɪ'sɪdjʊəs] *adj.* (tree) which loses its leaves in winter.

decimal ['desɪml] **1.** *adj.* (system of mathematics) based on the number 10; **d. point** = dot indicating the division between units and parts which are less than one unit (such as 2.05). **2.** *n.* figure expressed on the base of 10. **decimalize,** *v.* to change to decimals. **decimate,** *v.* to remove one out of ten of; to cut down/to remove/to kill in large numbers.

decipher [dɪ'saɪfə] *v.* to make out (sth badly written, or written in code). **decipherment,** *n.* act of deciphering.

decison [dɪ'sɪʒn] *n.* making up your mind; ability to make up your mind. **decisive** [dɪ'saɪsɪv] *adj.* firm (voice); (contest, etc.) which brings about a result. **decisively,** *adv.* in a decisive way; firmly.

deck [dek] *n.* (*a*) floor (of ship/bus). **flight deck** = (i) control cabin (of plane); (ii) flat surface on an aircraft carrier where aircraft land and take off. (*b*) *Am.* pack (of playing cards). (*c*) apparatus for playing records, tapes, cassettes. **deckchair,** *n.* collapsible canvas chair (for sitting in the sun). **decked,** *adj.* decorated/covered with.

deckle-edged [dekl'edʒd] *adj.* (paper) with a ragged edge.

declaim [dɪ'kleɪm] *v.* to recite in a loud voice. **declamatory** [dɪ'klæmətərɪ] *adj.* as if in a loud voice.

declare [dɪ'kleə] *v.* (*a*) to state (officially). (*b*) (*at customs*) to say what (dutiable goods) one has. (*c*) (*at cricket*) to stop your innings and ask the other team to bat. (*d*) (*at cards*) to say which suit is trumps. **declaration** [deklə-'reɪʃn] *n.* (official) statement.

decline [dɪ'klaɪn] **1.** *n.* downward trend. **2.** *v.* (*a*) to refuse (an invitation). (*b*) to become weaker. (*c*) (*in grammar*) to

show the different cases of (a word). **declension,** *n.* form of the different cases of a word.

declivity [dɪ'klɪvɪtɪ] *n.* slope downwards.

declutch [dɪ'klʌtʃ] *v.* to disengage the clutch in a car.

decode [diː'kəʊd] *v.* to translate (a message) out of code. **decoder,** *n.* person who decodes.

decoke [diː'kəʊk] *v. inf.* to clean carbon from (an engine).

decollate [dekəleɪt] *v.* to separate copies. **decollator,** *n.* machine which separates copies (of computer printouts).

decompose [diːkəm'pəʊz] *v.* to rot. **decomposition** [diːkɒmpə'zɪʃn] *n.* act of rotting.

decompression [diːkəm'preʃn] *n.* reducing the pressure in sth; **d. chamber** = room where divers stay to get used gradually to normal pressures after working in very deep water.

decongestant [diːkən'dʒestənt] *n.* medicine which unblocks, esp. a blocked nose.

decontaminate [diːkən'tæmɪneɪt] *v.* to remove infection/radioactivity from (sth). **decontamination** [diːkəntæmɪ-'neɪʃn] *n.* act of decontaminating.

decontrol [diːkən'trəʊl] *v.* to remove controls from sth.

decor ['deɪkɔː] *n.* (*a*) scenery (for a play). (*b*) interior decoration (of a room).

decorate ['dekəreɪt] *v.* (*a*) to paint (a building); to put new wallpaper in (a room); to put up flags/lights (to celebrate an occasion). (*b*) to award (s.o.) a medal. **decorations** [dekə-'reɪʃnz] *n.pl.* (*a*) flags/lights, etc., used to celebrate an occasion. (*b*) medals. **decorative** ['dekərətɪv] *adj.* pleasant to look at; serving as a decoration. **decoratively,** *adv.* in a decorative way. **decorator,** *n.* person who paints houses; **interior d.** = person who designs ways of decorating the inside of buildings.

decorum [dɪ'kɔːrʌm] *n.* being decorous. **decorous** ['dekərəs] *adj.* very well-behaved.

decoy 1. *n.* ['diːkɔɪ] object to attract and trap sth. **2.** *v.* [dɪ'kɔɪ] to attract and trap (sth/s.o.).

decrease 1. *n.* ['di:kri:s] fall; lessening. **2.** *v.* [di:'kri:s] to fall; to become less.

decree [dɪ'kri:] **1.** *n.* legal order which has not been voted by Parliament; **d. nisi** ['naisai]/**d. absolute** = granting by a judge of a provisional/complete divorce. **2.** *v.* to state as a legal order.

decrepit [dɪ'krepɪt] *adj.* falling to pieces; old and feeble (person). **decrepitude**, *n.* being decrepit.

decry [dɪ'kraɪ] *v.* to say that (sth) is bad.

dedicate ['dedɪkeɪt] *v.* to place (a church) under the patronage of a saint; to write a book for/to offer a book to (s.o.); to spend (all your life) on sth. **dedicated**, *adj.* (computer/program) reserved for a particular task. **dedication** [dedɪ'keɪʃn] *n.* (*a*) devotion. (*b*) inscription at the beginning of a book showing to whom it is dedicated.

deduce [dɪ'dju:s] *v.* to conclude (from examining evidence).

deduct [dɪ'dʌkt] *v.* to remove (from a sum of money). **deductible**, *adj.* which can be deducted. **deduction** [dɪ'dʌkʃn] *n.* (*a*) thing which is deduced; conclusion. (*b*) thing which is deducted; sum of money which is taken away.

deed [di:d] *n.* (*a*) (noble) act. (*b*) legal document; **the deeds of a house** = papers showing who owns the house; **d. poll** = legal document, signed by one party only, such as when s.o. changes his name.

deem [di:m] *v.* (*formal*) to consider.

deep [di:p] **1.** *adj.* (**-er, -est**) (*a*) which goes down a long way. (*b*) rich/dark (colour). (*c*) low-pitched/bass (voice). **2.** *adv.* a long way down. **3.** *n.* **the d.** = the sea. **deepen**, *v.* to go further down; to become deeper; to make (sth) deeper. **deep-freeze**, *n.* refrigerator for freezing food and keeping it frozen. **deep-fried**, *adj.* cooked in deep oil. **deeply**, *adv.* profoundly; very much. **deep-rooted**, *adj.* which goes down a long way. **deep-seated**, *adj.* solid/firm.

deer [dɪə] *n.* (*pl.* **deer**) wild animal which runs fast, and of which the male usually has horns. **deerhound**, *n.* large fast-running dog, bred for chasing deer. **deerstalker**, *n.* round tweed hat, with small peaks at the front and back.

deface [dɪ'feɪs] *v.* to spoil the surface of (sth); to write on (a wall); to mutilate (a statue). **defacement**, *n.* act of defacing.

de facto [di:'fæktəʊ] *adj.* existing in fact/real.

defamation [defə'meɪʃn] *n.* **d. of character** = saying bad things about s.o. **defamatory** [dɪ'fæmətrɪ] *adj.* which says bad things about s.o. **defame** [dɪ'feɪm] *v.* to say bad things about s.o.

default [dɪ'fɔ:lt] **1.** *n.* (*a*) failing to carry out the terms of a contract. (*b*) (*computers*) set way of working; **d. drive** = the drive which is set to be accessed first. **2.** *v.* to fail to carry out the terms of a contract. **defaulter**, *n.* person who defaults; (*in the army*) soldier who is being punished.

defeat [dɪ'fi:t] **1.** *n.* loss (of fight/vote). **2.** *v.* to beat (s.o. in a fight/vote). **defeatism**, *n.* feeling sure that you will lose. **defeatist**, *adj.* sure that you will lose.

defecate ['defəkeɪt] *v.* to pass waste matter from the bowels.

defect 1. *n.* ['di:fekt] fault. **2.** *v.* [dɪ'fekt] to leave the army/your country, to go over to the enemy side. **defection**, *n.* going over to the side of the enemy. **defective**, *adj.* faulty. **defector**, *n.* person who defects.

defence, *Am.* **defense** [dɪ'fens] *n.* (*a*) protection. (*b*) **the d.** = lawyers who speak on behalf of an accused person. **defenceless**, *adj.* unprotected. **defensibility**, *n.* being defensible. **defensible**, *adj.* which can be defended. **defensive. 1.** *adj.* which protects. **2.** *n.* **on the d.** = feeling one has to justify oneself. **defensively**, *adv.* in a defensive way.

defend [dɪ'fend] *v.* (*a*) to protect (from attack). (*b*) to speak on behalf of (an accused person). **defendant**, *n.* person who is accused of doing sth illegal/person who is sued in a civil law suit. **defender**, *n.* person who defends.

defer [dɪ'fɜ:] *v.* (**deferred**) (*a*) to put off/to put back. (*b*) **to d. to s.o./to s.o.'s opinion** = to accept the advice of s.o. who knows better. **deference** ['defərəns] *n.* respect. **deferential**, *adj.* respectful. **deferment**, *n.* postponement.

defiance [dɪˈfaɪəns] *n.* acting against (law/authority). **defiant**, *adj.* very proud and antagonistic.

defibrillator [diːˈfibrɪleɪtə] *n.* machine which stimulates a weak heart by giving it electric shocks.

deficiency [dɪˈfɪʃənsɪ] *n.* lack. **deficient**, *adj.* (in) lacking (sth). **mentally deficient** = below normal intelligence.

deficit [ˈdefɪsɪt] *n.* amount by which expenditure is larger than receipts (in a firm's/a country's accounts).

defile 1. *n.* [ˈdiːfaɪl] narrow pass between mountains. **2.** *v.* [dɪˈfaɪl] to dirty/to pollute. **defilement**, *n.* act of polluting.

define [dɪˈfaɪn] *v.* (*a*) to explain clearly/to give the meaning of. (*b*) to state the boundary of. **definable**, *adj.* which can be defined. **definite** [ˈdefɪnət] *adj.* very clear; **d. article** = 'the' (*as opposed to the indefinite article*, 'a' *or* 'an'). **definitely**, *adv.* certainly. **definition** [defɪˈnɪʃn] *n.* (*a*) clear explanation (of a word). (*b*) clearness (of a picture). **definitive** [dɪˈfɪnɪtɪv] *adj.* final/which cannot be improved.

deflate [dɪˈfleɪt] *v.* (*a*) to let the air out of (a tyre). (*b*) to reduce inflation in (the economy). **deflation** [dɪˈfleɪʃn] *n.* reducing inflation. **deflationary**, *adj.* which leads to deflation.

deflect [dɪˈflekt] *v.* to turn aside (an arrow/a bullet, etc.). **deflection**, *n.* act of deflecting.

defoliate [diːˈfəʊlɪeɪt] *v.* to remove the leaves of (a tree, etc.). **defoliation**, *n.* act of defoliating. **defoliant**, *n.* chemical used to defoliate.

deforestation [diːfɒresˈteɪʃn] *n.* removal of trees from an area of land.

deformed [dɪˈfɔːmd] *adj.* badly shaped. **deformation** [defɔːˈmeɪʃn] *n.* spoiling the shape of sth. **deformity**, *n.* badly shaped part of the body.

defraud [dɪˈfrɔːd] *v.* to cheat.

defray [dɪˈfreɪ] *v.* to pay (costs).

defreeze [diːˈfriːz] *v.* to thaw (frozen food).

defrock [diːˈfrɒk] *v.* to remove (a priest) from holy orders.

defrost [diːˈfrɒst] *v.* to melt the ice on (the inside of a refrigerator).

deft [deft] *adj.* (**-er, -est**) very agile/clever (with your hands). **deftly**, *adv.* in a deft way. **deftness**, *n.* being deft.

defunct [dɪˈfʌŋkt] *adj.* dead (person); (law) which is no longer applied.

defuse [diːˈfjuːz] *v.* to take the fuse out of (a bomb) so that it cannot explode; to make (a situation) less tense.

defy [dɪˈfaɪ] *v.* (*a*) to refuse to obey (law). (*b*) to challenge (s.o. **to** sth).

degenerate 1. *adj.* [dɪˈdʒenərət] which has degenerated/become depraved. **2.** *v.* [dɪˈdʒenəreɪt] (*a*) to become depraved. (*b*) to get worse. **degeneracy**, *n.* being degenerate. **degeneration** [dɪdʒenəˈreɪʃn] *n.* becoming degenerate; becoming worse.

degrade [dɪˈgreɪd] *v.* (*a*) to humiliate (s.o.); to make (s.o.) like an animal. (*b*) to make (a chemical compound) simpler. **degradable**, *adj.* which can be degraded. **degradation** [degrəˈdeɪʃn] *n.* becoming like an animal. **degrading**, *adj.* lowering; which humiliates/which makes a person like an animal.

degree [dɪˈgriː] *n.* (*a*) division of an angle or scale. (*b*) level; amount; **to a certain d.** = to some extent. (*c*) diploma (of a university).

dehiscence [diːˈhɪsəns] *n.* bursting of a seed pod.

dehumidifier [diːhjuːˈmɪdɪfaɪə] *n.* device which removes humidity from the air.

dehydrate [diːhaɪˈdreɪt] *v.* to remove water from (sth). **dehydration**, *n.* becoming dehydrated.

de-ice [diːˈaɪs] *v.* to remove the ice from (sth). **de-icer**, *n.* thing which de-ices.

deify [ˈdeɪfaɪ] *v.* to make (sth/s.o.) into a god. **deification** [deɪɪfɪˈkeɪʃn] *n.* making into a god.

deign [deɪn] *v.* to condescend (**to** to sth).

deity [ˈdeɪɪtɪ] *n.* god.

déjà vu [dɪʒæˈvuː] *adv.* feeling that you have already seen sth before.

dejected [dɪˈdʒektɪd] *adj.* depressed/unhappy. **dejectedly**, *adv.* in a gloomy way. **dejection** [dɪˈdʒekʃn] *n.* gloom/depression.

de jure [diːˈdʒʊərɪ] *adv.* correct according to the law.

dekko [ˈdekəʊ] *n. Sl.* **to have a d.** = to have a quick look.

delay [dɪˈleɪ] **1.** *n.* time during which one is late. **2.** *v.* (*a*) to make late. (*b*) to wait; to put (sth) off until later.

delectable [dɪ'lektəbl] *adj.* very pleasant; very attractive. **delectation** [dɪlek-'teɪʃn] *n.* pleasure/enjoyment.

delegate 1. *n.* ['delɪgət] person who represents others at a meeting. **2.** *v.* ['delɪgeɪt] to pass (authority/responsibility) on to a subordinate. **delegation** [delɪ'geɪʃn] *n.* (*a*) group of representatives. (*b*) passing of authority to a subordinate.

delete [dɪ'li:t] *v.* to cross out (a word/text). **deletion** [dɪ'li:ʃn] *n.* word/phrase which has been crossed out.

deleterious [dɪlɪ'tɪərɪəs] *adj.* (*formal*) harmful.

deliberate 1. *adj.* [dɪ'lɪbərət] (*a*) done on purpose. (*b*) slow and thoughtful (speech/manner). **2.** *v.* [dɪ'lɪbəreɪt] to debate/to discuss. **deliberately**, *adv.* (*a*) on purpose. (*b*) slowly and thoughtfully. **deliberation** [dɪlɪbə-'reɪʃn] *n.* (*a*) thought; consideration. (*b*) **the deliberations of a meeting** = the debate/discussion.

delicacy ['delɪkəsɪ] *n.* (*a*) sensitivity. (*b*) state of being delicate. (*c*) rare thing to eat. **delicate**, *adj.* (*a*) easily damaged; very thin. (*b*) liable to get illnesses. (*c*) very fine. **delicately**, *adv.* with care.

delicatessen [delɪkə'tesn] *n.* shop selling cold meat and foreign food, etc.

delicious [dɪ'lɪʃəs] *adj.* which tastes very good. **deliciously**, *adv.* in a delicious way.

delight [dɪ'laɪt] **1.** *n.* pleasure. **2.** *v.* to take pleasure (**in**). **delighted**, *adj.* very pleased. **delightful**, *adj.* very pleasant.

delineate [dɪ'lɪnɪeɪt] *v.* (*formal*) to draw. **delineation** [dɪlɪnɪ'eɪʃn] *n.* (*formal*) drawing.

delinquency [dɪ'lɪŋkwənsɪ] *n.* minor crime; **juvenile d.** = crimes committed by young people. **delinquent**, *adj.* & *n.* criminal.

delirious [dɪ'lɪrɪəs] *adj.* mad with fever/with happiness. **delirium**, *n.* madness caused by fever; great excitement.

deliver [dɪ'lɪvə] *v.* (*a*) to bring (sth) to s.o. (*b*) to make (a speech). (*c*) to help the mother give birth to (a baby). **deliverance**, *n.* (*formal*) rescue. **delivery**, *n.* (*a*) bringing sth to s.o. (*b*) birth (of a child).

dell [del] *n.* small hollow filled with trees.

delphinium [del'fɪnɪəm] *n.* garden plant with tall blue flowers.

delta ['deltə] *n.* (*a*) land around the mouth of a river made of mud brought by the river. (*b*) fourth letter of the Greek alphabet. **d. wing aircraft** = with wings forming a triangle.

delude [dɪ'lu:d] *v.* to make (s.o.) believe sth which is wrong. **delusion** [dɪ'lu:ʒn] *n.* wrong belief.

deluge ['delju:dʒ] **1.** *n.* flood. **2.** *v.* to flood (**with**).

de luxe [dɪ'lʌks] *adj.* very expensive; of very high quality.

delve [delv] *v.* to dig (**into** the past/archives, etc.).

demagogue ['deməgɒg] *n.* politician who appeals to the crowd for support. **demagoguery**, *n.* appealing for support from the crowd as a means of obtaining political power.

demand [dɪ'mɑ:nd] **1.** *n.* asking for sth; **it is in d.** = many people want it. **2.** *v.* to ask insistently for sth. **demanding**, *adj.* (job) which takes up much time and energy.

demarcation [di:mɑ:'keɪʃn] *n.* showing of boundaries; **d. dispute** = dispute between workers over who should be responsible for a certain type of work.

démarche ['deɪmɑ:ʃ] *n.* official, often diplomatic, approach to another party.

demean [dɪ'mi:n] *v* **to d. yourself** = to make yourself appear undignified or contemptible.

demeanour [dɪ'mi:nə] *n.* behaviour/manner.

demented [dɪ'mentɪd] *adj.* mad. **dementia** [dɪ'menʃə] *n.* (*formal*) madness.

demerara [demə'reərə] *n.* type of coarse brown sugar.

demerit [di:'merɪt] *n.* fault; unattractive point.

demi- ['demɪ] *prefix meaning* half.

demijohn ['demɪdʒɒn] *n.* large bottle for alcoholic drink.

demilitarized [di:'mɪlɪtəraɪzd] *adj.* (zone) which no longer has armed forces in it.

demise [dɪ'maɪz] *n.* (*formal*) death.

demist [di:'mɪst] *v.* to clear condensation from the windows of a car. **demister**, *n.* blower (in a car) to prevent the windows misting up.

demo ['deməʊ] *n. inf.* demonstration.

demob [di:'mɒb] **1.** *v.* (**demobbed**) *inf.* to demobilize. **2.** *n. inf.* demobilization.

demobilize [di:'məʊbɪlaɪz] *v.* to release (s.o.) from the armed forces. **demobilization** [di:məʊbɪlaɪ'zeɪʃn] *n.* being demobilized.

democracy [dɪ'mɒkrəsɪ] *n.* system of government by freely elected representatives of the people. **democrat** ['deməkræt] *n.* (*a*) person who believes in democracy. (*b*) **Democrat** = member of one of the two main political parties in the USA. **democratic** [demə'krætɪk] *adj.* referring to democracy. **democratically**, *adv.* in a democratic way.

demographic [demə'græfɪk] *adj.* referring to demography. **demography** [dɪ'mɒgrəfɪ] *n.* study of population figures.

demolish [dɪ'mɒlɪʃ] *v.* to knock down. **demolition** [demə'lɪʃn] *n.* knocking down.

demon ['di:mən] *n.* devil. **demoniacal** [di:mə'naɪəkl], **demonic** [di:'mɒnɪk] *adj.* like a devil.

demonstrate ['demənstreɪt] *v.* (*a*) to show. (*b*) to form a crowd to protest (**against** sth). **demonstrable**, *adj.* which can be demonstrated. **demonstration** [demən'streɪʃn] *n.* (*a*) showing. (*b*) march to protest against sth; crowd which is protesting against sth. **demonstrator**, *n.* person who marches/who forms part of a crowd to protest against sth; person who shows how to do sth. **demonstrative** [dɪ'mɒnstrətɪv] *adj* (person) who shows his feelings openly.

demoralize [dɪ'mɒrəlaɪz] *v.* to lower the morale/confidence of (s.o.). **demoralization** [dɪmɒrəlaɪ'zeɪʃn] *n.* lowering of morale. **demoralized**, *adj.* doubtful that you can win.

demote [di:'məʊt] *v.* to give (s.o.) a less important job. **demotion**, *n.* act of demoting.

demur [dɪ'mɜ:] *v.* (**demurred**) **to d. at** = to object to sth.

demure [dɪ'mjʊə] *adj.* quiet and serious (girl). **demurely**, *adv.* in a demure way.

demurrage [di:'mʌrɪdʒ] *n.* payment for keeping a ship in dock when unloading.

den [den] *n.* (*a*) place to hide away in. (*b*) *inf.* small room where you can hide away to work.

denationalize [di:'næʃnəlaɪz] *v.* to put (a nationalized industry) into private ownership. **denationalization** [dɪnæʃnlaɪ'zeɪʃn] *n.* act of denationalizing.

dendrochronology [dendrəʊkrɒ'nɒlədʒɪ] *n.* finding the age of wood by the study of the tree rings.

dengue ['deŋgɪ] *n.* tropical fever.

denial [dɪ'naɪəl] *n.* statement that sth is not true.

denigrate ['denɪgreɪt] *v.* to say that (an action) is worse than it is.

denim ['denɪm] *n.* thick cotton cloth; **denims** = clothes made of this cloth.

denizen ['denɪzən] *n.* (*formal*) inhabitant of a particular place.

denomination [dɪnɒmɪ'neɪʃn] *n.* (*a*) unit of money (on a banknote/coin). (*b*) religious sect; church. **denominational**, *adj.* belonging to a particular sect. **denominator** [dɪ'nɒmɪneɪtə] *n.* figure beneath the line in a fraction.

denote [dɪ'nəʊt] *v.* to mean.

dénouement [deɪ'nu:mɒŋ] *n.* ending (of a plot).

denounce [dɪ'naʊns] *v.* to blame/to accuse (s.o./sth) openly.

dense [dens] *adj.* (**-er, -est**) (*a*) very thick; crowded together. (*b*) stupid. **densely**, *adv.* thickly. **denseness**, *n.* being dense. **density**, *n.* (*a*) physical degree of mass per unit of volume. (*b*) **high d. of population** = many people per unit of area.

dent [dent] *n.* **1.** slight hollow (as made by a blow). **2.** *v.* to make a slight hollow in (sth).

dentist ['dentɪst] *n.* person who looks after teeth. **dental**, *adj.* referring to teeth; **d. floss** = thin thread for cleaning between teeth; **d. surgery** = dentist's office. **dentifrice**, *n.* toothpaste. **dentistry**, *n.* work of a dentist. **dentition**, *n.* arrangement of a person's teeth. **dentures** ['dentʃəz] *n.pl.* false teeth.

denude [dɪ'nju:d] *v.* to make (sth) bare; to remove all the covering from (sth).

denunciation [dɪnʌnsɪ'eɪʃn] *n.* public accusation/blame.

deny [dɪ'naɪ] *v.* to state that (sth) is not

correct; to prevent (s.o.) having sth; **to d. oneself** = not to eat/drink, etc., very much.

deodorant [dɪˈəʊdərənt] *n.* preparation which removes unpleasant smells. **deodorize**, *v.* to remove unpleasant smells from (sth).

deoxyribonucleic **acid** [diːɒksɪraɪbəʊnjuːˈkleɪkˈæsɪd] *n.* DNA, the basic genetic material in a cell.

depart [dɪˈpɑːt] *v.* to go away. **departed**. *n.* **the d.** = the dead. **departure** [dɪˈpɑːtʃə] *n.* leaving. **d. lounge** = large waiting room at an airport for passengers about to leave.

department [dɪˈpɑːtmənt] *n.* section of a large organization; **d. store** = large shop with many different sections. **département**, *n.* administrative division of France. **departmental** [dɪpɑːˈtmentl] *adj.* referring to a department.

depend [dɪˈpend] *v.* (*a*) (**on**) to be decided according to sth. (*b*) to rely (**on** sth). **dependable**, *adj.* that can be relied on. **dependant**, *n.* member of family supported by another. **dependence**, *n.* being dependent. **dependency**, *n.* country which is ruled by another. **dependent**, *adj.* (*a*) supported by s.o. else; relying on s.o. else. (*b*) addicted to (a drug).

depict [dɪˈpɪkt] *v.* (*formal*) to show. **depiction**, *n.* showing.

depilatory [dɪˈpɪlətrɪ] *adj. & n.* (substance) which removes hair from the body.

deplete [dɪˈpliːt] *v.* to run down/to use up (stores).

deplore [dɪˈplɔː] *v.* to be extremely sorry that sth has happened; to dislike (an action/an attitude). **deplorable**, *adj.* very bad (behaviour).

deploy [dɪˈplɔɪ] *v.* to spread out (soldiers, etc.) for action. **deployment**, *n.* act of deploying.

depopulate [diːˈpɒpjʊleɪt] *v.* to reduce the number of people living in an area. **depopulation** [diːpɒpjʊˈleɪʃn] *n.* act of being depopulated.

deport [dɪˈpɔːt] *v.* to expel (s.o.) from a country. **deportation** [diːpɔːˈteɪʃn] *n.* expulsion (of a foreigner). **deportment**, *n.* way of walking/sitting.

depose [dɪˈpəʊz] *v.* (*a*) to force (s.o.) to leave his position; to force (a king, etc.) to give up his throne. (*b*) to state (in court). **deposition** [depəˈzɪʃn] *n.* (*a*) forcing s.o. to leave his position. (*b*) statement (by a witness).

deposit [dɪˈpɒzɪt] **1.** *n.* (*a*) money placed (in a bank); money given to secure sth you want to buy; **d. account** = bank account where you leave money for some time to earn interest. (*b*) mineral layer (in the ground); sediment/ chemical left at the bottom of a container. **2.** *v.* to put (money) in a bank. **depositary**, *n.* person who receives something which is deposited for safe keeping. **depositor**, *n.* person with money in a bank. **depository**, *n.* place for storing furniture, etc.

depot [ˈdepəʊ] *n.* central warehouse; central garage; central barracks for a regiment.

depraved [dɪˈpreɪvd] *adj.* corrupted/ wicked. **depravity** [dɪˈprævɪtɪ] *n.* state of living a wicked life.

deprecate [ˈdeprəkeɪt] *v.* to disapprove of (sth).

depreciate [dɪˈpriːʃɪeɪt] *v.* to lose value. **depreciation** [dɪprɪʃɪˈeɪʃn] *n.* regular loss in value. **depreciatory**, *adj.* which depreciates.

depredation [deprəˈdeɪʃn] *n.* attack/ ruining.

depress [dɪˈpres] *v.* (*a*) to make miserable. (*b*) to push down (a button). **depressed**, *adj.* miserable. **depressing**, *adj.* gloomy. **depression** [dɪˈpreʃn] *n.* (*a*) miserable feeling. (*b*) low pressure area bringing bad weather. (*c*) economic crisis. (*d*) hollow (in the ground). **depressive**, *adj.* which makes s.o. depressed.

deprive [dɪˈpraɪv] *v.* **to d. s.o. of sth** = to take sth away from s.o. **deprivation** [deprɪˈveɪʃn] *n.* being deprived of sth. **deprived**, *adj.* (person) who has not enjoyed any of society's benefits.

dept. = department.

depth [depθ] *n.* (*a*) how deep sth is; distance downwards; **he's out of his d.** = (i) the water is too deep for him; (ii) it is too difficult for him to understand. (*b*) very deep point. **depth charge,** *n.* type of bomb dropped into the sea which explodes deep beneath the surface.

deputation [depjʊˈteɪʃn] *n.* group of people who speak on behalf of others. **depute. 1.** *n.* [ˈdepjuːt] (*in Scotland*) deputy. **2.** *v.* [dɪˈpjuːt] to give responsibility (**to** s.o.). **deputize** [ˈdepjʊtaɪz] *v.* to stand in (**for** s.o.). **deputy** [ˈdepjʊtɪ] *n.* person who can take the place of another person.

derail [dɪˈreɪl] *v.* to make (a train) leave the rails. **derailment,** *n.* leaving the rails. **derailleur** [dɪˈreɪljə] *n.* bicycle gear system, where the chain goes round a movable sprocket.

deranged [dɪˈreɪnʒd] *adj.* mad.

derby [ˈdɑːbɪ] *n.* (*a*) sporting contest between local teams. (*b*) *Am.* [ˈdɜːrbɪ] bowler hat.

deregulate [dɪˈregjuleɪt] *v.* to remove government restrictions over an industry. **deregulation,** *n.* removal of official restrictions.

derelict [ˈderəlɪkt] **1.** *n.* tramp/dosser. **2.** *adj.* ruined and abandoned. **dereliction** [derəˈlɪkʃən] *n.* neglecting (to do your duty).

derestricted [diːrɪˈstrɪktɪd] *adj.* (road) with no speed limit.

deride [dɪˈraɪd] *v.* to laugh at (s.o.). **derision** [dɪˈrɪʒn] *n.* mockery. **derisive** [dɪˈraɪsɪv] *adj.* mocking (laughter). **derisory** [dɪˈraɪzərɪ] *adj.* laughably small (amount).

de rigueur [dərɪˈgɜːə] *adv.* obligatory.

derive [dɪˈraɪv] *v.* to come originally (**from** sth). **derivation** [derɪˈveɪʃn] *n.* origin (of a word). **derivative** [dɪˈrɪvətɪv] *n.* thing which is derived.

dermatitis [dɜːməˈtaɪtɪs] *n.* disease of the skin. **dermatologist** [dɜːməˈtɒlədʒɪst] *n.* person who studies dermatology. **dermatology,** *n.* study of skin diseases.

derogatory [dɪˈrɒgətrɪ] *adj.* showing contempt.

derrick [ˈderɪk] *n.* large metal construction (like a crane); **oil d.** = metal frame which holds the drilling equipment for an oil well.

derris [ˈderɪs] *n.* powder used to kill insects.

derv [dɜːv] *n.* fuel used in diesel engines.

desalinate [diːˈsælɪneɪt] *v.* to remove salt (from sea water).

descant [ˈdeskænt] *n.* musical part which is played/sung much higher than the rest.

descend [dɪˈsend] *v.* (*a*) to go down (a staircase, etc.). (*b*) **to d. from s.o.** = to have s.o. as an ancestor. (*c*) **to d. upon** = to attack; *inf.* to visit unexpectedly. **descendant,** *n.* person whose family goes back to a certain ancestor. **descent,** *n.* (*a*) going down. (*b*) **he is of Irish descent** = his family was Irish.

describe [dɪˈskraɪb] *v.* to say what (sth/s.o.) is like. **description** [dɪˈskrɪpʃn] *n.* picture in words of what sth is like. **descriptive,** *adj.* which says what sth is like.

desecrate [ˈdesɪkreɪt] *v.* to use (a church/a grave) in a disrespectful way. **desecration,** *n.* act of desecrating.

desegregate [dɪˈsegrəgeɪt] *v.* to end the segregation of (a group of people, or institution). **desegregation,** *n.* action of desegregating.

deselect [disəˈlekt] *v.* to remove the approval of a local political party for a candidate or for an MP. **deselection,** *n.* removal of approval for an MP or a candidate.

desert 1. *adj. & n.* [ˈdezət] very dry, usu. sandy (place). **2.** *v.* [dɪˈzɜːt] to leave the armed forces without permission; to leave (s.o.) all by himself. **deserted,** *adj.* abandoned; with no inhabitants. **deserter,** *n.* person who leaves the armed forces without permission. **desertion,** *n.* act of deserting. **deserts** [dɪˈzɜːts] *n. pl.* (*formal*) **just d.** = rightful reward.

deserve [dɪˈzɜːv] *v.* to merit (sth). **deservedly** [dɪˈzɜːvɪdlɪ] *adv.* in a way which is right. **deserving,** *adj.* which ought to be supported/helped.

desiccate [ˈdesɪkeɪt] *v.* to dry.

design [dɪˈzaɪn] **1.** *n.* plan; drawing of sth, before it is constructed; **to have designs on** = to plan to attack/take (sth). **2.** *v.* to plan (sth). **designer,** *n.* artist who plans sth. **designing,** *adj.* crafty (person).

designate [ˈdezɪgneɪt] **1.** *v.* to appoint (s.o.) to a post. **2.** *suffix showing* person who has been appointed but has not started work; **the ambassador-designate. designation,** *n.* act of designating.

desire [dɪ'zaɪə] **1.** *n.* want. **2.** *v.* to want. **desirability,** *n.* being desirable. **desirable,** *adj.* which a lot of people want. **desirous,** *adj.* (**of**) wanting.

desist [dɪ'zɪst] *v.* (*formal*) (**from**) to stop doing (sth).

desk [desk] *n.* table for writing. **desktop publishing,** *n.* creating finished printed documents using a computer and a special program.

desolate ['desələt] *adj.* bleak inhospitable (place). **desolation** [desə'leɪʃn] *n.* bleakness; ruin (of a place).

despair [dɪ'speə] **1.** *n.* hopelessness. **2.** *v.* **he despaired of being rescued** = he had given up all hope of being rescued.

desperate ['desprət] *adj.* (*a*) hopeless. (*b*) wild (through being in despair). **desperately,** *adv.* urgently; wildly. **desperation** [despə'reɪʃn] *n.* hopelessness.

despicable [dɪ'spɪkəbl] *adj.* worthless/which you can look down on.

despise [dɪ'spaɪz] *v.* to look down on (s.o.)/to think (s.o.) is not worth much.

despite [dɪ'spaɪt] *prep.* in spite of.

despoil [dɪ'spɔɪl] *v.* to ruin, to plunder.

despondency [dɪ'spɒndənsɪ] *n.* discouragement. **despondent,** *adj.* discouraged.

despot ['despɒt] *n.* tyrant/dictator. **despotic** [dɪ'spɒtɪk] *adj.* like a dictator. **despotism** *n.* tyranny/dictatorship.

dessert [dɪ'zɜːt] *n.* sweet course (in a meal). **dessertspoon,** *n.* spoon for eating dessert.

destination [destɪ'neɪʃn] *n.* place a person/vehicle is going to. **destine** ['destɪn] *v.* to aim (s.o.) **for** a certain position. **destiny,** *n.* what may happen in the future.

destitute ['destɪtjuːt] *adj.* with no money or belongings. **destitution** [destɪ'tjuːʃn] *n.* being destitute.

destroy [dɪ'strɔɪ] *v.* to remove/to kill; to ruin completely. **destroyer,** *n.* medium-sized naval ship.

destruction [dɪ'strʌkʃn] *n.* complete ruining. **destructive** [dɪ'strʌktɪv] *adj.* which destroys. **destructiveness,** *n.* tendency to destroy things.

desultory ['dezəltrɪ] *adj.* haphazard/with no connecting links.

detach [dɪ'tætʃ] *v.* to separate; **detached house** = house which is not attached to another. **detachable,** *adj.* which you can separate. **detachment,** *n.* (*a*) indifference; lack of immediate interest. (*b*) small group of servicemen, etc.

detail ['diːteɪl] **1.** *n.* small item. **2.** *v.* (*a*) to list all the small items. (*b*) **to do sth to do s.o.** = to give a task or duty to s.o.

detain [dɪ'teɪn] *v.* (*a*) to keep (s.o. in prison). (*b*) to hold (s.o.) back; to stop (s.o.) from leaving. **detainee** [diːteɪ'niː] *n.* person held in prison.

detect [dɪ'tekt] *v.* to discover; to notice. **detection** [dɪ'tekʃn] *n.* discovery. **detective,** *n.* policeman who investigates crimes. **detector,** *n.* instrument which discovers sth.

détente [deɪ'tɑːnt] *n.* friendly atmosphere between two formerly hostile countries.

detention [dɪ'tenʃn] *n.* imprisonment; keeping s.o. from leaving; **d. centre** = place where young criminals are imprisoned for a short time.

deter [dɪ'tɜː] *v.* (**deterred**) to discourage (s.o. **from** doing sth).

detergent [dɪ'tɜːdʒənt] *n.* chemical used instead of soap for washing clothes or dishes.

deteriorate [dɪ'tɪərɪəreɪt] *v.* to go bad; to get worse. **deterioration** [dɪtɪərɪə'reɪʃn] *n.* worsening.

determine [dɪ'tɜːmɪn] *v.* (*a*) to fix (a date, etc.). (*b*) to decide finally (**to**). **determinant,** *n.* thing which determines. **determination** [dɪtɜːmɪ'neɪʃn] *n.* firm intention. **determined,** *adj.* resolved (**to**).

deterrent [dɪ'terənt] *n.* thing which discourages; **nuclear d.** = nuclear weapon which it is hoped will discourage the enemy from attacking.

detest [dɪ'test] *v.* to dislike intensely. **destestable,** *adj.* very unpleasant. **detestation** [diːtes'teɪʃn] *n.* strong dislike.

detonate ['detəneɪt] *v.* to set off (an explosive). **detonation** [detə'neɪʃn] *n.* explosion. **detonator,** *n.* small explosive charge which will set off a large explosion.

detour ['diːtʊə] *n.* roundabout road taken to avoid an obstacle/to see sth not on the direct route.

detract [dɪ'trækt] v. (**from**) to remove part of sth/to make sth less important. **detractor**, n. person who criticizes sth.

detriment ['detrɪmənt] n. hurt; damage; **to the d. of** = damaging to. **detrimental** [detrɪ'mentl] adj. which damages.

detritus [di:'traɪtəs] n. rubbish which is formed by the weathering of rock; any waste matter.

deuce [dju:s] n. (a) score in tennis when both players are at 40 points. (b) score of two (in cards).

deuterium [dju:'tɪərɪəm] n. heavy form of hydrogen.

Deutschmark ['dɔɪtʃmɑ:k] n. currency used in Germany.

devalue [di:'vælju:] v. to reduce value of (a currency) in relationship to that of other countries. **devaluation** [di:vælju-'eɪʃn] n. reducing the international value of currency.

devastate ['devəsteɪt] v. to wreck/to lay waste (countryside). **devastating**, adj overwhelming. **devastation** [devə-'steɪʃn] n. widespread damage.

develop [dɪ'veləp] v. (a) to use to good purpose. (b) to expand. (c) to start (a disease, etc.). (d) to produce and fix (a photograph) from film. (e) to grow. **developer**, n. (a) liquid for developing photographs. (b) person who builds property. **developing**, adj. growing; **d. countries** = countries which are becoming industrialized. **development**, n. (a) growth. (b) **developments** = what will happen.

deviate ['di:vɪeɪt] v. to swerve/to turn away (from a direct line). **deviation** [di:vɪ'eɪʃn] n. moving away from a direct or normal line. **deviance**, n. deviation from normal human behaviour. **deviant**, adj. & n. (person) who deviates from normal human behaviour.

device [dɪ'vaɪs] n. (a) small (useful) machine. (b) **left to his own devices** = left to do whatever he wanted. (c) emblem (on a coat of arms).

devil ['devl] n. (a) evil spirit; inf. **what the devil?** = what on earth? **d.'s advocate** = person who argues the opposite point of view, in order to oppose a widely held opinion. (b) inf. person;

lucky d.! **devilish**, adj. referring to the devil. **devilled**, adj. cooked in a spicy sauce. **devilment, devilry**, n. wicked behaviour.

devious ['di:vɪəs] adj. not straight-forward; roundabout. **deviously**, adv. in a devious way. **deviousness**, n. not being straightforward.

devise [dɪ'vaɪz] v. to think up; to invent.

devoid [dɪ'vɔɪd] adj. empty (**of**).

devolution [di:və'lju:ʃn] n. removing of power from the centre. **devolve** [dɪ'vɒlv] v. to pass on (responsibility) to a deputy.

devote [dɪ'vəʊt] v. **to d. time to sth** = spend time on sth. **devoted**, adj. (person) who spends all his time on sth. **devotee** [devə'ti:] n. (**of**) person who is very enthusiastic about sth. **devotion** [dɪ'vəʊʃn] n. (religious) attachment; **devotions** = prayers. **devotional**, adj. religious.

devour [dɪ'vaʊə] v. (formal) to eat (greedily).

devout [dɪ'vaʊt] adj. pious; deeply concerned with religion.

dew [dju:] n. water which forms at night on objects in the open air. **dewdrop**, n. drop of dew; inf. drop on the end of s.o.'s nose. **dew claw**, n. small claw on the side of a dog's foot. **dewlap**, n. skin which hangs in folds on the throat. **dewy**, adj. covered in dew. **dewy-eyed**, adj. innocent and sentimental.

dexterity [dek'sterətɪ] n. skill (with hands). **dextrous** ['dekstrəs] adj. clever (with one's hands).

dextrose ['dekstrəʊz] n. sweet substance found naturally.

dhow [daʊ] n. Arab sailing boat.

diabetes [daɪə'bi:ti:z] n. (no pl.) illness where the sugar content of the blood rises because of lack of insulin. **diabetic** [daɪə'betɪk] 1. adj. referring to diabetes; **d. food** = food with a low sugar content which can be eaten by people suffering from diabetes. 2. n. person suffering from diabetes.

diabolic(al) [daɪə'bɒlɪk(l)] adj. referring to the devil; evil.

diacritic [daɪə'krɪtɪk] n. sign written above a character to show pronunciation.

diadem ['daɪədem] n. crown.

diaeresis [daɪˈɪərɪsɪs] *n.* two dots (¨) put over a vowel to show that it is pronounced separately from another.

diagnose [daɪəgˈnəʊz] *v.* to identify (an illness). **diagnosis,** *n.* (*pl.* **-ses**) identification (of an illness). **diagnostic** [daɪəgˈnɒstɪk] *adj.* referring to diagnosis. **diagnostics,** *pl. n.* test to find faults in computer hardware/software.

diagonal [daɪˈægənl] *adj. & n.* (line) going from one corner to another slantwise. **diagonally,** *adv.* slantwise.

diagram [ˈdaɪəgræm] *n.* sketch/plan. **diagrammatic** [daɪəgrəˈmætɪk] *adj.* in the form of a diagram.

dial [ˈdaɪəl] **1.** *n.* round face (of a clock/meter/telephone). **2.** *v.* (**dialled**) to make a telephone number; **to call the police you must dial 999. dialling,** *n.* making a number on the telephone; **d. tone** = sound on the telephone which shows that you can dial; **d. code** = number which you dial to call a particular town or country.

dialect [ˈdaɪəlekt] *n.* variety of a language spoken in a particular area. **dialectal,** *adj.* referring to a dialect.

dialectic [daɪəˈlektɪk] *n.* reasoned investigation of philosophical truth.

dialogue [ˈdaɪəlɒg] *n.* conversation between two people/two groups.

dialysis [daɪˈælɪsɪs] *n.* cleaning of the blood by passing it through a filter.

diameter [daɪˈæmɪtə] *n.* distance across the centre of a circle. **diametrically** [daɪəˈmetrɪklɪ] *adv.* **d. opposed to** = completely against/opposite.

diamond [ˈdaɪəmənd] *n.* (*a*) very hard transparent precious stone; **d. wedding** = 60th wedding anniversary. (*b*) one of the four suits in a pack of cards.

dianthus [daɪˈænθəs] *n.* Latin name for carnations or pinks.

diaper [ˈdaɪəpə] *n. Am.* nappy.

diaphanous [daɪˈæfənəs] *adj.* (cloth) which is so thin that you can see through it.

diaphragm [ˈdaɪəfræm] *n.* (*a*) thin sheet which vibrates with noise. (*b*) thin wall of muscle separating the chest and the abdomen.

diarrhoea, *Am.* **diarrhea** [daɪəˈrɪə] *n.* illness of the intestines where your bowel movements are very fluid.

diary [ˈdaɪərɪ] *n.* (*a*) description of what has happened in your life day by day; **he has kept a d. for years.** (*b*) small book in which you write notes/appointments for each day of the week. **diarist,** *n.* person who writes a diary.

diastase [daɪəˈsteɪz] *n.* enzyme which breaks down starch and converts it to sugar.

diastole [daɪəˈstəʊl] *n.* phase in the beating of the heart when the heart swells and fills with blood.

diatom [ˈdaɪætəm] *n.* type of microscopic sea creature.

diatribe [ˈdaɪətraɪb] *n.* violent spoken or written criticism.

dibber, dibble [ˈdɪbə, ˈdɪbl] *n.* stick used to make holes in the ground for planting.

dice [daɪs] **1.** *n.* (*pl.* **dice**) small cube with one to six dots on each face (for games). **2.** *v.* (*a*) to cut up (vegetables, etc.) into very small cubes. (*b*) to gamble. **dicey,** *adj. inf.* dangerous/difficult.

dichotomy [daɪˈkɒtəmɪ] *n.* splitting into two (usu. contradictory) parts.

dickens [ˈdɪkɪnz] *n. inf.* **the d. of** = a lot of; **what the d.?** = what on earth?

dicker [ˈdɪkə] *v. inf.* **to d. about** = to hesitate.

dicky [ˈdɪkɪ] **1.** *n. inf.* (*a*) false shirt front. (*b*) folding back seat in a car. **2.** *adj. inf.* ill; not working properly.

dicotyledon [daɪkɒtɪˈliːdən] *n.* plant whose seedlings have two fleshy leaves.

dictate [dɪkˈteɪt] *v.* (*a*) to say (sth) to s.o. who writes down your words. (*b*) to tell s.o. what to do. **dictation** [dɪkˈteɪʃn] *n.* act of dictating (sth to be written down). **dictator,** *n.* person who rules a country alone. **dictatorial** [dɪktəˈtɔːrɪəl] *adj.* like a dictator. **dictatorship,** *n.* rule of a country by one person.

diction [ˈdɪkʃn] *n.* way of speaking.

dictionary [ˈdɪkʃənrɪ] *n.* (*a*) book which lists words in alphabetical order, giving their meanings or translations. (*b*) list of correctly spelled words in a spelling check program.

dictum [ˈdɪktəm] *n.* (*pl.* **-ta**) saying (made by a notable person).

did [dɪd] *v. see* **do.**

didactic [daɪˈdæktɪk] *adj.* which teaches.

diddle ['dɪdl] v. inf. to trick/to cheat.
die [daɪ] 1. n. metal stamp for making coins. 2. v. to stop living; inf. **I'm dying to read his book** = I am very eager to read his book; **I'm dying for a cup of tea** = I'd love a cup of tea; **the sound died away** = became fainter; **the wind died down** = became less strong; **the old customs are dying out** = not being continued. **diecast**, adj. cast from metal in a mould. **diehard**, adj. & n. inf. very reactionary (person).
dieldrin [daɪ'eldrɪn] n. powerful insecticide.
diesel ['di:zl] n. **d. engine** = engine which runs on thicker fuel than petrol; **d. oil** = oil used in diesel engines.
diet ['daɪət] 1. n. (a) kind of food you eat; **to be on a d.** = to eat only one sort of food/to eat less. (b) (in some countries) parliament. 2. v. to eat less food/only one sort of food. **dietary**, adj. referring to a diet. **dieter**, n. person who is on a diet. **dietetics**, n. study of food and its nutritional value. **dietician** [daɪə'tɪʃn] n. person who specializes in the study of diets.
differ ['dɪfə] v. **to d. from** = not to be the same as; **I beg to d.** = I must disagree.
difference ['dɪfrəns] n. way in which two things are not the same; **it doesn't make any d.** = it does not alter the situation. **different**, adj. not the same; **that is quite a d. thing** = it is not at all the same. **differential** [dɪfə'renʃl] 1. adj. showing up the difference; **d. equation**. 2. n. (a) part of the axle of a car which allows wheels to turn at different speeds at corners. (b) difference in salary between different grades of jobs. **differentiate**, v. to make/to tell the difference (between). **differentiation**, n. act of differentiating. **differently**, adv. not in the same way.
difficult ['dɪfɪkʌlt] adj. not easy. **difficulty**, n. thing which is not easy; **she got into difficulties when swimming** = she was in danger of drowning; **he is in financial difficulties** = he has problems to do with money.
diffidence ['dɪfɪdəns] n. being diffident. **diffident**, adj. shy; lacking confidence. **diffidently**, adv. shyly.
diffract [dɪ'frækt] v. to split light

into its different colours. **diffraction** [dɪ'frækʃn] n. splitting up of light into its different colours.
diffuse 1. adj. [dɪ'fju:s] vague/unclear; **d. lighting** = soft lighting, not giving any sharp shadows. 2. v. [dɪ'fju:z] to spread out; to send out; **diffused lighting** = soft lighting, not giving any sharp shadows. **diffusion**, n. act of diffusing.
dig [dɪg] 1. n. (a) poke; **he gave me a d. in the ribs** = he nudged me with his elbow. (b) satirical attack. (c) archaeological excavation. 2. v. (**dug; has dug**) to make a hole in the ground; **we dug up a Roman coin in the garden** = we found the coin when digging. **digger**, n. person/machine that digs. **digging**, n. action of making a hole in the ground. **dig in**, v. (a) to bury (manure) in the ground. (b) inf. to start eating. **digs**, n. pl. inf. furnished room(s) let to students, etc.
digest 1. n. ['daɪdʒest] summary. 2. v. [daɪ'dʒest] (a) to turn (food) into energy in the stomach and intestine; **I cannot d. my dinner** = I am feeling unwell after my dinner. (b) to ponder over (a piece of information). **digestible**, adj. which can be digested. **digestion**, n. action of turning food into energy. **digestive**, adj. which helps you to digest; **d. biscuit** = sweet wholemeal biscuit.
digit ['dɪdʒɪt] n. (a) single figure (from 0 to 9). (b) finger or toe. **digital**, adj. which involves figures; **d. watch** = watch where the time is shown by figures (such as 11:52); **d. computer** = computer which works on a varied signal. **digitize**, v. to convert information to digital form.
digitalin, digitalis [dɪdʒɪ'teɪlɪn, -ɪs] n. drugs made from foxgloves.
dignified ['dɪgnɪfaɪd] adj. solemn/important-looking. **dignify**, v. to honour (s.o.) with a title; to give dignity to (s.o.). **dignitary**, n. important person; **civic dignitaries** = the mayor, councillors, etc., of a town. **dignity**, n. (a) solemn/serious way of behaving; **it is beneath his d. to clean his own shoes** = he is too proud to clean them. (b) title (given to s.o. as an honour).
digress [daɪ'gres] v. to wander away from the subject when speaking. **di-**

gression, *n.* speech/writing which does not deal with the subject.

dihedral [dar'hi:drəl] *n.* angle at which an aircraft's wing varies from the horizontal.

dike [daɪk] *n.* (*a*) long wall of earth to keep out water. (*b*) long ditch.

diktat ['dɪktæt] *n.* official command.

dilapidated [dɪ'læpɪdeɪtɪd] *adj.* falling into ruin. **dilapidation,** *n.* being in ruins.

dilate [daɪ'leɪt] *v.* to make (eyes) grow larger; (*of the eyes*) to grow larger. **dilate upon,** *v.* to talk at length about. **dilatation** [dɪlə'teɪʃn], **dilation** [daɪ'leɪʃn] *n.* act of dilating. **dilator,** *n.* drug used to make a part of the body (such as the eyes) grow larger.

dilatory ['dɪlətərɪ] *adj.* slow (to act). **dilatoriness,** *n.* slowness.

dilemma [dɪ'lemə] *n.* serious problem, where a choice has to be made between several bad alternatives; **in a d.** = not knowing which course of action to follow.

dilettante [dɪlɪ'tæntɪ] *n.* person who is interested in a subject, but not very seriously.

diligence ['dɪlɪdʒəns] *n.* hard work/taking care. **diligent,** *adj.* hard-working.

dill [dɪl] *n.* herb used for flavouring fish and pickles.

dilly-dally ['dɪlɪ'dælɪ] *v.* to hang back; to loiter.

dilute [daɪ'lju:t] **1.** *v.* to add water to (another liquid) to make it weaker. **2.** *adj.* with water added. **dilution,** *n.* act of diluting.

dim [dɪm] **1.** *adj.* (**dimmer, dimmest**) (*a*) weak (light); **I have a d. recollection of it** = I can remember it vaguely. (*b*) rather stupid. **2.** *v.* (**dimmed**) to turn down (a light); **the house lights dimmed** = the lights in the theatre were turned down (as the play started). **dimly,** *adv.* vaguely; unclearly. **dimmer,** *n.* light switch which dims a light. **dimness,** *n.* weakness (of light); vagueness (of memory).

dime [daɪm] *n. Am.* ten cent coin.

dimension [dɪ'menʃn] *n.* measurement (in figures). **dimensional,** *adj.* **two-dimensional** = having two dimensions, flat; **three-dimensional** = having three dimensions/in the round.

diminish [dɪ'mɪnɪʃ] *v.* to make (sth) smaller; to become smaller. **diminution** [dɪmɪ'nju:ʃn] *n.* becoming smaller. **diminutive** [dɪ'mɪnjʊtɪv] **1.** *adj.* very small. **2.** *n.* word used to show that sth is small; **'Kate' is a d. of 'Catherine'.**

diminuendo [dɪmɪnjʊ'endəʊ] *n.* (*in music*) decreasing noise.

dimple ['dɪmpl] *n.* small hollow (in cheeks/in babies' fat elbows). **dimpled,** *adj.* with dimples.

din [dɪn] **1.** *n.* loud noise. **2.** *v.* (**dinned**) to force (a piece of information **into** s.o.'s head) by frequently repeating it.

dine [daɪn] *v.* to have dinner; **to d. out** = to have dinner away from home. **diner,** *n.* (*a*) person eating dinner. (*b*) dining car. (*c*) *Am.* small restaurant selling hot food. **dining car,** *n.* restaurant car (on a train). **dining room,** *n.* room where people usually eat.

ding-dong ['dɪŋdɒŋ] **1.** *n.* sound made by a bell. **2.** *adj. & n. inf.* vigorous (argument).

dinghy ['dɪŋgɪ] *n.* small boat.

dingo ['dɪŋgəʊ] *n.* Australian wild dog.

dingy ['dɪndʒɪ] *adj.* (**-ier, -iest**) dirty. **dinginess,** *n.* dirt.

dinkum ['dɪŋkəm] *adj.* (*in Australia*) *inf.* real.

dinner ['dɪnə] *n.* main meal (usu. the evening meal); **school d.** = meal served to children in school in the middle of the day; **d. break** = school break at the middle of the day; **d. table** = table (where people eat); **d. party** = dinner to which guests are invited; **d. service** = set of plates for eating a meal; **d. jacket** = formal (usu. black) jacket worn for dinner with a black bow tie.

dinosaur ['daɪnəsɔ:] *n.* large prehistoric reptile.

dint [dɪnt] *n.* **by d. of** = through; by means of.

diocese ['daɪəsɪs] *n.* area under the charge of a bishop. **diocesan** [daɪ'ɒsɪzn] *adj.* referring to a diocese.

dioxide [daɪ'ɒksaɪd] *n.* oxide with two parts of oxygen to one part of another substance.

dip [dɪp] **1.** *n.* (*a*) quick covering with liquid. (*b*) sudden drop (of a road/of land). (*c*) savoury paste, into which biscuits, etc., can be dipped as cocktail snacks. (d) short bathe/swim. (e) **sheep d.** = place where sheep are dipped in pesticide to kill ticks. **2.** v. **(dipped)** (a) to put (sth) quickly **into** a liquid. (b) to dive. (c) **to d. your headlights** = to lower the beam of your headlights when another car is approaching. (d) **to d. into a book** = to read a few lines here and there. **dipper,** n. (a) **big d.** = fairground railway which goes up and down steep slopes. (b) small brown bird which dives into water. **dipstick,** n. rod (in the engine of a car) which shows the level of oil in the engine.

diphtheria [dɪf'θɪərɪə] n. (no pl.) serious infectious disease of babies.

diphthong ['dɪfθɒŋ] n. two vowel sounds which are pronounced together.

diploma [dɪ'pləʊmə] n. certificate showing that you have passed an examination.

diplomacy [dɪ'pləʊməsɪ] n. art of negotiating between different parties, esp. between different countries. **diplomat** {'dɪpləmæt] n. person (such as an ambassador) who represents his country abroad. **diplomatic** [dɪplə-'mætɪk] adj. (a) representing one's country. (b) careful not to give offence. **diplomatically,** adv. in a diplomatic way. **diplomatist** [dɪ'pləʊmətɪst] n. diplomat.

dipsomania [dɪpsə'meɪnɪə] n. habitual drinking of alcohol. **dipsomaniac,** n. person who wants to drink alcohol all the time.

dire ['daɪə] adj. very serious; **d. necessity** = urgent necessity.

direct [daɪ'rekt/dɪ'rekt] **1.** v. (a) to aim towards a point. (b) to tell (s.o.) to do sth; to manage/organize (a film, etc.). **2.** adj. straight; **d. taxation** = taxes which you pay to the tax office; **d. hit** = hit on the target; **there is a d. flight to London** = the plane does not stop between here and London. **3.** adv. straight; without stopping. **direction** [daɪ'rekʃn] n. (a) point to which you are going/at which you are aiming. (b) instruction. (c) guiding (of the making of a film). **directional,** adj. going in one direction. **directive,** n. official instruction. **directly. 1.** adv. immediately; straight.

2. conj. **I will write the letter d. I get home** = as soon as I get home. **directness,** n. frankness (of a reply). **director** [daɪ'rektə] n. (a) person who is appointed by the shareholders to help run a firm; **managing d.** = person who is in charge of a firm. (b) person in charge of making a film/a play. **directorate,** n. group of directors. **directorship,** n. position of director. **directory,** n. list of people/businesses showing their telephone numbers and addresses; book giving lists of people/ businesses with their addresses and telephone numbers; **classified d.** = telephone directory where firms are classified into various groups.

dirge [dɜːdʒ] n. funeral song.

dirigible [dɪ'rɪdʒɪbl] n. large airship which can be steered.

dirk [dɜːk] n. short dagger.

dirndl ['dɜːndl] n. wide skirt gathered tight at the waist.

dirt [dɜːt] n. mud; earth; filth; **d. cheap** = extremely cheap. **dirtiness,** n. being dirty/not being clean. **dirt-track,** n. cinder-covered track for racing. **dirty. 1.** adj. (-ier, -iest) (a) not clean; covered with dirt. (b) **d. weather** = grey/drizzly weather; **d. trick** = low/unpleasant trick. **2.** v. to cover with dirt.

disability [dɪsə'bɪlɪtɪ] n. physical handicap. **disabled** [dɪs'eɪbld] **1.** adj. physically handicapped. **2.** n. **the d.** = physically handicapped people.

disabuse [dɪsə'bjuːz] v. to make (s.o.) see that he was wrong.

disadvantage [dɪsəd'vɑːntɪdʒ] n. handicap; drawback; lack of advantage. **disadvantaged,** adj. handicapped. **disadvantageous** [dɪsædvɑːn'teɪdʒəs] adj. which does not give an advantage; unfavourable.

disaffected [dɪsə'fektɪd] adj. discontented/rebellious.

disagree [dɪsə'griː] v. not to agree; **cabbage disagrees with me** = makes me feel ill. **disagreeable,** adj. unpleasant. **disagreement,** n. lack of agreement.

disallow [dɪsə'laʊ] v. to refuse to accept; **the team's second goal was disallowed** = was not counted.

disappear [dɪsə'pɪə] v. to vanish. **disappearance,** n. vanishing.

disappoint [dɪsə'pɔɪnt] v. to let (s.o.) down; not to turn out as expected. **disappointing,** adj. unsatisfactory; not coming up to expectations. **disappointment,** n. sadness because what was expected did not take place.

disapprove [dɪsə'pruːv] v. not to approve (of sth). **disapproval, disapprobation** [dɪsæprəu'beɪʃn] n. lack of approval. **disapprovingly,** adv. in a way which shows you do not approve.

disarm [dɪs'ɑːm] v. to remove weapons from (s.o.). **disarmament,** n. abolition of weapons by a country. **disarming,** adj. charming (manner) which prevents people from criticizing.

disarrange [dɪsə'reɪndʒ] v. to put (sth) into disorder.

disarray [dɪsə'reɪ] n. lack of order.

disaster [dɪ'zɑːstə] n. catastrophe; very bad accident; **air d.** = crash of an aircraft killing many people. **disastrous,** adj. very bad/catastrophic. **disastrously,** adv. very badly.

disband [dɪs'bænd] v. to send (soldiers) back home; to split up (a group of soldiers/musicians, etc.).

disbar [dɪs'bɑː] v. (**disbarred**) (formal) to remove (a lawyer) from the bar.

disbelief [dɪsbɪ'liːf] n. lack of belief. **disbeliever,** n. person who does not believe.

disbud [dɪs'bʌd] v. (**disbudded**) to remove some of the buds from (a plant).

disburse [dɪs'bɜːs] v. to pay out (money).

disc [dɪsk] n. round flat object, esp. a record for playing on a record-player; **slipped d.** = painful condition where one of the cushioning discs in the spine has become displaced; **d. brakes** = brakes in a car which are in the form of discs; **d. harrow** = type of harrow, formed of a series of metal discs; **d. jockey** = person who plays records on the radio/in a club, etc.

discard. 1. n. ['dɪskɑːd] thing which has been discarded. **2.** v. [dɪs'kɑːd] to put (sth) on one side; to reject.

discern [dɪ'sɜːn] v. to see/to make out. **discernible,** adj. which can be seen. **discerning,** adj. (person) who has good judgement. **discernment,** n. ability to judge correctly.

discharge 1. n. ['dɪstʃɑːdʒ] (a) liquid (coming out of a pipe, etc.); pus (coming out of a wound). (b) payment (of a debt). (c) release (of a prisoner). **2.** v. [dɪs'tʃɑːdʒ] (a) to unload (a cargo); to let off (a gun). (b) to send (s.o.) away; **he was discharged from hospital** = he was allowed to go home because he was better. (c) to release (a prisoner). (d) to pay (a debt); **discharged bankrupt** = person who has paid off his debts according to the requirements of the court.

disciple [dɪ'saɪpl] n. follower (of a religious leader).

discipline ['dɪsɪplɪn] **1.** n. keeping people under control. **2.** v. to control/to punish (s.o.). **disciplinarian** [dɪsɪplɪ'neərɪən] n. person who believes in strict discipline. **disciplinary** [dɪsɪ'plɪnərɪ] adj. (action) which keeps s.o. under control.

disclaim [dɪs'kleɪm] v. not to admit/to deny; **he disclaims all knowledge of the payment** = he says he knows nothing about the payment. **disclaimer,** n. statement in which you disclaim all knowledge of sth.

disclose [dɪs'kləuz] v. to reveal (a secret). **disclosure** [dɪs'kləuʒə] n. revealing (of a secret).

disco ['dɪskəu] n. (pl. **-os**) inf. discotheque; place where people dance to recorded music; dancing to pop/rock records.

discolour, Am. **discolor** [dɪs'kʌlə] v. to change the colour of (sth). **discoloration** [dɪskʌlə'reɪʃn] n. change of colour.

discomfort [dɪs'kʌmfət] n. lack of comfort.

disconcert [dɪskən'sɜːt] v. to surprise/to embarrass. **disconcerting,** adj. worrying/surprising.

disconnect [dɪskə'nekt] v. to undo (two things which are connected); **they disconnected the refrigerator** = they unplugged the refrigerator. **disconnected,** adj. disjointed; with no links.

disconsolate [dɪs'kɒnsələt] adj. very sad. **disconsolately,** adv. very sadly.

discontent [dɪskən'tent] n. state of not being satisfied. **discontented,** adj. not satisfied.

discontinue [dɪskən'tɪnjuː] v. not to continue to produce (sth). **discontinuity** [dɪskɒntɪ'njuɪtɪ] n. being discontinuous. **discontinuous,** adj. which stops and starts; intermittent.

discord ['dɪskɔːd] n. lack of agreement. **discordant** [dɪs'kɔːdənt] adj. (a) not in agreement. (b) out of harmony.

discotheque ['dɪskətek] n. place where people dance to recorded music.

discount 1. n. ['dɪskaʊnt] percentage less than the normal price; **d. store** = shop where goods are cheaper than elsewhere. 2. v. [dɪs'kaʊnt] (a) not to pay any attention to (sth). (b) to put a discount on (a price).

discourage [dɪs'kʌrɪdʒ] v. not to encourage; **to d. s.o. from doing sth** = to stop s.o. doing sth. **discouragement,** n. being discouraged; thing which stops you doing sth. **discouraging,** adj. not encouraging.

discourse 1. n. ['dɪskɔːs] (formal) talk/speech. 2. v. [dɪs'kɔːs] (formal) to speak.

discourteous [dɪs'kɜːtɪəs] adj. rude. **discourteously,** adv. rudely. **discourtesy,** n. rudeness.

discover [dɪs'kʌvə] v. to find (sth new). **discoverer,** n. person who finds sth. **discovery,** n. act of finding sth new.

discredit [dɪs'kredɪt] 1. n. doubt/lack of belief (in s.o.). 2. v. to make people doubt (s.o./sth); **he has been discredited** = no one believes him any more. **discreditable,** adj. not honourable (conduct). **discreditably,** adv. dishonourably.

discreet [dɪs'kriːt] adj. quiet; not allowing anyone to notice. **discreetly,** adv. quietly; without anyone noticing.

discrepancy [dɪs'krepənsɪ] n. lack of agreement (between figures/accounts).

discrete [dɪs'kriːt] adj. separate/not connected.

discretion [dɪs'kreʃn] n. wisdom/good sense; **I leave it to your d.** = I leave it for you to decide. **discretionary,** adj. (powers) used at s.o.'s discretion.

discriminate [dɪs'krɪmɪneɪt] v. to distinguish; **to d. between** = to treat (two things) differently; **to d. against** = to prefer (one thing to another). **discriminating,** adj. able to distinguish/judge. **discrimination** [dɪskrɪmɪ'neɪʃn] n. (a) judgement; **a man of d.** = of good taste. (b) preference (for or against sth); **racial d.** = preference for or against a race.

discursive [dɪs'kɜːsɪv] adj. not succinct/not to the point.

discus ['dɪskəs] n. (pl. -es) flat round disc which is thrown as a sport.

discuss [dɪs'kʌs] v. to talk about (a problem). **discussion** [dɪs'kʌʃn] n. talking about (a problem); **the question under d.** = the problem we are talking about.

disdain [dɪs'deɪn] 1. n. looking down; feeling that s.o./sth is inferior. 2. v. to look down on (sth); to refuse to do (sth) because it is beneath you. **disdainful,** adj. superior (air). **disdainfully,** adv. with a superior air.

disease [dɪ'ziːz] n. serious illness (of animals, plants, etc.). **diseased,** adj. sick.

disembark [dɪsɪm'baːk] v. to get off a ship. **disembarkation** [dɪsembaː-'keɪʃn] n. getting off a ship.

disembodied [dɪsɪm'bɒdɪd] adj. not connected to a body.

disembowel [dɪsɪm'baʊəl] v. to remove the intestines from (s.o.).

disenchanted [dɪsɪn'tʃaːntɪd] adj. (with) feeling that sth has not turned out as well as expected. **disenchantment,** n. feeling that sth has not turned out as well as expected.

disenfranchise [dɪsɪn'fræntʃaɪz] v. to take away the right to vote.

disengage [dɪsɪn'geɪdʒ] v. (a) to break off; **the troops disengaged** = the troops broke off the fighting. (b) to separate (the gears of a car).

disentangle [dɪsɪn'tæŋgl] v. to untie (knotted string, etc.).

disfavour, Am. **disfavor** [dɪs'feɪvə] n. shame; lack of favour; **the minister fell into d.** = he was disgraced; **the minister incurred the king's d.** = he fell into disgrace with the king.

disfigure [dɪs'fɪgə] v. to make ugly. **disfigurement,** n. act of disfiguring.

disfranchise [dɪs'fræntʃaɪz] v. to remove the right to vote from (s.o.). **disfranchisement,** n. removal of the right to vote.

disgorge [dɪs'gɔːdʒ] v. (a) to pour out. (b) to give up (things which have been stolen).

disgrace [dɪsˈɡreɪs] 1. *n.* shame; being out of favour with s.o.; **the minister fell into d.** = he was out of favour. 2. *v.* to bring shame on. **disgraceful,** *adj.* which you should be ashamed of. **disgracefully,** *adv.* in a disgraceful way.

disgruntled [dɪsˈɡrʌntld] *adj.* annoyed/discontented.

disguise [dɪsˈɡaɪz] 1. *n.* costume, wig, etc., to make a person look like s.o. else; **in d.** = dressed to look like s.o. else. 2. *v.* to dress so as to look like s.o. else; to make (sth) look/sound different; **there is no disguising the fact** = you cannot hide the fact.

disgust [dɪsˈɡʌst] 1. *n.* (at) strong dislike; feeling sick/very discontented. 2. *v.* to make (s.o.) feel sick. **disgusting,** *adj.* which makes you feel sick.

dish [dɪʃ] 1. *n.* (*pl.* **-es**) (*a*) large plate (for serving food); **to wash the dishes** = do the washing-up. (*b*) part of a meal; (plate of) prepared food. 2. *v.* **he is dishing up the food** = he is serving the meal; *inf.* **they are dishing out tickets** = they are handing out tickets. **dishcloth,** *n.* cloth for washing dishes. **dishwasher,** *n.* machine for washing dishes. **dishwater,** *n.* water which has been used for washing dishes. **dishy,** *adj. inf.* attractive (girl).

disharmony [dɪsˈhɑːmənɪ] *n.* not being in agreement/in harmony.

dishearten [dɪsˈhɑːtn] *v.* to discourage. **disheartening,** *adj.* discouraging.

dishevelled [dɪˈʃevəld] *adj.* uncombed (hair).

dishonest [dɪsˈɒnɪst] *adj.* not honest. **dishonestly,** *adv.* not honestly; illegally. **dishonesty,** *n.* lack of honesty.

dishonour, *Am.* **dishonor** [dɪsˈɒnə] 1. *n.* lack of honour. 2. *v.* (*a*) to treat rudely. (*b*) not to honour; **dishonoured cheque** = cheque which the bank will not pay. **dishonourable,** *adj.* not honourable; shameful. **dishonourably,** *adv.* in a dishonourable way.

disillusion [dɪsɪˈluːʒn] *n.* feeling of being let down/that sth has not turned out as you expected. **disillusioned,** *adj.* feeling that sth has not turned out as expected. **disillusionment,** *n.* feeling of being let down/that sth has not turned out as expected.

disincentive [dɪsɪnˈsentɪv] *n.* thing which discourages; **the low salary is a d. to work** = the salary does not encourage people to work.

disinclined [dɪsɪnˈklaɪnd] *adj.* not inclined; **she is feeling d. to go to work today** = she does not want to go to work today. **disinclination** [dɪsɪnklɪˈneɪʃn] *n.* not wanting to do sth.

disinfect [dɪsɪnˈfekt] *v.* to remove/to prevent infection. **disinfectant,** *n.* chemical liquid for fighting infection.

disinformation [dɪsɪnfəˈmeɪʃən] *n.* false information to confuse an enemy.

disingenuous [dɪsɪnˈdʒenjʊəs] *adj.* false; lacking frankness; pretending to be naive.

disinherit [dɪsɪnˈherɪt] *v.* to change your will so that s.o. will no longer inherit your money when you die.

disintegrate [dɪsˈɪntɪɡreɪt] *v.* to fall to pieces. **disintegration** [dɪsɪntɪˈɡreɪʃn] *n.* falling to pieces.

disinter [dɪsɪnˈtɜː] *v.* (**disinterred**) to dig up (sth) which has been buried.

disinterested [dɪsˈɪntrəstɪd] *adj.* not in favour of one side or the other; **he is a totally d. observer** = he is an impartial observer. **disinterestedness,** *n.* being disinterested.

disjointed [dɪsˈdʒɔɪntɪd] *adj.* without any links; unconnected.

disk [dɪsk] *n.* any round flat object, especially a piece of magnetized plastic used in computers to record information; **floppy d.** = small disk which can be inserted and removed from a computer; **hard d.** = disk with a large capacity, which is permanently fixed in a computer. **diskette,** *n.* small floppy disk. **disk drive,** *n.* device which spins a disk in a computer and controls the access of information.

dislike [dɪsˈlaɪk] 1. *n.* lack of liking; **to take a d. to** = to start to hate. 2. *v.* not to like; **I don't d. honey** = I rather like honey.

dislocate [ˈdɪsləkeɪt] *v.* (*a*) to put (an arm/leg, etc.) out of joint. (*b*) to disorganize. **dislocation** [dɪsləˈkeɪʃn] *n.* (*a*) disorganization. (*b*) putting an arm/leg, etc., out of joint.

dislodge [dɪsˈlɒdʒ] *v.* to detach/to remove.

disloyal [dɪs'lɔɪəl] *adj.* not loyal. **disloyalty,** *n.* being disloyal.

dismal ['dɪzməl] *adj.* miserable. **dismally,** *adv.* miserably; (to fail a test) very badly.

dismantle [dɪs'mæntl] *v.* to take to pieces.

dismay [dɪs'meɪ] **1.** *n.* horror/consternation. **2.** *v.* to strike (s.o.) with horror.

dismember [dɪs'membə] *v.* to cut up (a body) into parts; to take apart.

dismiss [dɪs'mɪs] *v.* (*a*) to send (s.o.) away. (*b*) to remove (s.o.) from a job. (*c*) to refuse (a request). **dismissal,** *n.* removal from a job.

dismount [dɪs'maʊnt] *v.* to get off a horse/bicycle, etc.

disobey [dɪsə'beɪ] *v.* not to obey. **disobedience** [dɪsə'biːdɪəns] *n.* lack of obedience. **disobedient,** *adj.* not obedient.

disorder [dɪs'ɔːdə] *n.* (*a*) lack of order; untidiness. (*b*) riot; disturbance. (*c*) illness. **disorderly,** *adj.* wild (crowd).

disorganize [dɪs'ɔːgənaɪz] *v.* to put (sth) out of its usual order.

disorientate [dɪs'ɔːrɪənteɪt] *v.* to make (s.o.) lose their sense of direction; to confuse (s.o.). **disorientation,** *n.* feeling lost.

disown [dɪs'əʊn] *v.* to refuse to acknowledge (sth) is yours.

disparage [dɪs'pærɪdʒ] *v.* to say that sth is bad. **disparagement,** *n.* act of disparaging. **disparaging,** *adj.* critical; saying that sth is bad.

disparate ['dɪspərət] *adj.* varied/different. **disparity** [dɪs'pærɪtɪ] *n.* difference.

dispassionate [dɪs'pæʃnət] *adj.* calm and without emotion. **dispassionately,** *adv.* calmly.

dispatch [dɪs'pætʃ] **1.** *n.* (*pl.* **-es**) (*a*) sending; **d. note** = note saying that goods have been sent. (*b*) speed (of doing sth). (*c*) message; **d. box** = box containing government papers; **d. rider** = motorcyclist who carries messages. **2.** *v.* (*a*) to send. (*b*) to finish quickly. (*c*) to kill off.

dispel [dɪs'pel] *v.* (**dispelled**) to clear away.

dispense [dɪs'pens] *v.* (*a*) to distribute. (*b*) to prepare and sell (medicine).

(*c*) **to d. with** = to do without. **dispensable,** *adj.* which can be dispensed with. **dispensary,** *n.* place where a chemist prepares medicines. **dispensation** [dɪspən'seɪʃn] *n.* permission not to follow a rule, etc. **dispenser,** *n.* automatic machine/box with a hole to allow one object to come out at a time. **dispensing,** *adj.* **d. chemist** = chemist who has the qualifications to prepare medicines.

disperse [dɪs'pɜːs] *v.* to clear away; to scatter in different directions. **dispersal, dispersion,** *n.* act of dispersing.

dispirited [dɪ'spɪrɪtɪd] *adj.* sad/discouraged; feeling disappointed.

displace [dɪs'pleɪs] *v.* to move (sth) from its usual place; **displaced persons** = refugees who have fled from their home lands. **displacement,** *n.* moving (of sth); amount of water removed by a ship, (hence) the volume of the ship.

display [dɪs'pleɪ] **1.** *n.* show/exhibition; **air d.** = exhibition of flying by various aircraft; **d. screen** = screen on which data is displayed. **d. unit** = special stand for showing goods for sale. **2.** *v.* to put (sth) on show.

displease [dɪs'pliːz] *v.* not to please. **displeasure** [dɪs'pleʒə] *n.* annoyance.

disport [dɪs'pɔːt] *v.* (*formal*) **to d. oneself** = to amuse oneself.

dispose [dɪs'pəʊz] *v.* **to d. of sth** = to get rid of sth. **disposable,** *adj.* which can be thrown away after use; **d. income** = amount of income left after the tax has been deducted. **disposal,** *n.* (*a*) **waste d. unit** = machine attached to a sink which grinds up waste. (*b*) **I am at your d.** = you can ask me to do anything you wish. **disposed,** *adj.* **he is well d. towards us** = he favours us. **disposition** [dɪspə'zɪʃn] *n.* (*a*) character. (*b*) act of passing property to another person.

dispossess [dɪspə'zes] *v.* **to d. s.o. of** = to remove possessions from s.o.

disproportion [dɪsprə'pɔːʃn] *n.* being out of proportion. **disproportionate,** *adj.* unusual; out of proportion. **disproportionately,** *adv.* in a disproportionate way.

disprove [dɪs'pruːv] *v.* to prove (sth) is wrong.

dispute [dɪs'pjuːt] **1.** *n.* argument. **2.**

v. to argue that (sth) is incorrect. **disputable,** *adj.* which can be disputed. **disputant,** *n.* person who disputes. **disputation,** *n.* (*formal*) argument.

disqualify [dɪs'kwɒlɪfaɪ] *v.* to rule that (s.o.) is incapable of doing sth/not qualified to do sth. **disqualification** [dɪskwɒlɪfɪ'keɪʃn] *n.* rule that s.o. is disqualified.

disquiet [dɪs'kwaɪət] *n.* worry. **disquieting,** *adj.* which makes you worried.

disquisition [dɪskwɪ'zɪʃn] *n.* (*formal*) long speech.

disregard [dɪsrɪ'gɑːd] **1.** *n.* (**for**) indifference (to sth); lack of worry (about sth). **2.** *v.* to take no notice of.

disrepair [dɪsrɪ'peə] *n.* **in d.** = needing to be repaired.

disrepute [dɪsrɪ'pjuːt] *n.* bad reputation. **disreputable** [dɪs'repjʊtəbl] *adj.* with a bad reputation; **he is a d. character** = a wicked person.

disrespect [dɪsrɪ'spekt] *n.* lack of respect. **disrespectful,** *adj.* lacking respect; rude.

disrobe [dɪs'rəʊb] *v.* (*formal*) to undress.

disrupt [dɪs'rʌpt] *v.* to break up/ to interrupt (a meeting). **disruption** [dɪs'rʌpʃn] *n.* breaking up; interruption (of a meeting). **disruptive,** *adj.* which disrupts.

dissatisfaction [dɪssætɪs'fækʃn] *n.* lack of satisfaction. **dissatisfied** [dɪs'sætɪsfaɪd] *adj.* not satisfied.

dissect [dɪ'sekt] *v.* to cut up (a dead body/plant) in order to examine the inside. **dissection,** *n.* cutting up (a body or plant).

dissemble [dɪ'sembl] *v.* (*formal*) to hide one's feelings.

disseminate [dɪs'semɪneɪt] *v.* to spread (news) around. **dissemination,** *n.* act of spreading news around.

dissension [dɪ'senʃn] *n.* lack of agreement. **dissent** [dɪ'sent] **1.** *n.* lack of agreement. **2.** *v.* **to d. from** = not to agree with. **dissenter,** *n.* person who does not agree (esp. with the established church).

dissertation [dɪsə'teɪʃn] *n.* short (university) thesis.

disservice [dɪs'sɜːvɪs] *n.* unintentional harm; **you do yourself a d.** = you are harming your reputation.

dissident ['dɪsɪdənt] *adj. & n.* (person) who does not agree with the opinion of his political party/with the state. **dissidence,** *n.* disagreement (with the state).

dissimilar [dɪ'sɪmɪlə] *adj.* not the same; **they are not d.** = they are quite alike.

dissimulate [dɪ'sɪmjʊleɪt] *v.* (*formal*) to hide one's feelings. **dissimulation,** *n.* (*formal*) hiding one's feelings.

dissipate ['dɪsɪpeɪt] *v.* to clear away; to get rid of. **dissipation** [dɪsɪ'peɪʃn] *n.* throwing away (a fortune); wild living.

dissociate [dɪ'səʊsɪeɪt] *v.* **to d. yourself from** = to say that you have nothing to do with. **dissociation,** *n.* act of dissociating oneself.

dissolute ['dɪsəljuːt] *adj.* depraved; undisciplined.

dissolve [dɪ'zɒlv] *v.* (*a*) to make (a solid substance) become part of a liquid; to become part of a liquid. (*b*) to bring to an end. **dissolution,** *n.* act of dissolving (Parliament, etc.). **dissolvent,** *n.* substance which can dissolve other substances.

dissonant ['dɪsənənt] *adj.* out of harmony.

dissuade [dɪ'sweɪd] *v.* **to d. s.o. from sth** = to persuade s.o. not to do sth. **dissuasion,** *n.* persuading s.o. not to sth.

distal ['dɪstəl] *adj.* away from the centre of the body.

distance ['dɪstəns] **1.** *n.* space from one point to another; **in the d.** = quite a long way away. **2.** *v.* **to d. yourself from** = to put yourself at a distance from. **distant,** *adj.* far away; **he is a d. relative** = he is related to me, but not of my close family. **distantly,** *adv.* in a distant way.

distaste [dɪs'teɪst] *n.* dislike. **distasteful,** *adj.* unpleasant.

distemper [dɪs'tempə] **1.** *n.* (*a*) water colour paint for walls. (*b*) sickness of dogs. **2.** *v.* to put distemper on (a wall).

distend [dɪs'tend] *v.* to swell. **distension,** *n.* swelling.

distil [dɪ'stɪl] *v.* (**distilled**) to make pure water/alcohol by heating and collecting the vapour; **distilled water** = pure water. **distillation,** *n.* act of distilling (water/alcohol). **distiller,** *n.* person who distils alcohol. **distillery,** *n.* factory for distilling alcohol.

distinct [dɪ'stɪŋkt] *adj.* (*a*) separate. (*b*) clear. **distinction** [dɪ'stɪŋkʃn] *n.* (*a*) difference. (*b*) special excellence. **distinctive**, *adj.* very noticeable; particular to one thing; which makes one thing different from others. **distinctly**, *adv.* clearly. **distinctness**, *n.* being distinct.

distinguish [dɪ'stɪŋgwɪʃ] *v.* (*a*) to see clearly; to make out (detail). (*b*) to make a difference (**between** two things). (*c*) **he distinguished himself** = he made himself noticed. **distinguishable**, *adj.* which can be distinguished. **distinguished,** *adj.* important/well-known (writer/painter, etc.).

distort [dɪ'stɔ:t] *v.* to twist; to give a false impression of. **distortion** [dɪ'stɔ:ʃn] *n.* twisting; giving a false impression.

distract [dɪ'strækt] *v.* to attract attention from. **distracted,** *adj.* wild (with worry/ grief). **distraction** [dɪ'strækʃn] *n.* (*a*) amusement. (*b*) worry; **he loved her to d.** = he was wild about her.

distrain [dɪs'treɪn] *v.* to seize goods to pay for debts.

distraught [dɪs'trɔ:t] *adj.* wild (with worry/grief, etc.).

distress [dɪ'stres] **1.** *n.* (*a*) great sorrow/pain. (*b*) difficulty; **d. signal** = signal sent out by ship/aircraft in difficulties. **2.** *v.* to make (s.o.) very sad. **distressing,** *adj.* very sad; worrying.

distribute [dɪ'strɪbju:t] *v.* to give to several people; **we d. Japanese cars** = we are the agents for Japanese cars. **distribution** [dɪstrɪ'bju:ʃn] *n.* giving to several people. **distributive** [dɪ'strɪbjutɪv] *adj.* which distributes. **distributor,** *n.* (*a*) company which sells goods for another (usu. overseas) company. (*b*) (*in a car engine*) mechanism which passes the electric spark to each sparking plug in turn.

district ['dɪstrɪkt] *n.* area/region; *Am.* **d. attorney** = government official, a lawyer who prosecutes cases in a certain region; **d. council** = section of local government which administers a district.

distrust [dɪs'trʌst] **1.** *n.* lack of trust. **2.** *v.* not to trust.

disturb [dɪ'stɜ:b] *v.* to bother/to worry (s.o.); to interrupt (s.o.). **disturbance,** *n.* (*a*) noise. (*b*) crackling noise (on radio). **disturbing,** *adj.* worrying.

disunited [dɪsju:'naɪtəd] *adj.* no longer united.

disuse [dɪs'ju:s] *n.* **to fall into d.** = not to be used any more. **disused** ['dɪsju:zd] *adj.* not used.

ditch [dɪtʃ] **1.** *n.* long trench for taking away water. **2.** *v.* (*a*) to make a ditch. (*b*) (*of aircraft*) to come down in the sea. (*c*) *inf.* to abandon; **he ditched his car and walked** = he left his car by the side of the road.

dither ['dɪðə] **1.** *n.* **all of a d.** = very agitated. **2.** *v.* not to be able to make up one's mind.

ditto ['dɪtəʊ] *n.* the same thing; printer's sign (") meaning that the same thing is to be repeated.

ditty ['dɪtɪ] *n.* little song.

diuretic [daɪjʊ'retɪk] *adj. & n.* (substance) which makes you produce more urine.

diurnal [daɪ'ɜ:nəl] *adj.* (*poetic*) daily.

divan [dɪ'væn] *n.* low couch; bed with a solid base and no back or ends.

dive [daɪv] **1.** *n.* (*a*) plunge downwards head first. (*b*) *inf.* disreputable bar/ club. **2.** *v.* (**dived,** *Am.* **dove** [dəʊv]) to plunge head first. **diver,** *n.* person who works underwater. **diving board,** *n.* plank at swimming pool from which people dive. **diving suit,** *n.* heavy suit for divers working at great depths.

diverge [daɪ'vɜ:dʒ] *v.* to split; to go in different ways. **divergence,** *n.* split/ difference. **divergent,** *adj.* which split/ which are different. **diverging,** *adj.* splitting; **d. opinions** = opinions which are quite different.

diverse [daɪ'vɜ:s] *adj.* varied. **diversification** [daɪvɜ:sɪfɪ'keɪʃn] *n.* act of diversifying. **diversify,** *v.* to vary; to do other sorts of work. **diversity,** *n.* great variety.

diversion [daɪ'vɜ:ʃn] *n.* (*a*) sending traffic another way. (*b*) amusement. (*c*) **to create a d.** = to do sth to distract s.o.'s attention from another thing which you do not want him to see. **divert,** *v.* (*a*) to send traffic another way. (*b*) to amuse. (*c*) **I am trying to d. his attention** = to distract his attention.

divest [daɪ'vest] *v.* (*formal*) **to d. s.o. of sth** = to take sth away from s.o.

divide [dɪ'vaɪd] *v.* (*a*) to cut into parts.

(b) to calculate how many of one number there are in another. (c) (*in the House of Commons*) to vote. **dividers**, *n. pl.* pair of compasses for measuring.

dividend ['dɪvɪdend] *n.* part of profits shared out among shareholders.

divine [dɪ'vaɪn] **1.** *adj.* referring to God. **2.** *v.* to predict the future; to search for hidden sources of water. **3.** *n.* (*formal*) learned priest. **divination** [dɪvɪ-'neɪʃn] *n.* predicting what will happen in the future. **diviner**, *n.* person who finds hidden sources of water. **divinity** [dɪ'vɪnɪtɪ] *n.* god; state of being a god.

division [dɪ'vɪʒn] *n.* (a) splitting up into parts; calculation of how many of one number there are in another; **long d.** = working out of a complicated division (such as 2894 divided by 19) on paper. (b) (*in British Parliament*) counting of votes. (c) important part (of army/firm). **divisional,** *adj.* referring to a division. **divisible** [dɪ'vɪzəbl] *adj.* which can be divided. **divisive,** *adj.* which produces quarrels. **divisor** [dɪ'vaɪzə] *n.* number which divides another.

divorce [dɪ'vɔːs] **1.** *n.* legal separation of husband and wife leaving each free to remarry. **2.** *v.* (a) to separate (two ideas, etc.). (b) to break off a marriage legally. **divorcee** [dɪvɔː'siː] *n.* person who is divorced.

divot ['dɪvət] *n.* small piece of turf.

divulge [daɪ'vʌldʒ] *v.* to reveal (a secret).

DIY [diːaɪ'waɪ] *abbrev. for* do it yourself; **a DIY shop** = shop selling paints/tools, etc.

dizzy ['dɪzɪ] *adj.* (**-ier, -iest**) feeling that everything is spinning round; **I feel d.** = my head is turning; **d. heights** = such great heights that they make your head turn. **dizzily,** *adv.* in a dizzy way. **dizziness,** *n.* feeling that everything is turning round you.

DJ ['diːdʒeɪ] *abbrev. for* disc jockey.

DNA [diːen'eɪ] *abbrev. for* deoxyribonucleic acid.

do [duː] **1.** *n.* (*pl.* **dos**) party; social gathering. **2.** *v.* (**did; done**) (a) to work at (sth); to make/to complete (sth); **I'm doing my hair** = I am combing my hair; **she was doing the washing; he hasn't done the dishes; can you do today's crossword? well done!** = congratulations, you have worked/run, etc., well! (b) **the potatoes aren't done yet** = aren't cooked yet; **the meat is done to a turn** = the meat is well cooked; *inf.* **I feel done in** = I am tired out. (c) to be satisfactory; **will this colour do? we will have to make do with paper plates** = we will have to accept paper plates because there is no alternative. (d) to go (at a certain speed). (e) (*used in negatives, questions and answers*) **it doesn't matter; we didn't laugh; do you live in England?—yes, I do; but your parents don't live there, do they?—no they do not.** (f) (*takes the place of another verb*) **can you swim as fast as he does? he speaks French better than I do; she arrived before we did.** (g) (*telling someone not to do something*) **don't throw that paper away!** (h) **how do you do?** = hello! (i) (*to emphasize*) **why don't you work?—I do work! why didn't she tell you?—she did tell me! do away, v. to do away with sth** = to abolish sth; **to do away with s.o.** = to murder s.o. **do down,** *v. inf.* to trick (s.o.). **do for,** *v. inf.* (a) to kill/to destroy. (b) to do housework for (s.o.). **do-gooder,** *n.* (*pl.* **do-gooders**) *inf.* person who tries to help others, but in an ineffectual or officious way. **do in,** *v. inf.* to kill. **doing,** *n.* (a) **it takes some d.** = it is quite difficult to do. (b) *inf.* **doings** = things. **do-it-yourself,** *n.* repairing/building/painting by yourself, without employing a professional. **do out,** *v.* to clean out (a room/a cupboard). **do up, v.** (a) to fasten. (b) to renovate; **they bought an old cottage and did it up. do with,** *v.* (a) *inf.* to need; **I could do with a drink.** (b) to concern; **it is nothing to do with me** = it is not my business; **it is to do with the new book** = it concerns/it is about the new book; **what have you done with my hat?** = where have you put my hat? **do without,** *v.* to manage without.

docile ['dəʊsaɪl] *adj.* quiet/not aggressive. **docility** [də'sɪlɪtɪ] *n.* being docile.

dock [dɒk] **1.** *n.* (a) artificial harbour; **the docks** = the whole harbour; **the ship is in d.** = is tied up at the quay; *inf.* **my car**

is in d. = being repaired; **dry d.** = dock where the water is pumped out to allow repairs to be done to a ship; (b) box in a law court, where the prisoner sits. (c) wild plant with very large leaves. **2.** v. (a) to put a ship into harbour; (of ship) to arrive in harbour. (b) to link two spacecraft together in space. (c) to cut off/to remove. **docker,** n. man who works in the docks. **dockyard,** n. place where ships are built.

docket ['dɒkɪt] **1.** n. paper showing the list of contents (of a packet which has been sent). **2.** v. to attach a docket to (sth).

doctor ['dɒktə] **1.** n. (shortened in names to **Dr**) person who looks after people's health; learned person with a superior degree from a university. **2.** v. (a) to look after (a patient/a sick animal). (b) to change figures in (accounts). (c) to castrate (an animal). **doctoral,** adj. referring to a doctorate. **doctorate** ['dɒktərət] n. higher degree from a university.

doctrine ['dɒktrɪn] n. statement of what a group of people believe. **doctrinaire** [dɒktrɪ'neə] adj. very dogmatic. **doctrinal** [dɒk'traɪnl] adj. referring to a doctrine.

document ['dɒkjumənt] n. paper with writing on it. **documentary** [dɒkju-'mentərɪ] **1.** n. factual film about a real subject. **2.** adj. referring to documents. **documentation,** n. all the documents which refer to sth.

dodder ['dɒdə] v. to walk uncertainly/to totter. **doddery,** adj. old and trembly.

doddle ['dɒdl] n. inf. **it's a d.** = it's very easy.

dodge [dɒdʒ] **1.** n. trick. **2.** v. to avoid/to get out of the way. **dodgems,** n. pl. amusement at a fairground, where small electric cars are driven round and bump into each other. **dodgy,** adj. inf. unsafe; unsure.

dodo ['dəudəu] n. large extinct bird; **as dead as a d.** = totally dead/finished.

doe ['dəu] n. female (deer/rabbit).

doff [dɒf] v. to take off (one's hat).

dog [dɒg] **1.** n. (a) carnivorous animal which barks, often kept as a pet; **let sleeping dogs lie** = not to disturb the existing state of affairs. (b) male fox.

(c) **the dogs** = dog races; **to go to the dogs** = to go to ruin. (d) **d. days** = very hot period in late summer. **2.** v. **(dogged) to d. s.o.'s footsteps** = to follow s.o. **dog-collar,** n. (a) leather band to go round a dog's neck. (b) inf. white collar worn by a clergyman. **dog-eared,** adj. (book) with its pages bent or torn. **dog-fish,** n. huss/small white sea fish. **dogged** ['dɒgɪd] adj. not giving in easily. **doggedly,** adv. in a dogged way. **doggo,** adv. inf. **to lie d.** = to stay quiet. **doghouse,** n. Am. kennel; inf. **in the d.** = in disgrace. **dogrose,** n. wild pink rose. **dogsbody,** n. person who always has all the worst jobs to do. **dog-tired,** adj. worn out. **dogwatch,** n. (in the navy) one of two watches in the evening. **dogwood,** n. shrub with bright red stems.

doggerel ['dɒgərəl] n. bad poetry.

dogma ['dɒgmə] n. official belief. **dogmatic** [dɒg'mætɪk] adj. insistent that what you say is right. **dogmatically,** adv. in a dogmatic way. **dogmatism,** n. insistence that you are right. **dogmatize,** v. to insist that you are right.

doily ['dɔɪlɪ] n. decorated paper/lace serviette to put under a cake on a plate.

doldrums ['dɒldrəmz] n. pl. **in the d.** = not making any progress.

dole [dəul] **1.** n. money given by the government to people without work; **on the d.** = unemployed and receiving government payments. **2.** v. **to d. out** = to hand out (in a half-hearted way).

doleful ['dəulful] adj. gloomy. **dolefully,** adv. gloomily.

doll [dɒl] n. toy which looks like a baby. **dolled up,** adj. inf. very smartly dressed. **dolly,** n. (a) inf. doll. (b) wheeled platform for a TV camera.

dollar ['dɒlə] n. money used in the USA and many other countries.

dollop ['dɒləp] n. inf. large lump (of sth soft).

dolmen ['dɒlmən] n. prehistoric tomb with a flat stone supported by uprights.

dolphin ['dɒlfɪn] n. mammal like a small whale living in the sea. **dolphinarium** [dɒlfɪ'neərɪəm] n. large aquarium, where people pay to watch dolphins perform tricks.

dolt [dəult] n. silly person.

domain [də'meɪn] n. (a) area controlled by s.o. (b) area of knowledge.

dome [dəʊm] *n.* semi-spherical roof. **domed,** *adj.* with a dome.

Domesday Book ['du:mzdeɪ bʊk] *n.* record of land and population in England, made for William I in 1086.

domestic [də'mestɪk] *adj.* (*a*) referring to the home; **d. science** = study of cooking and running a home; **d. animals** = animals which man keeps for wool/milk/meat, etc. (*b*) **d. flights** = flights inside a country. **domesticated** [də'mestɪkeɪtɪd] *adj.* (animal) trained to live in the house. **domesticity** [dɒme-'stɪsɪtɪ] *n.* life at home.

domicile ['dɒmɪsaɪl] *n.* (*formal*) place where s.o. lives. **domicilary,** *adj.* which takes place in the home. **domiciled,** *adj.* (*formal*) living; resident.

dominant ['dɒmɪnənt] *adj.* most important; supreme; commanding. **dominance,** *n.* being dominant. **dominate** ['dɒmɪneɪt] *v.* (*a*) to rule. (*b*) to be very obvious. **dominating,** *adj.* ruling; overshadowing. **domination** [dɒmɪ'neɪʃn] *n.* act of dominating. **domineer** [dɒmɪ'nɪə] *v.* to rule (s.o.); **a domineering wife** = a wife who rules her husband.

dominion [də'mɪnjən] *n.* (*a*) self-governing state in the Commonwealth. (*b*) rule (over a territory).

domino ['dɒmɪnəʊ] *n.* (*pl.* -oes) one of a set of small flat blocks, each divided into two sections, with up to six dots in each section; **d. theory** = theory that if one event occurs, others will inevitably follow.

don [dɒn] **1.** *n.* university teacher. **2.** *v.* (**donned**) to put on (a piece of clothing). **donnish,** *adj.* like a don.

donate [dəʊ'neɪt] *v.* to give. **donation** [dəʊ'neɪʃn] *n.* gift.

done [dʌn] *v. see* **do.**

donkey ['dɒŋkɪ] *n.* farm animal like a small horse but with long ears; *inf.* **I haven't seen him for donkey's years** = I have not seen him for a long time; **d. jacket** = thick woollen jacket with a wide leather strip across the shoulders, worn esp. by workmen; **d. work** = hard dull work.

donor ['dəʊnə] *n.* person who gives; **blood d.** = person who gives blood for blood transfusions.

doodle ['du:dl] *v.* to make meaningless drawings/patterns on paper.

doom [du:m] **1.** *n.* (*a*) fate. (*b*) unhappy ending/ruin. **2.** *v.* to condemn (s.o./sth). **Doomsday,** *n.* end of the world.

door [dɔ:] *n.* barrier of wood/metal, etc., which closes an entrance; **front d.** = main door of a house; **back d.** = door at the back of a house; **he lives two doors down the street** = he lives two houses away. **doorkeeper,** *n.* person who is on guard at a main door. **doorknob,** *n.* round handle for opening/shutting a door. **doorman,** *n.* (*pl.* -men) person who is in attendance at a door (of a restaurant/hotel, etc.). **doormat,** *n.* rough carpet in front of a door. **doorstep,** *n.* block of stone/wood, etc., forming the base of a doorway. **doorway,** *n.* space filled by a door.

dope [dəʊp] *n.* (*a*) *inf.* drug. (*b*) strong glue/varnish for making models. (*c*) *inf.* information. (*d*) *inf.* stupid fool. **dopey,** *adj. inf.* stupid/silly.

dormant ['dɔ:mənt] *adj.* sleeping; **account** = bank account which is not used; **d. plant** = plant which is not growing because it is winter; **d. volcano** = volcano which is not erupting, but which is not extinct.

dormer ['dɔ:mə] *n.* **d. (window)** = window with a small gable roof jutting out from a sloping roof.

dormitory ['dɔ:mɪtrɪ] *n.* long room full of beds.

dormouse ['dɔ:maʊs] *n.* (*pl.* **dormice**) small mouse-like animal.

dorsal ['dɔ:sl] *adj.* (muscle/fin) on the back of an animal.

DOS [dɒs] disk operating system.

dose [dəʊs] **1.** *n.* (*a*) quantity of medicine. (*b*) *inf.* attack of a disease. (*c*) *Sl.* attack of venereal disease. **2.** *v.* to give (s.o.) medicine. **dosage,** *n.* amount of medicine to be given.

doss [dɒs] *v. inf.* **to d. down** = to sleep on a rough bed/on the ground, etc. **dosser,** *n. inf.* tramp/vagrant. **dosshouse,** *n. inf.* cheap lodging for vagrants.

dossier ['dɒsɪə] *n.* collection of relevant papers.

dot [dɒt] **1.** *n.* small round spot; **he arrived on the d. of three** = exactly at three o'clock; *inf.* **since the year d.** = for ever. **2.** *v.* (**dotted**) to mark with small spots; **dotted line** = line made up of small spots; **the hillside is dotted with houses** = there are houses here and there on the hillside. **dot-matrix printer**, *n.* computer printer which forms letters from many small dots. **dotty**, *adj.* (**-ier, -iest**) *inf.* slightly mad.

dote [dəʊt] *v.* **to d. on s.o.** = to be very fond of s.o. **dotage**, *n.* feebleness of mind from old age.

dotterel ['dɒtərəl] *n.* type of field bird.

dottle ['dɒtl] *n.* mass of unburnt tobacco at the bottom of a pipe.

double ['dʌbl] **1.** *adj.* (*a*) with two parts; **d. bed** = bed for two people; **d. cream** = thick cream which can be whipped easily; **d. figures** = numbers from 10 to 99; **d. chin** = chin with a second fold of flesh beneath. (*b*) twice as big; **a d. whisky** = two measures of whisky; **it takes d. the time** = twice as long; **it is d. the distance** = twice as far. **2.** *adv.* **I am seeing d.** = I can see two things when there is only one there. **3.** *n.* (*a*) **at the d.** = at a run. (*b*) **he is my d.** = he and I look exactly alike. (*c*) **men's/women's/mixed doubles** = tennis matches for two men or two women or one man and one woman on each side. **4.** *v.* (*a*) to multiply by two. (*b*) **he doubled back** = he turned round and came back along the same way. (*c*) **she was doubled up in pain** = was bent forwards. **double-barrelled**, *adj.* (*a*) (gun) with two barrels. (*b*) (surname) with two parts linked with a hyphen. **double bass**, *n.* very large stringed musical instrument. **double-breasted**, *adj.* (jacket) which overlaps in front. **double-cross**, *v.* to trick (s.o.) when he thinks that you are working on his side. **double-crosser**, *n.* trickster/cheat. **double dealing**, *n.* trickery. **double-decker**, *n.* (*a*) bus with an upper as well as a lower deck. (*b*) *inf.* sandwich made with three slices of bread. **double Dutch**, *n. inf.* nonsense. **double-edged**, *adj.* (*a*) with two sharp edges. (*b*) which have two quite different meanings. **double glazing**, *n.* two panes of glass in windows, which insulate. **double-jointed**, *adj.* with very flexible finger joints. very flexibly. **double-park**, *v.* to park alongside a car

which is already parked at the side of the street. **double-parking**, *n.* parking alongside a car which is already parked at the side of the street. **double-quick**, *adj. & adv.* extremely fast. **double take**, *n.* second reaction which comes after a first. **double-talk**, *n.* words which mean sth quite different from what they seem. **doubly**, *adv.* twice.

doublet ['dʌblət] *n.* (*a*) tight-fitting jacket. (*b*) word of the same origin as another word.

doubt [daʊt] **1.** *n.* not being sure; **to have doubts about** = not to be sure; **no d.** = of course/certainly; **in d.** = uncertain. **2.** *v.* not to be sure of. **doubtful**, *adj.* uncertain. **doubtfully**, *adv.* hestitatingly. **doubtless**, *adv.* certainly.

douche [du:ʃ] *n.* spray of water to clean part of the body.

dough [dəʊ] *n.* (*a*) uncooked mixture of flour and water for making bread, etc. (*b*) *Sl.* money. **doughnut**, *n.* small round or ring-shaped cake cooked by frying in oil. **doughy**, *adj.* soft and wet (like uncooked dough).

doughty ['daʊtɪ] *adj.* (*poetic*) brave.

dour [dʊə] *adj.* gloomy/silent. **dourly**, *adv.* gloomily.

douse [daʊs] *v.* to throw water on (sth).

dove [dʌv] *n.* (*a*) white domesticated pigeon. (*b*) politician who is in favour of negotiating for peace. (*c*) [dəʊv] *v. Am. see* **dive. dovetail**, *v.* (*a*) to join (wood) together with a V-shaped joint. (*b*) to fit in neatly. **dovecote**, *n.* house for doves.

dowager ['daʊədʒə] *n.* widow of a nobleman who has kept her title.

dowdy ['daʊdɪ] *adj.* (**-ier, -iest**) badly-dressed (person); dull/unfashionable (clothes). **dowdily**, *adv.* in a dowdy way.

dowel ['daʊəl] *n.* round wooden peg like a nail for attaching pieces of wood together. **dowelling**, *n.* **a piece of d.** = a long round stick of wood from which dowels can be cut.

dower ['daʊə] *n.* share of property which belongs to a widow.

down [daʊn] **1.** *adv., adj. & prep.* (*a*) towards the bottom; **he fell d.** = fell to the ground; **d. with examinations!** = let's do away with examinations; **he**

tried to go up the d. escalator = the one which was going downwards. (b) at the bottom; **she is d. with influenza** = she has gone to bed with influenza; *inf.* **d. under** = in Australia and New Zealand; **inflation is d. again** = inflation is lower again. (c) **to pour d.** = to rain hard. **2.** *n.* (a) soft feathers (of a duck). (b) **the downs** = rounded chalk hills in the South of England. **3.** *v.* (a) to swallow quickly. (b) **to down tools** = to stop work/go on strike. **down-and-out,** *n.* tramp/person with no money who lives in the street. **down-at-heel,** *adj.* worn/shabby (clothes). **downcast,** *adj.* gloomy/depressed. **downfall,** *n.* collapse/ruin. **downgrade,** *v.* to reduce the status of (s.o.). **downhearted,** *adj.* depressed/gloomy. **downhill,** *adv.* towards the bottom (of a hill). **download,** *v.* to load data/program into a computer. **down-market** *adj.* aiming at the cheaper end of the market. **down payment,** *n.* part of a total cost paid in advance. **downpour,** *n.* heavy fall of rain. **downright. 1.** *adj.* complete/distinct. **2.** *adv.* completely/distinctly. **downside,** *n.* negative/pessimistic view. **downstage,** *adv.* towards the front of a stage. **downstairs,** *adv.* & *n.* onto/on a lower, esp. the ground, floor. **downstream,** *adj.* & *adv.* towards the mouth of a river. **down-to-earth,** *adj.* straightforward/matter-of-fact (way of speaking, etc.). **downtown,** *adv.* & *n.* (in/to the) central business district of a town. **downtrodden,** *adj.* oppressed/badly treated. **downward,** *adj.* (movement) towards the bottom. **downwards,** *adv.* towards the bottom. **downy,** *adj.* covered with down/with soft feathers.

Downing Street ['daʊnɪŋstriːt] *n.* residence of the British Prime Minister; *inf.* the British government.

Down's syndrome ['daʊnz'sɪndrəʊm] *n.* congenital defect, where the patient has slanting eyes, a wide flat face, and has difficulty in speaking.

dowry ['daʊrɪ] *n.* money or goods which a bride brings to her husband.

dowse [daʊz] *v.* to look for water using a forked twig which moves above water. **dowser,** *n.* person who dowses.

doyen ['dɔɪən] *n.* senior member of a group.

doyly ['dɔɪlɪ] *n.* doily.

doze [dəʊz] **1.** *n.* short sleep. **2.** *v.* to be half asleep; **he dozed off** = he went into a light sleep. **dozy,** *adj.* sleepy.

dozen ['dʌzn] *n.* twelve; **half a d. apples** = six apples; **dozens of people/times** = many people/times.

Dr ['dɒktə] *abbreviation for* Doctor.

drab [dræb] *adj.* lacking bright colours; brown, grey.

drachm [dræm] *n.* small measure used in pharmacy.

drachma ['drækmə] *n.* unit of money used in Greece.

draconian [drə'kəʊnɪən] *adj.* very severe/harsh (law, etc.).

draft [drɑːft] **1.** *n.* (a) rough plan (of a document). (b) *Am.* obligatory military service. (c) order for money to be paid by a bank. **2.** *v.* (a) to draw up a rough plan of. (b) *Am.* to call (s.o.) into service; *see also* **draught.**

drag [dræg] **1.** *n.* (a) long uphill climb; *Sl.* **what a d.!** = how boring! (b) *Sl.* wearing of women's clothes by a man; **he was in d.** (c) *inf.* one puff on a cigarette. **2.** *v.* **(dragged)** (a) to pull sth heavy along. (b) to hang back/to stay behind; to go slowly. (c) to pull a net along the bottom of (a lake) to try to find sth. **dragnet,** *n.* net used to drag a lake; full search for criminals. **drag on,** *v.* to continue slowly. **drag out,** *v.* to pull out; to make (a story) last a long time.

dragon ['drægən] *n.* mythological animal which breathes fire. **dragonfly,** *n.* common insect with brilliant transparent wings.

dragoon [drə'guːn] **1.** *n.* (old) soldier on horseback. **2.** *v.* to force.

drain [dreɪn] **1.** *n.* (a) pipe for carrying waste water; *inf.* **it's like pouring money down the d.** = it is a waste of money. (b) **d. on resources** = gradual loss of money; **brain d.** = emigration of professional people to work overseas for better pay. **2.** *v.* (a) to remove (a liquid). (b) to drink the contents of (a glass). **drainage,** *n.* system of pipes for taking away waste water. **draining,** *n.* removal of excess liquid; **d. board** = sloping surface next to a sink for draining water off dishes. **drainpipe,** *n.* pipe which takes away waste water.

drake [dreɪk] *n.* male duck.

dram [dræm] *n.* small drink (of spirits).

drama ['drɑːmə] *n.* (*a*) serious theatrical performance; **d. department** = department which deals with plays. (*b*) series of serious events. **dramatic** [drə'mætɪk] *adj.* (*a*) referring to drama. (*b*) surprising; giving a shock. **dramatically,** *adv.* very surprisingly. **dramatics,** *n. pl.* putting on plays. **dramatist** ['dræmətɪst] *n.* person who writes plays. **dramatization,** [dræmətaɪ'zeɪʃn] *n.* adaptation (of a novel) for the stage/ for the TV. **dramatize** ['dræmətaɪz] *v.* (*a*) to adapt (a novel) for the stage/for the TV. (*b*) to make (sth) seem much more dramatic than it really is.

drank [dræŋk] *v. see* **drink.**

drape [dreɪp] **1.** *n. Am.* **drapes** = curtains. **2.** *v.* to hang (clothes) around sth.

draper ['dreɪpə] *n.* person who sells cloth. **drapery,** *n.* (*a*) cloth goods. (*b*) thin cloth draped around s.o.

drastic ['dræstɪk] *adj.* severe/sudden. **drastically,** *adv.* suddenly.

draught, *Am.* **draft** [drɑːft] *n.* (*a*) pulling; **d. horse** = horse trained to pull heavy loads; **beer on d./d. beer** = beer which is pumped out of a barrel, by hand. (*b*) mouthful/swallow. (*c*) amount of a ship's bottom which is under water; **boat with a shallow draught** = boat which does not go very deep into the water. (*d*) breeze (in a room). (*e*) **draughts** = game played with black and white counters on a board with black and white squares. **draughtsman** ['drɑːftsmən] *n.* (*pl.* **-men**) person who draws plans. **draughtsmanship,** *n.* skill at drawing. **draughty,** *adj.* (**-ier, -iest**) full of breezes.

draw [drɔː] **1.** *n.* (*a*) lottery. (*b*) attraction. (*c*) **he is quick on the d.** = he pulls out his gun and shoots quickly. (*d*) game where neither side wins. **2.** *v.* (**drew, drawn**) (*a*) to make a picture with a pen or pencil. (*b*) to pull; **he drew the curtains** = he opened/closed the curtains; **to d. lots** = take a piece of paper/stick, etc., from a bundle, the

person taking the marked paper/stick being the one selected; **he drew a blank** = he was unsuccessful in his search. (*c*) to move (sth) closer, etc. (*d*) not to have a winner in a game; **the match was drawn** = neither side won. (*e*) to collect liquid; **to d. blood** = to cut s.o. so that they bleed. (*f*) to take (money) from an account. **draw aside,** *v.* to take (s.o.)/ to move to one side. **draw back,** *v.* **he drew back the curtains** = he opened the curtains; **she drew back** = she moved backwards. **drawback,** *n.* inconvenient thing; obstacle. **drawbridge,** *n.* bridge which can be raised or lowered to give access across water. **drawer,** *n.* sliding compartment in a desk or cupboard which you open by pulling on a handle; **chest of drawers** = piece of bedroom furniture made of several sliding compartments. **draw in,** *v.* **the days are drawing in** = becoming shorter. **drawing,** *n.* picture done with pen or pencil; **d. pin** = pin with a large flat head for pinning paper; **d. board** = large board used by designers, on which paper is laid for drawing on; **it was back to the d. board** = he had to start the project all over again. **drawing room,** *n.* sitting room; room for sitting and talking in, but not eating. **drawn,** *adj.* looking tired. **draw out,** *v.* to pull (sth) out; to make (sth) last a long time. **drawstring,** *n.* string which, when pulled, closes a bag. **draw up,** *v.* to make (a plan, etc.).

drawl [drɔːl] **1.** *n.* slow way of speaking. **2.** *v.* to speak slowly, dragging the words.

drawn [drɔːn] *v. see* **draw.**

dray [dreɪ] *n.* low flat lorry or cart for carrying barrels.

dread [dred] **1.** *n.* great fear. **2.** *v.* to fear greatly. **dreadful,** *adj.* awful. **dreadfully,** *adv.* awfully/extremely.

dream [driːm] **1.** *n.* (*a*) things which you think you see happening when you are asleep. (*b*) lovely thing. **2.** *v.* (**he dreamed/he dreamt** [dremt]) to think you see things happening while you are asleep; **I wouldn't d. of wearing pink socks** = I wouldn't ever think of wearing pink socks. **dreamer,** *n.* person who thinks a lot/who is out of touch with practical things. **dreamily,** *adv.* as in a dream. **dreamless,** *adj.* without dreams. **dream up,** *v.* to invent. **dreamy,** *adj.* like a dream.

dreary ['drɪərɪ] *adj.* (**-ier, -iest**) sad/gloomy; not interesting. **drearily,** *adv.* sadly/gloomily. **dreariness,** *n.* being dreary; dreary appearance.

dredge [dredʒ] *v.* (*a*) to scrape the bottom of (a river or lake) to remove sand or mud. (*b*) to sprinkle (a cake) with sugar, etc. **dredger,** *n.* (*a*) machine for removing sand or mud from the bottom of a river or lake; boat with such a machine in it. (*b*) container with holes in the top for sprinkling (sugar, etc.).

dregs [dregz] *n. pl.* sediment at the bottom of a bottle; rubbish.

drench [drentʃ] *v.* to soak; **drenched** = wet through.

dress [dres] **1.** *n.* (*pl.* **-es**) (*a*) piece of woman's/girl's clothing, covering more or less all the body. (*b*) special clothes; **d. rehearsal** = rehearsal where the actors wear their costumes; **d. circle** = first balcony of seats above the stalls in a theatre; **d. coat** = man's formal black coat. **2.** *v.* (*a*) to put on clothes. (*b*) to clean (a wound)/to put a bandage on (a wound). (*c*) to arrange a display in (a shop window). (*d*) to prepare (a chicken) for cooking. **dress down,** *v.* to criticize. **dresser,** *n.* (*a*) person in theatre who helps the actors with their costumes; **window d.** = person who arranges displays in shop windows. (*b*) piece of kitchen furniture with open shelves above and cupboards below. **dressing,** *n.* (*a*) putting on clothes; **d. room** = room for getting dressed, esp. room where an actor puts on his costume; **d. gown** = long robe worn over pyjamas or nightdress; **d. table** = bedroom table with mirrors. (*b*) sauce (for salad); **French d.** = sauce made of oil and vinegar. (*c*) bandage (for a wound). **dressmaker,** *n.* person who makes women's clothes. **dressmaking,** *n.* making of women's clothes by hand. **dress up,** *v.* to put on a costume. **dressy,** *adj.* very showily dressed; showy (clothes).

dressage ['dresɑːʒ] *n.* training of a horse which shows how obedient it is.

drew [druː] *v. see* **draw.**

drey [dreɪ] *n.* squirrel's nest.

dribble ['drɪbl] *v.* (*a*) to let drops of liquid run out of your mouth. (*b*) to kick a football along as you are running.

driblets, dribs and drabs ['drɪbləts, 'drɪbzən'dræbz] *n. pl.* little bits; **in dribs and drabs** = a little at a time.

drier ['draɪə] *n.* = **dryer.**

drift [drɪft] **1.** *n.* (*a*) general direction; **I got the general d. of his argument** = I understood the general sense of his argument. (*b*) pile of snow blown by the wind. (*c*) **North Atlantic D.** = current which crosses the North Atlantic. **2.** *v.* (*a*) to let yourself move. (*b*) (*of snow*) to pile up. **drifter,** *n.* person with no set plan in life/person who moves aimlessly from job to job. **driftwood,** *n.* (*no pl.*) wood which floats and blows on to the shore.

drill [drɪl] **1.** *n.* (*a*) machine for making holes (in wood/metal, etc.); **pneumatic d.** = machine driven by compressed air for making holes in roads. (*b*) military practice in marching, etc.; *inf.* **what's the d.?** = what do we do now? **fire d.** = practice in reaching the life boats on a ship/practice in evacuating a building in case of fire. (*c*) small furrow in the ground in which you sow seeds. (*d*) thick cotton cloth. **2.** *v.* (*a*) to make holes; **he is drilling for oil** = he is making holes in the ground in the hope of finding oil. (*b*) to do military practice.

drily ['draɪlɪ] *adv.* = **dryly.**

drink [drɪŋk] **1.** *n.* liquid which you swallow; alcohol; **soft drinks** = non-alcoholic drinks; **he has a d. problem** = he suffers from alcoholism; **he was much the worse for d.** = he was drunk. **2.** (**drank; has drunk**) to swallow (liquid); **he was drinking at the bar** = he was drinking alcohol at the bar; **she doesn't d.** = she never drinks alcohol; **let's d. to the success of the expedition** = let us raise our glasses and wish it success. **drinkable,** *adj.* nice to drink. **drinker,** *n.* person who drinks (too much alcohol). **drinking,** *n.* action of swallowing liquid; consumption of alcohol; alcoholism; **d. water** = water which is safe to drink.

drip [drɪp] **1.** *n.* (*a*) small drop of water.

(b) (in hospital) device which allows liquid to drip regularly into the bloodstream of a patient. **2.** v. (**dripped**) to fall in drops; **the tap is dripping** = drops of water are coming out of the tap which has not been turned off tightly enough; **drip-dry shirt** = shirt which does not crease if hung to dry while wet. **dripping**, n. fat left in a pan after roasting meat.

drive [draɪv] **1.** n. (a) ride in a motor vehicle. (b) way in which a car is propelled or guided; **car with front-wheel d.** = car where the engine is connected directly to the front wheels; **car with left-hand d.** = car where the driver sits on the left-hand side. (c) device in a computer which spins a disk. (d) short private road leading to a house. (e) stroke (in golf or cricket) where the ball is hit hard and far. (f) energy. (g) campaign (to collect money for charity). **2.** v. (**drove; has driven**) (a) to make a motor vehicle travel in a certain direction; **I will d. you to the airport** = I will take you to the airport in my car. (b) to force/to push; **he was driven to it** = he was forced to do it; **she drives a hard bargain** = she is a very tough businesswoman; **the pressure of work was driving her frantic** = making her become frantic. (c) (in golf or cricket) to hit the ball hard and far. **drive along**, v. to ride along a road in a motor vehicle. **drive at**, v. **what is he driving at?** = what is he trying to say? **drive away**, v. (a) to force (sth/s.o.) to go away. (b) to ride away in a motor vehicle. **drive back**, v. (a) to force back. (b) to go/to come back in a motor vehicle. **drive in**, v. (a) to force in. (b) to go in by car; **drive-in cinema/restaurant** = cinema/restaurant where you drive in in a car and watch a film or eat while still sitting in the car. **drive on**, v. to continue one's journey. **driver**, n. person who drives (a motor vehicle); Am. **driver's license** = permit which allows you to drive. **driveway**, n. short private road leading to a house. **driving. 1.** adj. (rain/snow) blown by the wind. **2.** n. action of driving a motor vehicle. **d. test** = test taken before you can have a driving licence; **d. school** = school where you

learn to drive; **d. licence** = permit which allows you to drive; **d. wheel** = wheel which moves a part of the machinery (in a machine)/steering wheel (in a car/lorry, etc.).

drivel ['drɪvl] n. rubbish.

driven ['drɪvn] v. see **drive**.

drizzle ['drɪzl] **1.** n. thin continuous rain. **2.** v. to rain in a thin mist. **drizzly**, adj. (weather) where it is raining in thin mist.

drogue [drəʊg] n. (a) funnel-shaped object, made of cloth, used to pull behind an aircraft for target practice. (b) parachute used as a brake.

droll [drəʊl] adj. funny in an odd way.

dromedary ['drɒmədərɪ] n. camel with only one hump.

drone [drəʊn] **1.** n. (a) male bee. (b) lazy person. (c) buzz (of an insect/an engine); monotonous noise. **2.** v. to buzz; to talk slowly and in a monotonous voice.

drool [druːl] v. (a) to slobber. (b) inf. to show excessive pleasure about something.

droop [druːp] v. to hang down; **his spirits drooped** = he was feeling miserable.

drop [drɒp] **1.** n. (a) tiny quantity of liquid which falls; **the doctor has given me some drops for my eyes** = liquid to be put in the eyes in small quantities. (b) small round jewel; small round sweet. (c) fall. (d) jumping by a group of people with parachutes. **2.** v. (**dropped**) to fall; to let (sth) fall; **the wind dropped** = stopped blowing hard; **she dropped a stitch** = she let a stitch slip in her knitting; inf. **d. me a line when you are in Paris** = send me a short letter when you are in Paris; **shall I d. you at your door?** = shall I drive you back and leave you at your door? **he has dropped the idea of going to live in Greece** = he has given up the idea; **the whole project has been dropped** = has been stopped; **d. it** = stop talking about it. **drop in**, v. to call on s.o. **drop-kick**, n. kick in football where you drop the ball to the ground and kick it as it is falling. **droplet**, n. little drop. **drop off**, v. to fall off; **he dropped off** = he fell asleep. **drop out**, v. to stop competing; **he has dropped out** =

he has given up his studies/has stopped living conventionally. **drop-out,** *n*. person who has stopped studying/stopped living conventionally. **dropper,** *n*. glass tube for putting drops in eyes, etc. **droppings,** *n. pl.* solid waste matter from birds/animals.

dropsy ['drɒpsɪ] *n.* disease where liquid forms in parts of the body. **dropsical,** *adj.* suffering from dropsy.

dross [drɒs] *n.* worthless rubbish.

drought [draʊt] *n.* long period when there is no rain/when the land is dry.

drove [drəʊv] **1.** *n.* large number (of people/animals). **2.** *v. see* **drive.**

drown [draʊn] *v.* (*a*) to die by being unable to breathe in water. (*b*) to flood (a field). (*c*) to cover up (a noise).

drowse [draʊz] *v.* to be half asleep. **drowsily,** *adv.* sleepily. **drowsiness,** *n.* feeling of wanting to go to sleep. **drowsy,** *adj.* sleepy.

drubbing ['drʌbɪŋ] *n.* beating.

drudge [drʌdʒ] *n.* person who does hard/boring work. **drudgery,** *n.* hard/boring work.

drug [drʌg] **1.** *n.* (*a*) medicine. (*b*) substance which affects the nerves, and which can be habit forming. **2.** *v.* (**drugged**) to give a drug to (s.o.); **his coffee had been drugged** = s.o. had put a drug in his coffee. **druggist,** *n.* chemist. **drugstore,** *n. Am.* chemist's shop and snack bar.

druid ['druːɪd] *n.* priest of the old Celtic religion.

drum [drʌm] **1.** *n.* (*a*) large round percussion instrument, covered with tightly stretched material and played with a stick; **d. major** = head of a military band. (*b*) large barrel; cylindrical container. **2.** *v.* (**drummed**) (*a*) to bang on a drum; to tap your fingers quickly on a surface. (*b*) **to d. up support** = to encourage people vigorously to give their support. (*c*) **to d. sth into s.o.** = to make s.o. learn sth by constantly repeating it. **drummer,** *n.* person who plays the drums. **drumstick,** *n.* (*a*) wooden stick for playing a drum. (*b*) lower part of a leg (of a cooked chicken/turkey, etc.).

drunk [drʌŋk] **1.** *adj.* excited/incapable because of drinking alcohol. **2.** *n.* per-

son who is drunk. **drunkard,** *n.* person who is often drunk. **drunken,** *adj.* referring to an excess of alcohol. **drunkenly,** *adv.* in a drunken way. **drunkenness,** *n.* (habit of) being drunk.

drupe [druːp] *n.* fruit with a large stone (like a peach).

dry [draɪ] **1.** *adj.* (**drier, driest**) (*a*) not wet; **he only had d. bread to eat** = bread with no butter or jam; **d. land** = solid land; **at the end of the film there wasn't a d. eye in the house** = the film made all the audience cry. (*b*) (*of wine*) not sweet. (*c*) (area) where alcohol is forbidden. (*d*) uninteresting/boring (book). (*e*) **d. sense of humour** = where you make jokes without seeming to know they are funny. **2.** *v.* to stop being wet; to wipe (sth) until it is dry. **dry-clean,** *v.* to clean (clothes) with chemicals. **dry-cleaner's,** *n.* shop where clothes are dry-cleaned. **dryer,** *n.* machine for drying; **spin d.** = machine which dries washing by spinning it round very fast. **dry-goods store,** *n. Am.* draper's shop. **dry ice,** *n.* solid carbon dioxide, used to produce very cold temperatures. **drying,** *n.* action of making something dry; **I'll do the d.** = I'll dry the dishes. **dryly,** *adv.* in a sharp, sarcastic way. **dryness,** *n.* state of being dry. **dry out,** *v.* to make (sth) dry. **dry rot,** *n.* disease in wood which makes the wood powdery. **dry run,** *n.* practice. **dry up,** *v.* to stop flowing; **he dried up in the middle of his speech** = he stopped talking and could not continue.

dryad ['draɪæd] *n.* mythological wood goddess.

DTP desktop publishing.

dual ['djʊəl] *adj.* double; in a pair; **he has d. nationality** = he is a citizen of two countries; **d. carriageway** = main road separated into two parts by a central grass bank or fence. **duality** [djʊˈælɪtɪ] *n.* being dual.

dub [dʌb] *v.* (**dubbed**) (*a*) to make (s.o.) a knight. (*b*) to add a dialogue to (a film) in another language from the original.

dubbin ['dʌbɪn] *n.* type of thick oil for making boots soft and waterproof.

dubious ['djuːbɪəs] *adj.* (*a*) doubtful/vague; suspicious. (*b*) hesitant. **dubi-**

ously, *adv.* doubtfully. **dubiety** [dju:-'baɪətɪ] *n.* doubt.

duchess ['dʌtʃes] *n.* wife/widow of a duke. **duchy,** *n.* land ruled by a duke.

duck [dʌk] **1.** *n.* (*a*) common water bird; female of this bird; meat of this bird used as food; **lame d.** = firm/person in financial difficulties. (*b*) score of zero (in cricket). (*c*) strong cotton cloth. **2.** *v.* (*a*) to lower your head quickly (to avoid hitting sth). (*b*) to push (s.o.) under water. (*c*) to avoid (an unpleasant job). **duckboards,** *n. pl.* boards placed as a path across wet ground. **ducking,** *n.* **he got a d.** = he fell/was pushed into the water. **duckling,** *n.* baby duck. **duckweed,** *n.* green weed which floats on the surface of ponds.

duct [dʌkt] *n.* tube for carrying air/liquid, etc.

ductile ['dʌktaɪl] *adj.* (metal) which can be pulled to form thin wires.

dud [dʌd] *n. inf.* failure; false coin/banknote; (shell) which will not explode; **d. cheque** = worthless cheque.

dude [dju:d] *n. Am.* dandy; visitor to a ranch.

dudgeon ['dʌdʒən] *n.* **in high d.** = very indignant.

due [dju:] **1.** *adj.* (*a*) expected; **when is the baby d.?** = when is the baby expected to be born? (*b*) (money which is) owed. (*c*) just/deserved. (*d*) **d. to** = caused by. (*e*) **in d. course** = subsequently. **2.** *adv.* **the plane flew d. west** = straight in a westerly direction. **3.** *n.* what is owed/deserved; **to give him his d. he works very hard** = to be just to him; **harbour dues** = money owed to the harbour authorities for using the harbour.

duel ['djuəl] *n.* fight between two people (with swords/guns). **duellist,** *n.* person who fights a duel.

duenna [dju:'enə] *n.* elderly Spanish lady, who acts as chaperone.

duet [dju'et] *n.* piece of music played/sung by two people.

duff [dʌf] **1.** *adj. inf.* rotten/no good. **2.** *n.* boiled pudding. **duffer,** *n. inf.* stupid person.

duffel, duffle ['dʌfl] *n.* **d. coat** = thick coat (often with a hood) fastened with toggles; **d. bag** = tubular bag which is closed by a string.

dug [dʌg] *v. see* **dig. dugout,** *n.* hole in the ground, made as a shelter for soldiers; **d. canoe** = boat made from a tree trunk which has been hollowed out.

duke [dju:k] *n.* highest rank of nobleman.

dulcet ['dʌlsɪt] *adj.* (voice, etc.) which sounds pleasant.

dulcimer ['dʌlsɪmə] *n.* musical instrument with strings hit with little hammers.

dull [dʌl] *adj.* (**duller, dullest**) (*a*) not exciting/not interesting. (*b*) gloomy (weather). (*c*) not sharp (sound). (*d*) not bright; gloomy (colour). (*e*) rather stupid. **dullard,** *n.* stupid person. **dullness,** *n.* (*a*) lack of excitement. (*b*) gloominess (of colour/weather). (*c*) boredom. (*d*) slowness; stupidity. **dully,** *adv.* in a dull way.

duly ['dju:lɪ] *adv.* properly; as you should.

dumb [dʌm] *adj.* (*a*) unable to speak. (*b*) stupid. **dumbbell** ['dʌmbel] *n.* bar with weights on each end used by weightlifters. **dumbfound** [dʌm'faʊnd] *v.* to surprise/to flabbergast; **I am dumbfounded at the news** = I am astonished by the news. **dumbly,** *adv.* silently/without saying anything.

dumdum ['dʌmdʌm] *n.* soft-nosed bullet which flattens out when it hits its target.

dummy ['dʌmɪ] *n.* (*a*) plastic teat sucked by babies. (*b*) false thing; **d. run** = practice. (*c*) **tailor's d.** = model of a person used to show clothes (in a shop window). (*d*) stupid fool.

dump [dʌmp] **1.** *n.* place to put rubbish; **what a d.!** = what an awful place. **2.** *v.* (*a*) to put (sth) heavily on the ground. (*b*) to throw away; to get rid of. (*c*) to sell (surplus goods) at a very cheap price (usu. overseas).

dumpling ['dʌmplɪŋ] *n.* small ball of dough served in stew; **apple dumplings** = apples baked in dough.

dumps [dʌmps] *n. pl. inf.* **down in the d.** = miserable.

dumpy ['dʌmpɪ] *adj.* short and squat.

dun [dʌn] **1.** *n.* debt collector. **2.** *adj.* dull brown colour. **3.** *v.* (**dunned**) to pester (a debtor) for money.

dunce [dʌns] *n.* stupid person.

dune [dju:n] *n.* **sand dunes** = grass-covered sandy ridges by the seashore.

dung [dʌŋ] *n.* solid waste matter (of animals).

dungarees [dʌŋgə'ri:z] *n. pl.* overalls/working clothes, usu. of thick blue cloth, worn over ordinary clothes.

dungeon ['dʌndʒən] *n.* dark and unpleasant underground prison.

dunk [dʌŋk] *v.* to dip (biscuit, etc.) into a liquid.

dunlin ['dʌnlɪn] *n.* small shore bird.

dunno [də'nəʊ] *v. inf.* = (I) **don't know.**

dunnock ['dʌnək] *n.* the hedge sparrow.

duo ['dju:əʊ] *n.* two people (usu. two performers).

duodecimal [dju:əʊ'desɪml] *adj.* (system of calculating) based on the number 12.

duodenum [dju:əʊ'di:nəm] *n.* part of the intestine immediately below the stomach. **duodenal,** *adj.* referring to the duodenum.

dupe [dju:p] **1.** *n.* person who has been tricked. **2.** *v.* to trick (s.o.).

duplex ['dju:pleks] *n. (pl.* **-es)** *Am.* two-family house; **d. apartment** = flat with rooms on two floors.

duplicate 1. *n. & adj.* ['dju:plɪkət] copy/double. **2.** *v.* ['dju:plɪkeɪt] to make a copy (of a letter, etc.); **you are just duplicating his work** = you are simply doing his work all over again. **duplicating,** *n.* action of making a copy. **duplication** [dju:plɪ'keɪʃn] *n.* copying; repetition. **duplicator,** *n.* machine which makes copies of documents.

duplicity [dju:'plɪsɪtɪ] *n.* dishonesty; tricking s.o.

durable ['djʊərəbl] *adj.* which lasts/which does not wear away. **durability** [djʊərə'bɪlɪtɪ] *n.* ability to last/not wear out. **durably,** *adv.* in a durable way.

duration [djʊ'reɪʃn] *n.* period of time for which sth lasts.

duress [djʊ'res] *n.* force/illegal threats used to make s.o. do sth.

during ['djʊərɪŋ] *prep.* for the time sth lasts.

durum ['djʊərəm] *n.* hard wheat, used for making pasta.

dusk [dʌsk] *n.* twilight/period in the evening just before it gets dark. **dusky,** *adj.* dark-skinned.

dust [dʌst] **1.** *n.* thin layer of dry dirt. **2.** *v.* (a) to remove dust from (sth). (b) to sprinkle (sugar) on a cake. **dustbin,** *n.* large container for household rubbish. **dust bowl,** *n.* area where the dry surface soil has been blown away. **dust cover,** *n.* paper cover round a book. **duster,** *n.* (a) cloth for removing dust; **feather d.** = brush made of feathers for removing dust. (b) *inf.* flag (on a ship). **dusting,** *n.* (a) removing of dust. (b) sprinkling (of sugar, etc.). **dust jacket,** *n.* paper cover round a book. **dustman,** *n. (pl.* **-men)** person employed by a town to remove household rubbish. **dustpan,** *n.* small wide shovel for scooping up dirt. **dust-up,** *n. inf.* quarrel. **dusty,** *adj.* **(-ier, -iest)** covered with dust; **d. answer** = unsatisfactory reply.

Dutch [dʌtʃ] **1.** *adj.* referring to Holland; **D. courage** = courage which comes from being drunk; **D. treat** = party where each person pays his share. **2.** *n.* (a) language spoken in Holland. (b) **the Dutch** = the people of Holland. (c) **to go d.** = to split the expenses. **Dutchman, Dutchwoman,** *(pl.* **-men, -women)** man/woman from Holland.

duty ['dju:tɪ] *n.* (a) what one has to do; service; **to be on d. all day; d. chemist** = the chemist's shop which is open on Sundays; **d. officer** = officer who is in charge at a particular time. (b) money which has to be paid; **d. free shop** = shop at an airport/on a boat where goods can be bought free of local tax. **dutiable,** *adj.* (goods) on which a customs duty must be paid. **dutiful,** *adj.* (person) who does what they should do. **dutifully,** *adv.* as one should.

duvet ['du:veɪ] *n.* bag stuffed with feathers, used as the only covering for a bed.

dwarf [dwɔ:f] **1.** *n.* person who is much smaller than normal; variety of plant or animal which is smaller than usual; **d. beans** = beans which form low bushes and do not climb. **2.** *v.* to make (sth) appear small.

dwell [dwel] *v.* **(dwelled/dwelt)** to live. **dweller,** *n. & suffix* person who lives (in a place). **dwelling,** *n.* house. **dwell on,** *v.* to refer at length to (a subject).

dwindle ['dwɪndl] v. to get less. **dwindling**, adj. which is getting less.

dye [daɪ] **1.** n. colour used to stain cloth; **fast d.** = colour which will not come out when washed. **2.** v. to stain with a colour. **dyeing**, n. staining (of cloth).

dying ['daɪɪŋ] adj. about to die.

dyke [daɪk] n. see **dike**.

dynamic [daɪ'næmɪk] adj. energetic/forceful (person). **dynamics**, n. pl. study of objects in movement.

dynamite ['daɪnəmaɪt] **1.** n. high explosive. **2.** v. to blow up with dynamite.

dynamo ['daɪnəməʊ] n. (pl. **-os**) small electricity generator.

dynasty ['dɪnəstɪ] n. several generations of one family, esp. a family of rulers.

dysentery ['dɪsəntrɪ] n. disease of the intestines.

dysfunction [dɪs'fʌŋkʃən] n. abnormal functioning of an organ.

dyslexia [dɪs'leksɪə] n. being dyslexic. **dyslexic**, adj. (child) who has great difficulty in reading and writing.

dyspepsia [dɪs'pepsɪə] n. inability to digest food properly. **dyspeptic**, adj. unable to digest food properly.

dystrophy ['dɪstrəfɪ] n. **muscular d.** = disease causing gradual weakening of the muscles. **dystrophic** [dɪs'trɒfɪk] adj. (lake) with acid peaty water.

Ee

each [iːtʃ] **1.** adj. every. **2.** pron. every person; everything. **3.** **e. other** = both of two people or things; **we write to e. other.**

eager ['iːgə] adj. very willing to do sth. **eagerly**, adv. in an eager way. **eagerness**, n. being eager.

eagle ['iːgl] n. large bird of prey. **eagle-eyed**, adj. (person) who can see very clearly/who notices small details.

ear ['ɪə] n. (a) part of the head, used for hearing; **middle e.** = space inside the head beyond the eardrum; **inner e.** = space inside the head, beyond the middle ear, which controls balance and hearing. (b) sense of hearing; sense of correct tone. (c) **e. of corn** = head of corn seeds. **earache** ['ɪəreɪk] n. pain in an ear. **eardrum**, n. tight skin inside the ear which resonates to sound waves

and so allows you to hear. **earlobe**, n. lobe on an ear. **earmark**, v. to reserve (sth such as money) for a special purpose. **earphone**, n. part of a pair of headphones which fits over one ear. **earring**, n. ring attached to the earlobe as an ornament. **earshot**, n. **within e./out of e.** = near enough to be heard/too far away to be heard.

earl [ɜːl] n. high-ranking nobleman.

early ['ɜːlɪ] (**-ier**, **-iest**) **1.** adv. before the proper time; at the beginning of a period of time; **the train left five minutes e.; e. in the afternoon. 2.** adj. which happens at the beginning of a period of time; which happens before the usual time; **at an e. date** = soon; **e. closing day** = day on which shops close in the afternoon.

earn [ɜːn] v. to be paid money for working. **earnings** ['ɜːnɪŋz] n. pl. amount of money earned; salary/wages.

earnest ['ɜːnɪst] **1.** adj. serious. **2.** n. (a) money paid as a guarantee. (b) **in e.** = seriously/really. **earnestly**, adv. seriously. **earnestness**, n. being earnest.

earth [ɜːθ] **1.** n. (a) planet on which we live; inf. **it costs the e.** = a great deal of money; **why on e. did you say that?** = what ever made you say that? (b) soil. (c) **e. wire** = electric wire which connects with the ground. (d) fox's hole; **to run s.o. to e.** = to find s.o. after a difficult search. **2.** v. to connect (electrical apparatus) to the ground. **earthen** ['ɜːθən] adj. made of clay. **earthenware**, n. & adj. (pottery) made of clay. **earthly**, adj. inf. **he hasn't an e. (chance)** = he has no chance at all. **earthquake**, n. shaking of the earth caused by a fault or underground volcanic activity. **earth-shattering**, adj. inf. momentous (news). **earth up**, v. to pile earth around a growing plant. **earthworks**, n. pl. walls of earth built as defences. **earthworm**, n. worm/small animal which looks like a very small snake and lives in earth. **earthy**, adj. (**-ier**, **-iest**) coarse/rude (humour).

earwig ['ɪəwɪg] n. small insect with curved pincers on its tail.

ease [iːz] **1.** n. absence of difficulty; **ill at e.** = nervous/uncomfortable. **2.** v. (a) to make less painful. (b) to make easy. (c) to make less tight. **ease off,** v. to become less. **ease up,** v. to slow down.

easel ['i:zl] n. vertical frame on legs (to support a blackboard/painting, etc.).

easement ['i:zmənt] n. right to use a path across someone else's property.

east [i:st] **1.** n. one of the points of the compass, the direction of the rising sun; the eastern part of a country; **the Far E.** = countries to the east of India; **the Middle E.** = countries to the east of Egypt and west of Pakistan; **the Near E.** = countries at the eastern end of the Mediterranean. **2.** adj. of the east; **E. Germany** = German Democratic Republic; **E. Anglia** = eastern part of England to the north-east of London. **3.** adv. towards the east. **eastbound,** adj. going towards the east. **easterly,** adj. (a) e. **wind** = wind from the east. (b) towards the east. **eastern,** adj. of the east. **easternmost,** adj. furthest east. **eastward,** adj. towards the east. **eastwards,** adv. towards the east.

Easter ['i:stə] n. Christian festival (in March or April); **E. Day** = Sunday celebrating Christ's rising from the dead; **E. egg** = chocolate or sugar egg eaten at Easter.

easy ['i:zɪ] (-ier, -iest) **1.** adj. not difficult; **the house is within e. reach of the station** = is conveniently close to the station; **my boss is very e. to get on with** = not difficult to work for. **2.** adv. **to take things e.** = to rest/to do only light work; **e. now!** = be careful/don't get excited! **go e. on/with the jam!** = don't take too much of it. **easily,** adv. without difficulty. **easiness,** n. state of being easy/of not being difficult. **easy chair,** n. large comfortable armchair. **easy-going,** adj. (person who is) easy to get on with/not very critical.

eat [i:t] v. (ate [et]; has eaten) to chew and swallow (food); **eating apple** = sweet apple; **I had him eating out of my hand** = he did everything I told him to do; **he had to e. his words** = to take back what he had said. **eatable,** adj. which can be eaten. **eatables,** n. pl. things to eat. **eat away,** v. (of acid) to corrode. **eater,** n. person who eats. **eat into,** v. to reduce gradually. **eat up,** v. to finish

eating; inf. **car that eats up petrol** = car that uses a lot of petrol.

eau de Cologne [əʊdəkə'ləʊn] n. liquid with a light scent.

eaves [i:vz] n. pl. edge of a roof overhanging the wall. **eavesdrop,** v. (eavesdropped) to listen to a conversation which you are not supposed to hear. **eavesdropper,** n. person who eavesdrops.

ebb [eb] **1.** n. (of tide) going down. **2.** v. (of tide) to go down.

ebony ['ebənɪ] n. black tropical wood.

ebullient [ɪ'bʌljənt] adj. very excited/full of life. **ebullience,** n. high spirits.

EC ['i:si:] n. European Community.

eccentric [ɪk'sentrɪk] adj. odd (person). **eccentrically,** adv. in an eccentric way. **eccentricity** [eksen'trɪsɪtɪ] n. being eccentric.

ecclesiastical [ɪkli:zɪ'æstɪkl] adj. belonging to the church.

ECG ['i:si:'dʒi:] electrocardiogram.

echelon ['eʃəlɒn] n. (a) arrangement of separate things in steps, and not in a straight line. (b) group of people at a certain level in an organization.

echo ['ekəʊ] **1.** n. (pl. echoes) repeated sound reverberating in a cave, etc.; **e. sounder** = device which measures depth by using echoes from the bottom of the sea. **2.** v. (of sound) to repeat.

éclair [eɪ'kleə] n. long cake made of pastry, filled with cream and covered with chocolate.

eclectic [ɪ'klektɪk] adj. taking ideas, etc., from several different sources.

eclipse [ɪ'klɪps] **1.** n. temporary disappearance of (part of) the sun or moon, because another body passes across them. **2.** v. (a) to hide (another planet) by passing in front of it. (b) to be more brilliant/successful than s.o.

ecology [ɪ'kɒlədʒɪ] n. study of the relationship between plants and animals and their environment. **ecological** [i:kə'lɒdʒɪkl] adj. referring to ecology. **ecologist,** n. person who studies ecology.

economy [ɪ'kɒnəmɪ] n. (a) saving (of money or resources); **e. pack** = cheaper packet of goods. (b) way in which a country makes money; financial state of a country. **economic** [i:kə'nɒmɪk] adj.

referring to economy. **economical,**
adj. which saves money or resources.
economically, *adv.* without waste.
economics, *n.* (*a*) study of the finance
of industry/of a country. (*b*) financial
structure. **economist** [ɪ'kɒnəmɪst] *n.*
person who specializes in the study of
finance. **economize,** *v.* to e. (on) = to
save/not to waste.

ecru [eɪ'kruː] *n.* pale fawn colour.

ecstasy ['ekstəsɪ] *n.* great happiness.
ecstatic [ɪk'stætɪk] *adj.* very happy.
ecstatically, *adv.* extremely happy.

ECT [iːsiː'tiː] electroconvulsive therapy.

ectoplasm ['ektəʊplæzəm] *n.* substance
said to come from the body of a person
in a trance.

ECU ['ekjuː] European Currency Unit.

ecumenical [iːkjuː'menɪkl] *adj.* referring to Christian unity/concerned with
joining together all Christian groups.

eczema ['eksɪmə] *n.* skin disease which
causes itchy red spots.

eddy ['edɪ] **1.** *n.* small swirl of water (in a
stream). **2.** *v.* to swirl around.

edelweiss ['eɪdəlveɪs] *n.* alpine plant
with white flowers.

edge [edʒ] **1.** *n.* (*a*) (sharp) side of flat
object; **the violin set my teeth on e.** =
made me shudder; **on e.** = nervous/
jumpy. (*b*) sharpened side of a knife/
axe, etc. (*c*) point at the outside of
sth; **a house at the e. of the forest. 2.**
v. (*a*) to creep sideways. (*b*) to put
along the edge; **a dress edged with silk.**
edgeways, edgewise, *adv.* sideways.
edging, *n.* material used to edge with.
edgy, *adj.* nervous/jumpy.

edible ['edɪbl] *adj.* which can be safely
eaten.

edict ['iːdɪkt] *n.* official order.

edifice ['edɪfɪs] *n.* large building.

edify ['edɪfaɪ] *v.* (*formal*) to instruct and
improve (s.o.). **edification** [edɪfɪ'keɪʃn]
n. instruction and improvement.

edit ['edɪt] *v.* to make notes on (a
text); to change (a text) to make it
more acceptable; to prepare (a text)
for publication; to cut up (a film/tape)
and stick it together in correct order
to make it ready to be shown/played.
edition [ɪ'dɪʃn] *n.* (*a*) number of books/
papers printed at the same time; **first
e.** = copy of the first printing of a

book. (*b*) form in which a book is
published. **editor,** *n.* (*a*) person who
makes notes on a text/who prepares
a text for publication. (*b*) director of
a newspaper or part of a newspaper;
the sports e. (*c*) computer program for
editing text. **editorial** [edɪ'tɔːrɪəl] **1.**
adj. referring to editors/to editing. **2.** *n.*
leading article written by the editor of
a newspaper.

educate ['edjʊkeɪt] *v.* to teach/to
instruct (s.o.); **an educated person** =
person who is cultivated. **education**
[edjʊ'keɪʃn] *n.* (system of) teaching/be-
ing taught; **adult e.** = teaching of adults;
further e. = teaching people who have
left school. **educational,** *adj.* referring to education/teaching/schools; **e.
publisher** = publisher who produces
school books. **educationist,** *n.* person
who specializes in the study of teaching
methods.

Edwardian [ed'wɔːdjən] *adj.* referring
to the time of Edward VII (1901–1910).

EEC [iːiː'siː] *n.* European Economic
Community.

eel [iːl] *n.* long thin fish like a snake.

eerie ['ɪərɪ] *adj.* (**eerier, eeriest**) frighten-
ing/weird. **eerily,** *adv.* in an eerie way.
eeriness, *n.* being eerie.

efface [ɪ'feɪs] *v.* to rub out. **effacement,**
n. rubbing out.

effect [ɪ'fekt] **1.** *n.* (*a*) result/influence;
**this rule takes e./comes into e. from
November 1st** = starts to be applied.
(*b*) meaning; **words to that e.** = words
with that meaning. (*c*) (*in theatre/
film/on radio*) **sound effects** = artificial or reproduced sounds (such as
thunder, horses, creaking doors). **2.**
v. to produce/to carry out. **effective,**
adj. (*a*) which produces a (good) result. (*b*) which takes effect; **a rule e.
from November 1st. effectively,** *adv.*
in a way which produces a good result.
effectual, *adj.* (*formal*) which produces
the intended effect. **effectually,** *adv.* in
an effectual way. **effectuate,** *v.* to carry
out (sth) effectively.

effeminate [ɪ'femɪnət] *adj.* (*of man*) behaving in a feminine way. **effeminacy,**
n. being effeminate.

effervesce [efə'ves] *v.* (*of liquid*) to
make bubbles giving off gas. **efferves-
cence,** *n.* bubbles in liquid; act of mak-

ing bubbles. **effervescent,** *adj.* which bubbles.

effete [e'fi:t] *adj.* weak/with no strength left.

efficacious [efɪ'keɪʃəs] *adj.* (medicine, etc.) which produces the correct result. **efficacy** ['efɪkəsɪ] *n.* being effective; power to produce the correct result.

efficiency [ɪ'fɪʃənsɪ] *n.* ability to produce the required result; **business e.** = ability to work effectively in business. **efficient,** *adj.* able to work well/to produce the required result. **efficiently,** *adv.* in an efficient way.

effigy ['efɪdʒɪ] *n.* statue/model of s.o.

effluent ['efluənt] *n.* sewage; liquid waste (from a factory). **effluvium,** *n.* hidden liquid which has a strong unpleasant smell.

effort ['efət] *n.* use of physical energy. **effortless,** *adj.* without apparently using any energy.

effrontery [ɪ'frʌntərɪ] *n.* rudeness.

effusive [ɪ'fju:sɪv] *adj.* too enthusiastic (in thanks). **effusively,** *adv.* very enthusiastically.

e.g. [i:'dʒi:] *abbreviation for* exempli gratia, *meaning* for example.

egalitarian [ɪgælɪ'teərɪən] *adj.* & *n.* (person) who believes in equality for everyone.

egg [eg] **1.** *n.* (*a*) ovum produced by a female animal. (*b*) hard-shelled cell, produced by a bird, esp. that of a hen. **2.** *v.* **to e. s.o. on** = to encourage s.o. to do sth. **eggcup,** *n.* holder for a boiled egg. **egghead,** *n.* *inf.* clever person. **eggplant,** *n.* aubergine/purple fruit eaten as vegetable. **eggshell,** *n.* shell around an egg; **e. finish** = slightly shiny matt finish to paintwork. **eggtimer,** *n.* device for timing how long an egg is boiled.

ego ['i:gəʊ] *n.* yourself; high opinion of yourself; **e. trip** = action which boosts your opinion of yourself. **egocentric** [egəʊ'sentrɪk] *adj.* thinking only about yourself. **egoism** ['egəʊɪzəm] *n.* thinking about oneself. **egoist,** *n.* person who only thinks of himself. **egotism** ['egəʊtɪzəm] *n.* talking only about oneself. **egotist,** *n.* person who only talks about himself. **egotistic(al)** [egəʊ'tɪstɪk(l)] *adj.* conceited.

egregious [ɪ'gri:dʒəs] *adv.* very bad; shocking.

egret ['i:grət] *n.* type of heron with beautiful white tail feathers.

Egyptian [ɪ'dʒɪpʃn] **1.** *adj.* referring to Egypt. **2.** *n.* person from Egypt.

eh [eɪ] *inter.* showing surprise/enquiry.

eider ['aɪdə] *n.* type of duck. **eiderdown** ['aɪdədaʊn] *n.* bed covering made of a large bag full of feathers.

eight [eɪt] (*a*) number 8. **he is e. (years old)**; **come to see us at e. (o'clock).** (*b*) eight people (the crew of a rowing boat). **eighteen,** number 18; **the e. hundreds** = the years between 1800 and 1899. **eighteenth, 18th,** *adj.* & *n.* referring to eighteen; **the e. century** = period from 1700 to 1799. **eighth, 8th,** *adj.* & *n.* referring to eight. **eightieth, 80th,** *adj.* & *n.* referring to eighty. **eighty,** number 80.

Eire ['eərə] *n.* Irish Republic.

eisteddfod [aɪ'stedfəd] *n.* Welsh literary and musical competition.

either ['aɪðə, 'i:ðə] **1.** *adj.* & *pron.* (*a*) one or the other; **I don't believe e. of you.** (*b*) both; **there are trees on e. side of our house. 2.** *conj.* & *adv.* (*showing choice*) **e. you come here or I go to you;** (*emphatic*) **he isn't French and he isn't English e.**

ejaculate [ɪ'dʒækjuleɪt] *v.* (*a*) (*formal*) to exclaim/to say (sth) suddenly. (*b*) (*of male*) to produce sperm. **ejaculation** [ɪdʒækjʊ'leɪʃn] *n.* act of ejaculating; sperm which has been ejaculated.

eject [ɪ'dʒekt] *v.* to throw out. **ejector seat,** *n.* seat in an aircraft which throws the pilot out in an emergency.

eke [i:k] *v.* **to e. out** = to economize (savings)/to try not to use up (resources).

elaborate 1. *adj.* [ɪ'læbərət] very detailed, very complicated. **2.** *v.* [ɪ'læbəreɪt] to go into details. **elaboration** [ɪlæbə'reɪʃn] *n.* being elaborate; detailed explanation. **elaborately,** *adv.* in a complicated/detailed way.

eland ['i:lənd] *n.* large S. African antelope.

elapse [ɪ'læps] *v.* (*of time*) to pass.

elastic [ɪ'læstɪk] **1.** *adj.* which stretch and contracts; not rigid; **e. band** of rubber for holding pap gether. **2.** *n.* piece of rubber which can stretch. **elasticate,** *v.* to fit with elastic. **elasticity** [ɪlæ'stɪsɪtɪ] *n.* ability to stretch.

elated [ɪ'leɪtɪd] *adj.* very excited and pleased. **elation** [ɪ'leɪʃn] *n.* feeling of excitement and pleasure.

elbow ['elbəʊ] *n.* joint in the arm. **elbowroom,** *n.* space to move about.

elder ['eldə] **1.** *adj.* older (person); **e. statesman** = statesman who is older (and wiser) than others. **2.** *n.* (*a*) older person. (*b*) common tree with white flowers and bunches of small purple berries. **elderberry,** *n.* (*a*) elder tree. (*b*) fruit of an elder. **elderly,** *adj.* quite old. **eldest,** *adj.* oldest (of a group).

El Dorado [eldɒ'rɑːdəʊ] *n.* legendary country of gold.

elect [ɪ'lekt] **1.** *v.* (*a*) to choose by voting. (*b*) **to e. to do sth** = to choose to do sth. **2.** *suffix showing* person who has been elected to a post, but who has not taken it up officially; **the mayor-elect. election** [ɪ'lekʃn] *n.* process of choosing by voting; **general e.** = election for the national Parliament. **electioneering,** *n.* working for an election campaign. **elective,** *adj.* which can be chosen. **elector,** *n.* person who is qualified to vote in an election. **electoral,** *adj.* referring to an election; **e. college** = group of people elected to elect s.o. (such as a president); **e. roll/register** = list of people who are qualified to vote in a certain area. **electorate,** *n.* all the people in a country who are qualified to vote.

electric [ɪ'lektrɪk] *adj.* (*a*) generating/ worked by electricity. (*b*) **the atmosphere was e.** = full of excitement. **electrical,** *adj.* referring to electricity. **electrically,** *adj.* by electricity. **electric chair,** *n.* chair used to execute criminals by passing a strong electric current through their bodies. **electrician** [elek'trɪʃn] *n.* person who works on electrical maintenance. **electricity** [elek'trɪsɪtɪ] *n.* form of energy used for power. **electrification** [ɪlektrɪfɪ'keɪʃn] *n.* changing to an electric source of power. **electrify** [ɪ'lektrɪfaɪ] *v.* (*a*) to convert to an electric source of power. (*b*) to startle

and excite. **electrocardiogram,** *n.* chart made by an electrocardiograph. **electrocardiograph,** *n.* device for recording the electric impulses made by a beating heart. **electroconvulsive therapy,** *n.* treatment of mental disorders by giving the patient small electric shocks. **electrocute,** *v.* to kill by electricity. **electrocution** [ɪlektrə-'kjuːʃn] *n.* killing by electricity. **electrode,** *n.* rod which leads the electric current into or out of a cell. **electroencephalogram,** *n.* chart made by an electroencephalograph. **electroencephalograph,** *n.* device for recording the electric impulses made by the brain. **electrolysis** [ɪlek'trɒlɪsɪs] *n.* (*a*) separation of the parts of a compound liquid by passing an electric current through it. (*b*) removal of unwanted hair by electric current. **electrolyte** [ɪ'lektrəlaɪt] *n.* chemical solution which can be broken into its parts by electrolysis. **electromagnet,** *n.* magnet made of material wound with a coil of wire with an electric current passing through it. **electromagnetic,** *adj.* made by an electromagnet. **electromotive,** *adj.* (force) which produces an electric current. **electron,** *n.* basic particle in an atom. **electronic** [ɪlek'trɒnɪk] *adj.* referring to electrons or electronics. **electronically,** *adv.* in an electronic way. **electronics,** *n.* science of conduction of electrons; industry which makes TV sets/radios/ calculators, etc. **electroplate,** *v.* to coat (a metal, usu. copper), with a thin layer of silver by means of electrolysis.

eleemosynary [eliːmɒʊ'saɪnərɪ] *adj.* referring to charity.

elegant ['elɪgənt] *adj.* well dressed; very fashionable. **elegance,** *n.* being elegant. **elegantly,** *adv.* fashionably.

elegy ['elədʒɪ] *n.* sad poem about s.o. who is dead. **elegiac** [elɪ'dʒaɪək] *adj.* sad and regretful.

element ['elɪmənt] *n.* (*a*) basic chemical substance. (*b*) basic part (of sth). (*c*) natural environment; **he's in his e. when he's talking about gardening.** (*d*) **the elements** = bad weather (wind/rain, etc.). (*e*) wire which heats in an electric heater/cooker, etc. **elementary**

[elɪ'mentrɪ] *adj.* basic/simple; **e. mathematics.**

elephant ['elɪfənt] *n.* very large African or Indian animal, with a trunk and tusks; **white e.** = expensive but useless thing. **elephantiasis** [elɪfən'taɪəsɪs] *n.* tropical disease where parts of the body become huge. **elephantine** [elɪ'fæntaɪn] *adj.* very large, heavy and difficult to move.

elevate ['elɪveɪt] *v.* to raise up. **elevation** [elɪ'veɪʃn] *n.* (a) raising. (b) (drawing of) one side of a building. (c) height (above sea-level). **elevator,** *n.* (a) device for lifting goods (*Am.* or people) inside a building; **grain e.** = large building for hoisting and storing grain. (b) part of the tail of an aircraft.

eleven [ɪ'levn] *adj. & n.* (a) number 11; **he arrived at (o'clock); he is e. (years old).** (b) eleven people (as in a sports team); **the England e. elevenses,** *n. pl. inf.* snack eaten in the mid-morning. **eleventh, 11th,** *adj. & n.* referring to eleven; **at the e. hour** = at the last minute; **the e. century** = period from 1000 to 1099.

elf [elf] *n.* (*pl.* **elves** [elvz]) small, usu. male, supernatural being. **elfin,** *adj.* referring to elves.

elicit [ɪ'lɪsɪt] *v.* to obtain (information) (**from** s.o.).

elide [ɪ'laɪd] *v.* to omit a sound when speaking. **elision** [ɪ'lɪʒn] *n.* omitting of a sound.

eligible ['elɪdʒɪbl] *adj.* able to be chosen (**for** sth); **e. bachelor** = man who has all the qualifications (esp. money) to be married. **eligibility** [elɪdʒə'bɪlɪtɪ] *n.* being eligible.

eliminate [ɪ'lɪmɪneɪt] *v.* (a) to remove (waste, etc.). (b) to exclude (s.o.) after a test. **elimination** [ɪlɪmɪ'neɪʃn] *n.* act of eliminating. **eliminator,** *n.* game, etc., which decides who is eliminated.

élite [ei'li:t] *n.* group of privileged people/the best people. **elitism,** *n.* rule by an élite.

elixir [ɪ'lɪksə] *n.* medicine which people imagine will cure everything.

Elizabethan [elɪzə'bi:θən] *adj.* referring to the time of Elizabeth I (1558–1603).

elk [elk] *n.* (*pl.* **elk**) large European deer with flat antlers.

ellipse [ɪ'lɪps] *n.* oval shape. **ellipsis,** *n.* absence of a word which is needed to complete the meaning of a phrase. **elliptic(al),** *adj.* (a) oval. (b) difficult to understand because of a missing word or phrase.

elm [elm] *n.* large deciduous tree; **Dutch e. disease** = disease which kills elms.

elocution [elə'kju:ʃn] *n.* clear and elegant way of speaking.

elongate ['i:lɒŋgeɪt] *v.* to stretch out to make longer. **elongation** [i:lɒŋ'geɪʃn] *n.* act of elongating.

elope [ɪ'ləup] *v.* to run away from home to get married (**with** s.o.). **elopement,** *n.* act of eloping.

eloquence ['eləkwəns] *n.* art of speaking well. **eloquent,** *adj.* good and persuasive (speech). **eloquently,** *adv.* in an eloquent way.

else [els] *adv.* (a) otherwise; **come in or e. stay out; you had better pay, or e.** = or I will force you to pay. (b) other; **anyone e.** = any other person; **nobody e.** = no other person; **anything e.** = any other thing; **nowhere e.** = no other place; **somewhere e.** *Am.* **some place e.** = in some other place. **elsewhere,** *adv.* somewhere else; in other places.

elucidate [ɪ'lu:sɪdeɪt] *v.* to make clear/to make easy to understand. **elucidation** [ɪlu:sɪ'deɪʃn] *n.* making clear.

elude [ɪ'lu:d] *v.* to escape/to avoid (capture). **elusion,** *n.* act of eluding. **elusive** [ɪ'lu:sɪv] *adj.* difficult to find.

elver ['elvə] *n.* baby eel.

em [em] *n.* space in printing equal to the width of the letter 'm'.

emaciated [ɪ'meɪsɪeɪtɪd] *adj.* extremely thin. **emaciation,** *n.* being emaciated.

email ['i:meɪl] *n.* electronic mail, a system of sending messages from one computer to another, using telephone lines.

emanate ['eməneɪt] *v.* to come **from**. **emanation,** *n.* thing which comes.

emancipate [ɪ'mænsɪpeɪt] *v.* to make (s.o.) free. **emancipation** [ɪmænsɪ'peɪʃn] *n.* setting free.

emasculate [ɪ'mæskjʊleɪt] *v.* to make feeble. **emasculation** [ɪmæskjʊ'leɪʃn] *n.* making feeble.

embalm [ɪm'bɑ:m] *v.* to treat (a dead body) with chemicals to prevent it decaying.

embankment [ɪm'bæŋkmənt] *n.* artificial bank (along a river); road along such a bank.

embargo [ɪm'bɑːgəʊ] **1.** *n.* (*pl.* -oes) official prohibition (**on** goods/traffic/information). **2.** *v.* to prohibit (sth) officially.

embark [ɪm'bɑːk] *v.* **1.** to go on board a ship; **the passengers embarked at Southampton. 2. to e. on sth** = to start doing sth. **embarkation** [embɑː'keɪʃn] *n.* act of going on board a ship or aircraft.

embarrass [ɪm'bærəs] *v.* to make (s.o.) feel uncomfortable (by rudeness/indecency, etc.). **embarrassment,** *n.* act of making s.o. feel uncomfortable.

embassy ['embəsɪ] *n.* home or offices of an ambassador.

embattled [ɪm'bætld] *adj.* under attack; constantly criticized.

embed [ɪm'bed] *v.* (**embedded**) to fix (sth) into a mass of concrete/flesh, etc.

embellish [ɪm'belɪʃ] *v.* to decorate/to make beautiful. **embellishments,** *n. pl.* decorations/beautiful improvements.

embers ['embəz] *n. pl.* pieces of wood/coal which are red hot.

embezzle [ɪm'bezl] *v.* to steal (money which you are looking after for s.o.). **embezzlement,** *n.* act of embezzling. **embezzler,** *n.* person who embezzles.

embittered [ɪm'bɪtəd] *adj.* (*of person*) made angry and sad (by disappointment/envy).

emblem ['embləm] *n.* design which is adopted as the characteristic of a country/team/town, etc. **emblematic** [emblə'mætɪk] *adj.* which acts as an emblem.

embody [ɪm'bɒdɪ] *v.* to show (an idea) in a physical form. **embodiment,** *n.* physical expression of an idea.

embolism ['embəlɪzəm] *n.* blocking of a blood vessel by a blood clot or a bubble of air.

emboss [ɪm'bɒs] *v.* to raise (a design) above a flat surface; **embossed letterhead** = address pressed on writing paper so that it stands above the surface.

embrace [ɪm'breɪs] *v.* (*a*) to hold and (s.o.) as a gesture of affection. (*b*) a convert to (a belief).

embrocation [embrə'keɪʃn] *n.* liquid which you rub into parts of the body which are stiff.

embroider [ɪm'brɔɪdə] *v.* to make artistic patterns by sewing with coloured threads. **embroidery,** *n.* art of sewing flower designs/patterns.

embroil [em'brɔɪl] *v.* to involve (s.o.) in a quarrel.

embryo ['embrɪəʊ] *n.* (*pl.* -os) earliest state of a living organism; rudimentary idea. **embryology,** *n.* study of embryos. **embryonic** [embrɪ'ɒnɪk] *adj.* original/in a very early state.

emend [iː'mend] *v.* to change/to make correct. **emendation** [iːmen'deɪʃn] *n.* change/correction.

emerald ['emrəld] *adj. & n.* green precious stone; colour of this stone.

emerge [ɪ'mɜːdʒ] *v.* to come out (**from** inside sth); to become apparent/known. **emergence,** *n.* act of emerging. **emergent,** *adj.* **e. nations** = countries which are slowly becoming economically independent.

emergency [ɪ'mɜːdʒənsɪ] *n.* dangerous state where decisions have to be taken quickly (such as fire/accident/breakdown of law and order); **state of e.** = when normal administrative processes are taken over by the police or armed forces; **e. exit** = door used when a fire breaks out; **e. operation** = operation carried out at short notice because the patient is seriously ill; **e. services** = the police, fire and ambulance services.

emeritus [ɪ'merɪtəs] *adj.* (professor) who has retired but keeps his title.

emery ['emərɪ] *n.* fine crystals used for polishing. **emery board,** *n.* thin stick of cardboard covered with fine crystals, used for filing fingernails. **emery paper,** *n.* fine sandpaper.

emetic [ɪ'metɪk] *n.* substance which makes you vomit.

emigrate ['emɪgreɪt] *v.* to leave a country to live in another. **emigrant,** *n.* person who emigrates. **emigration** [emɪ'greɪʃn] *n.* act of leaving a country to live in another. **emigré** ['emɪgreɪ] *n.* person who has emigrated for political reasons.

eminence ['emɪnəns] *n.* high place; high rank. **eminent** ['emɪnənt] *adj.* very highly respected because of position or work. **eminently,** *adv.* remarkably; particularly.

emir ['emɪə] *n.* Muslim ruler. **emirate,** *n.* country ruled by an emir.

emissary ['emɪsərɪ] *n.* person sent to negotiate on s.o.'s behalf.

emit [ɪ'mɪt] *v.* (**emitted**) to send out (a sound/smoke, etc.). **emission,** *n.* act of emitting; thing emitted.

emollient [ɪ'mɒlɪənt] *adj.* & *n.* (substance) which softens.

emolument [ɪ'mɒljʊmənt] *n.* (*formal*) payment/salary.

emotion [ɪ'məʊʃn] *n.* (strong) feeling. **emotional,** *adj.* showing emotion. **emotionally,** *adv.* in an emotional way. **emotive,** *adj.* which is likely to cause strong feeling.

empanel [ɪm'pænəl] *v.* to chose (a jury).

empathy ['empəθɪ] *n.* being able to share the feelings of another person, by imagining yourself as that person.

emperor ['emprə] *n.* ruler of an empire.

emphasize ['emfəsaɪz] *v.* to stress the importance of (sth). **emphasis** ['emfəsɪs] *n.* stress (usu. in speech). **emphatic** [ɪm'fætɪk] *adj.* using emphasis. **emphatically,** *adv.* in a forceful way.

empire ['empaɪə] *n.* large territories ruled by a central government.

empirical [em'pɪrɪkl] *adj.* based on practical experiment and not on theory.

emplacement [ɪm'pleɪsmənt] *n.* place where guns are set.

employ [ɪm'plɔɪ] *v.* (*a*) to give (s.o.) regular work. (*b*) to use. **employee** [emplɔɪ'iː] *n.* person who is employed. **employer,** *n.* person who gives work to people and pays them. **employment,** *n.* regular paid work.

emporium [ɪm'pɔːrɪəm] *n.* large shop.

empower [ɪm'paʊə] *v.* to give (s.o.) the authority to do sth.

empress ['emprəs] *n.* woman ruler of an empire; wife/widow of an emperor.

empty ['emtɪ] **1.** *adj.* with nothing inside. **2.** *n.* thing, usu. bottle, which has nothing in it. **3.** *v.* to make (sth) empty; to remove the (contents) from sth. **emptiness,** *n.* being empty. **empty-handed,** *adj.* with no results; having received nothing.

EMS [iːem'es] = European Monetary System.

emu ['iːmjuː] *n.* large Australian bird which cannot fly.

EMU [iːem'juː] = European Monetary Union.

emulate ['emjʊleɪt] *v.* to try to do as well as or better than (s.o.). **emulation** [emjʊ'leɪʃn] *n.* act of emulating.

emulsion [ɪ'mʌlʃn] *n.* mixture of two liquids which do not unite completely, such as oil and water; **e. paint** = paint made of colour added to an emulsion of oil and water. **emulsifier,** *n.* thing which emulsifies. **emulsify,** *v.* to make into an emulsion.

en [en] *n.* space in printing equal to the width of the letter 'n'.

enable [ɪ'neɪbl] *v.* to make it possible for s.o. to do sth.

enact [ɪ'nækt] *v.* to make (a law). **enactment,** *n.* making (of a law).

enamel [ɪ'næml] **1.** *n.* (*a*) very hard covering of colour. (*b*) hard coloured coating fixed to metal by heating. (*c*) hard coating on the teeth. **2.** *v.* (**enamelled**) to cover with very hard colour.

enamoured [ɪ'næməd] *adj.* **I'm not e. of her hair style** = I don't like it very much.

en bloc [ɒn'blɒk] *adv.* all together as a group.

encamped [ɪn'kæmpd] *adj.* in a camp. **encampment,** *n.* large camp.

encapsulate [ɪn'kæpsjʊleɪt] *v.* to put in a capsule; to put in a shortened form.

encase [ɪn'keɪs] *v.* to surround as if in a case.

enchant [ɪn'tʃɑːnt] *v.* to charm. **enchanting,** *adj.* very beautiful/magical. **enchantment,** *n.* magic spell.

encircle [ɪn'sɜːkl] *v.* to surround completely.

enclave ['enkleɪv] *n.* small group/small area completely surrounded by another quite different and larger group/mass.

enclose [ɪn'kləʊz] *v.* to put (an object) inside sth; **I am enclosing a bill with my letter. enclosure** [ɪn'kləʊʒə] *n.* (*a*) fenced area for keeping animals. (*b*) paper enclosed with a letter in an envelope.

encode [en'kəʊd] *v.* to put data/a message into code.

encomium [ɪn'kəʊmɪəm] *n.* (*formal*) praise.

encompass [ɪnˈkʌmpəs] *v.* to surround.

encore [ˈɒŋkɔː] **1.** *n.* (*a*) calling (by the audience) for a performer to repeat a song, a piece of music. (*b*) song/piece of music repeated at the request of the audience. **2.** *v.* to call for a song, etc., to be repeated.

encounter [ɪnˈkauntə] **1.** *n.* (*a*) meeting. (*b*) short conflict. **2.** *v.* to meet.

encourage [ɪnˈkʌrɪdʒ] *v.* to give (s.o.) the confidence to do sth. **encouragement,** *n.* giving s.o. the confidence to do sth. **encouraging,** *adj.* which encourages.

encroach [ɪnˈkrəutʃ] *v.* **to e. on** = to occupy space belonging to s.o. else. **encroachment,** *n.* act of encroaching.

encrust [ɪnˈkrʌst] *v.* to cover with a hard covering.

encumber [ɪnˈkʌmbə] *v.* (*formal*) to weigh down (s.o.) **with** sth. **encumbrance,** *n.* thing which encumbers.

encyclical [ɪnˈsɪklɪkl] *n.* solemn letter from the Pope.

encyclopaedia, encyclopedia [ɪnsaɪkləˈpiːdɪə] *n.* reference book which gives facts about things/people/events, etc. **encyclopaedic, encyclopedic,** *adj.* like an encyclopaedia.

end [end] **1.** *n.* (*a*) final part; *inf.* **no e. of** = very many; **to throw s.o. in at the deep e.** = to give s.o. a difficult job to start with; **to be at a loose e.** = to have nothing to do; **to make ends meet** = to have enough money to live on; **big e.** = end of the rod in a car engine which connects the piston to the camshaft. (*b*) final part of a period of time. (*c*) aim; **to this e.** = in order to do this. **2.** *v.* to finish. **endgame,** *n.* way of playing the last moves in chess game. **ending,** *n.* way a story, etc., finishes. **endless,** *adj.* with no apparent end. **endlessly,** *adv.* with no apparent end. **endpapers,** *n.* pages (usually left blank) at the beginning and end of a book. **endways,** *adv.* with the end first.

endanger [ɪnˈdeɪndʒə] *v.* to put in danger.

endear [ɪnˈdɪə] *v.* **to e. s.o. to s.o.** = to make s.o. loved by s.o. **endearment,** *n.* **term of e.** = word showing that you love.

endeavour, Am. endeavor [ɪnˈdevə] **1.** *n.* (*formal*) attempt. **2.** *v.* (*formal*) to try hard.

endemic [enˈdemɪk] *adj.* (disease) which is often found in a particular place.

endive [ˈendɪv] *n.* salad vegetable with curly leaves.

endocardium [endəuˈkɑːdɪəm] *n.* membrane lining the heart.

endocrine [ˈendəkraɪn] *adj.* **e. gland** = gland which makes hormones and passes them directly into the bloodstream without using ducts.

endorse [ɪnˈdɔːs] *v.* (*a*) to show approval; **to e. a cheque** = to sign it on the back to show it is yours. (*b*) **his driving licence was endorsed** = had a note attached to show he had been found guilty of a traffic offence. **endorsement,** *n.* (*a*) approval. (*b*) note which endorses a driving licence.

endow [ɪnˈdau] *v.* (*a*) to give a regular income to (a school/hospital, etc.). (*b*) **endowed with** = having (naturally) certain qualities. **endowment,** *n.* (*a*) giving of money (to a school, etc.) to provide a regular income. (*b*) **e. policy** = type of insurance policy where a sum of money is paid to the insured person on a certain date, or to his heirs if he dies.

endure [ɪnˈdjuə] *v.* (*a*) to suffer. (*b*) to stay/to last. **endurable,** *adj.* which can be endured. **endurance,** *n.* ability to suffer hardship; **e. test** = test of a machine/person to see if it/he works well under bad conditions.

enema [ˈenɪmə] *n.* liquid medicine put into the rectum with a syringe.

enemy [ˈenəmɪ] *n.* opponent (in war).

energy [ˈenədʒɪ] *n.* force/strength; **atomic e.** = power from atomic reactions. **energetic** [enəˈdʒetɪk] *adj.* using force; lively. **energetically,** *adv.* using much force. **energize,** *v.* to make (sth) vigorous.

enervate [ˈenəveɪt] *v.* to make (s.o.) lazy/sluggish.

enfeeble [ɪnˈfiːbl] *v.* to make (s.o.) feeble.

enfold [ɪnˈfəuld] *v.* to wrap (sth) up **in** sth.

enforce [ɪnˈfɔːs] *v.* to make sure (a law)

is obeyed. **enforceable,** *adj.* which can be enforced. **enforcement,** *n.* act of enforcing.

enfranchise [ɪn'fræntʃaɪz] *v.* to give (s.o.) the right to vote in elections.

engage [ɪn'geɪdʒ] *v.* (*a*) to attach together (legally); to employ (new staff). (*b*) to make parts of a machine fit into each other; **e. first gear** = put your car into first gear. (*c*) to be occupied (**in** doing sth). (*d*) to attack (the enemy). **engaged,** *adj.* (*a*) having officially stated one's intention to marry. (*b*) busy; occupied. **engagement,** *n.* (*a*) appointment. (*b*) statement of intention to marry; **e. ring** = ring given by man to woman when they agree to marry. (*c*) battle. **engaging,** *adj.* charming.

engender [ɪn'dʒendə] *v.* (*formal*) to produce.

engine ['endʒɪn] *n.* (*a*) machine/large motor which produces power. (*b*) locomotive/vehicle for pulling trains. **engined,** *adj.* with an engine; **single-engined aircraft. engine-driver,** *n.* person who drives a locomotive. **engineer** [endʒɪ'nɪə] **1.** *n.* (*a*) person who looks after technical equipment, esp. engines. (*b*) (*in army*) soldier who specializes in construction of bridges/defences, etc.; **civil e.** = person who specializes in construction of roads/bridges, etc. (*c*) *Am.* person who drives a locomotive. **2.** *v.* to arrange (sth) by plotting. **engineering,** *n.* science/study of technical equipment; **civil e.** = science of construction (esp. of roads/bridges, etc.).

English ['ɪŋglɪʃ] **1.** *adj.* referring to England; **I think he is E. although he speaks with an American accent. 2.** *n.* (*a*) **the E.** = the people of England. (*b*) language of England, the USA, Australia, and many other countries; **can you speak E.? what is that in E.? what's the E. for 'pommes frites'? Englishman, Englishwoman,** *n.* (*pl.* **-men, -women**) person from England.

engrave [ɪn'greɪv] *v.* to cut (a pattern/a letter) on to a hard surface. **engraver,** *n.* artist who engraves. **engraving,** *n.* picture printed from an engraved plate.

engross [ɪn'grəʊs] *v.* to draw up a legal document in its final form.

engrossed [ɪn'grəʊst] *adj.* **e. in** = very interested/busy in.

engulf [ɪn'gʌlf] *v.* to swallow up.

enhance [ɪn'hɑːns] *v.* to increase (beauty/value). **enhancement,** *n.* increase (in value, etc.).

enigma [ɪ'nɪgmə] *n.* mystery/puzzle. **enigmatic** [enɪg'mætɪk] *adj.* difficult to explain/difficult to understand.

enjoin [ɪn'dʒɔɪn] *v.* (*formal*) to command.

enjoy [ɪn'dʒɔɪ] *v.* to take pleasure in (sth); **to e. yourself** = to have a good time. **enjoyable,** *adj.* pleasing. **enjoyment,** *n.* pleasure.

enlarge [ɪn'lɑːdʒ] *v.* (*a*) to make bigger. (*b*) **to e. upon** = to give more details about. **enlargement,** *n.* bigger photograph (than the original negative). **enlarger,** *n.* device for enlarging photographs.

enlighten [ɪn'laɪtn] *v.* **to e. s.o. on/ about sth** = to give s.o. a clear picture of sth. **enlightened,** *adj.* free of prejudice; holding approved ideas. **enlightenment,** *n.* knowledge/absence of ignorance; **the Enlightenment** = period in the 18th century when many scientific discoveries were made.

enlist [ɪn'lɪst] *v.* (*a*) (*of soldier*) to join the armed forces. (*b*) **to e. s.o.'s help** = to get help from s.o. **enlistment,** *n.* joining the armed forces.

enliven [ɪn'laɪvn] *v.* to make more lively.

en masse [ɒn'mæs] *adv.* all together in a crowd.

enmity ['enmɪti] *n.* hatred **towards** s.o.

ennoble [ɪ'nəʊbl] *v.* to make (s.o.) a peer.

enormous [ɪ'nɔːməs] *adj.* very large. **enormity,** *n.* seriousness (of a crime). **enormously,** *adv.* very much.

enough [ɪ'nʌf] **1.** *adj.* sufficient; as much as is needed; **have you got e. money? 2.** *n.* sufficient quantity; **have you had e. to eat? 3.** *adv.* sufficiently; **it is not light e. to take pictures.**

enquire [ɪŋ'kwaɪə] *v.* **1.** to ask questions (about). **2.** to conduct an official investigation. **enquiry,** *n.* (*a*) question; asking for information; **enquiries (desk)** = place (in a shop, etc.) for dealing with questions. (*b*) official investigation.

enrage [ɪn'reɪdʒ] *v.* to make (s.o.) very annoyed.

enrapture [ɪn'ræptʃə] *v.* to charm (s.o.).

enrich [ɪn'rɪtʃ] v. to make richer. **enrichment**, n. making richer.

enrol, Am. **enroll** [ɪn'rəʊl] v. (**enrolled**) to admit (new members/new students); **he enrolled for a cookery class. enrolment**, n. action of admitting new members/students; list of all new students.

en route [ɒn'ruːt] adv. on the way.

ensconced [ɪn'skɒnst] adj. firmly settled.

ensemble [ɒn'sɒmbl] n. (a) group (of musicians/singers). (b) set of women's clothes which match. (c) group of things which fit together.

enshrine [ɪn'ʃraɪn] v. to enclose as if in a shrine.

ensign ['ensaɪn] n. (a) national flag used by a ship. (b) Am. junior naval officer.

enslave [ɪn'sleɪv] v. to make a slave of (s.o.).

ensnare [ɪn'sneə] v. to catch in a trap.

ensue [ɪn'sjuː] v. to follow. **ensuing**, adj. which follows.

en suite [ɒn'swiːt] adv. joined in a series.

ensure [ɪn'ʃʊə] v. to make sure of.

ENT [iːen'tiː] ear, nose and throat.

entail [ɪn'teɪl] v. to involve/to include.

entangle [ɪn'tæŋgl] v. to be caught up (in string/bushes/problems). **entanglement**, n. state of being entangled; **barbed wire e.** = mass of coiled barbed wire to protect soldiers.

entente [ɒn'tɒnt] n. peaceful agreement (between countries).

enter ['entə] v. (a) to go in/to come in. (b) to write down (a name, etc.). (c) to type information on a keyboard, and put it into a computer system. **enter for**, v. to put your name on a list as a competitor; **to e. for the marathon. enter into**, v. to take part in (an agreement).

enteritis [entə'raɪtɪs] n. infection of the intestines. **enteric** [en'terɪk] adj. referring to the intestines.

enterprise ['entəpraɪz] n. (a) new plan/adventure. (b) ability to plan. (c) method of working in business; **private e.** = business firms which are not State-owned. **enterprising**, adj. with initiative.

entertain [entə'teɪn] v. (a) to amuse. (b) to offer (s.o.) a meal. (c) to consider (a suggestion/an idea). **entertainer**, n. person/performer who entertains.

entertaining, adj. amusing. **entertainment**, n. (a) amusement. (b) hospitality; **e. allowance** = money allowed for entertaining guests to meals.

enthralling [ɪn'θrɔːlɪŋ] adj. extremely interesting.

enthrone [ɪn'θrəʊn] v. to put (s.o.) on a throne.

enthusiasm [ɪn'θjuːzɪæzəm] n. great interest. **enthuse** [ɪn'θjuːz] v. inf. to show great interest (over sth). **enthusiast**, n. person who shows great interest in sth. **enthusiastic** [ɪnθjuːzɪ'æstɪk] adj. showing great interest; **he was very e. about my book. enthusiastically**, adv. with enthusiasm.

entice [ɪn'taɪs] v. to attract/to tempt. **enticement**, n. act of enticing; thing which entices.

entire [ɪn'taɪə] adj. whole. **entirely**, adv. wholly; **I e. agree with you. entirety** [ɪn'taɪərətɪ] n. being whole; **he translated the book in its e.** = completely.

entitle [ɪn'taɪtl] v. (a) to give the right to; **he is entitled to ten days' holiday a year.** (b) to give a title to; **a book entitled 'War and Peace'. entitlement**, n. right to have.

entity ['entɪtɪ] n. thing which exists as a separate unit.

entomb [ɪn'tuːm] v. to bury.

entomology [entə'mɒlədʒɪ] n. study of insects. **entomological** [entəmə'lɒdʒɪkl] adj. referring to entomology. **entomologist** [entə'mɒlədʒɪst] n. person who studies insects.

entourage [ɒntʊ'rɑːʒ] n. group of people (secretaries/assistants/advisers, etc.) surrounding an important person.

entrails ['entreɪlz] n. pl. intestines of an animal.

entrance[1] ['entrəns] n. (act of) going in; (door for) going in; **main e.** = main doorway.

entrance[2] [ɪn'trɑːns] v. to bewitch. **entrancing**, adj. very attractive/beautiful.

entrant ['entrənt] n. person who enters for a race/a competition.

entreat [ɪn'triːt] v. to plead. **entreating**, adj. pleading. **entreatingly**, adv. pleadingly. **entreaty**, n. plea.

entrée ['ɒntreɪ] n. (a) freedom to go in. (b) small dish served before the main dish (in a formal meal).

entrench [ɪn'trenʃ] v. to put in trenches/ to dig in. **entrenched**, adj. **firmly e.** = (i) firmly established; (ii) holding firm opinions.

entrepreneur [ɒntrəprə'nɜː] n. (a) person who directs a company and speculates commercially. (b) contractor who acts as a middleman. **entrepreneurial** [ɒntrəprə'nɜːrɪəl] adj. speculative.

entrust [ɪn'trʌst] v. to **e. sth to s.o./to e. s.o. with sth** = to give s.o. the responsibility for sth.

entry ['entrɪ] n. (a) going in. (b) written information in a reference book/ accounts ledger/computer system.

entwine [ɪn'twaɪn] v. to twist around.

E number ['iːnʌmbə] n. classification number for food additives, used in the EC.

enumerate [ɪ'njuːməreɪt] v. to mention one by one/to make a list of. **enumeration**, n. list; act of enumerating.

enunciate [ɪ'nʌnsɪeɪt] v. to speak (words) clearly. **enunciation** [ɪnʌnsɪ-'eɪʃn] n. clear pronunciation.

envelop [ɪn'veləp] v. to cover/to surround with a covering. **envelope** ['envələʊp] n. paper covering for sending letters.

environment [ɪn'vaɪərənmənt] n. surroundings (in which you live). **environmental** [ɪnvaɪərən'mentl] adj. which refers to the surroundings of sth; **e. health officer** = official who monitors pollution, insanitary conditions, etc. in an area. **environs** [ɪn'vaɪərənz] n. pl. area surrounding a place.

envisage [ɪn'vɪzɪdʒ] v. to foresee; to plan (sth) which may take place.

envoy ['envɔɪ] n. person sent officially (by a country)/high-ranking diplomat.

envy ['envɪ] 1. n. feeling of wishing to have sth which s.o. else has/of wanting to be or do sth else. 2. v. to **e. s.o. sth** = to wish to have sth belonging to s.o.; to be unhappy because you want to be like s.o. else. **enviable**, adj. which one can envy. **envious**, adj. feeling envy.

enzyme ['enzaɪm] n. substance which can make other substances change (as in digestion).

epaulette, Am. **epaulet** ['epəlet] n. decorative strip on the shoulder of a uniform.

ephemeral [ɪ'fiːmərəl] adj. which disappears quickly/does not last long. **ephemera**, n. pl. printed papers (like tickets) which are thrown away after use.

epic ['epɪk] 1. n. long story/poem/film, esp. about war. 2. adj. long and difficult.

epicentre ['episentə] n. point on the surface of the earth which an earthquake reaches first.

epicure ['epɪkjʊə] n. person who is fond of, and knows a lot about, food. **epicurean** [epɪkjʊ'riːən] adj. & n. (referring to) an epicure.

epidemic [epɪ'demɪk] n. wave of disease which affects a lot of people.

epidermis [epɪ'dɜːmɪs] n. outer layer of skin.

epidural [epɪ'djʊərəl] adj. (anaesthetic) given in the spine.

epiglottis [epɪ'glɒtɪs] n. cartilage at the back of the throat which prevents food from being taken into the windpipe.

epigram ['epɪgræm] n. short, witty saying. **epigrammatic** [epɪgrə'mætɪk] adj. witty, like an epigram. **epigraph**, n. text used to illustrate sth. (as at the end of a book).

epilepsy ['epɪlepsɪ] n. disease which usu. gives convulsive fits. **epileptic** [epɪ'leptɪk] 1. adj. referring to epilepsy. 2. n. person who suffers from epilepsy.

epilogue ['epɪlɒg] n. short text at the end of a longer work; short moral programme at the end of a day's TV or radio programmes.

Epiphany [ɪ'pɪfənɪ] n. Christian festival on January 6th, celebrating the visit of the Kings to the Christ child.

episcopal [ɪ'pɪskəpl] adj. referring to bishops; (church) which has bishops. **episcopalian** [ɪpɪskə'peɪlɪən] adj. & n. (member) of an episcopal church.

episode ['epɪsəʊd] n. (a) short piece of action in longer story. (b) short period (in your life).

epistemology [epɪstə'mɒlədʒɪ] n. study of knowledge.

epistle [ɪ'pɪsl] n. (formal) long letter.

epitaph ['epɪtɑːf] n. writing on a gravestone.

epithet ['epɪθet] n. special name describing s.o.; **William I has the e. of 'the Conqueror'.**

epitome [ɪ'pɪtəmɪ] n. person who shows a particular quality very strongly. **epitomize**, v. to show (a quality) very strongly.

epoch ['iːpɒk] n. major period of time. **epoch-making**, adj. very important historically.

equable ['ekwəbl] adj. calm/not easily upset.

equal ['iːkwəl] 1. v. (equalled) to be exactly the same as/to add up to; **two plus two equals four.** 2. adj. (a) exactly the same as/level with something; **all things being e. =** having considered everything carefully. (b) **he wasn't e. to the task =** he wasn't strong enough/brave enough to do it. 3. n. person who is on the same level as s.o. else. **equality** [ɪ'kwɒlɪtɪ] n. state of being equal; **e. of opportunity =** state where everyone has the same chance of getting a job/ of doing well. **equalize** ['iːkwəlaɪz] v. to make equal; to score and make the points of both teams the same. **equalizer**, n. goal, etc., which makes the score equal. **equally**, adv. in exactly the same way.

equanimity [ekwə'nɪmɪtɪ] n. not getting flustered/calmness.

equate [ɪ'kweɪt] v. to see (two things) as equal. **equation** [ɪ'kweɪʒn] n. mathematical or chemical formula showing two parts are equal.

equator [ɪ'kweɪtə] n. imaginary line around the circumference of the earth which is the same distance from the North and South Poles. **equatorial** [ekwə'tɔːrɪəl] adj. referring to the equator.

equerry ['ekwərɪ] n. man who is in attendance on a king/queen.

equestrian [ɪ'kwestrɪən] adj. & n. (person) riding on a horse.

equidistant [iːkwɪ'dɪstənt] adj. at an equal distance from sth.

equilateral [iːkwɪ'lætərəl] adj. (triangle) with all sides of the same length.

equilibrium [iːkwɪ'lɪbrɪəm] n. state of being perfectly balanced.

equine ['ekwaɪn] adj. referring to horses.

equinox ['iːkwɪnɒks] n. time of the year when the day and night are of equal

length. **equinoctial** [iːkwɪ'nɒkʃl] adj. referring to an equinox.

equip [ɪ'kwɪp] v. (equipped) to provide (sth/s.o.) with arms/machinery/furniture; **well equipped =** with all the arms/machinery, etc., which are thought necessary. **equipment**, n. things which are provided to equip sth.

equity ['ekwɪtɪ] n. (a) state of justice; **in e. =** to be fair. (b) **equities =** ordinary shares (in a company). **equitable**, adj. fair/just. **equitably**, adv. in an equitable way.

equivalent [ɪ'kwɪvələnt] adj. & n. (thing) of the same value/same strength (as sth); **what is the British e. of the Secretary of State? equivalence**, n. being equivalent.

equivocate [ɪ'kwɪvəkeɪt] v. to mislead/ to give an ambiguous answer. **equivocal**, adj. uncertain/ambiguous. **equivocally**, adv. in an equivocal way. **equivocation**, n. ambiguous reply.

era ['ɪərə] n. long period of history; **the Victorian e.**

eradicate [ɪ'rædɪkeɪt] v. to wipe out/to destroy completely. **eradication** [ɪrædɪ'keɪʃn] n. wiping out.

erase [ɪ'reɪz] v. to rub out (writing)/to remove (recorded material) from a tape; to remove data on a disk. **eraser**, n. Am. rubber for erasing; **ink e. =** hand eraser for rubbing out ink. **erasure** [ɪ'reɪʒə] n. place where a piece of writing has been erased.

ere [eə] prep. (poetic) before.

erect [ɪ'rekt] 1. adj. straight upright. 2. v. to put up a mast/a building. **erectile**, adj. (tissue) which can become erect. **erection**, n. (a) action of putting up; thing which has been erected. (b) state where the penis becomes erect.

erg [ɜːg] n. unit of measurement of work.

ergonomics [ɜːgə'nɒmɪks] n. study of people at work and their working environment.

ergot ['ɜːgɒt] n. poisonous disease of rye.

erica ['erɪkə] n. heather.

ERM [iːaː'em] = Exchange Rate Mechanism.

ermine ['ɜːmɪn] n. white fur (from the winter coat of a stoat).

erode [ɪ'rəʊd] v. to wear away. **erosion** [ɪ'rəʊʒn] n. act of wearing away.

erogenous [ɪ'rɒdʒənəs] adj. very sensitive sexually.

erotic [ɪ'rɒtɪk] *adj.* strongly sexual. **eroticism**, *n.* erotic quality.

err [ɜː] *v.* to make a mistake/to be at fault; **he erred on the right side** = his mistake was to his advantage.

errand ['erənd] *n.* being sent out (esp. to buy sth); **to run errands for s.o.**

errant ['erənt] *adj.* (knight) wandering in search of adventure.

erratic [ɪ'rætɪk] *adj.* irregular/wild. **erratically**, *adv.* in a wild manner.

erratum [ɪ'rɑːtəm] *n.* (*pl.* **errata**) mistake in a printed book.

error ['erə] *n.* mistake; **in e.** = by mistake. **erroneous** [ɪ'rəʊnɪəs] *adj.* wrong. **erroneously**, *adv.* by mistake.

ersatz ['eəzæts] *adj.* artificial; imitated.

erstwhile ['ɜːstwaɪl] *adj.* former.

eructation [erʌk'teɪʃn] *n.* (*formal*) belching.

erudite ['erjuːdaɪt] *adj.* learned. **erudition** [erjuː'dɪʃn] *n.* learning/knowledge.

erupt [ɪ'rʌpt] *v.* (*of volcano*) to throw out lava, ash, etc.; (*of person*) to become angry suddenly. **eruption**, *n.* (*a*) (*of volcano*) throwing out of lava/ash. (*b*) appearance of spots on the skin.

erysipelas [erɪ'sɪpələs] *n.* red rash on the skin.

escalate ['eskəleɪt] *v.* to get worse/more violent; to increase steadily. **escalation** [eskə'leɪʃn] *n.* getting worse/bigger. **escalator**, *n.* moving stairs.

escalope [eskə'lɒp] *n.* thin slice of meat, esp. veal.

escapade ['eskəpeɪd] *n.* wild act.

escape [ɪ'skeɪp] **1.** *n.* (*a*) action of getting away from prison/from an awkward situation; **we had a narrow e.** = we were almost killed; **e. clause** = part of a contract which allows one party to avoid the obligations of the contract. (*b*) key/program which controls the actions of a computer. **2.** *v.* (*a*) to get away (**from** prison/**from** an awkward situation); **he escaped through the window.** (*b*) to avoid/to miss; **his name escapes me** = I cannot remember his name. **escapee** [eskeɪ'piː] *n.* person who has escaped from prison. **escapement**, *n.* device in a watch or clock which regulates the movement. **escapism**, *n.* retreat from reality. **escapist** *adj.*

& *n.* (person) who retreats from reality. **escapologist** [eskə'pɒlədʒɪst] *n.* performer who escapes from chains/sealed box, etc., before an audience.

escarpment [ɪ'skɑːpmənt] *n.* steep slope.

eschew [es'tʃuː] *v.* (*formal*) to avoid.

escort 1. *n.* ['eskɔːt] person or group of people accompanying s.o. **2.** *v.* [es'kɔːt] to accompany (s.o.).

Eskimo ['eskɪməʊ] *n.* & *adj.* (*pl.* **-o** or **-os**) one of a people living in the north of Canada and Greenland.

esophagus [ə'sɒfəgəs] *n. Am.* oesophagus.

esoteric [isəʊ'terɪk] *adj.* understood by very few people; difficult to understand.

espadrille [espə'driːj, -drɪl] *n.* canvas rope-soled shoe.

espalier [ɪ'spælɪə] *n.* artificial shape of a fruit tree, with a central stem and branches which form the shape of a ladder.

esparto [es'pɑːtəʊ] *n.* type of grass.

especial [e'speʃl] *adj.* particular. **especially**, *adv.* particularly/very.

espionage ['espɪənɑːʒ] *n.* spying; **industrial e.** = spying on a rival firm to try to find out trade secrets.

esplanade ['espləneɪd] *n.* level place (along a seafront) where people can walk.

espouse [es'paʊz] *v.* (*formal*) to support (a cause).

espresso [ɪ'spresəʊ] *n.* coffee made by forcing boiling water through ground coffee.

esprit de corps [espriːdə'kɔː] *n.* feeling of loyalty to a group (usually a military unit).

espy [ɪ'spaɪ] *v.* (*old*) to see.

Esq. [es'kwaɪə] *abbreviation for* esquire (*very polite form of address written after man's name on envelope*) **George Martin, Esq.**

essay. 1. *n.* ['eseɪ] piece of prose writing on a particular subject. **2.** *v.* [e'seɪ] (*formal*) to attempt. **essayist**, *n.* person who writes essays.

essence ['esəns] *n.* pure extract taken from sth; central part (of an argument). **essential** [ɪ'senʃl] *adj.* & *n.* (thing) which is very important/indispensable;

the bare essentials = the things which are absolutely necessary. **essentially,** *adv.* basically/for the most important part.

establish [ɪ'stæblɪʃ] *v.* (*a*) to set up/ to create. (*b*) to show sth to be true. **establishment,** *n.* (*a*) creation/setting up. (*b*) commercial firm. (*c*) **the E.** = (small) group of people in positions of authority or influence.

estate [ɪ'steɪt] *n.* (*a*) large area of land belonging to one person; **e. agent** = person who arranges the sale of houses and land; **housing e.** = area of houses or flats built at one time; **e. car/wagon** = long car, with room at the back for carrying luggage/equipment, etc. (*b*) property owned by a person at the time of death.

esteem [ɪ'stiːm] **1.** *n.* respect; **to hold s.o. in (high) e.** = to respect s.o. (very much). **2.** *v.* (*formal*) to consider; **I esteem it an honour. esteemed,** *adj.* highly respected. **estimable,** *adj.* which can be respected.

ester ['estə] *n.* compound of an acid and an alcohol.

estimate 1. *n.* ['estɪmət] calculation which shows the worth/cost/number of sth; price quoted by a supplier; **rough e.** = an approximate calculation. **2.** *v.* ['estɪmeɪt] to calculate (approximately) the cost/the number, etc., of sth; to calculate a price (before supplying the item). **estimation** [estɪ'meɪʃn] *n.* calculation of how much sth is worth; judgement of how valuable a person is.

ester ['estə] *n.* compound of an acid and an alcohol.

estrange [ɪ'streɪndʒ] *v.* to make unfriendly. **estrangement,** *n.* becoming estranged.

estuary ['estjʊərɪ] *n.* wide part of a river where the sea comes in at high tide.

etc. [et'setərə] *abbreviation for* et cetera *meaning* and so on/and the others. **etceteras** [et'setərəz] *n. pl.* other things.

etch [etʃ] *v.* to engrave on metal with acid. **etching,** *n.* picture reproduced from a metal plate which has been engraved with acid.

eternity [ɪ'tɜːnɪtɪ] *n.* never-ending period of time; *inf.* **it will take an e.** = it will take a very long time. **eternal,** *adj.*

everlasting. **eternally,** *adv.* for ever; *inf.* all the time.

ether ['iːθə] *n.* very volatile liquid which burns easily and is used as an anaesthetic.

ethereal [ɪ'θɪəriəl] *adj.* very light like a fairy.

ethics ['eθɪks] *n.* moral principles. **ethical,** *adj.* morally right.

ethnic ['eθnɪk] *adj.* relating to a particular race; **e. minority** = minority of a different racial origin than that of the majority. **ethnography,** *n.* writing about different races. **ethnological** [eθnə'lɒdʒɪkl] *adj.* referring to ethnology. **ethnologist** [eθ'nɒlədʒɪst] *n.* person who studies ethnology. **ethnology** [eθ'nɒlədʒɪ] *n.* study of the customs of different races.

ethos ['iːθɒs] *n.* beliefs or characteristics (esp. of a group of people).

ethyl ['eθɪl] *n.* liquid formed from ether and alcohol, used to add to petrol.

etiquette ['etɪket] *n.* correct way of behaving in society; **professional e.** = the rules of behaviour of a particular group of people.

etymology [etɪ'mɒlədʒɪ] *n.* way in which a word and its meaning have developed historically. **etymological** [etɪmə'lɒdʒɪkl] *adj.* referring to etymology.

eucalyptus [juːkə'lɪptəs] *n.* evergreen tree which gives a strong-smelling oil used to treat colds.

eucharist ['juːkərɪst] *n.* Christian ceremony of taking consecrated bread and wine. **eucharistic** [juːkə'rɪstɪk] *adj.* referring to the eucharist.

eugenics [juː'dʒenɪks] *n.* science of breeding strong human beings.

eulogy ['juːlədʒɪ] *n.* (*formal*) speech or writing praising s.o. **eulogize,** *v.* to praise (s.o.) strongly. **eulogistic** [juːlə'dʒɪstɪk] *adj.* which eulogizes.

eunuch ['juːnək] *n.* castrated man, usu. a servant.

euphemism ['juːfəmɪzəm] *n.* word or phrase used in place of a more offensive or unpleasant word. **euphemistic** [juːfə'mɪstɪk] *adj.* referring to euphemism. **euphemistically,** *adv.* as a euphemism.

euphonium [juː'fəʊnɪəm] *n.* large brass wind instrument.

euphony ['ju:fəni] *n.* pleasant sound.

euphoria [ju:'fɔ:rɪə] *n.* extreme happiness. **euphoric** [ju:'fɒrɪk] *adj.* very happy.

eureka [juː'riːkə] *interj. meaning* a discovery has been made.

Euro- ['jʊərəʊ] *prefix referring to* Europe; **Eurocurrency, Eurovision.**

European [jʊərə'piːən] *adj. & n.* (person) from Europe; **the E. Community** = group of twelve European countries linked together by the Treaty of Rome; **the E. Parliament** = the parliament to which members (MEPs) are elected from each country of the European Community; **the E. monetary system** = system of controlled exchange rates between some member states of the EC.

Eustachian [ju:'steɪʃn] *adj.* **E. tube** = tube which connects the middle ear to the throat.

euthanasia [ju:θə'neɪzɪə] *n.* painless killing of very sick or old persons to put them out of their misery.

eutrophic [ju:'trɒfɪk] *adj.* (lake) which is rich in nutrients.

evacuate [ɪ'vækjʊeɪt] *v.* (*a*) to make (people) leave a dangerous place; to remove (troops) from a place; to remove people from (a place). (*b*) to empty (the bowels). **evacuation** [ɪvækjʊ'eɪʃn] *n.* (*a*) leaving a dangerous place. (*b*) emptying of the bowels. **evacuee** [ɪvækjʊ'iː] *n.* person who has been evacuated.

evade [ɪ'veɪd] *v.* to avoid.

evaluate [ɪ'væljʊeɪt] *v.* to calculate value. **evaluation** [ɪvæljʊ'eɪʃn] *n.* act of calculating.

evanescent [ɪvə'nesənt] *adj.* (*formal*) which fades quickly.

evangelical [i:væn'dʒelɪkl] *adj.* referring to certain Protestant churches and their teaching of the Bible. **evangelist** [ɪ'vændʒəlɪst] *n.* (*a*) one of the four men who wrote the Gospels. (*b*) preacher.

evaporate [ɪ'væpəreɪt] *v.* (*a*) to turn liquid into vapour. (*b*) to disappear. **evaporation** [ɪvæpə'reɪʃn] *n.* process of turning liquid into vapour. **evaporated,** *adj.* **e. milk** = milk which has been reduced in volume by evaporation.

evasion [ɪ'veɪʒn] *n.* avoiding (a direct

answer). **evasive** [ɪ'veɪsɪv] *adj.* which tries to avoid. **evasively,** *adj.* trying to avoid a direct answer. **evasiveness,** *n.* trying to avoid a direct answer.

eve [i:v] *n.* night before; short time before; **on the e. of our departure** = just before we were due to leave; **Christmas E.** = 24th December/day before Christmas; **New Year's E.** = 31st December.

even ['i:vn] **1.** *adj.* (*a*) flat/level. (*b*) regular; **a man of very e. temper** = who never gets very excited. (*c*) equal (in a competition); **to get e. with s.o.** = try to have revenge on s.o.; **the company is just breaking e.** = it is making no profit, but no loss either. (*d*) **e. number** = number which can be divided by 2. **2.** *v.* (*a*) to flatten/to smooth (sth). (*b*) to make equal; **to e. things up** = to make things equal. **3.** *adv.* not only; **he doesn't e. like strawberries** = most people like strawberries, but he doesn't; **e. worse** = worse than before; **e. so** = however/ if you consider everything; **e. now** = right at this minute. **evenly,** *adv.* (*a*) in a level way. (*b*) equally; **they are e. matched** = they are equals (in competition). **evenness,** *n.* being even.

evening ['i:vnɪŋ] *n.* late part of the day, as night falls; **this e.** = today in the evening. **evening-dress,** *n.* clothes worn to special occasions in the evening (long dress for women, black clothes and black or white bow tie for men).

evensong ['i:vnsɒŋ] *n.* Anglican church service held in the evening.

event [ɪ'vent] *n.* (*a*) happening; **happy e.** = birth of a child; **in the course of events** = as things turned out; **in the e. of his refusing** = if he should refuse. (*b*) result; **in any e.** = whatever happens; **at all events** = in any case. (*c*) sporting competition; **field events** = jumping and throwing competitions; **track events** = running and hurdling. **eventful,** *adj.* exciting/full of unexpected happenings.

eventide [i:vn'taɪd] *n.* (*old*) evening.

eventual [ɪ'ventjʊəl] *adj.* final. **eventuality** [ɪventjʊ'ælɪtɪ] *n.* thing which might happen; **in that e.** = if that should happen. **eventually,** *adv.* in the end.

ever ['evə] *adv.* (*a*) at any time; **I hardly e. see her** = almost never see her;

louder than e. = louder than before. (b) always; **e. since then** = from that time onwards; **they lived happily e. after** = always, from then on; **I will love you for e. and e.** = always; **Scotland for e.!** = *excl.* to show support for Scotland or a Scottish team. (c) *inf.* **e. so** = extremely. (d) (*emphatic*) **what e. is the matter?** = what on earth is the matter? **what e. is it for?** = what can it be used for? **evermore,** *adv.* always. **evergreen** ['evəgriːn] 1. *adj.* (plant) which keeps its leaves all winter. 2. *n.* tree which keeps its leaves all winter. **everlasting** [evə'lɑːstɪŋ] *adj.* going on for ever.

every ['evrɪ] *adj.* each; all (taken separately); **e. other day** = each alternate day. **everybody,** *pron.* all people. **everyday,** *adj.* ordinary/very common. **everyone,** *pron.* everybody. **everything.** *pron.* all things. **everywhere,** *adv.* in all places.

evict [ɪ'vɪkt] *v.* to put (s.o.) out of their home. **eviction** [ɪ'vɪkʃn] *n.* act of putting s.o. out of their home.

evidence ['evɪdəns] *n.* (a) traces (of crime); (b) written or spoken report (at a trial); **the criminal turned State's/Queen's e.** = gave information to the court which proved that his accomplices were guilty. (c) **in e.** = visible. **evident,** *adj.* obvious. **evidently,** *adv.* obviously; presumably.

evil ['iːvl] 1. *adj.* very wicked. 2. *n.* wickedness; injustice.

evince [ɪ'vɪns] *v.* (*formal*) to show (a certain quality/feeling).

evoke [ɪ'vəuk] *v.* to call up (an image). **evocation** [ɪvəu'keɪʃn] *n.* act of evoking. **evocative** [ɪ'vɒkətɪv] *adj.* which calls up a sensation in the mind of the onlooker or reader.

evolve [ɪ'vɒlv] *v.* (a) to work out gradually (a scientific theory/a way of working). (b) to develop (gradually). **evolution** [iːvə'luːʃn] *n.* gradual development; **the theory of e.** = theory that man and other living organisms developed gradually from primitive forms of life. **evolutionary,** *adj.* referring to evolution.

ewe [juː] *n.* female sheep.

ewer ['juːə] *n.* large jug.

ex- [eks] *prefix meaning* (a) former; who used to be; **my ex-girlfriend.** (b) out of; **ex-factory** = (price) direct from the factory.

exacerbate [ɪg'zæsəbeɪt] *v.* (*formal*) to make worse/more painful. **exacerbation** [ɪgzæsə'beɪʃn] *n.* making worse.

exact [ɪg'zækt] 1. *adj.* precise. 2. *v.* to force (sth) **from** s.o. **exacting,** *adj.* (person) who demands a lot (of effort). **exaction,** *n.* (*formal*) demand (for money). **exactitude,** *n.* precision. **exactly,** *adv.* precisely; **e.!** = quite right.

exaggerate [ɪg'zædʒəreɪt] *v.* to make things seem larger/worse/better than they really are. **exaggeration** [ɪgzædʒə'reɪʃn] *n.* (statement, etc.) making things seem larger/worse/better; **without e.** = quite truthfully.

exalted [ɪg'zɔːltɪd] *adj.* in a high position in authority; very happy. **exaltation** [egzəl'teɪʃn] *n.* exalted feeling.

examine [ɪg'zæmɪn] *v.* to inspect (sth) to see if it is correct; to test (a student); to ask (a witness) questions. **exam** [ɪg'zæm] *n. inf.* written or spoken test. **examination** [ɪgzæmɪ'neɪʃn] *n.* inspection; written or spoken test. **examinee** [ɪgzæmɪ'niː] *n.* person being tested. **examiner** [ɪg'zæmɪnə] *n.* person who inspects or tests.

example [ɪg'zɑːmpl] *n.* case selected to show sth; **to set an e.** = to act well, so that others may copy you; **to make an e. of s.o.** = to punish s.o. so that others will learn not to do what he did; **for e.** = to name one thing out of many.

exasperate [ɪg'zɑːspəreɪt] *v.* to make (s.o.) furious. **exasperation** [ɪgzɑːspə-'reɪʃn] *n.* fury.

excavate ['ekskəveɪt] *v.* to dig (a hole in the ground); to carry out an archaeological investigation of (a place). **excavation** [ekskə'veɪʃn] *n.* large hole; archaeological investigation. **excavator,** *n.* machine for making holes in the ground.

exceed [ɪk'siːd] *v.* to go beyond (a limit). **exceedingly,** *adv.* very.

excel [ɪk'sel] *v.* (**excelled**) to be very good (**at** sth). **excellence** ['eksələns] *n.* very good quality. **Excellency,** *n.* title given to ambassadors. **excellent,** *adj.* very good.

except [ɪk'sept] **1.** *prep. & conj.* not
including; other than; **all went well
e. that James was sick** = apart from
the fact that. **2.** *v.* not to include
(sth). **exception** [ɪk'sepʃn] *n.* thing
not included; **he took e. to what
she said** = he was annoyed at what
she said. **exceptionable**, *adj.* not to
be approved of. **exceptional**, *adj.*
outstanding. **exceptionally**, *adv.* particularly.

excerpt ['eksɜːpt] **1.** *n.* small part (of a
larger piece of music/writing). **2.** *v.* to
make an excerpt.

excess [ɪk'ses] *n.* (*a*) too much (of sth);
in e. of = more than; **to e.** = too
much; **e. baggage** = more baggage than
one is allowed to carry. (*b*) **excesses**
= bad actions which are worse than
is normally acceptable. **excessive**, *adj.*
more than is normal. **excessively**, *adv.*
too much.

exchange [ɪks'tʃeɪndʒ] **1.** *n.* giving of
one thing for another; **he took my
old car in part e.** = he took my old
car as part of the payment for the
new one I was buying; **foreign e.** =
exchange of the money of one country
for that of another; **e. rate** = rate at
which one money is given for another;
telephone e. = place where telephone
calls are linked; **stock e.** = place
where stocks and shares are bought
and sold. **2.** *v.* to swap/to give (sth)
for sth else; **they exchanged addresses**
= each of them gave the other his
address. **exchangeable**, *adj.* which can
be exchanged.

exchequer [eks'tʃekə] *n.* British government department dealing with public money; **Chancellor of the E.** = British minister of finance.

excise 1. *n.* ['eksaɪz] tax on certain
goods. **2.** *v.* [ɪk'saɪz] to cut out. **excision**
[ɪk'sɪʒn] *n.* cutting out.

excite [ɪk'saɪt] *v.* to arouse (s.o./sth);
to make (s.o.) very emotional; **he
was excited at/by the thought of going
on holiday. excitability** [ɪksaɪtə'bɪlɪtɪ]
n. ease with which you are made
very excited. **excitable** [ɪk'saɪtəbl] *adj.*
easily excited. **excitement**, *n.* state
of being excited. **exciting**, *adj.* which
makes s.o. excited.

exclaim [ɪk'skleɪm] *v.* to say (sth) loudly
and suddenly. **exclamation** [eksklə-
'meɪʃn] *n.* shouting out; **exclamation
mark** = written sign (!) to show exclamation.

exclude [ɪk'sklu:d] *v.* to shut out (sth
from somewhere). **excluding**, *prep.*
without; other than; not including.
exclusion [ɪk'sklu:ʒn] *n.* act of shutting
out. **exclusive. 1.** *adj.* (*a*) very select;
not open to everyone. (*b*) **e. right** =
right to do sth which no one else is then
allowed to do. **2.** *adv.* not including.
exclusively, *adv.* solely/only.

excommunicate [ekskə'mju:nɪkeɪt] *v.*
to refuse communion to (a member of a church). **excommunication**
[ekskəmju:nɪ'keɪʃn] *n.* refusal of
communion.

excrement ['ekskrəmənt] *n.* solid waste
matter produced by the body.

excrescence [ɪk'skresns] *n.* ugly
growth/lump.

excrete [ɪk'skri:t] *v.* to produce (waste
matter). **excreta**, *n. pl.* (*formal*) waste
matter produced by the body.

excruciating [ɪk'skru:ʃɪeɪtɪŋ] *adj.* very
painful.

exculpate ['ekskʌlpeɪt] *v.* (*formal*) to
remove blame from (s.o.).

excursion [ɪk'skɜ:ʃn] *n.* short pleasure
trip; **e. ticket** = special cheap ticket.

excuse 1. *n.* [ɪk'skju:s] reason; apology.
2. *v.* [ɪk'skju:z] to pardon (s.o.); to
allow (s.o.) not to do sth; **e. me**
= I am sorry; **please may I be
excused?** = please may I go to the
lavatory? **excusable**, *adj.* which can
be pardoned. **excusably**, *adv.* in an
excusable way.

ex-directory ['eksdaɪ'rektrɪ] *adj.* (telephone number) which is not listed in the
telephone directory.

execrate ['eksɪkreɪt] *v.* (*formal*) to
curse/to hate (s.o.). **execrable**, *adj.* extremely bad. **execrably**, *adv.* extremely
badly.

execute ['eksɪkju:t] *v.* to carry out
(an official order), esp. to kill s.o.
who has been condemned to death.
executant [eg'zekjutənt] *n.* performer
(of a piece of music). **execution** [eksɪ-
'kju:ʃn] *n.* carrying out (of plan);
legal killing of person sentenced to

death. **executioner** [eksɪˈkjuːʃənə] *n.* official who executes people. **executive** [ɪgˈzekjutɪv] **1.** *adj.* which carries out plans; which puts things into practice; **e. committee** = committee which runs the business, etc. **2.** *n.* (*a*) person in business who makes decisions/plans, etc. (*b*) **Chief E.** = main administrator in an organization; main administrator in a town. (*c*) **the E.** = the part of a Government which carries out laws. **executor** [ɪgˈzekjutə] *n.* person who sees that a dead person's will is carried out. **executrix** [ɪgˈzekjutrɪks] *n.* woman who sees that a dead person's will is carried out.

exegesis [eksɪˈdʒiːsɪs] *n.* commentary (on the Bible).

exemplary [ɪgˈzemplərɪ] *adj.* which serves as an example. **exemplar,** *n.* perfect example. **exemplify,** *v.* to show as an example.

exempt [ɪgˈzempt] **1.** *adj.* not forced to obey (law, etc.). **2.** *v.* to free (s.o.) **from** having to obey a rule or law/**from** doing sth. **exemption** [ɪgˈzempʃn] *n.* (**from**) ruling that s.o. does not have to do sth.

exercise [ˈeksəsaɪz] **1.** *n.* use of physical or mental powers; **e. book** = book for writing out work at school. **2.** *v.* (*a*) to make (an animal) take exercise. (*b*) to use (power); **he exercised his right of veto.**

exert [ɪgˈzɜːt] *v.* to use (force/pressure, etc.). **exertion** [ɪgˈzɜːʃn] *n.* effort.

ex gratia [eksˈgreɪʃə] *adj.* (payment) made as a present, with no obligation implied.

exhale [eksˈheɪl] *v.* (*formal*) to breathe out.

exhaust [ɪgˈzɔːst] **1.** *n.* escape (of steam/gas); **e. (pipe)** = pipe in a car which carries away fumes from the engine. **2.** *v.* to wear out; to finish. **exhausted,** *adj.* (*a*) tired out. (*b*) completely used up. **exhaustion** [ɪgˈzɔːstʃn] *n.* state of being very tired. **exhaustive,** *adj.* very thorough. **exhaustively,** *adv.* thoroughly.

exhibit [ɪgˈzɪbɪt] **1.** *n.* object displayed (in court/at an exhibition). **2.** *v.* to display. **exhibition** [eksɪˈbɪʃn] *n.* display (of works of art, flowers, etc.). **exhibitionist,** *n.* person who acts in a

strange way so that people will look at him. **exhibitor,** *n.* person who displays sth at an exhibition.

exhilarate [ɪgˈzɪləreɪt] *v.* to make extremely happy. **exhilarating,** *adj.* which makes you full of energy. **exhilaration** [ɪgzɪləˈreɪʃn] *n.* extreme happiness.

exhort [ɪgˈzɔːt] *v.* (*formal*) to urge/to encourage (s.o. to do sth). **exhortation** [ɪgzɔːˈteɪʃn] *n.* encouragement.

exhume [ɪgˈzjuːm] *v.* to dig up (a dead person who has been buried). **exhumation** [eksjuˈmeɪʃn] *n.* act of digging up a dead body which has been buried.

exigent [ˈegzɪdʒənt] *adj.* (*formal*) very urgent. **exigency** [egˈzɪdʒənsɪ] *n.* (*formal*) urgent need.

exiguous [egˈzɪgjuəs] *adj.* very small.

exile [ˈegzaɪl] **1.** *n.* (*a*) banishment (from home country); **he went into e.** (*b*) person who is banished. **2.** *v.* to send (s.o.) away from his home country as a punishment.

exist [ɪgˈzɪst] *v.* to live/to be. **existence,** *n.* life/being. **existent, existing,** *adj.* actual/which is present at this moment.

exit [ˈegzɪt, ˈeksɪt] **1.** *n.* way out; going out; **he made his e. by the window** = he went out by the window; **emergency e.** = door used in emergency; **fire e.** = door used in case of fire. **2.** *v.* (*in a play*) goes out; **e. Mr Smith.**

ex libris [eksˈliːbrɪs] *n.* printed label stuck in a book to show who it belongs to.

exocrine [ˈeksəukriːn] *adj.* (gland) with ducts.

exodus [ˈeksədəs] *n.* departure/leaving (usu. of a crowd).

ex officio [eksɒˈfɪʃɪəu] *adv. & adj.* because of your position.

exonerate [ɪgˈzɒnəreɪt] *v.* to state that no blame should be attached to (s.o.). **exoneration** [ɪgzɒnəˈreɪʃn] *n.* statement that no blame is attached to s.o.

exorbitant [ɪgˈzɔːbɪtənt] *adj.* very high (price).

exorcize [ˈegzɔːsaɪz] *v.* to drive (a devil/a ghost) from a place. **exorcism** [ˈegzɔːsɪzəm] *n.* driving away a devil/a ghost. **exorcist,** *n.* person who exorcizes.

exotic [ɪgˈzɒtɪk] *adj.* unusual; referring to a tropical place; from a foreign place. **exotically,** *adv.* in an exotic way.

expand [ɪkˈspænd] *v.* to increase in size/ to become larger.

expanse [ɪkˈspæns] *n.* wide extent. **expansion** [ɪkˈspænʃn] *n.* increase in size. **expansive,** *adj.* (person) who talks freely. **expansiveness,** *n.* being expansive.

expatiate [ɪkˈspeɪʃɪeɪt] *v.* (*formal*) to talk at great length on sth.

expatriate 1. *n.* [ɪkˈspætrɪət] person who is not living in his home country. 2. *v.* [ɪkˈspætrɪeɪt] to send (s.o.) away from his home country.

expect [ɪkˈspekt] *v.* to think/to hope/ to assume sth is going to happen; **I e. she is tired; he expects me to do all the housework; is it going to rain?—I e. so; we're expecting visitors** = we are waiting for visitors to arrive; **she's expecting** = she is pregnant. **expectancy,** *n.* hope; **life e.** = number of years a person will probably live. **expectant,** *adj.* expecting; **e. mother** = pregnant woman. **expectantly,** *adv.* hopefully. **expectation** [ekspekˈteɪʃn] *n.* hope.

expectorant [ɪkˈspektərənt] *n.* cough medicine which makes you cough up phlegm. **expectorate,** *v.* (*formal*) to cough up phlegm.

expediency [ɪkˈspiːdɪənsɪ] *n.* most simple/straightforward way of doing sth. **expedient.** 1. *n.* simple way of doing sth. 2. *adj.* simple/straightforward.

expedite [ˈekspɪdaɪt] *v.* to make sth happen faster. **expedition** [ekspɪˈdɪʃn] *n.* (*a*) rapidity. (*b*) journey of exploration; **to go on an e. to the North Pole. expeditionary,** *adj.* (army) which is on a journey. **expeditious,** *adj.* prompt/ rapid. **expeditiously,** *adv.* rapidly.

expel [ɪkˈspel] *v.* (**expelled**) to throw (s.o.) out; to send (s.o.) away.

expendable [ɪkˈspendəbl] *adj.* which is not worth keeping after it has been used; **he is e.** = he can be sacked/left behind/killed.

expenditure [ɪkˈspendɪtʃə] *n.* amount spent.

expense [ɪkˈspens] *n.* amount of money spent; **e. account** = money which a businessman is allowed to spend on entertainment and personal expenses which are paid for by his firm; **they had a good laugh at his e.** = they laughed at him. **expensive,** *adj.* which costs a lot of money.

experience [ɪkˈspɪərɪəns] 1. *n.* thing lived through; wisdom gained by living through various situations; **I have no e. of travelling in the desert.** 2. *v.* to live through (sth). **experienced,** *adj.* wise from plenty of practice.

experiment [ɪkˈsperɪmənt] 1. *n.* scientific test. 2. *v.* to carry out a scientific test. **experimental** [ɪksperɪˈmentl] *adj.* used as part of a test. **experimentally,** *adv.* as an experiment. **experimentation,** *n.* carrying out of experiments.

expert [ˈekspɜːt] 1. *adj.* referring to s.o. who knows a great deal about a subject; **e. system** = computer program which has been devised for a particular purpose. 2. *n.* person who knows a great deal about a subject. **expertise** [ekspə-ˈtiːz] *n.* specialist knowledge.

expiate [ˈekspɪeɪt] *v.* (*formal*) to make amends for (a crime). **expiation** [ekspɪ-ˈeɪʃn] *n.* making amends.

expire [ɪkˈspaɪə] *v.* (*a*) to come to an end. (*b*) (*formal*) to die. **expiration, expiry,** *n.* coming to an end; **the e. date of a ticket.**

explain [ɪkˈspleɪn] *v.* to give reasons for (sth); to make (sth) clear. **explanation** [ekspləˈneɪʃn] *n.* reason for sth. **explanatory** [ɪkˈsplænətərɪ] *adj.* which gives reasons; which makes clear.

expletive [ɪkˈspliːtɪv] *n.* swear word.

explicable [ɪkˈsplɪkəbl] *adj.* which can be explained.

explicit [ekˈsplɪsɪt] *adj.* straightforward/ clear. **explicitly,** *adv.* clearly.

explode [ɪkˈspləʊd] *v.* (*a*) (*of bombs, etc.*) to go off/to blow up. (*b*) to make (bombs) go off; to destroy (a theory).

exploit 1. *n.* [ˈeksplɔɪt] great/daring achievement. 2. *v.* [ɪkˈsplɔɪt] to take commercial advantage of (sth); **to e. the mineral resources of the North Sea. exploitation** [eksplɔɪˈteɪʃn] *n.* taking advantage.

explore [ɪkˈsplɔː] *v.* to investigate/to travel and discover (esp. unknown lands). **exploration** [eksplə'reɪʃn] *n.* investigation (of unknown lands). **exploratory** [ɪk'splɒrətəri] *adj.* tentative/preliminary. **explorer,** *n.* person who explores unknown lands.

explosion [ɪk'spləʊʒn] *n.* blowing up (of bombs/oil tanks, etc.); **population e.** = rapid increase in population. **explosive** [ɪk'spləʊsɪv] **1.** *adj.* liable to blow up. **2.** *n.* material (like gunpowder) which can blow up.

exponent [ɪk'spəʊnənt] *n.* person who practises a certain belief/a certain art. **exponential** [ekspə'nenʃəl] *adj.* growing in proportion to the original number (i.e. growing faster as numbers increase).

export 1. *n.* ['ekspɔːt] goods sent to a foreign country for sale; **e. manager** = person in charge of sales to foreign countries. **2.** *v.* [ɪk'spɔːt] to send (goods) to a foreign country for sale. **exporter,** *n.* person or company which sells goods to foreign countries.

expose [ɪk'spəʊz] *v.* (*a*) to show. (*b*) to let light go on to a film. (*c*) to reveal (a scandal). **exposed,** *adj.* (*a*) open; **in a very e. position** = not sheltered from the wind. (*b*) **e. film** = where the pictures have been taken but not developed. **exposition** [ekspə'zɪʃn] *n.* detailed explanation. **exposure** [ɪk'spəʊʒə] *n.* (*a*) state of not being sheltered from cold/danger, etc. (*b*) time and amount of light needed for a picture to be taken on film; **e. meter** = device for calculating the exposure for a photograph. (*c*) revealing (of corruption, etc.). (*d*) direction in which (a house) faces.

exposé [ɪk'spəʊzeɪ] *n.* newspaper report revealing corruption/wrongdoing, etc.

expostulate [ɪk'spɒstjʊleɪt] *v.* (*formal*) to protest/to reason (**with** s.o.). **expostulation** ['ɪkspɒstjʊ'leɪʃn] *n.* protest.

expound [ɪk'spaʊnd] *v.* to explain in detail.

express [ɪk'spres] **1.** *adj.* done on purpose; **I did it with the e. intention of killing him. 2.** *adj.* & *n.* rapid (train/postal service). **3.** *v.* (*a*) to put into words; **I expressed myself badly** = I did not make clear what I wanted to say. (*b*) to put into symbols; **to e. a fraction**

in decimals. **expression** [ɪk'spreʃn] *n.* (*a*) way of showing feeling on the face. (*b*) phrase. **expressive,** *adj.* showing feeling. **expressly,** *adv.* on purpose. **expressway,** *n. Am.* fast road with few junctions.

expropriate [ɪk'sprəʊprɪeɪt] *v.* (*of the state/a local authority*) to take away (property) from a private owner. **expropriation** [ɪksprəʊprɪ'eɪʃn] *n.* taking of property away from a private owner.

expulsion [ɪk'spʌlʃn] *n.* act of being thrown out/sent away.

expunge [ek'spʌndʒ] *v.* (*formal*) to wipe out/to cross out.

expurgate ['ekspəgeɪt] *v.* to remove rude/offensive expressions from (a book). **expurgation** [ekspə'geɪʃn] *n.* act of expurgating.

exquisite [ɪk'skwɪzɪt] *adj.* very finely made/very refined. **exquisitely,** *adv.* finely.

exserviceman [eks'sɜːvɪsmən] *n.* (*pl.* **-men**) man who used to be a member of the armed forces.

extant [ɪk'stænt] *adj.* still in existence.

extempore [ɪk'stempəri] *adv.* & *adj.* without notes; **he spoke for ten minutes e.; an e. speech. extemporize,** *v.* to speak without preparation/without notes.

extend [ɪk'stend] *v.* (*a*) to stretch out; **extended family** = family group which includes distant relatives. (*b*) to make longer. **extendable, extensible,** *adj.* which can be extended. **extension,** *n.* (*a*) act of extending; thing added on. (*b*) subsidiary telephone in an office. **extensive,** *adj.* very widespread; very vast. **extensively,** *adv.* very greatly/widely. **extensor,** *n.* muscle which makes a joint become straight.

extent [ɪk'stent] *n.* degree; size; range; area.

extenuating [ɪk'stenjʊeɪtɪŋ] *adj.* which lessens or explains a crime; **e. circumstances. extenuation** [ɪkstenjʊ'eɪʃn] *n.* lessening (of the seriousness of a crime).

exterior [ɪk'stɪərɪə] **1.** *adj.* outside. **2.** *n.* outside; **the e. of a house.**

exterminate [ɪk'stɜːmɪneɪt] *v.* to kill (large number of living things). **extermination** [ɪkstɜːmɪ'neɪʃn] *n.* act of killing (large numbers).

external [ɪkˈstɜ:nl] *adj.* outside; **medicine for e. use only** = which must not be drunk or eaten. **externally,** *adv.* outside.

extinct [ɪkˈstɪŋkt] *adj.* (volcano) which no longer erupts; (species) which has died out. **extinction** [ɪkˈstɪŋkʃn] *n.* putting out (of a fire); dying out (of a species).

extinguish [ɪkˈstɪŋgwɪʃ] *v.* to put out (a fire). **extinguisher,** *n.* **fire e.** = apparatus for putting out fires.

extirpate [ˈekstɜ:peɪt] *v.* (*formal*) to destroy completely.

extol [ɪkˈstəʊl] *v.* (**extolled**) (*formal*) to praise very highly.

extort [ɪkˈstɔ:t] *v.* to get (money) from s.o. by threats. **extortion** [ɪkˈstɔ:ʃn] *n.* getting money from s.o. by threats. **extortionate,** *adj.* excessive (demands); very high (price).

extra [ˈekstrə] 1. *adj.* more than normal; additional. 2. *adv.* (*a*) more than usual; **e. strong string.** (*b*) in addition; **the service charge is e.** 3. *n.* (*a*) person (not a star) appearing in crowd scenes in a film. (*b*) sth more than usual. 4. **extra-** *prefix meaning* outside; **extracurricular** = outside the curriculum; **extramarital** = outside marriage; **extramural** = (course) for students who are not full members of a university; **extrasensory** = (perception) by other means than the five senses; **extraterritorial** = outside the territory.

extract 1. *n.* [ˈekstrækt] thing reduced from sth larger; **meat e.** = substance concentrated from meat. 2. *v.* [ɪkˈstrækt] to pull (sth) out; to produce (sth). **extraction** [ɪkˈstrækʃn] *n.* (*a*) pulling out (of a tooth); production (of coal, etc.). (*b*) origin; **he is of French e.** = his family originally was French. **extractor,** *n.* **e. fan** = fan which sucks air out.

extradite [ˈekstrədaɪt] *v.* to bring back (a criminal) to his home country for trial (by agreement with the country where he was arrested). **extraditable,** *adj.* (crime) for which you can be extradited. **extradition** [ekstrəˈdɪʃn] *n.* return of a criminal to his home country.

extraneous [ɪkˈstreɪnɪəs] *adj.* not directly connected with sth.

extraordinary [ɪkˈstrɔ:dnrɪ] *adj.* marvellous; quite different from everything else; strange/unusual. **extraordinarily,** *adv.* in an extraordinary way.

extrapolate [ɪkˈstræpəleɪt] *v.* to calculate (sth unknown) on the basis of available information. **extrapolation** [ɪkstræpəˈleɪʃn] *n.* calculating sth unknown on the basis of available information.

extravagance [ɪkˈstrævəgəns] *n.* excessive expense and luxury. **extravagant,** *adj.* (*a*) (person) who spends a lot of money. (*b*) expensive and luxurious. **extravagantly,** *adv.* in an extravagant way. **extravaganza** [ɪkstrævəˈgænzə] *n.* expensive and luxurious party/show/film.

extreme [ɪkˈstri:m] 1. *adj.* very great; excessive; **at the e. end** = right at the end. 2. *n.* **to go to extremes** = to do everything in an excessive way. **extremely,** *adv.* very; excessively. **extremist,** *n.* person who has extreme views (usu. about politics). **extremity** [ɪkˈstremɪtɪ] *n.* end point; **the extremities** = the hands and feet.

extricate [ˈekstrɪkeɪt] *v.* to get (s.o.) out of a difficult situation.

extrovert [ˈekstrəvɜ:t] *n.* person who is very outgoing and jolly. **extroverted** *adj.* referring to an extrovert.

extrude [ɪkˈstru:d] *v.* to squeeze out under pressure. **extrusion** [ɪkˈstru:ʒn] *n.* squeezing (of metal) under pressure.

exuberance [ɪgˈzju:bərəns] *n.* wild enthusiasm. **exuberant,** *adj.* wildly enthusiastic.

exude [ɪgˈzju:d] *v.* to send out/to give off (a smell/a feeling) in all directions; **he exudes self-confidence.**

exult [ɪgˈzʌlt] *v.* to rejoice/to be glad; **he exulted over his victim** = he showed great pleasure at having a victim. **exultant,** *adj.* full of triumph. **exultation,** *n.* great rejoicing.

eye [aɪ] 1. *n.* (*a*) part of the head, used for seeing; **keep your eyes open!** = watch out! **to set/clap eyes on sth** = to see sth (suddenly); **it catches the e.** = it is very noticeable; *inf.* **I'm up to my eyes in work** = I have masses of work to do; **to keep an e. on** = to guard; **they don't see e. to e.** = they do not agree. (b) inf. **private e.** = private detective. (c) small hole in a needle for passing the thread through; small loop for attaching a hook; bud on a potato through which sprouts grow. **2.** v. to look at (s.o./sth) carefully. **eyeball,** n. ball of the eye. **eyebath,** n. small cup for bathing the eye. **eyebrow,** n. small arch of hair above the eye. **eyeful,** n. inf. good look at sth. **eyelash,** n. one of the hairs growing round the rim of the eye. **eyelet,** n. small hole (as in a shoe, for passing the lace through). **eyelid,** n. covering for the eye. **eyeliner,** n. substance for drawing a line round the eye. **eye-opener,** n. thing which surprises you. **eyepiece,** n. lens at the end of a telescope through which you look. **eyeshade,** n. shade worn on the forehead for keeping bright light out of the eyes. **eyeshadow,** n. substance for colouring the skin round the eye. **eyesight,** n. (no pl.) ability to see; **his e. is failing** = he can see less well. **eyesore,** n. thing which is hideous/unpleasant to look at. **eyestrain,** n. (no pl.) tiredness of the eyes. **eyetooth,** n. (pl. -teeth) canine. **eyewash,** n. (no pl.) liquid for bathing the eyes; inf. **it's all e.** = it is rubbish. **eyewitness,** n. person who has seen sth happen.

eyrie, Am. **aerie** ['ɪərɪ] n. nest of an eagle; high and inaccessible house.

Ff

F symbol for fluorine.
fable ['feɪbl] n. moral story usu. about animals, making them seem like human beings.
fabric ['fæbrɪk] n. (a) material. (b) basic structure (of society). **fabricate** ['fæbrɪkeɪt] v. to invent (an untrue story); to forge (a paper). **fabrication** [fæbrɪ'keɪʃn] n. invention.
fabulous ['fæbjuləs] adj. (a) imaginary; as in a fable. (b) inf. marvellous/wonderful. **fabulously,** adv. inf. wonderfully.
façade [fə'sɑːd] n. front of a large building; outward appearance which is intended to give a false impression.
face [feɪs] **1.** n. (a) front part of the head; **f. to f.** = talking and looking at

each other; **to make a f.** = to make a rude expression; **to lose f.** = to feel humiliated. (b) front of an object. **2.** v. (a) to put a facing/an outward covering on (sth). (b) to turn your head towards; **the house faces east** = the house looks towards the east; **to f. up to** = to accept bravely. **facecloth, face flannel,** n. small piece of towelling for washing the face or body. **faceless,** adj. threateningly anonymous. **facelift,** n. operation to remove wrinkles from your face. **face pack,** n. cream which is left on the face to improve the skin. **face value,** n. value written on a coin/banknote/share certificate; **to take sth at face value** = to assume that the first/obvious meaning is the correct one. **facing,** n. material covering the surface of a building/the edges of a garment.
facet ['fæsɪt] n. (a) one of the flat sides on a cut gem. (b) aspect (of a problem, etc.).
facetious [fə'siːʃəs] adj. funny/joking (in an offensive way). **facetiously,** adv. not seriously/in a joking way. **facetiousness,** n. being facetious.
facial ['feɪʃl] **1.** adj. referring to a face. **2.** n. beauty treatment to make your face more beautiful.
facile ['fæsaɪl] adj. done too easily.
facility [fə'sɪlɪtɪ] n. (a) ease/absence of difficulty. (b) **facilities** = equipment which can be used (for sth). (c) large industrial/scientific building. **facilitate,** v. to make (sth) easy.
facsimile [fæk'sɪmɪlɪ] n. (a) perfect reproduction; perfect copy. (b) fax.
fact ['fækt] n. thing that is true; **in f./as a matter of f.** = really/actually.
faction ['fækʃn] n. group of people linked together in opposition to a leader/a government. **factional,** adj. referring to factions.
factor ['fæktə] n. (a) one of the numbers which produce a given number when multiplied. (b) thing which is influential/important. (c) person who buys debts at a discount and then tries to reclaim the full amount from the debtor.
factory ['fæktrɪ] n. building where things are made; **f. ship** = ship which freezes or cans fish which are caught by smaller fishing boats.

factotum [fæk'təʊtəm] *n.* person who does all types of work.

factual ['fæktjʊəl] *adj.* containing facts. **factually,** *adv.* in a factual way.

faculty ['fækəltɪ] *n.* (*a*) special ability. (*b*) division of a university. (*c*) *Am.* teaching staff (of a school/university/college, etc.).

fad [fæd] *n.* strange temporary mania. **faddist,** *n.* person who follows a fad. **faddy,** *adj. inf.* (person) who has odd likes and dislikes about food.

fade [feɪd] *v.* to lose colour, brightness or strength; to make (sth) lose colour.

faeces, *Am.* **feces** ['fiːsiːz] *n. pl.* (*formal*) solid waste matter from the body. **faecal,** *adj.* referring to faeces.

fag [fæg] **1.** *n.* (*a*) tiring/boring work. (*b*) *Sl.* cigarette. (*c*) *Sl.* male homosexual. **2.** *v.* to work hard; *Sl.* **fagged out** = tired out.

faggot ['fægət] *n.* (*a*) bundle of sticks for lighting a fire. (*b*) spiced meat ball. (*c*) *inf.* nasty old woman. (*d*) *Sl.* male homosexual.

Fahrenheit ['færənhaɪt] *adj.* (scale for) measuring heat where the boiling point of water is 212° and the freezing point 32°.

faience [faɪ'ɑːns] *n.* thick glazed earthenware.

fail [feɪl] **1.** *v.* (*a*) to be unsuccessful in doing sth. (*b*) to grow weaker. (*c*) not to pass (a candidate) in an examination. **2.** *n.* **without f.** = certainly. **failing. 1.** *n.* weakness/bad point. **2.** *prep.* **f. that** = if that does not work. **fail-safe,** *adj.* (machine) made so that if anything goes wrong it will stop working and so not be dangerous. **failure** ['feɪljə] *n.* (*a*) breakdown/stoppage; **heart f.** = dangerous condition when the heart has stopped beating; **power f.** = breakdown in electricity supplies. (*b*) thing which did not work out satisfactorily.

faint [feɪnt] **1.** *adj.* (*a*) not clear; difficult to see or hear; weak. **2.** *v.* to lose consciousness for a short time. **fainthearted,** *adj.* timid. **faintly,** *adv.* weakly. **faintness,** *n.* being faint.

fair [feə] **1.** *n.* (*a*) group of sideshows/amusements/food stalls, etc., set up in one place for a short time. (*b*) market for selling and advertising goods. **2.** *adj.*

(**-er, -est**) (*a*) light-coloured (skin, hair). (*b*) honest/correct. (*c*) not bad. (*d*) (*of weather*) dry and warm. **fairground,** *n.* place in the open air where a fair is held. **fairly,** *adv.* (*a*) quite/not completely. (*b*) justly/correctly. **fairness,** *n.* (*a*) light colouring. (*b*) honesty/correctness. **fairway,** *n.* (*a*) part of a golf course where the grass is kept cut. (*b*) navigable channel.

fairy ['feərɪ] *n.* (*a*) small supernatural creature who is able to work magic; **f. story** = story about fairies/princesses/giants, etc.; **f. godmother** = kind person who gives you gifts; **f. lights** = small coloured electric lights for decorating trees, etc.; **f. ring** = dark ring on grass, caused by a fungus. (*b*) *Sl.* male homosexual. **fairyland,** *n.* land where fairies are supposed to live. **fairytale,** *n.* fairy story; **a f. castle** = romantic castle like those in fairytales.

faith [feɪθ] *n.* belief/trust; **f. healer** = person who heals by prayer; **in good f.** = honourably, even though wrongly. **faithful,** *adj.* (*a*) trusting/loyal. (*b*) completely correct. **faithfulness,** *n.* being faithful. **faithfully,** *adv.* (*a*) loyally. (*b*) **yours f.** = used as an ending for business letters, when addressed to no specific person. **faithless,** *adj.* disloyal.

fake [feɪk] **1.** *n.* imitation/forgery; not the real thing. **2.** *v.* to make an imitation of (sth).

fakir ['feɪkɪə] *n.* Indian holy man.

falcon ['fɔːlkən] *n.* small bird of prey, sometimes trained to catch other birds in sport. **falconry,** *n.* sport of hunting with falcons.

fall [fɔːl] **1.** *n.* (*a*) drop/collapse. (*b*) *esp. Am.* the autumn. (*c*) **falls** = waterfall. (*d*) **f. from power** = loss of a powerful position. **2.** *v.* (**fell; has fallen**) to drop down. **fall back,** *v.* to retreat/to go back. **fall back on,** *v.* to use (sth) which was kept as a reserve. **fall down,** *v.* to drop to the ground. **fallen. 1.** *adj.* dropped. **2.** *n.* **the f.** = people who have been killed in battle/in a war. **fall for,** *v.* (*a*) to fall in love with (s.o.). (*b*) to be tricked by (sth). **fall in,** *v.* (*in the army*) to stand in line. **fall in with,** *v.* to join with (s.o.); to agree with (an idea). **fall off,** *v.* to become less. **fall**

out, v. (a) to drop. (b) to have an argument. **fallout,** n. radioactive dust from a nuclear explosion. **fall through,** v. to fail. **fall to,** v. to start to do sth (esp. eat or work).

fallacy ['fæləsɪ] n. false argument; error. **fallacious** [fə'leɪʃəs] adj. wrong. **fallibility** [fælɪ'bɪlɪtɪ] n. being fallible. **fallible** ['fælɪbl] adj. (person) who can make a mistake.

Fallopian [fə'ləʊpɪən] adj. **F. tube** = tube in a woman from an ovary to the womb.

fallow ['fæləʊ] adj. (land) which is purposely not used for crops for a time so that it can regain its goodness. **fallow deer,** n. small deer with white spots.

false [fɔːls] adj. (-er, -est) (a) not true. (b) not real; **f. teeth** = artificial teeth; **f. alarm** = signal for an emergency when there isn't one. **falsehood,** n. lie. **falsely,** adv. in a false way. **falseness,** n. being false. **falsification,** n. act of falsifying. **falsify,** v. to change (sth) thus making it invalid.

falsetto [fɒl'setəʊ] n. unnaturally high voice (used by a man singing).

falter ['fɔːltə] v. to move or speak hesitantly.

fame [feɪm] n. being well known. **famed,** adj. well known.

familiar [fə'mɪljə] adj. (a) heard or seen before; well known; **I am f. with that type of machine** = I know that type of machine. (b) very informal/(too) friendly. **familiarity** [fəmɪlɪ'ærɪtɪ] n. (a) (with) good knowledge of s.o./sth. (b) excessively informal way of speaking to s.o. **familiarization** [fəmɪljəraɪ'zeɪʃn] n. act of familiarizing. **familiarize** [fə'mɪljəraɪz] v. **to f. yourself with sth** = to become informed about sth. **familiarly,** adv. in a familiar way.

family ['fæmɪlɪ] n. (a) group of people who are closely related, esp. mother, father and their children; **f. planning** = birth control; **f. tree** = table of the family going back over many generations. (b) group of animals/plants, etc., which are closely related.

famine ['fæmɪn] n. very serious lack/shortage of food. **famished,** adj. inf. very hungry.

famous ['feɪməs] adj. well known.

fan [fæn] **1.** n. (a) object/machine for moving air, to make things cooler or warmer; **f. belt** = loop of rubber which turns a fan to cool the engine of a car. (b) passionate admirer; **a Liverpool f.** = a supporter of Liverpool football team. **2.** v. (**fanned**) to make the air move. **fan club,** n. organized group of admirers (of a pop star). **fan mail,** n. admiring letters received by a pop star, etc. **fan out,** v. to spread out (like a fan).

fanatic [fə'nætɪk] adj. & n. (person) who is madly enthusiastic about sth, esp. religion. **fanatical,** adj. too enthusiastic. **fanatically,** adv. in a fanatical way. **fanaticism,** n. being fanatical.

fancier ['fænsɪə] n. person who has an interest in (a certain type of animal); **pigeon f.** = person who breeds and races pigeons.

fancy ['fænsɪ] **1.** n. (a) imagination. (b) desire; **it took his f.** = made him want it. **2.** adj. pretty/decorated. **3.** v. (a) to imagine/to believe. (b) to like/to want to have; inf. **I think she fancies you** = she is attracted to you. **fancy dress,** n. unusual costume (worn to a party). **fanciful,** adj. imaginative.

fanfare ['fænfeə] n. piece of music played on trumpets to signal the entrance of an important person/the start of a show.

fang [fæŋ] n. animal's long tooth.

fanlight ['fænlaɪt] n. small window over a door or a large window.

fantasy ['fæntəsɪ] n. invented story/not a true story. **fantasize,** v. to imagine/to dream. **fantastic** [fæn'tæstɪk] adj. (a) strange/like a dream. (b) inf. wonderful/amazing. **fantastically,** adv. in a fantastic way.

far [fɑː] (**farther/further; farthest/furthest**) **1.** adv. (a) a long way away/not near; **so f.** = up to now. (b) much; **by f. the best.** **2.** adj. distant/not near. **faraway,** adj. distant/remote. **far-fetched,** adj. difficult to believe. **far-reaching,** adj. which has important results. **far-sighted,** adj. looking to the future.

farad ['færæd] n. unit of electrical capacity.

farce [fɑːs] n. comedy based on slapstick and ridiculous situation; absurd situation. **farcical,** adj. absurd.

fare [feə] **1.** *n.* (*a*) price to be paid for a journey; **return f.** = fare from one place to another and back again. (*b*) passenger in a bus/taxi. (*c*) food. **2.** *v.* to get on; to do (well/badly).

farewell [feə'wel] *inter.* & *n.* (*formal*) goodbye.

farinaceous [færɪ'neɪʃəs] *adj.* made of flour.

farm [fɑːm] **1.** *n.* land used for growing crops and keeping animals. **2.** *v.* to look after a farm; to grow crops/to keep animals for sale. **farmer,** *n.* man who looks after a farm. **farmhouse,** *n.* house where the farmer and his family live. **farming,** *n.* job of looking after a farm/growing crops/keeping animals for sale. **farm out,** *v.* to hand over (work/child, etc.) to another person. **farmstead,** *n.* small farm. **farmyard,** *n.* space outside a farmhouse, usu. surrounded by farm buildings or a wall.

farrago [fə'rɑːgəʊ] *n.* tangled mass.

farrier ['farɪə] *n.* blacksmith who shoes horses. **farriery,** *n.* business of a farrier.

farrow ['færəʊ] *v.* to have a litter of piglets.

fart [fɑːt] **1.** *n.* (*vulgar*) noise made when passing gas from the intestines through the anus. **2.** *v.* (*vulgar*) to make a fart.

farther ['fɑːðə] *adj.* & *adv.* to a greater distance; more distant. **farthest** ['fɑːðəst] *adj.* & *adv.* to the greatest distance; most distant.

farthing ['fɑːðɪŋ] *n.* (*old*) small coin, worth half a halfpenny.

fascia ['feɪʃə] *n.* (*a*) long board over the windows of a shop with the name of the shop written on it. (*b*) dashboard (of a car).

fascicle ['fæsɪkl] *n.* section of a large book, which is published in sections.

fascinate ['fæsɪneɪt] *v.* to attract/to charm. **fascinating,** *adj.* attractive/very interesting. **fascination** [fæsɪ'neɪʃn] *n.* attraction/charm. **fascinator,** *n.* person who fascinates.

fascism ['fæʃɪzəm] *n.* extreme right-wing political movement. **fascist,** *adj.* & *n.* (person) supporting fascism.

fashion ['fæʃn] **1.** *n.* (*a*) manner/way; **after a f.** = not very well. (*b*) most admired style at a particular moment. **2.** *v.* to make. **fashionable,** *adj.* in

fashion. **fashionably,** *adv.* (dressed) in a fashionable way.

fast [fɑːst] **1.** *adj.* & *adv.* (**-er, -est**) (*a*) quick; **my watch is five minutes f.** = my watch shows a time five minutes later than it really is; **f. film** = film which requires very short exposure times; **f. food** = food which is prepared and served quickly. (*b*) tightly fixed; **f. colours** = colours in clothing which do not run when washed; **to make sth f.** = to attach sth tightly. (*c*) **f. asleep** = soundly sleeping. **2.** *n.* period when you stop eating. **3.** *v.* to stop eating (for a time).

fasten ['fɑːsn] *v.* to fix tightly. **fastener,** *n.* device which fastens/attaches; **zip f.** = sliding fastener for attaching clothes, bags, etc. **fastening,** *n.* thing which fastens.

fastidious [fæ'stɪdɪəs] *adj.* hard to please; easily shocked. **fastidiously,** *adv.* in a fastidious way. **fastidiousness,** *n.* being fastidious.

fastness ['fɑːsnəs] *n.* (*pl.* **-es**) stronghold in mountains.

fat [fæt] **1.** *adj.* (**fatter, fattest**) (*a*) big and round; overweight; *inf.* **a f. lot of good** = very little good. (*b*) thick. (*c*) full of grease. **2.** *n.* (*a*) grease/white layer on an animal's body under the skin. (*b*) **cooking f.** = refined oil (either vegetable or animal) used in frying, etc. **fatness,** *n.* being fat. **fatstock,** *n.* cows/sheep, etc., fattened for food.

fate [feɪt] *n.* destiny; thing that is certain to happen as we think it has been decided by a power beyond human control. **fatal,** *adj.* deadly/causing death. **fatalism,** *n.* accepting fate. **fatalist,** *n.* person who accepts what happens, knowing that it is usually bad and cannot be avoided. **fatalistic** [feɪtə'lɪstɪk] *adj.* like a fatalist. **fatalities** [fə'tælɪtɪz] *n. pl.* deaths. **fatally,** *adv.* causing death. **fated,** *adj.* destined/condemned by fate. **fateful,** *adj.* (decision, etc.) important for its serious consequences in the future.

father ['fɑːðə] **1.** *n.* (*a*) male parent; **f. figure** = older man who is consulted for advice. (*b*) originator. (*c*) title given to a priest. **2.** *v.* to be the father of. **father-in-law,** *n.* (*pl.* **fathers-in-law**) father of your wife or husband. **fatherland,** *n.*

native country. **fatherless,** *adj.* with no father. **fatherly,** *adj.* like a father.

fathom ['fæðəm] 1. *n.* measure of depth of water (6 feet or 1.8 metres). 2. *v.* (*also* **fathom out**) to find the meaning of (a mystery).

fatigue [fə'ti:g] 1. *n.* (*a*) tiredness; **metal f.** = wearing out of metal used in a construction, causing weak points. (*b*) **fatigues** = (i) cleaning duty in the army; (ii) overalls worn when doing this. 2. *v.* to tire (s.o.) out.

fatten ['fætn] *v.* to make fat. **fattening,** *adj.* (foods) which make you fat. **fatty,** *adj.* (food/tissue) which has a lot of fat in it.

fatuous ['fætjʊəs] *adj.* stupid/silly. **fatuously,** *adv.* in a fatuous way. **fatuousness, fatuity** [fə'tjʊɪtɪ] *n.* being fatuous.

faucet ['fɔ:sɪt] *n.* *Am.* tap.

fault [fɔ:lt] 1. *n.* (*a*) mistake; **she's at f.** = has made a mistake. (*b*) imperfection/ thing which is not as it should be. (*c*) (*in geology*) break in a rock layer where a section of rock slips down and another section rises. (*d*) (*in tennis*) error in serving. 2. *v.* to criticize/to find (sth) wrong. **faultiness,** *n.* being faulty. **faultless,** *adj.* perfect. **faultlessly,** *adv.* perfectly. **faulty,** *adj.* (**-ier, -iest**) with mistakes or imperfections.

faun [fɔ:n] *n.* mythical creature, like a man with goat's legs and horns.

fauna ['fɔ:nə] *n.* wild animals (of an area).

faux pas [fəʊ'pɑ:] *n.* piece of embarrassing behaviour.

favour, *Am.* **favor** ['feɪvə] 1. *n.* (*a*) friendly act/kindness. (*b*) support for one group/one person at the expense of others; **out of f.** = disliked; **the score is 3-2 in his f.** = he is leading 3-2. (*c*) preference/liking; **to be in f. of** = to prefer. (*d*) ribbon/badge (worn by a supporter). 2. *v.* (*a*) to like/to prefer. (*b*) to make things easy for (s.o.). **favourable** ['feɪvrəbl] *adj.* helpful/ kind; good (impression). **favourably,** *adv.* in a favourable way. **favoured,** *adj.* preferred/liked. **favourite.** 1. *adj.* preferred/most liked. 2. *n.* (*a*) most liked thing/person. (*b*) horse, team, etc., which most people think will win.

favouritism, *n.* prejudice/preference for one thing/person.

fawn [fɔ:n] 1. *n.* young deer. 2. *adj.* brownish cream colour. 3. *v.* **to f. on s.o.** = to try to get s.o.'s favour by doing everything they ask.

fax [fæks]. 1. *n.* (*pl.* **faxes**) copy of a text or image sent by telephone. 2. *v.* to send an image by telephone.

FBI [efbi:'aɪ] *n.* *US* Federal Bureau of Investigation.

Fe *symbol for* iron.

fear ['fɪə] 1. *n.* terror/worry/feeling of being afraid; *inf.* **no f.!** = certainly not! 2. *v.* to be afraid of (sth). **fearful,** *adj.* terrible. **fearfully,** *adv.* terribly/very. **fearless,** *adj.* with no feeling of terror. **fearlessly,** *adv.* not feeling afraid. **fearsome,** *adj.* frightening.

feasible ['fi:zəbl] *adj.* (*a*) which can be done. (*b*) likely/probable. **feasibility** [fi:zə'bɪlɪtɪ] *n.* ability to be done; **f. study** = study to see if sth can be done. **feasibly,** *adv.* possibly.

feast [fi:st] 1. *n.* (*a*) special religious day when we remember a saint or special event. (*b*) very large meal. 2. *v.* (*a*) to eat expensive food. (*b*) to eat a very large meal.

feat [fi:t] *n.* unusually difficult act.

feather ['feðə] 1. *n.* one of many growths which form the covering of a bird's body; **light as a f.** = very light. 2. *v.* (*a*) **to f. one's nest** = to make a lot of money (usu. fraudulently). (*b*) to make the blade of an oar skim fast across the surface of the water. **feather-brained,** *adj.* silly and forgetful. **feathered,** *adj.* with feathers. **featherweight,** *n.* weight in boxing between bantamweight and lightweight. **feathery,** *adj.* light/delicate (like a-feather).

feature ['fi:tʃə] 1. *n.* (*a*) special part of the face (such as nose/mouth, etc.); important aspect. (*b*) important item in a news programme or article; important article on a special subject; (*c*) **f. film** = main long film. 2. *v.* to have as the main actor/as the main subject, esp. on film, TV, or in a newspaper; to appear as the main actor/subject in a film or on TV. **featureless,** *adj.* with no striking features.

February ['februəri] *n.* 2nd month of the year.

feces ['fi:si:z] *n. pl. Am. see* **faeces**.

feckless ['fekləs] *adj.* (person) who has no aim in life/who is incompetent.

fecund ['fekənd] *adj.* fertile/fruitful. **fecundity** [fi'kʌndɪtɪ] *n.* being fecund.

fed [fed] *v. see* **feed**. **fed up**, *adj. inf.* bored/tired (**with**).

federation [fedə'reɪʃn] *n.* group of states or societies which have joined together. **federal** ['fedərəl] *adj.* referring to a system where a group of semi-independent states exist under a central government. **federate** ['fedəreɪt] *v.* to join (states) together in a federation.

fee [fi:] *n.* money paid to doctors, schools and lawyers, etc.

feeble ['fi:bl] *adj.* (-er, -est) weak. **feeble-minded**, *adj.* of low intelligence. **feebleness**, *n.* weakness. **feebly**, *adv.* weakly.

feed [fi:d] **1.** *n.* (a) food given to animals. (b) meal, esp. given to babies. (c) means of putting material into a machine; **sheet f.** = device on a printer for inserting single sheets of paper. **2.** *v.* (**fed**) (a) to give food to (s.o./sth). (b) to eat. (c) to put (**in**). **feedback**, *n.* (a) return of a signal in an electronic circuit causing a high-pitched noise. (b) information/details about sth which has been done. **feeder**, *n.* (a) feeding bottle; device for feeding material into a machine. (b) baby's bib. (c) **f. school** = junior school which provides children for a senior school. **feeding**, *adj.* giving food; **f. bottle** = bottle used for giving milk, etc., to a baby. **feedlot**, *n.* fenced area of land where cattle are fattened.

feel [fi:l] **1.** *n.* touch, esp. with the fingers. **2.** *v.* (**felt**) (a) to touch, esp. with your fingers; **the knife felt cold; to f. one's way** = act cautiously until one has more experience. (b) to have a feeling/sensation; **he feels it would be unwise** = he thinks it would be unwise; **do you f. like a cup of tea?** = would you like a cup of tea? **to f. up to doing sth** = to feel strong enough to do it. **feeler**, *n.* antenna/long part on an insect's head with which it touches; **to put out a f.** = to explore sth/to see if sth is acceptable. **feeling**, *n.* (a) sense of touch. (b) thing felt inside/emotion.

feet [fi:t] *n. pl. see* **foot**.

feign [feɪn] *v.* (*formal*) to pretend.

feint [feɪnt] **1.** *n.* false attack; move to confuse your opponent. **2.** *adj.* (paper) with very pale lines drawn on it. **3.** *v.* to make a move to confuse your opponent.

feisty ['feɪstɪ] *adj. Am.* aggressive.

felicity [fə'lɪsɪtɪ] *n.* (*formal*) happiness. **felicitous**, *adj.* well chosen (words).

feline ['fi:laɪn] **1.** *adj.* referring to a cat; like a cat. **2.** *n.* member of the cat family.

fell [fel] **1.** *n.* high moorland in the North of England. **2.** *adj.* (*old*) cruel; **at one f. swoop** = swiftly. **3.** *v.* to cut down (a tree); to knock (s.o.) down; *see also* **fall**.

fellow ['feləu] *n.* (a) man. (b) person who is in the same group; **f. workers**. (c) member of a college (at Oxford and Cambridge). **fellowship**, *n.* (a) friendly feeling. (b) group of people with similar interests. (c) position of fellow (at Oxford and Cambridge).

felon ['felən] *n.* criminal. **felony**, *n.* serious crime.

felt [felt] **1.** *n.* thick, matted material made of wool; **f. tipped pen** = pen of which the writing end is made of hard felt. **2.** *v.* to cover (sth) with felt; *see also* **feel**. **felt-tip**, *n.* felt tipped pen.

female ['fi:meɪl] **1.** *adj.* (a) referring to women/girls. (b) referring to the sex which has young. **2.** *n.* (a) *inf.* woman/girl. (b) animal/insect/bird which gives birth to young or lays eggs; flower which produces seeds.

feminine ['femənɪn] *adj.* (a) belonging to a woman, like a woman. (b) (*in grammar*) referring to words which have a particular form to indicate the female gender. **femininity** [femɪ'nɪnətɪ] *n.* womanliness; female qualities. **feminism** ['femɪnɪzəm] *n.* being a feminist. **feminist**, *n.* person (usu. woman) who actively supports the right of women to equal status with men.

femoral ['fi:mərəl] *adj.* referring to the femur.

femur ['fi:mə] *n.* thigh bone.

fen [fen] *n.* large area of marsh.

fence [fens] *n.* (a) barrier of wood or wire, used to keep people or animals in or out of a place; **to sit on the f.** = to avoid giving a definite answer to a question. (b) *Sl.* person who takes stolen goods to resell them. **2.** *v.* (a) **to f. in/off** = to surround with a fence. (b) to fight with swords as a sport. **fencer,** *n.* person who fences. **fencing,** *n.* (a) material making up a fence. (b) sport of fighting with swords.

fend [fend] *v.* (a) **to f. off** = to push away. (b) **to f. for yourself** = to look after yourself.

fender ['fendə] *n.* (a) low guard around a fireplace to stop coal or wood falling out into the room. (b) rope mat/rubber tyre, etc., hung against the side of a boat to protect it from bumps. (c) *Am.* mudguard of a car.

fennel ['fenl] *n.* herb with a smell like aniseed.

feral ['fɪərəl] *adj.* (animal) which is wild (having once been domesticated).

ferment 1. *n.* ['fɜːmənt] upset/agitation. **2.** *v.* [fə'ment] to change by fermentation. **fermentation** [fɜːmen'teɪʃn] *n.* chemical change brought about in liquids, usu. leading to the production of alcohol.

fern [fɜːn] *n.* green plant often with feathery leaves which does not have flowers or seeds.

ferocious [fə'rəʊʃəs] *adj.* fierce/angry. **ferociously,** *adv.* in a ferocious way. **ferocity** [fə'rɒsɪtɪ] *n.* fierceness.

ferret ['ferɪt] **1.** *n.* small weasel-like animal half-tamed and used to drive rabbits or rats from holes. **2.** *v.* **to f. out** = to find out by endless searching.

Ferris wheel ['ferɪswiːl] *n.* large vertical wheel in a funfair, with seats.

ferroconcrete [ferəʊ'kɒŋkriːt] *n.* concrete reinforced with steel bars.

ferrous ['ferəs] *adj.* containing iron.

ferrule ['feruːl] *n.* metal cap on the end of an umbrella or stick.

ferry ['ferɪ] **1.** *n.* (a) (*also* **ferryboat**) boat which carries goods or people to and fro across a stretch of water. (b) place where a boat crosses a stretch of water. **2.** *v.* to take (s.o.) across in a boat; **the bus ferried people to and from the station** = took them back and forth. **ferryman,** *n.* (*pl.* **-men**) man in charge of a ferry.

fertile ['fɜːtaɪl, *Am.* 'fɜːtl] *adj.* rich enough to produce crops; (*of female*) able to produce young; **he has a f. imagination** = he is very imaginative/he can imagine things very easily. **fertility** [fə'tɪlətɪ] *n.* ability to produce crops or young. **fertilization** [fɜːtɪlaɪ'zeɪʃn] *n.* the act of fertilizing. **fertilize** ['fɜːtɪlaɪz] *v.* (a) to join male and female cells together, so that a new animal/plant will be made. (b) to spread fertilizer on. **fertilizer,** *n.* chemical or manure spread over the ground to make it richer and more able to produce crops.

fervour, *Am.* **fervor** ['fɜːvə] *n.* passion. **fervent, fervid,** *adj.* passionate. **fervently,** *adv.* in a fervent way.

fescue ['feskjuː] *n.* grass grown in meadows.

fester ['festə] *v.* (*of wound*) to become bad and produce pus.

festival ['festɪvl] *n.* (a) religious celebration which comes at the same time each year. (b) artistic celebration/entertainment which is put on at regular intervals; **arts f.** = competitions in music, drama, painting and handicrafts, etc. **festive,** *adj.* happy; fit for a celebration. **festivity** [fe'stɪvɪtɪ] *n.* celebration.

festoon [fe'stuːn] **1.** *n.* long chain of hanging decorations. **2.** *v.* to hang with decorations.

fetch [fetʃ] *v.* (a) to go and bring (s.o./sth) back. (b) to be sold at (a certain price). **fetch in,** *v.* to collect. **fetching,** *adj.* attractive/pretty. **fetch up,** *v. inf.* to arrive/to end up (in a certain place).

fête [feɪt] **1.** *n.* public celebration, usu. in the open air, with stalls, sideshows and competitions. **2.** *v.* to celebrate (the arrival of an important person, etc.).

fetid ['fiːtɪd] *adj.* bad-smelling (water/breath).

fetish ['fetɪʃ] *n.* (a) object worshipped by s.o. (b) obsession.

fetlock ['fetlɒk] *n.* back part of a horse's leg just above the hoof.

fetter ['fetə] *v.* to chain (a prisoner). **fetters,** *n. pl.* chains.

fettle ['fetl] *n.* **in fine f.** = in very good condition.

fetus ['fiːtəs] *n. Am. see* **foetus.**

feud [fjuːd] **1.** *n.* bitter quarrel. **2.** *v.* to quarrel bitterly all the time.

feudal ['fjuːdl] *adj.* **f. system** = medieval

system of holding land in return for services to an overlord or king. **feudalism,** *n.* feudal system.

fever ['fi:və] *n.* (*a*) state when the body's temperature is higher than normal. (*b*) **f. (pitch)** = great excitement. **feverish,** *adj.* suffering from a fever. **feverishly,** *adv.* excitedly; impatiently.

few [fju:] *adj. & n.* (*a*) (**-er, -est**) not many. **a f.** = some/several.

fey [feɪ] *adj.* otherworldly (person); not interested in practical things.

fez [fez] *n.* round hat worn in some Muslim countries.

fiancé, fiancée [fɪ'ɒnseɪ] *n.* man/woman who is engaged to be married.

fiasco [fɪ'æskəʊ] *n.* (*pl.* **-os**) total failure.

fib [fɪb] **1.** *n.* lie. **2.** *v.* (**fibbed**) to tell lies. **fibber,** *n.* person who tells lies.

fibre, Am. fiber ['faɪbə] *n.* small thread of material. (*b*) **moral f.** = strength of moral feelings. **fibreglass,** *n.* (*a*) glass fibre wool used as insulation (*b*) strong material made of woven threads of glass; plastic containing threads of glass. **fibre optics,** *n.* use of thin strands of material through which light can be passed, in order to convey messages or images over long distances. **fibroid,** *adj.* (growth, etc.) made of fibres. **fibrositis** [faɪbrəʊ'saɪtɪs] *n.* pain in tissues, muscles, etc. **fibrous,** *adj.* made of fibres.

fibula ['fɪbjʊlə] *n.* thin bone between the knee and the ankle behind the tibia.

fickle ['fɪkl] *adj.* changeable/not steady. **fickleness,** *n.* being fickle.

fiction ['fɪkʃn] *n.* (*a*) story that is not true. (*b*) novels. **fictional** *adj.* (character) who exists in fiction. **fictitious** [fɪk'tɪʃəs] *adj.* untrue/not real.

fiddle ['fɪdl] **1.** *n. inf.* (*a*) violin. (*b*) dishonest/illegal dealings; **on the f.** = trying to make money illegally. **2.** *v. inf.* (*a*) to play the fiddle. (*b*) to play idly **with** sth. (*c*) *inf.* to handle (money) in a dishonest way. **fiddler,** *n. inf.* violin player. **fiddlesticks,** *n. inf.* nonsense. **fiddly,** *adj. inf.* small and awkward to use.

fidelity [fɪ'delɪtɪ] *n.* faithfulness/accuracy (of a reproduction).

fidget ['fɪdʒɪt] **1.** *n.* person who cannot stay still. **2.** *v.* to move restlessly. **fidgety,** *adj.* restless.

field [fi:ld] **1.** *n.* (*a*) piece of cultivated land surrounded by fences or hedges. (*b*) large surface/area; **f. day** = busy and exciting time. (*c*) piece of ground for playing games; **f. events** = jumping and throwing competitions. (*d*) special area of study. (*e*) area of influence (of a magnet/of gravity/of a charged particle). **2.** *v.* (*in cricket*) (*a*) to stop (a ball hit by a batsman). (*b*) to be part of the side which is not batting. **fielder,** *n.* (*in cricket*) member of the side which is not batting. **field glasses,** *n. pl.* binoculars: **field hockey,** *n. Am.* hockey. **field marshal,** *n.* highest rank in the army. **fieldmouse,** *n.* (*pl.* **-mice**) small type of country mouse. **fieldsman,** *n.* (*pl.* **-men**) (*in cricket*) member of the side which is not batting. **fieldwork,** *n.* scientific research done outside, and not in a laboratory. **fieldworker,** *n.* person engaged in fieldwork.

fiend [fi:nd] *n.* devil; monster; *inf.* addict. **fiendish,** *adj.* devilish; very cruel.

fierce ['fɪəs] *adj.* ferocious/angry; which will attack anything; (*of fire*) very hot. **fiercely,** *adv.* strongly and angrily. **fierceness,** *n.* violence (of a battle); heat (of a fire).

fiery ['faɪərɪ] *adj.* burning/full of fire; angry.

fiesta [fɪ'estə] *n.* Spanish festival.

fife [faɪf] *n.* small metal flute played in military bands.

fifteen [fɪf'ti:n] *n.* (*a*) number 15. (*b*) group of fifteen people (as in a Rugby team). **fifteenth, 15th,** *adj. & n.* referring to fifteen.

fifth, 5th [fɪfθ] *adj. & n.* referring to five; **f. column** = enemy sympathizers inside a country under attack. **Fifth Amendment,** *n.* the Amendment to the Constitution of the USA which allows citizens not to give evidence in court which might incriminate themselves.

fifty ['fɪftɪ] number 50; **f.-f.** = each paying half of the cost. **fiftieth, 50th,** *adj.* referring to fifty.

fig [fɪg] *n.* juicy sweet fruit of the fig tree.

fight [faɪt] **1.** *n.* struggle/battle; boxing match. **2.** *v.* (**fought**) to hit out; to struggle **with** (s.o./sth). **fighter,** n. (a) person who fights. (b) fast attacking aircraft. **fighting,** n. action of struggling with s.o.

figment ['fɪgmənt] n. **f. of the imagination** = thing which has been imagined.

figure ['fɪgə, Am. 'fɪgjə] **1.** n. (a) written number (such as 28). (b) geometric shape such as a triangle or circle; drawing/diagram in a book. (c) shape of a person. (d) **f. of speech** = colourful expression used to illustrate a meaning. (e) pattern of movement (in skating/dancing). **2.** v. (a) **to f. out** = to try to understand; inf. **that figures** = that makes sense. (b) to appear (in a novel, etc.). **figurative** ['fɪgjʊrətɪv] adj. (usage of a word) which is not the literal meaning. **figuratively,** adv. in a figurative way. **figurehead,** n. (a) wooden figure carved on the front of a ship. (b) person who seems important but who has no real power. **figurine** ['fɪgjʊriːn] n. small figure (in china/wood, etc.).

filament ['fɪləmənt] n. thin wire (in an electric bulb).

filbert ['fɪlbət] n. type of hazel nut.

filch [fɪltʃ] v. to steal.

file [faɪl] **1.** n. (a) metal tool used for smoothing rough surfaces. (b) holder for papers and documents. (c) section of data on a computer. (d) line of people; **in single f.** = one behind the other. **2.** v. (a) to smooth (a surface) with a file. (b) to put (papers) away in a folder or case. (c) to walk in a line. **filing cabinet,** n. box with drawers for putting files in. **filings,** n. pl. small pieces of metal which come away when metal is filed smooth.

filial ['fɪlɪəl] adj. (formal) referring to a son or daughter.

filibuster ['fɪlɪbʌstə] **1.** n. attempt to prevent a law being passed by speaking for a very long time in the debate. **2.** v. to delay the passing of a law by speaking for a very long time in the debate.

filigree ['fɪlɪgriː] n. very decorative ornamental work done in precious metals.

Filipino [fɪlɪ'piːnəʊ] adj. & n. (pl. **-os**) (person) from the Philippines.

fill [fɪl] v. to put as much as possible into

(sth)/to make (sth) full; to become full; to drill a hole in (a bad tooth) and fill it up with metal, etc.; to find s.o. to do (a job). **filler,** n. material used to fill holes and cracks in walls/woodwork, etc. **fill in,** v. (a) to fill a hole. (b) to complete the blank spaces in (a form/document). (c) inf. **to f. s.o. in on** = to tell/to inform (s.o.). **filling,** n. thing that fills up sth else. **filling station,** n. place where you can buy petrol and oil. **fill out,** v. (a) to write everything that is asked for on (a form). (b) to get fatter. **fill up,** v. to fill (sth) until it is completely full; to become completely full; to complete (a form).

fillet ['fɪlɪt] **1.** n. good cut of meat or fish from which all the bones have been removed. **2.** v. to remove the bones from (a fish).

fillip ['fɪlɪp] n. sharp boost.

filly ['fɪlɪ] n. young female horse.

film [fɪlm] **1.** n. (a) moving picture shown on a screen. (b) roll of coated plastic put in a camera and used for taking photographs or moving pictures. (c) thin covering (of dust, etc.). **2.** v. to take pictures of (sth) with a cine-camera. **film star,** n. well-known film actor or actress. **filmstrip,** n. strip of film with several still pictures which are projected one after the other. **filmy,** adj. very thin/almost transparent.

filter ['fɪltə] **1.** n. (a) device/material for straining liquids or air, stopping any solids from passing through. (b) glass on a camera which allows only certain colours or intensities of light to pass through. **2.** v. (a) to pass through a filter. (b) to move gradually and quietly; **f. lane/lights** = traffic lane/lights only for cars turning. (c) **to f. through/down** = to go/come slowly through or down. **filter paper,** n. paper used for filtering liquids. **filter-tip cigarettes,** n. pl. cigarettes with a filter at the mouth end.

filth [fɪlθ] n. dirt; obscene words/books, etc. **filthy,** adj. (-ier, -iest) (a) very dirty. (b) very unpleasant and angry (temper). (c) obscene. **filthily,** adv. in a filthy way. **filthiness,** n. being filthy; filthy things.

filtrate ['fɪltreɪt] n. liquid which has been filtered. **filtration,** n. action of filtering.

FIMBRA ['fɪmbræ] Financial Intermediaries, Managers and Brokers Regulatory Association, the organization which regulates the working of investment advisers, insurance brokers, etc.

fin [fɪn] *n.* (*a*) thin limb on the body of a fish which it moves to swim. (*b*) piece shaped in a similar way on a bomb, rocket or aircraft.

finagle [fɪ'neɪgl] *v. Am. inf.* to work dishonestly; to get (sth) dishonestly.

final ['faɪnl] **1.** *adj.* coming at the end; last; **the decision is f.** = cannot be changed. **2.** *n.* (*a*) last competition in a tournament between several teams or competitors. (*b*) **finals** = last examinations at the end of a university course, after which you get your degree. **finalist,** *n.* person taking part in the final competition. **finality** [faɪ'nælɪtɪ] *n.* state of being at the end. **finalization** [faɪnəlaɪ'zeɪʃn] *n.* act of finalizing. **finalize** ['faɪnəlaɪz] *v.* to finish making plans for sth. **finally,** *adv.* at last; in the last place.

finale [fɪ'nɑːlɪ] *n.* last part of a piece of music/of a show.

finance ['faɪnæns] **1.** *n.* money, esp. belonging to the public or to a company. **2.** *v.* to provide money for. **financial** [fɪ'nænʃl] *adj.* concerning money; **f. year** = 12 month period for which accounts are calculated. **financially,** *adv.* regarding finance. **financier** [fɪ'nænsɪə] *n.* person who deals with money on a large scale.

finch [fɪntʃ] *n.* (*pl.* **-es**) small seed-eating bird.

find [faɪnd] **1** *n.* good thing which you have discovered. **2.** *v.* (**found**) to discover (sth hidden or lost); **to be found** = to exist; **to f. out** = to discover; to learn; **to f. s.o. out** = to discover s.o. is dishonest or naughty; **it has been found that** = it is a known fact that. **finder,** *n.* person who finds. **findings,** *n. pl.* facts discovered/recommendations.

fine [faɪn] **1.** *n.* money to be paid as a punishment for doing wrong. **2.** *adj.* (**-er, -est**) (*a*) pure. (*b*) lovely/good. (*c*) (*of weather*) good; with no rain. (*d*) very thin; very small. **3.** *inter.* **f.!** = all right/agreed. **4.** *v.*

(*a*) to make (sth) fine. (*b*) to punish by making s.o. pay a fine. **fine art,** *n.* painting/sculpture, etc. **finely,** *adv.* delicately/thinly/beautifully. **finery,** *n.* fine clothes.

finesse [fɪ'nes] *n.* skill (in dealing with awkward situations).

finger ['fɪŋgə] **1.** *n.* (*a*) one of the five parts at the end of a hand, usu. other than the thumb; **to keep your fingers crossed** = to hope that sth will happen as you want it; **to put your f. on sth** = to identify it; **to have a f. in every pie** = to be involved in every plan. (*b*) part of a glove into which a finger goes. (*c*) thing shaped like a finger. **2.** *v.* to touch with the fingers. **fingering,** *n.* use of the fingers when playing a musical instrument. **fingernail,** *n.* thin horny substance which grows at the end of the fingers. **fingerprint,** *n.* mark left by the end of the fingers. **fingerstall,** *n.* cover put over a finger which has been hurt. **fingertip,** *n.* end of the finger; **he has it at his fingertips** = he knows all about it.

finial ['fɪnɪəl] *n.* decoration on a gable.

finical, finicking, finickity, finicky ['fɪnɪkl, 'fɪnɪkɪŋ, fɪ'nɪkɪtɪ, 'fɪnɪkɪ] *adj. inf.* (*a*) awkward and detailed (work). (*b*) fussy (person) who dislikes things, esp. certain types of food.

finish ['fɪnɪʃ] **1.** *n.* (*a*) end. (*b*) way in which sth is completed; appearance of sth when it is finished. **2.** *v.* to end. **finish off,** *v.* (*a*) to complete. (*b*) to kill. **finish up,** *v.* (*a*) to end up. (*b*) to finish completely. **finish with,** *v.* **to f. with s.o.** = to stop being friendly with s.o.; **to f. with sth** = to need sth no longer.

finite ['faɪnaɪt] *adj.* with an end/with a limit; **f. verb** = verb which indicates a tense.

Finn [fɪn] *n.* person from Finland. **Finnish** ['fɪnɪʃ] **1.** *adj.* referring to Finland. **2.** *n.* language spoken in Finland.

fiord ['fɪɔːd] *n.* long arm of the sea among mountains in Norway.

fir [fɜː] *n.* **f. (tree)** = evergreen tree with needle-shaped leaves. **fir cone,** *n.* hard scaly fruit of the fir.

fire ['faɪə] **1.** *n.* (*a*) thing that is burning; **to catch f.** = to start burning because of sth else which is in flames; **to set f. to sth** =

to make sth start burning. (*b*) great enthusiasm or excitement. (*c*) shooting of guns. **2.** *v.* (*a*) to make (sth) burn. (*b*) to make (s.o.) excited. (*c*) to bake/to heat. (*d*) to shoot (a gun); **f. away** = ask your question. (*e*) to dismiss (s.o.) from a job. **fire alarm**, *n.* bell/siren which gives warning that a fire has started. **firearm**, *n.* any gun held in the hand. **firebrand**, *n.* agitator. **firebreak**, *n.* strip of land which has been cleared of trees, to prevent forest fires from spreading. **fire brigade**, *n.* people whose job is to put out fires. **firedamp**, *n.* explosive gas in a mine. **fire engine**, *n.* vehicle used by the fire brigade to carry pumps/hoses/ladders, etc., to put out fires. **fire escape**, *n.* stairs/ladder which can be used by people to get out of buildings on fire. **fire extinguisher**, *n.* portable cylinder filled with chemicals or foam to put out a small fire. **firefly**, *n.* type of insect which glows at night. **fireguard**, *n.* metal screen put in front of a fireplace. **firelight**, *n.* light from a fire. **firelighter**, *n.* block of inflammable material used to start a fire. **fireman**, *n.* (*pl.* **-men**) (*a*) man whose job it is to put out fires. (*b*) man who keeps the fire burning in a furnace/a steam train. **fireplace**, *n.* place where a fire is lit indoors. **fireproof**, *adj.* which will not burn. **fireside**, *n.* area around a fireplace in a room. **fire station**, *n.* centre where fire engines are based. **firewarden**, *n.* person whose job it is to look out for forest fires. **firewood**, *n.* (*no pl.*) wood for making fires. **firework**, *n.* small container holding chemicals which will sparkle or explode when lit.

firm [fɜ:m] **1.** *n.* business/company. **2.** *adj.* solid/fixed/strong. **3.** *adv.* **to stand f.** = to refuse to change your mind. **firmly**, *adv.* in a strong way.

firmament ['fɜ:məmənt] *n.* (*formal*) sky.

first [fɜ:st] **1.** *adj. & adv.* (*as a number can be written* **1st**) (*a*) at the beginning/coming before everything else; **at f.** = at the beginning. (*b*) for the first time. (*c*) in a first class seat. **2.** *n.* thing/person coming before everything else; **in f.** = in first gear; **a f. in Physics** = a first-

class degree. **first aid**, *n.* help given to a person who is hurt before a doctor or ambulance arrives. **First Amendment**, *n.* the Amendment to the Constitution of the USA which grants citizens freedom of speech. **first class**. **1.** *adj.* excellent; highest; most expensive. **2.** *adv.* (travel) with the most expensive seats. **first day cover**, *n.* special stamped envelope cancelled on the first day of issue of the stamp on it. **first floor**, *n.* storey above the ground floor in a building; *Am.* ground floor. **firsthand**, *adj. & adv.* direct from the original source. **First Lady**, *n.* wife of the President of the USA. **firstly**, *adv.* to start with. **first mate**, *n.* second-in-command of a merchant ship. **first night**, *n.* evening when a play is performed for the first time. **first-rate**, *adj.* excellent.

firth [fɜ:θ] *n.* (*in Scotland*) long arm of the sea.

fiscal ['fɪskl] *adj.* (*a*) referring to tax/government revenue. (*b*) (*in Scotland*) **procurator f.** = public prosecutor.

fish [fɪʃ] **1.** *n.* (*pl.* **fish**, *occasionally* **fishes**) cold-blooded animal with fins and scales, that lives in water; **he's like a f. out of water** = awkward, because he feels he is not in his usual surroundings. **2.** *v.* (*a*) to try to catch fish; *inf.* **to f. out** = to take out. (*b*) to try to get (information). **fishbone**, *n.* bone in a fish. **fishcake**, *n.* round cake of fish and potato mixed together. **fisherman**, *n.* (*pl.* **-men**) man who catches fish, either as his job or for sport. **fishery**, *n.* business of catching fish. **fish finger**, *Am.* **fish stick**, *n.* frozen finger-shaped piece of fish covered in breadcrumbs. **fish-hook**, *n.* metal hook at the end of a line which catches in the mouth of the fish. **fishing**, *n.* catching fish. **fishing boat**, *n.* boat used for fishing. **fishing rod**, *n.* long piece of wood to which is attached the line and hook. **fishing tackle**, *n.* all the equipment used by a fisherman. **fishmonger**, *n.* man who sells raw fish in a shop. **fishmonger's**, *n.* shop selling raw fish. **fishplate**, *n.* metal clamp which holds rails together. **fish shop**, *n.* shop selling (i) raw fish or (ii) (*also* **fish-and-chip shop**) cooked fish and chips. **fish slice**, *n.* flat utensil used for turning food and removing it from a frying pan. **fishy,** *adj.* (*a*) like a fish. (*b*) *inf.* suspicious/odd (story, etc.).

fission ['fɪʃn] *n.* breaking up of sth into parts; **nuclear f.** = breaking up of an atom in an explosion.

fissure ['fɪʃə] *n.* crack/split, esp. in a rock or in the ground.

fist [fɪst] *n.* tightly closed hand. **fistful,** *n.* amount you can hold in your fist. **fisticuffs,** *n. pl.* (*old*) fighting.

fit [fɪt] **1.** *n.* sudden sharp attack of illness, etc.; **by fits and starts** = at odd moments/with continual stoppages. **2.** *adj.* (**fitter, fittest**) (*a*) right/suitable. (*b*) capable. (*c*) healthy. **3.** *v.* (**fitted**) (*a*) to be the right size for. (*b*) to put in the right place. (*c*) to make suitable for. **fitful,** *adj.* irregular. **fitfully,** *adv.* irregularly. **fit in,** *v.* (*a*) to be suitable/to match (with). (*b*) to find room/ time for (s.o./sth). **fitment,** *n.* piece of furniture which is fixed in a room. **fitness,** *n.* being fit. **fit out, fit up,** *v.* to provide all the equipment/clothing necessary for. **fitted,** *adj.* suitable/right; which has been made to fit. **fitter,** *n.* (*a*) skilled mechanic who adjusts machines and their parts. (*b*) person who makes sure clothes fit. **fitting. 1.** *adj.* suitable/ right. **2.** *n.* (*a*) action of making sth fit/ of trying on a new piece of clothing; **f. room** = small room in a shop where you can try on clothes before you buy them. (*b*) size (of shoe, etc.). (*c*) thing which is fixed in a building but which could be removed.

five [faɪv] *n.* number 5. **fiver,** *n. inf.* five pound note; five dollar bill. **fives,** *n.* game in which a ball is hit off the walls of a court with the hands or a bat.

fix [fɪks] **1.** *n.* (*pl.* **-es**) (*a*) difficult position. (*b*) *Sl.* injection of a drug such as heroin. **2.** *v.* (*a*) to fasten/ to attach. (*b*) to arrange. (*c*) *Am.* to make/to prepare (a drink/meal, etc.). (*d*) to pass (a photographic plate) through a liquid to stop the image changing (*e*) to mend. **fixated,** *adj.* obsessed. **fixation** [fɪk'seɪʃn] *n.* obsession. **fixative** ['fɪksətɪv] *n.* substance which fixes the colours on a painting. **fixed,** *adj.* (*a*) attached firmly. (*b*) (price, etc.) arranged or agreed upon. **fixedly** ['fɪksɪdlɪ] *adv.* with eyes fixed on s.o. **fixer,** *n.* person who can arrange sth. **fixity,** *n.* state of being fixed. **fixture** ['fɪkstʃə] *n.* (*a*) (date for a) sports match. (*b*) **fixtures** = objects permanently fixed in a house (like radiators). **fix up,** *v.* to arrange.

fizz [fɪz] **1.** *n.* sound like a lot of bubbles. **2.** *v.* to bubble up. **fizzy,** *adj.* bubbly.

fizzle out ['fɪzl'aʊt] *v. inf.* to come to nothing/not to work.

fjord ['fjɔːd] *n.* fiord.

flabbergast ['flæbəgɑːst] *v.* to amaze.

flabby ['flæbɪ] *adj.* (**-ier, -iest**) (person) who is soft and fat. **flab,** *n. inf.* soft excess flesh. **flabbiness,** *n.* being flabby.

flaccid ['flæksɪd] *adj.* hanging loosely.

flag [flæg] **1.** *n.* (*a*) piece of material with the emblem of a country/club, etc., on it. (*b*) small paper badges sold in aid of charities. (*c*) large paving stone. (*d*) iris/marsh plant with long fat leaves and purple flowers. (*e*) mark inserted in a computer text. **2.** *v.* (**flagged**) (*a*) to grow tired. (*b*) **to f. down** = to wave to make (a taxi) stop. (*c*) to insert a mark in a computer file. **flag day,** *n.* day on which small paper flags are sold in aid of a charity. **flagpole, flagstaff,** *n.* tall pole on which large flags are flown. **flagship,** *n.* ship on which the admiral sails, and which therefore flies his special flag. **flagstone,** *n.* large flat stone used for pavements/floors.

flagellate ['flædʒəleɪt] *v.* (*formal*) to whip. **flagellation** [flædʒə'leɪʃn] *n.* (*formal*) whipping.

flagon ['flægən] *n.* large round container for liquids.

flagrant ['fleɪgrənt] *adj.* (crime) which is obvious. **flagrance,** *n.* being flagrant. **flagrantly,** *adv.* in a flagrant way.

flail [fleɪl] **1.** *n.* implement for threshing corn. **2.** *v.* to wave (your arms) about.

flair ['fleə] *n.* natural ability (**for** sth).

flak [flæk] *n.* (*no pl.*) gun fire against aircraft; sharp criticism.

flake [fleɪk] **1.** *n.* tiny, thin piece. **2.** *v.* to **f. off/away** = to fall off in little pieces; *Sl.* **to f. out** = to collapse with tiredness. **flaky,** *adj.* in thin pieces.

flamboyant [flæm'bɔɪənt] *adj.* brightly coloured; too bright. **flamboyance,** *n.*

being flamboyant. **flamboyantly,** *adv.* in a flamboyant way.

flame [fleɪm] *n.* bright tongue of fire. **flameproof, flame-resistant,** *adj.* specially treated so that it will not catch fire or melt. **flaming,** *adj.* (*a*) in flames. (*b*) **in a f. temper** = furious/in a very bad mood.

flamingo [flə'mɪŋɡəʊ] *n.* (*pl.* **-os**) water bird with long legs and neck, often with pink feathers.

flammable ['flæməbl] *adj.* easily set on fire/inflammable.

flan [flæn] *n.* open tart.

flange [flændʒ] *n.* rim/edge which sticks out on a pipe or wheel; **f. coupling** = joint with a rim sticking out.

flank [flæŋk] **1.** *n.* side (esp. of an animal, an army). **2.** *v.* to be at the side of (sth).

flannel ['flænl] *n.* (*a*) warm woollen material; **flannels** = flannel trousers. (*b*) small piece of towelling for washing the face or body. **flannelette,** *n.* warm cotton material, which feels like flannel.

flap [flæp] **1.** *n.* (*a*) hinged part (which hangs down). (*b*) *inf.* excitement and worry. (*c*) movement like that of a bird's wing. **2.** *v.* (**flapped**) to move up and down like a bird's wing. **flapjack,** *n.* flat cake made of oats, honey, etc.

flare ['fleə] **1.** *n.* (*a*) device which gives a sudden blaze of light (esp. as a signal). (*b*) widening bottom part (of a skirt/of trousers). **2.** *v.* (*a*) to burn brightly. (*b*) (*of a skirt/trousers*) to widen gradually. **flare up,** *v.* (*a*) to blaze suddenly. (*b*) to get angry.

flash [flæʃ] **1.** *n.* (*pl.* **-es**) (*a*) short sudden burst of light or emotion; **in a f.** = very quickly. (*b*) apparatus for taking photographs in the dark. (*c*) short item of news. (*d*) coloured marking on a uniform. **2.** *v.* (*a*) to light up quickly and suddenly. (*b*) to show (sth) quickly. (*c*) **to f. by/past** = to move/to pass by quickly. **flashback,** *n.* scene in a film, showing what happened at an earlier date. **flashbulb,** *n.* photographic light bulb which makes a short burst of light when you take a photograph. **flashcube,** *n.* square block of four flash bulbs. **flasher,** *n. inf.* man who exposes his private parts. **flashgun,** *n.* photographic device for holding a flashbulb. **flashily,** *adv.* in a flashy way. **flashiness,** *n.* being flashy. **flashing,** *n.* metal strip which covers a joint in a roof. **flashlight,** *n.* hand torch/lamp. **flashpoint,** *n.* temperature at which gas or petrol vapour will ignite/moment at which a revolution will break out. **flashy,** *adj.* showy and bright but of poor quality.

flask [flɑːsk] *n.* (small) bottle for liquids; **thermos f./vacuum f.** = insulated bottle for keeping liquids hot or cold.

flat [flæt] **1.** *adj. & adv.* (**flatter, flattest**) (*a*) level/smooth; punctured (tyre); **f. rate** = fixed charge which never changes. (*b*) (*of drink*) no longer sparkling. (*c*) (*of battery*) no longer producing electricity. (*d*) (*of music*) below the correct pitch. (*e*) definite (refusal). (*f*) **to go f. out** = as fast as you can go; **f. broke** = with no money at all. **2.** *n.* (*a*) place which is level; **f. racing** = horse racing on a level course, not over jumps. (*b*) *Am.* puncture/flat tyre. (*c*) accommodation made up of a set of rooms, usu. on one floor, in a building containing several such groups of rooms. (*d*) note in music which is a semitone lower. **flatfish,** *n.* type of fish with a flattened body. **flatlet,** *n.* small flat. **flatly,** *adv.* definitely. **flatten,** *v.* to make flat. **flatworm,** *n.* worm with a flat body.

flatter ['flætə] *v.* (*a*) to praise (s.o.) insincerely. (*b*) to make (s.o.) feel honoured. (*c*) **to f. yourself** = to deceive yourself/to persuade yourself that sth is true, when it is not. **flatterer,** *n.* person who flatters. **flattery,** *n.* insincere praise.

flatulence ['flætjʊləns] *n.* gas in the intestine. **flatulent,** *adj.* suffering from flatulence.

flaunt [flɔːnt] *v.* to display (sth) in a vulgar way to attract attention.

flautist ['flɔːtɪst] *n.* person who plays the flute.

flavour, *Am.* **flavor** ['fleɪvə] **1.** *n.* taste. **2.** *v.* to add spices and seasoning in cooking; to add a flavour to (sth). **flavouring,** *n.* substance added to food to give a particular taste.

flaw [flɔː] **1.** *n.* fault/mistake; defect. **2.** *v.* to spoil. **flawless,** *adj.* perfect.

flax [flæks] n. (no pl.) plant used for making linen cloth. **flaxen-haired,** adj. fair-haired.

flay [fleɪ] v. (a) to strip the skin off (an animal). (b) to beat (s.o.) harshly.

flea [fliː] n. tiny blood-sucking insect that jumps. **flea bite,** n. (a) place where a flea has bitten. (b) inf. very slight bother. **flea market,** n. market for secondhand goods.

fleck [flek] 1. n. small spot. 2. v. to mark (sth) with spots.

fled [fled] v. see **flee.**

fledgling ['fledʒlɪŋ] n. small bird ready to fly from the nest.

flee [fliː] v. (**fled**) to run away (**from**).

fleece [fliːs] 1. n. wool of a sheep. 2. v. Sl. to cheat (s.o.) and take their money. **fleecy,** adj. made of fleece; covered with fleece; looking like fleece.

fleet [fliːt] 1. n. (a) group of ships belonging together. (b) collection of vehicles. 2. adj. rapid (footsteps). **fleeting** ['fliːtɪŋ] adj. short and quick. **fleetingly,** adv. rapidly.

flesh [fleʃ] n. (a) soft part of the body covering the bones; **in the f.** = in reality (not on TV or in photographs); **a f. wound** = one which is not too deep; **his own f. and blood** = his relations/his family. (b) soft part of a fruit. **fleshy,** adj. fat/plump.

fleur-de-lys [flɜːdə'liːs] n. lily design, formerly the emblem of France.

flew [fluː] v. see **fly.**

flex [fleks] 1. n. flexible insulated cable for carrying electricity. 2. v. to bend. **flexibility** [fleksɪ'bɪlɪtɪ] n. ability to bend easily/to adapt to new circumstances. **flexible,** adj. (a) easy to bend. (b) adaptable. **flexibly,** adv. in a flexible way. **flexitime,** n. system where workers can start and stop their day's work at various times.

flibbertigibbet ['flɪbətɪdʒɪbɪt] n. silly, empty-headed woman.

flick [flɪk] 1. n. little sharp blow/tap. 2. v. to hit lightly. **flick knife,** n. knife with a blade which can fit inside the handle and which shoots out when a spring is released. **flick through,** v. to glance at (the pages of a book) very rapidly.

flicker ['flɪkə] 1. n. trembling/quivering. 2. v. to tremble/to quiver; to burn unsteadily.

flier ['flaɪə] n. see **fly.**

flight [flaɪt] n. (a) journey through the air; flying. (b) group of birds/aircraft flying together. (c) **f. of stairs** = group of stairs in one direction. (d) running away; **to put to f.** = to chase away; **to take f.** = to run away. **flight deck,** n. (a) flat surface on an aircraft carrier on which aircraft land and take off. (b) section at the front of a large aircraft where the pilots sit. **flightless,** adj. (bird) which cannot fly. **flight lieutenant,** n. rank in the air force below squadron leader. **flight recorder,** n. box carried on a plane where details of the flight are recorded automatically. **flighty** ['flaɪtɪ] adj. silly and empty-headed.

flimsy ['flɪmzɪ] adj. (of material) light and thin; poorly made; poor (excuse). **flimsily,** adv. in a flimsy way. **flimsiness,** n. being flimsy.

flinch [flɪntʃ] v. to move back in pain/fear.

fling [flɪŋ] 1. n. (a) wild dance. (b) **to have one's f.** = to let off one's high spirits. 2. v. (**flung**) to throw wildly.

flint [flɪnt] n. (a) very hard type of rock which makes sparks when struck. (b) small piece of metal which makes a spark to light a cigarette lighter. **flinty,** adj. hard/severe (look).

flip [flɪp] v. (**flipped**) to hit lightly; **to f. over** = to turn over quickly. **flip flops,** n. pl. rubber sandals held on by a strap between the toes. **flip side,** n. second side of a record.

flippant ['flɪpənt] adj. joking about things which should be taken seriously. **flippantly,** adv. in a flippant way.

flipper ['flɪpə] n. (a) limb of a sea animal used for swimming. (b) long flat piece of rubber which you can attach to your foot to help you swim faster.

flirt [flɜːt] 1. n. person, esp. woman, who flirts. 2. v. to play at attracting people of the opposite sex for amusement. **flirtation** [flɜː'teɪʃn] n. brief love affair. **flirtatious,** adj. (person) who flirts a lot.

flit [flɪt] 1. n. **to do a moonlight f.** = to escape quietly at night. 2. v. (**flitted**) (a) to move quickly and quietly. (b) to go away quietly without anyone noticing.

flitch [flɪtʃ] n. (pl. **-es**) side of bacon.

float [fləʊt] 1. n. (a) piece of cork, etc., attached to a fishing line which will float on the surface of the water. (b) decorated lorry in a procession; **milk f.** = low electric truck for delivering milk. (c) cash taken from a central supply and used for small expenses. 2. v. to (make sth) lie on the top of a liquid; to start up (a company) by selling shares in it; to let (a currency, such as the pound sterling) find its own exchange rate internationally and not fix it at a certain amount. **floating**, adj. resting on the surface of a liquid; **f. voter** = person who is uncertain which party to vote for in an election.

flock [flɒk] 1. n. (a) group of similar animals together, esp. sheep/goats/birds. (b) waste cotton. 2. v. to move in a group; **to f. together** = to come together in a group.

floe [fləʊ] n. large sheet of ice floating on the sea.

flog [flɒg] v. (**flogged**) (a) to beat hard, usu. with a whip. (b) Sl. to sell.

flood [flʌd] 1. n. large amount of water over land which is usu. dry. (b) large amount of (tears/letters, etc.). 2. v. to cover with water; **they flooded in** = came in large numbers. **floodgate**, n. part of a lock/sluice/dam in a river, which can be opened or shut and which helps control the flow of the water. **floodlight**. 1. n. powerful light often used for lighting the outside of a building or a football pitch at night. 2. v. (**floodlit**) to light with floodlights.

floor [flɔː] 1. n. (a) part of a room on which you walk. (b) storey/one level of rooms in a building. (c) part of an assembly room where people discuss; **to take the f.** = to start speaking in a discussion. 2. v. (a) to knock to the ground. (b) to amaze and puzzle (s.o.). **floorboard**, n. long flat piece of wood used for making wooden floors. **floorcloth**, n. cloth for washing floors. **floorshow**, n. cabaret entertainment.

flop [flɒp] 1. n. (a) inf. failure. (b) movement of sth falling limply. 2. v. (**flopped**) (a) to fall/to sit/to lie limply or heavily. (b) inf. to fail. **floppy**, adj. which hangs limply; **f. disk** = disk used in a computer.

flora ['flɔːrə] n. wild plants (of an area). **floral**, adj. referring to flowers.

floret ['flɒrɪt] n. little flower which is part of a flowerhead.

floribunda [flɒrɪ'bʌndə] n. type of rose with many small flowers.

florid ['flɒrɪd] adj. red (face).

florin ['flɒrɪn] n. (old) British coin worth two shillings.

florist ['flɒrɪst] n. person who sells flowers.

floss [flɒs] n. waste silk threads; **dental f.** = thin thread for pulling between the teeth to remove pieces of food; **candy f.** = molten sugar spun to make a fluffy mass.

flotation [fləʊ'teɪʃn] n. starting of a new company by selling shares in it.

flotilla [flə'tɪlə] n. small group of boats.

flotsam ['flɒtsəm] n. (no pl.) rubbish floating in the water.

flounce [flaʊns] 1. n. border of ruffled cloth (attached to a skirt, etc.). 2. v. **to f. out** = to go out of a room showing your impatience and annoyance. **flounced**, adj. with flounces.

flounder ['flaʊndə] 1. n. common edible flat fish. 2. v. (also **flounder about, around**) to move (in water) with difficulty; to be uncertain of an answer to a question.

flour ['flaʊə] n. grain crushed to powder, used for making bread/cakes, etc. **flourmill**, n. place where grain is ground into flour. **floury**, adj. like flour.

flourish ['flʌrɪʃ] 1. n. (pl. **-es**) (a) wide movement of the arm in the air. (b) large curve in handwriting. (c) fanfare (of trumpets). 2. v. (a) to grow well. (b) to wave (sth) in the air.

flout [flaʊt] v. to scorn/to disregard (sth).

flow [fləʊ] 1. n. movement of liquid/air, etc. 2. v. to move along smoothly. **flowchart**, n. diagram showing the stages in a process.

flower ['flaʊə] 1. n. colourful part of a plant which produces the seed. 2. v. to make flowers. **flowerbed**, n. part of a garden where flowers are grown. **flowerpot**, n. container to grow plants in. **flowery**, adj. (a) (also **flowered**) decorated with a pattern of flowers. (b) ornate (style).

flown [fləʊn] v. see **fly**.

flu [fluː] n. influenza/common illness like a bad cold, often with a high temperature.

fluctuate ['flʌktjʊeɪt] v. to move backwards and forwards/up and down. **fluctuation** [flʌktjʊ'eɪʃn] n. movement backwards and forwards/up and down.

flue [fluː] n. pipe leading to a chimney.

fluency ['fluːənsɪ] n. ease of speaking. **fluent**, adj. able to speak easily. **fluently**, adv. easily.

fluff [flʌf] **1.** n. soft pieces of wool or hair. **2.** v. inf. to do (sth) badly. **fluffiness**, n. being fluffy. **fluffy**, adj. like fluff; covered with fluff.

fluid ['fluːɪd] **1.** n. liquid. **2.** adj. (situation) which is not settled. **fluidity**, [fluː'ɪdɪtɪ] n. being fluid.

fluke [fluːk] n. (a) inf. chance/lucky event. (b) one of the two flat parts of a whale's tail/of an anchor. (c) type of flatworm.

flummox ['flʌməks] v. inf. to confuse (s.o.).

flung [flʌŋ] v. see **fling**.

flunk [flʌŋk] v. Am. inf. to fail (an examination/a candidate).

flunkey ['flʌŋkɪ] n. servant.

fluorescence [flʊə'resns] n. ability to send out a glow of light when an electric current is applied. **fluorescent**, adj. giving off light when electric current is applied.

fluorine ['flʊəriːn] n. (element: F) pale yellow-green gas. **fluoridation** [flʊəraɪ-'deɪʃn] n. adding fluoride to water (to prevent tooth decay). **fluoride** ['flʊəraɪd] n. compound of fluorine; f. **toothpaste** = toothpaste with small amount of fluoride added in order to prevent tooth decay.

flurry ['flʌrɪ] n. (a) hurried excitement. (b) sudden small amount of snow, rain or wind.

flush [flʌʃ] **1.** n. (pl. **-es**) (a) redness of the face. (b) rush of water. (c) (at cards) hand with all the cards of the same suit. **2.** v. (a) to go red in the face. (b) **to f. out** = to drive out of hiding. (c) **to f. a lavatory** = to wash it out by moving a handle which makes water rush through. **3.** adj. (a) f. **with** = level with. (b) inf. having plenty of money to spend.

fluster ['flʌstə] **1.** n. nervous worry. **2.** v. to worry/to confuse (s.o.).

flute [fluːt] n. (a) wind instrument played by blowing across a small hole at the end of a pipe. (b) long rounded groove. **fluted**, adj. decorated with grooves or scallops. **flutist**, n. Am. person who plays the flute.

flutter ['flʌtə] **1.** n. (a) light movement, esp. of wings. (b) inf. small gamble. **2.** v. (a) to move (wings, etc.) quickly and lightly. (b) to move softly and quickly.

fluvial ['fluːvɪəl] adj. referring to rivers.

flux [flʌks] n. (a) constant change. (b) substance used in soldering.

fly [flaɪ] **1.** n. (pl. **flies**) (a) small insect with two wings; f. **fishing** = sport of fishing with an imitation fly as bait. (b) (also **flies**) trouser front fastened by a zip or buttons. **2.** v. (**flew; has flown**) (a) to move through the air. (b) to move fast. (c) to put up (a flag). **3.** adj. inf. clever/sly. **flyblown**, adj. rotten (meat). **fly-by-night**, n. inf. unreliable company. **flycatcher**, n. bird which catches flies. **flier, flyer**, n. (a) person who pilots an aircraft. (b) paper advertising sth. **flying club**, n. club for people interested in flying aircraft. **flying doctor**, n. doctor who visits patients using an aircraft. **flying fish**, n. fish which jumps out of the water as it moves. **flying saucer**, n. unidentified flying object which people claim to see and which they think comes from another planet. **flying squad**, n. group of policemen who arrive quickly at the scene of a crime. **flying start**, n. good beginning to a race/a new job, etc. **flying visit**, n. very short visit. **flyleaf**, n. blank leaf of paper at the beginning and end of a book. **flyover**, n. road built to pass over another. **flypast**, n. flight of aircraft over a certain spot to celebrate sth. **flysheet**, n. extra roof for a tent. **flyweight**, n. lightest category of boxer. **flywheel**, n. large heavy wheel which turns, keeping an engine working at a steady pace.

foal [fəʊl] n. young horse.

foam [fəʊm] **1.** n. mass of small bubbles; f. **rubber** = rubber in blocks with many little holes in it, used for chair cushions, etc. **2.** v. to make froth. **foamy**, adj. covered with foam.

fob [fɒb] **1.** *n.* little ornament attached to a watch-chain. **2.** *v.* **(fobbed) to f. s.o. off with sth** = to deceive s.o. into accepting sth which they don't really want. **fob watch,** *n.* watch carried in a pocket, attached to the end of a chain.

fo'c'sle ['fəʊksl] *n.* front part of a ship where the crew lives.

focus ['fəʊkəs] **1.** *n.* (*a*) (*pl.* **foci** ['fəʊsaɪ] point where rays of light from an object meet; **in f.** = clearly visible; **out of f.** = blurred/not clear. (*b*) centre of attention. **2.** *v.* to adjust so as to be able to see clearly. **focal,** *adj.* referring to a focus.

fodder ['fɒdə] *n.* food for cows/sheep, etc.

foe [fəʊ] *n.* (*formal*) enemy/opponent.

foetus, *Am.* **fetus** ['fi:təs] *n.* unborn child/reptile/bird, etc., which is developing from an embryo. **foetal,** *adj.* referring to a foetus.

fog [fɒg] *n.* thick mist through which it is difficult to see. **fogginess,** *n.* being foggy. **foggy,** *adj.* misty. **foghorn,** *n.* hooter used in fog as a warning to ships. **foglamp,** *n.* car lamp used in fog.

fogey ['fəʊgɪ] *n.* **old f.** = reactionary old man.

foible ['fɔɪbl] *n.* odd way of behaving or thinking.

foil [fɔɪl] **1.** *n.* (*a*) thin metal sheet; **tin f./cooking f.** = foil used for wrapping food before cooking. (*b*) long thin sword with a button on the end used in the sport of fencing. (*c*) person who contrasts sharply with another and so makes the other's qualities stand out. **2.** *v.* to defeat; to prevent (a plot) being put into effect.

foist [fɔɪst] *v.* **to f. sth on s.o.** = to force s.o. to accept sth which they don't want.

fold [fəʊld] **1.** *n.* (*a*) small enclosure for sheep. (*b*) crease (in paper/cloth, etc.) **2.** *v.* (*a*) to bend (sth) so that one part is on top of another. (*b*) **to f. your arms** = to bend your arms together in front of your chest. **folder,** *n.* cardboard envelope for holding papers. **folding,** *adj.* able to be folded. **fold up,** *v.* (*a*) to bend (sth) over to make a smaller area than before. (*b*) *inf.* to finish/to end.

foliage ['fəʊlɪdʒ] *n.* leaves on a tree or plant. **foliar,** *adj.* referring to leaves.

folio ['fəʊlɪəʊ] *n.* (*a*) very large size of book. (*b*) page number.

folk [fəʊk] *n. pl.* people; **my f.** = my family. **folk dance,** *n.* traditional dance. **folklore,** *n.* traditional stories and beliefs. **folksong,** *n.* traditional song. **folkweave,** *n.* traditional peasant cloth.

follicle ['fɒlɪkl] *n.* small hole (in the skin) out of which a hair grows.

follow ['fɒləʊ] *v.* (*a*) to go after/to come after; to continue along (a road). (*b*) to act in accordance with (a rule). (*c*) to understand. **follower,** *n.* supporter. **following,** *adj.* which follows; next. **follow up,** *v.* to investigate/to research (sth) further.

folly ['fɒlɪ] *n.* silly behaviour.

foment [fə'ment] *v.* (*formal*) to stir up (trouble). **fomentation** [fəʊmen'teɪʃn] *n.* act of stirring up trouble.

fond [fɒnd] *adj.* loving; **I am f. of music** = I like music. **fondly,** *adv.* in a fond way. **fondness,** *n.* liking/love.

fondle ['fɒndl] *v.* to stroke lovingly.

fondue ['fɒndju:] *n.* dish of melted cheese into which pieces of bread are dipped, or of hot oil into which pieces of meat are dipped.

font [fɒnt] *n.* basin holding holy water for baptism in a church.

fontanelle [fɒntə'nel] *n.* soft membrane between the pieces of the skull of a baby.

food [fu:d] *n.* substances eaten by people and animals or taken in by plants; **f. poisoning** = illness caused by sth eaten. **foodstuff,** *n.* thing that can be eaten.

fool [fu:l] **1.** *n.* (*a*) idiot/stupid person. (*b*) type of creamed fruit dessert. **2.** *v.* (*a*) **to f. about/around** = to play around in a silly way. (*b*) to trick (s.o.). **foolhardy,** *adj.* brave, but taking unnecessary risks. **foolish,** *adj.* silly/stupid. **foolishly,** *adv.* stupidly. **foolishness,** *n.* silliness/stupidity. **foolproof,** *adj.* so simple that even an idiot could use it safely. **foolscap** ['fu:lskæp] *n.* large size of writing paper.

foot [fʊt] **1.** *n.* (*pl.* **feet**) (*a*) end part of the leg on which you stand; **on f.** = walking; **under f.** = on the ground; *inf.* **to put your f. in it** = to say sth embarrassing; **to put your f. down** =

to be firm/not to give in. (b) base/end of sth. (c) measure of length (= 30.5 cm); **three feet wide.** 2. v. (a) **to f. it** = to walk. (b) **to f. the bill** = to pay the bill. **foot and mouth disease,** n. disease of cows. **footage,** n. (no pl.) cine film which has been exposed. **football,** n. (a) game played between two teams with a ball which is kicked; **Rugby f.** = game played between two teams with an oval ball which can be kicked or passed by hand. (b) ball used in the game of football. **footballer,** n. person who plays football. **footbrake,** n. brake (on a machine or car) operated by the foot. **footbridge,** n. small bridge for people to walk across. **footfall,** n. footstep. **foothills,** n. pl. lower slopes. **foothold,** n. (a) place where you can put your foot when climbing. (b) small position on which you can build. **footing,** n. (a) safe place for your feet. (b) **to put things on a firm f.** = to base things firmly. **footlights,** n. pl. row of lights along the front of the stage in a theatre. **footloose,** adj. free to go anywhere; with no ties. **footman,** n. (pl. -men) male servant. **footnote,** n. explanation at the bottom of a page, referring to sth on the page. **footpath,** n. path for walkers. **footplate,** n. platform in a steam engine for the driver and his helper. **footprint,** n. mark left by the foot on the ground. **footslogging,** n, walking. **foot soldier,** n. soldier who travels on foot. **footsore,** adj. (person) with feet which hurt. **footstep,** n. sound of a foot touching the ground. **footstool,** n. small stool which supports the feet. **footwear,** n. (no pl.) boots and shoes. **footwork,** n. (no pl.) way of using your feet (esp. in sports).

footling ['fu:tlɪŋ] adj. silly/insignificant.

for [fɔ:]. 1. prep. (a) in exchange. (b) in support of. (c) used as. (d) because of. (e) in the direction of; **the train f. London.** (f) towards; **my love f. you.** (g) over a distance of/over a length of time; **f. miles; f. a fortnight.** (h) as a present to; belonging to; **a letter f. you.** (i) in the place of; **can you write this letter f. me?** (j) with the purpose of; **to go f. a walk; run f. the bus** = to catch the bus. (k) **f. all that** = in spite of everything; **as f.** =

regarding; **f. sale** = able to be bought; **f. example** = to name one thing out of many; **f. ever/f. good** = always; **f. the most part** = usually. 2. conj. because.

forage ['fɒrɪdʒ] 1. n. food for horses and cattle. 2. v. (a) to search for food/supplies. (b) to rummage/to look for sth. **forage cap,** n. soft cap shaped like an upturned boat.

foray ['fɒreɪ] n. sudden attack.

forbade [fə'bæd] v. see forbid.

forbearance [fɔ:'beərəns] n. patience. **forbearing,** adj. patient/long-suffering.

forbid [fə'bɪd] v. (forbade [fə'bæd]; forbidden) to tell (s.o.) not to do sth. **forbidding,** adj. sinister/looking dangerous.

force [fɔ:s] 1. n. (a) strength/power; **in f.** = (i) in large numbers; (ii) (law which is) operating/working. (b) organized group of people; **police f; the armed forces** = navy, army and air force. 2. v. (a) to move by using strength. (b) to compel/to make (s.o.) do sth. (c) to make (plants) grow faster/earlier than normal. **force back,** v. to push sth back very hard. **forced,** adj. (a) compelled; **f. landing** = quick landing of an aircraft because sth is wrong. (b) artificial/not real. **force-feed,** v. (force-fed) to feed (s.o. on hunger strike) by force. **forceful,** adj. strong/powerful. **forcefully,** adv. in a forceful way. **forcefulness,** n. being forceful. **force majeure,** n. thing which happens (such as a war) which cannot be controlled by parties to a contract. **forcemeat,** n. minced meat used as stuffing (for turkeys, etc.).

forceps ['fɔ:seps] n. (no pl.) pincers used by doctors in surgery.

forcible ['fɔ:sɪbl] adj. done by/with force. **forcibly,** adv. using force.

ford [fɔ:d] 1. n. shallow part of a river where you can cross by going through the water. 2. v. to cross a river by going through a shallow part. **fordable,** adj. (river) which can be forded.

fore [fɔ:] 1. n. front part of a ship; **f. and aft** = front and back of a ship. **to come to the f.** = to become prominent. 2. adj. front/before (used as a prefix in words such as **forearm, foresee**). **forearm.** 1. n. ['fɔ:rɑ:m] part of the arm between the hand and the elbow. **2.** *v.* [fɔː'ɑːm] to get ready for a fight in good time. **forebears,** *n. pl. (old)* ancestors. **foreboding** [fɔː'bəʊdɪŋ] *n.* feeling that sth evil will take place. **forecast. 1.** *n.* description of what will happen in the future. **2.** *v.* (forecast) to say what will happen in the future. **forecaster,** *n.* person who says what will happen in the future, esp. concerning the weather. **forecastle** ['fəʊksl] *n.* front part of a ship where the crew live. **foreclose** [fɔː'kləʊz] *v.* to take away property because the owner cannot pay back money which he has borrowed on its security. **foreclosure,** *n.* act of foreclosing. **forecourt,** *n.* courtyard in front of a building. **forefather,** *n.* ancestor. **forefinger,** *n.* index finger/ first finger next to the thumb. **forefoot,** *n.* front foot (of an animal). **forefront,** *n.* **to be in the f. of a campaign** = to be one of the leaders. **forego** [fɔː'gəʊ] *v.* (forewent, has foregone) to do without. **foregoing,** *adj.* which has gone before. **foregone,** *adj.* decided in advance; **it was a f. conclusion** = everyone knew. **foreground,** *n.* part of a picture/ scene nearest the viewer. **forehand,** *adj.* (*in tennis*) (stroke) played with the palm of the hand facing forwards. **forehead** ['fɒrɪd, 'fɔːhed] *n.* part of the head between the eyes and the hair. **foreknowledge,** *n.* knowledge in advance. **foreland,** *n.* headland. **foreleg,** *n.* front leg of an animal. **foreman,** *n.* (*pl.* **-men**) (*a*) (*in a factory*) workman in charge of several others. (*b*) **f. of a jury** = spokesman for the jury. **foremost,** *adj.* & *adv.* first/chief; **first and f.** = first of all. **forenoon,** *n.* morning. **forepaw,** *n.* front paw. **forerunner,** *n.* person/thing coming before another more important one. **foresee** [fɔː'siː] *v.* (foresaw; has foreseen) to feel in advance that sth will happen. **foreseeable,** *adj.* which can be foreseen. **foreshadow** [fɔː'ʃædəʊ] *v.* to be a sign of (sth to come). **foreshore,** *n.* part of a beach which is covered by the sea at each high tide. **foresight,** *n.* ability to see what will probably happen in the future; ability to plan for emergencies. **foreskin,** *n.* loose skin covering the end of the penis. **forestall** [fɔː'stɔːl] *v.* to anticipate/to stop (s.o. doing sth). **foretaste,** *n.* small bit of sth that will be had later on. **foretell** [fɔː-'tel] *v.* (foretold) to predict/to say what will happen in the future. **forethought,** *n.* thinking ahead. **forewarned,** *adj.* warned in advance. **foreword,** *n.* short section at the beginning of a book introducing it to the reader.

foreign ['fɒrən] *adj.* (*a*) not belonging to your own country. (*b*) strange; **f. exchange** = exchanging the money of one country for money of another; **f. to his nature** = very strange for him to do it. (*c*) **f. body** = thing from outside which lodges in your body. **foreigner,** *n.* person who does not belong to your country.

forensic [fə'rensɪk] *adj.* referring to the solving and punishment of crime; **f. medicine** = medicine concerned with crimes.

forest ['fɒrɪst] *n.* large area covered with trees. **forester, forest ranger,** *n.* person whose job it is to look after a forest. **forestry,** *n.* job of looking after a forest and its trees; science of growing and maintaining forests.

forever [fə'revə] *adv.* always.

forfeit ['fɔːfɪt] **1.** *n.* thing taken/lost as a punishment. **2.** *v.* to lose (sth), esp. as a punishment. **forfeiture** ['fɔːfɪtʃə] *n.* act of forfeiting.

forgather [fɔː'gæðə] *v.* (*formal*) to gather together.

forgave [fə'geɪv] *v. see* **forgive.**

forge [fɔːdʒ] **1.** *n.* blacksmith's workshop where he makes horseshoes and other iron objects. **2.** *v.* (*a*) to work (metal) in a forge. (*b*) to copy (sth) illegally. (*c*) **to f. ahead** = to go forward quickly. **forged,** *adj.* copied illegally. **forger,** *n.* person who copies sth illegally. **forgery,** *n.* (*a*) making an illegal copy. (*b*) illegal copy.

forget [fə'get] *v.* (forgot; has forgotten) not (to be able) to remember; to leave (sth) behind. **forgetful,** *adj.* often unable to remember. **forgetfulness,** *n.* being forgetful. **forget-me-not,** *n.* small blue-flowered plant.

forgive [fə'gɪv] *v.* (forgave [fə'geɪv]; has forgiven) to pardon/to stop being angry with (s.o.). **forgivable**, *adj.* able to be pardoned/understandable. **forgiveness**, *n.* pardon(ing).

forgo [fɔ:'gəʊ] *v.* (**forwent, has forgone**) to do without.

forgot [fə'gɒt] *v. see* **forget**.

fork [fɔ:k] **1.** *n.* (*a*) object with a handle at one end and sharp points at the other, used for picking things up. (*b*) place where a branch leaves a tree trunk. (*c*) place where two roads split. **2.** *v.* (*a*) to **f. over the soil** = to turn the soil over with a fork. (*b*) to turn off a road. (*c*) (*of a road*) to split into two parts. (*d*) *inf.* to **f. out** = to pay for sth, usu. unwillingly. **forked**, *adj.* divided into two. **forklift truck**, *n.* motor vehicle which can lift heavy loads on metal arms.

forlorn [fə'lɔ:n] *adj.* left alone and feeling sad; **f. hope** = very slight hope. **forlornly**, *adv.* sadly.

form [fɔ:m] **1.** *n.* (*a*) shape. (*b*) paper with blank spaces for you to fill in. (*c*) condition of an athlete/racing animal; **he's in good f.** = he's in a good mood/ he's very amusing. (*d*) structure/style of a piece of writing/a piece of music. (*e*) school class. (*f*) long wooden seat with no back. (*g*) custom/behaviour. (*h*) hare's nest. **2.** *v.* (*a*) to shape; to take shape. (*b*) to be. (*c*) to organize; **they formed a club. formation** [fɔ:'meɪʃn] *n.* shaping/forming of sth. **formative** ['fɔ:mətɪv] *adj.* referring to the early years of life when a person's character is being formed.

formal ['fɔ:ml] *adj.* (*a*) ceremonial/ done according to certain rules. (*b*) regular; clearly written (agreement). **formality** [fɔ:'mælɪtɪ] *n.* thing which has to be done to conform with the rules but which does not mean much. **formalization**, *n.* making formal. **formalize**, *v.* to make (an agreement) formal/regular. **formally**, *adv.* according to rules/ceremonially.

formaldehyde [fɔ:'mældɪhaɪd] *n.* gas used in solution to make formalin. **formalin**, *n.* solution used as a disinfectant and preservative.

format ['fɔ:mæt] **1.** *n.* (*a*) shape/size (in which sth is made). (*b*) dimensions of a page/book. **2.** *v.* (**formatted**) to arrange text on a computer, so that it is ready

for final printing; to set a computer disk so that it is ready to receive data.

forme [fɔ:m] *n.* frame in which type is fixed for printing.

former ['fɔ:mə] *adj.* (*a*) earlier. (*b*) first thing mentioned (of two). **formerly**, *adv.* at an earlier time.

formic ['fɔ:mɪk] *adj.* **f. acid** = acid found in the sting of ants.

formica [fɔ:'maɪkə] *n.* trade name for a hard plastic.

formidable ['fɔ:mɪdəbl] *adj.* frighteningly difficult; very impressive (person).

formula ['fɔ:mjʊlə] *n.* (*pl.* **-ae** [-i:]) (*a*) statement, usu. of a scientific fact and often by means of symbols. (*b*) **Formula I race** = car race where the cars all have engines of the largest classification. (*c*) *Am.* milky food for babies. **formulate**, *v.* (*a*) to express (sth) as a formula. (*b*) to express (an idea) clearly. **formulation**, *n.* expressing clearly.

fornicate ['fɔ:nɪkeɪt] *v.* to have sexual intercourse (when not married). **fornication**, *n.* act of fornicating.

forsake [fə'seɪk] *v.* (**forsook; has forsaken**) to leave behind. **forsaken**, *adj.* abandoned/deserted.

forswear [fɔ:'sweə] *v.* (*formal*) to swear not to do (sth).

forsythia [fɔ:'saɪθɪə] *n.* common garden shrub with yellow flowers.

fort [fɔ:t] *n.* strong building which can be defended against enemy attacks; **to hold the f.** = to be in charge while s.o. is away.

forte ['fɔ:tɪ] **1.** *n.* (*a*) loud piece of music. (*b*) particular ability. **2.** *adv.* played loudly.

forth [fɔ:θ] *adv.* (*formal*) forward; **back and f.** = backwards and forwards; **and so f.** = and so on. **forthcoming**, *adj.* (*a*) soon to appear. (*b*) *inf.* friendly/full of information. **forthright**, *adj.* direct/ blunt (way of speaking). **forthwith**, *adv.* immediately.

fortify ['fɔ:tɪfaɪ] *v.* to make strong; **fortified wine** = wine (like sherry/port) with extra alcohol added. **fortification** [fɔ:'tɪfɪ'keɪʃn] *n.* (*a*) making strong. (*b*) **fortifications** = walls/towers built to defend a city.

fortissimo [fɔːˈtɪsɪməʊ] adv. very loudly (in music).

fortitude [ˈfɔːtɪtjuːd] n. strength of mind/bravery, esp. when in pain.

fortnight, [ˈfɔːtnaɪt] n. two weeks. **fortnightly,** adj. & adv. once every two weeks.

fortress [ˈfɔːtrəs] n. (pl. -es) strong building/castle.

fortuitous [fɔːˈtjuɪtəs] adj. accidental/happening by chance. **fortuitously,** adv. by chance/accidentally.

fortune [ˈfɔːtjuːn] n. (a) luck/chance. (b) what will happen in the future. (c) large amount of money. **fortunate** [ˈfɔːtʃənət] adj. lucky. **fortunately,** adv. by good luck. **fortune-teller,** n. person who says what will happen in the future by looking at cards or lines on your hand.

forty [ˈfɔːtɪ] n. number 40; inf. **f. winks** = short sleep in the daytime. **fortieth, 40th,** adj. & n. referring to 40.

forum [ˈfɔːrəm] n. (a) place where matters of general interest can be discussed. (b) public discussion.

forward [ˈfɔːwəd] 1. adj. (a) towards the front. (b) advanced/well ahead. (c) too confident. 2. adv. (a) **from that day f. =** from then on. (b) to the front; **to look f. to sth** = to wait for sth with pleasure. 3. n. (in football, etc.) player in an attacking/front position. 4. v. (a) to send on (a letter) to another address. (b) to help (sth) progress. **forward-looking,** adj. thinking ahead/dealing with the future optimistically. **forwards,** adv. to the front.

fossick [ˈfɒsɪk] v. (Australian) to look for sth/to search.

fossil [ˈfɒsl] n. remains of an animal/plant left in a rock; inf. elderly old-fashioned person. **fossilization,** n. becoming fossilized. **fossilized** [ˈfɒsɪlaɪzd] adj. turned into a rock.

foster [ˈfɒstə] v. (a) to bring up (a child who is not your own). (b) to encourage (an idea, etc.). **foster-child,** n. (pl. -children) child brought up by parents who are not his own. **foster home,** n. family/home where a foster-child is brought up. **foster-mother,** n. mother who fosters a child. **foster-parents,** n. pl. parents who foster a child.

fought [fɔːt] v. see **fight**.

foul [faʊl] 1. adj. (-er, -est) (a) bad/dirty/unpleasant (taste, language, air, etc.). (b) against the rules of a game. (c) **f. play =** murder. (d) **to fall f. of =** to get into trouble with. 2. n. action against the rules of the game. 3. v. (a) to make dirty. (b) to do sth against the rules of the game. (c) **the boat fouled its anchor =** its anchor got stuck in weeds, etc; inf. **to f. sth up =** to make a mess of sth/to create a problem. **foully,** adv. in a foul way. **foulmouthed,** adj. with foul language. **foulness,** n. being foul.

found [faʊnd] v. (a) to establish/to begin (sth). (b) to base (a story, etc.). (c) to melt (metal); to make (sth) out of molten metal; see also **find**. **foundation** [faʊnˈdeɪʃn] n. (a) establishing/beginning. (b) **foundations =** base below ground on which a building is laid; **f. stone =** stone in a wall which records the start of building. (c) organization which provides money for certain projects. (d) **f. (cream) =** coloured cream put on the face under powder. **founder. 1.** n. person who establishes/begins sth; **f. member =** one of the first to establish a club, etc. **2.** v. (of a boat, scheme) to collapse/to sink. **foundling,** n. baby abandoned by its parents and found by s.o. else. **foundry,** n. works where things are made from molten metal, etc.

fount n. (a) [fɒnt] set of type of one particular size and design. (b) [faʊnt] (old) fountain.

fountain [ˈfaʊntɪn] n. jet of water in a street or garden; **f. pen =** pen which you can fill up with ink.

four [fɔː] n. (a) number 4; **on all fours =** on hands and knees. (b) four people (in a rowing boat). **fourfold,** adv. & adj. four times as much. **fourpart,** adj. (music) for four different voices. **fourposter (bed),** n. bed with a tall post at each corner and curtains. **foursome,** n. (a) activity/game played by four people. (b) group of four people. **fourteen,** n. number 14. **fourteenth, 14th,** adj. referring to fourteen. **fourth, 4th. 1.** adj. referring to four. **2.** n. quarter.

fowl [faʊl] n. (pl. fowl) domestic birds kept for food or eggs (chickens, ducks, turkeys and geese); **wild f.** = game birds which are shot for sport. **fowling piece,** *n.* gun for shooting wild fowl.

fox [fɒks] **1.** *n.* wild animal with reddish fur and a bushy tail. **2.** *v.* to puzzle/to trick. **fox cub,** *n.* young fox. **foxglove,** *n.* tall purple and white flower found in woods. **foxhound,** *n.* dog used for hunting foxes. **foxhunting,** *n.* chasing foxes to catch and kill them, usu. with dogs. **fox terrier,** *n.* type of small dog. **foxtrot,** *n.* type of ballroom dance. **foxy,** *adj.* crafty/cunning.

foyer ['fɔɪeɪ] *n.* large entrance hall at the front of a hotel/theatre.

fracas ['frækɑ:] *n.* noisy disturbance.

fraction ['frækʃn] *n.* (*a*) very small piece/amount. (*b*) (*in mathematics*) less than a whole number. **fractional,** *adj.* very small. **fractionally,** *adv.* by a very small amount.

fractious ['frækʃəs] *adj.* bad-tempered/crying (child). **fractiousness,** *n.* being fractious.

fracture ['fræktʃə] **1.** *n.* break (esp. in bones); **simple f.** = clean break of a bone; **compound f.** = one where the broken bone has pierced the skin. **2.** *v.* to break (a bone).

fragile ['frædʒaɪl] *adj.* easily broken/delicate; *inf.* feeling weak and ill after drinking too much alcohol. **fragility** [frə'dʒɪlɪtɪ] *n.* being easily broken.

fragment 1. *n.* ['frægmənt] small piece. **2.** *v.* [fræg'ment] to break into small pieces. **fragmentary,** *adj.* in pieces/not complete. **fragmentation,** *n.* breaking into small pieces.

fragrance ['freigrəns] *n.* pleasant smell. **fragrant,** *adj.* sweet-smelling.

frail [freɪl] *adj.* weak. **frailty,** *n.* weakness.

frame [freɪm] **1.** *n.* (*a*) supporting structure of a building/ship/aircraft/bicycle/glasses, etc.; **f. tent** = tent supported on a framework of poles; *Am.* **f. house** = wooden house. (*b*) bone structure of a person/animal; **f. of mind** = temper/mood. (*c*) border of wood/metal round a picture/mirror/window. (*d*) one picture in a length of cine film. (*e*) glass box for protecting young plants in a garden. **2.** *v.* (*a*) to put into words. (*b*) to put a border around (sth). (*c*) *inf.*

to make (an innocent person) appear guilty. **frame-up,** *n. inf.* arrangement whereby an innocent person is framed.

framework, *n.* (*a*) structure supporting a building, etc. (*b*) basis of a plan.

franc [fræŋk] *n.* unit of money in France, Belgium and Switzerland.

franchise ['fræntʃaɪz] **1.** *n.* (*a*) right to vote. (*b*) permit to sell a company's products in a certain region/to trade using a well-known brand name. **2.** *v.* to license a product to others who will use it for trade and pay a fee for its use. **franchisee,** *n.* person who runs a business under franchise. **franchisor,** *n.* person who licenses s.o. to operate a franchise.

Franco- ['fræŋkəʊ] *prefix meaning* between France and another country.

frank [fræŋk] **1.** *adj.* plain-speaking; (person) who says what he thinks. **2.** *v.* to stamp (a letter) on a special machine. **frankly,** *adv.* speaking truthfully. **frankness,** *n.* saying what you think.

frankfurter ['fræŋkfɜ:tə] *n.* long spiced sausage, which is boiled and sometimes eaten with a roll.

frankincense ['fræŋkɪnsens] *n.* gum from a tree, burnt as incense.

frantic ['fræntɪk] *adj.* worried and wildly excited. **frantically,** *adv.* in an excited and worried way.

fraternal [frə'tɜ:nl] *adj.* brotherly. **fraternally,** *adv.* in a fraternal way. **fraternity,** *n.* (*a*) society of men with similar interests; *Am.* **student f.** = student association for men. (*b*) brotherly feeling. **fraternization** [frætənaɪ'zeɪʃn] *n.* act of fraternizing. **fraternize** ['frætənaɪz] *v.* to become friendly (**with** s.o.).

fratricide ['frætrɪsaɪd] *n.* murder of your brother.

fraud [frɔ:d] *n.* (*a*) (piece of) dishonesty. (*b*) person pretending to be sth he is not; thing that is not what you expect. **fraudulence,** *n.* dishonesty. **fraudulent,** *adj.* dishonest.

fraught [frɔ:t] *adj.* (*a*) (**with**) full of (problems, danger). (*b*) *inf.* full of anxiety; worrying (situation).

fray [freɪ] **1.** *n.* fight; **ready for the f.** = ready to fight/ready to take part in the action. **2.** v. (*of material*) to become worn/to unravel so that threads are loose.

frazzle ['fræzl] n. state of exhaustion.

freak [friːk] n. (a) unusual type of person/animal/plant. (b) extraordinary change in the weather. (c) person who is fanatic about sth. **freakish**, adj. unusual/extraordinary. **freak out**, v. inf. to become very excited because of the effect of drugs.

freckle ['frekl] n. small brown mark on the skin, often caused by the sun. **freckled**, adj. covered in freckles.

free [friː] **1.** adj. (**freer, freest**) (a) not imprisoned/not tied down. (b) not occupied. (c) not costing any money. (d) able to do what you want; **to be f. with sth** = to give sth away generously. (e) **to be f. from/of sth** = to be without sth (usu. unpleasant). **2.** v. (a) to get (a person) out of prison. (b) to release from a difficult situation. **freedom**, n. state of being free; **f. of speech** = ability to say what you like. **free-for-all**, n. general fight/general argument among several people. **freehand**, adj. & adv. (drawing) drawn without the help of rulers/compasses, etc. **freehold**, n. & adj. right to own a property for ever. **freeholder**, n. person who owns a freehold property. **free house**, n. pub which is not owned by one brewery company but can sell any brand of drink. **freelance. 1.** adj. & n. independent (worker), not employed by one particular company. **2.** adv. (to work) independently. **3.** v. to work independently. **freeloader**, n. inf. person who lives on gifts which he cadges from other people. **freely**, adv. in a frank manner/without being tied. **Freemason**, n. member of a secret society. **freemasonry**, n. brotherhood/fraternity. **free-range**, adj. (hens) kept in the open, not in boxes. **free style**, n. (*in sport*) any style; (*in swimming*) any stroke, usu. crawl. **free trade**, n. system of trade agreements between countries where goods are imported and exported free of tax. **freeway**, n. Am. fast motorway with few junctions. **freewheel** [friː'wiːl] v. to go along on a bicycle without pedalling. **free will**, n. ability to decide for yourself.

freesia ['friːʒə] n. scented flower grown from a bulb.

freeze [friːz] **1.** n. (a) period of frost. (b) **wage f./price f.** = period of standstill in wages or prices. **2.** v. (**froze; has frozen**) (a) to change from liquid to solid because of the cold. (b) to become very cold. (c) to stay very still. (d) to store (food) at below freezing point. (e) to keep prices or wages at the present level. (f) to prevent the owner from using or selling (assets). **freezer**, n. deep-freeze/refrigerator for freezing food and keeping it frozen. **freezing point**, n. temperature at which a liquid becomes solid.

freight [freɪt] **1.** n. (a) transport of goods by air, sea or land. (b) goods transported; **f. train** = train used for transporting goods; Am. **f. car** = goods wagon. **2.** v. to transport (goods). **freighter**, n. aircraft/ship which carries goods. **freightliner**, n. train carrying goods in containers.

French [frentʃ] **1.** adj. referring to France; **F. window** = door made of glass usu. opening on to a garden; **F. beans** = beans grown on low bushes and eaten when green in their pods; **F. dressing** = salad dressing made of oil and vinegar; Am. **F. fries/F. fried potatoes** = chips; **to take F. leave** = to go away without permission; **F. horn** = brass instrument with a coiled tube. **2.** n. (a) language spoken in France and some other countries. (b) **the F.** = the people of France. **Frenchman, Frenchwoman**, n. (pl. **-men, -women**) person from France. **French polish**, v. to polish (wood) with a resin polish.

frenetic [frə'netɪk] adj. wildly excited.

frenzy ['frenzɪ] n. wild excitement. **frenzied**, adj. wildly excited. **frenziedly**, adv. in a frenzied way.

frequent 1. adj. ['friːkwənt] happening often/often seen. **2.** v. [frɪ'kwent] go go (somewhere) very often. **frequency**, n. (a) rate at which sth happens. (b) number of vibrations per second made by a radio wave. **frequently**, adv. often.

fresco ['freskəʊ] n. (pl. **-oes**) painting done on wet plaster on a wall.

fresh [freʃ] adj. (**-er, -est**) (a) new/not used; **f. air** = open air. (b) recent (news); newly-made (cakes). (*c*) not tinned or frozen. (*d*) quite strong (wind). (*e*) healthy-looking. (*f*) cheeky/rather rude. **freshen**, *v.* to become/to make fresh. **fresher, freshman**, *n.* (*pl.* **-men**) new student in his/her first year at college. **freshly**, *adv.* newly/recently. **freshness**, *n.* being fresh. **fresh water**, *n.* water in rivers or lakes. **freshwater**, *adj.* referring to river or lake water, not salt water.

fret [fret] **1**. *n.* raised metal strip crossing the neck of a guitar against which you press the strings. **2**. *v.* (**fretted**) to worry/be unhappy. **fretful**, *adj.* crying and unhappy (child). **fretfully**, *adv.* in a fretful way.

fretwork ['fretwɜːk] *n.* patterns in wood cut with a very fine saw. **fretsaw**, *n.* fine saw used for cutting patterns in wood.

Freudian ['frɔɪdɪən] *adj.* referring to Freud and his theories of psychoanalysis; **a F. slip** = a mistake in speaking which seems to show your real feelings, when you are trying to hide them.

friable ['fraɪəbl] *adj.* (earth) which can be crumbled easily.

friar ['fraɪə] *n.* member of a Christian religious order.

fricassée ['frɪkæseɪ] *n.* dish of pieces of meat cooked in a rich sauce.

friction ['frɪkʃn] *n.* (*a*) rubbing one thing against another. (*b*) disagreement between two or more people.

Friday ['fraɪdeɪ] *n.* fifth day of the week/day between Thursday and Saturday; **Good F.** = the Friday before Easter Day; **Man F.** = general helper.

fridge [frɪdʒ] *n. inf.* refrigerator/apparatus for keeping things cold.

fried [fraɪd] *v. see* **fry**.

friend [frend] *n.* person whom you know well and like; supporter (of a cause); **the Society of Friends** = religious society, also called the Quakers. **friendless**, *adj.* having no friends. **friendliness**, *n.* friendly feeling. **friendly**. **1**. *adj.* like a friend/kind/helpful. **2**. *n. inf.* game which does not count in a tournament. **friendship**, *n.* state of being friends.

frieze [friːz] *n.* decorative border round the top of walls, pillars, etc.

frigate ['frɪgət] *n.* small fast-moving naval ship.

fright [fraɪt] *n.* (*a*) fear. (*b*) *inf.* awful-looking person. **frightful**, *adj. inf.* terrible/awful. **frightfully**, *adv. inf.* extremely/terribly/very. **frightfulness**, *n.* unpleasantness.

frighten ['fraɪtn] *v.* to make (s.o.) afraid. **frightened**, *adj.* afraid/scared (of). **frightening**, *adj.* causing fear.

frigid ['frɪdʒɪd] *adj.* (*a*) very cold/icy. (*b*) unfriendly/not showing any warm feelings; (woman) not interested in sex. **frigidity** [frɪ'dʒɪdɪtɪ] *n.* (*a*) great cold. (*b*) coldness of feelings, esp. lack of interest in sex. **frigidly**, *adv.* in a cold way.

frill [frɪl] *n.* (*a*) piece of material gathered together and sewn on to a dress, etc. (*b*) **frills** = unnecessary ornaments. **frilled**, *adj.* with frills. **frilly, with many frills**.

fringe [frɪndʒ] *n.* (*a*) hair lying over the forehead. (*b*) edging of material consisting of loose threads hanging down (on a shawl/dress/carpet, etc.) (*c*) outer edge of an area; **f. benefits** = extra benefits on top of a salary (such as a free car, etc.); **f. theatre** = usu. experimental drama, often not using a traditional theatre building.

frippery ['frɪpərɪ] *n.* useless ornament.

frisk [frɪsk] *v.* (*a*) to jump (**about**). (*b*) to search (s.o.) by running your hands over him to see if he is carrying a weapon. **friskily**, *adv.* in a frisky way. **friskiness**, *n.* feeling full of life. **frisky**, *adj.* lively.

fritillary [frɪ'tɪlərɪ] *n.* type of small butterfly.

fritter ['frɪtə] **1**. *n.* piece of meat/fruit/vegetable dipped in a mixture of flour, egg and milk and fried. **2**. *v.* **f. away** = to waste (time, money).

frivolous ['frɪvələs] *adj.* silly/not serious. **frivolously**, *adv.* in a frivolous way. **frivolousness, frivolity** [frɪ'vɒlɪtɪ] *n.* silliness/lack of seriousness.

frizzle ['frɪzl] *v. inf.* (*a*) (*of hair*) to be very tightly curled. (*b*) to fry in hot fat.

frizzy ['frɪzɪ] *adj. inf.* tightly curled (hair). **frizz**, *v. inf.* to put (hair) into tight curls.

fro [frəʊ] *adv.* **to and f.** = backwards and forwards.

frock [frɒk] *n.* (*a*) dress/piece of female clothing covering more or less all the body. (b) long robe worn by monks or priests.

frog [frɒg] n. (a) small tailless reptile which lives on both land and water; **to have a f. in your throat** = to feel you have sth in your throat which stops you speaking clearly. (b) decorated fastening on a uniform. **frogman,** n. (pl. **-men**) underwater diver. **frogmarch,** v. to force (s.o., esp. a prisoner) to move by carrying him by his arms (and sometimes legs). **frogspawn,** n. (no pl.) transparent jelly containing frog's eggs.

frolic ['frɒlɪk] 1. n. happy game/party. 2. v. (**frolicked**) to play happily.

from [frɒm] prep. (a) (showing movement away) **the plane f. London.** (b) (showing where something started) **f. beginning to end; f. now on; f. time to time** = sometimes. (c) (showing difference) **I can't tell butter f. margarine.** (d) sent by; **a letter f. Peter.** (e) because of; **he died f. pneumonia.** (f) according to; **f. what I heard.**

frond [frɒnd] n. large leaf of a fern or palm tree.

front [frʌnt] 1. n. (a) part which faces forward; most prominent part; **in f. of** = before. (b) road which runs beside the sea in a seaside town. (c) line of an army nearest the enemy in battle. (d) (of weather) line separating cold and warm masses of air. (e) business used to hide an illegal activity. 2. adj. foremost/first (seat, door, etc.). 3. v. to face (**on to**). **frontage** ['frʌntɪdʒ] n. (a) length of a property along a road. (b) land between a building and the road. **frontal,** adj. of/in the front; belonging to the front.

frontier ['frʌntɪə] n. (a) boundary line between two countries or states. (b) **the frontiers of science** = the furthest point in human knowledge.

frontispiece ['frʌntɪspiːs] n. picture opposite the title page of a book.

frost [frɒst] n. (a) weather when the temperature is below the freezing point of water; **ten degrees of f.** = ten degrees below freezing. (b) white covering on the ground/trees, etc., when the temperature is below freezing. **frostbite,** n. damage to a part of the body due

to cold. **frostbitten,** adj. attacked by frostbite. **frosted,** adj. (a) covered in frost; damaged by frost. (b) (glass) which has a rough surface through which it is difficult to see. (c) (cake) covered with sugar. **frostily,** adv. coldly/in an unfriendly way. **frosting,** n. icing on a cake. **frosty,** adj. (a) very cold; covered with frost. (b) cold/unfriendly (manner).

froth [frɒθ] 1. n. mass of bubbles on top of a liquid. 2. v. to have masses of bubbles. **frothy,** adj. having bubbles on top.

frown [fraʊn] 1. n. pulling down the eyebrows as a sign of anger/puzzlement, etc. 2. v. to pull down the eyebrows; **to f. on (sth)** = to disapprove of sth.

frowsty ['fraʊztɪ] adj. smelling dirty and stale.

frowzy ['fraʊzɪ] adj. untidy and dirty.

froze [frəʊz] v. see **freeze.**

frozen ['frəʊzn] adj. (a) very cold. (b) at a temperature below freezing point; **f. food** = food stored at a temperature below freezing; see also **freeze.**

frugal ['fruːgl] adj. spending/costing very little money. **frugality** [fruːˈgælɪtɪ] n. being frugal. **frugally,** adv. in a frugal way.

fruit [fruːt] 1. n. (a) (pl. usu. **fruit**) part of a plant which contains the seeds and which is often eaten; **f. salad** = pieces of fresh fruit mixed and served cold. (b) product of (hard work). 2. v. to carry/to produce edible parts. **fruitcake,** n. cake with a lot of dried fruit in it. **fruiterer,** n. person who sells fruit. **fruitful,** adj. (work) which produces good results. **fruitfully,** adv. in a fruitful way. **fruition** [fruːˈɪʃn] n. **to come to f.** = to be accomplished with good results. **fruitless,** adj. producing no results. **fruitlessly,** adv. in a fruitless way. **fruit machine,** n. gambling machine where pictures of different fruits revolve when you pull a handle. **fruity,** adj. (a) tasting of fruit. (b) inf. deep and tuneful (voice).

frump [frʌmp] n. person, usu. a woman, who wears old-fashioned clothes. **frumpish,** adj. (wearing) out-of-date clothes.

frustrate [frʌˈstreɪt] v. to prevent (s.o.)

doing what he wants to do. **frustration** [frʌ'streɪʃn] n. feeling of anger and impatience when stopped from doing what you want.

fry [fraɪ] **1.** n. (pl. fry) baby fish; **small f.** = unimportant people. **2.** v. to cook in oil/fat. **frying pan,** n. shallow, open pan used for frying; **to jump out of the frying pan into the fire** = to go from one difficult situation to sth worse.

fuchsia ['fjuːʃə] n. garden plant with colourful hanging flowers.

fuddle ['fʌdl] v. to make (s.o.) feel hazy and confused.

fuddy-duddy ['fʌdɪdʌdɪ] n. inf. old-fashioned person.

fudge [fʌdʒ] **1.** n. soft sweet made from butter, sugar and milk. **2.** v. **to f. the issue** = to avoid making a decision on an issue.

fuel ['fjʊəl] **1.** n. substance (coal/gas/oil/wood, etc.) which can be burnt to give heat/power; **to add f. to the flames** = to make matters worse. **2.** v. (**fuelled**) to provide fuel for.

fug [fʌg] n. inf. stuffy/hot atmosphere. **fugginess,** n. being fuggy. **fuggy,** adj. stuffy/hot.

fugitive ['fjuːdʒətɪv] n. & adj. (person) who is running away.

fugue [fjuːg] n. piece of music where a tune is repeated in several patterns.

fulcrum ['fʊlkrəm] n. point on which a lever rests/on which a seesaw balances.

fulfil [fʊl'fɪl] v. (**fulfilled**) to complete (sth) satisfactorily. **fulfilment,** n. satisfactory ending.

full [fʊl] **1.** adj. (-er, -est) (a) containing as much as possible; **f. up** = with no more room; **I'm f. (up)** = I have eaten as much as I can; **f. skirt** = wide skirt made from lots of material. (b) all; as many (as possible). (c) complete; **f. stop** = dot (.) at the end of a sentence. (d) round and plump (face); **f. moon** = moon when completely round. **2.** n. **in f.** = completely/entirely; **to the f.** = completely. **full back,** n. (in games) defensive player near the goal. **fullblooded,** adj. (a) vigorous (argument). (b) (of horses) strongly typical. **full-blown,** adj. (a) (of a flower) wide open. (b) **he is a full-blown doctor** = he has passed all his examinations and is qualified. **full-grown,** adj. adult. **full-length,** adj. (a) from head to toe. (b) long (story/film). **fullness,** n. (a) state of containing as much as possible. (b) state when all is completed; **in the f. of time** = eventually/in the end. **full-scale,** adj. complete/total. **full time,** n. end of a sports match. **full-time,** adj. & adv. all the time. **fully,** adv. completely/entirely. **fully-fledged,** adj. experienced/qualified.

fulmar ['fʊlmɑː] n. grey and white northern seabird.

fulminate ['fʌlmɪneɪt] v. (formal) to protest angrily. **fulminations** [fʌlmɪ-'neɪʃnz] n. pl. angry protests.

fulsome ['fʊlsəm] adj. excessive/too much.

fumarole ['fjuːmərəʊl] n. hole in the side of a volcano through which smoke escapes.

fumble ['fʌmbl] v. (**with**) to touch/to feel clumsily. **fumbling,** adj. clumsy.

fume [fjuːm] **1.** n. pl. **fumes** = smoke/gas. **2.** v. to be angry.

fumigate ['fjuːmɪgeɪt] v. to clean (a room) by smoking out germs and insects. **fumigation** [fjuːmɪ'geɪʃn] n. smoking out germs/insects.

fun [fʌn] n. amusement/pleasure; **to make f. of/to poke f. at** = to laugh nastily at/to mock; **for f./in f.** = not seriously/as a joke. **funfair,** n. group of amusements, sideshows, etc., collected together.

function ['fʌŋkʃn] **1.** n. (a) job/duty. (b) gathering of people; party. **2.** v. (a) to work. (b) to serve (**as**). **functional,** adj. useful but not decorative. **functionally,** adv. in a functional way. **functionary,** n. official. **function key,** n. key on a computer keyboard which activates a set of instructions.

fund [fʌnd] **1.** n. (a) sum of money set aside for a special purpose. (b) collection. **2.** v. to provide money for (a special purpose).

fundamental [fʌndə'mentl] adj. basic/essential. **fundamentally,** adv. basically.

funeral ['fjuːnərəl] n. ceremony where a dead person is buried/cremated. **funerary,** adj. used in a funeral. **funereal** [fjuː'nɪərɪəl] adj. sad and gloomy.

fungus ['fʌŋgəs] n. (pl. **fungi** ['fʌŋgaɪ]) plant which has no green leaves or flowers and which frequently lives on other plants. **fungicide** ['fʌndʒɪsaɪd] n. chemical which kills fungus. **fungicidal,** adj. which kills fungus. **fungoid,** adj. like a fungus.

funicular [fə'nɪkjʊlə] n. **f. (railway)** = railway where cars held by cables travel up a slope.

funk [fʌŋk] **1.** n. inf. fear; **to be in a blue f.** = to be terrified. **2.** v. inf. to be afraid to do sth.

funnel ['fʌnl] **1.** n. (a) tube with a wide mouth and narrow bottom used when pouring liquids from one container into another. (b) chimney on a ship from which the smoke comes. **2. (funnelled)** v. to pass through a funnel/through a narrow space.

funny ['fʌnɪ] adj. (a) which makes people laugh. (b) odd/unusual; **I feel f.** = I feel ill. **funnily,** adv. oddly. **funny bone,** n. inf. part of the elbow which hurts sharply if it is hit.

fur [fɜː] **1.** n. (a) soft coat of an animal. (b) deposit in kettles/water pipes, etc. **2.** v. **(furred)** to become covered with a deposit. **furry,** adj. covered with fur.

furbish ['fɜːbɪʃ] v. to polish/to clean.

furious ['fjʊərɪəs] adj. very angry. **furiously,** adv. in a furious way.

furl [fɜːl] v. to roll up and tie securely.

furlong ['fɜːlɒŋ] n. measure of length (= 220 yards).

furlough ['fɜːləʊ] n. leave of absence (esp. from the armed forces).

furnace ['fɜːnəs] n. (a) large brick or metal oven which can be heated to a very high temperature; **blast f.** = furnace where iron is heated until it melts. (b) heater which warms the water for central heating.

furnish ['fɜːnɪʃ] v. (a) to provide with chairs/tables, etc.; **furnished rooms/flat** = rented place where the furniture is provided by the owner. (b) to supply **(with). furnishings,** n. pl. fittings in a house; **soft f.** = curtains, cushions, etc.

furniture ['fɜːnɪtʃə] n. (no pl.) tables/chairs/cupboards/beds, etc.; **a piece of f.** = one article of furniture.

furore, Am. **furor** [fjʊə'rɔːrɪ, fjuː'rɔː] n. outburst of anger/excitement.

furrier ['fʌrɪə] n. person who sells fur coats, etc.

furrow ['fʌrəʊ] **1.** n. long groove cut in the earth by a plough. **2.** v. to make furrows in (the land, etc.).

further ['fɜːðə] **1.** adv. & adj. (a) farther/to a greater distance/more distant. (b) additional; **College of F. Education** = college for people who have left school. **2.** v. to advance (a plan). **furtherance,** n. advancing (of a plan). **furthermore** [fɜːðə'mɔː] adv. also/in addition. **furthermost** ['fɜːðəməʊst] adj. most distant. **furthest,** adj. & adv. to the greatest distance/most distant.

furtive ['fɜːtɪv] adj. secret; as if hiding something. **furtively,** adv. in a furtive way. **furtiveness,** n. being furtive.

fury ['fjʊərɪ] n. fierce anger.

furze [fɜːz] n. gorse.

fuse [fjuːz] **1.** n. (a) length of string attached to a bomb which burns slowly when lit. (b) small piece of wire in an electrical circuit which melts and breaks if the circuit is overloaded, and so prevents further damage; **to blow a f.** = to overload the electric circuit and make the fuse break. **2.** v. (a) to break the electrical circuit. (b) **to f. together** = to join together (wires/companies), etc.). **fusebox,** n. box where the fuses are kept. **fusewire,** n. fine wire for putting into fuses.

fuselage ['fjuːzəlɑːʒ] n. body of an aircraft.

fusilier [fjuːzə'lɪə] n. rifleman in the army.

fusillade [fjuːzɪ'leɪd] n. rapid gunfire.

fusion ['fjuːʒn] n. (a) melting together of two pieces of metal. (b) joining together of two different things.

fuss [fʌs] **1.** n. agitated complaints about little things that do not matter; **to make a f. about sth** = to complain at length about sth unimportant; **to make a f. of s.o.** = to pay great attention to s.o. **2.** v. to be agitated; to show unnecessary care and attention (over little things). **fussily,** adv. in a fussy way. **fussiness,** n. being fussy. **fussy,** adj. (a) unnecessarily careful and demanding about little things. (b) disliking lots of things.

fusty ['fʌstɪ] *adj.* smelling of dampness. **fustiness**, *n.* being fusty.

futile ['fjuːtaɪl, *Am.* 'fjuːtl] *adj.* useless. **futility** [fjuː'tɪlɪtɪ] *n.* uselessness.

future ['fjuːtʃə] **1.** *n.* time which has not yet happened; **in f.** = from now on. **2.** *adj.* coming/not yet happened. **futures**, *n.* trade in something, such as foreign currency or commodities, for delivery at a later date. **futuristic** [fjuːtʃə'rɪstɪk] *adj.* oddly modern (art).

fuzz [fʌz] *n.* (*a*) fluffy hair. (*b*) *Sl.* **the f.** = the police. **fuzziness**, *n.* being fuzzy. **fuzzy**, *adj.* (*a*) fluffy and curly. (*b*) not clear/blurred.

Gg

g *abbrev. for* gram.

gab [gæb] *n. inf.* talk/chat; **the gift of the g.** = talent for speaking.

gabardine ['gæbədiːn] *n.* closely woven cotton material, used for making raincoats.

gabble ['gæbl] **1.** *n.* loud, unintelligible talk. **2.** *v.* to speak very quickly.

gable ['geɪbl] *n.* triangular upper part of a wall at the end of a roof. **gabled**, *adj.* with gables.

gad [gæd] *v.* (**gadded**) **to g. about** = to be constantly out and about. **gadabout**, *n.* person who is always out and about. **gadfly**, *n.* fly which attacks cows; irritating person.

gadget ['gædʒɪt] *n.* useful machine/tool. **gadgetry**, *n.* lots of gadgets.

Gaelic ['geɪlɪk, *in Scotland* 'gælɪk] *n.* language of Scots, Manx and Irish Celts.

gaff [gæf] **1.** *n.* stick with iron hook for catching large fish; *inf.* **to blow the g.** = to let out a secret. **2.** *v.* to catch with a gaff.

gaffe [gæf] *n.* blunder; indiscreet act or remark.

gaffer ['gæfə] *n. inf.* (*a*) old man. (*b*) boss.

gag [gæg] **1.** *n.* (*a*) soft object put into or tied round the mouth to stop s.o. speaking. (*b*) joke. **2.** *v.* (**gagged**) (*a*) to bind (s.o.) round the mouth; **to g. the press** = to impose censorship. (*b*) to retch/to choke.

gaga ['gaːgaː] *adj. inf.* senile/stupid.

gaggle ['gægl] *n.* flock (of geese).

gaiety ['geɪətɪ] *n.* happiness/cheerfulness. **gaily** ['geɪlɪ] *adv.* happily.

gain [geɪn] **1.** *n.* increase of possessions; profit. **2.** *v.* (*a*) to obtain/to get; **to g. the upper hand** = to get control. (*b*) **the clock gains five minutes a day** = it moves five minutes ahead of the correct time in every twenty-four hours. (*c*) **to g. on s.o./sth** = to get closer to a person or thing you are chasing. **gainful**, *adj.* which earns money; **gainful employment**. **gainfully**, *adv.* **g. employed** = doing work which earns money.

gainsay [geɪn'seɪ] *v.* (**gainsaid**) (*formal*) to deny (sth).

gait [geɪt] *n.* manner of walking.

gaiter ['geɪtə] *n.* covering of cloth or leather worn over the leg below the knee.

gal. *abbrev. for* gallon.

gala ['gaːlə] *n.* festive occasion; **swimming g.** = swimming competition.

galaxy ['gæləksɪ] *n.* collection of stars, found singly and in groups and clusters. **galactic** [gə'læktɪk] *adj.* belonging to a galaxy.

gale [geɪl] *n.* very strong wind.

galena [gə'liːnə] *n.* natural form of lead sulphide.

gall [gɔːl] **1.** *n.* (*a*) bile/bitter liquid produced by the liver to digest fat. (*b*) growth produced by insects on trees, esp. the oak. (*c*) painful swelling/blister (esp. on horses). (*d*) *inf.* rudeness/impudence. **2.** *v.* to annoy/to humiliate. **galling**, *adj.* humiliating; annoying. **gall-bladder**, *n.* bag in the body where bile is stored. **gallstone**, *n.* small stone-like substance which sometimes forms in the gall-bladder.

gallant ['gælənt] *adj.* (*a*) brave/chivalrous. (*b*) very polite towards women. **gallantly**, *adv.* in a gallant way. **gallantry** ['gæləntrɪ] *n.* bravery.

galleon ['gælɪən] *n.* large Spanish warship in the 16th century.

gallery ['gælərɪ] *n.* (*a*) room in which pictures are hung. (*b*) art museum. (*c*) shop selling pictures/antiques, etc. (*d*) (*in a church/hall, etc.*) balcony which runs around part of the main hall; (*in a theatre/cinema*) highest rows of seats; **to play to the g.** = to appeal to people who have no taste; **minstrels' g.** = balcony above the end of a castle dining hall from where musicians entertained the diners. (*d*) **shooting g.** = long, narrow room at one end of which is a target for shooting.

galley ['gælɪ] *n.* (*a*) low, flat, single-decked ship, rowed by slaves. (*b*) ship's kitchen. (*c*) (*in printing*) rectangular tray which holds type. **galley proof,** *n.* proof printed on long sheets of paper.

Gallic ['gælɪk] *adj.* French. **gallicism** ['gælɪsɪzəm] *n.* French word or phrase adopted into another language.

gallivant ['gælɪvænt] *v. inf.* to be always out and about looking for amusement.

gallon ['gælən] *n.* liquid measure equal to 4 quarts or 4.5 litres.

gallop ['gæləp] **1.** *n.* (*a*) fastest pace of a horse running with all feet off the ground in each stride. (*b*) fast ride on a horse. **2.** *v.* to run/to go fast; **he galloped through his speech** = spoke it very fast; **galloping inflation** = rapidly rising inflation.

gallows ['gæləuz] *n.* structure on which criminals are hanged.

Gallup poll ['gæləp'pəul] *n.* test of public opinion on an important topic, esp. of how a representative sample of the public will vote, in order to forecast an election result.

galore [gə'lɔ:] *adv.* (*always after the noun*) plenty; **apples g.**

galoshes [gə'lɒʃɪz] *n. pl.* plastic/rubber shoes worn over other shoes to protect them.

galumph [gə'lʌmf] *v. inf.* to walk about heavily.

galvanize ['gælvənaɪz] *v.* (*a*) **galvanized iron** = iron coated with zinc to protect it from rust. (*b*) to rouse by shock. **galvanization** [gælvənaɪ-'zeɪʃn] *n.* process of galvanizing. **galvanometer** [gælvə'nɒmɪtə] *n.* instrument for measuring small electric currents.

gambit ['gæmbɪt] *n.* (*a*) (*in chess*) opening move whereby a player sacrifices a minor piece in order to take a major one later. (*b*) opening move in some action.

gamble ['gæmbl] **1.** *n.* risk taken in the hope of getting good results. **it's**

a bit of a g. = you can't be sure it will succeed. **2.** *v.* to risk (money) on cards or sporting results; **to g. on sth happening** = to act in the hope that it will happen. **gambler,** *n.* person who gambles. **gambling,** *n.* risking money; betting on sth.

gambol ['gæmbl] *v.* (**gambolled**) to frisk about like a lamb.

game [geɪm] **1.** *n.* (*a*) contest played according to rules and decided by skill, strength or luck; **a g. of tennis/chess; to play the g.** = to act honourably; **the g.'s up** = we have been found out; **so that's his little g.** = now we know what his plans are. (*b*) (*in tennis/bridge, etc.*) single round. (*c*) wild animals and birds (deer, rabbits, pheasants, etc.) hunted for sport or food; **g. soup** = soup made from game; **big g.** = large wild animals (lions/elephants, etc.) shot for sport. **2.** *adj.* (*a*) willing/courageous. (*b*) lame (leg). **gamekeeper,** *n.* person employed to breed and look after game. **gamely,** *adv.* bravely. **gameness,** *n.* being game. **gamesmanship,** *n.* (*no pl.*) the art of winning by devious means, such as distracting your opponent. **gaming,** *n.* gambling.

gamete ['gæmi:t] *n.* plant or animal cell which can link with another to reproduce.

gamma ['gæmə] *n.* third letter of the Greek alphabet. **gamma globulin,** *n.* protein found in blood plasma. **gamma rays** *n. pl.* rays of short wavelength sent out by radioactive substances.

gammon ['gæmən] *n.* smoked or cured ham.

gammy ['gæmɪ] *adj. inf.* lame (leg).

gamut ['gæmət] *n.* (*a*) whole range of musical notes. (*b*) whole range or scope; **the whole g. of crime** = every type of crime imaginable.

gander ['gændə] *n.* male goose.

gang [gæŋ] **1.** *n.* band of people acting or going about together. **2.** *v.* **to g. up (with)** = to team up with; **to g. up on (s.o.)** = to take sides with one or more people against s.o. **gangland,** *n.* all gangs. **gangplank,** *n.* long piece of wood giving access to a boat from the shore. **gangster,** *n.* member of a gang of violent criminals. **gangway,** *n.* (*a*) (*in a theatre/cinema, etc.*) passage between rows of seats. (*b*) bridge from the shore to a ship.

gangling ['gæŋglɪŋ] *adj.* tall (person) with long arms and legs.

ganglion ['gæŋglɪən] *n.* (*a*) nucleus of nerves in the central nervous system. (*b*) small lump on a tendon.

gangrene ['gæŋgriːn] *n.* rotting of body tissue, caused by a blockage of the blood supply. **gangrenous** ['gæŋgrɪnəs] *adj.* affected by gangrene.

gannet ['gænɪt] *n.* large white sea bird.

gantry ['gæntrɪ] *n.* metal bridge for carrying lights/a crane, etc.

gaol [dʒeɪl] **1.** *n.* prison. **2.** *v.* to put (s.o.) in prison. **gaolbird,** *n.* person who has been sent to prison often. **gaoler,** *n.* person in charge of the prisoners in a gaol.

gap [gæp] *n.* (*a*) space/hole in a hedge/wall, etc. (*b*) gorge or pass (between mountains). (*c*) space/difference; **age g.** = difference in age; **generation g.** = difference in years between one generation and another, often resulting in intolerance between them.

gape [geɪp] *v.* to open your mouth wide. **gaping,** *adj.* wide open.

garage ['gærɪdʒ, 'gæraːʒ] **1.** *n.* (*a*) building for storing motor vehicles; **g. sale** = private sale of unwanted household goods (held in the garage of a house). (*b*) petrol station/place where motor vehicles are repaired. **2.** *v.* to put (a vehicle) into a garage.

garb [gaːb] *n.* (*no pl.*) (*formal*) clothing. **garbed,** *adj.* dressed (**in**).

garbage ['gaːbɪdʒ] *n.* refuse/rubbish; *Am.* **g. can** = dustbin.

garble ['gaːbl] *v.* to select certain items from speeches in order to give an unfair or malicious representation; to distort/confuse.

Garda ['gaːdə] *n.* (*pl.* **-ai**) (*in Republic of Ireland*) police.

garden ['gaːdn] **1.** *n.* piece of ground used for growing flowers, fruit, or vegetables; **g. centre** = place where plants, seeds and garden tools are sold; **g. of remembrance** = garden dedicated to the memory of the dead. **2.** *v.* to look after a garden. **gardener,** *n.* person who looks after a garden. **gardening,** *n.* looking after a garden.

gardenia [gaː'diːnɪə] *n.* shrub with fragrant white or yellow flowers.

gargantuan [gaː'gæntjʊən] *adj.* huge/enormous.

gargle ['gaːgl] **1.** *n.* antiseptic liquid used for washing the throat. **2.** *v.* to wash the throat by holding antiseptic liquid in it and breathing out at the same time.

gargoyle ['gaːgɔɪl] *n.* water spout on a medieval building, carved like a grotesque head.

garish ['geərɪʃ] *adj.* bright/showy/over-decorated. **garishly,** *adv.* very brightly.

garland ['gaːlənd] **1.** *n.* (*a*) circle of flowers or leaves worn as a decoration. (*b*) decoration made of linked paper/ribbon, etc. **2.** *v.* to hang with garlands.

garlic ['gaːlɪk] *n.* plant whose bulb has a strong smell and taste, used as a flavouring. **garlicky,** *adj.* tasting/smelling of garlic.

garment ['gaːmənt] *n.* article of clothing.

garner ['gaːnə] *v.* (*formal*) to collect and store.

garnet ['gaːnɪt] *n.* semi-precious dark red stone.

garnish ['gaːnɪʃ] **1.** *n.* thing used to decorate food. **2.** *v.* to decorate (esp. food).

garret ['gærət] *n.* attic room immediately under the roof of a house.

garrison ['gærɪsn] **1.** *n.* (*a*) troops stationed in a fortress/town, etc., in order to defend it. (*b*) fortress. **2.** *v.* to place troops on garrison duty in (a town).

garrotte [gə'rɒt] *v.* to strangle (s.o.) with a cord.

garrulous ['gærjʊləs] *adj.* talkative. **garrulously,** *adv.* in a garrulous way. **garrulousness, garrulity** [gæ'ruːlɪtɪ] *n.* being garrulous.

garter ['gaːtə] *n.* band worn above or below the knee to keep a stocking or sock up; **Order of the Garter** = highest order of English knighthood.

gas [gæs] **1.** *n.* (*a*) chemical substance like air, which is completely fluid and has no definite shape or volume. (*b*) substance, produced from coal or extracted naturally from the ground, which is used for cooking or heating; **to cook by g.; g. cooker** = cooker which uses gas;

natural g. = gas which is extracted from the earth. (*c*) substance used to make you unconscious while having a tooth removed, etc. (*d*) *Am.* petrol; *inf.* **to step on the g.** = to accelerate. (*e*) *inf.* unimportant talk. **2.** *v.* (**gassed**) (*a*) to poison (s.o.) by making them breathe gas. (*b*) *inf.* to talk about nothing in particular. **gaseous** ['gæsjəs] *adj.* referring to gas. **gasholder,** *n.* gasometer. **gasmask,** *n.* mask used as protection against poison gases. **gasoline,** *n. Am.* petrol. **gasometer** [gæ'sɒmɪtə] *n.* large container in which gas is stored. **gas station,** *n. Am.* place where you can buy petrol. **gassy,** *adj.* full of gas/full of bubbles. **gasworks,** *n.* place where gas is manufactured.

gash [gæʃ] **1.** *n.* long deep cut/wound. **2.** *v.* to make a gash.

gasket ['gæskɪt] *n.* piece of thin material used to seal two parts of an engine to prevent air/gas, etc., from escaping.

gasp [gɑːsp] **1.** *n.* sharp intake of breath. **2.** *v.* to struggle to breathe/to catch your breath in surprise.

gasteropod ['gæstərəpɒd] *n.* type of mollusc, like a snail or limpet.

gastric ['gæstrɪk] *adj.* referring to the stomach; **g. flu** = infection of the stomach. **gastrectomy,** *n.* operation to remove the stomach. **gastroenteritis** [gæstrəʊentə'raɪtɪs] *n.* illness of the stomach and intestines. **gastronome** ['gæstrənəʊm] *n.* expert on food and drink. **gastronomic** [gæstrə'nɒmɪk] *adj.* referring to food and drink. **gastronomy** [gæs'trɒnəmɪ] *n.* art of cooking.

gate [geɪt] *n.* (*a*) barrier, usu. made of wood or iron, closing an opening in a wall/fence, etc. (*b*) number of people who watch a football match/sports competition; money paid by spectators at a football match, etc. **gatecrash,** *v.* to go uninvited to (a party). **gatecrasher,** *n.* uninvited guest. **gated,** *adj.* (road) with gates. **gate-legged table,** *n.* table with hinged legs which fold like a gate. **gatepost,** *n.* post to which a gate is attached by hinges. **gateway,** *n.* gap in a wall/fence, etc., where a gate can be fitted.

gateau ['gætəʊ] *n.* (*pl.* **gateaux** ['gætəʊz]) large decorated cream cake.

gather ['gæðə] *v.* (*a*) to bring together/to collect. (*b*) to gain (speed). (*c*) to understand; **I g. that you are coming.** (*d*) to pull (material) into folds by means of tiny stitches. **gathering. 1.** *n.* (*a*) group of people who have come together. (*b*) swelling with pus. **2.** *adj.* imminent; **a g. storm. gather up,** *v.* to bring (things) together and pick them up.

gauche [gəʊʃ] *adj.* clumsy/tactless.

gaucho ['gaʊtʃəʊ] *n.* South American herdsman.

gaudy ['gɔːdɪ] *adj.* (**-ier, -iest**) too brightly coloured; showy; lacking in taste. **gaudily,** *adv.* showily. **gaudiness,** *n.* being gaudy.

gauge [geɪdʒ] **1.** *n.* (*a*) standard measure of width/thickness, etc. (*b*) distance between rails on a railway line. (*c*) instrument measuring depth/pressure, etc. **2.** *v.* (*a*) to measure exactly. (*b*) to estimate/to guess.

gaunt [gɔːnt] *adj.* lean/haggard. **gauntness,** *n.* being gaunt.

gauntlet ['gɔːntlət] *n.* strong glove with long wrist cover, for driving, fencing, etc.; **to fling/throw down the g.** = to issue a challenge; **to run the g.** = to go through a dangerous area.

gauss [gaʊs] *n.* unit for measuring the strength of a magnetic field.

gauze [gɔːz] *n.* thin/transparent material. **gauzy,** *adj.* thin (material).

gave [geɪv] *v. see* **give.**

gavel ['gævl] *n.* auctioneer's or chairman's hammer.

gawky ['gɔːkɪ] *adj.* (**-ier, -iest**) awkward/ungainly. **gawkiness,** *n.* being gawky.

gawp [gɔːp] *v. inf.* to stare rudely (**at**).

gay [geɪ] **1.** *adj.* (**-er, -est**) happy; full of fun. **2.** *adj. & n. inf.* homosexual. **gayness,** *n.* being gay.

gaze [geɪz] **1.** *n.* intent look. **2.** *v.* to look steadily for a long time.

gazebo [gə'ziːbəʊ] *n.* small summerhouse.

gazelle [gə'zel] *n.* kind of antelope.

gazette [gə'zet] *n.* official newspaper, giving details of public appointments, etc. **gazetteer** [gæzə'tɪə] *n.* geographical dictionary.

gazump [gə'zʌmp] *v.* **to g. s.o.** = to accept a higher price for a house which s.o. has already agreed to buy.

GBH [dʒiːbiːˈeɪtʃ] Grievous Bodily Harm.

GDP [dʒiːdiːˈpiː] gross domestic product.

gear [gɪə] **1.** *n.* (*a*) equipment; **landing g.** = undercarriage of an aircraft. (*b*) *inf.* clothing. (*c*) **gears** = arrangement of toothed wheels, levers, etc., connecting an engine/pedals, etc., with wheels; **in g.** = with the gears connected. **2.** *v.* **to g. sth to** = to fit/to match. **gearbox**, *n.* casing for gears in cars. **gearing**, *n.* ratio of debt to assets. **gearlever**, **gearstick**, *Am.* **gearshift**, *n.* handle by which the gears are changed in a car. **gearwheel**, *n.* toothed wheel connecting with another wheel of different diameter to change the power ratio of the engine.

gecko [ˈgekəʊ] *n.* (*pl.* **-os**) small tropical lizard.

gee [dʒiː] *inter. showing surprise.*

gee-gee [ˈdʒiːdʒiː] *n.* child's name for a horse.

geese [giːs] *n. pl. see* **goose**.

gee-up [ˈdʒiːʌp] *inter. used* to tell a horse to go faster.

geezer [ˈgiːzə] *n. Sl.* (old) man.

Geiger counter [ˈgaɪgəkaʊntə] *n.* device for detecting and recording radioactivity.

geisha [ˈgeɪʃə] *n.* Japanese hostess and dancing girl.

gel [dʒel] *n.* substance like a jelly. **gelatin(e)** [ˈdʒelətiːn] *n.* substance obtained after stewing skin, bones, etc., and used to make jellies. **gelatinous** [dʒəˈlætɪnəs] *adj.* like jelly.

geld [geld] *v.* to castrate.

gelding [ˈgeldɪŋ] *n.* castrated animal, esp. horse.

gelignite [ˈdʒelɪgnaɪt] *n.* nitroglycerine explosive.

gem [dʒem] *n.* precious stone. **gemmology** [dʒeˈmɒlədʒɪ] *n.* the science of gems.

Gemini [ˈdʒemɪnaɪ] *n.* one of the signs of the zodiac, shaped like twins.

gen [dʒen] *n. Sl.* information.

gender [ˈdʒendə] *n.* grammatical classification of objects roughly corresponding to the two sexes and absence of sex.

gene [dʒiːn] *n.* part of a chromosome which carries characteristics transmitted by the parent.

genealogical [dʒiːnɪəˈlɒdʒɪkl] *adj.* referring to genealogy. **genealogist** [dʒiːnɪˈælədʒɪst] *n.* person who studies genealogy. **genealogy**, *n.* study of family descent through the generations.

genera [ˈdʒenərə] *n. see* **genus**.

general [ˈdʒenrəl] **1.** *adj.* completely or approximately universal; including or affecting all or nearly all parts; **g. anaesthetic** = anaesthetic which makes the patient lose consciousness; **g. election** = election in which the whole country is involved; **in g.** = as a rule. **2.** *n.* superior officer immediately below a field marshal in the army. **generalissimo** [dʒenrəˈlɪsɪməʊ] *n.* commander-in-chief of several armed forces. **generality** [dʒenəˈrælɪtɪ] *n.* being general; **generalities** = general subjects (for a conversation). **generalization** [dʒenrəlaɪˈzeɪʃn] *n.* general statement. **generalize** [ˈdʒenrəlaɪz] *v.* to try to express sth as a general notion. **generally** [ˈdʒenrəlɪ] *adv.* as a rule. **general practitioner**, *n.* doctor who treats all illnesses/family doctor. **general-purpose**, *adj.* serving many purposes.

generate [ˈdʒenəreɪt] *v.* to bring into existence; to produce. **generation** [dʒenəˈreɪʃn] *n.* (*a*) bringing into existence. (*b*) all people born about the same time; **g. gap** = age difference between one generation and another, often resulting in intolerance between them. (*c*) period of years separating parents and children. (*d*) members of a family born about the same time. **generator** [ˈdʒenəreɪtə] *n.* apparatus for producing electricity by gas/petrol, etc.

generic [dʒəˈnerɪk] *adj.* referring to a genus/group/type. **generically**, *adv.* in a generic way.

generous [ˈdʒenərəs] *adj.* (*a*) **g. with sth** = willing to give sth. (*b*) large; **a g. helping. generosity** [dʒenəˈrɒsɪtɪ] *n.* willingness to give (money, etc.). **generously**, *adv.* in a generous way.

genesis [ˈdʒenəsɪs] *n.* origin/beginning.

genetics [dʒəˈnetɪks] *n.* study of heredity. **genetic**, *adj.* referring to genes/to genetics. **genetically**, *adv.* in a genetic way.

genial ['dʒi:nɪəl] *adj.* cheerful/kindly. **genially,** *adv.* cheerfully.

genie ['dʒi:nɪ:] *n.* in the Arabian Nights, a magic slave who appears from a bottle or lamp.

genital ['dʒenɪtl] **1.** *adj.* referring to the sex organs. **2.** *n.pl.* **genitals** = external sex organs.

genitive ['dʒenɪtɪv] *adj. & n.* (*in grammar*) **g. (case)** = form of a word showing possession.

genius ['dʒi:nɪəs] *n.* (*pl.* **-es**) (*a*) person with very great intelligence. (*b*) very great intelligence. (*c*) **evil g.** = bad spirit/person with a bad influence. (*d*) **g. for** = ability to do sth easily.

genocide ['dʒenəsaɪd] *n.* mass killing of a race.

genre ['ʒɑ:nrə] *n.* particular type (of art, etc.).

gent [dʒent] *n. inf.* gentleman. **gents,** *n. inf.* men's toilet.

genteel [dʒen'ti:l] *adj.* too refined. **genteelly,** *adv.* in a genteel way. **gentility** [dʒen'tɪlɪtɪ] *n.* refinement (of manners).

gentian ['dʒenʃn] *n.* small blue alpine flower.

gentile ['dʒentaɪl] *n.* person not of Jewish race.

gentle ['dʒentl] *adj.* (**-er, -est**) mild/tender/soft. **gentlefolk,** *n. pl.* (*old*) people of good breeding. **gentleman** ['dʒentlmən] *n.* (*pl.* **-men**) (*a*) man of good breeding and manners; **g.'s agreement** = agreement which is not written down. (*b*) (*polite way of referring to men*) **Well, gentlemen, shall we begin?** **gentlemanly,** *adj.* like a gentleman. **gentleness,** *n.* softness/carefulness. **gently** ['dʒentlɪ] *adv.* softly/carefully; **g. does it!** = be careful as you do it.

gentry ['dʒentrɪ] *n.* people of high class in society, below the aristocracy.

genuflect ['dʒenjuflekt] *v.* to bend the knee, esp. in worship. **genuflexion,** *n.* bending the knee.

genuine ['dʒenjuɪn] *adj.* authentic/true. **genuinely,** *adv.* truly. **genuineness,** *n.* being genuine.

genus ['dʒi:nəs] *n.* (*pl.* **genera** ['dʒenərə]) group of animals/plants which have common characteristics, and are distinct from all other groups.

geocentric [dʒi:əʊ'sentrɪk] *adj.* (astronomy, etc.) using the earth as the starting point when measuring distances.

geodesy [dʒi:'ɒdɪsɪ] *n.* science of measurement of the earth. **geodesic** [dʒi:əʊ'di:sɪk] *adj.* referring to geodesy; **g. dome** = dome made of set of polygons.

geography [dʒi'ɒgrəfɪ] *n.* science of the earth's surface/form/physical features/climate, etc. **geographer** [dʒi'ɒgrəfə] *n.* person who studies geography. **geographic(al)** [dʒiə'græfɪk(l)] *adj.* referring to geography. **geographically,** *adv.* in a geographical way.

geology [dʒi'ɒlədʒɪ] *n.* science of the earth's crust, esp. rock formations. **geological** [dʒiə'lɒdʒɪkl] *adj.* referring to geology. **geologically.** *adv.* in a geological way. **geologist** [dʒi'ɒlədʒɪst] *n.* person who studies geology.

geometry [dʒi'ɒmətrɪ] *n.* mathematical science of properties and relations of lines/surfaces/solids, etc., in space. **geometric(al)** [dʒiə'metrɪk(l)] *adj.* referring to geometry; **a g. design** = design of lines/curves, etc. **geometrically,** *adv.* in a geometrical way.

geophysics [dʒi:əʊ'fɪzɪks] *n.* study of the physical properties of the earth. **geophysicist,** *n.* person who studies geophysics.

Geordie ['dʒɔ:dɪ] *adj. & n.* (person) from Newcastle.

georgette [dʒɔ:'dʒet] *n.* thin silk cloth.

Georgian ['dʒɔ:dʒɪən] *adj.* referring to the reigns of George I to IV (1714–1830).

geostationary orbit [dʒi:əʊ'steɪʃənrɪ 'ɔ:bɪt] *n.* orbit of a satellite which remains over the same point on the earth's surface.

geothermal [dʒi:əʊ'θɜ:məl] *adj.* (energy) derived from the earth's heat.

geranium [dʒə'reɪnɪəm] *n.* perennial plant with white, pink or red flowers.

gerbil ['dʒɜ:bl] *n.* small desert rat which jumps, kept as a pet.

geriatrics [dʒerɪ'ætrɪks] *n.* branch of medical science dealing with old age and its diseases. **geriatric,** *adj.* for old people. **geriatrician** [dʒerɪə'trɪʃn] *n.* doctor specializing in geriatrics.

germ [dʒɜːm] n. (a) portion of organism capable of developing into a new one; **wheat g.** (b) micro-organism, often causing disease. **germicidal,** adj. which kills germs. **germicide,** n. substance which kills germs. **germ warfare,** n. war fought using germs as a weapon.

German ['dʒɜːmən] adj. referring to Germany; **G. measles** = mild disease which gives a red rash and which can affect the development of an unborn child if caught by a pregnant woman; Am. **G. shepherd** = alsatian dog. 2. n. (a) person from Germany. (b) language spoken in Germany, Austria and parts of Switzerland. **Germanic** [dʒɜː'mænɪk] adj. referring to the Germans. **Germano,** prefix meaning between Germany and another country.

germane [dʒɜː'meɪn] adj. relevant.

germinate ['dʒɜːmɪneɪt] v. (of seeds) to begin to grow/to sprout. **germination** [dʒɜːmɪ'neɪʃn] n. beginning of plant growth from a seed.

gerontology [dʒerɒn'tɒlədʒɪ] n. scientific study of old age and its problems.

gerrymander ['dʒerɪmændə] v. to alter the boundaries of constituencies to improve the chances of a political party in an election.

gerund ['dʒerʌnd] n. noun formed from the -ing form of a verb.

gestation [dʒe'steɪʃn] n. period between conception and birth.

gesticulate [dʒe'stɪkjuleɪt] v. to make expressive signs with the hands and arms. **gesticulation** [dʒestɪkju'leɪʃn] n. sign with arms or hands.

gesture ['dʒestʃə] 1. n. (a) movement of limb or body, esp. hands, to give an expression of feeling. (b) action which expresses some positive feeling; **token g.** = small action which symbolizes feelings. 2. v. to make a movement to express a feeling.

get [get] v. (got; has got; Am. has gotten) (a) to obtain. (b) to receive. (c) **to have got** = to possess. (d) inf. to understand; **you've got it!** = you've found the right answer/you understand correctly. (e) to cause to happen; to make (s.o.) do sth; **he got his shoes mended; she got the policeman to show her the way.** (f) **to have got to** = to be obliged to. (g) **to g.**

to = to arrive at. (h) inf. to start; **let's get going** = let's start now. (i) to catch (a disease). (j) to become; **he's getting too old for the job.** (k) to be doing sth; **she's getting dressed. get about,** v. (a) to go from place to place. (b) to be rumoured. **get across,** v. (a) to cross (a road). (b) to make (sth) understood. **get along,** v. (a) to manage. (b) inf. **get along with you!** = I don't believe you. (c) to be on friendly terms (with s.o.). **get at,** v. (a) to reach. (b) inf. to criticize. **get-atable,** adj. inf. easy to reach. **get away,** v. to manage to go away; to escape; **he got away with it** = he wasn't found out. **getaway,** n. escape; **g. car** = car used to escape in. **get back,** v. (a) to return. (b) to recover (sth). (c) **to get your own back on s.o.** = to have your revenge. **get by,** v. (a) to pass. (b) inf. to manage. **get down,** v. (a) to descend. (b) to fetch down. (c) to depress; to make (s.o.) gloomy. (d) to make (sth) be written. (e) **to get down to some hard work** = to start to work hard. **get in,** v. (a) to go inside (a car, etc.). (b) to be elected. **get into,** v. (a) to go inside (a car, etc.). (b) **to get into a temper** = to become angry; **to get into trouble** = to be in a difficult situation. **get off,** v. (a) to come down from. (b) **he got off lightly** = he received a light punishment. **get on,** v. (a) to mount (a bicycle, etc.). (b) to age; **he is getting on** = he is past middle age. (c) to succeed. (d) **to get on with s.o.** = to be friendly with s.o.; **they don't get on (together)** = they don't like each other. **get out,** v. (a) to bring out/to go out; **get out!** = leave the room. (b) **I've got out of the habit of eating chocolates** = I don't eat chocolates any more. (c) **to get out of (doing) sth** = to avoid doing sth. **get over,** v. (a) to overcome (a difficulty). (b) to recover from (an illness). (c) to climb over. **get round,** v. (a) to go round (a corner). (b) to flatter (s.o.). (c) **to get r. to (doing) sth** = to find time to do (sth). **get through,** v. (a) to pass (a test). (b) **to get through to s.o.** = to manage to get in contact with s.o. (by telephone). **get-together,** n. inf. meeting. **get up,** v. (a) to rise (from sitting or lying position); to get out of bed. (b) to organize (a petition). (*c*) **to get up to** = to reach. (*d*) **to get up to mischief** = to do sth naughty. **get-up,** *n.* odd clothes.

geyser ['giːzə] *n.* (*a*) hot spring of water. (*b*) gas apparatus for heating water.

ghastly ['gɑːstlɪ] *adj.* (**-ier, -iest**) horrible/frightful. **ghastliness,** *n.* being ghastly.

gherkin ['gɜːkɪn] *n.* small vegetable of the cucumber family, used for pickling.

ghetto ['getəʊ] *n.* (*pl.* **-os**) area in a city where deprived people live.

ghost [gəʊst] **1.** *n.* (*a*) spirit of a dead person; **g. story** = story about ghosts which aims at frightening the reader. (*b*) **the Holy G.** = third person of the Christian Trinity. (*c*) ghost writer. (*d*) **a g. of a smile** = very slight smile. **2.** *v.* to write (book/article/speech, etc.) for s.o. else who then takes the credit. **ghostly,** *adj.* like a ghost. **ghost writer,** *n.* person who writes a book for s.o. else who then takes the credit.

ghoul [guːl] *n.* evil ghost which haunts graves. **ghoulish** ['guːlɪʃ] *adj.* weird/bloodthirsty.

giant ['dʒaɪənt] **1.** *n.* (*a*) (*in fairy tales and myths*) huge human being. (*b*) abnormally tall person, animal or plant. (*c*) very powerful industrial organization. (*d*) extremely able person. **2.** *adj.* very large. **giantess** [dʒaɪən'tes] *n.* (*pl.* **-es**) female giant.

gibber ['dʒɪbə] *v.* to speak very fast, without any meaning. **gibberish** ['dʒɪbrɪʃ] *n.* (*no pl.*) fast unintelligible speech.

gibbet ['dʒɪbɪt] *n.* gallows/structure on which criminals were hanged.

gibbon ['gɪbən] *n.* long-armed ape.

gibe [dʒaɪb] **1.** *n.* sarcastic remark. **2.** *v.* to jeer/to mock.

giblets ['dʒɪbləts] *n.pl.* liver/heart, etc., of poultry, removed before the bird is cooked.

giddy ['gɪdɪ] *adj.* (**-ier, -iest**) dizzy; feeling as if everything is spinning round. **giddily,** *adv.* in a giddy way. **giddiness,** *n.* dizzy feeling.

gift [gɪft] *n.* (*a*) present/thing given; **g. token** = card given as a present, which allows the person who receives it to buy sth at a shop. (*b*) talent; **she has a g. for music. gifted,** *adj.* talented. **gift-wrap,**

v. (**gift-wrapped**) to wrap (sth) in coloured paper to give as a present.

gig [gɪg] *n.* (*a*) light carriage on two wheels. (*b*) *inf.* performance by popular musicians.

giga- ['gɪgə] *prefix* one thousand million.

gigantic [dʒaɪ'gæntɪk] *adj.* huge/colossal.

giggle ['gɪgl] **1.** *n.* little nervous laugh; **to have a fit of the giggles** = to be unable to stop giggling. **2.** *v.* to laugh little nervous laughs.

gigolo ['dʒɪgpləʊ] *n.* (*pl.* **-os**) man who is paid by a woman to be her lover.

gild [gɪld] *v.* to cover with a thin layer of gold.

gill [dʒɪl] *n.* liquid measure equal to a quarter of a pint (140 ml).

gillie ['gɪlɪ] *n.* (*in Scotland*) man who helps a huntsman or fisherman.

gills [gɪlz] *n.pl.* (*a*) breathing organs in fish and other aquatic creatures. (*b*) thin vertical folds on the underside of mushrooms.

gilt [gɪlt] **1.** *adj.* covered with a thin layer of gold. **2.** *n.* (*a*) young female pig. (*b*) **gilts** = safe government bonds. **gilt-edged,** *adj.* (investment) which will not lose its value.

gimbals ['gɪmbəlz] *n. pl.* device (of several rings balanced inside each other) to keep a compass level at sea.

gimcrack ['dʒɪmkræk] *adj.* cheap and badly made.

gimlet ['gɪmlət] *n.* small tool used for boring holes.

gimmick ['gɪmɪk] *n.* device adopted for the purpose of attracting attention or publicity.

gin [dʒɪn] *n.* (*a*) colourless alcoholic drink flavoured with juniper; glass of this drink. (*b*) trap for catching wild animals and game. (*c*) machine for cleaning raw cotton.

ginger ['dʒɪndʒə] **1.** *n.* plant with a hot-tasting root used in cooking and medicine. **2.** *adj.* (hair) of reddish colour. **gingerbread,** *n.* cake made with treacle and flavoured with ginger. **ginger ale, ginger beer,** *n.* fizzy ginger-flavoured drink. **gingerly, 1.** *adj.* cautious. **2.** *adv.* delicately/with caution. **ginger up,** *v.* to stimulate/to arouse.

gingham ['gɪŋəm] *n.* checked cotton cloth.

gingivitis [dʒɪndʒɪ'vaɪtɪs] *n.* swelling and bleeding of the gums.

ginkgo ['gɪŋgəʊ] *n.* Chinese tree, which is similar to trees which flourished millions of years ago.

gipsy ['dʒɪpsɪ] *n.* member of a wandering race.

giraffe [dʒɪ'rɑ:f] *n.* African animal with a very long neck and spotted skin.

gird [gɜ:d] *v.* (*formal*) (**girded/girt**) to tie a belt round (sth).

girder ['gɜ:də] *n.* iron/steel beam used as a support.

girdle ['gɜ:dl] *n.* (*a*) belt/sash. (*c*) corset. (*c*) **pelvic g.** = bones around the hips supporting the lower limbs. (*d*) (*in N. of England & Scotland*) griddle.

girl [gɜ:l] *n.* female child; young woman. **girlfriend**, *n.* female companion (esp. of a man). **Girl Guides**, *n.pl.* social/training organization for girls. **girlhood**, *n.* period when you are a girl (before becoming a woman). **girlie**, *adj. inf.* **girlie magazine** = one with photographs of naked young women. **girlish**, *adj.* like a young girl.

giro ['dʒaɪrəʊ] *n.* (*a*) (*also* **National Girobank**) banking system in which money can be transferred directly from one account to another without writing a cheque. (*b*) payment made through the giro system.

girt [gɜ:t] *v. see* **gird**.

girth [gɜ:θ] *n.* (*a*) circumference/distance round sth. (*b*) band of leather or cloth tied round the body of a horse to secure the saddle.

gist [dʒɪst] *n.* real point of a matter; basic essentials.

give [gɪv] **1.** *v.* (**gave; has given**) (*a*) to hand (sth) **to** s.o.; to transfer (sth) **to** s.o. (*b*) to utter (a cry). (*c*) to collapse; to bend. **2.** *n.* (*a*) suppleness; **the plank hasn't enough g.** (*b*) **g. and take** = agreement between two people/parties to make concessions. **give away**, *v.* (*a*) to hand over (sth) without asking for anything in return. (*b*) to betray/to tell (a secret). (*c*) to give (a bride) to the bridegroom. **give back**, *v.* to return. **give in**, *v.* to surrender/to yield. **given**, *adj.* (*a*) **she is g. to crying** = she cries frequently. (*b*) particular/which has been identified. (*c*) **g. name** = first

name/Christian name. **give off**, *v.* to let out. **give out**, *v.* (*a*) to distribute. (*b*) *inf.* to fail. (*c*) to make known. **give over**, *v. inf.* to stop. **giver**, *n.* person who gives. **give up**, *v.* to stop (doing sth); **I give up!** = I cannot think of the answer; **the murderer gave himself up** = surrendered to the police. **give way**, *v.* (*a*) to allow s.o. to go first. (*b*) to yield; to bend; to collapse.

gizzard ['gɪzəd] *n.* second stomach of a bird, where its food is ground up into tiny pieces.

glabrous ['glæbrəs] *adj.* smooth, with no hair.

glacé ['glæseɪ] *adj.* (cherries) preserved in sugar.

glacier ['glæsɪə] *n.* mass of ice which moves slowly down from a mountain. **glacial** ['gleɪʃl] *adj.* (*a*) referring to ice. (*b*) very cold; without emotion. **glaciation** [gleɪsɪ'eɪʃn] *n.* effect of ice on rocks.

glad [glæd] *adj.* pleased/happy. **gladden**, *v.* to make glad. **gladly**, *adv.* happily. **gladness**, *n.* happiness.

glade [gleɪd] *n.* (*formal*) clear open space in the midst of trees.

gladiator ['glædɪeɪtə] *n.* man who fought in an arena (in ancient Rome). **gladiatorial** [glædɪə'tɔ:rɪəl] *adj.* referring to gladiators.

gladiolus [glædɪ'əʊləs] *n.* (*pl.* **gladioli** [glædɪ'əʊlaɪ]) tall garden plant with sword-shaped leaves and bright flower spikes.

glair [gleːə] *n.* white of egg, used as a coating.

glamour, *Am.* **glamor** ['glæmə] *n.* (*a*) magic/enchantment. (*b*) outward charm/attractiveness (of a woman). **glamorize**, *v.* to make (sth) appear more appealing than it really is. **glamorous**, *adj.* attractive/enchanting.

glance [glɑːns] **1.** *n.* quick look. **2.** *v.* (*a*) to look briefly. (*b*) to slide off an object instead of striking it fully. **glancing**, *adj.* sliding off to the side; not straight.

gland [glænd] *n.* organ of the body which produces a liquid which controls bodily changes, such as growth. **glandular** ['glændjʊlə] *adj.* referring to glands; **g. fever** = severe illness which affects the glands.

glare ['gleə] **1.** *n.* (*a*) strong/fierce light. (*b*) fierce/fixed look. **2.** *v.* (*a*) to shine too brightly. (*b*) to look angrily **at** s.o. **glaring,** *adj.* **g. mistake** = very obvious mistake.

glasnost ['glæznɒst] *n.* openness, freedom of information.

glass [glɑːs] *n.* (*a*) substance made from sand and soda or potash, usu. transparent, used for making windows, etc. (*b*) vessel made of glass used esp. for drinking; contents of such a glass. (*c*) barometer. (*d*) **looking g.** = mirror; **stained g.** = coloured glass used frequently in the windows of a church. **glass blower,** *n.* person who blows and shapes molten glass into bottles, etc. **glasses,** *n.pl.* spectacles. **glass fibre,** *n.* strong material made of woven fibres of glass; plastic containing fibres of glass. **glasshouse,** *n.* (*a*) greenhouse. cultivation of plants. (*b*) *Sl.* military prison. **glassware,** *n.* (*no pl.*) articles made of glass. **glass wool,** *n.* soft substance, made from glass fibre, used as an insulating material in buildings. **glassy,** *adj.* (*a*) resembling glass. (*b*) dull/unseeing; **a g. stare.**

glaucoma [glɔːˈkəumə] *n.* disease of the eyes which can cause blindness.

glaze [gleɪz] **1.** *n.* shiny surface (on pottery). **2.** *v.* (*a*) to fit with glass; to put glass in (a window). (*b*) to cover with a shiny coating. **glazier** ['gleɪzɪə] *n.* person whose trade is to fit glass in windows. **glazing,** *n.* fitting with windows; **double g.** = windows with two sheets of glass a small distance apart, which help insulation.

gleam [gliːm] **1.** *n.* (*a*) short-lived weak light. (*b*) faint/temporary show of some quality. **2.** *v.* to shine.

glean [gliːn] *v.* to collect (grain) left after the harvest; to scrape together (news/information, etc.). **gleaner,** *n.* person who gleans. **gleanings,** *n. pl.* odd bits of information.

glee [gliː] *n.* (*a*) short song sung by several singers, (*b*) joy/gaiety. **gleeful,** *adj.* joyful. **gleefully,** *adv.* happily.

glen [glen] *n.* (*in Scotland*) narrow valley. **glengarry,** *n.* tartan forage cap with ribbons hanging at the back.

glib [glɪb] *adj.* fluent but insincere way

of speaking. **glibly,** *adv.* smoothly and insincerely.

glide [glaɪd] **1.** *n.* smooth movement. **2.** *v.* to move smoothly. **glider,** *n.* small aircraft without an engine that relies on wind currents for propulsion. **gliding,** *n.* sport of flying gliders.

glimmer ['glɪmə] **1.** *n.* (*a*) feeble light. (*b*) tiny quantity; faint/temporary show of (interest, etc.). **2.** *v.* to shine feebly/intermittently.

glimpse [glɪmps] **1.** *n.* quick/passing sight. **2.** *v.* to catch sight of (sth).

glint [glɪnt] **1.** *n.* flash/glitter/sparkle. **2.** *v.* to flash/to glitter (like metal).

glisten ['glɪsn] *v.* (*of something wet*) to shine/to sparkle.

glitter ['glɪtə] **1.** *n.* bright light/sparkle. **2.** *v.* to shine brightly/to sparkle.

gloaming ['gləumɪŋ] *n.* twilight.

gloat [gləut] *v.* **to g. over** = to take pleasure in (s.o.'s misfortune); to look at (sth) greedily.

globe [gləub] *n.* (*a*) **the g.** = the earth. (*b*) ball with a map of the world on it. (*c*) round object; glass ball which covers an electric light bulb; **g. artichoke** = tall green thistle-like plant of which you eat parts of the flower head. **global,** *adj.* world-wide. **globally,** *adv.* all over the world. **globetrotter,** *n.* tourist who travels all over the world.

globule ['glɒbjuːl] *n.* small round object (such as a drop of water). **globular,** *adj.* shaped like a globe. **globulin,** *n.* protein found in blood, which contains antibodies.

glockenspiel ['glɒknspiːl] *n.* musical instrument like a xylophone with metal bars.

gloom [gluːm] *n.* (*a*) darkness/obscurity. (*b*) despair/melancholy. **gloomily,** *adv.* in a gloomy way. **gloomy,** *adj.* (**-ier, -iest**) melancholy; pessimistic.

glory ['glɔːrɪ] **1.** *n.* (*a*) fame/renown. (*b*) magnificent sight. **2.** *v.* **to g. in** = to get great pleasure from/to pride oneself on. **glorification** [glɔːrɪfɪˈkeɪʃn] *n.* transforming into sth more splendid. **glorify,** *v.* to make glorious/to transform into sth more splendid. **glorious** ['glɔːrɪəs] *adj.* splendid. **gloriously,** *adv.* in a glorious way. **gloryhole,** *n.* cupboard/room where you can keep junk.

gloss [glɒs] 1. n. (a) shine on a surface; showy appearance; **g. paint** = paint which is shiny when dry. (b) comment about a text. 2. v. **to g. over** = to try to hide (a mistake, etc.). **glossiness,** n. being glossy. **glossy,** adj. & n. (**-ier, -iest**) **g. magazines/glossies** = colourful, expensive magazines printed on shiny paper.

glossary ['glɒsərɪ] n. short explanation of meanings of words, usu. found at the end of a book.

glottis ['glɒtɪs] n. space in the vocal cords, which makes sound when opened or closed. **glottal,** adj. referring to the glottis; **g. stop** = type of clicking sound made by closing the glottis.

glove [glʌv] n. article of clothing worn on the hand; **to handle s.o. with kid gloves** = to deal gently with s.o.; **hand in g. with s.o.** = closely associated with s.o.; **g. compartment** = small cupboard on the dashboard of a car, in which you can put small items. **gloved,** adj. wearing gloves.

glow [gləʊ] 1. n. (a) brightness/warmth. (b) blush/bloom. 2. v. to shine; to show warm colour. **glowing,** adj. shining/warm. **glow-worm,** n. female beetle which gives off a green light in the dark.

glower ['glaʊə] v. to frown.

gloxinia [glɒk'sɪnɪə] n. type of pot plant with large trumpet-shaped flowers.

glucose ['glu:kəʊz] n. natural sugar found in fruit.

glue [glu:] 1. n. substance which will stick things together. 2. v. to stick together. **gluey,** adj. sticky.

glum [glʌm] adj. (**glummer, glummest**) sullen; looking dejected/miserable.

glut [glʌt] 1. n. too much of (sth); supply exceeding demand. 2. v. **to be glutted** (**with**) = to have too much.

gluten ['glu:tən] n. protein left when starch is removed from flour. **glutinous** ['glu:tɪnəs] adj. sticky.

glutton ['glʌtn] n. (a) person who eats too much. (b) person with great enthusiasm **for** sth. **gluttonous,** adj. referring to overeating. **gluttony,** n. eating too much.

glycerine, Am. **glycerin** ['glɪsərɪn] n. colourless, sweet liquid (used in medicines/in explosives, etc.).

gm abbrev. for gram.

GMT [dʒi:em'ti:] abbreviation for Greenwich Mean Time.

gnarled [nɑ:ld] adj. twisted/rugged; covered with hard lumps.

gnash [næʃ] v. to grind (the teeth).

gnat [næt] n. small, two-winged fly which stings.

gnaw [nɔ:] v. to chew.

gneiss [naɪs] n. type of hard rock.

gnome [nəʊm] n. dwarf/mischievous ugly little man (in fairy stories); inf. **the gnomes of Zurich** = Swiss international bankers. **gnomic,** adj. concise and clever (saying).

GNP [dʒi:en'pi:] gross national product.

gnu [nu:] n. large South African antelope.

go [gəʊ] 1. n. (a) act of moving; inf. **he's always on the go** = always moving about. (b) inf. energy; **she's full of go.** (c) attempt/try. (d) **to try and make a go of it** = to try to make the business successful. 2. v. (**went; has gone**) (a) to move from one place to another; to travel. (b) to work; **my watch won't go.** (c) to leave; **from the word go** = from the start. (d) **to be going to do sth** = to intend to do sth; to be about to do sth. (e) to fit; **it's too big to go into the box.** (f) to become; **she went pale.** (g) to make a noise; **the guns went bang.** (h) to have a certain tune/certain words; **how does the song go?** (i) to fail; **the brakes went. go about,** v. (a) to try to do sth/to plan how to do sth. (b) (of sailing boat) to turn to sail in another direction. (c) to move around. **go ahead,** v. to start to do sth. **go-ahead. 1.** n. permission to start. **2.** adj. enterprising; active. **go along with,** v. to agree with (s.o./sth). **go back,** v. to return. **go back on,** v. not to keep (a promise). **go-between,** n. person who carries messages from one person to another. **go-cart,** n. flat wooden frame with four wheels for children to play with. **go down,** v. (a) to descend. (b) **to go down well** = to be accepted. **go for,** v. (a) to apply for. (b) to like. (c) to be sold. (d) to attack. **go-getter,** n. inf. energetic, ambitious person. **go-go dancer,** n. inf. person who performs an energetic (and usu. erotic) dance in a nightclub. **go in,** v. to enter;

the sun's gone in = is hidden by clouds. **go in for,** v. (a) to enter (for a test/examination). (b) to do (sth) as a hobby. **going. 1.** adj. (a) working. (b) **g. rate** = usual rate/current rate. **2.** n. (a) surface of a race track; **do it while the g. is good** = while you have the chance. (b) **goings-on** = unusual things which are happening. **go into,** v. (a) to enter. (b) (in maths) to divide. (c) to examine. **go-kart,** n. flat frame with four wheels and an engine, used as a small racing car. **go-karting,** n. racing in go-karts. **go off,** v. (a) to explode. (b) to turn bad. (c) to dislike; **I've gone off him** = I used to like him, but now I don't. **go on,** v. (a) to continue. (b) (showing disbelief) inf. **go on!** = I don't believe you! (c) to happen; **what's going on here?** (d) **to go on about sth** = to talk all the time; to nag. **go out,** v. (a) to leave. (b) to be shut off; to die. **go out with,** v. to go to parties/the cinema, etc. with (s.o. of the opposite sex). **go round,** v. (a) to turn. (b) to be enough for all. (c) to visit. **go-slow,** n. slowing down of production by workers as a protest. **go under,** v. (a) to drown. (b) to be ruined. **go up,** v. to rise; **to go up in flames** = to burn. **go with,** v. to match/to fit with. **go without,** v. not to have.

goad [gəʊd] **1.** n. long stick for driving cattle. **2.** v. **to g. s.o. into doing sth** = to urge/to drive s.o. on by annoying him.

goal [gəʊl] n. (a) object of effort/ambition; aim. (b) two posts between which a ball has to be driven to score a point in a game. (c) points won (in football/hockey, etc.). **goalkeeper,** inf. **goalie,** n. player who defends the goal. **goalmouth,** n. area just in front of the goal. **goalpost,** n. one of the two posts between which a ball is driven to score a goal.

goat [gəʊt] n. domestic animal with horns and a beard; **to separate the sheep from the goats** = to divide the good from the bad; inf. **to get s.o.'s g.** = to annoy s.o. **goatee** [gəʊ'tiː] n. small beard, like that of a goat.

gob [gɒb] n. Sl. **1.** mouth; **shut your g.!** = stop talking! **2.** v. Sl. to spit.

gobbet ['gɒbɪt] n. large lump (of fat).

gobble ['gɒbl] v. (a) to eat quickly and

greedily. (b) to make a noise like a turkey. **gobbledegook** ['gɒbldɪguːk] n. inf. meaningless official/technical language.

goblet ['gɒblət] n. metal or glass drinking cup without handles.

goblin ['gɒblɪn] n. (in fairy stories) mischievous ugly little man.

god [gɒd] n. (a) deity; superhuman power. (b) **God** = creator and ruler of the Universe, according to Christian/Jewish/Muslim, etc., belief. (c) thing which is worshipped. **godchild,** n. (pl. -children) child who was sponsored at baptism. **god-daughter,** n. girl who was sponsored at baptism. **goddess,** n. female ✦god. **godfather,** n. man who sponsors a child at baptism; inf. head of a mafia group. **god-fearing,** adj. sincerely religious. **godforsaken,** adj. bad/awful. **godlike,** adj. like a god. **godliness,** n. being godly. **godly,** adj. holy. **godmother,** n. woman who sponsors a child at baptism. **godparents,** n.pl. people who sponsor a child at baptism. **godsend,** n. blessing. **godson,** n. boy who was sponsored at baptism.

godown ['gəʊdaʊn] n. warehouse (in the Far East).

goggle ['gɒgl] v. to stare (at). **gogglebox,** n. inf. television. **goggles,** n.pl. protective spectacles against dust and glare.

goitre, Am. **goiter** ['gɔɪtə] n. disease in which the thyroid gland in the neck swells up.

gold [gəʊld] **1.** n. (a) (element: Au) precious yellow metal. (b) medal made of gold (won in a sports competition). **2.** adj. made of gold; **g. leaf** = thin covering of gold; **g. plate** = dishes made of gold. **goldcrest,** n. very small bird, with an orange crest on its head. **gold-digger,** n. (a) person who digs for gold. (b) inf. woman who marries a man for his money. **golden,** adj. made of gold; gold-coloured; **g. opportunity** = wonderful chance; **g. rule** = very important rule; **g. wedding** = fiftieth anniversary of marriage; **g. handshake** = sum of money presented when you leave work; **g. disc** = award given to a singer whose record has sold one million copies;

g. **handcuffs** = very attractive salary and benefits, with a penalty if the employee leaves. **goldfield,** *n.* land where gold is mined. **goldfinch,** *n.* brightly coloured song bird. **goldfish,** *n.* (*pl.* **goldfish**) small orange fish kept in ponds/bowls. **goldmine,** *n.* mine which produces gold; very profitable business. **goldsmith,** *n.* person who works in gold.

golf [gɒlf] *n.* game for two people, or two couples, where a small hard ball is struck with long-handled clubs into a series of holes, the object being to use as few strokes as possible. **golf club,** *n.* (*a*) wooden- or metal-headed stick for striking the golf ball. (*b*) group of people who play golf, and allow others to join them on payment of a fee; clubhouse where golfers meet. **golf course,** *n.* ground on which golf is played. **golfer,** *n.* person who plays golf.

golliwog [ˈgɒlɪwɒg] *n.* doll like a man with a black face and curly black hair.

gonad [ˈgəʊnæd] *n.* gland which produces gametes.

gondola [ˈgɒndələ] *n.* (*a*) boat used on the canals in Venice. (*b*) basket/passenger compartment hanging underneath a balloon. **gondolier** [gɒndəˈlɪə] *n.* man who pushes a gondola, using a pole.

gone [gɒn] *v. see* **go. goner** [ˈgɒnə] *n. inf.* dying person; dead person.

gong [gɒŋ] *n.* (*a*) metal disc with a turned rim which gives a resonant sound when struck, used esp. to call people to meals. (*b*) *Sl.* medal.

gonna [ˈgɒnə] *v. Sl.* = going to.

gonorrh(o)ea [gɒnəˈriːə] *n.* type of venereal disease.

goo [guː] *n. inf.* (*no pl.*) sticky stuff. **gooey,** *adj. inf.* sticky.

good [gʊd] **1.** *adj.* (**better, best**) (*a*) having the right qualities/satisfactory; **did you have a g. time?** = did you enjoy yourself? (*b*) able; **he is g. at French.** (*c*) right/proper; **it is a g. idea.** (*d*) morally excellent/virtuous; **he is a g. man.** (*e*) well behaved/not troublesome; **as g. as gold** = exceptionally well behaved. (*f*) efficient/suitable/competent; **he was as g. as his word** = he did what he

said he would do. (*g*) **g. morning! g. afternoon! g. evening!** *interjections used when meeting or leaving someone in the morning, afternoon or evening.* (*h*) valid/sound/thorough. (*i*) not less than; **she waited a g. half-hour.** (*j*) a lot of; **a g. many people; a g. deal of money.** (*k*) **as g. as** = practically/almost. **2.** *n.* (*a*) **the g.** = virtuous people. (*b*) profit/advantage; **what g. will it do him? to do g.** = to act kindly; **for g.** = permanently/forever; **he is up to no g.** = he is acting in a suspicious manner. (*c*) **goods** = movable property; **goods and chattels** = personal possessions; **goods train** = train which carries cargo not passengers. **goodbye** [gʊdˈbaɪ] *n. & inter. used when leaving someone.* **good-for-nothing,** *n.* useless, lazy person. **Good Friday,** *n.* Friday before Easter Day. **good-humoured,** *adj.* pleasant; in a happy mood. **goodish,** *adj.* quite good. **good-looking,** *adj.* handsome/pretty. **good-natured,** *adj.* kindly/pleasant. **goodness,** *n.* virtue/kindness/generosity; **thank g.!** = how glad I am! **goodnight,** *n. & inter. used when leaving someone late at night.* **goodwill,** *n.* (*a*) kindly feeling towards a person. (*b*) good reputation of a business. **goody,** *n. inf.* (*a*) good person. (*b*) **goodies** = good things/money/treasure. **goody-goody,** *adj. inf.* (person) who is too good.

goof [guːf] **1.** *n. Sl.* stupid person. **2.** *v.* to make a stupid mistake. **goofy,** *adj. inf.* stupid.

googly [ˈguːglɪ] *n.* (*in cricket*) ball which twists sharply in the opposite direction to that expected.

goon [guːn] *n.* silly fool.

goosander [guːˈsændə] *n.* type of wild duck.

goose [guːs] *n.* (*pl.* **geese**) (*a*) web-footed water bird, larger than a duck. (*b*) *inf.* silly person. **gooseberry** [ˈguːzbrɪ] *n.* small edible green fruit; bush which bears this fruit. **gooseflesh,** *n.* **goose-pimples,** *n.pl.* mass of small bumps on the skin caused by fear/by cold, etc. **goose-step. 1.** *n.* way of marching without bending the knees. **2.** *v.* (**goosestepped**) to march without bending the knees.

gopher ['gəufə] n. American rodent which lives in burrows.

gore [gɔ:] 1. n. (a) (formal) blood which has thickened after coming from a wound. (b) section of a skirt, shaped like a triangle. 2. v. to pierce with a horn. **gored,** adj. (skirt) with a gore.

gorge [gɔ:dʒ] 1. n. narrow opening between hills. 2. v. to eat greedily; **he gorged himself on chocolates.**

gorgeous ['gɔ:dʒəs] adj. magnificent/splendid; richly coloured. **gorgeously,** adv. splendidly.

gorgon ['gɔ:gən] n. fierce woman.

gorilla [gə'rɪlə] n. large, powerful African ape.

gormandize ['gɔ:məndaɪz] v. to eat far too much.

gormless ['gɔ:mləs] adj. inf. foolish/stupid.

gorse [gɔ:s] n. prickly yellow-flowered shrub.

gory ['gɔ:rɪ] adj. (-ier, -iest) covered in blood.

gosh [gɒʃ] inter. showing surprise.

goshawk ['gɒshɔ:k] n. type of trained hawk.

gosling ['gɒzlɪŋ] n. baby goose.

gospel ['gɒspl] n. record of Christ's life in the books of the four evangelists; **it's the g. truth** = it's absolutely true.

gossamer ['gɒsəmə] n. (a) very fine cobweb. (b) very fine material.

gossip ['gɒsɪp] 1. n. (a) idle chat, esp. about other people; **g. column** = section in a paper which gives news about the private lives of famous people. (b) person who spreads rumours. 2. v. to talk idly; to spread rumours. **gossipy,** adj. full of gossip.

got [gɒt] v. (a) see **get.** (b) **to have g. to do sth** = to be obliged/to have to do sth.

gothic ['gɒθɪk] adj. style of architecture with pointed arches used in Western Europe in 12th–16th centuries.

gotta ['gɒtə] v. Sl. = (have) got to.

gotten ['gɒtn] v. Am. see **get.**

gouache [gu'ɑ:ʃ] n. kind of thick watercolour paint.

gouge [gaʊdʒ] 1. n. kind of chisel used in carpentry. 2. v. to scoop out.

goulash ['gu:læʃ] n. Hungarian stew flavoured with paprika.

gourd ['gʊəd] n. dried fruit of a climbing plant, used as a bowl.

gourmand ['gʊəmənd] n. person who eats too much.

gourmet ['gʊəmeɪ] n. connoisseur of food and wine.

gout [gaʊt] n. painful inflammation of the joints, esp. the big toe. **gouty,** adj. afflicted with gout.

govern ['gʌvən] 1. v. (a) to rule with authority. (b) to influence/to determine. **governance,** n. (formal) way of governing. **governess,** n. female teacher, usu. in a private household. **government** ['gʌvənmənt] n. group of people ruling a country. **governmental** [gʌvən'mentl] adj. referring to a government. **governor,** n. person who rules (esp. a prison); **Governor-General** = person who represents the Queen at the head of a Commonwealth country.

gown [gaʊn] n. (a) (formal) dress. (b) long official robe (worn by a mayor/judge/person with a degree, etc.). (c) **dressing-gown** = long coat worn over night clothes.

GP ['dʒi'pi:] abbreviation for general practitioner; family doctor.

GPO [dʒi:pi:'əʊ] abbreviation for General Post Office.

grab [græb] 1. n. sudden seizing with the hands; **to make a g. for** = to try to seize. 2. v. (grabbed) to seize.

grace [greɪs] 1. n. (a) pleasing quality/attractiveness; **with good g.** = with a show of willingness. (b) short prayer of thanksgiving before or after a meal. (c) act of mercy; pardon from all sin. (d) favour shown by granting a delay; **ten days' g.** 2. v. to honour. **graceful,** adj. moving with ease. **gracefully,** adv. moving easily. **gracefulness,** n. ease of movement. **graceless,** adj. with no grace. **grace note,** n. note in music which need not be played, but which adds to the attraction of the piece.

gracious ['greɪʃəs] adj. kind/agreeable; elegant (way of living); **good g.!** = how surprising! **graciously,** adv. kindly. **graciousness,** n. being gracious.

grade [greɪd] 1. n. (a) degree/level/rank; **to make the g.** = to succeed. (b) mark in an exam. (c) Am. class (in school). 2. v. to arrange in grades/to sort out. **gradation** [grə'deɪʃn] n. series of steps, passing from one level to another. **grade crossing,** *n. Am.* place where a railway line crosses a road.

gradient ['greidiənt] *n.* amount of slope in a road, railway, etc.

gradual ['grædjuəl] *adj.* slow/progressive. **gradually,** *adv.* little by little.

graduate 1. *n.* ['grædjuət] person who has obtained a degree; **g. of London University.** 2. *v.* ['grædjueit] (*a*) to obtain a degree (**from** a university). (*b*) to regulate. (*c*) to mark in a scale; **graduated measuring glass** = one with quantities marked on it. **graduation** [grædju'eiʃn] *n.* (*a*) obtaining a degree. (*b*) act of marking a scale.

graffiti [grə'fiːtɪ] *n.pl.* unofficial drawings or writing on walls.

graft [grɑːft] 1. *n.* (*a*) shoot of a plant inserted into another plant from which it receives sap and of which it becomes part. (*b*) (*in surgery*) piece of transplanted living tissue. (*c*) *Sl.* hard work. (*d*) *Sl.* bribery; bribe. 2. *v.* to insert (part of a plant) into another plant so that it can grow; to attach (skin, etc.) to other parts of the body.

Grail [greil] *n.* **the Holy G.** = precious object (the cup used at the Last Supper) which was sought by medieval knights.

grain [grein] *n.* (*a*) seed of cereal. (*b*) small particle of sand/gold, etc. (*c*) texture of particles (in stone); lines of fibres in wood/material; **it goes against the g.** = it goes against natural instincts. (*d*) measurement of weight. **grainy,** *adj.* (wood) with a strongly marked grain.

gram [græm] *n.* measurement of weight, one thousandth part of a kilogram.

grammar ['græmə] *n.* (*a*) art and science of a language; rules of the forms of words and their relationship in a language. (*b*) book which explains/teaches the rules of a language. **grammarian** [grə'meəriən] *n.* specialist in the study of grammar. **grammar school,** *n.* (*old*) selective secondary school. **grammatical** [grə'mætikl] *adj.* conforming to the rules of grammar. **grammatically,** *adv.* according to the rules of grammar.

gramophone ['græməfəun] *n.* (*old*) machine on which records are played and which is wound up with a handle.

grampus ['græmpəs] *n.* sea animal similar to a dolphin; **to puff like a g.** = to have difficulty in breathing.

gran [græn] *n. inf.* grandmother.

granary ['grænəri] *n.* storehouse for grain; **g. loaf** = bread made with whole wheat grain.

grand [grænd] 1. *adj.* (**-er, -est**) (*a*) important/imposing. (*b*) final. (*c*) conducted with solemnity. (*d*) very good. 2. *n.* (*a*) *inf.* grand piano. (*b*) *Sl.* thousand pounds/dollars. **grandad,** *n. inf.* grandfather. **grandchild,** *n.* (*pl.* **-children**) child of a son or daughter. **granddaughter,** *n.* daughter of a son or daughter. **grandee** [græn'diː] *n.* proud aristocrat (usu. Spanish). **grandeur** ['grændʒə] *n.* splendour/majesty. **grandfather,** *n.* father of a mother or father; **g. clock** = tall clock standing on the floor. **grandiloquence** [græn'dıləkwəns] *n.* pompous/wordy speech. **grandiloquent,** *adj.* speaking in a pompous way. **grandiose** ['grændıəus] *adj.* very splendid. **grandly,** *adv.* in a grand way. **grandma** ['grænmɑː] *n. inf.* grandmother. **grandmaster,** *n.* chessplayer of international quality. **grandmother,** *n.* mother of a mother or father. **grandness,** *n.* being grand. **grandpa** ['grænpɑː] *n. inf.* grandfather. **grandparents,** *n.pl.* parents of a mother or father. **grand piano,** *n.* large horizontal piano. **Grand Prix** [grɒŋ'priː] *n.* motor/motorcycle race. **grandson,** *n.* son of a son or daughter. **grandstand,** *n.* building with a sloping bank of seats for spectators at a racecourse or sportsground.

grange [greindʒ] *n.* country house with farm buildings attached to it.

granite ['grænit] *n.* hard light-grey stone used for building.

granny ['græni] *n. inf.* grandmother; **g. flat** = part of a house converted into a separate flat for an old relative; **g. knot** = insecure type of reef knot.

grant [grɑːnt] 1. *n.* financial aid. 2. *v.* (*a*) to agree/to give consent; **to take sth for granted** = not to appreciate it any more. (*b*) to agree; **I g. you it is a difficult job** = I admit that it is difficult. **granted,** *adj.* admitted/understood.

granulate ['grænjuleit] *v.* to form

into grains. **granular,** *adj.* containing grains; like grains. **granule,** *n.* very small particle.

grape [greɪp] *n.* small green or purple fruit growing in clusters on a vine, eaten as fruit or made into wine. **grapefruit,** *n.* (*pl.* **grapefruit**) large round yellow citrus fruit. **grapevine,** *n.* climbing plant on which grapes grow. **I heard it on the g.** = I learnt the news by gossip/unofficially.

graph [grɑːf] *n.* mathematical diagram/curve. **graphic** ['græfɪk] *adj.* (*a*) referring to graphs/diagrams/signs, etc. (*c*) vivid (description). **graphical,** *adj.* referring to graphs/diagrams/signs, etc. **graphically,** *adv.* (*a*) using graphs/diagrams/signs, etc. (*b*) in a graphic way. **graphics,** *n.* pictures/charts on a printed document or on a computer screen. **graph paper,** *n.* paper with small squares for drawing graphs on.

graphite ['græfaɪt] *n.* naturally occurring form of carbon; lead (as used in a pencil).

graphology [græ'fɒlədʒɪ] *n.* science of discovering s.o.'s character from handwriting. **graphologist,** *n.* person who practises graphology.

grapnel ['græpnl] *n.* small anchor with several hooks.

grapple ['græpl] *v.* to wrestle/to fight (with). **grappling iron,** *n.* grapnel.

grasp [grɑːsp] **1.** *n.* (*a*) tight hold/grip. (*b*) understanding. **2.** *v.* (*a*) to seize; to grab tightly. (*b*) to understand. **grasp at,** *v.* to try to grab. **grasping,** *adj.* (person) who is eager to get more things.

grass [grɑːs] **1.** *n.* (*a*) low green plant of which the thin leaves and stalks are eaten by cattle, etc.; **don't let the g. grow under your feet** = waste no time in doing sth. (*b*) plant of a species related to grass (including bamboo, etc.). (*c*) lawn/piece of ground covered with grass. (*d*) *Sl.* police informer. (*e*) *Sl.* marijuana. **2.** *v.* (*a*) **to g. over** = to cover with grass. (*b*) *Sl.* to inform the police about a crime. **grasshopper,** *n.* green jumping insect with long back legs. **grassland,** *n.* prairie pasture. **grassroots,** *n.pl.* ordinary members of a political party/a trade union; common people; **g. reaction** = reac-

tion by the ordinary members (of a party, etc.). **grass-snake,** *n.* common snake. **grasswidow,** *n.* wife whose husband has temporarily gone away. **grasswidower,** *n.* husband whose wife has temporarily gone away. **grassy,** *adj.* covered with growing grass.

grate [greɪt] **1.** *n.* fireplace. **2.** *v.* (*a*) to reduce to small bits by rubbing on a rough surface. (*b*) to make a noise like two rough surfaces rubbing together. (*c*) to have an irritating effect upon. **grater,** *n.* instrument for grating cheese, etc. **grating. 1.** *n.* grille; framework of wooden or metal bars. **2.** *adj.* **a g. sound** = an irritating sound as of the rubbing together of rough surfaces.

grateful ['greɪtful] *adj.* thankful. **gratefully,** *adv.* thankfully.

gratify ['grætɪfaɪ] *v.* (*a*) to satisfy/to delight. (*b*) to please. **gratification** [grætɪfɪ'keɪʃn] *n.* satisfaction. **gratifying,** *adj.* pleasing/satisfying.

gratin ['grætæŋ] *n.* dish cooked with a crust, often of cheese, on top.

gratis ['grɑːtɪs] *adv.* free/without charge.

gratitude ['grætɪtjuːd] *n.* appreciation.

gratuity [grə'tjuːɪtɪ] *n.* (*a*) present of money. (*b*) sum of money given to s.o. on retirement. **gratuitous,** *adj.* unasked for; undeserved.

grave [greɪv] **1.** *n.* tomb/hole in the ground to put a dead body in; burial place; **to have one foot in the g.** = to be very near to death. **2.** *adj.* **(-er, -est)** serious/solemn. **gravedigger,** *n.* man who digs graves. **gravestone,** *n.* memorial stone placed on a grave. **graveyard,** *n.* cemetery/place where people are buried.

gravel ['grævl] *n.* mixture of sand and small stones.

graven ['greɪvn] *adj.* (*old*) carved.

gravitate ['grævɪteɪt] *v.* to move (**towards** sth). **gravitation** [grævɪ'teɪʃn] *n.* force of the earth's centre which attracts and causes objects to fall to the ground if dropped. **gravity** ['grævɪtɪ] *n.* (*a*) seriousness. (*b*) weight; **specific g.** = density of a substance divided by the density of water. (*c*) force attracting all objects to the earth's centre, causing objects to fall to the ground if dropped.

gravy ['greɪvɪ] *n.* (*no pl.*) (*a*) juices that drip from meat during cooking. (*b*) brown sauce served with meat. **gravy boat,** *n.* small wide jug for serving gravy.

gray [greɪ] *adj. & n.* (*usu. Am.*) = **grey**.

grayling ['greɪlɪŋ] *n.* (*a*) type of brown butterfly. (*b*) grey fish.

graze [greɪz] **1.** *n.* slight surface wound/scratch. **2.** *v.* (*a*) to feed on growing grass. (*b*) to wound slightly in passing. **grazing,** *n.* pasture.

grease [gri:s] **1.** *n.* (*a*) melted animal fat. (*b*) oily/fatty substance. **2.** *v.* (*a*) to cover/to coat with oil/fat, etc. (*b*) *inf.* **to g. s.o.'s palm** = to bribe s.o. **greasegun,** *n.* device for putting grease into machines. **greasepaint,** *n.* make-up used by actors. **greaseproof paper,** *n.* paper which will not let oil through. **greasy,** *adj.* smeared with grease; oily.

great [greɪt] **1.** *adj.* (**-er, -est**) (*a*) large/big. (*b*) extreme. (*c*) distinguished/grand. (*d*) remarkable. (*e*) *inf.* wonderful. **great-aunt,** *n.* aunt of a father or mother. **greatcoat,** *n.* thick army coat. **Great Dane,** *n.* breed of very large dog. **great-grandchildren,** *n.pl.* grandchildren of a son or daughter. **great-granddaughter,** *n.* granddaughter of a son or daughter. **great-grandfather,** *n.* grandfather of a father or mother. **great-grandmother,** *n.* grandmother of a father or mother. **great-grandparents,** *n.pl.* grandparents of a father or mother. **great-grandson,** *n.* grandson of a son or daughter. **greatly,** *adv.* very much. **greatness,** *n.* remarkable ability. **great-uncle,** *n.* uncle of a father or mother.

grebe [gri:b] *n.* type of diving bird with a long neck.

Grecian ['gri:ʃn] *adj.* referring to ancient Greece.

greed [gri:d] *n.* too great appetite; desire for more than is necessary. **greedily,** *adv.* with great appetite. **greediness,** *n.* being greedy. **greedy,** *adj.* (**-ier, -iest**) wanting to eat too much; **g. for** = always wanting (power, etc.).

Greek [gri:k] **1.** *adj.* referring to Greece. **2.** *n.* (*a*) person from Greece. (*b*) language spoken in Greece.

green [gri:n] **1.** *adj.* (**-er, -est**) (*a*) of a colour like grass; **g. light** = light which shows you can go ahead; **g. with envy** = very envious. (*b*) immature/gullible. (*c*) **g. bacon** = plain bacon which has not been smoked. (*d*) referring to a concern about the environment; **g. issues** = problems concerning the environment. **2.** *n.* (*a*) colour like that of grass. (*b*) piece of public land covered with grass. (*c*) piece of land covered with smooth grass on which you can play certain games. **greenback,** *n. inf. Am.* dollar bill. **green belt,** *n.* area of countryside round a town where building is prohibited. **green card,** *n.* (*a*) insurance certificate to insure a car being taken abroad. (*b*) work permit for s.o. who is going to live in the USA. **greenery,** *n.* vegetation. **greenfield site,** *n.* site for a factory in fields. **greenfinch,** *n.* bird with yellow and green plumage. **green fingers,** *n.pl.* skill in gardening. **greenfly,** *n.* (*pl.* **greenfly**) small green aphis. **greengage,** *n.* kind of green plum. **greengrocer,** *n.* person who sells fruit and vegetables. **greengrocer's, greengrocery,** *n.* shop selling fruit and vegetables. **greenhorn,** *n.* inexperienced person. **greenhouse,** *n.* shelter made of glass and wood or metal for cultivation of delicate plants; **g. effect** = warming effect on the atmosphere, caused by carbon dioxide in the upper atmosphere. **greenish,** *adj.* rather green. **greenmail,** *n.* buying shares in a company, threatening to take the company over, then selling the shares at a profit. **Green Paper,** *n.* official report by the government on proposals which are being studied. **Green Party,** *n.* political party which is mainly concerned with environmental questions. **green pound,** *n.* value of the pound as used in calculating the Common Market agricultural prices and subsidies relating to the UK. **greenroom,** *n.* room where actors can rest when they are off-stage. **greens,** *n.pl. inf.* cooked green vegetables. **Greens,** *n. pl.* the Green Party. **greenstick fracture,** *n.* fracture of a long bone in a child, where the bone bends, but does not break. **green thumb,** n. Am. skill in gardening.

greet [gri:t] v. to salute/to welcome. **greeting,** n. reception/way of welcoming s.o. **greetings,** n.pl. good wishes.

gregarious [grɪ'geərɪəs] adj. fond of company/sociable.

gremlin ['gremlɪn] n. imaginary imp, supposed to be responsible for faults in machinery.

grenade [grɪ'neɪd] n. small bomb thrown by hand. **grenadier** [grenə'dɪə] n. (a) (old) soldier who threw grenades. (b) member of the Grenadier Guards.

grenadine [grenə'di:n] n. red drink, made from pomegranate juice.

grew [gru:] v. see **grow.**

grey [greɪ] 1. adj. (-er, -est) of a colour between black and white; **g. matter** = active part of the brain; inf. intelligence. 2. n. colour between black and white. **grey-haired,** adj. with grey hair. **greyhound,** n. slender, long-legged, swift dog, often used for racing. **greyish,** adj. rather grey. **greylag,** n. common European wild goose.

grid [grɪd] n. (a) grating/frame of spaced parallel bars. (b) system of numbered squares on a map. (c) national electricity supply system. (d) **starting g.** = lines drawn on a track to show the start in a car/motorcycle race. **griddle,** n. iron plate placed over heat for cooking flat cakes. **gridiron,** n. (a) metal frame for cooking over an open fire. (b) Am. fóotball field.

grief [gri:f] n. deep sorrow; **to come to g.** = to meet with disaster. **grief-stricken,** adj. very sad.

grievance ['gri:vəns] n. real or imagined grounds for complaint; **to air one's grievances** = to tell everyone about one's complaints.

grieve [gri:v] v. to feel sad (for); **it grieves me** = it makes me sad. **grieve over,** v. to mourn; to feel sad because of (sth). **grievous,** adj. severe; **g. bodily harm** = severe injury to s.o.

griffin ['grɪfɪn] n. imaginary animal with a lion's head and eagle's wings.

griffon ['grɪfən] n. (a) type of small terrier. (b) type of vulture.

grill [grɪl] 1. n. (a) part of a cooker where food is cooked under a direct source

of heat; **charcoal g.** = gridiron over a bed of hot charcoal. (b) (also **grillroom**) restaurant where most food is cooked under a grill or on a charcoal grill. (c) **mixed g.** = collection of grilled food. (d) framework of metal/wooden bars. 2. v. (a) to cook under the grill. (b) inf. to interrogate (s.o.)/to ask (s.o.) searching questions.

grille [grɪl] n. grating; frame of spaced parallel bars; **radiator g.** = parallel bars in front of a radiator on a car.

grilse [grɪls] n. young salmon, returning to the river from the sea for the first time.

grim [grɪm] adj. (**grimmer, grimmest**) (a) sinister/severe. (b) bad/gloomy. **grimly,** adv. tenaciously; with determination. **grimness,** n. being grim.

grimace [grɪ'meɪs] 1. n. twisted expression on the face. 2. v. to make a grimace.

grime [graɪm] n. ingrained dirt. **griminess,** n. being grimy. **grimy,** adj. dirty.

grin [grɪn] 1. n. wide smile. 2. v. (**grinned**) to smile broadly; **to g. and bear it** = to accept things bravely.

grind [graɪnd] 1. n. boring/monotonous work; **the daily g.** = repetitive work to be done every day. 2. v. (**ground**) (a) to reduce to small pieces by crushing; **to g. corn/coffee.** (b) Am. to mince; **ground beef** = minced beef. (c) to rub surfaces together; **to g. your teeth** = to rub together the upper and lower teeth, usu. in anger; **to g. to a halt** = to stop. (d) to sharpen (a tool)/to smooth (sth rough); **to have an axe to g.** = to have a particular interest or point of view which makes your judgement biased. **grinder,** n. (a) machine for grinding. (b) Am. mincer. **grinding,** adj. terrible (poverty). **grindstone,** n. stone which turns to sharpen knives; **to keep s.o.'s nose to the g.** = to keep him working very hard.

gringo ['grɪŋgəʊ] n. inf. (esp. in Mexico) foreigner, usu. American.

grip [grɪp] 1. n. (a) firm hold; **to come to grips with** = to tackle; **to keep a g. on** = to remain in control of. (b) soft bag/hold-all for carrying clothes, etc. (c) pin for holding your hair in place. 2. v. (**gripped**) (a) to seize. (b) to hold (attention). **gripping,** adj. holding the attention.

gripe [graip] v. to moan/to complain **about** sth. **gripe water,** n. medicine given to babies to stop stomach pains.

grisly ['grɪzlɪ] adj. (**-ier, -iest**) causing horror/dread.

grist [grɪst] n. inf. **it's all g. to the mill** = it's all useful/it all helps.

gristle ['grɪsl] n. tough, whitish, flexible tissue in meat. **gristly,** adj. full of pieces of gristle.

grit [grɪt] **1.** n. (a) small particles of stone/sand. (b) inf. courage. (c) Am. **grits** = type of porridge made of maize or wheat. **2.** v. (**gritted**) (a) to make a surface of grit; to put grit on (an icy road) to prevent cars sliding. (b) **to g. your teeth** = to clench your teeth together, usu. in fear/determination. **grittiness,** n. being gritty. **gritty,** adj. full of grit.

grizzle ['grɪzl] v. (of children) to whimper/to cry fretfully.

grizzled ['grɪzld] adj. with grey hair. **grizzly** ['grɪzlɪ] **1.** adj. grey; grey-haired. **2.** n. **g. (bear)** = large, fierce North American bear.

groan [grəʊn] **1.** n. deep sound expressing pain/grief/disapproval. **2.** v. (a) to moan deeply. (b) **to g. under a weight** = to be heavily laden.

groats [grəʊts] n. pl. crushed oats.

grocer ['grəʊsə] n. dealer in tinned foods, butter, sugar, eggs, etc., and miscellaneous domestic supplies. **groceries,** n.pl. items on sale in a grocer's shop. **grocer's, grocery,** n. grocer's shop.

grog [grɒg] n. drink of spirits and water. **groggily,** adv. unsteadily. **groggy,** adj. unsteady.

groin [grɔɪn] n. (a) hollow where the thigh joins the belly. (b) place where two vaults join. **groined,** adj. (roof) with joined vaults.

groom [gruːm] **1.** n. (a) person who looks after horses. (b) bridegroom/new husband. **2.** v. to look after/to make smart; **well-groomed** = smart and well-dressed.

groove [gruːv] n. (a) channel/hollow. (b) routine; **to get into a g.** = to be stuck in a routine. **groovy,** adj. Sl. fine/fashionable.

grope [grəʊp] v. to feel with your hands as if you were blind.

grosbeak ['grəʊsbiːk] n. small bird with a large beak.

gross [grəʊs] **1.** n. (pl. **gross**) twelve dozen, 144. **2.** adj. (**-er, -est**) (a) bloated; horribly fat. (b) great/excessive; **g. injustice.** (c) total; **g. weight** = combined weight of container and contents; **g. income** = total income before tax is deducted. **grossly,** adv. greatly.

grotesque [grə'tesk] adj. outrageous/fantastic; strange and ugly.

grotto ['grɒtəʊ] n. (pl. **-oes**) picturesque cave; room decorated with shells to resemble a cave.

grotty ['grɒtɪ] adj. inf. dirty.

grouch [graʊtʃ] **1.** n. inf. grumble. **2.** v. inf. to grumble. **grouchy,** adj. inf. grumpy.

ground [graʊnd] **1.** n. (a) soil/earth. (b) surface of the earth; **to go to g.** = to hide away. (c) area of land; **to stand one's g.** = to maintain one's position/authority; **to lose g.** = to become less successful; **to break new g.** = to be the first to start a project; **to get (sth) off the g.** = to start (sth) successfully/to get a .project) going. (d) large area of land set aside for a particular purpose; **football g.** (e) **grounds** = land surrounding a large house. (f) reason; **grounds for complaint.** (g) **coffee grounds** = small pieces of ground coffee beans left after the coffee has been made. **2.** v. (a) to base. (b) to run (a boat) on to the land. (c) to keep (aircraft/pilot) on the ground. (d) see also **grind. grounding,** n. instruction. **groundless,** adj. without reason. **groundnut,** n. peanut. **groundsheet,** n. rubber/plastic cloth spread on the ground for sitting/sleeping on. **groundsman,** n. (pl. **-men**) person who looks after sports pitches or gardens. **ground rule,** n. basic rule of procedure. **groundspeed,** n. the speed of an aircraft over the ground. **groundswell,** n. (no pl.) large slow-moving waves. **groundwork,** n. basic work/preliminary work.

groundsel ['graʊnsl] n. common weed with small yellow flowers.

group [gruːp] **1.** n. (a) number of people

or animals gathered close together. (b) classification; **blood g.; age g.** (c) small number of people playing music together. (d) several different companies linked together in the same organization. **2.** v. **to g. (together)** = to form into groups. **group captain,** n. rank in the air force above wing commander. **grouper,** n. large tropical sea fish, used as food. **groupie,** n. Sl. girl follower of a pop group. **group practice,** n. several doctors who share patients between them and usu. work from the same offices.

grouse [graʊs] **1.** n. (a) (pl. **grouse**) reddish/black bird shot for sport and food. (b) inf. grumble. **2.** v. inf. to grumble (**about** sth). **grouser,** n. person who grouses.

grout [graʊt] v. to fill the spaces between tiles on a floor or wall with cement. **grouting,** n. cement used to fill spaces between tiles.

grove [graʊv] n. small group of trees.

grovel ['grɒvl] v. (**grovelled**) to humble yourself; to lie with your face on the ground.

grow [graʊ] **1.** v. (**grew** [gru:], has **grown**) (a) to develop/to exist as a living plant. (b) to increase in size/height. (c) to become/to evolve gradually. (d) to cultivate; **she grows roses. grower,** n. (a) person who cultivates. (b) plant that grows in a specified way; **a slow g. growing,** adj. getting bigger. **grown,** adj. developed to full size. **grown-up,** adj. & n. adult. **grow on,** v. inf. to become accepted; **this picture grows on you** = you gradually come to like it. **grow out of,** v. to become bigger/older (so that clothes no longer fit, etc.). **growth,** n. (a) development; increase in height/size. (b) lump of tissue in the body. **growth rate,** n. speed with which sth grows. **grow up,** v. to become adult.

growl [graʊl] **1.** n. sound made in the throat expressing anger. **2.** v. to murmur angrily.

grown [graʊn] v. see **grow**.

groyne [grɔɪn] n. long breakwater built into the sea.

grub [grʌb] **1.** n. (a) larva of an insect; short worm which grows into an insect. (b) Sl. food. **2.** v. (**grubbed**) (also to grub up) to dig. **grubbiness,** n. dirty appearance. **grubby,** adj. (-ier, -iest) dirty.

grudge [grʌdʒ] **1.** n. feeling of resentment/ill will (**against** s.o.). **2.** v. to be unwilling to give (s.o. sth). **grudging,** adj. reluctant.

gruel ['grʊəl] n. thin porridge.

gruelling ['grʊəlɪŋ] adj. exhausting/ tiring; very difficult.

gruesome ['gru:səm] adj. causing horror/dread.

gruff [grʌf] adj. (-er, -est) (a) deep/rough (voice). (b) stern (manner). **gruffly,** adv. in a gruff way. **gruffness,** n. being gruff.

grumble ['grʌmbl] **1.** n. moan/complaint. **2.** v. to complain (**about** sth). **grumbler,** n. person who complains. **grumbling,** adj. inf. **g. appendix** = appendix which hurts from time to time.

grumpy ['grʌmpɪ] adj. (-ier, -iest) bad-tempered. **grumpily,** adv. in a bad-tempered manner. **grumpiness,** n. being grumpy.

grunt [grʌnt] **1.** n. low sound, like that made by pigs. **2.** v. to make a low snorting sound.

guano ['gwɑ:nəʊ] n. (no pl.) droppings of sea-birds used as manure.

guarantee [gærən'ti:] **1.** n. (a) legal document promising that a machine will work for a certain time; **the car is still under g.** (b) person acting as a security. (c) thing given as security. **2.** v. to give assurance (**that** sth will happen). **guaranteed,** adj. assured. **guarantor** [gærən'tɔ:] n. person who promises to pay s.o.'s debts.

guard [gɑ:d] **1.** n. (a) watch/looking out; **to be on g./to keep g.** = to act as sentry; **to be on your g.** = to be prepared against attack/surprise, etc.; **to be caught off g.** = to be taken unawares. (b) soldier/policeman who protects s.o./a building; **g. of honour** = group of soldiers acting as a ceremonial escort to an important person. (c) **the Guards** = special regiments of elite soldiers. (d) person in charge of a train, who gives orders to the driver. (e) device to prevent injury or accident. **2.** v. (a) to defend/to protect; to watch (prisoners) carefully so that they cannot escape; **closely guarded secret** = secret which is carefully kept secret. (b) to be careful. **guarded,** adj. careful/noncommital (reply). **guardian,** n. keeper/protector responsible for the upbringing of a child. **guardianship,** n. protection. **guardroom,** n. building at the entrance to a military camp, used as a prison. **guardsman,** n. (pl. **-men**) soldier of the Guards.

guava ['gwɑːvə] n. orange-coloured tropical fruit.

gudgeon ['gʌdʒn] n. (a) small river fish. (b) pin joining a piston rod and connecting rod. (c) pin on which a hinge hangs.

guelder rose ['geldə'rəʊz] n. garden shrub with white pompom flowers.

guer(r)illa [gə'rɪlə] n. person (not a regular soldier) engaged in unofficial fighting; group of these soldiers.

guernsey ['gɜːnzɪ] n. (a) breed of cow, which gives rich milk. (b) thick pullover.

guess [ges] 1. n. rough estimate; **it is anybody's g.** = no one really knows. 2. v. (a) to estimate. (b) Am. to think. **guesstimate,** n. inf. rough calculation. **guesswork,** n. process of guessing.

guest [gest] n. (a) person entertained at another's house; **paying g.** = lodger/boarder; **g. artist/g. conductor** = person who is invited to play with/to conduct an orchestra. (b) person staying in a hotel. **guesthouse,** n. house where people pay for a bed and meals.

guff [gʌf] n. inf. words which mean nothing.

guffaw [gə'fɔː] 1. n. loud/coarse laugh. 2. v. to laugh loudly.

guide [gaɪd] 1. n. (a) person who shows the way/who describes buildings/works of art, etc., as you see them. (b) indication. (c) book of helpful advice. (d) member of the Girl Guides; **the Guides** = the Girl Guides/social/training organization for girls. 2. v. to conduct/to lead; **guided tour** = tour where the tourists are led by a guide; **guided missile** = missile which is led to the target by a controlling device. **guidance,** n. advice. **guidebook,** n. book of helpful advice/information. **guide dog,** n. dog which is specially trained to lead a blind person. **guide-**

lines, n. pl. advice how to proceed. **guiding,** adj. directing.

guild [gɪld] n. association of merchants or craftsmen. **guildhall,** n. hall where a guild used to meet, now usu. a town hall.

guile [gaɪl] n. treachery/cunning/trickery. **guileless,** adj. honest/straightforward.

guillemot ['gɪlɪmɒt] n. black and white sea bird.

guillotine ['gɪlətiːn] 1. n. (a) machine with a sharp blade for beheading criminals. (b) machine with a sharp blade for cutting paper. (c) arrangement to limit the length of a debate in Parliament so that a vote can be taken quickly. 2. v. (a) to cut the head off (s.o.) with a guillotine. (b) to cut (paper) with a guillotine.

guilt [gɪlt] n. having committed a crime; being aware that you have committed a crime. **guiltily,** adv. showing that you know you have done wrong. **guiltless,** adj. innocent. **guilty,** adj. (**-ier, -iest**) blameworthy/criminal; having done wrong.

guinea ['gɪnɪ] n. (old) coin worth 21 shillings.

guinea fowl ['gɪnɪfaʊl] n. small black bird with white spots, used for food.

guinea pig ['gɪnɪpɪg] n. (a) small furry animal with no tail, often kept as a pet. (b) person/animal used in a scientific experiment.

guise [gaɪz] n. (formal) appearance; **in the g. of** = pretending to be.

guitar [gɪ'tɑː] n. stringed musical instrument played with the fingers; **electric g.** = guitar which is connected to an amplifier. **guitarist,** n. person who plays a guitar.

gulch [gʌltʃ] n. gully.

gulf [gʌlf] n. (a) area of sea partly surrounded by coast. (b) wide difference (**between** points of view). **Gulf Stream,** n. warm current which crosses the Atlantic from West to East.

gull [gʌl] n. long-winged, web-footed sea bird.

gullet ['gʌlɪt] n. food tube from the mouth to the stomach.

gullible ['gʌlɪbl] adj. easily taken in/ready to believe anything. **gullibility** [gʌlɪ'bɪlɪtɪ] n. being gullible.

gully ['gʌlɪ] *n.* small ravine/water channel.

gulp [gʌlp] **1.** *n.* quick swallow. **2.** *v.* (*also* **to gulp down**) to swallow hastily.

gum [gʌm] **1.** *n.* (*a*) sticky substance produced by some trees. (*b*) thin glue. (*c*) flesh in which the teeth are set. (*d*) **(chewing) g.** = sweet sticky substance you chew but do not swallow. **2.** *v.* (**gummed**) to stick together; **gummed label** = label with dry glue, which sticks if moistened. **gumboil**, *n.* small abcess on a gum. **gumboot**, *n.* rubber boot. **gumdrop**, *n.* type of hard sweet. **gumshoe**, *n. Am. Sl.* private detective. **gum tree**, *n.* eucalyptus tree; *inf.* **up a g. t.** = in a difficult spot.

gumption ['gʌmpʃn] *n.* enterprising spirit/resourcefulness.

gun [gʌn] **1.** *n.* weapon which uses an explosive force to send out a bullet; **starting g.** = weapon used to make a bang to start a race; **grease g.** = instrument for injecting a small amount of grease into a part of an engine; **to stick to one's guns** = to maintain one's position; **to jump the g.** = to start doing sth before you should. **2.** *v.* (**gunned**) (*a*) to shoot at. (*b*) **to be gunning for s.o.** = to be trying to attack s.o. **gunboat**, *n.* small ship carrying heavy guns. **gun carriage**, *n.* vehicle which carries a heavy gun. **gundog**, *n.* dog trained to accompany hunters shooting birds. **gunfire**, *n.* firing of a gun. **gunman**, *n.* (*pl.* **-men**) armed robber. **gunner**, *n.* soldier in the artillery; person who fires a gun. **gunnery**, *n.* management of large guns. **gun metal**, *n.* dark grey metal, made of copper, tin, lead and zinc. **gunpowder**, *n.* explosive substance. **gunroom**, *n.* (*a*) room where you keep sporting guns. (*b*) compartment for junior officers in a warship. **gun runner**, *n.* person who brings guns into a country illegally. **gun running**, *n.* illegal importing of guns. **gunshot**, *n.* bullet from a gun; sound made by a gun being fired. **gunsmith**, *n.* manufacturer of guns. **gunwale** ['gʌnl] *n.* upper edge of ship's side.

gunge [gʌndʒ] *n. Sl.* sticky/dirty stuff.

gung-ho [gʌŋ'həʊ] *adj. inf.* wildly militaristic.

gunny ['gʌnɪ] *n.* thick material for making sacks.

guppy ['gʌpɪ] *n.* small tropical fish often kept as a pet.

gurgle ['gɜːgl] **1.** *n.* bubbling sound. **2.** *v.* to make a bubbling sound.

guru ['guːruː] *n.* notable thinker who has many disciples.

gush [gʌʃ] **1.** *n.* sudden stream/sudden rush of liquid. **2.** *v.* (*a*) to flow heavily. (*b*) to speak effusively; to praise too much. **gusher**, *n.* oil well where the oil comes out so strongly that it does not need to be pumped. **gushing**, *adj.* praising/talking extravagantly.

gusset ['gʌsɪt] *n.* triangle of cloth inserted in an article of clothing to make it larger. **gusseted**, *adj.* with gussets.

gust [gʌst] **1.** *n.* sudden violent rush of wind or rain. **2.** *v.* to blow in gusts. **gustily**, *adv.* in gusts. **gusty**, *adj.* windy.

gusto ['gʌstəʊ] *n.* (*no pl.*) zest/enthusiasm.

gut [gʌt] **1.** *n.* (*a*) lower part of the intestine; *inf.* **g. reaction** = natural/instinctive reaction; *inf.* **I hate his guts** = I dislike him a lot. (*b*) *inf.* **guts** = courage. (*c*) material made from the intestines of animals and used for violin and tennis racket strings. **2.** *v.* (**gutted**) (*a*) to take out the internal organs of (animal/fish). (*b*) to remove/to destroy (the contents of sth); **the house was gutted by fire. gutsy**, *adj. inf.* brave.

gutta-percha [gʌtə'pɜːʃə] *n.* soft rubbery substance from Malaya.

gutter ['gʌtə] **1.** *n.* shallow trough below the eaves of a house or at the side of a street to carry away rainwater; **g. press** = newspapers which specialize in scandals. **2.** *v.* (*of a candle*) to flicker so that the molten wax runs down the side. **guttering**, *n.* (*no pl.*) curved metal or plastic used to make gutters. **guttersnipe**, *n.* dirty child, living in the poor part of a town.

guttural ['gʌtərəl] *adj.* produced in the throat. **gutturally**, *adv.* spoken in the throat.

guy [gaɪ] **1.** *n.* (*a*) man/fellow. (*b*) rope. (*c*) figure of a man burnt on a bonfire in England on 5th November. **2.** *v.* to imitate (s.o.) in a funny way. **guyrope**, *n.* rope which holds a tent tight.

guzzle ['gʌzl] *v*. to eat or drink greedily. **guzzler,** *n*. person who eats greedily.

gym [dʒɪm], **gymnasium** [dʒɪm-'neɪzɪəm] *n*. hall for indoor athletics and exercises. **gymnast** ['dʒɪmnæst] *n*. expert in gymnastics. **gymnastic** [dʒɪm-'næstɪk] *adj*. referring to gymnastics. **gymnastics,** *n*. exercises on wall bars/ wooden horse, etc., to help develop muscles and physical coordination. **gymslip,** *n*. dark-coloured dress with no sleeves, worn by schoolgirls as part of their uniform.

gymkhana [dʒɪm'kɑːnə] *n*. competition for horse riding and racing; *Am*. display of car driving.

gynaecology [gaɪnə'kɒlədʒɪ] *n*. study of the diseases of women's reproductive system. **gynaecologist,** *n*. doctor specializing in diseases of women's reproductive system. **gynaecological** [gaɪnəkə'lodʒɪkl] *adj*. referring to women's diseases.

gypsophila [dʒɪp'sofɪlə] *n*. garden plant with masses of small white flowers.

gypsum ['dʒɪpsəm] *n*. sulphate of lime.

gypsy ['dʒɪpsɪ] *n. see* **gipsy.**

gyrate [dʒaɪ'reɪt] *v*. to turn round; to move rhythmically. **gyration** [dʒaɪ-'reɪʃn] *n*. circular movement. **gyratory** [dʒaɪ'reɪtərɪ] *adj*. turning round in a circle.

gyro- ['dʒaɪrəʊ] *prefix meaning* revolving; **gyro-compass** = compass which uses a gyroscope to avoid the shock of movement. **gyroscope** ['dʒaɪrəskəʊp] *n*. spinning wheel mounted so that it can rotate on any axis. **gyroscopic** [dʒaɪrə-'skopɪk] *adj*. rapidly spinning.

Hh

H *symbol for* hydrogen.

ha [hɑː] (*a*) *inter. showing surprise*. (*b*) *abbrev. for* hectare.

habeas corpus ['heɪbɪəs 'kɔːpəs] *n*. order to bring a prisoner to answer a charge in court.

haberdashery ['hæbədæʃrɪ] *n*. shop/ department selling buttons, ribbons, thread.

habit ['hæbɪt] *n*. (*a*) custom; regular way of doing sth; **from force of h.** = because it is sth you ordinarily do.

(*b*) dress; **riding h.** = special dress for horse riding. **habit-forming,** *adj*. (drug) which you can become addicted to. **habitual** [hə'bɪtjʊəl] *adj*. regular/ normal. **habitually,** *adv*. ordinarily/ in the usual way. **habituate,** *v*. to accustom (s.o.) to doing sth. **habitué** [hæ'bɪtjʊeɪ] *n*. regular client/visitor.

habitat ['hæbɪtæt] *n*. place where a certain animal or plant is usually found.

habitation [hæbɪ'teɪʃn] *n*. place/building where s.o. lives; **not fit for h.** = not fit to live in. **habitable** ['hæbɪtəbl] *adj*. fit to live in.

hack [hæk] **1.** *n*. (*a*) horse which is hired. (*b*) writer who is paid by the piece. (*c*) *Sl*. second-rate journalist. **2.** (*a*) *v*. to chop roughly. (*b*) to kick. (*c*) to enter a computer system illegally, using a modem. **hacker,** *n*. person who hacks into a computer system. **hacking,** *adj*. dry and unpleasant (cough).

hackles ['hæklz] *n. pl*. neck feathers (on a cock); hairs on the neck (of a dog); **to put s.o.'s h. up** = to make s.o. annoyed.

hackney ['hæknɪ] *n*. **h. carriage** = taxi. **hackneyed** ['hæknɪd] *adj*. (phrase) which is often used.

hacksaw ['hæksɔː] *n*. saw for cutting metal, which has a narrow blade attached to a frame.

had [hæd] *v. see* **have.**

haddock ['hædək] *n*. (*pl*. **haddock**) common white sea fish.

Hades ['heɪdiːz] *n*. hell.

haematite ['hiːmətaɪt] *n*. iron ore.

haemoglobin [hiːmə'gləʊbɪn] *n*. substance in red blood cells which contains iron and carries oxygen.

haemophilia [hiːmə'fɪlɪə] *n*. hereditary disease in males which prevents blood from clotting. **haemophiliac,** *n*. person suffering from haemophilia.

haemorrhage ['hemərɪdʒ] **1.** *n*. loss of much blood, usu. internally. **2.** *v*. to suffer a haemorrhage.

haemorrhoids ['hemərɔɪdz] *n. pl*. small swollen veins at the anus.

haft [hɑːft] *n*. handle (of a knife, etc.).

hag [hæg] *n*. witch; ugly old woman.

haggard ['hægəd] *adj*. thin/tired (face).

haggis ['hægɪs] *n*. Scottish food, made of sheep's heart, liver, etc., cooked with oatmeal in a bag.

haggle ['hægl] v. (**over**) to discuss a price to try to reduce it.

hagiography ['hægɪɒgrəfi] n. writing about saints.

ha-ha ['hɑːhɑː] **1.** inter. to show that you are amused. **2.** n. fence put at the bottom of a ditch.

haiku ['haɪkuː] n. very short Japanese poem.

hail [heɪl] **1.** n. (a) small pieces of ice which fall like frozen rain. (b) small missiles which fall. (c) call; **within h.** = near enough to be called. **2.** v. (a) to fall as small pieces of ice; to fall in small pieces. (b) to call out to (s.o.); to wave to (a taxi) to stop. (c) to come **from**. **hailstone**, n. small piece of ice falling from the sky. **hailstorm**, n. storm when hailstones fall from the sky.

hair ['heə] n. (a) single long thread growing on the body of a human or animal. (b) mass of hairs growing on the head; inf. **to let your h. down** = to relax/become less formal. **hairbrush**, n. special brush for keeping your hair tidy. **haircut**, n. making your hair shorter by cutting. **hairdo**, n. inf. style of a woman's hair. **hairdresser**, n. person who cuts/dyes/styles hair. **hairdresser's**, n. shop where people can have their hair cut and styled. **hairdressing**, n. cutting/dyeing/styling hair. **hairless**, adj. with no hair. **hairline**, n. (a) line where the hair meets the forehead. (b) very thin line/crack. **hairnet**, n. light net worn over the hair to keep it in place. **hairpiece**, n. small wig; piece of false hair. **hairpin**, n. bent piece of wire used to keep hair in place; **h. bend** = very sharp bend, as on a mountain road. **hair-raising**, adj. frightening. **hairspring**, n. spiral spring in a watch. **hairstyle**, n. way of dressing/cutting, etc., the hair. **hairy**, adj. (-**ier**, -**iest**) (a) covered with hairs. (b) Sl. frighteningly dangerous.

hake [heɪk] n. (pl. **hake**) common small white sea fish.

halcyon ['hælsɪən] adj. calm/beautiful (weather); carefree (days).

hale [heɪl] adj. **h. and hearty** = very healthy.

half [hɑːf] **1.** n. (pl. **halves** [hɑːvs]) (a) one of two equal parts; **first h.** = first part of a match; **to go halves** = each pays half. (b) midfield player in Rugby. (c) child's ticket which costs half the adult fare. **2.** adj. being divided into two equal parts; **h. an hour** = 30 minutes. **3.** adv. partly/not fully; **h. as tall** = smaller by half, 50 per cent of the size. **half-and-half**, adv. in two equal quantities. **half-back**, n. defence player in football/rugby. **half-baked**, adj. inf. (plan) which has not been well thought out; (person) who cannot plan. **half-breed**, n. person/animal with parents of different races. **half-brother**, n. brother who has one parent the same as you. **half-caste**, n. person with parents of two different races. **half-cock**, n. **to go off at half-cock** = have a bad start. **half-dozen**, n. six. **half-empty**, adj. partly empty/not completely empty. **half-fare**, n. fare reduced by half. **half-full**, adj. partly full/not completely full. **half-hardy**, adj. (plant) which can stand some cold but not hard frost. **half-hearted**, adj. lacking conviction/enthusiasm. **half-hourly**, adj. & adv. every thirty minutes. **half-life**, n. time taken for a substance to lose half its radioactivity. **half-mast**, n. **the flags are at half-mast** = the flags are flying halfway up the flagpole as a sign of mourning. **half-nelson**, n. hold in wrestling, where the victor twists the arm of the victim below his back. **half-open**, adj. partly open/not completely open. **halfpenny** ['heɪpnɪ] n. (pl. -**pennies** = coins, -**pence** = price) coin worth half a penny. **half-sister**, n. sister who has one parent the same as you. **half-term**, n. short holiday in the middle of a term. **half-timbered**, adj. (house) whose walls are made of wooden beams with brick or plaster walls between. **half-time**, n. short rest in the middle of a game. **half-tone**, n. photograph reproduced by means of dots of varying sizes. **half-track**, n. vehicle driven by caterpillar tracks behind and by ordinary wheels in front. **half-volley**, n. (in tennis) hitting the ball just after it has bounced. **halfway**, adv. in the middle of a distance or length; **to meet s.o. h.** = to compromise with s.o. **halfwit**, *n.* idiot. **half-witted**, *adj.* stupid. **half-year**, *n.* six months. **half-yearly**, *adj. & adv.* (taking place) every six months.

halibut ['hælɪbət] *n.* (*pl.* **halibut**) large white flatfish living in the sea.

halitosis [hælɪ'təʊsɪs] *n.* bad-smelling breath.

hall [hɔ:l] *n.* (*a*) large room; large building for public meetings; **h. of residence** = large building where students live in a college. (*b*) (**entrance**) **h.** = room or passage through which you enter a house. (*c*) large house, usu. in the country.

hallelujah [hælɪ'lu:jə] *inter. meaning* praise to God.

hallmark ['hɔ:lmɑ:k] *n.* mark put on gold and silver to show that it has the correct purity. **hallmarked**, *adj.* (silver spoon, etc.) with a hallmark stamped on it.

hallo [hə'ləʊ] *inter. showing a greeting.*

halloo [hə'lu:] **1.** *n.* call to dogs when hunting. **2.** *v.* to shout halloo.

hallow ['hæləʊ] *v.* to bless (sth)/to declare (sth) holy; **hallowed ground** = ground (near a church) which has been blessed. **Hallowe'en** [hæləʊ'i:n] *n.* 31st October, the eve of All Saints' Day, when witches and ghosts are said to roam about.

hallucination [həlu:sɪ'neɪʃn] *n.* seeing things which are not there; thing seen when you hallucinate. **hallucinate** [hə'lu:sɪneɪt] *v.* to see things which are not there. **hallucinatory** [hə'lu:sɪnətrɪ] *adj.* (drug) which causes hallucinations. **hallucinogen** [hə'lu:sɪnədʒən] *n.* substance which gives you hallucinations. **hallucinogenic**, *adj.* which causes hallucinations.

halo ['heɪləʊ] *n.* (*pl.* **-oes**) glow of light (round the moon/round the head of a saint).

halogen ['hælədʒən] *n.* one of a group of chemical elements (including chlorine/fluorine/iodine).

halt [hɔ:lt] **1.** *n.* (*a*) complete stop; **to come to a h.** = to stop; **to call a h. to** = to bring to a stop. (*b*) very small railway station. **2.** *v.* to stop. **halting**, *adj.* hesitant.

halter ['hɔ:ltə] *n.* rope put round an-

imal's neck to lead it; **h. neck dress** = dress with a piece of material going round the back of the neck, leaving the arms and back bare.

halve [hɑ:v] *v.* (*a*) to divide into two equal parts. (*b*) to reduce by half. **halves**, *n. pl. see* **half**.

halyard ['hæljəd] *n.* rope used to pull up a flag/sail.

ham [hæm] **1.** *n.* (*a*) salted or smoked meat from a pig's leg usu. eaten cold. (*b*) *inf.* bad actor. (*c*) *inf.* amateur radio operator working from home. **2.** *v.* (**hammed**) to act badly. **ham-fisted**, **ham-handed**, *adj.* clumsy.

hamburger ['hæmbɜ:gə] *n.* flat cake of minced beef, cooked and eaten as a sandwich in a toasted roll.

hamlet ['hæmlət] *n.* small village.

hammer ['hæmə] **1.** *n.* (*a*) heavy metal tool for knocking nails into wood/posts into the ground, etc. (*b*) object which hits sth as part of a machine. (*c*) metal ball which is thrown in sporting contests. **2.** *v.* to hit hard, as with a hammer. **hammer out**, *v.* (*a*) to make (sth) flat with a hammer. (*b*) **to h. out an agreement** = to come to an agreement after long difficult discussions. **hammer toe**, *n.* deformed toe which bends downwards.

hammock ['hæmək] *n.* hanging bed made of a strong cloth or net.

hamper ['hæmpə] **1.** *n.* large basket. **2.** *v.* to stop/to hinder/to get in the way.

hamster ['hæmstə] *n.* small rodent, often kept as a pet.

hamstring ['hæmstrɪŋ] *n.* tendon behind the knee. **hamstrung**, *adj.* incapacitated; unable to do anything.

hand [hænd] **1.** *n.* (*a*) part of the body at the end of each arm; **to have a h. in sth** = to help to make sth happen; **to give a h./lend a h. with** = to help with; **at h.** = near; **in h.** = in reserve; **on h.** = readily available; **out of h.** = uncontrollable. (*b*) workman; sailor; **an old h.** = very experienced person. (*c*) cards which have been dealt you in a game. (*d*) one of pointers on a clock or dial. (*e*) round of applause. (*f*) unit of measurement of the height of a horse. **2.** *v.* to pass (sth) **to s.o. by hand. handbag**, *n.* woman's bag for carrying money, handkerchief and other belongings. **handbill,** *n.* small poster. **handbook,** *n.* book which gives instructions or information. **handbrake,** *n.* lever in a vehicle which works the brakes. **handclap,** *n.* **slow h.** = regular slow beating of the hands to show impatience/boredom. **handcuff,** *v.* to attach (s.o.'s hands) with handcuffs. **handcuffs,** *n. pl.* metal rings linked by a chain for attaching a prisoner's hands together. **handful,** *n.* as much as you can hold in your hand; small number; person who is difficult to control. **handgun,** *n.* small gun which is carried in the hand. **handicap. 1.** *n.* (*a*) physical/mental disability; thing which puts you at a disadvantage. (*b*) penalty imposed on good sportsmen to make it harder for them to win. **2.** *v.* (**handicapped**) to put at a disadvantage; **the mentally handicapped** = people with a disability of the mind. **handicapper,** *n.* person who calculates a sportsman's handicap. **handicraft,** *n.* work done by hand; **handicrafts** = artistic work done by hand (such as knitting/pottery, etc.). **handily,** *adv.* in a handy way. **hand in,** *v.* to give in by hand. **handiwork,** *n.* work done by a particular person. **handkerchief** ['hæŋkətʃiːf] *n.* square piece of cloth or paper for wiping your nose. **handmade,** *adj.* made by hand, not by machine. **hand on,** *v.* to pass on by hand. **hand out,** *v.* to distribute. **handout,** *n.* (*a*) money which is given out. (*b*) printed information sheet given out to people. **hand over,** *v.* to give (sth) to s.o. **handpicked,** *adj.* carefully selected. **handrail,** *n.* bar which you hold on to (next to a staircase, escalator, etc.). **hand round,** *v.* to pass round by hand. **handset,** *n.* the part of a telephone which is held in the hand. **handshake,** *n.* greeting when you grasp hands. **handspring,** *n.* gymnastic exercise where you turn a somersault on your hands and land on your feet. **handstand,** *n.* **to do a h.** = to balance on your hands with your feet in the air. **handwriting,** *n.* writing done by hand. **handwritten,** *adj.* written by hand, not typed or printed. **handy,** *adj.* (**-ier, -iest**) useful; in a convenient

place. **handyman,** *n.* (*pl.* **-men**) person who can do any sort of work, esp. repairs in the house.

handle ['hændl] **1.** *n.* part of an object which you hold in the hand; *inf.* **to fly off the h.** = to lose your temper. **2.** *v.* (*a*) to move (goods) around (by hand). (*b*) to deal with (sth); **handling charge** = charge which has to be paid to s.o. who has delivered or dealt with sth. **handlebar(s),** *n.* (*pl.*) bar on the front of a bicycle or motorcycle which steers the front wheel.

handsome ['hænsəm] *adj.* (*a*) good-looking. (*b*) fine/large (profit). **handsomely,** *adv.* elegantly; generously.

hang [hæŋ] **1.** *n.* (*a*) way in which sth hangs/drops/falls; *inf.* **to get the h. of sth** = to understand how sth works. (*b*) *inf.* **he doesn't give/care a h.** = he doesn't worry about it at all. **2.** *v.* (**hung**) (*a*) to attach/to be attached above the ground to a nail or by a string/chain, etc. (*b*) to stick (wallpaper) on a wall. (*c*) (**hanged**) to kill (s.o.) by tying a rope round his neck and suspending him off the ground. **hang about, hang around,** *v. inf.* to wait/to wander aimlessly in a certain place. **hang back,** *v.* to stay behind the others. **hangdog,** *adj. inf.* sheepish (expression). **hang down,** *v.* to hang in a long piece. **hanger,** *n.* object for hanging sth; **coat h.** = piece of wood/plastic/metal which is placed inside a coat to hang it up. **hanger-on,** *n.* (*pl.* **hangers-on**) person who stays near s.o. in the hope of getting money or food. **hang fire,** *v.* to be slow in happening/in taking effect. **hang glider,** *n.* huge kite used in hang gliding. **hang gliding,** *n.* sport of floating through the air by hanging on to a huge kite made of a metal frame covered with plastic. **hanging,** *n.* carpet/tapestry which is hung on a wall as decoration. **hangman,** *n.* (*pl.* **-men**) executioner who kills people by hanging them. **hangnail,** *n.* torn skin at the root of a fingernail. **hang on,** *v.* (*a*) **to h. on to sth** = to clutch (sth)/to keep (sth). (*b*) *inf.* to wait. **hang out,** *v. inf.* to live (in a place). **hangover,** *n.* (*a*) unpleasant effects of having drunk too much alcohol. **hang up,** *v.* to hang (sth) on a hook; to replace (a telephone receiver). **hang-up**, n. (pl. **hang-ups**) Sl. thing which worries you and prevents you from acting normally.

hangar ['hæŋə] n. large shed for keeping aircraft in.

hank [hæŋk] n. wool coiled into a loose loop.

hanker ['hæŋkə] v. **to h. after/for** = to want (very much). **hankering**, n. desire.

hanky ['hæŋkɪ] n. inf. handkerchief.

hankypanky [hæŋkɪ'pæŋkɪ] n. inf. trouble/bad behaviour; trickery.

Hansard ['hænsɑːd] n. official report of what is said in Parliament.

haphazard [hæp'hæzəd] adj. done at random/unplanned. **haphazardly**, adv. at random; without any plan.

hapless ['hæpləs] adj. (formal) unfortunate/unlucky.

happen ['hæpn] v. (a) to take place; **what has happened to him?** = (i) what is he doing now? (ii) what harm has come to him? (b) to take place by chance. **happening**, n. event/thing which takes place. **happenstance**, n. **by h.** = by a coincidence.

happy ['hæpɪ] adj. (-ier, -iest) glad/full of joy. **happily**, adv. joyfully/gladly. **happiness**, n. joy/gladness. **happy-go-lucky**, adj. easy-going/carefree.

hara-kiri [hærə'kɪrɪ] n. Japanese form of suicide.

harangue [hə'ræŋ] **1.** n. loud speech. **2.** v. to make a loud speech to (s.o.).

harass ['hærəs, Am. hə'ræs] v. to bother/ to worry (s.o.). **harassment**, n. bothering/worrying; many small attacks on an enemy.

harbinger ['hɑːbɪndʒə] n. (formal) thing which shows that sth else is approaching.

harbour, Am. **harbor** ['hɑːbə] **1.** n. port/ safe place where ships can tie up to load or unload. **2.** v. (a) to keep (a grudge) against s.o. (b) to protect (a criminal). (c) to hold (germs) and allow them to spread.

hard [hɑːd] **1.** adj. (-er, -est) (a) firm/ not soft. (b) h. **currency** = one which does not lose its value compared to other currencies. (c) difficult; h. **lines/ h. luck** = bad luck; h. **labour** =

punishment involving difficult manual work. (d) strict/severe. (e) (of water) containing calcium, which makes it difficult to form a lather. (f) strong (drink); (drug) which makes you become addicted; h. **drinker** = person who drinks a lot of alcohol. **2.** adv. (a) strongly. (b) with difficulty. **hard-and-fast**, adj. strict/absolute (rule). **hardback**, n. book with a stiff cover. **hardboard**, n. artificial board made of small shreds of wood stuck together. **hard-boiled**, adj. (a) (egg) which has been boiled until the white and yolk are set solid. (b) (person) without much feeling/who is not easily shocked. **hard by**, adv. close. **hardcore**. **1.** n. (a) packed rubble used in making paths. (b) central part (of a group). **2.** adj. referring to a central group. **hard disk**, n. solid disk, fixed in a computer. **harden**, v. to make hard; **hardened criminal** = regular/permanent criminal. **harden off**, v. to bring (tender plants) into the open air. **hard hat**, n. protective helmet worn by construction workers, etc. **hard-headed**, adj. practical/sensible. **hard-hearted**, adj. cruel. **hardliner**, n. person who is very antagonistic/stern towards s.o./an enemy, etc. **hardly**, adv. almost not. **hardness**, n. being solid/hard/not soft; difficulty; strictness. **hard of hearing**, adj. (person) who is quite deaf. **hard sell**, n. strenuous efforts to sell sth. **hardship**, n. suffering caused by lack of sth. **hard shoulder**, n. strip along the edge of a motorway where vehicles can park if they have broken down. **hard up**, adj. inf. with no money. **hardware**, n. (no pl.) (a) tools, pots and pans; h. **shop** = shop selling pans/ hammers/nails/paint, etc.; **military h.** = guns, tanks, and other military equipment. (b) physical parts/machinery of a computer. **hard-wearing**, adj. which does not wear out easily. **hardwood**, n. wood which comes from deciduous trees. **hardworking**, adj. (person) who works hard. **hardy**, adj. (-ier, -iest) which can survive in difficult conditions; (plant) which can stay out of doors all the year round.

hare ['heə] **1.** n. common field mammal, like a large rabbit. **2.** v. to run fast. **hare-brained,** *adj.* mad/senseless (plan). **harebell,** *n.* wild flower shaped like a little blue bell. **harelip,** *n.* split in the upper lip from birth.

harem ['ha:'ri:m] *n.* women in a Muslim household; women's quarters in a Muslim house.

haricot ['hærɪkəʊ] *n.* **h. (bean)** = dry white bean eaten cooked.

hark [ha:k] **1.** *old inter. meaning* listen. **2.** *v.* **to h. back to** = to go back to (a subject talked about earlier).

harlequin ['ha:lɪkwɪn] *n.* character in old pantomime, wearing a mask and a suit of diamond-patterned cloth.

harlot ['ha:lət] *n.* (*formal*) prostitute.

harm [ha:m] **1.** *n.* damage. **2.** *v.* to damage/to hurt. **harmful,** *adj.* which hurts/ which causes damage. **harmless,** *adj.* which causes no damage/which does not hurt.

harmony ['ha:mənɪ] *n.* (*a*) musical sounds which do not clash. agreeable effect (of music/colour, etc.). (*b*) general agreement. **harmonic** [ha:-'mɒnɪk]. **1.** *adj.* referring to harmony. **2.** *n.* higher note which is heard when a note is played. **harmonica** [ha:-'mɒnɪkə] *n.* mouth organ. **harmonious** [ha:'məʊnɪəs] *adj.* (sounds) which are in agreement/which sound well together. **harmoniously,** *adv.* in a harmonious way. **harmonium** [ha:-'məʊnɪəm] *n.* musical instrument like an organ where the sound comes from air pumped through reeds. **harmonization,** [ha:mənaɪ'zeɪʃn] *n.* act of harmonizing. **harmonize,** *v.* (*a*) to agree together. (*b*) to form chords out of the main tune of a piece of music.

harness ['ha:nəs] **1.** *n.* (*a*) leather straps which attach a horse to a cart; **he is still in h.** = he is still working. (*b*) straps for attaching a parachute to s.o.; straps which have a lead attached to control a small child. **2.** *v.* (*a*) to attach (a horse) to a cart. (*b*) to use (natural resources/ atomic power, etc.) for making energy.

harp [ha:p] **1.** *n.* large upright musical instrument, with many strings which are plucked with the fingers. **2.** *v.* **to h. on about** = keep talking about. **harpist,** *n.* person who plays a harp.

harpoon [ha:'pu:n] **1.** *n.* long barbed spear used to kill whales. **2.** *v.* to kill (a whale) with a harpoon.

harpsichord ['ha:psɪkɔ:d] *n.* old musical instrument, like a piano, but with strings which are plucked.

harpy ['ha:pɪ] *n.* (*a*) cruel mythical monster, with a woman's body and an eagle's claws. (*b*) cruel person (esp. woman).

harrier ['hærɪə] *n.* (*a*) dog/person who hunts hares. (*b*) long-distance runner. (*c*) type of falcon.

harrow ['hærəʊ] **1.** *n.* large rake pulled by a tractor for breaking up heavy soil. **2.** *v.* to break up soil with a harrow. **harrowing,** *adj.* very sad, causing mental pain.

harry ['hærɪ] *v.* to bother/to worry (s.o.) by continual attacks.

harsh [ha:ʃ] *adj.* (**-er, -est**) (*a*) cruel/ sharp (punishment, etc.). (*b*) rough/unpleasant (voice, etc.). **harshly,** *adv.* in a harsh way. **harshness,** *n.* cruelty/ roughness.

hart [ha:t] *n.* male deer.

harum-scarum [heərəm'skeərəm] *adj. & n.* wild (young person).

harvest ['ha:vɪst] **1.** *n.* (*a*) cutting/ picking of ripe crops. (*b*) period of the year when crops are picked. **2.** *v.* to cut/ to pick ripe crops. **harvester,** *n.* person/ machine which cuts crops.

has [hæz] *v. see* **have. has-been** ['hæzbi:n] *n.* (*pl.* **has-beens**) *inf.* person/thing no longer as well known/important as before.

hash [hæʃ] **1.** *n.* (*a*) minced meat; *inf.* **he made a h. of it** = he did it badly. (*b*) *inf.* hashish. (*c*) **h. (sign)** = printed sign **2.** (**#**) used in computers as an indicator. *v.* to mince (meat, etc.); *Am.* **hash(ed) brown potatoes** = fried grated potatoes.

hashish ['hæʃɪʃ] *n.* hemp used as a drug.

hasp [ha:sp] *n.* metal bar, which closes a door or lid by fitting over a loop which is locked with a padlock.

hassle ['hæsl] **1.** *n. inf.* bother/struggle to do sth. **2.** *v. inf.* to struggle/to argue.

hassock ['hæsək] *n.* cushion for kneeling on in a church.

haste [heɪst] *n.* speed; **to make h.** = to hurry up. **hasten** ['heɪsn] *v.* to make (sth) go faster/come faster; to hurry up. **hastily,** *adv.* rapidly. **hastiness,** *n.* being hasty. **hasty**, *adj.* (**-ier, -iest**) rapid and with not enough preparation.

hat [hæt] *n.* piece of clothing worn on the head; **keep it under your h.** = keep it secret; **h. trick** = three goals, etc., scored by the same person in the same game. **hatband**, *n.* piece of ribbon which goes round a hat. **hatless**, *adj.* not wearing a hat.

hatch [hætʃ] 1. *n.* opening in a ship's deck; opening in the floor or wall of an aircraft; **service h.** = small opening in a wall for passing food from a kitchen to a dining room. 2. *v.* (*a*) to warm (eggs) until baby birds appear; (*of a baby bird*) to break out of the egg; to plan (a plot). (*b*) to indicate shade in a sketch by drawing parallel lines close together. **hatchback**, *n.* type of car with a sloping back and a large rear door which opens upwards. **hatchery**, *n.* place where eggs are kept until they develop into young. **hatchway**, *n.* opening in a ship's deck.

hatchet ['hætʃɪt] *n.* small axe; *inf.* **to bury the h.** = to make peace; *Sl.* **h. man** = person brought into a firm to sack some of the staff. **hatchet-faced**, *adj.* (person) with a grim pointed face.

hate [heɪt] 1. *n.* great dislike. 2. *v.* to dislike intensely. **hateful**, *adj.* horrible/unpleasant. **hatred**, *n.* great dislike.

hatter ['hætə] *n.* person who makes men's hats.

haughty ['hɔːtɪ] *adj.* (**-ier, -iest**) very proud. **haughtily**, *adv.* proudly. **haughtiness**, *n.* being haughty.

haul [hɔːl] 1. *n.* (*a*) catch (of fish); **the burglars made a good h.** = they stole a lot of valuable property. (*b*) distance travelled. 2. *v.* to pull with difficulty. **haulage**, *n.* moving of goods by road; **h. contractor** = person who arranges for goods to be moved by road. **haulier**, *n.* haulage contractor.

haulm [hɔːm] *n.* stems of peas/beans/potatoes.

haunch [hɔːnʃ] *n.* thigh and loin (of an animal); **the dog was sitting on its haunches** = sitting in a squatting position.

haunt [hɔːnt] 1. *n.* place where s.o. goes frequently. 2. *v.* to go to (a place) frequently; (*of ghosts*) to appear in (a place). **haunted**, *adj.* (house) where a ghost appears.

have [hæv] *v.* (**I have, he has; I had, he had**) (*a*) (*also* **have got**) to possess. **the house has (got) no telephone.** (*b*) to take (a meal/a bath). (*c*) to play; **will you h. a game of tennis?** (*d*) to get (sth) done. (*f*) (*making the past tense of verbs*) **h. you finished your work?** (*g*) (*showing compulsion to do something*) **you will h. to sing that song again; you had better say nothing.** **have got**, *v.* **to have got to do sth** = to be obliged/to have to do sth. **have had**, *v. inf.* **he's had it** = he is finished/he has missed an opportunity. **have on**, *v.* (*a*) to be wearing. (*b*) to be busy/occupied; **have you anything on tonight?** (*c*) *inf.* to trick (s.o.); **they're having you on. have out**, *v.* (*a*) **to have a tooth out** = to get a tooth removed by a dentist. (*b*) **to have it out with s.o.** = to sort out a quarrel with s.o. **have up**, *v. inf.* to call (s.o.) to a court; **he has been had up for speeding.**

haven ['heɪvn] *n.* safe port; safe place; **tax h.** = country where taxes are low.

haver ['heɪvə] *v.* to hesitate.

haversack ['hævəsæk] *n.* bag carried on the back.

havoc ['hævək] *n.* damage; **to play h. with** = do a lot of damage to.

haw [hɔː] 1. *n.* small red berry on the hawthorn. 2. *v. see* **hum. hawfinch**, *n.* largest European finch.

hawk [hɔːk] 1. *n.* (*a*) bird of prey; **she has eyes like a h.** = she has very good eyesight/notices every detail. (*b*) person who is in favour of military attacks on an enemy/who is prepared to take a hard line in international relations. 2. *v.* (*a*) to sell goods from door to door. (*b*) to clear your throat. **hawker**, *n.* person who sells things from place to place.

hawse [hɔːz] *n.* bow of a ship, with holes for the anchor cable. **hawser** ['hɔːzə] *n.* thick rope for attaching a boat to the quay.

hawthorn ['hɔːθɔːn] *n.* common hedge shrub with white flowers and red berries.

hay [heɪ] *n.* long dried grass used to feed cattle in winter; **to make h. while the sun shines** = to enjoy yourself/to make money while you can. **hayfever**, *n.* running nose/eyes, etc., caused by an allergy to pollen or dust. **hayfield**, *n.*

field of grass which will be cut to make hay. **haymaking,** *n.* cutting of the hay. **hayseed,** *n. inf.* silly country person. **haystack,** *n.* bales of hay stored in a large heap built like a house. **haywire,** *adj. inf.* **he's gone h.** = he's gone mad.

hazard ['hæzəd] **1.** *n.* (*a*) risk. (*b*) rough ground (on a golf course). **2.** *v.* to risk; **he hazarded a guess** = he made a rough guess. **hazardous,** *adj.* dangerous/risky.

haze [heɪz] *n.* light mist. **hazily,** *adv.* vaguely. **haziness,** *n.* being hazy. **hazy,** *adj.* (*-ier, -iest*) (*a*) misty. (*b*) vague.

hazel ['heɪzl] **1.** *n.* tree which bears small nuts. **2.** *adj. & n.* light brown (colour). **hazel nut,** *n.* nut from a hazel tree.

he [hiː] (*a*) *pronoun referring to a male person or animal;* **he is my father.** (*b*) *prefix meaning* male; **he-goat. he-man,** *n.* (*pl.* **he-men**) strong/virile man.

He *symbol for* helium.

head [hed] **1.** *n.* (*a*) part of the body with brain, eyes, ears, mouth, etc., attached to the rest of the body by the neck; **the horse won by a h.** = by the length of a head; **h. over heels** = over and over. (*b*) brain; **a good h. for figures; a bad h. for heights.** (*c*) top; leafy part (of a cabbage); foam (on the top of a glass of beer). (*d*) first one (of a lot/ a procession). (*e*) most important person; **h. waiter.** (*f*) top side of a coin; side of a coin with the head of a king on it; **to play heads or tails** = to spin a coin and try to guess which side will be on top. (*g*) part of a machine which records/picks up data on a tape recorder/computer. (*h*) (*no pl.*) number of animals; **fifty h. of sheep. 2.** *v.* (*a*) to be first/to lead. (*b*) to go **towards.** (*c*) to hit (a ball) with your head. **headache,** *n.* (*a*) pain in the head. (*b*) complicated problem. **headboard,** *n.* board/panel at the top of a bed. **headdress,** *n.* ornamental covering for the head. **header,** *n.* (*a*) dive. (*b*) hitting a ball with the head. **head first,** *adv.* with one's head first. **headgear,** *n.* hat or cap. **headhunt,** *v.* to look for candidates for important jobs. **headhunter,** *n.* (*a*) member of a tribe which cuts off the heads of enemies and collects them. (*b*) *inf.* person who tries

to find suitably qualified candidates for important jobs. **heading,** *n.* words at the top of a text. **headlamp,** *n.* main light on the front of a car/bicycle, etc. **headland,** *n.* (*a*) promontory. (*b*) land at the edge of a field, where the tractor turns. **headless,** *adj.* with no head. **headlight,** *n.* main light on the front of a car/bicycle, etc. **headline,** *n.* words in large capitals in a newspaper; **news headlines** = short summary of the main items of news on TV/radio. **headlong,** *adj. & adv.* rushing/non-stop; with your head first. **headmaster,** *n.* man in charge of a school. **headmistress,** *n.* woman in charge of a school. **head off,** *v.* to prevent (sth) from taking place. **head-on,** *adj. & adv.* with the front; head first. **headphones,** *n. pl.* apparatus for listening to radio/records, etc., which fits over your ears. **headquarters,** *n. pl.* main offices (of an army/of a firm). **headrest,** *n.* cushion/part of a seat for leaning your head on. **headroom,** *n.* space to pass upright. **headscarf,** *n.* (*pl.* **-scarves**) square piece of cloth worn by women to cover their hair. **headset,** *n.* apparatus for listening to radio/records, etc., which fits over your ears with a band across the top of your head. **headship,** *n.* position of headmaster/headmistress. **headstone,** *n.* gravestone. **headstrong,** *adj.* obstinate/self-willed. **headway,** *n.* progress/movement forward. **headwind,** *n.* wind blowing in your face. **headword,** *n.* main word in a dictionary. **heady,** *adj.* (*-ier, -iest*) (drink) which is likely to make you drunk; (news) which is likely to make you excited.

heal [hiːl] *v.* to make (a person/a wound) become healthy; to become healthy. **healing,** *n.* making healthy.

health [helθ] *n.* (*a*) state of the body where there is no sickness; **your h.!/ good h.!** = wish said when drinking; **h. farm** = clinic in the country where people who eat or drink too much go to slim; **h. foods** = natural foods (such as yoghurt/nuts, etc.) which are good for your health; **h. service** = governmentrun service providing medical treatment for everyone; **h. visitor** = person who visits sick people in their homes. (*b*) general state of the body. **healthily,** *adv.* in a healthy way. **healthiness,** *n.* being healthy. **healthy,** *adj.* (*a*) full of good health/not ill. (*b*) which gives good health. (*c*) strong (dislike, etc.).

heap [hi:p] **1.** *n.* large pile; *inf.* **heaps** = lots. **2.** *v.* to put in a pile.

hear ['hɪə] *v.* (**heard** [hɜ:'d]) to sense sounds by the ear; to listen to (sth); **he's never heard of it** = does not know about it; **he won't h. of it** = he will not allow it. **hearer,** *n.* person who hears. **hear hear!** *inter.* used to show agreement. **hearing,** *n.* (*a*) ability to hear; **h. aid** = small device for improving the hearing of s.o. who is nearly deaf. (*b*) listening to s.o. (*c*) court case. **hearsay,** *n.* what people say, rather than what is true.

heard [hɜ:d] *v. see* **hear.**

hearse [hɜ:s] *n.* vehicle for carrying a coffin.

heart [ha:t] *n.* (*a*) organ in an animal which pumps blood round the body; **h. attack** = severe illness when the heart stops temporarily; **h. failure** = dangerous condition when the heart has stopped beating; **to learn by h.** = learn by memory so that you can repeat it. (*b*) centre of the emotions; **with all my h.** = with great emotion. (*c*) centre (of a town/forest). (*d*) courage; **to lose h.** = to become discouraged; **to take h.** = to be encouraged. (*e*) **hearts** = one of the four suits of playing cards. **heartbeat,** *n.* sound of the heart pumping blood. **heart-breaking** *adj.* which makes you very sad/upset. **heart-broken,** *adj.* extremely sad/disappointed. **heartburn,** *n.* burning feeling in the chest and stomach after eating indigestible food. **hearten,** *v.* to encourage. **heartfelt,** *adj.* sincere. **heartily,** *adv.* vigorously; warmly. **heartiness,** *n.* being hearty. **heartland,** *n.* central part of a country. **heartless,** *adj.* cruel. **heartlessly,** *adv.* in a heartless way. **heart-rending,** *adj.* pitiful. **heartsearching,** *n.* deep thought about how to deal with a problem. **heartstrings,** *n. pl.* deepest feelings (of pity/love, etc.). **heart-throb,** *n.* popular film-star, etc. **heart-to-heart,** *adj.* earnest private (con-

versation). **heartwarming,** *adj.* which encourages/pleases. **hearty,** *adj.* (**-ier, -iest**) vigorous/strong; large (meal/appetite).

hearth [ha:θ] *n.* base of a fireplace; a fireplace. **hearthrug,** *n.* small rug placed in front of a fireplace.

heat [hi:t] **1.** *n.* (*a*) great warmth. (*b*) qualifying round in a competition; **dead h.** = race where two competitors come in equal first. (*c*) (*of female animal*) **on h.** = sexually excited. **2.** *v.* to warm to a higher temperature; **heated discussion** = discussion where people become quite angry. **heatedly,** *adv.* angrily. **heater,** *n.* apparatus for warming. **heating,** *n.* making sth warm; means of heating; **central h.** = heating system for a whole building from one source. **heatwave,** *n.* period of very hot weather.

heath [hi:θ] *n.* (*a*) area of wild country covered with low shrubs. (*b*) heather. **heathland,** *n.* wild country covered with low shrubs.

heathen ['hi:ðn] *adj. & n.* (person) who is not a Christian; (person) who is not a member of any important religious group.

heather ['heðə] *n.* wild plant with small purple or white bell-shaped flowers, which grows on moors and mountains.

heave [hi:v] **1.** *n.* hard pull. **2.** *v.* (**heaved**) (*a*) to pull hard. (*b*) (**hove**) **to h. to** = to stop a ship; **to h. in sight** = to appear. (*c*) *inf.* to throw. (*d*) to breathe noisily.

heaven ['hevn] *n.* paradise/place where God and the angels live; **the heavens** = the sky; **good heavens!** = how surprising! **heavenly,** *adj.* (*a*) belonging to heaven. (*b*) *inf.* beautiful; very fine. **heaven-sent,** *adj.* lucky.

heavy ['hevɪ] *adj.* (**-ier, -iest**) (*a*) weighing a lot; (meal) which is very filling and indigestible. (*b*) strong/great. (*c*) rough (sea). (*d*) full (timetable, etc.). (*e*) **h. drinker** = person who drinks a lot of alcohol. **heavily,** *adv.* (*a*) as if weighing a lot. (*b*) greatly; **h. underlined** = with thick lines put underneath. (*c*) (to sleep) soundly. **heaviness,** *n.* being heavy. **heavy-duty,** *adj.* (machine, etc.) specially made for rough work. **heavy industry,** *n.* industry which makes large products (like steel/ships/cars, etc.). **heavy water,** *n.* water containing deuterium in place of hydrogen. **heavyweight,** *n.* heaviest category of boxer.

Hebrew ['hi:bru:] *n.* (*a*) member of Jewish people living in ancient Palestine. (*b*) language of the Jews.

heckle ['hekl] *v.* to call out; to interrupt a public speaker. **heckler,** *n.* person who interrupts a speaker at a meeting. **heckling,** *n.* interrupting a speaker.

hect-, hecto- ['hekt(əʊ)] *prefix meaning* one hundred. **hectolitre,** *n.* one hundred litres.

hectare ['hekta:] *n.* (measure of) area of 10,000 square metres (approx. 2.4 acres).

hectic ['hektɪk] *adj.* very busy/active. **hectically,** *adv.* in a hectic way.

hector ['hektə] *v.* to bully/to intimidate. **hectoring,** *adj.* bullying (tone of voice).

hedge [hedʒ] **1.** *n.* (*a*) screen/fence made of growing shrubs. (*b*) protection (**against**). **2.** *v.* (*a*) to surround with a hedge. (*b*) to avoid answering a question. (*c*) **to h. your bets** = to arrange things so that you will be protected against losing. **hedgehog,** *n.* small mammal covered with prickles. **hedgerow,** *n.* long hedge, esp. by the side of a country road. **hedge sparrow,** *n.* common sparrow found in the country.

hedonist ['hi:dənɪst] *n.* person who lives for pleasure. **hedonistic,** *adj.* like a hedonist.

heed [hi:d] **1.** *n.* **to take h. of/to pay h. to** = to pay attention to. **2.** *v.* to pay attention to. **heedless,** *adj.* careless/imprudent; without paying attention. **heedlessly,** *adv.* in a heedless way.

heel [hi:l] **1.** *n.* (*a*) back part of the foot; back part of a sock/stocking into which the heel of the foot goes; **to take to one's heels** = to run away. (*b*) raised block under the back of a shoe. (*c*) *Sl.* unpleasant person. **2.** *v.* (*a*) (*in Rugby*) to kick (the ball) backwards. (*b*) to put a new heel on (a shoe). (*c*) (*of a ship*) **to h. over** = to lean to one side.

hefty ['heftɪ] *adj.* (**-ier, -iest**) large/strong.

hegemony [hɪ'gemənɪ] *n.* leadership by one country.

heifer ['hefə] *n.* young cow.

height [haɪt] *n.* (*a*) measurement of how tall or high sth is. (*b*) highest point. **heighten,** *v.* to increase/to make more noticeable.

heinous ['heɪnəs] *adj.* wicked (crime).

heir, heiress ['eə, eə'res] *n.* person who is going to inherit money, etc., from s.o. **heirloom,** *n.* valuable object which has belonged to a family for years.

held [held] *v. see* **hold.**

helical ['helɪkl] *adj. see* **helix.**

helicopter ['helɪkɒptə] *n.* type of aircraft with revolving blades on top, enabling it to take off vertically. **helipad,** *n.* small marked area where a helicopter may land. **heliport,** *n.* place where helicopters land and take off.

heliograph ['hi:lɪəgra:f] *n.* apparatus for signalling, using mirrors which flash in the sun.

heliotrope ['hi:lɪətrəʊp] *n. & adj.* plant with purple flowers; purple (colour).

helium ['hi:lɪəm] *n.* (*element:* He) light gas which does not burn.

helix ['hi:lɪks] *n.* spiral shape. **helical** ['helɪkl] *adj.* spiral.

hell [hel] *n.* (*a*) place where devils live and wicked people are punished after death. (*b*) *inf.* **a h. of a noise** = a very loud noise; **one h. of a party** = a very good party; **to give s.o. h.** = to make life difficult for s.o.; *Sl.* **what the h.?** = what on earth? **hell-bent on,** *adj. inf.* very determined to do sth. **hellish,** *adj.* like hell; *inf.* unbearable.

hellebore ['helɪbɔ:] *n.* winter plant with greenish white flowers.

Hellenic [he'lenɪk] *adj.* referring to Greece.

hello [hə'ləʊ] *inter. showing a greeting.*

helm [helm] *n.* wheel or handle connecting to the rudder of a ship; **at the h.** = in charge. **helmsman,** *n.* (*pl.* **-men**) person who is steering a ship.

helmet ['helmət] *n.* metal or plastic hat used as a protection; **crash h.** = helmet worn by motorcyclists.

help [help] **1.** *n.* (*a*) aid/assistance. (*b*) person who helps. **2.** *v.* (*a*) to aid (s.o.)/to come to s.o.'s assistance. (*b*) **to h. yourself** = to serve yourself; *inf.* **to h. yourself to** = to steal. (*c*) **can't h. doing sth** = can't stop (doing sth)/

can't avoid (sth). **helper,** *n.* person who helps. **helpful,** *adj.* (person) who helps; (thing) which is useful. **helpfully,** *adv.* in a helpful way. **helpfulness,** *n.* being helpful. **helping. 1.** *adj.* which helps. **2.** *n.* serving/portion (of food). **helpless,** *adj.* weak/unable to help yourself. **helplessly,** *adv.* unable to help. **helplessness,** *n.* being helpless. **helpmate,** *n.* helper. **help out,** *v.* to come to (s.o.'s) assistance in an emergency.

helter-skelter ['heltə'skeltə] **1.** *adv.* in a confused rush. **2.** *n.* (*in a fairground*) tower with a spiral slide round it.

hem [hem] **1.** *n.* sewn edge on a piece of cloth/a skirt/tablecloth/ handkerchief, etc. **2.** *v.* (**hemmed**) (*a*) to sew a hem. (*b*) **to h. in** = to enclose. **hemline,** *n.* bottom edge of a dress/ skirt, etc. **hemstitch. 1.** *n.* stitch used in a hem. **2.** *v.* to sew a hem using a hemstitch.

hemi- ['hemi] *prefix* half. **hemiplegia,** *n.* paralysis affecting one side of the body.

hemisphere ['hemisfiə] *n.* half a sphere, esp. half of the earth's globe; **northern h./southern h.** = parts of the earth north and south of the equator. **hemispherical** [hemi'sferikl] *adj.* shaped like half a sphere.

hemlock ['hemlɒk] *n.* (*a*) common poisonous plant. (*b*) type of American evergreen tree.

hemoglobin [hi:mə'gləubin] *n. see* **haemoglobin.**

hemophilia [hi:mə'filiə] *n. see* **haemophilia.**

hemorrhage ['hemərɪdʒ] *n. see* **haemorrhage.**

hemorrhoids ['hemərɔidz] *n. pl. see* **haemorrhoids.**

hemp [hemp] *n.* tropical plant, which gives rough fibres for making sacks/ ropes, etc., and which also provides a drug. **hempen,** *adj.* (*formal*) made of hemp.

hen [hen] *n.* (*a*) female chicken. (*b*) female bird; *inf.* **h. party** = party for women only. **henhouse,** *n.* wooden hut for keeping chickens in. **henpecked,** *adj.* (husband) whose wife nags him continuously and tells him what to do.

hence [hens] *adv.* (*a*) from this time; **five years h.** (*b*) for this reason. **henceforth, henceforward,** *adv.* from now on.

henchman ['hentʃmən] *n.* (*pl.* **-men**) helper/accomplice (of a criminal).

henna ['henə] *n.* red dye used to colour hair. **hennaed** ['henəd] *adj.* (hair) coloured with henna.

hepatitis [hepə'taitis] *n.* disease of the liver.

heptagon ['heptəgən] *n.* geometrical figure with seven sides. **heptagonal** [hep'tægənl] *adj.* seven-sided.

her [hɜ:] **1.** *pronoun referring to a female; object form of* she; **have you seen her? 2.** *adj.* belonging to a female; **have you seen her brother?**

herald ['herəld] **1.** *n.* messenger sent to announce sth; officer dealing with hearaldry. **2.** *v.* to be a sign that sth is approaching; to announce. **heraldic** [he'rældik] *adj.* referring to heraldry. **heraldry** ['herəldri] *n.* study of coats of arms.

herb [hɜ:b] *n.* tasty or pungent plant used in cooking or as a medicine. **herbaceous border** [hɜ:'beiʃəs 'bɔ:də] *n.* flowerbed planted with flowers which sprout up again every year. **herbage,** *n.* grass or other green plants. **herbal,** *adj.* containing/using herbs. **herbalist,** *n.* person who sells herbs as medicines. **herbarium,** *n.* collection of wild plants. **herbicide,** *n.* substance which kills weeds. **herbivore** ['hɜ:bivɔ:] *n.* animal which eats plants. **herbivorous** [hɜ:'bivərəs] *adj.* (animal) which eats plants.

herculean [hɜ:kju:'li:ən] *adj.* showing great strength; (task) which needs great effort.

herd [hɜ:d] **1.** *n.* group of animals; **h. instinct** = tendency of people to do what others do. **2.** *v.* to form/to make into a group. **herdsman,** *n.* (*pl.* **-men**) man who looks after a herd of cows, etc.

here ['hiə] *adv.* to/in this place. **hereabouts,** *adv.* round about here/in this area. **hereafter,** *adv.* from this time on. **hereby,** *adv.* (*formal*) in this way. **hereto,** *adv.* to this. **herewith** [hiə'wiθ] *adv.* with this.

heredity [hi'rediti] *n.* passing on of characteristics from parent to child. **hereditament,** *n.* property which can be inherited. **hereditary,** *adj.* which is passed on from parent to child; (title such as Lord, etc.) which is passed from father to son.

heresy ['herəsɪ] n. heretical belief. **heretic,** n. person who does not hold generally accepted religious beliefs. **heretical** [hə'retɪkl] adj. (belief) which is not generally accepted/which is condemned by the church.

heritage ['herɪtɪdʒ] n. thing which is passed on from one generation to the next.

hermaphrodite [hɜː'mæfrədaɪt] n. animal/plant which is both male and female.

hermetic [hɜː'metɪk] adj. sealed; airtight. **hermetically,** adv. (sealed) tightly so that no air can get in.

hermit ['hɜːmɪt] n. person who lives alone and refuses to see other people; **h. crab** = small crab which lives in empty sea shells. **hermitage,** n. place where a hermit lives.

hernia ['hɜːnɪə] n. state where part of the bowel has pushed through a weak place in the wall of the abdomen.

hero, heroine ['hɪərəʊ, 'herəʊɪn] n. (pl. -oes) person who does brave deeds; main character in a book/film, etc. **heroic** [hɪ'rəʊɪk] adj. brave/like a hero. **heroically,** adv. like a hero. **heroism** ['herəʊɪzəm] n. bravery.

heroin ['herəʊɪn] n. drug made from poppies.

heron ['herən] n. common water bird with long legs and neck.

herpes ['hɜːpiːz] n. disease which gives blisters on the skin.

herring ['herɪŋ] n. common sea fish; **red h.** = distraction/false lead. **herringbone,** adj. (pattern) in a zigzag. **herring gull,** n. common large grey and white gull.

hers [hɜːz] adj. belonging to her. **herself** [hɜː'self] pronoun referring to a female subject; she was washing h.; all by h.; she wrote to me h.

hertz [hɜːts] n. (no pl.) standard unit of frequency of radio waves.

hesitate ['hezɪteɪt] v. to stop for a moment; to be unable to decide. **hesitance, hesitancy,** n. being hesitant. **hesitant,** adj. doubtful/undecided. **hesitantly,** adv. in a hesitant way. **hesitation** [hezɪ'teɪʃn] n. indecision/doubt.

hessian ['hesɪən] n. rough cloth like sacking.

heterogeneous [hetərəʊ'dʒiːnjəs] adj. of varied sorts.

heterosexual [hetərəʊ'seksjʊəl] adj. & n. (person) who is attracted to people of the opposite sex.

het up ['het 'ʌp] adj. inf. excited; anxious.

heuristic [hjuː'rɪstɪk] adj. which encourages science.

hew [hjuː] v. (**hewn**) to carve/to cut.

hexagon ['heksəgən] n. geometrical figure with six sides. **hexagonal** [hek'sægənl] adj. six-sided.

hexameter [hek'sæmɪtə] n. line of poetry with six beats.

hey [heɪ] inter. showing a greeting/surprise.

heyday ['heɪdeɪ] n. period of greatest glory/success/power.

Hg symbol for mercury.

hi [haɪ] esp. Am. inter. showing a greeting.

hiatus [haɪ'eɪtəs] n. (pl. -uses) gap/interruption.

hibernate ['haɪbəneɪt] v. (of animals) to sleep during the winter. **hibernation** [haɪbə'neɪʃn] n. spending the winter asleep.

hibiscus [hɪ'bɪskəs] n. tropical shrub with large trumpet-shaped flowers.

hiccup, hiccough ['hɪkʌp] 1. n. repeated spasm in the throat like a small cough. 2. v. (**hiccupped**) to make a loud noise because of a hiccup.

hick [hɪk] n. Am. inf. stupid person from the country.

hickory ['hɪkərɪ] n. American tree like a walnut.

hid, hidden [hɪd, 'hɪdn] v. see hide.

hide [haɪd] 1. n. (a) leather; whole skin of an animal. (b) camouflaged place where you can sit and watch birds, etc. 2. v. (**hid, has hidden**) to be out of sight; to put (a thing) somewhere so that no one can see it. **hide-and-seek,** n. children's game, where some hide and the others try to find them. **hidebound,** adj. unwilling to change ideas/narrowminded. **hide-out,** n. secret place where you cannot be found. **hiding,** n. (a) putting yourself/sth out of sight. (b) inf. beating/whipping.

hideous ['hɪdɪəs] adj. horribly ugly.

hideously, *adv.* in a hideous way. **hideousness,** *n.* being hideous.

hierarchy ['haɪərɑːkɪ] *n.* arrangement in a system of ranks/grades. **hierarchical** [haɪə'rɑːkɪkl] *adj.* arranged in a set system of ranks.

hieroglyphics [haɪərəʊ'glɪfɪks] *n. pl.* system of picture writing used by the Ancient Egyptians. **hieroglyph,** *n.* symbol used in hieroglyphics.

hi-fi ['haɪ'faɪ] *adj. & n. inf.* high fidelity radio/stereo (equipment).

higgledy-piggledy [hɪgldɪ'pɪgldɪ] *adv.* in disorder/all over the place.

high [haɪ] **1.** *adj.* (**-er, -est**) (*a*) going far above; tall. (*b*) great (rank, price, etc.); **h. fidelity** = (radio equipment) which gives excellent reproduction of sound. (*c*) shrill (note). (*d*) (*of meat*) going rotten. (*e*) main; most important. (*f*) powerful (explosive). (*g*) *inf.* influenced by drugs. **2.** *adv.* (**-er, -est**) (*a*) far above. (*b*) to a great degree. **3.** *n.* (*a*) high-pressure zone in the atmosphere. (*b*) **an all-time h.** = the highest point ever reached. (*c*) *inf.* state of intoxication produced by a drug, etc. **highball,** *n. Am.* whisky and soda. **highbrow,** *adj. & n.* intellectual (person). **high chair,** *n.* small chair with very long legs for a baby to sit in to eat. **High Church,** *adj. & n.* (section of the Anglican Church) which regards ritual as very important. **High Commissioner,** *n.* title given to the ambassador of a Commonwealth country. **High Court,** *n.* main civil court in England and Wales. **high-falutin,** *adj. inf.* which sounds/looks imposing. **high-fidelity,** *adj.* which produces sound of a very high quality. **high flyer,** *n.* very intelligent/very ambitious person. **high-handed,** *adj.* (action) done without considering other people. **highland,** *adj.* coming from the highlands/from a mountain region. **Highlander,** *n.* person who lives in the Highlands of Scotland. **Highlands,** *n. pl.* mountain region, esp. in northern Scotland. **highlight. 1.** *n.* most interesting event. **2.** *v.* to accentuate/to draw attention to. **highly,** *adv.* very/greatly. **highly-strung,** *adj.* very emotional/excitable. **high-minded,** *adj.* noble/very serious. **highness,** *n.* (*a*) being high/being above other things. (*b*) title given to princes, etc. **high-pitched,** *adj.* sharp/shrill (sound); steep (roof). **high-powered,** *adj.* very powerful (engine). **high priest,** *n.* most important priest. **high-rise,** *adj.* (building) with many floors. **highroad,** *n.* main road. **high school,** *n.* secondary school. **high seas,** *n. pl.* the oceans. **high season,** *n.* most popular season for holiday travel. **high-speed,** *adj.* which goes/works very fast. **high-spirited,** *adj.* lively. **high spot,** *n.* most enjoyable part of an entertainment. **High Street,** *n.* main shopping street. **high tea,** *n.* (*in North of England and Scotland*) large meal of tea, cold meat, cakes, etc., eaten in the early evening. **highwater mark,** *n.* highest point (reached by the tide/by sth advancing). **highway,** *n.* main road; **h. code** = official rules for people travelling on public roads. **highwayman,** *n.* (*pl.* **-men**) person who attacked travellers and robbed them.

hijack ['haɪdʒæk] *v.* to take control of (an aircraft/a train, etc.) with passengers on board, by threatening the pilot/driver. **hijacker,** *n.* person who hijacks.

hike [haɪk] **1.** *n.* (*a*) strenuous walk. (*b*) *Am.* increase (in price, etc.). **2.** *v.* (*a*) to go for a strenuous walk. (*b*) *Am.* to increase (prices, etc.). **hiker,** *n.* person who goes for long walks. **hiking,** *n.* walking as a relaxation.

hilarious [hɪ'leərɪəs] *adj.* very funny/very happy. **hilariously,** *adv.* in a very funny way. **hilarity** [hɪ'lærɪtɪ] *n.* great laughter.

hill [hɪl] *n.* rise in the land, lower than a mountain. **hillbilly,** *n. Am.* person who lives in the country; **h. music** = country style music. **hillock,** *n.* little hill. **hillside,** *n.* side of a hill. **hilly,** *adj.* (**-ier, -iest**) (region) with many hills.

hilt [hɪlt] *n.* protective shield on the handle of a sword; **to the h.** = totally.

him [hɪm] *pronoun referring to a male; object form of* he; **have you seen h.?** **himself** [hɪm'self] *pronoun referring to a male subject;* he was washing h.; he is all by h.; he wrote to me h.

hind [haɪnd] **1.** *n.* female deer. **2.** *adj.* **h. legs** = back legs (of an animal).

hinder ['hɪndə] v. to prevent (s.o.) from doing sth. **hindrance,** n. obstacle.

hindmost ['haɪndməʊst] adj. furthest back.

hindsight ['haɪndsaɪt] n. knowing facts about an event in the past which could have been useful if they had been known at the time.

Hindu ['hɪnduː] adj. & n. (person) following the main religion of India. **Hindi,** n. language spoken in the central part of India.

hinge [hɪndʒ] 1. n. (a) metal bracket on which a door/a window hangs and opens. (b) **stamp h.** = small piece of gummed paper for sticking stamps into a stamp album. 2. v. to centre/to depend (on). **hinged.** adj. with hinges.

hint [hɪnt] 1. n. (a) hidden suggestion/clue. (b) sign. (c) **hints** = helpful advice. 2. v. to suggest/to insinuate.

hinterland ['hɪntəlænd] n. area inland from a sea port/around a large town.

hip [hɪp] n. (a) projecting bone where the legs join the body; wide part of the body where the legs join it. (b) fruit of a wild rose. (c) **h. h. hooray!** = words used to give a cheer. **hipped,** adj. (roof) which breaks at an angle. **hipsters,** n. pl. trousers which only reach to the hips and not the waist.

hippie ['hɪpɪ] n. inf. person who lives/dresses in a different way from the majority of people in society.

hippopotamus, inf. **hippo** [hɪpə-'pɒtəməs, 'hɪpəʊ] n. (pl. **-muses, -mi** [-maɪ]; **-os**) very large African animal living in water and mud.

hire ['haɪə] 1. n. renting (of a car, etc.) usu. for a short time; **h. purchase** = system where you buy sth by paying instalments. 2. v. to rent (a car, etc.); to engage (staff); **he hires out cars** = he has cars which people can rent. **hireling,** n. person who is hired to do a job. **hirer,** n. person who hires.

hirsute ['hɜːsjuːt] adj. covered with long hair.

his [hɪz] adj. (a) belonging to a male. (b) belonging to him; **a friend of h.**

Hispano [hɪs'pɑːnəʊ] 1. prefix meaning between Spain and another country. 2. n. Am. Spanish-speaking immigrant.

hiss [hɪs] 1. n. whistling sound like an 's', made by snakes/by gas escaping, etc.; similar sound made to show you do not like sth. 2. v. to make a hissing sound.

histamine ['hɪstəmiːn] n. substance which causes an allergy.

histology [hɪ'stɒlədʒɪ] n. science of body cells. **histologist,** n. person who specializes in histology.

history ['hɪstərɪ] n. (a) study of the past; story of what happened in the past. (b) **natural h.** = study of animals and plants. **historian** [hɪ'stɔːrɪən] n. person who studies or writes about the past. **historic** [hɪ'stɒrɪk] adj. (event) which is so important that it will be remembered. **historical,** adj. referring to history; **h. novel** = novel set in the past. **historically,** adv. as in the past.

histrionic [hɪstrɪ'ɒnɪk] adj. referring to acting. **histrionics,** n. pl. dramatic behaviour.

hit [hɪt] 1. n. (a) blow; **he scored three hits** = he hit the target three times. (b) song/play, etc. which is very popular. 2. v. (**hit; has hit**) (a) to knock against; to touch (sth) hard. (b) to affect (badly). **hit and miss,** adj. erratic/careless. **hit back,** v. to defend yourself against attack. **hit-man,** n. (pl. **-men**) person employed to kill/to hurt s.o. **hit off,** v. inf. **to hit it off with s.o.** = to get on well with s.o. **hit-or-miss,** adj. erratic/careless. **hit out,** v. (at) to try to attack (s.o.). **hit (up)on,** v. to discover.

hitch [hɪtʃ] 1. n. awkward delay/unexpected stoppage. 2. v. (a) to jerk up/to pull up. (b) to hitch-hike. (c) to attach with a rope; inf. **to get hitched** = to get married. **hitch-hike,** v. to get a free ride in s.o.'s car, stopping the car by pointing your thumb. **hitch-hiker,** n. person who hitch-hikes.

hither ['hɪðə] adv. (formal) to this place; **h. and thither** = all over the place. **hitherto,** adv. up till now.

HIV ['eɪtʃaɪ'viː] human immunodeficiency virus.

hive [haɪv] 1. n. (a) box in which bees make their nest. (b) **hives** = sore red patches on the skin, usu. on the face. 2. v. **to h. off** = to split off.

HMSO abbrev. for Her Majesty's Stationery Office.

hoard [hɔːd] 1. n. mass/store (of money/

food, etc.) which has been collected.
2. *v.* to collect and store (money/food,
etc.). **hoarder,** *n.* person who buys food
when supplies are low. **hoarding,** *n.*
(*a*) buying food, etc., when supplies are
low. (*b*) fence made of rough planks.
(*c*) large advertising board in the street.

hoarfrost ['hɔːfrɒst] *n.* white frost which
covers trees/plants, etc.

hoarse [hɔːs] *adj.* rough (voice).
hoarsely, *adv.* in a hoarse voice.
hoarseness, *n.* roughness/harshness
(of voice).

hoary ['hɔːrɪ] *adj.* (**-ier, -iest**) (*a*) (*formal*)
white-haired. (*b*) *inf.* very old (joke).

hoax [həʊks] **1.** *n.* trick. **2.** *v.* to trick/to
deceive. **hoaxer,** *n.* person who hoaxes.

hob [hɒb] *n.* (*a*) metal stand where a
kettle can be put by the side of a fire.
(*b*) flat top to a cooker.

hobble ['hɒbl] *v.* (*a*) to attach the legs of
(a horse) so that it cannot move easily.
(*b*) to walk with difficulty.

hobby ['hɒbɪ] *n.* pastime; thing done as
a relaxation. **hobbyhorse,** *n.* subject
which s.o. always talks about.

hobgoblin [hɒb'gɒblɪn] *n.* goblin.

hobnail ['hɒbneɪl] *n.* large nail used to
protect the soles of boots. **hobnailed,**
adj. (boots) with large metal nails.

hobnob ['hɒbnɒb] *v.* (**hobnobbed**) *inf.*
to be on friendly terms (**with** s.o. important).

hobo ['həʊbəʊ] *n. Am.* person with no
home or money.

hock [hɒk] *n.* (*a*) middle joint of an animal's leg; lower part of a leg of an animal used for food. (*b*) German white
wine. (*c*) *Sl.* **in h.** = pawned.

hockey ['hɒkɪ] *n.* (*a*) = team game
played on grass with long curved sticks
and a hard ball. (*b*) *Am.* ice hockey.

hocus-pocus ['həʊkəs'pəʊkəs] *n.* (*a*)
meaningless words (used by conjurers).
(*b*) trickery.

hod [hɒd] *n.* (*a*) wooden container on the
end of a pole, used by builders for carrying bricks. (*b*) metal container for coal.

hoe [həʊ] **1.** *n.* garden tool with a blade
on the end of a long handle. **2.** *v.* to take
out weeds/to loosen the soil with a hoe.

hog [hɒg] **1.** *n.* castrated male pig; *inf.* **to
go the whole h.** = to do sth completely.
2. *v.* (**hogged**) (*a*) to eat/to drink like a
pig. (*b*) to monopolize.

hogg [hɒg] *n.* young female sheep.

Hogmanay ['hɒgmə'neɪ] *n.* Scottish festival on 31st December.

hogshead ['hɒgzhed] *n.* (*a*) large barrel.
(*b*) measure of about 50 gallons.

hoick [hɔɪk] *v. inf.* to pull (out).

hoi polloi [hɔɪpə'lɔɪ] *n.* the ordinary
people.

hoist [hɔɪst] **1.** *n.* apparatus for lifting;
goods lift. **2.** *v.* to lift up.

hoity-toity ['hɔɪtɪ'tɔɪtɪ] *adj. inf.* snobbish; superior (air).

hold [həʊld] **1.** *n.* (*a*) grip. (*b*) influence/
power. (*c*) part of a ship/aircraft where
cargo is carried. **2.** *v.* (**held**) (*a*) to have
in your hand, etc. (*b*) to contain. (*c*) to
make (sth) take place. (*d*) to keep in
(one's breath, a liquid). (*e*) to stay. (*f*) **to
h. office** = to have a post (in a government). **holdall,** *n.* large travelling bag.
hold back, *v.* to keep back; not to go
forward. **hold down,** *v.* to keep (sth)
down; to work hard to keep (a job).
holder, *n.* person or thing which holds.
hold forth, *v.* to talk at great length.
holding, *n.* number of shares which you
own; **h. company** = company formed to
control shares in other companies. **hold
off,** *v.* not to act. **hold on,** *v.* (*a*) to
cling on to/to take a grip on (sth). (*b*)
to wait. **hold out,** *v.* (*a*) to offer. (*b*)
to last. **hold over,** *v.* to postpone (sth).
hold up, *v.* (*a*) to raise. (*b*) to support.
(*c*) to hinder/to delay. (*d*) to attack and
rob. **hold-up,** *n.* (*a*) delay; breakdown.
(*b*) armed attack. **hold with,** *v. inf.* to
accept/to agree with.

hole [həʊl] **1.** *n.* opening/space. **2.** *v.* (*a*)
to make a hole in. (*b*) (*in golf*) to send
(the ball) into the hole. **hole up,** *v. inf.*
to hide away.

holiday ['hɒlɪdeɪ] **1.** *n.* period when you
do not work. **2.** *v.* to go on holiday.
holidaymaker, *n.* person on holiday
away from home.

holiness ['həʊlɪnəs] *n. see* **holy.**

holistic [hɒ'lɪstɪk] *adj.* (attitude) which
considers many sides to a problem;
(medical treatment) which deals with
the environment of the patient as well
as the illness itself.

holler ['hɒlə] *v. inf.* to shout.

hollow ['hɒləʊ] **1.** *n.* low-lying land;
small depression in a flat surface. **2.** *adj.*

empty/with nothing inside; meaningless (success). **3.** *v.* **to h. out** = to make (sth) hollow.

holly ['hɒlɪ] *n.* very prickly evergreen bush with red berries.

hollyhock ['hɒlɪhɒk] *n.* common garden flower which produces very tall spikes of blossom.

holm oak ['hɒlməʊk] *n.* evergreen oak found in temperate climates.

holocaust ['hɒləkɔ:st] *n.* destruction by fire.

holograph ['hɒləgrɑ:f] *n.* letter, etc., written by s.o. by hand, not typed. **hologram**, *n.* three-dimensional picture produced by lasers. **holography**, *n.* science of making holograms.

holster ['həʊlstə] *n.* leather pouch for carrying a revolver.

holy ['həʊlɪ] *adj.* (**-ier, -iest**) sacred (place); very pious (person); **h. orders** = being a priest. **holiness**, *n.* being holy; **his H.** = title given to the Pope. **Holy Week**, *n.* the week which ends with Easter Sunday.

homage ['hɒmɪdʒ] *n.* (*a*) respect; **to pay h. to s.o.** = to show s.o. signs of respect. (*b*) (*formal*) duty/service (to a feudal lord).

home [həʊm] **1.** *n.* (*a*) place where you live/place where you come from originally. (*b*) (*in sports*) **at h.** = playing on a local sports ground. (*c*) house where children are looked after. (*d*) top left-hand corner of a computer screen. **2.** *adv.* to/at the place where you live; **to strike h.** = to hit the target. **3.** *adj.* (*a*) referring to the place where you live. (*b*) not foreign/internal; **h. trade** = ·trade inside the country. (*c*) (*in sports*) referring to the local team/the local sports ground; (match) played by the local team on their own ground. **4.** *v.* **to h. in on** = to go to a target. **Home Counties**, *n. pl.* the counties around London. **homegrown**, *adj.* (vegetables) grown in the garden, not bought; (industry) which is developed in a country, and not imported. **home help**, *n.* person who helps an invalid with housework in the home. **homeland**, *n.* land which is the home of a people. **homeless**, *adj.* with nowhere to live. **homeliness**, *n.* being

homely. **homely**, *adj.* (*a*) simple; not ostentatious. (*b*) plain/ugly (person). **home-made**, *adj.* made at home/not bought. **Home Office**, *n.* Government department which deals with internal problems of law and order in England and Wales. **home run**, *n.* (*in baseball*) run made by a batter who touches all the bases. **Home Secretary**, *n.* Minister in charge of the Home Office. **homesick**, *adj.* unhappy because of wanting to go home. **homesickness**, *n.* feeling of being homesick. **homestead**, *n.* farmhouse and the fields around it. **homeward**, *adj. & adv.* going towards home. **homewards**, *adv.* towards home. **homework**, *n.* work which children take from school to be done at home in the evening. **homing**, *adj.* **h. pigeon** = pigeon trained to return to the place where it usually lives; **h. device** = device (on a missile) which guides it to the target.

homicide ['hɒmɪsaɪd] *n.* murder. **homicidal** [hɒmɪ'saɪdl] *adj.* likely to murder.

homily ['hɒmɪlɪ] *n.* sermon/talk to encourage s.o. to be less wicked.

homoeopathy, *Am.* **homeopathy** [həʊmɪ'ɒpəθɪ] *n.* method of curing sick people by accustoming them to very small quantities of drugs which would normally make them ill. **homoeopath**, *Am.* **homeopath** ['həʊmjəpæθ] *n.* doctor who practices homoeopathy. **homoeopathic**, *Am.* **homeopathic**, *adj.* referring to homoeopathy.

homogeneous [hɒməʊ'dʒi:nɪəs] *adj.* of the same sort/quality (as other things). **homogeneity** [hɒməʊdʒə-'ni:ətɪ] *n.* being homogeneous.

homogenize [hə'mɒdʒənaɪz] *v.* to mix various parts until they become a single whole; to mix the cream into milk. **homogenization** [hɒmɒdʒənaɪ-'zeɪʃn] *n.* treatment of milk so that the cream does not separate.

homonym ['hɒmənɪm] *n.* word which is spelt the same as another word with a different meaning.

homophone ['hɒməfəʊn] *n.* word which is pronounced the same as another, but spelt differently.

homosexual [həʊməʊ'seksjʊəl] *adj. & n.* (person) who is attracted to persons

of the same sex as himself/herself.
homosexuality [həʊməʊseksjʊˈælɪtɪ]
n. being homesexual.

hone [həʊn] *v.* to smooth/to sharpen (a blade).

honest [ˈɒnɪst] *adj.* truthful; not cheating or stealing. **honestly,** *adv.* truthfully. **honesty,** *n.* (*a*) truthfulness. (*b*) garden flower with silvery seed cases, used as a winter decoration.

honey [ˈhʌnɪ] *n.* sweet substance produced by bees. **honey-bee,** *n.* type of bee which makes honey. **honeycomb,** *n.* construction of wax cells in which bees store honey; pattern of six-sided shapes like bees' cells. **honeycombed,** *adj.* full of little holes. **honeydew,** *n.* type of melon which has green flesh. **honeyed,** *adj.* sweet/flattering (words). **honeymoon. 1.** *n.* holiday taken by man and wife immediately after their wedding. **2.** *v.* to go on a honeymoon. **honeysuckle,** *n.* common climbing plant with scented yellow and pink flowers.

honk [ˈhɒŋk] **1.** *n.* noise made by a goose/by a car horn. **2.** *v.* to make a noise like a goose/a car horn.

honorarium [ɒnəˈreərɪəm] *n.* money paid to s.o. for work which is usually done free.

honorary [ˈɒnərərɪ] *adj.* (*a*) (person) who is not paid a salary. (*b*) given as a mark of respect.

honour, *Am.* **honor** [ˈɒnə] **1.** *n.* (*a*) self-respect. (*b*) mark of respect; title given as a mark of respect. (*c*) **honours degree** = university degree taken after a more difficult course of study. (*d*) title given to a judge. **2.** *v.* (*a*) to respect; to give a title/medal to (s.o.) as a mark of respect. (*b*) to pay (a bill); (*of a bank*) to pay (a cheque). **honourable,** *adj.* that can be respected. **honourably,** *adv.* in a way which you can respect.

hooch [huːtʃ] *n. Sl.* alcoholic drink.

hood [hʊd] *n.* (*a*) loose covering for the head, attached to a coat. (*b*) folding roof on a car or pram. (*c*) *Am.* lid covering the engine of a car. (*d*) *Sl.* gangster. **hooded,** *adj.* wearing a hood.

hoodlum [ˈhuːdləm] *n.* thug/violent hooligan.

hoodwink [ˈhʊdwɪŋk] *v.* to trick.

hoof [huːf] *n.* (*pl.* **hooves**) hard part of the foot of a horse, etc. **hoofed,** *adj.* (animal) which has hooves.

hoo-ha [ˈhuːhɑː] *n. inf.* fuss/bother.

hook [hʊk] **1.** *n.* (*a*) bent piece of metal used for holding or pulling, etc.; **to get s.o. off the h.** = to release s.o. from a difficult situation; **by h. or by crook** = by any means available; **h. and eye** = small hook and loop for fastening clothing. (*b*) very small, bent piece of metal used for catching fish. (*c*) (*in boxing/cricket*) blow/stroke made with the arm bent. **2.** *v.* (*a*) to hang on a hook; to attach with a hook. (*b*) to catch (a fish) with a hook. **hooked,** *adj.* (*a*) shaped like a hook. (*b*) caught with/on a hook. (*c*) *inf.* **h. on** = very interested in (a book, etc.); addicted to (drugs). **hooker,** *n.* (*a*) (*in Rugby*) forward in the centre of the front line of the scrum, whose job is to hook the ball backwards to his own side. (*b*) *inf.* prostitute. **hook-up,** *n.* radio or T.V. link. **hookworm,** *n.* type of parasitic worm.

hookah [ˈhʊkə] *n.* tobacco pipe where the smoke is cooled by being passed through water.

hookey [ˈhʊkɪ] *n. Am.* child who avoids going to school; **to play h.** = to avoid going to school.

hooligan [ˈhuːlɪgən] *n.* rowdy wild person. **hooliganism,** *n.* wild behaviour.

hoop [huːp] *n.* large ring of wood or metal. **hoop-la,** *n.* game where you throw hoops over little pegs.

hoopoe [ˈhuːpuː] *n.* large cream-coloured bird with a crest.

hooray [hʊˈreɪ] *inter. showing great pleasure/excitement.*

hoot [huːt] **1.** *n.* (*a*) call of an owl; **hoots of laughter** = sound like an owl call, made when you are laughing. (*b*) sound made by a car horn. **2.** *v.* (*a*) (*of an owl*) to call; **to h. with laughter** = laugh hilariously. (*b*) to sound the horn of a car. **hooter,** *n.* (*a*) warning siren. (*b*) car horn.

Hoover [ˈhuːvə] **1.** *n.* trademark for a type of vacuum cleaner. **2.** *v.* **to h.** = to clean with a vacuum cleaner.

hop [hɒp] **1.** *n.* (*a*) little jump; *inf.* **to catch s.o. on the h.** = find s.o. unexpectedly. (*b*) short flight (in a plane). (*c*) bitter fruit used in making beer; climbing plant which bears this fruit. **2.** *v.* (**hopped**) to jump on one leg; (*of birds*) to jump with both feet together; *inf.* **hop it!** = go away. **hopfield,** *n.* field where hops are grown. **hop-picker,** *n.* person who picks hops.

hope [həʊp] **1.** *n.* expectation/wanting sth to happen. **2.** *v.* to expect that sth will happen; to want sth to happen. **hopeful,** *adj.* full of hope/confident; likely to happen. **hopefully,** *adv.* (*a*) confidently. (*b*) **h. the rain will stop** = let's hope/I hope it will stop. **hopeless,** *adj.* with no hope; **he's h. at chess** = he plays very badly. **hopelessly,** *adv.* with no hope. **hopelessness,** *n.* being hopeless.

hopper ['hɒpə] *n.* very large funnel for channelling loose material (like sand/corn, etc.).

hopsack ['hɒpsæk] *n.* thick rough material.

hopscotch ['hɒpskɒtʃ] *n.* children's game in which you hop over marked squares on the ground.

horde [hɔːd] *n.* crowd/mass.

horizon [hə'raɪzn] *n.* (*a*) line where the earth seems to meet the sky. (*b*) layer of soil.

horizontal [hɒrɪ'zɒntl] *adj.* lying flat/not upright. **horizontally,** *adv.* lying flat.

hormone ['hɔːməʊn] *n.* substance produced by glands in the body, which causes various physical reactions. **hormonal,** *adj.* referring to hormones.

horn [hɔːn] *n.* (*a*) hard bony growth on the head of some animals. (*b*) feeler on a snail's head. (*c*) brass musical instrument shaped like an animal's horn. (*d*) instrument on a car, etc., which makes a loud warning noise. **horned,** *adj.* with horns. **horn in (on),** *v. inf.* to join (a meeting) uninvited. **hornpipe,** *n.* vigorous dance danced by sailors. **hornrimmed,** *adj.* (spectacles) with tortoiseshell frames. **horny,** *adj.* hard/rough (hands).

hornbeam ['hɔːnbiːm] *n.* common hedgerow tree.

hornet ['hɔːnɪt] *n.* large red wasp.

horology [hɒ'rɒlədʒɪ] *n.* study of time and clocks.

horoscope ['hɒrəskəʊp] *n.* description of a person's character/forecasting of what will happen to a person in the future, based on the position of the stars when he or she was born.

horrendous [hɒ'rendəs] *adj.* quite horrible.

horrible ['hɒrəbl] *adj.* terrible/frightening. **horribly,** *adv.* frighteningly/badly. **horrid** ['hɒrɪd] *adj.* nasty/unpleasant. **horrific** [hə'rɪfɪk] *adj.* frightening/shocking. **horrifically,** *adv.* in a horrific way. **horrify** ['hɒrɪfaɪ] *v.* to make (s.o.) very frightened/to shock (s.o.).

horror ['hɒrə] *n.* terror/feeling of being very frightened; **h. film** = film which aims to frighten the spectators; *inf.* **little h.** = very naughty child. **horror-stricken, horror-struck,** *adj.* very frightened.

hors-d'œuvre [ɔː'dɜːv] *n. pl.* cold food served at the beginning of a meal.

horse [hɔːs] **1.** *n.* (*a*) large animal with hooves, which is used for riding or pulling vehicles; **h. racing** = racing of horses; **dark h.** = person you know nothing about and who may win; *inf.* **straight from the horse's mouth** = from a very reliable source. (*b*) apparatus made of wood over which you jump in gymnastics. (*c*) **clothes h.** = wooden frame used for drying clothes. **2.** *v.* **to h. around/about** = to play roughly. **horseback,** *n.* **on h.** = riding on a horse. **horsebox,** *n.* enclosed box on wheels for transporting horses. **horse-chestnut,** *n.* type of large tree; shiny inedible nut of this tree. **horsefly,** *n.* large fly which bites animals. **horsehair,** *n.* hair from the mane or tail of a horse, used for padding furniture. **horse laugh,** *n.* loud unpleasant laugh. **horseman,** *n.* (*pl.* -**men**) man riding a horse; man who often rides on horses. **horseplay,** *n.* rough fighting/rough games. **horsepower,** *n.* unit formerly used when calculating the power of a car engine. **horseradish,** *n.* plant with a large root used to make a sharp sauce. **horserider,** *n.* person who rides a horse. **horse sense,** *n. inf.* commonsense. **horseshoe,** *n.* curved metal strip nailed to the hooves of horses. **horsetail,** *n.* common leafless weed.

horse trading, *n.* bargaining between parties before coming to an agreement. **horsewoman,** *n.* (*pl.* **-women**) woman riding a horse; woman who often rides on horses. **horsy,** *adj.* (*a*) looking like a horse. (*b*) interested in horses.

horticulture ['hɔːtɪkʌltʃə] *n.* science of gardening. **horticultural** [hɔːtɪ-'kʌltʃərəl] *adj.* referring to horticulture. **horticulturist,** *n.* person who specializes in gardening.

hose [həʊz] **1.** *n.* (*a*) (*also* **hosepipe**) long, flexible tube. (*b*) stockings/socks; **panty h.** = tights/stockings and briefs in one piece. **2.** *v.* (*also* **hose down**) to spray with water, etc., from a hose. **hosiery** ['həʊzjərɪ] *n.* knitted pieces of clothing (esp. socks/gloves).

hospice ['hɒspɪs] *n.* place where poor or terminally ill people can live.

hospitable [hɒ'spɪtəbl] *adj.* welcoming. **hospitably,** *adv.* in a welcoming way. **hospitality** [hɒspɪ'tælɪtɪ] *n.* welcome to visitors; giving visitors food, drink, etc.

hospital ['hɒspɪtl] *n.* place where sick people are treated. **hospitalize,** *v.* to put (s.o.) in hospital.

host [həʊst] **1.** *n.* (*a*) man who invites guests. (*b*) hotel keeper. (*c*) animal/plant on which other animals/plants live. (*d*) large number. (*e*) (*in church*) consecrated bread. **2.** *v.* to be the host at (a reception/a conference/TV show). **hostess,** *n.* (*a*) woman who invites guests. (*b*) **air h.** = woman who looks after passengers on an aircraft.

hosta ['hɒstə] *n.* common garden plant which grows in shade.

hostage ['hɒstɪdʒ] *n.* person kept prisoner until the demands of the captor are met.

hostel ['hɒstl] *n.* (*a*) building providing rooms for homeless families/students, etc. (*b*) **youth h.** = building where young walkers, etc. may stay the night cheaply.

hostile ['hɒstaɪl, *Am.* 'hɒstl] *adj.* referring to an enemy; unfriendly. **hostility** [hɒ'stɪlɪtɪ] *n.* (*a*) dislike (of a plan)/opposition (to a plan). (*b*) **hostilities** = warfare.

hot [hɒt] **1.** *adj.* (**hotter, hottest**) (*a*) very warm; *inf.* **to get into h. water** = to get into trouble; **to make things h.**

for s.o. = make life unbearable. (*b*) highly spiced. (*c*) very strong; **h. line** = direct telephone link between heads of state; **he's in the h. seat** = his job involves him in awkward decisions. (*d*) *inf.* very recent (news); (goods) which have just been stolen. **2.** *v.* (**hotted**) *inf.* **to h. up** = to warm up (cold food); **things are hotting up** = things are getting more dangerous/more exciting. **hot air,** *n.* *inf.* useless excited talk. **hotbed,** *n.* place where sth unpleasant breeds rapidly. **hot-blooded,** *adj.* (person) with a violent temper. **hot dog,** *n.* hot frankfurter eaten in a long roll with pickles or onions. **hotfoot,** *adv.* running fast. **hothead,** *n.* impetuous person. **hothouse,** *n.* heated greenhouse. **hotplate,** *n.* piece of metal heated usu. by electricity, used to heat food. **hotpot,** *n.* meat stew with potatoes on top. **hot-tempered,** *adj.* (person) with a violent temper. **hot-water bottle,** *n.* container filled with hot water which is placed in a bed to warm it.

hotchpotch ['hɒtʃpɒtʃ] *n.* mixture/jumble.

hotel [həʊ'tel] *n.* building where you can buy food and drink, and rent a room for the night. **hotelier** [həʊ'telɪə] *n.* person who runs a hotel.

hound [haʊnd] **1.** *n.* large hunting dog. **2.** *v.* to chase (s.o.)/to victimize (s.o.).

hour ['aʊə] *n.* (*a*) period of time lasting sixty minutes; *inf.* **they took hours to do it** = a very long time. (*b*) particular point in time; **on the h.** = at 9, 10, etc., o'clock exactly. **hourglass,** *n.* timing device made of two glass containers joined by a narrow tube, through which sand falls. **hourly,** *adj.* & *adv.* every hour.

house 1. *n.* [haʊs, *pl.* 'haʊzɪz] (*a*) building in which people live; *inf.* **they get on like a h. on fire** = they are very friendly. (*b*) dynasty/royal family. (*c*) commercial firm. (*d*) audience (at a play); members (of a parliament). (*e*) **public h.** = inn/building with a licence to sell drinks; **drinks are on the h.** = drinks offered free by the innkeeper. (*f*) (*in a school*) division of the school to which one group of children belongs for competitions or for boarding. (*g*) **the House** = one of the two parts of the British Parliament; a debating group. **2.** *v.* [hauz] to provide accommodation for (s.o./sth). **house-agent,** *n.* person who arranges the sale of houses. **house arrest,** *n.* **under h. arrest** = not allowed to leave one's house which is being guarded by the police. **houseboat,** *n.* large boat which is used for living in. **housebound,** *adj.* not able to leave the house. **housebreaker,** *n.* burglar/person who breaks into a house to steal. **housebreaking,** *n.* breaking into a house to steal. **housecoat,** *n.* light coat/dressing gown worn by women in the house. **housecraft,** *n.* skill at looking after a house. **household,** *n.* family/people who live together in the same house; **h. word** = saying which everybody uses. **householder,** *n.* head of a family/person who owns/who is in charge of a house. **housekeeper,** *n.* woman employed to look after a house. **housekeeping,** *n.* looking after a house; **h. money** = money set aside for paying food/heating, etc., in a house. **housemaid,** *n.* girl who looks after the cleaning of a house. **houseman,** *n.* doctor working and usu. living in a hospital. **housemaster, housemistress,** *n.* person in charge of a house in a school. **House of Commons,** *n.* lower house of the British Parliament. **House of Lords,** *n.* upper house of the British Parliament. **House of Representatives,** *n.* lower house of the US Congress. **house physician,** *n.* doctor working and usu. living in a hospital. **house plant,** *n.* plant which is kept in the house. **houseproud,** *adj.* taking great pride in the appearance of one's house. **houseroom,** *n. inf.* **I wouldn't give it h.** = I don't like it, and wouldn't have in in my house. **Houses of Parliament,** *n.* building in which the two parts of the British Parliament meet. **house surgeon,** *n.* doctor working and usu. living in a hospital. **house-trained,** *adj.* (animal) trained not to pass excreta in the house. **housewarming,** *n.* party to celebrate moving into a new house. **housewife,** *n.* (*pl.* **-wives**)

woman who spends her time looking after a house and usu. has no outside work. **housework,** *n.* general cleaning work in a house. **hous(e)y-hous(e)y,** *n.* bingo. **housing** [hauzɪŋ] *n.* (*a*) providing accommodation for people; **h. estate** = area of houses and flats built at one time. (*b*) covering for part of a machine.

hove [həuv] *v. see* **heave.**

hovel ['hɒvl] *n.* small dirty house.

hover ['hɒvə] *v.* (*a*) to fly/to hang in the air without moving forward. (*b*) to hang (**around** s.o.). **hovercraft,** *n.* vehicle which moves over water or land on a cushion of air. **hoverfly,** *n.* small insect which hovers.

how [hau] *adv.* (*a*) in what way/to what extent; **h. are you?** (*b*) the means of; **tell me h. to do it.** (*c*) (*showing surprise*) **h. green the trees are! how do you do?** *inter. showing greeting.* **however** [hau'evə] *adv.* (*a*) to whatever extent. (*b*) in spite of this.

howdah ['haudɑ:] *n.* seat on an elephant's back.

howitzer ['hauɪtsə] *n.* short gun which fires shells high into the air.

howl [haul] **1.** *n.* loud wail. **2.** *v.* to make a loud wailing noise. **howl down,** *v.* to stop (s.o.) making a speech by shouting at him. **howler,** *n. inf.* bad mistake. **howling,** *n.* loud wailing.

hoyden ['hɔɪdn] *n.* boisterous girl. **hoydenish,** *adj.* like a hoyden.

HP ['eɪtʃ'pi:] hire purchase.

HQ ['eɪtʃ'kju:] *n.* headquarters.

hub [hʌb] *n.* (*a*) centre of a wheel where it is connected to the axle. (*b*) centre of activity/business. **hub cap,** *n.* metal plate covering the centre of a car wheel.

hubble-bubble ['hʌblbʌbl] *n. inf.* hookah.

hubbub ['hʌbʌb] *n.* confused sound of voices.

huddle ['hʌdl] **1.** *n.* **to go into a h.** = to meet together to discuss sth in secret. **2.** *v.* to crowd together.

hue [hju:] *n.* (*a*) colour. (*b*) **h. and cry** = loud noise showing anger/alarm.

huff [hʌf] *n.* **in a h.** = in a bad temper. **huffy,** *adj. inf.* bad-tempered.

hug [hʌg] **1.** *n.* throwing your arms round s.o. **2.** *v.* (**hugged**) (*a*) to throw your arms around (s.o.). (*b*) to keep close to (sth).

huge [hju:dʒ] *adj.* very large/enormous. **hugely,** *adv. inf.* enormously.

hugger-mugger ['hʌgəmʌgə] *adv. inf.* (*a*) in secret. (*b*) in a mess.

hulk [hʌlk] *n.* (*a*) rotten old ship which is no longer used for sailing. (*b*) large and clumsy thing/person. **hulking,** *adj.* big and awkward.

hull [hʌl] **1.** *n.* (*a*) main body of a ship. (*b*) pea or bean pod. **2.** *v.* to take (peas) out of their pods.

hullabaloo [hʌləbə'lu:] *n.* loud disorderly noise.

hullo [hə'ləʊ] *inter. showing a greeting.*

hum [hʌm] **1.** *n.* low buzzing noise. **2.** *v.* (**hummed**) (*a*) to make a continual low buzzing noise. (*b*) to sing the tune of a song without using the words. (*c*) *inf.* to give off an unpleasant smell. (*d*) **to h. and haw** = not to make up your mind. **hummingbird,** *n.* very small brightly coloured tropical bird which hovers.

human ['hju:mən] **1.** *adj.* referring to mankind; **a h. being** = a person; **h. immunodeficiency virus** = virus which causes AIDS; **h. nature** = general characteristics of people. **2.** *n.* person. **humane** [hju:'meɪn] *adj.* kind/gentle. **humanely,** *adv.* kindly/gently. **humanism** ['hju:mənɪzəm] *n.* concern with human beings rather than with religions. **humanist,** *n.* person who believes in humanism. **humanistic,** *adj.* referring to humanism. **humanitarian** [hju:mænɪ'teərɪən] *adj.* kind towards other humans. **humanity** [hju:'mænɪtɪ] *n.* (*a*) all people. (*b*) great kindness. (*c*) **the humanities** = arts subjects (not sciences). **humanization,** *n.* act of humanizing. **humanize,** *v.* to make (more) human. **humankind,** *n.* people, seen as a biological group. **humanly,** *adv.* **we will do everything h. possible** = all we can.

humble ['hʌmbl] **1.** *adj.* (**-er, -est**) modest/not proud; **to eat h. pie** = to admit you were wrong. **2.** *v.* to make (s.o.) less proud/less important. **humbleness,** *n.* being humble.

humbug ['hʌmbʌg] *n.* (*a*) confidence trick. (*b*) person who tricks s.o./who pretends to be sth which he is not. (*c*) kind of hard striped sweet.

humdinger [hʌm'dɪŋə] *n. Am. inf.* marvellous person/thing.

humdrum ['hʌmdrʌm] *adj.* dull/ordinary.

humerus ['hju:mərəs] *n.* bone in the top part of the arm.

humid ['hju:mɪd] *adj.* damp. **humidifier** [hju:'mɪdɪfaɪə] *n.* machine which dampens the air (in a house). **humidity** [hju:'mɪdɪtɪ] *n.* dampness.

humiliate [hju:'mɪlɪeɪt] *v.* to make (s.o.) feel unimportant/humble/ashamed. **humiliation** [hju:mɪlɪ'eɪʃn] *n.* making s.o. feel unimportant/humble/ashamed. **humility** [hju:'mɪlɪtɪ] *n.* humbleness/being humble.

hummock ['hʌmək] *n.* low hump in the ground.

humour, *Am.* **humor** ['hju:mə] **1.** *n.* (*a*) seeing the funny aspects of sth. (*b*) general feeling/mood. **2.** *v.* to do what s.o. wants in order to keep him happy. **humorist,** *n.* person who makes jokes; writer of funny stories or articles. **humorous,** *adj.* funny/amusing. **humorously,** *adv.* in a humorous way.

hump [hʌmp] **1.** *n.* lump on the back; small rounded bump in the ground. **2.** *v. inf.* to carry (on your shoulder). **humpbacked,** *adj.* (person) with a hump; (bridge) with a very high arch.

humus ['hju:məs] *n.* good soil made rich with decayed animal or vegetable matter.

hunch [hʌntʃ] **1.** *n. inf.* feeling that sth is going to happen. **2.** *v.* to bend low. **hunchback,** *n.* person with a hunched back.

hundred ['hʌndrəd] *n.* number 100; **hundreds of** = very many. **hundredfold,** *adv.* a hundred times. **hundredth, 100th,** *adj.* referring to a hundred. **hundredweight,** *n.* weight of 112 pounds (approx. 50 kilos).

hung [hʌŋ] *v. see* hang; **h. parliament** = one where no party has an absolute majority; **h. jury** = jury which cannot reach a majority decision. **hung over,** *adj. inf.* feeling ill after drinking too much alcohol. **hung up,** *adj. inf.* suffering from an emotional disturbance.

Hungarian [hʌŋ'geərɪən] **1.** *adj.* referring to Hungary. **2.** *n.* (*a*) person from Hungary. (*b*) language spoken in Hungary.

hunger ['hʌŋgə] *n.* wanting/needing to eat. **hunger strike,** *n.* refusing to eat to force s.o. to do sth. **hungrily,** *adv.* in a hungry way. **hungry,** *adj.* feeling hunger.

hunk [hʌŋk] *n.* large rough piece (of bread/cheese).

hunt [hʌnt] **1.** *n.* (*a*) chasing of wild animals for sport; group of people who meet regularly to chase wild animals, esp. foxes. (*b*) search (for s.o.). **2.** *v.* (*a*) to look for (s.o./sth). **hunt down,** *v.* to track (a person/an animal) and catch them. **hunter,** *n.* person who chases wild animals; horse used in hunting; **bargain h.** = person who is looking for bargains in shops. **hunting,** *n.* (*a*) chasing wild animals. (*b*) looking for sth. **hunting ground,** *n.* (*a*) place where wild animals are often found. (*b*) place where things are often found. **huntsman,** *n.* (*pl.* **-men**) man who hunts wild animals; man who looks after a pack of hunting hounds.

hurdle ['hɜːdl] *n.* (*a*) moveable fence for keeping sheep in. (*b*) small fence which has to be jumped over in a race. (*c*) obstacle. **hurdler,** *n.* person who takes part in hurdling. **hurdling,** *n.* running a race where you have to jump over fences.

hurdy-gurdy ['hɜːdɪ'gɜːdɪ] *n.* machine which produces music if a handle is turned.

hurl [hɜːl] *v.* to throw hard. **hurling,** *n.* game similar to hockey, played in Ireland.

hurly-burly ['hɜːlɪ'bɜːlɪ] *n.* rough activity.

hurrah, hurray [hʊ'rɑː, hʊ'reɪ] *inter.* *showing great pleasure/excitement.*

hurricane ['hʌrɪkən] *n.* violent tropical storm, esp. in the West Indies; **h. lamp** = lamp with a glass shield round the flame.

hurry ['hʌrɪ] **1.** *n.* rush. **2.** *v.* (*also* **hurry up**) (*a*) to go fast. (*b*) to make (s.o.) go faster. **hurried,** *adj.* quick/rushed. **hurriedly,** *adv.* quickly.

hurt [hɜːt] **1.** *n.* pain. **2.** *v.* (**hurt**) to give (s.o.) pain/to make (s.o.) sad. **hurtful,**

adj. which is painful to the feelings/ which makes s.o. sad.

hurtle ['hɜːtl] *v.* to move quickly/to rush dangerously.

husband ['hʌzbənd] **1.** *n.* man who is married to a certain woman. **2.** *v.* (*formal*) to look after carefully/not to waste (your resources). **husbandry,** *n.* farming; **animal h.** = rearing of animals on a farm.

hush [hʌʃ] **1.** *n.* quiet. **2.** *v.* to make quiet. **hush-hush,** *adj.* *inf.* secret. **hush money,** *n.* money paid to s.o. to stop them revealing a secret. **hush up,** *v.* to suppress (a scandal).

husk [hʌsk] **1.** *n.* hard outside covering of a seed. **2.** *v.* to take the husk off (a seed).

husky ['hʌskɪ] **1.** *adj.* (**-ier, -iest**) rough/ hoarse (voice). **2.** *n.* dog which pulls sledges in the Arctic. **huskily,** *adv.* in a husky voice. **huskiness,** *n.* hoarseness of the voice.

huss [hʌs] *n.* (*pl.* **huss**) small white sea fish.

hussar ['hʌzɑː] *n.* soldier on horseback.

hussy ['hʌsɪ] *n.* **brazen h.** = wicked girl/ woman.

hustings ['hʌstɪŋz] *n.* **at the h.** = during an election campaign.

hustle ['hʌsl] **1.** *n.* rush/violent activity. **2.** *v.* to push/to hurry (roughly). **hustler,** *n.* person who gets things going/who hurries business along.

hut [hʌt] *n.* small rough house, usu. made of wood.

hutch [hʌtʃ] *n.* wooden box to keep rabbits in.

hyacinth ['haɪəsɪnθ] *n.* strongly-scented spring flower grown from a bulb.

hybrid ['haɪbrɪd] *adj. & n.* (plant/animal, etc.) produced from two different species.

hydatid ['haɪdætɪd] *adj.* (cyst) caused by a tapeworm.

hydrangea [haɪ'dreɪndʒə] *n.* garden shrub with large blue or pink flowers.

hydrant ['haɪdrənt] *n.* water pipe in a street to which a hose can be attached; **fire h.** = one to which firemen can attach fire hoses.

hydrate ['haɪdreɪt] *n.* chemical compound with water.

hydraulic [haɪ'drɔːlɪk] *adj.* worked by

fluid. **hydraulically,** *adv.* using hydraulic force. **hydraulics,** *n.* study of fluids used mechanically.

hydro ['haɪdrəʊ] *n.* (*pl.* **-os**) *inf.* (*a*) hotel and clinic which specializes in the use of water to cure people. (*b*) hydroelectric station.

hydro- ['haɪdrəʊ] *prefix meaning* water.

hydrocarbon [haɪdrəʊ'kɑːbn] *n.* organic compound of hydrogen and carbon.

hydrochloric [haɪdrəʊ'klɒrɪk] *adj.* (acid) made of hydrogen and chlorine.

hydroelectric [haɪdrəʊɪ'lektrɪk] *adj.* referring to hydroelectricity. **hydroelectricity** [haɪdrəʊelek'trɪsɪtɪ] *n.* electricity produced by water power.

hydrofoil ['haɪdrəfɔɪl] *n.* boat which skims over the water on thin legs.

hydrogen ['haɪdrədʒən] *n.* (*element:* H) common gas which combines with oxygen to form water; **h. bomb** = extremely powerful nuclear bomb.

hydrographer [haɪ'drɒgrəfə] *n.* person who makes maps of the sea or sea bed.

hydrolysis [haɪ'drɒlɪsɪs] *n.* decomposition of a chemical substance by water.

hydrometer [haɪ'drɒmɪtə] *n.* device for measuring the relative density of water.

hydrophobia [haɪdrə'fəʊbɪə] *n.* rabies; fear of water (usu. a symptom of rabies).

hydroplane ['haɪdrəpleɪn] *n.* powerful flat-bottomed motorboat which skims over the surface of the water.

hydroponics [haɪdrə'pɒnɪks] *n.* science of growing plants in water, without using soil.

hydrostatic [haɪdrəʊ'stætɪk] *adj.* referring to fluids at rest.

hydrotherapy [haɪdrə'θerəpɪ] *n.* treatment of sick people with water.

hyena [haɪ'iːnə] *n.* fierce dog-like African animal.

hygiene ['haɪdʒiːn] *n.* keeping clean and free of germs. **hygienic** [haɪ'dʒiːnɪk] *adj.* (which keeps) clean and free of germs. **hygienically,** *adv.* in a hygienic way. **hygienist,** person who specializes in (esp. dental) hygiene.

hygrometer [haɪ'grɒmɪtə] *n.* instrument for measuring humidity.

hymen ['haɪmen] *n.* thin tissue which covers the entrance to the vagina of

a girl who has never had sexual intercourse.

hymn [hɪm] *n.* religious song. **hymnal** ['hɪmnl], **hymn-book,** *n.* book of hymns.

hype [haɪp] **1.** *n.* *inf.* excessive publicity. **2.** *v.* to publicize (a product) excessively.

hyper- ['haɪpə] *prefix meaning* to a great degree; **hyperactive** = very active.

hyperbola [haɪ'pɜːbələ] *n.* type of curve. **hyperbolic** [haɪpə'bɒlɪk] *adj.* referring to a hyperbola.

hyperbole [haɪ'pɜːbəlɪ] *n.* exaggerated comparison. **hyperbolical** [haɪpə'bɒlɪkl] *adj.* referring to hyperbole.

hypercritical [haɪpə'krɪtɪkl] *adj.* extremely critical.

hypermarket ['haɪpəmɑːkɪt] *n.* very large supermarket.

hypersensitive [haɪpə'sensɪtɪv] *adj.* very easily offended.

hypertension [haɪpə'tenʃn] *n.* very high blood pressure.

hyphen ['haɪfn] *n.* short line (-) which joins two words or separates one word into parts. **hyphenate,** *v.* to join (words) with a hyphen or separate (one word) into parts with a hyphen. **hyphenation** [haɪfə'neɪʃn] *n.* act of hyphenating.

hypnosis [hɪp'nəʊsɪs] *n.* putting s.o. into a trance, so that they obey your orders; **under h.** = while in a trance. **hypnotic** [hɪp'nɒtɪk] *adj.* referring to hypnosis. **hypnotically,** *adv.* in a hypnotic way. **hypnotism** ['hɪpnətɪzəm] *n.* use of hypnosis as a medical process or for amusement. **hypnotist,** *n.* person who practises hypnosis. **hypnotize,** *v.* to put (s.o.) into a trance.

hypo ['haɪpəʊ] *n.* substance used for fixing the picture when developing a photograph.

hypo- ['haɪpəʊ] *prefix meaning* under/below.

hypocaust ['haɪpəʊkɔːst] *n.* Roman heating system, where hot air flowed under a raised floor.

hypochondria [haɪpə'kɒndrɪə] *n.* being permanently worried about your health. **hypochondriac,** *n.* person who is always worried about his health.

hypocrisy [hɪ'pɒkrəsɪ] *n.* pretending to

be the opposite of what you really are/to feel the opposite of what you really feel. **hypocrite** ['hɪpəkrɪt] *n.* hypocritical person. **hypocritical** [hɪpə'krɪtɪkl] *adj.* referring to hypocrisy.

hypodermic [haɪpə'dɜːmɪk] *adj.* **h. syringe/needle** = medical instrument used for injections just below the surface of the skin.

hypotension [haɪpəʊ'tenʃn] *n.* very low blood pressure.

hypotenuse [haɪ'pɒtənjuːz] *n.* longest side of a right-angled triangle.

hypothermia [haɪpə'θɜːmɪə] *n.* state where the temperature of the body is abnormally low.

hypothesis [haɪ'pɒθəsɪs] *n.* (*pl.* **-theses** [-θəsiːz]) suggestion that sth is true, though without proof. **hypothetical** [haɪpə'θetɪkl] *adj.* suggested as true, but not necessarily so. **hypothetically,** *adv.* in a hypothetical way.

hysterectomy [hɪstə'rektəmɪ] *n.* surgical operation to remove a woman's womb.

hysteria [hɪ'stɪərɪə] *n.* nervous excitement leading to wild fits of laughing or crying. **hysterical** [hɪ'sterɪkl] *adj.* suffering from hysteria; laughing/crying in a wild manner. **hysterically,** *adv.* in an uncontrollable way. **hysterics,** *n. pl.* attack of hysteria.

Ii

I, i [aɪ] **to dot one's i's and cross one's t's** = to be very careful to settle the final details.

I [aɪ] *pronoun referring to the speaker.*

I *symbol for* iodine

iamb ['aɪæmb] *n.* Greek poetic measure, formed of a short and a long syllable. **iambic,** *adj.* referring to iambs.

Iberian [aɪ'bɪərɪən] *adj.* referring to Spain and Portugal.

ibex ['aɪbeks] *n.* (*pl.* **ibex(es)**) mountain goat with large curved horns.

ibid, ibidem ['ɪbɪd(em)] *adv.* in the same way.

ibis ['aɪbɪs] *n.* tropical water bird with long legs and a curved bill.

i/c ['aɪ'siː] *abbrev. for* in charge.

ice [aɪs] **1.** *n.* (*a*) frozen water; **to break the i.** = to bring an embarrassing silence

to an end; **to keep sth on i.** = not do anything about it for the moment. (*b*) ice cream. (*c*) **dry i.** = frozen carbon dioxide. **2.** *v.* (*a*) to cool with ice. (*b*) to freeze. (*c*) to cover with sugar icing. **ice age,** *n.* geological period when parts of the world were covered with ice. **ice axe,** *n.* axe used by mountaineers to cut footholds in ice. **iceberg,** *n.* large floating mass of ice at sea; **tip of the i.** = small part of sth (usu. unpleasant) which makes you eventually discover the rest. **icebox,** *n.* (*a*) box containing ice to keep food or drink cool. (*b*) *Am.* refrigerator. **ice-breaker,** *n.* boat specially strengthened to break up ice in shipping lanes. **ice cream,** *n.* frozen sweet made of cream and flavouring. **icefield,** *n.* large area of ice floating on the sea. **icefloe,** *n.* sheet of ice floating in the sea. **ice hockey,** *n.* form of hockey played on ice. **icehouse,** *n.* house for storing ice during the summer. **Icelander,** *n.* person from Iceland. **Icelandic. 1.** *adj.* referring to Iceland. **2.** *n.* language spoken in Iceland. **icicle,** *n.* long hanging piece of ice formed by dripping water in cold weather. **icily,** *adv.* in a cold/unfriendly way. **iciness,** *n.* bitter coldness (of weather/of greeting). **icing,** *n.* sugar topping for a cake; **i. sugar** = very fine sugar for covering cakes. **icy,** *adj.* (**-ier, -iest**) (*a*) covered with ice. (*b*) very cold/unwelcoming.

ichneumon fly [ɪk'njuːmən 'flaɪ] *n.* insect, whose larvae live on other insects.

icon ['aɪkən] *n.* (*a*) picture of Christ or a saint in the Eastern Christian church. (*b*) little pictorial symbol on a computer screen. **iconoclast** [aɪ'kɒnəklæst] *n.* person who attacks beliefs which are held by many people. **iconoclastic** [aɪkɒnə'klæstɪk] *adj.* which attacks beliefs which are held by many people. **iconography,** *n.* the study of icons; the study of pictures of a particular subject.

id [ɪd] *n.* the basic unconscious drives in a person.

I'd [aɪd] *short for* **I would/I had/I should.**

idea [aɪ'dɪə] *n.* thought/plan in the mind; **I had no i.** = I did not know.

ideal [aɪ'dɪəl] **1.** *n.* summit of perfection;

man of ideals = person who has standards of perfection. **2.** *adj.* perfect; very suitable. **idealism,** *n.* aiming at achieving an ideal. **idealist,** *n.* person who aims at achieving an ideal; impractical person. **idealistic** [aɪdɪəˈlɪstɪk] *adj.* aiming at an ideal; too perfect. **idealize,** *v.* to make (s.o./sth) seem perfect. **ideally,** *adv.* if everything were perfect.

identify [aɪˈdentɪfaɪ] *v.* (*a*) to say who s.o. is/what sth is. (*b*) to state that sth belongs to you. (*c*) **to i. with** = to feel you have the same characteristics as (s.o.); to have a feeling of sympathy for (s.o./sth). **identical,** *adj.* (**with/to**) exactly the same as. **identically,** *adv.* in exactly the same way. **identifiable,** *adj.* which can be identified. **identification** [aɪdentɪfɪˈkeɪʃn] *n.* saying who s.o. is/who sth belongs to; **i. parade** = line of people at a police station from whom a witness is asked to identify the criminal. **identikit,** *n.* method of making a portrait of a criminal using pieces of photographs or drawings of different faces to form a composite picture. **identity,** *n.* (*a*) who s.o. is; **i. card** = card which shows a photograph of the holder, with the name, date of birth and other details; **i. parade** = identification parade. (*b*) being the same/being identical.

ideogram [ˈɪdɪəʊɡræm] *n.* picture/character which represents a word.

ideology [aɪdɪˈɒlədʒɪ] *n.* theory of life based on political or economic philosophy rather than religious belief. **ideological** [aɪdɪəˈlɒdʒɪkl] *adj.* referring to ideology.

ides [aɪdz] *npl.* in the Latin calendar, the 15th of some months and the 13th of others.

idiocy [ˈɪdɪəsɪ] *n. see* **idiot.**

idiom [ˈɪdɪəm] *n.* (*a*) characteristic way of speaking/of writing. (*b*) particular expression where the words do not have their literal meaning. **idiomatic** [ɪdɪəˈmætɪk] *adj.* referring to a particular way of speaking.

idiosyncrasy [ɪdɪəʊˈsɪŋkrəsɪ] *n.* particular way of behaving. **idiosyncratic** [ɪdɪəʊsɪŋˈkrætɪk] *adj.* odd/peculiar; particular to one person.

idiot [ˈɪdɪət] *n.* (*a*) mentally deficient person. (*b*) person who is stupid. **idiocy,** *n.* stupidity. **idiotic** [ɪdɪˈɒtɪk] *adj.* stupid. **idiotically,** *adv.* in a stupid way.

idle [ˈaɪdl] **1.** *adj.* (**idler, idlest**) (*a*) lazy. (*b*) not working. (*c*) aimless/not worthwhile. **2.** *v.* (*a*) not to work; to spend time doing nothing. (*b*) (*of an engine*) to run gently. **idleness,** *n.* laziness. **idler,** *n.* person who idles. **idly,** *adv.* (*a*) lazily. (*b*) without being involved.

idol [ˈaɪdl] *n.* (*a*) statue of a god. (*b*) favourite person. (*c*) star performer (who is worshipped by fans). **idolater,** *n.* person who worships idols. **idolatry** [aɪˈdɒlətrɪ] *n.* worship of idols. **idolize,** *v.* to worship.

idyll [ˈɪdɪl] *n.* pleasant/happy scene. **idyllic** [ɪˈdɪlɪk] *adj.* pleasant/happy (in a romantic way). **idyllically,** *adv.* in an idyllic way.

i.e. [ˈaɪˈiː] *abbrev. for* id est, *meaning* that is.

if [ɪf] **1.** *conj.* (*a*) (*showing what might happen*) **if it rains the ground gets wet.** (*b*) (*showing supposition*) **if only to please him.** (*c*) (*exclamation*) **if only I had known!** (*d*) whether; **do you know if the plane is late?** (*e*) although; **he is nice, if rather lazy.** (*f*) at any time when. **2.** *n. inf.* undecided question.

igloo [ˈɪɡluː] *n.* dome-shaped shelter built by Eskimos out of blocks of snow.

igneous [ˈɪɡnɪəs] *adj.* (rock) which was originally formed from solidified lava.

ignite [ɪɡˈnaɪt] *v.* to set fire to; to catch fire. **ignition** [ɪɡˈnɪʃn] *n.* (*in a car*) electrical device which makes the spark which fires the petrol; **i. key** = key used to switch on the ignition.

ignoble [ɪɡˈnəʊbl] *adj.* (*formal*) unworthy.

ignominy [ˈɪɡnəmɪnɪ] *n.* shame/disgrace. **ignominious** [ɪɡnəˈmɪnɪəs] *adj.* shameful. **ignominiously,** *adv.* in an ignominious way.

ignore [ɪɡˈnɔː] *v.* not to notice (on purpose). **ignoramus** [ɪɡnəˈreɪməs] *n.* (*pl.* **-es**) person who is stupid/who knows nothing. **ignorance** [ˈɪɡnərəns] *n.* not knowing. **ignorant** [ˈɪɡnərənt] *adj.* not knowing/stupid. **ignorantly,** *adv.* stupidly.

iguana [ɪɡjuˈɑːnə] kind of large tropical lizard.

ileum ['ɪlɪəm] n. long part of the small intestine.

ilium ['ɪlɪəm] n. top part of the hip bone.

ilk [ɪlk] n. inf. sort/type.

ill [ɪl] **1.** adj. (**worse, worst**) (a) sick; not well. (b) bad. **2.** n. bad thing. **3.** adv. badly. **ill-advised,** adj. not recommended. **ill-bred,** adj. badly brought up; with bad manners. **ill-fated,** adj. fated to fail. **ill-feeling,** n. resentment; dislike. **ill-gotten,** adj. illegally acquired. **ill-mannered,** adj. badly behaved/with bad manners/rude. **illness,** n. sickness. **ill-starred,** adj. fated to fail. **ill-treat,** v. to treat (animals/children) badly. **ill will,** n. **to bear s.o. ill will** = to want sth bad to happen to s.o.

I'll [aɪl] short for I will/I shall.

illegal [ɪ'li:gl] adj. against the law. **illegality,** n. being illegal. **illegally,** adv. against the law.

illegible [ɪ'ledʒɪbl] adj. (writing) which cannot be read. **illegibility,** n. being illegible. **illegibly,** adv. in an illegible way.

illegitimate [ɪlɪ'dʒɪtəmət] adj. (a) (person) born of unmarried parents. (b) against the law. **illegitimately,** adv. in an illegitimate way. **illegitimacy,** n. being illegitimate.

illicit [ɪ'lɪsɪt] adj. against the law/illegal. **illicitly,** adv. in an illicit way.

illiteracy [ɪ'lɪtərəsɪ] n. inability to read and write. **illiterate,** adj. & n. (person) who cannot read or write.

illogical [ɪ'lɒdʒɪkl] adj. not sensible/not reasonable. **illogically,** adv. in an illogical way. **illogicality** [ɪlɒdʒɪ'kælɪtɪ] n. being illogical.

illuminate [ɪ'lu:mɪneɪt] v. (a) to light up. (b) to draw coloured initials/pictures in a manuscript. **illuminating,** adj. which throws light on (a subject). **illumination** [ɪlu:mɪ'neɪʃn] n. (a) floodlighting; decoration. (b) coloured initial illustration in a manuscript.

illusion [ɪ'lu:ʒn] n. impression which is not true; **optical i.** = thing which appears different from what it really is because the eye is being deceived. **illusionist,** n. person who entertains with optical illusions. **illusive,** adj. false. **illusory,** adj. which is an illusion.

illustrate ['ɪləstreɪt] v. (a) to add pictures to. (b) to give/to be an example of. **illustration** [ɪlə'streɪʃn] n. (a) picture (in a book). (b) example. **illustrative** ['ɪləstrətɪv] adj. which illustrates/which is an example. **illustrator** ['ɪləstreɪtə] n. person who draws the pictures for a book.

illustrious [ɪ'lʌstrɪəs] adj. very famous.

I'm [aɪm] short for I am.

image ['ɪmɪdʒ] n. (a) portrait/statue; inf. **he's the spitting i. of his father** = he looks exactly like his father. (b) idea which other people have of a person/a company. (c) picture produced by a lens/seen in a mirror. (d) comparison/symbol used esp. in poetry. **imagery,** n. using comparison/symbols (in writing) as a way of making people imagine things.

imagine [ɪ'mædʒɪn] v. to picture (sth) in your mind. **imaginable,** adj. which you can imagine. **imaginary,** adj. false/not real. **imagination** [ɪmædʒɪ'neɪʃn] n. ability to picture things in your mind. **imaginative** [ɪ'mædʒɪnətɪv] adj. (artist) with a strong imagination; (drawing/poem) which shows a lot of imagination. **imaginatively,** adv. in an imaginative way.

imago [ɪ'mɑ:gəʊ] n. final form of an insect (such as a butterfly) after the larval and pupal stages.

imam ['ɪmæm] n. Muslim priest.

imbalance [ɪm'bæləns] n. lack of balance.

imbecile ['ɪmbəsi:l] n. (a) mentally deficient person. (b) stupid person. **imbecility** [ɪmbə'sɪlɪtɪ] n. being mentally deficient.

imbibe [ɪm'baɪb] v. (formal) to drink.

imbricated ['ɪmbrɪkeɪtɪd] adj. overlapping.

imbroglio [ɪm'brəʊljəʊ] n. (pl. **-os**) complicated plot.

imbue [ɪm'bju:] v. (formal) to fill with a feeling.

IMF [aɪem'ef] abbrev. for International Monetary Fund.

imitate ['ɪmɪteɪt] v. to copy/to do like (s.o.). **imitation** [ɪmɪ'teɪʃn] n. copy; act of imitating. **imitative** ['ɪmɪtətɪv] adj. which copies. **imitator** ['ɪmɪteɪtə] n. person who copies.

immaculate [ɪˈmækjʊlət] *adj.* extremely clean/tidy. **immaculacy**, *n.* being immaculate. **immaculately**, *adv.* extremely tidily.

immanent [ˈɪmənənt] *adj.* existing as an inherent part.

immaterial [ɪməˈtɪərɪəl] *adj.* not important.

immature [ɪməˈtʃʊə] *adj.* not mature/not fully grown/not fully developed. **immaturity**, *n.* not being mature.

immeasurable [ɪˈmeʒrəbl] *adj.* which cannot be measured/very large. **immeasurably**, *adv.* enormously.

immediate [ɪˈmiːdjət] *adj.* (*a*) close/nearest. (*b*) very soon. **immediacy**, *n.* being immediate. **immediately**, *adv.* & *conj.* straight away.

immemorial [ɪməˈmɔːrɪəl] *adj.* **from time i.** = from very ancient times.

immense [ɪˈmens] *adj.* huge/very wide/enormous. **immensely**, *adv.* very much. **immensity**, *n.* vastness/huge size.

immerse [ɪˈmɜːs] *v.* to plunge (sth) in a liquid. **immersion** [ɪˈmɜːʃn] *n.* plunging (into a liquid); **i. heater** = heater inside a water tank.

immigrate [ˈɪmɪɡreɪt] *v.* to come to settle in a country. **immigrant**, *n.* person who comes to a country to settle. **immigration** [ɪmɪˈɡreɪʃn] *n.* settling in a new country; **i. office** = office dealing with immigrants; **i. controls** = restrictions placed by a country on the numbers of immigrants.

imminent [ˈɪmɪnənt] *adj.* which is about to happen. **imminence**, *n.* being about to happen.

immobile [ɪˈməʊbaɪl] *adj.* without moving; unable to move. **immobility** [ɪməˈbɪlɪtɪ] *n.* state of not moving. **immobilization** [ɪməʊbɪlaɪˈzeɪʃn] *n.* stopping sth moving. **immobilize** [ɪˈməʊbɪlaɪz] *v.* to stop (sth) moving.

immoderate [ɪˈmɒdərət] *adj.* extravagant/not moderate. **immoderately**, *adv.* in an immoderate way.

immodest [ɪˈmɒdɪst] *adj.* not modest.

immolate [ˈɪməʊleɪt] *v.* (*poetic*) to sacrifice.

immoral [ɪˈmɒrəl] *adj.* not concerned with the principles of good behaviour. **immorality** [ɪməˈrælɪtɪ] *n.* lack of morality. **immorally**, *adv.* in an immoral way.

immortal [ɪˈmɔːtl] **1.** *adj.* like a god; who never dies. **2.** *n.* god. **immortality** [ɪmɔːˈtælɪtɪ] *n.* being immortal/never dying. **immortalize** [ɪˈmɔːtəlaɪz] *v.* to make (s.o.) be remembered forever.

immovable [ɪˈmuːvəbl] *adj.* which cannot be moved. **immovably**, *adv.* in an immovable way.

immune [ɪˈmjuːn] *adj.* (**to**) (person) who cannot catch a disease. **immunity**, *n.* (*a*) protection (**against** a disease). (*b*) protection against arrest; **parliamentary/diplomatic i.** = protection of members of parliament/diplomats against being arrested. **immunization** [ɪmjunaɪˈzeɪʃn] *n.* giving protection against a disease. **immunize** [ˈɪmjunaɪz] *v.* to give protection **against** a disease. **immunology**, *n.* study of immunity.

immure [ɪˈmjʊə] *v.* to shut (s.o.) in prison.

immutable [ɪˈmjuːtəbl] *adj.* (*formal*) which cannot be changed/which does not change. **immutability**, *n.* being immutable. **immutably**, *adv.* in an immutable way.

imp [ɪmp] *n.* small devil; wicked child.

impact [ˈɪmpækt] *n.* forceful shock/effect. **impacted** [ɪmˈpæktɪd] *adj.* (tooth) which is stuck in the jaw and cannot grow.

impair [ɪmˈpeə] *v.* to harm. **impairment**, *n.* harm.

impala [ɪmˈpɑːlə] *n.* large African antelope.

impale [ɪmˈpeɪl] *v.* to jab a sharp object through (s.o.'s body).

impalpable [ɪmˈpælpəbl] *adj.* (*formal*) which cannot be touched.

impart [ɪmˈpɑːt] *v.* (*formal*) to pass on/to communicate (sth **to** s.o.).

impartial [ɪmˈpɑːʃl] *adj.* not biased. **impartiality**, *n.* being impartial. **impartially**, *adv.* in an impartial way.

impassable [ɪmˈpɑːsəbl] *adj.* which you cannot go through or across.

impasse [ˈæmpæs] *n.* deadlock/state where two sides cannot agree.

impassioned [ɪmˈpæʃnd] *adj.* very deeply felt/excited (speech).

impassive [ɪmˈpæsɪv] *adj.* expressionless. **impassively**, *adv.* in an impassive way.

impatient [ɪmˈpeɪʃnt] *adj.* (*a*) (**with**) not patient; unable to wait for sth. (*b*) in a hurry (to do sth). **impatience**, *n.* lack of patience. **impatiently**, *adv.* in a hurried way/not patiently.

impeach [ɪmˈpiːtʃ] *v.* to charge (s.o.) with treason or crime against the state. **impeachment**, *n.* act of impeaching.

impeccable [ɪmˈpekəbl] *adj.* perfect/perfectly correct. **impeccably**, *adv.* perfectly.

impecunious [ɪmpɪˈkjuːnɪəs] *adj.* (*formal*) with no money.

impede [ɪmˈpiːd] *v.* to get in the way of (sth); to prevent (sth) happening. **impedance** [ɪmˈpiːdəns] *n.* resistance to an electric current. **impediment** [ɪmˈpedɪmənt] *n.* obstacle; **speech i.** = stammer, etc., which prevents you speaking clearly. **impedimenta**, *n. pl.* heavy/awkward baggage or equipment.

impel [ɪmˈpel] *v.* (**impelled**) to push/to force.

impending [ɪmˈpendɪŋ] *adj.* imminent/about to happen.

impenetrable [ɪmˈpenɪtrəbl] *adj.* which you cannot go through or into. **impenetrability**, *n.* being impenetrable.

impenitent [ɪmˈpenɪtənt] *adj.* not penitent/not sorry for having done sth wrong.

imperative [ɪmˈperətɪv] *adj.* (*a*) urgent/obligatory. (*b*) (*in grammar*) **verb in the i.** = verb used as a command.

imperceptible [ɪmpəˈseptɪbl] *adj.* which you can hardly notice. **imperceptibly**, *adv.* scarcely noticeably.

imperfect [ɪmˈpɜːfɪkt] *adj.* not perfect/not complete. **imperfection** [ɪmpəˈfekʃn] *n.* flaw.

imperial [ɪmˈpɪərɪəl] *adj.* (*a*) referring to an empire. (*b*) (weights/measures) used in the UK and the British Commonwealth. **imperialism**, *n.* belief in the good of building an empire. **imperialist. 1.** *n.* person who builds an empire. **2.** *adj.* (*also* **imperialistic**) referring to imperialism.

imperil [ɪmˈperɪl] *v.* (**imperilled**) (*formal*) to put in danger.

imperious [ɪmˈpɪərɪəs] *adj.* arrogant (way of giving orders). **imperiously**, *adv.* in an imperious way.

impermanent [ɪmˈpɜːmənənt] *adj.* not permanent/not lasting.

impermeable [ɪmˈpɜːmɪəbl] *adj.* which liquids cannot go through.

impersonal [ɪmˈpɜːsnl] *adj.* (*a*) without a personal touch. (*b*) (verb) used without a person or thing as the subject. **impersonally**, *adv.* in an impersonal way.

impersonate [ɪmˈpɜːsəneɪt] *v.* to imitate (s.o.)/to disguise yourself as (s.o.). **impersonation**, *n.* act of impersonating. **impersonator**, *n.* person who impersonates.

impertinence [ɪmˈpɜːtɪnəns] *n.* rudeness/insolence. **impertinent**, *adj.* rude/insolent. **impertinently**, *adv.* in an impertinent way.

imperturbable [ɪmpəˈtɜːbəbl] *adj.* calm. **imperturbability**, *n.* being imperturbable. **imperturbably**, *adv.* calmly.

impervious [ɪmˈpɜːvɪəs] *adj.* (**to**) which liquids cannot go through.

impetigo [ɪmpɪˈtaɪɡəʊ] *n.* contagious disease of the skin (esp. in children).

impetuous [ɪmˈpetjʊəs] *adj.* thoughtless/hasty (act); (person) who rushes to do sth without thinking. **impetuosity** [ɪmpetjʊˈɒsɪtɪ] *n.* rushing to do sth without thinking. **impetuously** [ɪmˈpetjʊəslɪ] *adv.* without thinking.

impetus [ˈɪmpɪtəs] *n.* (*pl.* -es) movement forward.

impinge [ɪmˈpɪndʒ] *v.* (**on**) to affect.

impious [ˈɪmpɪəs] *adj.* not pious/not religious. **impiety** [ɪmˈpaɪətɪ] *n.* being impious.

impish [ˈɪmpɪʃ] *adj.* like an imp.

implacable [ɪmˈplækəbl] *adj.* who/which cannot be satisfied. **implacably**, *adv.* in an implacable way.

implant [ɪmˈplɑːnt] **1.** *n.* tissue which has been implanted. **2.** *v.* to fix (sth) in deeply.

implausible [ɪmˈplɔːzəbl] *adj.* not likely to be true.

implement 1. *n.* [ˈɪmplɪmənt] tool/instrument. **2.** *v.* [ˈɪmplɪment] to put into effect. **implementation** [ɪmplɪmənˈteɪʃn] *n.* putting into effect.

implicate [ˈɪmplɪkeɪt] *v.* **to i. s.o. in sth** = to suggest that s.o. was connected with sth. **implication** [ɪmplɪˈkeɪʃn] *n.* (*a*) suggestion (that s.o. is connected with a crime). (b) thing which is implied.

implicit [ɪmˈplɪsɪt] adj. which is not definitely said, but is suggested. **implicitly,** adv. without questioning.

implore [ɪmˈplɔː] v. to beg (s.o. to do sth).

imply [ɪmˈplaɪ] v. to suggest.

impolite [ɪmpəˈlaɪt] adj. rude/not polite. **impolitely,** adv. rudely, **impoliteness,** n. lack of politeness.

impolitic [ɪmˈpɒlɪtɪk] adj. (formal) not wise.

imponderables [ɪmˈpɒndrəblz] n. pl. things whose importance you cannot easily calculate.

import. 1. n. [ˈɪmpɔːt] (a) **imports** = goods which are brought into a country; **i. duty** = tax paid on goods brought into a country; **i. controls** = rules limiting goods which can be brought into a country. (b) (formal) meaning (of words). 2. v. [ɪmˈpɔːt] to bring goods into a country. **importation** [ɪmpɔːˈteɪʃn] n. act of importing; goods imported. **importer** [ɪmˈpɔːtə] n. person or country which imports.

importance [ɪmˈpɔːtns] n. seriousness/ serious effect/influence. **important,** adj. (a) serious/with a serious effect/ which matters a great deal. (b) with great influence/holding an influential position. **importantly,** adv. seriously/ with a serious effect.

importune [ɪmˈpɔːtjuːn] v. (formal) to pester/to bother (s.o.). **importunate** [ɪmˈpɔːtjunət] adj. pestering/bothering.

impose [ɪmˈpəʊz] v. (a) to inflict. (b) **to i. on** = cause trouble/inconvenience. **imposing,** adj. grand/solemn. **imposition** [ɪmpəˈzɪʃn] n. (a) making people pay a tax; laying down (of conditions). (b) taking advantage (of s.o.). (c) unfair duty; punishment (in school).

impossible [ɪmˈpɒsɪbl] adj. (a) which cannot be done. (b) awkward/difficult (person/situation). **impossibility,** n. being impossible. **impossibly,** adv. in an impossible way; inf. greatly.

impostor [ɪmˈpɒstə] n. person who pretends to be s.o. else. **imposture** [ɪmˈpɒstʃə] n. pretending to be s.o. else.

impotence [ˈɪmpətəns] n. (a) lack of strength. (b) (of man) inability to have

sexual intercourse. **impotent,** adj. (a) weak. (b) (of man) unable to have sexual intercourse. **impotently,** adv. without being able to act.

impound [ɪmˈpaʊnd] v. to take (sth) away and put it in a safe place.

impoverish [ɪmˈpɒvərɪʃ] v. to make poor. **impoverishment,** n. making poor.

impracticable [ɪmˈpræktɪkəbl] adj. (plan) which cannot work; (road) which cannot be used.

impractical [ɪmˈpræktɪkl] adj. (plan) which is not easy to put into practice; (person) who is not good at doing things with his hands.

imprecation [ɪmprɪˈkeɪʃn] n. (formal) oath/curse.

imprecise [ɪmprɪˈsaɪs] adj. not precise/ not accurate. **imprecision,** n. lack of precision.

impregnable [ɪmˈpregnəbl] adj. (castle) which cannot be captured. **impregnability,** n. being impregnable.

impregnate [ˈɪmpregneɪt] v. (a) to soak (with sth). (b) to make pregnant. **impregnation,** n. act of impregnating.

impresario [ɪmprɪˈsɑːrɪəʊ] n. (pl. -os) person who organizes concerts and operas.

impress [ɪmˈpres] v. (a) to make (s.o.) admire/respect s.o./sth. (b) **to i. sth on s.o.** = to make him understand. (c) to stamp (a pattern on sth). **impression** [ɪmˈpreʃn] n. (a) effect on s.o.'s mind. (b) imitation of how s.o. talks/behaves. (c) mark (of a pattern). (d) printing (of a book). **impressionable,** adj. (person) who is easily influenced (by others). **impressionism,** n. art movement where painters tried to convey an impression of reality, in particular of light. **impressionist.** 1. adj. referring to impressionism. 2. n. painter in the impressionist movement. **impressionistic** [ɪmpreʃəˈnɪstɪk] adj. vague/ sketchy. **impressive** [ɪmˈpresɪv] adj. which commands respect. **impressively,** adv. in an impressive way.

imprest [ˈɪmprest] n. system of purchasing by a government department.

imprimatur [ɪmprɪˈmɑːtə] n. official permission to print a book.

imprint. 1. n. [ˈɪmprɪnt] (a) mark made

by sth pressed down. (*b*) name of publishing firm printed in a book. **2.** *v.* [ɪmˈprɪnt] to stamp/to mark.

imprison [ɪmˈprɪzn] *v.* to put/to keep in prison. **imprisonment**, *n.* putting/keeping in prison.

improbable [ɪmˈprɒbəbl] *adj.* not probable; unlikely. **improbability**, *n.* lack of probability. **improbably**, *adv.* not likely.

impromptu [ɪmˈprɒmptjuː] *adj.* & *adv.* without any rehearsal or practice.

improper [ɪmˈprɒpə] *adj.* (*a*) rude. (*b*) (word) used in a wrong way. **improperly**, *adv.* (*a*) not correctly. (*b*) (word which is used) wrongly. **impropriety** [ɪmprəˈpraɪətɪ] *n.* being improper; improper action.

improve [ɪmˈpruːv] *v.* to make/to get better. **improvement**, *n.* thing which makes better/is better.

improvident [ɪmˈprɒvɪdənt] *adj.* (person) who spends too much money or who does not plan for the future. **improvidence**, *n.* being improvident. **improvidently**, *adv.* not thinking about saving for the future.

improvise [ˈɪmprəvaɪz] *v.* to do/to make (sth) without preparation. **improvisation** [ɪmprəvaɪˈzeɪʃn] *n.* making sth without any preparation.

imprudent [ɪmˈpruːdənt] *adj.* careless/not prudent. **imprudently**, *adv.* in an imprudent way.

impudent [ˈɪmpjudənt] *adj.* rude/cheeky. **impudence**, *n.* rudeness/cheekiness. **impudently**, *adv.* rudely/cheekily.

impugn [ɪmˈpjuːn] *v.* (*formal*) to attack (s.o.'s character/the truth of a statement).

impulse [ˈɪmpʌls] *n.* (*a*) shock (which makes sth move/work). (*b*) sudden feeling/decision; **i. buying** = buying goods on the basis of a sudden decision. **impulsive** [ɪmˈpʌlsɪv] *adj.* acting on a sudden decision/without thinking. **impulsively**, *adv.* in an impulsive way. **impulsiveness**, *n.* being impulsive.

impunity [ɪmˈpjuːnɪtɪ] *n.* **with i.** = without risk of punishment.

impure [ɪmˈpjʊə] *adj.* not pure. **impurities** [ɪmˈpjʊərɪtɪz] *n. pl.* substances which make sth impure.

impute [ɪmˈpjuːt] *v.* to attribute (sth **to** s.o.); to say that (sth) is caused by (s.o./sth). **imputation**, *n.* saying that s.o. is at fault.

in [ɪn] **1.** *prep.* & *adv.* (*a*) (*showing place*) **in Russia; in bed.** (*b*) (*showing time*) **in autumn; in January; long skirts are in** = fashionable. (*c*) **one in ten** = one out of ten. (*d*) (*showing state*) **dressed in pink; in public;** *inf.* **all in** = tired out; **all in price** = including everything. **2.** *n.* **the ins and outs** = the intricate details. **3.** *adj. inf.* fashionable. **in for**, *adv.* to **be in for sth** = to be about to get sth. **in on**, *adv.* **to be in on (a secret)** = to know a secret. **in-tray**, *n.* file/basket for incoming letters.

inability [ɪnəˈbɪlɪtɪ] *n.* being unable (**to**).

inaccessible [ɪnəkˈsesɪbl] *adj.* impossible to reach.

inaccurate [ɪnˈækjʊrət] *adj.* not exact/not accurate. **inaccurately**, *adv.* not accurately. **inaccuracy**, *n.* not being exact; lack of accuracy.

inactive [ɪnˈæktɪv] *adj.* not active/not doing anything. **inaction, inactivity** [ɪnækˈtɪvɪtɪ] *n.* lack of action/doing nothing.

inadequate [ɪnˈædɪkwət] *adj.* (*a*) not enough/insufficient. (*b*) not competent enough. **inadequacy**, *n.* being inadequate. **inadequately**, *adv.* not enough; insufficiently.

inadmissible [ɪnədˈmɪsəbl] *adj.* (evidence) not allowed to be presented in a court.

inadvertent [ɪnədˈvɜːtənt] *adj.* said/done by mistake, not on purpose. **inadvertence**, *n.* being inadvertent; thing done inadvertently. **inadvertently**, *adv.* by mistake.

inadvisable [ɪnədˈvaɪzəbl] *adj.* unwise/not recommended.

inalienable [ɪnˈeɪljənəbl] *adj.* (*formal*) which cannot be taken away or refused.

inane [ɪˈneɪn] *adj.* stupid. **inanity** [ɪnˈænɪtɪ] *n.* being stupid.

inanimate [ɪnˈænɪmət] *adj.* not alive.

inapplicable [ɪnəˈplɪkəbl] *adj.* unsuitable/which does not apply (**to**).

inappropriate [ɪnəˈprəʊprɪət] *adj.* (**to**) not appropriate/not suitable/not fitting the circumstances.

inaptitude [ɪnˈæptɪtjuːd] *n.* (**for**) unsuitableness; lack of ability.

inarticulate [ɪnɑːˈtɪkjʊlət] *adj.* (*a*) not speaking clearly. (*b*) unable to speak.

inartistic [ɪnɑːˈtɪstɪk] *adj.* not artistic; not concerned with the arts.

inasmuch as [ɪnəzˈmʌtʃæz] *conj.* (*formal*) seeing that/owing to the fact that.

inattentive [ɪnəˈtentɪv] *adj.* not paying attention/not attentive. **inattention,** *n.* not paying attention.

inaudible [ɪnˈɔːdɪbl] *adj.* which cannot be heard. **inaudibly,** *adv.* so quietly that it cannot be heard.

inaugurate [ɪnˈɔːgjʊreɪt] *v.* to swear in (a new president); to open officially (a new building/a festival, etc. **inaugural,** *adj.* (speech) given at an opening ceremony; first (use); opening (ceremony). **inauguration** [ɪnɔːgjʊˈreɪʃn] *n.* swearing in (of a new president); official opening.

inauspicious [ɪnɔːˈspɪʃəs] *adj.* unlucky/ not giving hope for the future.

inboard [ˈɪnbɔːd] *adj.* inside a boat.

inborn [ˈɪnbɔːn] *adj.* (feelings/ideas) which a person has had since birth.

inbred [ˈɪnbred] *adj.* (feelings/ideas) which a person has had since a very young age. **inbreeding,** *n.* breeding between closely related persons/animals, etc.

Inc. [ɪnˈkɔːpəreɪtɪd] *Am. short for* incorporated.

incalculable [ɪnˈkælkjʊləbl] *adj.* which cannot be calculated/so large that it cannot be measured.

in camera [ɪnˈkæmərə] *adv.* in secret; not in public.

incandescent [ɪnkænˈdesnt] *adj.* which burns with a very bright light. **incandescence,** *n.* very bright light.

incantation [ɪnkænˈteɪʃn] *n.* magic words.

incapable [ɪnˈkeɪpəbl] *adj.* (*a*) (**of**) not able; **drunk and i.** = so drunk that you cannot stand up. (*b*) not capable; not competent. **incapability** [ɪnkeɪpəˈbɪlɪti] *n.* incompetence/not being capable.

incapacity [ɪnkəˈpæsɪti] *n.* lack of strength/ability to do sth. **incapacitate,** *v.* to make (s.o.) unable to do sth.

incarcerate [ɪnˈkɑːsəreɪt] *v.* (*formal*) to put/to keep in prison. **incarceration** [ɪnkɑːsəˈreɪʃn] *n.* putting/keeping in prison.

incarnate [ɪnˈkɑːnət] *adj.* in human form. **incarnation** [ɪnkɑːˈneɪʃn] *n.* appearance in human form.

incautious [ɪnˈkɔːʃəs] *adj.* not prudent. **incautiously,** *adv.* rashly.

incendiary [ɪnˈsendjəri] **1.** *adj.* which causes fire. **2.** *n.* (*a*) bomb which causes fire. (*b*) person who sets fire to buildings.

incense. 1. *n.* [ˈɪnsens] spice powder which when burnt gives a strong smell. **2.** *v.* [ɪnˈsens] to make (s.o.) annoyed.

incentive [ɪnˈsentɪv] *n.* thing which encourages; **i. bonus** = extra money paid when production is increased.

inception [ɪnˈsepʃn] *n.* beginning.

incessant [ɪnˈsesnt] *adj.* unceasing/ continuous.

incest [ˈɪnsest] *n.* sexual intercourse with a close member of the family. **incestuous** [ɪnˈsestjʊəs] *adj.* referring to incest.

inch [ɪnʃ] **1.** *n.* (*pl.* **-es**) measure of length (2.54 cm.). **2.** *v.* to go (slowly).

inchoate [ɪnˈkəʊeɪt] *adj.* (*formal*) not fully developed.

incident [ˈɪnsɪdənt] *n.* (*a*) minor happening. (*b*) (usu. violent) action/disturbance. **incidence,** *n.* rate. **incidental** [ɪnsɪˈdentl] *adj. & n.* (thing) which happens in connection with sth else, but forming an unimportant part; subsidiary; **i. music** = background music which accompanies a film; **i. expenses** = secondary expenses. **incidentally,** *adv.* by the way.

incinerate [ɪnˈsɪnəreɪt] *v.* to destroy by burning. **incineration** [ɪnsɪnəˈreɪʃn] *n.* destruction by burning. **incinerator,** *n.* furnace for burning rubbish.

incipient [ɪnˈsɪpɪənt] *adj.* which is beginning/coming.

incise [ɪnˈsaɪz] *v.* to make a cut in (esp. a stone). **incision** [ɪnˈsɪʒn] *n.* cut. **incisive** [ɪnˈsaɪsɪv] *adj.* sharp/ cutting. **incisively,** *adv.* sharply. **incisor** [ɪnˈsaɪzə] *n.* sharp front tooth for cutting.

incite [ɪnˈsaɪt] *v.* to encourage (s.o. **to** do sth). **incitement,** *n.* encouragement (**to**).

incivility [ɪnsɪˈvɪlɪti] *n.* (*formal*) rudeness.

inclement [ɪnˈklemənt] *adj.* (*formal*) (of weather) bad.

incline 1. *n.* ['ınklaın] slope. **2.** *v.*
[ın'klaın] (*a*) to slope. (*b*) to encourage
(s.o.) to do sth. (*c*) to tend. (*d*) to bend/
to bow. **inclination** [ınklı'neıʃn] *n.* (*a*)
(angle of) slope. (*b*) slight bow (of the
head). (*c*) tendency. **inclined** *adj.* (*a*)
sloping. (*b*) likely (**to** do sth).

include [ın'kluːd] *v.* to count (s.o./sth)
along with others. **inclusion** [ın'kluːʒn]
n. counting s.o./sth in among others.
inclusive, *adj.* which includes everything; **from Monday to Friday i.** =
including both Monday and Friday.

incognito [ınkɒg'niːtəʊ] *adv. & n.* **to
travel i.** = under a false name or
identity; **he kept his i.** = people did not
find out who he really was.

incoherent [ınkəʊ'hıərənt] *adj.* not
coherent; not linked; which does not
make sense. **incoherence**, *n.* being incoherent. **incoherently**, *adv.* not in a
coherent way; in a way which does not
make sense.

income ['ıŋkʌm] *n.* money which you
receive; **i. tax** = tax on income;
unearned i. = income from invest-
ments/rents.

incoming ['ınkʌmıŋ] **1.** *adj.* which is
arriving/coming in; **i. calls** = telephone
calls received. **2.** *n. pl.* **incomings** =
revenue.

incommode [ınkɒ'məʊd] *v.* (*formal*) to
inconvenience (s.o.).

incommunicado [ınkəmjuːnı'kɑːdəʊ]
adv. not allowed to see or write to any
person.

incomparable [ın'kɒmprəbl] *adj.*
which cannot be compared to anything
else. **incomparably**, *adv.* vastly; so
much that it cannot be compared.

incompatible [ınkəm'pætıbl] *adj.*
(**with**) which cannot live/work/fit together. **incompatibility** [ınkəmpætə-
'bılıtı] *n.* being incompatible (**with**).

incompetent [ın'kɒmpıtənt] *adj.* not
good at doing sth/not competent. **in-
competence**, *n.* lack of competence.
incompetently, *adv.* in an incompetent way.

incomplete [ınkəm'pliːt] *adj.* not com-
plete/not finished. **incompletely**, *adv.*
not completely.

incomprehensible [ınkɒmprı'hensıbl]
adj. which cannot be understood.

incomphehension, *n.* lack of understanding.

inconceivable [ınkən'siːvəbl] *adj.*
which cannot be imagined.

inconclusive [ınkən'kluːsıv] *adj.* not
final; without a definite result. **incon-
clusively**, *adv.* in an inconclusive way.

incongruous [ın'kɒŋgrʊəs] *adj.* which
does not fit with the rest; which seems
out of place. **incongruity**, *n.* being out
of place.

inconsequential [ınkɒnsı'kwenʃl] *adj.*
not of any importance.

inconsiderable [ınkən'sıdərəbl] *adj.*
small.

inconsiderate [ınkən'sıdərət] *adj.* not
thinking of other people. **inconsider-
ately**, *adv.* not thinking about other
people.

inconsistent [ınkən'sıstənt] *adj.* (*a*)
which does not follow/which contra-
dicts. (*b*) (person) who changes his
mind frequently. **inconsistency**, *n.*
lack of consistency.

inconsolable [ınkən'səʊləbl] *adj.* (person) who cannot be comforted.

inconspicuous [ınkən'spıkjʊəs] *adj.*
not very noticeable. **inconspicuously**,
adv. without being noticed.

inconstant [ın'kɒnstənt] *adj.* (*formal*)
not constant; unfaithful. **inconstancy**,
n. lack of constancy.

incontestable [ınkən'testəbl] *adj.*
which cannot be argued with.

incontinent [ın'kɒntınənt] *adj.* unable
to control your bladder or bowels.
incontinence, *n.* being incontinent.

incontrovertible [ınkɒntrə'vɜːtəbl]
adj. (fact) with which you must agree.

inconvenience [ınkən'viːnıəns] **1.**
n. awkwardness. **2.** *v.* to bother
(s.o.). **inconvenient**, *adj.* awkward;
not handy. **inconveniently**, *adv.*
awkwardly.

incorporate [ın'kɔːpəreıt] *v.* (*a*) to
bring into one main part. (*b*) to form an
official body. (*c*) *Am.* to form a large
firm. **incorporation** [ınkɔːpə'reıʃn] *n.*
act of incorporating.

incorrect [ınkə'rekt] *adj.* not correct/
false. **incorrectly**, *adv.* wrongly/falsely.

incorrigible [ın'kɒrıdʒəbl] *adj.* (person)
who cannot be corrected/improved.
incorrigibly, *adv.* in an incorrigible
way.

incorruptible [ɪnkə'rʌptəbl] *adj.* (person) who cannot be corrupted/be persuaded to behave dishonestly. **incorruptibility** [ɪnkərʌptɪ'bɪlɪtɪ] *n.* being incorruptible.

increase 1. *n.* ['ɪnkriːs] growth/expansion; rise (in salary). 2. *v.* [ɪn'kriːs] to rise/to grow/to expand. **increasing,** *adj.* growing. **increasingly,** *adv.* more and more.

incredible [ɪn'kredɪbl] *adj.* which it is difficult to believe. **incredibly,** *adv.* unbelievably.

incredulous [ɪn'kredjʊləs] *adj.* (person) who does not believe. **incredulity** [ɪnkrə'djuːlɪtɪ] *n.* lack of belief. **incredulously,** *adv.* as if you do not believe.

increment ['ɪnkrəmənt] *n.* regular automatic addition (to salary). **incremental** [ɪnkrɪ'mentl] *adj.* referring to increments.

incriminate [ɪn'krɪmɪneɪt] *v.* to show that (s.o.) took part in a crime, etc. **incriminating,** *adj.* which shows that s.o. took part in a crime. **incriminatory** [ɪn'krɪmɪnətərɪ] *adj.* which incriminates.

incrustation [ɪŋkrʌs'teɪʃn] *n.* layer (of dirt, etc.) encrusted on a surface.

incubate ['ɪnkjubeɪt] *v.* to keep (eggs) warm until they hatch; to have (the germs of a disease) in your body. **incubation** [ɪŋkju'beɪʃn] *n.* keeping eggs warm until they hatch; **i. period** = period during which a disease develops in your body. **incubator,** *n.* warm box in which eggs are kept until they hatch; sterilized receptacle for keeping very small babies in until they are strong.

incubus ['ɪŋkjubəs] *n.* nightmare; problem which causes great worry.

inculcate ['ɪnkʌlkeɪt] *v.* (*formal*) to fix (ideas, etc.) in the mind of a young person.

incumbent [ɪn'kʌmbənt] 1. *n.* person who holds a post, esp. priest in charge of a parish. 2. *adj.* (*formal*) **it is i. on you** = it is your responsibility. **incumbency,** *n.* period when s.o. holds a post/when a priest is in charge of a parish.

incur [ɪn'kɜː] *v.* (**incurred**) to run (a risk); to be liable to; to bring (sth) on yourself.

incurable [ɪn'kjʊərəbl] *adj.* which cannot be made better. **incurably,** *adv.* in a way which cannot be made better.

incurious [ɪn'kjʊərɪəs] *adj.* not curious/ not showing any curiosity.

incursion [ɪn'kɜːʃn] *n.* movement into sth; attack on sth.

indebted [ɪn'detɪd] *adj.* owing sth **to** s.o. **indebtedness,** *n.* being indebted.

indecent [ɪn'diːsnt] *adj.* not decent/ rude. **indecency,** *n.* being indecent. **indecently,** *adv.* not decently; in a way which shocks.

indecipherable [ɪndɪ'saɪfrəbl] *adj.* (writing/message) that cannot be read/ understood.

indecision [ɪndɪ'sɪʒn] *n.* (state of) not being able to decide; hesitating. **indecisive** [ɪndɪ'saɪsɪv] *adj.* without a positive result; which/who cannot decide anything.

indecorous [ɪn'dekərəs] *adj.* (*formal*) slightly rude.

indeed [ɪn'diːd] *adv.* (a) really/truly. (b) in fact. (c) *inter. meaning* really! **i. not!** = of course not!

indefatigable [ɪndɪ'fætɪgəbl] *adj.* tireless/who cannot be tired out. **indefatigably,** *adv.* tirelessly.

indefensible [ɪndɪ'fensɪbl] *adj.* which cannot be defended/excused.

indefinable [ɪndɪ'faɪnəbl] *adj.* which cannot be defined/explained.

indefinite [ɪn'defɪnɪt] *adj.* vague; not definite; **i. article** = 'a' (*as opposed to the definite article* 'the'). **indefinitely,** *adv.* for an indefinite period.

indelible [ɪn'delɪbl] *adj.* which cannot be rubbed out. **indelibly,** *adv.* permanently (marked).

indelicate [ɪn'delɪkət] *adj.* rude/not polite. **indelicacy,** *n.* being indelicate.

indemnify [ɪn'demnɪfaɪ] *v.* to pay (s.o.) for damage. **indemnity,** *n.* (a) payment (for loss/damage). (b) guarantee (of payment) against loss/damage.

indent [ɪn'dent] *v.* (a) to start a line several spaces in from the left-hand margin. (b) (*in commerce*) to put in an order for (sth). **indentation** [ɪnden'teɪʃn] *n.* inward cut along an edge; deep bay/inlet on a coastline. **indented,** *adj.* with a jagged edge.

indentures [ɪn'dentʃəz] *n. pl.* contract by which a person is apprenticed to a master craftsman.

independent [ɪndɪ'pendənt] *adj.* free/

not ruled by anyone else; not needing/not relying on anyone else; (candidate) not belonging to a political party; **i. school** = private school, not run by the state. **independence**, *n.* freedom; not needing/not relying on anyone else. **independently**, *adv.* freely; separately.

indescribable [ɪndɪ'skraɪbəbl] *adj.* which cannot be described. **indescribably**, *adv.* in a way which cannot be described.

indestructible [ɪndɪ'strʌktəbl] *adj.* which cannot be destroyed.

indeterminable [ɪndɪ'tɜ:mɪnəbl] *adj.* which cannot be decided/solved.

indeterminate [ɪndɪ'tɜ:mɪnət] *adj.* vague/not precise.

index ['ɪndeks] **1.** *n.* (*pl.* **-dexes, -dices** [-dɪsi:z]) (*a*) **i. (finger)** = first finger (next to the thumb). (*b*) classified list (showing the contents/references in a book). (*c*) **cost of living i.** = regular government statistics which show the rises and falls in the cost of living. **2.** *v.* (*a*) to write an index for (a book). (*b*) to relate (pensions, etc.) to the cost of living index. **indexer**, *n.* person who compiles indexes. **indexing**, *n.* (*a*) (*also* **indexation**) relating sth to the cost of living index. (*b*) compiling of an index. **index-linked**, *adj.* calculated according to the cost of living index.

Indian ['ɪndjən] **1.** *adj.* referring to India; referring to the indigenous people of America; **in I. file** = in line/one behind the other; **I. ink** = black ink which cannot be removed by washing; **I. summer** = period of hot weather in autumn. **2.** *n.* (*a*) person from India. (*b*) member of one of the indigenous tribes of America.

indiarubber [ɪndjə'rʌbə] *n.* rubber for rubbing out pencil marks.

indicate ['ɪndɪkeɪt] *v.* to show/to point out. **indication** [ɪndɪ'keɪʃn] *n.* sign/pointer. **indicative** [ɪn'dɪkətɪv] *adj.* (*a*) typical/which indicates. (*b*) (tense of a verb) which shows that the action actually took place/is taking place. **indicator**, *n.* (*a*) thing which indicates; flashing light (on a car) which shows which way you intend to turn. (*b*) large board which shows details of train times.

indict [ɪn'daɪt] *v.* to accuse (s.o.) of a crime. **indictable**, *adj.* (offence) which you can be charged with. **indictment** [ɪn'daɪtmənt] *n.* detailed accusation.

indifferent [ɪn'dɪfrənt] *adj.* (*a*) not caring; not interested. (*b*) ordinary/mediocre; not special. **indifference**, *n.* lack of interest. **indifferently**, *adv.* (*a*) not bothering. (*b*) in a mediocre way.

indigenous [ɪn'dɪdʒənəs] *adj.* (**to**) which is born in/belongs to (a place).

indigent ['ɪndɪdʒənt] *adj.* (*formal*) very poor. **indigence**, *n.* great poverty.

indigestion [ɪndɪ'dʒestʃn] *n.* not being able to digest food; pain caused when the body is unable to digest food. **indigestible**, *adj.* which cannot be digested; which causes pain because the body cannot digest it.

indignant [ɪn'dɪgnənt] *adj.* feeling offended/angry. **indignantly**, *adv.* in an indignant way. **indignation** [ɪndɪg'neɪʃn] *n.* being indignant.

indignity [ɪn'dɪgnɪti] *n.* rudeness/offence to dignity.

indigo ['ɪndɪgəʊ] *n.* blue dye; deep blue colour.

indirect [ɪndɪ'rekt, ɪndaɪ'rekt] *adj.* (*a*) not direct/oblique; (tax) added to the price of goods and not paid directly to the government. (*b*) (speech) reporting what s.o. has said. **indirectly**, *adv.* not directly.

indiscreet [ɪndɪ'skri:t] *adj.* revealing/not discreet. **indiscretion** [ɪndɪ'skreʃn] *n.* (*a*) lack of discretion/being careless about what you do or say. (*b*) doing sth careless.

indiscriminate [ɪndɪ'skrɪmənət] *adj.* widespread/not selective. **indiscriminately**, *adv.* (*a*) in every direction. (*b*) without selecting/without choosing.

indispensable [ɪndɪ'spensəbl] *adj.* which you cannot do without.

indisposed [ɪndɪ'spəʊzd] *adj.* (*a*) slightly ill. (*b*) unwilling. **indisposition** [ɪndɪspə'zɪʃn] *n.* (*a*) slight illness. (*b*) unwillingness.

indisputable [ɪndɪ'spju:təbl] *adj.* which cannot be argued over. **indisputably**, *adv.* certainly.

indissoluble [ɪndɪ'sɒljʊbl] *adj.* which cannot be destroyed/dissolved.

indistinct [ɪndɪ'stɪŋkt] *adj.* vague/

unclear. **indistinctly,** adv. vaguely/unclearly.

indistinguishable [ɪndɪ'stɪŋgwɪʃəbl] adj. which cannot be told apart from sth.

individual [ɪndɪ'vɪdjuəl] **1.** n. (a) single person. (b) inf. person. **2.** adj. (a) single. (b) belonging to a particular person. (c) for one person. **individualist,** n. person who emphasizes that he is unique and not a member of a group. **individualistic,** adj. like an individualist. **individuality** [ɪndɪvɪdju'ælɪtɪ] n. quality which makes each person different from all others. **individually,** adv. singly/as a single person.

indivisible [ɪndɪ'vɪzəbl] adj. which cannot be divided/separated. **indivisibly,** adv. in a way which prevents it being divided/separated.

indoctrinate [ɪn'dɒktrɪneɪt] v. to teach (s.o.), esp. political ideas. **indoctrination** [ɪndɒktrɪ'neɪʃn] n. teaching s.o., esp. political ideas.

indolence ['ɪndələns] n. laziness. **indolent,** adj. lazy.

indomitable [ɪn'dɒmɪtəbl] adj. which cannot be overcome.

indoor ['ɪndɔː] adj. done/found inside a building. **indoors** [ɪn'dɔːz] adv. inside a building.

indubitable [ɪn'djuːbɪtəbl] adj. which cannot be doubted. **indubitably,** adv. certainly/definitely.

induce [ɪn'djuːs] v. (a) to persuade (s.o.) to do sth. (b) to provoke (sth)/to make (sth) happen; to make (a birth) happen. **inducement,** n. thing which helps persuade you to do sth.

induct [ɪn'dʌkt] v. to place (s.o., esp. a priest) in office. **induction** [ɪn'dʌkʃn] n. (a) entry of a person into a new job; installation of a new priest; **i. course** = training course for s.o. in a new job. (b) creation of electricity in an object by placing it near a magnet or near sth which is electrically charged. **inductive,** adj. (reasoning) based on known facts.

indulge [ɪn'dʌldʒ] v. (a) to spoil (s.o.). (b) (**in**) to give way to (sth enjoyable). **indulgence,** n. being indulgent; indulgent action. **indulgent,** adj. kind/soft; too generous. **indulgently,** adv. kindly; too generously.

industry ['ɪndəstrɪ] n. (a) all manufacturing processes. (b) hard work/steady work. **industrial** [ɪn'dʌstrɪəl] adj. referring to manufacturing work; **i. action** = strike or protest by workers; **i. estate** = group of factories built together. **industrialist,** n. owner/director of a factory. **industrialization** [ɪndʌstrɪəlaɪ'zeɪʃn] n. changing of a society from agricultural to industrial. **industrialize** [ɪn'dʌstrɪəlaɪz] v. to create industries (where there were none before). **industrially,** adv. (made) by industry. **industrious,** adj. (person) who works steadily and hard. **industriously,** adv. in an industrious way.

inebriate [ɪ'niːbrɪət] adj. (formal) (person) who is often drunk. **inebriated,** adj. drunk. **inebriation,** n. drunken state.

inedible [ɪn'edɪbl] adj. which you cannot eat.

ineducable [ɪn'edjukəbl] adj. (person) who cannot be educated.

ineffable [ɪn'efəbl] adj. (formal) so wonderful that it cannot be properly described.

ineffective [ɪnɪ'fektɪv] adj. which does not have any effect.

ineffectual [ɪnɪ'fektjuəl] adj. (attempt) which is unsuccessful; (person) who is weak/incapable of asserting his authority.

inefficient [ɪnɪ'fɪʃnt] adj. not efficient; not competent. **inefficiency,** n. incompetence/lack of efficiency. **inefficiently,** adv. in an inefficient way.

inelegant [ɪn'elɪgənt] adj. not elegant.

ineligible [ɪn'elɪdʒəbl] adj. (person) who is not qualified (**for** sth, **to** do sth).

inept [ɪn'ept] adj. stupid (remark); incapable (person). **ineptitude,** n. stupidity/silliness; being unable to do sth.

inequality [ɪnɪ'kwɒlɪtɪ] n. lack of equality.

inequitable [ɪn'ekwɪtəbl] adj. unjust/not fair.

ineradicable [ɪnɪ'rædɪkəbl] adj. which cannot be eradicated/removed.

inert [ɪ'nɜːt] adj. unmoving; (gas) which does not react with other substances. **inertia** [ɪ'nɜːʃə] n. (a) lack of motion in a body. (b) continuous movement of a body, unless checked by a force.

(c) laziness; **i. selling** = method of selling goods through the post where it is assumed that they have been bought if they are not returned.

inescapable [ɪnɪ'skeɪpəbl] *adj.* which you cannot avoid.

inessential [ɪnɪ'senʃl] *adj. & n.* (thing) which is not absolutely necessary.

inestimable [ɪn'estɪməbl] *adj.* which cannot be estimated/calculated.

inevitable [ɪn'evɪtəbl] *adj.* which cannot be avoided. **inevitability** [ɪnevɪtə'bɪlɪtɪ] *n.* being inevitable. **inevitably,** *adv.* of course.

inexact [ɪnɪg'zækt] *adj.* not exact/not correct. **inexactitude,** *n.* error.

inexcusable [ɪnɪk'skjuːzəbl] *adj.* which cannot be excused/forgiven. **inexcusably,** *adv.* in an inexcusable way.

inexhaustible [ɪnɪg'zɔːstəbl] *adj.* which cannot be used up.

inexorable [ɪn'eksərəbl] *adj.* which cannot be changed/influenced.

inexpedient [ɪnɪk'spiːdɪənt] *adj.* (action) which is not expedient.

inexpensive [ɪnɪk'spensɪv] *adj.* cheap/not expensive.

inexperience [ɪnɪk'spɪərɪəns] *n.* lack of experience. **inexperienced,** *adj.* with no experience/lacking experience.

inexpert [ɪn'ekspɜːt] *adj.* **(at)** not expert/not skilled.

inexplicable [ɪnɪk'splɪkəbl] *adj.* which cannot be explained. **inexplicably,** *adv.* in a way which cannot be explained.

inexpressible [ɪnɪk'spresɪbl] *adj.* which cannot be expressed in words.

in extremis [ɪneks'triːmɪs] *adv.* at the very end; *(of person)* when near to death.

inextricable [ɪneks'trɪkəbl] *adj.* which you cannot get out of. **inextricably,** *adv.* in an inextricable way.

infallible [ɪn'fæləbl] *adj.* always correct/true; (person) who never makes mistakes. **infallibility** [ɪnfælɪ'bɪlɪtɪ] *n.* being infallible. **infallibly,** *adv.* unfailingly/always.

infamous ['ɪnfəməs] *adj.* very wicked (person/action). **infamy,** *n. (formal)* great wickedness.

infant ['ɪnfənt] *n.* young child; **i. prodigy** = small child who is exceptionally good at sth, such as music/chess, etc. **infancy,** *n.* young childhood. **infanticide** [ɪn'fæntɪsaɪd] *n.* killing of a baby. **infantile** ['ɪnfəntaɪl] *adj.* referring to a small child; childish.

infantry ['ɪnfəntrɪ] *n.* section of an army which fights on foot.

infatuated [ɪn'fætjʊeɪtɪd] *adj.* mad (about); wildly in love (with). **infatuation** [ɪnfætjʊ'eɪʃn] *n.* blind love for someone.

infect [ɪn'fekt] *v.* to make diseased. **infection,** *n.* (a) making diseased. (b) disease which spreads. **infectious,** *adj.* (disease) which can be passed from one person to another.

infer [ɪn'fɜː] *v.* **(inferred)** (a) to deduce **(from).** (b) to imply/to hint. **inference** ['ɪnfərəns] *n.* conclusion/deduction.

inferior [ɪn'fɪərɪə] **1.** *adj.* not as good. **2.** *n.* person of a lower rank/subordinate. **inferiority** [ɪnfɪərɪ'ɒrɪtɪ] *n.* state of being not as good as s.o. else; **i. complex** = exaggerated idea that one is not as good as others.

infernal [ɪn'fɜːnl] *adj. inf.* like hell/hellish. **infernally,** *adv. inf.* extremely.

inferno [ɪn'fɜːnəʊ] *n.* **(-os)** blaze of fire.

infertile [ɪn'fɜːtaɪl, *Am.* ɪn'fɜːtl] *adj.* not fertile/not capable of having young; (land) which is not rich enough to produce crops. **infertility** [ɪnfə'tɪlɪtɪ] *n.* being unable to have young.

infest [ɪn'fest] *v.* to cover/to swarm over in large numbers. **infestation** [ɪnfes'teɪʃn] *n.* being covered with pests.

infidel ['ɪnfɪdəl] *n.* person who is opposed to Christianity.

infidelity [ɪnfɪ'delɪtɪ] *n.* being unfaithful.

infighting ['ɪnfaɪtɪŋ] *n.* bitter argument between members of a group.

infiltrate ['ɪnfɪltreɪt] *v.* to enter (a political group) secretly. **infiltration** [ɪnfɪl'treɪʃn] *n.* act of infiltrating. **infiltrator** ['ɪnfɪltreɪtə] *n.* person who infiltrates.

infinite ['ɪnfɪnət] *adj.* endless/with no end. **infinitely,** *adv.* completely; much more. **infinitesimal** [ɪnfɪnɪ'tesɪml] *adj.* tiny/microscopic. **infinitive** [ɪn'fɪnɪtɪv] *adj. & n.* form of the verb using 'to'. **infinity,** *n.* never-ending space.

infirm [ɪn'fɜːm] *adj.* sick/weak (person). **infirmary,** *n.* (a) hospital. (b) sickbay in a factory or school. **infirmity,** *n.* physical weakness.

inflame [ɪnˈfleɪm] *v.* (*a*) (*formal*) to make violent. (*b*) to cause inflammation in. **inflammable** [ɪnˈflæməbl] *adj.* which catches fire easily. **inflammation** [ɪnfləˈmeɪʃn] *n.* swelling/ redness caused by infection. **inflammatory** [ɪnˈflæmətərɪ] *adj.* (speech) which makes people behave violently.

inflate [ɪnˈfleɪt] *v.* to blow up (balloon/ tyre); to increase (prices, etc.) artificially. **inflatable,** *adj.* which can be blown up. **inflation** [ɪnˈfleɪʃn] *n.* economic state where prices and wages are rising to keep pace with each other. **inflationary,** *adj.* (policy) which tends to increase inflation.

inflect [ɪnˈflekt] *v.* to change the ending of (a word, e.g. when used in the plural). **inflection, inflexion,** *n.* ending of a word which changes to indicate the plural, the gender, etc.

inflexible [ɪnˈfleksəbl] *adj.* which cannot be bent/altered; (person) who cannot be persuaded to change his mind. **inflexibility** [ɪnfleksɪˈbɪlɪtɪ] *n.* not being able to bend/to adapt. **inflexibly,** *adv.* in an unbending way.

inflict [ɪnˈflɪkt] *v.* **to i. pain/damage on** = to cause pain/damage to; **to i. oneself on s.o.** = force s.o. to accept one's presence. **infliction** [ɪnˈflɪkʃn] *n.* (act of) inflicting.

inflorescence [ɪnfləˈresəns] *n.* group of flowers arranged on one stem.

inflow [ˈɪnfləʊ] *n.* flowing in.

influence [ˈɪnfluəns] **1.** *n.* (**on**) ability to make s.o./sth change; effect on others. **2.** *v.* to make (s.o./sth) change. **influential** [ɪnfluˈenʃl] *adj.* so powerful as to cause change; having an effect on others.

influenza [ɪnfluˈenzə] *n.* virus disease like a bad cold with a high temperature.

influx [ˈɪnflʌks] *n.* (*pl.* **-es**) entry (of a crowd of people).

inform [ɪnˈfɔːm] *v.* to tell officially; to give details; **to i. against s.o.** = to tell (the police, etc.) about s.o. **informant,** *n.* person who passes on information/ who gives details. **informatics,** *n.* study of information processing. **information** [ɪnfəˈmeɪʃn] *n.* details/knowl-

edge. **informative** [ɪnˈfɔːmətɪv] *adj.* which tells you a lot/which conveys much detailed information. **informed,** *adj.* up-to-date/reliable. **informer,** *n.* person who informs against his accomplices.

informal [ɪnˈfɔːml] *adj.* not formal/relaxed; not following any rules; not official. **informally,** *adv.* not formally/ unofficially. **informality** [ɪnfɔːˈmælɪtɪ] *n.* lack of any special ceremony.

infra dig [ˈɪnfrəˈdɪg] *adv. inf.* beneath one's dignity.

infra-red [ɪnfrəˈred] *adj.* (heat rays) which are invisible and have a longer wave-length than visible red heat rays.

infrastructure [ˈɪnfrəstrʌktʃə] *n.* basic structure; supporting framework.

infrequent [ɪnˈfriːkwənt] *adj.* not frequent; not happening very often. **infrequency,** *n.* lack of frequency. **infrequently,** *adv.* not very often/not frequently.

infringe [ɪnˈfrɪndʒ] *v.* to break (a law). **infringement,** *n.* breaking (of a law).

infuriate [ɪnˈfjʊərɪeɪt] *v.* to make furious.

infuse [ɪnˈfjuːz] *v.* to pour hot water (on tea/lime flowers) to make a drink. **infusion** [ɪnˈfjuːʒn] *n.* drink made by pouring hot water on dried leaves.

ingenious [ɪnˈdʒiːnɪəs] *adj.* very clever (device/person). **ingenuity** [ɪndʒəˈnjuːɪtɪ] *n.* cleverness/skill in inventing new techniques.

ingénue [ænʒeɪˈnjuː] *n.* supposedly simple girl.

ingenuous [ɪnˈdʒenjuəs] *adj.* naive/ innocent; lacking experience. **ingenuousness,** *n.* being ingenuous.

ingest [ɪnˈdʒest] *v.* (*formal*) to take into the body (as food).

inglenook [ˈɪŋgəlnʊk] *n.* seat at the side of a very large fireplace.

inglorious [ɪnˈglɔːrɪəs] *adj.* (*formal*) dishonourable/not glorious.

ingot [ˈɪŋgət] *n.* bar (of gold, etc.).

ingrained [ˈɪŋgreɪnd] *adj.* fixed.

ingratiate [ɪnˈgreɪʃɪeɪt] *v.* **to i. oneself with s.o.** = make oneself liked by s.o. **ingratiating,** *adj.* which will help you worm your way into s.o.'s favour.

ingratitude [ɪnˈgrætɪtjuːd] *n.* lack of gratitude; not being grateful.

ingredient [ɪn'gri:dɪənt] *n.* substance which goes to make sth.

ingress ['ɪngres] *n.* (*formal*) entry.

ingrowing ['ɪngrəʊɪŋ] *adj.* (toenail) which grows into the flesh.

inhabit [ɪn'hæbɪt] *v.* to live in. **inhabitable,** *adj.* (place) which can be lived in. **inhabitant,** *n.* person who lives in a place.

inhale [ɪn'heɪl] *v.* to draw (sth) into the lungs when breathing. **inhalant, inhalation,** *n.* medicine which has to be inhaled. **inhaler,** *n.* device which makes a vapour which has to be inhaled.

inherent [ɪn'hɪərənt] *adj.* natural/inborn. **inherently,** *adv.* naturally.

inherit [ɪn'herɪt] *v.* (*a*) to take over (money, etc.) from a person who has died; to have (characteristics) passed on from a parent. (*b*) to take over (a client/a problem) from a predecessor. **inheritance,** *n.* money/goods which you receive on the death of s.o. **inheritor,** *n.* person who inherits.

inhibit [ɪn'hɪbɪt] *v.* to restrain (s.o.) **from** doing sth. **inhibition** [ɪnhɪ'bɪʃn] *n.* thing which prevents you from expressing yourself freely/from letting yourself go. **inhibitory,** *adj.* which inhibits.

inhospitable [ɪnhɒ'spɪtəbl] *adj.* not welcoming.

in-house [ɪn'haʊs] *adj. & adv.* inside an office or factory.

inhuman [ɪn'hju:mən] *adj.* not human; savage/brutal. **inhumane** [ɪnhju:'meɪn] *adj.* not humane; showing barbarity. **inhumanity** [ɪnhju:'mænɪtɪ] *n.* cruelty/barbarity. **inhumanly,** *adv.* savagely/brutally.

inimical [ɪ'nɪmɪkl] *adj.* (*formal*) unfriendly.

inimitable [ɪ'nɪmɪtəbl] *adj.* which cannot be imitated.

iniquitous [ɪ'nɪkwɪtəs] *adj.* (*formal*) wicked. **iniquity,** *n.* wickedness.

initial [ɪ'nɪʃl] **1.** *adj.* first. **2.** *n.* **initials** = first letters (of name). **3.** *v.* (**initialled**) to write your initials on (a document) to show you have read and approved it. **initially,** *adv.* in the first place/at the beginning.

initiate [ɪ'nɪʃɪeɪt] *v.* (*a*) to start (sth) going. (*b*) to introduce (s.o.) **into** a secret society; to show (s.o.) the basic

information about sth. **initiation** [ɪnɪʃɪ'eɪʃn] *n.* introduction to a secret society.

initiative [ɪ'nɪʃɪətɪv] *n.* decision to get sth going; ability to decide. **initiator,** *n.* person who starts (a project).

inject [ɪn'dʒekt] *v.* to pump a liquid into (sth/s.o.) under pressure; to put (sth new) into. **injection,** *n.* act of injecting; liquid which has been injected.

injudicious [ɪndʒu:'dɪʃəs] *adj.* (*formal*) unwise.

injunction [ɪn'dʒʌŋkʃn] *n.* (*a*) order (by a court) preventing s.o. from doing sth. (*b*) instruction.

injure ['ɪndʒə] *v.* to hurt/to wound; **the injured party** = the party in a court case who has been offended. **injured,** *n. pl.* people who have been wounded. **injurious** [ɪn'dʒu:ərɪəs] *adj.* which can injure. **injury,** *n.* hurt/wound.

injustice [ɪn'dʒʌstɪs] *n.* lack of justice; not being fair.

ink [ɪŋk] **1.** *n.* liquid for writing with a pen. **2.** *v.* to write with a pen and ink; to mark with ink. **ink pad,** *n.* pad of cloth soaked in ink for inking date stamps, etc. **inkwell,** *n.* pot to put ink in. **inky,** *adj.* (black) like ink; covered with ink.

inkling ['ɪŋklɪŋ] *n.* suspicion/idea.

inlaid [ɪn'leɪd] *v. see* **inlay.**

inland ['ɪnlænd] *adj. & adv.* (to/of) the interior of a country; **the I. Revenue** = government department dealing with tax.

in-laws ['ɪnlɔːz] *n. pl. inf.* parents related to you by marriage.

inlay [ɪn'leɪ] **1.** *n.* thing which is inlaid. **2.** *v.* (**inlaid**) to insert small pieces of stone/wood/metal in (a surface) to create a pattern.

inlet ['ɪnlet] *n.* (*a*) small branch of water off a large stretch of water. (*b*) **i. pipe** = pipe for introducing a liquid.

inmate ['ɪnmeɪt] *n.* resident (of a house); person living in a home for old people/in a prison.

inmost ['ɪnməʊst] *adj.* deepest (thoughts, etc.).

inn [ɪn] *n.* small hotel; public house. **innkeeper,** *n.* person who runs an inn. **Inns of Court,** *n.* four societies of barristers in London.

innards ['ɪnədz] *n. pl. inf.* intestines; inside workings (of a machine).

innate [ɪ'neɪt] *adj.* inborn/natural.

inner ['ɪnə] *adj.* inside; **i. room** = room leading off another room; **i. tube** = light tube containing air inside a tyre; **i. ear** = space inside the head, beyond the middle ear, which controls balance and hearing. **innermost**, *adj.* furthest inside.

innings - ['ɪnɪŋz] *n.* (*pl.* **innings**) (*in cricket*) time when a team/a player bats. **he's had a good i.** = he's been a long time at his job/he's lived a long time.

innocent ['ɪnəsnt] *adj.* not guilty; lacking experience/knowledge. **innocence**, *n.* lack of guilt. **innocently**, *adv.* in a way which shows lack of experience/knowledge.

innocuous [ɪ'nɒkjuəs] *adj.* inoffensive/harmless.

innovate ['ɪnəveɪt] *v.* to introduce changes/new methods. **innovation** [ɪnə'veɪʃn] *n.* invention which is new; change (in doing sth). **innovative** ['ɪnəveɪtɪv] *adj.* which breaks new ground/which changes everything. **innovator**, *n.* person who introduces changes.

innuendo [ɪnjʊ'endəʊ] *n.* (*pl.* **-oes**) remark which suggests criticism.

innumerable [ɪ'njuːmərəbl] *adj.* countless/which cannot be counted.

inoculate [ɪ'nɒkjʊleɪt] *v.* **to i. s.o. against** = to prevent s.o. catching a disease by injecting him with a vaccine. **inoculation** [ɪnɒkjʊ'leɪʃn] *n.* injection to stop you catching a disease.

inoffensive [ɪnə'fensɪv] *adj.* mild/harmless.

inoperable [ɪn'ɒprəbl] *adj.* which cannot be operated on.

inoperative [ɪn'ɒprətɪv] *adj.* which is not in operation/which is not working.

inopportune [ɪn'ɒpətjuːn] *adj.* awkward/badly timed.

inordinate [ɪn'ɔːdɪnət] *adj.* excessive. **inordinately**, *adv.* excessively.

inorganic [ɪnɔː'gænɪk] *adj.* not relating to living organisms; **i. chemistry** = chemistry dealing with substances which are not organic.

in-patient ['ɪnpeɪʃnt] *n.* patient who stays in a hospital.

input ['ɪnpʊt] *n.* (*a*) electric current put into an apparatus. (*b*) data/information

fed into a computer. (*c*) **inputs** = goods or services bought which are subject to VAT.

inquest ['ɪŋkwest] *n.* legal inquiry into a death.

inquire [ɪŋ'kwaɪə] *v.* (*a*) to ask questions (**about** sth). (*b*) to conduct an official investigation (**into**). **inquirer**, *n.* person who inquires. **inquiring**, *adj.* interested in finding out information. **inquiringly**, *adv.* in a questioning way. **inquiry**, *n.* (*a*) formal investigation (**into**). (*b*) question.

inquisition [ɪŋkwɪ'zɪʃn] *n.* (*a*) asking very thorough questions, usu. using threats or force. (*b*) (*old*) Catholic tribunal for discovering heretics. **inquisitor** [ɪŋ'kwɪzɪtə] *n.* person who asks very thorough questions.

inquisitive [ɪŋ'kwɪzətɪv] *adj.* curious/asking questions. **inquisitively**, *adv.* curiously/inquiringly. **inquisitiveness**, *n.* being inquisitive.

inquorate [ɪn'kwɔːreɪt] *adj.* without a quorum.

inroads ['ɪnrəʊdz] *n. pl.* **to make i. into** **sth** = to use up a large quantity of sth.

inrush ['ɪnrʌʃ] *n.* sudden quick movement inwards.

insalubrious [ɪnsə'luːbrɪəs] *adj.* not healthy.

insane [ɪn'seɪn] *adj.* mad. **insanely**, *adv.* madly. **insanity** [ɪn'sænɪtɪ] *n.* madness.

insanitary [ɪn'sænɪtərɪ] *adj.* not clean/not hygienic.

insatiable [ɪn'seɪʃəbl] *adj.* which cannot be satisfied. **insatiably**, *adv.* in a way which cannot be satisfied.

inscribe [ɪn'skraɪb] *v.* to write (officially) (in a book/on a stone). **inscription** [ɪn'skrɪpʃn] *n.* writing inscribed on a stone, etc.

inscrutable [ɪn'skruːtəbl] *adj.* mysterious/which you cannot understand.

insect ['ɪnsekt] *n.* small six-legged animal with a body in three parts. **insecticide** [ɪn'sektɪsaɪd] *n.* liquid/powder which kills insects. **insectivorous** [ɪnsek'tɪvərəs] *adj.* (animal) which eats insects.

insecure [ɪnsɪ'kjʊə] *adj.* not safe; wobbly/not firmly fixed. **insecurely**, *adv.* not firmly. **insecurity**, *n.* feeling of not being safe.

inseminate [in'semineit] v. to introduce male seed into (a female). **insemination** [insemi'neiʃn] n. artificial i. = introduction of sperm from a male into a female by a doctor or veterinary surgeon.

insensate [in'senseit] adj. without any feeling.

insensible [in'sensəbl] adj. (a) not conscious. (b) with no feeling. (c) very small (change).

insensitive [in'sensitiv] adj. not sensitive. **insensitivity** [insensi'tiviti] n. lack of sensitivity/lack of awareness of how other people feel.

inseparable [in'seprəbl] adj. which cannot be separated; (of people) always together.

insert. 1. n. ['insɜːt] thing which is put in. **2.** v. [in'sɜːt] to put (sth) in. **insertion** [in'sɜːʃn] n. act of putting sth in; thing which is put in.

inset ['inset] **1.** n. small piece which is put into sth larger. **2.** adj. with sth fixed into it.

inshore [in'ʃɔː] adj. & adv. near a coast.

inside [in'said] **1.** n. (a) inner part; **i. out** = with the inner part facing outwards; **to know i. out** = to know very well. (b) (in games) **i. left/right** = forward player next to the wings. **2.** adj. (a) indoors; which is in the interior. (b) (information) known only to people working in a certain organization. **3.** adv. (a) to/in the interior. (b) inf. in prison. **4.** prep. (a) to/in the interior of (sth). (b) within; **i. three hours** = in less than three hours. **insider**, n. person who works in an organization and therefore knows secret information; **i. dealing** = illegal buying or selling of shares by people who have secret information about a company.

insidious [in'sidiəs] adj. quietly treacherous; working secretly to do harm. **insidiously**, adv. quietly and dangerously. **insidiousness**, n. being insidious.

insight ['insait] n. (a) clear thought. (b) deep knowledge; clear understanding.

insignia [in'signiə] n. pl. badges/chains/crowns, etc., which symbolize an office.

insignificant [insig'nifikənt] adj. unimportant. **insignificance**, n. being insignificant.

insincere [insin'siə] adj. not sincere/false. **insincerity** [insin'seriti] n. lack of sincerity.

insinuate [in'sinjueit] v. (a) to suggest (by dropping hints); **to i. oneself** = work one's way gradually (into a favourable position). **insinuation** [insinju'eiʃn] n. (usu. cruel) hint/suggestion.

insipid [in'sipid] adj. watery/not strong; with no flavour/no excitement. **insipidity** [insi'piditi] n. being insipid.

insist [in'sist] v. **to i. on sth being done** = to state firmly that sth should be done. **insistence**, n. firm demands. **insistent**, adj. demanding firmly. **insistently**, adv. in a way which demands attention.

in situ [in'sitjuː] adv. on the site; in its original place.

insole ['insəul] n. soft pad which you put inside a shoe to make it more comfortable or fit better.

insolent ['insələnt] adj. rude. **insolence**, n. rudeness. **insolently**, adv. rudely.

insoluble [in'sɒljubl] adj. (a) (substance) which will not dissolve, usu. in water. (b) (problem) which cannot be solved. **insolubility** [insɒlju'biliti] n. inability (of a chemical) to dissolve.

insolvent [in'sɒlvənt] adj. bankrupt/unable to pay one's debts. **insolvency**, n. being insolvent.

insomnia [in'sɒmniə] n. chronic inability to sleep. **insomniac**, n. person who suffers from insomnia.

insouciant [in'suːsiənt] adj. not caring about anything. **insouciance**, n. being insouciant.

inspect [in'spekt] v. to examine closely. **inspection** [in'spekʃn] n. examining sth closely. **inspector**, n. senior official who examines; **school i.** = official of the department of education who examines the teaching in schools; **police i.** = officer in the police force. **inspectorate**, n. all inspectors (in a certain area) taken as a group.

inspire [in'spaiə] v. to make (s.o.) feel a certain sensation. **inspiration** [inspi'reiʃn] n. (a) sudden urge to write poems/to compose music, etc. (b) sudden good idea.

instability [instə'biliti] n. lack of stability/not being steady.

install [ɪn'stɔ:l] *v.* to put (a person into a job/a machine into a workshop). **installation** [ɪnstə'leɪʃn] *n.* (*a*) putting (a machine in place); (*b*) group of machines which have been put in place.

instalment, *Am.* **installment** [ɪn'stɔ:lmənt] *n.* part (of sth which is being delivered in parts); regular payment (of part of a total sum). *Am.* **i. plan** = hire purchase.

instance ['ɪnstəns] **1.** *n.* example/case; **for i.** = as an example. **2.** *v.* to give as an example.

instant ['ɪnstənt] **1.** *n.* moment/second. **2.** *adj.* immediate; **i. coffee** = coffee powder to which you add hot water to make coffee rapidly. **instantaneous** [ɪnstən'teɪnɪəs] *adj.* immediate. **instantaneously,** *adv.* immediately. **instantly,** *adv.* straight away/immediately.

instead [ɪn'sted] *adv.* in the place of/rather than (sth).

instep ['ɪnstep] *n.* arched part of a foot.

instigate ['ɪnstɪgeɪt] *v.* to provoke/to start (sth). **instigation** [ɪnstɪ'geɪʃn] *n.* suggestion. **instigator,** *n.* person who stirs up trouble/who provokes action.

instil [ɪn'stɪl] *v.* (**instilled**) to put (an idea, etc.) into s.o.'s mind gradually.

instinct ['ɪnstɪŋkt] *n.* feeling/ability for doing sth which you have from birth and have not learnt. **instinctive** [ɪn'stɪŋktɪv] *adj.* natural/inborn (reaction). **instinctively,** *adv.* because of a natural impulse.

institute ['ɪnstɪtju:t] **1.** *n.* (*a*) organization set up for a purpose. (*b*) building which houses such an organization. **2.** *v.* to set up/to start. **institution** [ɪnstɪ'tju:ʃn] *n.* (*a*) setting up (of an organization). (*b*) organization/society set up for a purpose. (*c*) permanent feature; longstanding custom. **institutional,** *adj.* referring to an institution; **i. buying** = buying of shares by insurance companies, etc. **institutionalize,** *v.* to make (sth) into an institution; to put (s.o.) into an institution (such as an old people's home, etc.).

instruct [ɪn'strʌkt] *v.* (*a*) to teach. (*b*) to order. (*c*) to give orders to (a solicitor) to start legal proceedings.

instruction [ɪn'strʌkʃn] *n.* (*a*) teaching. (*b*) **instructions** = orders; indication of how sth is to be used. **instructive,** *adj.* which teaches. **instructor, instructress,** *n.* teacher (esp. of sport).

instrument ['ɪnstrumənt] *n.* (*a*) piece of equipment. (*b*) legal document (esp. in international law). (*c*) **musical i.** = device which is blown/hit/plucked, etc., to make a musical note. **instrumental** [ɪnstru'mentl] *adj.* (*a*) responsible/playing an important role (**in** getting sth done). (*b*) referring to a musical instrument. **instrumentalist,** *n.* person who plays a musical instrument.

insubordinate [ɪnsə'bɔ:dɪnət] *adj.* unruly; not obeying orders. **insubordination** [ɪnsəbɔ:dɪ'neɪʃn] *n.* not obeying orders.

insubstantial [ɪnsəb'stænʃl] *adj.* not substantial/not solid.

insufferable [ɪn'sʌfrəbl] *adj.* intolerable/which you cannot bear. **insufferably,** *adv.* intolerably.

insufficient [ɪnsə'fɪʃnt] *adj.* not sufficient/not enough. **insufficiency,** *n.* lack. **insufficiently,** *adv.* not enough.

insular ['ɪnsjulə] *adj.* (*a*) referring to an island. (*b*) narrow-minded. **insularity** [ɪnsju'lærɪtɪ] *n.* prejudice/narrowness of opinions.

insulate ['ɪnsjuleɪt] *v.* to cover so as to prevent heat/electricity/sound escaping or entering. **insulation** [ɪnsju'leɪʃn] *n.* act of insulating; material which insulates. **insulator** ['ɪnsjuleɪtə] *n.* material/device which insulates.

insulin ['ɪnsjulɪn] *n.* hormone which regulates the use of sugar by the body, and is used to treat diabetes.

insult. 1. *n.* ['ɪnsʌlt] rude word said to or about a person. **2.** *v.* [ɪn'sʌlt] to say rude things about (s.o.). **insulting,** *adj.* rude.

insuperable [ɪn'sju:prəbl] *adj.* which cannot be overcome.

insupportable [ɪnsə'pɔ:təbl] *adj.* unbearable/which cannot be borne.

insure [ɪn'ʃuə] *v.* to agree with a company that if you pay them a regular sum, they will compensate you for loss or damage to property or persons; **to i. a jewel for £10,000. insurance,** *n.* agreement with a company by which you are paid compensation for loss or damage in return for regular payments of money; **i. policy** = document with the details of an insurance; **i. broker** = person who arranges an insurance; **life i.** = insurance paying a sum of money when s.o. dies; **National I.** = government-run insurance which provides for state medical care, unemployment payments, etc. **insurer,** *n.* person/company which insures.

insurgent [ɪn'sɜːdʒənt] *adj. & n.* (person) in a state of revolt.

insurmountable [ɪnsə'maʊntəbl] *adj.* which cannot be overcome.

insurrection [ɪnsə'rekʃn] *n.* uprising/revolution.

intact [ɪn'tækt] *adj.* in one piece/not broken.

intaglio [ɪn'tɑːlɪəʊ] *n.* design cut into a surface (as of a precious stone).

intake ['ɪnteɪk] *n.* thing which is taken in; group of new students/soldiers, etc.

intangible [ɪn'tændʒəbl] *adj.* which cannot be touched/which cannot be defined.

integral ['ɪntɪgrəl] *adj.* forming (part of) a whole. **integer** ['ɪntɪdʒə] *n.* whole number (not a fraction). **integrate** ['ɪntɪgreɪt] *v.* to link to form a whole; to make (people) full members of society; **integrated circuit** = electronic circuit on a microchip. **integration** [ɪntɪ'greɪʃn] *n.* (act of) integrating.

integrity [ɪn'tegrɪtɪ] *n.* honesty.

integument [ɪn'tegjʊmənt] *n.* (*formal*) skin.

intellect ['ɪntəlekt] *n.* ability to think or reason; brainpower. **intellectual** [ɪntə'lektjʊəl] **1.** *adj.* referring to the intellect; good at using the brain. **2.** *n.* person who believes that brainpower is very important/who uses his brain to make a living. **intellectually,** *adv.* referring to intelligence.

intelligence [ɪn'telɪdʒəns] *n.* (*a*) quickness of understanding/mental ability; **i. quotient** = number showing how intelligent you are compared to others. (*b*) secret information. **intelligent,** *adj.* clever/mentally able. **intelligently,** *adv.* in an intelligent way. **intelligentsia** [ɪntelɪ'dʒensɪə] *n.* intellectual class of society.

intelligible [ɪn'telɪdʒəbl] *adj.* which can be understood. **intelligibility** [ɪntelɪgə-'bɪlɪtɪ] *n.* being intelligible.

intemperate [ɪn'temprət] *adj.* wild/not moderate.

intend [ɪn'tend] *v.* to plan to do (sth)/to mean.

intense [ɪn'tens] *adj.* (**-er, -est**) very strong/vigorous (action); extremely serious (person). **intensely,** *adv.* strongly. **intensification,** *n.* becoming stronger. **intensify,** *v.* to grow stronger/to make (sth) stronger. **intensity,** *n.* strength/violence (of pain). **intensive,** *adj.* very concentrated; **i. care unit** = section of a hospital dealing with seriously ill patients who need a lot of attention. **intensively,** *adv.* very strongly.

intent [ɪn'tent] **1.** *adj.* determined/absorbed. **2.** *n.* **with i. to defraud** = with the aim of deceiving; **to all intents and purposes** = virtually/in nearly every way. **intently,** *adv.* fixedly.

intention [ɪn'tenʃn] *n.* aim. **intentional,** *adj.* done on purpose. **intentionally,** *adv.* on purpose.

inter [ɪn'tɜː] *v.* (**interred**) (*formal*) to bury.

inter- ['ɪntə-] *prefix meaning* between.

interact [ɪntə'rækt] *v.* to have an effect on each other. **interaction** [ɪntər'ækʃn] *n.* effect of two things on each other. **interactive,** *adj.* (computer program) which allows the user to communicate with the computer.

inter alia [ɪntə'ɑːlɪə] among other things.

interbreed [ɪntə'briːd] *v.* (**interbred**) to breed (with an adult of another strain).

intercede [ɪntə'siːd] *v.* to plead; to make an appeal. **intercession** [ɪntə'seʃn] *n.* pleading (on behalf of s.o.).

intercept [ɪntə'sept] *v.* to stop (sth) as it is passing. **interception** [ɪntə'sepʃn] *n.* stopping (of sth which is passing). **interceptor,** *n.* person/aircraft which intercepts.

interchange ['ɪntətʃeɪndʒ] **1.** *n.* (*a*) exchange (of ideas). (*b*) large road junction where motorways cross. **2.** *v.* to exchange one thing for another. **interchangeable** [ɪntə'tʃeɪndʒəbl] *adj.* which can be substituted for each other.

intercity [ɪntəˈsɪtɪ] *adj.* (train/plane) between two cities.

intercom [ˈɪntəkɒm] *n.* radio for speaking to people over a short distance.

interconnected [ɪntəkəˈnektɪd] *adj.* which connect with each other.

intercontinental [ɪntəkɒntɪˈnentl] *adj.* from one continent to another.

intercourse [ˈɪntəkɔːs] *n.* (*a*) reproductive act between a male and a female. (*b*) (*formal*) communication between people.

interdict [ˈɪntədɪkt] *n.* (*formal*) order forbidding sth.

interest [ˈɪntrəst] **1.** *n.* (*a*) percentage return on investment; percentage payable on a loan. (*b*) financial share. (*c*) particular attention. (*d*) thing which you pay attention to. (*e*) advantage. **2.** *v.* to attract s.o.'s attention. **interested,** *adj.* with a personal (usu. financial) interest in sth. **interesting,** *adj.* which attracts attention.

interface [ˈɪntəfeɪs] *n.* area where two different systems meet and interact.

interfere [ɪntəˈfɪə] *v.* (*a*) to meddle/to get involved (**in/with**). (*b*) to affect the reception of radio/TV programmes. **interference,** *n.* (*a*) involvement/meddling. (*b*) noise which affects radio/TV programmes. **interferon,** *n.* protein which fights a virus.

interim [ˈɪntərɪm] *adj.* & *n.* (report) given halfway through an investigation; **in the i.** = meanwhile.

interior [ɪnˈtɪərɪə] *adj.* & *n.* inner part (of a building/car); **ministry of the i.** = ministry dealing with affairs inside a country.

interject [ɪntəˈdʒekt] *v.* to make a sudden exclamation. **interjection** [ɪntəˈdʒekʃn] *n.* exclamation; word used to show surprise.

interlace [ɪntəˈleɪs] *v.* to weave together.

interlard [ɪntəˈlɑːd] *v.* to insert comments into (a text).

interleave [ɪntəˈliːv] *v.* to put (sth) between the pages of a book.

interlock [ɪntəˈlɒk] *v.* to fit together.

interlocutor [ɪntəˈlɒkjʊtə] *n.* person who speaks to s.o. else.

interloper [ˈɪntələʊpə] *n.* person who comes in/who intrudes.

interlude [ˈɪntəluːd] *n.* quiet time between two lively periods; rest period between parts of a performance.

intermarry [ɪntəˈmærɪ] *v.* to marry within the same family group. **intermarriage,** *n.* act of intermarrying.

intermediary [ɪntəˈmiːdjərɪ] *adj.* & *n.* (person) who goes between two others/who acts as messenger.

intermediate [ɪntəˈmiːdjət] *adj.* halfway between two extremes.

interment [ɪnˈtɜːmənt] *n.* (*formal*) burial.

intermezzo [ɪntəˈmetzəʊ] *n.* (*pl.* **-os**) short piece (of music) linking two other pieces.

interminable [ɪnˈtɜːmɪnəbl] *adj.* never-ending. **interminably,** *adv.* without coming to an end.

intermingle [ɪntəˈmɪŋgl] *v.* to mix together.

intermission [ɪntəˈmɪʃn] *n.* (*a*) interval (in a play/film/concert). (*b*) **without i.** = without a break/without stopping.

intermittent [ɪntəˈmɪtənt] *adj.* which takes place from time to time. **intermittently,** *adv.* (taking place) from time to time/on and off.

intern. 1. *n.* [ˈɪntɜːn] junior doctor who works and lives in a hospital. **2.** *v.* [ɪnˈtɜːn] to put (prisoners) in a prison without trial. **internee** [ɪntɜːˈniː] *n.* prisoner in a detention camp who has not been tried. **internment,** *n.* putting prisoners in a prison or camp without trial.

internal [ɪnˈtɜːnl] *adj.* inside; **i. telephone** = private telephone inside a building; **i. combustion engine** = engine in which the fuel is burnt inside a closed space (as in the cylinders in a car engine). **internally,** *adv.* inside.

international [ɪntəˈnæʃnl] **1.** *adj.* between countries. **2.** *n.* (*a*) sportsman who has played for his country's team against another country. (*b*) game/sporting competition between two countries. **internationally,** *adv.* (done) between countries.

internecine [ɪntəˈniːsaɪn] *adj.* (*formal*) (two things) which destroy each other.

internode [ˈɪntənəʊd] *n.* space between two joints in a plant. **internodal** *adj.* between joints.

interphone [ˈɪntəfəʊn] *n.* short-distance internal telephone.

interplanetary [ɪntə'plænətrɪ] *adj.* between planets.

interplay ['ɪntəpleɪ] *n.* reaction between two forces.

Interpol ['ɪntəpɒl] *n.* international police system.

interpolate [ɪn'tɜːpəleɪt] *v.* to add (words) in between others. **interpolation** [ɪntɜːpə'leɪʃn] *n.* adding of words between existing words in a text; word(s) thus added.

interpose ['ɪntəpəʊz] *v.* to place (sth) in between.

interpret [ɪn'tɜːprɪt] *v.* (*a*) to explain (sth) to s.o. who does not understand. (*b*) to translate aloud what is spoken from one language into another. **interpretation** [ɪntɜːprɪ'teɪʃn] *n.* (*a*) meaning. (*b*) translating aloud from one language to another. **interpreter,** *n.* person who translates aloud from one language to another.

interregnum [ɪntə'regnəm] *n.* period between the reigns of successive kings; period of inactivity between one management and another.

interrelated [ɪntərɪ'leɪtɪd] *adj.* (several things) which are related.

interrogate [ɪn'terəgeɪt] *v.* to question severely. **interrogation** [ɪntərə'geɪʃn] *n.* severe questioning (of a prisoner). **interrogative** [ɪntə'rɒgətɪv] *adj. & n.* questioning; **i. pronoun** = pronoun which asks a question. **interrogator** [ɪn'terəgeɪtə] *n.* person who questions (a prisoner) closely.

interrupt [ɪntə'rʌpt] *v.* to break into (a speech); to stop (sth) continuing. **interruption** [ɪntə'rʌpʃn] *n.* (act of) interrupting; thing which interrupts.

intersect [ɪntə'sekt] *v.* to cut across; to cut across (each other). **intersection,** *n.* place where lines cut across each other; crossroads.

intersperse [ɪntə'spɜːs] *v.* to scatter.

interstate [ɪntə'steɪt] *adj.* (*a*) between two countries. (*b*) *Am.* between two states.

interstellar [ɪntə'stelə] *adj.* between stars.

interstice [ɪn'tɜːstɪs] *n.* small space in between other things.

intertwine [ɪntə'twaɪn] *v.* to twist (things) together; to be twisted together.

interval ['ɪntəvl] *n.* period/gap (between two points/between two acts in a play); (in music) difference in pitch.

intervene [ɪntə'viːn] *v.* to come/to arrive in between. **intervention** [ɪntə'venʃn] *n.* coming between; entry into sth.

interview ['ɪntəvjuː] **1.** *n.* (*a*) discussion (on radio/TV/in the newspaper) between an important or interesting person and a journalist. (*b*) questioning (by one or more people) of a person applying for a job. **2.** *v.* (*a*) to ask (a famous/interesting person) questions in order to show his answers publicly. (*b*) to ask questions of (a person applying for a job). **interviewee** [ɪntəvjuː'iː] *n.* person who is being/who is going to be interviewed. **interviewer,** *n.* person who asks the questions at an interview.

interweave [ɪntə'wiːv] *v.* (**interwove; interwoven**) to weave/to bind together.

intestate [ɪn'testeɪt] *adj.* not having made a will.

intestine [ɪn'testɪn] *n.* long tube in the body through which food passes from the stomach to the anus. **intestinal,** *adj.* referring to the intestine.

intimate. 1. *adj.* ['ɪntɪmət] (*a*) very close (friend); detailed (knowledge). (*b*) sexual (relationship). **2.** *n.* ['ɪntɪmət] close friend. **3.** *v.* ['ɪntɪmeɪt] to announce ; to suggest. **intimacy,** *n.* close relationship (with s.o.). **intimately,** *adv.* closely. **intimation** [ɪntɪ'meɪʃn] *n.* suggestion.

intimidate [ɪn'tɪmɪdeɪt] *v.* to frighten (s.o.) by threats. **intimidating,** *adj.* frightening. **intimidation** [ɪntɪmɪ'deɪʃn] *n.* frightening by threats.

into ['ɪntʊ] *prep.* (*a*) (movement) towards the inside. (*b*) so as to become; to develop as; **the tadpole changed i. a frog; he burst i. tears.** (*c*) dividing; **four i. three won't go.**

intolerable [ɪn'tɒlərəbl] *adj.* which you cannot bear. **intolerably,** *adv.* unbearably.

intolerant [ɪn'tɒlərənt] *adj.* (person) who cannot bear people with different ideas from his own. **intolerance,** *n.* not accepting other people's points of view.

intonation [ɪntə'neɪʃn] *n.* rise or fall of the voice (in speech or singing).

intone [ɪn'təʊn] *v.* to recite (psalms, etc.) in a singing voice.

intoxicate [ɪn'tɒksɪkeɪt] v. to make (s.o.) drunk. **intoxicant,** n. substance which intoxicates. **intoxicating,** adj. which makes you drunk; exciting. **intoxication** [ɪntɒksɪ'keɪʃn] n. drunkenness.

intra- ['ɪntrə-] prefix meaning within.

intractable [ɪn'træktəbl] adj. very difficult to deal with; (problem) which is impossible to solve.

intransigent [ɪn'trænsɪdʒənt] adj. firm; obstinate/not shifting your position/not changing your mind. **intransigence,** n. firmness/being obstinate.

in transit [ɪn'trænzɪt] adv. (goods) which are being transported.

intransitive [ɪn'trænsɪtɪv] adj. (verb) which has no object.

intrauterine [ɪntrə'juːtərɪn] adj. inside the uterus; **i. device** = contraceptive device which is placed inside a woman's uterus.

intravenous [ɪntrə'viːnəs] adj. (injection) made into a vein.

intrepid [ɪn'trepɪd] adj. fearless/very brave. **intrepidity** [ɪntrə'pɪdɪti] n. being intrepid.

intricate ['ɪntrɪkət] adj. very complicated; made of many different parts. **intricacy,** n. complexity. **intricately,** adv. in an intricate way.

intrigue [ɪn'triːg] **1.** n. secret plot. **2.** v. (a) to plot. (b) to make (s.o.) interested.

intrinsic [ɪn'trɪnzɪk] adj. forming a basic part of sth. **intrinsically,** adv. basically.

introduce [ɪntrə'djuːs] v. (a) to present (s.o.) to another person/to people who did not know him previously. (b) to announce (a TV/radio programme, etc.). (c) to make (sth) go in; to bring (sth) in. **introduction** [ɪntrə'dʌkʃn] n. (a) act of presenting sth; thing which presents sth. (b) making s.o. known to another person/to people who did not know him previously. (c) piece at the beginning of a book which explains the rest of the book. (d) elementary book about a subject. **introductory,** adj. (words) which introduce; **i. offer** = offer of a new range of goods at a specially low price.

introit ['ɪntrɔɪt] n. music sung at the beginning of a church service.

introspective [ɪntrə'spektɪv] adj. inward-looking; thinking a lot about yourself. **introspection** [ɪntrə'spekʃn] n. looking inwards at yourself.

introvert ['ɪntrəvɜːt] n. person who thinks mainly about himself. **introverted,** adj. (person) who thinks mainly about himself.

intrude [ɪn'truːd] v. to enter where you are not wanted. **intruder,** n. person who has intruded. **intrusion** [ɪn'truːʒn] n. act of intruding. **intrusive** [ɪn'truːsɪv] adj. unwanted.

intuition [ɪntjuː'ɪʃn] n. thinking of sth/knowing sth naturally without it being explained. **intuitive** [ɪn'tjuːɪtɪv] adj. based on intuition. **intuitively,** adv. in an intuitive way.

Inuit ['ɪnjuːɪt] n. Eskimos.

inundate ['ɪnʌndeɪt] v. to flood. **inundation** [ɪnʌn'deɪʃn] n. flood.

inure [ɪn'juə] v. (formal) to accustom **to** sth unpleasant.

invade [ɪn'veɪd] v. to attack and enter (a country) with an army. **invader,** n. person who enters a country with an army.

invalid. 1. adj. & n. ['ɪnvəlɪd] sick/disabled (person); **i. carriage** = small vehicle for one disabled person. **2.** v. ['ɪnvəliːd] **to i. s.o. out** = to make s.o. retire because of ill health. **3.** adj. [ɪn'vælɪd] not valid/not legal. **invalidation** [ɪnvælɪ'deɪʃn] n. making invalid. **invalidate** [ɪn'vælɪdeɪt] v. to make (sth) invalid. **invalidity,** n. being an invalid.

invaluable [ɪn'væljuəbl] adj. extremely valuable.

invariable [ɪn'veərɪəbl] adj. always the same/not changing. **invariably,** adv. always.

invasion [ɪn'veɪʒn] n. (a) entering a country with armed forces. (b) **i. of privacy** = illegal entering of a person's home in a way which destroys his private life.

invective [ɪn'vektɪv] n. insulting speech/abuse.

inveigh [ɪn'veɪ] v. (formal) to speak violently (**against** sth).

inveigle [ɪn'veɪgl] v. to trick (s.o.) **into** doing sth.

invent [ɪn'vent] v. to create (a new process/new machine); to think up (an excuse). **invention** [ɪn'venʃn] n. (a) creation (of new process/new machine). (b) new machine. **inventive,** adj. creative. **inventiveness,** n. ability to invent. **inventor,** n. person who invents new processes/new machines.

inventory ['ɪnvəntrɪ] n. list (of contents of a house, etc.); Am. stock (in a warehouse).

inverse ['ɪnvɜːs] adj. & n. opposite/contrary. **inversion** [ɪn'vɜːʃn] n. turning sth round in a contrary way. **invert** [ɪn'vɜːt] v. to turn (sth) upside down/back to front; **inverted commas** = printing sign ("") which indicates speech.

invertebrate [ɪn'vɜːtɪbreɪt] adj. & n. (animal) without a backbone.

invest [ɪn'vest] v. to put (money) into savings/property, etc., so that it will increase in value. **investment,** n. money placed so that it will increase in value. **investor,** n. person who puts money into savings or property.

investigate [ɪn'vestɪgeɪt] v. to study/to examine. **investigation** [ɪnvestɪ'geɪʃn] n. examination. **investigator,** n. detective; person who investigates.

investiture [ɪn'vestɪtʃə] n. ceremony where s.o. is given a medal/where s.o. is installed in office.

inveterate [ɪn'vetərət] adj. obstinate/hardened.

invidious [ɪn'vɪdɪəs] adj. which is likely to offend people unreasonably.

invigilate [ɪn'vɪdʒɪleɪt] v. to supervise an examination. **invigilator,** n. supervisor of an examination.

invigorate [ɪn'vɪgəreɪt] v. to make strong/vigorous; to make (s.o.) feel livelier.

invincible [ɪn'vɪnsəbl] adj. which cannot be defeated. **invincibility** [ɪnvɪnsə'bɪlɪtɪ] n. being unbeatable.

inviolable [ɪn'vaɪələbl] adj. which cannot be violated. **inviolability** [ɪnvaɪələ'bɪlɪtɪ] n. being inviolable.

invisible [ɪn'vɪzəbl] adj. which cannot be seen. **invisibility** [ɪnvɪzə'bɪlɪtɪ] n. not being able to be seen.

invite [ɪn'vaɪt] v. (a) to ask (s.o.) to do sth. (b) to ask for (comments, etc.). **invitation** [ɪnvɪ'teɪʃn] n. asking (s.o. to do sth). **inviting,** adj. attractive.

in vitro [ɪn'viːtrəʊ] adj. (experiment) which is carried out in a laboratory.

invocation [ɪnvə'keɪʃn] n. (formal) calling on s.o. for help/support.

invoice ['ɪnvɔɪs] 1. n. note sent to ask for payment for services or goods. 2. v. to send a note asking for payment for services or goods. **invoicing,** n. sending of an invoice.

invoke [ɪn'vəʊk] v. to call on (s.o./sth) for help/support.

involuntary [ɪn'vɒləntrɪ] adj. not voluntary/not willingly done. **involuntarily,** adv. not willingly.

involve [ɪn'vɒlv] v. (a) to bring (s.o./sth) into (a dispute/a scheme). (b) to make necessary. **involved,** adj. intricate/complicated. **involvement,** n. contact/collaboration.

invulnerable [ɪn'vʌlnərəbl] adj. which cannot be successfully attacked.

inward ['ɪnwəd] adj. on/to the inside. **inwardly,** adv. on the inside. **inwards,** adv. towards the inside.

iodine ['aɪədiːn] n. (element: I) substance which is used in solution, e.g. as a disinfectant. **iodize,** v. to fill with iodine.

ion ['aɪən] n. atom with an electric charge. **ionize,** v. to produce ions; to become ions. **ionosphere** [aɪ'ɒnəsfɪə] n. part of the atmosphere surrounding the earth which reflects radio waves back to earth.

iota [aɪ'əʊtə] n. very small piece.

IOU [aɪəʊ'juː] n. paper promising that you will pay back money which you have borrowed.

ipecacuanha [ɪpɪkækjuːˈɑːnə] n. drug made from the root of a plant, used as an emetic and also as cough medicine.

ipso facto ['ɪpsəʊ'fæktəʊ] adv. because of this fact.

IQ ['aɪ'kjuː] abbrev. for intelligence quotient.

IRA ['aɪɑːˈeɪ] abbrev. for Irish Republican Army; Am. Individual Retirement Account.

Iranian [ɪ'reɪnjən] 1. adj. referring to Iran. 2. n. person from Iran.

Iraqi [ɪ'rɑːkɪ] 1. adj. referring to Iraq. 2. n. (pl. -is) person from Iraq.

irascible [ɪ'ræsɪbl] adj. easily becoming angry. **irascibility** [ɪræsɪ'bɪlɪtɪ] n. being irascible.

ire ['aɪə] n. (formal) anger. **irate** [aɪ'reɪt] adj. very angry.

iridescent [ɪrɪ'desnt] adj. with changing/shimmering colours. **iridescence**, n. being iridescent.

iris ['aɪərɪs] n. (pl. -es) (a) plant with tall flat leaves and usu. yellow or purple flowers. (b) part of the eye which is coloured.

Irish ['aɪərɪʃ] 1. adj. referring to Ireland. 2. n. (a) Celtic language spoken in parts of Ireland. (b) **the I.** = people from Ireland. **Irishman, Irishwoman**, n. (pl. -men, -women) person from Ireland.

irk [ɜːk] v. to annoy/to bother. **irksome** ['ɜːksəm] adj. annoying/bothersome.

iron ['aɪən] 1. n. & adj. (element: Fe) (a) common grey metal which can be made into a magnet; **i. ore** = iron in its natural state. (b) electric household instrument for smoothing the creases from clothes. (c) **in irons** = imprisoned with iron chains round one's ankles. (d) metal frame to support a weak leg. (e) golf club with a metal head. 2. v. to press (cloth) with an iron; **to i. out** = to sort out (a problem/difficulty). **Iron Age**, n. period when man first used iron. **Iron Curtain**, n. border formerly existing between Communist countries in Eastern Europe and non-communist Western Europe. **ironing**, n. (a) pressing clothes with an electric iron. (b) clothes which need pressing. **ironing board**, n. high narrow table used for ironing clothes. **iron lung**, n. machine which encloses a patient's body, and in which pressure is increased and reduced to make the patient breathe. **ironmonger**, n. person who runs a hardware shop, selling tools, paint, pans, etc. **ironmonger's, ironmongery**, n. hardware shop. **ironwork**, n. (decorative) locks/handles/gates, etc., made of iron. **ironworks**, n. factory which produces iron.

irony ['aɪərənɪ] n. (a) way of referring to sth where you say the opposite of what you mean. (b) quality of happening at the wrong moment, as if deliberately planned. **ironic(al)** [aɪ'rɒnɪk(l)] adj. mocking/slightly funny. **ironically**, adv. in a mocking way.

irradiate [ɪ'reɪdɪeɪt] v. (of heat/light/rays) to shine on (sth). **irradiation** [ɪreɪdɪ'eɪʃn] n. act of irradiating.

irrational [ɪ'ræʃnl] adj. not rational/not sensible/against common-sense. **irrationally**, adv. in an irrational way.

irreconcilable [ɪrekən'saɪləbl] adj. which cannot be made to agree.

irrecoverable [ɪrɪ'kʌvərəbl] adj. which cannot be recovered.

irredeemable [ɪrɪ'diːməbl] adj. (loss) which cannot be made good; (pledge) which cannot be redeemed.

irreducible [ɪrɪ'djuːsəbl] adj. which cannot be reduced.

irrefutable [ɪrɪ'fjuːtəbl] adj. (argument) which cannot be disproved.

irregular [ɪ'regjulə] 1. adj. (a) not regular; not level; not happening at the same time. (b) not according to the rules; (verb) which has forms which do not fit the usual patterns of grammar. 2. n. pl. **irregulars** = soldiers who do not form part of the regular army. **irregularity** [ɪregju'lærɪtɪ] n. thing which goes against the rules/the law. **irregularly**, adv. not regularly.

irrelevant [ɪ'reləvənt] adj. (to) not relevant/which has no connection to the subject. **irrelevance**, n. having no connection with the subject.

irreligious [ɪrɪ'lɪdʒəs] adj. not religious; not showing respect for religion.

irreparable [ɪ'reprəbl] adj. which cannot be repaired. **irreparably**, adv. in a way which cannot be repaired.

irreplaceable [ɪrɪ'pleɪsəbl] adj. which cannot be replaced; (thing) for which there is no substitute.

irrepressible [ɪrɪ'presəbl] adj. which cannot be held back.

irreproachable [ɪrɪ'prəutʃəbl] adj. perfect/which cannot be criticized.

irresistible [ɪrɪ'zɪstəbl] adj. which cannot be resisted; which you cannot help accepting.

irresolute [ɪ'rezəluːt] adj. undecided; (person) who hesitates/cannot decide. **irresolutely**, adv. not knowing what to do. **irresolution**, n. being irresolute.

irrespective [ɪrɪ'spektɪv] prep. taking no account (of).

irresponsible [ɪrɪ'spɒnsəbl] adj. wild/senseless; not responsible. **irresponsibly**, adv. with no sense of responsibility.

irretrievable [ɪrɪ'triːvəbl] *adj.* which cannot be found again. **irretrievably,** *adv.* hopelessly.

irreverent [ɪ'revrənt] *adj.* not serious; disrespectful. **irreverence,** *n.* being irreverent. **irreverently,** *adv.* not in a serious way; disrespectfully.

irreversible [ɪrɪ'vɜːsəbl] *adj.* (decision) which cannot be changed.

irrevocable [ɪ'revəkəbl] *adj.* (decision) which cannot be changed.

irrigate ['ɪrɪgeɪt] *v.* (*a*) to water (land) by using canals and pumps. (*b*) to wash (a wound) with a flow of water. **irrigation** [ɪrɪ'geɪʃn] *n.* watering of fields (by using canals and pumps).

irritate ['ɪrɪteɪt] *v.* (*a*) to annoy. (*b*) to prickle/to burn. **irritability** [ɪrɪtə'bɪlɪtɪ] *n.* being irritable. **irritable** ['ɪrɪtəbl] *adj.* easily annoyed. **irritably,** *adv.* in a bad-tempered way. **irritant,** *n.* thing which annoys/causes a burning feeling. **irritating,** *adj.* which annoys. **irritation** [ɪrɪ'teɪʃn] *n.* annoyance; thing which annoys/which causes a burning feeling.

irrupt [ɪ'rʌpt] *v.* (*formal*) to appear/to come in suddenly. **irruption** [ɪ'rʌpʃn] *n.* sudden appearance.

is [ɪz] *v. see* **be.**

isinglass ['aɪzɪŋglɑːs] *n.* type of gelatine.

Islam ['ɪzlæm] *n.* religion of the Muslims. **Islamic** [ɪz'læmɪk] *adj.* referring to Islam.

island ['aɪlənd] *n.* piece of land entirely surrounded by water; **traffic i.** = small raised piece of pavement in the centre of the road where pedestrians can safely stand. **islander,** *n.* person who lives on an island. **isle** [aɪl] *n.* island. **islet,** *n.* small island.

isn't ['ɪznt] *v.* short for **is not.**

isobar ['aɪsəʊbɑː] *n.* line on a weather map showing places of equal barometric pressure.

isolate ['aɪsəleɪt] *v.* (*a*) to put (sth/ s.o.) in a place alone; **isolated attack** = single attack, not repeated. (*b*) to separate (a chemical) substance from a compound. **isolation** [aɪsə'leɪʃn] *n.* cutting off from communication with other people; **i. hospital** = hospital for people suffering from dangerous diseases. **isolationism,** *n.* policy of not communicating with other countries.

isolationist, *n.* person who advocates isolationism.

isomer ['aɪsəmə] *n.* chemical compound with the same molecular formula as another, but with a different arrangement of atoms.

isometric [aɪsəʊ'metrɪk] *adj.* (exercises) using muscles acting against each other or a fixed object.

isosceles [aɪ'sɒsɪliːz] *adj.* **i. triangle** = triangle with two sides of the same length.

isotherm ['aɪsəʊθɜːm] *n.* line on a weather map showing places with equal temperatures.

isotope ['aɪsətəʊp] *n.* one of two or more forms of a chemical element which have atoms which are chemically similar but with different atomic weights.

Israeli [ɪz'reɪlɪ] **1.** *adj.* referring to Israel. **2.** *n.* (*pl.* **-is**) person from Israel.

issue ['ɪʃuː] **1.** *n.* (*a*) result. (*b*) problem; **to make an i. of** = have a big discussion about; **the point at i.** = the question which is being discussed; **to take i. with** = disagree with. (*c*) publication (of a book); putting on sale (new stamps); putting into circulation (new coins/ notes); giving out (of uniforms/official permits, etc.). (*d*) one copy of a newspaper or magazine. (*e*) (*old*) children. **2.** *v.* (*a*) to come out. (*b*) to put (new stamps) on sale; to publish (books); to put (new banknotes) into circulation; to give out/to hand out (uniforms/official permits, etc.).

isthmus ['ɪsməs] *n.* (*pl.* **-es**) narrow piece of land connecting two larger pieces of land.

it [ɪt] *pronoun referring to a thing.* (*a*) (*standing in the place of thing just mentioned*) **put it down; it's here.** (*b*) (*referring to nothing in particular*) **it's raining;** *inf.* **you're for it** = you are going to be in trouble.

Italian [ɪ'tæljən] **1.** *adj.* referring to Italy. **2.** *n.* (*a*) person from Italy. (*b*) language spoken in Italy.

italic [ɪ'tælɪk] *adj. & n.* sloping (letter); *this is printed in italics.* **italicize** [ɪ'tælɪsaɪz] *v.* to print in italics.

itch [ɪtʃ] **1.** *n.* (*pl.* **-es**) tickling sensation. **2.** *v.* to tickle; to be very eager (to do sth). **itching,** *n.* tickling sensation.

itchy, *adj.* tickly; making you feel you want to scratch; **i. feet** = desire to change jobs/to travel.

item [ˈaɪtəm] *n.* thing (in a list); **news items** = separate pieces of news on a news programme. **itemize,** *v.* to make a detailed list of (things).

itinerary [ɪˈtɪnərərɪ] *n.* route; list of places to be visited on a tour. **itinerant,** *adj.* wandering/travelling.

its [ɪts] *adj.* belonging to a thing/to it.

it's [ɪts] *short for* **it is/it has.**

itself [ɪtˈself] *pronoun referring to a thing/ to it. (a) (referring to an object)* **all by i.; the dog has hurt i.** *(b) (for emphasis)* **the television i.**

IUD [aɪjuːˈdiː] *abbrev. for* intrauterine device.

I've [aɪv] *short for* **I have.**

ivory [ˈaɪvərɪ] *adj. & n.* (made of) whitish substance from an elephant's tusk; **i. tower** = imaginary place where an intellectual can keep away from contact with the everyday world.

ivy [ˈaɪvɪ] *n.* evergreen plant which climbs up walls and trees.

Jj

jab [dʒæb] **1.** *n.* (a) sharp blow (often with a pointed object). *(b) inf.* injection. **2.** *v.* (**jabbed**) to poke firmly (esp. with a pointed object).

jabber [ˈdʒæbə] **1.** *n.* quick, indistinct talk. **2.** *v.* to speak quickly and indistinctly.

jacaranda [dʒækæˈrændə] *n.* tropical tree with scented pale purple flowers.

jack [dʒæk] *n.* (a) instrument for raising a heavy object (esp. a motor vehicle). *(b) (in playing cards)* the card between the queen and the ten. *(c)* male of certain mammals. *(d) (at bowls)* small white ball for players to aim at. *(e)* flag; **the Union J.** = flag of the United Kingdom. *(f)* single-pin electric plug. **jackboot,** *n.* high military boot. **jackbooted,** *adj.* wearing jackboots. **jackhammer,** *n.* power drill held in the hand. **jack-in-the-box,** *n.* box from which a toy figure springs up when the lid is opened. **jack-knife, 1.** *n.* (*pl.* **-knives**) type of large folding knife. **2.** *v.* (*of vehicle pulling a trailer*) to fold in half in an accident. **jack-of-all-trades,** *n.* person who is reasonably good at a large number of jobs. **jack up,** *v.* (a) to raise with a jack. *(b) inf.* to raise (profits or prices).

jackal [ˈdʒækl] *n.* wild dog, which feeds chiefly on dead flesh.

jackass [ˈdʒækæs] *n.* **laughing j.** = kookaburra.

jackdaw [ˈdʒækdɔː] *n.* type of small crow.

jacket [ˈdʒækɪt] *n.* (a) short coat. *(b)* outer casing or covering; loose paper cover for a book. *(c)* skin (of a potato). **jacketed,** *adj.* with a jacket.

jackpot [ˈdʒækpɒt] *n.* **to win/to hit the j.** = to win a high prize in a lottery/to enjoy particular success in sth.

Jacobean [dʒækəˈbiːən] *adj.* referring to the time of James I (1601–1625).

Jacobite [ˈdʒækəbaɪt] *adj. & n.* (person) who supported James II or his descendants in exile.

jade [dʒeɪd] *n.* hard, usu. green, precious stone. **jade-green,** *adj.* of the bluish-green colour of jade.

jaded [ˈdʒeɪdɪd] *adj.* worn out/tired.

jag [dʒæg] *n. Sl.* drinking session.

jagged [ˈdʒægɪd] *adj.* with an irregular, rough, spiky edge.

jaguar [ˈdʒægjʊə] *n.* large wild cat of Central and South America.

jail [dʒeɪl] **1.** *n.* prison. **2.** *v.* to put (s.o.) in prison. **jailbird,** *n.* person who has been sent to prison often. **jailer,** *n.* person who guards prisoners in jail.

jalopy [dʒəˈlɒpɪ] *n. inf.* dilapidated old car.

jam [dʒæm] **1.** *n.* (a) stoppage/blockage caused by too many things in too small a space. *(b) inf.* **in a j.** = in a difficult situation. *(c)* sweet food made by boiling together fruit, sugar, etc.; **money for j.** = money very easily earned. **2.** *v.* (**jammed**) (a) (*of machine*) to stop/to stick so that it cannot move. *(b)* to crowd/to force (things) into a small space. *(c)* to make (a radio broadcast) impossible to understand by broadcasting noise on the same wavelength. **jamming,** *n.* making a radio broadcast impossible to understand. **jammy,** *adj.* sticky with jam. **jam-packed,** *adj. inf.* packed full. **jam session,** *n.* impromptu jazz concert.

Jamaican [dʒəˈmeikən] 1. *adj.* referring to Jamaica. 2. *n.* person from Jamaica.

jamb [dʒæm] *n.* side post of a door or window.

jamboree [dʒæmbəˈriː] *n.* large meeting (esp. of Scouts); big festival/party.

jangle [ˈdʒæŋgl] 1. *n.* harsh clanging noise. 2. *v.* (*a*) to make a harsh clanging noise. (*b*) to disturb/to irritate (the nerves).

janitor [ˈdʒænɪtə] *n.* caretaker, esp. in a school or college.

January [ˈdʒænjʊərɪ] *n.* 1st month of the year.

Japanese [dʒæpəˈniːz] 1. *adj.* referring to Japan. 2. *n.* (*a*) (*pl.* **Japanese**) person from Japan. (*b*) language spoken in Japan.

japonica [dʒəˈpɒnɪkə] *n.* flowering quince bush.

jar [dʒɑː] 1. *n.* container for jam, etc., often of glass and usu. cylindrical; **a j. of jam; jam j.** = special jar for putting jam in. 2. *v.* (**jarred**) (*a*) to make a nasty/unpleasant sound. (*b*) **to j. on s.o.'s nerves** = to annoy. (*c*) to bump/to give a shock to. (*d*) to sound/to look unpleasant.

jardinière [ʒɑːdɪnɪˈeə] *n.* ornamental container for plants.

jargon [ˈdʒɑːgən] *n.* special form of language used by a trade/profession or particular group of people.

jasmine [ˈdʒæzmɪn] *n.* shrub with sweet-smelling white or yellow flowers.

jasper [ˈdʒæspə] *n.* coloured quartz.

jaundice [ˈdʒɔːndɪs] *n.* sickness which makes the skin turn yellow, due to a disorder of the liver or bile. **jaundiced,** *adj.* (*a*) suffering from jaundice. (*b*) miserable/dispirited; envious; resentful.

jaunt [dʒɔːnt] *n.* short excursion. **jaunting car,** *n.* (*in Ireland*) light two-wheeled carriage.

jaunty [ˈdʒɔːntɪ] *adj.* (**-ier, -iest**) cheerful/lively. **jauntily,** *adv.* cheerfully. **jauntiness,** *n.* lively manner.

javelin [ˈdʒævlɪn] *n.* long spear used in battle or in sport.

jaw [dʒɔː] 1. *n.* (*a*) arrangement of bones which allow the mouth to open and shut. (*b*) **jaws** = two parts of a tool which grip. 2. *v. inf.* to talk (too much). **jawbone,** *n.* one of the two bones forming a jaw.

jay [dʒei] *n.* brightly coloured bird of the crow family. **jaywalker,** *n.* pedestrian who does not take care when crossing the street. **jaywalking,** *n.* crossing a street without taking care.

jazz [dʒæz] *n.* type of music with strong rhythm, originally played by American negroes. **jazz up,** *v. inf.* to make bright/attractive. **jazzy,** *adj.* bright (colour).

jealous [ˈdʒeləs] *adj.* (**of**) feeling sorrow/anger because you want sth which belongs to s.o. else. **jealously,** *adv.* in a jealous way. **jealousy,** *n.* jealous feeling.

jeans [dʒiːnz] *n. pl.* (often blue) trousers made of a type of strong cotton.

jeep [dʒiːp] *n.* trademark for a strongly built vehicle used for travelling over rough ground.

jeer [ˈdʒɪə] 1. *n.* mocking/laughing in a nasty way. 2. *v.* (**at**) to mock/to laugh at (s.o.) in a nasty way.

Jehovah [dʒɪˈhəʊvə] *n.* God of Israel.

jejune [dʒɪˈdʒuːn] *adj.* naive.

jell [dʒel] *v.* (*of liquid*) to become a jelly. (*b*) (*of plan*) to become definite. **jelly** [ˈdʒelɪ] *n.* (*a*) semi-solid substance, esp. type of sweet food made of gelatine/water/fruit flavouring, etc. (*b*) type of jam made of fruit juice boiled with sugar. **jellied** [ˈdʒelɪd] *adj.* cooked/preserved in a jelly. **jelly bean,** *n. Am.* sweet of coloured jelly, shaped like a bean. **jellyfish,** *n.* sea creature with jelly-like body. **jelly roll,** *n. Am.* swiss roll.

jemmy [ˈdʒemɪ] *n.* flat iron bar with a curved end, used by burglars to open doors or windows.

jenny [ˈdʒenɪ] *n.* female donkey.

jeopardize [ˈdʒepədaɪz] *v.* to put in danger/at risk. **jeopardy** [ˈdʒepədɪ] *n.* danger/risk.

jeremiad [dʒerɪˈmaɪəd] *n.* (*formal*) long complaint about your problems.

jerk [dʒɜːk] 1. *n.* (*a*) sudden uneven movement; sharp pull. (*b*) *Am. Sl.* stupid person. 2. *v.* to make a sudden movement; to pull sharply. **jerkily,** *adv.* with an abrupt/sudden movement. **jerkiness,** *n.* being jerky. **jerky,** *adj.* abrupt/sudden.

jerkin [ˈdʒɜːkɪn] *n.* short coat with no sleeves.

jerrican ['dʒerɪkæn] *n.* large metal container for water/petrol, etc.

jerry-builder ['dʒerɪbɪldə] *n.* person who builds cheap, poorly constructed, buildings. **jerry-built,** *adj.* (building) which is cheaply built.

jersey ['dʒɜːzɪ] *n.* (*a*) close-fitting warm upper garment; special shirt of a football team, etc. (*b*) **j.** (**cloth**) = type of loosely woven, usu. woollen, cloth. (*c*) type of cow.

jest [dʒest] **1.** *n.* joke; thing done/said for amusement only. **2.** *v.* to make jokes. **jester,** *n.* person who plays jokes, esp. someone employed to do this at a royal court.

jet [dʒet] **1.** *n.* (*a*) type of black mineral which can be highly polished; **j. black** = very black. (*b*) long narrow spray of liquid or gas. (*c*) opening to allow gas to escape. (*d*) jet-propelled aircraft; **j. lag** = tiredness felt by travellers who fly by jet across time zones; **j. set** = wealthy people who frequently travel by jet. **2.** *v.* (**jetted**) *inf.* to travel by jet. **jet engine,** *n.* engine which is propelled by a jet. **jet-propelled,** *adj.* pushed forward by a backward movement of jets of gas. **jet propulsion,** *n.* being jet-propelled. **jetstream,** *n.* (*a*) wind in the upper atmosphere. (*b*) stream of gases coming from a jet engine.

jetsam ['dʒetsəm] *n.* (*no pl.*) things which have been thrown into the water from a boat.

jettison ['dʒetɪzn] *v.* to throw out (unwanted things) from a ship/balloon, etc.

jetty ['dʒetɪ] *n.* wall built into water, where boats can tie up.

Jew [dʒuː] *n.* person descended from the Hebrews of ancient Palestine. **Jewess,** *n.* Jewish woman. **Jewish,** *adj.* referring to Jews. **Jewry,** *n.* the Jews.

jewel ['dʒuːəl] *n.* (*a*) precious stone. (*b*) ornament to be worn, made from precious stones and/or precious metals, or of imitation stones. **jewelled,** *adj.* covered with jewels. **jeweller,** *n.* person who makes/sells jewellery. **jewellery,** *n.* ornaments to be worn, made of precious stones/metals.

jib [dʒɪb] **1.** *n.* (*a*) triangular sail in front of a boat. (*b*) arm of a crane. **2.** *v.* (**jibbed**)

(*a*) (*of horse*) to refuse (a fence, etc.). (*b*) **to j. at** = to refuse to do sth.

jibe [dʒaɪb] *n.* & *v. see* **gibe.**

jiffy ['dʒɪfɪ] *n. inf.* very short time.

jig [dʒɪg] **1.** *n.* (*a*) type of fast lively dance; music for this dance. (*b*) instrument for guiding a tool and holding the material being worked on. **2.** *v.* (**jigged**) to jump up and down; to move about jerkily.

jigger, *n.* (*a*) small insect which lives in sand. (*b*) measure for serving alcohol.

jigsaw, *n.* (*a*) type of saw with very fine blade for cutting out shapes. (*b*) **j.** (**puzzle**) = puzzle of irregularly shaped pieces of wood/cardboard which when fitted together form a picture. **jiggery-pokery** ['dʒɪgərɪ'pəʊkərɪ] *n. inf.* tricks.

jiggle ['dʒɪgl] *v. inf..* to move rapidly/nervously.

jilt [dʒɪlt] *v.* to (encourage and then) reject (a lover).

jingle ['dʒɪŋgl] **1.** *n.* (*a*) sound made by small pieces of metal knocking together. (*b*) verse with a very simple rhyme and/or rhythm; catchy tune advertising a product. **2.** *v.* to make a tinkling sound (like pieces of metal).

jingoism ['dʒɪŋgəʊɪzəm] *n.* excessive love for your country and hatred for others. **jingoistic** [dʒɪŋgəʊ'ɪstɪk] *adj.* full of jingoism.

jinks [dʒɪŋks] *n. pl.* **high jinks** = wild amusement.

jinx [dʒɪŋks] *n.* (*pl.* **-es**) *inf.* bad luck.

jitters ['dʒɪtəz] *n. pl.* **to have the j.** = to be (unnecessarily) nervous/flustered. **jittery,** *adj.* nervous/flustered.

jive [dʒaɪv] **1.** *n.* type of fast rhythmic dance; music for this dance. **2.** *v.* to dance to jive music.

job [dʒɒb] *n.* (*a*) piece of work; **to make a good j. of sth** = to do it well; *inf.* **it's a good j. that** = it's lucky that; **to give sth up as a bad j.** = to stop making useless efforts to do sth; *inf.* **just the j.** = exactly what is needed; **odd jobs** = pieces of work, esp. repairs in the house; **odd j. man** = person who does odd jobs. (*b*) difficult task; **I had a j. to eat my meal** = it was difficult. (*c*) position in employment; **to be out of a j.** = to be unemployed; **jobs for the boys** = giving of employment to your supporters. (*d*) *inf.* crime, esp.

a theft. **jobber,** *n. Am.* wholesaler. **jobbing,** *adj.* (*of a workman*) (person) who is paid for each job separately. **job centre,** *n.* government office which displays available vacant jobs. **jobless,** **1.** *adj.* with no job. **2.** *n.* **the j.** = people who have no jobs. **job lot,** *n.* group of miscellaneous items sold together.

jockey ['dʒɒkɪ] **1.** *n.* person who rides horses in races. **2.** *v.* **to j. for position** = to try to improve your position, esp. by cheating or trickery. **jockstrap** ['dʒɒkstræp] *n.* support for genitals, worn by male sportsmen.

jocose [dʒə'kəʊs] *adj.* humorous. **jocular** ['dʒɒkjʊlə] *adj.* good humoured; treating things as a joke. **jocularity** [dʒɒkjʊ'lærɪtɪ] *n.* good humour. **jocularly,** *adv.* in a joking way.

jocund ['dʒɒkənd] *adj.* (*formal*) cheerful.

jodhpurs ['dʒɒdpəz] *n. pl.* special trousers for horse riding which are narrow below the knee.

joey ['dʒəʊɪ] *n.* (*in Australia*) *inf.* young kangaroo.

jog [dʒɒg] **1.** *n.* (*a*) rather slow pace. (*b*) light blow, esp. from the elbow. **2.** *v.* (**jogged**) (*a*) to move at a steady, but rather slow pace. (*b*) to run at an easy pace, esp. for exercise. (*c*) to shake/to push lightly; **it jogged his memory** = it made him remember. **jogger,** *n.* person who jogs for exercise. **jogging,** *n.* running at an easy pace for exercise. **jogtrot,** *n.* rather slow, easy pace.

joggle ['dʒɒgl] *v. inf.* to move rapidly/nervously.

john [dʒɒn] *n. Sl.* toilet.

join [dʒɔɪn] **1.** *n.* place/line where two things come together. **2.** *v.* (*a*) to come together/to be united; to bring together. (*b*) to (meet and) go along with; to meet and do sth together; **to j. forces** = to do sth by combined effort. (*c*) to become a member of (a club). **joiner,** *n.* person who constructs things from wood, esp. furniture and house fittings. **joinery,** *n.* joiner's trade. **join in,** *v.* to take part. **join up,** *v.* to become a member of the armed forces.

joint [dʒɔɪnt] **1.** *n.* (*a*) (place where) two or more pieces are attached, esp. in building or carpentry. (*b*) place where

bones come together, allowing movement; **out of j.** = dislocated. (*c*) large piece of meat, esp. for roasting. (*d*) *inf.* low-class night club or gambling den. (*e*) *Sl.* cigarette containing marijuana. **2.** *v.* (*a*) to cut up (a chicken, etc.) into pieces. (*b*) to provide with joints. **3.** *adj.* together/combined; shared by two or more; **j. account** = bank account shared by two people; **j. author** = author who writes a book with another. **jointed,** *adj.* having joints. **jointly,** *adv.* together; by combined effort.

joist [dʒɔɪst] *n.* beam which supports a ceiling or floorboards.

joke [dʒəʊk] **1.** *n.* thing said or done for amusement, to cause laughter; **practical j.** = action which makes s.o. uncomfortable for the amusement of others. **2.** *v.* to tell or make jokes; to say or do sth for amusement; **I was only joking** = I did not mean it seriously. **joker,** *n.* (*a*) person who jokes. (*b*) extra card in a pack used as a bonus in certain games. **jokingly,** *adv.* in a joking way.

jolly ['dʒɒlɪ] **1.** *adj.* (**-ier, -iest**) merry/happy. **2.** *adv. inf.* very. **3.** *v. inf.* **to j. s.o. along** = to encourage s.o. by keeping him happy. **jollification** [dʒɒlɪfɪ'keɪʃn] *n.* enjoyment/being jolly. **jollity,** *n.* merriness.

jolt [dʒəʊlt] **1.** *n.* abrupt shake/shock; violent jerk. **2.** *v.* (*a*) to move with a jumping movement. (*b*) to push/to shake abruptly. (*c*) to give a sudden shock to.

jonquil ['dʒɒŋkwɪl] *n.* narcissus.

joss stick ['dʒɒsstɪk] *n.* stick with incense painted on it, which burns slowly giving off a pleasant smell.

jostle ['dʒɒsl] *v.* to push/to bump (esp. with the elbows).

jot [dʒɒt] **1.** *n.* very small amount. **2.** *v.* (**jotted**) **to j. sth down** = to make (quick) notes. **jotter,** *n.* small pad of paper for making notes. **jottings,** *n. pl.* (random) notes.

joule [dʒuːl] *n.* standard unit of work and energy.

journal ['dʒɜːnl] *n.* (*a*) diary. (*b*) periodical, esp. on a learned subject. (*c*) book for recording each day's business. **journalese** [dʒɜːnə'liːz] *n.* style used by bad journalists. **journalism**

['dʒɜ:nəlızəm] n. profession of writing for newspapers or periodicals. **journalist**, n. person who writes for newspapers or periodicals.

journey ['dʒɜ:nı] n. (a) long trip. (b) long distance travelled; **it's two days' j. from here.** 2. v. (formal) to make a long trip. **journeyman**, n. (pl. **-men**) craftsman who works for s.o.

joust [dʒaʊst] v. to fight with spears on horseback (as an entertainment).

jovial ['dʒəʊvıəl] adj. good-humoured/merry. **joviality** [dʒəʊvı'ælıtı] n. good humour. **jovially**, adv. in a jovial way.

jowl [dʒaʊl] n. jaw/cheek; **cheek by j.** = very close together.

joy [dʒɔı] n. (cause of) very great happiness. **joyful**, adj. very happy. **joyfully**, adv. very happily. **joyless**, adj. very sad. **joyous**, adj. very happy. **joyride**, n. excursion for pleasure, esp. in a stolen car. **joystick**, n. (a) rod which controls the movements of an aircraft. (b) device with a movable arm, which moves a cursor on a computer screen.

JP ['dʒeı'pi:] abbreviation for Justice of the Peace.

jubilant ['dʒu:bılənt] adj. full of happiness/triumph. **jubilantly**, adv. triumphantly. **jubilation** [dʒu:bı'leıʃn] n. great happiness/triumph.

jubilee ['dʒu:bıli:] n. (celebration of the) anniversary of an important event; **silver/golden/diamond j.** = celebration 25/50/60 years after an event took place.

Judaism ['dʒu:deıızəm] n. religion of the Jews.

Judas tree ['dʒu:dəstri:] n. ornamental tree with pink flowers.

judder ['dʒʌdə] 1. n. shaking (of a machine). 2. v. (of a machine) to shake.

judge [dʒʌdʒ] 1. n. (a) person appointed to make decisions, esp. in a higher court of law. (b) person who decides which is the best entry in a competition. (c) person with good judgement; **he's a good j. of character.** 2. v. (a) to make decisions in a court of law/competition, etc. (b) to have as your opinion; to estimate. **judgement**, n. (a) making a decision. (b) sentence of a court; legal decision. (c) ability to see things clearly/to make good decisions; **against my better j.** = although I felt it was not the right thing to do.

judicial [dʒu:'dıʃl] adj. referring to a legal process/to a court of law. **judicature** ['dʒu:dıkətʃə] n. (a) judicial system. (b) judiciary. **judicially**, adv. legally. **judiciary** [dʒu:'dıʃərı] n. all the judges in a country. **judicious**, adj. based on/having good judgement. **judiciously**, adv. in a well judged way.

judo ['dʒu:dəʊ] n. modern form of Japanese wrestling.

jug [dʒʌg] n. (a) container with a handle, used for pouring liquids. (b) Sl. jail. **jugged hare**, n. hare soaked in wine and cooked slowly.

juggernaut ['dʒʌgənɔ:t] n. (a) overpowering force to which people sacrifice themselves. (b) inf. very large lorry.

juggle ['dʒʌgl] v. (a) to throw and catch several objects, so that most of them are in the air at the same time. (b) (with) to change things around very quickly, esp. in order to deceive. **juggler**, n. person who juggles.

jugular ['dʒʌgjʊlə] n. & adj. **j. (vein)** = main vein in the neck.

juice [dʒu:s] n. (a) liquid from fruit/vegetables/meat, etc; **to stew in your own j.** = to suffer the consequences of your own mistakes. (b) inf. petrol; electricity. **juiciness**, n. state of being full of juice. **juicy**, adj. full of juice.

jujitsu [dʒu:'dʒıtsu:] n. traditional Japanese unarmed combat.

juju ['dʒu:dʒu:] n. African magic charm.

jujube ['dʒu:dʒu:b] n. type of soft sweet.

jukebox ['dʒu:kbɒks] n. coin-operated record-playing machine.

julep ['dʒu:ləp] n. Am. drink made of alcohol and water, usu. with a mint flavour.

July [dʒʊ'laı] n. 7th month of the year. **Julian calendar**, n. calendar instituted by Julius Caesar, slightly longer than the present-day calendar.

jumble ['dʒʌmbl] 1. n. mixture/confusion; **j. sale** = sale of second-hand goods, usu. for charity. 2. v. (**up**) to mix; to confuse.

jumbo ['dʒʌmbəʊ] n. (pl. **-os**) (a) child's name for an elephant. (b) anything very large, esp. a very large aircraft holding several hundred people.

jump [dʒʌmp] 1. n. (a) leap (in the air); (in sports) **long j./high j.** = competition to see how far/how high you can leap. (b) sudden movement. (c) (in sports) obstacle to be jumped over. 2. v. (a) to move suddenly, esp. upwards. (b) to move by jumping; **to j. over the stream; to j. a page** = to miss out a page. (c) to make a sudden movement, esp. from some emotion; **to j. to conclusions** = to make a decision too quickly; **to j. the gun** = to begin before your turn/before the correct time; **to j. the queue** = to go ahead of your turn. **jump at,** v. to seize (an opportunity) eagerly. **jumped-up,** adj. (person) who has been promoted faster than his qualities merit. **jumper,** n. (a) person who jumps. (b) warm knitted upper garment. **jump jet,** n. aircraft which can take off vertically. **jump lead,** n. cable which allows two car batteries to be connected to help a car to start. **jump rope,** n. Am. skipping rope. **jump suit,** n. one-piece suit, with trousers attached to the shirt. **jumpy,** adj. (-ier, -iest) inf. nervous; excited.

junction ['dʒʌŋkʃn] n. joining (place), esp. of railway lines/roads; **j. box** = box where several electric wires join.

juncture ['dʒʌŋktʃə] n. (formal) point in time.

June [dʒu:n] n. 6th month of the year.

jungle ['dʒʌŋgl] n. (a) almost impassable tropical forest. (b) confused mass; place or circumstances where progress is difficult; **blackboard j.** = schools with uncontrollable pupils; **concrete j.** = area of tall impersonal buildings.

junior ['dʒu:nɪə] 1. adj. (a) younger; **John Smith J.** = son of John Smith Senior. (b) for younger children; **j. school** = school for children from 7 to 11 years old. (c) lower in rank. 2. n. (a) person who is younger/lower in rank. (b) Am. third-year student.

juniper ['dʒu:nɪpə] n. shrub with evergreen leaves and dark berries, used as flavouring for gin.

junk [dʒʌŋk] n. (a) large Chinese sailing boat. (b) useless articles/rubbish; **j. bonds** = bonds giving a high interest, based on the security of a company which is the target of a takeover bid. (c) (inferior) second-hand goods. (d) Sl. drugs, esp. heroin. **junk food,** n. bad commercially prepared food with little nutritional value. **junkie,** n. Sl. drug addict. **junk shop,** n. shop selling junk.

junket ['dʒʌŋkɪt] 1. n. (a) sweet food made of curdled milk. (b) feast/celebration. (c) pleasure trip made by an official at public expense. 2. v. to have a celebration, esp. by eating and drinking. **junketing,** n. great celebrations, esp. at public expense.

junta ['dʒʌntə] n. group of soldiers who seize power and rule a country.

jurisdiction [dʒuərɪs'dɪkʃn] n. (legal) power.

jurisprudence [dʒuərɪs'pru:dəns] n. study of the law.

jurist ['dʒuərɪst] n. person who specializes in law.

jury ['dʒuərɪ] n. (a) group of citizens sworn to decide a verdict on the strength of evidence in a court of law. (b) group of judges in a competition. **juror, juryman,** n. (pl. **-men**) member of a jury. **jurybox** n. place where the jury sits.

just [dʒʌst] 1. adj. showing no favour; true/correct. 2. adv. (a) exactly; very nearly/almost; **j. by the door; it's j. about ready** = almost ready; **that's j. it** = that is exactly the problem. (b) (used to indicate the immediate past or future) **he's j. arrived; I'm j. going.** (c) only; **we're j. good friends.** (d) **j. now** = (i) at the present moment; (ii) a short time ago. (e) **j. as** = (i) exactly when; (ii) exactly in the manner that. **justly,** adv. fairly; with justice. **justness,** n. fairness.

justice ['dʒʌstɪs] n. (a) quality of being fair; **to do j. to** = to treat (sth) as it deserves; **the portrait doesn't do her j.** = it is not a good likeness. (b) **to bring to j.** = to bring legal proceedings against. (c) (esp. as title) judge/magistrate. **Justice of the Peace,** n. local magistrate. **justiciary,** n. judges/magistrates taken as a group.

justify ['dʒʌstɪfaɪ] v. (a) to show that sth is fair/to prove that sth is right. (b) to space characters so that the right margin is even. **justifiable,** adj. which can be justified. **justifiably,** adv. in a way which can be justified. **justification** [dʒʌstɪfɪ'keɪʃn] n. (a) reason which shows that sth is fair. (b) making a right margin even.

jut [dʒʌt] v. (**jutted**) **to j.** (**out**) = to stick out, usu. horizontally.

jute [dʒuːt] n. fibre of plants used for making sacks, etc.

juvenile ['dʒuːvənaɪl] **1.** adj. of/for young people; **j. delinquent** = young person who is guilty of a crime. **2.** n. young person. **juvenilia** [dʒuːvə'nɪlɪə] n. works written by a famous writer when a child.

juxtapose [dʒʌkstə'pəʊz] v. to place side by side/very close together. **juxtaposition** [dʒʌkstəpə'zɪʃn] n. being side by side/very close together.

Kk

K 1. symbol for potassium. **2.** abbrev. for one thousand.

kaftan ['kæftæn] n. long Arab-style gown.

kale [keɪl] n. (no pl.) type of cabbage with wrinkled leaves.

kaleidoscope [kə'laɪdəskəʊp] n. tube with mirrors which reflect small pieces of coloured glass and make patterns which can be seen through a viewer. **kaleidoscopic** [kəlaɪdə'skɒpɪk] adj. like a kaleidoscope/with bright changing colours; frequently changing.

kamikaze [kæmɪ'kɑːzɪ] n. & adj. suicidally daring (air attack).

kangaroo [kæŋɡə'ruː] n. large Australian animal, which carries its young in a pouch; **k. court** = illegal court set up by terrorists/strikers, etc., to judge one of their members.

kaolin ['keɪəlɪn] n. fine white clay, used for making porcelain, and sometimes in medicine.

kapok ['keɪpɒk] n. kind of cotton wool, used for stuffing cushions.

kaput [kə'pʊt] adj. inf. finished; broken.

karat ['kærət] n. Am. measure of purity of gold.

karate [kə'rɑːtɪ] n. Japanese style of fighting, where you hit with the side of the hand.

karma ['kɑːmə] n. in Buddhism, the way in which a person acts which will affect his future life.

kayak ['kaɪæk] n. (a) Eskimo canoe, covered with sealskins. (b) small canoe with a narrow opening for the canoeist.

kebab [kɪ'bæb] n. small cubes of meat grilled on a skewer.

kedgeree [kedʒə'riː] n. spicy mixture of rice, fish and eggs.

keel [kiːl] **1.** n. lowest timber in a ship, on which the framework is built; **on an even k.** = stable/steady. **2.** v. **to k. over** = to fall over.

keen [kiːn] **1.** adj. (**-er, -est**) (a) (**on**) eager/willing. (b) sharp. (c) sensitive/acute (sense). (d) inf. **k. prices** = very competitive prices. **2.** v. to wail/to cry (because s.o. has died). **keenly,** adv. sharply. **keenness,** n. being keen.

keep [kiːp] **1.** n. (a) central tower/strongest part of a castle. (b) maintenance; **she doesn't earn her k.** = she doesn't earn enough money to pay for her food and lodging. (c) inf. **for keeps** = for ever. **2.** v. (**kept** [kept]) (a) to continue to have/to possess. (b) to continue; **he kept running.** (c) to pay regard to (a promise, etc.). (d) to own/to manage (animals). (e) to maintain. (f) to support financially. (g) to have for sale. (h) to detain/to restrain. (i) to conceal. (j) to reserve. (k) to prevent (s.o. **from** doing sth). (l) to remain; **let's k. in touch** = we mustn't lose contact with each other; **she kept him company** = she stayed with him. (m) **to k. a diary** = to write notes every day about what you have done. (n) to continue to stay in good condition; **raspberries don't k.** = go rotten quickly. **keeper,** n. (a) person in charge of animals in a zoo; person in charge of a museum. (b) fruit which stays in good condition for a long time. **keeping,** n. (a) custody. (b) **in k. with** = in harmony with. **keep in with,** v. to stay on friendly terms with (s.o.). **keep on,** v. to continue (to do sth); **he kept on running. keep on at,** v. inf. to criticize without stopping; **she keeps on at me about painting the kitchen** = she tells me all the time that I should paint the kitchen. **keepsake,** n. memento; thing kept to remind you of the giver. **keep up,** v. to continue. **keep up with,** v. (a) to keep yourself informed about. (b) to go forward at the same pace; **to keep up with the Joneses** = to try to maintain the same social level as your neighbours.

keg [keg] n. small barrel; **k. beer** = beer kept in pressurized metal kegs.

kelp [kelp] n. large seaweed.

kelvin ['kelvɪn] n. standard unit of temperature.

ken [ken] 1. n. knowledge; **beyond our k.** = out of our normal range of knowledge. 2. v. (**kenned**) (*in Scotland*) to know.

kennel ['kenl] 1. n. shelter for a dog; **kennels** = place where dogs can be left when their owners go away/where dogs are bred. 2. v. (**kennelled**) to keep in a kennel.

kentledge ['kentlɪdʒ] n. iron used as ballast.

Kenyan ['kenjən] 1. adj. referring to Kenya. 2. n. person from Kenya.

kept [kept] v. see **keep**.

kerb [kɜːb] n. stone edging to a pavement/path.

kerchief ['kɜːtʃɪf] n. large square scarf worn over your head.

kerfuffle [kə'fʌfl] n. inf. fuss/bother.

kernel ['kɜːnl] n. (a) softer part inside the hard shell of a nut. (b) essential part/centre.

kerosene ['kerəsiːn] n. paraffin.

kestrel ['kestrəl] n. type of small falcon.

ketch [ketʃ] n. (pl. **-es**) two-masted sailing boat.

ketchup ['ketʃəp] n. sauce made from tomatoes and spices.

kettle ['ketl] n. metal container, with a lid and a spout, used for boiling water; **a pretty k. of fish** = an awkward state of affairs. **kettledrum**, n. large drum with a round bottom.

key [kiː] 1. n. (a) piece of metal for turning locks. (b) solution/explanation. (c) system of musical notes related to each other. (d) part of a piano/flute/typewriter/computer, etc., which you press down to make the instrument work. (e) seed case, shaped like a key. 2. adj. most important (thing/person). 3. v. (a) to link to/to make suitable for. (b) to type (words/figures) on a keyboard. **keyboard 1.** n. set of keys on a piano/typewriter/computer, etc. 2. v. to input data into a computer, using a keyboard. **keyed up,** adj. nervous/tense (before an examination/a battle, etc.). **keyhole,** n. hole in a lock into which a key is put. **keynote,** n. (a) dominating musical note. (b) main theme in a speech; **k. speech** =

main speech (at a conference). **keypad,** n. small set of keys on a computer; **numeric k.** = set of numbered keys on a computer keyboard, used for various functions. **key ring,** n. ring for carrying several keys together. **keystone,** n. central supporting block of stone or brick in an arch; important idea on which everything else is based.

kg abbrev. for kilogram.

khaki ['kɑːkɪ] adj. & n. dull yellow-brown (colour); the colour of soldiers' uniforms.

kibbutz [kɪ'bʊts] n. (pl. **-tzim** [-'tsiːm]) farming settlement in Israel.

kibosh ['kaɪbɒʃ] n. Sl. **to put the k. on sth** = to stop sth happening.

kick [kɪk] 1. n. (a) blow with the foot. (b) inf. thrill/excitement; **he did it for kicks** = to give himself a thrill. 2. v. to strike with the foot. **kickback,** n. (a) recoil (of a gun). (b) Sl. bribe/illegal commission paid to s.o. who helps a business deal. **kick off,** v. to start a game of football. **kick-off,** n. start (of a football game). **kick start(er),** n. pedal to start a motorcycle engine. **kick up,** v. inf. to make (a fuss/a row).

kid [kɪd] 1. n. (a) young goat. (b) inf. child. 2. v. (**kidded**) inf. to make (s.o.) believe sth that is not true; **I'm only kidding** = I don't mean it; **no kidding?** = is it really true? **kiddy,** n. inf. child.

kidnap ['kɪdnæp] v. (**kidnapped**) to steal (a child); to carry (a person) off by force illegally. **kidnapper,** n. person who kidnaps. **kidnapping,** n. carrying away of a person by force.

kidney ['kɪdnɪ] n. one of a pair of organs in animals that extract impurities from the blood; this organ used as food; **k. bean** = type of bean with reddish seeds; **k. machine** = device by which a patient's blood can be purified when his kidneys do not function properly.

kill [kɪl] 1. n. putting an animal to death for sport; **to be in at the k.** = to be there at the end of the affair. 2. v. to put to death; to make (s.o./an animal/a plant) die; **he was killing himself with laughter** = he was laughing very heartily; **k. time** = to spend time doing very little while waiting for sth; **to k. two birds with one stone** = to get two successful results from one action; *inf.* **my feet are killing me** = my feet hurt. **killer,** *n.* person who kills; **k. whale** = medium-sized black and white carnivorous whale. **killing. 1.** *adj. inf.* very funny. **2.** *n.* (*a*) putting to death. (*b*) large profit (on the stock market). **killjoy,** *n.* person who stops others enjoying themselves. **kill off,** *v.* to get rid of (sth) by killing.

kiln [kıln] *n.* oven for baking pottery or bricks.

kilo ['ki:ləʊ] **1.** *prefix meaning* one thousand. **2.** *n.* (*pl.* **-os**) kilogram.

kilobyte ['kıləʊbaıt] *n.* storage unit of computer data equal to 1,024 bytes.

kilocycle ['kıləʊsaıkl] *n.* one thousand cycles as a frequency of radio waves.

kilogram ['kıləʊgræm] *n.* one thousand grams.

kilohertz ['kıləʊhɜ:ts] *n.* one thousand hertz.

kilometre, *Am.* **kilometer** [kı'lɒmıtə] *n.* one thousand metres.

kilovolt ['kıləʊvɒlt] *n.* one thousand volts.

kilowatt ['kıləwɒt] *n.* one thousand watts.

kilt [kılt] *n.* pleated skirt, usu. of tartan cloth, worn by men in Scotland, and also by women. **kilted,** ['kıltıd] *adj.* wearing a kilt.

kimono [kı'məʊnəʊ] *n.* (*pl.* **-os**) long, loose robe worn by Japanese women.

kin [kın] *n.* **next of k.** = nearest relative(s); *see also* **kith.**

kind [kaınd] **1.** *n.* type/variety; **two of a k.** = two the same; **it's nothing of the k.** = not at all true; **payment in k.** = payment in goods or natural produce, not in money; *inf.* **k. of sorry** = rather sorry. **2.** *adj.* (**-er, -est**) amiable/thoughtful; friendly/thinking of others. **kind-hearted,** *adj.* thoughtful about other people. **kindliness,** *n.* being kindly. **kindly,** *adj.* & *adv.* thoughtful/pleasant; in a thoughtful/pleasant way; **she doesn't take k. to** = she doesn't like; **k. shut the door** = please shut the door. **kindness,** *n.* being kind.

kindergarten ['kındəgɑ:tn] *n.* school for very young children.

kindle ['kındl] *v.* to make a fire; to catch fire. **kindling,** *n.* (*no pl.*) small pieces of wood used to start a fire.

kindred ['kındrıd] *adj.* similar; **k. spirit**

= person with whom you have sth in common.

kinetic [kı'netık] *adj.* produced by moving; (energy) which a body has in motion.

king [kıŋ] *n.* (*a*) male sovereign or hereditary ruler of a country. (*b*) main piece in chess/draughts; (*in cards*) card following the queen. **kingcup,** *n.* large buttercup. **kingdom,** *n.* (*a*) land ruled over by a king. (*b*) part of the world of nature. (*c*) **until k. come** = until the end of the world. **kingfisher,** *n.* small brilliant blue bird that dives for fish. **kingly,** *adj.* like a king. **kingpin,** *n.* central bolt; central person in an organization. **king-size(d),** *adj.* very large.

kink [kıŋk] **1.** *n.* (*a*) knot/twist in a length of cord, wire or rope. (*b*) peculiar mental state. **2.** *v.* to make a kink in (sth). **kinky,** *adj. Sl.* sexually odd/peculiar.

kinship ['kınʃıp] *n.* family relationship. **kinsfolk,** *n. pl.* relatives. **kinsman, kinswoman,** *n.* (*pl.* **-men, -women**) relative.

kiosk ['ki:ɒsk] *n.* small outdoor cabin for the sale of newspapers/sweets, etc.; telephone booth.

kip [kıp] **1.** *n. Sl.* short sleep. **2.** *v.* (**kipped**) *Sl.* to sleep.

kipper ['kıpə] *n.* split smoked herring. **kippered,** *adj.* smoked (fish).

kirk [kɜ:k] *n.* (*in Scotland*) church.

kirsch [ki:əʃ] *n.* cherry brandy.

kiss [kıs] **1.** *n.* (*pl.* **-es**) touching with the lips; **she blew him a k.** = signalled to send him a kiss from a distance; **k. of life** = resuscitation by breathing into a person's mouth; **k. of death** = act which ruins (a business, etc.). **2.** *v.* to touch with the lips. **kisser,** *n. Sl.* mouth.

kit [kıt] *n.* (*a*) clothes and personal equipment, usu. packed for travelling; **first aid k.** = supplies for the emergency treatment of injuries. (*b*) box containing pieces which can be put together to make a model/a piece of furniture, etc. **kitbag,** *n.* round bag for carrying a soldier's clothes and equipment. **kit out,** *v.* (**kitted out**) to supply with clothes and equipment.

kitchen ['kıtʃın] *n.* room in which food is cooked. **kitchenette,** *n.* very small kitchen. **kitchen garden,** *n.* fruit and vegetable plot in a garden.

kite [kaɪt] n. (a) large bird of prey of the falcon family. (b) toy made of light wood and paper or cloth which is flown in a strong wind on the end of a string; **k. mark** = mark put on British goods to show that they have met standards; **he's just flying a k.** = he's putting forward an idea to see how people react to it.

kith [kɪθ] n. **k. and kin** = friends and relatives.

kitsch [kɪtʃ] n. lack of artistic taste; tasteless artistic production.

kitten ['kɪtn] n. young cat; inf. **to have kittens** = to be afraid/nervous. **kittenish**, adj. playful/like a kitten.

kittiwake ['kɪtɪweɪk] n. type of gull.

kitty ['kɪtɪ] n. joint fund.

kiwi ['kiːwiː] n. non-flying bird, native of New Zealand. **kiwi fruit**, n. small tropical fruit, with a hairy skin and green flesh.

Kleenex ['kliːneks] n. (pl. -es) trademark for a paper handkerchief.

kleptomania [kleptə'meɪnɪə] n. irresistible tendency to steal. **kleptomaniac**, n. person who cannot stop stealing.

km abbrev. for kilometre.

knack [næk] n. talent/ability.

knacker ['nækə] n. person who buys and kills useless horses. **knackered**, adj. inf. tired out.

knapsack ['næpsæk] n. canvas/leather bag carried on the back.

knave [neɪv] n. (a) (old) trickster. (b) (in cards) jack/card between the ten and the queen.

knead [niːd] v. to press with the hands.

knee [niː] n. joint between your thigh and lower leg; **she was sitting on his k.** = sitting on his thighs. **kneecap. 1.** n. bone in front of the knee. **2.** v. to punish (s.o.) by shooting him in the kneecap. **knee-deep**, adj. up to the knees (in). **knees-up**, n. inf. jolly dance.

kneel [niːl] v. (**knelt** [nelt]) to go on your knees. **kneel down**, v. to go down on your knees. **kneeler**, n. hard cushion for kneeling on.

knell [nel] n. (formal) sound of a bell, rung at a solemn ceremony such as a funeral.

knelt [nelt] v. see **kneel**.

knew [njuː] v. see **know**.

knickerbockers ['nɪkəbɒkəz] n. pl. trousers which are gathered at the knees. **knickers** ['nɪkəz] n. pl. undergarment worn by a woman or girl on the lower part of the body.

knick-knack ['nɪknæk] n. small/light article; trinket.

knife [naɪf] **1.** n. (pl. **knives** [naɪvz]) cutting blade with a sharpened edge fixed into a handle; **to have your k. into s.o.** = to try to hurt/to behave nastily towards s.o.; **on a k. edge** = in a difficult position, where the outcome is not sure. **2.** v. (**knifed**) to stab (s.o.) with a knife.

knight [naɪt] **1.** n. (a) man honoured by a king for personal merit or services to his country (and taking the title **Sir**). (b) (in medieval times) brave soldier often devoted to the service of a lady. (c) piece in a chess set with a horse's head. **2.** v. to make (s.o.) a knight. **knighthood**, n. title of knight.

knit [nɪt] v. (a) (**knitted**) to make (a garment) out of wool, etc., by linking two threads together with the aid of two long needles; **to k. one's brows** = to frown. (b) (**knit**) (of broken bone) to join together again. **knitter**, n. person who knits. **knitting**, n. woollen garment which is in the process of being made. **knitting machine**, n. machine for knitting. **knitting needle**, n. long needle for knitting. **knitwear**, n. knitted woollen garments.

knives [naɪvz] n. see **knife**.

knob [nɒb] n. (a) rounded bump; round lump. (b) round handle of door/drawer. **knobbly, knobby**, adj. bumpy; covered with knobs.

knock [nɒk] **1.** n. sharp blow; sound of a sharp blow. **2.** v. (a) to strike (sth) with a hard blow; **he knocked on/at the door** = hit the door with his knuckles to call attention. (b) inf. to criticize; **knocking copy** = publicity material which criticizes a rival's products. (c) (of car engine) to make a regular/sharp noise because of misfiring. **knock about**, v. (a) to drift aimlessly. (b) **to knock (s.o.) about** = to beat (s.o.). **knock back**, v. inf. (a) to cost (s.o.) a sum. (b) to surprise (s.o.). (c) to swallow quickly. **knock down**, v. (a) to hit (s.o./sth) to the ground. (b) to sell (an item) at an auction to a purchaser. **knock-down**, adj. very low (price). **knocker**, n. knob or ring hinged to a door which can be struck against it to call attention. **knocking,** *n.* series of sharp blows; noise made by an engine which is misfiring. **knock-kneed,** *adj.* having knees that touch each other when walking. **knock off,** *v.* (*a*) to hit (sth) so that it falls off. (*b*) *inf.* **he knocked off work at 4.30** = he stopped working at 4.30. (*c*) **the vendor knocked £10 off the price of the car** = he reduced the price of the car by £10. **knock out,** *v.* to hit (s.o.) so hard that he loses consciousness. **knockout,** *n.* (*a*) hitting s.o. so hard that he loses consciousness. (*b*) **k. competition** = contest where several teams compete against each other and are eliminated in turn. **knock up,** *v.* (*a*) to waken. (*b*) to make very tired. (*c*) to score. (*d*) *Am. inf.* to make pregnant. (*e*) *inf.* to put (sth) together rapidly. **knock-up,** *n.* practice before a tennis match.

knoll [nɒl] *n.* small hill.

knot [nɒt] **1.** *n.* (*a*) looping the ends of string/rope, etc., and fastening them together; small group (of people); **to tie yourself in knots** = to get into difficulties. (*b*) hard round place in a piece of wood where a branch used to join it. (*c*) measurement by which a ship's/an aircraft's speed is calculated (= one nautical mile per hour). (*c*) type of small shore bird. **2.** *v.* (**knotted**) to tie in a knot. **knotty,** *adj.* (**-ier, -iest**) difficult (problem).

know [nəʊ] **1.** *n.* **to be in the k.** = to be well informed about sth which is not generally known. **2.** *v.* (**knew** [njuː]**; has known**) (*a*) to have in your mind because of learning or experience; **do you k. French?** = do you speak French? (*b*) to recognize (s.o.). (*c*) to be acquainted with; **I k. him by sight/ by name.** (*d*) **to k. what it is like to** = to have personal experience of; **to k. your own mind** = to be clear and firm in your views. **know-all,** *n.* person who claims he knows everything. **know-how,** *n.* *inf.* knowledge about how sth is made/ is done. **knowing,** *adj.* understanding; having knowledge. **knowingly,** *adv.* deliberately. **knowledge** ['nɒlɪdʒ] *n.* (*a*) what s.o. knows. (*b*) what is generally known. **knowledgeable,** *adj.*

(person) who knows a lot about sth. **know of,** *v.* to be aware of.

knuckle ['nʌkl] *n.* (*a*) finger joint; **near the k.** = verging on the indecent. (*b*) (*on an animal*) joint on the leg (esp. when used as food). **knuckle down,** *v.* to apply yourself seriously to work. **knuckle duster,** *n.* metal instrument worn on the knuckles, either as a protection or as a weapon. **knuckle under,** *v.* to give in/to submit.

KO *abbrev. for* knock out.

koala [kəʊ'ɑːlə] *n.* **k. (bear)** = small Australian animal which carries its young in a pouch and lives in trees.

kohl [kəʊl] *n.* powder used to make eyelids darker.

kohlrabi [kəʊl'rɑːbiː] *n.* vegetable with a thick purplish stem which is eaten.

kookaburra ['kʊkəbʌrə] *n.* large Australian kingfisher.

kop [kɒp] *n.* (*in South Africa*) small hill.

Koran [kɒ'rɑːn] *n.* holy book of the Muslims.

Korean [kə'rɪən]. **1.** *adj.* referring to Korea. **2.** *n.* (*a*) person from Korea. (*b*) language spoken in Korea.

kosher ['kəʊʃə] *adj.* (food) prepared according to Jewish law.

kowtow [kaʊ'taʊ] *v.* to show great respect (**to**).

kraal [krɑl] *n.* (*in South Africa*) village with a fence round it.

Kremlin ['kremlɪn] *n.* the Russian government.

krill [krɪl] *n.* (*pl.* **krill**) minute shrimps living in the sea.

krypton ['krɪptɒn] *n.* (*element:* Kr) rare gas.

kudos ['kjuːdɒs] *n.* glory/renown.

kudu ['kuːduː] *n.* small African antelope.

kumquat ['kʌmkwɒt] *n.* very small orange.

kung fu [kuːŋ'fuː] *n.* Chinese style of fighting.

Ll

L,l [el] **L plates** = signs with a red L on them, attached to a car, etc., to show that the driver is a learner.

lab [læb] *n. short for* **laboratory.**

label ['leɪbl] **1.** *n.* (*a*) piece of paper/card, etc., attached to sth to indicate price/

contents/name/address, etc. (b) name under which sth is generally known. **2.** v. (**labelled**) (a) to put a label on. (b) to name/to describe.

labial ['leɪbɪəl] adj. referring to the lips.

laboratory [ləˈbɒrətrɪ, Am. 'læbrətɔːrɪ] n. place where scientific experiments/ research are carried out.

laborious [ləˈbɔːrɪəs] adj. (a) involving a great deal of work. (b) (style) showing signs of effort. **laboriously,** adv. in a laborious way.

labour, Am. **labor** ['leɪbə] **1.** n. (a) (hard) work; **hard l.** = prison sentence involving heavy manual work. (b) workers/the workforce. (c) **Labour/ the Labour Party** = socialist political party linked with the trade unions and concerned with the welfare of workers. (d) (pains of) childbirth. **2.** v. (a) to work (hard). (b) **to l. under a delusion** = to have a (persistently) wrong impression; **to l. the point** = to argue/to discuss sth too long. (c) (of engine, etc.) to work with difficulty. **laboured,** adj. (a) (of style) heavy/ clumsy. (b) (of breathing) heavy/difficult. **labourer,** n. person who does heavy manual work. **Labourite,** n. inf. member of the Labour Party. **laboursaving,** adj. (of machine/gadget) which lessens work.

labrador ['læbrədɔː] n. type of large dog, usu. black or yellow.

laburnum [ləˈbɜːnəm] n. tree with bright yellow flowers and poisonous seeds in pods.

labyrinth ['læbɪrɪnθ] n. maze; place where it is difficult to find your way about. **labyrinthine** [læbəˈrɪnθaɪn] adj. like a labyrinth.

lace [leɪs] **1.** n. (a) thin strip of material for tying up a shoe, etc. (b) decorative cloth with open patterns of threads. **2.** v. (a) to tie with a lace. (b) to pour a little alcohol into (sth).

lacerate ['læsəreɪt] v. (formal) to wound/ to tear (flesh). **laceration** [læsəˈreɪʃn] n. tearing; place where flesh has been torn.

lachrymose ['lækrɪməʊs] adj. (formal) (person) who tends to cry. **lachrymal,** adj. (gland) which produces tears.

lack [læk] **1.** n. not having sth. **2.** v. not to have (enough of) sth. **lacking,** adj. not enough/without.

lackadaisical [lækəˈdeɪzɪkl] adj. not showing any vigour/any enthusiasm.

lackey ['lækɪ] n. servant who obeys without questioning.

lacklustre, Am. **lackluster** ['læklʌstə] adj. dull/not brilliant.

laconic [ləˈkɒnɪk] adj. using few words. **laconically,** adv. in a laconic way.

lacquer ['lækə] **1.** n. (a) type of hard shiny varnish/paint, often used on metals. (b) spray for keeping your hair in place. **2.** v. to coat with lacquer.

lacrosse [ləˈkrɒs] n. team game played with a ball and a curved stick with a net at the end.

lactic ['læktɪk] adj. referring to milk. **lactation** [lækˈteɪʃn] n. (of female) production of milk. **lactose,** n. sugar occurring in milk.

lacuna [ləˈkjuːnə] n. (pl. -ae) gap/space.

lacustrine ['lækuːstriːn] adj. referring to lakes.

lacy ['leɪsɪ] adj. (-ier, -iest) like lace; made of a network of fine threads.

lad [læd], **laddie** ['lædɪ] n. inf. boy; young man.

ladder ['lædə] **1.** n. (a) object made of horizontal bars between two uprights, used for climbing. (b) long hole in a stocking. **2.** v. (of stocking, etc.) to get a ladder.

laden ['leɪdn] adj. (**with**) carrying a (heavy) load; (of ship) containing a cargo. **lading,** n. (a) loading of ships. (b) cargo.

ladle ['leɪdl] **1.** n. large deep spoon for serving soup, etc. **2.** v. (also **ladle out**) to serve with a ladle.

lady ['leɪdɪ] n. (a) woman, esp. of high social standing or with good manners. (b) (as title) **Lady** = feminine equivalent of Lord; title of wife or sometimes daughter of a peer; title of wife of a knight or baronet. (c) **Our Lady** = the Virgin Mary. **ladies,** n. inf. women's toilet. **ladybird,** Am. **ladybug,** n. type of small beetle, usu. red with black spots. **Lady Day,** n. 25th March. **ladykiller,** n. inf. man who is attractive to women. **ladylike,** adj. wellmannered/polite (as a lady should be). **lady's finger,** n. okra. **ladyship,** n. (form of address to a titled lady) Your Ladyship.

lag [læg] **1.** *n.* (*a*) (*in time*) space/interval, esp. between two parts of an event. (*b*) *Sl.* **old l.** = person who has been put in prison many times. **2.** *v.* (**lagged**) (*a*) to go/fall/be behind. (*b*) to cover (a heating appliance, pipes, etc.) to prevent heat loss or to prevent freezing. **laggard** ['lægəd] *n.* person who is behind the others. **lagging**, *n.* material for wrapping round pipes.

lager ['lɑːgə] *n.* type of light beer.

lagoon [lə'guːn] *n.* area of sea water almost completely surrounded by land, esp. by a coral island.

laid [leɪd] *v. see* **lay. laid-back,** *adj. inf.* unhurried/relaxed.

lain [leɪn] *v. see* **lie.**

lair ['leə] *n.* resting place of a wild animal.

laird ['leəd] *n.* (*in Scotland*) owner of a country estate.

laissez-faire [leseɪ'fɛə] *adj.* (economy) where the government does not interfere on principle.

laity ['leɪtɪ] *n.* people who have not been trained as priests.

lake [leɪk] *n.* (*a*) (large) inland stretch of water. **wine l.** = large quantity of wine stockpiled because of overproduction. (*b*) type of reddish dye.

lakh [læk] *n.* (*in India*) one hundred thousand rupees.

lam [læm] *v. inf.* to hit.

lama ['lɑːmə] *n.* Buddhist priest, esp. in Tibet. **lamasery,** *n.* monastery for lamas.

lamb [læm] **1.** *n.* (*a*) young sheep. (*b*) flesh of sheep used as food. **2.** *v.* to give birth to a lamb. **lambing** ['læmɪŋ] *n.* giving birth to lambs. **lambswool,** *n.* (*no pl.*) very soft wool.

lambast(e) [læm'beɪst] *v.* to criticize (s.o.) sharply.

lame [leɪm] **1.** *adj.* (**-er, -est**) (*a*) unable to walk properly. (*b*) weak/unsatisfactory. **2.** *v.* to injure (s.o.) so that he cannot walk properly. **lame duck,** *n.* person/company in difficulties and having to rely on outside support. **lamely,** *adv.* in a weak way. **lameness,** *n.* being lame.

lamé ['lɑːmeɪ] *n.* cloth with gold or silver threads.

lamella [læ'melə] *n.* (*pl.* **-ae**) thin scale.

lament [lə'ment] **1.** *n.* (*a*) song/music for mourning. (*b*) expression of grief; complaint. **2.** *v.* to be very sad about (the death of s.o.). **lamentable** ['læməntəbl] *adj.* very bad. **lamentably,** *adv.* very badly. **lamentation** [læmən'teɪʃn] *n.* expression of great sorrow.

laminated ['læmɪneɪtɪd] *adj.* (*a*) formed in thin layers. (*b*) covered with a thin layer of plastic. **lamination** [læmɪ'neɪʃn] *n.* process of covering with a thin plastic film.

Lammas ['læməs] *n.* August 1st.

lamp [læmp] *n.* object which produces light. **lamplight,** *n.* light from a lamp. **lamp-post,** *n.* tall post which holds a street lamp. **lampshade,** *n.* (decorative) cover to put over a lamp.

lampoon [læm'puːn] **1.** *n.* writing which makes s.o. seem ridiculous. **2.** *v.* to ridicule (s.o.) in writing.

lamprey ['læmprɪ] *n.* edible fish, like an eel.

lance [lɑːns] **1.** *n.* type of long spear. **2.** *v.* to cut (a wound/an abscess, etc.) with a lancet. **lance-corporal,** *n.* non-commissioned officer below the rank of corporal. **lancer,** *n.* soldier in a regiment which used to be armed with lances. **lancet,** *n.* (*a*) pointed two-edged surgical knife. (*b*) tall thin pointed window.

land [lænd] **1.** *n.* (*a*) solid part of the earth's surface. (*b*) earth/soil; **to go back to the l.** = to go back to being a farmer again. (*c*) country. (*d*) estate owned by s.o. (*e*) **Land** = one of the states making up the Federal Republic of Germany. **2.** *v.* (*a*) to come to land; to bring to land; **to l. on one's feet** = enjoy easy success. (*b*) to bring a fish out of water and on to the land; to obtain (a good job). (*c*) to give/to deal (a blow). (*d*) **to l. (up) in** = to arrive/to reach. **landed,** *adj.* owning land. **landfall,** *n.* seeing land for the first time from sea or air. **landfill,** *n.* disposing of rubbish in holes in the ground. **landing,** *n.* (*a*) (*esp. of aircraft*) touching land; **l. gear** = wheels on which an aircraft lands. (*b*) space at the top of a flight of stairs. **landing-net,** *n.* net at the end of a long pole, for taking fish out of water. **landing stage,** *n.* (floating) platform where passengers can leave boats. **landlady,**

n. (*a*) woman from whom you rent a house/room, etc. (*b*) woman who keeps a hotel or inn, etc. **landlocked,** *n.* (sea/harbour) surrounded by land. **landlord,** *n.* (*a*) man from whom you rent a house/room, etc. (*b*) man who keeps a hotel or inn, etc. **landlubber,** *n. inf.* person who is not used to going on ships. **landmark,** *n.* (*a*) object on land which you can see easily, esp. one used by ships to find out their position. (*b*) outstanding/important event, etc. **landmine,** *n.* mine hidden in the ground. **landowner,** *n.* person who owns a country estate. **landrace,** *n.* native species. **landscape** ['lændskeɪp] **1.** *n.* (*a*) scenery/appearance of the countryside; **l. gardening** = making a garden more beautiful by making artificial lakes, hills, planting trees, etc. (*b*) painting of a country scene. **2.** *v.* to improve (a garden) by creating small hills/lakes, planting trees, etc. **landscape gardener,** *n.* person who designs the layout of large gardens/pieces of land. **landslide,** *n.* (*a*) slipping of large amounts of earth, etc., down a hillside. (*b*) overwhelming event, esp. an electoral victory in which one party is totally defeated. **landslip,** *n.* landslide. **landward,** *adj. & adv.* towards the land. **landwards,** *adv.* towards the land.

landau ['lændɔː] *n.* horse-drawn carriage with a folding top.

lane [leɪn] *n.* (*a*) narrow road, often in the country. (*b*) way/road for traffic, usu. in a particular direction; **shipping lanes** = routes followed by ships; **bus l.** = part of a road where only buses may drive.

language ['læŋgwɪdʒ] *n.* (*a*) way of speaking of a country/a group of people; **l. laboratory** = room with tape recorders where students can study foreign languages. (*b*) way of speaking; **bad l.** = swearing. (*c*) human speech. (*d*) means of communication, esp. signs, letters and other symbols used to instruct a computer.

languid ['læŋgwɪd] *adj.* slow-moving/lacking energy. **languidly,** *adv.* lazily. **languish** ['læŋgwɪʃ] *v.* to become weak/ill, often because of sorrow. **languor**

['læŋgə] *n.* (*a*) lack of energy. (*b*) tender emotional mood. **languorous,** *adj.* slow-moving/lazy.

lank [læŋk] *adj.* (*a*) (*of hair*) straight/dull/lifeless. (*b*) (*of person*) thin/drooping. **lankiness,** *n.* being lanky. **lanky,** *adj.* (**-ier, iest**) tall/thin/awkward (person).

lanolin ['lænəlɪn] *n.* fat from sheep's wool used in skin creams.

lantern ['læntən] *n.* lamp with a covering to protect it, which can be carried in the hand.

lanyard ['lænjəd] *n.* string worn around your neck or shoulder with a whistle, etc., on it.

lap [læp] **1.** *n.* (*a*) your body from waist to knees, when you are sitting; **in the l. of luxury** = in great luxury. (*b*) circuit/round (of a racecourse). (*c*) part of a long journey. **2.** *v.* (**lapped**) (*a*) (*of animal*) to drink with the tongue. (*b*) (**up**) to take in greedily. (*c*) (*of waves*) to wash against (the shore/the edge of sth). (*d*) to go so fast that you are a whole lap ahead of (another competitor). (*e*) to fold (sth) so that it overlaps. **lapdog,** *n.* small pet dog. **laptop,** *n.* small computer which can be held on the lap.

lapel [lə'pel] *n.* part of collar of coat, etc., which folds back.

lapidary ['læpɪdərɪ] *adj.* (*a*) referring to stones (esp. precious stones). (*b*) very short and precise (statement).

lapis lazuli [læpɪs'læzjʊlaɪ] *n.* bright blue stone.

lapse [læps] **1.** *n.* (*a*) failure to do sth properly. (*b*) interval of time, esp. when sth does not take place. **2.** *v.* (*a*) to fail/to cease to do sth. (*b*) to cease to be valid. (*c*) to fall **into** a lower/less active state.

lapwing ['læpwɪŋ] *n.* bird found in fields and moors.

larboard ['laːbəd] *n.* (*old*) port side (of ship).

larceny ['laːsnɪ] *n.* crime of stealing.

larch [laːtʃ] *n.* (*pl.* **-es**) cone-bearing tree which loses its leaves in winter.

lard [laːd] **1.** *n.* melted down pig fat used in cooking. **2.** *v.* to cover (meat) with bacon or lard; to fill (a speech) with quotations, etc.

lardy cake, *n.* type of bread, made with fat and covered with sticky sugar.

larder ['lɑːdə] n. room/cupboard for storing food.

large [lɑːdʒ] adj. (**-er, -est**) (a) (very) big. (b) **at l.** = (i) free/not imprisoned; (ii) in general. **largely,** adv. mostly/for the most part. **large-scale,** adj. in a large way/involving large numbers of people or large sums of money.

largesse [lɑːˈdʒes] n. generous gift of money.

largo ['lɑːgəʊ] adv. & n. (piece of music) which is played slowly.

lariat ['lærɪət] n. lasso.

lark [lɑːk] 1. n. (a) bird which sings and flies high in the sky. (b) inf. piece of fun/joke. 2. v. inf. **to l.** (**about**) = to fool around/play jokes. **larkspur,** n. plant with tall spikes of flowers.

larrikin ['lærɪkɪn] n. (in Australia) hooligan.

larrup ['lærəp] v. inf. to beat (s.o.) up.

larva ['lɑːvə] n. (pl. **-vae** [-viː]) early stage of development of an insect, different in form from the adult.

larynx ['lærɪŋks] n. (pl. **-es**) upper part of the windpipe, where sounds are made by the voice. **laryngitis** [lærɪnˈdʒaɪtɪs] n. inflammation of the larynx causing a sore throat.

lasagne [ləˈzænjə] n. type of pasta which is made of wide flat strips.

lascivious [ləˈsɪvɪəs] adj. full of sexual desire. **lasciviously,** adv. in a lascivious way. **lasciviousness,** n. being lascivious.

laser ['leɪzə] n. instrument which produces a highly concentrated beam of light.

lash [læʃ] 1. n. (pl. **-es**) (a) stroke with a whip. (b) flexible part of a whip. (c) eyelash. 2. v. (a) to beat (sth) with a whip. (b) to make a movement like beating with a whip. (c) to fasten/to tie down tightly with rope/string. **lashing,** n. (a) whipping. (b) tying/binding with rope, etc. **lashings,** n. pl. inf. plenty. **lash out,** v. (a) **to lash out at** = to become (unexpectedly) very angry at/to try to hit. (b) inf. **to lash out on** = to become (unexpectedly) very extravagant and spend a large sum of money.

lass [læs], **lassie** ['læsɪ] n. (pl. **-es**) (in N. England & Scotland) inf. girl; young woman.

Lassa fever ['læsəˈfiːvə] n. fatal viral disease which originated in Africa.

lassitude ['læsɪtjuːd] n. (formal) tiredness.

lasso [ləˈsuː] 1. n. (pl. **-os**) rope with looped end for catching horses/cattle, etc. 2. v. to catch (animals) with a lasso.

last [lɑːst] 1. adj. (a) placed/coming at the end (of a list/line/period of time); **l. thing at night** = at the very end of the day; **l. but one** = the one before the end one; **l. but not least** = at the end of a list, but not because it is the least important; **the l. straw** = final piece of trouble which makes everything seem unbearable; **the l. word in hats** = the very latest fashion; **the l. person I would want to go on holiday with** = the most unlikely person. (b) most recent; **l. Monday; l. week.** 2. n. (a) shape on which a shoe is made or repaired. (b) final thing/period/sight; **at (long) l.** = in the end/after a long time; **to the l.** = till the very end. 3. adv. (a) at the end. (b) most recently. 4. v. to continue (to exist); to remain in good condition. **lasting,** adj. which continues for a long time. **lastly,** adv. at the end/finally. **Last Post,** n. trumpet call sounded at a military funeral. **Last Supper,** n. last meal take by Christ with his disciples.

latch [lætʃ] 1. n. (pl. **-es**) fastening for a door, etc., consisting of a small bar which fits into a catch; **the door is on the l.** = is held shut by a latch but is not locked. 2. v. (a) to close with a latch. (b) inf. **to l. on to sth** = to seize/to take up. **latchkey,** n. key for a front door; **l. child** = child who has a key to the house and lets himself in when he comes home from school because both parents are at work.

late [leɪt] 1. adj. (**-er, -est**) (a) at a time after that decided/intended; **the train is ten minutes l.** (b) at/towards the end of a period of time. (c) at/towards/past the end of a season. (d) **latest** = last/most recent. (e) (formal) referring to s.o. who has died; **my l. father.** 2. adv. (**-er, -est**) (a) after the appointed time. (b) after a certain time. **latecomer,** n. person who arrives after others/after the appointed time. **lately,** adv. during recent days/weeks. **lateness,** n. being late.

latent ['leɪtənt] adj. present but not developed.

lateral ['lætərəl] adj. referring to the side; (fin) on the side of a fish's body; **l. thinking** = solving problems by unusual means. **laterally**, adv. towards the side.

laterite ['lætəraɪt] n. hard clay, like rock.

latex ['leɪteks] n. milky juice from a rubber tree.

lath [lɑːθ] n. narrow thin strip of wood.

lathe [leɪð] n. machine for holding and turning wood/metal, so that it can be shaped.

lather ['lɑːðə] **1.** n. (a) mass of (soap) bubbles. (b) (esp. on horse) frothy sweat; **to get in a l.** = to get upset/flustered. **2.** v. (a) to make (sth) form a lather; to form a lather. (b) to cover with lather.

Latin ['lætɪn] **1.** n. (a) language formerly spoken by the Romans. (b) person from Italy, Spain, Portugal or South America. **2.** adj. (a) referring to the language of ancient Rome. (b) referring to Italy, Spain, Portugal and South America; **L. America** = countries in South and Central America where Spanish or Portuguese is spoken.

latitude ['lætɪtjuːd] n. (a) breadth of view/tolerance/scope. (b) position on the earth's surface measured in degrees north or south of the equator; **northern latitudes** = in areas north of the equator.

latrine [lə'triːn] n. lavatory in a military camp or prison.

latter ['lætə] **1.** adj. (a) second thing mentioned (of two). (b) recent; of the final part/period. **latterly**, adv. recently.

lattice ['lætɪs] n. pattern (of pieces of wood in a fence, etc.) made of crisscross diagonal lines; **l. window** = window with small panes and lead frames forming a crisscross pattern.

laud [lɔːd] v. (formal) to praise. **laudable**, adj. worthy of praise. **laudably**, adv. in a laudable way. **laudatory**, adj. which praises.

laudanum ['lɔːdnəm] n. opium in alcohol, used as a sedative.

laugh [lɑːf] **1.** n. sound made to express amusement/happiness; **to do sth for a l.** = to do it for amusement only/as a joke. **2.** v. (a) to make sounds which express amusement/happiness; **to l. up one's sleeve** = to laugh secretly. (b) **to l. at** = to make fun of. **laughable**, adj. only worth laughing at; ridiculous. **laughing gas**, n. gas which makes you laugh when you breathe it, used esp. by dentists as an anaesthetic. **laughing stock**, n. person whom everyone makes fun of. **laughter**, n. (sound/act of) laughing.

launch [lɔːntʃ] **1.** n. (pl. **-es**) (a) type of small motor boat. (b) act of launching (boat/rocket/new project, etc.). **2.** v. (a) to put a (boat/ship) into the water, esp. for the first time. (b) to send off (a rocket into the air). (c) to give (sth/s.o.) a start. **launching pad**, n. starting platform for a rocket, etc. **launch out**, v. to start doing sth expensive or ambitious.

laundry ['lɔːndrɪ] n. (a) place where clothes/sheets, etc., are washed. (b) clothes/sheets, etc. for washing, or which have been washed. **launder**, v. (a) to wash clothes. (b) inf. to pass (illegal profits, etc.) into the conventional banking system. **laund(e)rette**, Am. **laundromat** ['lɔːndret, 'lɔːndrəmæt] n. trademark for a shop with coin-operated washing machines for public use. **laundress**, n. woman who washes laundry.

laureate ['lɔːrɪət] n. person who has been awarded a prize; **Poet L.** = leading poet who is asked to write commemorative verse for special occasions.

laurel ['lɒrəl] n. tree with smooth shiny evergreen leaves; **to rest on your laurels** = to enjoy your past success, without trying to gain more.

lav [læv] n. inf. lavatory.

lava ['lɑːvə] n. molten material flowing from a volcano which becomes solid when it cools.

lavatory ['lævətrɪ] n. (a) small room for getting rid of waste matter from the body, usu. with a flushing bowl. (b) bowl with a seat and a flushing system, for getting rid of waste matter from the body.

lavender ['lævɪndə] n. (a) plant with sweet-smelling bluish-purple flowers. (b) bluish-purple colour.

lavish ['lævɪʃ] **1.** *adj.* (*a*) generous/ample (helping of food, etc.). (*b*) extravagant/ over-generous. **2.** *v.* (**on** s.o.) to give (over-)generously. **lavishly,** *adv.* in a lavish way. **lavishness,** *n.* being lavish.

law [lɔː] *n.* (*a*) rules by which a country is governed and the people controlled. (*b*) rule/controlling force; **to lay down the l.** = to state sth in a dogmatic way; **to be a l. unto yourself** = to do exactly what you want, regardless of rules or of anyone else. (*c*) process of upholding the rules of a country. **law-abiding,** *adj.* obeying the law. **law centre,** *n.* local office whose staff offer legal advice free of charge. **lawcourt,** *n.* court where a judge/magistrate hears cases. **lawful,** *adj.* according to law/ legal. **lawfully,** *adv.* in a lawful way. **lawless,** *adj.* wild/uncivilized; paying no attention to law. **lawlessness,** *n.* being lawless. **lawsuit,** *n.* legal case. **lawyer,** *n.* person who has studied law and can advise people on legal matters.

lawn [lɔːn] *n.* (*a*) (area of) short grass in a garden; **l. tennis** = tennis played on grass. (*b*) very fine cotton material. **lawnmower,** *n.* machine for cutting grass.

lax [læks] *adj.* (**-er, -est**) loose/not rigid. **laxative,** *adj. & n.* (substance) which helps to open the bowels. **laxity, laxness,** *n.* being loose/not being rigid.

lay [leɪ] **1.** *adj.* (*a*) (person) who is not trained as a priest. (*b*) not belonging to a profession or specialization. **2.** *n.* (*old*) short narrative poem. **3.** *v.* (**laid**) (*a*) to place/to put, often in a horizontal position. (*b*) to place in the right position; **to l. a carpet.** (*c*) to cause (dust) to settle/to subside. (*d*) (*of bird*) to produce (an egg). (*e*) to make (a bet). (*f*) to set/to place dishes, etc. on (a table); **l. the table for three.** (*g*) to set (a trap/a scene). (*h*) *see also* **lie. layabout,** *n. inf.* person who does no work and wanders about idly. **lay aside, lay by,** *v.* to put (sth) away for future use. **layby,** *n.* place at the side of a road where vehicles can park. **lay down,** *v.* (*a*) to put (sth) down/to give (sth) up. (*b*) to state clearly in writing. **layer. 1.** *n.* (*a*) (horizontal) thickness of sth. (*b*) **good l.** = hen which produces many

eggs. (*c*) shoot which is layered. **2.** *v.* to make a new plant by attaching a shoot to the ground so that it takes root. **lay figure,** *n.* large doll used by artists as a model. **lay in,** *v.* to make a store/ to store up. **lay into,** *v. inf.* to attack/ to hit (s.o.). **layman,** *n.* (*pl.* **-men**) person who does not belong to a particular profession or specialization. **lay off,** *v.* (*a*) to dismiss (workers) temporarily. (*b*) *inf.* to stop doing sth. **lay-off,** *n.* temporary dismissal from work. **lay on,** *v.* to put on/in; to provide. **lay out,** *v.* (*a*) to place in an orderly way, esp. on a table, etc. (*b*) to make a design for (a garden/a book, etc.). (*c*) to spend (money). (*d*) to prepare (a corpse) for burial. **layout,** *n.* design, esp. of a garden/a book. **lay up,** *v.* (*a*) to store (away). (*b*) **to be laid up** = to be ill in bed.

layette [leɪ'et] *n.* clothes for a new-born baby.

lazy ['leɪzɪ] *adj.* (**-ier, -iest**) not wanting to do any work. **laze,** *v.* to do nothing or very little. **lazily,** *adv.* in a lazy way. **laziness,** *n.* being lazy. **lazybones,** *n. inf.* person who does not like work/who does nothing.

lb [paʊnd] *abbrev. for* pound (in weight).

LCD *abbrev. for* liquid crystal display.

lea [liː] *n.* (*in poetry*) meadow.

leach [liːtʃ] *v.* to remove a substance from soil, etc., by passing water through it.

lead¹ [led] *n.* (*a*) (*element:* Pb) heavy soft bluish-grey metal. (*b*) weight at the end of a rope, used for measuring the depth of water, *inf.* **to swing the l.** = to avoid doing any work. (*c*) writing part of a pencil. **leaden** ['ledn] *adj.* of/like lead; **l. sky** = dull grey sky.

lead² [liːd] **1.** *n.* (*a*) front position/first action; **to go into the l./to take the l.** (*b*) (*in cards*) right to play first. (*c*) strap to keep a dog in control. (*d*) electric wire, etc., which joins an appliance to its source of power. (*e*) (actor who plays a) main role. (*f*) amount by which one is ahead. **2.** *v.* (**led** [led]) (*a*) to go/to be ahead; to show the way; to go towards. (*b*) to be the first/to have the most important place. (*c*) to make (sth) have; to have; **it led me to think**

she **was lying** = made me think. (d) to be at the head of/to direct. (e) (in cards) to play as first card; to play first. (f) to go in a particular direction. **leader** ['li:də] n. (a) person who manages/directs others. (b) main article in a newspaper which expresses the editor's opinion. (c) chief player, esp. of the violin, in an orchestra. (d) main barrister in a group of lawyers. **Leader of the House,** n. minister who is responsible for the administration of legislation in the House of Commons. **Leader of the Opposition,** n. head of the main party which opposes a government. **leadership,** n. being the person who manages/directs others. **leading,** adj. which leads; most important; **l. article** = main article in a newspaper, giving views on topics of current interest; **l. aircraftman/seaman** = junior rank in the air force/in the navy; **l. lady/man** = actress/actor taking the main role; **l. question** = question which is worded in order to get a particular answer. **lead on,** v. to go ahead, so that others will follow; to encourage (s.o.) to go on, esp. to do sth stupid. **lead time,** n. time between placing an order and receiving the goods. **lead up to,** v. to prepare the way for sth (in conversation).

leaf [li:f] **1.** n. (pl. **leaves** [li:vz]) (a) flat, usu. green, part of a plant, growing from a stem or branch; **trees in l.** = with leaves. (b) sheet of paper forming two pages of a book; **to turn over a new l.** = to change your ways/to try to improve; **to take a l. out of s.o.'s book** = to follow s.o.'s example. (c) flat folding part (of a table). (d) very thin sheet of metal, etc. **2.** v. **to l. through the pages of a book** = to turn them over rapidly without reading. **leaflet,** n. sheet of paper, often folded, giving information as an advertisement. **leaf mould,** n. compost made of rotted leaves. **leafy,** adj. covered with leaves.

league [li:g] **1.** n. (a) group joined together for some purpose; **in l. with s.o.** = working with s.o. against s.o. else. (b) association of sports clubs which play against each other. (c) (old) measure of distance (about 5 km). **2.** v.

to join together/to form a group for a particular purpose.

leak [li:k] **1.** n. (a) hole through which liquid/gas, etc., can escape or enter; **the ship sprang a l.** = got a hole. (b) escape of secret information. **2.** v. (a) (of liquid/gas, etc.) to flow away/to escape. (b) (of container) to allow liquid/gas, etc., to escape or enter. (c) to pass on (secret information). **leakage,** n. (a) action of leaking. (b) amount of liquid, etc., which has escaped. **leaky,** adj. which leaks.

lean [li:n] **1.** adj. (-er, -est) (a) thin/with little flesh. (b) (of meat) with little fat. (c) poor/unproductive. **2.** n. meat with little fat. **3.** v. (**leaned/lent** [lent]) (a) to support (yourself/sth) (on sth/s.o.). (b) to stand/to be in a position at an angle. (c) to have a tendency **towards. leaning,** n. tendency **towards**/interest in. **leanness,** n. being thin. **lean over,** v. to bend (in a particular direction); **to lean over backwards to help** = make every effort to help. **lean-to,** n. (small) building supported against the wall of a larger building.

leap [li:p] **1.** n. (a) jump. (b) upward/forward movement; **to advance by leaps and bounds** = to make rapid progress; **l. in the dark** = action where you are unsure of the consequences. **2.** v. (**leaped/leapt** [lept]) (a) to jump. (b) to rise suddenly. **leap at,** v. to seize/to accept eagerly. **leapfrog. 1.** n. game in which one person jumps over the bent back of another. **2.** v. (**leapfrogged**) to jump over s.o.'s bent back. **leap year,** n. every fourth year, in which February has 29 days.

learn [lə:n] v. (**learned/learnt** [lə:nd, lə:nt]) (a) to gain knowledge of (sth)/of how to do (sth). (b) to hear (news, etc.). **learned** ['lə:nɪd] adj. (a) (person) who has much knowledge. (b) (journal) for specialists. **learner,** n. person who is learning. **learning,** n. (a) gaining knowledge of sth/of how to do sth. (b) great study/knowledge.

lease [li:s] **1.** n. letting/renting of a building/piece of land, etc., for a specified period; **it's given him a new l. of life** = it's made him want to make a fresh start/to live more fully. **2.** v. (a) (also

lease out) to take/to give on a lease. (*b*) to hold on a lease. **leasehold. 1.** *n.* (holding of) property on a lease. **2.** *adj.* held on a lease. **leaseholder,** *n.* person who holds a property on a lease.

leash [liːʃ] *n.* (*pl.* **-es**) strap/cord to keep a dog in control.

least [liːst] **1.** *adj.* & *n.* (of) the smallest/most unimportant (amount). **2.** *adv.* in the smallest way.

leather [ˈleðə] *n.* skin of certain animals, used to make shoes/bags, etc. **leather-jacket,** *n.* grub of a fly. **leathery,** *adj.* (tough) like leather.

leave [liːv] **1.** *n.* (*a*) permission. (*b*) time off; permission to be away. (*c*) **to take l. of** = to say goodbye to; **to take l. of one's senses** = to become quite mad. **2.** *v.* (**left** [left]) (*a*) to go away (from). (*b*) to allow to remain behind/to forget to take; **l. me alone** = don't pester me; **l. it to me** = let me deal with it. (*c*) to abandon. (*d*) to give (sth) to s.o. in your will. (*e*) to have at the time of one's death. **leave behind,** *v.* to forget to take (s.o./sth) with you. **leave off,** *v.* to stop. **leave out,** *v.* to forget/to omit (sth).

leaven [ˈlevn] **1.** *n.* substance which causes a dough to rise; thing which causes a change for the better. **2.** *v.* to add leaven to (dough); to cause a change.

Lebanese [lebəˈniːz] **1.** *adj.* referring to the Lebanon. **2.** *n.* (*pl.* **Lebanese**) person from the Lebanon.

lecher [ˈletʃə] *n.* man who frequently indulges in sex. **lecherous,** *adj.* indulging in sex. **lechery,** *n.* indulgence in sex.

lectern [ˈlektən] *n.* stand with a sloping surface on which you can put a book/papers, etc., from which you are going to read aloud in public.

lecture [ˈlektʃə] **1.** *n.* (*a*) talk, esp. to students or other group of people on a particular subject. (*b*) (long) scolding. **2.** *v.* to give a lecture (**on** sth). **lecturer,** *n.* (*a*) person who gives a talk on a particular subject. (*b*) teacher in a university or college. **lectureship,** *n.* position as lecturer.

led [led] *v. see* **lead**².

ledge [ledʒ] *n.* flat (narrow) part which sticks out from a cliff or building.

ledger [ˈledʒə] *n.* book in which accounts are kept. **ledger line,** *n.* leger line.

lee [liː] *n.* side of a ship sheltered from the wind; **l. shore** = shore towards which the wind is blowing. **leeward,** *adj.,* *adv.* & *n.* (side of a ship) sheltered from the wind. **leeway,** *n.* (*a*) time which has been lost; **to make up l.** = to make up for lost time/opportunity. (*b*) extra time/extra space.

leech [liːtʃ] *n.* (*pl.* **-es**) (*a*) type of worm which sucks blood. (*b*) (*old inf.*) doctor.

leek [liːk] *n.* vegetable related to the onion, with white stem and long green leaves.

leer [ˈlɪə] **1.** *n.* nasty sideways look, often expressing sexual desire. **2.** *v.* to look with a leer (**at** s.o.).

lees [liːz] *n. pl.* sediment left at the bottom of a wine bottle, etc.

left [left] **1.** *n.* (*a*) side of the body which normally has the weaker hand. (*b*) left hand/fist. (*c*) (*in politics*) group/policy supporting the rights of the workers. **2.** *adj.* (*a*) of/on the side of the body which normally has the weaker hand; **l. bank** = bank of a river, etc., on your left when facing down stream. (*b*) of the left (in politics). **3.** *adv.* on/to the left. **4.** *see also* **leave. left-handed,** *adj.* using the left hand more than the right. **leftist,** *adj.* & *n.* (person) who is on the left of the socialist party. **left-luggage office,** *n.* place where suitcases, etc., can be left and collected later for a fee. **leftovers,** *n. pl.* what is not used, esp. food which has not been eaten. **left-wing,** *adj.* politically on the left. **left-winger,** *n.* person who is on the left politically.

leg [leg] **1.** *n.* (*a*) part of the body on which a person or animal walks; **to be on one's last legs** = to be almost exhausted; **to give s.o. a l. up** = to help him to climb to a higher position; **to pull s.o.'s l.** = to joke by telling him sth untrue. (*b*) leg of an animal used for food. (*c*) part of a garment which covers the leg. (*d*) part of a piece of furniture which supports. (*e*) section of a race/journey. **2.** *v. inf.* **to l. it** = to walk. **legged** [legd, ˈlegɪd] *suffix meaning* with legs; **four-legged animal. leggings,** *n. pl.* thick coverings for the lower legs. **leggy,** *adj.* with long legs. **legless,** *adj.* (*a*) without any legs. (*b*) *Sl.* drunk. **leg-pull,** *n. inf.* hoax. **leg warmers,** *n. pl.* knitted garments for the legs, like long socks with no feet.

legacy ['legəsɪ] *n.* what is left to a person (after s.o.'s death). **legatee** [legə'ti:] *n.* person who receives a legacy.

legal ['li:gl] *adj.* (*a*) in accordance with/ obeying the law; **l. aid** = free legal representation given to people without enough money to pay lawyers' fees; **l. tender** = money which must legally be accepted if you give it in payment. (*b*) referring to the (processes of the) law. **legalistic** [li:gə'lɪstɪk] *adj.* too concerned with the law. **legality** [lɪ'gælɪtɪ] *n.* being allowed by law. **legalize,** *v.* to authorize (sth) by law. **legally,** *adv.* in accordance with the law.

legate ['legət] *n.* official envoy (from the Pope). **legation** [lɪ'geɪʃn] *n.* group of officials who represent their government in a foreign country; building where they live and work.

legend ['ledʒənd] *n.* (*a*) story from the past which may not be based on fact. (*b*) key to symbols used on a map. **legendary,** *adj.* referring to a legend.

legerdemain [ledʒədə'meɪn] *n.* trickery; conjuring.

leger line ['ledʒə'laɪn] *n.* small line on a musical score, written above or below the normal five lines.

legible ['ledʒɪbl] *adj.* clear/able to be (easily) read. **legibility** [ledʒɪ'bɪlɪtɪ] *n.* being easily read. **legibly,** *adv.* in a legible way.

legion ['li:dʒən] *n.* (*a*) division of an army. (*b*) association/body, esp. of soldiers; **the Foreign L.** = private army, organized by France, which serves overseas. (*c*) very large number. **legionnaire,** *n.* member of a legion, such as the Foreign Legion; **legionnaires' disease** = disease, similar to pneumonia, caused by bacteria in air-conditioning systems.

legislate ['ledʒɪsleɪt] *v.* to make laws. **legislation** [ledʒɪ'sleɪʃn] *n.* (making of) laws. **legislative** ['ledʒɪslətɪv] *adj.* referring to laws/law-making. **legislator,** *n.* person who makes laws. **legislature** ['ledʒɪslətʃə] *n.* law-making body.

legitimacy [lɪ'dʒɪtɪməsɪ] *n.* being in accordance with the law. **legitimate,** *adj.* (*a*) legal/lawful; (child) born to married parents. (*b*) reasonable/ justifiable. **legitimately,** *adv.* in accordance with the law; correctly. **legitimize,** *v.* to make legitimate.

legume ['legju:m] *n.* plant (like a pea or bean) which has seeds in pods. **leguminous** [le'gju:mɪnəs] *adj.* (plant) which has seeds in pods.

leisure ['leʒə] *n.* time free to do what you want; **at your l.** = when there is an opportunity/without hurry; **l. pursuits** = pastimes. **leisured,** *adj.* having plenty of leisure; **l. classes** = people who do not need to work to earn money. **leisurely,** *adj.* without hurry.

leitmotiv ['laɪtməʊti:f] *n.* theme (in music) which reappears and which shows a special feeling/state.

lemming ['lemɪŋ] *n.* small Scandinavian mammal which travels in groups and is said to fall blindly over cliffs into the sea.

lemon ['lemən] *n.* pale yellow sour-tasting fruit; tree which bears such fruit; **l. curd** = cream made with eggs and lemons, used to spread on bread. **lemonade** [lemə'neɪd] *n.* usu. fizzy lemon-flavoured drink.

lemur ['li:mə] *n.* monkey-like animal with a long tail.

lend [lend] *v.* (**lent**) (*a*) to give (sth to s.o.) for a certain period of time; **will you l. me your book for a day or two?** (*b*) to give/to contribute (to); **to l. a hand** = to help; **to lend itself to** = to be suitable for. **lender,** *n.* person who lends (money). **lending library,** *n.* section of a library from which books may be taken away for a time.

length [leŋθ] *n.* (*a*) measurement of how long sth is from end to end; **he won the race by a l.** = by the length of a horse/ man/boat, etc.; **throughout the l. and breadth of the country** = all over the country. (*b*) piece of sth of a particular length; **a l. of rope.** (*c*) being long; **a stay of some l.** = quite a long stay; **at l.** = (i) at last; (ii) for a long time. (*d*) **to go to great lengths** = to make great efforts. **lengthen,** *v.* to make/to become longer. **lengthily,** *adv.* for a long time/at length. **lengthiness,** n. being long. **lengthways, lengthwise,** adv. along the length/along the longest side. **lengthy,** adj. (-ier, -iest) (very) long.

lenience, leniency ['li:njəns(ɪ)] n. being merciful/not being strict. **lenient,** adj. showing mercy/not strict or severe. **leniently,** adv. in a lenient way.

lens [lenz] n. (pl. -es) (a) piece of glass/plastic, etc., curved so as to cause light rays to join or spread out, and used in spectacles/telescopes/cameras, etc. (b) part of the eye. (c) **contact l.** = small lens worn on the eyeball to help you to see.

lent [lent] v. see **lend.**

Lent [lent] n. (in the Christian church) period before Easter when many Christians eat less/give up some luxury. **Lenten,** adj. referring to Lent.

lentil ['lentl] n. small round dried seed used as food.

Leo ['li:əʊ] n. one of the signs of the Zodiac, shaped like a lion. **leonine** ['li:əʊnaɪn] adj. referring to a lion.

leopard ['lepəd] n. large spotted animal of the cat family. **leopardess,** n. female leopard.

leotard ['lɪəʊtɑ:d] n. skintight one-piece costume worn by ballet dancers.

leper ['lepə] n. person who has leprosy. **leprosy,** n. serious infectious skin disease which slowly destroys flesh and nerves. **leprous,** adj. like leprosy.

lepidoptera [lepɪ'dɒptərə] n. pl. group of insects, including butterflies and moths.

leprechaun ['leprəkɔ:n] n. (in Ireland) wicked little elf.

lesbian ['lezbɪən] adj. & n. (woman) who is sexually attracted to other women. **lesbianism,** n. state of being lesbian.

lesion ['li:ʒn] n. wound; change in body tissue.

less [les] 1. adj. & n. (of a) smaller quantity/size/value. 2. prep. minus/with a certain amount taken away. 3. adv. in a smaller amount/to a smaller degree. **lessen,** v. to make (sth) become less; to reduce. **lesser,** adj. smaller.

lessee [le'si:] n. person who holds a lease/who pays rent. **lessor** [le'sɔ:] n. person who gives a lease/who receives rent.

lesson ['lesn] n. (a) period of time in school, etc., during which you are taught. (b) means by which you learn; **he's learnt his l.** = he is wiser; **to teach s.o. a l.** = to make s.o. wiser/to punish s.o. (c) part of the Bible which is read in church.

lest [lest] conj. (a) (formal) in order to avoid. (b) for fear that.

let [let] 1. v. (**let**) (a) to permit/to allow. (b) to lend (a house, etc.) for a period of time in return for money. 2. v. (showing command/suggestion) **let's hurry; don't let's start yet.** 3. n. inf. period of lease of a property. **let alone,** adv. even less. **let down,** v. (a) to take down/to lower. (b) to fail to help/to disappoint. **letdown,** n. disappointment. **let go,** v. (a) to lose hold (of sth). (b) to allow (s.o.) to leave. **let in,** v. (a) to allow to come in. (b) **to let yourself in for** = to allow yourself to get involved in (a difficult situation). **let off,** v. (a) to make (a gun, etc.) fire. (b) **to let s.o. off** = not to punish s.o. after all. **let on,** v. inf. to tell a secret. **let out,** v. (a) to allow to go out/to escape. (b) to lend for a period of time in return for money. (c) to make (a garment, etc.) wider. **letout,** n. way of avoiding doing sth which you ought to do. **let up,** v. to stop/to become less. **let-up,** n. stopping/slackening.

lethal ['li:θl] adj. deadly/causing death.

lethargy ['leθədʒɪ] n. (feeling of) unwillingness to do anything; lack of energy. **lethargic** [lə'θɑ:dʒɪk] adj. feeling/appearing unwilling to do anything; lacking energy.

let's [lets] short for **let us.**

letter ['letə] 1. n. (a) written/printed symbol representing a sound of speech; **to the l.** = to the last detail. (b) piece of writing sent from one person/organization to another to pass on information. (c) **letters** = literary learning. 2. v. to mark with letters. **letterbox,** n. box where letters are posted; hole in a door through which letters are delivered. **letterhead,** n. printed heading on writing paper. **lettering,** n. (a) writing letters. (b) letters in an inscription, etc. **letterpress,** n. method of printing using metal letters.

lettuce ['letɪs] *n.* green vegetable whose leaves are often used in salads.

leucocyte ['lju:kəsaɪt] *n.* white blood cell.

leukaemia, *Am.* **leukemia** [lu:'ki:mɪə] *n.* serious, often fatal, illness, which increases the white cells in the blood.

levee ['levɪ] *n. Am.* embankment built along the bank of a river which is liable to flood.

level ['levl] **1.** *n.* (*a*) flat/horizontal position; **on the l.** = (i) in a flat position; (ii) *inf.* straight/honest. (*b*) position in relation to height and depth; position on a scale/in a list. (*c*) instrument for testing whether sth is horizontal or not. **2.** *adj.* (*a*) flat/even/horizontal. (*b*) (**with**) at the same level as. (*c*) calm/even; *inf.* **to do one's l. best** = one's very best. **3.** *v.* (**levelled**) (*a*) to make/to become level; **they levelled the house to the ground** = they destroyed it completely. (*b*) to point/to aim (an accusation) at s.o. **level crossing,** *n.* place where a road crosses a railway line without a bridge or tunnel. **level-headed,** *adj.* calm/able to act sensibly. **leveller,** *n.* person who believes everyone should be equal in status. **level with,** *v. inf.* to speak frankly.

lever ['li:və] **1.** *n.* instrument such as a bar which helps to raise a heavy object, or to move part of a machine, etc.; **gear l.** = handle in a car which changes the gears. **2.** *v.* to move with a lever. **leverage,** *n.* (*a*) force of a lever. (*b*) influence which you can use to reach your aims. **leveraged buyout,** *n.* buying a company, using the company's assets as security for the money borrowed to buy it.

leveret ['levrət] *n.* young hare.

leviathan [lɪ'vaɪəθən] *n.* huge powerful monster or machine.

levitate ['levɪteɪt] *v.* (*of person/heavy body*) to rise into the air. **levitation** [levɪ'teɪʃn] *n.* rising into the air.

levity ['levɪtɪ] *n.* disrespectful way of considering serious things.

levy ['levɪ] **1.** *n.* (*a*) demand for/collection of (a tax/a number of soldiers). (*b*) tax/number of soldiers (which has been collected). **2.** *v.* to demand/to collect (a tax/a number of soldiers).

lewd [lu:d] *adj.* (**-er, -est**) indecent/rude. **lewdly,** *adv.* in a lewd way. **lewdness,** *n.* lewd action.

lexicon ['leksɪkən] *n.* dictionary. **lexicography** [leksɪ'kɒgrəfɪ] *n.* writing of dictionaries. **lexicographer,** *n.* person who writes dictionaries.

ley [leɪ] *n.* field which is used for pasture.

liable ['laɪəbl] *adj.* (*a*) (legally) responsible (**for** sth). (*b*) (**for**) obliged/bound to do. (*c*) apt/likely (**to** do sth). **liability** [laɪə'bɪlɪtɪ] *n.* (*a*) (legal) responsibility. (*b*) obligation; **he couldn't meet his liabilities** = he couldn't pay his debts. (*c*) tendency to do sth. (*d*) *inf.* **he's a l.** = he causes problems.

liaison [lɪ'eɪzən] *n.* joining/relationship/connection; **l. officer** = person responsible for dealings with another group. **liaise,** *v.* to join with others, esp. for discussion (**with s.o.**).

liar ['laɪə] *n.* person who tells lies.

lib [lɪb] *n. inf.* short for **liberation.**

libation [laɪ'beɪʃn] *n.* (*formal*) drink offered to a god.

libel ['laɪbl] **1.** *n.* untrue statement(s) in writing, damaging to s.o.'s character. **2.** *v.* (**libelled**) to damage s.o.'s character in writing. **libellous,** *adj.* (writing) which libels s.o.

liberal ['lɪbrəl] **1.** *adj.* (*a*) wide in views/meaning, etc. (*b*) ample/generous. (*c*) (*in politics*) **Liberal** = having views/policies based on freedom of individuals, democratic reform, etc. **2.** *n.* (*in politics*) **Liberal** = member or supporter of a Liberal party or policy. **liberalism,** *n.* (*in politics*) liberal views/policies. **liberality** [lɪbə'rælɪtɪ] *n.* (*a*) being open-minded. (*b*) generosity. **liberalization** [lɪbərəlaɪ'zeɪʃn] *n.* act of liberalizing. **liberalize** ['lɪbərəlaɪz] *v.* to make (laws, etc.) more liberal; to become more liberal. **liberally,** *adv.* in a liberal way.

liberate ['lɪbəreɪt] *v.* to set/to make (s.o./sth) free (**from** sth). **liberation** [lɪbə'reɪʃn] *n.* setting free. **liberator,** *n.* person who sets s.o. free. **libertarian** [lɪbə'teərɪən] *n.* person who believes in freedom of thought and action. **libertine** ['lɪbəti:n] *n.* man who is sexually immoral. **liberty** ['lɪbətɪ] *n.* freedom; **at l.** = free/not in captivity;

to take liberties = to do sth without permission; **to take liberties with sth/s.o.** = to treat sth./s.o. too familiarly.

libido [lɪ'biːdəʊ] n. (pl. -os) sexual urge. **libidinous,** adj. full of sexual urge.

Libra ['liːbrə] n. one of the signs of the zodiac, shaped like a pair of scales.

library ['laɪbrərɪ] n. (a) place where books are stored (to be read/borrowed/ consulted). (b) collection of books; **record l.** = collection of records available for borrowing. **librarian** [laɪ'breərɪən] n. person who works in a library. **librarianship,** n. art of being a librarian.

libretto [lɪ'bretəʊ] n. (pl. -os) words of an opera. **librettist,** n. person who writes a libretto.

Libyan ['lɪbjən] 1. adj. referring to Libya. 2. n. person from Libya.

lice [laɪs] n. pl. see **louse.**

licence, Am. **license** ['laɪsəns] n. (a) (document giving) official permission to have/to do sth. (b) freedom, esp. when used too much or wrongly. (c) **poetic l.** = use of language in poetry which would not be acceptable in prose. **license** ['laɪsəns] 1. n. Am. see **licence.** 2. v. to give (s.o.) official permission to do sth; **licensed grocer** = one allowed by law to sell alcoholic drink. **licensee** [laɪsən'siː] n. holder of a licence, esp. landlord of a public house. **licentiate** [laɪ'senʃɪət] n. person who has been licensed to practise a profession. **licentious** [laɪ'senʃəs] adj. indulging in sex or other pleasures beyond what is normally permitted. **licentiousness,** n. excessive indulgence in sex.

lichen ['laɪkən] n. flat grey/yellow/green plant which grows on stones or on other plants.

licit ['lɪsɪt] adj. legal.

lick [lɪk] 1. n. (a) stroke with the tongue. (b) thin coating (of paint). (c) inf. speed. (d) inf. **a l. and a promise** = a quick wash. 2. v. (a) to taste/to stroke with the tongue; **to l. s.o.'s boots** = to behave very humbly towards him to gain favour; **to l. into shape** = to train (s.o.) into proper ways. (b) to beat/ to hit. (c) inf. to defeat (in a game). **licking,** n. (a) stroking with the tongue. (b) beating. (c) inf. defeat.

licorice ['lɪkərɪs] n. Am. see **liquorice.**

lid [lɪd] n. (a) covering for a container, often with a handle; inf. **that's put the l. on it** = that's made it impossible. (b) eyelid/covering of the eye.

lido ['liːdəʊ] n. (pl. -os) swimming pool and terraces round it.

lie [laɪ] 1. n. (a) statement which is not true; **to give the l. to** = to prove (sth) is wrong. (b) position/direction in which sth is situated; **the l. of the land** = state of affairs. 2. v. (a) (lied, lying) to say something which is not true. (b) (lay, lying, has lain) to be in a horizontal position; **he lay dead on the ground.** (c) to be; **see how the land lies** = see what the condition/position of sth is. **lie down,** v. to put yourself in a horizontal position (on sth); **they won't take that lying down** = they won't accept it without protest. **lie-down,** n. inf. short rest. **lie in,** v. to stay in bed longer than usual. **lie-in,** n. inf. **to have a lie-in** = to stay in bed longer than usual. **lie low,** v. to hide.

lieder ['liːdə] n. German romantic song.

liege [liːdʒ] n. (old) lord (to whom people give service).

lien ['lɪən] n. legal right to take and hold s.o.'s goods until a debt is paid.

lieu [ljuː] n. **in l. of** = instead of.

lieutenant [lef'tenənt, Am. luː'tenənt] n. (a) rank in the armed forces (in the army below captain, in the navy below lieutenant-commander); **l.-colonel** = rank in the army below colonel; **l.-commander** = rank in the navy below commander; **flight l.** = rank in the air force below squadron leader. (b) main helper; henchman.

life [laɪf] n. (pl. lives [laɪvz]) (a) state of being alive; **run for your lives** = as fast as you can; **I can't for the l. of me understand** = I can't understand at all; **not on your l.** = not under any circumstances. (b) liveliness/energy. (c) living things; **is there l. on Mars?** (d) (length of) time you are alive; **in early l.** = when he was a child; **l. insurance** = insurance paid if you die; **l. imprisonment** = imprisonment for the rest of your life. (e) story of s.o.'s life. **lifebelt,** n. cork-filled ring to keep s.o. afloat. **lifeboat,** n. boat used to rescue people at sea. **life cycle,** n. life of an animal/

plant through various stages. **lifeguard,** *n.* person who rescues people who get into difficulties while swimming. **life jacket,** *n.* cork-filled coat to keep s.o. afloat. **lifeless,** *adj.* (*a*) not alive. (*b*) not lively. **lifelike,** *adj.* (*of a picture, etc.*) looking like the real person/thing. **lifeline,** *n.* rope thrown to a drowning person; help given to s.o. in difficulties. **lifelong,** *adj.* lasting your whole life. **life preserver,** *n.* (*a*) short stick, used in self-defence. (*b*) *Am.* lifebelt/life jacket. **lifer,** *n.* person who is serving a sentence of life imprisonment. **life-saving,** *n.* rescuing people from drowning. **life-size(d),** *adj.* (statue/painting, etc.) which is the same size as the real thing or person. **life style,** *n.* way in which s.o. or a group of people live their daily lives. **lifetime,** *n.* time when you are alive; **the chance of a l.** = the best chance you are ever likely to get.

lift [lɪft] **1.** *n.* (*a*) (act of) raising. (*b*) ride in a car. (*c*) mechanical device for carrying people or goods from one floor of a building to another; **ski l.** = device to take skiers to the top of a ski slope. **2.** *v.* (*a*) to raise (to a higher position). (*b*) to pick up (potatoes) out of the ground. (*c*) to take away/to remove (a ban). (*d*) *inf.* to steal. (*e*) (*of fog/clouds*) to rise. **lift-off,** *n.* vertical take-off of a space rocket.

ligament ['lɪgəmənt] *n.* tough tissue which holds bones together.

ligature ['lɪgətʃuə] *n.* thread used for tying in surgical operations; link between two printed letters.

light [laɪt] **1.** *n.* (*a*) brightness which allows you to see; **don't stand in my l.** = between me and the source of light. (*b*) bulb/object which gives light. (*c*) **in the l. of what he said** = in consideration of it; **to throw l. on sth** = make it clearer; **to come to l.** = be discovered. (*d*) appearance/aspect. (*e*) means of making a cigarette, etc., catch fire. (*f*) *pl.* **lights** = (i) lungs of certain animals used as food; (ii) traffic lights. **2.** *v.* (**lit**) (*a*) to make (sth) light. (*b*) to give light to. **3.** *adj.* (**-er, -est**) (*a*) having a lot of light, allowing you to see well. (*b*) pale (colour). (*c*) not heavy; **she's**

a l. sleeper = wakens easily. (*d*) not serious; **to make l. of** = to treat as unimportant. **4.** *adv.* (to travel) with little luggage. **lighten,** *v.* (*a*) to make lighter/not so dark. (*b*) to make lighter/not so heavy. **lighter,** *n.* (*a*) small instrument for making cigarettes, etc., burn. (*b*) boat used for loading other boats. **lighterman,** *n.* (*pl.* **-men**) man who works on a lighter. **light-fingered,** *adj.* (person) who is likely to steal. **light-headed,** *adj.* dizzy; feeling excited. **light-hearted,** *adj.* cheerful/without a care. **light heavyweight,** *n.* weight in boxing between middleweight and heavyweight. **lighthouse,** *n.* tall building containing a light to guide ships. **lighting-up time,** *n.* time at which street lamps and car lights have to be switched on. **lightly,** *adv.* in a light way; **l. dressed** = wearing thin clothes; **to get off l.** = with little or no punishment. **lightness,** *n.* being light. **light on,** *v.* to find. **light pen,** *n.* pen with a tip which is sensitive to light, and which can 'read' lines or images and transfer them to a computer. **lightship,** *n.* ship which carries a large light, acting as a floating lighthouse. **light up,** *v.* (*a*) to give light to (sth). (*b*) to become bright. (*c*) to start to smoke. (*d*) to switch car lights on as it gets dark. **lightweight, 1.** *n.* (*a*) weight in boxing between featherweight and welterweight. (*b*) person without much influence. **2.** *adj.* (*a*) light (clothes). (*b*) not very influential/important. **light year,** *n.* distance travelled by light during one year (about six million million miles).

lightning ['laɪtnɪŋ] **1.** *n.* flash of electricity in the sky, followed by thunder; **like l.** = very fast; **l. conductor** = rod for carrying a lightning charge straight to the ground to prevent damage to buildings. **2.** *adj.* extremely fast; **l. strike** = strike taking place without warning.

lignite ['lɪgnaɪt] *n.* brown coal.

like [laɪk] **1.** *adj.* (nearly) the same/similar. **2.** *prep.* in the same way as/the same as/similar to; **I feel l. some chocolate** = I would like to eat some chocolate. **3.** *n.* similar thing(s). **4.** *adv.* (**as**) **l. as not** = probably. **5.** *conj.* in the same way as. **6.** *v.* (*a*) to have pleasant feelings about. (*b*) to desire/to want. **likeable**, *adj.* pleasant. **likelihood**, *n.* probability. **likely. 1.** *adj.* (**-ier, -iest**) (*a*) probable. (*b*) suitable (for)/apt (to). **2.** *adv.* probably; **not l.!** = certainly not. **like-minded**, *adj.* (person) who has the same opinions. **liken** ['laɪkən] *v.* **to l. sth to sth** = to compare, by showing how one thing is similar to another. **likeness**, *n.* thing which looks like s.o./ sth. **likes**, *n. pl.* (*a*) **l. and dislikes** = things you like and don't like. (*b*) *inf.* **the l. of him** = people like him. **likewise**, *adv.* (*a*) in the same way. (*b*) similarly/the same. **liking**, *n.* pleasant feeling towards s.o.; fondness for s.o./ sth.

lilac ['laɪlək] *n.* (*a*) tree with clusters of (pale) purple or white flowers. (*b*) pale purple colour.

lilliputian [lɪlɪ'pjuːʃn] *adj.* very small.

lilt [lɪlt] **1.** *n.* song/way of speaking with a light well-marked rhythm. **2.** *v.* to sing/ to play a tune with a light well-marked rhythm. **lilting**, *adj.* (song) which has a lilt.

lily ['lɪlɪ] *n.* type of white flower which grows from a bulb. **lily-of-the-valley**, *n.* spring plant with small white flowers growing in clusters.

lima bean ['liːməbiːn] *n.* bean with flat pale seeds.

limb [lɪm] *n.* (*a*) leg/arm/wing; **danger to life and l.** = danger that you may be hurt. (*b*) branch of a tree; **out on a l.** = in a difficult/exposed situation.

limber ['lɪmbə] *v.* **to l. up** = to do exercises to warm your muscles before taking part in a sporting contest.

limbo ['lɪmbəʊ] *n.* (*a*) place between heaven and hell, where unbaptized people are said to go when they die. (*b*) position of not being accepted or rejected; being halfway between two stages. (*c*) **l. dancing** = West Indian dance where the dancer bends his body backwards parallel to the floor to pass under a horizontal bar.

lime [laɪm] *n.* (*a*) white substance containing calcium, used in making cement. (*b*) small yellowish-green tropical fruit like a lemon; tree which bears such fruit. (*c*) northern deciduous

tree with smooth leaves and yellowish flowers. **lime green**, *adj. & n.* green colour of lime. **limelight**, *n.* attention/ publicity. **limestone**, *n.* light-coloured stone containing calcium.

limerick ['lɪmərɪk] *n.* type of amusing five-line poem.

limey ['laɪmɪ] *adj. & n. Sl.* English (person).

limit ['lɪmɪt] **1.** *n.* furthest point/extent; boundary; end (beyond which you cannot go); *inf.* **that's the l.** = too much. **2.** *v.* to put a limit on/to keep within limits; not to allow (sth) to go beyond a certain point; **limited company** = private company in which the members only have to pay debts up to the amount of capital they have put in. **limitation** [lɪmɪ'teɪʃn] *n.* (*a*) act of limiting. (*b*) thing which stops you going further; **to know your limitations** = to know what you are capable of doing.

limousine [lɪmə'ziːn] *n.* large luxurious car, with a partition between the driver and the passenger.

limp [lɪmp] **1.** *n.* way of walking unevenly. **2.** *v.* to walk with an uneven step. **3.** *adj.* without stiffness/soft; without energy. **limply**, *adv.* in a limp way. **limpness**, *n.* being limp.

limpet ['lɪmpɪt] *n.* cone-shaped shellfish which clings to rocks.

limpid ['lɪmpɪd] *adj.* clear. **limpidity** [lɪm'pɪdɪtɪ] *n.* (*formal*) being clear.

linchpin ['lɪnʃpɪn] *n.* (*a*) pin which goes through an axle to hold a wheel on. (*b*) very important person/piece of machinery.

linctus ['lɪŋktəs] *n.* cough syrup.

lindane ['lɪndeɪn] *n.* powerful insecticide.

linden ['lɪndən] *n.* (*formal*) lime tree.

line [laɪn] **1.** *n.* (*a*) (long) thin mark; **to draw the l. at** = to stop short of/not to do; **to be on the right lines** = to be doing things the right way. (*b*) long wire/cord; **hard lines** = bad luck. (*c*) **telephone l.** = cable along which telephone messages are sent; **the l.'s bad** = it is difficult to make out what s.o. is saying; **crossed l.** = two telephone conversations which intermingle by error. (*d*) row of people/ cars/words, etc.; *inf.* **to drop s.o. a l.** = to send a short letter; **l. printer** =

computer printer which prints each line separately. (*e*) *Am.* queue. (*f*) tracks on which trains run. (*g*) shipping/air company. (*h*) sequence of ancestors/descendants. (*i*) **lines** = shape/outline; general design. (*j*) direction; method; course of action; **in l. with** = according to/following (a decision); **to take a hard l.** = to be aggressive/not to weaken in any way. (*k*) type of work/goods. **2.** *v.* (*a*) to put lines on. (*b*) to form a line (along the edge of a street). (*c*) to put a layer of material inside (a piece of clothing); **to l. one's pockets** = to make money (usu. dishonestly). **lineage** ['lɪnɪɪdʒ] *n.* line of descendants (from an ancestor). **lineal** ['lɪnɪəl] *adj.* (descendant) in direct line. **lineaments,** *n. pl.* outline of the face/features. **linear** ['lɪnɪə] *adj.* referring to lines/to length. **liner,** *n.* (*a*) thing used for lining; **bin l.** = plastic bag for putting inside a dustbin. (*b*) large passenger ship. **linesman,** *n.* (*pl.* **-men**) (*a*) man who looks after electric/telephone/railway lines. (*b*) person who stays on the sideline in a game to see if the ball goes over the line. **line up,** *v.* to form a line/a queue. **line-up,** *n.* row/list of people. **lining,** *n.* layer of material inside sth.

linen ['lɪnɪn] *n.* (*a*) cloth made from flax. (*b*) (**household**) **l.** = sheets/pillowcases/tablecloths, etc. (*c*) underwear; **to wash your dirty l. in public** = tell shameful personal secrets.

ling [lɪŋ] *n.* (*a*) type of small edible fish. (*b*) heather.

linger ['lɪŋgə] *v.* (*a*) to wait/to remain/to stay longer than necessary/expected. (*b*) (*of sick person*) to remain alive.

lingerie ['lænʒərɪ] *n.* women's underwear.

lingo ['lɪŋgəʊ] *n. Sl.* language.

lingua franca [lɪŋgwə'fræŋkə] *n.* language used by speakers of various languages as a common means of communication.

lingual ['lɪŋgwəl] *adj.* referring to the tongue.

linguist ['lɪŋgwɪst] *n.* (*a*) person who knows foreign languages well. (*b*) person who studies linguistics. **linguistic** [lɪŋ'gwɪstɪk] *adj.* (*a*) referring to language(s). (*b*) referring to the science of language. **linguistics,** *n.* science of language.

liniment ['lɪnɪmənt] *n.* oily substance which you rub on the skin to lessen pains.

link [lɪŋk] **1.** *n.* (*a*) ring which forms part of a chain. (*b*) thing which connects two parts. **2.** *v.* to join. **linkage,** *n.* act of linking. **linkman,** *n.* (*pl.* **-men**) person who speaks between sections of TV programmes.

links [lɪŋks] *n. pl.* golf course.

linnet ['lɪnɪt] *n.* small singing bird.

lino ['laɪnəʊ] *n. inf.* linoleum. **linocut** ['laɪnəʊkʌt] *n.* design printed from a block of linoleum which has been cut into a pattern. **linoleum** [lɪ'nəʊlɪəm] *n.* hard smooth floor covering.

linseed ['lɪnsiːd] *n.* seed of flax.

lint [lɪnt] *n.* soft cloth used for putting on wounds.

lintel ['lɪntl] *n.* piece of wood/stone over a door or window.

lion ['laɪən] *n.* large wild animal of the cat family, the male of which has a long mane; **the l.'s share** = the biggest part. **lioness,** *n.* female lion. **lionize,** *v.* to treat (s.o.) as very important.

lip [lɪp] *n.* (*a*) one of two fleshy parts round the outside of the mouth; **to keep a stiff upper l.** = not to show emotion in time of trouble; **to smack one's lips over** = to express great enjoyment of. (*b*) *Sl.* cheek/rudeness. (*c*) edge of a bowl/cup, etc. **lipped,** *adj.* with lips. **lip-read,** *v.* (**lip-read** ['lɪpred]) (*of a deaf person*) to follow speech by watching the movements of the lips of the person speaking. **lip salve,** *n.* ointment to prevent lips cracking. **lip service,** *n.* **to pay lip service to sth** = to give a false impression of respecting/obeying sth. **lipstick,** *n.* (stick of) substance for colouring the lips.

lipid ['lɪpɪd] *n.* fatty substance in the tissue in human bodies.

liquefy ['lɪkwɪfaɪ] *v.* to become liquid; to make (sth) become liquid. **liquefaction** [lɪkwɪ'fækʃn] *n.* making/becoming liquid.

liqueur [lɪ'kɜː] *n.* strong alcoholic drink.

liquid ['lɪkwɪd] **1.** *n.* substance which flows easily like water, and which is neither a gas nor a solid. **2.** *adj.* (*a*) which is neither gas nor solid, and which flows easily; **l. crystal display** = display panel, where the figures appear black. (*b*) (*of assets, etc.*) able to be changed easily into cash. (*c*) (*of sounds*) pure/clear. **liquidate,** *v.* (*a*) to close (a company) which cannot pay its debts. (*b*) to pay (a debt). (*c*) *inf.* to kill. **liquidation** [lɪkwɪˈdeɪʃn] *n.* closing of a company which cannot pay its debts. **liquidator,** *n.* person named to close a company. **liquidity** [lɪˈkwɪdɪtɪ] *n.* (*in finance*) being able to change assets into cash. **liquidize,** *v.* to reduce fruit to liquid. **liquidizer,** *n.* machine which liquidizes.

liquor [ˈlɪkə] *n.* (*a*) alcoholic drink. (*b*) liquid produced in cooking.

liquorice, *Am.* **licorice** [ˈlɪkərɪs] *n.* black substance from the root of a plant, used in medicine and in sweets.

lira [ˈlɪrə] *n.* unit of money used in Italy.

lisle [laɪl] *n.* fine cotton (used to make stockings).

lisp [lɪsp] **1.** *n.* speech defect in which 's' is pronounced as 'th'. **2.** *v.* to speak with a lisp.

lissom [ˈlɪsəm] *adj.* lithe/supple.

list [lɪst] **1.** *n.* (*a*) number of items written/spoken one after another; **wine l.** = list of wines available in a restaurant; **to be on the sick l.** = to be reported sick; **to be on the danger l.** = to be dangerously ill; **l. price** = price of sth as shown in a catalogue. (*b*) (*of ship*) leaning to one side. (*c*) **to enter the lists** = to be a candidate in an election. **2.** *v.* (*a*) to say/to write (a number of items) one after the other. (*b*) (*of ship*) to lean over to one side.

listen [ˈlɪsn] *v.* to pay attention (**to s.o./sth**) in order to hear. **listener,** *n.* person who listens.

Listeria [lɪsˈtiːərɪə] *n.* bacteria found in some foods and in domestic animals, which can cause infections such as meningitis.

listless [ˈlɪstləs] *adj.* (feeling) dull, without interest or energy. **listlessly,** *adv.* in a way which shows lack of interest. **listlessness,** *n.* lack of interest/energy.

lit [lɪt] *v. see* **light.**

litany [ˈlɪtənɪ] *n.* form of prayer with repeated responses, used in churches.

litchi [ˈlaɪtʃɪ] *n.* small Chinese fruit, with a red skin and large stone.

liter [ˈliːtə] *n. Am.* litre.

literacy [ˈlɪtərəsɪ] *n.* ability to read and write. **literal 1.** *adj.* keeping to the exact meaning of the original words. **2.** *n.* typesetting mistake. **literally,** *adv.* in a literal way; (*to emphasize*) **his eyes were l. popping out of his head. literalness,** *n.* being literal. **literary,** *adj.* referring to literature. **literate** [ˈlɪtərət] *adj.* (*a*) able to read and write. (*b*) well educated, esp. in literary subjects. **literati** [lɪtəˈrɑːtiː] *n. pl.* literary people. **literature** [ˈlɪtrɪtʃə] *n.* (*a*) books/writing, esp. novels, poetry, drama, biography, etc. (*b*) what has been written on a particular subject. (*c*) written information about sth.

lithe [laɪð] *adj.* supple/bending easily.

lithograph [ˈlɪθəɡrɑːf] **1.** *n.* painting/drawing, etc., reproduced by lithography. **2.** *v.* to print by lithography. **lithographic** [lɪθəˈɡræfɪk] *adj.* of lithography. **lithography** [lɪˈθɒɡrəfɪ] *n.* method of printing using oil and ink on a flat surface such as a stone/a sheet of metal, etc.

litigate [ˈlɪtɪɡeɪt] *v.* to go to law; to bring a lawsuit against s.o. **litigant,** *n.* person involved in a lawsuit. **litigation** [lɪtɪˈɡeɪʃn] *n.* (*a*) bringing a lawsuit against s.o. (*b*) lawsuit. **litigious** [lɪˈtɪdʒəs] *adj.* always ready to go to law.

litmus [ˈlɪtməs] *n.* blue substance which is turned red by an acid and back to blue by an alkali. **litmus paper,** *n.* paper containing litmus, used to test for acids and alkalis.

litre, *Am.* **liter** [ˈliːtə] *n.* measurement for liquids (almost 2 pints).

litter [ˈlɪtə] **1.** *n.* (*a*) rubbish left on streets. (*b*) (*old*) stretcher/bed on which a person is carried. (*c*) bedding of straw, etc., for animals. (*d*) (*of animals*) group of young born at one time. **2.** *v.* (*a*) to drop rubbish about. (*b*) (*of animals*) to produce young.

little [ˈlɪtl] **1.** *adj.* (**less, least**) (*a*) small; **his l. sister** = his younger sister. (*b*) **a l.** = small amount of. (*c*) not much. **2.** *n.* small amount; **l. by l.** = gradually. **3.** *adv.* (*a*) (by) a small amount; **I see him very l.** = not very often. (*b*) **he l.**

thought he would win = he had no idea that he would win.

littoral ['lɪtɒrəl] *adj. & n.* (referring to the) coast.

liturgy ['lɪtədʒɪ] *n.* form of public service in church. **liturgical** [lɪ'tɜːdʒɪkl] *adj.* referring to liturgy.

live. 1. *adj.* [laɪv] (*a*) in a living state. (*b*) burning. (*c*) (*of broadcast*) not recorded. (*d*) carrying an electric current; (ammunition) which has not been defused; *inf.* **l. wire** = very lively and energetic person. **2.** *v.* [lɪv] (*a*) to be alive/to have life; **l. and let l.** = be tolerant. (*b*) to have your (place of) residence. (*c*) to lead a certain type of life; **he lives in style;** *inf.* **to l. it up** = to lead a life of wild parties, etc. (*d*) **to l. on** = to get food/money, etc., from. **live down,** *v.* to cause (a disgrace) to be forgotten; **he'll never l. it down** = it will never be forgotten. **live in,** *v.* to live in the building where you work. **livelihood** ['laɪvlɪhʊd] *n.* (way of getting) your means of living. **liveliness** ['laɪvlɪnəs] *n.* being lively. **livelong** ['lɪvlɒŋ] *adj.* (*formal*) **the l. day** = all the day. **lively** ['laɪvlɪ] *adj.* (**-ier, -iest**) bright/wide-awake/(very) active. **liven,** *v.* to make lively. **livestock** ['laɪvstɒk] *n.* animals kept on a farm. **liveware,** *n. inf.* people who work with computers. **living** ['lɪvɪŋ] **1.** *adj.* alive. **2.** *n.* (*a*) (way of) life. (*b*) means of subsistence. (*c*) **the l.** = people who are alive. (*d*) position as parish priest. **living room,** *n.* room in a house for general use.

liver ['lɪvə] *n.* organ in the lower part of the body which helps the digestion by producing bile; animal's liver used as food. **liverish,** *adj.* feeling rather sick and unwell; irritable.

livery ['lɪvrɪ] *n.* (*a*) special clothing of a group of servants/of an organization. (*b*) care of horses for payment; **l. stable** = place where horses may be looked after and may also be hired. **liveried,** *adj.* wearing a livery.

livid ['lɪvɪd] *adj.* (*a*) of the dark grey colour of lead. (*b*) extremely angry.

lizard ['lɪzəd] *n.* type of reptile with four legs and scales.

llama ['lɑːmə] *n.* thick-haired camel-like animal found in South America.

Lloyd's [lɔɪdz] *n.* central London insurance market.

lo [ləʊ] *inter.* (*old*) look!

load [ləʊd] **1.** *n.* (*a*) heavy object(s) which have to be carried. (*b*) (*on vehicle*) what has to be/what is being transported. (*c*) amount of material transported. (*d*) amount of power carried by an electric circuit. (*e*) thing which is difficult to bear; **that's a l. off my mind** = I feel much less worried. (*f*) *inf.* **loads of** = plenty/lots. **2.** *v.* (*a*) to put (esp. sth heavy) **into/on to.** (*b*) to put ammunition into (a gun)/to put film into (a camera); to put a disk/program into a computer. (*c*) **to l. s.o. with** = to give large quantities to. **loaded,** *adj.* (*a*) *inf.* having a lot of money. (*b*) **l. question** = question which is worded in such a way so as to trap the person who answers. (*c*) (dice) which has a secret weight in it. **loader,** *n.* person who loads.

loaf [ləʊf] **1.** *n.* (*pl.* **loaves** [ləʊvz]) (*a*) (large) piece of bread baked separately. (*b*) *Sl.* head; **use your l.** = use your brains. **2.** *v.* to wander about/to waste time doing nothing. **loafer,** *n.* (*a*) person who does nothing all day. (*b*) *Am.* light casual shoe with no laces.

loam [ləʊm] *n.* fertile soil which crumbles easily. **loamy,** *adj.* crumbly fertile (soil).

loan [ləʊn] **1.** *n.* (*a*) lending. (*b*) thing lent (esp. a sum of money from a bank). **2.** *v.* to lend.

loath [ləʊθ] *adj.* very unwilling.

loathe [ləʊð] *v.* to hate very much. **loathing,** *n.* feeling of hate/disgust (**for**). **loathsome,** *adj.* disgusting/horrible.

lob [lɒb] **1.** *n.* ball which is hit high into the air. **2.** *v.* (**lobbed**) to throw/hit (a ball) slowly in a high curve.

lobby ['lɒbɪ] **1.** *n.* (*a*) entrance hall/corridor. (*b*) corridor where Members of Parliament go to vote. (*c*) hall in the House of Commons used esp. for interviews with members of the public; **l. correspondent** = journalist who reports on parliamentary matters, after confidential briefings from ministers. **2.** *v.* to try to influence (s.o.) (esp. in order to get a bill through Parliament).

lobe [ləʊb] *n.* (*a*) lower curved part of

the ear. (b) division of the lungs/brain/
liver, etc. **lobar,** adj. referring to a lobe.
lobotomy [lə'bɒtəmɪ] n. operation to
remove a lobe.
lobelia [lɒ'biːlɪə] n. low plant with blue
flowers.
lobster ['lɒbstə] n. shellfish with a long
body, two large claws, and eight legs,
used as food. **lobster pot,** n. cage left
in the sea to catch lobsters.
local ['ləʊkl] **1.** adj. referring to a place/
district; near at hand; **l. anaesthetic** =
which numbs a particular area of the
body; **l. authority** = section of elected
government which runs a district. **2.**
n. (a) person who lives in a district,
esp. the district where you live. (b) inf.
nearest public house. **locale** [ləʊ'kɑːl]
n. place where sth takes place. **locality**
[ləʊ'kælɪtɪ] n. area/district. **localize**
['ləʊkəklaɪz] v. to set in a particular
place; to be confined to a particular
area. **locally,** adv. in the (same) district.
locate [ləʊ'keɪt] v. (a) to find (the position of). (b) **to be located** = to be
in a particular position. **location** [ləʊ-
'keɪʃn] n. (a) finding the position of sth.
(b) place/position. (c) **on l.** = (filming)
which takes place in a real setting, not
in a studio.
loch [lɒx] n. (in Scotland) lake; arm of
the sea.
lock·[lɒk] **1.** n. (a) device for closing a
door/container, etc., by means of a key;
under l. and key = shut up firmly. (b)
part in a gun by which it is fired; **l., stock
and barrel** = (everything) all together.
(c) amount by which the wheels of a car
are able to turn. (d) section of a canal/
river with barriers which can be opened
or closed to control the flow of water,
thus allowing boats to move up or down
to different levels. (e) bundle of hair
hanging together. **2.** v. (a) to close (a
door/a box, etc.) with a key. (b) to fix/
to become fixed in a certain position.
lockable, adj. which can be locked.
locker, n. small cupboard for personal
belongings which you can close with
a key; **l. room** = room in a sports
stadium where players change and leave
their clothes in lockers. **lockjaw,** n. disease where your jaws become closed
tight together. **lock-keeper,** n. person

who looks after a lock in a canal/river.
locknut, n. second nut, used to keep
the first nut in place. **lock out,** v. to
prevent (s.o.) from going in by locking
the door. **lockout,** n. industrial dispute in which employees are kept out
of the factory until they agree to certain terms. **locksmith,** n. person who
makes/repairs locks. **lock up,** v. (a)
to close (a building) by locking doors.
(b) to keep (a person/animal) inside by
locking doors, etc. **lockup,** n. (a) (old)
prison cell. (b) **l. garage/shop** = garage/
shop which can be locked and which is
not part of the owner's house.
locket ['lɒkɪt] n. small ornamental case
to hold a picture/lock of hair, etc., worn
round the neck.
locomotive [ləʊkə'məʊtɪv] **1.** adj. referring to movement. **2.** n. engine of a
train. **locomotion,** n. (power of) movement.
locum (tenens) ['ləʊkəm('tenenz)] n.
person who does the work of a doctor/
clergyman, while the latter is away.
locus ['ləʊkəs] n. (pl. **loci** ['ləʊsaɪ]) point,
line, curve, etc., in a technical diagram.
locust ['ləʊkəst] n. insect, like a large
grasshopper, which destroys crops.
lode [ləʊd] n. vein of metal ore.
lodestar, n. pole star. **lodestone,** n.
magnetic iron ore.
lodge [lɒdʒ] **1.** n. (a) small house at the
gates of a large building. (b) house in
the country used for shooting parties.
(c) (meeting place for a) group of
freemasons, etc. (d) home of beavers.
2. v. (a) to rent a room (in a boarding
house). (b) to be/to remain. (c) (formal)
to make/to place (a complaint). **lodger,**
n. person who rents a room. **lodging,**
n. (a) accommodation. (b) **lodgings** =
rented rooms.
loess ['ləʊəs] n. yellow powdery earth
found in China, North America, etc.
loft [lɒft] n. (a) top part of a house
immediately under the roof. (b) **organ
l.** = gallery for an organ in a church,
etc. (c) **hay l.** = top part of a barn used
for storing hay.
lofty ['lɒftɪ] adj. (-ier, -iest) (a) very high.
(b) arrogant/proud. **loftily,** adv. in a
proud way.
log [lɒg] **1.** n. (a) thick piece of a tree

trunk/large branch; **to sleep like a l.** = very soundly; **as easy as falling off a l.** = very easy. (*b*) device for calculating the speed of a ship. (*c*) daily detailed record of speed/position/happenings, esp. on a ship. (*d*) *short for* **logarithm. 2.** *v.* (**logged**) (*a*) to write down details of (sth which has happened) in a logbook. (*b*) to cover a (distance)/to spend (time). **logbook,** *n.* (*a*) (*on ship, etc.*) book with record of a journey. (*b*) official record book showing details of the owners of a car. **logging,** *n. Am.* cutting trees for timber.

loganberry ['ləʊɡənberɪ] *n.* soft fruit, a cross between a blackberry and a raspberry.

logarithm ['lɒɡərɪðm] *n.* one of a set of numbers listed in such a way as to help with calculations by adding and subtracting instead of multiplying and dividing. **logarithmic** [lɒɡə'rɪθmɪk] *adj.* referring to logarithms.

loggerheads ['lɒɡəhedz] *n.* **to be at l.** = to quarrel constantly.

loggia ['lɒdʒɪə] *n.* (*in southern Europe*) covered gallery which is open on one side.

logic ['lɒdʒɪk] *n.* science of reasoning; power of reasoning clearly. **logical,** *adj.* (*a*) clearly reasoned. (*b*) (*of person*) able to reason clearly. **logically,** *adv.* in a logical/reasonable way.

logistics [lɒ'dʒɪstɪks] *n.* organization of the movement of supplies/people, etc.

logo ['lɒɡəʊ] *n.* (*pl.* **-os**) symbol/design used by a company to identify its products.

loin [lɔɪn] *n.* (*a*) (meat from the) back of an animal. (*b*) **loins** = part of the body between the hips. **loincloth,** *n.* long cloth wrapped round the hips.

loiter ['lɔɪtə] *v.* to wander about slowly/aimlessly; to stand about. **loiterer,** *n.* person who wanders/who is standing about.

loll [lɒl] *v.* (*a*) to sit/stand/lie in a lazy way. (*b*) (*of tongue*) to hang out.

lollipop ['lɒlɪpɒp] *n.* sweet on the end of a stick; *inf.* **l. man/woman** = person employed to stop traffic to let schoolchildren cross a street.

lollop ['lɒləp] *v. inf.* to walk with long clumsy steps.

lolly ['lɒlɪ] *n.* (*a*) *inf.* lollipop; **ice l.** = lump of flavoured ice on the end of a stick. (*b*) *Sl.* money.

lone [ləʊn] *adj.* alone; lonely; **l. wolf** = person who likes to be alone. **lonely,** *adj.* (*a*) with few or no people. (*b*) feeling sad because of being alone. **loneliness,** *n.* being alone; feeling sad because you are alone. **loner,** *n.* person who prefers to be alone. **lonesome,** *adj.* lonely/sad because of being alone.

long [lɒŋ] **1.** *adj.* (**-er, -est**) (*a*) measured in space from end to end; not short. (*b*) measured in time; **they stayed for a l. time. 2.** *adv.* for a long time; **all night l.** = for the whole night. (*b*) **as l. as** = while. (*c*) **so/as l. as** = provided that. **3.** *n.* long time; **before l.** = in a short time; **for l.** = for a long time. **4.** *v.* **to l. for** = to want very much. **long-distance,** *adj.* (*a*) (*in sport*) (race) run between two places which are far apart. (*b*) (telephone call) made over a long distance. **longhand,** *n.* ordinary writing (not shorthand). **long-haul,** *adj.* (flight) between continents. **longhorn,** *n.* type of cow with long horns. **longing,** *n.* great desire (**for** sth). **long johns,** *n. pl. inf.* long underpants. **long-lived,** *adj.* (person) who lives for a long time. **long-playing,** *adj.* (record) which plays for about 20 minutes each side. **long-range,** *adj.* which covers a long distance. **longshoreman,** *n.* (*pl.* **-men**) *Am.* person who works at a port, loading or unloading ships. **long shot,** *n.* attempt which has little chance of being successful. **long-sighted,** *adj.* able to see things at a distance more clearly than things which are close. **longstanding,** *adj.* which has been arranged some time before. **long-suffering,** *adj.* patient/tolerating much. **long-term,** *adj.* lasting/planned to last for a long time. **long wave,** *n.* radio wave longer than 1000 metres. **long-winded,** *adj.* (person) who talks too much in a boring way; (talk) which lasts too long.

longevity [lɒn'dʒevɪtɪ] *n.* very long life.

longitude ['lɒndʒɪtjuːd] *n.* position on the earth's surface measured in degrees east or went of an imaginary line running through Greenwich, London.

longitudinal, *adj.* which runs length-wise. **longitudinally,** *adv.* from end to end.

loo [lu:] *n. inf.* lavatory.

loofah ['lu:fə] *n.* type of long sponge, made from a dried pod.

look [lʊk] **1.** *n.* (*a*) turning your eyes (often quickly) to see sth. (*b*) search (**for** sth). (*c*) appearance; the way sth/s.o. appears. (*d*) **good looks** = beauty/pleasing personal appearance. **2.** *v.* (*a*) (**at**) to make efforts to see; **l'. here!** = I object. (*b*) to stare at; **he looked me straight in the face.** (*c*) to seem/to have the appearance of; **he looks ill; she looks the part** = looks right for the job. **look after,** *v.* to take care of. **look ahead,** *v.* to make plans for the future. **lookalike,** *n. inf.* person who looks like s.o. famous. **look at,** *v.* to make efforts to see/to examine/to consider. **look back,** *v.* (*a*) to turn round to see what is behind you. (*b*) **after that they never looked back** = they were very successful. **look back on,** *v.* to think about (sth) in the past. **look down,** *v.* **to look down on s.o./to look down your nose at s.o.** = to think you are better than s.o. **looker-on,** *n.* (*pl.* **lookers-on**) person who is watching (without taking part). **look for,** *v.* to try to find. **look forward,** *v.* (**to**) to think about (sth) in the future (usu. with pleasure). **look in (on),** *v. inf.* to visit (s.o.) briefly. **look-in,** *n. inf.* chance/opportunity (to share in sth). **looking glass,** *n.* mirror. **look into,** *v.* to examine/to find out about. **look on,** *v.* (*a*) to watch without taking part. (*b*) to consider/to think of sth as. **look out,** *v.* (*a*) (**on**) to have a view towards. (*b*) (**for**) to keep looking in order to find. (*c*) (**for**) to be careful of. **lookout,** *n.* (*a*) place from which you can see what is happening. (*b*) careful attention. (*c*) future hope. (*d*) affair; **that's his l.** = he must deal with it himself. (*e*) person who watches. **look over,** *v.* to examine. **look round,** *v.* (*a*) to turn to see behind you. (*b*) to examine all of a place. **look through,** *v.* (*a*) to examine the whole of (sth) (often quickly). (*b*) to pretend not to see. **look to,** *v.* (*a*) to expect (help) from. (*b*) (*formal*) to take care of. **look up,** *v.* (*a*) to turn your eyes in an upward direction. (*b*) to get better. (*c*) to try to find (sth) in a reference book, etc. (*d*) to get in contact with. **look up to,** *v.* to consider with respect/admiration.

loom [lu:m] **1.** *n.* machine on which cloth is woven. **2.** *v.* to appear/to come into sight (gradually).

loon [lu:] *n.* grebe.

loony ['lu:nɪ] *adj. & n. inf.* mad (person). **loony bin,** *n. inf.* lunatic asylum.

loop [lu:p] **1.** *n.* (*a*) curve formed by a piece of thread/ribbon, etc. which crosses over itself. (*b*) thing of this shape. **2.** *v.* to make a loop/loops; **l. back the curtain** = to tie it back with a cord; (*of aircraft*) **to l. the loop** = to fly in a complete circle vertically, turning upside down at the top. **loophole,** *n.* (*a*) narrow hole in a wall for shooting through. (*b*) means of escape/of avoiding (a law).

loose [lu:s] **1.** *adj.* (**-er, -est**) (*a*) not (fully) attached/not fixed; **to be at a l. end** = to have nothing special to do. (*b*) not tight. (*c*) with pieces separated. (*d*) **l. change** = money in coins only. (*e*) (translation) which is not very exact. (*f*) of doubtful morals. **2.** *v.* to make (sth) become untied/to let (sth) go. **3.** *adv.* not tightly. **loosebox,** *n.* stable where a horse can move about. **loosely,** *adv.* (*a*) not tightly. (*b*) in an inexact way. **looseleaf,** *adj.* (book) of which the pages can be removed and replaced. **loosen,** *v.* to make (sth) less tight. **looseness,** *n.* being loose.

loot [lu:t] **1.** *n.* (*a*) things which have been taken. (*b*) *Sl.* money. **2.** *v.* to steal. **looter,** *n.* person who steals (esp. from shops during a riot).

lop [lɒp] *v.* (**lopped**) to cut off (esp. tree branches).

lope [ləʊp] **1.** *n.* running with long strides. **2.** *v.* to run with long (slow) strides.

lop-eared ['lɒpɪəd] *adj.* (rabbit) with drooping ears.

lopsided [lɒp'saɪdɪd] *adj.* with one side larger/lower/heavier than the other.

loquacious [lɒ'kweɪʃəs] *adj.* (person) who talks a lot/too much. **loquaciousness, loquacity** [lɒ'kwæsɪtɪ] *n.* talking too much.

lord [lɔːd] **1.** *n.* (*a*) nobleman/ruler. (*b*) title for certain peers; **House of Lords** = upper chamber of the British Parliament. (*c*) **the Lord** = Jesus Christ. (*d*) title for men in certain positions (such as bishops/judges, etc.). (*e*) expression of surprise/shock; **Good Lord! 2.** *v.* **to l. it over s.o.** = to behave as if you are superior. **lordliness**, *n.* (*a*) nobility. (*b*) pride. **lordly**, *adj.* (*a*) referring to the nobility. (*b*) proud/arrogant. **lordship**, *n.* (*form of address to a lord*) **Your Lordship.**

lore [lɔː] *n.* (*no pl.*) traditional beliefs and knowledge.

lorgnette [lɔːˈnjet] *n.* glasses which you hold in front of your eyes with a handle.

lorry [ˈlɒrɪ] *n.* large motor vehicle for carrying goods. **lorry driver**, *n.* person who drives a lorry.

lose [luːz] *v.* (**lost** [lɒst]) (*a*) to stop having/owning (sth); **she lost her gloves** = did not know where they were; **they lost sight of it** = could no longer see it; **that joke was lost on him** = he did not understand it. (*b*) to fail to win. (*c*) to cause the loss of. (*d*) **to get lost/to l. your way** = to be/become unable to find the way to where you were going; *Sl.* **get lost!** = go away! (*e*) **to l. weight** = to become lighter. (*f*) (*of clock/watch*) to become/to go slow. **loser**, *n.* person who does not win; **he's a bad l.** = behaves badly when he loses a game. **lost** [lɒst] *adj.* which has been lost; **to give sth up for l.** = have no hope of ever having it again; **he looks l.** = looks bewildered. **lost property office**, *n.* place where articles which people have left on trains/buses, etc., are stored, and where they can be claimed by the loser.

loss [lɒs] *n.* (*pl.* **-es**) (*a*) no longer having sth. (*b*) thing/amount which you no longer have; **they sold it at a l.** = for less than they paid for it; *inf.* **that's a dead l.** = no use at all. (*c*) **to be at a l. what to do** = not to know what to do. **loss leader**, *n.* article which is sold at a loss to attract customers.

lost [lɒst] *v. see* **lose.**

lot [lɒt] *n.* (*a*) *inf.* **a lot (of)/lots (of)** = a large amount/number (of); **I've seen quite a l. of him lately** = seen him many times. (*b*) **the l.** = everything. (*c*) set of things (for selling); thing/group of things together offered at an auction sale. (*d*) **bad l.** = wicked person. (*e*) *esp. Am.* piece of land; **parking l.** = place where cars can be parked. (*f*) fate/fortune. (*g*) **to draw lots** = to decide sth by taking pieces of paper from a box/throwing dice, etc.

loth [ləʊθ] *adj.* very unwilling.

lotion [ˈləʊʃn] *n.* liquid used to soothe/to soften/to heal the skin.

lottery [ˈlɒtrɪ] *n.* game of chance in which tickets are sold with prizes given for certain numbers.

lotus [ˈləʊtəs] *n.* tropical water plant, with large flowers.

loud [laʊd] **1.** *adj.* (**-er, -est**) (*a*) having a sound which is (too) easily heard. (*b*) (*of colours, etc.*) too striking/showy. **2.** *adv.* in a way which is easily heard. **loud-hailer**, *n.* megaphone operated by electricity. **loudly**, *adv.* in a way which is easily heard; **she was loudly dressed** = in bright/clashing colours. **loud-mouthed**, *adj.* talking in a way which is too easily heard. **loudness**, *n.* being (too) easily heard. **loudspeaker**, *n.* part of a radio, etc., which allows sound to be heard.

lough [lɒk] *n.* (*in Ireland*) lake.

lounge [laʊndʒ] **1.** *n.* (*a*) room for sitting in. (*b*) **l. (bar)** = comfortable/expensive bar in a hotel; **departure l.** = room at an airport where passengers wait to board their planes. (*c*) sitting around doing nothing or very little. **2.** *v.* to sit/to lie doing nothing or very little. **lounger**, *n.* person who lounges. **lounge suit**, *n.* (man's) informal suit.

louring [ˈlaʊərɪŋ] *adj.* gloomy/threatening(-looking).

louse [laʊs] *n.* (*pl.* **lice** [laɪs]) small insect which lives on human and animal bodies. **lousy** [ˈlaʊzɪ] *adj.* (*a*) covered with lice. (*b*) *inf.* horrible/unfair.

lout [laʊt] *n.* loutish person. **loutish**, *adj.* awkward/rude/ill-mannered.

louvre, *Am.* **louver** [ˈluːvə] *n.* sloping wooden strips in a frame which overlap and only allow some light to enter. **louvered**, *adj.* with louvres.

love [lʌv] **1.** *n.* (*a*) great liking/respect for s.o./sth; **to do sth for the l. of it** = without looking for profit; **it can't be had for**

l. **nor money** = not at all/by any means; **there's no l. lost between them** = they hate each other. (b) great liking/passion for s.o., esp. strong sexual feeling towards s.o.; **to be in l./to fall in l. with s.o.; to make l. (to s.o.)** = have sexual intercourse with; l. **story** = one about sexual love; l. **affair** = (often short) sexual relationship. (c) person whom you love. (d) inf. form of address, esp. to a woman or child. (e) (in tennis, etc.) score of zero. **2.** v. (a) to have strong feelings of affection for. (b) to have great liking/passion, esp. strong sexual feelings for (s.o.). (c) to like very much. **lovable,** adj. pleasant/easy to love. **lovebird,** n. budgerigar. **love-child,** n. illegitimate child. **loveless,** adj. without love. **loveliness,** n. being very attractive. **lovelorn,** adj. sad because you love s.o. who does not love you. **lovely,** adj. (-ier, -iest) (a) beautiful. (b) inf. very pleasant. **lover,** n. (a) person (esp. a man) who is in love. (b) person who loves (sth). **lovesick,** adj. unhappy because of being in love. **loving,** adj. affectionate/ showing love. **lovingly,** adv. in a loving way.

low [ləʊ] **1.** adj. (-er, -est) (a) at/ near/towards the bottom; in a position below (others); l. **voice** = not easily heard. (b) coarse/mean; inferior. (c) feeling depressed/ill, etc. **2.** adv. in a low direction/way/position; **to lie l.** = to keep hidden; **supplies are running l.** = are becoming scarce. **3.** n. (a) low-pressure zone in the atmosphere, bringing bad weather. (b) **sales are at an all-time l.** = the lowest point ever. **4.** v. to make a sound like a cow. **lowbrow,** adj. & n. (person) without intellectual interests. **Low Church,** n. section of Anglican church which stress prayer and preaching, but not ceremony. **lowdown. 1.** adj. mean/bad/ to be despised. **2.** n. inf. **to give the lowdown (on sth)** = the details (esp. confidential). **lower. 1.** adj. further down; l. **deck** = deck under another deck; l. **case** = small (letter), not a capital; **Lower House** = more important of two parts of a parliament. **2.** v. (a) to make (sth) reach a po-

sition further down; l. **your voice** = speak more quietly. (b) **to l. yourself (so far as to)** = to do sth of which you should be ashamed. **low frequency,** n. radio frequency which is low and can be heard. **low-grade,** adj. of poor quality. **low-key,** adj. quiet/without excitement. **lowland,** adj. coming from a low-lying region. **lowlands,** n. pl. low-lying region. **lowliness,** n. being lowly. **lowly,** adj. (-ier, -iest) humble/modest. **low-lying,** adj. (region) which is at a low altitude/almost at sea level. **low season,** n. season when there are few tourists.

lowering ['laʊərɪŋ] adj. gloomy/threatening(-looking).

loyal ['lɔɪəl] adj. **(to)** faithful/supporting (s.o./sth). **loyalist,** n. person who is loyal. **loyally,** adv. in a loyal way. **loyalty,** n. being faithful.

lozenge ['lɒzɪndʒ] n. (a) diamond shape (esp. as used in heraldry). (b) sweet; medicine tablet.

LP [el'piː] abbreviation for long-playing record.

Ltd ['lɪmɪtɪd] short for limited.

lubricate ['luːbrɪkeɪt] v. to cover (sth) with oil or grease to make it run smoothly. **lubricant,** adj. & n. (substance) which makes sth run smoothly. **lubrication** [luːbrɪ'keɪʃn] n. covering with oil or grease.

lucerne [luˈsɜːn] n. plant like clover used as fodder for cattle.

lucid ['luːsɪd] adj. (a) clear/easily understood. (b) able to think clearly. **lucidity** [luːˈsɪdɪtɪ] n. being clear. **lucidly,** adv. in a lucid way.

luck [lʌk] n. (a) chance/fortune; **hard l.!** = I'm sorry you are unlucky; **as l. would have it** = as it happened; **to be down on your l.** = have bad luck. (b) good fortune; **to be out of l.** = have bad luck. **luckily,** adv. by good fortune. **luckless,** adj. with no luck/unlucky. **lucky,** adj. (-ier, -iest) (a) having good fortune/success. (b) having good fortune associated with it; **13's my l. number.**

lucre ['luːkə] n. inf. **(filthy) l.** = money. **lucrative** ['luːkrətɪv] adj. bringing in (much) money/profit.

ludicrous ['luːdɪkrəs] adj. causing laughter; ridiculous.

ludo ['lu:dəʊ] *n.* game played on a board with dice and counters.

luff [lʌf] *v.* to sail towards the wind.

lug [lʌg] 1. *n.* small projecting piece on the side of a jar, etc., for carrying it or for attaching sth to it. 2. *v.* (**lugged**) to pull (sth heavy) along. **lughole**, *n. Sl.* ear.

luggage ['lʌgɪdʒ] *n.* (*no pl.*) suitcases/bags, etc., for carrying your belongings when travelling; **l. rack** = space for bags, etc., above seats in a train, etc.

lugger ['lʌgə] *n.* small sailing boat.

lugubrious [lə'gu:brɪəs] *adj.* very miserable/mournful. **lugubriously**, *adv.* in a lugubrious way.

lukewarm ['lu:kwɔ:m] *adj.* (*a*) slightly warm, but not hot. (*b*) without enthusiasm.

lull [lʌl] 1. *n.* quiet(er)/calm(er) interval. 2. *v.* to make calmer/to soothe. **lullaby** ['lʌləbaɪ] *n.* song/piece of music designed to make a child sleep.

lumbago [lʌm'beɪgəʊ] *n.* pain in the lower part of the back. **lumbar** ['lʌmbə] *adj.* referring to the lower part of the back.

lumber ['lʌmbə] 1. *n.* (*a*) old articles which are not in use at the moment; junk; **l. room** = room in which you keep boxes/unwanted articles. (*b*) *Am.* wood which has been cut. 2. *v.* (*a*) *inf.* (**with**) to give (s.o.) things he doesn't really want. (*b*) to move with a slow heavy step/pace. **lumberjack**, *n.* person who cuts down trees. **lumber jacket**, *n.* short thick working coat.

lumen ['lu:mɪn] *n.* unit of measurement of light.

luminous ['lu:mɪnəs] *adj.* giving out light (in the dark). **luminary**, *n.* learned person. **luminiscence**, *n.* sending out light without heat. **luminosity** [lu:mɪ'nɒsɪtɪ] *n.* being luminous.

lump [lʌmp] 1. *n.* (*a*) (often shapeless) mass; **sugar l.** = solid cube of sugar; **l. sum** = money (paid) in one amount/not divided up. (*b*) swelling on the body. (*c*) *inf.* heavy, clumsy person. 2. *v.* (*a*) **to l. together** = to put together in one place/in one group. (*b*) *inf.* **he can l. it** = he'll just have to tolerate it. **lumpy**, *adj.* (**-ier, -iest**) having solid parts.

lunacy ['lu:nəsɪ] *n.* madness. **lunatic**, *adj. & n.* mad (person).

lunar ['lu:nə] *adj.* referring to the moon; **l. month** = period from one new moon to the next.

lunch [lʌnʃ] 1. *n.* (*pl.* **-es**) midday meal. 2. *v.* (*formal*) to have lunch. **luncheon** ['lʌnʃən] *n.* (*formal*) midday meal; **l. meat** = tinned meat loaf; **l. voucher** = ticket given to an employee to buy food with. **lunch hour, lunchtime**, *n.* period when the midday meal is usually eaten.

lung [lʌŋ] *n.* one of two organs in the chest, with which you breathe; **iron l.** = machine which allows a person to breathe if his lungs are not working properly. **lung fish**, *n.* type of fish which breathes through lungs.

lunge [lʌndʒ] 1. *n.* sudden forward movement. 2. *v.* to make a sudden movement forward.

lupin ['lu:pɪn] *n.* garden flower with tall flower spikes.

lupine ['lu:paɪn] *adj.* referring to a wolf.

lurch [lɜ:tʃ] 1. *n.* (*pl.* **-es**) (*a*) sudden (unsteady) movement. (*b*) *inf.* **to leave in the l.** = to leave/fail in time of trouble or crisis. 2. *v.* to move with a sudden unsteady movement. **lurcher**, *n.* dog used to retrieve game.

lure ['ljʊə] 1. *n.* (*a*) small object used to attract fish, etc., in order to catch them. (*b*) thing which traps/attracts. 2. *v.* to attract, esp. into sth bad.

lurid ['ljʊərɪd] *adj.* (*a*) (light, etc.) which glows in an unpleasant sinister way. (*b*) (*of book/film*) sensational/meant to shock. **luridly**, *adv.* in a lurid way. **luridness**, *n.* being lurid.

lurk [lɜ:k] *v.* to hide/to remain hidden.

luscious ['lʌʃəs] *adj.* good to taste.

lush [lʌʃ] 1. *adj.* (plants) growing thickly/richly. 2. *n. Sl.* drunkard. **lushness**, *n.* being lush.

lust [lʌst] 1. *n.* (*a*) strong sexual desire. (*b*) great desire for sth. 2. *v.* **to l.** (**after**) = to have a great desire for. **lustful**, *adj.* full of sexual desire.

lustre, *Am.* **luster** ['lʌstə] *n.* shine/brilliance. **lustrous**, *adj.* brilliant.

lusty ['lʌstɪ] *adj.* (**-ier, -iest**) strong/healthy. **lustily**, *adv.* strongly. **lustiness**, *n.* great strength/health.

lute [lu:t] *n.* old stringed musical instrument played like a guitar.

luv [lʌv] *n. inf.* (*form of address*) love.

luxuriance [lʌg'ʒuːrɪəns] n. great quantity/abundance. **luxuriant**, adj. growing abundantly. **luxuriantly**, adv. in a luxuriant way. **luxuriate**, v. to enjoy freely/to laze happily.

luxury ['lʌkʃəri] n. (a) great comfort. (b) thing which is pleasant to have but not necessary. **luxurious** [lʌg'ʒʊrɪəs] adj. very comfortable; very expensive. **luxuriously**, adv. in a luxurious way. **luxuriousness**, n. being comfortable/expensive.

lych-gate ['lɪtʃgeɪt] n. gate with a roof at the entrance to a churchyard.

lye [laɪ] n. water mixed with ashes, used for washing.

lying ['laɪɪŋ] v. see **lie**.

lymph [lɪmf] n. liquid found in animal tissues. **lymphatic** [lɪm'fætɪk] adj. referring to lymph.

lynch [lɪntʃ] v. (of a mob) to kill (s.o.) without trial (esp. by hanging).

lynx [lɪŋks] n. (pl. **-es**) spotted short-tailed animal of the cat family. **lynx-eyed**, adj. with very good eyesight.

lyre ['laɪə] n. old stringed musical instrument. **lyrebird**, n. tropical bird with tail feathers shaped like a lyre.

lyric ['lɪrɪk] adj. & n. (a) (poem, etc.) concerned with feeling. (b) (poem, etc.) intended to be sung. **lyrical**, adj. (a) (poem) using suitable language to express feelings. (b) inf. eager/enthusiastic. **lyrically**, adv. in a lyrical way. **lyricism** ['lɪrɪsɪzəm] n. quality of a poem which expresses feelings. **lyricist**, n. person who writes the words of a song. **lyrics**, n. pl. words of a song.

Mm

m abbrev. for metre; mile.

ma [mɑː] n. inf. mother.

ma'am [mɑːm] n. short for madam (now only used to address the Queen).

mac [mæk] n. inf. raincoat.

macabre [mə'kɑːbr] adj. causing horror; gruesome.

macadam [mə'kædəm] n. road surface made of small pieces of broken stone. **macadamized**, adj. covered with macadam.

macaroni [mækə'rəʊnɪ] n. Italian food, made of short thick tubes of flour paste.

macaroon [mækə'ruːn] n. small sweet almond biscuit.

macaw [mə'kɔː] n. brightly coloured South American parrot.

mace [meɪs] n. (a) heavy bar of wood/metal used in ceremonies to symbolize authority. (b) spice made from the outside of a nutmeg.

macerate ['mæsəreɪt] v. to soak in a liquid until soft.

Mach (number) ['mæk('nʌmbə)] n. figure showing the speed of supersonic aircraft in relation to the speed of sound; at M. one = at the speed of sound.

machete [mə'tʃetɪ] n. jungle knife used in South America.

Machiavellian [mækɪə'velɪən] adj. sly/clever (in political plotting).

machination [mækɪ'neɪʃn] n. plot.

machine [mə'ʃiːn] 1. n. (a) device in which power from a motor drives wheels/gears, etc. (b) organization. 2. v. to make/to shape with a machine; to sew with a sewing machine. **machine gun**, n. gun which automatically fires many bullets one after the other. **machinery**, n. (no pl.) mechanism; (working parts of) machines. (b) organization. **machine tools**, n. pl. tools operated by a motor and used to shape metal/wood, etc. **machining**, n. working with a machine. **machinist**, n. person who works a machine, esp. a sewing machine.

machismo [mə'kɪzməʊ] n. exaggerated sense of male pride. **macho** ['mætʃəʊ] adj. (man) who is aggressively male.

mackerel ['mækrəl] n. (pl. **mackerel**) common sea fish.

mackintosh ['mækɪntoʃ] n. raincoat.

macramé [mə'krɑːmeɪ] n. (no pl.) knotted string articles.

macro- ['mækrəʊ] prefix meaning very large/covering a wide area.

macrobiotic [mækrəʊbaɪ'ɒtɪk] adj. referring to a health-giving diet of cereals/vegetables, etc.

macrocosm ['mækrəʊkɒzəm] n. large complete system; the universe.

mad [mæd] adj. (**madder, maddest**) (a) not sane; wild/silly; inf. **like m.** = (i) very fast; (ii) very enthusiastically; **he's m. with/at you** = angry with you; **m. cow disease** = bovine spongiform encephalopathy, a disease affecting the brains of cattle. (*b*) very enthusiastic (**about** s.o./sth). (*c*) (dog) suffering from rabies. **madcap**, *adj. & n.* wild (person). **madden**, *v.* to make mad; to exasperate/to annoy. **maddening**, *adj.* exasperating. **madhouse**, *n.* place which is full of noise and people rushing about. **madly**, *adv.* like a madman. **madman**, *n.* (*pl.* **-men**) lunatic; **he drove like a m.** = he drove very fast/furiously. **madness**, *n.* being mad; lunacy. **madwoman**, *n.* (*pl.* **-women**) female lunatic.

madam ['mædəm] *n.* (*a*) formal way of addressing a woman. (*b*) woman who keeps a brothel.

madder ['mædə] *n.* plant which gives a red dye.

made [meɪd] *v. see* **make**.

madeira [mə'dɪərə] *n.* (*a*) sweet dessert wine. (*b*) **m. cake** = type of plain cake.

madonna [mə'dɒnə] *n.* (picture/statue of) the Virgin Mary.

madrigal ['mædrɪgl] *n.* group song popular in the sixteenth and seventeenth centuries.

maelstrom ['meɪlstrəm] *n.* violent whirlpool in the sea; violent confusion.

maestro ['maɪstrəʊ] *n.* (*pl.* **-os**) *inf.* musical genius; conductor.

mafia ['mæfɪə] *n.* secret (Italian) organization dealing in crime.

mag [mæg] *short for* magazine; magnetic.

magazine [mægə'ziːn] *n.* (*a*) (illustrated) paper which appears at regular intervals. (*b*) radio/TV programme made up from various items on the same theme, broadcast regularly. (*c*) box containing ammunition/film/slides which clips on to a gun/a camera/ projector. (*d*) room/building used as a store for explosives.

magenta [mə'dʒentə] *n. & adj.* dark red-purple (colour).

maggot ['mægət] *n.* white grub (of a bluebottle) which lives in rotting meat. **maggoty**, *adj.* full of maggots.

Magi ['meɪdʒaɪ] *n. pl.* wise men who brought gifts to the infant Christ.

magic ['mædʒɪk] **1.** *n.* spells/conjuring tricks, etc., which do not appear to follow normal scientific rules; **as if by m.** = suddenly/from nowhere; **black m.** =

evil spells designed to harm people. **2.** *adj.* enchanted. **magical**, *adj.* produced by magic; fairy-like. **magically**, *adv.* by magic. **magician** [mə'dʒɪʃn] *n.* wizard/ conjuror.

magisterial [mædʒɪ'stɪərɪəl] *adj.* with an air of authority. **magisterially**, *adv.* in a commanding way.

magistrate ['mædʒɪstreɪt] *n.* judge in a minor court.

magma ['mægmə] *n.* (*a*) molten rock under the earth's crust. (*b*) paste.

Magna Carta ['mægnə 'kɑːtə] *n.* charter, signed by King John in 1215, which gave basic rights to some subjects.

magnanimous [mæg'nænɪməs] *adj.* very generous. **magnanimity** [mægnə'nɪmɪtɪ] *n.* great generosity. **magnanimously**, *adv.* in a magnanimous way.

magnate ['mægneɪt] *n.* important businessman.

magnesium [mæg'niːzɪəm] *n.* (*element:* Mg) metal which burns with a brilliant white light. **magnesia**, *n.* white powder made from magnesium used in medicines.

magnet ['mægnət] *n.* thing which attracts, esp. a metal object which attracts iron and steel and points roughly north and south when suspended. **magnetic** [mæg'netɪk] *adj.* having a power of attraction; **m. pole/m. north** = the point to which the needle of a compass points; **m. field** = area around a magnet which is under its influence; **m. mine** = floating bomb which is attracted to a passing ship; **m. tape** = plastic tape for recording music/information, etc. **magnetically**, *adv.* by a magnet. **magnetism** ['mægnətɪzəm] *n.* (*a*) natural attractive power of magnets. (*b*) personal power of attraction. **magnetize**, *v.* to make (a piece of metal) into a magnet.

magneto [mæg'niːtəʊ] *n.* (*pl.* **-os**) device in an engine which produces electricity used for ignition.

magnificent [mæg'nɪfɪsnt] *adj.* very fine/splendid/very luxurious. **magnificence**, *n.* splendour/luxury. **magnificently**, *adv.* in a magnificent way.

magnify ['mægnɪfaɪ] *v.* to make (something) appear larger; **magnifying glass** = lens which makes small objects appear larger. **magnification** [mægnıfı'keıʃn] *n.* making something appear larger; degree to which things appear larger. **magnifier**, *n.* thing which magnifies.

magnitude ['mægnıtjuːd] *n.* size; (*of stars*) brightness.

magnolia [mæg'nəʊlıə] *n.* (*a*) large tree with huge flowers. (*b*) very pale pink colour.

magnum ['mægnəm] *n.* very large bottle (of wine, esp. champagne).

magpie ['mægpaı] *n.* common large black and white bird.

maharajah [maːhə'raːdʒə] *n.* Indian prince. **maharani** [maːhə'raːniː] *n.* Indian princess.

mahatma [mə'hætmə] *n.* (*in India*) title given to a holy man.

mahjong [maː'dʒɒŋ] *n.* Chinese game played with small counters.

mahogany [mə'hɒgənı] *n.* dark wood used for making furniture.

maid [meıd] *n.* female servant; **old m.** = middle-aged unmarried woman. **maiden. 1.** *n.* (*formal*) unmarried girl/ woman. **2.** *adj.* (*a*) unmarried (woman); **m. aunt** = unmarried aunt; **m. name** = surname of a woman before she is married. (*b*) first; **m. voyage/flight** = first voyage of a new ship/of a new aircraft; **m. speech** = first speech of a Member of Parliament. **maidenhair**, *n.* type of fern. **maidenhood**, *n.* (*formal*) being a maiden. **maidenly**, *adj.* (*formal*) like a maiden. **maiden (over)**, *n.* (*in cricket*) over where no runs are scored.

mail [meıl] **1.** *n.* (*a*) letters delivered. (*b*) postal services; **m. order** = ordering and buying by post; **m. merge** = computer program which allows the same letter to be written to many different addresses. (*c*) **chain m.** = type of armour made of small interlocking metal rings. **2.** *v.* to send (sth) by the postal services. **mailbag**, *n.* large canvas bag for carrying mail. **mailbox**, *n. Am.* letterbox. **mailing list**, *n.* list of names and addresses of people to whom information can be sent. **mailman**, *n.* (*pl.* -men) *Am.* man who delivers letters.

maim [meım] *v.* to wound; to make lame.

main [meın] **1.** *n.* (*a*) (*formal*) **with might and m.** = with all your strength. (*b*) **in the m.** = generally speaking. (*c*) central pipe for distributing water/gas, etc. (*d*) **the mains** = electric power. **2.** *adj.* most important; **to have an eye to the m. chance** = to watch out for the best way of making money/of improving your position. **mainland** ['meınlənd] *n.* large solid mass of land. **mainly**, *adv.* mostly/in a very important way. **mainmast**, *n.* most important mast on a ship. **mainsail** ['meınsl] *n.* most important sail on a ship. **mainspring**, *n.* (*a*) central spring of a watch. (*b*) most important force which makes you do sth. **mainstay**, *n.* principal support. **mainstream**, *n.* most important trend in a form of art.

maintain [meın'teın] *v.* (*a*) to keep (order); to keep (doing sth). (*b*) to keep sth in working order. (*c*) to state/to assert. **maintenance**, *n.* (*a*) keeping. (*b*) money for upkeep.

maisonette [meızə'net] *n.* flat on two floors.

maître d'hôtel ['metrədəʊ'tel], *Am.* **maître d'** [metrə'diː] *n.* head waiter.

maize [meız] *n.* tall cereal crop.

majesty ['mædʒəstı] *n.* (*a*) greatness. (*b*) form of address to a King or Queen. **majestic** [mə'dʒestık] *adj.* grand/ stately. **majestically**, *adv.* grandly.

major ['meıdʒə] **1.** *n.* (*a*) army officer above a captain. (*b*) (*formal*) legally adult person. **2.** *adj.* (*a*) bigger; more important; **the m. part of the work** = most of the work. (*b*) musical key where there are semitones between the third and fourth, and between the seventh and eighth notes. **3.** *v.* to specialize in a subject as an undergraduate. **majordomo**, *n.* chief servant in a large house. **majorette** [meıdʒə-'ret] *n.* girl bandleader or marcher. **major-general**, *n.* senior army officer below a lieutenant-general. **majority** [mə'dʒɒrıtı] *n.* (*a*) larger part. (*b*) larger number of voters; **the government has a m. of one** = has one vote more than the opposition. (*c*) legally adult age.

make [meık] **1.** *n.* (*a*) brand; country of origin (of an object). (*b*) *inf.* **he's on the m.** = all he wants to do is to make money. **2.** *v.* (**made**) (*a*) to prepare; to do; to construct; **to m. the beds** = to tidy the beds after they have been slept in. (*b*) to earn; **I m. £50 a week.** (*c*) to add up to; to score. (*d*) to cause (s.o.) to be; **he made himself comfortable.** (*e*) to force (s.o.) to do sth; **make away with,** *v.* to remove (sth)/to make (sth) disappear. **make-believe,** *n.* pretending/believing sth is true when it is not. **make do,** *v.* (**with**) to put up with (sth)/to use (sth) even if it is not suitable. **make for,** *v.* to aim; to go towards. **make good,** *v.* (*a*) to put (sth) right. (*b*) to carry out (a promise). (*c*) to become successful. **make of,** *v.* to consider; **what do you make of it?** = what do you think of it? **make off with,** *v.* to run away with (sth)/to steal (sth). **make out,** *v.* (*a*) to draw up (a list); to write (a cheque). (*b*) to distinguish/to see properly. (*c*) to assert/to maintain. (*d*) *inf.* to succeed. **make over,** *v.* to transfer. **maker,** *n.* person who makes sth. **makeshift,** *adj. & n.* (thing) used temporarily in place of sth else. **make up,** *v.* (*a*) to complete/to fill up; **I can't make up my mind** = I can't decide; **to make up for lost time** = to act specially quickly. (*b*) to put lipstick/powder, etc., on your face. (*c*) to invent. (*d*) **to make it up** = to become friends again. (*e*) **to make it up to s.o.** = to compensate s.o. for sth lost/damaged, etc. **make-up,** *n.* (*a*) composition. (*b*) character. (*c*) lipstick/cream/powder, etc., used to beautify your face. **makeweight,** *n.* small quantity added to make up the weight of sth. **making,** *n.* formation; **it was 3 years in the m.** = it took 3 years to make; **it has the makings of** = it may develop into.

malacca [mæl'ækə] *n.* tropical cane used to make walking sticks.

malachite ['mæləkaɪt] *n.* green stone.

maladjusted [mælə'dʒʌstɪd] *adj.* (person) who does not fit into society. **maladjustment,** *n.* being maladjusted.

maladministration [mælədmɪnɪ'streɪʃn] *n.* incompetent administration.

maladroit [mælə'drɔɪt] *adj.* (*formal*) clumsy.

malady ['mælədɪ] *n.* (*formal*) illness.

malaise [mæ'leɪz] *n.* (*formal*) awkward feeling; slight sickness.

malapropism ['mæləprɒpɪzəm] *n.* incorrect use of a word which sounds similar to the correct one.

malaria [mə'leərɪə] *n.* tropical fever caused by a parasite carried by mosquitoes. **malarial,** *adj.* referring to malaria.

Malaysian [mə'leɪʒn] **1.** *adj.* referring to Malaysia. **2.** *n.* person from Malaysia. **Malay,** *n. & adj.* (person) from Malaysia; language spoken in Malaysia.

malcontent ['mælkəntent] *n.* (*formal*) dissatisfied person.

male [meɪl] **1.** *adj.* (*a*) referring to men/boys. (*b*) referring to the sex which fertilizes eggs produced by females. **2.** *n.* (*a*) man/boy. (*b*) animal/insect of the sex which does not give birth to offspring.

malefactor ['mælɪfæktə] *n.* (*formal*) criminal.

malevolence [mə'levələns] *n.* (*formal*) ill-will; desire to hurt others. **malevolent,** *adj.* wishing (s.o.) ill.

malfeasance [mæl'fiːzəns] *n.* (*formal*) an unlawful act.

malformation [mælfɔ:'meɪʃn] *n.* being wrongly shaped/badly formed. **malformed,** *adj.* badly formed/shaped.

malfunction [mæl'fʌŋkʃn] **1.** *n.* bad/incorrect working (of a machine/of the heart, etc.). **2.** *v.* to work badly.

malice ['mælɪs] *n.* unfriendly feelings; **out of m.** = to be spiteful. **malicious** [mə'lɪʃəs] *adj.* wicked/intentionally spiteful; wanting to hurt others. **maliciously,** *adv.* in a malicious way.

malign [mə'laɪn] *v.* to say bad things about (s.o.); **he has been much maligned** = people have criticized him a lot. **malignancy** [mə'lɪgnənsɪ] *n.* being malignant. **malignant** [mə'lɪgnənt] *adj.* (*a*) wishing harm to someone. (*b*) likely to be fatal. **malignity,** *n.* malignant feeling.

malinger [mə'lɪŋgə] *v.* to pretend to be ill (to avoid work). **malingerer,** *n.* person who pretends to be ill.

mall [mɔ:l] *n. Am.* shopping precinct or covered shopping arcade.

mallard ['mælɑ:d] *n.* common wild duck.

malleable ['mælɪəbl] *adj.* soft/which can be moulded into shape. **malleability,** *n.* being malleable.

mallet ['mælɪt] *n.* large wooden hammer.

mallow ['mæləʊ] *n.* wild flower growing in marshy ground.

malnutrition [mælnjuː'trɪʃn] *n.* lack of enough good food.

malodorous [mæl'əʊdərəs] *adj.* (*formal*) which smells bad.

malpractice [mæl'præktɪs] *n.* illegal use of your position/authority to gain money.

malt [mɔːlt] *n.* grain which has been prepared for making beer or whisky by being allowed to sprout and then dried. **malted,** *adj.* tasting of malt.

Maltese [mɒl'tiːz] *adj. & n.* (person) from Malta.

maltreat [mæl'triːt] *v.* to treat (s.o.) badly. **maltreatment,** *n.* rough treatment.

mama [mə'mɑː] *n.* child's name for mother.

mamba ['mæmbə] *n.* poisonous African snake.

mambo ['mæmbəʊ] *n.* South American dance.

mamma [mə'mɑː] *n.* = **mama.**

mammal ['mæml] *n.* type of animal which gives birth to live young and suckles them with milk. **mammalian** [mə'meɪlɪən] *adj.* referring to mammals. **mammary,** *adj.* referring to the breast.

mammon ['mæmən] *n.* evil wealth.

mammoth ['mæməθ] **1.** *n.* very large prehistoric hairy elephant. **2.** *adj.* huge.

man [mæn] **1.** *n.* (*pl.* **men**) (*a*) human being. (*b*) person; **the m. in the street** = the ordinary citizen; **no man's land** = land between two armies which belongs to neither side. (*c*) male human adult. (*d*) husband. (*e*) servant; ordinary soldier/worker. (*f*) piece (in chess, etc.). **2.** *v.* (**manned**) to provide with men; to be the workforce for (a machine/an office, etc.). **man-eater,** *n.* animal which eats people. **man-eating,** *adj.* (animal) which eats people. **manfully,** *adv.* like a man; in a strong/forceful way. **manhandle,** *v.* (*a*) to move (something large and heavy) by hand. (*b*) to handle someone roughly. **manhole,** *n.* hole in the road or pavement through which you go down into the sewers/into a coal store, etc. **manhood,** *n.* (*no pl.*) state of

being an adult male. **man-hour,** *n.* work done by one man in one hour. **manhunt,** *n.* search (for a criminal). **mankind** [mæn'kaɪnd] *n.* (*no pl.*) the human race. **manliness,** *n.* virility/male characteristics. **manly,** *adj.* virile/with very strong male features; brave. **man-made,** *adj.* artificial (material, etc.). **mannish,** *adj.* (woman) who looks/dresses like a man. **manpower,** *n.* work force/number of workmen. **man-of-war,** *n.* (*a*) (*old*) battleship. (*b*) **Portuguese man-of-war** = type of very large jellyfish. **manservant,** *n.* male servant. **man-sized,** *adj.* of the right size for one man. **manslaughter,** *n.* killing s.o. without intending to do so.

manacle ['mænəkl] **1.** *n.* one of two steel rings connected by a chain, which attach the wrists of a prisoner together. **2.** *v.* to attach (a prisoner's) wrists together.

manage ['mænɪdʒ] *v.* (*a*) to direct. (*b*) to arrange to do sth; to succeed in doing sth; **can she m. all by herself?** = can she cope/can she do the work all by herself? **manageable,** *adj.* which can be managed/directed. **management,** *n.* (*a*) handling of (a tool); directing (of work). (*b*) group of people who direct workers; **under new m.** = with a new owner/manager. **manager,** *n.* (*a*) head of a department in a commercial firm. (*b*) person who manages/directs; director of a theatre; organizer of a sports team/singer, etc.; person who runs a shop. **manageress** [mænɪdʒə'res] *n.* (*pl.* **-es**) woman who runs a shop. **managerial** [mænə'dʒɪərɪəl] *adj.* referring to a manager; **discussions at m. level** = discussions among managers. **managing director,** *n.* overall director of a firm.

manatee [mænə'tiː] *n.* large plant-eating sea mammal.

mandamus [mæn'deɪməs] *n.* order from a higher court to a lower court.

mandarin ['mændərɪn] *n.* (*a*) small orange with a soft easily-peeled skin. (*b*) important government official. (*c*) **Mandarin** = principal form of the Chinese language.

mandate ['mændeɪt] *n.* power given to a person to act on behalf of s.o. else; **the government has a m. from the people to**

cut taxes = people approved of the plan to cut taxes when they voted for the government. **mandated**, *adj.* (territory) which is entrusted to a country to administer. **mandatory** ['mændətərɪ] *adj.* obligatory/compulsory.

mandible ['mændɪbl] *n.* lower jawbone (of birds/insects, etc.).

mandolin ['mændəlɪn] *n.* stringed instrument like a small guitar.

mandrel ['mændrəl] *n.* the turning central shaft of a lathe.

mandrill ['mændrɪl] *n.* large baboon.

mane [meɪn] *n.* long hair on neck of a lion or horse; long untidy hair.

maneuver [məˈnuːvə] *n.* & *v.* Am. see **manœuvre**.

manganese ['mæŋgəniːz] *n.* (element: Mn) grey metal.

mange [meɪndʒ] *n.* disease of the skin of animals, which makes the hair fall out. **mangy**, *adj.* dirty/diseased.

mangel-wurzel ['mæŋglwɜːzl] *n.* beet used as food for cattle.

manger ['meɪndʒə] *n.* box for food for horses/cows, etc.

mangle ['mæŋgl] 1. *n.* device with rollers for squeezing the water out of clothes. 2. *v.* (*a*) to squeeze water out of (clothes) by passing them through a mangle. (*b*) to tear; to chop up; to mess up.

mango ['mæŋgəʊ] *n.* (*pl.* **-oes**) large tropical fruit with a big stone.

mangrove ['mæŋgrəʊv] *n.* kind of tropical tree growing in wet areas.

mania ['meɪnɪə] *n.* madness; exaggerated passion (**for** sth). **maniac**, *n.* mad person. **maniacal** [məˈnaɪəkl] *adj.* mad. **manic** ['mænɪk] *adj.* referring to mania.

manicure ['mænɪkjʊə] 1. *n.* looking after the hands; **to have a m.** = to have your hands cleaned and nails trimmed. 2. *v.* to look after the hands. **manicure set**, *n.* small box or bag with scissors/nail file, etc. **manicurist**, *n.* person who looks after people's hands.

manifest ['mænɪfest] 1. *adj.* (*formal*) obvious/plain to see. 2. *n.* list of goods in a shipment. 3. *v.* (*formal*) to appear/ to show. **manifestation** [mænɪfe-ˈsteɪʃn] *n.* appearance. **manifestly**, *adv.* (*formal*) obviously. **manifesto**

[mænɪˈfestəʊ] *n.* (*pl.* **-os**) programme of action outlined by a political party.

manifold ['mænɪfəʊld] 1. *adj.* (*formal*) of varying sorts. 2. *n.* **exhaust m.** = tubes of an exhaust pipe of a car.

manikin ['mænɪkɪn] *n.* very small man.

manilla [məˈnɪlə] *n.* thick brown paper (used for envelopes).

manioc ['mænɪɒk] *n.* tropical plant from which a flour is made.

manipulate [məˈnɪpjʊleɪt] *v.* to handle; to falsify (accounts) to make them seem more profitable. **manipulation** [mənɪpjʊˈleɪʃn] *n.* handling (of machinery); falsification (of accounts). **manipulator**, *n.* person who manipulates.

manna ['mænə] *n.* unexpected help/ food.

mannequin ['mænɪkɪn] *n.* person or dummy wearing clothes to show them to possible buyers.

manner ['mænə] *n.* (*a*) way of behaving/ acting; (*b*) **manners** = way of acting in public. (*c*) sort; **in a m. of speaking** = in a sort of way. **mannered**, *adj.* full of mannerisms. **mannerism**, *n.* affected way of acting/odd way of doing sth. **mannerly**, *adj.* well-behaved.

manœuvre, *Am.* **maneuver** [məˈnuːvə] 1. *n.* (*a*) action of moving sth. (*b*) **manœuvres** = military exercises. 2. *v.* (*a*) to move (sth) heavy/ awkward. (*b*) to work to put yourself in a good position. **manœuvrability** [mənuːvrəˈbɪlɪtɪ] *n.* ability to be easily manœuvred. **manœuvrable**, *adj.* which can be manœuvred/moved.

manometer [mæˈnɒmɪtə] *n.* instrument for measuring pressure.

manor ['mænə] *n.* (land surrounding) a country house; **m. house** = country house.

mansard ['mænsɑːd] *n.* **m. (roof)** = roof where the top part slopes more gently than the bottom.

manse [mæns] *n.* (*in Scotland*) church minister's house.

mansion ['mænʃən] *n.* very large private house; **mansions** = large block of flats.

mantelpiece ['mæntlpiːs] *n.* shelf above a fireplace.

mantis ['mæntɪs] *n.* **praying m.** = large tropical insect.

mantle ['mæntl] *n.* (*a*) cloak. (*b*) gauze cover for a gas lamp.

manual ['mænjʊəl] **1.** *adj.* (*a*) done by hand. (*b*) (car) where the gears are changed by hand. **2.** *n.* (*a*) book of instructions. (*b*) keyboard of an organ. **manually,** *adv.* (done) by hand.

manufacture [mænjʊ'fæktʃə] **1.** *n.* making of a commercially produced product. **2.** *v.* to make (products) commercially; **manufacturing town** = industrial town. **manufacturer,** *n.* person/company producing industrial products.

manure [mə'njʊə] **1.** *n.* dung of animals used as a fertilizer on land. **2.** *v.* to spread manure on (land).

manuscript ['mænjʊskrɪpt] *adj.* & *n.* (document/novel/poem) written by hand or typed, etc., but not printed.

Manx [mæŋks] *adj.* & *n.* (person, etc.) from the Isle of Man.

many ['menɪ] *adj.* & *n.* (**more, most**) great number; **a good m. prisoners** = quite a large number; **m. a time** = often.

Maori ['maʊrɪ] **1.** *adj.* referring to the original natives of New Zealand. **2.** *n.* (*a*) language spoken by the native race of New Zealand. (*b*) member of the native race of New Zealand.

map [mæp] **1.** *n.* diagram of a town/country as if seen from above; **street m.** = diagram showing streets with their names; **physical m.** = diagram showing mountains/rivers, etc.; **political m.** = diagram showing the borders of countries/administrative districts, etc. **2.** *v.* (**mapped**) to draw a diagram of (a town or country); **to m. out a route** = to plan a journey in advance. **mapping,** *n.* art of making maps; **m. pen** = pen with a very fine nib.

maple ['meɪpl] *n.* northern tree, with sweet sap; **m. sugar/m. syrup** = sugar/syrup made from the sap of the maple tree.

mar [maː] *v.* (**marred**) to spoil.

marabou ['mærəbuː] *n.* large stork, with a heavy bill.

maracas [mæ'rækəs] *n. pl.* percussion instrument, formed of a pair of gourds with dried seeds inside them.

maraschino [mærə'skiːnəʊ] *n.* (*pl.* **-os**) cherry used to make liqueur or jam.

marathon ['mærəθən] *n.* long distance race; (sth) which lasts a long time.

maraud [mə'rɔːd] *v.* to raid; to go about looking for plunder. **marauder,** *n.* person who raids. **marauding,** *adj.* (person) who raids.

marble ['maːbl] *n.* (*a*) very hard type of limestone which can be brilliantly polished. (*b*) small glass ball for playing with. **marbled,** *adj.* with streaks of different colours.

March [maːtʃ] *n.* 3rd month of the year.

march [maːtʃ] **1.** *n.* (*pl.* **-es**) (*a*) military walking in step; **route m.** = long training march; **m. past** = ceremonial parade of soldiers; **quick m.** = rapid walking pace; **slow m.** = slow walking pace. (*b*) **protest m.** = mass of people walking in a line to protest about sth. (*c*) music for marching. (*d*) progress/advance of time/events. (*e*) **the marches** = border region. **2.** *v.* (*a*) to walk in step; **quick m.!** = order to walk at a rapid pace; **the police marched him off to prison** = removed him quickly to prison. (*b*) to walk quickly and purposefully. (*c*) to walk in a protest march. **marcher,** *n.* person who marches.

mare ['meə] *n.* female horse; **mare's tails** = thin wispy clouds showing a change in the weather; **mare's nest** = discovery which turns out to be useless.

margarine [maːdʒə'riːn] *n.* mixture of animal or vegetable fat which is used instead of butter. **marge** [maːdʒ] *n. inf.* margarine.

margin ['maːdʒɪn] *n.* (*a*) edge/border (of a page). (*b*) extra space/time; **leave a m. for error** = allow extra space/time in case you have made a mistake in your calculations; **safety m.** = space/time left to allow for safety. (*c*) money received which is more than money paid. **marginal,** *adj.* (*a*) (note) in a margin. (*b*) (parliamentary seat) where there is very little difference in the votes of the opposing parties. (*c*) slight. **marginally,** *adv.* slightly.

marguerite [maːgə'riːt] *n.* common large white daisy.

marigold ['mærɪgəʊld] *n.* common garden plant with yellow flowers.

marijuana [mærɪ'hwaːnə] *n.* drug made from hemp.

marina [mə'ri:nə] *n.* harbour for yachts/ motor boats, etc.

marinade [mærɪ'neɪd] **1.** *n.* mixture of wine and herbs, etc., in which meat or fish is soaked before cooking. **2.** *v.* (*also* **marinate**) to soak (meat or fish) in a mixture of wine and herbs.

marine [mə'ri:n] **1.** *adj.* referring to the sea. **2.** *n.* (*a*) **the merchant m.** = the merchant navy. (*b*) soldier serving on a ship. **mariner** ['mærɪnə] *n.* sailor.

marionette [mærɪə'net] *n.* string puppet.

marital ['mærɪtl] *adj.* referring to marriage.

maritime ['mærɪtaɪm] *adj.* referring to the sea.

marjoram ['mɑ:dʒərəm] *n.* common herb used as flavouring.

mark [mɑ:k] **1.** *n.* (*a*) spot/stain; thing which can be seen. (*b*) target; **wide of the m.** = far from correct. (*c*) sign; **punctuation m.** = printing sign (such as full stop/comma, etc.). (*d*) number of points given to a student. (*e*) starting line in a race; **on your marks** = get ready at your places. (*f*) line indicating a point reached. (*g*) unit of money in Germany. **2.** *v.* (*a*) to make a sign on (sth). (*b*) to correct and give points to. (*c*) **to m. time** = (i) to march on one spot; (ii) to stay in one place/not to advance. (*d*) to follow closely (an opposing player in football/Rugby, etc.). **mark down,** *v.* to lower the price of (sth). **marked,** *adj.* obvious/noticeable; **a m. man** = man who has been selected by the enemy as a probable target. **markedly** ['mɑ:kɪdlɪ] *adv.* obviously. **marker,** *n.* thing which marks; person who notes the scores in a competition, etc.; **m. buoy** = buoy used to indicate a dangerous spot; **m. pen** = coloured felt pen which makes a wide mark. **marking,** *n.* (*a*) making marks; **m. ink** = black ink which will not wash off. (*b*) **markings** = spots/stripes, etc., on a bird or animal. (*c*) correcting (exercises/homework, etc). **mark out,** *v.* to indicate the boundaries of (a land); to select. **marksman,** *n.* (*pl.* **-men**) person who shoots well. **marksmanship,** *n.* ability to shoot well. **mark up,** *v.* to increase the price of (sth). **mark-up,** *n.* amount added to the cost price to give the selling price.

market ['mɑ:kɪt] **1.** *n.* (*a*) selling of produce (from stalls); place where produce is sold (from stalls); **m. day** = special day when a market is held. (*b*) sale; **on the m.** = for sale. (*c*) place where a product is required/could be sold; need for a product; **m. research** = examination of the possible sales of a product before it is launched; **the Common M.** = the European Economic Community; **black m.** = illegal selling at high prices. **2.** *v.* to sell (products). **marketable,** *adj.* which can be sold easily. **market garden,** *n.* small farm growing vegetables/fruit for sale in a nearby town. **market gardener,** *n.* person who runs a market garden. **marketing,** *n.* selling techniques (publicity/packaging, etc.) for a product. **marketplace,** *n.* place where a market is held/where goods are sold.

marl [mɑ:l] *n.* soil which is a mixture of clay and lime.

marlinespike ['mɑ:lɪnspaɪk] *n.* pointed hook, used for unravelling rope.

marmalade ['mɑ:məleɪd] *n.* jam made from oranges/lemons or grapefruit.

marmoset [mɑ:mə'zet] *n.* small American monkey.

marmot ['mɑ:mət] *n.* small burrowing animal.

maroon [mə'ru:n] **1.** *adj. & n.* deep purple red (colour). **2.** *n.* firework used as a distress signal by ships. **3.** *v.* to abandon in an awkward place.

marquee [mɑ:'ki:] *n.* very large tent.

marquetry ['mɑ:kətrɪ] *n.* (making) patterns on the surface of wood with inlaid pieces of different-coloured wood or ivory.

marram grass ['mærəm'grɑ:s] *n.* type of grass used to stabilize sand dunes.

marriage ['mærɪdʒ] *n.* (*a*) state of being legally joined as husband and wife. (*b*) ceremony of being married. **marriageable,** *adj.* suitable to become married.

marrow ['mærəʊ] *n.* (*a*) soft interior of bones. (*b*) large green vegetable growing on a creeping plant. **marrowfat pea,** *n.* type of pea with large seeds.

marry ['mærɪ] *v.* (*a*) to make (two people) husband and wife. (*b*) to become married to (s.o.). **married,** *adj.* joined as husband and wife; **m. name** = name taken by a woman when she gets married.

marsala [mɑːˈsɑːlə] *n.* sweet Italian wine.

marsh [mɑːʃ] *n.* (*pl.* **-es**) wet/swampy land; **m. marigold** = common yellow flower growing in marshes; **m. mallow** = common pink flower growing in marshes. **marshmallow,** *n.* soft and sticky white or pink sweet. **marshy,** *adj.* (**-ier, -iest**) swampy/wet (land).

marshal [ˈmɑːʃl] **1.** *n.* (*a*) very high-ranking military officer; **M. of the Royal Air Force** = highest rank in the Royal Air Force. (*b*) organizer (of a race/a show). (*c*) *Am.* police chief. **2.** *v.* (**marshalled**) to set out (facts) in order; to organize (a race/a show). **marshalling yard,** *n.* railway yard where wagons are sorted out into trains.

marsupial [mɑːˈsuːpɪəl] *adj. & n.* (animal) which carries its young in a pouch.

mart [mɑːt] *n.* market.

martello tower [mɑːˈteləʊˈtauə] *n.* round fort, built by the sea in the 19th century.

marten [ˈmɑːtɪn] *n.* small wild flesh-eating animal like a weasel.

martial [ˈmɑːʃl] *adj.* referring to war; **m. music** = marches played by military bands; **m. law** = maintenance of law by the army instead of the police; **m. arts** = oriental fighting techniques using swords/sticks, etc.

Martian [ˈmɑːʃn] *n.* being which is said to inhabit the planet Mars.

martin [ˈmɑːtɪn] *n.* small dark bird similar to a swallow.

martinet [mɑːtɪˈnet] *n.* very strict person.

martingale [ˈmɑːtɪŋgeɪl] *n.* strap to hold a horse's head down.

martini [mɑːˈtiːnɪ] *n.* drink made of gin/vodka and vermouth.

martyr [ˈmɑːtə] **1.** *n.* person killed because of his religious beliefs; **a m. to** = suffering a lot from. **2.** *v.* to kill (s.o.) for their religious beliefs. **martyrdom,** *n.* death for one's beliefs.

marvel [ˈmɑːvl] **1.** *n.* object of wonder. **2.** *v.* (**marvelled**) to show wonder/sur-prise (**at** s.o./sth). **marvellous,** *adj.* wonderful/amazing.

Marxism [ˈmɑːksɪzəm] *n.* political theory of the philosopher Marx, on which communism is based. **Marxist,** *adj. & n.* (person) who follows Marxism.

marzipan [ˈmɑːzɪpæn] *n.* paste made from almonds, used for making sweets or covering cakes.

mascara [mæˈskɑːrə] *n.* liquid/paste for making eyelashes dark.

mascot [ˈmæskət] *n.* object/animal which brings good luck.

masculine [ˈmæskjʊlɪn] *adj.* (*a*) male/manly. (*b*) (*in grammar*) referring to words which have a particular form to indicate the male gender. **masculinity** [mæskjʊˈlɪnɪtɪ] *n.* manliness.

maser [ˈmeɪzə] *n.* device which amplifies microwaves.

mash [mæʃ] **1.** *n.* (*a*) mixture of things crushed together. (*b*) *inf.* mashed potatoes. (*c*) food mixture for horses. (*d*) mixture used as the base for making beer. **2.** *v.* to crush (sth) into a paste. **masher,** *n.* device for crushing. **mashie,** *n.* type of heavy metal golf club.

mask [mɑːsk] **1.** *n.* covering to disguise/to protect the face. **2.** *v.* to cover up/to hide. **masked,** *adj.* wearing a mask. **masking tape,** *n.* tape used to cover an area which is not being painted.

masochist [ˈmæsəkɪst] *n.* person who enjoys being hurt. **masochism,** *n.* enjoyment at being hurt. **masochistic,** *adj.* referring to masochism.

mason [ˈmeɪsn] *n.* (*a*) person who builds with stone. (*b*) member of a secret society of freemasons. **masonic** [məˈsɒnɪk] *adj.* referring to freemasons. **masonry** [ˈmeɪsnrɪ] *n.* art of building with stone; large stones in a building.

masquerade [mɑːskəˈreɪd] **1.** *n.* (*a*) dance/party where people wear masks. (*b*) pretence/hiding of the truth. **2.** *v.* (**as**) to pretend to be (s.o.).

mass [mæs] **1.** *n.* (*pl.* **-es**) (*a*) Catholic communion service; **high m.** = mass with full ceremony; **low m.** = mass without ceremony; **Requiem M.** = (music for) a mass for the dead. (*b*) (*in physics*) solid body. (*c*) (*in physics*) amount of

matter in a body. (*d*) large number/
large quantity; **m. murderer** = killer of
a large number of people; **m. meeting**
= meeting of a lot of people; **m. production** = production of a large number of products; **m. media** = means of
communicating (TV/radio/newspapers)
which reach a large number of people.
(*e*) **the masses** = the common people. 2.
v. to group together into a mass. **mass-
produce,** *v*. to produce a large number
of (products) at the same time.

massacre ['mæsəkə] 1. *n*. killing of a lot
of people/animals. 2. *v*. to kill a lot of
people/animals.

massage ['mæsɑːʒ] 1. *n*. rubbing of
the body to relieve pain or to reduce
weight. 2. *v*. to rub (s.o.'s body)
to relieve pain or to reduce weight.
masseur [mæ'sɜː] *n*. man who massages. **masseuse** [mæ'sɜːz] *n*. woman
who massages.

massive ['mæsɪv] *adj*. very large. **mas-
sively,** *adv*. very much. **massiveness,**
n. being massive.

mast [mɑːst] *n*. (*a*) tall pole on a ship
to carry the sails. (*b*) tall metal construction to carry an aerial. (*c*) (*no pl.*)
seeds of beech/oak, etc., trees.

mastectomy [mæ'stektəmɪ] *n*. operation to remove a breast.

master ['mɑːstə] 1. *n*. (*a*) person in
control; captain (of a ship). (*b*) male
teacher; person with a second degree
from a university. (*c*) head of a college.
(*d*) skilled person; **an old m.** = painting by a great painter of the past.
2. *adj*. controlling; **m. key** = main
key; **m. switch** = switch which controls
all other switches; **m. tape** = main
tape from which copies are made; **m.
bedroom** = main bedroom. 3. *v*. to
become skilled at (sth); to gain control of (sth). **master-at-arms,** *n*. (*in
the navy*) petty officer in charge of
small arms and discipline. **masterful,**
adj. commanding/like a commander.
masterfully, *adv*. in a commanding
way. **masterly,** *adj*. clever; like an expert. **mastermind.** 1. *n*. very clever
person. 2. *v*. to be the brains behind (a plan). **masterpiece,** *n*. very
fine painting/book/piece of music, etc.
masterstroke, *n*. very clever action.

mastery, *n*. control over s.o.; complete
understanding of a subject; great skill
at a game.

mastic ['mæstɪk] *n*. gum from certain
trees.

masticate ['mæstɪkeɪt] *v*. (*formal*) to
chew. **mastication** [mæstɪ'keɪʃn] *n*.
chewing.

mastiff ['mæstɪf] *n*. large fierce breed of
dog.

mastoid ['mæstɔɪd] *n*. (*a*) bone just behind the ear. (*b*) *inf*. **mastoids** = inflammation of the mastoid.

masturbate ['mæstəbeɪt] *v*. to rub the
sex organs to excite them. **mastur-
bation** [mæstə'beɪʃn] *n*. exciting the sex
organs by rubbing.

mat [mæt] *n*. (*a*) small piece of carpet/
woven straw, etc. used as a floor covering; **bath m.** = small carpet to step on
to when getting out of a bath. (*b*) small
piece of cloth/wood/glass put under a
plate on a table. **matted,** *adj*. stuck together (like a mat). **matting,** *n*. (material for making) large mats; **coconut
m.** = floor covering made from coconut
fibres.

matador ['mætədɔː] *n*. bullfighter who
fights on foot.

match [mætʃ] 1. *n*. (*pl*. **-es**) (*a*) equal
(person/thing); **they are a good m.** =
they go well together. (*b*) game; **test m.**
= international cricket match. (*c*) small
piece of wood/cardboard with a chemical tip which lights when rubbed against
a rough surface. (*d*) marriage. 2. *v*. (*a*)
to be equal to. (*b*) to fit/to go with.
match board, *n*. tongue-and-groove
board, with a projecting tongue along
one edge and a corresponding groove
along the other. **matchbox,** *n*. small
box containing matches. **matchless,**
adj. with no equal. **matchmaker,**
n. person who arranges a marriage.
matchstick, *Am*. **matchstalk,** *n*. stick
of wood forming a match; **m. men** =
sketches of people drawn with single
lines for each limb. **matchwood,** *n*.
small pieces of wood.

mate [meɪt] 1. *n*. (*a*) one of a pair of animals; husband or wife. (*b*) *inf*. friend/
companion. (*c*) workman's helper. (*d*)
(*in merchant navy*) officer. (*e*) (*in chess*)
position where the king cannot move,

and the game ends. **2.** *v.* (*a*) (*of animals*) to breed. (*b*) (*in chess*) to put (your opponent's king) in a position from which he cannot escape. **matey**, *adj. inf.* friendly.

material [mə'tɪərɪəl] **1.** *n.* (*a*) substance which can be used for making sth. (*b*) useful implements; **writing materials =** pens/pencils/ink/paper, etc. (*c*) cloth. (*d*) subject matter/notes (for a book, etc.). **2.** *adj.* (*a*) referring to physical things. (*b*) important. **materialism**, *n.* interest only in physical things/belief that only physical things are important. **materialist**, *n.* person who believes in materialism. **materialistic**, *adj.* referring to materialism. **materialize**, *v.* to become real/to appear. **materially**, *adv.* greatly/noticeably.

maternal [mə'tɜ:nl] *adj.* referring to a mother; **m. grandfather** = father of your mother. **maternally**, *adv.* like a mother. **maternity**, *n.* becoming a mother; giving birth; **m. leave** = paid leave from a job while you are having a baby.

mathematics [mæθə'mætɪks] *n.* science of numbers and measurements. **mathematical**, *adj.* referring to mathematics. **mathematically**, *adv.* by mathematics. **mathematician** [mæθəmə'tɪʃn] *n.* expert at mathematics. **maths**, *Am.* **math**, *n. inf.* mathematics.

matinée ['mætɪneɪ] *n.* afternoon performance of a play or film.

matins ['mætɪnz] *n. pl.* prayers said in the morning.

matriarch ['meɪtrɪɑ:k] *n.* woman who leads a family/a group. **matriarchal** [meɪtrɪ'ɑ:kl] *adj.* referring to a matriarch; (society) where women rule families. **matriarchy**, *n.* matriarchal society.

matricide ['mætrɪsaɪd] *n.* murder of one's mother.

matriculate [mə'trɪkjʊleɪt] *v.* to pass an examination which allows you to join a university; to become a member of a university. **matriculation** [mətrɪkjʊ'leɪʃn] *n.* joining a university after passing an examination; examination which you need to pass in order to join a university.

matrimony ['mætrɪmənɪ] *n.* state of being married. **matrimonial** [mætrɪ'məʊnɪəl] *adj.* referring to marriage.

matrix ['meɪtrɪks] *n.* (*pl.* **-trices** [-trɪsiː]) (*a*) plan/pattern from which copies are made. (*b*) mathematical arrangement of figures in a series of columns.

matron ['meɪtrən] *n.* (*a*) (*formal*) senior nursing officer in charge of a hospital. (*b*) woman (usu. a nurse) who looks after children in a boarding school. (*c*) middle-aged married woman. **matronly**, *adj.* like a matron.

matt [mæt] *adj.* dull/not shiny.

matter ['mætə] **1.** *n.* (*a*) substance/material. (*b*) thing/business; **that's quite another m.** = that's quite different. (*c*) problem. (*d*) **no m. what** = any. **2.** *v.* to be important. **matter-of-fact**, *adj.* practical.

mattock ['mætək] *n.* type of pickaxe with a wide blade, used for breaking up soil.

mattress ['mætrəs] *n.* (*pl.* **-es**) thick, soft part of a bed made of a canvas case with various fillings; **sprung m.** = mattress with springs inside.

mature [mə'tjʊə] **1.** *adj.* ripe; older; reasonable/adult (attitude); (student) who is older than normal. **2.** *v.* to ripen. **maturation**, *n.* becoming mature. **maturity**, *n.* ripeness/readiness.

maudlin ['mɔ:dlɪn] *adj.* weeping/silly through drink.

maul [mɔ:l] *v.* to attack/handle roughly. **maulstick**, *n.* stick used by a painter to hold his hand steady.

maunder ['mɔ:ndə] *v.* to mumble disconnected phrases.

Maundy Thursday ['mɔ:ndɪ'θɜ:zdɪ] *n.* Thursday before Easter Sunday.

mausoleum [mɔ:zə'lɪəm] *n.* important burial building.

mauve [məʊv] *adj. & n.* light pinkish-purple (colour).

maverick ['mævərɪk] *n.* (*a*) *Am.* animal which has not been branded and is running loose. (*b*) person who does not fit in to the usual pattern.

maw [mɔ:] *n.* (*of animal*) large mouth; stomach.

mawkish ['mɔ:kɪʃ] *adj.* silly/falsely sentimental.

maxilla [mæk'sɪlə] *n.* upper jawbone. **maxillary**, *adj.* referring to the upper jaw.

maxim ['mæksɪm] *n.* wise saying.

maximum ['mæksɪməm] *adj. & n.* greatest possible (number/amount); **at the m.** = at most. **maximize** ['mæksɪmaɪz] *v.* to make as large as possible.

May [meɪ] *n.* (a) 5th month of the year; **M. Day** = May 1st. (b) **may** = hawthorn/wild shrub growing in hedges and flowering in May. **mayday,** *n.* international distress signal. **mayfly,** *n.* small fly which appears in summer. **maypole,** *n.* tall pole around which people dance on the first of May.

may [meɪ] *v.* (**might**) (a) *used with other verbs to mean* it is possible; **might as well** = it would be better if; **you might have left it on the train** = perhaps you left it on the train; **much good m. it do you!** = I hope it does you a lot of good (though I doubt if it will). (b) *used with other verbs to mean* it is allowed. **maybe,** *adv.* perhaps; **maybe not** = possibly not.

mayhem ['meɪhem] *n.* wild confusion.

mayonnaise [meɪə'neɪz] *n.* cream sauce made with egg yolks and oil.

mayor ['meə] *n.* elected leader of a town. **mayoress** ['meəres] *n.* wife of a mayor; woman mayor.

maze [meɪz] *n.* network of puzzling paths in which you can get lost.

Mb megabyte.

me [mi:] *pron. referring to the speaker.*

mead [mi:d] *n.* alcoholic drink made from honey.

meadow ['medəʊ] *n.* large green field. **meadowsweet,** *n.* common wild plant with many little white flowers.

meagre, *Am.* **meager** ['mi:gə] *adj.* (a) scanty/few. (b) thin. **meagreness,** *n.* small amount.

meal [mi:l] *n.* (a) food taken at a sitting. (b) coarse flour. **mealtime,** *n.* time when you usually eat. **mealy,** *adj.* floury. **mealy-mouthed,** *adj.* not straightforward; (person) who tries not to offend and so doesn't say what he thinks.

mean [mi:n] **1.** *n.* (a) middle; average; middle point between two extremes. (b) **means** = way/method of doing sth; **by no means** = not at all; **by all means** = certainly. (c) **means** = money/resources; **it's beyond my means** = it's too expensive for me; **means test** = inquiry into the amount of money earned by s.o. in order to calculate how much state benefit he should receive. **2.** *adj.* (**-er, -est**) (a) average/ middle. (b) miserable/low; **he has no m. opinion of himself** = he thinks a lot of himself; **m. trick** = unkind trick. (c) miserly. (d) *Sl.* very good. **3.** *v.* (**meant** [ment]) (a) to intend; **he means well** = he has good intentions; **do you m. Richard?** = are you talking about Richard?; **you are meant to** = you are supposed to. (b) to signify/to show. **meaning. 1.** *n.* signification. **2.** *adj.* significant. **meaningful,** *adj.* full of meaning/significant. **meaningfully,** *adv.* significantly. **meaningless,** *adj.* not signifying anything. **meanly,** *adv.* poorly. **meanness,** *n.* miserliness; dislike of sharing things/of spending money. **mean-spirited,** *adj.* sly/unpleasant.

meander [mɪ'ændə] **1.** *n.* bend in a river. **2.** *v.* to wind/to wander about. **meandering,** *adj.* wandering/ very winding (path).

meant [ment] *v. see* **mean.**

meantime ['mi:ntaɪm] **1.** *n.* **in the m.** = between two events. **2.** *adv.* during this time.

meanwhile ['mi:nwaɪl] *adv.* during this time.

measles ['mi:zlz] *n.* children's disease which gives you a red rash; **German m.** = mild disease which gives a red rash and which can affect an unborn child if caught by a pregnant woman. **measly,** *adj. inf.* miserable/small.

measure ['meʒə] **1.** *n.* (a) quantity; size; **made to m.** = made specially to fit. (b) unit for showing the size/quantity of sth. (c) thing for showing the size/ quantity of sth; small metal cup; long tape with centimetres/inches marked on it. (d) action; **as a precautionary m.** = as a precaution. (e) seam/layer of coal. (f) plan of a new law/a bill. (g) time (in music); rhythm (in poetry). **2.** *v.* to be of a certain size/length/quantity, etc.; to find out the length/quantity of (sth). **measurable,** *adj.* which can be measured. **measured,** *adj.* regular; **with m. tread** = in a slow and stately

way. **measureless,** *adj.* so large that
it cannot be measured. **measurement,**
n. (*a*) finding out the size/length/quan-
tity of sth. (*b*) quantity/size, etc., found
out when you measure. **measure up
to,** *v.* to be able to do (a difficult job).
measuring, *n.* finding out the size/
length/quantity of sth; **m. tape** = long
tape with centimetres/inches marked on
it; **m. glass/jug** = glass jar with quantities marked on it by lines.

meat [mi:t] *n.* flesh of an animal which is
eaten. **meat ball,** *n.* minced meat rolled
into a ball and cooked. **meaty,** *adj.* (*a*)
with a lot of meat. (*b*) with a lot of de-
tails/information.

mecca ['mekə] *n.* place which attracts a
large number of people.

mechanic [mɪ'kænɪk] *n.* person who
works on engines. **mechanical,** *adj.* referring to a machine; **m. gestures** =
gestures done automatically as if you
were a machine. **mechanically,** *adv.* by
machine; like a machine; automatically.
mechanics, *n.* (*a*) the study of force
and power. (*b*) the study of machines.
(*c*) way in which sth works. **mechanism** ['mekənɪzəm] *n.* (*a*) working
parts (of a machine). (*b*) way in which
sth works. **mechanization** [mekənaɪ-
'zeɪʃn] *n.* introduction of machines
to take the place of manual labour.
mechanize ['mekənaɪz] *v.* to introduce
machines in place of manual labour.
mechanized, *adj.* (soldiers/regiment)
with armoured vehicles.

medal ['medl] *n.* metal disc, usu. attached to a ribbon, made to commemorate an important occasion or
battle; **gold/silver/bronze m.** = medal
for first/second/third place in competitions. **medallion** [mɪ'dæljən] *n.* large
medal. **medallist** ['medəlɪst] *n.* person
who has won a medal in a sports competition, etc.

meddle ['medl] *v.* (**in/with**) to interfere;
to get involved with. **meddler,** *n.*
person who likes to meddle. **med-
dlesome,** *adj.* (person) who interferes.
meddling. 1. *n.* interfering. **2.** *adj.*
(person) who is always interfering.

media ['mi:dɪə] *n.* pl. (*a*) means
of communicating information; **the
(mass) m.** = newspapers/TV/radio,

etc; **m. resources centre** = centre for
communicating information by tele-
vision/films/tapes, etc. (*b*) *see also*
medium.

mediaeval [medɪ'i:vl] *adj. see*
medieval.

median ['mi:dɪən] *adj. & n.* (point)
which is in the middle/(line) which goes
through the middle. **medial,** *adj.* in the
middle.

mediate ['mi:dɪeɪt] *v.* to intervene/to try
to bring peace between two opponents.
mediation [mi:dɪ'eɪʃn] *n.* attempt to
make two opponents agree. **mediator,**
n. person who tries to make two
opponents agree.

medical ['medɪkl] **1.** *adj.* referring to the
study of disease; **the m. profession** =
all doctors; **m. officer of health** = person responsible for the health services
of a town, etc. **2.** *n. inf.* examination
of the body by a doctor. **medic,** *n. inf.*
doctor. **medically,** *adv.* in a medical
way. **medicament,** *n.* (*formal*) medicine. **medicate,** *v.* to add a medicine to
(sth). **medication,** *n.* drug.

medicine ['medsɪn] *n.* (*a*) study of disease, ill health and their cure. (*b*) liquid/
powder/pill taken to cure an illness;
m. ball = large heavy ball used for
physical exercises; **m. chest** = cupboard
for keeping medicines in. **medicinal**
[me'dɪsɪnl] *adj.* used to treat an illness.
medicinally, *adv.* (used) as a medicine.
medicine man, *n.* witch doctor.

medieval [medɪ'i:vl] *adj.* referring to
the Middle Ages.

mediocre [mi:dɪ'əʊkə] *adj.* ordinary/not
good or bad. **mediocrity** [mi:dɪ'ɒkrɪtɪ]
n. (*a*) not being good or bad/ordinari-
ness. (*b*) very ordinary person with no
special talents.

meditate ['medɪteɪt] *v.* (**on/about**) to
think deeply about (sth). **meditation**
[medɪ'teɪʃn] *n.* long deep (often religious) thought. **meditative,** *adj.*
thoughtful.

medium ['mi:dɪəm] **1.** *adj.* middle/
average. **2.** *n.* (*pl.* **media/mediums**) (*a*)
middle point; **happy m.** = compromise.
(*b*) type of paint used by an artist. (*c*)
means of doing sth/of communicating
sth. (*d*) person who thinks the spirits of
dead people can talk through him/her.

medlar ['medlə] *n.* fruit like a brown apple; tree which bears this fruit.

medley ['medlɪ] *n.* mixture.

medulla ['medjulə] *n.* bone marrow; the soft inner part of any organ.

meek [mi:k] *adj.* (-er, -est) quiet/ humble. **meekly,** *adv.* quietly/humbly. **meekness,** *n.* quietness/humility.

meerschaum ['mɪəʃəm] *n.* white substance, used to make tobacco pipes.

meet [mi:t] **1.** *n.* gathering of huntsmen. **2.** *v.* (met) (*a*) to come together. (*b*) to become acquainted with s.o.; **we have already met** = we know each other already. (*c*) to satisfy (needs). **meeting,** *n.* (*a*) coming together. (*b*) group of people who meet for a special purpose; **Annual General M. (AGM)** = yearly assembly of all the members of a club/society/of all the shareholders in a company. **meet with,** *v.* (*a*) to find/to come up against; to have (an accident). (*b*) *Am.* to meet (s.o.).

mega- ['megə] *prefix meaning* (*a*) very large. (*b*) one million.

megabyte ['megəbaɪt] *n.* unit of storage for a computer, equal to 1,048,576 bytes.

megacycle ['megəsaɪkl], **megahertz** ['megəhɜ:ts] *n.* frequency of radio waves of one million cycles per second.

megalith ['megəlɪθ] *n.* huge stone set up by prehistoric man.

megalomania [megələ'meɪnɪə] *n.* mad belief that you are more important/ more powerful than you really are. **megalomanic,** *n.* person suffering from megalomania.

megaphone ['megəfəʊn] *n.* metal trumpet which makes the voice sound louder.

megaton ['megətʌn] *n.* force of an explosion equal to the force produced by exploding one million tons of TNT.

meiosis [mi:'əʊsɪs] *n.* splitting of cells.

melancholy ['melənkəlɪ] **1.** *n.* great sadness. **2.** *adj.* very sad. **melancholia,** [melən'kəʊlɪə] *n.* (*formal*) melancholy state. **melancholic** [melən'kɒlɪk] *adj.* very sad.

melanin ['melənɪn] *n.* pigment which colours the hair and skin. **melanoma,** *n.* cancer caused by sunlight.

mêlée ['meleɪ] *n.* crowd of struggling people.

mellifluous [me'lɪflʊəs] *adj.* soothing/ pleasant (sound).

mellow ['meləʊ] **1.** *adj.* ripe (fruit); (wine) which has matured; soft/rich (voice); calm and relaxed (older person). **2.** *v.* to grow ripe/to mature; to become soft/rich; **he has mellowed** = he is much less angry/unpleasant than he used to be. **mellowness,** *n.* ripeness/ maturity.

melodrama ['melədra:mə] *n.* extremely exciting but badly-written play which emphasizes violently alternating passions. **melodramatic** [melədrə'mætɪk] *adj.* arousing violent emotions. **melodramatically,** *adv.* in a melodramatic way.

melody ['melədɪ] *n.* tune. **melodic** [mɪ'lɒdɪk] *adj.* referring to tunes. **melodious** [mə'ləʊdɪəs] *adj.* tuneful. **melodiously,** *adv.* in a tuneful way.

melon ['melən] *n.* large round fruit of a creeping plant; **water m.** = very large type of melon with red flesh and black seeds.

melt [melt] *v.* to change from solid to liquid by heating; **rioters melted away when the police appeared** = they disappeared; **to m. down scrap metal** = to heat it and make it into blocks so that it can be used again; **my heart melted at the sight of the puppies** = became softened/less angry. **melting point,** *n.* temperature at which a solid becomes liquid. **melting pot,** *n.* (*a*) pot in which metals can be melted. (*b*) place where people of different origins come to live together.

member ['membə] *n.* (*a*) person who belongs to a group; **M. of Parliament** = person elected to the lower house of a parliament. (*b*) limb on a human body. **membership,** *n.* (*a*) belonging to a group; **m. card** = card which shows you belong (to a club/party). (*b*) all the members of a group.

membrane ['membreɪn] *n.* thin layer of tissue in the body.

memento [mə'mentəʊ] *n.* (*pl.* **-oes**) thing kept to remind you of sth; souvenir.

memo ['meməʊ] *n.* (*pl.* **-os**) note/short message between people working in the same organization; **m. pad** = pad of paper for writing short notes.

memoir ['memwɑ:] *n.* (*a*) *pl.* **memoirs** = written account of what you can remember of your life. (*b*) short official/scientific note.

memorandum [memə'rændəm] *n.* (*pl.* **-da**) note/short message.

memory ['memərɪ] *n.* (*a*) ability to remember; **he recited the poem from m.**; **if my m. serves me right** = if I can remember it correctly. (*b*) what you remember; **in m. of** = to remind us of. (*c*) capacity for storing information (in a computer). **memorable,** *adj.* which you cannot forget/very striking. **memorial** [mɪ'mɔ:rɪəl] **1.** *adj.* which reminds you of sth/s.o.; **m. service** = church service to remember someone who has died. **2.** *n.* monument to remind you of sth/s.o. **memorize,** *v.* to learn (sth) by heart.

men [men] *n. pl. see* **man.**

menace ['menəs] **1.** *n.* threat; bad thing; **that child's a m.** = very naughty. **2.** *v.* to threaten; **menacing clouds** = clouds which threaten to bring rain. **menacingly,** *adv.* in a threatening way.

menage [me'nɑ:ʒ] *n.* household.

menagerie [mɪ'nædʒərɪ] *n.* small zoo; collection of more or less wild animals.

mend [mend] **1.** *n.* (*a*) place where a piece of clothing has been repaired. (*b*) *inf.* **on the m.** = getting better. **2.** *v.* to repair; to be repaired. **mender,** *n.* person who mends. **mending,** *n.* (*a*) repairing. (*b*) clothes which need repairing.

mendacity [men'dæsɪtɪ] *n.* (*formal*) telling lies. **mendacious** [men'deɪʃəs] *adj.* not truthful.

mendicant ['mendɪkənt] *adj.* (person) who begs.

menfolk ['menfəʊk] *n. pl.* all the men (in a family/group, etc.).

menhir ['menhɪə] *n.* tall standing stone, erected by prehistoric people.

menial ['mi:nɪəl] *adj.* low; badly paid; **m. tasks** = dirty jobs which a servant might do.

Ménière's disease ['meɪnɪeəzdɪ'si:z] *n.* disease of the middle ear, causing dizziness.

meningitis [menɪn'dʒaɪtɪs] *n.* inflammation of the membrane covering the brain.

meniscus [me'nɪskəs] *n.* curved surface of a drop of water.

menopause ['menəpɔ:z] *n.* period of life (around the age of 50) when women become no longer capable of bearing children; **male m.** = difficult period in a man's life (around the age of 50).

menstruate ['menstrʊeɪt] *v.* (*of women*) to lose blood through the vagina at regular periods. **menstrual,** *adj.* referring to the regular monthly loss of blood through the vagina. **menstruation** [menstrʊ'eɪʃn] *n.* monthly loss of blood through the vagina.

mensuration [mensjʊə'reɪʃn] *n.* study of measurement.

menswear ['menzweə] *n.* (*no pl.*) clothes for men.

mental ['mentl] *adj.* referring to the mind; **m. arithmetic** = calculations done in the head; **m. age** = way of showing the development of a person's mind, by expressing it as the age at which such development is normal; **m. hospital** = hospital for those who suffer from illnesses of the mind. **mentality** [men'tælɪtɪ] *n.* (*a*) mental power. (*b*) way of thinking which is typical of s.o./of a group. **mentally,** *adv.* concerning the brain; **m. defective** = well below normal intelligence.

menthol ['menθɒl] *n.* white substance which tastes strongly of mint. **mentholated,** *adj.* treated with menthol; with menthol added.

mention ['menʃn] **1.** *n.* reference to sth. **2.** *v.* to refer to (sth); **not to m.** = not forgetting/as well as.

mentor ['mentɔ:] *n.* (*formal*) person who teaches/helps another (younger) person.

menu ['menju:] *n.* (*a*) list of food available in a restaurant. (*b*) list of options available on a computer program.

meow [mi:'aʊ] *Am.* = **miaow.**

MEP [emi:'pi:] *n.* Member of the European Parliament.

mercantile ['mɜ:kəntaɪl] *adj.* referring to commerce.

mercenary ['mɜ:sənərɪ] **1.** *adj.* (person) who is interested in money. **2.** *n.* person who serves foreigners as a soldier for money.

mercerize ['mɜːsəraɪz] *v.* to make (cotton cloth) shiny.

merchant ['mɜːtʃənt] *n.* businessman; person who buys and sells; **m. navy** = commercial ships of a country; **m. seaman** = seaman in the merchant navy; **m. bank** = bank which lends money to companies, not individuals. **merchandise, 1.** *n.* goods for sale. **2.** *v.* to sell (goods) by wide and varied advertising. **merchantman, merchant ship,** *n.* (*pl.* **-men**) commercial ship.

mercury ['mɜːkjərɪ] *n.* (*element:* Hg) liquid metal used in thermometers/barometers, etc. **mercurial** [mɜː-'kjʊərɪəl] *adj.* (person) whose temper changes frequently.

mercy ['mɜːsɪ] *n.* (*a*) compassion/pity; kindness towards unfortunate people; **to have m. on** = to forgive/not to want to punish/harm s.o.; **m. killing** = euthanasia, killing of s.o. who is very ill or in pain; (*b*) gift (of fate); **we must be thankful for small mercies** = we must be grateful that everything has turned out fairly well so far. **merciful,** *adj.* (person) who forgives/who is kind. **mercifully,** *adv.* thankfully; in a forgiving/kindly way. **merciless,** *adj.* harsh/cruel. **mercilessly,** *adv.* without mercy. **mercilessness,** *n.* lack of pity; hardness (of character).

mere ['mɪə] **1.** *n.* small lake. **2.** *adj.* simply/only; **he's a m. boy** = only a boy; **the m. sight of grass makes me sneeze** = simply the sight of grass makes me sneeze. **merely,** *adv.* only/simply.

meretricious [merɪ'trɪʃəs] *adj.* showy and cheap.

merganser [mɜː'gænzə] *n.* type of large duck, with a crest.

merge [mɜːdʒ] *v.* to join together (**with** sth). **merger,** *n.* amalgamation/joining of two companies.

meridian [mə'rɪdɪən] *n.* imaginary line drawn from the North Pole to the South Pole; **the Greenwich m.** = line passing through Greenwich (near London) from which longitude is calculated.

meringue [mə'ræŋ] *n.* sweet baked dessert made of egg whites and sugar.

merino [mə'riːnəʊ] *n.* (*pl.* **-os**) type of long-haired sheep/fine wollen material.

merit ['merɪt] **1.** *n.* value/quality/excellence; **to go into the merits of** = to examine the good and bad points of. **2.** *v.* to be worthy of/to deserve (sth). **meritorious** [merɪ'tɔːrɪəs] *adj.* (*formal*) which is valuable/which should be rewarded.

mermaid ['mɜːmeɪd] *n.* mythical creature, half woman and half fish. **merman,** *n.* mythical creature, half man and half fish.

merry ['merɪ] *adj.* (**-ier, -iest**) (*a*) happy; **to make m.** = to have a good time; **the more the merrier** = the more there are the happier everything is. (*b*) *inf.* slightly drunk. **merrily,** *adv.* happily. **merriment,** *n.* fun. **merry-go-round,** *n.* roundabout with wooden horses, etc., in a funfair. **merrymaker,** *n.* person who is enjoying himself. **merrymaking,** *n.* festivity/celebration.

mesh [meʃ] **1.** *n.* (*pl.* **-es**) space between the threads of a net. **2.** *v.* (*of a cogwheel*) to link together with another toothed wheel.

mesmerize ['mezməraɪz] *v.* to hypnotize.

mess [mes] **1.** *n.* (*pl.* **-es**) (*a*) dirt; disorder/confusion; **they made a m. of the repair job** = they did the repair job badly. (*b*) group of soldiers/sailors who eat together; room where officers eat and sleep. **2.** *v.* (**with**) to eat together. **mess about,** *v.* (*a*) to spend your spare time doing sth. (*b*) to waste time. (*c*) *inf.* **to mess s.o. about** = to disrupt s.o.'s way of life/to treat s.o. badly. **messily,** *adv.* in a messy way. **mess up,** *v. inf.* (*a*) to dirty. (*b*) to ruin/to spoil. **messy,** *adj.* (**-ier, -iest**) dirty; disorderly.

message ['mesɪdʒ] *n.* news/information sent; *inf.* **he got the m.** = he understood. **messenger,** *n.* person who brings a message.

messiah [mɪ'saɪə] *n.* (*a*) person whom the Jews expect will come to free them. (*b*) Jesus Christ. **messianic** [mesɪ'ænɪk] *adj.* referring to the Messiah.

Messrs ['mesəz] *n. used formally as plural of* Mr.

met [met] *v. see* **meet**.

Met [met] *n.* **the Met** = the Metropolitan Police.

meta- ['metə] *prefix meaning* change.

metabolism [me'tæbəlɪzəm] *n.* processes by which plants and animals use food to create energy. **metabolic** [metə'bɒlɪk] *adj.* referring to metabolism.

metacarpus ['metə'ka:pəs] *n.* the bones in the hand.

metal ['metl] *n.* usu. solid mineral substance which can conduct heat and electricity. **metalled,** *adj.* (road) covered with small stones set in tar. **metallic** [mə'tælɪk] *adj.* referring to metal; **m. sheen** = shine such as you get on polished metal. **metallurgist** [me'tælədʒɪst] *n.* person who studies metals. **metallurgy** [me'tælədʒɪ] *n.* study of metals. **metalwork,** *n.* making things with metal; pieces of metal made into a construction/a work of art.

metamorphosis [metə'mɔ:fəsɪs] *n.* (*pl.* **-phoses** [-fəsi:z]) change, esp. an insect's change of form. **metamorphose** [metə'mɔ:fəʊz] *v.* to change from one state to another.

metaphor ['metəfə] *n.* way of describing sth by suggesting it has the properties of sth else. **metaphorical** [metə'fɒrɪkl] *adj.* like a metaphor. **metaphorically,** *adv.* in a metaphorical way.

metaphysics [metə'fɪzɪks] *n.* philosophical study of truth/knowledge/existence, etc. **metaphysical,** *adj.* referring to metaphysics.

metatarsus [metə'ta:səs] *n.* the bones in the foot.

metathesis [me'tæθəsɪs] *n.* change of sounds in a word, where letters are transposed.

mete out ['mi:t'aʊt] *v.* to give (punishment).

meteor ['mi:tɪə] *n.* small object which flashes through space and shines brightly as it burns up on entering the earth's atmosphere. **meteoric** [mi:tɪ'ɒrɪk] *adj.* like a meteor/very rapid. **meteorite** ['mi:tɪəraɪt] *n.* lump of rock/iron which falls to earth from space.

meteorology [mi:tɪə'rɒlədʒɪ] *n.* study of climate and weather. **meteorological** [mi:tɪərə'lɒdʒɪkl] *adj.* referring to the climate and weather; **m. station** = research station which notes weather conditions. **meteorologist** [mi:tɪə'rɒlədʒɪst] *n.* person who studies climate and weather.

meter ['mi:tə] **1.** *n.* (*a*) device for counting how much time/water/gas, etc., has been used; **parking m.** = device into which you put money to pay for parking. (*b*) *Am.* metre. **2.** *v.* to count by a meter.

methane ['mi:θeɪn] *n.* colourless gas, which easily catches fire and is found naturally in the ground.

methanol ['meθənɒl] *n.* methyl alcohol.

method ['meθəd] *n.* (*a*) way of doing sth. (*b*) well-organized system. **methodical** [mɪ'θɒdɪkl] *adj.* ordered/regulated. **methodically,** *adv.* in a well-organized way. **Methodist,** *n. & adj.* (person) following the teaching of Wesley. **methodology,** *n.* methods used in a certain process or study.

methyl ['meθɪl] *n.* **m. alcohol** = poisonous alcohol found in wood. **methylated spirits,** *inf.* **meths** ['meθɪleɪtɪd'spɪrɪts, meθs] *n.* alcohol used for lighting or heating.

meticulous [me'tɪkjʊləs] *adj.* attentive to detail (**about** doing sth). **meticulously,** *adv.* carefully/paying attention to details. **meticulousness,** *n.* being meticulous.

metier ['metɪeɪ] *n.* profession; occupation one is good at.

metre, *Am.* **meter** ['mi:tə] *n.* (*a*) standard measurement of length (approximately 39.4 inches). (*b*) regular rhythm in poetry. **metric** ['metrɪk] *adj.* (*a*) referring to metre as a measurement; **the m. system** = system of measurement based on metres, litres, etc. (*b*) referring to metre as rhythm. **metrical,** *adj.* (poem) written in a regular rhythm. **metricate** ['metrɪkeɪt] *v.* to express in metres/centimetres, etc. **metrication** [metrɪ'keɪʃn] *n.* changing of a measuring system to the metric system.

metronome ['metrənəʊm] *n.* device which beats time regularly, used when practising/playing music.

metropolis [mə'trɒpəlɪs] *n.* (*pl.* **-es**) large capital city. **metropolitan** [metrə'pɒlɪtən] **1.** *adj.* referring to a large capital city; **the M. Police** = the police force of Greater London. **2.** *n.* chief bishop in the Orthodox Church.

mettle ['metl] *n.* vigour/strength of character (of a person); **to put s.o. on his m.** = to make s.o. try to do his best.

mettlesome, *adj.* (*formal*) vigorous/ active.

mew [mju:] **1.** *n.* soft cry which a cat makes. **2.** *v.* to make a soft cry like a cat.

mews [mju:z] *n.* (*a*) row of former stables or garages converted into houses. (*b*) stables.

Mexican ['meksɪkən] **1.** *adj.* referring to Mexico. **2.** *n.* person from Mexico.

mezzanine ['metsəni:n] *n.* floor between the ground floor and the first floor.

mezzo-soprano ['metsəusə'prɑːnəu] *n.* singer or voice lower in pitch than a soprano.

mezzotint ['medzəutɪnt] *n.* print made from a plate which has rough and smooth areas.

Mg *symbol for* magnesium.

mg *abbrev. for* milligram.

miaow, *Am.* **meow** [mi:'au] **1.** *n.* call of a cat. **2.** *v.* to call like a cat.

miasma [mɪ'æzmə] *n.* unpleasant/poisonous air.

mica ['maɪkə] *n.* type of mineral which splits into thin glittering layers.

mice [maɪs] *n. pl. see* **mouse.**

Michaelmas ['mɪkəlməs] *n.* 29th September; **M. daisy** = common autumn garden flower.

mickey ['mɪkɪ] *n. inf.* **to take the m. out of** = to make fun of.

micro- ['maɪkrəu] **1.** *prefix meaning* (*a*) very small. (*b*) one millionth. **2.** *n.* microcomputer.

microbe ['maɪkrəub] *n.* germ; tiny living organism.

microchip ['maɪkrəutʃɪp] *n.* small piece of silicon used in electronics.

microcomputer [maɪkrəukʌm'pju:tə] *n.* small computer for office or personal use.

microclimate ['maɪkrəu'klaɪmət] *n.* climate of a small area.

microcosm ['maɪkrəkɒzəm] *n.* miniature version.

microfiche ['maɪkrəfi:ʃ] *n.* index card made of microfilms.

microfilm ['maɪkrəfɪlm] **1.** *n.* film on which sth is photographed in very small scale; **m. reader** = apparatus with an enlarger and a display screen for reading microfilms. **2.** *v.* to make a very small-scale photograph of.

micrometer [maɪ'krɒmɪtə] *n.* instrument for measuring very small distances.

micron ['maɪkrɒn] *n.* one millionth of a metre.

microorganism [maɪkrəu'ɔːgənɪzm] *n.* tiny living organism.

microphone ['maɪkrəfəun] *n.* apparatus for capturing sound and passing it to a loudspeaker or recording apparatus.

microprocessor [maɪkrəu'prəusesə] *n.* small central processing unit using microchips.

microscope ['maɪkrəskəup] *n.* apparatus which enlarges things which are very small. **microscopic** [maɪkrə-'skɒpɪk] *adj.* so small as to be visible only through a microscope.

microwave ['maɪkrəweɪv] *n.* very short electric wave; **m. oven** = small oven which cooks very rapidly using microwaves.

mid- [mɪd] *prefix meaning* middle. **midday,** *n.* twelve o'clock noon. **midland,** *adj. & n.* (referring to the) central part of a country; **the Midlands** = the central part of England. **midnight,** *n.* twelve o'clock at night. **midriff,** *n.* front part of the body above the waist and below the chest. **midshipman,** *n.* (*pl.* -men) trainee officer in the Royal Navy. **midst,** *n.* middle; **in our m.** = among us. **midstream,** *n.* middle part of a river. **midsummer,** *n.* middle of the summer; **Midsummer's Day** = June 24th. **midway,** *adv.* halfway. **Midwest,** *n.* central northern part of the United States. **midwinter,** *n.* middle of the winter.

midden ['mɪdn] *n.* heap of dung.

middle ['mɪdl] **1.** *adj.* in the centre; halfway between two things; **m. sized** = neither big nor small; **m. class** = professional class (between the upper class and the lower/working class); **the M. Ages** = historical period between the Dark Ages and the Renaissance (about 1000 to 1500 AD). **2.** *n.* (*a*) centre; central point. (*b*) waistline. **middle-aged,** *adj.* not young and not old (between 40 and 60 years of age). **Middle**

East, *n.* area between Egypt and Pakistan. **Middle Eastern,** *adj.* referring to the Middle East. **middleman,** *n.* (*pl.* **-men**) businessman who buys from one source to sell to another. **middle-of-the-road,** *adj.* centre/moderate (politics). **middleweight,** *n.* weight in boxing between welterweight and light heavyweight. **middling,** *adj.* neither good nor bad; not very large or small.

midge [mɪdʒ] *n.* small stinging flying insect.

midget ['mɪdʒɪt] *n.* very small person; **m. submarine** = submarine which can only carry one or two people.

midwife ['mɪdwaɪf] *n.* (*pl.* **-wives** ['-waɪvz]) person (usu. a woman) trained to help deliver a baby. **midwifery** ['mɪdwɪfrɪ] *n.* work of helping deliver babies.

mien [miːn] *n.* way in which a person behaves or looks.

miff [mɪf] *v. inf.* to offend/to annoy (s.o.).

might [maɪt] **1.** *v. see* **may. 2.** *n.* force/strength. **mighty. 1.** *adj.* (**-ier, -iest**) (*a*) strong. (*b*) great; *inf.* **you're in a m. hurry** = you are very impatient. **2.** *adv. inf.* very. **mightily,** *adv.* greatly.

mignonette [mɪnjə'net] *n.* scented garden plant.

migraine ['miːgreɪn] *n.* recurrent very bad headache.

migrate [maɪ'greɪt] *v.* to move from one place to another with the seasons. **migrant** ['maɪgrənt] *adj. & n.* (bird) which moves from one place to another with the seasons; (workman) who moves from one job to another or from one country to another. **migration** [maɪ'greɪʃn] *n.* movement of birds from one country to another. **migratory** ['maɪgrətərɪ] *adj.* referring to migration.

mike [maɪk] *n. inf.* microphone.

milch [mɪltʃ] *adj.* **m. cow** = cow kept for milk.

mild [maɪld] *adj.* (**-er, -est**) (*a*) soft/not severe (punishment). (*b*) not harsh (weather). (*c*) not strong/powerful. **mildly,** *adv.* softly/kindly; **to put it m.** = not to say anything ruder. **mildness,** *n.* kindness/softness; warmness (of winter weather).

mildew ['mɪldjuː] **1.** *n.* powdery fungus on plants/paper/leather, etc. **2.** *v.* to become covered with mildew. **mildewed,** *adj.* covered with mildew.

mile [maɪl] *n.* measure of length (1,760 yards/1.61 kilometres); *inf.* **miles of string** = very long piece of string; **it's miles too big** = much too big. **mileage,** *n.* (*a*) distance travelled in miles; **car with a low m.** = car which has not travelled as much as is normal. (*b*) *inf.* **to get a lot of m. out of** = to gain benefit from. **mileometer** [maɪ'lɒmɪtə] *n.* dial showing number of miles travelled. **miler,** *n.* person who runs in a 1 mile race. **milestone,** *n.* stone showing distance in miles; important point (history, etc.).

milieu ['miːljəː] *n.* surroundings/environment.

militant ['mɪlɪtənt] *adj. & n.* (person) who supports a policy of violence; (person) who is very active in supporting a cause/a political party. **militancy,** *n.* activity/vigour (in supporting a political party/a cause).

military ['mɪlɪtrɪ] **1.** *adj.* referring to the army. **2.** *n.* **the m.** = the army. **militarism,** *n.* belief in the use of the army to solve political problems. **militarist,** *n.* person who believes in militarism. **militaristic,** *adj.* believing that the army should be used to solve political problems. **militate,** *v.* to work actively (**against**). **militia** [mɪ'lɪʃə] *n.* emergency army; police force organized like an army.

milk [mɪlk] **1.** *n.* white liquid produced by female mammals for feeding their young, esp. the milk produced by cows; **m. shake** = milk mixed with flavouring and ice cream; **m. chocolate** = pale brown chocolate (flavoured with milk); **m. teeth** = first set of teeth produced by a child. **2.** *v.* (*a*) to take the milk from (an animal). (*b*) to get all the money from (s.o.). **milker,** *n.* (*a*) person who milks. (*b*) **good m.** = cow which produces a lot of milk. **milk float,** *n.* slow van which delivers milk to houses. **milking,** *n.* taking milk from a cow; **m. machine** = machine which milks cows automatically. **milkman,** *n.* (*pl.* **-men**) person who delivers the milk to houses each morning. **milky,** *adj.* (**-ier, -iest**) tasting like milk; cloudy like milk; containing milk; **the M. Way** = luminous band in the night sky composed of many stars.

mill [mɪl] **1.** *n.* (*a*) machine for grinding corn into flour; building which contains such a machine; *inf.* **he's been through the m.** = (i) he has been fully trained; (ii) he has suffered a great deal. (*b*) small instrument for grinding. (*c*) large factory. **2.** *v.* (*a*) to grind (corn, etc.). (*b*) to put vertical lines around the edge of a coin. **mill about, mill around,** *v.* to move in various directions. **miller,** *n.* man who runs a flour mill. **millpond,** *n.* water dammed to provide power for a watermill; **like a m.** = perfectly calm. **millstone,** *n.* (*a*) large grooved stone used to grind corn. (*b*) great obstacle which causes trouble.

millenium [mɪ'leniəm] *n.* (*pl.* **-ia**) (*a*) period of a thousand years. (*b*) period of great happiness.

millepede ['mɪlɪpiːd] *n.* millipede.

millet ['mɪlɪt] *n.* grain used for food.

milli- ['mɪlɪ] *prefix meaning* one thousandth.

millibar ['mɪlɪbɑː] *n.* unit of atmospheric pressure.

milligram ['mɪlɪgræm] *n.* one thousandth of a gram.

millimetre, *Am.* **millimeter** ['mɪlɪmiːtə] *n.* one thousandth of a metre.

milliner ['mɪlɪnə] *n.* person who makes/sells women's hats. **millinery,** *n.* hats and ribbons.

million ['mɪljən] number 1,000,000. **millionaire** [mɪljə'neə] *n.* person who has more than a million pounds; **dollar m.** = person who has more than a million dollars. **millionth, 1,000,000th, 1.** *adj.* referring to a million. **2.** *n.* one of a million parts.

millipede ['mɪlɪpiːd] *n.* small creeping animal with a large number of legs.

milometer [maɪ'lɒmɪtə] *n.* mileometer.

milt [mɪlt] *n.* sperm from a male fish.

mime [maɪm] **1.** *n.* (*a*) actor who does not speak, but conveys a story/emotions through gesture. (*b*) gesture used to convey a story/emotions. (*c*) story conveyed by gestures. **2.** *v.* to convey a story/emotions through gesture.

mimic ['mɪmɪk] **1.** *n.* person who imitates. **2.** *v.* (**mimicked**) to imitate. **mimicry,** *n.* imitation.

mimosa [mɪ'məʊzə] *n.* semi-tropical tree with yellow, scented flowers.

minaret [mɪnə'ret] *n.* tower attached to a mosque.

mince [mɪns] **1.** *n.* meat which has been ground up into very small pieces. **2.** *v.* (*a*) to grind up (meat/vegetables) until they are in very small pieces; **he didn't m. his words** = he said what he had to say in a straightforward way. (*b*) **to m. along** = to walk along in a very affected manner, taking small steps. **mincemeat,** *n.* mixture of apples, spices, dried fruit, etc.; **to make m. out of** = to defeat/destroy completely. **mince pie,** *n.* small pie filled with mincemeat and eaten at Christmas. **mincer,** *n.* machine for grinding up meat, etc. **mincing,** *adj.* (*a*) affected (way of walking). (*b*) **m. machine** = mincer.

mind [maɪnd] **1.** *n.* power of thinking; memory; **bear him in m.** = remember him; **to make up your m.** = to decide what to do; **I'm in two minds about going** = I can't decide whether to go or not; **I've a good m. to do it myself** = I would very much like to do it myself; **he's changed his m. twice already** = he has changed his decision/his point of view; **what do you have in m.?** = what are you thinking of? **state of m.** = general opinion/mood/feeling; **he's got sth on his m.** = he is worried about sth; **try to take her m. off the subject** = try to stop her thinking about the subject; **not in his right m.** = mad. **2.** *v.* (*a*) to be careful about. (*b*) to bother about/to be busy about; **m. your own business** = don't interfere in my affairs; **never m.** = don't bother/don't worry. (*c*) to object to/to be annoyed by; **would you m. shutting the door?** = please shut the door; **I wouldn't m. a cup of tea** = I would rather like a cup of tea. (*d*) to look after (sth) while the owner is away. **mind-boggling,** *adj. inf.* very surprising. **minded,** *adj.* interested (in doing sth); **commercially m.** = businesslike. **minder,** *n.* (*a*) person who looks after sth (while

the owner is away). (*b*) bodyguard.
mindful, *adj.* remembering/thinking of
sth. **mindless**, *adj.* without thinking/
stupid. **mind reader**, *n.* person who
seems to be able to guess what s.o. else
is thinking.

mine [maɪn] **1.** *n.* (*a*) deep hole in
the ground for digging out minerals;
he is a m. of information = he is
full of information. (*b*) explosive device which is planted underground or
underwater. **2.** *v.* (*a*) to excavate/to dig
for minerals. (*b*) to plant mines underground or under water. **3.** *pron.* belonging to me; **he's a friend of m.** =
one of my friends. **minefield**, *n.* area
of land/sea full of mines. **minelayer**,
n. ship which specializes in planting
mines under water. **miner**, *n.* person
who works in a mine; **m.'s lamp** = special lamp worn by a miner on his helmet.
minesweeper, *n.* ship which specializes in removing mines placed under
water by the enemy. **mineworker**, *n.*
worker in a mine. **mining**, *n.* (*a*) action of extracting minerals. (*b*) placing
mines underground or under water.

mineral ['mɪnrəl] *adj.* & *n.* (non-living
substance) which is extracted from the
earth; **m. water** = (i) water from a
spring; (ii) non-alcoholic fizzy drink; **m.
rights** = permission to dig out minerals.
mineralogist [mɪnə'rælədʒɪst] *n.* scientist who studies minerals. **mineralogy**,
n. study of minerals.

minestrone [mɪnɪ'strəʊnɪ] *n.* type of
Italian vegetable soup.

mingle ['mɪŋgl] *v.* to mix.

mingy ['mɪndʒɪ] *adj.* *inf.* mean/not
generous (**with** money, etc.).

mini ['mɪnɪ] **1.** *n.* (*a*) trade name for a
very small British car. (*b*) miniskirt. **2.**
adj. & *prefix.* very small. **minibus**, *n.*
small bus holding about twelve people.
minicomputer, *n.* small computer, but
larger than a micro. **minimarket**, *n.*
small self-service store. **miniskirt**, *n.*
very short skirt.

miniature ['mɪnɪtʃə] **1.** *n.* very small
model/portrait/painting. **2.** *adj.* very
small. **miniaturize**, *v.* to produce a very
small version of (sth).

minim ['mɪnɪm] *n.* note in music lasting
for two crotchets or half as long as a
semibreve.

minimum ['mɪnɪməm] *adj.* & *n.* (*pl.*
-ma) smallest possible (quantity).
minimal, *adj.* smallest possible. **min-
imize**, *v.* to reduce to the smallest
amount; to make (sth) seem very small.

minion ['mɪnjən] *n.* low-grade assistant
(who flatters his boss).

minister ['mɪnɪstə] **1.** *n.* (*a*) member of a
government in charge of a department;
the M. of Defence. (*b*) Protestant clergyman. **2.** *v.* **to m. to s.o.'s needs** =
to look after s.o./to take care of s.o.
ministerial [mɪnɪ'stɪərɪəl] *adj.* referring
to a government minister. **ministering**,
adj. (angel) who looks after the needs
of people. **ministration** [mɪnɪ'streɪʃn]
n. care given by a priest. **ministry**, *n.*
(*a*) government; **the Labour Ministry
of 1945.** (*b*) government department;
offices of a government department; **the
Ministry of Defence.** (*c*) work of a priest/
priesthood.

mink [mɪŋk] *n.* (*a*) small animal whose
fur is very valuable; **m. farm** = farm
where these animals are reared. (*b*) *inf.*
mink coat.

minnow ['mɪnəʊ] *n.* small freshwater
fish.

minor ['maɪnə] **1.** *adj.* (*a*) lesser; less important; **Asia M.** = Turkey. (*b*) (musical key) where there are semitones
between the second and third, and between the fifth and sixth notes. **2.** *n.*
young person under the age of 18.
minority [maɪ'nɒrɪtɪ] *n.* (*a*) number/
quantity less than half of a total; **the
men are in the m.** = there are more
women than men; **m. government** =
with fewer members of parliament than
the oppposition. (*b*) period when a person is less than 18 years old.

minster ['mɪnstə] *n.* (*usu. in names*)
large, important church.

minstrel ['mɪnstrəl] *n.* (*old*) travelling
singer or musician. (*b*) one of a group of
performers made up to look like black
people.

mint [mɪnt] **1.** *n.* (*a*) factory where
coins are made; **in m. condition** =
perfect/exactly as when it was made;
inf. **a m. of money** = a great deal
of money. (*b*) common herb used as
flavouring. (*c*) small white sweet tasting
of peppermint. **2.** *v.* to make coins.

minuet [mɪnjʊ'et] *n.* slow stately dance.

minus ['maɪnəs] **1.** *prep.* less; *inf.* **he came m. his wife** = without his wife. **2.** *n.* sign (–) meaning less; **m. 10 degrees** (–10°).

minuscule ['mɪnəskjuːl] *adj.* very small.

minute[1] ['mɪnɪt] *n.* (*a*) one sixtieth part of an hour or of a degree in an angle; **ten minutes past three** = 3.10; **five minutes to four** = 3.55; **m. hand** = long hand on watch or clock; **m. steak** = thin slice of beef which can be cooked quickly. (*b*) very short space of time; **he'll be here any m. now** = any time now. (*c*) **minutes** = notes of what is said at a meeting. **minutebook,** *n.* book in which minutes of meetings are kept. **minuted,** *adj.* put in the minutes of a meeting.

minute[2] [maɪ'njuːt] *adj.* very small. **minutely** [maɪ'njuːtlɪ] *adv.* in great detail. **minuteness** [maɪ'njuːtnəs] *n.* very small size. **minutiae** [mɪ'njuːʃiː] *n. pl.* very small details.

minx [mɪŋks] *n.* naughty girl.

miracle ['mɪrəkl] *n.* marvellous thing which happens apparently by the power of God; very wonderful happening. **miraculous** [mɪ'rækjʊləs] *adj.* wonderful/inexplicable. **miraculously,** *adv.* wonderfully/inexplicably.

mirage ['mɪrɑːʒ] *n.* imaginary image caused by heat (such as water and palm trees seen in a desert).

mire ['maɪə] *n.* (*formal*) muddy place; mud.

mirror ['mɪrə] **1.** *n.* glass backed by metal which reflects an image; **driving m./rear-view m.** = mirror inside a car which enables the driver to see what is behind without turning his head; **m. image** = exact copy, but reversed as in a mirror. **2.** *v.* to reflect as in a mirror.

mirth [mɜːθ] *n.* (*formal*) gaiety/happiness.

mis- [mɪs] *prefix meaning* wrongly.

misadventure [mɪsəd'ventʃə] *n.* unlucky accident.

misanthrope,   misanthropist ['mɪzənθrəʊp, mɪ'zænθrəpɪst] *n.* person who dislikes the human race. **misanthropic** [mɪzən'θrɒpɪk] *adj.* (person) who dislikes the human race. **misanthropy** [mɪ'zænθrəpɪ] *n.* dislike of the human race.

misapply [mɪsə'plaɪ] *v.* to use (sth) wrongly.

misapprehend [mɪsæprɪ'hend] *v.* not to understand. **misapprehension** [mɪsæprɪ'henʃən] *n.* not understanding; **labouring under a m.** = not understanding the situation correctly.

misappropriate [mɪsə'prəʊprɪeɪt] *v.* to use (public money) for your own purposes. **misappropriation** [mɪsəprəʊprɪ'eɪʃn] *n.* using public money for your own purposes.

misbehave [mɪsbɪ'heɪv] *v.* to act badly/to behave badly. **misbehaviour,** *n.* bad behaviour.

miscalculate [mɪs'kælkjʊleɪt] *v.* to calculate wrongly. **miscalculation** [mɪskælkjʊ'leɪʃn] *n.* mistake in calculating.

miscarry [mɪs'kærɪ] *v.* (*a*) (*of plan*) to go wrong. (*b*) to produce a baby which is not sufficiently developed to live. **miscarriage** ['mɪskærɪdʒ] *n.* (*a*) failure (of a scheme); **m. of justice** = wrong decision by a court. (*b*) loss of a baby during pregnancy.

miscast [mɪs'kɑːst] *v.* (**miscast**) to cast (an actor/actress) in a part which is unsuitable.

miscellaneous [mɪsə'leɪnɪəs] *adj.* varied/mixed. **miscellany** [mɪ'selənɪ] *n.* collection of varied things (usu. varied pieces of writing).

mischance ['mɪstʃɑːns] *n.* (*formal*) bad luck.

mischief ['mɪstʃɪf] *n.* bad behaviour/bad action; **they mean m.** = they are intending to do damage; **to make m.** = to make trouble/to make two people angry with each other; **the boy is always getting into m.** = he's always doing something naughty. **mischief-maker,** *n.* person who tries to start trouble. **mischievous** ['mɪstʃɪvəs] *adj.* wicked/naughty. **mischievously,** *adv.* in a mischevous way. **mischievousness,** *n.* tendency to cause trouble.

misconception [mɪskən'sepʃən] *n.* mistaken idea.

misconduct [mɪs'kɒndʌkt] *n.* bad conduct/bad behaviour; **professional m.** = behaviour which is not acceptable in a member of a profession.

misconstrue [mɪskən'struː] *v.* not

to understand. **misconstruction** [mɪskən'strʌkʃn] *n.* wrong interpretation of an action.

miscount [mɪs'kaʊnt] *v.* to count wrongly.

miscreant ['mɪskrɪənt] *n.* wicked person/criminal.

misdeed [mɪs'di:d] *n.* wicked action.

misdemeanour, Am. misdemeanor [mɪsdɪ'mi:nə] *n.* (not very serious) unlawful act.

misdirect [mɪsdaɪ'rekt] *v.* to give wrong directions to.

miser ['maɪzə] *n.* person who hoards money and refuses to spend it. **miserliness,** *n.* dislike of spending money. **miserly,** *adj.* not wanting to spend money.

miserable ['mɪzrəbl] *adj.* sad/unhappy; awful/bad/unpleasant (weather); very low (salary). **miserably,** *adv.* sadly/unhappily.

misericord [mɪ'zerɪkɔ:d] *n.* seat in a medieval church which folds back to show carving on its underside.

misery ['mɪzərɪ] *n.* sadness; suffering; **her life was sheer m.** = was very unhappy; **to put a dog out of its m.** = to kill a dog because it is in pain; **to put s.o. out of his m.** = to tell s.o. the result/not to keep s.o. waiting any longer.

misfire [mɪs'faɪə] *v.* not to fire properly; **the car engine is misfiring** = is not igniting the petrol at the right time; **his plan misfired** = went wrong.

misfit ['mɪsfɪt] *n.* person who does not fit in with a group/fit into society.

misfortune [mɪs'fɔ:tju:n] *n.* bad luck.

misgiving [mɪs'gɪvɪŋ] *n.* doubt/fear.

misguided [mɪs'gaɪdɪd] *adj.* badly advised; wrongly judged; foolish.

mishap ['mɪshæp] *n.* slight accident.

mishmash ['mɪʃmæʃ] *n.* disorderly collection; jumble.

misinform [mɪsɪn'fɔ:m] *v.* to give (s.o.) wrong information.

misinterpret [mɪsɪn'tɜ:prɪt] *v.* to interpret wrongly, not to understand correctly. **misinterpretation** [mɪsɪntɜ:prɪ'teɪʃn] *n.* wrong interpretation; misunderstanding.

misjudge [mɪs'dʒʌdʒ] *v.* to judge wrongly; to form a wrong opinion about (s.o./sth).

mislay [mɪs'leɪ] *v.* (**mislaid**) to put (sth) down and not to remember where you have put it.

mislead [mɪs'li:d] *v.* (**misled**) to give (s.o.) wrong information/to make (s.o.) make a mistake. **misleading,** *adj.* wrong/erroneous; likely to cause a mistake.

mismanage [mɪs'mænɪdʒ] *v.* to manage wrongly/badly. **mismanagement,** *n.* bad management.

mismatch [mɪs'mætʃ] **1.** *n.* bad match. **2.** *v.* to match (two opponents) badly.

misnomer [mɪs'nəʊmə] *n.* wrong name/wrong term.

misogynist [mɪ'sɒdʒɪnɪst] *n.* man who dislikes women. **misogyny,** *n.* hatred of women.

misplace [mɪs'pleɪs] *v.* to put in the wrong place.

misprint ['mɪsprɪnt] *n.* error in printing.

mispronounce [mɪsprə'naʊns] *v.* to pronounce wrongly. **mispronunciation** [mɪsprənʌnsɪ'eɪʃn] *n.* pronouncing wrongly.

misquote [mɪs'kwəʊt] *v.* to quote wrongly/incorrectly. **misquotation** [mɪskwəʊ'teɪʃn] *n.* incorrect quotation.

misread [mɪs'ri:d] *v.* (**misread** [mɪs'red]) to read wrongly; to make a mistake when reading.

misrepresent [mɪsreprɪ'zent] *v.* to show (sth) wrongly; to give a wrong idea of (sth); to distort (facts). **misrepresentation** [mɪsreprɪzen'teɪʃn] *n.* distortion of what s.o. said or wrote.

misrule [mɪs'ru:l] **1.** *n.* bad rule/bad government. **2.** *v.* to rule badly.

miss [mɪs] **1.** *n.* (*pl.* **-es**) (*a*) failure to hit; **we'll give it a m.** = we will not do it/not go to see it. (*b*) title of unmarried woman; **Miss Jones.** (*c*) title given to schoolmistress/used to call a waitress, etc. **2.** *v.* (*a*) not to hit/see, etc.; **you didn't m. much** = there wasn't much to see/the performance was not very good. (*b*) **he just missed being killed** = he was very nearly killed. (*c*) to regret the absence of (s.o./sth). **missing,** *adj.* absent/lost; stolen. **miss out,** *v.* to omit/to leave (sth) out. **miss out on,** *v. inf.* not to enjoy (sth) because of being absent.

missal ['mɪsl] *n.* book containing the text of the Catholic mass and other prayers.

missel ['mɪsl] *n.* **m. thrush** = type of woodland thrush.

misshapen [mɪs'ʃeɪpn] *adj.* deformed/oddly shaped.

missile ['mɪsaɪl, *Am.* 'mɪsl] *n.* (*a*) weapon which is thrown. (*b*) explosive rocket which can be guided to its target.

mission ['mɪʃn] *n.* (*a*) aim/purpose for which s.o. is sent; **her m. in life is to help orphans** = her calling/her chosen task. (*b*) house/office of a missionary. (*c*) group of people sent somewhere with a particular aim. (*d*) embassy or consulate. **missionary** ['mɪʃənrɪ] *adj.* & *n.* (person) whose duty is to try to convert people to his religion.

missive ['mɪsɪv] *n.* (*formal*) letter.

misspell [mɪs'spel] *v.* (**mispelled/mispelt**) to spell wrongly. **mispelling,** *n.* spelling mistake.

misspent [mɪs'spent] *adj.* (youth) which has been wasted.

misstatement [mɪs'steɪtmənt] *n.* wrong statement of facts.

missus ['mɪsɪz] *n. inf.* wife.

mist [mɪst] 1. *n.* thin fog/haze. 2. *v.* to get covered with mist; **to m. up** = to become covered with condensation. **mistiness,** *n.* being misty. **misty,** *adj.* (-ier, iest) (*a*) full of mist. (*b*) vague (memory).

mistake [mɪs'teɪk] 1. *n.* error; wrong action. 2. *v.* (**mistook; mistaken**) (*a*) to understand (sth) wrongly. (*b*) **to m. s.o. for s.o.** = to assume (s.o.) is s.o. else. **mistaken,** *adj.* wrong. **mistakenly,** *adv.* by mistake/in error.

mister ['mɪstə] *n. inf.* form of address to a man.

mistime [mɪs'taɪm] *v.* to choose the wrong time/an inconvenient time to do something.

mistletoe ['mɪzltəʊ] *n.* parasitic plant which grows on oaks or apple trees, used as a Christmas decoration.

mistook [mɪs'tʊk] *v. see* **mistake.**

mistreatment [mɪs'tri:tmənt] *n.* bad treatment (of prisoners, etc.).

mistress ['mɪstrəs] *n.* (*pl.* -es) (*a*) woman in charge/who employs/teaches; **she's her own m.** = she is independent. (*b*) woman who has a sexual relationship with a man without being married to him.

mistrust [mɪs'trʌst] 1. *n.* wariness/lack of trust. 2. *v.* not to trust (s.o.)/to be doubtful about (s.o.). **mistrustful,** *adj.* not trusting.

misunderstand [mɪsʌndə'stænd] *v.* (**misunderstood**) not to understand. **misunderstanding,** *n.* wrong understanding/disagreement.

misuse 1. *n.* [mɪs'ju:s] wrong use. 2. *v.* [mɪs'ju:z] to use (sth) in a wrong way; to treat (s.o.) badly.

mite [maɪt] *n.* (*a*) very small child. (*b*) very small creature like a spider, living in stale food.

miter ['maɪtə] *n. Am.* = **mitre.**

mitigate ['mɪtɪgeɪt] *v.* to make (a crime) less serious. **mitigation** [mɪtɪ'geɪʃn] *n.* making less serious.

mitosis [maɪ'təʊsɪs] *n.* cell division.

mitre, *Am.* **miter** ['maɪtə] *n.* (*a*) hat worn by bishops and archbishops. (*b*) (*in woodwork*) type of sloping joint/sloping edge. **mitred,** *adj.* sloping (joint/edge).

mitt, mitten [mɪt, 'mɪtn] *n.* (*a*) glove without separate fingers, esp. a glove to wash with or to hold hot dishes with. (*b*) glove which leaves the fingers bare.

mix [mɪks] 1. *n.* (*pl.* -es) blend/mingling of several things. 2. *v.* to blend/to mingle. **mixed,** *adj.* made up of different things put together; **a mixed marriage** = marriage between two people of different races; (*in tennis*) **mixed doubles** = doubles match where a man and woman play against another man and woman; **mixed school** = school with both boys and girls; **I have very mixed feelings about the project** = in some ways I am for it and in others I am against it; **it's a mixed blessing** = in some ways it a good thing, but in others it is not. **mixer,** *n.* (*a*) machine for mixing. (*b*) person who fits in well with other people. **mixture** ['mɪkstʃə] *n.* blend/mingling together; **cough m.** = liquid medicine to cure a cough. **mix up,** *v.* (*a*) to confuse; **I always mix him up with his brother** = I always think he is his brother. (*b*) to involve. (*c*) **the speaker got all mixed up** = he got confused/lost his notes. **mix-up,** *n. inf.* confusion.

mizzenmast ['mɪzənma:st] *n.* mast

nearest the stern of a ship. **mizzen,** *n.* sail on a mizzenmast.

ml *abbrev. for* millilitre.

mm *abbrev. for* millimetre.

Mn *symbol for* manganese.

mnemonic [nɪˈmɒnɪk] *adj.* & *n.* (rhyme) which helps you to remember certain facts.

Mo *symbol for* molybdenum.

moan [məʊn] **1.** *n.* (*a*) low groan. (*b*) general complaint. **2.** *v.* (*a*) to make a low groan. (*b*) to complain (**about** sth). **moaner,** *n. inf.* person who complains.

moat [məʊt] *n.* wide ditch with water in it, surrounding a castle/old house. **moated,** *adj.* with a moat.

mob [mɒb] **1.** *n.* (*a*) crowd of unruly people. (*b*) *inf.* criminal gang. **2.** *v.* (**mobbed**) to surround in a wild crowd. **mobster,** *n. inf.* member of a criminal gang.

mobile [ˈməʊbaɪl, *Am.* ˈməʊbl] **1.** *adj.* which can move; **he is not very m.** = he can't walk easily; **m. library** = library in a van which travels around from place to place. **2.** *n.* artistic creation using pieces of metal/ paper, etc., which when hung up can move. **mobility** [məʊˈbɪlɪtɪ] *n.* ability to move. **mobilization** [məʊbɪlaɪˈzeɪʃn] *n.* grouping of people together (esp. to join the armed forces). **mobilize** [ˈməʊbɪlaɪz] *v.* to group (people) together (esp. to join the armed forces).

moccasins [ˈmɒkəsɪnz] *n. pl.* soft leather shoes.

mocha [ˈmɒkə] *n.* (*a*) type of coffee from Arabia. (*b*) coffee and chocolate flavouring.

mock [mɒk] **1.** *adj.* false/imitation; **m. examinations** = trial examinations carried out before the real ones. **2.** *v.* to laugh at (s.o./sth). **mockery,** *n.* (*a*) laughing at (s.o./sth). (*b*) thing which is only a bad imitation. **mocking,** *adj.* & *n.* laughing at (s.o./sth). **mockingbird,** *n.* bird from the southern United States which imitates the song of other birds. **mock-up,** *n.* scale model of a new product for testing purposes.

mod [mɒd] *adj. inf. short for* **modern.** **mod cons,** *n. pl.* modern conveniences (in a house).

mode [məʊd] *n.* way (of doing sth).

modal, *adj.* & *n.* (verb such as **can, must,** etc.) which is used with other verbs, and not alone.

model [ˈmɒdl] **1.** *n.* & *adj.* (*a*) small-scale copy. (*b*) thing which you can take as a perfect example to be copied; **artist's m.** = person whose job is to sit while an artist draws pictures of him/ her. (*c*) person whose job is to wear new clothes to show them to customers. (*d*) style of car, etc., produced in a particular period. **2.** *v.* (**modelled**) (*a*) to make a model; to make shapes (of clay); **modelling clay** = special clay for sculpture. (*b*) **he modelled his way of walking on that of his father** = he imitated his father's way. (*c*) to wear (new clothes) to show to customers.

modem [ˈməʊdem] *n.* device for sending data by telephone, linking a computer to the telephone lines.

moderate 1. *adj.* & *n.* [ˈmɒdərət] (*a*) not excessive; middling. (*b*) (person) without a violent political bias. **2.** *v.* [ˈmɒdəreɪt] to diminish/to make less strong. **moderately,** *adv.* quite/not excessively. **moderation** [mɒdəˈreɪʃn] *n.* not an excessive use; calming down. **moderator,** *n.* (*a*) chairman of a church meeting. (*b*) examiner from outside the school/college, etc., who checks that examination standards are high enough. (*c*) chairman of a learned discussion.

modern [ˈmɒdn] *adj.* of the present day; not ancient; **m. languages** = languages which are spoken today. **modernity** [məˈdɜːnɪtɪ] *n.* being modern. **modernization** [mɒdənaɪˈzeɪʃn] *n.* act of modernizing. **modernize** [ˈmɒdənaɪz] *v.* to make modern; to renovate.

modest [ˈmɒdɪst] *adj.* (*a*) not boasting. (*b*) not demanding/not excessive; **a m. flat** = one which does not look expensive. **modestly,** *adv.* in a modest way. **modesty,** *n.* (*a*) not being boastful. (*b*) not being excessive/ demanding.

modicum [ˈmɒdɪkəm] *n.* small quantity.

modify [ˈmɒdɪfaɪ] *v.* (*a*) to change/to alter (sth) to fit a different use. (*b*) to reduce. **modification** [mɒdɪfɪˈkeɪʃn] *n.* change. **modifier,** *n.* thing which modifies; word which qualifies another word.

modish ['məʊdɪʃ] *adj.* fashionable.

modulate ['mɒdjʊleɪt] *v.* to change the pitch of a note/a musical key. **modulation** [mɒdjʊ'leɪʃn] *n.* change of pitch.

module ['mɒdjuːl] *n.* section of a larger combination; **lunar m.** = section of a spacecraft which lands on the moon. **modular,** *adj.* made of various modules.

modus operandi ['məʊdəsɒpə'rændɪ] *n.* way of working.

modus vivendi ['məʊdəsvɪ'vendɪ] *n.* informal way of working together.

moggy ['mɒgɪ] *n. Sl.* cat.

mogul ['məʊgəl] *n. inf.* (*a*) **film m.** = boss of a film company. (*b*) bump on a ski slope.

mohair ['məʊheə] *n.* very soft wool from a type of goat.

moke [məʊk] *n. inf.* donkey.

moist [mɔɪst] *adj.* (**-er, -est**) slightly wet/damp. **moisten** ['mɔɪsn] *v.* to make moist. **moistness,** *n.* being moist. **moisture** ['mɔɪstʃə] *n.* slight wetness. **moisturizer** ['mɔɪstʃəraɪzə] *n.* cream which makes the skin softer. **moisturizing,** *adj.* (cream) which makes the skin softer.

molar ['məʊlə] *n.* large back tooth used for grinding food.

molasses [mə'læsɪz] *n.* thick black raw syrup removed from unrefined sugar.

mold [məʊld] *Am.* = mould.

mole [məʊl] *n.* (*a*) small black mammal which lives underground. (*b*) small dark spot on the skin. (*c*) *inf.* member of an organization who is in the pay of the opponent/enemy. (*d*) stone jetty/pier used as a breakwater. (*e*) standard measurement of the amount of a substance. **molehill,** *n.* little heap of earth pushed up by a mole; **to make a mountain out of a m.** = to make a fuss about sth which is really trivial. **moleskin,** *n.* skin of a mole used for making clothes.

molecule ['mɒlɪkjuːl] *n.* smallest unit into which a substance can be divided. **molecular** [mə'lekjʊlə] *adj.* referring to molecules: **m. weight** = mass of one molecule of a substance compared to that of one atom of carbon.

molest [mə'lest] *v.* to attack/to beat (s.o.). **molestation** [mɒlɪs'teɪʃn] *n.* (*formal*) act of molesting.

mollify ['mɒlɪfaɪ] *v.* to make (s.o.) feel less annoyed. **mollification** [mɒlɪfɪ'keɪʃn] *n.* act of mollifying.

mollusc, *Am.* **mollusk** ['mɒləsk] *n.* animal with no backbone, but usu. with a shell (such as snails/oysters, etc.).

mollycoddle ['mɒlɪkɒdl] *v.* to spoil (s.o.)/to treat (s.o.) too softly.

Molotov cocktail ['mɒlətɒf'kɒkteɪl] *n.* handmade bomb, made of a bottle filled with petrol, with a short wick.

molt [məʊlt] *Am.* = moult.

molten ['məʊltən] *adj.* not solid; melted.

molybdenum [mɒ'lɪbdənəm] *n.* (*element:* Mo) whitish metal.

moment ['məʊmənt] *n.* (*a*) very short space of time; **at any m.** = very soon; **at the m.** = just now; **for the m.** = for the time being. (*b*) importance. **momentarily,** *adv.* for a short space of time. **momentary,** *adj.* shortlived/passing. **momentous** [mə'mentəs] *adj.* very important.

momentum [mə'mentəm] *n.* impetus; movement forwards; **to gain/to lose m.** = to progress faster/slower.

monarch ['mɒnək] *n.* king or queen; ruler. **monarchic(al)** [mə'nɑːkɪk(l)] *adj.* referring to a monarchy. **monarchist** ['mɒnəkɪst] *n.* supporter of a monarchy. **monarchy** ['mɒnəkɪ] *n.* system of government with a hereditary ruler such as a king or queen.

monastery ['mɒnəstrɪ] *n.* group of buildings where monks live. **monastic** [mɒ'næstɪk] *adj.* referring to a monastery/to monks.

Monday ['mʌndɪ] *n.* first day of the week/day between Sunday and Tuesday.

monetary ['mʌnɪtərɪ] *adj.* referring to money or currency. **monetarism,** *n.* belief that inflation can be checked by reducing the amount of money available in the economy. **monetarist,** *n.* person who believes in monetarism.

money ['mʌnɪ] *n.* coins or notes which are used for buying and selling; **to come into m.** = to inherit money; **we were offered our m. back** = a refund of what we had already paid; **we ran out of m.** = we had no money left. **moneybox,** *n.* box that can be locked and in which you can keep money.

moneyed, adj. rich. **moneylender,** n. person who lends money. **money order,** n. order for passing money from one person to another via the post office. **money-spinner,** n. inf. book/record, etc., which sells very well.

mongol ['mɒŋgəl] adj. & n. (person) born with mongolism. **mongolism** n. defect in a person from birth, of which the symptoms are slanting eyes, flattened skull and low intelligence.

mongoose ['mɒŋguːs] n. small tropical mammal which kills snakes.

mongrel ['mʌŋgrəl] adj. & n. not purebred (dog)/(dog) of mixed breeds.

monitor ['mɒnɪtə] 1. n. (a) person who watches/surveys the progress of sth. (b) senior pupil (in a school) who has a particular duty to perform. (c) apparatus for checking the progress of sth, esp. the screen of a computer or a small television screen in a television studio. 2. v. to check/to survey (the progress of sth); **monitoring station** = radio station specially for listening to foreign broadcasts and obtaining information from them.

monk [mʌŋk] n. man who is a member of a religious group and lives in a monastery. **monkish,** adj. like a monk.

monkey ['mʌŋkɪ] 1. n. usu. a tropical mammal which looks rather like a man, but which normally has a tail; inf. naughty child; **m. nut** = peanut; **m. puzzle tree** = type of tropical pine tree with spiky branches; **m. wrench** = large spanner with an adjustable grip. 2. inf. **to m. about** = to play/to mess around.

mono ['mɒnəʊ] 1. prefix meaning single. 2. n. & adj. not stereophonic; (machine/record) which reproduces sound through a single channel.

monochrome ['mɒnəkrəʊm] adj. & n. (in a) single colour, usu. black and white.

monocle ['mɒnəkl] n. eye glass/single lens worn to correct sight.

monocular [mɒ'nɒkjuːlə] adj. (vision) as with one eye, with no sense of depth.

monogamy [mə'nɒgəmɪ] n. system of marriage to one person at a time. **monogamous,** adj. (marriage) to one husband or wife.

monogram ['mɒnəgræm] n. design

based on the initials of your name. **monogrammed,** adj. with your initials on it.

monograph ['mɒnəgrɑːf] n. short book about a specialized subject.

monolith ['mɒnəlɪθ] n. single standing stone. **monolithic** [mɒnə'lɪθɪk] adj. solid/heavy; changeless.

monologue ['mɒnəlɒg] n. long speech by one actor alone on the stage.

monomania [mɒnə'meɪnɪə] n. mania about a single thing.

mononucleosis [mɒnənjuːklɪ'əʊsɪs] n. Am. glandular fever.

monophonic [mɒnə'fɒnɪk] adj. not stereophonic; (record) with sound coming from a single channel.

monoplane ['mɒnəpleɪn] n. plane with one pair of wings.

monopoly [mə'nɒpəlɪ] n. system where one person or company supplies all needs in one area without any competition. **monopolization** [mənɒpələ'zeɪʃn] n. creating of a monopoly. **monopolize** [mə'nɒpəlaɪz] v. to create a monopoly; to use (sth) entirely for yourself; **to m. the conversation** = to do all the talking and not let anyone else speak.

monorail ['mɒnəreɪl] n. train which runs on a single rail.

monosyllable ['mɒnəsɪləbl] n. word which only has one syllable. **monosyllabic** [mɒnəsɪ'læbɪk] adj. (word) with only one syllable; (conversation) using only monosyllables.

monotheism [mɒnəʊ'θiːɪzəm] n. belief that there is only one god.

monotone ['mɒnətəʊn] n. flat/level tone of voice. **monotonous** [mə'nɒtənəs] adj. not varied/not changing/boring. **monotonously,** adv. in a monotonous way. **monotony,** n. lack of variety.

monoxide [mə'nɒksaɪd] n. chemical compound containing one atom of oxygen.

monsignor [mɒn'siːnjə] n. title given to an important priest in the Roman Catholic church.

monsoon [mɒn'suːn] n. (a) season of wind and rain in the tropics. (b) wind blowing in the Indian Ocean.

monster ['mɒnstə] 1. n. (a) horrible/

strange creature. (b) very large and terrifying animal/thing. (c) cruel/wicked person. **2.** adj. very large. **monstrosity** [mɒn'strɒsɪtɪ] n. horrible/strange/ugly thing. **monstrous** ['mɒnstrəs] adj. huge/ugly/horrible.

montage [mɒn'tɑ:ʒ] n. picture/piece of music, etc., made of several items brought together; action of putting several items together to make a picture/piece of music, etc.

month [mʌnθ] n. one of the twelve periods which form a year. **monthly. 1.** adj. & adv. occurring every month. **2.** n. magazine which appears each month.

monument ['mɒnjumənt] n. (a) (to s.o.) stone/building/statue, etc., erected in memory of s.o. who is dead. (b) building which is very old. **monumental** [mɒnju'mentl] adj. (a) very large. (b) referring to a monument; **m. mason** = person who makes gravestones.

moo [mu:] **1.** n. sound made by a cow. **2.** v. to make a sound like a cow.

mooch [mu:tʃ] v. (about) to go about aimlessly.

mood [mu:d] n. (a) general feeling. (b) bad temper. (c) group of forms of a verb which indicates a fact, a possibility or a condition. **moodily,** adv. in a moody way. **moodiness,** n. gloomy feeling; quick change from good to bad temper. **moody,** adj. (-ier, -iest) often gloomy/often bad-tempered; changing quickly from good to bad temper.

moon [mu:n] n. satellite which travels round a planet, esp. the one which travels round the earth each month and shines with reflected light from the sun; **once in a blue m.** = very rarely. **moonbeam,** n. ray of light from the moon. **moonlight 1.** n. light from the moon. **2.** v. to do a second job (for cash). **moonlighter,** n. person who does a second job for cash. **moonlighting,** n. inf. doing a second job (usu. in the evening) apart from your regular work. **moonlit,** adj. lit by light from the moon. **moonshine,** n. inf. (a) nonsense. (b) illegal alcohol. **moonstone,** n. semi-precious stone with a white shine.

moor ['mʊə, mɔ:] **1.** n. uncultivated land covered with low shrubs. **2.** v. to attach (a boat) to a quayside/to a buoy. **moorhen,** n. common water bird. **mooring,** n. (a) action of attaching a boat. (b) **moorings** = place where a boat is moored; ropes, etc., used to moor a boat. **moorland,** n. area of uncultivated land covered with low shrubs.

moose [mu:s] n. (pl. **moose**) American elk.

moot [mu:t] **1.** adj. **m. point** = question which is open to discussion. **2.** v. to raise (a question/a suggestion).

mop [mɒp] **1.** n. brush for washing floors with a head made of soft string or foam rubber; **m. of hair** = long and untidy hair. **2.** v. (**mopped**) (a) to wash the floor, using a mop. (b) to wipe. **mop up,** v. (a) to clear up (liquid) using a mop. (b) to clear up (pockets of resistance).

mope [məup] v. to be miserable/gloomy.

moped ['məuped] n. two-wheeled cycle with a low-powered motor.

moquette [mɒ'ket] n. thick cloth for covering chairs, etc.

moraine [mə'reɪn] n. heap of gravel, etc., left by a glacier.

moral ['mɒrəl] **1.** adj. (a) referring to right and wrong in human behaviour. (b) referring to good human behaviour; **m. support** = encouragement without active help. **2.** n. lesson to be drawn from a story. **3. morals** = personal character and way of behaving. **moralist,** n. person who criticizes low moral standards. **morality** [mə'rælɪtɪ] n. correct way of behaving; sense of moral standards. **moralize** ['mɒrəlaɪz] v. to draw a lesson from a story or event. **morally,** adv. according to correct human behaviour.

morale [mə'rɑ:l] n. feeling of confidence.

morass [mə'ræs] n. (pl. **-es**) (a) deep swamp/marsh. (b) mass of things which prevent any progress.

moratorium [mɒrə'tɔ:rɪəm] n. (pl. **-ia**) temporary ban.

moray eel [mɒreɪ'i:l] n. type of large eel.

morbid ['mɔ:bɪd] adj. (a) interested in death/unpleasant things. (b) connected with disease. **morbidity** [mɔː'bɪdɪtɪ] *n.* sickly interest in death/unpleasant things. **morbidly,** *adv.* in a morbid way.

mordant ['mɔːdənt] *adj.* (*formal*) cruel (sarcasm).

more [mɔː] **1.** *adj.* extra/additional. **2.** *n.* extra/additional amount. **3.** *adv.* (*a*) additionally/to a larger extent. (*b*) (*forming comparative*) she is m. intelligent than her brother. (*c*) not any m. = no longer; **m. or less** = approximately/practically. **moreover** [mɔː-'rəʊvə] *adv.* besides; in addition.

morganatic [mɔːgə'nætɪk] *adj.* **m. marriage** = marriage of a king or queen to s.o. of lower rank who does not take their title.

morgue [mɔːg] *n.* building where dead bodies are kept before burial.

moribund ['mɒrɪbʌnd] *adj.* dying; going out of existence.

Mormon ['mɔːmən] *adj. & n.* (member) of a Christian sect, founded in the USA.

mornay ['mɔːneɪ] *adj.* cooked with a cheese sauce.

morning ['mɔːnɪŋ] *n.* early part of the day, before 12 noon; **4 in the m.** = 4 a.m.; **the m. train** = the train which leaves every morning.

morocco [mə'rɒkəʊ] *n.* fine soft leather.

moron ['mɔːrɒn] *n.* (*a*) adult with the intelligence of a child. (*b*) stupid person. **moronic** [mə'rɒnɪk] *adj.* stupid.

morose [mə'rəʊs] *adj.* gloomy and bad-tempered. **morosely,** *adv.* in a morose way. **moroseness,** *n.* being morose.

morphia, morphine ['mɔːfɪə, 'mɔːfiːn] *n.* drug which kills pain and makes you go to sleep.

morphology [mɔː'fɒlədʒɪ] *n.* (*a*) study of the way in which words change in the plural, or according to gender or conjugation. (*b*) study of the forms of plants or animals. **morphological** [mɔːfə'lɒdʒɪkl] *adj.* referring to morphology.

morris ['mɒrɪs] *n.* **m. dance** = old English dance, danced by men in white clothes with bells on their legs.

morrow ['mɒrəʊ] *n.* (*old*) next day.

Morse code [mɔːs'kəʊd] *n.* system of dots and dashes for sending messages.

morsel ['mɔːsl] *n.* small piece.

mortal ['mɔːtl] **1.** *adj.* (*a*) causing death;

m. enemy = deadly enemy. (*b*) referring to the body; **m. remains** = corpse. **2.** *n.* human being. **mortality** [mɔː-'tælɪtɪ] *n.* (*a*) human state. (*b*) **m. rate** = number of deaths (as a percentage of population). **mortally,** *adv.* so as to cause death.

mortar ['mɔːtə] *n.* (*a*) cement mixture for holding together bricks or stones when building. (*b*) bowl for crushing things with a pestle. (*c*) short cannon. **mortar-board,** *n.* black cap with a square top worn at ceremonies by people with university degrees.

mortgage ['mɔːgɪdʒ] **1.** *n.* agreement whereby s.o. lends money on the security of a property; money lent on the security of property; **second m.** = further loan obtained on a property which is already mortgaged. **2.** *v.* to give (a property) as security for a loan. **mortgagee** [mɔːgɪ'dʒiː] *n.* person who loans money on mortgage. **mortgagor** [mɔːgɪ'dʒɔː] *n.* person who borrows money on a mortgage.

mortice ['mɔːtɪs] *n.* hole cut in the end of a piece of wood into which another piece (a tenon) fits to form a joint; **m. lock** = lock which is fitted into a door.

mortician [mɔː'tɪʃn] *n. Am.* undertaker.

mortify ['mɔːtɪfaɪ] *v.* to humiliate. **mortification** [mɔːtɪfɪ'keɪʃn] *n.* feeling of shame/humiliation.

mortise ['mɔːtɪs] *n.* = **mortice.**

mortuary ['mɔːtjʊərɪ] *n.* place where dead bodies are kept before burial.

mosaic [mə'zeɪɪk] *n.* tiny pieces of coloured stone stuck to a wall or floor in patterns.

Moslem ['mɒzləm] *adj. & n.* = **Muslim.**

mosque [mɒsk] *n.* religious building for Muslims.

mosquito [məs'kiːtəʊ] *n.* (*pl.* -oes) small flying insect which sucks blood; **m. net** = thin net spread over a bed to prevent mosquitoes biting at night.

moss [mɒs] *n.* (*pl.* -es) primitive green plant growing in compact low clumps on the ground or on stones. **mossy,** *adj.* covered with moss.

most [məʊst] **1.** *adj.* the largest number/ largest quantity (of sth). **2.** *n.* the largest number/largest quantity; **to make the m. of** = get as much profit/value from sth as possible. **3.** *adv.* to the largest extent. (*a*) (*forming superlative*) **the m. intelligent child.** (*b*) (*intensive*) very. **mostly,** *adv.* in most cases/most often.

MOT [eməʊ'tiː] *n.* **MOT (test)** = mechanical test for cars over three years old.

motel [məʊ'tel] *n.* hotel for car drivers where there is a parking space for every room.

motet [məʊ'tet] *n.* music for a small group of unaccompanied singers.

moth [mɒθ] *n.* flying insect with large wings like a butterfly, but flying mainly at night; **clothes m.** = type of moth of which the grub eats wool or fur. **mothball,** *v. inf.* to store (a ship, etc.) in working order for future use. **mothballs,** *n. pl.* balls of a chemical substance put among clothes to keep moths away; **in m.** = stored for future use. **motheaten,** *adj.* full of holes made by moths; old and decrepit.

mother ['mʌðə] **1.** *n.* female parent; **m. country** = country where you or your ancestors were born; **m. tongue** = first language a child speaks; **M. Superior** = woman head of a religious community. **2.** *v.* to look after (s.o.) very attentively. **motherhood,** *n.* being a mother. **Mothering Sunday,** *n.* festival commemorating mothers. **mother-in-law,** *n.* (*pl.* **mothers-in-law**) mother of your wife or husband; **mother-in-law's tongue** = type of house plant with a few tall stiff vertical leaves. **motherless,** *adj.* with no mother. **motherly,** *adj.* maternal/like a mother. **mother of pearl,** *n.* shiny substance found on the inside of oyster shells.

motif [məʊ'tiːf] *n.* distinctive repeating pattern in a design/in a piece of music.

motion ['məʊʃn] **1.** *n.* (*a*) movement/act of moving; **in m.** = moving. (*b*) gesture/movement; **to go through the motions** = to do sth for the sake of appearances, without believing in it. (*c*) bowel movement. (*d*) proposal which is to be put to the vote (at a meeting); **to second a m.** = to support the person who proposed the motion. **2.** *v.* to make a gesture. **motionless,** *adj.* still/not moving.

motive ['məʊtɪv] **1.** *n.* reason for doing

sth. **2.** *adj.* which makes sth move. **motivate** ['məʊtɪveɪt] *v.* to make (s.o.) do sth; to encourage (s.o.) to do sth; **highly motivated** = eager. **motivation** [məʊtɪ'veɪʃn] *n.* reason for doing sth/encouragement to do sth.

motley ['mɒtlɪ] *adj.* varied; of varied sorts of colours.

motocross ['məʊtəʊkrɒs] *n.* motorcycle race over rough ground.

motor ['məʊtə] **1.** *n.* (*a*) machine which causes motion; engine. (*b*) car; **m. show** = show where new models of cars are shown to the public. **2.** *v.* to travel in a car. **3.** *adj.* (*a*) using a motor; **motor mower.** (*b*) (nerve) which links the brain to the muscles, so causing motion; **m. neurone disease** = disease of the nerves which control the muscles. **motorbike,** *n. inf.* motorcycle. **motorboat,** *n.* small boat with a motor. **motorcade,** *n. Am.* official procession of cars. **motorcar,** *n.* car. **motorcycle,** *n.* two-wheeled cycle powered by a motor. **motorcyclist,** *n.* person riding a motorcycle. **motoring,** *n.* driving of a car; **school of m.** = driving school. **motorist,** *n.* driver of a car. **motorize,** *v.* to provide (sth) with an engine; to equip (s.o.) with motor transport. **motorway,** *n.* special road for high-speed traffic with very few exit and entry points.

mottled ['mɒtld] *adj.* spotted with different colours.

motto ['mɒtəʊ] *n.* (*pl.* **-oes**) (*a*) short phrase which is used to sum up an attitude. (*b*) amusing phrase on a piece of paper inside a Christmas cracker.

mould, *Am.* **mold** [məʊld] **1.** *n.* (*a*) soft earth; **leaf m.** = soft earth formed from dead leaves. (*b*) hollow shape into which a liquid is poured, so that when the liquid becomes hard it takes that shape; **jelly m.** = shape for making jelly. (*c*) greyish powdery fungus. **2.** *v.* to shape (sth). **moulder.** **1.** *n.* person who moulds. **2.** *v.* to rot away. **mouldiness,** *n.* being mouldy/rotten. **moulding,** *n.* thing which has been moulded. **mouldy,** *adj.* rotten/covered with mould.

moult, *Am.* **molt** [məʊlt] *v.* to lose feathers/fur.

mound [maʊnd] n. small heap/hill.

mount [maʊnt] **1.** n. (a) (usu. in names) mountain. (b) cardboard frame for a picture. (c) horse/donkey, etc., on which a rider sits. **2.** v. (a) to climb on to (sth); to rise; **mounted police** = police on horseback. (b) **to m. guard over** = to stand on guard to protect sth. (c) to set (sth) in a cardboard frame/in a metal ring/brooch, etc. (d) to organize (an expedition). **Mountie,** n. inf. member of the Royal Canadian Mounted Police. **mount up,** v. to rise/to increase.

mountain ['maʊntn] n. (a) very high land; **m. sheep** = sheep which are specially bred to live on mountains; **m. ash** = common northern tree with red berries. (b) large amount; **butter m.** = large quantity of butter stockpiled by governments because of overproduction. **mountaineer** [maʊntə'nɪə] n. person who climbs mountains for pleasure. **mountaineering,** n. climbing of mountains as a sport. **mountainous,** adj. (area) full of mountains; very high (waves).

mountebank ['maʊntɪbæŋk] n. person who persuades people to pay money by talking cleverly.

mourn [mɔːn] v. to regret (sth). **mourner,** n. person who grieves for s.o. who has died; **the mourners** = people attending a funeral. **mournful,** adj. very sad. **mournfully,** adv. in a very sad way. **mourning,** n. (a) period of time when one grieves over the death of a relative or friend. (b) dark clothes worn as a mark of respect for someone who has died.

mouse [maʊs] n. (pl. mice [maɪs]) (a) small rodent with long tail, often living in houses. (b) device which is held in the hand and moved across a flat surface, used to control a cursor on a computer monitor. **mousehole,** n. small hole in which mice live. **mouser,** n. **the cat is a good m.** = good at catching mice. **mousetrap,** n. trap for catching mice; inf. **m. cheese** = strong/old/inferior cheese. **mousy,** adj. (a) small and insignificant (person). (b) brownish-grey (colour).

moussaka ['muːsækæ] n. Greek dish, made of aubergines and minced meat.

mousse [muːs] n. light food made of whipped eggs, cream and flavouring.

moustache, Am. **mustache** [mə'staːʃ, Am. 'mʌstæʃ] n. hair grown on the upper lip.

mouth 1. n. [maʊθ] (a) part of the head through which you take in food and drink and through which you speak. (b) wide entrance; **m. of a river** = place where a river enters the sea. **2.** v. [maʊð] to move the mouth as if speaking, without making any sound; to speak without being heard. **mouthful,** n. (a) quantity contained in the mouth. (b) inf. complicated word/phrase. **mouthorgan,** n. small musical instrument played by blowing, with a series of small valves giving different notes. **mouthpiece,** n. (a) part of a musical instrument which goes into the mouth. (b) person who speaks on behalf of s.o. **mouthwash,** n. antiseptic solution for cleaning the inside of the mouth. **mouthwatering,** adj. very delicious.

move [muːv] **1.** n. (a) action of changing place; movement; **get a m. on!** = hurry up; inf. **we must make a m.** = we must leave. (b) movement (of a piece in chess); **what's the next m.?** = what do we have to do next? (c) changing of place of residence. **2.** v. (a) to change the position (of sth); to change position; **don't m.!** = stand still! inf. **we must be moving** = we must leave. (b) to leave one place to go to live in another. (c) to change the feelings (of s.o.). (d) to propose (a motion in a debate). **movable, moveable** adj. which can be moved. **move about,** v. (a) to change (sth) from one place to another. (b) to wander about. **move away,** v. to change to another place further away; to change (sth) to a position further away; **we are moving away from London** = we are leaving London to live in another town. **move back,** v. (a) to go backwards; to change (sth) to a place further back. (b) to return to a previous place. **move forward,** v. to go forward; to make (s.o.) go to a place further forward. **move in,** v. to settle with furniture in a new house. **movement,** n. (a) action of changing position/of not being still. (b) mechanism (of a clock).

(*c*) main part of a large piece of music. (*d*) group of people working towards a certain aim. **move off**, *v*. to go away; **the train moved off** = began to leave. **move on**, *v*. to go forward; to make (s.o.) go forward. **mover**, *n*. (*a*) person who moves furniture from one house to another. (*b*) person who proposes a motion in a debate. **movie**, *n*. *Am*. cinema film. **moving**, *adj*. (*a*) which changes position/which is not still; **m. staircase** = escalator. (*b*) which affects your feelings.

mow [məʊ] *v*. (**has mown**) to cut (grass). **mow down**, *v*. to kill/to slaughter. **mower**, *n*. (*a*) person who cuts grass. (*b*) machine which cuts grass; **motor m.** = lawnmower powered by a motor.

MP [em'pi:] *n*. Member of Parliament.

mpg *abbrev. for* miles per gallon.

mph *abbrev. for* miles per hour.

Mr ['mɪstə] *n*. title given to a man.

Mrs ['mɪsɪz] *n*. title given to a married woman.

Ms [mʌz, mɪz] *n*. title given to a woman (married or unmarried).

much [mʌtʃ] **1.** *adj*. a lot of. **2.** *adv*. (**more/most**) to a great extent/very; **m. the most expensive** = by far the most expensive; *inf*. **it's a bit m.!** = it's quite unreasonable! **m. to my amazement** = to my great surprise. **3.** *n*. a lot; *inf*. **not up to m.** = not very good.

muck [mʌk] **1.** *n*. dirt; manure. **2.** *v*. to **m. out a stable** = to clean a stable; *inf*. **to m. about with** = to play about with; *inf*. **to m. up** = to ruin; *inf*. **m. in together** = cooperate in the work. **muckraking**, *n*. discovering and publishing scandalous stories about famous people. **mucky**, *adj*. (**-ier, -iest**) dirty; covered with muck.

mucus ['mju:kəs] *n*. shiny substance which coats the inside of cavities of the body. **mucous**, *adj*. referring to mucus; **m. membrane** = wet membrane which lines inside passages of the body.

mud [mʌd] *n*. very wet earth. **muddiness**, *n*. being muddy. **muddy**, **1.** *adj*. (**-ier, -iest**) full of mud; covered with mud. **2.** *v*. to put mud on sth; **to m. the waters** = to stir up trouble/confusion. **mudflap**, *n*. flap hanging behind the wheel of a car to prevent mud and

water being splashed. **mudflats**, *n. pl.* flat muddy land covered by the sea at high tide. **mudguard**, *n*. strip of metal over the wheel on a bicycle to stop mud and water being splashed. **mudpack**, *n*. paste put on the face to improve the texture of the skin. **mudslinging**, *n*. insults.

muddle ['mʌdl] **1.** *n*. confusion/mixture. **2.** *v*. to confuse/to mix up. **muddleheaded**, *adj*. confused. **muddle through**, *v*. to get through one's business/to succeed in a muddled way.

muesli ['mju:zlɪ] *n*. breakfast food of flakes of cereal/dried fruit, etc., eaten with milk.

muezzin [mu:'ezɪn] *n*. person who calls Muslims to prayer.

muff [mʌf] **1.** *n*. warm covering for a particular part of the body, esp. the hands. **2.** *v*. to do (sth) badly.

muffin ['mʌfɪn] *n*. small round cake eaten warm with butter.

muffle ['mʌfl] *v*. (*a*) to wrap up in clothes. (*b*) to deaden (a loud noise). **muffler**, *n*. (*a*) long scarf. (*b*) *Am*. silencer (on car exhaust).

mufti ['mʌftɪ] *n. inf.* **in m.** = in civilian clothes; not in uniform.

mug [mʌg] **1.** *n*. (*a*) large glass/cup with a handle. (*b*) *inf*. stupid person/person who is easily taken in. (*c*) *inf*. face. **2.** *v*. (**mugged**) (*a*) *inf*. **to m. up a subject** = to study a subject very hard at the last minute. (*b*) to attack and rob (in the street). **mugger**, *n*. person who attacks and robs s.o. in the street. **mugging**, *n*. robbery with violence (in the street). **mug shot**, *n. inf*. photograph of s.o.'s face.

muggins ['mʌgɪnz] *n. inf*. silly fool.

muggy ['mʌgɪ] *adj. inf*. warm and wet (weather).

mulatto [mju:'lætəʊ] *n*. (*pl.* **-os**) person of mixed Negro and White race.

mulberry ['mʌlbərɪ] *n*. soft purple fruit; tree which bears this fruit.

mulch [mʌltʃ] **1.** *n*. (*pl.* **-es**) covering of manure/rotten leaves, etc., spread on the ground to improve the soil. **2.** *v*. to spread mulch on (the ground).

mulct [mʌlkt] *v*. to take money away from (s.o.).

mule [mju:l] *n*. (*a*) hybrid between a

donkey and a horse; obstinate person. (*b*) light shoe with an open heel.
muleteer [mjʊləˈtɪə] *n.* person who drives mules carrying loads. **mulish,** *adj.* obstinate/difficult to deal with.
mull [mʌl] *v.* to heat (wine) with spices/ sugar, etc. **mull over,** *v.* to ponder/to think about (sth).
mullah [ˈmʊlə] *n.* Muslim religious thinker.
mullet [ˈmʌlɪt] *n.* small sea fish.
mulligatawny [mʌlɪgəˈtɔːnɪ] *n.* hot soup made with curry.
mullion [ˈmʌljən] *n.* vertical (wooden/ metal) bar between panes of glass in a window.
multi- [ˈmʌltɪ] *prefix meaning* many.
multicoloured [ˈmʌltɪkʌləd] *adj.* with many colours.
multifarious [mʌltɪˈfeərɪəs] *adj.* very varied/in many different types.
multilateral [mʌltɪˈlætərəl] *adj.* between more than two partners.
multimillionaire [mʌltɪmɪljəˈneə] *n.* person who has several million pounds.
multinational [mʌltɪˈnæʃnl] *adj. & n.* (company) which operates in several different countries.
multiple [ˈmʌltɪpl] **1.** *adj.* many/repeated; **m. store** = company with many shops in several towns; **m. sclerosis** = disease of the nervous system, which gets progressively worse. **2.** *n.* (*a*) number which contains another number several times exactly. (*b*) repeated groups of the same number of sth; **sold in multiples of five** = you can buy five, ten, fifteen, etc. **multiplication** [mʌltɪplɪˈkeɪʃn] *n.* action of multiplying; **m. sign** (×) = sign used to show that numbers are to be multiplied; **m. tables** = lists of figures to learn by heart how each number is multiplied. **multiplicity** [mʌltɪˈplɪsɪtɪ] *n.* vast and varied mass. **multiply** [ˈmʌltɪplaɪ] *v.* (*a*) to calculate the sum of several numbers repeated a stated number of times. (*b*) to increase in number.
multiracial [mʌltɪˈreɪʃl] *adj.* (society) whose members come from various races.
multistorey [ˈmʌltɪstɔːrɪ] *adj.* with many storeys.
multitude [ˈmʌltɪtjuːd] *n.* great number/

crowd. **multitudinous** [mʌltɪˈtjuːdɪnəs] *adj.* in very large numbers.
mum [mʌm] **1.** *adj.* silent; **he kept m.** = he didn't say a word. **2.** *n. inf.* mother.
mumble [ˈmʌmbl] **1.** *n.* speech which you can't understand because it is indistinct. **2.** *v.* not to speak distinctly.
mumbo-jumbo [mʌmbəʊˈdʒʌmbəʊ] *n.* nonsense/meaningless talk.
mummer [ˈmʌmə] *n.* (*old*) member of a group acting a traditional Christmas play.
mummy [ˈmʌmɪ] *n.* (*a*) *inf.* mother. (*b*) corpse preserved with ointments and bandages as in Ancient Egypt. **mummify,** *v.* to preserve (a dead body) in a perfect state.
mumps [mʌmps] *n.* infectious illness with swelling on either side of the neck.
munch [mʌnʃ] *v.* to chew (sth crisp or dry) with large regular movements of the jaws.
mundane [mʌnˈdeɪn] *adj.* ordinary.
municipal [mjuːˈnɪsɪpl] *adj.* referring to a town; **m. gardens** = park which belongs to a town; **m. buildings** = town hall. **municipality** [mjuːnɪsɪˈpælɪtɪ] *n.* self-governing town.
munificence [mjuːˈnɪfɪsns] *n.* (*formal*) great generosity. **munificent,** *adj.* (*formal*) extremely generous.
munitions [mjuːˈnɪʃnz] *n. pl.* weapons and ammunition.
mural [ˈmjʊərəl] **1.** *adj.* referring to walls. **2.** *n.* painting on a wall.
murder [ˈmɜːdə] **1.** *n.* (*a*) illegal killing of s.o. (*b*) *inf.* awful or unpleasant thing. **2.** *v.* (*a*) to kill (s.o.) illegally. (*b*) *inf.* to ruin (a song) by singing it badly. **murderer,** *n.* person who has committed a murder. **murderess** [ˈmɜːdrəs] *n.* woman who has committed a murder. **murderous** [ˈmɜːdərəs] *adj.* likely to kill.
murk [mɜːk] *n.* (*formal*) darkness/ gloominess. **murkiness,** *n.* being dark/ gloomy. **murky** [ˈmɜːkɪ] *adj.* (-ier, -iest) dark/gloomy (water).
murmur [ˈmɜːmə] **1.** *n.* low whisper of voices/low sound. **2.** *v.* to speak in a low voice; to complain in a low voice. **murmuring,** *n.* (*a*) speaking in a low voice. (*b*) **murmurings** = grumblings/ complaints.

muscat ['mʌskət] *n.* type of sweet grape; wine made from this grape.

muscatel [mʌskə'tel] *n.* type of sweet black grape, usually dried.

muscle ['mʌsl] **1.** *n.* spring-like parts of the body which allow the limbs to move; **he's flexing his muscles** = he's preparing to fight/to do sth great. **2.** *v. inf.* **to m. in on sth** = to push yourself forward to take part in sth which is organized by s.o. else. **muscular** ['mʌskjʊlə] *adj.* referring to muscles; **m. dystrophy** = disease causing gradual weakening of the muscles.

muse [mju:z] **1.** *n.* (*formal*) goddess who inspires poets, musicians, etc. **2.** *v.* to think deeply; to daydream.

museum [mju:'zɪəm] *n.* building in which a collection of valuable or rare objects are put on show permanently.

mush [mʌʃ] *n.* soft half-liquid mess. **mushiness,** *n.* being mushy. **mushy,** *adj.* (*a*) soft and partly liquid. (*b*) *inf.* very sentimental.

mushroom ['mʌʃru:m] **1.** *n.* edible round white fungus. **2.** *v.* to spring up rapidly.

music ['mju:zɪk] *n.* sounds made by playing instruments or singing; **to face the m.** = to face criticism. **musical. 1.** *adj.* referring to music; (person) who likes music/plays music a lot; **m. chairs** = (i) game where people try to sit on chairs when the music stops, with one chair and one person less each time; (ii) *inf.* continual movement from office to office/from job to job. **2.** *n.* (*also* **musical comedy**) play with songs and popular music. **musical-box,** *n.* small box with a clockwork motor which plays a tune when the box is opened. **musically,** *adv.* in a musical way. **music hall,** *n.* theatre specializing in variety shows. **musician** [mju:'zɪʃn] *n.* person who plays music professionaly/skillfully. **musicology** [mju:zɪ'kɒlədʒɪ] *n.* academic study of music. **musicologist,** *n.* specialist in the study of music.

musk [mʌsk] *n.* perfume obtained from glands of a deer. **musk ox,** *n.* large wild ox, found in North America. **musk-rat,** *n.* musquash. **musk-rose,** *n.* old-fashioned scented rose. **musky,** *adj.* with a smell like musk.

muskeg ['mʌskeg] *n.* (*in Canada*) marsh.

musket ['mʌskɪt] *n.* early portable gun with a long barrel. **musketeer,** *n.* soldier who was armed with a musket.

Muslim ['muzlɪm] *adj. & n.* (person) following the religion of the prophet Mohammed.

muslin ['mʌzlɪn] *n.* very fine thin cotton cloth.

musquash ['mʌskwɒʃ] *n.* American water rat with fine fur.

muss [mʌs] *v. Am. inf.* to ruffle (hair, etc.).

mussel ['mʌsl] *n.* mollusc with a dark blue shell, whose soft parts can be eaten.

must [mʌst] **1.** *v.* (*a*) *used with verbs to mean* it is necessary. (*b*) *used with verbs to mean* it is probable; **it m. be the doctor** = it cannot be anyone else. **2.** *n.* (*a*) *inf.* very necessary thing. (*b*) grape juice.

mustache ['mʌstæʃ] *n. Am.* = **moustache.**

mustang ['mʌstæŋ] *n.* wild American horse.

mustard ['mʌstəd] *n.* (*a*) sharp-tasting yellow powder made from crushed seeds; paste made from this powder; **m. gas** = poisonous gas which burns the skin; **m. yellow** = dull yellow colour. (*b*) plant whose seeds make mustard powder; **m. and cress** = seedlings of the mustard plant, together with seedlings of cress, eaten as a salad.

muster ['mʌstə] **1.** *n.* gathering; parade and inspection of soldiers; **to pass m.** = to be acceptable. **2.** *v.* to gather together.

musty ['mʌstɪ] *adj.* (**-ier, -iest**) smelling damp/rotten/stale; smelling old. **mustiness,** *n.* rotten/stale smell.

mutate [mju:'teɪt] *v.* to change genetically. **mutability** [mju:tə'bɪlɪtɪ] *n.* being mutable. **mutable,** *adj.* which is likely to change/which can be changed. **mutant** ['mju:tənt] *n.* animal/plant which has changed genetically. **mutation** [mju:'teɪʃn] *n.* genetic change.

mute [mju:t] **1.** *adj.* (*a*) silent/dumb (person). (*b*) (letter) which is not pronounced. **2.** *n.* (*a*) person who cannot speak/who is dumb; **deaf m.** = person who cannot hear or speak. (*b*) device used to soften the sound of a musical instrument. **3.** *v.* to soften the sound of (a musical instrument). **mutely,** *adv.* silently.

mutilate ['mju:tɪleɪt] *v.* to cut off a limb/ an ear, etc., from (s.o.); to damage (an object). **mutilation** [mju:tɪ'leɪʃn] *n.* loss of a limb; great damage.

mutiny ['mju:tɪnɪ] **1.** *n.* uprising, esp. of soldiers/sailors, etc., against the orders of their officers. **2.** *v.* to refuse to carry out orders/to rise up against officers. **mutineer** [mju:tɪ'nɪə] *n.* person who mutinies. **mutinous** ['mju:tɪnəs] *adj.* likely to mutiny/rebellious. **mutinously,** *adv.* in a mutinous way.

mutt [mʌt] *n. Sl.* (*a*) idiot/stupid person. (*b*) dog.

mutter ['mʌtə] **1.** *n.* low indistinct way of speaking. **2.** *v.* to mumble/to speak in a low and indistinct voice. **muttering,** *n.* speaking indistinctly.

mutton ['mʌtn] *n.* meat of a sheep.

mutual ['mju:tjʊəl] *adj.* felt/done by two people to each other; between two people; belonging to two people; **our m. friend** = the friend of both of us; **by m. consent** = with the agreement of both parties. **mutually,** *adv.* to two people; by two people.

Muzak ['mju:zæk] *n.* trademark for system of playing recorded music in public places.

muzzle ['mʌzl] **1.** *n.* (*a*) nose of an animal. (*b*) straps placed round the mouth of a dog to prevent it biting. (*c*) mouth of a gun. **2.** *v.* to tie up the mouth of (a dog) to prevent it biting; **to m. the press** = to stop newspapers from printing what they want.

muzzy ['mʌzɪ] *adj. inf.* dizzy/in a daze. **muzziness,** *n.* feeling muzzy.

my [maɪ] *adj.* belonging to me.

myalgia [maɪ'ældʒɪə] *n.* muscle pain.

mycology [maɪ'kɒlədʒɪ] *n.* study of fungi. **mycological** [maɪkə'lɒdʒɪkl] *adj.* referring to mycology.

myelitis [maɪə'laɪtɪs] *n.* inflammation of the spinal cord.

mynah (bird) ['maɪnə'(bɜ:d)] *n.* black tropical bird which can be taught to talk.

myopia [maɪ'əʊpɪə] *n.* short-sightedness/not being able to see things which are far away. **myopic** [maɪ'ɒpɪk] *adj.* short-sighted.

myriad ['mɪrɪəd] (*formal*) **1.** *n.* very large number. **2.** *adj.* very many.

myrrh [mɜ:] *n.* sweet-smelling resin used to make incense, etc.

myrtle ['mɜ:tl] *n.* evergreen plant with scented flowers.

myself [maɪ'self] *pronoun referring to* me. **all by m.** = on my own.

mystery ['mɪstrɪ] *n.* thing which cannot be explained; state of not being able to be explained. **mysterious** [mɪ'stɪərɪəs] *adj.* secret/which cannot be explained. **mysteriously,** *adv.* secretly/in a way which cannot be explained.

mystic ['mɪstɪk] **1.** *n.* person who attempts to make contact with God through prayer/meditation, etc. **2.** *adj.* in contact with God. **mystical,** *adj.* in contact with God by some process which cannot be understood. **mysticism** ['mɪstɪsɪzəm] *n.* religion based on attempts to contact God by prayer and meditation.

mystify ['mɪstɪfaɪ] *v.* to puzzle/to bewilder. **mystification** [mɪstɪfɪ'keɪʃn] *n.* puzzle/bewilderment.

mystique [mɪ'sti:k] *n.* mysterious atmosphere about a person or thing.

myth [mɪθ] *n.* (*a*) ancient folk story about gods. (*b*) untrue, but commonly held, notion. **mythical,** *adj.* (*a*) referring to ancient tales of gods. (*b*) untrue/not existing. **mythological** [mɪθə'lɒdʒɪkl] *adj.* referring to mythology. **mythology** [mɪ'θɒlədʒɪ] *n.* study of myths; ancient folk stories from a particular source.

myxomatosis [mɪksəmə'təʊsɪs] *n.* fatal disease of rabbits.

Nn

N *symbol for* nitrogen.

Na *symbol for* sodium.

nab [næb] *v.* (**nabbed**) (*a*) *inf.* to snatch/ to pull away (sth) suddenly/to steal. (*b*) *inf.* to catch (s.o.) in the act/to pounce on (s.o.).

nadir ['neɪdɪə] *n.* lowest point.

naevus ['ni:vəs] *n.* birthmark.

naff [næf] *adj. Sl.* worthless.

nag [næg] **1.** *n. inf.* horse. **2.** *v.* (**nagged**) to try to persuade (s.o.) by saying the same thing again and again/to criticize without seeming to stop. **nagging**, *adj.* persistent (pain, etc.).

naiad ['naɪæd] *n.* goddess living in a stream.

nail [neɪl] **1.** *n.* (*a*) hard covering at the ends of fingers and toes; **n. scissors** = curved scissors for cutting nails. (*b*) small metal spike with a pointed end, used to hold things together; **hard as nails** = very tough; *inf.* **to hit the n. on the head** = to make an accurate judgement/to say the right answer; *inf.* **to pay on the n.** = to pay immediately/promptly/on the spot. **2.** *v.* to attach with nails.

naive [naɪ'iːv] *adj.* inexperienced and innocent. **naively**, *adv.* in a naive way. **naivety**, *n.* being naive.

naked ['neɪkɪd] *adj.* with no clothes on; with no covering; **n. flame** = flame with no protective shield; **invisible to the n. eye** = which can only be seen using a telescope/microscope. **nakedly**, *adv.* with no covering. **nakedness**, *n.* being naked.

namby-pamby ['næmbɪpæmbɪ] *adj.* weak and silly.

name [neɪm] **1.** *n.* (*a*) title/word which you use to call people/things; **Christian n./first n.** = particular name given to someone as a child; **he put his n. down to join the club** = he applied to join; **to call s.o. names** = to insult s.o. (*b*) **in n. only** = according to the name used, but not really in fact. (*c*) **to give a bad n.** = a bad reputation; **to make a n. for oneself** = acquire a high reputation. **2.** *v.* (*a*) to call by a name; to give a name to. (*b*) to specify; **to n. the day** = to fix the date for a wedding. (*c*) to appoint s.o. to a post. **nameless**, *adj.* with no name; (word/name) not to be used because of disgust or in order to remain anonymous. **namely**, *adv.* that is to say. **namesake**, *n.* person with the same name as another.

nan, nana [næn, 'nænə] *n.* child's name for grandmother.

nanny ['nænɪ] *n.* (*a*) nurse paid to look after children in their own home. (*b*) **n. goat** = female goat.

nano- ['nænəʊ] *prefix* one thousand millionth.

nap [næp] **1.** *n.* (*a*) short sleep. (*b*) raised surface of cloth, such as velvet. (*c*) card game. (*d*) tip for the winner of a horse race. **2.** *v.* to sleep for a short time; **to catch s.o. napping** = to find s.o. off guard.

napalm ['neɪpɑːm] *n.* inflammable substance used in incendiary bombs.

nape [neɪp] *n.* back of the neck.

naphtha ['næfθə] *n.* oil derived from coal/petroleum, used to light fires/clean clothes, etc. **napthalene** ['næfθəliːn] *n.* strong-smelling white chemical used to make mothballs.

napkin ['næpkɪn] *n.* (*a*) square piece of cloth or paper used to protect clothes and wipe your mouth at mealtimes. (*b*) (*formal*) nappy.

nappy ['næpɪ] *n.* towel used to cover a baby's bottom.

narcissus [nɑː'sɪsəs] *n.* (*pl.* **-issi** [-ɪsaɪ]) white flower similar to a daffodil. **narcissism**, *n.* great love for your own appearance. **narcissistic** [nɑːsɪ'sɪstɪk] *adj.* loving your own appearance.

narcotic [nɑː'kɒtɪk] *adj. & n.* (substance) which can make you feel sleepy or become unconscious; *Am.* **narcotics squad** = police department dealing with drug offences.

nark [nɑːk] **1.** *n. Sl.* police spy. **2.** *v. Sl.* to annoy.

narrate [nə'reɪt] *v.* to write/to speak about events; to tell (a story). **narration** [nə'reɪʃn] *n.* speaking/writing about events. **narrative** ['nærətɪv] **1.** *n.* what is actually written or told. **2.** *adj.* describing events which took place. **narrator** [nə'reɪtə] *n.* person who gives an actual account; person who reads a story.

narrow ['nærəʊ] **1.** *adj.* (*a*) not wide; **n. squeak/n. escape** = escape at the last minute from an awkward or dangerous situation. (*b*) **n. majority** = very small margin of votes. (*c*) restricted (opinions). **2.** *v.* to make/to become less wide; to make/to become smaller. **narrowboat**, *n.* long boat used on canals. **narrowly**, *adv.* nearly/only just. **narrow-minded**, *adj.* not capable of seeing many points of view/not tolerant. **narrowness**, *n*. being narrow. **narrows**, *n. pl.* narrow stretch of water.

narwhal ['nɑ:wəl] *n*. type of whale which lives in the Arctic and has a long tusk.

nary ['neɪrɪ] *adj*. (*old*) not one.

nasal ['neɪzl] *adj*. referring to the nose; spoken as if through the nose. **nasally**, *adv*. in a nasal way.

nasturtium [nə'stɜ:ʃəm] *n*. creeping plant with large orange or yellow flowers.

nasty ['nɑ:stɪ] *adj*. (**-ier, -iest**) unpleasant/disagreeable; **to turn n.** = to become hostile/unfriendly; *inf*. **n. piece of work** = unpleasant person. **nastily**, *adv*. in a nasty way. **nastiness**, *n*. being nasty; nasty happening.

natal ['neɪtl] *adj*. referring to birth.

nation ['neɪʃn] *n*. people of a particular country. **national** ['næʃnl] **1.** *adj*. belonging to the people of a particular country; **N. Health Service** = British system of free medical care; **N. Insurance** = system of regular payments by workers and employers, to pay for free medical care and other benefits; **n. park** = large area of unspoilt land, managed by the state as a public amenity. **2.** *n*. person of a particular country. **nationalism** ['næʃnəlɪzəm] *n*. feeling of pride in one's nation; desire for independence for a country. **nationalist**, *n*. person who supports nationalism. **nationalistic**, *adj*. referring to nationalism. **nationality** [næʃə-'nælɪtɪ] *n*. citizenship of a country. **nationalization** [næʃnəlaɪ'zeɪʃn] *n*. conversion of private industries to ownership by the state. **nationalize** ['næʃnəlaɪz] *v*. to put a (private industry) under central government ownership and control. **nationally**, *adv*. in a national way; (done) all over the nation. **national park**, *n*. area of wild land run by the state where building/ tourism, etc. are controlled. **national service**, *n*. temporary conscription into the armed forces. **nationwide** ['neɪʃnwaɪd] *adj*. all over the country.

native ['neɪtɪv] **1.** *n*. (*a*) person born in a particular country. (*b*) uncivi-

lized original inhabitant. (*c*) plant/animal which originally comes from a particular country. **2.** *adj*. (*a*) natural; (qualities) with which a person is born. (*b*) unaltered/undeveloped. (*c*) belonging to those born in a country. (*d*) **n. to** = (plant/animal) which originally comes from a certain country.

nativity [nə'tɪvɪtɪ] *n*. birth, esp. that of Jesus Christ; **n. play** = play describing the events surrounding the birth of Jesus Christ.

natter ['nætə] **1.** *n. inf*. friendly informal conversation/chat. **2.** *v. inf*. to have a friendly informal chat.

natty ['nætɪ] *adj*. (**-ier, -iest**) (*a*) smart/ tidy (personal appearance). (*b*) cleverly designed (gadget).

natural ['nætʃrəl] **1.** *adj*. (*a*) based on inner knowledge or instinct; not learnt. (*b*) normal/not artificial. (*c*) not surprising/not unexpected. (*d*) dealing with (the study of) nature; **n. gas** = gas which is found in the earth. (*e*) (*in music*) (note) which is neither sharp nor flat. **2.** *n*. person who is naturally suitable for a job/a part in a play, etc. **natural history**, *n*. (*also* **natural science**) study of nature. **naturalism**, *n*. (*in art/ literature*) showing things as they really are. **naturalist**, *n*. person who studies animals or plants. **naturalistic**, *adj*. (art, etc.) which shows things as they really are. **naturalization** [nætʃərəlaɪ-'zeɪʃn] *n*. act of naturalizing; being naturalized. **naturalize** ['nætʃərəlaɪz] *v*. (*a*) to introduce (a plant or animal) into another country. (*b*) to let cultivated plants become wild. (*c*) to grant (s.o.) citizenship of a country other than that in which he was born. **naturally** ['nætʃrəlɪ] *adv*. (*a*) in a natural/unstudied way. (*b*) as you would expect/of course. **naturalness**, *n*. being natural.

nature ['neɪtʃə] *n*. (*a*) character (of a person/thing/animal); **human n.** = attitude and behaviour which are typical of human beings. (*b*) kind/class (of thing). (*c*) world of plants and animals; **the laws of n.** = what happens in the world of plants and animals; **n. study** = the study of plant or animal life in a junior school. **-natured,** *suffix showing a* characteristic; **good-natured.**

naturism, *n.* belief in the physical and mental advantages of going about naked. **naturist,** *n.* nudist.

naught [nɔːt] *n.* (*formal*) nothing.

naughty ['nɔːtı] *adj.* (**-ier, -iest**) bad/ disobedient (child). **naughtily,** *adv.* wickedly. **naughtiness,** *n.* wickedness/ bad behaviour.

nausea ['nɔːzıə] *n.* feeling of sickness/ of extreme dislike. **nauseate,** *v.* to make (s.o.) loathe/dislike very much. **nauseating,** *adj.* horrible/which makes you sick. **nauseous,** *adj.* (*a*) which nauseates. (*b*) *Am.* feeling unwell.

nautical ['nɔːtıkl] *adj.* referring to ships, sailing and boating; **n. mile** = measure of length at sea (2025 yards or 1.85 kilometres).

nautilus [nɔːˈtıləs] *n.* large type of shell fish.

naval ['neıvl] *adj.* referring to ships and esp. to a navy; **n. engagement** = battle at sea; **n. base** = port for warships; **n. college** = establishment for training naval officers.

nave [neıv] *n.* main part of a church.

navel ['neıvl] *n.* small hollow in the middle of your stomach where the umbilical cord was attached; **n. orange** = large seedless orange with a small hollow at the bottom.

navigate ['nævıgeıt] *v.* to guide/to steer (a ship or aircraft); to tell the driver of a car, etc., which way to go. **navigability** [nævıgəˈbılıtı] *n.* being navigable. **navigable,** *adj.* (*a*) steerable/seaworthy. (*b*) (river) deep enough for ships to sail in it. **navigation** [nævıˈgeıʃn] *n.* guiding/steering a ship/ an aircraft along a certain course; **inland n.** = travel by boat along rivers or canals. **navigator** ['nævıgeıtə] *n.* person who guides/steers a ship or an aircraft; person who tells the driver of a car which way to go.

navvy ['nævı] *n.* labourer.

navy ['neıvı] **1.** *n.* (*a*) all a country's warships and crews. (*b*) **Merchant N.** = all cargo ships of a country. **2.** *adj. & n.* **n.** (blue) = dark blue.

nay [neı] *adv.* (*old*) no.

n.b. [en'biː] *short for* nota bene, *meaning* please note.

NCO [ensiːˈəʊ] *n.* non-commissioned officer.

neap [niːp] *n.* **n. tide** = tide which does not rise or fall very much, midway between the spring tides.

Neapolitan [nıəˈpɒlıtən] *adj.* referring to Naples; **N. ice cream** = ice cream made of layers of different colours and flavours.

near ['nıə] (**-er, -est**) **1.** *adv.* close/at only a little distance in space or time. **2.** *prep.* close by (an object); not far away in time. **3.** *adj.* **n. relations** = closest relations; **n. side** = side closest to the kerb (in a car); **n. miss** = (i) sth which is not quite successful; (ii) narrow escape. **4.** *v.* to draw near to/to approach. **nearby,** *adj.* which is situated close by. **near by,** *adv.* close by. **Near East,** *n.* countries at the eastern end of the Mediterranean. **nearly,** *adv.* (*a*) almost. (*b*) closely; **not n. big enough** = far too small. **nearness,** *n.* closeness. **near-sighted,** *adj.* short-sighted/ only able to see clearly things which are near.

neat [niːt] *adj.* (**-er,-est**) (*a*) tidy/clean. (*b*) (alcohol) with no water added. (*c*) apt/precise (words). (*d*) skilful/well handled. **neatly,** *adv.* in a neat way. **neatness,** *n.* tidy/clean appearance.

nebula ['nebjulə] *n.* (*pl.* **-ae** [-liː]) cloud of dust in space which shines like a star at night. **nebulous** ['nebjuləs] *adj.* vague.

necessary ['nesəsərı] **1.** *n.* what is essential/what must be done; *inf.* **the n.** = the required amount of money. **2.** *adj.* essential/which cannot be avoided. **necessarily** [nesə-ˈserəlı] *adv.* in an unavoidable way; **taking the train isn't n. dearer than the bus** = it can be cheaper. **necessitate** [nıˈsesıteıt] *v.* to make essential/to compel. **necessitous,** *adj.* (*formal*) poor. **necessity,** *n.* (*a*) need/compulsion. (*b*) absolutely essential thing.

neck [nek] **1.** *n.* (*a*) part of the body connecting the head to the shoulders; *inf.* **to be up to your n. in work** = have a lot of work to do; **to breathe down s.o.'s n.** = to watch s.o. very closely/to follow close behind s.o.; **to win by a n.** = win a race by a very short distance; **to**

finish n. and n. = to be equal winners; *inf.* **a pain in the n.** = a troublesome person/thing; **to save your n.** = escape hanging/punishment; *inf.* **to get it in the n.** = to be severely criticized; *inf.* **to stick your n. out** = take a chance/to be asking for trouble. (*b*) narrow passage leading to a wider area; *inf.* **in this n. of the woods** = in this part of the world. (*c*) part of a garment which goes round your neck. (*d*) part of an animal eaten as food; **best end of n.** = joint of lamb consisting of the ribs nearest the neck. **2.** *v. inf.* to fondle/caress. **necklace,** *n.* string of beads/pearls, etc., worn round the neck. **necklet,** *n.* ornament worn tightly round the neck. **neckline,** *n.* edge of a dress, etc., round the neck. **necktie,** *n. esp. Am.* band of material worn round the neck and tied in front with a knot.

necromancy ['nekrəmænsı] *n.* art of black magic/of predicting the future by speaking to the dead. **necromancer,** *n.* person who practises necromancy.

necropolis [ne'krɒpəlɪs] *n.* large ancient cemetery.

nectar ['nektə] *n.* (*a*) sweet substance produced by flowers. (*b*) any extremely pleasant drink.

nectarine ['nektəri:n] *n.* fruit like a peach with a smooth skin.

née [neɪ] *adj.* with the maiden name of; **Mrs Smith, n. Taylor.**

need [ni:d] **1.** *n.* (*a*) what is necessary. (*b*) **in n. of** = requiring. (*c*) time of difficulty/poverty; **a friend in n. is a friend indeed** = a person who helps you when you are in difficulties is a real friend. **2.** *v.* to be necessary/to be required. **needful,** *adj.* (*old*) necessary. **needless,** *adj.* unnecessary/not called for. **needs.** **1.** *n. pl.* actual requirements. **2.** *adv.* **if n. must** = if it has to be done. **needy,** *adj.* (**-ier, -iest**) in need of/requiring help or food.

needle ['ni:dl] *n.* (*a*) thin metal/plastic/wooden tool with a sharp point at one end; **it's like looking for a n. in a haystack** = it's a hopeless task. (*b*) **hypodermic n.** = needle used for injections. (*c*) hand/pointer (on a dial); **compass n.** = the indicator on the dial of a compass. (*d*) leaf of a pine

tree. **2.** *v.* to irritate/to provoke (s.o.).

needlestick, *n.* pricking the finger accidentally on a hypodermic needle. **needlewoman,** *n.* woman who is good at sewing. **needlework,** *n.* sewing done with needle and thread.

ne'er do well ['neədu:wel] *n.* person who is good for nothing.

nefarious [nɪ'feərɪəs] *adj.* (*formal*) very wicked.

negate [nɪ'geɪt] *v.* to oppose/to cancel out (sth). **negation** [nɪ'geɪʃn] *n.* what is cancelled out/negated. **negative** ['negətɪv] **1.** *n.* (*a*) reply indicating no. (*b*) reverse image of a photograph. (*c*) one of the terminals in a battery. **2.** *adj.* (*a*) meaning no; showing opposition/refusal. (*b*) without good/positive qualities. (*c*) minus/less than zero. **3.** *v.* to contradict/to oppose (sth). **negatively,** *adv.* in a way which suggests opposition.

neglect [nɪ'glekt] **1.** *n.* disregard/lack of care or attention. **2.** *v.* (*a*) to fail to look after/to fail to maintain. (*b*) to omit to do (sth which should be done). **neglected,** *adj.* not looked after. **neglectful,** *adj.* **to be n. of** = forget about. **negligence** ['neglɪdʒəns] *n.* absence of proper care and attention. **negligent,** *adj.* not giving proper care and attention. **negligible,** *adj.* not significant/not worth regarding.

négligé ['neglɪʒeɪ] *n.* woman's light dressing gown.

negotiate [nɪ'gəʊsɪeɪt] *v.* (*a*) to discuss so as to make an agreement with s.o. (*b*) to make a financial arrangement. (*c*) to overcome an obstacle/difficulty. **negotiable** [nɪ'gəʊsɪəbl] *adj.* which can be overcome; **not n.** = not exchangeable for cash. **negotiation** [nɪgəʊsɪ'eɪʃn] *n.* discussing/arranging by discussion. **negotiator** [nɪ'gəʊsɪeɪtə] *n.* person who discusses to try to reach an agreement.

negro, negress ['ni:grəʊ, 'ni:grəs] *adj. & n.* (*pl.* **-oes**) member of a dark-skinned race of people originating in Africa. **negroid,** *adj.* having the characteristics of negroes.

neigh [neɪ] **1.** *n.* sound made by a horse. **2.** *v.* to make a sound like a horse.

neighbour, *Am.* **neighbor** ['neɪbə] *n.*

(a) person who lives in a nearby house/road/country. (b) person sitting beside.

neighbourhood, n. (a) district and its people; **n. watch scheme** = scheme where people living in an area are encouraged to look out for criminals. (b) **in the n. of** = around/near to (in space or amount). **neighbouring,** adj. next to each other. **neighbourly,** adj. in a friendly/helpful way.

neither ['naɪðə, 'niːðə] 1. adv. & conj. **n. . . . nor** = not one . . . and not the other. 2. adj. & pron. not either of two things or persons.

nelson ['nelsən] n. (in wrestling) way of holding the opponent, with the arms under his armpits and the hands on the back of his neck.

nem. con. ['nem'kɒn] adv. with no one voting against.

nemesis ['nemɪsɪs] n. (no pl.) just punishment from which you cannot escape.

neo- ['niːəʊ] prefix meaning new.

neolithic [niːəʊ'lɪθɪk] adj. belonging to the late Stone Age.

neologism [nɪ'ɒlədʒɪzəm] n. newly-invented word.

neon ['niːɒn] n. (element: Ne) colourless gas often used in tubes to make illuminated signs.

neophyte ['niːəʊfaɪt] n. beginner; person who is learning.

nephew ['nefjuː] n. son of your brother or sister.

nephritis [nef'raɪtɪs] n. kidney disease.

nepotism ['nepətɪzəm] n. giving members of your family jobs for which they are not necessarily qualified.

nerve [nɜːv] 1. n. (a) one of many thin threads forming part of the body's system for conveying messages to and from the brain; **in a state of nerves** = in a tense/anxious state; **to get on s.o.'s nerves** = to irritate/annoy s.o. (b) courage/confidence; inf. **he's got a n.** = he's cheeky/rude; **to have the n. to** = to be so rude as to. (c) **to strain every n.** = to make tremendous efforts. 2. v. **to n. yourself** = to summon up strength/confidence. **nervelessness,** n. lack of energy/limpness. **nerve-racking,** adj. disturbing. **nervous,** adj. (a) **the n. system** = the pattern of nerve fibres in the body; **n. breakdown** = physical and mental collapse caused by worry. (b) timid/easily disturbed/easily upset. **nervously,** adv. in a worried/frightened way. **nervousness,** n. being nervous. **nervy,** adj. inf. not relaxed/irritable.

nest [nest] 1. n. (a) place built by birds to lay their eggs; **to feather your n.** = to make a lot of money (usu. fraudulently). (b) hiding place/collecting place for people or animals. (c) **n. of tables** = tables of different sizes fitting under each other. 2. v. (of birds) to build a nest. **nest egg,** n. investment/money put aside for future use. **nestling** ['neslɪŋ] n. small bird not yet ready to leave the nest.

nestle ['nesl] v. (a) to settle down comfortably. (b) to have close and loving contact.

net [net] 1. n. loosely woven material; piece of this material used for fishing/catching/fencing, etc. 2. v. (netted) (a) to catch in a net. (b) to make a true profit; **to n. a big profit** = to make a lot of money. 3. adj. (price/weight) left after taking away the weight of the container/the tax paid, etc.; **n. profit** = actual gain after expenses have been paid; **n. weight** = true weight without the wrappings. **netball,** n. team game (usu. played by women) where the ball has to be thrown so that it goes through a ring placed high up at the end of the court. **netting,** n. material made of string/wire loosely woven into a regular pattern of holes. **network,** n. interconnecting system (of railways, etc.); radio/TV system; interconnected computer system.

nether ['neðə] adj. (formal) lower; **n. regions** = bottom part. **nethermost,** adj. lowest.

netsuke ['netskɪ] n. carved ivory toggle, formerly used in Japan.

nettle ['netl] 1. n. (stinging) **n.** = weed with stinging leaves. 2. v. to anger/to irritate. **nettlerash,** n. skin rash caused by an allergy.

neural ['njʊərəl] adj. referring to nerves. **neuralgia** [njʊ'rældʒə] n. nerve pains in the face or head. **neuralgic,** adj. referring to neuralgia. **neuritis** [njʊ'raɪtɪs] n. inflammation of nerves. **neurological**

[njʊərə'lɒdʒɪkl] *adj.* referring to neurology. **neurologist** [njʊ'rɒlədʒɪst] *n.* person who studies the nervous system. **neurology** [njʊ'rɒlədʒɪ] *n.* study of the body's nervous system. **neurone,** *n.* cell in the nerve system which passes on impulses. **neurosis** [njʊ'rəʊsɪs] *n.* (*pl.* **-oses** [-əʊsi:z]) mental illness caused by a nervous disorder. **neurotic** [njʊ'rɒtɪk] *adj.* unbalanced (behaviour). **neurotically,** *adv.* in an unbalanced way.

neuter ['nju:tə] **1.** *adj.* (*in grammar*) not having a masculine or feminine gender. **2.** *v.* to castrate. **neutral. 1.** *adj.* (*a*) not favouring or supporting either side in a dispute. (*b*) not having a distinctive colour. (*c*) neither acid or alkali. **2.** *n.* (*a*) citizen of a neutral country. (*b*) **the car is in n.** = not in gear. **neutrality** [njʊ'trælɪtɪ] *n.* being uncommitted/neutral; not taking sides. **neutralization** [nju:trəlaɪ'zeɪʃn] *n.* act of neutralizing. **neutralize** ['nju:trəlaɪz] *v.* to cancel out by using an opposite. **neutrally,** *adv.* in a neutral way. **neutron,** *n.* basic particle with no electric charge; **n. bomb** = nuclear bomb which kills people but does little damage to buildings.

never ['nevə] *adv.* (*a*) not ever/not at any time. (*b*) (*for emphasis*) not at all. (*c*) (*exclamation of surprise*) surely not; **well I n.!** how surprising! **never-ending,** *adj.* which does not stop. **nevermore,** *adv.* (*formal*) not any more. **never-never,** *n. inf.* hire-purchase system. **nevertheless** [nevəðə'les] *adv.* despite all that/all the same. **never-to-be-forgotten,** *adj.* memorable.

new [njuː] *adj.* (**-er, -est**) (*a*) completely different/not thought of before/ not met before. (*b*) changed/different. (*c*) fresh/unused; **to turn over a n. leaf** = become better/start again. (*d*) most recent; **n. moon** = moon when it is a thin crescent. (*e*) just bought/just acquired. **newborn,** *adj.* just born. **newcomer,** *n.* person who has just come to an area. **newfangled,** *adj.* unpleasant and newly invented. **new-laid,** *adj.* (*of eggs*) freshly laid/just laid. **newly,** *adv.* most recently; **newly-weds** = people

who have just got married. **newness,** *n.* being recent/fresh; not having been used. **news** [njuːz] *n.* spoken or written information about events; **it's in the n.** = it is of topical interest; **to break the n. to s.o.** = to tell s.o. bad/ unwelcome news; **no n. is good n.** = the absence of bad news means things may be going well. **newsagent,** *n.* person who runs a shop which sells newspapers. **newsagent's,** *n.* shop selling newspapers. **newscaster,** *n.* person who reads the news on television. **news flash,** *n.* short news item. **newsletter,** *n.* printed sheet giving news to members of a church/club, etc. **newsman,** *n.* (*pl.* **-men**) journalist. **newspaper,** *n.* daily/weekly paper containing information and news. **newsprint,** *n.* paper for printing newspapers and magazines. **newsreel,** *n.* short film about current events shown in a cinema. **news vendor,** *n.* person who sells newspapers in the street. **newsworthy,** *adj.* (events) worth recording/mentioning in papers or on television. **newsy,** *adj. inf.* full of news. **New World,** *n.* North and South America. **new year,** *n.* the year which has just started; period just after 1st January. **New Year's Day,** *n.* 1st January. **New Year's Eve,** *n.* 31st December.

newel ['njuːəl] *n.* post at the top or bottom of stairs, to which the banisters are attached.

newt [njuːt] *n.* small, lizard-like animal which can live either in or out of water.

newton ['njʊtən] *n.* standard measurement of force.

next [nekst] **1.** *adj.* (*a*) (*of time/sequence*) coming after. (*b*) (*of place*) closest to/ nearest; **she lives n. door** = in the house/ flat next to this one. **2.** *adv.* coming after in place/time; **what n.?** = what other amazing or absurd things can we expect? **it costs n. to nothing** = it costs very little. **3.** *n.* person/thing following; **the week after n.** = not the next week but the following one. **next-door,** *adj.* living next door. **next-of-kin,** *n.* (*no pl.*) nearest relative(s).

nexus ['neksəs] *n.* link/connecting point for ideas, organizations, etc.

Ni *symbol for* nickel.

nib [nɪb] *n.* pointed writing end of a pen.

nibble ['nɪbl] **1.** *n.* bite/very small amount eaten. **2.** *v.* to take very small, cautious bites. **nibble away,** *v.* to remove gradually/in little pieces.

nice [naɪs] *adj.* (**-er, -est**) (*a*) generally pleasant. (*b*) precise; subtle. **nice-looking,** *adj.* pretty/pleasant to look at. **nicely,** *adv.* in a satisfactory/good manner. **niceness,** *n.* quality of being agreeable. **nicety,** *n.* fine/exact detail.

niche [niːʃ] *n.* (*a*) hollow in a wall or pillar to put a statue/vase/decoration in; **to find your n./to find a n. for yourself** = to find a completely satisfying or suitable role/job. (*b*) special place in a market.

nick [nɪk] **1.** *n.* (*a*) small dent/notch (usu. to mark a place); *inf.* **in the n. of time** = just in time. (*b*) *Sl.* prison. (*c*) *Sl.* **in good n.** = in good form. **2.** *v.* (*a*) to make a small notch/cut. (*b*) *Sl.* to steal. (*c*) *Sl.* to catch/arrest.

nickel ['nɪkl] **1.** *n.* (*a*) (*element: Ni*) silver-coloured metal. (*b*) *Am.* 5-cent coin. **2.** *v.* (**nickelled**) to coat with nickel.

nickname ['nɪkneɪm] **1.** *n.* abbreviated or pet name. **2.** *v.* to give (s.o.) a nickname.

nicotine ['nɪkətiːn] *n.* poisonous brown liquid obtained from tobacco.

niece [niːs] *n.* daughter of your brother or sister.

nifty ['nɪftɪ] *adj. inf.* quick and agile; clever (gadget).

Nigerian [naɪ'dʒɪərɪən] **1.** *adj.* referring to Nigeria. **2.** *n.* person who comes from Nigeria.

niggardly ['nɪgədlɪ] *adj.* mean; very small (amount).

niggle ['nɪgl] *v.* to be fussy about relatively unimportant details; **to be niggled by s.o.** = to be annoyed/upset by s.o.'s spiteful or petty criticism. **niggling,** *adj.* unimportant/insignificant.

nigh [naɪ] *adv.* (*formal*) near.

night [naɪt] *n.* last part of each day; period of darkness from sunset to sunrise; **last n.** = yesterday after dark; **the first n.** = the official opening performance of a play or entertainment; **n. out** = evening spent outside the home.

nightcap, (*a*) (*old*) cap worn in bed. (*b*) bed-time drink. **nightclothes,** *n. pl.* clothes worn in bed. **nightclub,** *n.* club only open at night. **nightdress,** *n.* dress worn by women and girls in bed. **nightfall,** *n.* time when night starts. **nightgown,** *n.* (*old*) nightdress. **nightie,** *n. inf.* nightdress. **nightingale,** *n.* small brown singing bird. **nightjar,** *n.* dark-coloured bird which flies by night. **night life,** *n.* entertainment which takes place in a town at night. **nightlight,** *n.* small dim light or candle left burning at night. **nightly,** *adv.* every night. **nightmare,** *n.* (*a*) vivid frightening dream. (*b*) horrible event. **nightmarish,** *adj.* vividly frightening. **night school,** *n.* school which has classes for adults in the evening. **nightshade,** *n.* poisonous plant. **nightshirt,** *n.* long shirt worn by men in bed. **night soil,** *n.* human excreta, used as manure. **night-time,** *n.* period of night; **night-time flight** = flight during the hours of darkness. **nightwatchman,** *n.* (*pl.* **-men**) (*a*) man who guards a building at night. (*b*) (*in cricket*) batsman who starts his innings just before the end of the day's play and continues the following morning.

nihilism ['nɪhɪlɪzəm] *n.* belief that nothing which exists is good. **nihilist,** *n.* person who believes in nihilism.

nil [nɪl] *n.* nothing/zero.

nimble ['nɪmbl] *adj.* (**-er, -est**) agile/fast-moving; physically fit and alert. **nimbly,** *adv.* in an expert way.

nimbus ['nɪmbəs] *n.* (*a*) dark raincloud. (*b*) shining halo.

nincompoop ['nɪnkəmpuːp] *n.* silly person/fool.

nine [naɪn] *n.* number 9; **n. times out of ten** = in most cases; *inf.* **dressed up to the nines** = wearing your most elaborate clothes; **possession is n. tenths of the law** = it is easy to claim ownership of something which is already in your possession. **ninepins,** *n. pl.* skittles; **they went down like n.** = they fell down/caught the disease very easily. **nineteen,** *n.* number 19; **the n. hundreds** = the years after 1900. **nineteenth, 19th,** *adj. & n.* referring to nineteen; **the n. century** = period from

1800 to 1899. **ninetieth, 90th,** *adj. & n.* referring to ninety. **ninety,** *n.* number 90; **she's in her nineties** = she is between 90 and 99 years old. **ninth, 9th,** *adj. & n.* referring to nine; **the n. century** = period from 800 to 899.

ninny ['nɪnɪ] *n.* idiot.

nip [nɪp] **1.** *n.* (*a*) small amount of alcohol. (*b*) short sharp bite/pinch; **a n. in the air** = a sudden/sharp burst of cold weather. **2.** *v.* (**nipped**) (*a*) to bite/ to pinch sharply or suddenly. (*b*) *inf.* to go out very quickly. **nipper,** *n. inf.* (*a*) small child. (*b*) **nippers** = pincers. **nippy,** *adj. inf.* (*a*) agile/fast-moving. (*b*) cold.

nipple ['nɪpl] *n.* (*a*) small projection on the tip of a breast from which, in females, the mother's milk comes. (*b*) projection/bump on a surface. (*c*) small hole in a machine for greasing.

nirvana [nɪə'vɑːnə] *n.* (*for Buddhists*) happy state after death when the dead person's soul joins the divine soul.

nisi ['naɪsaɪ] *see* **decree.**

Nissen hut ['nɪsən'hʌt] *n.* army shed with a semi-circular roof of corrugated iron.

nit [nɪt] *n.* (*a*) egg of a louse. (*b*) *Sl.* idiot. **nit-picking,** *n. inf.* petty criticism/finding small faults to criticise. **nitwit,** *n. inf.* idiot.

nitrogen ['naɪtrədʒən] *n.* (*element:* N) gas which makes up four-fifths of the atmosphere. **nitroglycerine,** *n.* liquid explosive. **nitrate,** *n.* salt of nitric acid. **nitric acid,** *n.* acid containing nitrogen. **nitrous,** *adj.* containing nitrogen.

nitty-gritty [nɪtɪ'grɪtɪ] *n. inf.* basic details (of an argument).

NLQ *abbrev. for* near letter quality.

no. *abbrev. for* number.

no [nəʊ] **1.** *n. & adv.* showing the negative/opposite of yes; **the noes have it** = most people have voted no. **2.** *adj.* none of/not any of; **it's n. distance** = not at all far/a very short distance away; **it's n. joke** = not funny but serious; **n. admission** = entrance not allowed; *inf.* **n. way** = certainly not. **3.** *adv.* not/not at all; **n. sooner said than done** = it will be done immediately; **he's n. more** = he is dead. **no claims bonus,** *n.* reduction in insurance premiums

because no claims have been made. **no-go area,** *n.* section of a town where the police/soldiers cannot go.

nob [nɒb] *n. Sl.* (*a*) head. (*b*) upper-class person.

nobble ['nɒbl] *v. inf.* to give drugs to (a horse) to prevent it running well in a race; to try to influence (s.o.).

noble ['nəʊbl] **1.** *n.* person of high rank by title or birth. **2.** *adj.* (**-er, -est**) of high rank/dignified; worthy or praise/ splendid. **nobility,** *n.* (*a*) titled members of society/the aristocracy. (*b*) high-mindedness. **nobleman,** *n.* (*pl.* **-men**) noble. **noble-mindedness,** *n.* high-mindedness/worthy thoughts. **nobleness,** *n.* being noble; nobility. **noblewoman,** *n.* (*pl.* **-women**) woman of high rank. **nobly,** *adv.* in a noble fashion/heroically.

nobody ['nəʊbədɪ] **1.** *n.* person of no importance. **2.** *pron.* no one/no person.

nocturnal [nɒk'tɜːnl] *adj.* referring to the night; (animals which are) most active at night. **nocturne** ['nɒktɜːn] *n.* painting/piece of music conveying a feeling of night.

nod [nɒd] **1.** *n.* forward movement of the head as a greeting/as a sign of agreement; *inf.* **it went through on the n.** = it was agreed without any discussion. **2.** *v.* (**nodded**) to show agreement/to give permission/to agree by a forward movement of the head; **to n. off** = to fall asleep; **nodding acquaintance** = (i) person you know only slightly; (ii) slight knowledge.

node [nəʊd] *n.* (*a*) place where leaves grow from a plant's stem. (*b*) knob on a root/branch/human joint. (*c*) point where curves cross. **nodal,** *adj.* central/ at the point where lines meet. **nodule** ['nɒdjuːl] *n.* small node.

Noel [nəʊ'el] *n.* Christmas.

nog [nɒg] *n.* **egg n.** = drink made of alcohol and raw eggs. **noggin,** *n.* small quantity of alcohol.

noise [nɔɪz] **1.** *n.* loud (usu. unpleasant) sound; **to make a n. about sth** = to make a fuss/to complain; *inf.* **a big n.** = an important person. **2.** *v.* **to n. sth abroad** = to make sth public/to spread the news. **noiseless,** *adj.* without any sound. **noiselessly,** *adv.* in a silent

way. **noisily,** adv. in a noisy/loud way.
noisy, adj. (**-ier, -iest**) making a lot of
noise; loud.
nomad ['nəʊmæd] adj. & n. (member)
of a wandering tribe with no fixed
home. **nomadic** [nəʊ'mædɪk] adj. not
staying in one place/travelling.
no-man's-land ['nəʊmænzlænd] n.
territory between two armies which
belongs to neither side.
nom-de-plume [nɒmdə'pluːm] n.
name used by an author in place of his
own.
nomenclature [nə'menklətʃə] n. (formal) system of naming.
nominal ['nɒmɪnl] adj. (a) referring to
names. (b) in name rather than in fact;
n. fee = very small amount of money/
token payment. **nominally,** adv. in
name rather than in fact.
nominate ['nɒmɪneɪt] v. tr. to name/
to propose. **nomination** [nɒmɪ'neɪʃn]
n. act of nominating; suggested name.
nominator, n. person who nominates.
nominee [nɒmɪ'niː] n. person who is
nominated; **n. account** = bank account
held on behalf of s.o.
nominative ['nɒmɪnətɪv] n. form of a
noun when it is the subject of a verb.
non- [nɒn] prefix meaning not/the
opposite.
nonagenarian [nɒnədʒə'neərɪən] adj.
& n. (person) who is between 90 and
99 years old.
non-aggression [nɒnə'greʃn] n. agreement not to engage in war.
non-alcoholic [nɒnælkə'hɒlɪk] adj. not
intoxicating/not containing alcohol.
non-aligned [nɒnə'laɪnd] adj. (country)
which is not linked to a large and powerful bloc of countries. **non-alignment,**
n. policy of being non-aligned.
nonchalant ['nɒnʃələnt] adj. casual/
unexcited. **nonchalance,** n. being
calm/unmoved. **nonchalantly,** adv. in
a nonchalant way.
non-combatant [nɒn'kɒmbətənt] adj.
& n. (person) who does not fight;
doctor/priest, etc., attached to an army.
non-commissioned [nɒnkə'mɪʃnd]
adj. **non-commissioned officer** = soldier
of a lower rank than a commissioned
officer.
non-committal [nɒnkə'mɪtl] adj. not

favouring a definite course of action/
not agreeing with either side in an argument.
non compos mentis [nɒnkɒmpɒs-
'mentɪs] adj. mad.
nonconformist [nɒnkən'fɔːmɪst] adj.
& n. (person) who does not act in the
same way as most people; **Nonformist**
= (person) who does not hold the views
of the established church/member of a
Protestant church separated from the
Church of England. **nonconformity,** n.
being nonconformist.
nondescript ['nɒndɪskrɪpt] adj. very or-
dinary/without individual qualities.
none [nʌn] **1.** pron. (a) not any (of); **n.
of your cheek!** = don't be rude. (b) no
person/no one. **2.** adv. (used with **the**
and comparative or **too**) not at all; **n. too
good; n. the worse for the accident.**
nonentity [nɒ'nentɪtɪ] n. person of no
importance.
nonetheless [nʌnθə'les] adv.
nevertheless.
non-event [nɒnɪ'vent] n. happening
which was expected to be important but
which turns out not to be.
nonexistent [nɒnɪg'zɪstənt] adj. not
having any existence in fact/not real.
non-fiction ['nɒnfɪkʃn] n. (no pl.) books
which are not fiction/which are factual.
non-intervention [nɒnɪntə'venʃən] n.
act of not interfering.
non-iron [nɒn'aɪən] adj. not needing
ironing.
non-payment [nɒn'peɪmənt] n. failing
to pay what is due.
non-plussed [nɒn'plʌst] adj. puzzled/
confused.
non-profit-making [nɒn'prɒfɪtmeɪkɪŋ]
adj. (organization such as a charity)
which is not allowed to make a profit.
non-refundable [nɒnrɪ'fʌndəbl] adj.
which will not be refunded.
non-resident [nɒn'rezɪdənt] adj. & n.
(person) not living in/not staying very
long in a place; **a non-resident's work
permit** = permit which allows s.o. from
another country to work.
non-returnable [nɒnrɪ'tɜːnəbl] adj.
(bottle) on which there is no deposit and
which the manufacturers do not want
back.
nonsense ['nɒnsəns] n. foolish ideas/

ridiculous behaviour. **nonsensical** [nɒn'sensɪkl] *adj.* absurd.

non sequitur [nɒn'sekwɪtə] *n.* phrase which does not follow logically from what has gone before; conclusion drawn incorrectly from the evidence.

non-skid [nɒn'skɪd] *adj.* which prevents skidding.

non-smoker ['nɒnsməʊkə] *n.* (*a*) person who does not smoke. (*b*) place where smoking is not allowed. **nonsmoking,** *adj.* where smoking is not allowed.

non-starter [nɒn'stɑːtə] *n.* (*a*) horse which is not ready to start at the beginning of a race. (*b*) *inf.* project/plan which is never going to be accepted.

non-stick ['nɒnstɪk] *adj.* (pan) covered with a substance which prevents food from sticking when cooking.

non-stop ['nɒnstɒp] **1.** *adj.* not stopping/travelling directly from point to departure to terminus. **2.** *adv.* ceaselessly/without stopping.

non-union [nɒn'juːnɪən] *adj.* not belonging to a union.

non-violence [nɒn'vaɪələns] *n.* absence of physical violence/of aggression.

noodles ['nuːdlz] *n. pl.* strips of paste for cooking. **noodle,** *n. Sl.* fool.

nook [nʊk] *n.* small hiding place; **in every n. and cranny** = in every little hole and corner.

noon [nuːn] *n.* midday. **noonday,** *n.* **the n. sun** = the sun at noon.

no one ['nəʊwʌn] *pron.* nobody/no person.

noose [nuːs] *n.* rope knotted to form a loop which can be tightened by pulling.

nor [nɔː] *conj.* (*a*) (*usu. followed by verb then subject*) not either/and not. (*b*) **neither. . n.** = not one. . .and not the other.

Nordic ['nɔːdɪk] *adj.* referring to Scandinavia.

norm [nɔːm] *n.* normal/standard pattern.

normal ['nɔːml] *adj.* usual/regular/ expected. **normality** [nɔː'mælɪtɪ] *n.* being normal/not having unusual features. **normally,** *adv.* in the usual way.

Norman ['nɔːmən] *adj. & n.* (person) from Normandy; (architecture, etc.) developed in England after the conquest by the Normans in 1066.

Norse [nɔːs] **1.** *adj.* referring to ancient Scandinavian. **2.** *n.* ancient Scandinavian language. **Norseman,** *n.* (*pl.* -men) person from ancient Scandinavia.

north [nɔːθ] **1.** *n.* one of the points of the compass, the direction to the right when you are facing the setting sun. **2.** *adv.* towards the north; **3.** *adj.* referring to the north. **n. wind** = wind which blows from the north. **northbound,** *adj.* going towards the north. **north-east,** *n.* direction halfway between east and north. **northeasterly,** *adj.* towards/from the northeast. **northeastern,** *adj.* referring to the north-east. **northerly** ['nɔːðəlɪ] *adj. & n.* in/to/from the north; (wind) from the north. **northern** ['nɔːðn] *adj.* referring to the north. **northerner,** *n.* person who lives in/comes from the north. **northward,** *adj.* towards the north. **northernmost,** *adj.* furthest north. **northwards,** *adv.* towards the north. **north-west,** *n.* direction halfway netween west and north. **northwesterly,** *adj.* towards/from the northwest. **north-western,** *adj.* referring to the north-west.

Norwegian [nɔː'wiːdʒən] **1.** *adj.* referring to Norway. **2.** *n.* (*a*) person from Norway. (*b*) language spoken in Norway.

nose [nəʊz] **1.** *n.* (*a*) part of the face used for breathing in air and smelling; **as plain as the n. on your face** = very obvious; **to speak through your n.** = speak as if your nose is blocked; *inf.* **I paid through the n. for it** = I paid far too much for it; **I did it under his very n.** = did it right in front of him but he didn't notice; **to poke your n. into** = to interfere unasked; **to cut off your n. to spite your face** = to do sth when you are angry which in fact harms you; **follow your n.** = go straight on; **to keep s.o.'s n. to the grindstone** = to make s.o. work hard all the time; **to look down your n. at s.o.** = to regard s.o. as inferior; **to turn up your n. at sth** = to reject sth as not good enough. (*b*) good sense of smell; **a good n. for** = an instinct for finding sth. (*c*) front end of a vehicle. **2.** *v.* (*a*) to discover by smell. (*b*) *inf.* to detect/to discover. (*c*) (*of boat*) to go in gently. **nose about, nose around,** *v.* to look/to search around. **nosebag,** *n.* bag of food hung around an animal's neck. **nosebleed,** *n.* flow of blood from the nose. **nose cone,** *n.* round pointed part at the top of a rocket. **nosedive. 1.** *n.* steep downward dive of an aircraft. **2.** *v.* to dive down steeply. **nosegay,** *n.* small bunch of flowers. **nosey, nosy,** *adj.* (**-ier, -iest**) *inf.* curious/interested in the affairs of other people; **n. parker** = very inquisitive person. **nosily,** *adv.* in a nosey way.

nosh [nɒʃ] *n. Sl.* food.

nostalgia [nɒ'stældʒɪə] *n.* longing for/sentimental recollection of the past. **nostalgic,** *adj.* encouraging nostalgia. **nostalgically,** *adv.* in a nostalgic way.

nostril ['nɒstrl] *n.* one of the two holes in the nose to admit air and smells.

nostrum ['nɒstrəm] *n.* quack medicine.

not [nɒt] *adv.* (*a*) (*used with verbs to make the action negative; short form* **n't**) he will not come/he won't come. (*b*) (*used to make negative words/phrases/sentences*) I **think not** = I don't think so. (*c*) (*providing emphasis by a form of contrast*) **not yours but mine.** (*d*) (*used to show the opposite*) **not a few** = many; **not too well** = badly; **not sorry to leave** = glad to leave; **not without reason** = with good reason. **not half,** *adv. inf.* extremely.

nota bene ['nəʊtə'beneɪ] note well, pay attention to this.

notable ['nəʊtəbl] **1.** *adj.* worth noticing; large. **2.** *n.* important person. **notability** [nəʊtə'bɪlɪtɪ] *n.* (*a*) being important. (*b*) notable/important person. **notably,** *adv.* significantly/particularly.

notary (public) ['nəʊtərɪ('pʌblɪk)] *n.* person who has authority to see that legal documents are correctly written and who witnesses their signing.

notation [nəʊ'teɪʃn] *n.* system of symbols used to show notes in music/to show mathematical signs.

notch [nɒtʃ] **1.** *n.* (*pl.* **-es**) small cut (usu. V-shaped) used to mark/to record. **2.** *v.* to mark with notches; **to n. up** = to score (a goal/a victory).

note [nəʊt] **1.** *n.* (*a*) music sound. (*b*) written sign which indicates a musical sound. (*c*) key on a piano, etc.; **to strike**

the right n. = to play the correct note/to provide the appropriate tone/atmosphere/words in a particular situation. (*d*) very short letter; very brief written/printed document. (*e*) banknote/piece of paper money. (*f*) notice/attention/importance; **of n.** = important; **to take n. of** = to pay attention to/to be aware of. (*g*) indication. **2.** *v.* (*a*) to write down. (*b*) to pay attention to. **notebook,** *n.* book in which you write notes. **notecase,** *n.* wallet or container for banknotes. **noted,** *adj.* famous/well-known. **notepad,** *n.* pad of paper for notes. **notepaper,** *n.* writing paper for letters. **noteworthy,** *adj.* deserving attention.

nothing ['nʌθɪŋ] **1.** *n.* (*a*) not anything; **to say n. about** = to keep silent about; **there's n. in it** = no truth in it; **to make sth out of n.** = to exaggerate sth; *inf.* **n. doing!** = I refuse; **to get sth for n.** = get sth free; **there's n. else for it** = there's no alternative; **to think n. of it** = make it seem easy; **to have n. to do with** = not to associate with/not to become involved in; **it's n. to do with you** = not your concern; **to come to n.** = be unsuccessful. (*b*) (*used with an adj. following*) not anything. (*c*) (*used as a comparison/to suggest something inferior*) **that's n. to what I saw. 2.** *adv.* in no way/not at all; **n. daunted** = not intimidated. **nothingness,** *n.* void/nothing at all.

notice ['nəʊtɪs] **1.** *n.* (*a*) advance information/warning; warning to leave one's job; **n. to quit** = legal document telling s.o. to leave premises. (*b*) **to take n. of** = to pay attention to. (*c*) written account/announcement; written information. (*d*) review in a newspaper. **2.** *v.* to pay attention to. **noticeable,** *adj.* easily seen. **noticeably,** *adv.* in a noticeable way. **noticeboard,** *n.* flat piece of wood, etc., on a wall, on which notices can be pinned.

notify ['nəʊtɪfaɪ] *v.* to announce/to declare/to advise/to inform. **notifiable,** *adj.* which has to be notified to the authorities. **notification** [nəʊtɪfɪ'keɪʃn] *n.* formal information.

notion ['nəʊʃn] *n.* (*a*) vague awareness/idea/thought. (*b*) *Am.* **notions** = shop or department selling buttons/thread/ribbons, etc. **notional,** *adj.* vague but assumed to be correct. **notionally,** *adv.* in a notional way.

notorious [nəʊˈtɔːrɪəs] *adj.* well known (usu. for doing sth bad). **notoriety** [nəʊtəˈraɪətɪ] *n.* bad/unfavourable reputation. **notoriously,** *adv.* unfavourably significant.

notwithstanding [nɒtwɪθˈstændɪŋ] (*formal*) **1.** *prep.* despite. **2.** *adv.* all the same/anyway.

nougat [ˈnuːɡɑː] *n.* type of white sweet made with nuts, honey and egg whites.

nought [nɔːt] *n.* zero/nothing; the sign 0; **to come to n.** = be unsuccessful; **noughts and crosses** = game for two players where each puts a cross or a nought in one of nine squares in turn, the object being to be the first to make a line of three noughts or three crosses.

noun [naʊn] *n.* word used as a name of a person or thing.

nourish [ˈnʌrɪʃ] *v.* (*a*) to provide (sth) with food so that it will grow. (*b*) to keep alive (ideas/feelings). **nourishing,** *adj.* providing nourishment. **nourishment,** *n.* food which enables plants/animals to grow.

nous [naʊs] *n. inf.* common sense/ordinary intelligent reaction.

nova [ˈnəʊvə] *n.* star which suddenly becomes much brighter and then fades away.

novel [ˈnɒvl] **1.** *n.* long fictional story in the form of a book. **2.** *adj.* new/original. **novelette** [nɒvəˈlet] *n.* short novel with no literary merit. **novelist** [ˈnɒvəlɪst] *n.* person who writes novels. **novelty,** *n.* (*a*) new/original thing. (*b*) small/unusual toy or trinket. (*c*) newness.

November [nəˈvembə] *n.* 11th month of the year.

novice [ˈnɒvɪs] *n.* (*a*) beginner; inexperienced person. (*b*) person who is intending to join a religious order but who has not yet taken the vows. **noviciate,** *n.* state of being a novice in a religious order.

now [naʊ] **1.** *adv.* (*a*) at this moment. (*b*) immediately/beginning from this time. (*c*) **just n.** = in the immediate past. (*d*) (*when relating events*) then/next/by that time. **2.** *inter.* showing warning/

criticism; **n. then! 3.** *conj.* as a result of/since. **4.** *n.* this time; the present time. **nowadays** [ˈnaʊədeɪz] *adv.* at the present day/in these modern times.

nowhere [ˈnəʊweə] *adv.* not in/at/to any place; **n. near completion** = far from being finished; **I got n.** = I was totally unsuccessful in what I was trying to do.

noxious [ˈnɒkʃəs] *adj.* unpleasant/harmful.

nozzle [ˈnɒzl] *n.* special fitting at the end of a pipe or hose for controlling what comes out.

nth [enθ] *adj.* to a very great extent.

nuance [ˈnjuːɑːns] *n.* shade of meaning or colour.

nub [nʌb] *n.* central point.

nubile [ˈnjuːbaɪl] *adj.* (*of a young woman*) very attractive physically.

nucleus [ˈnjuːklɪəs] *n.* (*pl.* **-lei**) (*a*) vital central part around which things collect. (*b*) central part of an atom. **nuclear,** *adj.* concerned with/belonging to a nucleus, esp. of an atom; **n. energy** = energy produced by nuclear power; **n. family** = family group consisting of the parents and children; **n. reactor** = device for producing atomic energy; **n. power** = power from atomic energy; **n. submarine** = driven by nuclear power. **nucleonics** [njuːklɪˈɒnɪks] *n.* study of the application of nuclear energy.

nude [njuːd] **1.** *n.* (*a*) naked person. (*b*) **in the n.** = naked. **2.** *adj.* naked/bare. **nudism,** *n.* belief in the physical and mental advantages of going about naked. **nudist,** *n.* person who believes in going about naked; **n. colony** = club/camp for those who wish to go about naked. **nudity,** *n.* not wearing any clothes/nakedness.

nudge [nʌdʒ] **1.** *n.* slight push/prod with the elbow to attract attention. **2.** *v.* to attract attention, usu. by pushing with the elbow.

nugatory [ˈnjuːɡətrɪ] *adj.* (*formal*) worthless; useless.

nugget [ˈnʌɡɪt] *n.* lump of gold in its natural state. **n. of information** = piece of useful information.

nuisance [ˈnjuːsns] *n.* annoying or disagreeable person/thing; **public n.** = action which bothers other people in such a way as to be against the law.

null [nʌl] *adj.* without significance/cancelled out; **n. and void** = no longer valid. **nullify**, *v.* to cancel out/to make invalid. **nullity**, *n.* nothingness/thing that is null.

numb [nʌm] **1.** *adj.* without feeling or sensation/unable to move. **2.** *v.* to make incapable of movement or feeling. **numbly**, *adv.* not moving because of being numb. **numbness**, *n.* having no feeling or sensation/being incapable of action. **numbskull**, *n. inf.* stupid person.

number ['nʌmbə] **1.** *n.* (a) name of a figure; total of objects or persons; **one of their n.** = one of them; *inf.* **to take care of n. one** = to look after yourself/your own interests. (b) **numbers** = many in quantity. (c) (*in grammar*) term indicating whether a noun is singular or plural. (d) copy of a periodical/a song/a piece of played music; **back n.** = thing which is out of date; *inf.* **his number's up** = he's dying. **2.** *v.* (a) to count/to include among/to total; **his days are numbered** = he hasn't much time to live. (b) to put a number/figure on. **numberless**, *adj.* which cannot be counted. **numberplate**, *n.* plate on the front and back of a vehicle, showing its registration number.

numeral ['njuːmərəl] *n.* actual sign representing a number. **numeracy**, *n.* ability to calculate mathematically/ability to work out sums. **numerate** ['njuːmərət] *adj.* able to calculate mathematically. **numeration** [njuːmə-'reɪʃn] *n.* calculation. **numerator**, *n.* figure above the line in a fraction. **numeric keypad**, *n.* set of numbered keys on a computer keyboard. **numerical** [njuː'merɪkl] *adj.* referring to numbers; **in n. order** = in order of numbers. **numerically**, *adv.* by/in number. **numerous** ['njuːmərəs] *adj.* many/a lot of.

numismatics [njuːmɪz'mætɪks] *n.* study of coins. **numismatist** [njuː'mɪzmətɪst] *n.* person who collects/studies coins.

nun [nʌn] *n.* woman who is a member of a religious order living in a separate community or convent. **nunlike**, *adj.* very calm/good/restrained. **nunnery**, *n.* convent/community where nuns live.

nuncio ['nʌnsɪəʊ] *n.* ambassador sent by the Pope to a foreign country.

nuptial ['nʌpʃl] *adj.* (*formal*) referring to marriage/wedding ceremonies. **nuptials**, *n. pl.* wedding.

nurse [nɜːs] **1.** *n.* (a) (usu. female) person trained and employed to look after the sick; **night n.** = nurse who is on duty at night. (b) woman employed to look after children. **2.** *v.* (a) to look after (a sick person). (b) to look after very carefully; **to n. a constituency** = to look after the needs of electors in the hope that they will vote for you at the next election. (c) to think about/to ponder over. (d) to hold close. **nursemaid**, *n.* young woman who is paid to look after children. **nursery**, *n.* (a) room/building where babies or young children are looked after; **day n.** = place where babies are looked after during the day time; **n. school** = school for very young children; **n. rhyme** = little poem telling a simple story told or sung to young children. (b) place where people are brought up or trained; **n. slopes** = gentle slopes where you can learn to ski. (c) place where young plants are grown. **nurseryman**, *n.* (*pl.* -men) man who looks after young plants. **nursing**. **1.** *adj.* (person) who nurses/looks after; **n. mother** = mother who breast-feeds her baby; **n. staff** = hospital nurses; **n. home** = small (usu. private) hospital; **n. officer** = person in charge of the nurses in a hospital. **2.** *n.* profession of looking after the sick.

nurture ['nɜːtʃə] *v.* (*formal*) to protect and bring up carefully.

nut [nʌt] **1.** *n.* (a) fruit with an edible centre inside a hard shell; **to crack nuts** = to open the shells to get at the edible centres; *inf.* **a tough n. to crack** = a hard person/a difficult problem. (b) small metal ring used for tightening a bolt; **wing n.** = nut with two projecting pieces for turning. (c) *inf.* head; **he's off his n.** = he's mad. (d) *inf.* **nuts about** = very keen on/enthusiastic about. (e) small lump (of butter). **2.** *v.* **to go nutting** = to gather nuts. **nutcase**, *n. inf.* mad person. **nutcrackers**, *n. pl.* pincers for cracking nuts. **nuthatch**, *n.* small grey and brown bird which climbs up tree trunks. **nutmeg,** *n.* seed of a tropical tree, used as a spice. **nutshell,** *n.* hard outside covering of a nut; **in a n.** = giving all the important details as briefly as possible. **nutty,** *adj.* (*a*) tasting of/full of nuts. (*b*) *inf.* crazy/very enthusiastic (**about** s.o./sth).

nutriment ['nju:trɪmənt] *n.* thing which nourishes. **nutrient,** *adj.* & *n.* (food) which feeds/nourishes. **nutrition** [nju:'trɪʃn] *n.* giving/receiving of nourishment. **nutritious** [nju:'trɪʃəs] *adj.* nourishing/providing food which is necessary for growth. **nutritive** ['nju:trətɪv] **1.** *n.* food which is necessary for growth. **2.** *adj.* providing food/nourishment.

nuzzle ['nʌzl] *v.* to press the nose up to/ to snuggle up to.

nylon ['naɪlɒn] *n.* very tough synthetic material. **nylons,** *n.* *pl.* women's stockings.

nymph [nɪmf] *n.* (*a*) young girl; minor goddess. (*b*) young insect, esp. young dragonfly. **nymphet,** *n.* sexually desirable young girl. **nymphomania** [nɪmfə-'meɪnɪə] *n.* (*in woman*) uncontrollably strong sexual desire. **nymphomaniac,** *n.* woman who has uncontrollable sexual desires.

Oo

O, o [əʊ] zero/nothing.
O *symbol for* oxygen.
oaf [əʊf] *n.* stupid/clumsy/unfeeling person. **oafish,** *adj.* like an oaf.
oak [əʊk] *n.* type of large deciduous tree; wood of this tree. **oak apple,** *n.* round growth on oak trees caused by an insect. **oaken,** *adj.* (*formal*) made of oak.
oakum ['əʊkəm] *n.* (*no pl.*) loose pieces of old rope formerly used for stuffing into the seams of wooden ships.
OAP [əʊeɪ'pi:] *n.* *short for* old age pensioner.
oar [ɔ:] *n.* long pole with a flat end, used for moving a boat along; *inf.* **to stick your o. in** = to interfere. **oarlock,** *n.* *Am.* rowlock. **oarsman,** *n.* (*pl.* -men) person who rows a boat. **oarsmanship,** *n.* being skilled at rowing.
oasis [əʊ'eɪsɪs] *n.* (*pl.* -ses [-si:z]) (*a*) place in the desert with water,

where plants grow. (*b*) place which is pleasantly different from its surroundings.
oasthouse ['əʊsthaʊs] *n.* building for drying hops.
oatcake ['əʊtkeɪk] *n.* dry biscuit made of oatmeal.
oath [əʊθ] *n.* (*a*) swearing that you are telling the truth. (*b*) promise. (*c*) swear word.
oatmeal ['əʊtmi:l] *n.* coarse flour made from oats.
oats [əʊts] *n.* *pl.* cereal plant whose grain is used as food; **to sow one's wild o.** = behave in a very free and unruly way when young.
obbligato [ɒblɪ'gɑ:təʊ] *n.* (*pl.* -os) (*in music*) important accompanying part played by a solo instrument.
obdurate ['ɒbdjʊrət] *adj.* stubborn/ unyielding/unmoving. **obduracy,** *n.* being obdurate.
obedience [ə'bi:dɪəns] *n.* being obedient. **obedient,** *adj.* (person) who does what he is told to do. **obediently,** *adv.* in an obedient way.
obeisance [əʊ'beɪsəns] *n.* sign of respect, such as a bow or curtsey.
obelisk ['ɒbəlɪsk] *n.* four-sided pillar which becomes narrower towards the top.
obese [ə'bi:s] *adj.* very fat. **obesity** [ə'bi:sɪtɪ] *n.* being obese.
obey [ə'beɪ] *v.* to do what you are told to do (by s.o.).
obfuscate ['ɒbfʌskeɪt] *v.* (*formal*) to make (sth) difficult to understand.
obituary [ə'bɪtjʊərɪ] *n.* written report of s.o.'s death, usu. with details of his life; **o. column** = part of a newspaper which gives obituaries.
object 1. *n.* ['ɒbdʒekt] (*a*) thing; **o. lesson** = (i) lesson using an object as a teaching aid; (ii) thing which makes a course of action very clear. (*b*) aim; target/purpose. (*c*) person/ thing to which feeling, etc., is directed. (*d*) (*in grammar*) noun/pronoun, etc., which follows directly from a verb or preposition. (*e*) **money is no o.** = is no obstacle/problem. **2.** *v.* [əb'dʒekt] (**to**) to refuse to agree; to express unwillingness towards/disapproval (of).
objection [ɒb'dʒekʃn] *n.* act of objecting; reason against. **objectionable,**

(a) adj. causing disapproval. (b) (esp. of person) very unpleasant. **objective** [ɒb'dʒektɪv] **1.** adj. (a) (in grammar) referring to the object. (b) referring to the external world. (c) considering matters from a general viewpoint and not just your own. **2.** n. (a) aim/object in view. (b) lens in a microscope which is nearest to the object being examined. **objectively**, adv. in an objective way/without being influenced by your own feelings. **objectivity**, n. being objective. **objector**, n. person who objects; **conscientious o.** = person who refuses to join the armed forces because he feels war is wrong.

objet d'art [ɒbʒei'dɑː] n. ornament.

oblate ['ɒbleɪt] n. person who has vowed to do religious work.

oblige [ə'blaɪdʒ] v. (a) to make (s.o.) feel it is their duty to do sth. (b) to force (s.o.) to do sth. (c) to do sth useful for/helpful to (s.o.). (d) **to be obliged to s.o.** = to owe s.o. gratitude. **obligate** ['ɒblɪgeɪt] v. to oblige. **obligation** [ɒblɪ'geɪʃn] n. (a) duty; legal bond. (b) duty to be grateful; **under an o. to s.o.** = morally obliged to help s.o. **obligatory** [ə'blɪgətərɪ] adj. necessary according to rules or laws. **obliging**, adj. ready to help. **obligingly**, adv. in an obliging way.

oblique [ə'bliːk] adj. (a) at a slant; **o. angle** = angle which is not a right angle. (b) from the side; not direct. **obliquely**, adv. in an oblique way.

obliterate [ə'blɪtəreɪt] v. to wipe out/to destroy. **obliteration** [ɒblɪtə'reɪʃn] n. act of obliterating; being obliterated.

oblivion [ə'blɪvɪən] n. forgetting totally; being completely forgotten. **oblivious**, adj. forgetful/unaware.

oblong ['ɒblɒŋ] n. & adj. (referring to a) rectangular shape with two pairs of equal sides, one pair being longer than the other.

obloquy ['ɒbləkwɪ] n. (formal) criticism.

obnoxious [ɒb'nɒkʃəs] adj. very unpleasant/offensive.

oboe ['əʊbəʊ] n. high-pitched woodwind instrument. **oboist**, n. person who plays the oboe.

obscene [ɒb'siːn] adj. offending moral standards/sensitive feelings; indecent.

obscenely, adj. in an obscene way. **obscenity** [ɒb'senɪtɪ] n. (a) being obscene. (b) obscene word.

obscure [əb'skjuə] **1.** adj. (a) (of place) dark/gloomy. (b) not clear. (c) not well-known. **2.** v. to hide, esp. by covering. **obscurely**, adv. in an obscure way. **obscurity**, n. being obscure.

obsequious [əb'siːkwɪəs] adj. too humble; showing too much respect for/obedience to (s.o.). **obsequies** ['ɒbsɪkwɪz] n. pl. funeral ceremonies. **obsequiously**, adv. in an obsequious way. **obsequiousness**, n. being obsequious.

observe [əb'zɜːv] v. (a) to follow/to obey (a law/rule/custom). (b) to watch/to look (at). (c) to notice. (d) to remark/to note. **observance**, n. (act of) observing. **observant**, adj. noticing (many details). **observation** [ɒbzə'veɪʃn] n. (a) (act of) observing; **under o.** = being carefully watched. (b) calculation of position of a ship. (c) remark. **observatory**, n. place from which stars and planets can be watched. **observer**, n. person who attends a meeting and watches (esp. without taking part).

obsess [ɒb'ses] v. to fill s.o.'s thoughts. **obsession** [əb'seʃn] n. idea/subject which fills your mind constantly. **obsessive**, adj. caused by an obsession. **obsessively**, adv. in an obsessive way.

obsidian [ɒb'sɪdɪən] n. hard glasslike volcanic rock.

obsolete ['ɒbsəliːt] adj. (word, custom) no longer in general use. **obsolescence**, n. being obsolescent. **obsolescent** [ɒbsə'lesənt] adj. going out of use/out of fashion.

obstacle ['ɒbstəkl] n. thing which is in the way/which prevents progress. **obstacle race**, n. race in which various obstacles have to be passed.

obstetric(al) [ɒb'stetrɪk(l)] adj. referring to obstetrics or childbirth. **obstetrician** [ɒbstə'trɪʃn] n. doctor who specializes in obstetrics. **obstetrics**, n. branch of medicine dealing with childbirth.

obstinate ['ɒbstɪnət] adj. (a) sticking to your opinion/course of action, etc. against all arguments. (b) which will not go away. **obstinacy,** *n.* being obstinate. **obstinately,** *adv.* in an obstinate way.

obstreperous [ɒb'strepərəs] *adj.* behaving in an uncontrolled/wild/loud way.

obstruct [əb'strʌkt] *v.* to get in the way of (sth); to prevent/to hinder the progress of (sth). **obstruction** [ɒb'strʌkʃn] *n.* (*a*) act of obstructing. (*b*) thing which gets in the way. **obstructive,** *adj.* which obstructs; which aims to cause an obstruction.

obtain [ɒb'teɪn] *v.* (*a*) to get. (*b*) to exist as a rule. **obtainable,** *adj.* which can be obtained.

obtrude [əb'tru:d] *v.* (*formal*) to come/to put in the way; to form an obstacle. **obtrusion** [əb'tru:ʒn] *n.* (*a*) (act of) obtruding. (*b*) thing which is in the way. **obtrusive** [əb'tru:sɪv] *adj.* (thing) which sticks out/which is in the way.

obtuse [əb'tju:s] *adj.* (*a*) stupid/dull (person). (*b*) **o. angle** = angle of between 90° and 180°. **obtusely,** *adv.* in an obtuse way. **obtuseness,** *n.* being obtuse.

obverse ['ɒbvɜːs] *n.* side of a coin with the head on it/the main side of a coin.

obviate ['ɒbvɪeɪt] *v.* to avoid/to get round.

obvious ['ɒbvɪəs] *adj.* clear; easily seen/easily noticed. **obviously,** *adv.* in an obvious way/clearly. **obviousness,** *n.* being obvious.

ocarina [ɒkə'ri:nə] *n.* wind instrument, made of a small pot, with holes to be covered by the fingers.

occasion [ə'keɪʒn] **1.** *n.* (*a*) thing which causes sth else. (*b*) (time of a) happening; **on o.** = from time to time. (*c*) special event. **2.** *v.* to cause (sth) to happen. **occasional,** *adj.* happening now and then/not often. **occasionally,** *adv.* sometimes/not often.

Occident ['ɒksɪdənt] *n.* (*formal*) the West; Western countries. **occidental** [ɒksɪ'dentl] *adj.* referring to the Occident.

occiput ['ɒksɪpʌt] *n.* back of the head. **occipital** [ɒk'sɪpɪtəl] *adj.* referring to the back of the head.

occlude [ɒ'klu:d] *v.* (*formal*) to shut up. **occlusion,** *n.* (*a*) movement of warm air upwards, caused by the arrival of

colder air. (*b*) blockage in a blood vessel.

occult ['ɒkʌlt] *adj. & n.* (referring to the) supernatural; magic.

occupy ['ɒkjupaɪ] *v.* (*a*) to fill/to take up (space or time). (*b*) to take/to have possession of. (*c*) to take possession and remain in control of. (*d*) to give work/activity to. **occupancy,** *n.* being occupied. **occupant,** *n.* person who occupies a place/who is in a certain seat. **occupation** [ɒkju'peɪʃn] *n.* (*a*) (act of) occupying; being occupied. (*b*) job/position/employment. **occupational,** *adj.* referring to an occupation; **o. therapy** = treating sick people by encouraging them to do special activities. **occupier,** *n.* person who lives in (a house).

occur [ə'kɜː] *v.* (**occurred**) (*a*) to take place/to happen. (*b*) (**to**) to come into one's thoughts. (*c*) to be (found). **occurrence** [ə'kʌrəns] *n.* happening.

ocean ['əʊʃn] *n.* large expanse of sea surrounding the land masses of the earth; a part of this sea. **oceanic** [əʊsɪ'ænɪk] *adj.* referring to the ocean. **oceanography** [əʊʃə'nɒgrəfɪ] *n.* study of the sea.

ocelot ['ɒsɪlɒt] *n.* leopard-like animal found in Central and South America.

ochre, *Am.* **ocher** ['əʊkə] *n.* yellow/red natural material used for colouring; dull yellow colour.

o'clock [ə'klɒk] *adv. phrase used with numbers meaning* the exact hour; **at six o'clock; the six o'clock train.**

octagon ['ɒktəgən] *n.* geometrical figure with eight sides. **octagonal** [ɒk'tægənl] *adj.* eight-sided.

octane ['ɒkteɪn] *n.* **o. number/o. rating** = number given to types of petrol to indicate their quality.

octave ['ɒktɪv] *n.* (*in music*) space between the first and last notes of an eight-note scale.

octavo [ɒk'teɪvəʊ] *n.* size of a book, when a sheet of paper is folded to make sixteen pages.

octet [ɒk'tet] *n.* group of eight people, esp. musicians; piece of music for such a group.

October [ɒk'təʊbə] *n.* 10th month of the year.

octogenarian [ɒktədʒə'neərɪən] *adj. & n.* (person) who is between 80 and 89 years old.

octopus [ˈɒktəpəs] *n.* (*pl.* **-es**) sea animal with eight arms.

ocular [ˈɒkjʊlə] *adj.* referring to the eyes/ to sight. **oculist,** *n.* doctor who specializes in care of the eyes.

odd [ɒd] *adj.* (**-er, -est**) (*a*) (number) which cannot be divided exactly by two. (*b*) approximately/a little more than. (*c*) occasional; referring to various individual things/items; (*in an auction*) **o. lots** = groups of different items for sale. (*d*) referring to a member of a set or pair, when separated from the rest. (*e*) strange/peculiar. **oddball,** *n. Am. inf.* eccentric person. **oddity,** *n.* (*a*) being odd. (*b*) odd thing/person. **oddly,** *adv.* in an odd way; for odd reasons. **oddments,** *n. pl.* bits and pieces; items left over. **oddness,** *n.* being odd. **odds,** *n. pl.* (*a*) difference between the amount which has been bet and the amount to be won; **o. of 10 to 1.** (*b*) more than an equal chance; **the o. are against it.** (*c*) **it makes no o.** = it makes no difference. (*d*) **to be at o. with s.o.** = to quarrel constantly. (*e*) **o. and ends** = bits and pieces.

ode [əʊd] *n.* long poem often addressed to a person or thing.

odious [ˈəʊdiəs] *adj.* hateful/horrible. **odiously,** *adv.* in an odious way. **odiousness,** *n.* being odious. **odium,** *n.* great unpopularity/hatred.

odometer [əʊˈdɒmitə] *n.* device for measuring the distance a vehicle travels.

odontology [ɒdɒnˈtɒlədʒi] *n.* study of teeth.

odour, *Am.* **odor** [ˈəʊdə] *n.* (*a*) scent/ smell. (*b*) **to be in good/bad o. with** = to be in/out of favour with. **odorous,** *adj.* with a strong scent. **odourless,** *adj.* without any smell.

odyssey [ˈɒdɪsɪ] *n.* long voyage of adventure.

oedema [ɪˈdiːmə] *n.* excess liquid gathering in tissues, causing a swelling.

Oedipus complex [ˈiːdɪpəsˈkɒmpleks] *n.* feeling (in a man) of hatred for his father and love for his mother.

oesophagus, *Am.* **esophagus** [əˈsɒfəgəs] *n.* part of the throat down which food passes from the mouth to the stomach.

oestrogen [ˈiːstrədʒən] *n.* female hormone, controlling bodily changes in the reproductive cycle.

of [ɒv] *prep.* (*a*) belonging to/connected with. (*b*) being a part/a quantity. (*c*) (who/which) is; **a child of ten.** (*d*) by/ from; **south of the border; made of wool.** (*e*) about/concerning.

off [ɒf] **1.** *adv.* (*a*) away (from); **they're o.** = they've started running; **day o.** = day away from work. (*b*) not on; **the deal is o.** = has been cancelled; (*in restaurant*) **chicken is o.** = not available. (*c*) no longer fresh. (*d*) **well/badly o.** = having plenty/not enough (money). (*e*) **right/straight o.** = immediately; **on and o.** = from time to time. (*f*) (*with verbs*) completely; **to finish o. 2.** *prep.* (*a*) (away) from. (*b*) (*at sea*) a certain distance from. (*c*) branching from. (*d*) disliking/not wanting (food). **3.** *adj.* away; not on; **o. day** = one on which you are less successful; **o. season** = less busy season. **offbeat,** *adj. inf.* rather odd/unusual. **offchance,** *n.* slight possibility. **off-colour,** *adj.* not well. **offhand,** *adv. & adj.* (*a*) without preparation/without thinking carefully. (*b*) (*also* **offhanded**) rude/without courtesy. **offhandedly,** *adv.* rudely. **off-licence,** *n.* (shop, etc., which has) a licence to sell alcoholic drinks to be taken away. **off-line,** *adj.* (computer) which is not connected to a network or to a main system. **offload,** *v.* (**on to**) to pass a load to sth/s.o. else. **off-peak,** *adj.* away from the busiest/most used times. **off-putting,** *adj. inf.* causing (mild) annoyance. **offseason,** *adj. & n.* (period, usually winter) when prices are lower because fewer people travel. **offset. 1.** *n.* [ˈɒfset] method of printing from a plate to a rubber surface and then to paper. **2.** *v.* [ɒfˈset] (**offset**) to balance (one thing) against another. **offshoot** [ˈɒfʃuːt] *n.* small side shoot of a plant; thing which branches from sth else. **offshore,** *adj.* (away) from/ at a distance from the shore. **off side,** *n.* (*in a car*) side nearest the middle of the road. **offside** [ɒfˈsaɪd] **1.** *adv.* (*in football*) between the ball and the opposing team's goal. **2.** *adj.* referring to the side of a car nearest to the middle of the road. **offspring** [ˈɒfsprɪŋ] *n.*

child; young (of an animal). **offstage,** *adv. & adj.* not on the stage/unseen by the audience.

offal ['ɒfl] *n.* internal organs (heart, etc.) of animals, used as food.

offence [ə'fens] *n.* (*a*) state of offending; being offended; **to take o. at** = to be offended by. (*b*) crime; (act of) offending (esp. against a law). **offend** [ə'fend] *v.* to be/to go against (the law/ opinions/wishes/feelings). **offender,** *n.* person who offends (esp. **against** a law). **offensive. 1.** *adj.* (*a*) which is unpleasant. (*b*) (*in army*) which is used in an attack. **2.** *n.* (military) attack; **to take the o.** = to start the attack. **offensively,** *adv.* in an offensive way. **offensiveness,** *n.* being offensive.

offer ['ɒfə] **1.** *n.* (act of) indicating that you will do/give sth; thing which is offered; **on o.** = offered; **special o.** = goods which are put on sale at a reduced price. **2.** *v.* (*a*) to say/to indicate that you will do/give (sth). (*b*) to make/to express (an opinion, etc.). **offering,** *n.* thing which is offered. **offertory,** *n.* (*a*) offering of wine and bread in the communion service. (*b*) collection of money taken while the wine and bread are being offered.

office ['ɒfɪs] *n.* (*a*) room/building where business or professional activity is carried out; *Am.* **doctor's o.** = room where a doctor sees his patients. (*b*) position/function. (*c*) (*esp. in titles*) organization; government department. (*d*) help/services. **officer,** *n.* (*a*) person who holds an official position. (*b*) person who holds one of the commissioned ranks in the armed forces, etc. (*c*) **police o.** = policeman. **official** [ə'fɪʃl] **1.** *adj.* referring to an organization which is recognized by a government, etc. **2.** *n.* person holding a recognized position. **officialdom,** *n.* bureaucracy. **officialese,** *n. inf.* clumsy language used by bureaucrats. **officially,** *adv.* in an official way. **officiate** [ə'fɪʃɪeɪt] *v.* (*a*) (*of clergyman*) (**at**) to perform a religious ceremony. (*b*) to act as chairman, etc. **officious,** *adj.* too ready to interfere or to offer help. **officiously,** *adv.* in an officious way. **officiousness,** *n.* being officious.

offing ['ɒfɪŋ] *n.* **in the o.** = coming/ available soon.

often ['ɒfn] *adv.* many times; in many instances. **oftentimes,** *adv. Am.* often.

ogee ['əʊdʒi:] *n.* S-shaped curve in architecture; an arch with two S-shaped curves, joining at a point.

ogle ['əʊgl] *v.* to leer/look at (s.o.) with sexual desire.

ogre ['əʊgə] *n.* cruel giant who eats human beings; cruel terrifying person.

oh [əʊ] *inter. expressing surprise/shock.*

ohm [əʊm] *n.* standard measure of electrical resistance.

oil [ɔɪl] **1.** *n.* (*a*) thick smooth-running liquid of various kinds (used in cooking/heating/engineering/painting). (*b*) liquid found mainly underground and used to produce power. (*c*) picture painted with oil paints. **2.** *v.* to put oil on/in (esp. to make a machine run more smoothly); **to o. the wheels** = to help to make things run more smoothly; *inf.* **well-oiled** = rather drunk. **oil-bearing,** *adj.* (rocks, etc.) which contain oil. **oilfield,** *n.* area where oil is found. **oiliness,** *n.* being oily. **oilrig,** *n.* structure for drilling for oil. **oilskin(s),** *n.* (clothing of) material made waterproof with oil. **oilslick,** *n.* thin covering of oil on the surface of the sea. **oiltanker,** *n.* large ship/large lorry for carrying oil. **oily,** *adj.* (**-ier, -iest**) (*a*) like oil; covered with oil. (*b*) (*of manner*) too smooth and pleasant; insincere.

ointment ['ɔɪntmənt] *n.* smooth healing or soothing substance spread on the skin.

OK, okay [əʊ'keɪ] *inf. inter. & adj.* all right. **2.** *n.* sign of approval. **3.** *v.* to give a sign of approval to.

okapi [ɒ'kɑ:pi:] *n.* African animal, like a large black horse, with white stripes on its rear legs.

okra ['ɒkrə] *n.* tropical plant with edible green pods.

old [əʊld] *adj.* (**-er, -est**) (*a*) having great age; **o. wives' tale** = belief based on tradition rather than on fact. (*b*) having been in use for a long time. (*c*) being of a particular age. (*d*) having been in a certain state/having been done for a long time. (*e*) former.

(*f*) term showing vagueness/affection/disrespect, etc.; *inf.* **the o. man** = boss/headmaster/father. **Old Bailey,** *n.* central criminal court in London. **old boy network,** *n.* system where men who were at school together help each other get ahead in later life. **olden,** *adj.* (*formal*) old (times). **old-fashioned,** *adj.* not in fashion; out of date. **oldie,** *n. inf.* old-fashioned/out of date thing. **oldish,** *adj.* rather old. **old maid,** *n.* older woman who has never married. **old-time,** *adj.* not of the present/done in an old-fashioned way. **old timer,** *n.* former worker/soldier, etc. **Old World,** *n.* Europe, Asia and Africa.

oleaginous [ɒliˈæʒɪnəs] *adj.* (*formal*) oily.

oleander [ɒliˈændə] *n.* tropical shrub with pink flowers.

olfactory [ɒlˈfæktərɪ] *adj.* (*formal*) referring to the sense of smell.

oligarchy [ˈɒlɪɡɑːkɪ] *n.* (country with a) government by a few powerful people.

olive [ˈɒlɪv] *n.* (*a*) small black or green fruit which produces oil and is used as food; tree which bears this fruit; **o. branch** = sign of peace. (*b*) **o. (green)** = dull green colour of unripe olives; **o. skin** = yellowish skin.

Olympic [əˈlɪmpɪk] *adj. & n.* **the O. Games/the Olympics** = international athletic competition held every four years. **Olympiad,** *n.* major international sporting competition. **Olympian,** *adj.* like a god; rather supercilious.

ombudsman [ˈɒmbədzmən] *n.* (*pl.* **-men**) official who investigates complaints by members of the public against a government department.

omega [ˈəʊmɪɡə] *n.* last letter of the Greek alphabet.

omelette, *Am.* **omelet** [ˈɒmlət] *n.* cooked egg mixture often with savoury substances added.

omen [ˈəʊmən] *n.* thing giving an indication of the future. **ominous** [ˈɒmɪnəs] *adj.* threatening bad results. **ominously,** *adv.* in an ominous way.

omit [əˈmɪt] *v.* (**omitted**) (*a*) to leave out. (*b*) (**to**) not to do sth. **omission** [əˈmɪʃn] *n.* (*a*) act of omitting. (*b*) thing omitted.

omnibus [ˈɒmnɪbəs] **1.** *n.* (*old*) bus. **2.** *n. & adj.* (book) which includes several books all together.

omnidirectional [ɒmnɪdaɪˈrekʃənəl] *adj.* (aerial which can capture signals) from any direction.

omnipotence [ɒmˈnɪpətəns] *n.* quality of being all-powerful. **omnipotent,** *adj.* all-powerful.

omnipresent [ˈɒmnɪprezənt] *adj.* which is everywhere.

omniscient [ɒmˈnɪsɪənt] *adj.* (person) who knows everything. **omniscience,** *n.* knowing everything.

omnivorous [ɒmˈnɪvərəs] *adj.* eating everything; (animal) which eats both plants and other animals.

on [ɒn] **1.** *prep.* (*a*) touching the top/outer surface of sth. (*b*) in/at. (*c*) with; **have you any money on you?** (*d*) belonging to/a member of; **on the staff.** (*e*) indicating a means of moving; **on foot.** (*f*) engaged in; **on business.** (*g*) from/by; **to live on a small income.** (*h*) (*indicating a time*) **on Sundays; on application** = when you apply; **on sale** = for sale; (*i*) approximately; **just on a year ago.** (*j*) because of; **to congratulate s.o. on his success.** (*k*) about/concerning; **a book on Wales.** (*l*) towards/against; **an attack on s.o.** (*m*) *inf.* paid by; **on foot.** (*f*) engaged (*n*) (*as a bet*) **to put £10 on a horse** = to bet £10 that the horse will win. **2.** *adv.* (*a*) in position; **put the kettle on;** *inf.* **it's just not on** = cannot be allowed. (*b*) in action; open; **the light is on.** (*c*) happening; **what's on at the cinema?** (*d*) being worn; **put your shoes on** (*e*) (in a) continuing (way); **they worked on.** (*f*) (*indicating passing of time*) **later on.** (*g*) *inf.* **on at s.o.** = scolding/criticizing. (*h*) **on and off** = not continuously/with breaks in between; **on and on** = without stopping. (*i*) *inf.* **to have s.o. on** = to tell s.o. a lie as a joke.

onager [ˈɒnədʒə] *n.* wild Asian donkey.

once [wʌns] **1.** *adv.* (*a*) for one time. (*b*) at all/ever. (*c*) at a (particular) time in the past. (*d*) **at o.** = (i) immediately; (ii) at the same time. **2.** *conj.* as soon as. **once-over,** *n. inf.* quick examination.

oncoming [ˈɒnkʌmɪŋ] *adj.* coming towards you.

one [wʌn] **1.** *n.* number 1. (*a*) first number; *inf.* **look after number o.** = look after yourself first. (*b*) single unit in quantity or number. (*c*) *inf.* **a quick o.** =

a quick drink; she **hit him o.** = hit him a blow. **2.** *adj.* (*a*) single (example of). (*b*) the only. (*c*) the same; **it's all o. to me.** **3.** *pron.* (*a*) thing/person indicated. (*b*) example of a type. **4.** *indefinite adj.* (on) a certain; **o. night. 5.** *indefinite pron.* (*a*) (*pl.* **some/any**) an example of sth. (*b*) (*formal*) anyone/an indefinite person. **one-armed bandit,** *n.* gambling machine worked by a handle. **one-horse town,** *n. inf.* small town where very little happens. **one-legged** ['wʌn-'legɪd] *adj.* with only one leg. **one-night stand,** *n.* performance (of a play/of a show) for one night only. **one-off,** *adj.* done/made once only. **oneself,** *pronoun referring to a person as an indefinite subject.* **one-sided,** *adj.* treating or giving justice to one side only. **one-time,** *adj.* former. **one-track mind,** *n.* mind which concentrates on one thing at a time. **oneupmanship,** *n.* art of putting yourself at an advantage over others. **one-way,** *adj.* (street) for traffic in one direction only; (ticket) for a single journey only.

onerous ['ɒnərəs] *adj.* causing much (tiring) effort.

onion ['ʌnjən] *n.* strong-smelling vegetable with a round white bulb.

online ['ɒnlaɪn] *adv. & adj.* linked directly to a computer.

onlooker ['ɒnlʊkə] *n.* person who watches.

only ['əʊnlɪ] **1.** *adj.* (the) single/(the) one without any others. **2.** *adv.* (*a*) and not anyone/anything else. (*b*) as recently as. (*c*) **if o.** = expressing a strong wish/desire; **o. too** = very. **3.** *conj.* but.

onomastics [ɒnə'mæstɪks] *n.* study of names.

onomatopoeia [ɒnəmætə'pi:ə] *n.* making/using words which imitate a sound. **onomatopoeic,** *adj.* using onomatopoeia.

onrush ['ɒnrʌʃ] *n.* rushing in/on.

onset ['ɒnset] *n.* beginning (of an attack, etc.)

onslaught ['ɒnslɔːt] *n.* sudden severe attack.

onto ['ɒntu:] *prep.* on to.

ontology [ɒn'tɒlədʒɪ] *n.* study of reality. **ontological** [ɒntə'lɒdʒɪkl] *adj.* referring to reality.

onus ['əʊnəs] *n.* responsibility (for a difficult task)

onward ['ɒnwəd] **1.** *adj.* forward. **2.** *adv.* (*also* **onwards**) forward.

onyx ['ɒnɪks] *n.* (*pl.* **-es**) multicoloured precious stone.

oodles ['u:dlz] *n. pl. inf.* lots (**of**).

ooh [u:] *inter. showing surprise/shock.*

ooze [u:z] **1.** *n.* slimy mud. **2.** *v.* to flow slowly and gently.

opacity [ə'pæsɪtɪ] *n.* state of being opaque.

opal ['əʊpl] *n.* semi-precious stone with varied or changing colours. **opalescence,** *n.* being opalescent. **opalescent,** *adj.* shining like an opal.

opaque [əʊ'peɪk] *adj.* which you cannot see through.

OPEC ['əʊpek] *n.* (= Organization of Petroleum Exporting Countries) group of countries who produce and export oil.

open ['əʊpn] **1.** *adj.* (*a*) not closed. (*b*) which you can enter. (*c*) without limits. (*d*) **o. to** = without protection (from sth). (*e*) ready to accept/to be accepted. (*f*) with no attempt (being made) to hide sth. (*g*) with space between the parts. (*h*) with no fixed idea(s)/conditions. (*i*) (competition) without restrictions. **2.** *v.* (*a*) to become open. (*b*) to start (up)/to set going. (*c*) to have an exit (**on to**). **3.** *n.* unlimited area outdoors. **open-air,** *adj.* not in a building. **opencast,** *adj.* (mine) dug on the surface of the ground. **open-ended,** *adj.* with no definite end. **opener,** *n.* device for opening sth. **openhanded,** *adj.* generous. **openheart,** *adj.* (surgery) with the chest cut open to expose the heart. **opening. 1.** *n.* (*a*) act of opening. (*b*) beginning. (*c*) place where sth opens. (*d*) opportunity, such as a job vacancy. **2.** *adj.* which opens. **open letter,** *n.* letter published as an article in a newspaper and not sent to the addressee. **openly,** *adv.* in an open way. **open mind,** *n.* to **have an o. m.** = not to have a fixed opinion on sth. **openness,** *n.* quality of being open. **open out,** *v.* to open (fully); to spread out widely. **open-plan,** *adj.* (offices) with no walls between them. **open prison,** *n.* prison with few restrictions.

open up, v. (a) to open (completely). (b) to bring into use. **open verdict,** n. verdict by a coroner's jury, which describes the death, but does not state if a crime is involved. **openwork,** n. pattern (on a shoe, etc.) with holes in it.

opera ['ɒprə] n. (a) dramatic performance with music, in which the words are partly or wholly sung. (b) company which performs operas. **opera glasses,** n. pl. small binoculars for looking at performers on the stage. **opera house,** n. theatre in which opera is performed. **operatic** [ɒpə'rætɪk] adj. of/like/for opera. **operetta** [ɒpə'retə] n. opera with a light-hearted story in which some of the words are spoken.

operate ['ɒpəreɪt] 1. v. (a) to act. (b) to (cause to) work. (c) **to o. on a patient** = to treat a patient by cutting open the body. **operable** ['ɒpərəbl] adj. which can be operated on. **operation** [ɒpə-'reɪʃn] n. (a) (act of) operating; being operated on; **to come into o.** = begin to be applied. **operational,** adj. referring to the working of sth. (b) ready for use. **operative** ['ɒpərətɪv] 1. adj. in operation. 2. n. worker, esp. one who operates a machine, etc. **operator** ['ɒpəreɪtə] n. (a) person who works instruments, etc. (b) person who carries things out/organizes things; inf. **smart o.** = clever businessman.

ophthalmic [ɒf'θælmɪk] adj. referring to (the medical treatment of) the eye. **ophthalmologist** [ɒfθæl'mɒlədʒɪst] n. doctor who specializes in diseases of the eye. **ophthalmology,** n. study of the eye.

opiate ['əʊpɪət] n. drug which sends you to sleep.

opinion [ə'pɪnjən] n. (a) (of) what a person thinks/feels about sth; **public o.** = what people think/feet about sth. (b) view; piece of (usu. expert) advice. **opinionated,** adj. (person) with rigid opinions/who thinks he is always right.

opium ['əʊpɪəm] n. drug which puts you to sleep, made from a type of poppy.

opossum [ə'pɒsəm] n. small North American animal which carries its young in a pouch.

opponent [ə'pəʊnənt] n. person/group which is against you.

opportune ['ɒpətjuːn] adj. coming (by chance) at the right time. **opportunely,** adv. in an opportune way; at the right time. **opportunism,** n. being an opportunist. **opportunist,** n. person who takes advantage of opportunities, esp. at the expense of others. **opportunity** [ɒpə'tjuːnɪtɪ] n. chance/circumstances which allow you to do sth.

oppose [ə'pəʊz] v. to act against (s.o./ sth); to try to prevent. **opposed to,** adj. (a) against. (b) in contrast.

opposite ['ɒpəzɪt] 1. adj. (a) facing. (b) at/in/towards the other side of sth; **o. number** = person who is in a similar position in another organization. (c) belonging to a completely different type/ position. 2. n. thing which is completely different. 3. prep. in an opposite position to. **opposition** [ɒpə'zɪʃn] n. (a) (act of) opposing. (b) (esp. in politics) the party/group which opposes the government. (c) rivalry.

oppress [ə'pres] v. (a) to cause to suffer, esp. by harsh rule. (b) to cause depression/sadness in. **oppression** [ə'preʃn] n. (act of) oppressing; being oppressed. **oppressive,** adj. oppressing. **oppressively,** adv. in an oppressive way. **oppressiveness,** n. being oppressive. **oppressor,** n. person who oppresses.

opprobrium [ə'prəʊbrɪəm] n. (formal) disgrace; (cause of) strong disapproval. **opprobrious,** adj. disgraceful; rude.

opt [ɒpt] v. (for) to decide (in favour of). **opt out,** v. (of) to decide not to (take part).

optical ['ɒptɪkl] adj. referring to the eyes/to the eyesight; referring to optics; **o. fibres** = fine threads of glass, used for transmitting light signals. **optic,** adj. referring to the eye/to sight. **optically,** adv. referring to optics. **optician** [ɒp'tɪʃn] n. person who prescribes/ makes/sells spectacles or contact lenses, etc. **optics,** n. science of light; **fibre o.** = use of optical fibres to transmit signals.

optimal ['ɒptɪməl] adj. best.

optimism ['ɒptɪmɪzəm] n. belief that everything is as good as it can be/ will work out for the best; confident/ cheerful attitude. **optimist** ['ɒptɪmɪst] *n.* person who believes everything will work out for the best. **optimistic** [ɒptɪ'mɪstɪk] *adj.* feeling that everything will work out for the best; giving cause for optimism. **optimistically,** *adv.* in an optimistic way.

optimum ['ɒptɪməm] 1. *n.* best way. 2. *adj.* best.

option ['ɒpʃn] *n.* (*a*) choice/alternative possibility. (*b*) **o. on sth** = opportunity to buy/sell sth within a certain time or at a certain price. **optional,** *adj.* which may or may not be chosen.

optometrist [ɒp'tɒmətrɪst] *n. Am.* optician. **optometry,** *n.* science of eyesight.

opulence ['ɒpjuləns] *n.* being opulent. **opulent,** *adj.* rich/luxurious/splendid. **opulently,** *adv.* in an opulent way.

opus ['əupəs] *n.* (*pl.* **-es** or **opera**) (*a*) piece of music which is given a number. (*b*) large work of art.

or [ɔ:] *conj.* (*a*) the opposite/the alternative/the other (possibility). (*b*) approximately. (*c*) **or (else)** = if not.

oracle ['ɒrəkl] *n.* (*a*) (*in Ancient Greece*) place where the gods answered questions about the future; person who answered questions about the future. (*b*) very wise and knowing person. **oracular** [ɒ'rækjulə] *adj.* referring to an oracle.

oral ['ɔ:rl] 1. *adj.* (*a*) by speaking. (*b*) taken by the mouth. 2. *n.* examination where you answer questions by speaking. **orally,** *adv.* (*a*) in/by speech. (*b*) by the mouth.

orange ['ɒrɪndʒ] 1. *n.* usu. sweet citrus fruit, reddish yellow when ripe; tree which bears this fruit. 2. *adj. & n.* colour of an orange. **orangeade** [ɒrɪndʒ'eɪd] *n.* fizzy orange-flavoured drink.

orang-utang [ɔræŋu:'tæŋ] *n.* large red ape found in South-East Asia.

oration [ə'reɪʃn] *n.* (*formal*) speech. **orator** ['ɒrətə] *n.* person who is able to speak forcefully and persuasively to large numbers of people; person making a speech. **oratorical** [ɒrə'tɒrɪkl] *adj.* full of eloquence. **oratory** ['ɒrətərɪ] *n.* (*a*) eloquent/forceful public speaking. (*b*) private chapel.

oratorio [ɒrə'tɔ:rɪəu] *n.* (*pl.* **-os**) piece of music for orchestra, choir and soloists, often telling a religious story.

orb [ɔ:b] *n.* (*a*) spherical object (such as a planet or an eyeball). (*b*) ornamental globe with a cross on top used by a king as a symbol of state power.

orbit ['ɔ:bɪt] 1. *n.* (*a*) curved track (of an object moving through space). (*b*) extent of influence. 2. *v.* to move in an orbit round sth.

orchard ['ɔ:tʃəd] *n.* field with fruit trees.

orchestra ['ɔ:kəstrə] *n.* (*a*) large group of musicians who play together. (*b*) part of a theatre, usu. next to the stage, where the musicians sit; **o. stalls** = seats in a theatre very close to where the orchestra sits. **orchestral** [ɔ:'kestrəl] *adj.* referring to an orchestra. **orchestrate** ['ɔ:kɪstreɪt] *v.* (*a*) to arrange (a piece of music) for an orchestra. (*b*) to organize (a demonstration, etc.). **orchestration** [ɔ:kɪ'streɪʃn] *n.* (act of) orchestrating; being orchestrated.

orchid, orchis ['ɔ:kɪd, 'ɔ:kɪs] *n.* flowering plant with showy flowers.

ordain [ɔ:'deɪn] *v.* (*a*) to make (s.o.) a priest/a clergyman in a formal ceremony. (*b*) (*formal*) to order/to command (that sth be done).

ordeal [ɔ:'di:l] *n.* painful test of strength/courage; difficult period.

order ['ɔ:də] 1. *n.* (*a*) command/demand that sth should be done. (*b*) obeying of rules or laws without unrest or violence. (*c*) demand/request for goods from a customer; goods supplied to a customer; *inf.* **a tall o.** = a difficult task. (*d*) organization of items in succession. (*e*) good/correct arrangement; **in o.** = correct/valid; **out of o.** = not working. (*f*) arrangement of an army. (*g*) rules for an assembly/meeting. (*h*) organization of monks/priests, etc.; **in holy orders** = being a priest. (*i*) organization of knighthood; group of people to whom a certain honour has been given. (*j*) type/kind/classification/rank. (*k*) paper which authorizes the transfer of money. (*l*) **in o. to/that** = so that/for the purpose of. 2. *v.* (*a*) to command/to demand/to say (that sth should be done). (*b*) to demand/to request (goods/services, etc.). (*c*) to arrange/to put in order. **orderliness** ['ɔ:dəlnəs] *n.* (*a*) being in good order/tidiness. (*b*) being quiet/being orderly. **orderly. 1.** *adj.* (*a*) in good order; tidy or well-arranged. (b) well-behaved. **2.** n. person whose duty it is to carry out routine tasks (in a hospital or in the armed services).

ordinal ['ɔːdɪnl] n. & adj. (referring to a) number indicating the position in a series.

ordinance ['ɔːdɪnəns] n. laws/rule made by an authority.

ordinary ['ɔːdnrɪ] adj. normal/not unusual; typical of its class/not having any special characteristics; **out of the o.** = extraordinary. **ordinarily,** adv. in the usual way/usually.

ordination [ɔːdɪ'neɪʃn] n. (act/ceremony of) ordaining s.o. as a priest.

ordnance ['ɔːdnəns] n. (a) heavy guns. (b) (government department dealing with) military supplies. **ordnance survey,** n. government department which produces detailed maps.

ore [ɔː] n. material found in the earth from which metals are obtained.

oregano [ɒrɪ'gɑːnəʊ] n. spicy herb used in cooking.

organ ['ɔːgən] n. (a) part of the body with a special function. (b) periodical which gives the views of a group/of an organization. (c) musical instrument with keyboard(s) and many pipes through which air is pumped to make a sound. **organic** [ɔː'gænɪk] adj. (a) referring to an organ/to organs. (b) referring to living things; **o. chemistry** = concerned with carbon compounds; **o. farming** = using only natural fertilizers. (c) having an organized/structure. **organically** [ɔː'gænɪklɪ] adv. in an organic way. **organism** ['ɔːgənɪzəm] n. living thing. **organist,** n. person who plays the organ. **organization** [ɔːgənaɪ'zeɪʃn] n. (a) (act of) arranging; being arranged. (b) organized group or institution. **organize** ['ɔːgənaɪz] v. to arrange/to put into a special form of order; to put into good order. **organizer,** n. person who arranges things.

organdie [ɔː'gændɪ] n. very thin stiff cotton cloth.

orgasm ['ɔːgæzəm] n. climax of sexual excitement.

orgy ['ɔːdʒɪ] n. uncontrolled indulgence in drinking/dancing; uncontrolled state or activity.

oriel ['ɔːrɪəl] n. **o. window** = upstairs window which projects from the wall.

orient ['ɔːrɪənt] **1.** n. **the O.** = the East/Eastern countries. **2.** v. to put in a certain direction. **oriental** [ɔːrɪ'entl] **1.** adj. referring to the Orient. **2.** n. person from the Orient. **orientalist,** n. person who studies the East. **orientate** ['ɔːrɪənteɪt] v. to put in a certain direction. **orientation** [ɔːrɪən'teɪʃn] n. (act of) orientating/putting in a certain position/direction. **orienteering** [ɔːrɪən'tɪərɪŋ] n. sport of finding your way across country by means of maps and compasses.

orifice ['ɒrɪfɪs] n. (formal) hole/opening.

origami [ɒrɪ'gɑːmɪ] n. (no pl.) art of folding coloured paper to make shapes.

origin ['ɒrɪdʒɪn] n. beginning/root; where sth/s.o. comes from. **original** [ə'rɪdʒɪnl] **1.** adj. (a) from its beginning(s); from earliest times. (b) new/different; created for the first time/not a copy. (c) showing ideas not based on those of other people. **2.** n. (a) thing from which other things are copied/translated, etc. (b) unusual person. **originality** [ɒrɪdʒɪ'nælɪtɪ] n. (a) being original/new/different. (b) ability to create sth which has never been done before. **originally,** adv. (a) in an original way. (b) at or from the beginning. **originate** [ə'rɪdʒɪneɪt] v. (a) to bring into existence for the first time. (b) to begin/to have its beginning. **origination** [ərɪdʒɪ'neɪʃn] n. act of originating. **originator,** n. person who originates.

oriole ['ɒrɪəl] n. bird with black and yellow feathers.

ormolu ['ɔːmǝluː] n. (no pl.) decorations made of bronze covered with gold leaf.

ornament. 1. n. ['ɔːnəmənt] thing used as decoration. **2.** v. ['ɔːnəmənt] to decorate/to help to make more beautiful. **ornamental** [ɔːnə'mentl] adj. acting as an ornament; being pretty rather than useful. **ornamentation** [ɔːnəmən'teɪʃn] n. act of ornamenting; group of ornaments.

ornate [ɔː'neɪt] adj. having (too) much ornament.

ornery ['ɔːnərɪ] adj. Am. inf. bad-tempered.

ornithology [ɔːnɪˈθɒlədʒɪ] n. study of birds. **ornithological** [ɔːnɪθəˈlɒdʒɪkl] adj. referring to ornithology. **ornithologist** [ɔːnɪˈθɒlədʒɪst] n. person who studies birds.

orotund [ˈɒrətʌnd] adj. pompously calm.

orphan [ˈɔːfn] 1. n. child who has no parents. 2. v. to make (s.o.) an orphan. **orphanage** [ˈɔːfənɪdʒ] n. home where orphans are looked after.

orrery [ˈɒrərɪ] n. mechanical model of the solar system.

orris root [ˈɒrɪsˈruːt] n. perfume from the dried roots of a type of iris.

orthodontics [ɔːθəˈdɒntɪks] n. treatment to correct badly formed teeth.

orthodox [ˈɔːθədɒks] adj. (a) holding the generally accepted beliefs of a religion/a philosophy, etc. (b) (Jews) who observe traditional practices very strictly; **the O. Church** = the Christian Church of Eastern Europe. **orthodoxy**, n. being orthodox.

orthography [ɔːˈθɒgrəfɪ] n. (correct) spelling. **orthographical** [ɔːθəˈgræfɪkl] adj. referring to orthography.

orthopaedic [ɔːθəˈpiːdɪk] adj. referring to diseases and deformities of bones. **orthopaedics**, n. branch of medicine dealing with bones, etc. **orthopaedist**, n. doctor who specializes in orthopaedics.

orthoptics [ɔːˈθɒptɪks] n. correction of squints.

oryx [ˈɒrɪks] n. large rare Arabian antelope.

oscillate [ˈɒsɪleɪt] v. to swing from one side to the other. **oscillation** [ɒsɪˈleɪʃn] n. (act of) oscillating. **oscilloscope** [ɒˈsɪləskəʊp] n. device which shows oscillations on a screen.

osier [ˈəʊzɪə] n. type of willow tree whose branches are used to make baskets/furniture, etc.

osmosis [ɒzˈməʊsɪs] n. movement of liquid into another liquid through the porous walls of a container.

osprey [ˈɒsprɪ] n. large bird of prey which eats fish.

ossicle [ˈɒsɪkəl] n. small bone in the middle ear.

ossify [ˈɒsɪfaɪ] v. to make into bone; to make rigid. **ossification** [ɒsɪfɪˈkeɪʃn] n. act of ossifying.

ostensible [ɒˈstensɪbl] adj. which shows on the surface; which is meant to seem real. **ostensibly**, adv. seemingly.

ostentatious [ɒstenˈteɪʃəs] adj. showy/aiming to impress. **ostentation**, n. showing off in a luxurious way which is intended to impress. **ostentatiously**, adv. in an ostentatious way.

osteoarthritis [ɒstɪəʊɑːˈθraɪtɪs] n. painful disease of the joints.

osteopath [ˈɒstɪəpæθ] n. person who treats diseases of the bones and muscles by moving or massaging the patient's limbs. **osteopathic** [ɒstɪəˈpæθɪk] adj. referring to osteopathy. **osteopathy** [ɒstɪˈɒpəθɪ] n. treatment of diseases of the bones and muscles by moving or massaging limbs.

ostracism [ˈɒstrəsɪzəm] n. being cut off from a group/from society. **ostracize** [ˈɒstrəsaɪz] v. to force/to keep (s.o.) out of a group.

ostrich [ˈɒstrɪtʃ] n. (pl. -es) large, fast-running, flightless bird found in Africa.

other [ˈʌðə] 1. adj. (a) different/not the one already mentioned/not the same. (b) second of two; **every o. week** = every second week. (c) (expressing a vague idea) **the o. day** = a day or two ago. 2. pron. (a) different person/different thing. (b) (used to contrast two things or groups) **one after the o.** 3. adv. **o. than** = apart from. **otherwise**, adv. (a) in a different way/situation. (b) in other respects. (c) if not/or else. **otherworldly**, adj. (person) who is not interested in material things/who is vague and impractical.

otiose [ˈəʊtɪəʊs] adj. (formal) superfluous/unwanted.

otitis [əʊˈtaɪtɪs] n. inflammation of the ear.

otter [ˈɒtə] n. fish-eating mammal with webbed feet living mainly by rivers.

ottoman [ˈɒtəmən] n. box for storing goods with a padded seat on top.

ouch [aʊtʃ] inter. showing reaction to pain.

ought [ɔːt] v. (past tense: ought to have) used with other verbs (a) (expressing duty or obligation) **you o. to go** = it is your duty to go. (b) (expressing something which is vaguely desirable) **you o. to hear that concert.** (c) (expressing *something which is probable*) **that horse o. to win.**

ounce [aʊns] *n.* measure of weight (28 grams).

our ['aʊə] *adj.* belonging to us. **ours** ['aʊəz] *pron.* thing(s)/person(s) belonging to us. **ourselves** [aʊə'selvz] *pron. referring to the subject* we.

oust [aʊst] *v.* to force s.o. to leave a place/position.

out [aʊt] **1.** *adv.* (*a*) not in (a building, etc.); **the men are o.** = on strike. (*b*) away from the starting point (of sth). (*c*) (in a direction) away from the inside/from the starting point. (*d*) having appeared/become known; **the hawthorn is o.** = in flower; **her book is just o.** = has just been published. (*e*) **o. loud** = so that it can be heard. (*f*) not in the right position/state; **o. of practice** = not having done enough practice; (*in cricket*) **he is 62 not o.** = he has scored 62 and has not been bowled/caught, etc. (*g*) mistaken. (*h*) (*of fire/light*) no longer burning; (*of hairstyle/dress*) no longer fashionable. (*i*) finished; having reached the end. **2.** *n.* **to know the ins and outs of** = to know sth in all its details. **out-and-out,** *adj. & adv.* complete(ly)/total(ly). **outback,** *n.* (*in Australia*) area(s) away from centres of population. **outbid,** *v.* (**outbid**) (*at auction*) to bid a higher sum than (s.o.). **outboard,** *adj.* (engine) which is attached to the outside of a boat. **outbreak,** *n.* sudden occurrence of an illness or unrest. **outbuildings,** *n. pl.* buildings standing apart from the main building. **outburst,** *n.* sudden display of (violent) emotion. **outcast,** *n. & adj.* (person who has been) rejected by/driven away from a society or a group. **outclass,** *v.* to be much better than. **outcome,** *n.* result. **outcrop,** *n.* rock which sticks out of the surface of the ground. **outcry,** *n.* loud protest from a number of people. **outdated,** *adj.* old-fashioned. **outdo,** *v.* (**outdid; outdone**) to do better than. **outdoor,** *adj.* in the open air. **outdoors,** *adv. & n.* (in/to) the open air. **outer,** *adj.* further out; on the outside; beyond the limits; **o. space** = space beyond the earth's atmosphere. **outermost,** *adj.* furthest out.

outfall, *n.* pipe which takes sewage out to sea. **outfit,** *n.* (*a*) set of equipment needed for a particular purpose. (*b*) set of clothing. (*c*) *inf.* organization. **outfitter,** *n.* supplier of (esp. men's) clothing. **outflank,** *v.* to go by the side of (an enemy). **outflow,** *n.* quantity which flows out. **outgoing,** *adj.* (*a*) which is going out. (*b*) open/lively (personality). **outgoings,** *n. pl.* money spent. **outgrow,** *v.* (**outgrew; outgrown**) to grow too big for (clothes); to leave behind as one grows up. **outhouse,** *n.* building standing apart from a main building. **outing,** *n.* trip, usu. for pleasure. **outlandish,** *adj.* strange/different from the usual. **outlast,** *v.* to live/to last longer than. **outlaw. 1.** *n.* person who has been outlawed. **2.** *v.* to declare (s.o.) to be beyond (the protection of) the law. **outlay,** *n.* expenditure. **outlet,** *n.* (*a*) means by which sth can escape. (*b*) place where sth can be sold or distributed. **outline. 1.** *n.* line showing the outer edge(s) of sth; broad description without much detail. **2.** *v.* to make a broad description of (a plan, etc.). **outlive,** *v.* to live longer than. **outlook,** *n.* view from a building/of the world/of the future. **outlying,** *adj.* away from the centre/from the main part. **outmanœuvre,** *Am.* **outmaneuver,** *v.* to beat s.o. by acting/working more cleverly. **outmoded,** *adj.* old-fashioned. **outnumber,** *v.* to be greater in number than. **out of,** *prep.* (*a*) outside of; away from; **o. of your mind** = mad. (*b*) from; **one o. of ten.** (*c*) made from. (*d*) because of. (*e*) no longer having; **o. of print** = with no printed copies left; **o. of stock** = with no stock left. **out of date,** *adj.* (*a*) no longer in fashion (*b*) no longer valid. **out of pocket,** *adj.* having paid expenses personally. **out of the way,** *adj.* (*a*) very far from the centre. (*b*) unusual/extraordinary. **outpatient,** *n.* person who attends a hospital without staying overnight. **outpost,** *n.* small garrison of soldiers in a distant part of an occupied territory. **outpourings,** *n. pl.* flood (of complaints/of emotional speech). **output,** *n.* amount which a firm/machine/person produces; information produced by a computer; **outputs** = goods or services sold, on which VAT is charged. **outrank,** *v.* to be of a higher rank than (s.o.). **outreach,** *n.* services of a local authority provided outside the offices of the authority. **outrider** ['autraɪdə] *n.* guard on a motorcycle or horse, riding beside a car/carriage in a procession. **outrigger,** *n.* long piece with a float at the end, which is attached to the side of a boat to make it more stable. **outright** ['autraɪt] *adv. & adj.* (*a*) complete(ly); all at once. (*b*) straight out/without pretending. **outset** ['autset] *n.* beginning. **outshine** [aut'ʃaɪn] *v.* (**outshone**) to do much better than (s.o.). **outside** [aut'saɪd] **1.** *n.* (*a*) outer surface (of sth); what is beyond the outer surface/ edge of sth. (*b*) **at the o.** = at the most. **2.** *adj.* (*a*) on the outer surface. (*b*) the most (possible). (*c*) from the outside/from another group, etc. **3.** *adv. & prep.* beyond the outer surface/edge of (sth). **outsider,** *n.* (*a*) person who does not belong to a group, etc. (*b*) horse which is not expected to win. **outsize** ['autsaɪz] *n. & adj.* (of) size which is larger than the normal or usual range. **outskirts** ['autskɜːts] *n. pl.* outer edges of a town, etc. **outsmart** [aut'smaːt] *v.* to trick (s.o.) by being cleverer. **outspoken** [aut'spəʊkən] *adj.* speaking (too) frankly. **outstanding** [aut'stændɪŋ] *adj.* (*a*) excellent; of unusual quality; of very high standard. (*b*) not yet fulfilled/incomplete. **outstandingly,** *adv.* to an outstanding degree. **outstay** [aut'steɪ] *v.* to stay longer than. **outstretched,** *adj.* (arm, etc.) which is stretched out. **outstrip,** *v.* (**outstripped**) to run past (s.o.); to do better than (s.o.). **out to,** *adj.* trying to/aiming for. **out tray,** *n.* basket for correspondence which is to be sent out. **outvote** [aut'vəʊt] *v.* to defeat by having more votes than. **outward** ['autwəd] *adj. & adv.* (*a*) towards the outside; away from the centre or starting point. (*b*) on the outside. **outwardly,** *adv.* (appearing) on the outside. **outwards,** *adv.* towards the outside. **outweigh** [aut'weɪ] *v.* to be more important than (sth). **outwit**

[aut'wɪt] *v.* (**outwitted**) to trick (s.o.) by being cleverer. **outwork,** *n.* work which a company pays s.o. to do at home. **outworker,** *n.* person who does outwork. **outworn,** *adj.* (*formal*) worn out (cliché, etc.). **outrage** ['autreɪdʒ] **1.** *n.* offence; vigorous attack (esp. against moral standards). **2.** *v.* to shock/to be a cause of moral indignation. **outrageous** [aut'reɪdʒəs] *adj.* causing (moral) indignation/shock. **outrageously,** *adv.* in an outrageous way.

outré ['uːtreɪ] *adj.* strange/weird.
ouzel ['uːzl] *n.* type of diving bird.
ova ['əʊvə] *n. pl. see* **ovum.**
oval ['əʊvl] *n. & adj.* (of) a long rounded shape; egg-shaped(d).
ovary ['əʊvərɪ] *n.* one of the two organs of a female mammal in which eggs are produced. **ovarian** [əʊ'veərɪən] *adj.* referring to ovaries.
ovation [ə'veɪʃn] *n.* great applause.
oven ['ʌvn] *n.* enclosed box which can be heated for cooking/for baking pottery, etc. **ovenware,** *n.* (*no pl.*) dishes which can be put in a hot oven.
over ['əʊvə] **1.** *prep.* (*a*) on the top (surface) of. (*b*) higher than. (*c*) across/ to the other side of. (*d*) from the top of. (*e*) on the other/on the far side of. (*f*) everywhere in. (*g*) during. (*h*) more than. (*i*) better than. (*j*) about. **2.** *adv.* (*a*) in all parts of (sth). (*b*) repeatedly. (*c*) above the top of (sth). (*d*) downwards from a previous vertical position. (*e*) into another position; **please turn o.** = turn the page. (*f*) to the other side of. (*g*) more/ higher in number. (*h*) in excess/left behind. (*i*) past/finished. (*j*) *prefix meaning* too (much); **overexcited; overtired.** **3.** *n.* one of the sections of a cricket match, during which one bowler bowls six times. **overall. 1.** *adj.* covering; taking in all aspects. **2.** *n.* (*a*) light coat worn by women at work. (*b*) **overalls** = man's one-piece suit worn to protect the other clothes. **overarm,** *adv.* (*in cricket*) (to bowl) with the arm higher than the shoulder. **overawe** [əʊvə'ɔː] *v.* to frighten. **overbalance,** *v.* to (cause to) lose balance. **overbearing,** *adj.* trying to dominate others. **overblown,**

adj. (rose) which has almost finished flowering; (claim) which is excessive. **overboard,** *adv.* into the water from the edge of a ship, etc.; *inf.* **to go o. for** = to be enthusiastic about. **overbook,** *v.* to book more places than there are rooms/seats. **overcast,** *adj.* (*of sky*) heavy/dull/cloudy. **overcharge,** *v.* to charge too much for sth. **overcoat,** *n.* (full-length) coat for outdoor wear. **overcome,** *v.* (overcame; has overcome) to gain victory over (an enemy/ a problem/an emotion). **overcrowded,** *adj.* containing too many people/ animals, etc. **overdo,** *v.* (overdid; overdone) (*a*) to do too much; to exaggerate. (*b*) to cook too much. **overdose,** *n.* too large a dose (of a drug). **overdraft,** *n.* amount by which a bank account is overdrawn; amount which the bank allows you to borrow. **overdraw,** *v.* (overdrew; overdrawn) to take out money (from a bank account) when there is no money there. **overdrive,** *n.* mechanism in a car which gives an extra gear above the top gear. **overdue,** *adj.* (debt) which has not been paid at the correct time; (book) which should have been returned to the library; (visit) which should have been made; (plane, etc.) which is late. **overeat,** *v.* (overate; overeaten) to eat too much. **overeating,** *n.* eating too much. **overestimate,** *v.* to estimate too much; to think (sth) is larger than it is. **overexposed,** *adj.* (film) which has been exposed too much. **overfed,** *adj.* given too much to eat. **overfishing,** *n.* catching more fish than is allowed. **overflow. 1.** *v.* (*a*) to flow over the top. (*b*) to occupy greater space. **2.** *n.* (*a*) liquid which has overflowed. (*b*) pipe to catch overflowing liquid. (*c*) amount or number which will not fit a given space. **overgrown,** *adj.* covered (**with** plants, etc.). **overhanging,** *adj.* which juts out over. **overhaul. 1.** [əʊvə'hɔːl] *v.* (*a*) to examine carefully, repairing where necessary. (*b*) to overtake (another ship). **2.** *n.* ['əʊvəhɔːl] (act of) overhauling. **overhead. 1.** *adv.* above. **2.** *adj.* (*a*) above; **o. projector** = projector which projects a picture from

a flat surface onto a screen. (*b*) **o. expenses** = general expenses incurred by a business as a whole, such as salaries/heating/rent, etc. **3.** *n. Am.* overhead expenses. **overheads,** *n. pl.* overhead expenses. **overhear** [əʊvə-'hiə] *v.* (overheard [əʊvə'hɜːd]) to hear accidentally (what you are not meant to hear). **overheat,** *v.* to heat too much. **overjoyed,** *adj.* very happy. **overkill,** *n.* excess of weapons/excessive strength for what is required. **overland,** *adv.* & *adj.* by land. **overlap. 1.** *v.* (overlapped) to cover a section of (sth). **2.** *n.* amount by which sth overlaps. **overleaf,** *adv.* on the other side of a page. **overload,** *v.* to put too heavy a load on (sth). **overlook,** *v.* (*a*) not to notice. (*b*) to pretend not to notice; to pay no attention to. (*c*) to look out on to. **overlord,** *n.* person in supreme command. **overly,** *adv.* too much. **overmanning,** *n.* having more workers than are needed for the job. **overmuch,** *adv.* too much. **overnight. 1.** *adv.* until morning. **2.** *adj.* for the night. **overpass,** *n.* road which crosses over the top of another road. **overpay,** *v.* (overpaid) to pay (s.o.) too much. **overpayment,** *n.* paying too much. **overplay,** *v.* **to o. your hand** = to attempt (to gain) too much in negotiations. **overpower,** *v.* to gain control of (s.o.) by force. **overpowering,** *adv.* very strong. **overproduction,** *n.* excess production. **overrate,** *v.* to estimate/to value (sth) higher than it is. **overreach,** *v.* **to o. yourself** = to go too far (and fail in what you are trying to do). **overreact,** *v.* to react very violently. **override,** *v.* (overrode; overridden) (*a*) to pay no attention to (an order, etc.). (*b*) to be more important than other things. **overrider,** *n.* rubber pad fixed to the bumper of a car. **overripe,** *adj.* too ripe. **overrule,** *v.* to rule/to order against. **overrun,** *v.* (overran; overrun) (*a*) to go into/to attack all parts of. (*b*) to continue beyond (a time limit). **overseas,** *adv.* & *adj.* across the sea. **oversee,** *v.* (oversaw; overseen) to superintend/supervise. **overseer,** *n.* person who supervises other people at work. **overshadow,** *v.* to hide/

to make less conspicuous by greater brilliance. **overshoes,** *n. pl.* rubber/plastic shoes worn over ordinary shoes to protect them. **overshoot,** *v.* (overshot) to go beyond a natural stopping place. **oversight,** *n.* not doing sth because of forgetfulness/not noticing. **oversleep,** *v.* (overslept; has overslept) to sleep longer than you meant to. **overspend,** *n.* (overspent) to spend more than you should. **overspill,** *n.* excess population which is moved from one area to another. **overstate,** *v.* to state too strongly/with too much detail. **overstatement,** *n.* act of overstating; what is overstated. **overstay,** *v.* to o. your welcome = to stay for such a long time that you are no longer welcome. **oversteer,** *v.* (of vehicle) to turn more sharply than the driver intends. **overstep,** *v.* (overstepped) to go further than you ought to. **overstuffed,** *adj.* well padded (sofa). **oversubscribed,** *adj.* (shares) which more people applied for than there were available. **overtake,** *v.* (overtook; overtaken) to reach and go past (s.o. ahead of you); to pass (another car) which is going more slowly than you. **overtax,** *v.* to demand too much tax from; **to o. one's strength** = to do more than one is physically capable of. **over-the-counter market,** *n.* stock market which deals in shares not listed on a main Stock Exchange. **overthrow. 1.** *n.* removal (of a government/dictator) from power. **2.** *v.* (overthrew; overthrown) to defeat. **overtime. 1.** *n.* (*a*) time worked beyond normal working hours. (*b*) money paid for working beyond normal hours. **2.** *adv.* beyond normal hours. **overtones,** *n. pl.* suggestion of sth which is different from the general content. **overturn** [əʊvə'tɜːn] *v.* to (cause to) fall over/to turn upside down. **overview,** *n.* general view (of a subject). **overweening** [əʊvə'wiːnɪŋ] *adj.* excessive/arrogant (pride). **overweight** [əʊvə'weɪt] *adj.* too heavy. **overwhelm** [əʊvə'welm] *v.* (*a*) to conquer (completely). (*b*) **overwhelmed with work** = having more work than you can do. **overwhelming,** *adj.* enormous; greater than all others.

overwork [əʊvə'wɜːk] **1.** *n.* too much work. **2.** *v.* to (cause to) work too hard. **overwrought** [əʊvə'rɔːt] *adj.* very agitated/under a lot of stress.

overt [əʊ'vɜːt] *adj.* open/not hidden.

overture ['əʊvətʃə] *n.* (*a*) (short) piece of music played at the beginning of an opera/concert, etc. (*b*) **to make overtures to s.o.** = to try to begin a conversation/negotiations with s.o.

oviduct ['əʊvɪdʌkt] *n.* tube through which ova are passed to the womb.

oviparous [ɒ'vɪpərəs] *adj.* which lays eggs.

ovoid ['əʊvɔɪd] *adj.* shaped like an egg.

ovum ['əʊvəm] *n.* (*pl.* ova ['əʊvə]) female egg which can develop inside the mother's body when fertilized. **ovulate** ['ɒvjʊleɪt] *v.* to produce female eggs. **ovulation,** *n.* producing female eggs. **ovule,** *n.* part of a plant where the seeds develop.

ow [aʊ] *inter. showing pain.*

owe [əʊ] *v.* (*a*) to be obliged; to be due to pay (s.o.). (*b*) **to o. sth to** = to have sth because of (s.o./sth). **owing to,** *prep.* because of.

owl [aʊl] *n.* bird of prey which is mainly active at night. **owlish,** *adj.* like an owl.

own [əʊn] **1.** *v.* (*a*) to have/to possess. (*b*) to recognize as belonging to you. (*c*) to admit; to say that sth is true. (*d*) *inf.* **to o. up to sth** = to admit/to say that you have done sth wrong. **2.** *adj.* belonging to yourself (alone). **3.** *n.* (*a*) **my o./his o.** = mine/his; **of your o.** = belonging to you; **to come into your o.** = to have the success which you deserve; *inf.* **to get your o. back** = have your revenge; **to hold your o.** = to remain firm against some threat. (*b*) **on your o.** = alone/by yourself. **owner,** *n.* person who owns. **ownership,** *n.* state of owning.

ox [ɒks] *n.* (*pl.* oxen) (*a*) large animal of the cow family. (*b*) castrated bull. **oxbow,** *n.* curved lake formed in a bend of a river where the current no longer runs. **oxeye,** *n.* daisy with large flowers. **oxtail,** *n.* tail of the ox used as food.

oxalis [ɒk'sælɪs] *n.* type of flower, which produces a poisonous substance.

oxide ['ɒksaɪd] *n.* chemical compound of oxygen. **oxidation, oxodization** [ɒksɪ-

'deɪʃn, ɒksɪdaɪ'zeɪʃn] *n.* act of oxidizing.
oxidize ['ɒksɪdaɪz] *v.* to (cause to) combine with oxygen.
oxyacetylene [ɒksɪə'setɪliːn] *n. & adj.* (referring to a) mixture of oxygen and acetylene.
oxygen ['ɒksɪdʒən] *n.* (*element:* O) gas which forms part of the earth's atmosphere and is essential for plant and animal life.
oyez ['ɒ'jez] *int.* hear this.
oyster ['ɔɪstə] *n.* type of double-shelled shellfish highly valued as food; **o. bed** = part of the sea floor where oysters are found. **oystercatcher,** *n.* common black and white bird which lives on the seashore.
oz *abbrev. for* ounce.
ozone ['ɒvzəʊn] *n.* (*a*) harmful form of oxygen; **o. hole** = gap which forms in the ozone layer, allowing harmful radiation from the sun to reach the earth; **o. layer** = layer of ozone in the stratosphere, formed by the action of sunlight on oxygen, which acts as protection against harmful rays from the sun. (*b*) *inf.* refreshing sea air.

Pp

P *symbol for* phosphorus.
pa [pɑː] *n. inf. child's name for* father.
p.a. *abbrev. for* per annum.
pace [peɪs] **1.** *n.* (*a*) stride/step; distance covered by one step. (*b*) speed; **to keep p. with** = keep up with; (*of a runner*) **to set the p.** = to decide how fast a race should be run. **2.** *v.* (*a*) to walk; to measure by walking. (*b*) to set the pace for (a runner, etc.). **pacemaker,** *n.* (*a*) runner who sets the pace in a race; person who runs alongside a runner to encourage him to run faster. (*b*) electric device which makes heartbeats regular.
pachyderm ['pækɪdɜːm] *n.* animal with a thick skin (such as an elephant).
pacify ['pæsɪfaɪ] *v.* to calm. **pacific** [pə'sɪfɪk] *adj.* peaceful/calm. **pacifically,** *adv.* in a pacific way. **pacification** [pæsɪfɪ'keɪʃn] *n.* calming (of people in revolt). **pacifier** ['pæsɪfaɪə] *n. Am.* dummy (for babies). **pacifism,** *n.* opposition to war. **pacifist,** *n.* person who believes in pacifism.

pack [pæk] **1.** *n.* (*a*) bundle of things. (*b*) rucksack/bag carried on the back. (*c*) group of animals/people; **the p.** = the forwards in a rugby team. (*d*) articles put in a box for selling. (*e*) **face p.** = cream which is spread on your face and left on for a time to clean the skin. (*f*) **ice p.** = bag of ice placed on the forehead to cure a headache, etc. **2.** *v.* (*a*) to put (things) in order in a case/box. (*b*) to squeeze (many things) into a small area. **package. 1.** *n.* (*a*) bundle of things/parcel. (*b*) **p. deal** = deal where several items are agreed at the same time; **p. tour** = tour which is organized and paid for in advance. **2.** *v.* to wrap/to present (goods) in an attractive way. **packaging,** *n.* wrapping of goods in an attractive way. **packer,** *n.* person who packs goods. **packet,** *n.* (*a*) small parcel; small box. (*b*) *inf.* large amount of money. **pack ice,** *n.* mass of ice covering the sea. **packing,** *n.* (*a*) putting things into containers; **p. case** = special wooden box for packing goods (esp. for transport). (*b*) material used to protect goods which are being packed. (*c*) **to send s.o. p.** = to send s.o. away. **pack off,** *v.* to send (s.o.) away. **pack up,** *v.* to put things away (before closing a shop/before leaving a place).
pact [pækt] *n.* agreement/treaty.
pad [pæd] **1.** *n.* (*a*) soft part under the feet of some animals; soft protective cushion. (*b*) (*in cricket*) protective guards for the batsman's leg. (*c*) set of sheets of paper lightly attached. (*d*) **launching p.** = area from which a rocket is launched. (*e*) *Sl.* room/flat. **2.** *v.* (**padded**) (*a*) to soften (sth hard) by using soft material; to walk about softly; **to p. out** = to make (a speech/an article) longer by inserting irrelevant material. **padding,** *n.* (*a*) words added to pad out a speech or article. (*b*) soft material used to make cushions, etc.
paddle ['pædl] **1.** *n.* (*a*) short oar used to propel a canoe. (*b*) round bat used in table tennis. (*c*) walk in shallow water. (*d*) device with a knob, used for moving a cursor on a computer screen. **2.** *v.* (*a*) to make (a boat) move forward using a paddle. (*b*) to walk about in very shallow water. **paddle**

steamer, *n.* boat driven by large wheels on either side. **paddle wheel,** *n.* wheel on a paddle steamer. **paddling pool,** *n.* small shallow pool for little children.

paddock ['pædək] *n.* small field for horses.

paddy ['pædɪ] *n.* (*a*) *inf.* fit of bad temper. (*b*) (*also* **paddy field**) field where rice is grown.

padlock ['pædlɒk] **1.** *n.* small portable lock with a hook which can be unlocked and twisted to pass through a ring to lock a gate/a box, etc. **2.** *v.* to lock with a padlock.

padre ['pɑːdrɪ] *n.* (Army) chaplain.

paean ['piːən] *n.* (*formal*) great song praising s.o.

paediatrician [piːdɪə'trɪʃn] *n.* doctor who specializes in paediatrics. **paediatric** [piːdɪ'ætrɪk] *adj.* referring to the medical care of children. **paediatrics,** *n.* science of treatment of children's diseases.

pagan ['peɪgn] *adj. & n.* (person) who does not believe in one of the established religions; (person) who is not a Christian.

page [peɪdʒ] **1.** *n.* (*a*) one of the sides of a sheet of paper in a book or magazine. (*b*) messenger boy in a hotel. (*c*) small boy who accompanies the bride at a wedding. **2.** *v.* to call (s.o.) over a loudspeaker in a hotel, etc. **pageboy,** *n.* (*a*) (*old*) boy attendant on a medieval lord. (*b*) **p. hairstyle** = woman's hair cut quite short and straight.

pageant ['pædʒənt] *n.* grand display of people in costume. **pageantry,** *n.* grand ceremonies where people wear showy costumes.

paginate ['pædʒɪneɪt] *v.* to number the pages in a book. **pagination** [pædʒɪ'neɪʃn] *n.* act of paginating.

pagoda [pə'gəʊdə] *n.* tall tower made of several storeys, found in the Far East.

paid [peɪd] *v. see* **pay.**

pail [peɪl] *n.* bucket.

pain [peɪn] **1.** *n.* (*a*) sensation of being hurt. (*b*) **to take pains over sth/to do sth** = to take care. (*c*) **on p. of death** = at the risk of being sentenced to death. **2.** *v.* to hurt. **pained,** *adj.* sad/sorrowful (expression). **painful,** *adj.* which hurts. **painfully,** *adv.* in a pain-

ful way. **painkiller,** *n.* painkilling drug. **painkilling,** *adj.* (drug) which stops part of your body hurting. **painless,** *adj.* which does not hurt. **painlessly,** *adv.* in a painless way. **painstaking,** *adj.* careful/well-done (work).

paint [peɪnt] **1.** *n.* liquid in various colours used to colour. **2.** *v.* (*a*) to cover with colour. (*b*) to make a picture of (s.o./sth). **painter,** *n.* (*a*) person who paints pictures. (*b*) person who paints houses/cars, etc. (*c*) rope for tying up a boat. **painting,** *n.* (*a*) making pictures. (*b*) painted picture. **paintwork,** *n.* (*no pl.*) painted surfaces (doors/windows, etc.).

pair [peə] **1.** *n.* (*a*) two things taken together; two people. (*b*) two things joined together to make one. (*c*) agreement between two MPs from opposite parties, by which both can be absent from the House of Commons at the same time. **2.** *v.* (*a*) to join together in twos. (*b*) to mate.

paisley ['peɪzlɪ] *n.* pattern on textiles, of curved shapes.

pajamas [pə'dʒɑːməz] *n. pl. Am.* pyjamas.

Pakistani [pækɪ'stɑːnɪ] **1.** *adj.* referring to Pakistan. **2.** *n.* person from Pakistan.

pal [pæl] *n. inf.* friend. **pally,** *adj. inf.* friendly.

palace ['pæləs] *n.* large building where a king/queen/president, etc., lives.

palanquin ['pælənkwɪn] *n.* seat with a roof, carried by bearers.

palate ['pælət] *n.* top part of the inside of the mouth. **palatable,** *adj.* nice to eat/tasting good.

palatial [pə'leɪʃl] *adj.* magnificent/like a palace.

palaver [pə'lɑːvə] *n. inf.* fuss/bother.

pale [peɪl] **1.** *adj.* (**-er, -est**) light-coloured. **2.** *n.* **beyond the p.** = doing things which are not acceptable in society. **3.** *v.* (*a*) to lose colour; to become light. (*b*) to become less important. **paleness,** *n.* light colour.

paleography [pælɪ'ɒgrəfɪ] *n.* study of ancient writing.

paleolithic [pælɪəʊ'lɪθɪk] *adj.* referring to the early part of the Stone Age. **paleontology** [pælɪɒn'tɒlədʒɪ] *n.* study of fossils.

Palestinian [pælɪ'stɪnɪən] *adj. & n.* (person) from Palestine.

palette ['pælət] *n.* (*a*) flat board on which an artist mixes his colours; **p. knife** = long flat knife with a rounded end. (*b*) range of colours available, esp. on a computer graphics program.

palimony ['pælɪmənɪ] *n.* alimony paid to a friend when parting after years of life together.

palindrome ['pælɪndrəʊm] *n.* word or phrase which is spelt the same backwards and forwards.

paling(s) ['peɪlɪŋ(z)], **palisade** [pælɪ'seɪd] *n.* fence made of pointed pieces of wood.

pall [pɔːl] **1.** *n.* (*a*) (*formal*) thick layer (of smoke). (*b*) cloth put over a coffin. **2.** *v.* to become less interesting. **pallbearer**, *n.* person who walks beside a coffin in a funeral procession.

pallet ['pælɪt] *n.* (*a*) flat platform on which goods can be stacked and moved from place to place. (*b*) straw-filled mattress.

palliasse ['pælɪæs] *n.* straw-filled mattress.

palliate ['pælɪeɪt] *v.* to try to reduce (a vice/pain); to cover up (a mistake). **palliative** ['pælɪətɪv] *adj. & n.* (thing) which reduces pain.

pallid ['pælɪd] *adj.* pale (face).

pallor ['pælə] *n.* paleness (of face).

palm [pɑːm] *n.* (*a*) soft inside surface of your hand. (*b*) tall tropical tree with long leaves at the top. **palmist,** *n.* person who tells the future by palmistry. **palmistry**, *n.* telling what will happen to you in the future from the lines in the palm of your hand. **palm off,** *v. inf.* (**on**) to give (sth bad) to s.o. without his knowing. **Palm Sunday,** *n.* Sunday before Easter Sunday. **palmy,** *adj.* (**-ier, -iest**) pleasant.

palpable ['pælpəbl] *adj.* which can be felt/which can be easily seen. **palpably**, *adv.* in a palpable way. **palpation** [pæl'peɪʃn] *n.* examination of part of the body by feeling it with the hand.

palpitate ['pælpɪteɪt] *v.* to beat very quickly. **palpitations** [pælpɪ'teɪʃnz] *n. pl.* rapid beating of the heart.

palsy ['pɔlzɪ] *n.* (*a*) paralysis. (*b*) trembling (of the hands, etc.). **palsied,** *adj.* with trembling limbs.

paltry ['pɔːltrɪ] *adj.* (**-ier, -iest**) insignificant.

paludism ['pæljuːdɪzm] *n.* malaria.

pampas ['pæmpəs] *n. pl.* grass-covered plains in South America; **p. grass** = type of tall ornamental grass.

pamper ['pæmpə] *v.* to spoil (a child/a dog) by giving them too much food/by treating them too well.

pamphlet ['pæmflət] *n.* small book with only a few pages, which is not bound with a hard cover. **pamphleteer** [pæmflə'tɪə] *n.* person who writes political pamplets.

pan- [pæn] *prefix meaning* over a wide area; **pan-American** = covering the whole of America.

pan [pæn] **1.** *n.* (*a*) metal cooking container with a handle. (*b*) metal dish; one of the dishes on a pair of scales. (*c*) bowl of a lavatory. **2.** (**panned**) (*a*) to move a camera sideways to take in a wider view. (*b*) *inf.* to criticize. (*c*) **to p. for gold** = to sift mud in a stream, hoping to find gold in it. **pancake** ['pænkeɪk] *n.* thin soft flat cake made of flour, milk, eggs, etc. **pan out,** *v. inf.* to turn out/to succeed.

panacea [pænə'siːə] *n.* thing which cures everything/which solves every problem.

panache [pə'næʃ] *n.* showy way of doing things.

panama [pænə'mɑː] *n.* hat made of fine straw.

panatella [pænə'telə] *n.* long thin cigar.

panchromatic [pænkrə'mætɪk] *adj.* (film) which is sensitive to all colours.

pancreas ['pæŋkrɪəs] *n.* (*pl.* **-es**) gland which produces insulin, and also a liquid which helps digest food.

panda ['pændə] *n.* (**giant**) **p.** = large black and white Chinese animal; **p. car** = police car which patrols the streets.

pandemic [pæn'demɪk] *adj.* (disease) which occurs over the whole world/over a large area.

pandemonium [pændɪ'məʊnɪəm] *n.* great uproar and confusion.

pander ['pændə] *v.* to give in (**to** low tastes).

pane [peɪn] *n.* sheet of glass (in a window, etc.).

panegyric [pænɪ'dʒɪrɪk] *n.* (*formal*) speech in praise of s.o.

panel ['pænl] **1.** *n.* (*a*) flat surface which is higher/lower/thicker, etc., than the rest of the surface. (*b*) section of different-coloured material. (*c*) group of people who answer questions/who judge a competition; group of doctors in the same practice. **2.** *v.* (**panelled**) to cover with sheets of wood. **panel beater,** *n.* person who repairs car bodies. **panel game,** *n.* game (on radio/TV) where a group of people answer questions/guess answers, etc. **panelling,** *n.* sheets of wood used to cover walls, etc. **panellist,** *n.* member of a panel answering questions/judging a competition.

pang [pæŋ] *n.* sudden sharp pain.

panic ['pænɪk] **1.** *n.* terror/fright. **2.** *v.* (**panicked**) to become frightened. **panic-stricken,** *adj.* wild with fright. **panicky,** *adj.* likely to panic.

panicle ['pænɪkl] *n.* cluster of flowers which hangs down.

pannier ['pænɪə] *n.* one of a pair of bags carried on the side of an animal or a bicycle.

panoply ['pænəplɪ] *n.* fine show/grand display of costume, etc.

panorama [pænə'rɑːmə] *n.* wide expanse of landscape. **panoramic** [pænə-'ræmɪk] *adj.* wide.

pansy ['pænzɪ] *n.* (*a*) small multicoloured garden flower. (*b*) *inf.* effeminate man.

pant [pænt] *v.* to breathe fast.

pantechnicon [pæn'teknɪkən] *n.* large lorry for moving furniture.

pantheism ['pænθɪɪzəm] *n.* belief that God and the universe are one and the same; worship of many gods.

panther ['pænθə] *n.* large black leopard.

panties ['pæntɪz] *n. inf.* women's brief undergarment worn on the lower part of the body.

pantile ['pæntaɪl] *n.* curved tile for a roof.

pantograph ['pæntəgrɑːf] *n.* metal frame on the roof of an electric locomotive which rises to touch an overhead electric wire to pick up electricity.

pantomime ['pæntəmaɪm] *n.* Christmas theatrical entertainment on a traditional fairy-tale subject.

pantry ['pæntrɪ] *n.* cool cupboard or room for keeping food in.

pants [pænts] *n. pl.* (*a*) *inf.* brief undergarment worn on the lower part of the body. (*b*) *inf.* trousers.

panty hose ['pæntɪ'həʊz] *n. pl.* women's tights.

pap [pæp] *n.* soft food for invalids.

papa [pə'pɑː] *n. child's name for* father.

papacy ['peɪpəsɪ] *n.* position of pope. **papal,** *adj.* referring to the pope.

papaw ['pɔːpɔː], **papaya** [pə'pæjə] *n.* yellow fruit from a tropical tree.

paper ['peɪpə] **1.** *n.* (*a*) thin material made from rags or wood pulp, used for printing/writing, etc. (*b*) sheet of paper. (*c*) newspaper. (*d*) scientific/ learned article. **2.** *v.* to cover (the walls of a room) with paper. **paperback,** *n.* book with a paper cover. **paper boy,** *n.* boy who delivers ewspapers to houses. **paperchase,** *n.* game where people follow a trail of bits of paper. **paperclip,** *n.* piece of bent wire for holding pieces of paper together. **paperknife,** *n.* (*pl.* **-knives**) long knife for cutting paper (esp. for opening envelopes). **paper round,** *n.* group of streets/houses where one paper boy delivers newspapers. **paperweight,** *n.* heavy block put on papers to prevent them from being blown away. **paperwork,** *n.* office work. **papery,** *adj.* thin like paper.

papier mâché [pæpɪeɪ'mæʃeɪ] *n.* mixture of wet paper, used to make models, etc.

papist ['peɪpɪst] *n.* (*rude*) Roman Catholic.

papoose [pə'puːs] *n.* Red Indian baby.

paprika ['pæprɪkə] *n.* red spice made from powdered sweet peppers.

papyrus [pə'paɪrəs] *n.* reed growing in the Middle East, used by the ancient Egyptians to make a type of paper.

par [pɑː] *n.* (*a*) equal level; **to be on a p. with** = to be equal to. (*b*) **to buy shares at p.** = at their face value. (*c*) (*in golf*) number of strokes usu. needed to hit the ball into the hole; **below p.** = not very well.

parable ['pærəbl] *n.* usu. religious story with a moral.

parabola [pə'ræbələ] *n.* curve like the path of an object which is thrown

into the air and comes down again.
parabolic [pærə'bɒlɪk] *adj.* referring to a parabola.

paracetamol [pærə'setəmɒl] *n.* drug used to relieve headaches/colds, etc.

parachute ['pærəʃu:t] **1.** *n.* large piece of thin material shaped like an umbrella, with cords and a harness attached, which allows you to float down safely from an aircraft. **2.** *v.* to jump from an aircraft with a parachute. **parachutist,** *n.* person who jumps regularly with a parachute.

parade [pə'reɪd] **1.** *n.* (*a*) military display/march past; **p. ground** = square area on a military camp where parades are held. (*b*) series of bands/decorated cars, etc., passing in a street; **fashion p.** = display of new clothes by models. (*c*) wide street (where people like to walk up and down). **2.** *v.* to march past in ordered lines.

paradigm ['pærədaɪm] *n.* example to be copied.

paradise ['pærədaɪs] *n.* ideal place where good people are supposed to live after death; any beautiful place.

paradox ['pærədɒks] *n.* thing which appears to contradict itself but may really be true. **paradoxical** [pærə'dɒksɪkl] *adj.* contradictory. **paradoxically,** *adv.* in a paradoxical way.

paraffin ['pærəfɪn] *n.* thin oil for lamps/heaters, etc.; **liquid p.** = refined oil taken as a medicine; **p. wax** = solid white substance used for making candles.

paragon ['pærəgən] *n.* perfect model (of virtue, etc.).

paragraph ['pærəgrɑ:f] *n.* section of several lines of prose, usu. starting with a short blank space at the beginning of a new line.

parakeet [pærə'ki:t] *n.* kind of small tropical parrot.

parallax ['pærəlæks] *n.* difference in the position of an object when it is seen from different points.

parallel ['pærəlel] **1.** *adj.* (*a*) (**to/with**) (lines) which are side by side and remain the same distance apart without ever touching. (*b*) similar. **2.** *n.* (*a*) geometrical line which runs parallel to another. (*b*) line running round the globe fom east to west parallel to the equator. (*c*) closely similar situation; thing which can be compared. **3.** *v.* to be similar to. **parallelogram** [pærə'leləgræm] *n.* four-sided figure where each side is parallel to the one opposite.

paralyse, *Am.* **paralyze** ['pærəlaɪz] *v.* to make unable to move. **paralysis** [pə'ræləsɪs] *n.* being unable to move. **paralytic** [pærə'lɪtɪk] **1.** *adj.* (*a*) unable to move. (*b*) *Sl.* very drunk. **2.** *n.* paralysed person.

paramedical [pærə'medɪkl] *adj.* helping in medical treatment. **paramedic,** *n. inf.* person who is not a doctor, but who helps give medical treatment.

parameter [pə'ræmɪtə] *n.* figure which shows the upper or lower level of some expected result; data which defines the limits of sth.

paramilitary [pærə'mɪlɪtrɪ] *adj.* organized in the same way as the army, but not a part of it.

paramount ['pærəmaunt] *adj.* extreme/supreme.

paramour ['pærəmu:ə] *n.* (*old*) lover; mistress.

paranoia [pærə'nɔɪə] *n.* type of mental disease where you feel extremely important or think everyone is against you. **paranoiac,** *adj. & n.* (person) who suffers from paranoia. **paranoid,** *adj. & n.* (person) suffering from paranoia.

parapet ['pærəpet] *n.* small wall at the edge of a ledge/bridge, etc.

paraphernalia [pærəfə'neɪlɪə] *n.* (*no pl.*) mass of bits and pieces; equipment.

paraphrase ['pærəfreɪz] **1.** *n.* writing which repeats sth in different words. **2.** *v.* to repeat (what s.o. has said or written) using different words.

paraplegia [pærə'pli:dʒə] *n.* paralysis of the legs and lower part of the body. **paraplegic,** *adj. & n.* (person) who suffers from paraplegia.

parapsychology [pærəsaɪ'kɒlədʒɪ] *n.* study of unexplained psychological phenomena.

paraquat ['pærəkwæt] *n.* dangerous weedkiller.

parasite ['pærəsaɪt] *n.* animal/plant which lives on other animals or plants; person who does no useful work.

parasitic [pærə'sɪtɪk] *adj.* (insect, etc.) which lives off others.

parasol ['pærəsɒl] *n.* light umbrella to keep off the rays of the sun.

parastatal [pærə'steɪtl] *n.* government-run organization in Africa.

paratrooper ['pærətru:pə] *n.* soldier who is a parachutist. **paratroops,** *n. pl.* paratroopers.

paratyphoid [pærə'taɪfɔɪd] *n.* fever which is similar to typhoid, but less dangerous.

parboil ['pɑ:bɔɪl] *v.* to half-cook (food) in boiling water.

parcel ['pɑ:sl] **1.** *n.* (*a*) package (to be sent by post, etc.). (*b*) small area of land. **2.** *v.* (**parcelled**) to wrap and tie (something) up to send. **parcel out,** *v.* to divide up between several people.

parch [pɑ:tʃ] *v.* to dry.

parchment ['pɑ:tʃmənt] *n.* (*a*) skins of animals which have been treated and which can be used for writing on. (*b*) fine quality yellowish paper.

pardon ['pɑ:dn] **1.** *n.* (*a*) forgiveness. (*b*) freeing s.o. from prison or from punishment. **2.** *v.* (*a*) to forgive. (*b*) to allow (s.o.) to leave prison; not to punish (s.o.). **pardonable,** *adj.* which can be excused. **pardonably,** *adv.* in a way which can be excused.

pare ['peə] *v.* to cut the skin/peel (off a fruit/vegetable, etc.); to cut back (expenses). **parings,** *n. pl.* pieces of skin cut off a fruit/vegetable, etc.

parent ['peərənt] *n.* father or mother; (organization) which rules another. **parentage,** *n.* origin. **parental** [pə'rentl] *adj.* referring to parents. **parenthood,** *n.* being a parent.

parenthesis [pə'renθəsɪs] *n.* (*pl.* **-ses** [-si:z]) (*a*) phrase in the middle of a sentence which is placed in brackets or between dashes. (*b*) **parentheses** = (round) brackets. **parenthetic(al)** [pærən'θetɪk(l)] *adj.* which is not part of a main sentence.

pargetting ['pɑ:dʒetɪŋ] *n.* decorated plaster on the outside of a house.

pariah [pə'raɪə] *n.* person who is thrown out by civilized society.

parietal [pə'raɪətl] *adj.* referring to the walls of cavities in the body.

pari passu [pæri 'pæsu:] *adv.* equally/with equal shares.

parish ['pærɪʃ] *n.* (*pl.* **-es**) (*a*) administrative area round a church and under the care of a clergyman. (*b*) administrative district in a county. **parishioner** [pə'rɪʃənə] *n.* person who lives in or belongs to a parish.

parity ['pærɪti] *n.* equality.

park [pɑ:k] **1.** *n.* (*a*) open public place usu. with grass and trees; **business p.** = area with buildings specially built for businesses; **national p.** = large area of countryside kept in a natural state. (*b*) **car p.** = place where cars can be left temporarily. **2.** *v.* to leave (one's car) in a particular place; **no parking** = don't leave your car here; **parking meter** = device into which you put money to pay for parking; *Am.* **parking lot** = car park.

parka ['pɑ:kə] *n.* warm jacket with a hood.

parkin ['pɑ:kɪn] *n.* hard ginger cake.

Parkinson's disease ['pɑ:kɪnsənzdɪ-'zi:z] *n.* progressive disease, which affects the parts of the brain which control movement.

parky ['pɑ:kɪ] *adj. inf.* chilly (weather).

parlance ['pɑ:ləns] *n.* (*formal*) way of speaking.

parley ['pɑ:lɪ] **1.** *n.* discussion between enemies with a view to agreeing peace terms. **2.** *v.* to discuss peace terms with an enemy.

parliament ['pɑ:ləmənt] *n.* group of elected representatives who vote the laws of a country; **Act of P.** = decision which has been passed by parliament and which becomes law. **parliamentarian** [pɑ:ləmən'teərɪən] *n.* (experienced and knowledgeable) member of a parliament. **parliamentary** [pɑ:lə'mentəri] *adj.* referring to parliament.

parlour, *Am.* **parlor** ['pɑ:lə] *n.* (*a*) sitting room. (*b*) **beauty p.** = place where women can have their hair done and their faces made up.

parlous ['pɑ:ləs] *adj.* bad/dangerous (state).

parochial [pə'rəʊkɪəl] *adj.* (*a*) referring to a parish. (*b*) restricted (view); narrow-minded (person).

parody ['pærədɪ] **1.** *n.* imitation in order to make fun of s.o./sth. **2.** *v.* to imitate in order to make fun.

parole [pə'rəʊl] **1.** *n.* **prisoner on p.** = prisoner let out of prison before the end of his sentence on condition that he behaves well. **2.** *v.* to let (a prisoner) out of prison on condition that he behaves well.

paroxysm ['pærəksɪzəm] *n.* wild fit (of anger, etc.).

parquet ['pɑːkeɪ] *n.* flooring of small wooden blocks.

parricide ['pærɪsaɪd] *n.* murder of your own father; person who kills his father.

parrot ['pærət] *n.* colourful tropical bird with a large curved beak. **parrot-fashion**, *adv.* (repeating words) without really understanding them.

parry ['pærɪ] *v.* to prevent (a blow) from hitting you.

parse [pɑːz] *v.* to describe the grammatical function of each word in a sentence.

parsec ['pɑːsek] *n.* unit of measurement in astronomy (3.26 light years).

parsimony ['pɑːsɪmənɪ] *n.* (*formal*) miserliness. **parsimonious** [pɑːsɪ'məʊnɪəs] *adj.* miserly. **parsimoniously,** *adv.* in a parsimonious way.

parsley ['pɑːslɪ] *n.* green herb used in cooking.

parsnip ['pɑːsnɪp] *n.* vegetable with a long white edible root.

parson ['pɑːsn] *n.* clergyman in charge of a parish in the Church of England. **parsonage,** *n.* house of a parson.

part [pɑːt] **1.** *n.* (*a*) piece/bit; **in p.** = not completely; **spare parts** = replacement pieces (for a machine); **parts of speech** = types of words according to usage (noun/verb, etc.). (*b*) role; **take p. in** = to be active in; **to take sth in good p.** = without being offended by it. (*c*) **for my p.** = as far as I am concerned. **2.** *adv.* not entirely; **part-cooked. 3.** *v.* to separate. **parting,** *n.* (*a*) separation in the hair. (*b*) leaving. **partly,** *adv.* not entirely. **part-time,** *adj. & adv.* not for the whole working day. **part with,** *v.* to give away.

partake [pɑː'teɪk] *v.* (**partook; partaken**) (*formal*) (**of**) to eat (food).

parterre ['pɑːteə] *n.* formal arrangement of flowerbeds.

partial ['pɑːʃl] *adj.* (*a*) (**to**) biased/with a liking for. (*b*) not complete. **partiality** [pɑːʃɪ'ælɪtɪ] *n.* strong bias **for. partially,** *adv.* (*a*) in a biased way. (*b*) not completely.

participate [pɑː'tɪsɪpeɪt] *v.* to take part **in** (sth). **participant,** *n.* person who participates. **participation** [pɑːtɪsɪ'peɪʃn] *n.* taking part in sth. **participatory,** *adj.* in which you participate.

participle ['pɑːtɪsɪpl] *n.* part of a verb, used either to form compound tenses or as an adjective or noun. **participial** [pɑːtɪ'sɪpɪəl] *adj.* referring to a participle.

particle ['pɑːtɪkl] *n.* very small piece; minor part of speech.

particoloured, *Am.* **particolored** ['pɑːtɪkʌləd] *adj.* with one part in one colour, and the other part in another.

particular [pə'tɪkjʊlə] **1.** *adj.* (*a*) special; referring to one thing or person; **in p.** = as a special point. (*b*) fussy. **2.** *n.* detail. **particularity** [pɑːtɪkju'lærɪtɪ] *n.* particular quality. **particularize** [pɑːtɪkjʊlə'raɪz] *v.* to list details. **particularly,** *adv.* specially.

partisan [pɑːtɪ'zæn] *adj. & n.* (*a*) (person) who strongly supports a certain point of view. (*b*) (guerrilla) fighting against an army which has occupied his country. **partisanship,** *n.* being a partisan.

partition [pɑː'tɪʃn] **1.** *n.* (*a*) division into parts. (*b*) thin wall between two spaces, esp. splitting a large room into two. **2.** *v.* to divide (by means of a partition).

partner ['pɑːtnə] *n.* (*a*) person who has a part share in a business. (*b*) person who plays/dances with s.o. **partnership,** *n.* business association between two or more people where the risks and profits are shared.

partridge ['pɑːtrɪdʒ] *n.* large brown and grey bird, shot for sport and food.

parturition [pɑːtjʊ'rɪʃn] *n.* giving birth.

party ['pɑːtɪ] *n.* (*a*) enjoyable meeting of several people on invitation. (*b*) group of people. (*c*) person involved (esp. in legal matters); **third p.** = third person, in addition to the two principal people involved; **third-party insurance** = insurance against injuring s.o. not named in the insurance policy. (*d*) **p. line** = a shared telephone line; **p. wall** = wall which forms part of two houses. (*e*) (**political**) **p.** = official group of people with the same political ideas; **p. line** = official doctrine.

paschal ['pæskəl] *adj.* referring to passover or Easter.

pass [pɑːs] **1.** *n.* (*pl.* **-es**) (*a*) lower area between two mountain peaks. (*b*) (*in football, etc.*) moving the ball to another player. (*c*) acceptance at an examination. (*d*) bus/train season ticket; permit to go in or out. (*e*) **to make a p. at s.o.** = to try to start a sexual relationship with s.o. **2.** *v.* (*a*) to go past. (*b*) to move (sth) **to** s.o. (*c*) to get through (an examination/inspection). (*d*) vote by a majority for (a motion). (*e*) **to p. comments** = to make comments. (*f*) **to p. water** = to urinate. **passable,** *adj.* fairly good. **passably,** *adv.* fairly well. **passage** ['pæsɪdʒ] *n.* (*a*) corridor. (*b*) section of a text. (*c*) **sea p.** = journey by sea. **passageway,** *n.* corridor. **pass away,** *v.* to die. **passbook,** *n.* book which records how much money you put in or take out of your savings account in a bank or with a building society. **passenger** ['pæsɪndʒə] *n.* (*a*) traveller (in a vehicle). (*b*) weak member of a team. **passer-by** [pɑːsə'baɪ] *n.* (*pl.* **passers-by**) person who is walking past. **pass for,** *v.* to be thought to be. **passing,** *adj.* (*a*) not permanent. (*b*) which is going past. **pass key,** *n.* main key which opens several doors. **pass off,** *v.* (*a*) to take place. (*b*) **to pass oneself off as** = to pretend to be. **pass on,** *v.* to die. **pass out,** *v. inf.* to faint. **pass over,** *v.* (*a*) to go past above. (*b*) **to pass s.o. over for promotion** = to miss s.o. who should have been promoted. **passover** ['pɑːsəʊvə] *n.* Jewish festival which celebrates the freeing of the Jews from captivity in Egypt. **passport,** *n.* official document allowing you to pass from one country to another. **pass up,** *v. inf.* not to take (an opportunity). **password,** *n.* secret word which you say to go past a guard or to access a computer file.

passé ['pæseɪ] *adj.* old-fashioned.

passim ['pæsɪm] *adv.* throughout.

passion ['pæʃn] *n.* violent emotion/enthusiasm. **passionate,** *adj.* violently

emotional. **passionately,** *adv.* violently. **passionflower,** *n.* climbing plant with green and purple flowers. **passionfruit,** *n.* (*no pl.*) edible tropical fruit.

passive ['pæsɪv] *adj.* (*a*) not resisting; which allows things to happen; **p. resistance** = resisting (the police, etc.) by refusing to obey orders but not using violence. (*b*) (verb) which shows that the subject is being acted upon. **passively,** *adv.* not offering any resistance/not doing anything positive. **passiveness,** *n.* being passive. **passivity** [pə'sɪvɪtɪ] *n.* being passive.

past [pɑːst] **1.** *adj.* (time) which has gone by. **2.** *n.* time which has gone by. **3.** *prep.* after; beyond. **past master,** *n.* expert.

pasta ['pæstə] *n.* (*pl.* **pasta**). Italian food made of flour and water, such as spaghetti/macaroni, etc.

paste [peɪst] **1.** *n.* (*a*) thin glue, usu. made of flour and water. (*b*) soft substance. (*c*) imitation jewel. **2.** *v.* to glue (paper, etc.). **pasteboard,** *n.* cardboard.

pastel ['pæstl] *n.* (*a*) coloured crayon like chalk; **p. colours** = soft, light shades. (*b*) picture done with coloured crayons like chalk.

pastern ['pæstɜːn] *n.* part of a horse's foot above the hoof.

pasteurize ['pɑːstʃəraɪz] *v.* to kill the germs in (milk) by heating. **pasteurization** [pɑːstʃəraɪ'zeɪʃn] *n.* action of pasteurizing.

pastiche [pæ'stiːʃ] *n.* poem/piece of music, etc., which is a deliberate imitation of the style of another artist.

pastille ['pæstl] *n.* small sweet made of fruit-flavoured jelly.

pastime ['pɑːstaɪm] *n.* hobby/way of passing your spare time.

pastor ['pɑːstə] *n.* clergyman. **pastoral,** *adj.* (*a*) referring to shepherds. (*b*) referring to moral guidance.

pastry ['peɪstrɪ] *n.* (*a*) paste made of flour, fat and water which is used to make pies, etc. (*b*) cooked pie crust. (*c*) **pastries** = sweet cakes made of pastry filled with cream/fruit, etc.

pasture ['pɑːstʃə] **1.** *n.* grassy area where cows and sheep can graze. **2.**

v. to put (cows and sheep) to graze. **pasturage,** *n.* (*no pl.*) land used for pasturing.

pasty 1. *adj.* ['peɪstɪ] white (face). **2.** *n.* ['pæstɪ] pastry folded round a filling of meat and vegetables.

pat [pæt] **1.** *n.* (*a*) light hit; **a p. on the back** = praise. (*b*) small piece (of butter). **2.** *v.* (**patted**) to give (s.o./sth) a pat. **3.** *adj. & adv.* (answer) given promptly.

patch [pætʃ] **1.** *n.* (*pl.* **-es**) (*a*) small piece of material used for covering up holes; *inf.* **not a p. on** = not nearly as good as. (*b*) small area. **2.** *v.* to repair by attaching a piece of material over a hole. **patchily,** *adv.* in a patchy way. **patchiness,** *n.* being patchy. **patch up,** *v.* to end (a quarrel). **patchwork,** *n.* small pieces of material sewn together in patterns. **patchy,** *adj.* in small areas; not the same all through.

pate [peɪt] *n.* (*old*) head.

pâté ['pæteɪ] *n.* paste made of cooked meat or fish finely minced.

patella [pə'telə] *n.* (*formal*) kneecap.

patent ['peɪtənt] **1.** *n.* (*also* ['pætnt]) official confirmation that you have the right to make or sell a new invention. **2.** *adj.* (*a*) covered by an official patent; **p. medicine** = medicine made under a trade name by one company. (*b*) **p. leather** = extremely shiny leather. (*c*) obvious. **3.** *v.* to obtain a patent for. **patentee** [peɪtən'tiː] *n.* person who has obtained a patent. **patently,** *adv.* obviously/clearly.

paternity [pə'tɜːnɪtɪ] *n.* being a father. **paternal,** *adj.* referring to a father; like a father; **my p. grandfather** = my father's father. **paternalism,** *n.* paternalistic way of ruling a country/a company. **paternalistic** [pətɜːnə'lɪstɪk] *adj.* (way of ruling/of managing) which is kindly but does not give enough freedom or responsibility to individuals. **paternally,** *adv.* in a paternal way.

path [pɑːθ] *n.* (*a*) narrow way for walking/cycling, etc. (*b*) way in which sth moves. **pathway,** *n.* track for walking along.

pathetic [pə'θetɪk] *adj.* which makes you feel pity or contempt. **pathetically,** *adv.* in a pathetic way.

pathogen ['pæθədʒən] *n.* germ which causes a disease. **pathogenic,** *adj.* which causes a disease.

pathology [pə'θɒlədʒɪ] *n.* study of disease. **pathological** [pæθə'lɒdʒɪkl] *adj.* (*a*) referring to pathology. (*b*) caused by mental or physical disease. (*c*) unhealthy (interest). **pathologist** [pə'θɒlədʒɪst] *n.* doctor specializing in the study of disease; doctor who examines dead bodies to discover the cause of death.

pathos ['peɪθɒs] *n.* quality in sth which makes you feel pity.

patience ['peɪʃns] *n.* (*a*) being patient. (*b*) card game for one person. **patient. 1.** *adj.* (*a*) (person) who can wait for a long time/who remains calm/who doesn't lose his temper. (*b*) careful/painstaking. **2.** *n.* person who is in hospital or being treated by a doctor/dentist, etc. **patiently,** *adv.* calmly.

patina ['pætɪnə] *n.* green sheen on old bronze objects; shine on old wooden furniture, etc.

patio ['pætɪəʊ] *n.* (*pl.* **-os**) paved area outside a house for sitting or eating.

patisserie [pə'tiːsərɪ] *n.* shop selling continental style cakes and pastries.

patois ['pætwɑː] *n.* dialect spoken in a small area.

patrial ['peɪtrɪəl] *n.* person who has the right to live in a country because one of his parents or grandparents was born there.

patriarch ['peɪtrɪɑːk] *n.* (*a*) bishop/high dignitary of an Eastern church. (*b*) respected old man. **patriarchal,** *adj.* referring to a patriarch.

patrician [pə'trɪʃn] *adj. & n.* (referring to an) aristocrat.

patricide ['pætrɪsaɪd] *n.* murder of your own father; person who kills his father.

patrimony ['pætrɪmənɪ] *n.* inheritance/property which has been passed from father to son for generations.

patriot ['peɪtrɪət] *n.* person who fights for/who is proud of his country. **patriotic** [pætrɪ'ɒtɪk] *adj.* proud of your country; willing to fight for your country. **patriotically,** *adv.* in a patriotic way. **patriotism** ['peɪtrɪətɪzəm] *n.* pride in your country.

patrol [pə'trəʊl] **1.** *n.* (*a*) keeping guard

by walking or driving up and down. (b) group of people keeping guard; **p. car** = police car which drives up and down the streets. (c) group of Scouts or Guides. **2.** v. (**patrolled**) to keep guard by walking or driving up and down. **patrolman**, n. (pl. **-men**) esp. Am. policeman.

patron ['peɪtrən] n. (a) person who protects or supports s.o./sth; **p. saint** = saint who is believed to protect a special group of people. (b) regular customer (of a shop); person who goes regularly to the theatre. **patronage** ['pætrənɪdʒ] n. giving support/encouragement (to an artist, etc.). **patroness,** n. woman patron. **patronize** ['pætrənaɪz] v. (a) to support/to encourage (an artist, etc.). (b) to act in a condescending way to (s.o.). (c) to go regularly to (a shop/ public house/theatre). **patronizing,** adj. condescending; (tone) which makes s.o. feel inferior.

patronymic [pætrə'nɪmɪk] n. name which is derived from the name of a father.

patten ['pætən] n. wooden clog with high sole and heel.

patter ['pætə] **1.** n. (a) soft repeated tapping noise. (b) rapid talk by a conjuror/salesman/trickster to distract attention from what he is really doing. **2.** v. to make a soft repeated tapping noise.

pattern ['pætən] n. (a) model/example which you should copy; paper which shows how to cut out cloth to make a piece of clothing; **knitting p.** = instructions on how to knit sth. (b) design of repeated lines/pictures, etc. **patterned,** adj. with a repeated design.

patty ['pætɪ] n. small pie.

paucity ['pɔːsɪtɪ] n. (formal) small number/too little (**of** sth).

paunch [pɔːnʃ] n. (pl. **-es**) fat stomach.

pauper ['pɔːpə] n. poor person.

pause [pɔːz] **1.** n. short stop in work, etc. **2.** v. to stop doing sth for a short time.

pave [peɪv] v. to cover (a road/path, etc.) with a hard surface; **to p. the way** = to prepare the way. **pavement,** n. (a) hard path at the side of a road. (b) Am. hard road surface. **paving stone,** n. large flat stone slab used for making paths/courtyards, etc.

pavilion [pə'vɪljən] n. (a) small building for sportsmen to rest in between games. (b) building for an exhibition.

paw [pɔː] **1.** n. (a) hairy foot of an animal with claws. (b) inf. hand. **2.** v. to tap with a paw/hands, etc.; inf. to fondle.

pawky ['pɔːkɪ] adj. humorous in a dry way. **pawkiness,** n. dry humour.

pawl [pɔːl] n. metal piece which catches in the teeth of a ratchet wheel.

pawn [pɔːn] **1.** n. (a) smallest piece on the chessboard. (b) person used by s.o. more powerful. (c) **in p.** = (object) left in exchange for money which has been borrowed. **2.** v. to leave (an object) in exchange for borrowing money (which you claim back when the money is repaid). **pawnbroker,** n. person who lends money in exchange for valuables left with him. **pawnshop,** n. shop where goods can be pawned.

pay [peɪ] **1.** n. wages/salary; **in the p. of** = paid by. **2.** v. (**paid**) (a) to give money for sth; **to put paid to** = to end. (b) to be worth while. (c) to suffer punishment **for.** (d) to make (a visit/a call). (e) to make/to show (attention, etc.). **payable,** adj. which must be paid. **pay-as-you-earn,** n. system of collecting income tax direct from salaries. **pay back,** v. (a) to return money to (s.o.). (b) to get your revenge on (s.o.). **pay bed,** n. bed in a public hospital for which you pay. **paycheck,** n. Am. salary payment. **payee,** n. person who receives money. **payer,** n. person who pays money. **payload,** n. load carried by an aircraft or rocket. **paymaster,** n. officer who pays soldiers. **payment,** n. giving money for sth. **pay off,** v. (a) to remove (a debt) by paying the money owed. (b) inf. to be successful. **pay-off,** n. inf. (a) reward. (b) final success. **payola,** n. Am. bribery. **pay out,** v. (a) to give money to s.o. (b) to unroll a rope. **payroll,** n. list of people who receive wages. **pay up,** v. to pay what you owe.

PAYE [piːeɪwaɪ'iː] n. pay-as-you-earn system.

Pb symbol for lead.

PC ['piː'siː] personal computer; police constable.

PCB [piːsiː'biː] printed circuit board.

pea [piː] *n.* climbing plant of which the round green seeds are eaten as vegetables; **sweet peas** = plant of the pea family grown for its scented flowers. **pea-green**, *adj.* bright green. **pea-jacket**, *n.* double-breasted wool jacket, worn by sailors. **pea-souper**, *n.* thick yellow fog.

peace [piːs] *n.* (a) state of not being at war; **p. dividend** = money which becomes available for government expenditure as defence spending is reduced following a reduction in international tension. (b) calm/quiet. **peaceable**, *adj.* liking peace; not quarrelsome. **peaceably**, *adv.* calmly/without quarrelling. **peaceful**, *adj.* (a) calm. (b) liking peace; **p. coexistence** = living side by side without making war. **peacefully**, *adv.* (a) calmly. (b) without making war. **peacefulness**, *n.* being peaceful. **peacemaker**, *n.* person who tries to bring about peace.

peach [piːtʃ] 1. *n.* (*pl.* -es) (a) sweet fruit, with a large stone and velvety skin; tree which bears peaches. (b) pinkish-yellow colour. 2. *v. inf.* **to p. on s.o.** = to inform (the police) about s.o.

peacock ['piːkɒk], **peahen** [piːˈhen] *n.* (a) large bird, of which the cock has a huge tail with brilliant blue and green feathers. (b) type of brown butterfly with round purple spots.

peak [piːk] 1. *n.* (a) top of a mountain. (b) highest point; **p. period** = period of the day when most electricity is used/when most traffic is on the roads, etc. (c) front part of a cap which juts out. 2. *v.* to reach a high point. **peaked**, *adj.* (cap) with a peak. **peaky**, *adj.* looking ill.

peal [piːl] 1. *n.* (a) set of bells of different sizes; sound of bells ringing. (b) loud reverberating noise. 2. *v.* (a) to ring a peal of bells. (b) (*of thunder*) to roll/to make a loud noise.

peanut ['piːnʌt] *n.* (a) nut which grows in the ground in pods like a pea; **p. butter** = paste made from crushed peanuts. (b) *inf.* **peanuts** = very little money.

pear ['peə] *n.* elongated fruit with one end fatter than the other; tree which bears pears. **pear-shaped**, *adj.* shaped like a pear.

pearl [pɜːl] *n.* precious round white gem formed inside an oyster; **p. barley** = barley grains which have been rolled until they are shaped like pearls. **pearl-diver**, *n.* person who dives to the bottom of the sea to look for oysters with pearls in them. **pearly**, *adj.* shiny like a pearl.

peasant ['pezənt] *n.* farm labourer or small farmer living in a backward region. **peasantry**, *n.* (*no pl.*) peasants (seen as a class in society).

peat [piːt] *n.* decayed vegetable matter cut out of a bog and used as fuel or in gardening. **peaty**, *adj.* smelling/tasting like peat.

pebble ['pebl] *n.* small round stone. **pebble-dash**, *n.* covering for outside walls, where small stones are stuck into wet cement. **pebbly**, *adj.* covered with pebbles.

pecan ['piːkæn] *n.* nut from a tree which grows in the south of the USA.

peccadillo [pekəˈdɪləʊ] *n.* (*pl.* -oes) (*formal*) slight error/fault.

peccary ['pekərɪ] *n.* wild South American pig.

peck [pek] 1. *n.* (a) bite with a bird's beak. (b) *inf.* little kiss. (c) (*old*) measurement of quantity of grain. 2. *v.* (a) to bite with a beak; **pecking order** = unwritten order of importance of people in a firm/office, etc. (b) *inf.* to give (s.o.) a little kiss. **pecker**, *n. Sl.* **keep your p. up** = keep cheerful/optimistic. **peckish**, *adj. inf.* a bit hungry.

pectin ['pektɪn] *n.* jelly-like substance in fruit which helps jam to set hard.

pectoral ['pektərəl] 1. *adj.* (*formal*) referring to the chest; **p. cross** = cross worn by a priest round the neck. 2. *n.* muscle in the chest.

peculate ['pekjʊleɪt] *v.* (*formal*) to embezzle money. **peculation** [pekjʊˈleɪʃn] *n.* embezzlement.

peculiar [pɪˈkjuːljə] *adj.* (a) odd/strange. (b) belonging to one particular place or person. **peculiarity**, *n.* being peculiar; strange feature/detail which stands out. **peculiarly**, *adv.* oddly/strangely.

pecuniary [pɪˈkjuːnjərɪ] *adj.* referring to money.

pedagogical [pedəˈɡɒdʒɪkl] *adj.* referring to teaching. **pedagogue** ['pedəgɒg] n. unpleasant pedantic teacher.

pedal ['pedl] **1.** n. lever worked by your foot; **p. bin** = rubbish bin with a lid worked by a pedal. **2.** v. (**pedalled**) to make (a bicycle) go by pushing on the pedals.

pedant ['pedənt] n. pedantic person. **pedantic** [pɪ'dæntɪk] adj. paying too much attention to detail/showing off knowledge. **pedantically**, adv. in a pedantic way. **pedantry** ['pedəntrɪ] n. being pedantic.

peddle ['pedl] v. to go about trying to sell sth. **peddler,** n. (a) person who sells dangerous drugs. (b) Am. pedlar.

pederast ['pedəræst] n. person who practises pederasty. **pederasty,** n. homosexual relations with boys.

pedestal ['pedɪstl] n. base (for a statue).

pedestrian [pə'destrɪən] **1.** n. person who goes about on foot; **p. crossing** = place where pedestrians can cross a road; **p. precinct** = street or group of streets closed to traffic so that people can walk about freely. **2.** adj. (a) referring to pedestrians. (b) heavy/unimaginative.

pediatrician [piːdɪə'trɪʃn] n. doctor who specializes in pediatrics. **pediatrics** [piːdɪ'ætrɪks] n. science of treatment of children's diseases.

pedicure ['pedɪkjʊə] n. looking after the feet.

pedigree ['pedɪgriː] n. table of ancestors of a person/animal; **p. bull** = bull with a certificate showing it is pure bred.

pediment ['pedɪmənt] n. triangular part at the top of the front of a classical building.

pedlar ['pedlə] n. person who goes about trying to sell small articles.

pedometer [pe'dɒmɪtə] n. instrument which measures how far you have walked.

peduncle [pə'dʌŋkl] n. stalk of an inflorescence.

pee [piː] **1.** n. inf. (a) waste water from the body. (b) passing waste water from the body. **2.** v. inf. to pass waste water from the body.

peek [piːk] **1.** n. inf. quick look. **2.** v. inf. to look **at** sth quickly.

peel [piːl] **1.** n. outer skin of a fruit, etc. **2.** v. (a) to take the outer skin off (a fruit/a vegetable). (b) to come off in layers. **peeler,** n. special instrument for peeling vegetables. **peelings,** n. pl. bits of skin from vegetables. **peel off,** v. (a) (of peel/paint) to come off. (b) inf. to take off (clothes).

peep [piːp] **1.** n. (a) short/quick look. (b) cheep. **2.** v. to look quickly and secretly. **peephole,** n. small hole in a door which you can look through to see who is outside.

peer ['pɪə] **1.** n. (a) member of the nobility. (b) person of the same rank/class as another; **p. group** = group of people of equal (social) status. **2.** v. to look at sth hard when you cannot see very well. **peerage,** n. (no pl.) all nobles, taken as a group. **peeress,** n. woman peer. **peerless,** adj. excellent/which has no equal.

peeved [piːvd] adj. inf. annoyed/bothered. **peevish,** adj. bad-tempered/complaining. **peevishly,** adv. in a peevish way. **peevishness,** n. being peevish.

peewit ['piːwɪt] n. lapwing.

peg [peg] **1.** n. small wooden or metal stake/pin; **off the p.** = ready made. **2.** v. (**pegged**) (a) to attach with a peg. (b) to hold (prices, etc.) stable. **peg away at,** v. inf. to go on with (piece of work). **peg out,** v. Sl. to die.

pejorative [pə'dʒɒrətɪv] adj. disapproving/showing that you feel sth is bad.

pekinese [piːkɪ'niːz], inf. **peke** [piːk] n. breed of low flat-faced dogs.

pelagic [pə'lædʒɪk] adj. referring to the top and middle layers of the sea.

pelargonium [peləˈgəʊnɪəm] n. flowering plant, the geranium.

pelican ['pelɪkən] n. large white water bird, with a pouch under its beak in which it keeps the fish it has caught; **p. crossing** = pedestrian crossing with traffic lights worked by the pedestrians.

pellet ['pelɪt] n. (a) small ball. (b) small lead ball, used in shotguns. **pelleted,** adj. (seeds) made into pellets.

pellicle ['pelɪkl] n. thin layer of skin.

pell-mell [pel'mel] adv. in disorder.

pellucid [pə'luːsɪd] adj. very transparent.

pelmet ['pelmɪt] *n.* decorative strip of wood/cloth, etc., over a window which hides the curtain fittings.

pelt [pelt] **1.** *n.* (*a*) skin of an animal with fur on it. (*b*) **at full p.** = going fast. **2.** *v.* (*a*) **to p. s.o. with** = to fling things at s.o. (*b*) **the rain was pelting down** = pouring down.

pelvis ['pelvɪs] *n.* (*pl.* **-es**) bones in the lower part of the body forming the hips. **pelvic,** *adj.* referring to the pelvis.

pemmican ['pemɪkən] *n.* dried meat, used by explorers as rations.

pen [pen] **1.** *n.* (*a*) small fenced area for sheep. (*b*) writing instrument using ink; **p. name** = name used by a writer which is not his own; **p. friend** = person whom you have never met, but with whom you exchange letters. (*c*) female swan. **2.** *v.* (**penned**) (*a*) to enclose (sheep) in a pen. (*b*) to write with a pen.

penal ['pi:nl] *adj.* referring to a legal punishment; **p. system** = system of punishments relating to various crimes. **penalization** [pi:nəlaɪ'zeɪʃn] *n.* act of penalizing. **penalize,** *v.* to punish. **penalty** ['penltɪ] *n.* (*a*) punishment. (*b*) punishment in sport, esp. a kick at goal awarded to the opposite side in football. (*c*) disadvantages.

penance ['penəns] *n.* punishment which a person accepts to make amends for a sin.

pence [pens] *n. see* **penny.**

penchant ['pɑ: nʃɑ:ŋ] *n.* liking (**for** sth).

pencil ['pensl] **1.** *n.* instrument for writing, made of wood with a graphite centre. **2.** *v.* (**pencilled**) to write with a pencil. **pencil sharpener,** *n.* instrument for sharpening pencils.

pendant ['pendənt] *n.* ornament which hangs from a chain round the neck. **pendent,** *adj.* hanging.

pending ['pendɪŋ] *adj. & prep.* awaiting; until; **p. tray** = tray for papers and letters waiting to be dealt with.

pendulum ['pendjʊləm] *n.* weight on the end of a rod or chain which swings from side to side, such as that which makes a clock work. **pendulous,** *adj.* which hangs down heavily.

penetrate ['penɪtreɪt] *v,* go into/through. **penetrability** [penɪtrə'bɪlɪtɪ] *n.* ability to be penetrated. **penetrable,** *adj.* which can be penetrated. **penetrating,** *adj.* deep/searching (look); very profound (questions). **penetration** [penɪ'treɪʃn] *n.* (*a*) getting into sth. (*b*) deep understanding.

penguin ['peŋgwɪn] *n.* Antarctic bird which swims well but cannot fly.

penicillin [penɪ'sɪlɪn] *n.* substance made from a mould, used to kill bacteria.

peninsula [pə'nɪnsjʊlə] *n.* large piece of land jutting into the sea. **peninsular,** *adj.* referring to a peninsula.

penis ['pi:nɪs] *n.* (*pl.* **-es**) part of the male body used for urinating and for sexual intercourse.

penitent ['penɪtənt] *adj. & n.* (person) who is sorry for having done sth wrong. **penitence,** *n.* being penitent. **penitential** [penɪ'tenʃl] *adj.* referring to penance. **penitentiary** [penɪ'tenʃərɪ] *n. Am.* prison.

penknife ['pennaɪf] *n.* (*pl.* **-knives** [-naɪvz]) small folding pocket knife.

pennant ['penənt] *n.* long thin flag.

pennon ['penən] *n.* small forked flag.

penny ['penɪ] *n.* (*pl.* **pennies** = *coins;* **pence** = *price*) small coin (the smallest unit in some currencies); (*in Britain*) one hundredth part of a pound; **the penny's dropped** = he's understood at last. **penniless,** *adj.* with no money.

penology [pi:'nɒlədʒɪ] *n.* study of punishment and crime.

pension ['penʃn] **1.** *n.* money paid regularly to s.o. who has retired from work/to a widow, etc.; **old age p.** = money paid regularly by the state to people over a certain age. **2.** *v.* **to p. s.o. off** = to make s.o. stop working and live on a pension. **pensionable,** *adj.* (person) who has the right to have a pension; (job) which gives you the right to have a pension; (age) at which a pension begins to be paid. **pensioner,** *n.* person who gets a pension.

pensive ['pensɪv] *adj.* thoughtful. **pensively,** *adv.* thoughtfully. **pensiveness,** *n.* being pensive.

pent [pent] *adj.* **pent-up emotions** = violent emotions which are repressed.

pentagon ['pentəgən] *n.* (*a*) geometrical figure with five sides. (*b*) **the Pentagon** = the US ministry of defence. **pentagonal** [pen'tægənl] *adj.* five-sided.

pentameter [pen'tæmitə] *n.* line of poetry with five beats.

pentathlon [pen'tæθlən] *n.* athletic competition where competitors have to compete in five different sports.

penthouse ['penthaus] *n.* flat on the top of a high building.

penultimate [pe'nʌltimət] *adj.* next to last.

penumbra [pe'nʌmbrə] *n.* edge of a shadow where only part of the light is cut off.

penury ['penjuri] *n.* (*formal*) (*a*) extreme poverty. (*b*) great lack. **penurious** [pɪ'njuəriəs] *adj.* very poor.

peony ['piəni] *n.* perennial summer flower with large scented flowerheads.

people ['pi:pl] **1.** *n.* (*a*) (*pl.*) persons; human beings; **country p.** = persons who live in the country. (*b*) citizens (of a town or country). **2.** *v.* to fill with people.

pep [pep] **1.** *n. inf.* vigour; **p. pill** = medicine taken to make you more lively and active; **p. talk** = talk designed to encourage people to work hard/to win a match, etc. **2.** *v. inf.* **to p. s.o. up** = to make s.o. livelier and more active.

pepper ['pepə] **1.** *n.* (*a*) sharp spice used in cooking. (*b*) green or red fruit used as a vegetable. **2.** *v.* (**with**) to sprinkle/ to throw (things) at. **peppercorn**, *n.* dried seed of pepper; **p. rent** = nominal/ very low rent. **peppermill**, *n.* small grinder used for grinding peppercorns. **peppermint**, *n.* (*a*) common plant with a sharp mint flavour. (*b*) sweet flavoured with peppermint. **peppery**, *adj.* (*a*) (soup, etc.) with too much pepper in it. (*b*) very easily angered.

peptic ['peptik] *adj.* referring to the digestive system; **p. ulcer** = ulcer in the stomach.

per [pɜ:] *prep.* (*a*) out of; **ten p. thousand.** (*b*) in; **sixty kilometers p. hour.** (*c*) for; **p. annum** = in each year; **p. capita** = for each person.

perambulate [pə'ræmbjuleit] *v.* (*formal*) to walk about slowly. **perambulation**, *n.* slow walk. **perambulator**, *n.* (*formal*) pram.

perceive [pə'si:v] *v.* to notice through the senses; to become aware of. **perceptible** [pə'septibl] *adj.* which

can be seen/heard/smelled, etc. **perceptibly**, *adv.* noticeably. **perception** [pə'sepʃn] *n.* ability to notice. **perceptive**, *adj.* acute; able to notice quickly. **perceptively**, *adv.* in a perceptive way. **perceptiveness, perceptivity**, *n.* being perceptive.

per cent [pə'sent] *adv. & n.* out of each hundred. **percentage** [pə'sentidʒ] *n.* proportion shown as part of a hundred. **percentile** [pə'sentail] *n.* one of a hundred equal groups into which a large number can be divided.

perch [pɜ:tʃ] **1.** *n.* (*a*) (*pl.* **-es**) branch/ ledge on which a bird can sit. (*b*) (*pl.* **perch**) type of freshwater fish. **2.** *v.* to sit on a perch; to be set in a high place.

perchance [pə'tʃɑ:ns] *adv.* (*old*) perhaps.

percipient [pə'sipiənt] *adj.* perceptive/ able to notice quickly. **percipience**, *n.* being percipient.

percolate ['pɜ:kəleit] *v.* to filter (through). **percolation** [pɜ:kə'leiʃn] *n.* filtering. **percolator**, *n.* coffee pot where the water boils up and filters through coffee.

percussion [pə'kʌʃn] *n.* (*a*) action of hitting together; **p. instruments** = musical instruments which are hit (drums/ triangles, etc.); **p. cap** = piece of paper with a small amount of explosive powder which explodes when hit. (*b*) **the p.** = section of an orchestra with percussion instruments.

peregrinations [perigri'neiʃnz] *n. pl.* (*formal*) travelling/wandering.

peregrine ['perigrin] *n.* type of falcon.

peremptory [pə'remptəri] *adj.* abrupt (tone)/curt (refusal). **peremptorily**, *adv.* in a peremptory way.

perennial [pə'reniəl] **1.** *adj.* which continues from year to year. **2.** *n.* plant which flowers every year without needing to be sown again. **perennially**, *adv.* always.

perestroika [peri'strɔikə] *n.* reconstruction (of the Soviet economy).

perfect 1. *adj.* ['pɜ:fikt] (*a*) without any mistakes/flaws. (*b*) total (stranger). (*c*) **p. (tense)** = past tense of a verb which shows that the action has been completed. **2.** *v.* [pə'fekt] to make perfect. **perfection** [pə'fekʃn] *n.* state

of being perfect; **to p.** = perfectly.
perfectionist, n. person who insists
that perfection is possible/that everything has to be perfect. **perfectly**
['pɜːfɪktlɪ] adv. completely.

perfidy ['pɜːfɪdɪ] n. (formal) treachery.
perfidious [pə'fɪdɪəs] adj. (formal)
treacherous.

perforate ['pɜːfəreɪt] v. to make a hole
in/to pierce. **perforation** [pɜːfə'reɪʃn]
n. (a) action of making a hole. (b) small
hole.

perforce [pə'fɔːs] adv. (old) because it
is necessary.

perform [pə'fɔːm] v. (a) to carry out
an action. (b) to act in public. **performance,** n. (a) working of a machine;
action of a sportsman. (b) public show.
performer, n. person who gives a public show.

perfume 1. n. ['pɜːfjuːm] (a) pleasant
smell. (b) liquid scent. 2. v. [pə'fjuːm]
(a) to give a pleasant smell to (sth).
(b) to pour perfume on. **perfumery,** n.
shop which makes and sells perfumes.

perfunctory [pə'fʌŋktərɪ] adj. rapid and
superficial. **perfunctorily,** adv. in a
perfunctory way.

pergola ['pɜːgələ] n. framework of wood
over which climbing plants can be
trained.

perhaps [pə'hæps] adv. possibly/maybe.

pericardium [perɪ'kɑːdɪəm] n. membrane round the heart. **pericarditis,** n.
inflammation of the pericardium.

perihelion [perɪ'hiːlɪɒn] n. point where
a planet is nearest to the sun.

peril ['perəl] n. great danger. **perilous,**
adj. very dangerous. **perilously,** adv. in
a perilous way.

perimeter [pə'rɪmɪtə] n. outside line
round an enclosed area.

period ['pɪərɪəd] n. (a) length of time;
p. furniture = antique furniture from
a certain time; **p. piece** = piece of
antique furniture, etc. (b) class time in
a school. (c) full stop/dot (.) used in
writing to mark the end of a sentence.
(d) regular monthly flow of blood from
a woman's womb. **periodic** [pɪːrɪ'ɒdɪk]
adj. repeated after a regular length
of time; **p. table** = list of chemical
elements arranged in order of their
atomic numbers. **periodical. 1.** adj.

periodic; repeated after a regular length
of time. 2. n. magazine which appears
regularly. **periodically,** adv. from time
to time.

peripatetic [perɪpə'tetɪk] adj. (person)
who wanders from place to place; **p.
violin teacher** = teacher who goes from
school to school teaching children to
play the violin.

periphery [pə'rɪfərɪ] n. edge. **pe-
ripheral, 1.** adj. minor/not very important. 2. n. **peripherals** = items of
hardware (such as printers) which are
attached to a computer.

periphrasis [pə'rɪfrəsɪs] n. (pl. -ses) way
of saying sth which is not straightforward. **periphrastic** [perɪ'fræstɪk]
adj. not straightforward (expression).

periscope ['perɪskəup] n. long tube
with mirrors which allows s.o. in a
submerged submarine to look above the
surface of the water.

perish ['perɪʃ] v. (a) (formal) to die.
(b) to rot. (c) inf. **I'm perished** = I'm
cold. **perishable,** adj. (food) which can
go bad easily; **perishables** = perishable
food.

peristalsis [perɪ'stælsɪs] n. regular
movement of the muscles in the
intestine.

peritonitis [perɪtə'naɪtɪs] n. inflammation of the lining of the abdomen.

periwig ['perɪwɪg] n. large wig, worn in
the 17th and 18th centuries.

periwinkle ['perɪwɪŋkl] n. (a) small
creeping plant with blue flowers. (b)
edible snail which lives in salt water.

perjure ['pɜːdʒə] v. **to p. yourself** = to
tell lies in a court of law when you
have sworn to tell the truth. **perjurer,**
n. person who has committed perjury.
perjury, n. crime of perjuring yourself.

perk [pɜːk] 1. v. **to p. up** = to become
more alert/more interested. 2. n. inf.
valuable extras which you are given
by your employer in addition to your
salary. **perky,** adj. inf. lively/interested.

perm [pɜːm] 1. n. inf. (a) curls or a
wave put into your hair artificially. (b)
combination of football teams on a
football pools coupon. 2. v. inf. (a) to
put a wave or curl into (s.o.'s hair).
(b) to select several football teams
in various combinations on a football
pools coupon.

permafrost ['pɜːməfrɒst] *n.* (*no pl.*) soil in the Arctic which remains permanently frozen, even in summer.

permanent ['pɜːmənənt] *adj.* lasting for ever/supposed to last for ever; **p. secretary** = chief civil servant in a government department. **permanence, permanency,** *n.* state of being permanent. **permanently,** *adv.* always.

permanganate [pə'mæŋgəneɪt] *n.* salt containing manganese; **p. of potash** = dark purple crystals used for disinfecting.

permeate ['pɜːmɪeɪt] *v.* to filter; to spread right through. **permeability** [pɜːmɪə'bɪlɪti] *n.* being permeable. **permeable,** *adj.* which lets liquid pass through. **permeation** [pɜːmɪ'eɪʃn] *n.* act of permeating.

permissible [pə'mɪsəbl] *adj.* which can be allowed. **permission** [pə'mɪʃn] *n.* freedom which you are given to do sth. **permissive** [pə'mɪsɪv] *adj.* free; allowing many things to be done which formerly were not allowed. **permissiveness,** *n.* being permissive.

permit 1. *n.* ['pɜːmɪt] paper which allows you to do sth. 2. *v.* [pə'mɪt] (**permitted**) to allow.

permutation [pɜːmjuː'teɪʃn] *n.* grouping of several items together in varied combinations; combination of various items in a different order.

pernicious [pə'nɪʃəs] *adj.* harmful/evil.

pernickety [pə'nɪkəti] *adj. inf.* very fussy.

peroration [perə'reɪʃn] *n.* (*formal*) very long speech.

peroxide [pə'rɒksaɪd] *n.* chemical used for bleaching hair or killing germs.

perpendicular [pɜːpən'dɪkjʊlə] *adj.* & *n.* (line) standing vertically/at right angles to a base; style of late medieval English church architecture. **perpendicularly,** *adv.* in a perpendicular way.

perpetrate ['pɜːpɪtreɪt] *v.* (*formal*) to commit (a crime). **perpetration** [pə'pɪtreɪʃn] *n.* act of perpetrating. **perpetrator,** *n.* person who commits (a crime).

perpetual [pə'petjʊəl] *adj.* continuous/without any end. **perpetually,** *adv.* always. **perpetuate,** *v.* to make (sth) continue for ever. **perpetuity** [pɜːpɪ'tjuːɪti] *n.* (*formal*) **in p.** = for ever/without any end.

perplex [pə'pleks] *v.* to confuse/to puzzle. **perplexity,** *n.* bewilderment/puzzled state.

perquisite ['pɜːkwɪzɪt] *n.* (*formal*) valuable extra which is given to you by your employer in addition to your salary.

perry ['peri] *n.* alcoholic drink made from fermented pear juice.

per se [pɜː'seɪ] *adv.* in itself.

persecute ['pɜːsɪkjuːt] *v.* to torment/to treat cruelly. **persecution** [pɜːsɪ'kjuːʃn] *n.* relentless killing (because of religious beliefs); **p. mania** = mental disease where you feel that everyone is persecuting you. **persecutor** ['pɜːsɪkjuːtə] *n.* person who persecutes.

persevere [pɜːsɪ'vɪə] *v.* (**with/in**) to continue doing sth (in spite of obstacles). **perseverance,** *n.* act of persevering.

Persian ['pɜːʃn] 1. *adj.* referring to Persia. 2. *n.* (*a*) person from Persia. (*b*) cat with long silky fur.

persiflage [pɜːsɪ'flɑːʒ] *n.* (*formal*) frivolous talk.

persist [pə'sɪst] *v.* (**in**) to continue doing sth (in spite of obstacles); to continue to exist. **persistence,** *n.* obstinacy; refusal to stop doing sth. **persistent,** *adj.* continual. **persistently,** *adv.* in a persistent way.

person ['pɜːsn] *n.* (*a*) human being; **he appeared in p.** = appeared himself. (*b*) (*in grammar*) one of the three forms of verbs or pronouns which indicate who the speaker is; **first p.** = I or we; **second p.** = you; **third p.** = he, she, it, they. **persona** [pə'səʊnə] *n.* a person's character as seen by others. **personable,** *adj.* attractive/good-looking/having a pleasant character. **personage,** *n.* important person. **personal,** *adj.* (*a*) referring to a person; (letter) addressed so that you and no one else may open it; **p. computer** = small computer used by a person at home. (*b*) rude (remarks). (*c*) (*in grammar*) **p. pronoun** = pronoun which refers to s.o., such as 'I', 'he', 'she', etc. **personality** [pɜːsə'nælɪti] *n.* (*a*) character. (*b*) famous person; **p. cult** = publicity given to a political leader, making him into a kind of god. (*c*) legal status. **personalized,**

adj. with your name or initials printed on it. **personally,** *adv.* (*a*) from your own point of view. (*b*) in person. (*c*) **don't take it p.** = don't think it was meant to criticize you. **persona non grata** [pɜː'səʊnɒnɒn'grɑːtə] *n.* person (esp. a diplomat) who is not acceptable to a foreign country. **personification** [pəsɒnɪfɪ'keɪʃn] *n.* good example of an abstract quality in a person. **personify** [pə'sɒnɪfaɪ] *v.* to be a good example of. **personnel** [pɜːsə'nel] *n.* staff/people employed by a company; **p. manager** = manager who looks after pay/sick leave/administration, etc., for all the staff.

perspective [pə'spektɪv] *n.* (*a*) (*in art*) way of drawing objects/scenes, so that they appear to have depth or distance; **to put things in p.** = to show things in an objective way. (*b*) way of looking at sth.

perspex ['pɜːspeks] *n.* trademark for a type of tough clear plastic.

perspicacious [pɜːspɪ'keɪʃəs] *adj.* (person) who understands clearly. **perspicacity** [pɜːspɪ'kæsɪtɪ] *n.* clearness of understanding.

perspicuity [pɜːspɪ'kjuːɪtɪ] *n.* clearness of expression. **perspicuous** [pə'spɪkjʊəs] *adj.* clearly expressed.

perspire [pə'spaɪə] *v.* to sweat. **perspiration** [pɜːspə'reɪʃn] *n.* sweat.

persuade [pə'sweɪd] *v.* to get s.o. to do what you want by explaining or pleading. **persuasion** [pə'sweɪʒn] *n.* (*a*) act of persuading. (*b*) firm (usu. religious) belief. **persuasive** [pə'sweɪzɪv] *adj.* which persuades. **persuasively,** *adv.* in a persuasive way. **persuasiveness,** *n.* being persuasive.

pert [pɜːt] *adj.* cheeky.

pertain [pə'teɪn] *v.* (*formal*) to be relevant.

pertinacious [pɜːtɪ'neɪʃəs] *adj.* obstinate. **pertinacity** [pɜːtɪ'næsɪtɪ] *n.* obstinateness/stubbornness.

pertinent ['pɜːtɪnənt] *adj.* relevant; to the point. **pertinence,** *n.* being pertinent. **pertinently,** *adv.* in a pertinent way.

perturb [pə'tɜːb] *v.* to make (s.o.) anxious. **perturbation** [pɜːtə'beɪʃn] *n.* anxiety/bother.

peruse [pə'ruːz] *v.* (*formal*) to read carefully. **perusal,** *n.* reading.

Peruvian [pə'ruːvɪən] **1.** *adj.* referring to Peru. **2.** *n.* person from Peru.

pervade [pə'veɪd] *v.* to spread everywhere. **pervasive** [pə'veɪsɪv] *adj.* penetrating. **pervasiveness,** *n.* penetrating everywhere.

perverse [pə'vɜːs] *adj.* obstinately awkward; continuing to do sth even if it is wrong. **perversely,** *adv.* in an obstinate way. **perverseness,** *n.* contrariness. **perversion** [pə'vɜːʃn] *n.* corruption (of s.o. to do sth evil). **perversity,** *n.* being perverse. **pervert. 1.** *n.* ['pɜːvɜːt] person who commits unnatural sexual acts. **2.** *v.* [pə'vɜːt] (*a*) to corrupt (s.o.) to do evil. (*b*) **to p. the course of justice** = to influence a court so that justice is not done.

pervious ['pɜːvɪəs] *adj.* *Am.* (membrane) which allows liquid to pass through.

peseta [pe'seɪtə] *n.* unit of currency used in Spain.

peso ['peɪzəʊ] *n.* unit of currency used in many S. American countries.

pessary ['pesərɪ] *n.* (*a*) medicine put in the vagina. (*b*) contraceptive device placed in the vagina.

pessimism ['pesɪmɪzəm] *n.* belief that only bad things will happen. **pessimist** ['pesɪmɪst] *n.* pessimistic person. **pessimistic** [pesɪ'mɪstɪk] *adj.* gloomy/believing that only bad things will happen. **pessimistically,** *adv.* gloomily.

pest [pest] *n.* (*a*) troublesome plant, animal, or often an insect. (*b*) *inf.* person who annoys. **pester,** *v.* to bother (s.o.). **pesticide** ['pestɪsaɪd] *n.* poison to kill pests.

pestilence ['pestɪləns] *n.* (*formal*) plague/disease. **pestilential** [pestɪ'lenʃl] *adj.* like a plague/very unpleasant.

pestle ['pesl] *n.* round-headed heavy tool for crushing things in a bowl.

pet [pet] **1.** *n.* animal kept in the home to give pleasure. **2.** *adj.* (*a*) favourite; **p. name** = special name given to s.o. you are fond of. (*b*) tame (animal). **3.** *v.* (**petted**) to caress/to fondle.

petal ['petl] *n.* one of several colourful leaf-like parts of a flower.

petard [pə'tɑːd] *n.* (*formal*) **to be hoist with your own p.** = to be caught in a trap which you have set for s.o. else.

peter ['pi:tə] v. **to p. out** = to come to an end/to fade away.

petersham ['pi:təʃəm] n. thick ribbon used to put inside the waist of skirts/trousers, etc.

petite [pə'ti:t] adj. (of a woman) small and dainty.

petit four [pəti'fʊə] n. small fancy cake or biscuit eaten at parties.

petition [pə'tɪʃn] 1. n. (a) official request (often signed by many people). (b) legal request. 2. v. to ask (s.o.) for sth/to make an official request. **petitioner,** n. person who makes a petition.

petrel ['petrəl] n. sea bird which flies long distances.

petrify ['petrɪfaɪ] v. (a) to turn to stone. (b) to strike (s.o.) still with fear. **petrifaction,** n. act of petrifying.

petrochemical [petrəʊ'kemɪkl] adj. & n. (chemical) produced from petroleum or natural gas.

petrodollar [petrəʊ'dɒlə] n. dollar which is earned by a country selling oil.

petrol ['petrəl] n. inflammable liquid produced from petroleum and used as a fuel to drive motor engines, etc. **petroleum** [pə'trəʊliəm] n. raw mineral oil (from the earth); **p. products** = substances (like petrol/plastics, etc.) which are made from petroleum. **petrology,** n. study of rocks.

petticoat ['petɪkəʊt] n. piece of women's underwear/light skirt worn under another skirt.

pettifogging ['petɪfɒgɪŋ] adj. (a) dealing with small useless details. (b) dishonest (lawyer).

petty ['petɪ] adj. (a) insignificant/unimportant; **p. cash** = small amounts of cash (in an office); **p. officer** = non-commissioned officer in the Royal Navy; **p. sessions** = magistrate's court. (b) with a narrow point of view. **pettiness,** n. (a) unimportance. (b) narrowness of outlook.

petulant ['petjʊlənt] adj. irritable/bad-tempered. **petulance,** n. irritability. **petulantly,** adv. in a petulant way.

petunia [pɪ'tju:nɪə] n. common summer garden flower.

pew [pju:] n. long bench seat in a church; inf. **take a p.** = sit down.

pewter ['pju:tə] n. alloy, usu. a mixture of tin and lead, used for making mugs/plates, etc.

pH [pi:'eɪtʃ] n. **pH factor** = measurement of how much acidity or alkalinity there is (in the soil, etc.).

phalanx ['fælæŋks] n. (a) tight mass of people (esp. marching forward). (b) bone in a finger or toe.

phallus ['fæləs] n. (pl. -es) (formal) penis in erection. **phallic,** adj. referring to a phallus; **p. symbol** = thing which resembles a penis, and is taken to symbolize male sex.

phantasm ['fæntæzəm] n. seeing sth in the imagination/seeing ghosts. **phantasmagoria** [fæntæzmə'gɒrɪə] n. mass of ghostly shapes.

phantom ['fæntəm] n. ghost.

pharisaic(al) [færɪ'seɪk(l)] adj. unpleasantly good and religious.

pharmaceutical [fɑ:mə'sju:tɪkl] adj. referring to medicines. **pharmacist** ['fɑ:məsɪst] n. person who makes and sells medicines. **pharmacology** [fɑ:mə'kɒlədʒɪ] n. study of medicines. **pharmacopoeia** [fɑ:məkə'pi:ə] n. collection of drugs; book which lists drugs. **pharmacy,** n. study of medicines; shop which makes and sells medicines.

pharynx ['færɪŋks] n. (pl. -es) passage at the back of the nose leading to the oesophagus. **pharyngitis** [færɪn'dʒaɪtɪs] n. inflammation of the pharynx.

phase [feɪz] 1. n. period; stage in development of sth. 2. v. to **p. in/out** = to introduce/to remove gradually.

pheasant ['fezənt] n. large bright-coloured bird with a long tail, shot for sport and food.

phenobarbitone [fi:nəʊ'bɑ:bɪtəʊn] n. drug which makes the patient sleep.

phenol ['fi:nɒl] n. carbon derivative, used in medicine.

phenomenon [fe'nɒmɪnən] n. (pl. -mena) thing which happens naturally; esp. remarkable thing/happening. **phenomenal,** adj. remarkable. **phenomenally,** adv. remarkably.

phial ['faɪl] n. (formal) small bottle.

philanderer [fɪ'lændərə] n. man who flirts with women.

philanthropy [fɪ'lænθrəpɪ] n. love of/

caring for human beings, shown esp. by giving money to charity. **philanthropic** [fɪlən'θrɒpɪk] *adj.* kind (towards human beings). **philanthropist** [fɪ'lænθrəpɪst] *n.* person who is philanthropic.

philately [fɪ'lætəlɪ] *n.* stamp collecting. **philatelic** [fɪlə'telɪk] *adj.* referring to stamp collecting. **philatelist,** *n.* person who studies or collects stamps.

-phile [faɪl] *suffix meaning* (person) who likes; **Francophile** = person who likes the French.

philharmonic [fɪlɑ:'mɒnɪk] *adj.* liking music (used in names of orchestras/ concert halls, etc.).

philistine ['fɪlɪstaɪn] *adj. & n.* (person) who is unsympathetic to the arts.

philodendron [fɪlə'dendrən] *n.* tropical climbing plant, often used as a house plant.

philology [fɪ'lɒlədʒɪ] *n.* study of (the history of) language. **philological** [fɪlə-'lɒdʒɪkl] *adj.* referring to philology. **philologist** [fɪ'lɒlədʒɪst] *n.* expert in philology.

philosophy [fɪ'lɒsəfɪ] *n.* study of the meaning of human existence; study of the methods and limits of human knowledge; general way of thinking. **philosopher,** *n.* person who studies the meaning of human existence. **philosophical** [fɪlə'sɒfɪkl] *adj.* (*a*) thoughtful; calm. (*b*) referring to philosophy. **philosophically,** *adv.* thoughtfully; calmly. **philosophize,** *v.* to think seriously (like a philosopher).

philtre ['fɪltə] *n.* (*old*) magic potion to make s.o. fall in love.

phlebitis [flɪ'baɪtɪs] *n.* inflammation of a vein.

phlegm [flem] *n.* (*a*) slimy substance in the throat, etc., when you have a cold. (*b*) calmness. **phlegmatic** [fleg'mætɪk] *adj.* calm/not easily annoyed. **phlegmatically,** *adv.* in a phlegmatic way.

phlox [flɒks] *n.* (*pl.* **phlox**) common perennial flower.

-phobe [fəʊb] *suffix meaning* (person) who does not like; **xenophobe** = person who dislikes foreigners.

phobia ['fəʊbɪə] *n.* abnormal terror/ hatred of something.

phoenix ['fi:nɪks] *n.* mythical bird, said to die by burning and reappear from its ashes.

phone [fəʊn] **1.** *n.* telephone. **2.** *v.* to call (s.o.) by telephone. **phone book,** *n.* book which lists people's names, addresses and phone numbers. **phone box,** *n.* small cabin for a public telephone.

phonetic [fə'netɪk] **1.** *adj.* referring to spoken sounds. **2.** *n. pl.* **phonetics** = (i) study of sounds of a language; (ii) written signs which indicate sounds. **phonetically,** *adv.* using phonetics; (language spoken) in a way which closely follows the written letters. **phonetician** [fəʊnə'tɪʃn] *n.* person who studies phonetics. **phonics** ['fɒnɪks] *n.* method of teaching reading, using letters as guides to pronunciation. **phonology** [fə'nɒlədʒɪ] *n.* study of sounds of speech.

phon(e)y ['fəʊnɪ] **1.** *adj.* (**-ier, -iest**) *inf.* false. **2.** *n. inf.* person who pretends to be richer/more famous, etc., than he really is.

phonograph ['fəʊnəgrɑ:f] *n. Am.* gramophone.

phosphate ['fɒsfeɪt] *n.* chemical compound containing phosphorus, often used as a fertilizer.

phosphorescence [fɒsfə'resns] *n.* ability to shine in the dark after being exposed to light. **phosphorescent,** *adj.* which shines in the dark after being exposed to light. **phosphorus** ['fɒsfərəs] *n.* (*element:* P) poisonous yellow substance which shines in the dark.

photo ['fəʊtəʊ] **1.** *n.* (*pl.* **-os**) *inf.* photograph. **2.** **photo-** *prefix meaning* (i) light; (ii) photograph. **photochemical,** *adj.* (chemical reaction) which is caused by light. **photocopy** ['fəʊtəʊkɒpɪ] **1.** *n.* copy (of a document) made by photographing it. **2.** *v.* to copy (sth) photographically and make a print of it. **photocopier,** *n.* machine which takes photocopies. **photoelectric** [fəʊtəʊ-'lektrɪk] *adj.* referring to electricity controlled by light; **p. cell** = cell which converts light into electricity or which operates a machine when a beam of light is broken. **photo finish** ['fəʊtəʊfɪnɪʃ] *n.* very close end of a race when a photograph is used to decide who is the winner. **photogenic** [fəʊtəʊ-

'dʒiːnɪk] *adj.* (person) who looks well in photographs. **photograph** ['fəʊtəgrɑːf] **1.** *n.* picture taken by a camera by means of exposing sensitive film to light. **2.** *v.* to take a picture with a camera. **photographer** [fə'tɒgrəfə] *n.* person who takes photographs. **photographic** [fəʊtəʊ'græfɪk] *adj.* referring to photography; **p. memory** = ability to remember things in exact detail, as if seen. **photography** [fə'tɒgrəfɪ] *n.* (art of) taking pictures on sensitive film with a camera. **photogravure,** *n.* engraving of a photograph. **photo opportunity,** *n.* arranged situation where a famous person can be filmed or photographed by journalists. **photostat** ['fəʊtəʊstæt] **1.** *n.* trademark for a type of photographic copy. **2.** *v.* (**photostatted**) to make a photographic copy of. **photosynthesis,** *n.* process by which plants use sunlight to form carbohydrates.

phrase [freɪz] **1.** *n.* (*a*) expression; short sentence; group of words taken together; **p. book** = book of translations of common expressions. (*b*) group of notes in a piece of music. **2.** *v.* to express/to word (a sentence, etc.). **phrasal** ['freɪzl] *adj.* referring to a phrase; (verb) making a phrase. **phraseology** [freɪzɪ'ɒlədʒɪ] *n.* way of expressing sth; choice of words and phrases.

phrenology [fre'nɒlədʒɪ] *n.* study of the outside shape of the skull.

phut [fʌt] *adv. inf.* **to go p.** = to stop working.

physical ['fɪzɪkl] *adj.* (*a*) referring to matter/energy, etc.; **p. geography** = study of rocks and earth, etc.; **p. chemistry** = study of chemical substances. (*b*) referring to the human body; **p. exercise** = exercise of the body. **physically,** *adv.* referring to the body or to the laws of nature.

physician [fɪ'zɪʃn] *n.* doctor.

physics ['fɪzɪks] *n.* study of matter/energy, etc. **physicist** ['fɪzɪsɪst] *n.* person who studies physics.

physiognomy [fɪzɪ'ɒnəmɪ] *n.* human face.

physiology [fɪzɪ'ɒlədʒɪ] *n.* study of the way in which living things work.

physiological [fɪzɪə'lɒdʒɪkl] *adj.* referring to physiology. **physiologist,** *n.* person who studies physiology.

physiotherapy [fɪzɪəʊ'θerəpɪ] *n.* treatment of an illness, pain, etc., by exercise or rubbing. **physiotherapist,** *n.* person who practises physiotherapy.

physique [fɪ'ziːk] *n.* shape of a person's body.

pi [paɪ] *n.* letter of the Greek alphabet (ρ), symbolizing the quantity 3.14159, which is used to calculate the circumference of a circle from a known radius.

piano ['pjænəʊ] *n.* (*pl.* **-os**) musical instrument with keys which makes notes by striking wires with hammers; **grand p.** = large piano with horizontal wires. **pianist** ['pɪənɪst] *n.* person who plays the piano. **pianoforte** ['pjænəʊfɔːtɪ] *n.* (*old*) piano. **pianola** [pɪə'nəʊlə] *n.* trademark for a piano which plays music mechanically from a reel of perforated paper.

piazza [pɪ'ætsə] *n.* Italian square, often surrounded by arcades.

pibroch ['piːbrɒk] *n.* mournful bagpipe music.

pica ['paɪkə] *n.* measure of type.

picaresque [pɪkə'resk] *adj.* fancifully romantic (story).

piccalilli [pɪkə'lɪlɪ] *n.* pickle made of vegetables, such as cauliflower, onions, etc., in a mustard sauce.

piccolo ['pɪkələʊ] *n.* (*pl.* **-os**) small wind instrument, like a little flute.

pick [pɪk] **1.** *n.* (*a*) heavy tool (for breaking hard ground/concrete, etc.) with a long handle and a curved metal bar with pointed ends. (*b*) selected group; **to take your p.** = choose which one you want. **2.** *v.* (*a*) to break up (hard ground/concrete, etc.) with a pick. (*b*) to remove things with your fingers/with a pointed tool; to clean the inside of (your nose) with your fingers. (*c*) to eat very daintily and without any appetite. (*d*) to choose. (*e*) to collect (ripe fruit); to cut (flowers). (*f*) to open (a lock) with a piece of wire. (*g*) to steal from (s.o.'s pocket). (*h*) **to p. s.o.'s brains** = to ask for ideas/information. **pickaxe,** *Am.* **pickax,** *n.* pick. **picker,** *n.* person who picks. **pickings,** *n. pl.* bits and pieces left which people can pick up.

pick-me-up, *n. inf.* tonic. **pick off**, *v.* to defeat/kill (an enemy) one by one. **pick on**, *v.* to select (s.o.) as a target for criticism/for bullying. **pick out**, *v.* to select/to choose. **pickpocket**, *n.* person who steals things from people's pockets. **pick up**, *v.* (*a*) to take (sth) which is on the ground. (*b*) to learn (a language, etc.) unsystematically. (*c*) to give (s.o.) a lift in a car; (*of a bus*) to take (passengers) on board; (*of police*) to arrest/to take to a police station; to start an acquaintanceship with (s.o.) by chance. (*d*) to get stronger. **pick-up**, *n.* (*a*) *inf.* person who has been picked up. (*b*) needle and arm of a record player. (*c*) light van with an open back.

picket ['pɪkɪt] **1.** *n.* (*a*) guard. (*b*) pointed stake. (*c*) striking workman/union official who stands at the entrance to a factory to try to prevent other workmen from going to work; **p. line** = line of pickets preventing other workmen going to work. **2.** *v.* to post strikers at the entrance of a factory to try to prevent workers going to work.

pickle ['pɪkl] **1.** *n.* (*a*) vegetables preserved in vinegar, etc. (*b*) *inf.* naughty child. **2.** *v.* to preserve (vegetables, etc.) in vinegar. **pickled**, *adj. inf.* drunk.

picnic ['pɪknɪk] **1.** *n.* (*a*) excursion with a meal eaten in the open air. **2.** *v.* (**picknicked**) to eat a picnic. **picnicker**, *n.* person who goes on a picnic.

pictorial [pɪk'tɔːrɪəl] *adj.* referring to pictures.

picture ['pɪktʃə] **1.** *n.* (*a*) painting/drawing, etc.; *inf.* **to put s.o. in the p.** = to tell them all the relevant details. (*b*) image (on a TV screen, etc.). (*c*) **the pictures** = cinema. **2.** *v.* to imagine. **picturesque** [pɪktʃə'resk] *adj.* which would make a good picture; very artistic.

piddle ['pɪdl] *v. inf.* (*child's language*) to urinate. **piddling**, *adj. inf.* very small.

pidgin ['pɪdʒɪn] *n.* simple language made from several languages, used as a lingua franca; **p. (English)** = simplified form of English used in the Far East.

pie [paɪ] *n.* cooked dish, usu. of pastry with a filling of meat or fruit; **p. in the sky** = unattainable ideal. **pie-chart**, *n.* diagram shaped like a circle with

segments showing how sth is divided up. **pie-eyed**, *adj. inf.* drunk.

piebald ['paɪbɔːld] *adj.* (horse) with black and white patches.

piece [piːs] **1.** *n.* (*a*) small part/bit; **he went to pieces** = he lost control of himself/had a nervous breakdown. (*b*) short composition in music. (*c*) one of the figures used in chess, but not usu. a pawn. (*d*) gun. **2.** *v.* **to p. together** = to join separate parts together. **piecemeal**, *adv.* in bits; a bit at a time; separately. **piece rate**, *n.* rate of pay for a product produced. **piecework**, *n.* work for which you are paid by the amount of work done and not by the hour.

pièce de résistance [pɪesdəreisis'tɑŋs] *n.* main item.

pied [paɪd] *adj.* having two colours, usu. black and white.

pied-à-terre [pjeɪdæ'teə] *n.* small flat/house which you use to live in from time to time when visiting a place.

pier ['pɪə] *n.* (*a*) construction going out into the water, used as a landing place for ships. (*b*) pillar (of a bridge).

pierce ['pɪəs] *v.* to make a hole. **piercing**, *adj.* very loud, shrill (cry); very sharp/severe (cold or wind).

piety ['paɪətɪ] *n.* being pious; great respect for religion.

piffle ['pɪfl] *n. inf.* nonsense.

pig [pɪg] *n.* (*a*) farm animal which gives pork/bacon, etc.; various wild species of this animal. (*b*) *inf.* dirty/greedy person. (*c*) large block of metal; **p. iron** = iron in rough moulded blocks. (*d*) *Sl.* policeman. **piggery**, *n.* place where pigs are kept. **piggy**, *n.* child's name for a pig. **piggyback**, *n. adj. & adv.* carrying s.o. on your back with his arms round your neck. **piggybank**, *n.* child's money box in the shape of a pig. **pigheaded**, *adj. inf.* obstinate. **piglet**, *n.* little pig. **pigmeat**, *n.* meat from a pig. **pigskin**, *n.* leather made from the skin of a pig. **pigsty**, *n.* shed where pigs are kept. **pigtail**, *n.* hair hanging down in a plait at the back of the head.

pigeon ['pɪdʒɪn] *n.* common greyish bird. **pigeonhole. 1.** *n.* small square space used for filing papers/letters, etc. **2.** *v.* (*a*) to file letters/papers, etc. (often as the best way to forget them). (b) to put (s.o./sth) into a particular category. **pigeon-toed,** adj. with the feet turned inwards, towards each other.

pigment ['pɪgmənt] **1.** n. colouring matter. **2.** v. to colour with pigment. **pigmentation** [pɪgmən'teɪʃn] n. colouring of the skin.

pigmy ['pɪgmɪ] n. *see* **pygmy.**

pike [paɪk] n. (a) (pl. **pike**) large ferocious freshwater fish. (b) (old) weapon, like a spear with a broad blade.

pikelet ['paɪklət] n. (in north of England) crumpet.

pikestaff ['paɪkstɑ:f] n. **as plain as a p.** = very easy to see.

pilaff ['pɪlæf] n. Indian dish of meat with savoury rice.

pilaster [pɪ'læstə] n. rectangular column, usu. attached to a wall.

pilau ['pɪlaʊ] n. *see* **pilaff.**

pilchard ['pɪltʃəd] n. small fish similar to a herring.

pile [paɪl] **1.** n. (a) heap; inf. **he's made his p.** = his fortune. (b) large stake/ concrete shaft driven into the earth to provide a foundation. (c) thickness of tufts of wool in a carpet. (d) **piles** = haemorrhoids. **2.** v. **to p. (up)** = to heap up. **piledriver,** n. machine for forcing piles into the earth. **pile-up,** n. series of cars which have smashed into each other.

pilfer ['pɪlfə] v. to steal small objects or small amounts of money. **pilferer,** n. person who pilfers. **pilferage, pilfering,** n. stealing small objects or amounts of money.

pilgrim ['pɪlgrɪm] n. person who goes to visit a holy place. **pilgrimage,** n. journey to visit a holy place/a famous place.

pill [pɪl] n. small round tablet of medicine; inf. **she's on the p.** = she takes contraceptive tablets. **pillbox,** n. (a) round box for pills. (b) concrete shelter for a small gun.

pillage ['pɪlɪdʒ] **1.** n. plundering by soldiers. **2.** v. (of soldiers) to plunder/ to steal goods (from a captured town, etc.).

pillar ['pɪlə] n. (a) column. (b) strong supporter. **pillar box,** n. round red metal container into which you can post letters; **pillar-box red** = bright red.

pillion ['pɪljən] n. rear saddle for a passenger on a motorcycle; **p. passenger** = person riding on the pillion seat; **to ride p.** = to ride on the pillion seat.

pillory ['pɪlərɪ] **1.** n. wooden stand with holes for the head and hands, where criminals were placed so that the public could throw things at them. **2.** v. to make (s.o.) appear ridiculous or foolish in public.

pillow ['pɪləʊ] n. bag full of soft material which you put your head on in bed. **pillowcase, pillowslip,** n. cloth bag to cover a pillow with.

pilot ['paɪlət] **1.** n. (a) person who guides ships into harbour or through dangerous channels; **p. scheme** = small scheme used as a test before starting a full-scale scheme. (b) person who flies an aircraft. (c) **p. light** = small gas light on a cooker/water-heater, etc., from which the main gas jets are lit. **2.** v. (a) to guide (a ship). (b) to fly (an aircraft). **pilot officer,** n. lowest rank of officer in the air force.

pimento, Am. **pimiento** [pɪ'mentəʊ, Am. pɪmɪ'entəʊ] n. (pl. **-os**) green or red fruit with a hot spicy taste used as a vegetable.

pimp [pɪmp] **1.** n. man who organizes and makes money from prostitutes. **2.** v. to work as a pimp.

pimpernel ['pɪmpənel] n. wild plant with small red flowers.

pimple ['pɪmpl] n. small bump on the surface of the skin. **pimply,** adj. covered with pimples.

pin [pɪn] **1.** n. (a) small sharp metal stick with a round head, used for attaching clothes/papers, etc., together; **safety p.** = type of bent pin where the sharp point is held by a metal shield; **pins and needles** = prickling feeling in your hand or foot after it has been numb for a time. (b) blunt wooden or metal bolt used for fastening things together. **2.** v. (**pinned**) (a) to attach with a pin; **to p. s.o. down** = to get him to say what he really thinks/to make his mind up. (b) to hold fast. **pinball,** n. table game where a ball has to be rolled into holes. **pincushion,** n. round pad in which you can stick pins. **pin money,** n. inf. money earned by a woman for part-time work. **pinpoint,** v. to indicate exactly. **pinprick,** n. slight annoyance. **pinstripe,** n. dark cloth with a very thin white line in it. **pintable,** n. table for playing pinball. **pin-up,** n. inf. photograph of a pretty girl which you can pin up on a wall.

pinafore ['pɪnəfɔ:] n. apron worn to cover a dress.

pince-nez ['pænsneɪ] n. pl. glasses which clip on to your nose.

pincers ['pɪnsəz] n. pl. (a) (**pair of**) p. = scissor-shaped tool for holding sth tight. (b) claws of a crab/lobster.

pinch [pɪnʃ] 1. n. (pl. -es) (a) squeezing tightly/nipping between finger and thumb; **at a p.** = if really necessary; **to feel the p.** = find you have less money than you need. (b) small quantity of sth held between finger and thumb. 2. v. (a) to squeeze tightly, using the finger and thumb. (b) to hold tight and hurt. (c) inf. to steal. (d) Sl. to arrest.

pine [paɪn] 1. n. type of evergreen tree; **wood** from a pine tree. 2. v. (to) waste away (because you want sth). **pineapple** ['paɪnæpl] n. large tropical fruit, shaped like a pine cone with stiff prickly leaves on top. **pine cone,** n. fruit of a pine tree. **pine marten,** n. small carnivorous animal, living in coniferous forests. **pinewood,** n. a wood of pine trees. **pineal gland,** n. small gland, shaped like a pine cone, found in the brain.

ping [pɪŋ] 1. n. noise made when a small bell/a glass, etc., is hit. 2. v. to make a ping. **pinger,** n. inf. bell which makes a ping.

ping pong ['pɪŋpɒŋ] n. inf. table tennis.

pinion ['pɪnjən] 1. n. (a) large outer feather on a bird's wing. (b) toothed wheel or cogwheel. 2. v. to tie up (s.o.'s arms) tightly.

pink [pɪŋk] 1. adj. & n. (colour) like pale red or flesh colour. 2. n. (a) scented garden flower like a small carnation. (b) red jacket worn by a huntsman; **in the p.** = very well/prosperous. 3. v. (of an engine) to make a knocking noise when misfiring. **pinking shears,** n. pl. large scissors used by dressmakers, which give a zigzag edge to a cut.

pinnacle ['pɪnəkl] n. topmost point (of a pointed rock, of s.o.'s career); tall, thin stone spire or tower.

pint [paɪnt] n. liquid measure (= .568 of a litre or of a gallon). **pinta,** n. inf. pint of milk.

pioneer [paɪə'nɪə] 1. n. (a) person who is among the first to try to do sth/who is the first to explore/settle in a new land. (b) soldier who prepares the way for the main army. 2. v. to be first to do (sth).

pious ['paɪəs] adj. showing great respect for religion. **piously,** adv. in a pious way.

pip [pɪp] 1. n. (a) small seed. (b) star on the shoulder showing an officer's rank. (c) short high-pitched call used on radio to show a time signal. 2. v. to beat; **to p. s.o. at the post** = to beat him at the last minute.

pipe [paɪp] 1. n. (a) tube. (b) instrument for smoking tobacco. (c) thin metal flute; **the pipes** = bagpipes. 2. v. to send (water/gas, etc.) along a pipe; **piped music** = recorded music played continuously (in a restaurant, etc.). **pipe down,** v. inf. to stop talking. **pipedream,** n. plan which is impossible to carry out. **pipeline,** n. very large tube for carrying oil/natural gas, etc., over long distances; **in the p.** = being worked on/on the way. **piper,** n. person who plays the bagpipes. **pipe up,** v. inf. to start talking (esp. in a high-pitched voice). **piping.** 1. n. (a) collection of tubes; section of metal tube. (b) decoration like white tubes on a cake/on a dress. 2. adv. **p. hot** = extremely hot.

pipette [pɪ'pet] n. thin glass measuring tube used in laboratories.

pipit ['pɪpɪt] n. small singing bird.

pippin ['pɪpɪn] n. type of sweet apple.

piquant ['pi:kənt] adj. nice sharp (flavour); pleasantly interesting/amusing. **piquancy,** n. being piquant. **piquantly,** adv. in a piquant way.

pique [pi:k] 1. n. resentment/annoyance. 2. v. (a) to make (s.o.) resentful. (b) to arouse s.o.'s curiosity.

piqué ['pikeɪ] n. cotton material with ribs.

piranha [pɪ'rɑ:nə] n. small tropical fish which attacks animals, including man.

pirate ['paɪərət] 1. n. (a) robber (esp. at

sea). (*b*) person who copies a patented invention or a copyright work. (*c*) person who takes money from s.o. else; **p. radio** = illegal radio station. **2.** *v.* to publish books/make recordings which are copied from those of another publisher without having the right to do so. **piracy,** *n.* robbery (at sea); illegal publishing of books/making of records. **piratical** [paɪˈrætɪkl] *adj.* referring to a pirate.

pirouette [pɪruˈet] **1.** *n.* spinning round on one foot when dancing. **2.** *v.* to spin round on one foot.

piscatorial [pɪskəˈtɔːrɪəl] *adj.* referring to fishing.

Pisces [ˈpaɪsiːz] *n.* one of the signs of the zodiac, shaped like fish.

pisciculture [pɪsɪˈkʌltʃə] *n.* raising fish for food.

piss [pɪs] **1.** *n. inf. & vulgar* (*a*) waste water from the body. (*b*) passing waste water from the body. **2.** *v. inf. & vulgar* to pass waste water from the body.

pistachio [pɪˈstæʃɪəʊ] *n.* (*pl.* **-os**) small green tropical nut.

piste [piːst] *n.* track for skiing.

pistil [ˈpɪstɪl] *n.* female part of a flower, which produces seeds.

pistol [ˈpɪstl] *n.* small gun which is held in the hand.

piston [ˈpɪstn] *n.* (*in an engine*) metal disc which moves up and down in a cylinder; **p. rod** = rod which is attached to a piston and which drives other parts of the engine.

pit [pɪt] **1.** *n.* (*a*) deep, dark hole in the ground. (*b*) coalmine. (*c*) hole in the floor of a garage (for inspecting the underside of a car); (*at car races*) place where the cars are inspected and repaired. (*d*) back part of the ground floor of a theatre. (*e*) depths of your stomach. (*f*) *Am.* stone of some fruit. **2.** *v.* (**pitted**) (*a*) to try (your strength) **against.** (*b*) to take the stone out of (a fruit). (*c*) to mark with a hole. **pithead,** *n.* entrance to a coalmine shaft.

pitch [pɪtʃ] **1.** *n.* (*pl.* **-es**) (*a*) black substance which comes from tar and is used for waterproofing boats/roofs, etc. (*b*) level of tone in music. (*c*) ground on which a game is played; place in the street where a trader sells

his wares. (*d*) height (of anger/of excitement). (*e*) angle of a sloping roof. (*f*) **sales p.** = smooth talk, aimed at selling sth. **2.** *v.* (*a*) to put up (a tent). (*b*) to throw (a ball). (*c*) to set the level of a musical tone. (*d*) (*of boat*) to rock with the front and back going up and down. **pitch-black, pitch dark,** *adj.* very black; very dark. **pitchblende,** *n.* mineral which produces radium. **pitched,** *adj.* **p. battle** = battle fought on a selected piece of ground; fierce argument. **pitcher** [ˈpɪtʃə] *n.* (*a*) large earthenware jug. (*b*) person who pitches a ball. **pitchfork. 1.** *n.* large fork for moving bales of hay. **2.** *v.* to put (s.o.) suddenly **into** an awkward position. **pitch into,** *v.* to attack. **pitchpine,** *n.* type of pine which produces strong resin.

pitfall [ˈpɪtfɔːl] *n.* trap/danger.

pith [pɪθ] *n.* (*a*) soft part in the centre of a plant stem; soft white stuff under the skin of a lemon/an orange, etc. (*b*) important part (of an argument). **pithily,** *adv.* in a pithy way. **pithy,** *adj.* (**-ier, -iest**) (*a*) (wood) with a soft centre. (*b*) concise; full of serious meaning.

piton [ˈpiːtɒn] *n.* metal peg used in rock-climbing.

pittance [ˈpɪtns] *n.* low wage.

pitterpatter [ˈpɪtəpætə] *n.* series of small sounds.

pituitary [pɪˈtjuːɪtrɪ] *adj.* **p. gland** = gland in the brain which produces hormones which control the development and function of the body.

pity [ˈpɪtɪ] **1.** *n.* feeling of sympathy for s.o. unfortunate; **to take p. on s.o.** = to be sorry for s.o. **2.** *v.* to feel sympathy for (s.o.). **piteous** [ˈpɪtɪəs], **pitiable,** *adj.* which deserves pity. **pitiful,** *adj.* (*a*) deserving pity; sad. (*b*) inadequate. **pitifully,** *adv.* in a pitiful way. **pitiless,** *adj.* showing no pity.

pivot [ˈpɪvət] **1.** *n.* point on which sth turns. **2.** *v.* to turn on a point; to depend on sth. **pivotal,** *adj.* of great importance.

pixel [ˈpɪksəl] *n.* tiny element of colour or light on a TV screen or computer monitor.

pixie [ˈpɪksɪ] *n.* small fairy.

pizza [ˈpiːtsə] *n.* Italian savoury dish,

consisting of a flat round piece of dough cooked with tomatoes, onions, etc., on top. **pizzeria,** *n.* shop which sells pizzas.

pizzicato [pɪtsɪ'kɑːtəʊ] *n.* & *adv.* (music) played by plucking the strings instead of using the bow.

placard ['plækɑːd] **1.** *n.* poster. **2.** *v.* to stick posters up.

placate [plə'keɪt] *v.* to calm (s.o.); to make (s.o.) less angry. **placatory,** *adv.* which placates.

place [pleɪs] **1.** *n.* (*a*) location/spot. (*b*) house/home. (*c*) open area. (*d*) name of a smart street in a town. (*e*) set position; **to take p.** = to happen/to be held. (*f*) rank (in a series); **in the first p.** = first of all. (*g*) job. (*h*) one of the first three positions in a horse race. **2.** *v.* (*a*) to put. (*b*) to give (an order). (*c*) to put in a set position. (*d*) to remember who s.o. is. **placemat,** *n.* mat which a person's plate is put on. **placement,** *n.* placing s.o. in a job. **place setting,** *n.* set of knife/fork/spoon, etc. for one person.

placebo [plə'siːbəʊ] *n.* (*pl.* -os) harmless substance given to a patient instead of a drug to make him believe he is receiving treatment.

placenta [plə'sentə] *n.* tissue in the womb which nourishes the unborn baby.

placid ['plæsɪd] *adj.* (-er, -est) calm. **placidity** [plə'sɪdɪtɪ] *n.* calmness. **placidly,** *adv.* calmly.

placket ['plækɪt] *n.* opening with buttons at the waist of a skirt.

plagiarism ['pleɪdʒərɪzəm] *n.* copying what s.o. else has written. **plagiarist,** *n.* author who copies the work of s.o. else. **plagiarize,** *v.* to copy the work of (another author).

plague [pleɪg] **1.** *n.* (*a*) fatal infectious disease transmitted by fleas from rats. (*b*) great quantity of pests. **2.** *v.* to annoy/to bother (s.o.).

plaice [pleɪs] *n.* (*pl.* **plaice**) common flat sea fish.

plaid [plæd] *n.* (*in Scotland*) long piece of (tartan) cloth.

plain [pleɪn] **1.** *adj.* (-er, -est) (*a*) obvious/easy to understand. (*b*) simple/uncomplicated; **p. cover** = envelope without any company name on it. (*c*) not pretty. (*d*) **p. chocolate** = dark chocolate, made without milk; **p. flour** = white flour with no baking powder in it. **2.** *n.* large flat area of country. **plainclothes,** *n. pl.* ordinary/everyday clothes (not uniform). **plainly,** *adv.* (*a*) obviously. (*b*) simply. **plainness,** *n.* (*a*) clearness. (*b*) simpleness. **plainsong,** *n.* medieval music for church services. **plain-spoken,** *adj.* (person) who speaks in a straightforward way.

plaintiff ['pleɪntɪf] *n.* person who starts a legal action against s.o. else.

plaintive ['pleɪntɪv] *adj.* sad.

plait [plæt] **1.** *n.* (hair/wool, etc.) with three strands woven into a long rope. **2.** *v.* to weave hair, etc., to form a plait.

plan [plæn] **1.** *n.* (*a*) scheme; **according to p.** = as we had intended. (*b*) drawing of the way sth is to be built or constructed. (*c*) map of streets. **2.** *v.* (**planned**) (*a*) to draw up a scheme to construct sth. (*b*) to scheme/to propose to do sth. **planner,** *n.* person who draws up schemes; **town p.** = person who designs how a town should develop. **planning,** *n.* making plans; **family p.** = decision by parents on how many children to have.

plane [pleɪn] **1.** *n.* (*a*) flat surface. (*b*) aircraft. (*c*) tool for smoothing wood. (*d*) tree often grown in towns, of which bark comes off in large pieces. **2.** *adj.* level/flat. **3.** *v.* to smooth (wood) flat with a plane.

planet ['plænɪt] *n.* body which revolves round a star, esp. round the sun. **planetarium** [plænɪ'teərɪəm] *n.* domed building in which you sit and watch as pictures of the stars are projected against the ceiling. **planetary** ['plænɪtrɪ] *adj.* referring to the planets.

plangent ['plændʒnt] *adj.* sad resonant (music).

plank [plæŋk] *n.* (*a*) long flat piece of wood used in building. (*b*) proposal in a political programme. **planking,** *n.* series of planks.

plankton ['plæŋktn] *n.* tiny organisms living in the sea.

plant [plɑːnt] **1.** *n.* (*a*) thing which grows in the ground, is usu. green, and cannot move from one place to another. (*b*) factory. (*c*) machinery. **2.** *v.* (*a*) to put (a plant) into the ground. (*b*) to put in a special position. (*c*) to put (sth) secretly; to put (stolen goods) secretly on s.o., in order to make it look as if he stole them. **plantation** [plɑ:n'teɪʃn] n. (a) area of trees specially planted. (b) tropical estate growing a particular crop. **planter,** n. (a) person in charge of a plantation. (b) decorative container to hold plants in pots.

plantain ['plæntɪn] n. (a) common weed. (b) tropical fruit.

plaque [plæk] n. (a) decorative plate hung on a wall; stone/metal/earthenware plate with an inscription. (b) deposit which forms on the teeth.

plasma ['plæzmə] n. liquid part of blood.

plaster ['plɑ:stə] 1. n. (a) mixture of fine sand and lime which when mixed with water is used for covering walls of houses. (b) white paste, used to make moulds/to make coverings to hold broken arms and legs in place. (c) **sticking p.** = adhesive cloth/tape used for holding bandages in place/for covering small wounds. 2. v. (a) to cover with plaster. (b) to cover thickly as if with plaster. **plaster-cast,** n. (a) block of plaster put round a broken leg, etc. (b) mould made by covering sth with plaster. (c) copy of a statue made in plaster. **plastered,** adj. Sl. drunk. **plasterer,** n. person who covers walls with plaster.

plastic ['plæstɪk] 1. n. artificial substance, which can be moulded into any shape; **p. bomb** = explosive material which can be moulded in the hand. 2. adj. soft/pliable; **p. surgery** = operation to replace damaged skin or to improve s.o.'s appearance. **plasticity** [plæs'tɪsɪtɪ] n. state of being plastic.

plate [pleɪt] 1. n. (a) thin flat sheet of metal/glass, etc. (b) flat dish for putting food on. (c) dishes made of gold or silver. (d) thin layer of gold/silver on a less precious metal; objects made of this. (e) book illustration on shiny paper. (f) piece of plastic with false teeth attached which fits into your mouth. 2. v. to cover with a thin layer of gold or silver. **plateful,** n. quantity held by a plate. **plate glass,** n. glass in very large sheets. **platelayer,** n. railway worker who sets the rails in place/who repairs rails.

plateau ['plætəʊ] n. (pl. -eaux [-əʊz]) high flat area of land.

platelet ['pleɪtlət] n. small cell in the blood which helps blood to clot.

platen ['plætən] n. roller round which the paper goes in a typewriter.

platform ['plætfɔ:m] n. (a) raised floor space for speakers in a hall. (b) raised pavement by the side of the rails in a railway station so that passengers can get on and off trains easily. (c) proposals put forward by the leaders of a political party before an election.

platinum ['plætɪnəm] n. (element: Pt) rare light-coloured precious metal; **p. blonde** = woman with silvery blonde hair.

platitude ['plætɪtju:d] n. ordinary saying, esp. one which the speaker thinks is very important.

platonic [plə'tɒnɪk] adj. (love between man and woman) which is not sexual.

platoon [plə'tu:n] n. small group of soldiers/part of a company.

platter ['plætə] n. large serving plate.

platypus ['plætɪpəs] n. (pl. -es) Australian mammal which lays eggs.

plaudits ['plɔ:dɪts] n. pl. applause.

plausible ['plɔ:zɪbl] adj. which sounds as though it is correct when it often is not. **plausibly,** adv. in a plausible way. **plausibility** [plɔ:zɪ'bɪlɪtɪ] n. being plausible.

play [pleɪ] 1. n. (a) way of amusing yourself; sport. (b) theatrical performance; script of a theatrical performance. (c) freedom to move. 2. v. (a) to amuse yourself/to pass the time in a pleasant way. (b) to take part in a game. (c) to perform on a musical instrument. (d) to act a part in a theatrical performance. (e) to aim. (f) to let a fish which has been caught on a hook swim until it is tired and can easily be landed. (g) (of fountain, etc.) to work. (h) to make (a record-player) work; to make (a beam of light) hit sth. **play at,** v. (a) to work in a slack way. (b) (of children) to pretend to be. **play back,** v. to listen to (sth) which you have just recorded on tape. **playboy,** n. rich man who spends his time amusing himself rather than working. **play down,** v. to make (sth) seem less important. **player,** n. person who plays. **playfellow**, *n.* child another child plays with. **playful**, *adj.* liking to play. **playfully**, *adv.* in a playful way. **playfulness**, *n.* being playful. **playground**, *n.* area, esp. round school buildings, where children can play. **playgroup**, *n.* group of small children who play together under supervision. **playhouse**, *n.* theatre. **playing card**, *n.* one of a set of fifty-two cards, marked in four designs, used for playing various games. **playing field**, *n.* area of grass where sports can be played. **playmate**, *n.* playfellow. **play off**, *v.* **to p. s.o. off against s.o.** = to try to benefit by making two people oppose each other. **play on**, *v.* to take advantage by exciting (s.o.'s sympathy). **playpen**, *n.* type of cage in which babies can be left to play safely. **plaything**, *n.* toy. **playtime**, *n.* time in nursery school when children can play. **play up**, *v. inf.* to make trouble. **playwright**, *n.* person who writes plays.

plaza ['plɑːzə] *n.* open area in a town.

Plc [piːel'siː] *n.* short for public limited company.

plea [pliː] *n.* (*a*) answer to a charge in court; **p. bargaining** = arrangement where an accused person pleads guilty to some charges so as to be let off others. (*b*) (*formal*) request. (*c*) excuse.

plead [pliːd] *v.* (*a*) to answer a charge in a law court. (*b*) to give an excuse. (*c*) **to p. with s.o.** = to try to change s.o.'s mind by asking again and again.

pleasant ['pleznt] *adj.* (**-er**, **-est**) agreeable/which pleases. **pleasantly**, *adv.* in a pleasant way. **pleasantry**, *n.* joke; pleasant remark.

please [pliːz] *v.* (*a*) to make (s.o.) happy/satisfied; **p. yourself** = do as you like. (*b*) *polite expression after an order or request, meaning* if you would like. **pleased**, *adj.* happy; satisfied. **pleasing**, *adj.* which pleases. **pleasurable** ['pleʒərəbl] *adj.* pleasant. **pleasure** ['pleʒə] *n.* amusement/happiness.

pleat [pliːt] **1.** *n.* vertical fold (in a skirt, etc.). **2.** *v.* to iron vertical folds in.

plebiscite ['plebɪsɪt] *n.* general vote by the inhabitants of a country on an important issue.

plebs [plebz] *n. pl. inf.* ordinary people.

plebeian [pliː'biːən] *adj.* common/ordinary; of the working class.

plectrum ['plektrəm] *n.* small stick for plucking the strings of a guitar, etc.

pledge [pledʒ] **1.** *n.* (*a*) object given to the lender when borrowing money, and which will be returned to the borrower when the money is paid back. (*b*) promise; **to take the p.** = to swear never to drink alcohol again. **2.** *v.* (*a*) to give (sth) as a pledge when borrowing money. (*b*) to promise. (*c*) to drink (a toast).

plenary ['pliːnərɪ] *adj.* complete; **p. session** = session of a conference where all the delegates meet together.

plenipotentiary [plenɪpə'tenʃərɪ] *adj. & n.* (person) who has full powers to act on behalf of his country.

plenteous ['plentɪəs] *adj.* (*formal*) more than enough.

plenty ['plentɪ] *n.* large quantity. **plentiful**, *adj.* abundant; in large quantities.

plenum ['pleɪnəm] *n.* general meeting.

pleonasm ['plɪənæzəm] *n.* use of more words than necessary.

pleonastic [plɪə'næstɪk] *adj.* (expression) where some words are superfluous.

plethora ['pleθərə] *n.* (*formal*) too many (of).

pleura ['pluərə] *n.* membrane covering the lungs. **pleurisy**, *n.* disease of the membrane covering the lungs.

plexus ['pleksəs] *n.* network of nerves.

pliable ['plaɪəbl], **pliant** ['plaɪənt] *adj.* which can be bent easily; (person) who can be easily persuaded. **pliability**, **pliancy**, *n.* being pliable/pliant.

pliers ['plaɪəz] *n. pl.* (**pair of**) **p.** = tool shaped like scissors for pinching, twisting or cutting wire.

plight [plaɪt] **1.** *n.* bad state. **2.** *v.* (*formal*) to promise.

Plimsoll line ['plɪmsɒllaɪn] *n.* line along the side of a ship which shows the level of the water when the ship is loaded.

plimsolls ['plɪmsɒlz] *n. pl.* canvas shoes worn when doing gymnastics.

plinth [plɪnθ] *n.* pedestal on which a statue stands.

plod [plɒd] *v.* (**plodded**) (*a*) to walk heavily. (*b*) to work steadily. **plodder**, *n.* person who works steadily but rather slowly.

plonk [plɒŋk] 1. *n. inf.* (*a*) dull sound. (*b*) inferior wine. 2. *v. inf.* to put (sth) down heavily.

plop [plɒp] 1. *n.* noise made by a stone falling into water. 2. *v.* (**plopped**) to make a noise like a stone falling into water.

plot [plɒt] 1. *n.* (*a*) small area of land for building/for growing vegetables, etc. (*b*) basic story of a book/play/film. (*c*) wicked plan. 2. *v.* (**plotted**) (*a*) to mark on a map; to draw a graph. (*b*) to draw up a wicked plan. **plotter,** *n.* person who plots.

plough, *Am.* **plow** [plaʊ] 1. *n.* (*a*) farm machine for turning over soil. (*b*) **snow p.** = machine like a tractor with a large blade in front, used for clearing snow from streets, railway lines, etc. 2. *v.* (*a*) to turn over the soil. (*b*) to work slowly. **plough back,** *v.* to invest (profits) back in a business. **ploughman,** *n.* (*pl.* -**men**) farm worker who drives a plough; **ploughman's lunch** = bread, cheese and pickles. **ploughshare,** *n.* blade of a plough.

plover [ˈplʌvə] *n.* type of wading bird (found in fields and moors).

plow [plaʊ] *n. & v. Am. see* **plough.**

ploy [plɔɪ] *n.* clever trick.

pluck [plʌk] 1. *n.* courage. 2. *v.* (*a*) to pull out feathers or eyebrows. (*b*) to pick (flowers, etc.). (*c*) to pull and release the strings of a guitar to make a sound; **to p. up courage** = to get ready to face a danger. **pluckily,** *adv.* in a plucky way. **plucky,** *adj.* (-**ier, -iest**) brave.

plug [plʌg] 1. *n.* (*a*) disc which covers a hole, esp. the hole for waste water in a bath/sink, etc. (*b*) device with pins which go into the holes in an electric socket, and allow the current to pass through; (*in a car*) **sparking p.** = device which passes the electric spark through the petrol vapour. (*c*) *inf.* piece of publicity. (*d*) piece of tobacco which you chew. 2. *v.* (**plugged**) (*a*) to block up (a hole). (*b*) *inf.* to publicize. (*c*) *inf.* to shoot. **plug away,** *v. inf.* to work hard (at). **plughole,** *n.* hole in a bath/washbasin through which the dirty water runs away. **plug in,** *v.* to push an electric plug into a socket.

plum [plʌm] *n.* (*a*) gold, red or purple fruit with a smooth skin and a large stone; tree which bears this fruit; **p. pudding** = rich boiled fruit pudding, usu. eaten at Christmas; *inf.* **p. job** = very good job. (*b*) deep purple colour.

plumage [ˈpluːmɪdʒ] *n.* feathers on a bird.

plumb [plʌm] 1. *adj.* straight; vertical. 2. *n.* lead weight for testing if sth is straight. 3. *v.* (*a*) to measure (the depth of water) by using a plumbline. (*b*) to reach the bottom (of feeling of despair). (*c*) to fix the plumbing in (a house). 4. *adv.* (*a*) exactly (in the middle). (*b*) *Am.* completely. **plumber,** *n.* person who installs water pipes, etc. **plumb in,** *v.* to attach (a washing machine) permanently to the water system. **plumbing,** *n.* system of water pipes in a house. **plumbline,** *n.* rope with a weight on the end, dropped over the side from a ship to find how deep the water is or held beside a wall to see if it is vertical.

plume [pluːm] *n.* tall feather (worn in a hat, etc.); tall column of smoke. **plumed,** *adj.* with a plume.

plummet [ˈplʌmɪt] *v.* to fall sharply.

plummy [ˈplʌmɪ] *adj.* rich/full (voice).

plump [plʌmp] 1. *adj.* (-**er, -est**) fat and tender; round fat (person). 2. *v.* (*a*) **p. up** = to shake (squashed cushions) until they are fat. (*b*) *inf.* **to p. for** = to decide on. (*c*) to throw (oneself) down. **plumpness,** *n.* fatness.

plunder [ˈplʌndə] 1. *n.* booty/goods seized, esp. in war. 2. *v.* to seize goods by force.

plunge [plʌndʒ] 1. *n.* dive; **to take the p.** = suddenly decide to do sth. 2. *v.* to dive deeply; to throw yourself into. **plunger,** *n.* (*a*) device which goes up and down in a cylinder. (*b*) handle with a soft rubber head, for clearing blocked pipes by suction.

pluperfect [pluːˈpɜːfɪkt] *adj. & n.* (tense) showing sth which took place before a time in the past.

plural [ˈplʊərəl] *adj. & n.* (*in grammar*) form of a word showing more than one. **pluralism,** *n.* political system where several political parties are allowed to exist. **plurality** [plʊəˈrælɪtɪ] *n. Am.* majority.

plus [plʌs] 1. *prep.* in addition to. 2. *adj.*

& n. (a) sign (+) meaning more than. (b) inf. favourable sign. **plus-fours,** n. pl. baggy golfing trousers, attached at the calf.

plush [plʌʃ] **1.** n. soft-pile cloth for furnishings. **2.** adj. (**-er, -est**) inf. luxurious.

plutocrat ['plu:təkræt] n. person who is very rich and powerful. **plutocracy** [plu:'tɒkrəsɪ] n. government by the very rich.

plutonium [plu:'təʊnɪəm] n. (element: Pu) radioactive substance, used to produce nuclear power.

ply [plaɪ] **1.** n. (a) thickness of wood in plywood. (b) strand of wool. **2.** v. (a) to go backwards and forwards. (b) to p. **s.o. with** = to force s.o. to eat/drink sth. **plywood,** n. sheet made of several thin sheets of wood stuck together.

p.m. [pi:'em] adv. in the afternoon/after midday.

PM [pi:'em] n. **1.** = Prime Minister. **2.** = postmortem.

pneumatic [nju:'mætɪk] adj. driven by compressed air. **pneumatically,** adv. using compressed air.

pneumonia [nju:'məʊnɪə] n. illness caused by inflammation of the lungs.

PO ['pi:'əʊ] = post office.

poach [pəʊtʃ] v. (a) to cook (eggs without their shells/fish, etc.) in gently boiling water. (b) to catch game illegally. (c) to entice workers to leave their jobs and work for another employer. **poacher,** n. person who catches game illegally.

pochard ['pɒtʃəd] n. type of diving duck.

pocket ['pɒkɪt] **1.** n. (a) small bag attached to the inside of a coat/trousers, etc., for holding money/keys, etc.; **p. dictionary** = small dictionary which you can keep in your pocket; **p. money** = money given each week to a child to spend as he pleases. (b) **to be in p.** = to have made a profit; **to be out of p.** = to have lost money. (c) hole with a small bag at each corner and side of a billiard table. (d) small patch/small group in a certain place. **2.** v. (a) to put in your pocket. (b) to send (a billiard ball) into a pocket. **pocketbook,** n. small wallet. **pocketful,** n. amount contained in a pocket.

pockmarked ['pɒkmɑ:kt] adj. covered with round scars.

pod [pɒd] n. long case in which peas/beans, etc., are formed.

podgy ['pɒdʒɪ] adj. inf. (**-ier, -iest**) fat.

podium ['pəʊdɪəm] n. raised platform (for winning sportsmen/orchestral conductors, etc., to stand on).

podsol ['pɒdsɒl] n. type of pale acid soil.

poem ['pəʊɪm] n. piece of writing, in a particular rhythm, often with lines of a regular length which rhyme. **poet, poetess,** n. person who writes poems. **poetic(al)** [pəʊ'etɪk(l)] adj. referring to poetry; imaginative/rhythmic (as in a poem). **poetically,** adv. in a poetic way. **poetry** ['pəʊətrɪ] n. writing of poems; poems taken as a type of literature.

pogrom ['pɒgrəm] n. official persecution/massacre (esp. of Jews).

poignant ['pɔɪnjənt] adj. moving/sad (thought). **poignancy,** n. sadness. **poignantly,** adv. sadly/in a way which moves you to sadness.

poinsettia [pɔɪn'setɪə] n. plant with large green leaves, turning red at the top, used as a Christmas decoration.

point [pɔɪnt] **1.** n. (a) sharp end (of a pin, etc.). (b) dot; **decimal p.** = dot used to indicate the division between units and decimals (such as 3.25). (c) place/spot; **p. of no return** = place where you can only go on and not go back. (d) reason/purpose. (e) meaning/argument. (f) specific time; **on the p. of** = just about to. (g) headland. (h) mark in games or competitions; mark on a scale. (i) movable rails which allow trains to cross from one line to another. (j) electric socket; (in an engine) electrical contacts. **2.** v. (a) to aim (a gun/your finger) **at** s.o./sth. (b) to sharpen to a point. (c) to fill the spaces in between bricks with mortar. **point-blank,** adj. & adv. (a) at very close range. (b) sharply/directly. **point-duty,** n. (of a policeman) **to be on point-duty** = to direct the traffic. **pointed,** adj. (a) with a sharp end. (b) obviously unfriendly (remark). **pointedly,** adv. in an unfriendly way. **pointer,** n. (a) dog which is trained to point out game with its nose. (b) arrow/rod which points. **pointless,** adj. meaningless.

pointlessly, *adv.* meaninglessly. **point out,** *v.* to indicate/to show. **point-to-point,** *n.* type of horse race held over a rough track in the country. **point up,** *v.* to make (sth) seem even more obvious.

poise [pɔɪz] **1.** *n.* balance/graceful way of holding your head or of standing upright. **2.** *v.* to balance. **poised,** *adj.* ready (**to kill/for** action).

poison ['pɔɪzn] **1.** *n.* substance which kills or makes you ill if it is swallowed or if it gets into the bloodstream. **2.** *v.* to kill with poison. **poisoner,** *n.* person who poisons. **poisonous,** *adj.* which can kill or harm with poison.

poke [pəʊk] *v.* (*a*) to push with your finger/with a stick. (*b*) **to p. about for** = to search. **poker,** *n.* (*a*) long metal rod for stirring up a fire. (*b*) card game in which the players gamble. **poker face,** *n.* expression which shows no emotion. **pokerfaced,** *adj.* showing no emotion.

poky ['pəʊkɪ] *adj.* (**-ier, -iest**) *inf.* cramped/small (room).

polar ['pəʊlə] *adj.* referring to the North/South Poles. **polar bear,** *n.* white bear which lives in the Arctic. **polarize** ['pəʊləraɪz] *v.* to divide into two opposite groups. **polarization** [pəʊləraɪ'zeɪʃn] *n.* attraction around two opposite poles; division into main groups.

polder ['pɒldə] *n.* land which has been reclaimed from the sea.

pole [pəʊl] *n.* (*a*) one of the points at each end of the earth's axis. (*b*) one of the two opposing ends of a magnet; **they are poles apart** = they are very different/ they will never come to an agreement. (*c*) long wooden/metal rod; **p. vaulting** = sport where you have to jump over a high bar with the help of a long pole. (*d*) **Pole** = person from Poland. **poleaxe. 1.** *n.* (*old*) large axe used in battle. **2.** *v.* to knock (s.o.) down. **pole star,** *n.* star which appears to be near to the North Pole.

polecat ['pəʊlkæt] *n.* small wild flesh-eating animal, like a weasel.

polemic [pə'lemɪk] *n.* argument/attack on s.o.'s views. **polemical,** *adj.* controversial/likely to start an argument.

police [pə'liːs] **1.** *n.* group of people who keep law and order in a country; **p. constable** = ordinary member of the police; **p. force** = group of police in a certain area; **p. station** = local office of a police force. **2.** *v.* to keep law and order in (a town, etc.). **policeman, policewoman,** *n.* (*pl.* **-men, -women**) member of the police. **police state,** *n.* country which is terrorized by the police.

policy ['pɒlɪsɪ] *n.* (*a*) way of acting. (*b*) written agreement with an insurance company.

poliomyelitis [pəʊlɪəʊmaɪə'laɪtɪs] *inf.* **polio** ['pəʊlɪəʊ] *n.* disease of the nerves in the spinal cord, sometimes causing paralysis.

polish ['pɒlɪʃ] **1.** *n.* (*pl.* **-es**) (*a*) shiny surface. (*b*) rubbing to make sth shiny. (*c*) substance used to make things shiny. **2.** *v.* to rub (sth) to make it shiny. **polished,** *adj.* (*a*) shiny. (*b*) made perfect by practice. (*c*) polite (manners). **polisher,** *n.* machine which polishes. **polish off,** *v.* to finish off (a job) quickly/to eat (a meal) quickly. **polish up,** *v. inf.* to improve.

Polish ['pəʊlɪʃ] **1.** *adj.* referring to Poland. **2.** *n.* language spoken in Poland.

Politburo [pɒ'lɪtbjuːrəʊ] *n.* central committee of a communist party.

polite [pə'laɪt] *adj.* (**-er, -est**) not rude; courteous. **politely,** *adv.* courteously; in a well-mannered way. **politeness,** *n.* good manners.

politics ['pɒlɪtɪks] *n.* study of how to govern a country. **politic** ['pɒlɪtɪk] *adj.* wise/careful. **political** [pə'lɪtɪkl] *adj.* referring to government/party politics; **p. party** = organized group of people who believe in one particular method of ruling a country. **politically,** *adv.* as far as politics are concerned. **politician** [pɒlɪ'tɪʃn] *n.* person who works in politics, esp. a member of parliament.

polka ['pɒlkə] *n.* type of lively dance; **p. dots** = small round dots (as a pattern on cloth).

poll [pəʊl] **1.** *n.* (*a*) vote/voting. (*b*) number of votes. (*c*) **opinion p.** = questioning of a sample group of people to guess at the views of the whole population on a question. **2.** *v.* (*a*) to vote. (b) to get a number of votes in an election. (c) to cut the horns off (a cow); **polling**, n. voting; elections; **p. booth** = small cabin in which each voter writes his vote; **p. station** = place where you vote in an election. **poll tax**, n. tax which is levied equally on each person.

pollard ['pɒləd] v. to cut the branches of (a tree) back to the main trunk.

pollen ['pɒln] n. usu. yellow powder in flowers which fertilizes them; **p. count** = number showing the amount of pollen in the air (which can cause hayfever). **pollinate** ['pɒlɪneɪt] v. to fertilize with pollen. **pollination** [pɒlɪ'neɪʃn] n. fertilizing with pollen.

pollute [pə'luːt] v. to make dirty. **pollutant**, n. substance which pollutes. **polluter**, n. person or company which pollutes; **p. pays principle** = rule that the person who causes pollution should pay for it to be cleared. **pollution** [pə'luːʃn] n. making dirty.

polo ['pəʊləʊ] n. (a) ball game in which the two teams ride on ponies; **water p.** = ball game played by two teams in the water. (b) **p. neck pullover** = pullover with a high rolled neck.

polony [pə'ləʊnɪ] n. red sausage made of cooked pork.

poltergeist ['pɒltəgaɪst] n. ghost which knocks things over/makes loud sounds, etc.

poly- ['pɒlɪ] prefix meaning several.

polyanthus [pɒlɪ'ænθəs] n. common garden flower, like a primrose with a large flower head.

polychrome ['pɒlɪkrəʊm] adj. with several colours.

polyester [pɒlɪ'estə] n. type of synthetic fibre used esp. in clothing.

polygamy [pə'lɪgəmɪ] n. custom of having several wives at the same time. **polygamist**, n. man with several wives. **polygamous**, adj. referring to polygamy.

polyglot ['pɒlɪglɒt] adj. & n. (person) who speaks several languages; (dictionary, etc.) written in several languages.

polygon ['pɒlɪgən] n. geometrical figure with many sides. **polygonal** [pə'lɪgənl] adj. with many sides.

polymer ['pɒlɪmə] n. chemical com-

pound whose molecule is made of several single similar molecules. **polymerization**, n. act of polymerizing. **polymerize**, v. to make/to become a polymer.

polyp ['pɒlɪp] n. (a) small primitive water animal shaped like a tube. (b) growth inside the human body.

polystyrene [pɒlɪ'staɪriːn] n. light plastic used as a heat insulator or as packing material.

polysyllable ['pɒlɪsɪləbl] n. word with several syllables. **polysyllabic** [pɒlɪsɪ'læbɪk] adj. (word) with several syllables.

polytechnic [pɒlɪ'teknɪk] n. educational establishment for school-leavers, giving degrees, esp. in technical subjects.

polytheism [pɒlɪ'θiːɪzm] n. belief in the existence of many gods.

polythene ['pɒlɪθiːn] n. type of almost transparent plastic used in thin sheets.

polyunsaturated [pɒlɪʌn'sætjʊreɪtɪd] adj. (fat) which does not form cholesterol in the blood.

polyurethane [pɒlɪ'jʊərɪθeɪn] n. type of plastic used in paints.

pom [pɒm], **pommy** ['pɒmɪ] adj. & n. (in Australia) inf. (person) from Britain.

pomander [pə'mændə] n. (box containing) dried scented herbs; **p. ball** = dried orange with cloves stuck into it.

pomegranate ['pɒmɪgrænɪt] n. tropical fruit with red flesh and many seeds.

pommel ['pɒml] n. high front part of a saddle.

pomp [pɒmp] n. splendid ceremony. **pomposity** [pɒm'pɒsɪtɪ] n. being pompous. **pompous** ['pɒmpəs] adj. very solemn/too dignified.

pompom ['pɒmpɒm] n. small tufted ball of wool worn as an ornament on a hat, etc.

ponce [pɒns] **1.** n. Sl. man who lives off the money earned by prostitutes. **2.** v. Sl. **to p. about** = to prance about in an effeminate way.

poncho ['pɒnʃəʊ] n. (pl. **-os**) cloak made of a single large piece of material, with a hole in the centre for your head.

pond [pɒnd] n. small lake.

ponder ['pɒndə] v. to think deeply. **ponderous**, adj. very heavy and slow-moving. **ponderously**, *adv*. in a ponderous way.

pong [pɒŋ] 1. *n*. *Sl*. unpleasant smell. 2. *v*. *Sl*. to make an unpleasant smell.

pontiff ['pɒntɪf] *n*. the Pope. **pontifical** [pɒn'tɪfɪkl] *adj*. referring to the Pope. **pontificate** [pɒn'tɪfɪkeɪt] *v*. to speak/to write in a pompous way.

pontoon [pɒn'tu:n] *n*. (*a*) boat used to support a floating temporary bridge; **p. bridge** = one built on pontoons. (*b*) card game.

pony ['pəʊnɪ] *n*. small horse. **pony tail**, *n*. hairstyle where the hair is tied at the back and falls loosely. **pony-trekking**, *n*. holiday sport riding ponies across country.

poodle ['pu:dl] *n*. type of curly-haired dog, usu. clipped in a curious way.

poof [pu:f] *n*. *Sl*. homosexual.

pooh-pooh [pu:'pu:] *v*. *inf*. to ridicule (an idea).

pool [pu:l] 1. *n*. (*a*) small lake. (*b*) area of water or other liquid. (*c*) **swimming p.** = enclosed tank of water for swimming. (*d*) common supply of money/ food, etc., for a group of people. (*e*) group where people share facilities; **car p.** = arrangement where several people share cars; **typing p.** = group of typists working for several departments. (*f*) **football pools** = system of gambling where you have to forecast the results of football matches. (*g*) *Am*. game similar to snooker. 2. *v*. to group (resources) together. **poolroom**, *n*. *Am*. public room where you can play pool.

poop [pu:p] *n*. high raised stern of a ship.

poor ['pʊə, pɔ:] *adj*. (**-er**, **-est**) (*a*) having little or no money; **p. in** = with very little (of sth). (*b*) not very good. **poorly.** 1. *adv*. (*a*) in quite a bad way. (*b*) without money. 2. *adj*. ill. **poorness**, *n*. bad quality.

pop [pɒp] 1. *n*. (*a*) noise like a cork coming out of a bottle. (*b*) *inf*. father. (*c*) *inf*. popular song. (*d*) *inf*. fizzy drink. 2. *v*. (**popped**) (*a*) to make a pop. (*b*) *inf*. to go quickly. (*c*) to put quickly. (*d*) to ask (a question) quickly. 3. *adj*. *inf*. popular. **popcorn**, *n*. sweet corn which has been heated until it bursts. **popgun**, *n*. toy gun which makes a pop.

Pope [pəʊp] *n*. the head of the Roman Catholic Church.

poplar ['pɒplə] *n*. common tall and slender tree.

poplin ['pɒplɪn] *n*. strong cotton cloth used for making shirts.

poppadom ['pɒpədɒm] *n*. (*in Indian food*) thin fried cake.

popper ['pɒpə] *n*. *inf*. snap fastener.

poppet ['pɒpɪt] *n*. *inf*. nice girl.

poppy ['pɒpɪ] *n*. common flower, red when wild.

populace ['pɒpjʊləs] *n*. ordinary people.

popular ['pɒpjʊlə] *adj*. (*a*) referring to the ordinary people. (*b*) liked by a lot of people. **popularity** [pɒpjʊ'lærɪtɪ] *n*. being popular. **popularization** [pɒpjʊlərəɪ'zeɪʃn] *n*. act of popularizing. **popularize** ['pɒpjʊləraɪz] *v*. to make (sth) understood/liked by a lot of people. **popularly**, *adv*. generally; by most people.

populate ['pɒpjʊleɪt] *v*. to put people to live in (a place). **population** [pɒpjʊ'leɪʃn] *n*. number of people who live in a place. **populous** ['pɒpjʊləs] *adj*. thickly populated.

porbeagle ['pɔ:bi:gl] *n*. type of shark.

porcelain ['pɔ:slɪn] *n*. fine china.

porch [pɔ:tʃ] *n*. (*pl*. **-es**) shelter over a doorway.

porcine ['pɔ:saɪn] *adj*. like a pig.

porcupine ['pɔ:kjʊpaɪn] *n*. rodent with long sharp spikes covering its body.

pore [pɔ:] 1. *n*. small hole in the skin through which sweat passes. 2. *v*. **to p. over** = to look at (a book, etc.) very closely.

pork [pɔ:k] *n*. (*no pl*.) meat from a pig. **porker**, *n*. *inf*. pig.

pornography [pɔ:'nɒgrəfɪ] *n*. pornographic films/books/art. **porn** [pɔ:n] *n*. *inf*. pornography; **hard/soft p.** = extremely indecent/less indecent pornographic material. **pornographic** [pɔ:nə'græfɪk] *adj*. (book, etc.) which deals with sex in an indecent way.

porous ['pɔ:rəs] *adj*. (solid) which allows liquid to pass through. **porosity** [pɔ:'rɒsɪtɪ] *n*. being porous.

porphyry ['pɔ:fɪrɪ] *n*. type of stone with crystals in it.

porpoise ['pɔ:pəs] *n*. large sea mammal which tends to swim in groups.

porridge ['pɒrɪdʒ] *n*. (*no pl*.) oatmeal cooked in water.

port [pɔːt] n. (a) harbour. (b) town with a harbour. (c) left side (when looking forward on board a ship/aircraft). (d) strong sweet wine from Portugal. (e) opening in a ship's side for a gun. (f) opening in a computer for plugging in an attachment.

portable ['pɔːtəbl] 1. adj. which can be carried. 2. n. machine, such as a small computer, which can be carried.

portage [pɔː'tɑːʒ] n. transporting a boat across country.

portal ['pɔːtl] n. imposing entrance.

portcullis [pɔːt'kʌlɪs] n. (pl. -es) gate which was dropped to close the entrance to a medieval castle.

portend [pɔː'tend] v. (formal) to warn (that sth unpleasant is going to happen).

portent ['pɔːtənt] n. (formal) warning (that sth unpleasant is going to happen). **portentous** [pɔː'tentəs] adj. important/significant; warning that sth unpleasant is going to happen.

porter ['pɔːtə] n. (a) person who carries luggage for travellers. (b) doorkeeper (in a hotel). (c) person who does general work in a hospital. (d) (in Ireland) type of black beer. **porterage**, n. charge for carrying sth. **porterhouse (steak)**, n. piece of best quality steak.

portfolio [pɔːt'fəʊliəʊ] n. (pl. -os) (a) large cardboard case for carrying paintings, etc. (b) collection of shares. (c) minister's job in government.

porthole ['pɔːthəʊl] n. round window in the side of a ship.

portico ['pɔːtɪkəʊ] n. (pl. -oes) roof supported by columns forming a porch in front of the entrance to a building.

portion ['pɔːʃn] 1. n. (a) part. (b) serving of food. 2. v. **to p. out** = to share out.

portly ['pɔːtlɪ] adj. (-ier, -iest) rather fat.

portmanteau [pɔːt'mæntəʊ] n. trunk for carrying clothes.

portrait ['pɔːtreɪt] n. painting/photograph of a person. **portraiture** ['pɔːtrətʃə] n. art of painting portraits. **portray** [pɔː'treɪ] v. to paint/to describe (a scene or a person). **portrayal**, n. painting; description of a scene or person.

Portuguese [pɔːtjʊ'giːz] 1. adj. referring to Portugal; **P. man-of-war** = type of very large jelly fish. 2. n. (a) person

from Portugal. (b) language spoken in Portugal.

pose [pəʊz] 1. n. (a) way of standing/sitting. (b) way of behaving which is just a pretence. 2. v. (a) **to p. for s.o.** = to stand/to sit still while s.o. paints/photographs you. (b) to pretend to be. (c) to set (a problem); to put (a question). **poser**, n. inf. difficult question. **poseur** [pəʊ'zɜː] n. person who behaves in a false way.

posh [pɒʃ] adj. (-er, -est) inf. very smart.

position [pə'zɪʃn] 1. n. (a) way of standing/sitting. (b) place. (c) job. 2. v. to place.

positive ['pɒzɪtɪv] 1. adj. (a) meaning yes. (b) certain; sure/convinced. (c) registering the existence of sth. (d) plus/more than zero. 2. n. (a) photograph printed from a negative, where the light and dark appear as they are in nature. (b) one of the terminals in a battery. **positively**, adv. absolutely. **positron**, n. positive electron.

posse ['pɒsɪ] n. group of armed men/police.

possess [pə'zes] v. (a) to own. (b) to occupy s.o.'s mind; **what possessed him?** = why did he do it? **possession** [pə'zeʃn] n. (a) ownership. (b) thing you own. **possessive**, adj. (a) (in grammar) (word) which indicates possession. (b) (person) who treats another person as if he owns him. **possessively**, adv. in a possessive way. **possessor**, n. owner.

possible ['pɒsɪbl] adj. (a) which can happen. (b) likely. **possibility** [pɒsɪ'bɪlɪtɪ] n. (a) chance; being likely. (b) **the plan has possibilities** = may well work. **possibly**, adv. (a) which may happen. (b) perhaps.

possum ['pɒsəm] n. inf. **to play p.** = to pretend to sleep/to be dead so as to trick an opponent.

post [pəʊst] 1. n. (a) wooden/concrete stake fixed in the ground. (b) place where a sentry is on duty. (c) job/position. (d) small settlement far from civilization. (e) **the last p.** = bugle call to commemorate the dead. (f) mail; letters, etc., sent by mail. 2. v. (a) to send (s.o.) on duty. (b) to send (a letter, etc.) by mail; **to keep s.o. posted** =

to keep s.o. informed. (c) to stick up (a notice). **postage**, n. payment for sending a letter by mail; **p. stamp** = piece of paper which you buy and stick on a letter, etc., to pay for it to be sent to its destination. **postal**, adj. referring to the post; **p. order** = order to pay money, which can be bought and cashed at a post office. **postbag**, n. letters sent to a radio/TV show. **postbox**, n. box in a wall into which you can put letters, which will then be collected and sent on by the post office. **postcard**, n. card (sometimes with a picture) which you send through the post. **postcode**, n. system of letters or numbers to indicate a town or street in an address, to help with the sorting of mail. **poster**, n. large notice stuck up on a wall, etc.; large picture/advertisement stuck on a wall. **poste restante** [pəʊst-'rɛstɑ̃ːnt] n. service where letters can be addressed to s.o. at a post office where he can collect them. **post free**, adv. without paying for postage. **posthaste**, adv. very fast. **postman**, n. (pl. -men) person who delivers letters to houses. **postmark. 1.** n. mark stamped on a letter to show when it was sent off. **2.** v. to stamp (a letter) with a postmark. **postmaster, postmistress**, n. person in charge of a post office. **post office**, n. (a) building where mail is received/stamps sold, etc. (b) organization which runs the postal services. **postpaid**, adj. (reply) with postage paid by the sender.

post- [pəʊst] prefix meaning later than/after. **postdate**, v. to put a date on (a cheque) which is later than the day on which you actually write it. **postgraduate**, n. person who has a first degree from a university and who is studying for a further degree. **posthumous** ['pɒstjʊməs] adj. after death; **p. son** = son born after his father's death. **posthumously**, adv. after death. **post mortem** [pəʊst-'mɔːtəm] adj. & n. (examination) to find out the cause of death. **postnatal**, adj. referring to the time just after the birth of a child. **postpone** [pəs'pəʊn] v. to put off until later. **postponement**, n. putting off until later. **postprandial**, adj. after dinner. **postscript, post scriptum**, n. additional note at the end of a letter. **postwar**, adj. referring to the period after the war.

posterior [pɒ'stɪərɪə] n. behind/buttocks. **posterity** [pɒ'sterɪtɪ] n. generations which will follow.

postern ['pɒstən] n. (old) small gate.

postulate ['pɒstjʊleɪt] **1.** n. basis upon which sth is postulated. **2.** v. to suppose (that sth is true). **postulant**, n. person who is a candidate to join a religious order.

posture ['pɒstʃə] **1.** n. way of sitting/standing, etc. **2.** v. to take up a particular position for effect.

posy ['pəʊzɪ] n. small bunch of flowers.

pot [pɒt] **1.** n. (a) container made of glass or clay; inf. **pots of money** = lots of money. (b) inf. **to go to p.** = to become ruined/useless. (c) Sl. marijuana. **2.** v. (**potted**) (a) to put in a pot. (b) (in billiards) to send (a ball) into one of the pockets. **potbelly**, n. inf. fat stomach. **potboiler**, n. worthless novel written rapidly for money. **potbound**, adj. (of plant) with roots too large for the pot. **pot-hole**, n. (a) hole in rock worn away by water. (b) hole in a road surface. **pot-holer**, n. person who climbs down pot-holes as a sport. **potholing**, n. sport of climbing inside potholes. **potluck**, n. **to take p.** = to take whatever comes, with no possibility of choice. **potsherd**, n. piece of broken pot. **potshot**, n. inf. **to take a p. at s.o.** = to try to shoot s.o. without aiming properly. **potted**, adj. (a) preserved in a pot. (b) condensed. **potting shed**, n. shed in a garden where you put plants in pots.

potable ['pɒtəbl] adj. which can be drunk safely.

potash ['pɒtæʃ] n. potassium salts.

potassium [pə'tæsɪəm] n. (element: K) light white metallic substance.

potato [pə'teɪtəʊ] n. (pl. -oes) common vegetable, formed under the soil; **sweet p.** = yam.

poteen [pɒ'tiːn] n. illegal Irish whiskey.

potency ['pəʊtənsɪ] n. strength. **potent**, adj. strong.

potentate ['pəʊtənteɪt] n. Eastern ruler.

potential [pə'tenʃl] **1.** adj. possible.

2. *n.* (*a*) possibility of developing into sth valuable. (*b*) (*in physics*) electrical property which governs the flow of an electric charge. **potentiality,** *n.* being potential. **potentially,** *adv.* possibly. **potentiometer,** *n.* instrument for measuring differences in electrical potential.

potion ['pəʊʃn] *n.* liquid mixture to make you sleep, etc.

potpourri [pəʊpu:'ri:] *n.* (*a*) dried flowers/herbs kept in a bowl to scent a room. (*b*) general mixture of bits and pieces.

potter ['pɒtə] 1. *n.* person who makes pots out of clay. 2. *v.* **to p. about** = not to do anything in particular/to do little jobs. **pottery,** *n.* (*a*) potter's workshop. (*b*) pots; articles made of clay, earthenware.

potty ['pɒtɪ] *inf.* 1. *n.* child's chamberpot. 2. *adj.* (**-ier, -iest**) mad.

pouch [paʊtʃ] *n.* (*pl.* **-es**) (*a*) small bag for carrying coins/ammunition, etc. (*b*) bag in the skin in front of some marsupials where the young live and grow for some time after birth.

pouffe [pu:f] *n.* padded seat shaped like a drum.

poultice ['pəʊltɪs] 1. *n.* hot wet dressing put on a wound. 2. *v.* to dress (a wound) with a poultice.

poultry ['pəʊltrɪ] *n.* (*no pl.*) common farm birds such as ducks/hens, reared for eggs or to be eaten. **poulterer** ['pəʊltərə] *n.* shopkeeper who specializes in selling poultry.

pounce [paʊns] 1. *n.* act of pouncing. 2. *v.* to jump (**on** sth).

pound [paʊnd] 1. *n.* (*a*) measure of weight (= approx. 0.45 kilogram). (*b*) standard unit of money in Great Britain and several other countries. (*c*) place where stray animals or illegally-parked cars are put. 2. *v.* (*a*) to smash into little pieces; to hit hard. (*b*) to run heavily. (*c*) (*of heart*) to beat fast. **poundage** ['paʊndɪdʒ] *n.* rate charged for each pound.

pour [pɔ:] *v.* (*a*) to flow out/down. (*b*) to transfer liquid from one container to another.

pout [paʊt] 1. *n.* (*a*) sulky expression where the lips stick out. (*b*) type of fish.

2. *v.* to make a sulky expression with the lips.

poverty ['pɒvətɪ] *n.* being poor; **the p. of** = the lack of.

powder ['paʊdə] 1. *n.* very fine dry grains (like flour); (**face**) **p.** = scented flour-like substance for putting on the face; **p. compact** = small box containing face powder; **p. room** = women's toilet. 2. *v.* to put powder on. **powdered,** *adj.* covered with powder. **powdery,** *adj.* fine/like powder.

power ['paʊə] *n.* (*a*) strength. (*b*) ability. (*c*) driving force; **p. pack** = portable source of electricity; **p. point** = wall plug which supplies electricity. (*d*) (*in mathematics*) number of times a number is multiplied by itself. (*e*) (*in physics*) strength of a lens. (*f*) (*also* **power base**) political/social strength (of a person/a group). (*g*) political control. **powerboat,** *n.* boat which has a powerful engine, used for racing. **power drill,** *n.* powerful electric drill. **powered,** *adj.* driven/worked. **powerful,** *adj.* very strong. **powerless,** *adj.* unable to do anything. **power station, power plant,** *n.* works where electricity is produced. **power steering,** *n.* steering (in a car) which is powered by the engine.

powwow ['paʊwaʊ] *n. inf.* meeting to discuss some problem.

p.p. [pi:'pi:] *adv.* on behalf of (s.o.) who is absent.

PR [pi:'ɑ:] *n.* public relations; proportional representation.

practicable ['præktɪkəbl] *adj.* which can be done/which can be put into practice. **practicability** [præktɪkə'bɪlɪtɪ] *n.* ability to be put into practice.

practical ['præktɪkl] 1. *adj.* interested in practice/action rather than ideas; referring to practice rather than theory; **p. joke** = trick played on s.o. to make other people laugh. 2. *n. inf.* examination/test to show how well s.o. can work in practice. **practicality,** *n.* way in which sth works in practice. **practically,** *adv.* (*a*) in practice. (*b*) almost.

practice ['præktɪs] 1. *n.* (*a*) actual application; **to put sth into p.** = to apply sth/to use sth. (*b*) habit. (*c*) repeated exercise; **out of p.** = not capable because of lack of exercise. (*d*) business of a doctor/dentist/lawyer. (*e*) **practices** = ways of doing things. **2.** *v. Am. see* **practise.**

practise, *Am.* **practice** ['præktɪs] *v.* (*a*) to put sth into practice. (*b*) to do repeated exercises. (*c*) to carry on a job as a doctor or lawyer. **practised,** *adj.* skilled.

practitioner [præk'tɪʃənə] *n.* doctor; **general p.** = doctor who treats all patients/all illnesses.

pragmatic [præg'mætɪk] *adj.* dealing with fact/practical matters, not concerned with theory. **pragmatically,** *adv.* in a pragmatic way. **pragmatism** ['prægmətɪzəm] *n.* pragmatic approach (to a problem). **pragmatist,** *n.* person who is pragmatic.

prairie ['preərɪ] *n.* grass-covered plain in North America; **p. dog** = small American mammal, living in burrows; **p. oyster** = mixture of raw egg, tomato juice and spices, taken to cure a hangover.

praise [preɪz] **1.** *n.* admiration/expression of approval. **2.** *v.* to express strong approval of (sth). **praiseworthy,** *adj.* which should be praised.

praline ['prɑːliːn] *n.* sweet made of crushed nuts and honey.

pram [præm] *n. inf.* small carriage in which you can push a baby.

prance [prɑːns] *v.* to jump about/to move lightly.

prank [præŋk] *n.* trick.

prattle ['prætl] **1.** *n.* children's chatter. **2.** *v.* to chatter in a childish way.

prawn [prɔːn] *n.* shellfish like a large shrimp.

praxis ['præksɪs] *n.* practice.

pray [preɪ] *v.* to speak to God; to ask God for sth; (*formal*) **p. be seated** = please sit down. **prayer,** *n.* act of speaking to God; request.

pre- [prɪ] *prefix meaning* before.

preach [priːtʃ] *v.* (*a*) to give a sermon in church. (*b*) to recommend/to advise; to give moral advice. **preacher,** *n.* person who gives a sermon.

preamble [priː'æmbl] *n.* introduction/remarks at the beginning (of a speech/treaty, etc.).

prearrange [priːə'reɪndʒ] *v.* to arrange in advance.

precarious [prɪ'keərɪəs] *adj.* likely to fall; uncertain. **precariously,** *adv.* unsafely.

precaution [prɪ'kɔːʃn] *n.* care taken in advance (to avoid sth unpleasant). **precautionary,** *adj.* (measure) taken to avoid sth unpleasant.

precede [prɪ'siːd] *v.* to take place before (sth). **precedence** ['presɪdəns] *n.* **to take p. over** = to go before/to be more important than. **precedent** ['presɪdənt] *n.* thing which has happened before, and which can be a guide as to what should be done. **preceding** [prɪ'siːdɪŋ] *adj.* which comes before.

precentor [prɪ'sentə] *n.* person in charge of the music in a cathedral.

precept ['priːsept] *n.* (*a*) command; guiding rule. (*b*) order for local taxes to be paid.

precinct ['priːsɪŋkt] *n.* area surrounded by a wall; administrative district of a town; **shopping p./pedestrian p.** = area of a town which is closed to traffic.

precious ['preʃəs] *adj.* worth a lot of money; of great value.

precipice ['presɪpɪs] *n.* high cliff (not usu. near the sea). **precipitous** [prɪ'sɪpɪtəs] *adj.* very steep.

precipitate 1. *n.* [prɪ'sɪpɪtət] chemical substance which settles at the bottom of a liquid. **2.** *v.* [prɪ'sɪpɪteɪt] (*a*) to make sth happen suddenly. (*b*) to settle at the bottom of a liquid. **3.** *adj.* [prɪ'sɪpɪtət] rushed/hurried. **precipitately,** *adv.* in a rushed way. **precipitation** [prɪsɪpɪ-'teɪʃn] *n.* (*a*) (*formal*) great hurry. (*b*) quantity of rain/snow, etc., which falls on a certain place.

précis ['preɪsɪ] **1.** *n.* (*pl.* **précis** ['preɪsiːz]) summary of the main points of a text. **2.** *v.* to summarize.

precise [prɪ'saɪs] *adj.* (*a*) exact. (*b*) careful. **precisely,** *adv.* (*a*) exactly. (*b*) in a careful way. **precision** [prɪ'sɪʒn] *n.* accuracy.

preclude [prɪ'kluːd] *v.* to prevent.

precocious [prɪ'kəuʃəs] *adj.* (child) who is surprisingly advanced for its age. **precociously,** *adv.* in a precocious way. **precociousness, precocity** [prɪ'kɒsɪtɪ] *n.* being precocious.

preconceive [priːkən'siːv] *v.* to have an idea or belief from the beginning/before sth starts. **preconception** [pri:kən'sepʃn] *n.* preconceived idea.

precondition [pri:kən'dıʃn] *n.* condition which is set in advance.

precursor [prı'kɜ:sə] *n.* thing which leads to an invention/person who goes in advance. **precursory,** *adj.* which is in advance.

predate ['pri:deıt] *v.* to come before in date.

predator ['predətə] *n.* animal which lives by eating other animals. **predatory,** *adj.* (animal) which eats other animals; (person) who lives off other people.

predecease [pri:dı'si:s] *v.* (*formal*) to die before (s.o.). **predecessor** ['pri:dısesə] *n.* person who has held the same job, etc., before you.

predestine [pri:'destın] *v.* to decide the fate of (s.o.) in advance. **predestination** [pri:destı'neıʃn] *n.* being predestined.

predetermine [pri:dı'tɜ:mın] *v.* to decide in advance.

predicament [prı'dıkəmənt] *n.* troubles/difficult situation.

predicate 1. *n.* ['predıkət] (*in grammar*) statement about the subject. 2. *v.* ['predıkeıt] (*formal*) to base a supposition on (sth).

predicative [prı'dıkətıv] *adj.* (adjective, etc.) which makes a statement about a noun.

predict [prı'dıkt] *v.* to foretell/to tell in advance what will happen. **predictable,** *adj.* which could be predicted. **predictably,** *adv.* in a way which could have been predicted. **prediction** [prı'dıkʃn] *n.* foretelling.

predilection [pri:dı'lekʃn] *n.* liking/preference.

predispose [pri:dı'spəuz] *v.* to make (s.o.) favour sth in advance. **predisposition** [pri:dıspə'zıʃn] *n.* being predisposed.

predominate [prı'domıneıt] *v.* to be bigger/stronger/more numerous. **predominance,** *n.* being predominant. **predominant** [prı'domınənt] *adj.* most striking/obvious. **predominantly,** *adv* in a predominant way.

pre-eminent [pri:'emınənt] *adj.* excellent/much better than everything

else. **pre-eminence,** *n.* being preeminent.

pre-empt [pri:'empt] *v.* to get an advantage by doing sth before anyone else. **pre-emption,** *n.* act of preempting. **pre-emptive,** *adj.* which gains an advantage by acting before anyone else.

preen [pri:n] *v.* (*of bird*) to smooth its feathers; **to p. yourself** = to smarten yourself up; **to p. yourself on sth** = to congratulate yourself.

prefabricated [pri:'fæbrıkeıtıd] *adj.* built in advance; (house) built out of pieces which are assembled on the site. **prefab** ['pri:fæb] *n. inf.* prefabricated house. **prefabrication** [pri:fæbrı'keıʃn] *n.* building in advance.

preface ['prefəs] 1. *n.* piece written (usu. by the author) to introduce a book. 2. *v.* to say/to write sth as an introduction. **prefatory** ['prefətrı] *adj.* which acts as a preface.

prefect ['pri:fekt] *n.* (*a*) school pupil chosen to be in charge of others. (*b*) high official.

prefer [prı'fɜ:] *v.* (**preferred**) (*a*) **to p. sth to sth** = to like (to do) sth better than sth else. (*b*) (*formal*) to promote (s.o.). **preferable** ['prefrəbl] *adj.* which you would prefer. **preferably,** *adv.* if possible. **preference** ['prefrəns] *n.* liking for one thing more than another. **preferential** [prefə'renʃl] *adj.* showing one thing is preferred to another. **preferment** [prı'fɜ:mənt] *n.* promotion to a more important post.

prefix ['pri:fıks] 1. *n.* (*pl.* **-es**) part of a word put in front of another. 2. *v.* to put some word in front of another/to preface.

pregnancy ['pregnənsı] *n.* state of being pregnant; **p. test** = test to see if a woman is pregnant. **pregnant,** *adj.* carrying an unborn child; **p. pause** = pause while everyone waits for sth to happen/for s.o. to speak.

prehensile [pri:'hensaıl] *adj.* which can grasp/hold on to sth.

prehistory [pri:'hıstərı] *n.* time before written history. **prehistorian** [pri:hı'stɔ:rıən] *n.* person who specializes in the study of prehistory. **prehistoric** [pri:hı'stɒrık] *adj.* belonging to prehistory.

prejudge [pri:'dʒʌdʒ] v. to judge (sth) without hearing all the facts.

prejudice ['predʒədɪs] 1. n. (usu. unjust) feeling against s.o... 2. v. (a) to make (s.o.) unfriendly towards s.o./sth. (b) to harm. **prejudiced**, adj. unfairly biassed (**against** s.o.). **prejudicial** [predʒu'dɪʃl] adj. which might be damaging.

prelate ['prelət] n. person of high rank in a church.

preliminary [prɪ'lɪmɪnərɪ] adj. which goes before. **preliminaries**, n. pl. things which have to be done before sth can take place. **prelims** ['pri:lɪmz] n. pl. inf. (a) first few pages of a book before the text starts. (b) examinations which decide if you may study at a university.

prelude ['prelju:d] n. thing (esp. piece of music) which introduces sth more important; short piece of music on one theme.

premarital [prɪ'mærɪtəl] adj. before marriage.

premature [premə'tjuə] adj. which happens before the right time; (baby) born less than nine months after conception. **prematurely**, adv. before the right time.

premeditate [pri:'medɪteɪt] v. to think over/to plan in advance. **premeditation** [pri:medɪ'teɪʃn] n. planning in advance.

premier ['premɪə] 1. n. Prime Minister. 2. adj. first/most important. **première** ['premɪeə] n. first performance of a film/play, etc. **premiership**, n. being Prime Minister; time when s.o. is Prime Minister.

premise ['premɪs] n. premiss.

premises ['premɪsɪz] n. pl. building and land around it.

premiss ['premɪs] n. (pl. **-es**). statement which is the basis for reasoning.

premium ['pri:mɪəm] n. (a) annual amount paid for an insurance policy. (b) **at a p.** = scarce, and therefore valuable; **to put a p. on sth** = to show that sth is useful/valuable. (c) bonus; **p. offer** = specially attractive price. **premium bond**, n. British government bond which pays no interest but gives you the chance of winning a monthly prize.

premolar [pri:'məulə] n. tooth between the canines and the molars.

premonition [premə'nɪʃn] n. feeling that sth is going to happen. **premonitory** [prɪ'mɒnɪtrɪ] adj. warning (sign).

prenatal [pri:'neɪtl] adj. referring to the time before the birth of a child.

preoccupation [pri:ɒkju'peɪʃn] n. only thinking about one thing. **preoccupied**, adj. thinking only about one thing; worried. **preoccupy**, v. to make (s.o.) think about only one thing and worry about it.

prep [prep] adj. inf. (a) homework. (b) **p. school** = preparatory school. (c) preparing a patient for an operation.

prepare [prɪ'peə] v. to get ready. **preparation** [prepə'reɪʃn] n. (a) getting ready. (b) substance which has been mixed. **preparatory** [prɪ'pærətrɪ] adj. which prepares; **p. school** = private school for children up to the age of 13. **prepared**, adj. ready (**to**).

prepay ['pri:peɪ] v. (**prepaid**) to pay in advance; **prepaid telegram** = telegram where the answer has been paid for in advance. **prepayment**, n. paying in advance.

preponderate [prɪ'pɒndəreɪt] v. (formal) to be in a majority. **preponderance** [prɪ'pɒndərəns] n. large number. **preponderant**, adj. in a majority.

preposition [prepə'zɪʃn] n. word which is used with a noun/pronoun to show how it is linked to another word.

prepossessing [pri:pə'zesɪŋ] adj. pleasant.

preposterous [prɪ'pɒstərəs] adj. silly/absurd.

preprogrammed [pri:'prəugræmd] adj. (chip) which has been programmed in the factory.

prerequisite [pri:'rekwɪzɪt] n. thing which you must have before you can do sth.

prerogative [prɪ'rɒgətɪv] n. privilege belonging to one person or group.

presbyopia [prezbɪ'əupɪə] n. gradual failing sight (in an old person).

presbytery ['prezbɪtərɪ] n. (a) Roman Catholic priest's house. (b) court of a church made of ministers and important laymen. **Presbyterian** [prezbɪ'ti:ərɪən] adj. & n. (member) of a Protestant church, ruled by a group of laymen.

prescient ['presɪənt] adj. (formal) (person) who can tell what is likely to take place in the future. **prescience,** *n.* being prescient.

prescribe [prɪ'skraɪb] *v.* to order (sth) to be done; to tell s.o. to use (sth). **prescription** [prɪ'skrɪpʃn] *n.* paper on which a doctor has written out particulars of the medicine to be taken by the patient. **prescriptive,** *adj.* which prescribes.

presence ['prezns] *n.* (*a*) being present. (*b*) **p. of mind** = sense/calmness; ability to act quickly. (*c*) impressive appearance/way of acting (on the stage).

present 1. *adj.* ['preznt] (*a*) being at the place/at the time. (*b*) being here now. (*c*) (*in grammar*) (tense) which describes what is happening now. 2. *n.* ['preznt] *n.* (*a*) at the time we are in now; **at p.** = now. (*b*) gift. 3. *v.* [prɪ'zent] (*a*) to give. (*b*) to put on (a play/show). (*c*) to introduce (s.o. into society/an artist to the audience). (*d*) **to p. oneself** = to arrive/to come. **presentable** [prɪ'zentəbl] *adj.* (person) who is suitable to appear in company. **presentation** [prezən'teɪʃn] *n.* act of giving. **present-day,** *adj.* modern. **presenter,** *n.* person who presents a TV show. **presently,** *adv.* (*a*) soon. (*b*) *Am.* & *in Scotland* now.

presentiment [prɪ'zentɪmənt] *n.* feeling that sth unpleasant will soon happen.

preserve [prɪ'zɜːv] 1. *n.* (*a*) place where game/fish, etc., are protected so that they can be killed for sport. (*b*) **preserves** = jam/pickles, etc. 2. *v.* (*a*) (*formal*) to keep/to protect. (*b*) to treat (food) so that it keeps for a long time. **preservation** [prezə'veɪʃn] *n.* protecting; **p. order** = court order to prevent a building being demolished. **preservative** [prɪ'zɜːvətɪv] *n.* substance used to make food keep/to stop food from going bad. **preserver,** *n.* person/thing that preserves; *see also* **life preserver. preserving pan,** *n.* very large pan for making jam/chutney, etc.

preside [prɪ'zaɪd] *v.* to sit at the head of the table (at a meeting). **presidency** ['prezɪdnsɪ] *n.* job of president. **president** ['prezɪdənt] *n.* head of a republic; chief member of a club; (*esp. Am.*) head

of a business firm. **presidential** [prezɪ'denʃl] *adj.* referring to a president. **presidium** [prɪ'sɪdɪəm] *n.* ruling committee (in a communist country).

press [pres] 1. *n.* (*pl.* **-es**) (*a*) machine which squeezes. (*b*) **printing p.** = machine for printing books/newspapers, etc. (*c*) newspapers and magazines taken as a whole. (*d*) crowd. 2. *v.* (*a*) to push down; to push against; to squeeze. (*b*) to iron the creases from (clothes). (*c*) to force (s.o.) to do sth. (*d*) **to p. on/forward** = to continue/to go ahead. **pressed,** *adj.* **I'm p. for time** = I haven't much time; **I'd be hard p. to do it** = I would find it difficult. **press conference,** *n.* interview given by a famous person to several journalists. **press cutting,** *n.* piece cut out from a newspaper with an article which is relevant to s.o/sth. **pressgang.** 1. *n.* (*old*) group of people who forced men to join the Royal Navy. 2. *v.* to force (s.o.) **into** doing sth. **pressing.** 1. *adj.* urgent. 2. *n.* record/series of records. **press stud,** *n.* round fastening, where two parts are pressed to clip together. **press-up,** *n.* exercise where you lie flat on the floor and push yourself up with your hands. **pressure** ['preʃə] *n.* (*a*) act of squeezing/pushing down; **to put p. on s.o. to do sth** = to try to force s.o. to do sth. (*b*) force pushing down/moving/being heavy, etc.; **blood p.** = force with which the blood is driven round the body; **p. group** = group of people who try to influence the government, etc. (*c*) stress. **pressure cooker,** *n.* type of saucepan with a tight-fitting lid, which cooks food rapidly under pressure. **pressurization** [preʃəraɪ'zeɪʃn] *n.* keeping an aircraft cabin at a constant atomsopheric pressure. **pressurize,** *v.* to put under pressure; **to p. s.o. into doing sth** = to try to force (s.o.) to do sth. **pressurized,** *adj.* (aircraft cabin) kept at a constant atmospheric pressure.

prestige [pre'stiːʒ] *n.* admiration aroused by s.o. because of rank or qualifications or job. **prestigious** [pre'stɪdʒəs] *adj.* which brings prestige.

presto ['prestəʊ] *adv.* (*in music*) rapidly; **hey p.!** = words used by magicians when carrying out magic tricks.

prestressed [ˌpriːˈstrest] *adj.* which has been stressed in advance.

presume [prɪˈzjuːm] *v.* (*a*) to suppose/ to assume. (*b*) (**to**) to take the liberty of doing sth. (*c*) (*formal*) **to p. (up)on s.o.'s good nature** = to take unfair advantage of s.o.'s kindness. **presumably,** *adv.* probably; as you would expect. **presumption** [prɪˈzʌmpʃn] *n.* (*a*) thing which is assumed to be true. (*b*) rudeness. **presumptive,** *adj.* which is presumed to be true; **heir p.** = heir (to a throne) who may be displaced by the birth of s.o. with a better right. **presumptuous** [prɪˈzʌmptjʊəs] *adj.* rude/bold. **presumptuously,** *adv.* in a presumptuous way.

presuppose [priːsəˈpəʊz] *v.* to assume in advance (that sth is true/that certain conditions are met). **presupposition** [priːsəpəˈzɪʃn] *n.* thing which is assumed in advance.

pretax [ˈpriːtæks] *adj.* before tax is paid.

pretend [prɪˈtend] *v.* (*a*) to make believe so as to deceive s.o. (*b*) (**to**) to be bold enough to claim. **pretence,** *Am.* **pretense** [prɪˈtens] *n.* making believe. **pretender,** *n.* person who has (false) claims to sth, usu. person who claims to be king. **pretension** [prɪˈtenʃn] *n.* claim. **pretentious** [prɪˈtenʃəs] *adj.* very showy; claiming to be more important than you are. **pretentiousness,** *n.* being pretentious.

preternatural [priːtəˈnætʃrəl] *adj.* supernatural; extraordinary.

pretext [ˈpriːtekst] *n.* excuse.

pretty [ˈprɪtɪ] **1.** *adj.* (**-ier, -iest**) pleasant to look at; attractive. **2.** *adv. inf.* quite. **prettily,** *adv.* daintily. **prettiness,** *n.* attractiveness/pleasantness.

pretzel [ˈpretsəl] *n.* hard salty biscuit, made in the shape of a knot.

prevail [prɪˈveɪl] *v.* (*formal*) (*a*) **to p. upon** = to persuade. (*b*) to be usual/common. **prevailing,** *adj.* usual/common; **p. wind** = wind which usually blows from a certain direction. **prevalence** [ˈprevələns] *n.* being widespread. **prevalent,** *adj.* widespread.

prevaricate [prɪˈværɪkeɪt] *v.* (*formal*) to try not to tell the truth. **prevarication** [prɪværɪˈkeɪʃn] *n.* act of prevaricating; lie. **prevaricator,** *n.* person who prevaricates.

prevent [prɪˈvent] *v.* to stop (sth) happening; **to p. s.o. from** = to stop (s.o.) doing sth. **preventable,** *adj.* which could be prevented. **prevention** [prɪˈvenʃn] *n.* preventing. **preventative, preventive** [prɪˈvent(ət)ɪv] *adj.* which prevents.

preview [ˈpriːvjuː] *n.* showing of a film/ an exhibition, etc., before it is open to the general public.

previous [ˈpriːvɪəs] **1.** *adj.* former, earlier. **2.** *adv.* **p. to** = before. **previously,** *adv.* before.

pre-war [ˈpriːwɔː] *adj. & adv.* existing/ happening before a war.

prey [preɪ] **1.** *n.* animal eaten by another; **birds of p.** = birds which eat other birds/ animals. **2.** *v.* **to p. (up)on** = to attack animals and eat them; **sth is preying on his mind** = sth is worrying him.

price [praɪs] **1.** *n.* quantity of money which has to be paid to buy sth; **at a p.** = if you are willing to pay a lot. **2.** *v.* to give (sth) a price. **priceless,** *adj.* (*a*) extremely valuable. (*b*) very funny (joke). **pricey,** *adj. inf.* expensive.

prick [prɪk] **1.** *n.* pain caused by sth sharp. **2.** *v.* (*a*) to jab with sth sharp; to make small holes in (sth). (*b*) **to p. up your ears** = to listen attentively. (*c*) **to p. out seedlings** = to plant small seedlings in the open ground after they have been grown in boxes. **prickle,** *n.* thorn/sharp point (on a plant/hedgehog, etc.). **prickliness,** *n.* being prickly. **prickly,** *adj.* (*a*) covered with prickles; **p. pear** = type of cactus; **p. heat** = skin rash caused by hot climate. (*b*) (person) who takes offence easily.

pride [praɪd] **1.** *n.* (*a*) pleasure in your own abilities/achievements/ possessions. (*b*) very high opinions of yourself. (*c*) group of lions. **2. to p. oneself on** = to be extremely proud of.

priest [priːst] *n.* person who has been ordained to serve God/to interpret the wishes of God/to carry out formal religious duties; **parish p.** = priest who is in charge of a parish. **priestess,** *n.* female priest. **priesthood,** *n.* job of being a priest. **priestly,** *adj.* referring to priests.

prig [prɪg] *n.* very moral and conceited person. **priggish,** *adj.* very moral and conceited. **priggishness,** *n.* being priggish.

prim [prɪm] *adj.* (**primmer, primmest**)
very correct/unbending. **primly,** *adj.* in
a prim way. **primness,** *n.* being prim.

prima ballerina [priːmæbælə'riːnə] *n.*
leading woman dancer in a ballet
company. **prima donna** [priːmə'dɒnə]
n. leading woman singer in opera; person who is conceited and liable to
outbursts of emotion.

primacy ['praɪməsɪ] *n.* being in first
place, being most important.

prima facie [praɪmə'feɪʃɪ] *adv. & adj.*
based on what seems right at first sight.

primal ['praɪml] *adj.* (*formal*) primeval.

primary ['praɪmərɪ] 1. *adj.* basic; **p.
colours** = basic colours (red, yellow
and blue) which go to make up all
the other colours; *Am.* **p. election** =
first election to choose a candidate to
represent a political party in a main
election; **p. school** = school for small
children (up to the age of eleven). 2. *n.
Am.* primary election. **primarily,** *adv.*
mainly/mostly.

primate *n.* (*a*) ['praɪmət] leading bishop.
(*b*) ['praɪmeɪt] **the primates** = members
of the highest level of mammals (apes,
human beings, etc.).

prime [praɪm] 1. *adj.* (*a*) most important.
(*b*) of best quality. (*c*) **p. number** =
number (such as 2, 5, 11, etc.) which
can only be divided by itself or by
1. 2. *n.* period when you are at your
best. 3. *v.* (*a*) to get (sth) prepared; to
give (wood/metal) a first coat of special
paint, before giving the top coat. (*b*) to
put water into (a water pump)/oil into
(a machine) so as to start it working. (*c*)
to give (s.o.) drinks/information. **Prime
Minister,** *n.* head of the government in
Britain and other countries. **primer,** *n.*
(*a*) special paint to cover an unpainted
surface. (*b*) elementary text book.

primeval [praɪ'miːvl] *adj.* referring to
the period at the beginning of the world.

primitive ['prɪmɪtɪv] *adj.* (*a*) referring to
very early/prehistoric times. (*b*) rough/
crude.

primogeniture [praɪməʊ'dʒenɪtʃə] *n.*
rule by which the eldest son is the heir.

primordial [praɪ'mɔːdjəl] *adj.* (*formal*)
which existed at the beginning (a long
time ago).

primrose ['prɪmrəʊz] *n.* small pale
yellow wild spring flower.

primula ['prɪmjʊlə] *n.* garden flower,
like a primrose, but with many colours.

prince [prɪns] *n.* son of a king; male
ruler of a small state; male member
of a royal family. **princely,** *adj.* like
a prince; large (sum of money/salary).
princess, *n.* daughter of a king; female
member of a royal family; female ruler
of a small state; wife of a prince.

principal ['prɪnsɪpl] 1. *adj.* main/most
important. 2. *n.* (*a*) head (of a school/
a college); main actor (in a play). (*b*)
money on which interest is paid/capital
which has been invested. **principality**
[prɪnsɪ'pælɪtɪ] *n.* land ruled by a prince.
principally, *adv.* mainly.

principle ['prɪnsɪpl] *n.* (*a*) law/general
rule; **in p.** = in agreement with the
general rule. (*b*) personal sense of
truth; **on p.** = because of what you
believe.

print [prɪnt] 1. *n.* (*a*) mark made on
sth; *see also* **footprint, fingerprint.** (*b*)
letters printed on a page; **the small p.**
= conditions on a contract, usu. written in very small letters. (*c*) picture
which has been printed; photograph
which has been reproduced on paper;
cloth with a design printed on it. 2.
v. (*a*) to mark letters on paper by a
machine. (*b*) to write capital letters or
letters which are not joined together.
(*c*) to reproduce a photograph/pattern,
etc. **printed circuit,** *n.* electronic circuit
where the connections are printed on
a board; **p.c. board** = flat board on
which metal strips are printed to form a
circuit. **printer,** *n.* (*a*) person who prints
books/newspapers, etc. (*b*) machine
which prints automatically. **printing,** *n.*
art of printing books/newspapers, etc.;
p. press = machine which prints books,
etc. **printout,** *n.* printed information
from a computer.

prior ['praɪə] 1. *adj. & adv.* before;
previous; **p. to** = before. 2. *n.* male
head of a priory. **prioress,** *n.* woman
head of a priory. **priority** [praɪ'ɒrɪtɪ] *n.*
(*a*) right to be first. (*b*) thing which
has to be done first. **priory** ['praɪərɪ] *n.*
building where monks or nuns live.

prise [praɪz] *v.* **to p. up** = to lift up with
the help of a lever; **to p. out** = to pull
out using a lever.

prism ['prɪzəm] *n.* glass block usu. with a triangular cross-section, which splits white light up into the colours of the rainbow. **prismatic** [prɪz'mætɪk] *adj.* referring to a prism.

prison ['prɪzn] *n.* place where people are kept by law after they have been found guilty of a crime. **prisoner,** *n.* person who is in prison; **p. of war** = soldier/ airman, etc., who has been captured by the enemy.

prissy ['prɪsɪ] *adj.* (**-ier, -iest**) unpleasantly proud of being good.

pristine ['prɪstiːn] *adj.* (*formal*) fresh/ unspoilt.

private ['praɪvət] **1.** *adj.* (*a*) belonging to one person, not to everyone; **p. means** = personal income from investments; **p. parts** = sex organs; **p. eye** = detective employed by an ordinary person. (*b*) belonging to certain people, but not to the state or the general public; **p. view** = preview of an exhibition for certain invited guests. **2.** *n.* (*a*) **in p.** = being away from other people. (*b*) ordinary soldier of the lowest rank. (*c*) **privates** = private parts. **privacy** ['prɪvəsɪ] *n.* being away from other people. **privateer,** *n.* armed ship which belongs to a private individual. **privately,** *adv.* (*a*) in private. (*b*) (owned) by private individuals. **privatization** [praɪvətaɪ-'zeɪʃn] *n.* act of privatizing. **privatize** ['praɪvətaɪz] *v.* to return (a nationalized industry) to private ownership.

privation [praɪ'veɪʃn] *n.* lack of money/ food, etc.

privet ['prɪvɪt] *n.* common shrub, used for garden hedges.

privilege ['prɪvɪlɪdʒ] *n.* favour/right granted to some people but not to everyone. **privileged,** *adj.* having a privilege.

privy ['prɪvɪ] **1.** *adj.* (*formal*) **to be p. to a secret** = to know the details of a secret. **2.** *n. inf.* rough toilet outside a house. **Privy Council,** *n.* group of important people who advise a king or queen.

prize [praɪz] **1.** *n.* (*a*) money or object given to a winner. (*b*) ship captured in war. **2.** *v.* (*a*) to value. (*b*) *Am.* to prise. **prizefight,** *n.* (*old*) boxing match where the winner wins money. **prizefighter,** *n.* boxer.

pro [prəʊ] **1.** *prefix meaning* in favour of. **2.** *n.* (*a*) **pros and cons of a case** = arguments for and against it. (*b*) *inf.* professional sportsman/actor, etc.

probable ['prɒbəbl] *adj.* likely. **probability** [prɒbə'bɪlɪtɪ] *n.* likelihood. **probably,** *adv.* likely.

probate ['prəʊbeɪt] *n.* proving in law that a document (esp. a will) is valid.

probation [prə'beɪʃn] *n.* (*a*) period when s.o. is being tested. (*b*) period when a criminal is supervised instead of being put in prison; **p. officer** = official who looks after prisoners on probation. **probationary,** *adj.* (period) when s.o. is being tested. **probationer,** *n.* criminal who is on probation.

probe [prəʊb] **1.** *n.* (*a*) instrument used by doctors to examine wounds, etc. (*b*) thorough investigation. (*c*) **space p.** = spacecraft sent into space for scientific purposes. **2.** *v.* to examine (sth) deeply.

probity ['prəʊbɪtɪ] *n.* (*formal*) total honesty.

problem ['prɒbləm] *n.* thing which is difficult to solve. **problematic(al)** [prɒblə'mætɪk(l)] *adj.* doubtful; likely to cause a problem.

proboscis [prəʊ'bɒsɪs] *n.* (*pl.* **-es**) long sucking tube coming from the head of an animal (such as the trunk of an elephant/the sting of a mosquito).

proceed [prə'siːd] *v.* to continue/to go further. **procedural** [prə'siːdʒərəl] *adj.* referring to procedure. **procedure** [prə'siːdʒə] *n.* (*a*) way in which sth ought to be carried out. (*b*) medical treatment. **proceed against,** *v.* to start a lawsuit against (s.o.). **proceedings,** *n. pl.* report of what takes place at a meeting. **proceeds** ['prəʊsiːdz] *n. pl.* money which you receive when you sell sth.

process ['prəʊses] **1.** *n.* (*pl.* **-es**) (*a*) method of making sth. (*b*) **in the p. (of)** = while doing sth. **2.** *v.* (*a*) to make manufactured goods using raw materials; **processed cheese** = cheese which has been treated so that it will keep for a long time. (*b*) to prepare (figures) for a computer; to sort out (information). (*c*) [prə'ses] *inf.* to walk in a procession. **processing,** *n.* treating raw materials; sorting out information. **procession** [prə'seʃn] n. group of people marching (with a band, etc.) in line. **processional,** adj. referring to a procession. **processor,** n. machine/person who processes; computer device which processes information.

proclaim [prə'kleɪm] v. to state officially and in public. **proclamation** [prɒklə-'meɪʃn] n. official public statement.

proclivity [prə'klɪvɪtɪ] n. (formal) tendency.

procrastinate [prəʊ'kræstɪneɪt] (formal) v. to delay/to put sth off until later. **procrastination** [prəkræstɪ'neɪʃn] n. delaying/putting off.

procreate ['prəʊkrɪeɪt] v. (formal) to produce (young). **procreation,** n. act of procreating.

proctor ['prɒktə] n. university official who keeps law and order.

procure [prə'kjʊə] v. (formal) (a) to obtain. (b) to provide (girls) for sex. **procurable,** adj. which can be obtained. **procurator** ['prɒkjʊreɪtə] n. (in Scotland) **p. fiscal** = public prosecutor. **procurement,** n. obtaining.

prod [prɒd] 1. n. poke; **give him a p.** = nudge him/try to get him to act. 2. v. (**prodded**) to poke with a finger/stick, etc.

prodigal ['prɒdɪgl] adj. wasteful; (person) who spends a lot. **prodigality** [prɒdɪ'gælɪtɪ] n. being prodigal. **prodigally,** adv. wastefully.

prodigy ['prɒdɪdʒɪ] n. remarkable person or thing. **prodigious** [prə'dɪdʒəs] adj. remarkable/enormous. **prodigiously,** adv. remarkably/enormously.

produce 1. n. ['prɒdjuːs] things grown on the land. 2. v. [prə'djuːs] (a) to bring out. (b) to make/to manufacture. (c) to put on (a play/a film). (d) to yield (crops, etc.). **producer** [prə'djuːsə] n. (a) person who puts on a play/a film. (b) person/country which makes/grows sth. **product** ['prɒdʌkt] n. (a) thing which is manufactured/produced. (b) result. (c) (in mathematics) result of multiplying two numbers. **production** [prə'dʌkʃn] n. (a) manufacturing. (b) putting on a play/film. **productive** [prə'dʌktɪv] adj. which produces. **productivity** [prɒdʌk-'tɪvɪtɪ] n. rate of output/of production (in a factory); **p. bonus** = bonus paid for increased output.

profane [prə'feɪn] adj. not religious; blasphemous. **profanely,** adv. in a profane way. **profanity** [prə'fænɪtɪ] n. rudeness; swearing/blasphemy.

profess [prə'fes] v. to declare. **professed,** adj. declared. **professedly** [prə'fesɪdlɪ] adv. openly. **profession** [prə'feʃn] n. (a) work which needs special training/skill/knowledge. (b) declaration (of belief in sth). **professional.** 1. adj. (a) referring to a profession; expert; **p. footballer** = footballer who is paid to play. 2. n. (a) expert. (b) sportsman who is paid to play. **professionalism,** n. (a) expertise/skill. (b) being a professional sportsman. **professionally,** adv. in a professional way. **professor,** n. (a) chief teacher in a subject at a university. (b) teacher of music/art, etc. **professorial** [prɒfə'sɔːrɪəl] adj. referring to a professor. **professorship,** n. position of professor at a university.

proffer ['prɒfə] v. (formal) to offer.

proficient [prə'fɪʃnt] adj. (at) very capable (of doing sth). **proficiency,** n. skill in doing sth. **proficiently,** adv. in a capable way.

profile ['prəʊfaɪl] n. (a) view of s.o.'s head from the side; **to maintain a low p.** = to be quiet/unobtrusive. (b) short biography/description of a famous person (in a newspaper).

profit ['prɒfɪt] 1. n. money gained; **p. margin** = percentage of money gained against money paid out. 2. v. to gain. **profitability** [prɒfɪtə'bɪlɪtɪ] n. ability to produce a profit. **profitable** ['prɒfɪtəbl] adj. likely to produce a profit. **profitably,** adv. at a profit. **profiteer** [prɒfɪ'tɪə] 1. n. person who makes too much profit. 2. v. to make too much profit. **profiteering,** n. making too much profit.

profligate ['prɒflɪgət] adj. & n. (formal) (person) who is very extravagant/who leads a wild life. **profligacy** ['prɒflɪgəsɪ] n. extravagance/spending money wildly.

proforma [prəʊ'fɔːmə] adj. & n. (invoice) sent asking the purchaser to pay in advance.

profound [prə'faʊnd] adj. very serious/very deep (understanding/thought).

profoundly, *adv.* extremely. **profundity** [prə'fʌndɪtɪ] *n.* depth (of thought or understanding). **profuse** [prə'fju:s] *adj.* abundant/excessive. **profusely,** *adv.* excessively/too much. **profuseness,** *n.* being profuse. **profusion** [prə'fju:ʒn] *n.* very large quantity.

progeny ['prɒdʒənɪ] *n.* (*no pl.*) (*formal*) children/offspring. **progenitor** [prəʊ'dʒenɪtə] *n.* ancestor; animal/plant from which others are descended.

progesterone [prəʊ'dʒestərəʊn] *n.* hormone which stops women ovulating, and helps the uterus in the first stages of pregnancy.

prognathous [prɒg'neɪθəs] *adj.* with a lower jaw which is longer than the upper.

prognosticate [prɒg'nɒstɪkeɪt] *v.* (*formal*) to foretell. **prognosis** [prɒg'nəʊsɪs] *n.* forecast. **prognostication,** *n.* (*formal*) forecast.

programme, *Am.* **program** ['prəʊgræm, *Am.* 'prəʊgrəm] **1.** *n.* (*a*) list of items in an entertainment. (*b*) show/item on TV or radio. **2.** *v.* to arrange shows on TV/radio. **program** ['prəʊgræm] **1.** *n.* instructions given to a computer. **2.** *v.* to give instructions to (a computer); **programming language** = system of signs and words used to program a computer. **programmable,** *adj.* (device) which can be programmed. **programmer,** *n.* (*a*) person who arranges shows on TV/radio. (*b*) person who programs a computer.

progress 1. *n.* ['prəʊgres] (*pl.* **-es**) movement forwards; **work in p.** = work which is being done. **2.** *v.* [prə'gres] to advance. **progression** [prə'greʃn] *n.* advance/movement forwards. **progressive,** *adj.* (*a*) (movement) in stages. (*b*) advanced (ideas). **progressively,** *adv.* by stages.

prohibit [prə'hɪbɪt] *v.* to forbid. **prohibition** [prəʊhɪ'bɪʃn] *n.* forbidding (esp. the sale of alcohol). **prohibitive** [prə'hɪbɪtɪv] *adj.* (price) which is so high that you cannot pay it.

project 1. *n.* ['prɒdʒekt] (*a*) plan. (*b*) work planned by students on their own. **2.** *v.* [prə'dʒekt] (*a*) to plan. (*b*) to throw (a picture on a screen). **projectile**

[prə'dʒektaɪl] *n.* thing which is thrown/shot. **projecting,** *adj.* sticking/jutting/standing out. **projection,** *n.* (*a*) thing planned/forecast. (*b*) (*in geography*) picture of the shape of the earth on a flat surface. (*c*) thing which stands/sticks out. (*d*) action of projecting a picture on a screen. **projectionist,** *n.* person who operates a projector in a cinema. **projector,** *n.* apparatus for throwing pictures on a screen.

prolapse ['prəʊlæps] *n.* state where an organ in the body moves out of place.

prolegomena [prəʊle'gɒmɪnə] *pl. n.* (*formal*) introduction.

proletariat [prəʊlɪ'teərɪət] *n.* working class. **proletarian,** *adj. & n.* (member) of the working class.

prolific [prə'lɪfɪk] *adj.* producing many children; very productive. **prolifically,** *adv.* in a prolific way. **proliferate** [prə'lɪfəreɪt] *v.* to produce shoots/young, etc., rapidly. **proliferation** [prəlɪfə'reɪʃn] *n.* rapid spread.

prolix ['prəʊlɪks] *adj.* (*formal*) long-winded/using too many words. **prolixity** [prəʊ'lɪksɪtɪ] *n.* being prolix.

prologue ['prəʊlɒg] *n.* piece spoken as the introduction of a play or poem; preliminary section in a book.

prolong [prə'lɒŋ] *v.* to lengthen. **prolongation** [prəʊlɒŋ'geɪʃn] *n.* lengthening. **prolonged,** *adj.* lasting for a long time.

promenade [prɒmə'nɑ:d] **1.** *n.* (*a*) terrace along the seashore where you can walk; (*on a ship*) **p. deck** = deck where passengers can stroll about. (*b*) **p. concerts** = inexpensive concerts of classical music where part of the audience stands and can walk about. **2.** *v.* to walk about. **prom** [prɒm] *n. inf.* promenade; **p. concerts/the proms** = promenade concerts. **promenader,** *n.* (*a*) person who promenades. (*b*) person who goes to a promenade concert.

prominence ['prɒmɪnəns] *n.* (*a*) standing out; thing which stands out. (*b*) fame. **prominent,** *adj.* (*a*) standing out/easily seen. (*b*) famous. **prominently,** *adv.* so as to be easily seen.

promiscuous [prə'mɪskjʊəs] *adj.* (person) who does not prefer one thing to another, esp. who has sexual relations with many people. **promiscuity** [promɪ'skju:ɪtɪ] *n.* having sexual relations with many people. **promiscuously,** *adv.* in a promiscuous way.

promise ['promɪs] **1.** *n.* (*a*) act of promising that you will definitely do sth. (*b*) **to show p.** = to make people feel that you will do well in the future. **2.** *v.* (*a*) to give your word that you will definitely do sth. (*b*) to show signs of what may happen in the future. **promising,** *adj.* (person) who is likely to succeed.

promissory ['promɪsərɪ] *adj.* (note) in which you promise to pay s.o. money on a certain date.

promontory ['promɑntərɪ] *n.* piece of land jutting out into the sea.

promote [prə'məʊt] *v.* (*a*) to give (s.o.) a better job. (*b*) to advertise. (*c*) to encourage. **promoter,** *n.* person who promotes; person who organizes a boxing match, etc. **promotion** [prə'məʊʃn] *n.* (*a*) advancement to a better job. (*b*) advertising (a new product). **promotional,** *adj.* (material) used in advertising.

prompt [prompt] **1.** *adj.* (**-er, -est**) done at once; quick/rapid. **2.** *v.* (*a*) to suggest to (s.o.) that he should do sth. (*b*) to tell an actor words which he has forgotten. **3.** *n.* message to a computer user, telling him to do sth. **prompter,** *n.* person who prompts an actor. **promptitude,** *n.* being prompt. **promptly,** *adv.* immediately; rapidly. **promptness,** *n.* quickness.

promulgate ['promʌlgeɪt] *v.* (*formal*) to make (a law) known to the public. **promulgation** [proml'geɪʃn] *n.* (*formal*) announcement of a law.

prone [prəʊn] *adj.* (*a*) (lying) flat. (*b*) likely (**to**).

prong [proŋ] *n.* one of the sharp points of a fork; point of an attack. **pronged,** *adj.* with prongs.

pronoun ['prəʊnaʊn] *n.* (*in grammar*) word which stands in place of a noun.

pronounce [prə'naʊns] *v.* (*a*) to speak a series of sounds which form a word; to speak clearly. (*b*) to declare in a formal way. **pronounced,** *adj.* noticeable. **pronouncement,** *n.* official/formal

statement. **pronunciation** [prənʌnsɪ-'eɪʃn] *n.* way of pronouncing words.

pronto ['prontəʊ] *adv. inf.* immediately.

proof [pru:f] **1.** *n.* (*a*) thing which proves/which shows that sth is true. (*b*) percentage of alcohol in a drink. (*c*) test sheet of printing which has to be corrected by the author before the book can be produced; copy of a photograph/lithograph, etc., for the artist to examine to see if it is acceptable. **2.** *adj.* (**against**) safe from/not affected by. **3.** *v.* to paint with a protective coat. **proofread,** *v.* to read and correct proofs.

-proof [pru:f] *suffix* safe against/ protected against.

prop [prop] **1.** *n.* (*a*) support; stick which holds sth up. (*b*) **props** = articles used in the production of a play/film. (*c*) (*in Rugby*) forward in the front row of the scrum. **2.** *v.* (**propped**) to support.

propaganda [propə'gændə] *n.* spreading of (frequently false) political ideas. **propagandist,** *n.* person who spreads political ideas.

propagate ['propəgeɪt] *v.* (*a*) to make (new plants) by sowing seed/taking cuttings. (*b*) to spread (ideas). **propagation** [propə'geɪʃn] *n.* act of propagating. **propagator,** *n.* small glass-covered box for growing new plants.

propane ['prəʊpeɪn] *n.* colourless gas used for heating and cooking.

propel [prə'pel] *v.* (**propelled**) to send forward. **propellant,** *n.* fuel used to propel. **propeller,** *n.* mechanism with blades which turns rapidly to drive boats and aircraft.

propensity [prə'pensɪtɪ] *n.* (*formal*) tendency/leaning.

proper ['propə] *adj.* (*a*) right. (*b*) thorough (cleaning, etc.). (*c*) (*in grammar*) **p. noun** = noun which is a name of a person/a country, etc. (*d*) very correct. (*e*) (thing) itself exactly. **properly,** *adv.* (*a*) rightly/correctly. (*b*) thoroughly.

property ['propətɪ] *n.* (*a*) thing which belongs to s.o. (*b*) building or buildings. (*c*) **properties** = articles used in the production of a play/film; **p. man** = person responsible for all the articles used in a play/film. (*d*) quality.

prophecy ['prɒfəsɪ] n. act of prophesying; thing prophesied. **prophesy** ['prɒfɪsaɪ] v. to foretell what will happen in the future. **prophet** ['prɒfɪt] n. person who foretells what will happen; religious leader. **prophetess**, n. woman prophet. **prophetic(al)** [prə'fetɪk(l)] adj. which is like a prophecy. **prophetically**, adv. in a prophetic way.

prophylaxis [prɒfɪ'læksɪs] n. prevention of a disease. **prophylactic** [prɒfɪ-'læktɪk] adj. & n. (substance) which prevents disease.

propinquity [prɒ'pɪŋkwɪtɪ] n. (formal) closeness/nearness.

propitiate [prə'pɪʃɪeɪt] v. (formal) to appease/to make (s.o.) less angry. **propitiation** [prəpɪʃɪ'eɪʃn] n. act of appeasing. **propitiatory** [prə'pɪʃɪətərɪ] adj. which tries to appease/to make less angry. **propitious** [prə'pɪʃəs] adj. favourable. **propitiously**, adv. in a propitious way.

proponent [prɒ'pəʊnənt] n. person who proposes sth.

proportion [prə'pɔːʃn] n. (a) part (of a total). (b) relationship between a part and a total; **in p.** = in the right amount. (c) **proportions** = the relative height/length (of a building/picture, etc.). **proportional**, adj. which is directly related; **p. representation** = system of voting where the votes cast for each party are more or less accurately reflected in the number of seats each party has. **proportionally**, adv. in proportion. **proportionate**, adj. which is in proportion. **proportionately**, adv. in proportion.

propose [prə'pəʊz] v. (a) to suggest/to make a suggestion. (b) **to p. to s.o.** = to ask s.o. to marry you. **proposal**, n. (a) suggestion/thing which is suggested. (b) asking s.o. to marry you. **proposer**, n. person who proposes (a motion). **proposition** [prɒpə'zɪʃn] n. (a) thing which has been proposed. (b) **tough p.** = problem which is difficult to solve.

propound [prə'paʊnd] v. (formal) to put forward (an idea).

proprietor [prə'praɪətə] n. owner. **proprietary** [prə'praɪətrɪ] adj. (a) referring to a proprietor. (b) **p. medicine** = medicine which is sold under a brand name and manufactured by a particular company. (c) (in S. Africa, Australia) **p. company** = private limited company. **proprietress**, n. woman proprietor. **proprietorial**, adj. like a proprietor.

propriety [prə'praɪətɪ] n. decency; good behaviour.

propulsion [prə'pʌlʃn] n. moving forward.

pro rata [prəʊ'rɑːtə] adv. & adj. in proportion.

prorogue [prəʊ'rəʊg] v. to end a session of parliament. **prorogation**, n. end of a session of parliament.

prosaic [prə'zeɪk] adj. ordinary; not poetic; rather dull. **prosaically**, adv. in a prosaic way.

proscenium [prə'siːnɪəm] n. part of a stage in a theatre which sticks out beyond the curtain; **p. arch** = arch above the front part of a stage in a theatre.

proscribe [prəʊ'skraɪb] v. (formal) to forbid by law. **proscription** [prɒs-'krɪpʃn] n. (formal) act of proscribing.

prose [prəʊz] n. writing which is not in verse. **prosy**, adj. wordy/dull in style.

prosecute ['prɒsɪkjuːt] v. to bring (s.o.) to court to answer a charge. **prosecution** [prɒsɪ'kjuːʃn] n. (a) court case against s.o. (b) people who have accused s.o. of a crime in a court. **prosecutor** ['prɒsɪkjuːtə] n. person who prosecutes; **public p.** = government lawyer who accuses a criminal in a law court on behalf of the state.

proselyte ['prɒsɪlaɪt] n. person recently converted to a religion. **proselytize**, v. to try to convert (people) to a religion.

prosody ['prɒsədɪ] n. rules of writing poetry.

prospect 1. n. ['prɒspekt] (a) view. (b) **to have sth in p.** = to expect sth to happen. (c) **prospects** = future possibilities. (d) person who may become a customer. **2.** v. [prə'spekt] to search (a land for minerals). **prospective**, adj. which may happen in the future. **prospector**, n. person who searches for minerals. **prospectus** [prə'spektəs] n. paper giving information about sth in the hope of attracting clients/customers.

prosper ['prɒspə] v. to succeed; to become rich. **prosperity** [prɒsˈperɪtɪ] n. being rich. **prosperous** [ˈprɒspərəs] adj. wealthy/rich.

prostate [ˈprɒsteɪt] n. gland round the bladder in men.

prosthesis [ˈprɒsθəsɪs] n. (pl. **-ses**) (formal) artificial leg/arm, etc.

prostitute [ˈprɒstɪtjuːt] 1. n. person who receives money for sexual intercourse. 2. v. to use (your talents) in a low/unworthy way. **prostitution** [prɒstɪˈtjuːʃn] n. offering sexual intercourse for payment.

prostrate 1. adj. [ˈprɒstreɪt] (lying) flat. 2. v. [prəˈstreɪt] **to p. oneself before s.o.** = to fall down (in front of s.o. as a mark of respect, fear, etc.); **he was prostrated by malaria** = he had to stay lying down. **prostration** [prɒˈstreɪʃn] n. lying down/ falling down in front of s.o.

protagonist [prəˈtægənɪst] n. main character in a play/book, etc.; leader of one side in a conflict.

protean [ˈprəʊtɪən] adj. which changes easily.

protect [prəˈtekt] v. to defend against attack; to shield against dirt/germs, etc. **protection** [prəˈtekʃn] n. (a) shelter. (b) defence. **protective,** adj. which protects. **protectively,** adv. in a protective way. **protector,** n. person/ thing which protects. **protectorate,** n. country which is protected (and usu. controlled) by another country.

protégé [ˈprɒteʒeɪ] n. person (usu. young) who is supported in work with money or advice by s.o. else.

protein [ˈprəʊtiːn] n. compound which is an essential part of living cells; one of the elements in food which is necessary to keep the human body working properly.

pro tempore, pro tem [prəʊ-ˈtempɒreɪ, ˈprəʊˈtem] adv. temporarily.

protest 1. n. [ˈprəʊtest] statement that you object or disapprove; **p. march** = march in procession to show that you protest against sth. 2. v. [prəˈtest] (a) to object/to raise a violent objection (**against**). (b) to state solemnly. **Protestant** [ˈprɒtɪstənt] adj. & n. (member) of a Western Christian church which is not part of the Roman Catholic Church. **Protestantism,** n. beliefs of

the Protestant church. **protestation** [prɒtɪˈsteɪʃn] n. violent statement of protest.

protocol [ˈprəʊtəkɒl] n. (a) correct (diplomatic) behaviour. (b) draft agreement.

proton [ˈprəʊtɒn] n. nucleus of a hydrogen atom, found in all atoms.

protoplasm [ˈprəʊtəplæzəm] n. basic jelly-like substance in all living matter.

prototype [ˈprəʊtətaɪp] n. first model of a new machine.

protozoa [prəʊtəʊˈzəʊə] n. pl. simplest types of living creatures.

protracted [prəˈtræktɪd] adj. very lengthy. **protraction,** n. being protracted. **protractor,** n. semicircular device, used for measuring angles in geometry.

protrude [prəˈtruːd] v. to stick out. **protrusion,** n. thing which protrudes.

protuberance [prəˈtjuːbərəns] n. bump/swelling. **protuberant,** adj. which swells outwards.

proud [praʊd] adj. (**of**) full of pride; thinking a lot of yourself/of sth belonging to you; inf. **he did himself p.** = he gave himself a large meal. **proudly,** adv. with pride; with great satisfaction.

prove [pruːv] v. (a) to demonstrate that sth is right. (b) to turn out. **provable,** adj. which can be proved. **proven** [ˈprəʊvn] adj. (a) which has been shown to be right. (b) (in Scotland) **not p.** = decision to release a prisoner because his guilt cannot be proved or disproved.

provenance [ˈprɒvənəns] n. (formal) origin.

provender [ˈprɒvəndə] n. (no pl.) (formal) food.

proverb [ˈprɒvɜːb] n. saying which has a moral/which teaches you sth. **proverbial** [prəˈvɜːbɪəl] adj. mentioned in a proverb; well-known. **proverbially,** adv. in a proverbial way.

provide [prəˈvaɪd] v. (a) to supply; **to p. for** = earn enough to feed and clothe. (b) to take care of. **provider,** n. person who provides. **provided that, providing,** conj. on condition that.

providence [ˈprɒvɪdəns] n. (lucky) fate. **provident,** adj. careful to think about the future and keep money/stores for use in time of need. **providential**

[provɪ'denʃnl] *adj*. lucky. **providentially,** *adv*. luckily.

province ['provɪns] *n*. (*a*) large administrative division of a country; **the provinces** = parts of a country away from the capital. (*b*) area of knowledge; area of responsbility. **provincial** [prə'vɪnʃl] **1.** *adj*. referring to a province/to the provinces; narrow-minded/not very civilized. **2.** *n*. person from the provinces.

provision [prə'vɪʒn] **1.** *n*. (*a*) thing that is provided; **to make p. for** = to see that sth is allowed for in the future. (*b*) *pl*. **provisions** = food. (*e*) condition in a document. **2.** *v*. to stock up with food. **provisional,** *adj*. temporary; conditional. **provisionally,** *adv*. temporarily.

proviso [prə'vaɪzəu] *n*. (*pl*. **-os**) condition.

provoke [prə'vəuk] *v*. (*a*) to incite (s.o.) to do sth violent. (*b*) to make (a reaction) start. **provocation** [provə'keɪʃn] *n*. action of provoking. **provocative** [prɒ'vɒkətɪv] *adj*. likely to provoke a violent response. **provocatively,** *adv*. in a provocative way. **provoking,** *adj*. annoying.

provost ['provəst] *n*. (*a*) person in charge of a college. (*b*) (*in Scotland*) mayor. (*c*) **p. marshal** = head of a group of military police.

prow [prau] *n*. front end of a ship.

prowess ['praues] *n*. (*formal*) skill.

prowl [praul] **1.** *n*. **on the p.** = creeping about. **2.** *v*. to creep about quietly. **prowler,** *n*. person who creeps about, esp. a burglar.

proximate ['prɒksɪmət] *adj*. (*formal*) nearest/closest. **proximity** [prɒk'sɪmɪtɪ] *n*. closeness.

proxy ['prɒksɪ] *n*. (*a*) document giving s.o. the power to act/to vote on your behalf. (*b*) person who acts/votes on your behalf.

prude [pru:d] *n*. prudish person. **prudery, prudishness,** *n*. state of being prudish. **prudish,** *adj*. with strict principles and easily shocked.

prudence ['pru:dns] *n*. great care/caution. **prudent,** *adj*. very careful/very cautious. **prudential** [pru:'denʃl] *adj*. (*formal*) showing prudence. **prudently,** *adv*. in a prudent way.

prune [pru:n] **1.** *n*. dried plum. **2.** *v*. to cut branches off (a tree); to cut back (a tree/shrub) to keep it in good shape or to encourage it to produce flowers; to cut back (expenditure, etc.); to cut out (parts of a book, etc.).

prurient ['pruərɪənt] *adj*. which causes indecent thoughts. **prurience,** *n*. being prurient.

prussic acid ['prʌsɪk 'æsɪd] *n*. type of poisonous acid.

pry [praɪ] *v*. (*a*) to look inquisitively into sth. (*b*) *Am*. to lift open with a lever.

PS [pi:'es] *short for* post scriptum, additional note at the end of a letter.

psalm [sɑ:m] *n*. religious song from the Bible. **psalmist,** *n*. person who wrote the psalms. **psalter** ['sɔ:ltə] *n*. book of psalms with music, for use in church.

PSBR *short for* Public Sector Borrowing Requirement.

psephology [se'fɒlədʒɪ] *n*. study of elections/voters. voting patterns and opinion polls of voters. **psephologist,** *n*. person who specializes in psephology.

pseud [sju:d] *n*. *inf*. person who is not really as he pretends to be.

pseudo- ['sju:dəu] *prefix meaning* false.

pseudonym ['sju:dənɪm] *n*. false/invented name. **pseudonymous** [sju:-'dɒnɪməs] *adj*. (writer) using a pseudonym.

psittacosis [psɪtə'kəusɪs] *n*. serious disease, caught by people from birds.

psoriasis [sɔ:'raɪəsɪs] *n*. itching disease which causes red patches on the skin.

psychedelic [saɪkə'delɪk] *adj*. so full of bright moving colours that you become hallucinated.

psychiatry [saɪ'kaɪətrɪ] *n*. study of mental disease. **psychiatric** [saɪkɪ'ætrɪk] *adj*. referring to psychiatry. **psychiatrist** [saɪ'kaɪətrɪst] *n*. person who studies and treats mental disease.

psychic ['saɪkɪk] *adj*. & *n*. (person) in contact with supernatural forces. **psychical,** *adj*. in contact with supernatural forces.

psychoanalysis [saɪkəuə'næləsɪs] *n*. treatment of mental disorder by discussion. **psychoanalyse,** *v*. to treat (s.o.) by psychoanalysis. **psychoanalyst** [saɪkəu'ænəlɪst] *n*. person who treats patients by psychoanalysis.

psychology [saɪˈkɒlədʒɪ] n. study of the human mind. **psychological** [saɪkə-ˈlɒdʒɪkl] adj. referring to psychology. **psychologically**, adv. mentally. **psychologist** [saɪˈkɒlədʒɪst] n. person who studies the human mind.

psychopath [ˈsaɪkəpæθ] n. psychopathic criminal. **psychopathic** [saɪkə-ˈpæθɪk] adj. mentally unstable in a dangerous way.

psychosis [saɪˈkəʊsɪs] n. (pl. **-oses** [-əʊsiːz]) mental illness which changes the patient's personality. **psychotic** [saɪˈkɒtɪk] adj. & n. (person) suffering from a psychosis.

psychosomatic [saɪkəʊsəˈmætɪk] adj. (physical illness) created by a mental state.

psychotherapy [saɪkəʊˈθerəpɪ] n. treatment of mental disorder by psychological means.

Pt symbol for platinum.

PTA Parent Teacher Association.

ptarmigan [ˈtɑːmɪgən] n. type of mountain bird.

pterodactyl [terəʊˈdæktɪl] n. prehistoric flying dinosaur.

PTO [piːtiːˈəʊ] short for please turn over.

Pu symbol for plutonium.

pub [pʌb] n. inf. public house/inn; **p. crawl** = going from inn to inn having a drink in each.

puberty [ˈpjuːbətɪ] n. period of adolescence when a person becomes sexually mature.

pubic [ˈpjuːbɪk] adj. referring to the area around the sexual organs.

public [ˈpʌblɪk] **1.** adj. (a) referring to the people in general; **p. holiday** = holiday for everyone; **p. house** = inn/place where you can buy and drink alcohol. (b) **p. school** = (in Britain) private fee-paying school which is not part of the state system; (in the USA) a state school. **2.** n. people in general; **in p.** = in the open; in front of everyone. **publican**, n. person who runs a public house. **publication** [pʌblɪˈkeɪʃn] n. (a) making public/publishing. (b) book/paper which has been published. **publicist** [ˈpʌblɪsɪst] n. person who attracts people's attention to a product. **publicity** [pʌbˈlɪsɪtɪ] n. advertising; attracting people's attention to a prod-

uct. **publicize**, v. to attract people's attention to sth/to make publicity for sth. **publicly**, adv. in public. **public relations**, n. maintaining good relations between an organization and the public. **public service**, n. working for the state; all government agencies and their personnel. **Public Sector Borrowing Requirement**, n. the amount of money the government needs to borrow, in order to run its services. **public-spirited**, adj. (person) who acts energetically for the good of the community.

publish [ˈpʌblɪʃ] v. to make publicly known; to bring out (a book/newspaper) for sale. **publisher**, n. person who produces books/newspapers for sale. **publishing**, n. producing books/newspapers for sale; **p. house** = firm which publishes books.

puce [pjuːs] adj. dark purplish red.

puck [pʌk] n. small disc which is hit in ice hockey.

pucker [ˈpʌkə] **1.** n. wrinkle/fold. **2.** v. to wrinkle (your brow).

puckish [ˈpʌkɪʃ] adj. mischievous/full of playful tricks.

pudding [ˈpʊdɪŋ] n. (a) dessert/sweet course at the end of the meat. (b) sweet food which has been cooked or boiled. (c) **black p.** = dark sausage made of blood.

puddle [ˈpʌdl] n. small pool of water (e.g. one left after rain).

pudgy [ˈpʌdʒɪ] adj. soft and fat.

puerile [ˈpjʊəraɪl] adj. childish/stupid. **puerility** [pjʊəˈrɪlɪtɪ] n. being puerile.

puff [pʌf] **1.** n. (a) small breath. (b) **powder p.** = light pad for powdering the skin. (c) **p. pastry** = light sort of pastry. (d) piece of publicity. **2.** v. to blow. **puffball**, n. type of round white fungus. **puffed (out)**, adj. inf. out of breath. **puffiness**, n. being puffy. **puffy**, adj. swollen (face).

puffin [ˈpʌfɪn] n. black and white bird with a large coloured beak, living near the sea.

pug [pʌg] n. type of small dog, with a flat face. **pugnosed**, adj. with a flattened nose.

pugilist [ˈpjuːdʒɪlɪst] n. (formal) fighter/boxer. **pugilism**, n. (formal) boxing.

pugnacious [pʌg'neɪʃəs] (*formal*) *adj.* (person) who likes fighting; quarrelsome. **pugnaciously,** *adv.* in a pugnacious way. **pugnacity** [pʌg'næsɪtɪ] *n.* being pugnacious.

puisne ['pjuːnɪ] *adj.* (judge) in the High Court.

puissance ['pwiːsɑːns] *n.* test in show-jumping, where a horse has to jump very high fences.

puke [pjuːk] *v. inf.* **to p. (up)** = to vomit.

pukka ['pʌkə] *adj. inf.* real; of good quality.

pulchritude ['pʌlkrɪtjuːd] *n.* (*formal*) beauty.

pule [pjuːl] *v.* (*of children*) to wail/to whimper.

pull [pʊl] **1.** *n.* (*a*) act of dragging/moving sth towards you. (*b*) *inf.* influence. (*c*) handle (which has to be pulled). (*d*) deep inhaling (of a cigarette). **2.** *v.* (*a*) to move (sth) by dragging; to move (sth) towards you. **to p. a face** = make a grimace. (*c*) to strain (a muscle). **pull down,** *v.* to bring (sth) down by pulling. **pull in,** *v.* to drive close to the side of the road (and stop). **pull-in,** *n. inf.* transport café. **pull off,** *v.* (*a*) to take off (a piece of clothing/a handle, etc.) by pulling. (*b*) *inf.* to succeed in doing (sth). (*c*) to drive off a road and stop. **pull out,** *v.* (*a*) to bring (sth) out by pulling. (*b*) to drive away from the side of the road; to drive towards the middle of the road. **pull round, pull through,** *v.* to recover from an illness. **pull together,** *v.* **he pulled himself together** = he became calmer/he controlled his emotions. **pull up,** *v.* (*a*) to stop (in a vehicle). (*b*) to raise by pulling; *inf.* **to p. one's socks up** = to do better/try harder.

pullet ['pʊlɪt] *n.* young chicken.

pulley ['pʊlɪ] *n.* apparatus for lifting heavy weights with a grooved wheel round which a rope runs.

pullman ['pʊlmən] *n.* (*a*) luxurious railway carriage. (*b*) *Am.* sleeping car (on a train).

pullover ['pʊləʊvə] *n.* piece of clothing made of wool, etc., covering the top part of the body and which you pull on over your head.

pulmonary ['pʌlmənrɪ] *adj.* referring to the lungs.

pulp [pʌlp] **1.** *n.* squashy mass. **2.** to crush to a pulp. **pulpy,** *adj.* in a pulp.

pulpit ['pʊlpɪt] *n.* enclosed platform in a church where the priest preaches.

pulsar ['pʌlsə] *n.* invisible star which sends out radio signals.

pulse [pʌls] *n.* **1.** (*a*) regular beat of the heart. (*b*) dried seed of peas/beans. **2.** *v.* to pulsate. **pulsate** [pʌl'seɪt] *v.* throb regularly. **pulsation** [pʌl'seɪʃn] *n.* regular throbbing.

pulverize ['pʌlvəraɪz] *v.* to crush to powder. **pulverization** [pʌlvəraɪ'zeɪʃn] *n.* crushing to powder.

puma ['pjuːmə] *n.* large wild American cat.

pumice (stone) ['pʌmɪs('stəʊn)] *n.* block of light grey porous lava used for rubbing stains off your skin.

pummel ['pʌml] *v.* (**pummelled**) to hit s.o. with many blows.

pump [pʌmp] **1.** *n.* (*a*) machine for forcing liquids or air. (*b*) soft shoe. **2.** *v.* (*a*) to force (liquid/air) with a pump. (*b*) *inf.* to ask (s.o.) searching questions. **pump priming,** *n.* investment by the government in new projects, to stimulate the economy.

pumpkin ['pʌmpkɪn] *n.* large round orange-coloured vegetable.

pun [pʌn] **1.** *n.* play with words of different meanings. **2.** *v.* (**punned**) to make puns. **punster,** *n.* a person who is always making puns.

punch [pʌntʃ] **1.** *n.* (*pl.* **-es**) (*a*) blow with the fist; **p. line** = last sentence of a story/joke which gives the point. (*b*) metal tool for making holes. (*c*) drink made of wine or spirits and spices. **2.** *v.* (*a*) to hit (s.o.) with your fist. (*b*) to make holes in (sth) with a punch. **Punch and Judy,** *n.* form of children's puppet show, with traditional characters. **punch bowl,** *n.* (*a*) bowl for mixing wine and spices to make punch. (*b*) small valley surrounded by hills. **punch-drunk,** *adj.* suffering from brain damage from being punched on the head too often. **punch-up,** *n. inf.* fight.

punctilious [pʌŋk'tɪlɪəs] *adj.* attentive to detail/extremely fussy. **punctiliously,** *adv.* in a punctilious way. **punctiliousness,** *n.* being punctilious.

punctual ['pʌŋktjʊəl] *adj.* on time. **punctuality** [pʌŋktjʊ'ælɪtɪ] *n.* being on time/never being late. **punctually,** *adv.* on time.

punctuate ['pʌŋktjʊeɪt] *v.* (*a*) to split a sentence using punctuation marks. (*b*) to interrupt. **punctuation** [pʌŋktjʊ'eɪʃn] *n.* splitting of a sentence using punctuation marks; **p. marks** = signs used in writing (such as full stop, comma, dash) to show how a sentence is split up.

puncture ['pʌŋktʃə] **1.** *n.* hole in a tyre; very small hole. **2.** *v.* to make a small hole in (sth).

pundit ['pʌndɪt] *n.* expert (esp. in political matters).

pungent ['pʌndʒənt] *adj.* sharp (taste, smell); sarcastic (comment). **pungency,** *n.* being pungent. **pungently,** *adv.* in a pungent way.

punish ['pʌnɪʃ] *v.* to make (s.o.) suffer because of sth he has done. **punishable,** *adj.* (offence) for which you can be punished. **punishment,** *n.* treatment given to punish s.o. **punitive** ['pju:nətɪv] *adj.* which aims to punish.

punk [pʌŋk] **1.** *n. inf.* (*a*) wild hooligan. (*b*) follower of punk rock. **2.** *adj. inf.* bad/inferior. **punk rock,** *n.* loud music played by people wearing outrageous costumes.

punnet ['pʌnɪt] *n.* small box made of plastic or thin pieces of wood for holding soft fruit.

punt [pʌnt] **1.** *n.* (*a*) long flat-bottomed boat, propelled with a pole. (*b*) (*Ireland*) pound (in currency). **2.** *v.* (*a*) to push (a punt) with a pole. (*b*) to kick a ball which is in the air. (*c*) to bet on a horse race. **punter,** *n.* (*a*) person who gambles, esp. on horseraces. (*b*) person who pushes a punt along with a pole.

puny ['pju:nɪ] *adj.* (**-ier, -iest**) weak/feeble; very small.

pup [pʌp] **1.** *n.* young of certain animals, esp. young dog; **p. tent** = small ridge tent. **2.** *n. v.* (**pupped**) to have pups.

pupa ['pju:pə] *n.* (*pl.* **-pae** [-pi:]) resting period in the life of an insect when it is changing from a grub/caterpillar to a butterfly/beetle. **pupal,** *adj.* referring to a pupa. **pupate** [pju:'peɪt] *v.* (*of caterpillar*) to turn into a pupa.

pupil ['pju:pl] *n.* (*a*) child at a school; person learning from a teacher. (*b*) hole in the central part of the eye, through which the light passes.

puppet ['pʌpɪt] *n.* doll which moves and which is used to give a performance; **p. show** = performance given using puppets; **p. state** = country controlled by another country. **puppeteer** [pʌpɪ'tɪə] *n.* man who gives a performance using puppets.

puppy ['pʌpɪ] *n.* young dog; **p. fat** = fatness in young children and adolescents.

purblind ['pɜ:blaɪnd] *adj.* partly blind.

purchase ['pɜ:tʃəs] **1.** *n.* (*a*) thing bought. (*b*) ability to grip/ability to lift sth by using a lever. **2.** *v.* to buy; **purchasing power** = quantity that can be bought with a certain amount of money. **purchaser,** *n.* person who buys sth.

purdah ['pɜ:də] *n.* seclusion of women (in Eastern countries).

pure ['pjʊə] *adj.* (**-er, -est**) (*a*) very clean; not mixed with other things. (*b*) innocent; with no faults. **purely,** *adv.* only/solely.

purée ['pjʊəreɪ] **1.** *n.* semi-liquid pulp (of a vegetable/fruit). **2.** *v.* to make (sth) into a purée.

purgatory ['pɜ:gətrɪ] *n.* place where you suffer temporarily after death; (place of) suffering.

purge [pɜ:dʒ] **1.** *n.* (*a*) medicine which clears the bowels. (*b*) removal of political opponents. **2.** *v.* (*a*) to clear out (waste matter). (*b*) **to p. one's contempt** = to apologize to a court. (*c*) to remove (political opponents). **purgative** ['pɜ:gətɪv] *adj. & n.* (medicine) which clears the bowels.

purify ['pjʊərɪfaɪ] *v.* to clean/to make pure. **purification** [pjʊərɪfɪ'keɪʃn] *n.* making pure. **purifier,** *n.* machine that purifies. **purist** ['pjʊərɪst] *n.* person who insists on everything being done in the correct way. **purity,** *n.* being pure/absolutely clean.

puritan ['pjʊərɪtən] *n.* puritanical person. **puritanical** [pjʊərɪ'tænɪkl] *adj.* very strict concerning morals.

purl [pɜ:l] *v.* to knit putting your needle into the back of the loop.

purlieus ['pɜ:lju:z] *pl. n.* (*formal*) surroundings.

purloin [pɜːˈlɔɪn] v. (formal) to steal.

purple [ˈpɜːpl] adj. & n. reddish-blue (colour). **purplish,** adj. quite purple.

purport [pɜːˈpɔːt] (formal) 1. n. meaning. 2. v. to mean.

purpose [ˈpɜːpəs] n. aim/plan; use; **on p.** = according to what was planned; intentionally. **purpose-built,** adj. built specially for a purpose. **purposeful,** adj. intentional; with an aim in view; (person) with set aims. **purposefully,** adv. in a purposeful way. **purposefulness,** n. being purposeful. **purposely,** adv. on purpose/intentionally.

purr [pɜː] 1. n. (a) noise made by a cat when pleased. (b) low noise made by a powerful engine. 2. v. (a) (of cat) to make a noise to show pleasure. (b) (of engine) to make a low noise.

purse [pɜːs] 1. n. (a) small bag for carrying money. (b) handbag. 2. **to p. your lips** = to pinch/to press your lips together to show you are displeased. **purser,** n. officer on a ship who deals with the money, supplies and the passengers' accommodation.

pursue [pəˈsjuː] v. (a) to chase (s.o./sth). (b) to continue to do (sth). **pursuance,** n. (formal) **in p. of** = while carrying out (duties). **pursuant to,** adv. relating to. **pursuer,** n. person who chases s.o. **pursuit** [pəˈsjuːt] n. (a) chase; **in p. of** = looking for. (b) (formal) career/occupation.

purulent [ˈpjʊərʊlənt] adj. (formal) full of pus.

purvey [pɜːˈveɪ] v. (formal) to supply (goods). **purveyor,** n. person who supplies goods.

purview [ˈpɜːvjuː] n. general scope of a document.

pus [pʌs] n. yellowish liquid which gathers in infected wounds/spots.

push [pʊʃ] 1. n. (-es) (a) act of pressing sth so that it moves away from you. (b) energy; inf. determination to do well. (c) inf. **at a p.** = if necessary. (d) inf. **to give s.o. the p.** = to dismiss s.o. from a job. 2. v. (a) to press; to move (sth) by pressing. (b) inf. **I am pushed for time** = I haven't much time to spare. (c) Sl. to sell (drugs) illegally. **pushbike,** n. inf. bicycle. **push button,** n. switch which is operated by pushing. **pushchair,** n. light folding carriage for pushing a child in. **pusher,** n. Sl. person who sells drugs illegally. **pushful, pushing,** adj. ambitious; eager to get what you want. **push off,** v. inf. to get going/to start a journey; **push off!** = go away! **pushover,** n. inf. easy task; person who is easily influenced. **push-up,** n. Am. press-up. **pushy,** adj. inf. wanting to succeed/ambitious.

pusillanimous [pjuːsɪˈlænɪməs] adj. (formal) timid/afraid. **pusillanimity** [pjuːsɪləˈnɪmɪtɪ] n. being pusillanimous.

puss [pʊs], **pussy** [ˈpʊsɪ], **pussycat** [ˈpʊsɪkæt] n. familiar words for a cat. **pussyfoot,** v. inf. **to p. about** = to dither/to be undecided.

pustule [ˈpʌstjuːl] n. blister/spot (on the skin).

put [pʊt] v. (**put; putting**) (a) to place; inf. **to stay p.** = to stay where you are. (b) to express in words. (c) to estimate **at.** (d) **to p. a stop to** = to stop. (e) (in sports) to throw (the shot). **put across,** v. to explain (sth) in a convincing way. **put away,** v. to clear (things) away. **put back,** v. to place (sth) where it was before. **put by,** v. to save. **put down,** v. (a) to place at a lower level/on the ground. (b) to let (passengers) get off. (c) to note. (d) to kill (a sick animal). (e) **to p. your foot down** = (i) to be very strict/firm; (ii) (in a car) to go faster. **put in,** v. (a) to place inside. (b) **he p. in three hour's work** = he worked for three hours. (c) **to p. in for a job** = to apply. **put off,** v. (a) to delay. (b) to frighten/to embarrass (s.o.) so that they can't do sth. **put on,** v. (a) to place. (b) to get dressed in (a piece of clothing). (c) to switch on (a light, etc.). (d) to add (weight). **put out,** v. (a) to place outside. (b) to stretch out (one's hand, etc.). (c) to switch off (a light, etc.). (d) inf. **to be p. out** = to be annoyed. (e) (of ships) **to p. out to sea** = to leave harbour. **put up,** v. (a) to fix upright; to build. (b) to raise. (c) to offer. (d) to find a place for (s.o.) to sleep. (e) **to p. up with s.o./sth** = to accept s.o./sth, even if they are unpleasant/noisy, etc. (f) **to p. s.o. up to sth** = to encourage s.o. to do sth. **put-upon,** adj. forced to do sth unpleasant.

putative [ˈpjuːtətɪv] adj. (formal) **the p.**

author = the person who is supposed to be the author.

putrefy ['pju:trɪfaɪ] v. to rot. **putrefaction** [pjutrɪ'fækʃn] n. rotting. **putrescent**, adj. which is rotting. **putrid**, adj. rotten; smelling rotten.

putsch [putʃ] n. armed overthrow of a government.

putt [pʌt] **1.** n. short shot (on a green) in golf. **2.** v. to hit a short shot in golf. **putter. 1.** n. golf club for putting. **2.** v. Am. **to p. around** = not to do anything in particular/to do little jobs here and there.

puttee ['pʌti] n. long piece of cloth wound round the leg to act as protection.

putty ['pʌti] n. soft substance which hardens after a time, used esp. for sealing the glass in windows.

puzzle ['pʌzl] **1.** n. (a) problem; thing which is difficult to solve. (b) game where you have to solve a problem. **2.** v. to perplex/to mystify; to be a problem. **puzzlement**, n. being puzzled. **puzzling**, adj. which does not make sense/which is a problem.

PVC [pi:vi:'si:] n. type of plastic.

pygmy ['pɪgmɪ] adj. & n. (type of animal) which is smaller than normal; very short (person).

pyjamas [pɪ'dʒɑ:məz] n. pl. light shirt and trousers worn in bed.

pylon ['paɪlən] n. tall metal tower for carrying electric cables.

pyorrhea [paɪə'rɪə] n. infection of the gums round the teeth.

pyramid ['pɪrəmɪd] n. shape with a square base and four sides rising to meet at a point. **pyramidal** [pɪ'ræmɪdl] adj. shaped like a pyramid.

pyre ['paɪə] n. ceremonial fire; **funeral p.** = pile on which a dead body is cremated.

pyrethrum [paɪ'ri:θrəm] n. insecticide made from a flower.

pyrites [paɪ'raɪti:z] n. yellowish chemical substance containing a metal.

pyromaniac [paɪrəʊ'meɪnɪæk] n. person who sets fire to buildings/who is mad about fire.

pyrotechnics [paɪrəʊ'teknɪks] n. pl. science of fireworks. **pyrotechnic(al)**, adj. referring to fireworks.

Pyrrhic victory ['pɪrɪk 'vɪktrɪ] n. victory

which costs the victor too much effort/too many losses.

python ['paɪθn] n. large snake which kills its prey by crushing.

pyx [pɪks] n. box in church where consecrated bread and wine are kept.

Qq

QC [kju:'si:] n. (short for **Queen's Counsel**) title given to an important lawyer.

qua [kweɪ] prep. taken by itself.

quack [kwæk] **1.** n. (a) sound made by a duck. (b) inf. unqualified doctor. **2.** v. to make a noise like a duck.

quad [kwɒd] n. inf. quadrangle. **quadrangle** ['kwɒdræŋgl] n. open square surrounded by buildings (in a school/college).

quadrant ['kwɒdrənt] n. (a) quarter of a circle. (b) instrument used for measuring angles.

quadraphonic [kwɒdrə'fɒnɪk] adj. (sound) which is reproduced through four loudspeakers.

quadratic [kwɒd'rætɪk] adj. (equation) involving the square of the unknown quantity.

quadrennial [kwɒd'renɪəl] adj. happening every four years.

quadrilateral [kwɒdrɪ'lætərəl] adj. & n. (shape) with four sides.

quadruped ['kwɒdruped] n. animal with four legs.

quadruple [kwɒ'dru:pl] v. to multiply four times. **quadruplets** ['kwɒdruplets] n. pl. four babies born at the same birth. **quadruplicate** [kwɒ'dru:plɪkət] n. **in q.** = in four copies. **quads** [kwɒdz] n. pl. inf. quadruplets.

quaff [kwɒf] v. to drink with large gulps.

quagmire ['kwɒgmaɪə] n. bog/area of dangerous marsh.

quail [kweɪl] **1.** n. small game bird. **2.** v. to shrink back in fear; to shudder (at sth).

quaint [kweɪnt] adj. (-er, -est) picturesque/oddly old-fashioned. **quaintly**, adv. in a quaint way. **quaintness**, n. old-fashioned oddness.

quake [kweɪk] **1.** n. inf. earthquake. **2.** v. to shake (with fear/cold). **Quaker**, n. inf. member of a Christian religious society, known as the Society of Friends.

qualify ['kwɒlɪfaɪ] v. (a) **to q. as** = to study for and obtain a diploma which allows you to do a certain type of work. (b) **to q. for** = to pass a test/a section of a competition and so proceed to the next step. (c) to modify; to attach conditions. **qualification** [kwɒlɪfɪ'keɪʃn] n. (a) proof that you have studied for and obtained a diploma; **what are his qualifications?** = what sort of diploma does he have? (b) modification/condition which limits. **qualifier,** n. (a) person who qualifies. (b) round of a sporting competition which qualifies a team to go to the next round.

quality ['kwɒlɪtɪ] n. (a) worth. (b) characteristics. **qualitative,** adj. referring to quality.

qualm [kwɑːm] n. feeling of guilt/worry.

quandary ['kwɒndrɪ] n. puzzle/problem; **in a q.** = puzzled/not knowing what to do.

quango ['kwæŋgəʊ] n. (pl. -os) large national body (such as a government commission which investigates a special problem) where the directors are appointed by the government, but without direct government control.

quantify ['kwɒntɪfaɪ] v. to calculate in quantitities/in amounts. **quantifiable,** adj. which can be quantified.

quantity ['kwɒntɪtɪ] n. amount; **a q. of waste paper** = a lot; **an unknown q.** = person/thing you know nothing about; **q. surveyor** = person who estimates how much material is needed for a building. **quantitative,** adj. referring to quantity.

quantum ['kwɒntəm] n. **q. theory.** = theory in physics that energy exists in fixed amounts.

quarantine ['kwɒrəntiːn] 1. n. period of time when an animal/a person (usu. coming from another country) has to be kept apart to avoid the risk of passing on disease. 2. v. to put (s.o./an animal) in quarantine.

quark [kwɑːk] n. smallest particle.

quarrel ['kwɒrəl] 1. n. argument; **to pick a q. with s.o.** = to start an argument. 2. v. (**quarrelled**) to argue (about/over sth). **quarrelling,** n. arguments. **quarrelsome,** adj. argumentative/often getting into quarrels.

quarry ['kwɒrɪ] 1. n. (a) place where stone, etc., is dug out of the ground. (b) animal which is being hunted; person/thing which is being looked for. 2. v. to dig (stone) out of the ground.

quart [kwɔːt] n. measure of liquid (= 2 pints).

quarter ['kwɔːtə] 1. n. (a) one of four parts. (b) period of fifteen minutes before or after the hour. (c) period of three months. (d) area. (e) **quarters** = accommodation for people in the armed forces. (f) Am. 25 cent coin. 2. v. (a) to cut into four equal parts. (b) to place (soldiers) in lodgings. **quarter day,** n. day which marks the beginning of a three month period for accounting purposes. **quarterdeck,** n. top deck of a ship near the stern. **quarter-final,** n. (in sport) one of four matches in a competition, the winners of which go into the semi-finals. **quarterlight,** n. small, usu. triangular, window in a car. **quarterly,** adj., adv. & n. (magazine) which appears every three months. **quartermaster,** n. (in Army) officer in charge of stores; (in Navy) petty officer in charge of signals.

quartet(te) [kwɔː'tet] n. (a) four people. (b) four musicians playing together. (c) piece of music for four musicians.

quarto ['kwɔːtəʊ] adj. & n. size of paper one quarter of a standard sheet.

quartz [kwɔːts] n. hard crystalline mineral, used for making watches because of its very regular vibrations.

quasar ['kweɪsɑː] n. distant star which gives off intense radiation.

quash [kwɒʃ] v. to annul (a legal sentence).

quasi- ['kweɪzaɪ] prefix meaning almost.

quatrain ['kwɒtreɪn] n. stanza of poetry with four lines.

quaver ['kweɪvə] 1. n. (a) musical note lasting half as long as a crotchet. (b) tremble (in the voice). 2. v. to tremble (of voice). **quavering,** adj. trembling (voice).

quay [kiː] n. stone jetty/place where ships tie up to load or unload. **quayside,** n. **at the q.** = next to the quay.

queasy ['kwiːzɪ] adj. feeling sick. **queasiness,** n. being queasy.

queen [kwi:n] n. (a) wife of a king; woman ruler of a country; **q. mother** = mother of a king or queen who is the widow of a king. (b) (at cards) card between the jack and the king. (c) important piece in chess. (d) **q. ant/bee** = leading ant/bee in a colony. (e) the best/the most perfect woman. (f) Sl. male homosexual. **queenly**, adj. like a queen. **Queen Mother**, n. mother of a king or queen.

queer ['kwɪə] 1. adj. (-er, -est) (a) odd/strange. (b) Sl. adj. & n. homosexual. (c) ill. 2. v. to make sth go wrong; **to q. s.o.'s pitch** = to upset s.o.'s plans. **queerness**, n. strangeness/oddness.

quell [kwel] v. to calm (a riot); to hold back (your feelings).

quench [kwenʃ] v. **to q. your thirst** = to have a drink.

quern [kwɜːn] n. mill for grinding flour by hand.

querulous ['kwerjʊləs] adj. bad-tempered/peevish; always complaining. **querulously**, adv. in a querulous way. **querulousness**, n. being querulous.

query ['kwɪəri] 1. n. (a) question. (b) question mark. 2. v. to doubt whether sth is true; to ask a question.

quest [kwest] n. (formal) search.

question ['kwestʃn] 1. n. (a) sentence which requires an answer; **q. mark** = sign (?) which shows that a question is being asked. (b) problem; **the human rights q.** (c) matter; **there is no q. of** = it is impossible; **the matter in q.** = which is being discussed; **it's out of the q.** = it's unthinkable. 2. v. (a) to ask (s.o.) questions. (b) to doubt. **questionable**, adj. doubtful. **questioner**, n. person who asks questions. **questionnaire** [kwestʃən'neə] n. printed list of questions given to people to answer.

queue [kju:] 1. n. line of people/cars, etc., waiting one behind the other for sth; **to jump the q.** = to go in front of people standing in a queue. 2. (also **queue up**) to form a queue.

quibble ['kwɪbl] 1. n. argument about details. 2. v. to argue about details/to argue over the meaning of words. **quibbler**, n. person who argues about details.

quiche [ki:ʃ] n. open tart with a filling of eggs/meat/vegetables, etc.

quick [kwɪk] 1. adj. (-er, -est) (a) fast/rapid. (b) **she has a q. temper** = she loses her temper easily. 2. n. live flesh (esp. flesh around fingernails/toenails); **he was cut to the q.** = he was very hurt. **quick-acting**, adj. (medicine) which takes effect rapidly. **quicken**, v. (a) to make (sth) go faster. (b) to stimulate (appetite). **quickie**, n. inf. (a) quick drink/question, etc. (b) quick divorce. **quicklime**, n. lime. **quickly**, adv. rapidly. **quickness**, n. being quick. **quicksand**, n. dangerous area of soft sand where you can sink in easily. **quicksilver**, n. mercury. **quickstep**, n. dance with quick steps. **quick-tempered**, adj. (person) who loses his temper easily. **quick-witted**, adj. intelligent (person)/(person) who understands quickly.

quid [kwɪd] n. (a) Sl. pound (in money). (b) lump of chewing tobacco.

quid pro quo [kwɪdprəʊ'kwəʊ] n. something done in return for something else.

quiescent [kwaɪ'esnt] adj. (formal) calm. **quiescence**, n. calmness.

quiet ['kwaɪət] 1. n. (a) absence of noise; calm/tranquillity. (b) **to do sth on the q.** = in secret. 2. adj. (-er, -est) (a) calm/making no noise. (b) simple; **q. wedding** = with few guests; **q. colour scheme** = where the colours aren't bright. 3. v. to calm; to stop (s.o.) being noisy. **quieten**, v. to calm; to stop (s.o.) being noisy. **quietly**, adv. (a) without making any noise. (b) secretly. **quietness**, n. calm/tranquility. **quietude**, n. (formal) quietness.

quiff [kwɪf] n. hair combed upwards and backwards from a man's forehead.

quill [kwɪl] n. long feather (formerly used as a pen).

quilt [kwɪlt] n. padded cover for a bed. **quilted**, adj. made with a pad sewn between two layers of cloth.

quince [kwɪns] n. hard fruit used for making jelly; tree producing this fruit.

quinine ['kwɪniːn] n. drug made from the bark of a tropical tree, used to treat malaria.

quinquennial [kwɪn'kwenɪəl] adj. happening every five years.

quins [kwɪnz] *n. pl. inf.* quintuplets.
quinsy ['kwɪnzɪ] *n.* infection of the tonsils.
quintessence [kwɪn'tesns] *n.* essential part (of sth); perfect example. **quintessential** [kwɪntɪ'senʃl] *adj.* which is a perfect example.
quintet(te) [kwɪn'tet] *n.* (*a*) group of five musicians playing together. (*b*) piece of music for five musicians.
quintuple ['kwɪntjʊpl] *v.* to multiply five times. **quintuplets**, *n. pl.* five babies born at the same birth.
quip [kwɪp] **1.** *n.* joke/clever remark. **2.** *v.* (**quipped**) to make a joke/a clever remark.
quire ['kwaɪə] *n.* 24 sheets of paper.
quirk [kwɜːk] *n.* oddity/strange event.
quisling ['kwɪzlɪŋ] *n.* person who betrays his country by helping the enemy who is occupying it.
quit [kwɪt] *v.* (**quit/quitted**) (*a*) *inf.* to leave (a job/house, etc.). (*b*) *Am. inf.* to stop. **quits**, *adj.* **to be q.** = to be equal. **quittance,** *n.* (*formal*) receipt. **quitter,** *n. inf.* person who gives up easily.
quite [kwaɪt] *adv.* (*a*) completely. (*b*) fairly/relatively; **q. a few** = several.
quiver ['kwɪvə] **1.** *n.* (*a*) tremor/slight shake. (*b*) holder for arrows. **2.** *v.* to tremble.
quixotic [kwɪk'sɒtɪk] *adj.* strange/impractical (person). **quixotically,** *adv.* in a quixotic way.
quiz [kwɪz] **1.** *n.* (*pl.* **quizzes**) series of questions; TV/radio programme where people are asked questions. **2.** *v.* (**quizzed**) to ask (s.o.) questions. **quizmaster,** *n.* person who asks the questions in a TV/radio quiz.
quizzical ['kwɪzɪkl] *adj.* amused.
quod [kwɒd] *n. Sl.* prison.
quoin [kɔɪn] *n.* block of stone making a corner of a building.
quoit [kwɔɪt] *n.* large ring used in a game to throw over pegs.
quorum ['kwɔːrəm] *n.* number of people who have to be present to make a vote valid. **quorate,** *adj.* with a quorum present.
quota ['kwəʊtə] *n.* fixed amount of goods which can be supplied/share; fixed number.
quote [kwəʊt] **1.** *n.* (*a*) passage quoted;

quotation. (*b*) estimate. (*c*) *inf.* **quotes** = inverted commas (" "). **2.** *v.* (*a*) to repeat a number (as a reference); to repeat a text of an author; **can I q. you?** = can I repeat what you have said? (*b*) to indicate the beginning of a quotation (when speaking). (*c*) to give an estimate for work to be done. **quotable,** *adj.* which can be quoted; suitable to be quotable. **quotation** [kwəʊ'teɪʃn] *n.* (*a*) passage quoted. (*b*) estimate. (*c*) **q. marks** = inverted commas (" ").
quoth [kwəʊθ] *v.* (*old*) said.
quotient ['kwəʊʃnt] *n.* result when one number is divided by another.
q.v. [kjuː'viː] *abbreviation for* quod vide, *meaning* which see.
qwerty ['kwɜːtɪ] *n.* normal English keyboard for a typewriter or computer.

Rr

R [ɑː] **the three Rs** = basic subjects in primary school (reading, writing, arithmetic).
Ra *symbol for* radium.
rabbi ['ræbaɪ] *n.* Jewish priest. **rabbinical** [rə'bɪnɪkl] *adj.* referring to a rabbi.
rabbit ['ræbɪt] **1.** *n.* common wild grey animal with long ears and short white tail which lives in burrows. **2.** *v. inf.* (*also* **rabbit on**) to talk at great length (**about**).
rabble ['ræbl] *n.* crowd/unruly mass of people.
rabid ['ræbɪd] *adj.* (*a*) suffering from rabies. (*b*) wild/fanatic. **rabidity** [rə'bɪdɪtɪ] *n.* being rabid. **rabies** ['reɪbiːz] *n.* hydrophobia.
raccoon [rə'kuːn] *n.* type of small North American flesh-eating wild animal.
race [reɪs] **1.** *n.* (*a*) competition to see who is the fastest; **to run a r.** (*b*) rush of water in a narrow channel. (*c*) group of human beings with similar physical characteristics; **r. relations** = relations between different racial groups in the same country. (*d*) species/breed of plant/animal, etc. **2.** *v.* (*a*) to run/to drive, etc., to see who is the fastest. (*b*) to go very fast. **racecourse,** *n.* grassy track where horse races are run. **racehorse,** *n.* horse specially bred

and trained to run in races. **racer,** *n.* (*a*) person who is running in a race. (*b*) special bicycle/car for racing. **racetrack,** *n.* grassy track where horse races are run. **racial** ['reɪʃl] *adj.* referring to race; **r. discrimination/prejudice** = discrimination/prejudice against s.o. because of race. **racialism,** *n.* racism. **racialist,** *adj. & n.* racist. **racially,** *adv.* in a racial way. **racing,** *n.* competitions to see who is fastest. **racism,** *n.* prejudice against a group of people because of their race. **racist,** *adj. & n.* (person) who treats s.o. differently because of race. **racy,** *adj.* (**-ier, -iest**) vigorous (style of writing).

raceme [rə'siːm] *n.* flowers growing along a stem.

rack [ræk] **1.** *n.* (*a*) frame to hold things (such as letters/pieces of toast); **roof r.** = grid attached to the roof of a car for carrying luggage. (*b*) **to go to r. and ruin** = to become dilapidated. (*c*) **r. of lamb** = joint of roast lamb, formed of a series of chops. **2.** *v.* (*a*) **to r. your brains** = to think very hard. (*b*) to cause pain (to). (*c*) to draw (wine, beer) off the dregs. **rack and pinion,** *n.* toothed wheel which connects with a toothed bar to drive a machine (esp. a mountain railway) forward. **rack railway,** *n.* railway with engines driven by a toothed wheel connecting with a central toothed rail. **rack rent,** *n.* (*a*) yearly rent. (*b*) very high rent.

racket ['rækɪt] **1.** *n.* (*a*) instrument made of a light frame with tight strings across it, used for hitting the ball in tennis, squash and badminton. (*b*) *inf.* loud noise. (*c*) *inf.* illegal profit-making deal. **racketeer** [rækɪ'tɪə] *n.* swindler/ gangster. **racketeering,** *n.* crime of running a racket. **rackety,** *adj.* (car) which makes a lot of noise.

raconteur [rækɒn'tɜː] *n.* person who is good at telling stories.

racquet ['rækɪt] *n.* (sports) racket.

radar ['reɪdɑː] *n.* system by which you can detect objects and judge their position by sending radio signals to them which are reflected back as dots on a small screen.

radiate ['reɪdɪeɪt] *v.* to send out/to give off (rays/heat); to spread out (from

a central point). **radial,** *adj.* which spreads out from a central point; (tyre) with grooves which give a better grip of the road surface. **radiance,** *n.* brightness. **radiant,** *adj.* bright (smile); (heat) which radiates. **radiantly,** *adv.* in a radiant way. **radiation** [reɪdɪ'eɪʃn] *n.* sending out/giving off (rays, heat). **radiator** ['reɪdɪeɪtə] *n.* (*a*) water-filled metal panel for heating. (*b*) water-filled metal panel for cooling a car engine.

radical ['rædɪkl] **1.** *adj.* thorough/complete; basic (difference); **r. party** = a party which believes in the necessity of making great changes in the system of running a country. **2.** *n.* member of a radical party. **radically,** *adv.* in a radical way.

radicle ['rædɪkl] *n.* small root (on a pea or bean).

radio ['reɪdɪəʊ] **1.** *n.* (*pl.* **-os**) system for sending out/receiving messages using atmospheric waves; apparatus which sends out/receives messages using atmospheric waves. **2.** *v.* to send (a message) using a radio. **radioactive** [reɪdɪəʊ'æktɪv] *adj.* (substance) which give off harmful radiation through the breaking up of its atoms. **radioactivity** [reɪdɪəʊæk'tɪvɪtɪ] *n.* giving off of harmful radiation due to the breaking up of atoms. **radiocarbon,** *n.* radioactive form of carbon; **r. dating** = calculating the age of sth. by measuring the amount of radiocarbon that has decayed. **radiogram,** *n.* (*old*) piece of furniture containing a radio and a record-player. **radiographer** [reɪdɪ'ɒgrəfə] *n.* person who takes X-ray photographs. **radiography,** *n.* making X-ray photographs. **radioisotope,** *n.* radioactive isotope, used in radiation treatment. **radiologist,** *n.* person who studies X-rays. **radiology** [reɪdɪ'ɒlədʒɪ] *n.* science of X-rays and their use in medicine. **radiotelephone,** *n.* long-distance telephone (from a ship) which uses radio. **radiotherapy** *n.* use of X-rays to treat disease.

radish ['rædɪʃ] *n.* small red root vegetable, eaten raw.

radium ['reɪdɪəm] *n.* (*element:* Ra) radioactive metal used in treating cancer.

radius ['reɪdɪəs] *n.* (*pl.* **radii** ['reɪdɪaɪ]) (*a*) distance from the centre of a circle to the circumference. (*b*) one of the two bones in the lower part of the arm.

radon ['reɪdɒn] *n.* (*element:* Rn) natural radioactive gas occurring in certain types of soil and construction materials.

raffia ['ræfɪə] *n.* (*no pl.*) strips from a palm leaf used to make baskets, etc.

raffish ['ræfɪʃ] *adj.* vulgar and showy; rather disreputable. **raffishness**, *n.* being raffish.

raffle ['ræfl] **1.** *n.* lottery where you buy a numbered ticket in the hope of winning a prize. **2.** *v.* to offer (a prize) for a lottery.

raft [rɑːft] *n.* flat boat made of pieces of wood/logs tied together.

rafter ['rɑːftə] *n.* sloping beam which holds up a roof.

rag [ræg] **1.** *n.* (*a*) piece of torn cloth; **dressed in rags** = wearing old, torn clothes; *inf.* **the r. trade** = dressmaking trade. (*b*) *inf.* newspaper. (*c*) piece of ragtime music. **2.** *v.* (**ragged** [rægd]) to play jokes on (s.o.). **ragbag**, *n.* collection of mismatched items. **rag-day**, *n.* day when students dress up to collect money for charity. **ragamuffin**, *n.* dirty boy wearing ragged clothes. **rag doll**, *n.* doll made of bits of cloth. **ragged** ['rægɪd] *adj.* (*a*) torn; uneven (edge). (*b*) (person) wearing rags. **rag rug**, *n.* rug made of strips of torn cloth sewn together. **ragtime**, *n.* music written with a strongly syncopated rhythm.

rage [reɪdʒ] **1.** *n.* violent anger; *inf.* **all the r.** = very fashionable. **2.** *v.* to be violently angry; to be violent.

raglan ['ræglən] *n.* style of coat where the sleeves continue straight to the collar, with no seam on the shoulder.

ragout ['ræguː] *n.* meat and vegetable stew.

raid [reɪd] **1.** *n.* sudden attack. **2.** *v.* to make a sudden attack on/a sudden visit to. **raider**, *n.* person who takes part in a raid.

rail [reɪl] **1.** *n.* (*a*) bar of wood/metal (in a fence, etc.). (*b*) **rails** = metal bars along which trains run; **live r.** = rail which conducts electricity for electric trains. (*c*) railway; **by r.** = on a train. (*d*) small bird which lives near water.

2. *v.* **to r. against** = to speak violently against. **railhead**, *n.* end of a railway line. **railings**, *n. pl.* fence made of bars of metal. **raillery**, *n.* making fun of s.o. **railroad. 1.** *n. Am.* railway. **2.** *v. inf.* to force (sth) hurriedly. **railway**, *n.* track with two metal rails along which trains run; train system of a country. **railwayman**, *n.* (*pl.* **-men**) man who works on the railways.

raiment ['reɪmənt] *n.* (*old*) clothing.

rain [reɪn] **1.** *n.* water falling from clouds in drops. **2.** *v.* to fall like rain. **rainbow**, *n.* coloured arch which appears in the sky when the sun's light falls on rain. **rain check**, *n. Am.* agreement to have/to do sth later; **I'll take a rain check on that** = I'll not accept your offer now, but I will take it up again later. **raincoat**, *n.* waterproof coat. **raindrop**, *n.* drop of rain. **rainfall**, *n.* amount of rain which falls in a certain place over a certain period. **rain forest**, *n.* thick, lush tropical jungle where it rains frequently. **rainwater**, *n.* water which has fallen as rain, and has been collected. **rainy**, *adj.* (**-ier, -iest**) with a lot of rain.

raise [reɪz] **1.** *n. Am.* increase in salary. **2.** *v.* (*a*) to lift; to make (sth) higher. (*b*) to bring up (a subject) for discussion. (*c*) to rear (animals/a family). (*d*) to collect.

raisin ['reɪzn] *n.* dried grape.

raison d'être [reɪzɒnˈdetr] *n.* reason for the existence of sth.

raj [rɑːdʒ] *n.* **the r.** = British rule in India. **rajah** ['rɑːdʒə] *n.* Indian ruler.

rake [reɪk] **1.** *n.* (*a*) tool with a long handle and bent metal teeth, used for smoothing earth/for gathering fallen leaves, etc. (*b*) immoral man. (*c*) angle of slope. **2.** *v.* (*a*) to smooth/to gather using a rake. (*b*) to slope. **rake-off**, *n. inf.* illegal payment paid as a commission. **rake up**, *v.* to start talking again about (sth which had been forgotten). **rakish**, *adj.* (that) worn at a slant/tilted sideways.

rally ['rælɪ] **1.** *n.* (*a*) gathering of members of a group/association/political party. (*b*) car competition where cars have to cross difficult country in a certain time. (*c*) return to strength (of s.o. who is ill). (*d*) long series of shots in tennis. **2.** v. (a) to gather together. (b) to recover (temporarily) from an illness/a setback.

ram [ræm] **1.** n. (a) male sheep. (b) heavy machine for pressing down hard. **2.** v. (**rammed**) (a) to batter sth down hard. (b) to hit (another ship/car, etc.,) hard.

RAM [ræm] n. random access memory, memory in a computer which allows access to data.

Ramadan [ræmə'dæn] n. 9th month of the year, when Muslims fast.

ramble ['ræmbl] **1.** n. walk for pleasure in the country. **2.** v. (a) to go for a walk. (b) to talk on and on in a confused way. **rambler,** n. (a) person who goes for walks in the country. (b) type of rose which climbs. **rambling,** adj. (a) confused (speech). (b) (house) which is full of rooms and corridors.

rambutan [ræmbu:'tæn] n. small reddish fruit found in S.E. Asia.

ramekin ['ræməkɪn] n. small dish for baking food in an oven; food cooked in this way.

ramification [ræmɪfɪ'keɪʃn] n. part of a large complicated system.

ramp [ræmp] n. (a) slightly sloping surface joining two different levels; slight hump in a road surface. (b) inf. swindle.

rampage [ræm'peɪdʒ] **1.** n. **to go on the r.** = to go about breaking things/creating disorder. **2.** v. **to r. about** = to create disorder.

rampant ['ræmpənt] adj. (crime) which is widespread and uncontrollable.

rampart ['ræmpɑːt] n. defensive wall.

ramrod ['ræmrɒd] n. **to stand stiff as a r.** = to stand very straight.

ramshackle ['ræmʃækl] adj. dilapidated/falling to pieces.

ran [ræn] v. see **run.**

ranch [rɑːntʃ] n. (in America) farm where horses or cattle are reared. **rancher,** n. person who owns/runs a ranch.

rancid ['rænsɪd] adj. bad/stale (butter). **rancidity,** n. being rancid.

rancour, Am. **rancor** ['ræŋkə] n. bitterness/dislike. **rancorous,** adj. bitter/hateful.

rand [rɒnt] n. money used in South Africa.

random ['rændəm] adj. & n. done aimlessly/without any planning; **at r.** = aimlessly/ with no selection; **r. sample** = sample for testing taken without any selection. **randomness,** n. being random.

randy ['rændɪ] adj. (**-ier, -iest**) eager to have sexual intercourse. **randiness,** n. being randy.

rang [ræŋ] v. see **ring.**

range [reɪndʒ] **1.** n. (a) series (of buildings/mountains) in line. (b) large open pasture; **free-range hens** = chickens which are allowed to run about in fields. (c) choice/series (of colours, etc.). (d) distance which a shell/bullet can reach; distance which an aircraft can fly without refuelling; distance for which you can see/hear. (e) old-fashioned kitchen stove which burns wood or coal. **2.** v. to spread/to vary. **rangefinder,** n. device (on a gun/camera) for calculating the distance of an object. **ranger,** n. person who looks after a forest or park. **rangy,** adj. with long legs.

rank [ræŋk] **1.** n. (a) row of soldiers. (b) **other ranks** = ordinary soldiers; **he rose from the ranks** = from being an ordinary soldier he became an officer; **the r. and file** = ordinary people. (c) position in society/in the army. (d) **taxi r.** = place where taxis wait in line. **2.** v. to classify/to be classified in order of importance. **3.** adj. (**-er, -est**) (a) (plants) which grow luxuriantly. (b) complete/total. (c) with an unpleasant smell. **rankness,** n. being rank.

rankle ['ræŋkl] v. to cause bitterness.

ransack ['rænsæk] v. to search/to turn over (a room) to find sth.

ransom ['rænsəm] **1.** n. payment asked for before a hostage is set free; **to hold s.o. to r.** = to demand payment before s.o. is set free. **2.** v. to pay a ransom for (s.o.).

rant [rænt] v. to declaim/to shout violently.

rap [ræp] **1.** n. (a) tap/sharp blow; inf. **to take the r.** = to accept responsibility. (b) form of West Indian music where the singer improvises. **2.** v. (**rapped**) (a) to tap/to give a sharp blow. (b) to sing rap music.

rapacious [rə'peɪʃəs] adj. greedy. **rapacity** [rə'pæsɪtɪ] n. greed.

rape [reɪp] 1. n. (a) act of having sexual intercourse with s.o. against their will. (b) vegetable with yellow flowers, whose seeds are used to produce oil. 2. v. to have sexual intercourse with (s.o.) against their will. **rapist,** n. person who rapes s.o.

rapid ['ræpɪd] 1. adj. fast. 2. n. pl. **rapids** = place where a river runs fast over boulders and down a steep slope. **rapidity** [rə'pɪdɪtɪ] n. speed. **rapidly,** adv. fast.

rapier ['reɪpɪə] n. long, thin sword for thrusting.

rapport [ræ'pɔː] n. understanding/close link.

rapprochement [ræ'prɒʃmɒŋ] n. becoming closer (of former enemies).

rapt [ræpt] adj. **with r. attention** = very attentively. **raptly,** adv. attentively.

raptor ['ræptə] n. bird of prey.

rapture ['ræptʃə] n. delight; **to go into raptures over** = to be delighted by. **rapturous,** adj. excited and delighted (applause, etc.). **rapturously,** adv. in a rapturous way.

rare [reə] adj. (-er, -est) (a) very unusual. (b) (meat) which is very lightly cooked. **rarely,** adv. hardly ever. **rarefied** ['reərɪfaɪd] adj. (air) which is not very dense. **rarity,** n. (a) (also **rareness**) uncommonness. (b) rare object.

rarebit ['reəbɪt] n. **Welsh r.** = cooked cheese on toast.

raring ['reərɪŋ] adj. inf. **r. to go** = eager to go.

rascal ['rɑːskəl] n. naughty person/child. **rascally,** adj. wicked.

rash [ræʃ] 1. n. red area/red spots on the skin; **heat r.** = spots caused by hot weather. 2. adj. (-er, -est) not cautious/thoughtless; done without thinking. **rashly,** adv. without thinking. **rashness,** n. being rash/acting rashly.

rasher ['ræʃə] n. slice (of bacon).

rasp [rɑːsp] 1. n. rough metal file used for smoothing surfaces. 2. v. to make a grating noise.

raspberry ['rɑːzbrɪ] n. (a) common red soft fruit growing on tall canes; bush which bears this fruit. (b) inf. rude noise made with the mouth to show derision.

Rastafarian [ræstə'feərɪən] adj. & n. (member) of a West Indian sect.

rat [ræt] 1. n. (a) common grey rodent, living in cellars/sewers/on ships. (b) sly unpleasant person. 2. v. (ratted) (a) to hunt rats. (b) inf. **(on)** to go back on a promise/to betray (s.o.). **rat race,** n. competition for success in the business world. **ratty,** adj. inf. annoyed/short-tempered.

ratafia [rætə'fɪə] n. biscuit/drink flavoured with almonds.

ratchet (wheel) ['rætʃət('wiːl)] n. wheel with teeth and a catch to prevent it from turning backwards.

rate [reɪt] 1. n. (a) number expressed as a proportion of one quantity to another; **birth r./death r.** = number of births/deaths per 1000 of population. (b) frequency at which sth is done/level of cost (as compared to a previous level). (c) speed. (d) **first r.** = very good; **second r.** = rather bad. (e) **at any r.** = in any case. (f) **business rates** = local taxes on businesses. 2. v. to value. **rateable,** adj. **r. value** = value of a house as calculated for local taxes. **ratepayer,** n. company/person who pays local business taxes. **rating,** n. (a) valuing. (b) **TV ratings** = comparative estimates of audiences for competing TV shows. (c) **naval r.** = ordinary seaman.

rather ['rɑːðə] adv. (a) relatively/quite. (b) (used with **would** to show preference) **I'd r. stay** = I would prefer to stay; **I'd r. not** = I would prefer not to. (c) **r. than** = in preference to.

ratify ['rætɪfaɪ] v. to approve (a treaty) officially. **ratification** [rætɪfɪ'keɪʃn] n. official approval.

ratio ['reɪʃɪəʊ] n. (pl. -os) proportion.

ratiocinate [rætɪ'ɒsɪneɪt] v. to think coherently.

ration ['ræʃn] 1. n. amount of food/supplies allowed. 2. v. to allow only a certain amount of food/supplies. **rationing,** n. allowing only a certain amount of food/supplies.

rational ['ræʃənl] adj. reasonable/based on reason. **rationale** [ræʃə'nɑːl] n. set of reasons which are the basis of a system/of a series of actions. **rationality,** n. being rational. **ration-**

alization [ræʃnəlaɪ'zeɪʃn] *n.* act of rationalizing. **rationalize** [ræʃnə'laɪz] *v.* (*a*) to find a reason for usu. unreasonable actions. (*b*) to streamline/ to modernize (old-fashioned production methods). **rationally,** *adv.* based on reason.

rattan [rə'tæn] *n.* tropical cane, used to make furniture.

rattle ['rætl] **1.** *n.* (*a*) (wooden) instrument which makes a loud repeated noise. (*b*) repeated clattering noise. **2.** *v.* (*a*) to make a repeated clattering noise. (*b*) *inf.* to worry/to upset. **rattle off,** *v. inf.* to speak rapidly. **rattlesnake,** *n.* American poisonous snake which makes a rattling noise with its tail. **rattling,** *adj. inf.* very (good).

raucous ['rɔːkəs] *adj.* rough/hoarse (cough/cry). **raucously,** *adv.* in a raucous way. **raucousness,** *n.* being raucous.

raunchy ['rɔːntʃɪ] *adj.* (**-ier, -iest**) *Am.* coarse/openly obscene.

ravage ['rævɪdʒ] *v.* to devastate/to ruin (a town, etc.). **ravages,** *n. pl.* damage.

rave [reɪv] *v.* (*a*) to be wildly mad. (*b*) *inf.* to be fanatical (about sth). **raving,** *adj.* wild (madman). **ravings,** *n. pl.* wild mad talk.

ravel ['rævl] *v.* (*a*) to disentangle (sth which is twisted). (*b*) to tangle/to make sth knotted and twisted.

raven ['reɪvn] *n.* large black bird of the crow family.

ravenous ['rævənəs] *adj.* very hungry. **ravenously,** *adv.* extremely (hungry).

ravine [rə'viːn] *n.* deep narrow valley.

ravioli [rævɪ'əʊlɪ] *n.* Italian dish of small pasta squares filled with a meat stuffing.

ravish ['rævɪʃ] *v.* (*a*) to steal by force. (*b*) to enchant. **ravishing,** *adj.* very beautiful/very delightful.

raw [rɔː] **1.** *adj.* (**-er, -est**) (*a*) uncooked. (*b*) basic/untreated (sewage/ data); untrained (recruits). (*c*) cold and damp (weather). (*d*) **r. deal** = bad/ unfair treatment. (*e*) exposed/sensitive; **to touch a r. nerve** = to touch a sensitive spot. **2.** *n.* (*a*) sensitive spot. (*b*) wild natural state. **rawhide,** *n.* leather which has not been tanned. **rawness,** *n.* being raw.

ray [reɪ] *n.* (*a*) beam of light/heat; small quantity (of hope); **X-rays** = rays which go through the soft tissue, and allow the bones and organs in the body to be photographed. (*b*) large, flat sea fish.

rayon ['reɪɒn] *n.* trade name for artificial silk.

raze [reɪz] *v.* **to r. to the ground** = to demolish completely.

razor ['reɪzə] *n.* instrument with a very sharp blade for removing hair. **razorbill,** *n.* type of black and white sea bird. **razor-sharp,** extremely sharp (blade/mind, etc.).

razzle ['ræzl] *n. inf.* **to go on the r.** = to have a good time.

razzmatazz ['ræzmətæz] *n. inf.* energetic publicizing (in an election campaign).

Rd. *short for* road.

re [riː] *prep.* concerning.

re- [riː] *prefix meaning* again.

reach [riːtʃ] **1.** *n.* (*pl.* **-es**) (*a*) distance you can travel easily; distance you can stretch out your hand. (*b*) straight section of a river. **2.** *v.* (*a*) to stretch out. (*b*) to arrive at. (*c*) to come to (an agreement). **reachable,** *adj.* which can be reached.

react [rɪ'ækt] *v.* to do/to say sth in reply to words or an action; **to r. against** = show opposition to; **acids r. with metals** = change their chemical composition. **reaction** [rɪ'ækʃn] *n.* act of reacting; thing done/said in reply; **what was his r.?** = what did he say/ do? **reactionary,** *adj. & n.* (person) who is opposed to any political change/ to any reforms. **reactivate,** *v.* to make (sth) work again. **reactive,** *adj.* which is active chemically. **reactor,** *n.* device for producing atomic energy.

read [riːd] **1.** *n. inf.* looking at and understanding writtten or printed words. **2.** *v.* (**read, has read** [red]) (*a*) to look at and understand written words; to speak aloud words which are written; **to r. between the lines** = to understand a hidden meaning which is not immediately apparent. (*b*) to study (a subject) at university. (*c*) to interpret; **to r. s.o.'s palm** = to interpret the lines on a hand as indications of what will happen in the future. **readability,** *n.* being readable. **readable,** *adj.* (*a*) legible/

which can be read. (*b*) (story) which is a pleasure to read. **reader,** *n.* (*a*) person who reads. (*b*) senior teacher at a university. (*c*) school book to help children to read. (*d*) apparatus for reading microfilms. (*e*) person who reads manuscripts/proofs to check them. **reading,** *n.* (*a*) act of looking at and understanding printed words. (*b*) interpretation. (*c*) one of the stages of the discussion of a Bill in Parliament. **reading room,** *n.* room (in a library) specially for reading.

readdress [riːəˈdres] *v.* to put another address on (an envelope/parcel).

readjust [riːəˈdʒʌst] *v.* to adjust again; to put back to the original position. **readjustment,** *n.* act of readjusting.

ready [ˈredɪ] *adj.* (**-ier, -iest**) (*a*) prepared (**to**). (*b*) fit to be used. (*c*) quick/rapid; **he has a r. reply to anything** = he always has an answer. (*d*) **r. cash** = cash which is immediately available. **readily,** *adv.* willingly. **readiness,** *n.* willingness; **to hold sth in r.** = to keep sth ready for use. **ready-cooked,** *adj.* (food) which has been cooked in advance. **ready-made, ready-to-wear,** *adj.* (clothes) which are made by mass production, to fit any person of a certain size.

reagent [rɪˈeɪdʒənt] *n.* substance used in a chemical reaction.

real [rɪəl] *adj.* true/not imitation; (sth) which exists. (*b*) **r. estate** = land or buildings which are bought or sold. (*c*) **r. tennis** = medieval form of tennis played with a hard ball in a court with high walls. **realism,** *n.* (*a*) facing facts/accepting life as it is. (*b*) showing things (in writing/painting) as they really are. **realist,** *n.* (*a*) artist/writer who shows things as they really are. (*b*) person who accepts life as it really is, and doesn't idealize it. **realistic** [rɪəˈlɪstɪk] *adj.* (*a*) which looks as if it is real. (*b*) accepting life as it really is. **realistically,** *adv.* in a realistic way. **reality** [rɪˈælɪtɪ] *n.* what is real/not imaginary. **really,** *adv.* truly. **real time,** *n.* action of a computer which takes place at the same time as the problem it is solving.

realign [riːəˈlaɪn] *v.* to set in a new direction; to set in a new group. **realignment,** *n.* change in a series of alliances between countries or political parties.

realize [ˈrɪəlaɪz] *v.* (*a*) to come to understand clearly. (*b*) to sell property for (money). (*c*) to make real; to make (sth) come true. **realization** [rɪəlaɪˈzeɪʃn] *n.* (*a*) gradual understanding. (*b*) conversion of property into money. (*c*) carrying out of a plan.

realm [relm] *n.* (*a*) kingdom. (*b*) general area.

Realpolitik [reɪˈælpɒlɪtɪk] *n.* politics based on real situations, not on moral principles.

realtor [ˈrɪəltə] *n. Am.* estate agent. **realty,** *n. Am.* real estate.

ream [riːm] *n.* (*a*) 480 sheets of paper. (*b*) **reams** = very large quantity (of paper).

reanimate [rɪˈænɪmeɪt] *v.* to bring back to life.

reap [riːp] *v.* to harvest (corn, etc.). **reaper,** *n.* person/machine which harvests corn.

reappear [riːəˈpɪə] *v.* to appear again. **reappearance,** *n.* second appearance.

reappraisal [riːəˈpreɪzl] *n.* fresh examination of sth to see if your former opinion was correct.

rear [rɪə] **1.** *n.* back part; **to bring up the r.** = march behind. **2.** *adj.* at the back; **r.-view mirror** = mirror in a car so that you can see what is behind you without turning round. **3.** *v.* (*a*) to breed/to raise (animals). (*b*) to lift (part of the body). (*c*) (*of horse, etc.*) to stand up on its back legs. **rear-admiral,** *n.* high-ranking naval officer (beneath vice-admiral). **rearguard,** *n.* soldiers defending the back part of an army. **rearmost,** *adj.* furthest at the back.

rearm [rɪˈɑːm] *v.* to arm/to stock up with weapons again. **rearmament** [rɪˈɑːməmənt] *n.* arming again.

rearrange [riːəˈreɪndʒ] *v.* to arrange again. **rearrangement,** *n.* new arrangement.

reason [ˈriːzn] **1.** *n.* (*a*) cause/explanation for why sth happens. (*b*) power of thought; commonsense. **2.** *v.* (*a*) to think/to plan carefully and logically. (*b*) **to r. with s.o.** = to try to calm s.o./to make s.o. change his mind. **reasonable,** *adj.* (*a*) not extravagant/moderate. (*b*) sensible. **reasonably,** *adv.* in a reasonable way. **reasoning,** *n.*

putting your mind to use; **I don't follow your r.** = I can't see how you reached this conclusion.

reassemble [rɪə'sembl] v. (a) to put back together. (b) to gather together again.

reassure [rɪə'ʃʊə] v. to calm (s.o.)/to make (s.o.) less afraid/less doubtful. **reassurance**, n. act of reassuring.

rebate ['riːbeɪt] n. (a) reduction in the amount of money which should be paid; money which is returned to the person who paid it. (b) groove cut into a piece of wood to hold the tongue on another piece.

rebel 1. n. ['rebəl] person who fights against the government/against the person in charge. 2. v. [rɪ'bel] (**rebelled**) to fight (**against** s.o./sth). **rebellion** [rɪ'beljən] n. revolt/fight against the government/against authority. **rebellious** [rɪ'beljəs] adj. fighting against the government/against authority.

rebore 1. n. ['riːbɔː] cleaning the cylinders on a car. 2. v. [riː'bɔː] vtr. to clean the cylinders of a car.

rebound 1. n. ['riːbaʊnd] bouncing back; **on the r.** = (i) as it bounces back; (ii) while still shocked by a disappointment. 2. v. [riː'baʊnd] to bounce back.

rebuff [rɪ'bʌf] 1. n. refusal. 2. v. to refuse.

rebuild [riː'bɪld] v. (**rebuilt**) to build again.

rebuke [rɪ'bjuːk] (formal) 1. n. blame/reproof. 2. v. to blame/to scold.

rebus ['riːbuːs] n. trick, where pictures are used to represent words.

rebut [rɪ'bʌt] v. (**rebutted**) to reject/to disprove (an argument). **rebuttal**, n. act of rebutting.

recalcitrant [rɪ'kælsɪtrənt] adj. (formal) difficult/disobedient. **recalcitrance**, n. being recalcitrant.

recall [rɪ'kɔːl] 1. n. calling back; **gone beyond r.** = gone and cannot be called back. 2. v. (a) to call/to summon back (an ambassador/defective cars); to ask Parliament to meet again. (b) to remember.

recant [rɪ'kænt] v. to admit that your former beliefs were wrong. **recantation** [rɪkæn'teɪʃn] n. act of recanting.

recapitulate [riːkə'pɪtjʊleɪt], inf. **recap** ['riːkæp] v. to repeat the main points of an argument. **recapitulation** [riːkəpɪtjʊ'leɪʃn] inf. **recap**, n. repeating the main points.

recapture [riː'kæptʃə] 1. n. act of recapturing. 2. v. to catch again (an escaped prisoner); to take again (a seat in an election).

recast [riː'kɑːst] v. to make again; to write (a statement) again in a different way.

recce ['rekɪ] n. inf. reconnaissance trip.

recd. abbrev. for received.

recede [rɪ'siːd] v. to go away/to retreat. **receding**, adj. (forehead) which slopes backwards; (hair) which begins to disappear from the front of the forehead.

receipt [rɪ'siːt] n. (a) receiving; **on r. of** = when you receive. (b) paper showing that you have paid/that you have received sth. (c) **receipts** = money taken in a business.

receive [rɪ'siːv] v. (a) to get sth which has been sent; inf. **he was on the receiving end of a lot of criticism** = he had to suffer a lot of criticism. (b) to greet/to welcome; to entertain. **receiver**, n. (a) person who accepts stolen goods. (b) official put in charge of a bankrupt company. (c) part of a telephone which you can lift and listen to. (d) part of a radio which receives broadcast programmes.

recent ['riːsənt] adj. which took place not very long ago. **recently**, adv. not long ago/only a short time ago.

receptacle [rɪ'septəkl] n. container.

reception [rɪ'sepʃn] n. (a) welcome. (b) (in a hotel) desk where you check in. (c) big party held to welcome special guests. (d) quality of sound of a radio/TV broadcast. **receptionist**, n. person in a hotel/doctor's office, etc., who meets visitors and answers the telephone. **receptive**, adj. eager to take in new ideas. **receptiveness**, **receptivity** [risep'tiviti] n. being receptive. **receptor**, n. cell at the end of a nerve, which receives impulses.

recess [rɪ'ses] n. (pl. **-es**) (a) alcove/part of the wall of a room which is set back. (b) official holiday of the law courts or parliament. (*c*) *Am.* recreation period at school. (*d*) inaccessible part. **recessed,** *adj.* set back. **recessive,** *adj.* (*of genes*) not likely to predominate.

recession [rɪ'seʃn] *n.* collapse of world economy/of trade.

recherché [re'ʃeəʃeɪ] *adj.* chosen with care.

recidivist [rə'sɪdɪvɪst] *n.* hardened criminal/person who commits a crime repeatedly.

recipe ['resɪpɪ] *n.* (*a*) instructions for cooking. (*b*) effective way to do sth; **it's a r. for disaster** = it's bound to lead to disaster.

recipient [rɪ'sɪpɪənt] *n.* person who receives.

reciprocate [rɪ'sɪprəkeɪt] *v.* to do the same thing in return. **reciprocal. 1.** *adj.* mutual; **r. trade agreement** = agreement on two-way trade between countries. **2.** *n.* (*in maths*) quantity produced when 1 is divided by a figure. **reciprocally,** *adv.* in a reciprocal way. **reciprocity** [resɪ'prɒsɪtɪ] *n.* principle that if one country buys goods from another, the second country will reciprocate.

recite [rɪ'saɪt] *v.* to speak (verse, etc.) aloud in public. **recital,** *n.* reciting in public sth which has been written. (*b*) performance of music by one or a few musicians. **recitation** [resɪ'teɪʃn] *n.* thing recited from memory; recital. **recitative** [resɪtə'tiːv] *n.* (*in an opera*) speech sung in a rhythmic way.

reckless ['rekləs] *adj.* foolish/rash/not thinking. **recklessly,** *adv.* in a reckless way. **recklessness,** *n.* foolishness/ rashness.

reckon ['rekn] *v.* (*a*) to calculate/to estimate; (*b*) to think. (*c*) **to r. on** = to count on/to depend on. (*d*) **to r. with** = to have to deal with. **reckoner,** *n.* book with tables to help calculations. **reckoning,** *n.* calculation; **day of r.** = time when you have to pay for your mistakes.

reclaim [rɪ'kleɪm] *v.* to make (useless land) fit for use; to take back (land) from the sea. **reclamation** [reklə'meɪʃn] *n.* reclaiming (of land).

recline [rɪ'klaɪn] *v.* to lie back.

recluse [rɪ'kluːs] *n.* person who lives alone and hidden away.

recognize ['rekəgnaɪz] *v.* (*a*) to know (s.o./sth) because you have seen him/ it before. (*b*) to admit (a mistake). (*c*) to admit (the value of sth). (*d*) **to r. a government** = to accept that a new government is the legal authority in a country; **to r. a union** = to agree that a union can represent workers in a factory. **recognition** [rekəg'nɪʃn] *n.* recognizing; **he's changed beyond all r.** = so much that you can't recognize him. **recognizable** [rekəg-'naɪzəbl] *adj.* which can be recognized. **recognizance** [re'kɒgnɪzəns] *n.* money given as a pledge to a court that s.o. will obey the conditions laid down by the court.

recoil 1. *n.* ['riːkɔɪl] sudden movement backwards of a gun when it is fired. **2.** *v.* [rɪ'kɔɪl] to move backwards suddenly; to shrink back from sth unpleasant.

recollect [rekə'lekt] *v.* to remember. **recollection** [rekə'lekʃn] *n.* remembering.

recommend [rekə'mend] *v.* (*a*) to advise s.o. to do sth. (*b*) to praise (sth/ s.o.). **recommendation** [rekəmen-'deɪʃn] *n.* (*a*) advice. (*b*) praise; thing which is in your favour.

recompense ['rekəmpens] **1.** *n.* payment for sth done/for the time lost, etc. **2.** *v.* to pay s.o. for sth done/for time lost, etc.

reconcile ['rekənsaɪl] *v.* (*a*) to make two enemies become friendly. (*b*) **to reconcile oneself to** = to accept. (*c*) to make (two accounts/statements) agree. **reconciliation** [rekənsɪlɪ'eɪʃn] *n.* bringing together of two enemies, so that they become friends; making two accounts/statements agree.

recondite [rɪ'kɒndaɪt] *adj.* (*formal*) obscure (information).

recondition [rɪkən'dɪʃn] *v.* to overhaul thoroughly.

reconnaissance [rɪ'kɒnɪsns] *n.* survey of land for military information.

reconnoitre, *Am.* **reconnoiter** [rekə-'nɔɪtə] *v.* to make a survey to get information/to make a reconnaissance.

reconsider [riːkən'sɪdə] *v.* to think over again.

reconstitute [rɪ'kɒnstɪtjut] *v.* to form (sth) again as it was before.

reconstruct [riːkənˈstrʌkt] v. (a) to build again. (b) to work out how (a crime) must have been committed. **reconstruction,** n. act of reconstructing; thing reconstructed.

reconvene [riːkənˈviːn] v. to meet again.

record 1. n. [ˈrekɔːd] (a) report of sth which has happened; **he is on r. as saying** = he is accurately reported as saying; **she spoke off the r.** = in private/what she said is not to be made public. (b) note/written account. (c) flat plastic disc on which sound is fixed by a recording instrument. (d) description of s.o.'s past career. (e) sporting achievement which is better than any other; **at r. speed** = very fast. **2.** v. [rɪˈkɔːd] (a) to report; to make a note; **recorded delivery** = postal service where you must sign a receipt to show you have received a parcel/a letter, etc. (b) to fix sound on a plastic disc or tape. **record-breaking,** adj. which breaks records. **recorder** [rɪˈkɔːdə] n. (a) judge in certain courts. (b) instrument which records. (c) wooden flute held forwards when played. **recording,** n. (a) act of fixing sounds on tape/on disc. (b) music/speech which has been recorded. **recordist,** n. person who records sounds on tape or disc. **record-player,** n. machine for playing back music/speech, etc., from a record.

recount 1. n. [ˈriːkaunt] counting votes again (when the result is very close). **2.** v. (a) [rɪˈkaunt] to tell (a story). (b) [riːˈkaunt] to count again.

recoup [rɪˈkuːp] v. **to r. your losses** = to get back money which you have lost.

recourse [rɪˈkɔːs] n. **to have r. to sth** = to use sth in an emergency.

recover [rɪˈkʌvə] v. (a) to get back (sth which has been stolen/lost). (b) (from) to get well again after an illness. (c) (from) to get over (a shock). (d) [riːˈkʌvə] to put a new cover (on a chair). **recoverable,** adj. which can be got back. **recovery,** n. (a) getting back (stolen property). (b) getting well again. (c) return to good condition.

recreation [rekrɪˈeɪʃn] n. pleasant occupation for your spare time; **r. ground** = public sports ground. **recreational,** adj. referring to recreation.

recriminate [rɪˈkrɪmɪneɪt] v. to accuse (s.o.) who has accused you. **recrimination** [rɪkrɪmɪˈneɪʃn] n. accusation made by s.o. who is accused. **recriminatory** [rɪˈkrɪmɪnətrɪ] adj. (remarks) which accuse s.o.

recrudescence [riːkruːˈdesəns] n. (formal) breaking out again (of a disease).

recruit [rɪˈkruːt] **1.** n. new soldier; new member of a club, etc. **2.** v. to encourage (s.o.) to join the army/a club, etc. **recruitment,** n. encouraging people to join the army/a club, etc.

rectal [ˈrektəl] adj. referring to the rectum.

rectangle [ˈrektæŋgl] n. four-sided shape with right angles and two sets of opposite and equal sides. **rectangular** [rekˈtæŋgjʊlə] adj. like a rectangle.

rectify [ˈrektɪfaɪ] v. to correct/to make right. **rectifiable,** adj. which can be corrected. **rectification** [rektɪfɪˈkeɪʃn] n. correction.

rectilinear [rektɪˈlɪnɪə] adj. with straight lines.

rectitude [ˈrektɪtjuːd] n. (esp. moral) correctness.

recto [ˈrektəʊ] n. right/main side (of a piece of paper, page of a book, etc.).

rector [ˈrektə] n. (a) priest in charge of a parish. (b) official representative of the students at a Scottish university. (c) (in Scotland) head of a school/college/university. **rectory,** n. house of a rector.

rectum [ˈrektəm] n. lower part of the intestine, leading to the anus.

recumbent [rɪˈkʌmbənt] adj. (formal) lying down.

recuperate [rɪˈkjuːpəreɪt] v. to recover/to get better after an illness of a loss. **recuperation** [rɪkjuːpəˈreɪʃn] n. getting better. **recuperative,** adj. which helps recuperation.

recur [rɪˈkɜː] v. (recurred) to happen again. **recurrence** [rɪˈkʌrəns] n. reappearance/happening again. **recurrent** [rɪˈkʌrənt], **recurring** [rɪˈkɜːrɪŋ] adj. (a) which happens again. (b) (decimal figure) which is repeated for ever.

recusant [ˈrekjʊzənt] adj. & n. (old) (person) who refused to accept the Anglican Church.

recycle [riːˈsaɪkl] v. to process (waste material) so that it can be used again.

red [red] *adj. & n.* (**redder, reddest**) (colour) like blood or fire; *inf.* **see r.** = get very angry; *inf.* **to be in the r.** = to be in debt; **r. carpet** = official welcome; **r. tape** = official rules which stop you doing sth quickly; **r. herring** = false track/sth which leads you away from the main problem; *inf.* **the Reds** = the Communists. **red-blooded,** *adj.* strong, vigorous. **redbreast,** *n.* robin. **red-brick,** *adj.* (British university) built in the nineteenth century. **Red Crescent,** *n.* organization similar to the Red Cross, working in Muslim countries. **Red Cross,** *n.* international organization which cares for the sick and injured, and also organizes relief work. **red currant,** *n.* common red soft fruit growing in small clusters; bush which bears this fruit. **redden,** *v.* to turn red/to blush. **reddish,** *adj.* rather red. **Red Flag,** *n.* flag of the communist party. **red-handed,** *adj.* **they caught him red-handed** = as he was committing a crime. **redhead,** *n.* person with red hair. **red-hot,** *adj.* (*of metal*) very hot. **Red Indian,** *n.* Indian from North America. **red-letter day,** *n.* very special day. **redness,** *n.* being red. **redshank,** *n.* large sandpiper. **redstart,** *n.* small singing bird with red feathers beneath the tail. **redwood,** *n.* type of very tall coniferous tree growing on the west coast of North America.

redecorate [ri:'dekəreɪt] *v.* to decorate/ to paint again.

redeem [rɪ'di:m] *v.* (*a*) to buy back (sth which you have pledged to borrow money); to pay off (a debt). (*b*) to compensate. (*c*) to save from sin. **Redeemer,** *n.* Jesus Christ. **redeeming,** *adj.* which compensates. **redemption** [rɪ'dempʃn] *n.* (*a*) payment of a debt. (*b*) being saved from sin.

redeploy [ri:dɪ'plɔɪ] *v.* to move (workers/soldiers) from one place to another. **redeployment,** *n.* act of redeploying.

redirect [ri:daɪ'rekt] *v.* to send (a letter) on to another address.

redolent ['redələnt] *adj.* which smells (of sth); which reminds you (of sth). **redolence,** *n.* being redolent.

redouble [ri:'dʌbl] *v.* **to r. your efforts** = to try even harder.

redoubt [rɪ'daʊt] *n.* small fort. **redoubtable** [rɪ'daʊtəbl] *adj.* formidable/bold.

redound [rɪ'daʊnd] *v.* (*formal*) **it will r. to your credit** = will make you more admired.

redress [rɪ'dres] **1.** *n.* compensation done to make up for something wrong. **2.** *v.* to correct/to compensate/to repair; **to r. the balance** = to make things equal again.

reduce [rɪ'dju:s] *v.* (*a*) to make smaller/ lower; **to r. s.o. to the ranks** = to punish an officer by making him an ordinary soldier; **to r. weight/***inf.* **to r.** = to get thinner. (*b*) to force (s.o.) to do sth humiliating. **reducible,** *adj.* which can be reduced. **reduction** [rɪ'dʌkʃn] *n.* lowering (of price/speed/standards).

redundant [rɪ'dʌndənt] *adj.* more than necessary; **to be made r.** = to lose your job because you are not needed any more. **redundancy,** *n.* losing a job because you are no longer needed.

reduplicate [rɪ'djʊplɪkeɪt] *v.* to repeat (sth).

re-echo [ri:'ekəʊ] *v.* to echo again.

reed [ri:d] *n.* (*a*) marsh plant with tall stem. (*b*) part of a wind instrument which vibrates to make a note. **reediness,** *n.* being reedy. **reedy,** *adj.* (*a*) high-pitched (voice). (*b*) (marsh) which is full of reeds.

reef [ri:f] **1.** *n.* (*a*) ridge of rock in the sea. (*b*) **r. knot** = type of flat knot which does not come undone easily. **2.** *v.* to reduce the size of (a sail) by rolling part of it up. **reefer,** *n.* (*a*) sailor's short coat. (*b*) *Sl.* marijuana cigarette.

reek [ri:k] **1.** *n.* strong smell. **2.** *v.* to smell strongly (**of**).

reel [ri:l] **1.** *n.* (*a*) spool for winding thread/string/film round. (*b*) vigorous Scottish dance. **2.** *v.* (*a*) to wind round a reel. **to r. off** = to quote at length. (*c*) to stagger.

reelect [ri:ɪ'lekt] *v.* to elect again. **reelection** [ri:ɪ'lekʃn] *n.* being reelected.

reemploy [ri:em'plɔɪ] *v.* to employ (s.o.) again.

reenter [ri:'entə] *v.* to enter again. **reentry** [ri:'entrɪ] *n.* entering again.

ref [ref] *n. inf.* (*in sports*) referee.

refectory [rɪ'fektərɪ] *n.* eating hall (in

a school, etc.); **r. table** = long narrow dining table.

refer to [rɪ'fɜː'tuː] v. (**referred**) (a) to mention. (b) to look into sth for information. (c) to pass (a problem) to s.o. to decide. (d) to tell (s.o.) to see s.o. else. **referee** [refə'riː] 1. n. (a) (in sports) person who sees that the game is played according to the rules/who judges between two sides. (b) person who gives a report on your character. 2. v. to act as a referee in a sports match. **reference** ['refrəns] n. (a) (to) mention; **with r. to** = concerning/about. (b) direction for further information; **r. book** = book (such as dictionary/encyclopedia) where you can look up information; **r. library** = library of reference books. (c) report on s.o.'s character, etc. **referral** [rɪ'fɜːrl] n. act of referring.

referendum [refə'rendəm] n. (pl. **-da/-dums**) vote by all the people of a country to decide a problem of national importance.

refill 1. n. ['riːfɪl] container with a fresh quantity of liquid/ink, etc.; another drink. 2. v. [riː'fɪl] to fill again.

refine [rɪ'faɪn] v. to make better/more pure. **refined**, adj. very elegant/polite. **refinement**, n. (a) elegance. (b) improvement. **refiner**, n. business/person that refines. **refinery**, n. factory where sth is refined.

refit 1. n. ['riːfɪt] repairs (to a ship). 2. v. [riː'fɪt] (**refitted**) to repair (a ship).

reflate [riː'fleɪt] v. to stimulate (an economy which has previously been deflated). **reflation** [riː'fleɪʃn] n. action of stimulating a deflated economy. **reflationary**, adj. likely to cause reflation.

reflect [rɪ'flekt] v. (a) to send back (light/heat/an image). (b) to think back into the past/to ponder. (c) **to r. on** = to be a criticism of. **reflection, reflexion** [rɪ'flekʃn] n. (a) sending back of light/heat; reflected image (in a mirror). (b) thought; **on r.** = on thinking more about it. (c) criticism. **reflective**, adj. thoughtful. **reflector**, n. apparatus which reflects.

reflex ['riːfleks] 1. n. (pl. **-es**) automatic action/instinctive response. 2. adj. (a)

which is automatic; **r. action** = action done instinctively. (b) which returns as a reflection; **r. camera** = camera where the picture is reflected from the lens to the viewfinder exactly as it will appear on the photograph; **r. angle** = angle of more than 180°. **reflexive** [rɪ'fleksɪv] adj. (in grammar) verb or pronoun which refers back to the subject.

refloat [riː'fləʊt] v. to float again (a ship which has gone aground).

reflux ['riːflʌks] n. flowing back.

reform [rɪ'fɔːm] 1. n. improving/improvement. 2. v. (a) to correct/to improve. (b) to become good/to stop committing crime. **reformation** [refə'meɪʃn] n. act of reforming; **the Reformation** = religious movement in sixteenth century Europe which brought about the creation of the Protestant churches. **reformatory** [rɪ'fɔːmətrɪ] n. type of prison school where young criminals are sent in the hope that they will be reformed. **reformer**, n. person who tries to improve (a system).

refract [rɪ'frækt] v. to bend (rays of light, etc.) as they pass through the surface of water. **refraction** [rɪ'frækʃn] n. bending of light as it goes from one substance to another (such as into water). **refractive**, adj. producing refraction. **refractor**, n. object/substance which refracts.

refractory [rɪ'fræktərɪ] adj. difficult/disobedient.

refrain [rɪ'freɪn] 1. n. chorus which is repeated after each section of a song or poem. 2. v. **to r. from** = not to do sth.

refresh [rɪ'freʃ] v. to make fresh again; to make less tired; **let me r. your memory** = help you to remember sth which you seem to have forgotten. **refresher**, n. fee paid to a lawyer for appearing again in court a second day; **r. course** = lessons which bring your knowledge of your job up to date. **refreshing**, adj. (a) which refreshes. (b) new and invigorating. **refreshment**, n. **refreshments** = food and drink; **r. room** = room at a railway station where food and drink are served.

refrigerator [rɪ'frɪdʒəreɪtə] n. cooling

cupboard for keeping things (esp. food) cold. **refrigerant,** *n.* substance used to make other substances very cold. **refrigerated,** *adj.* kept cold. **refrigeration** [rɪfrɪdʒə'reɪʃn] *n.* keeping things cold.

refuel [ri:'fjʊəl] *v.* (**refuelled**) to put more fuel into (a ship/plane/car, etc.).

refuge ['refjuːdʒ] *n.* place to hide/to shelter; **to take r.** = to shelter. **refugee** [refjuː'dʒiː] *n.* person who has been driven out of his own country and needs shelter; **political r.** = person who has left his country for political reasons.

refund 1. *n.* ['riːfʌnd] repayment of money. **2.** *v.* [rɪ'fʌnd] to pay back (money).

refurbish [ri'fɜːbɪʃ] *v.* to polish up again.

refuse 1. *n.* ['refjuːs] rubbish. **2.** *v.* [rɪ'fjuːz] (*a*) to say that you do not accept/that you will not do sth. (*b*) not to give s.o. (permission). **refusal** [rɪ'fjuːzl] *n.* (*a*) saying no; **to meet with a flat r.** = to be refused completely. (*b*) **to give s.o. first r. of sth** = to let them have first choice of buying sth.

refute [rɪ'fjuːt] *v.* to prove that (sth) is wrong. **refutation** [refjuː'teɪʃn] *n.* proof that sth is wrong.

regain [riː'geɪn] *v.* to get back.

regal ['riːgl] *adj.* referring to a king/queen; royal. **regalia** [rɪ'geɪlɪə] *n. pl.* robes/crown, etc., worn by a king/queen/mayor. **regally,** *adv.* like a king/queen.

regale [rɪ'geɪl] *v.* to entertain.

regard [rɪ'gɑːd] **1.** *n.* (*a*) concern. (*b*) esteem. (*c*) **regards** = best wishes. **2.** *v.* (*a*) to consider. (*b*) **as regards** = concerning. **regarding,** *prep.* concerning. **regardless,** *adj.* paying no attention to; **carry on r.** = carry on in spite of everything.

regatta [rɪ'gætə] *n.* series of boat races (for either yachts or rowing boats).

regenerate [rɪ'dʒenəreɪt] *v.* to start up again. **regeneration** [rɪdʒenə'reɪʃn] *n.* growing again/starting again.

regent ['riːdʒənt] *n.* person who rules in place of a king or queen. **regency,** *n.* period when a regent is ruling.

reggae ['regeɪ] *n.* type of West Indian music.

regicide ['redʒɪsaɪd] *n.* person who kills a king.

régime [re'ʒiːm] *n.* system of government/administration.

regimen ['redʒɪmən] *n.* planned course of action to improve your health.

regiment ['redʒɪmənt] **1.** *n.* group of soldiers, usu. commanded by a colonel or lieutenant-colonel. **2.** *v.* to keep (s.o.) under strict discipline. **regimental** [redʒɪ'mentl] *adj.* belonging to a regiment. **regimentals,** *n. pl.* military uniform of a certain regiment. **regimentation** [redʒɪmen-'teɪʃn] *n.* very strict discipline.

Regina [rɪ'dʒaɪnə] *n.* the Queen, i.e. the State in court cases.

region ['riːdʒən] *n.* area; (*in Scotland*) large administrative area; **the London r.** = area around London; **in the r. of £10,000** = about £10,000. **regional,** *adj.* referring to a region.

register ['redʒɪstə] **1.** *n.* (*a*) list (of names). (*b*) range of notes covered by a voice/a musical instrument. (*c*) **cash r.** = device which records sales/money taken in a shop. (*d*) (*in printing*) fitting of several printing plates in such a way that various colours correspond exactly on the paper. (*e*) level of language (such as formal/colloquial, etc.). **2.** *v.* (*a*) to write (a name) officially in a list; **to r. at a hotel** = to write your name and address when you arrive at the hotel. (*b*) to put into s.o.'s special care. (*c*) to record (a temperature, etc.). **registered,** *adj.* which has been officially recorded. **register office,** *n.* registry office. **registrar** ['redʒɪstrɑː] *n.* (*a*) person who keeps official records; person who keeps the records of a university. (*b*) specialist doctor in training. **registration** [redʒɪ'streɪʃn] *n.* act of registering; **r. plate** = number plate of a car; **r. number** = official number of a car. **registry** ['redʒɪstrɪ] *n.* place where official records are kept; **r. office** = office where records of births, marriages and deaths are kept/place where you can be married in a civil ceremony.

Regius Professor ['riːdʒɪəsprə'fesə] *n.* professor whose post was founded by the king.

regress [rɪ'gres] *v.* to go back to an earlier, and usu. worse, condition.

regression, *n.* going back. **regressive,** *adj.* which regresses.

regret [rɪ'gret] **1.** *n.* sorrow; **much to my r.** = I am very sorry. **2.** *v.* (**regretted**) to be sorry that sth has happened. **regretful,** *adj.* sorry/sad. **regretfully,** *adv.* sadly. **regrettable,** *adj.* which must be regretted. **regrettably,** *adv.* in a regrettable way.

regular ['regjʊlə] **1.** *adj.* (*a*) habitual/done at the same time each day. (*b*) usual/ordinary. (*c*) **r. army** = permanent, professional army; **r. officer** = professional officer. (*d*) (*in grammar*) **r. verb** = verb which has no unusual parts. **2.** *n.* (*a*) *inf.* customer who always shops in a particular shop/who always drinks in a certain bar, etc. (*b*) professional soldier. **regularity** [regjʊ-'lærɪtɪ] *n.* being regular. **regularization** [regjʊlərɑɪ'zeɪʃn] *n.* act of regularizing. **regularize** ['regjʊlərɑɪz] *v.* to make legal. **regularly,** *adv.* in a regular way. **regulate** ['regjʊleɪt] *v.* to adjust (a machine) so that it works regularly. **regulation** [regjʊ'leɪʃn] *n.* act of regulating; rule. **regulator,** *n.* person/instrument which regulates a machine. **regulo** ['regjuːləʊ] *n.* system of numbers indicating temperatures on a gas cooker.

regurgitate [rɪ'gɜːdʒɪteɪt] *v.* (*formal*) to spout out (food which has already been swallowed/information which has already been learnt). **regurgitation** [rɪgɜːdʒɪ'teɪʃn] *n.* act of regurgitating.

rehabilitate [riːhə'bɪlɪteɪt] *v.* to train (a disabled person/an ex-prisoner, etc.) to lead a normal life and fit into society. **rehabilitation** [riːhəbɪlɪ'teɪʃn] *n.* act of rehabilitating.

rehash 1. *n.* ['riːhæʃ] thing rehashed. **2.** *v.* [riː'hæʃ] to bring out (an old story/book, etc.) in more or less the same form as before.

rehearse [rɪ'hɜːs] *v.* to practise (a play/a concert, etc.) before a public performance. **rehearsal** [rɪ'hɜːsəl] *n.* practice of a play/concert, etc., before a public performance; **dress r.** = last rehearsal of a play, etc., when everyone is in costume.

rehouse [riː'haʊz] *v.* to put (s.o.) into a new house or flat.

reign [reɪn] **1.** *n.* period when a king/queen/emperor rules; **r. of terror** = period when law and order have broken down. **2.** *v.* to rule.

reimburse [riːɪm'bɜːs] *v.* to pay (s.o.) back the money he has spent. **reimbursement,** *n.* act of reimbursing; money reimbursed.

rein [reɪn] **1.** *n.* strap which controls a horse; **to keep on a tight r.** = under strict control. **2.** *v.* **to r. in** = to pull on the reins to control (a horse).

reincarnate [riːɪn'kɑːneɪt] *v.* (*formal*) to make (the soul of a dead person) be born again in another body. **reincarnation** [riːɪnkɑː'neɪʃn] *n.* survival of a person's soul born again in another body after death.

reindeer ['reɪndɪə] *n.* (*pl.* **reindeer**) type of deer which lives in the Arctic.

reinforce [riːɪn'fɔːs] *v.* to strengthen/to consolidate; **reinforced concrete** = concrete strengthened with metal rods. **reinforcement,** *n.* (*a*) act of reinforcing. (*b*) **reinforcements** = new soldiers to support others already fighting.

reinstate [riːɪn'steɪt] *v.* to put (s.o.) back into a post which he used to hold. **reinstatement,** *n.* putting s.o. back into a post.

reinsure [riːɪn'ʃʊə] *v.* to spread the risk of insurance, by insuring part of the risk with another insurer.

reinvest [riːɪn'vest] *v.* to invest again.

reiterate [riː'ɪtəreɪt] *v.* to repeat. **reiteration** [riːɪtə'reɪʃn] *n.* repetition.

reject 1. *n.* ['riːdʒekt] thing which has been thrown away as not satisfactory; **rejects** = substandard goods sold at a reduced price. **2.** *v.* [rɪ'dʒekt] to refuse to accept (sth); to throw (sth) away as not satisfactory. **rejection** [rɪ'dʒekʃn] *n.* refusal.

rejig [riː'dʒɪg] *v.* (**rejigged**) *inf.* to arrange in a different way.

rejoice [rɪ'dʒɔɪs] *v.* to be very happy. **rejoicing,** *n.* great happiness; **rejoicings** = celebrations.

rejoin [rɪ'dʒɔɪn] *v.* (*a*) to join again. (*b*) (*formal*) to reply. **rejoinder,** *n.* (*formal*) reply.

rejuvenate [rɪ'dʒuːvəneɪt] *v.* to make (s.o.) young again; to give (sth) new strength. **rejuvenation** [rɪdʒuːvə-'neɪʃn] *n.* act of rejuvenating.

rekindle [riːˈkɪndl] v. to light again.

relapse [rɪˈlæps] **1.** n. becoming ill again (after a temporary improvement); getting back into old bad habits. **2.** v. to become ill again; to get back into old bad habits.

relate [rɪˈleɪt] v. (a) to tell (a story). (b) to connect (two things). (c) to have a successful relationship (**with** s.o.). **related,** adj. (a) linked. (b) belonging to the same family. **relation** [rɪˈleɪʃn] n. (a) story. (b) linking/links (between two things); **public relations** = maintaining good connections with the public, esp. to put across a point of view/to publicize a product. (c) member of a family. **relationship,** n. link/connection; being related.

relative [ˈrelətɪv] **1.** n. person who is related to s.o.; member of a family. **2.** adj. (a) which is compared to sth; **their r. poverty** = their poverty compared with really wealthy people or with the wealth they used to have. (b) (in grammar) **r. pronoun** = pronoun (such as 'who' and 'which') which connects two clauses. **relatively,** adv. comparatively/more or less. **relativity** [reləˈtɪvɪtɪ] n. (in physics) relationship between objects and time and speed.

relax [rɪˈlæks] v. (a) to slacken/to decrease tension; to make less strict. (b) to rest from work. **relaxation** [riːlækˈseɪʃn] n. (a) slackening of a rule, etc. (b) rest. **relaxed,** adj. inf. happy/not upset.

relay 1. n. [ˈriːleɪ] (a) shift of people working. (b) **r. race** = running race by teams in which one runner passes a baton to another who then runs on. **2.** v. [rɪˈleɪ] to pass on (a message); to pass on (a TV/radio broadcast) through a relay station. **relay station,** n. transmitting station which receives signals from a main transmitter and broadcasts them further.

release [rɪˈliːs] **1.** n. (a) setting free. (b) new record/piece of information which is made public. **2.** v. (a) to set free. (b) to make public.

relegate [ˈrelɪgeɪt] v. to put into a worse position; to move (a team) down from one football division to a lower one. **relegation** [relɪˈgeɪʃn] n. moving into a worse position.

relent [rɪˈlent] v. to change your mind about a strict decision you have taken/to be less strict. **relentless,** adj. pitiless. **relentlessly,** adv. with no pity.

relevant [ˈrelɪvənt] adj. which relates/has to do with sth being spoken of. **relevance,** n. being relevant.

reliable [rɪˈlaɪəbl] adj. which can be relied on/which can be trusted. **reliably,** adv. in a way which can be trusted. **reliability** [rɪlaɪəˈbɪlɪtɪ] n. being reliable. **reliance,** n. trust/confidence. **reliant,** adj. which relies on sth.

relic [ˈrelɪk] n. object which has been left over from the past; holy remains (such as the bones of a saint). **relict,** n. (formal) widow.

relief [rɪˈliːf] n. (a) reducing pain/tension. (b) help; **famine r. fund** = money collected to help victims of a famine; **r. road** = road built to help traffic congestion. (c) person/thing that takes over from another. **a r. nurse.** (d) carving in which the details of design stand out; **in r.** = standing out/prominent; **r. map** = map where mountains are drawn so that an impression of height is given. **relieve** [rɪˈliːv] v. (a) to reduce (pain/tension); **to r. oneself** = to urinate or defecate. (b) to help. (c) to take over from (s.o.). (d) to remove a weight from (s.o.).

religion [rɪˈlɪdʒən] n. belief in gods or in one God; system of worship. **religious,** adj. referring to religion. **religiously,** adv. regularly/at a fixed time of day.

relinquish [rɪˈlɪŋkwɪʃ] v. (formal) to leave/to let go.

reliquary [ˈrelɪkweri] n. container for holy relics.

relish [ˈrelɪʃ] **1.** n. (pl. -es) (a) seasoning/flavour; spicy pickles/spicy sauce. (b) enjoyment. **2.** v. to enjoy.

relocate [riːləˈkeɪt] v. to set (offices) in a new location. **relocation** [riːləˈkeɪʃn] n. act of relocating.

reluctant [rɪˈlʌktənt] adj. not eager/not willing. **reluctantly,** adv. not willingly. **reluctance,** n. lack or eagerness.

rely [rɪˈlaɪ] v. (on) to trust.

remain [rɪˈmeɪn] v. (a) to stay. (b) **it remains to be seen** = we will see in due course. **remainder. 1.** n. (a) what is left over. (b) **remainders** = books which are sold off cheaply. **2.** *v.* to sell off (new books) cheaply. **remains,** *n. pl.* (*a*) dead body. (*b*) things left over/left behind.

remand [rɪ'mɑ:nd] *v.* to order (a prisoner) to appear at a later hearing of a trial when more evidence will be produced; **r. home** = place where young criminals can be kept while awaiting trial.

remark [rɪ'mɑ:k] **1.** *n.* comment/observation; **to pass remarks about** = make rude comments. **2.** *v.* to notice/to comment. **remarkable,** *adj.* unusual/which you might comment on. **remarkably,** *adv.* unusually.

remedy ['remədɪ] **1.** *n.* thing which may cure. **2.** *v.* to make (sth) better/to put (sth) right. **remedial** [rɪ'mi:dɪəl] *adj.* which cures/which makes sth better; **r. class** = class of special instruction for students who are weak in a subject.

remember [rɪ'membə] *v.* (*a*) to call back into your mind (sth which you have seen/read/heard, etc., before). (*b*) to send good wishes to s.o. (*c*) **he remembered me in his will** = he left me sth in his will. **remembrance,** *n.* memory.

remind [rɪ'maɪnd] *v.* **to r. s.o. of sth** = to make (s.o.) remember sth. **reminder,** *n.* thing which reminds you of sth.

reminiscence [remɪ'nɪsəns] *n.* memory of sth from the past. **reminisce** [remɪ'nɪs] *v.* to talk about memories of the past. **reminiscent,** *adj.* which reminds you of the past.

remiss [rɪ'mɪs] *adj.* careless.

remission [rɪ'mɪʃn] *n.* pardon (for your sins); cutting short a prison sentence.

remit 1. *n.* ['ri:mɪt] orders; area of responsibility. **2.** *v.* [rɪ'mɪt] (**remitted**) (*a*) to pardon (sins); to cut short (a prison sentence). (*b*) to send (money). **remittance,** *n.* sending money; money which is sent.

remnant ['remnənt] *n.* piece/quantity left over.

remonstrate ['remənstreɪt] *v.* to protest **against** sth. **remonstrance** [rɪ'mɒnstrəns] *n.* act of remonstrating.

remorse [rɪ'mɔ:s] *n.* regret about sth wicked which you have done. **remorseful,** *adj.* full of remorse. **remorseless,**

adj. pitiless/cruel. **remorselessly,** *adv.* in a remorseless way.

remote [rɪ'məʊt] *adj.* (**-er, -est**) (*a*) distant; **r. control** = control (of a model plane, etc.) by radio signals. (*b*) slight (possibility). (*c*) uncommunicative (person). **remotely,** *adv.* distantly. **remoteness,** *n.* being remote.

remould ['ri:məʊld] **1.** *v.* to mould again. **2.** *n.* tyre which has had its tread remoulded.

remount [ri:'maʊnt] *v.* to get back on to (a horse/bicycle, etc.).

remove [rɪ'mu:v] **1.** *n.* grade; **one r. from** = one grade up/down from. **2.** *v.* (*a*) to take away. (*b*) to dismiss (s.o.) from a job. **removable,** *adj.* which can be removed. **removal,** *n.* moving of a home; **r. van** = van in which your furniture is moved from one house to another. **remover,** *n.* (*a*) person who moves furniture from one house to another. (*b*) thing which removes; **paint r.** = liquid which removes old paint.

remunerate [rɪ'mju:nəreɪt] *v.* (*formal*) to pay (s.o.). **remuneration** [rɪmju:nə'reɪʃn] *n.* payment. **remumerative** [rɪ'mju:nərətɪv] *adj.* well paid.

renaissance [re'neɪsəns] *n.* rebirth/starting again; **the Renaissance** = artistic movement in late medieval Europe based on a renewal of interest in the Greek and Roman civilizations.

renal ['ri:nl] *adj.* referring to the kidneys.

renascent [rɪ'neɪsənt] *adj.* which is rising again.

rend [rend] *v.* (**rent**) (*old*) to tear.

render ['rendə] *v.* (*a*) to give (back); to send in (an account). (*b*) to translate. (*c*) **to r. (down)** = to melt (fat). (*d*) to cover (a wall) with a coating of cement. (*e*) to make (s.o.) be (speechless, etc.). **rendering,** *n.* translation; performance (of a song, etc.).

rendezvous ['rɒndeɪvu:] **1.** *n.* meeting place/appointment; meeting. **2.** *v.* (**rendezvoused** ['rɒndeɪvu:d]) to arrange to meet.

rendition [ren'dɪʃn] *n.* performance (of a song, etc.).

renegade ['renɪgeɪd] *adj. & n.* (person) who gives up a faith/a belief to adopt another; (person) who leaves one group to join another.

renege [rɪ'neɪg] v. **to r. on** = not to do sth which you had promised to do.

renew [rɪ'njuː] v. to start again; to replace (sth old) with sth new. **renewable**, adj. which can be renewed. **renewal**, n. act of renewing.

rennet ['renɪt] n. substance which when added to milk makes it curdle and so form cheese.

renounce [rɪ'naʊns] v. to give up officially. **renouncement**, n. act of renouncing.

renovate ['renəveɪt] v. to make (sth) like new. **renovation** [renə'veɪʃn] n. making like new. **renovator**, n. person/machine that renovates.

renown [rɪ'naʊn] n. fame. **renowned**, adj. famous (**for** sth).

rent [rent] **1.** n. (a) money paid for the hire of a flat/house/office, etc. (b) tear/slit (in cloth). **2.** v. (a) to pay money to hire (a house/flat, etc.). (b) to hire out (a house/flat, etc.) for money. (c) see also **rend. rental**, n. rent/money paid to hire a room/flat/office, etc.

renunciation [rɪnʌnsɪ'eɪʃn] n. giving up/renouncing of a claim.

reopen [riː'əʊpən] v. (a) to open again. (b) to start to investigate a case again.

reorganize [riː'ɔːgənaɪz] v. to organize in a new way. **reorganization** [riːɔːgənaɪ'zeɪʃn] n. act of reorganizing.

reorientate [riː'ɔːrɪənteɪt] v. to set (s.o.) in another direction.

rep [rep] n. inf. (a) travelling salesman. (b) repertory theatre. (c) strong corded material used in upholstery.

repaid [riː'peɪd] v. see **repay**.

repair [rɪ'peə] **1.** n. (a) mending. (b) **to be in a good state of r./in good r.** = to be in good condition. **2.** v. (a) to mend. (b) (old) to go. **repairer**, n. person who mends. **repairable**, adj. which can be mended. **reparation** [repə'reɪʃn] n. thing/money which makes up for a wrong.

repartee [repɑː'tiː] n. series of witty answers in a conversation.

repast [rɪ'pɑːst] n. (formal) meal.

repatriate [riː'pætrieɪt] v. to bring/to send (s.o.) back to their home country. **repatriation** [rɪpætrɪ'eɪʃn] n. act of repatriating.

repay [riː'peɪ] v. (**repaid**) (a) to pay back.

(b) to be worth; **it repays close examination** = it's worth examing carefully. **repayable**, adj. which can be repaid. **repayment**, n. paying back.

repeal [rɪ'piːl] **1.** n. abolition of a law, so that it is no longer valid. **2.** v. to do away with (a law).

repeat [rɪ'piːt] **1.** n. & adj. performance which is repeated. **2.** v. to say/to do (sth) again. **repeatable**, adj. which can be repeated. **repeatedly** [rɪ'piːtɪdlɪ] adv. over and over again. **repeater**, n. old pocket watch which rings the hours; gun which can fire several times without being reloaded.

repel [rɪ'pel] v. (**repelled**) (a) to drive back (an attack). (b) to disgust/to be so unpleasant that you drive people away. **repelling**, adj. disgusting. **repellent**, adj. & n. (thing) which drives away/which repels; **insect r.** = spray which keeps insects away.

repent [rɪ'pent] v. to be very sorry. **repentance**, n. great regret. **repentant**, adj. full of repentance.

repercussion [rɪpɜː'kʌʃn] n. result/effect.

repertoire ['repətwɑː] n. works which s.o. can play/sing by heart; works which a theatre company has ready for performance.

repertory ['repətrɪ] n. (a) **r. theatre** = theatre with a permanent group of actors who play a series of plays, changing them at regular intervals. (b) store (of information/stories, etc.).

repetition [repɪ'tɪʃn] n. act of repeating; thing which is repeated. **repetitious**, **repetitive** [rɪ'petɪtɪv] adj. which repeats sth too frequently.

replace [riː'pleɪs] v. (a) to put (sth) back in place. (b) to put (sth) in place of sth else. **replaceable**, adj. which can be replaced. **replacement**, n. (a) putting back; replacing sth with sth else. (b) thing which is used to replace; **r. parts** = spare parts (of an engine) used to replace parts which have worn out.

replay ['riːpleɪ] n. (a) football match which is played again because the first match was a draw. (b) **action r.** = section of a sporting event which is shown again on TV at a slower speed, so that the action can be appreciated.

replenish [rɪ'plenɪʃ] v. to fill up again. **replenishment**, n. act of replenishing; thing which replenishes.

replete [rɪ'pli:t] adj. (formal) full and satisfied.

replica ['replɪkə] n. exact copy.

reply [rɪ'plaɪ] 1. n. answer. 2. v. to answer.

report [rɪ'pɔ:t] 1. n. (a) description/story of what has happened. (b) comments by teachers on a child's progress in school; comments by a commission on a problem. (c) explosion. 2. v. (a) to write a description of what happened; **you must r. the burglary to the police** = give them the details. (b) to make a complaint about (s.o.). (c) to present oneself officially; **to r. for work.** (d) **to r. to** = be responsible to. **reportage** [repɔ:'tɑ:ʒ] n. reporting of news (esp. for a magazine or TV). **reportedly**, adv. according to what has been reported. **reporter**, n. journalist who writes articles for a newspaper on events.

repose [rɪ'pəʊz] 1. n. (formal) calm/resting. 2. v. (formal) (a) to rest. (b) to place (trust) in s.o.

repository [rɪ'pɒzɪtrɪ] n. (a) warehouse where you can store furniture; store (of information, etc.). (b) Am. store for nuclear waste.

repossess [ri:pə'zes] v. (of shop) to take back (goods) when the purchaser cannot pay the hire-purchase payments.

repoussé [rə'pu:seɪ] adj. & n. (metalwork) which is hammered into relief from the back.

reprehend [reprɪ'hend] v. to criticize. **reprehensible** adj. which can be criticized. **reprehensibly**, adv. in a reprehensible way.

represent [reprɪ'zent] v. (a) to mean/to show. (b) to speak on behalf of (s.o./a group of people). (c) to sell goods on behalf of (s.o.). **representation** [reprɪzen'teɪʃn] n. (a) being represented. (b) **representations** = complaints/protests. **representative** [reprɪ'zentətɪv] 1. adj. typical. 2. n. person who represents; travelling salesman; (in the United States) member of the lower house of Congress; **the House of Representatives.**

repress [rɪ'pres] v. to keep down/to control. **repressed**, adj. kept under strict control. **repression** [rɪ'preʃn] n. keeping under control. **repressive**, adj. severe/sharp.

reprieve [rɪ'pri:v] 1. n. pardon given to a prisoner. 2. v. to pardon.

reprimand ['reprɪmɑ:nd] 1. n. severe rebuke. 2. v. to criticize (s.o.) severely.

reprint 1. n. ['ri:prɪnt] book which has been printed again. 2. v. [ri:'prɪnt] to print (a book) again.

reprisal [rɪ'praɪzl] n. punishment of people in revenge for sth.

repro ['ri:prəʊ] n. proof which is photographed to make a printing film.

reproach [rɪ'prəʊtʃ] 1. n. (a) thing which is a disgrace. (b) **beyond r.** = blameless. (c) rebuke. 2. v. **to r. s.o. with sth** = to blame s.o. for sth. **reproachful**, adj. which blames. **reproachfully**, adv. in a reproachful way.

reprobate ['reprəbeɪt] n. wicked person/scoundrel.

reprocessing [ri:'prəʊsesɪŋ] n. treatment of used nuclear fuel, to extract useful substances.

reproduce [ri:prə'dju:s] v. (a) to copy. (b) to produce young. **reproduction** [ri:prə'dʌkʃən] n. (a) copy (of a painting, etc.); **the r. is bad on this record** = the quality of the sound is bad. (b) production of young. **reproductive**, adj. (organs) which produce young.

reprographics [riprəʊ'græfɪks] n. pl. pictures which are reproduced in a book.

reproof [rɪ'pru:f] n. (formal) blame/criticism. **reprove** [rɪ'pru:v] v. (formal) to criticize/to blame (someone). **reproving**, adj. criticizing.

reptile ['reptaɪl] n. cold-blooded animal which lays eggs and is covered with scales. **reptilian** [rep'tɪlɪən] adj. like a reptile.

republic [rɪ'pʌblɪk] n. system of government where there may be elected representatives or where the head of state is an elected or nominated president. **republican**, adj. & n. referring to a republic; (supporter) of a republic. **Republican**, adj. & n. Am. (member) of one of the two main political parties in the USA. **republicanism**, n. belief in the republic as a means of government.

repudiate [rɪ'pju:dɪeɪt] v. to reject/to refuse to accept. **repudiation** [rɪpju:dɪ'eɪʃn] n. rejection.

repugnant [rɪ'pʌgnənt] adj. unpleasant/nasty. **repugnance**, n. feeling of distaste/dislike.

repulse [rɪ'pʌls] v. to push back. **repulsion** [rɪ'pʌlʃn] n. (a) act of repulsing. (b) feeling of dislike/distaste. **repulsive**, adj. unpleasant/nasty.

repute [rɪ'pju:t] n. reputation/general opinion; **I only know her by r.** = I have never met her, but I know what people think of her. **reputable** ['repjʊtəbl] adj. well thought of/with a good reputation. **reputation** [repjʊ'teɪʃn] n. general opinion (of s.o.). **reputed** [rɪ'pju:tɪd] adj. supposed. **reputedly** [rɪ'pju:tɪdlɪ] adv. according to most people.

request [rɪ'kwest 1. n. asking/demand; **on r.** = if asked for; **r. stop** = bus stop where buses stop only if you signal to them. 2. v. to ask/to demand politely.

requiem ['rekwɪəm] v. mass for the dead; music to be sung at a requiem.

require [rɪ'kwaɪə] v. (a) to demand/to request. (b) to need. **requirement**, n. what is needed.

requisition [rekwɪ'zɪʃn] 1. n. official order. 2. v. to demand/to order that sth should be handed over; to demand and take (supplies) for an army; to order (supplies) for a school. **requisite** ['rekwɪzɪt] adj. & n. (thing) which is necessary. etc.

reredos ['rɪədɒs] n. carved screen behind an altar.

rerun ['ri:rʌn] n. second showing of a film on TV.

resale [ri:'seɪl] n. selling to s.o. goods which you have bought.

rescind [rɪ'sɪnd] v. to annul/to cancel (a law).

rescue ['reskju:] 1. n. saving; **r. squad** = group of people who are going to save s.o. 2. v. to save. **rescuer**, n. person who rescues or tries to rescue.

research [rɪ'sɜ:tʃ] 1. n. scientific study/trying to find out facts. 2. v. to study/to try to find out facts. **researcher**, n. person who researches.

resemble [rɪ'zembl] v. to be similar to. **resemblance**, n. looking like s.o.

resent [rɪ'zent] v. to feel annoyed at a real or imaginary injury. **resentful,** adj. annoyed. **resentfully,** adv. in a resentful way. **resentment,** n. annoyance.

reserve [rɪ'zɜ:v] 1. n. (a) quantity kept back for future special use; **in r.** = waiting to be used. (b) (in sport) extra player; **reserves** = part-time troops kept to help the regular army if necessary. (c) **nature r.** = area of land where animals and vegetation are protected. (d) shyness; not speaking openly. (e) (at an auction) price which an item must reach before the owner will allow it to be sold. 2. v. to keep back for a special use; to book (a seat/a table). **reservation** [rezə'veɪʃn] n. (a) booking (of a seat/table). (b) doubt. (c) national park; area where indigenous tribes live. **reserved,** adj. (a) booked. (b) shy; (person) who does not speak openly. **reservist** [rɪ'zɜ:vɪst] n. part-time soldier who is a member of the army reserves.

reservoir ['rezəvwɑ:] n. (a) large (usu. artificial) lake where water is kept for pumping to a town. (b) container (for storing liquids); mass (of information/facts) which can be used if necessary.

reshuffle [ri:'ʃʌfl] 1. n. reorganization (of ministers in a government). 2. v. (a) to shuffle again. (b) to reorganize (the ministers in a government).

reside [rɪ'zaɪd] v. (formal) to live/to have a house. **residence** ['rezɪdəns] n. (a) place where you live. (b) act of living in a place; **hall of r.** = block of flats where students live. **residency,** n. (old) house of a colonial governor. **resident** ['rezɪdənt] 1. adj. (a) living permanently in a place. (b) permanently fixed in a computer. 2. n. person who lives in a place. **residential** [rezɪ'denʃl] adj. (part of a town) with houses rather than shops or factories.

residue ['rezɪdju:] n. what is left over. **residual** [re'zɪdjuəl] adj. remaining. **residuary,** adj. (formal) residual (part of an estate).

resign [rɪ'zaɪn] v. (a) to give up a job. (b) **to r. yourself to** = to accept. **resignation** [rezɪg'neɪʃn] n. (a) giving up a job; **he tendered/handed in his r.** = he resigned. (b) acceptance that sth has to happen. **resigned,** adj. accepting that sth has to happen. **resignedly** [rɪˈzaɪnɪdlɪ] adv. patiently/calmly/without complaining.

resilient [rɪˈsɪlɪənt] adj. (material) which easily returns to its original shape (after being crushed); (person) who is strong/able to recover easily from a blow. **resilience**, n. being resilient.

resin [ˈrezɪn] n. sticky sap, esp. from pine trees. **resinous**, adj. like resin; made of resin.

resist [rɪˈzɪst] v. to oppose/not to give in to (sth). **resistance**, n. (a) opposition/fight against sth; **r. movement** = movement of ordinary people against an invader; **he took the line of least r.** = he did it the easiest way. (b) (in physics) force which opposes sth; ability not to conduct electricity/heat, etc. **resistant**, adj. which resists. **resistivity**, n. ability to resist the flow of an electric current. **resistor**, n. device which increases the resistance to an electric current/which prevents a current from flowing.

resit [riːˈsɪt] v. to take (an examination) again after failing.

resolute [ˈrezəluːt] adj. determined/having made up your mind. **resolutely**, adv. in a resolute way. **resolution** [rezəˈluːʃn] n. (a) decision reached at a meeting; proposal to be decided at a meeting. (b) (also **resoluteness**) determination (to do sth)/strength of character. (c) solving (of a problem). (d) splitting up into chemical parts. (e) clearness of a computer image (calculated as the number of pixels per unit of area).

resolve [rɪˈzɒlv] 1. n. determination (to do sth). 2. v. (a) to decide to do sth. (b) to solve (a problem). (c) to split up into chemical parts.

resonant [ˈrezənənt] adj. which sounds/rings/echoes loudly. **resonance**, n. deep loud ringing tone.

resort [rɪˈzɔːt] 1. n. (a) place where people go on holidays. (b) **as a last r./in the last r.** = when everything else fails. 2. v. **to r. to** = to use sth in a difficult situation/when everything else has failed.

resound [rɪˈzaʊnd] v. to make a loud, echoing, deep noise. **resounding**, adj. great/complete.

resource [rɪˈsɔːs] n. source of supply for what is needed/used; **natural resources** = minerals/oil/trees; **r. centre** = area in a school which provides books/equipment for school work; **left to his own resources** = left to look after himself. **resourceful**, adj. good at looking after yourself/at dealing with problems. **resourcefully**, adv. in a resourceful way. **resourcefulness**, n. being resourceful.

respect [rɪˈspekt] 1. n. (a) admiration/regard. (b) concern/detail; **with r. to** = concerning; **in some respects** = in some ways. (c) **respects** = polite good wishes. 2. v. (a) to admire/to honour (s.o.). (b) to pay attention to (sth). **respectability** [rɪspektəˈbɪlɪtɪ] n. being respectable. **respectable** [rɪˈspektəbl] adj. (a) proper/worthy of respect. (b) quite large/fairly large. **respectably**, adv. properly. **respecter**, n. person who respects others. **respectful**, adj. full of respect. **respectfully**, adv. showing respect. **respecting**, prep. concerning. **respective**, adj. referring to each one separately. **respectively**, adv. referring to each one separately.

respire [resˈpaɪə] v. (formal) to breathe. **respiration** [respɪˈreɪʃn] n. breathing in of air; **to give s.o. artificial r.** = to force s.o. (who is almost dead from drowning) to breathe. **respirator** [ˈrespɪreɪtə] n. device which helps you to breathe, esp. a mask worn as protection against gas, smoke, etc. **respiratory**, adj. referring to breathing.

respite [ˈrespaɪt] n. rest; **without r.** = without stopping.

resplendent [rɪˈsplendənt] adj. very splendid.

respond [rɪˈspɒnd] v. to reply/to react (to); **he responded to treatment** = he began to get better. **respondent**, n. defendant in a law suit, esp. in a divorce case. **response**, n. (a) answer. (b) reply made by the congregation to the priest in a church service. **responsibility** [rɪspɒnsɪˈbɪlɪtɪ] n. (a) being responsible; **he has taken on a lot of r.** = he has agreed to be responsible for many things. (b) thing which you are responsible for. **responsible**, adj. (a) (for) causing. (b) (person) taking decisions for sth/directing sth. (c)

r. to s.o. = being under the authority of s.o. who expects you to carry out the work well. (*d*) trustworthy (person). (*e*) **r. position** = post where decisions have to be taken. **responsibly,** *adv.* in a responsible way. **responsive,** *adj.* (person) who reacts quickly/who shows sympathy. **responsiveness,** *n.* sensitivity.

rest [rest] **1.** *n.* (*a*) sleep/calm state; **to set s.o.'s mind at r.** = to calm s.o.'s worries. (*b*) stop; **the car came to r. at the bottom of the hill** = stopped moving. (*c*) (*in music*) short break between notes. (*d*) support; **arm r.** = part of a chair which you put your arms on; **head r.** = cushion to support your head (usu. attached to a seat in a car). (*e*) **the r.** = remains/what is left over/other people. **2.** *v.* (*a*) to sleep/to be calm. (*b*) to make (sth) be calm. (*c*) **to let the matter r.** = not to deal with the problem any more. **restful,** *adj.* calm/which makes you feel calm. **restless,** *adj.* agitated; always on the move. **restlessly,** *adv.* in a restless way. **restlessness,** *n.* being restless. **restroom,** *n. Am.* toilet/lavatory.

restaurant ['restrɒnt] *n.* place where you can buy a meal; **self-service r.** = where you serve yourself; **r. car** = carriage on a train where you can have a meal. **restaurateur** [restəræ'tɜ:] *n.* person who runs a fashionable restaurant.

restitution [resti'tju:ʃn] *n.* compensation/paying back.

restive ['restiv] *adv.* nervous/agitated. **restiveness,** *n.* agitation.

restore [rɪs'tɔ:] *v.* (*a*) to give back. (*b*) to repair/to make (sth) new again. **restoration** [restə'reɪʃn] *n.* (*a*) giving back. (*b*) reparing sth/making sth look like new again. **restorative** [rɪ'stɒrətɪv] *adj.* & *n.* (medicine) which makes you stronger. **restorer,** *n.* person who restores old paintings, etc.; **hair r.** = liquid which is supposed to make your hair grow again.

restrain [rɪ'streɪn] *v.* to hold back; to prevent/to try and stop. **restrained,** *adj.* controlled/calm. **restraint,** *n.* control; **with great r.** = without losing your temper; **lack of r.** = (excessive) freedom; **wage r.** = keeping wage increases under control.

restrict [rɪ'strɪkt] *v.* to limit. **restricted,** *adj.* limited; **r. area** = (i) area where cars must obey a speed limit; (ii) area where only certain people are allowed. **restriction** [rɪ'strɪkʃn] *n.* limitation. **restrictive,** *adj.* which restricts/limits.

result [rɪ'zʌlt] **1.** *n.* (*a*) thing which happens because of sth; outcome. (*b*) score (in a game); marks (in an exam). **2.** *v.* **to r. from** = to happen because of sth which has been done; **to r. in** = to produce as an effect. **resultant,** *adj.* which results.

resume [rɪ'zju:m] *v.* to start again after an interruption. **resumption** [rɪ'zʌmpʃn] *n.* starting again.

résumé ['rezu:meɪ] *n.* (*a*) short summing up of the main points. (*b*) *Am.* curriculum vitae.

resurface [ri:'sɜ:fəs] *v.* (*a*) to put a new surface (on a road). (*b*) to reappear on the surface.

resurgent [rɪ'sɜ:dʒənt] *adj.* which is rising again/becoming more powerful again. **resurgence,** *n.* reappearance/rising again.

resurrect [rezə'rekt] *v.* to bring back to use; to start up again. **resurrection** [rezə'rekʃn] *n.* bringing back to life.

resuscitate [rɪ'sʌsɪteɪt] *v.* to bring (someone who is almost dead) back to life. **resuscitation** [rɪsʌsɪ'teɪʃn] *n.* bringing back to life.

retail ['ri:teɪl] **1.** *n.* selling small quantities of goods to an ordinary customer; **r. outlet** = shop which sells goods direct to the customer. **2.** *v.* (*a*) to sell (goods) direct to customers who will not sell them again; **to r. at** = to sell for (a certain price). (*b*) to pass on (gossip). **retailer,** *n.* shopkeeper who sells goods to users.

retain [rɪ'teɪn] *v.* to keep; **to r. a lawyer to act for you** = to agree with a lawyer that he will act for you (and to pay him in advance); **retaining wall** = wall which holds back a mass of earth/the water in a reservoir, etc. **retainer,** *n.* (*a*) money paid in advance to s.o. for work he will do later. (*b*) (old) servant.

retaliate [rɪ'tælɪeɪt] *v.* to hit back/to attack (s.o.) in revenge. **retaliation** [rɪtælɪ'eɪʃn] *n.* **in r. for** = as a reprisal for. **retaliatory** [rɪ'tælɪətrɪ] *adj.* (measures) taken in retaliation.

retard [rɪ'tɑːd] v. to make slow/to keep sth late. **retardation** [rɪtɑː'deɪʃn] n. act of retarding. **retarded**, adj. mentally slower than s.o. of the same age. **retardedness**, n. being retarded.

retch [retʃ] v. to have spasms in the throat as if you were about to vomit.

retention [rɪ'tenʃn] n. keeping/holding. **retentive**, adj. (memory) which retains well.

rethink [riː'θɪŋk] **1.** n. inf. second thought about a problem. **2.** v. (**rethought**) to think again/to reconsider.

reticent ['retɪsənt] adj. uncommunicative/not willing to talk about sth. **reticence**, n. unwillingness to talk.

retina ['retɪnə] n. layer on the inside of the surface of the eye, which is sensitive to light.

retinue ['retɪnjuː] n. group of people following an important person.

retire [rɪ'taɪə] v. (a) to stop work (and take a pension); to make (s.o.) stop work (and take a pension). (b) to go away into a place by yourself. (c) **to r. to bed for the night** = to go to bed. **retirement**, n. (a) act of retiring from work. (b) period of life when you are retired. **retiring**, adj. quiet and reserved (person).

retort [rɪ'tɔːt] **1.** n. (a) sharp reply. (b) glass bottle with a long, thin bent neck used for distilling. **2.** v. to reply sharply.

retouch [riː'tʌtʃ] v. to improve (a picture/a photograph) by adding or removing lines by hand.

retrace [riː'treɪs] v. to go back to the origins of (sth); **to r. one's steps** = go back over the same path again.

retract [rɪ'trækt] v. to pull back; to withdraw (sth said). **retractable**, adj. (undercarriage of a plane) which folds up into the body of the plane. **retraction** [rɪ'trækʃn] n. pulling back; folding up. **retractor**, n. surgical instrument used to hold back the flesh during an operation.

retread 1. n. ['riːtred] tyre which has had its surface renewed. **2.** v. [riː'tred] to renew the surface of a tyre.

retreat [rɪ'triːt] **1.** n. (a) withdrawing of an army from a battle. (b) quiet place. (c) period of calm meditation (in a religious establishment). **2.** v. to withdraw from a battle.

retrench [rɪ'trentʃ] v. to economize/to cut back on expenditure. **retrenchment**, n. reduction of expenditure.

retrial [riː'traɪəl] n. second trial.

retribution [retrɪ'bjuːʃn] n. well-deserved punishment. **retributive** [re'trɪbjuːtɪv] adj. acting as a punishment.

retrieve [rɪ'triːv] v. to get back (sth) which was lost; to bring back (sth). **retrievable**, adj. which can be retrieved. **retrieval**, n. getting back; **r. system** = system (in a catalogue/in a computer program) to allow information to be retrieved. **retriever**, n. type of dog trained to fetch birds which have been shot.

retroactive [retrəʊ'æktɪv] adj. which takes effect from a time in the past; **r. to last April** = which takes effect from last April.

retrograde ['retrəgreɪd] adj. backward; **r. step** = step which makes things worse than they were before.

retrogress [retrəʊ'gres] v. to move backwards. **retrogression**, n. moving backwards.

retrorocket ['retrəʊrɒkɪt] n. rocket which slows down a space vehicle/a plane.

retrospect ['retrəspekt] n. **in r.** = when you look back. **retrospective** [retrə'spektɪv] adj. & n. which looks back on past events; (exhibition) of works of art covering the whole career of an artist.

retroussé [rə'truːseɪ] adj. turned up (nose).

retsina [re'tsiːnə] n. Greek wine flavoured with resin.

return [rɪ'tɜːn] **1.** n. (a) going back/coming back; **on my r. home** = when I got back home; **r. ticket** = ticket which allows you to go to one place and come back; **many happy returns of the day** = best wishes for a happy birthday; **by r. of post** = by the next post service back. (b) profit/income from money invested. (c) sending back; **on sale or r.** = sale where the wholesaler will take the product back if the retailer cannot sell it. (d) report of results of an election; **income-tax r.** = statement of income, etc., to the tax office. (e) (in tennis, etc.) sending back of a ball. (f) **r. match** = match played between two teams who have played each other recently. (*g*) key on a computer keyboard which shows that data has been completely entered. **2.** *v.* (*a*) to come back/to go back. (*b*) to give back/to send back. (*c*) to elect (s.o.) to parliament. **returnable,** *adj.* which can be returned. **returning officer,** *n.* official who is responsible for an election in a constituency.

reunion [riː'juːnɪən] *n.* meeting of people who have not met for a long time. **reunite** [riːjuː'naɪt] *v.* to join (two things) together again.

reusable [riː'juːzəbl] *adj.* which can be used again.

rev [rev] **1.** *n. inf.* revolution. **2.** *v.* (**revved**) *inf.* (*also* **rev up**) to make (a car engine) go quickly while the car is standing still.

Rev ['revrənd] *short for* Reverend.

revalue [riː'væljuː] *v.* to value again (usu. at a higher value). **revaluation** [rɪvæljuː'eɪʃn] *n.* revaluing/recalculating the value.

revamp [riː'væmp] *v. inf.* to improve the appearance of (sth which is slightly old-fashioned).

Revd ['revrənd] *short for* Reverend.

reveal [rɪ'viːl] *v.* to show (sth) which was hidden. **revelation** [revə'leɪʃn] *n.* surprise.

reveille [rɪ'vælɪ] *n.* (*in the army*) signal to soldiers to get up in the morning.

revel ['revəl] **1.** *n.* **revels** = merrymaking/happy celebrations. **2.** *v.* (**revelled**) to take delight (**in**); to have a happy time. **reveller,** *n.* person who is celebrating. **revelry,** *n.* celebration.

revenge [rɪ'vendʒ] **1.** *n.* action to harm s.o. in return for harm he has caused you. **2.** *v.* to harm s.o. in return for harm he has caused you. **revengeful,** *adj.* wanting revenge.

revenue ['revənjuː] *n.* money which is received; taxes which a government receives.

reverberate [rɪ'vɜːbəreɪt] *v.* to echo/to ring out loudly in an echo. **reverberation** [rɪvɜːbə'reɪʃn] *n.* echoing.

revere [rɪ'vɪə] *v.* to worship/to respect (s.o.) very highly. **reverence** ['revrəns] *n.* (*a*) great respect. (*b*) bow (as a mark of respect). **reverend,** *adj.* (*a*) worthy

of respect. (*b*) **Reverend** = title given to priests; **Reverend Mother** = title given to he head of a convent. **reverent,** *adj.* showing respect. **reverential,** *adj.* extremely respectful. **reverently,** *adv.* in a reverent way.

reverie ['revərɪ] *n.* daydream.

revers [rɪ'vɪə] *n.* edge of a coat collar, etc., which is turned back to form the lapel.

reversal [rɪ'vɜːsəl] *n.* change to sth opposite; **r. of fortune** = bad luck.

reverse [rɪ'vɜːs] **1.** *adj.* opposite; **in r. order** = backwards. **2.** *n.* (*a*) the opposite. (*b*) gear of a car which makes you go backwards. (*c*) defeat (in battle). **3.** *v.* (*a*) to do the opposite; to make a car go backwards; (*on the phone*) **to r. the charges** = to ask the person you are calling to pay for the call. (*b*) to change a decision to the opposite. **reversible,** *adj.* cloth/coat which can be worn with either side out. **reversion** [rɪ'vɜːʃn] *n.* return to an original state/to an original owner. **reversionary,** *adj.* (property) which passes to another owner on the death of the existing one.

revert [rɪ'vɜːt] *v.* to go back/to come back (**to**); **to r. to type** = to go back to an original state; **to r. to a subject** = to start talking about the subject again.

revetment [rɪ'vetmənt] *n.* stone facing to a wall.

review [rɪ'vjuː] **1.** *n.* (*a*) written opinion of a book/play/film, etc. (*b*) magazine which contains articles about new books/films/plays. (*c*) general examination. (*d*) general inspection of soldiers/naval vessels, etc. **2.** *v.* (*a*) to write your opinion of (a book/play/film, etc.). (*b*) to inspect (soldiers/naval vessels). (*c*) to consider generally. **reviewer,** *n.* person who writes opinions of books/play/films.

revile [rɪ'vaɪl] *v.* (*formal*) to insult; to criticize sharply.

revise [rɪ'vaɪz] *v.* (*a*) to read/to study a lesson again. (*b*) to correct/to change. **revision** [rɪ'vɪʒən] *n.* act of revising; thing revised. **revisionism,** *n.* revising the original pure concept (of a political movement, esp. communism).

revive [rɪ'vaɪv] *v.* to come back/to bring back to life again. **revival,** *n.* bringing

back to life; renewal of interest in sth.
revivalist, *n.* person who leads a religious revival.

revoke [rɪ'vəʊk] *v.* to cancel. **revocation** [revə'keɪʃn] *n.* act of revoking.

revolt [rɪ'vəʊlt] **1.** *n.* uprising against authority. **2.** *v.* (*a*) to rise up against authority. (*b*) to disgust. **revolting,** *adj.* (*a*) in revolt. (*b*) disgusting/which makes you feel ill.

revolution [revə'luːʃn] *n.* (*a*) rotation/turning around a central point. (*b*) uprising against a government. **revolutionary. 1.** *adj.* (*a*) aiming to change things completely/very new. (*b*) referring to a political revolution. **2.** *n.* person who takes part in an uprising against a government. **revolutionize,** *v.* to change completely.

revolve [rɪ'vɒlv] *v.* (*a*) to turn round. (*b*) to be centred on. **revolver,** *n.* small hand gun with a cartridge chamber which turns after each shot is fired. **revolving,** *adj.* which turns round.

revue [rɪ'vjuː] *n.* stage show with satirical sketches/songs, etc.

revulsion [rɪ'vʌlʃn] *n.* (*formal*) disgust.

reward [rɪ'wɔːd] **1.** *n.* money/present given to s.o. as a prize or for information. **2.** *v.* to give (s.o.) money/a present as a prize or for giving information. **rewarding,** *adj.* which gives moral satisfaction.

rewrite ['riːraɪt] **1.** *n.* *inf.* act of rewriting. **2.** *v.* (**rewrote, rewritten**) to write (sth) again in different words.

Rex [reks] *n.* the King, i.e. the State, in legal cases.

Rh. *abbrev. for* rhesus.

rhapsody ['ræpsədɪ] *n.* poetry/music/song showing great excitement/passion. **rhapsodical** [ræp'sɒdɪkl] *adj.* excited/passionate. **rhapsodize,** *v.* (over) to praise (sth) extravagantly.

rheostat ['rɪəstæt] *n.* device for making lights fade by cutting down the flow of electric current gradually.

rhesus ['riːsəs] *adj.* **r. monkey** = small monkey, often used in laboratories for scientific research; **r. factor** = substance in the blood (or absent from it) which can affect newborn babies and people having blood transfusions; **r. positive** = having a rhesus factor; **r. negative** = with no rhesus factor.

rhetoric ['retərɪk] *n.* art of speaking forcefully and eloquently. **rhetorical** [rɪ'tɒrɪkl] *adj.* referring to rhetoric; **r. question** = question to which you do not expect an answer.

rheumatism ['ruːmətɪzəm] *n.* disease causing pains in the joints or muscles. **rheumatic** [ruː'mætɪk] *adj.* referring to rheumatism; **r. fever** = serious disease of children and young people where your joints swell. **rheumaticky,** *adj. inf.* rheumatic. **rheumatics,** *n. pl. inf.* rheumatism. **rheumatoid arthritis,** *n.* continuing disease of the joints where they become stiff, swollen and painful.

rhinestone ['raɪnstəʊn] *n.* imitation colourless precious stone.

rhinoceros [raɪ'nɒsərəs], *inf.* **rhino** ['raɪnəʊ] *n.* (*pl.* **-es, -os**) huge Asiatic or African animal with a thick skin and one or two horns on its head.

rhizome ['raɪzəʊm] *n.* thick stem which lies on the ground like a root and produces shoots.

rhododendron [rəʊdə'dendrən] *n.* large evergreen shrub with clusters of huge colourful flowers.

rhombus ['rɒmbəs] *n.* shape with four equal sides but with no right angles. **rhomboid. 1.** *adj.* shaped like a rhombus/diamond-shaped. **2.** *n.* four-sided shape with opposite sides equal in length and no right angles.

rhubarb ['ruːbaːb] *n.* garden plant with large poisonous leaves, whose stalks are cooked as a dessert.

rhyme [raɪm] **1.** *n.* (*a*) sameness of sounds between two words (used in poetry). (*b*) little piece of poetry; **nursery r.** = (often nonsensical) piece of poetry for children. **2.** *v.* (**with**) to have the same sound as; **rhyming slang** = slang devised in London, where words are replaced by words or phrases which rhyme with them.

rhythm ['rɪðəm] *n.* regular beat in music/poetry, etc. **rhythmic(al)** ['rɪðmɪk(l)] *adj.* with a regular beat. **rhythmically,** *adv.* in a rhythmical way.

rib [rɪb] **1.** *n.* (*a*) one of several bones forming a cage across the chest. (*b*) piece of meat with the rib attached to it; **spare ribs** = cooked pork ribs in a savoury sauce. (*c*) curved timber which is part of the structure of a ship; one of the spokes of an umbrella. (*d*) thicker part in a leaf. (*e*) thicker line of stitches in knitting. **2.** *v. inf.* to tease (s.o.). **ribbed**, *adj.* with ribs. **rib-cage**, *n.* all the ribs in an animal.

ribald ['rɪbəld] *adj.* rude (song/joke). **ribaldry**, *n.* rude jokes.

ribbon ['rɪbn] *n.* long flat thin piece of material for tying or decoration; **typewriter r.** = flat piece of material covered with ink, which is struck by the letters in a typewriter; **r. development** = building of lines of houses along the side of a road stretching into the countryside.

riboflavin [raibəu'fleivin] *n.* type of vitamin B.

ribonucleic acid [ri:bəunju:'kleɪk 'æsɪd] *n.* substance in cells which takes information from the DNA and converts it to enzymes and proteins.

rice [raɪs] *n.* common tropical cereal, grown in wet ground or water; **brown r.** = rice which still has its outer covering; **wild r.** = plant of North America, which resembles rice; **r. pudding** = dessert made of rice, milk and sugar; **r. paper** = very thin paper which you can eat and which is used in cooking.

rich [rɪtʃ] **1.** *adj.* (**-er, -est**) (*a*) having a great deal of money. (*b*) (food) with a lot of cream/fat/eggs, etc. in it. (*c*) deep and resonant (voice); dark (colour). (*d*) fertile (soil). (*e*) **r. in** = with many resources. **2.** *n.* **the r.** = rich people. **riches** ['rɪtʃɪz] *n.* wealth. **richly**, *adv.* splendidly; **you richly deserve it** = you deserve it very much. **richness**, *n.* wealth; being rich.

Richter scale ['rɪxtə'skeɪl] *n.* scale for measuring earthquakes.

rick [rɪk] **1.** *n.* (*a*) large pile of straw or hay built like a house. (*b*) sprain. **2.** *v.* to twist/sprain (ankle, back).

rickets ['rɪkɪts] *n.* disease of children (caused by lack of vitamins) where bones become bent. **rickety**, *adj.* wobbly (chair).

rickshaw, ['rɪkʃɔ:] *n.* light wheeled chair pulled by a man.

ricochet ['rɪkəʃeɪ] *v.* (**ricocheted** ['rɪkəʃeɪd]) to bounce off a surface at an angle.

rid [rɪd] *v.* (**rid**) to clear away; **to get r. of sth** = to dispose of sth/to throw sth away. **riddance**, *n.* **good r.** = I am glad to get rid of it.

-ridden [rɪdn] *suffix meaning* filled with/affected by.

riddle ['rɪdl] **1.** *n.* (*a*) guessing game where you have to guess the answer to a deliberately puzzling question. (*c*) large sieve for separating soil from stones. **2.** *v.* (*a*) to put (soil) through a sieve. (*b*) **to r. with bullets** = to shoot many times. **riddled with**, *adj.* full of.

ride [raɪd] **1.** *n.* trip/journey on horseback/on a bicycle/in a car, etc.; *Sl.* **he was taken for a r.** = (i) they tricked him; (ii) they murdered him. **2.** *v.* (**rode, has ridden**) (*a*) to go for a trip on horseback/on a bicycle/in a car, etc. (*b*) (*of ships*) **to r. at anchor** = to float; **the ships rode out the storm** = they remained at anchor during the storm. (*c*) **to r. a blow** = to move backwards to make a blow softer. **rider**, *n.* (*a*) person who rides. (*b*) additional clause to a contract. **riderless**, *adj.* (horse) with no rider. **ride up**, *v.* (*of dress, etc.*) to move upwards through movement of the body. **riding**, *n.* (*a*) sport of going on horseback; **r. school** = school where you learn to ride a horse. (*b*) (*Canada*) constituency. **riding lights**, *n. pl.* lights on a ship at anchor.

ridge [rɪdʒ] *n.* long narrow raised part; **r. tent** = tent made of two sloping sides and a horizontal pole. **ridged**, *adj.* with ridges.

ridicule ['rɪdɪkju:l] **1.** *n.* mocking/laughing at s.o.; **to hold s.o. up to r.** = to laugh at s.o. **2.** *v.* to laugh at (s.o./sth). **ridiculous**, *adj.* silly/which can be laughed at. **ridiculously**, *adv.* in a silly way. **ridiculousness**, *n.* silliness.

rife [raɪf] *adj.* common.

riffle ['rɪfl] *v.* to flick (**through** the pages of a book).

riffraff ['rɪfræf] *n.* (*no pl.*) worthless ordinary people.

rifle ['raɪfl] **1.** *n.* hand gun with a long barrel with spiral grooves inside. **2.** *v.* (*a*) to search and to steal from. (*b*) to make spiral grooves inside a gun barrel.

rift [rɪft] *n.* split/crack.

rig [rɪg] **1.** *n.* (*a*) way in which a ship's sails

are arranged. (b) metal construction for drilling for minerals. (c) inf. set of clothes. 2. v. (rigged) (a) to fit out a ship with sails. (b) to arrange a dishonest result. **rigging**, n. ropes on a ship. **rig-out**, n. inf. set of clothes. **rig up**, v. inf. to arrange/to construct (sth) quickly.

rigg [rɪg] n. small white sea fish.

right [raɪt] 1. adj. (a) good/honest. (b) correct; **quite r.!** = perfectly correct! (c) **to get on the r. side of s.o.** = to make s.o. favour you; inf. **on the r. side of forty** = less than forty years old. (d) **r. angle** = angle of 90°. (e) straight/in order; **is he in his r. mind?** = is he sane? **she's all r. again** = she's better. (f) not left; referring to the hand which most people use for writing. 2. n. (a) what is correct/good; **in the r.** = not to be criticized. (b) legal title to sth; **she has no r. to be here** = she should not be here; **civil rights** = legal entitlements of every citizen; **by rights** = if things were done properly. (c) the right-hand side/the right-hand direction; **the r.** = political parties which are conservative. 3. adj. (a) **r. on** = straight on. (b) **r. away** = immediately. (c) completely; **it serves you r.** = you deserved it. (e) to the right-hand side. 4. v. to correct; to make (sth) return to its correct position. 5. inter. (a) agreed/OK. (b) inf. do you understand? **right-angled**, adj. with a 90° angle. **righteous** ['raɪtʃəs] adj. virtuous/very good. **righteously**, adv. in a righteous way. **righteousness**, n. virtue/goodness. **rightful**, adj. legally correct. **rightfully**, adv. in a rightful way. **right-hand**, adj. referring to the right hand; **right-hand man** = most particular helper. **right-handed**, adj. (person) who uses the right hand for writing/working, etc. **rightist**, n. member of a conservative political group. **rightly**, adv. correctly; **I can't r. say** = I am not very sure. **right-minded**, adj. (person) who has correct ideas/who thinks in the way most people think. **rightness**, n. correctness. **right of way**, n. (a) right to walk over s.o. else's property. (b) right (of one vehicle) to go first at a crossroads. **right-wing**, adj. belonging to the conservative political parties.

right-winger, n. person who is on the right politically.

rigid ['rɪdʒɪd] adj. stiff/unbending/inflexible. **rigidly**, adv. stiffly. **rigidity** [rɪ'dʒɪdɪtɪ] n. being rigid.

rigmarole ['rɪgmərəʊl] n. long incoherent speech/meaningless jumble of words.

rigour, Am. **rigor** ['rɪgə] n. severity (of the law, etc.); harshness (of the climate). **rigor mortis** [-'mɔːtɪs] n. stiffening of a body after death. **rigorous**, adj. very strict. **rigorously**, adv. in a rigorous way.

rile [raɪl] v. inf. to annoy.

rill [rɪl] n. small stream.

rim [rɪm] n. edge of a wheel/of a cup; frame of spectacles. **rimless**, adj. (spectacles) with no frame. **rimmed**, adj. with a rim.

rime [raɪm] n. white frost.

rind [raɪnd] n. skin on fruit/meat/cheese.

ring [rɪŋ] 1. n. (a) circular piece of metal/wood, etc., with a hole in the centre. (b) anything shaped like a circle; inf. **to run rings around s.o.** = to do things more efficiently than s.o. (c) group of people (usu. criminals). (d) centre of a circus where performances take place; square place where a boxing/wrestling match takes place. (e) sound of a bell. (f) call on the telephone. 2. v. (rang, has rung) (a) to make a sound of a bell; inf. **it rings a bell** = it reminds me of sth. (b) **my ears are ringing** = there is a sound like that of bells in my ears. (c) to telephone; **to r. s.o. up** = to call s.o. on the telephone; **to r. back** = to phone in reply to a phone call; **to r. off** = to stop the telephone call/to put down the receiver. 3. v. (ringed) (a) to put a ring on the leg of a wild bird for marking purposes. (b) to mark with a circle. **ringer**, n. (a) person who rings church bells. (b) inf. **dead r.** = person/horse exactly similar to another. **ringleader**, n. chief of a gang or group/person who organizes a crime. **ringlet**, n. long curl (of hair). **ringmaster**, n. master of ceremonies in a circus. **ring road**, n. bypass/road which goes round a town. **ringside**, adj. by the side of a ring. **ringworm**, n. disease of the skin which causes round red patches.

rink [rɪŋk] *n.* place where you can roller-skate or skate on ice; ice for skating.

rinse [rɪns] **1.** *n.* (*a*) putting soapy washing/soapy hair through clean water to remove the soap. (*b*) coloured liquid for rinsing hair. **2.** *v.* to put (soapy/dirty things) into clean water to remove the soap/the dirt.

riot ['raɪət] **1.** *n.* (*a*) disorder among crowds of people; **to run r.** = to become disordered/to get out of control; **to read s.o. the r. act** = to warn s.o. to stop being disorderly. (*b*) mass (of sounds/colours). (*c*) very amusing film/play, etc. **2.** *v.* to take part in a riot/to get out of control. **rioter,** *n.* person who takes part in a riot. **rioting,** *n.* riots/outbreaks of civil disorder. **riotous,** *adj.* wild/out of control. **riotously,** *adv.* in a riotous way. **riot police,** *n.* police specially equipped to deal with rioters.

rip [rɪp] **1.** *n.* tear (in cloth). **2.** *v.* (**ripped**) to tear; *inf.* **to let r.** = to allow sth to go freely. **ripcord,** *n.* cord you pull to make a parachute open. **rip off,** *v.* (*a*) to tear off. (*b*) *Sl.* **to rip s.o. off** = to cheat s.o./to make s.o. pay too much. **rip-off,** *n. Sl.* bad deal/thing which costs too much. **rip-roaring,** *adj.* wild/noisy (party); great (success). **ripsaw,** *n.* saw with large teeth, for rough cutting.

RIP [ɑːraɪˈpiː] *short for* Rest in Peace, Requiescat in Pace.

riparian [rɪˈpeərɪən] *adj.* (*formal*) referring to the banks of a river.

ripe [raɪp] *adj.* (**-er, -est**) ready to eat/to be harvested; **to a r. old age** = until very old; **the time is r. for sth** = it is the right time to do sth. **ripen,** *v.* to become ripe. **ripeness,** *n.* readiness; state of being ripe.

riposte [rɪˈpɒst] **1.** *n.* quick, sharp reply. **2.** *v.* to make a quick, sharp reply.

ripple ['rɪpl] **1.** *n.* little wave. **2.** *v.* to make little waves.

rise [raɪz] **1.** *n.* (*a*) movement upwards; slope upwards. (*b*) increase in salary. (*c*) **to give r. to sth** = to start sth. **2.** *v.* (**rose, has risen**) (*a*) to move upwards; to get up; to get out of bed. (*b*) (*of court*) to stop meeting. (*c*) (*of a river*) to start. (*d*) **to r. in revolt/to r. against s.o.** = to riot/to rebel. **riser,** *n.* (*a*) **early r.** = person who gets up early in

the morning. (*b*) vertical board holding up the tread of a staircase. **rising. 1.** *adj.* which is moving upwards/which is increasing; **r. generation** = new generation which will follow the present one; **r. forty** = nearly forty years old. **2.** *n.* (*a*) movement upwards. (*b*) rebellion/revolt.

risible ['rɪzɪbl] *adj.* laughable.

risk [rɪsk] **1.** *n.* possible harm; dangerous chance; **they run the r. of being caught** = they may well be caught. **2.** *v.* to chance/to do sth which may possibly harm. **riskily,** *adv.* in a risky way. **riskiness,** *n.* being risky. **risky,** *adj.* (**-ier, -iest**) dangerous/which may cause harm.

risotto [rɪˈsɒtəʊ] *n.* Italian dish of cooked rice with meat/fish/vegetables in it.

risqué ['riːskeɪ] *adj.* slightly indecent.

rissole ['rɪsəʊl] *n.* fried ball of meat/fish, etc.

rite [raɪt] *n.* religious ceremony; **last rites** = communion for s.o. who is dying. **ritual** ['rɪtjʊəl] *adj. & n.* (referring to) a religious ceremony. **ritually,** *adv.* in a ritual way.

rival ['raɪvl] **1.** *n. & adj.* (person) who competes. **2.** *v.* (**rivalled**) to compete with s.o.; to be of similar quality. **rivalry,** *n.* competition.

riven ['rɪvn] *adj.* (*formal*) split.

river ['rɪvə] *n.* large stream of water which goes into another stream, or into the sea. **riverside,** *adj.* on the banks of a river.

rivet ['rɪvɪt] **1.** *n.* nail which fastens metal plates together. **2.** *v.* (*a*) to fasten metal plates together. (*b*) to attract s.o.'s attention.

Riviera [rɪvɪˈeərə] *n.* beautiful south coast.

rivulet ['rɪvjʊlət] *n.* little stream.

Rn *symbol for* radon.

RNA [ɑːenˈeɪ] *abbrev. for* ribonucleic acid.

roach [rəʊtʃ] *n.* (*a*) (*pl.* **roach**) small freshwater fish. (*b*) (*pl.* **roaches**) *inf.* cockroach.

road [rəʊd] *n.* (*a*) path for cars and other vehicles; way of getting somewhere; **the r. to success** = the path which leads to success; **on the r.** = travelling from place to place (as a salesman/worker). (b) **roads** = part of the sea near a port where ships can lie at anchor. **roadblock,** n. barrier put across a road by the police. **roadhog,** n. inf. fast dangerous driver. **roadhouse,** n. hotel by a main road. **roadie,** n. inf. person who organizes a travelling pop group. **roadmender,** n. person who repairs the road surface. **roadside,** n. by the side of a road. **roadstead,** n. part of the sea near a port where ships can lie at anchor. **roadway,** n. main surface of a road. **roadworks,** n. pl. repairs to a road. **roadworthiness,** n. being roadworthy. **roadworthy,** adj. in a fit state to be driven on a road.

roam [rəʊm] v. to wander.

roan [rəʊn] adj. & n. (brown horse) with grey hairs in its coat.

roar [rɔː] **1.** n. loud, deep call; loud shouting. **2.** v. to make a loud call. **roaring. 1.** adj. wild (success); **to do a r. trade in** = to sell sth rapidly. **2.** n. sound of loud, deep calls.

roast [rəʊst] **1.** n. meat which has been/which will be cooked in an oven. **2.** v. to cook over a fire/in an oven. **3.** adj. which has been roasted; **r. beef. roasting,** adj. (chicken) which is ready to be roasted.

rob [rɒb] v. **(robbed)** to steal from s.o. **robber,** n. person who steals money from s.o. **robbery,** n. stealing.

robe [rəʊb] n. **1.** long, loose dress (for men or women); Am. dressing gown. **2.** v. to dress in a robe.

robin ['rɒbɪn] n. common small brown bird with a red breast; **round r.** = letter of complaint signed by many people.

robot ['rəʊbɒt] n. machine which works like a man; (in science fiction) machine which looks a little like a man and which can act like one. **robotics** [rəʊ'bɒtɪks] n. science of electronic robots.

robust [rə'bʌst] adj. strong/vigorous. **robustly,** adv. in a robust way. **robustness,** n. being robust.

rock [rɒk] **1.** n. (a) stone/solid part of the earth's surface. (b) large piece of stone; inf. **on the rocks** = (i) bankrupt; (ii) (whisky) with ice; **r. plant** = alpine plant. (c) hard pink sweet shaped like a stick, often with the name of a town printed in it. (d) music with a strong rhythm. **2.** v. to sway from side to side; to make (sth) sway from side to side; inf. **don't r. the boat** = don't disturb what has been arranged. **rock bottom,** n. the lowest point. **rock cake,** n. small cake with currants in it. **rocker,** n. (a) semicircular wooden piece which a rocking chair stands on. (b) Am. rocking chair; inf. **off one's r.** = mad. (c) type of electric switch which rocks. **rockery,** n. garden planted around a collection of rocks. **rocking,** adj. swaying; **rocking-horse** = child's wooden horse on rockers; **rocking-chair** = chair which rocks backwards and forwards on rockers. **rock salmon,** n. dogfish. **rocky,** adj. (a) full of rocks. (b) inf. wobbly.

rocket ['rɒkɪt] **1.** n. (a) type of firework which, when lit, flies up into the sky; spacecraft; type of bomb which is shot through space at an enemy. (b) engine driven by burning gas, which powers a spacecraft or bomb. (c) inf. **to give s.o. a r.** =to criticize/reprimand s.o. **2.** v. to shoot upwards very fast. **rocketry,** n. (no pl.) science of space rockets.

rococo [rə'kəʊkəʊ] adj. & n. ornate flowery (style of architecture of the 18th century).

rod [rɒd] n. (a) long stick. (b) **fishing r.** = long stick with a line attached, used for fishing.

rode [rəʊd] v. see **ride.**

rodent ['rəʊdənt] n. animal which chews and gnaws (such as a mouse/rat, etc.).

rodeo [rəʊ'deɪəʊ] n. (pl. **-os**) display of skill by cowboys.

roe [rəʊ] n. (a) fish eggs. (b) type of small deer. **roebuck,** n. male roe deer.

roentgen ['rʌntjən] adj. referring to X-rays.

roger ['rɒdʒə] inter. & signal meaning message received and understood.

rogue [rəʊg] adj. & n. (a) wicked/dishonest person. (b) **r. elephant** = (i) elephant driven out of the herd by the other elephants; (ii) person who does not behave in the same way as others. **roguery,** n. roguish behaviour. **roguish,** adj. wicked/dishonest.

roisterer ['rɔɪstərə] n. person who celebrates noisily. **roistering,** n. noisy celebrations.

role [rəʊl] *n.* part played by s.o. (in a play or in real life).

roll [rəʊl] **1.** *n.* (*a*) thing which has been turned over and over to make a tube; **swiss r.**/*Am.* **jelly r.** = cake rolled up with jam or cream in it; **sausage r.** = small pastry with a sausage inside. (*b*) very small loaf of bread. (*c*) list of names; **r. of honour** = list of prizewinners/list of soldiers who have died during a war. (*d*) movement from side to side. (*e*) rumble (of drums). **2.** *v.* (*a*) to make a tube out of sth flat. (*b*) to flatten by using a roller. (*c*) to make (sth) move forward by turning it over and over; *inf.* **rolling in money** = having a great deal of money. (*d*) to rock from side to side. (*e*) **to r. one's r's** = when speaking the letter 'r', to make the tip of the tongue vibrate. (*f*) to make a low rumbling noise. (*g*) *Am. inf.* to attack and rob (s.o.). **rollcall,** *n.* calling names from a list. **roller,** *n.* (*a*) round object which rolls; **steam r.** = machine for flattening new road surfaces. (*b*) large wave in the sea. (*c*) **r. towel** = continuous towel hanging on a horizontal bar. (*d*) plastic tube used for rolling hair into curls. **roller coaster,** *n. Am.* fairground railway which goes up and down steep slopes. **roller-skate. 1.** *n.* device with wheels which you strap to your foot so as to glide along fast. **2.** *v.* to glide on roller-skates. **roller-skating,** *n.* sport of going on roller-skates. **rollng,** *adj.* (countryside) which is a mass of small hills; **r. pin** = wooden roller with handles, for flattening pastry; **r. stock** = carriages/wagons/engines used on a railway; **r. stone** = person who never lives long in one place. **rollmop,** *n.* herring fillet, spiced and rolled. **roll on/ roll off,** *n.* ferry where cars, lorries and buses can drive straight on and off the ship. **roll-top,** *adj.* **r. desk** = desk with a cover made of slats of wood which slide upwards to open it.

rollicking ['rɒlɪkɪŋ] *adj.* noisy and jolly.

roly-poly ['rəʊlɪ'pəʊlɪ] *n.* (*a*) cooked pudding made of pastry rolled round jam. (*b*) *adj. & n. inf.* fat (person).

ROM [rɒm] *n.* read-only memory, computer memory with data programmed into it, which can only be read, but not changed.

Roman ['rəʊmən] *adj.* referring to Rome; **roman** = printing type with straight letters; **R. candle** = type of firework giving a brilliant fountain of light; **R. numerals** = numbers written in the Roman style (I, II, III, IV, etc.). **Roman Catholic,** *adj. & n.* (person) belonging to the Christian church of which the Pope is the head. **Roman Catholicism,** *n.* beliefs of the Roman Catholic church.

romance [rə'mæns] **1.** *n.* (*a*) **r. language** = language which has derived from Latin. (*b*) love affair. (*c*) love story. (*d*) story remote from daily life. **2.** *v.* to invent/to make up a story. **romantic** [rə'mæntɪk] *adj.* (*a*) full of mystery and romance. (*b*) (literary/artistic style) which is very imaginative/based on personal emotions. **romantically,** *adv.* in a romantic way. **romanticism,** *n.* romantic literary style. **romanticize,** *v.* to turn (sth) into a romantic story.

Romanesque [rəʊmə'nesk] *adj. & n.* architectural style with round arches and vaults found in Europe in the early Middle Ages.

Romanian [ruː'meɪnɪən] **1.** *adj.* referring to Romania. **2.** *n.* (*a*) person from Romania. (*b*) language spoken in Romania.

Romany ['rəʊmənɪ] *n.* (*a*) gipsy. (*b*) language spoken by gipsies.

romp [rɒmp] **1.** *n.* energetic children's game. **2.** *v.* to play about energetically; **to r. home** = win easily. **rompers,** *n.* one-piece suit for a baby.

rondo ['rɒndəʊ] *n.* (*pl.* **-os**) piece of music where the the same theme is repeated several times.

rood [ruːd] *n.* **r. screen** = screen built across a church, separating the chancel from the nave.

roof [ruːf] **1.** *n.* (*a*) covering over a building. (*b*) top of the inside of the mouth. (*c*) top of a car/bus/lorry, etc.; **sunshine r.** = roof which you can open in fine weather; **r. rack** = grid fixed to the roof of a car for carrying luggage. **2.** *v.* to put a roof on (a building).

rook [rʊk] **1.** *n.* (*a*) large black bird of the crow family. (*b*) (*in chess*) piece shaped like a castle. **2.** *v. Sl.* to cheat. **rookery,** *n.* place where rooks nest; colony of penguins/seals.

rookie ['rʊkɪ] *n. inf.* new recruit in the armed forces/in the police.

room [ruːm] **1.** *n.* (*a*) one of the divisions inside a house. (*b*) space; **to make r. for** = squeeze up to give space for; **there's r. for improvement** = things could be improved. **2.** *v.* to live in furnished rooms. **rooming-house,** *n. Am.* house with furnished rooms to let. **room-mate,** *n.* person with whom you share a room. **roomy,** *adj.* (**-ier, -iest**) spacious.

roost [ruːst] **1.** *n.* perch for a bird; **to rule the r.** = be in charge/be the boss. **2.** *v.* to perch. **rooster,** *n.* cockerel.

root [ruːt] **1.** *n.* (*a*) part of a plant which goes down into the ground, and which takes nourishment from the soil; part of a hair/a tooth which goes down into the skin; **to take r.** = to start to grow; **to put down roots** = to begin to feel at home in a place. (*b*) source. (*c*) (*in language*) word which is a base for other words. (*d*) **square r.** = number which if multiplied by itself gives the number you have; **cube r.** = number which if multiplied by itself twice gives the number you have. **2.** *v.* to put down/to make roots; **deeply rooted fear** = fear which is very strongly felt. (*b*) (**for**) to dig (sth) up/to look for (sth); *Am.* **to r. for a team** = to cheer a team on. **root beer,** *n. Am.* dark fizzy drink, flavoured with roots. **root crop,** *n.* crop which is grown for its edible roots (such as carrots, turnips, etc.). **rootless,** *adj.* with no roots. **rootstock,** *n.* plant on which another is grafted. **root up, root out,** *v.* to pull up (a plant) by its roots; to remove (sth) completely.

rope [rəʊp] **1.** *n.* thick string/thick cord; *inf.* **he knows the ropes** = he knows all about it/how to go about doing it. **2.** *v.* to tie together with a rope; **to r. s.o. in** = to get s.o. to help/to join; **to r. off** = to stop people going into a place by putting a rope around it. **ropy,** *adj.* (**-ier, -iest**) *inf.* of bad quality; not healthy.

rosary ['rəʊzərɪ] *n.* string of beads used by Catholics when saying prayers.

rose [rəʊz] **1.** *n.* (*a*) scented flower

which grows on a prickly bush. (*b*) pink colour; *inf.* **see through r. coloured spectacles** = see things as being very good, when they are not. (*c*) piece of metal/plastic with many holes in it, which is attached to the spout of a watering can, so that the water comes out in a spray. **2.** *v. see* **rise. roseate** ['rəʊzɪət] *adj.* deep pink. **rosebud,** *n.* flower bud of a rose. **rose window,** *n.* large round decorated window found usu. in the west wall of a church. **rosewood,** *n.* fragrant hard red wood, used for making furniture. **rosiness,** *n.* being rosy. **rosy,** *adj.* (**-ier, -iest**) (*a*) bright pink. (*b*) very favourable.

rosé [rəʊ'seɪ] *n.* pink wine.

rosemary ['rəʊzmərɪ] *n.* common evergreen herb with scented leaves.

rosette [rə'set] *n.* ribbon bunched to look like a flower, used as a decoration or as a badge.

rosin ['rɒzɪn] *n.* solid resin used to rub a violin bow.

roster ['rɒstə] *n.* list of duties which have to be done and the people who have to do them.

rostrum ['rɒstrəm] *n.* raised stand for a speaker.

rot [rɒt] **1.** *n.* (*a*) decay; **dry r.** = decay in house timbers caused by a fungus; **the r. has set in** = things are beginning to go badly. (*b*) nonsense. **2.** *v.* (**rotted**) to decay; to go bad. **rotten,** *adj.* decayed; *inf.* **to feel r.** = (i) to feel ill; (ii) to feel ashamed. **rotter,** *n. inf.* bad person.

rota ['rəʊtə] *n.* list of duties which have to be done in turn and the people who have to do them.

rotate [rəʊ'teɪt] *v.* to turn round. **rotary** ['rəʊtərɪ] *adj.* which turns/rotates; **r. printing press** = one where the paper passes round large rollers. **rotation** [rəʊ'teɪʃn] *n.* turning/taking turns; **r. of crops** = growing different crops in turn. **rotatory,** *adj.* turning (motion). **rotor,** *n.* piece of machinery which rotates; the blades of a helicopter.

rote [rəʊt] *n.* learning by heart.

rotisserie [rəʊ'tiːsərɪ] *n.* electric machine for turning meat on a spit in front of heat.

rotund [rə'tʌnd] *adj.* round/fat. **rotunda,** *n.* circular building with a dome. **rotundity,** *n.* being rotund.

rouble ['ruːbl] *n.* unit of money of the Soviet Union.

rouge [ruːʒ] *n.* pink cream/powder which you put on your face to give yourself more colour. **rouged,** *adj.* wearing rouge.

rough [rʌf] **1.** *adj.* (**-er, -est**) (*a*) not smooth/bumpy/uneven; **to give s.o. a r. time** = treat s.o. badly; **r. house** = fight. (*b*) unfinished; approximate (translation). **2.** *n.* (*a*) area of long grass on a golf course. (*b*) unfinished design. (*c*) hooligan. **3.** *adv.* (*a*) brutally/harshly. (*b*) **to sleep r.** = without a proper bed. **4.** *v.* **to r. out** = to make a rough design; **to r. it** = to live uncomfortably; **to r. s.o. up** = to beat/to attack s.o. **roughage,** *n.* coarse stuff, such as bran, which you eat to help digestion. **rough and ready,** *adj.* approximate; not beautifully finished. **rough and tumble,** *n.* violent life; violent game. **roughcast,** *n.* covering for the outside of the walls of a house, made of small stones. **rough diamond,** *n.* person who is uncultivated but pleasant. **roughen,** *v.* to make/to become rough. **roughly,** *adv.* in a rough way. **roughneck,** *n.* rowdy hooligan. **roughness,** *n.* being rough. **roughshod,** *adj.* **to ride r. over s.o.'s feelings** = to pay no attention to s.o.'s feelings.

roulette [ruːˈlet] *n.* game of chance where bets are made on the number of a box where a small ball will stop in a rotating wheel; **Russian r.** = game played with a revolver containing a single bullet which is spun round and then fired at the player's head.

round [raʊnd] **1.** *adj.* (**-er, -est**) (*a*) circular/shaped like a circle. (*b*) **r. trip** = trip to a destination and back. (*c*) exact (number). **2.** *n.* (*a*) circle. (*b*) **r. of toast** = piece(s) of toast from one slice of bread; **r. of sandwiches** = sandwiches from two slices of bread. (*c*) regular route; **newspaper r.** = number of houses where a boy regularly delivers newspapers; **r. of golf** = going round all the holes in a golf course. (*d*) part of a contest/of a boxing match. (*e*) **r. of drinks** = series of drinks bought by one person; **r. of applause** = burst of clapping. (*f*) one bullet; one shell. (*g*)

song for several voices, each starting at a different point. **3.** *adv.* (*a*) in a circle. (*b*) completely; **all year r.** = during the whole year. (*c*) surrounding; **he looked r.** = (i) he looked around him; (ii) he looked behind him. (*d*) from one to another; **he handed r. the cups of tea** = he handed a cup to each person; **is there enough cake to go r.?** = enough for everybody; **come r. for a drink** = come to my house. **4.** *prep.* in a circle/around (sth). **5.** *v.* (*a*) (*also* **round off**) to make round. (*b*) to go round (a corner). (*c*) **to r. on s.o.** = to attack s.o.; **to r. up** = to gather together. (*d*) to make a whole number; **to r. a number up** = to increase it to the nearest whole number above. **roundabout. 1.** *n.* (*a*) place where several roads meet and the traffic moves in a circle. (*b*) type of children's amusement in a park, a heavy *wooden wheel which you push to turn round and then sit on; (*in a fair*) a revolving machine (with wooden horses) on which you can ride. **2.** *adj.* not straight. **rounded,** *adj.* with smooth/round corners or edges. **rounders,** *n.* team game played with a bat and ball, where the batsman has to run round the pitch to score. **Roundhead,** *n.* supporter of Parliament in the English Civil War. **roundhouse,** *n.* circular building for repairing railway engines. **roundly,** *adv.* sharply/critically; totally. **roundsman,** *n.* man who delivers food to houses. **roundup,** *n.* gathering together.

rouse [raʊz] *v.* to wake (s.o.) who is sleeping; to get (s.o.) to act. **rousing,** *adj.* loud/exciting.

roustabout ['raʊstəbaʊt] *n.* labourer on an oil rig.

rout [raʊt] **1.** *n.* complete defeat (of an army). **2.** *v.* (*a*) to defeat completely. (*b*) to search; **to r. s.o. out** = to pull s.o. out from where he is hidden.

route [ruːt] **1.** *n.* way to be followed to get to a destination; **bus r.** = normal way which a bus follows; **r. march** = training march by soldiers. **2.** *v.* to send (s.o.) along a route.

routine [ruːˈtiːn] **1.** *n.* (*a*) normal/regular way of doing things; **daily r.** = things which you do every day. (*b*) instructions which carry out a task as part of a computer program. **2.** *adj.* normal/everyday. **routinely,** *adv.* (done) as a routine.

roux [ru:] *n.* mixture of fat and flour cooked to make a base for a sauce.

rove [rəʊv] *v.* to wander.

row¹ [rəʊ] **1.** *n.* (*a*) line (of chairs, etc.). (*b*) short trip in a rowing boat. **2.** *v.* to make a boat go forward by using oars. **rowboat,** *n. Am.* rowing boat. **rower,** *n.* person who rows. **rowing,** *n.* making a boat move by the use of oars; **r. boat** = small boat for rowing.

row² [raʊ] **1.** *n.* (*a*) loud noise. (*b*) sharp argument. **2.** *v.* to make a row.

rowan ['rəʊən] *n.* mountain ash.

rowdy ['raʊdɪ] **1.** *adj.* making a great deal of noise. **2.** *n.* rough person, who makes a lot of noise. **rowdily,** *adv.* in a rowdy way. **rowdiness,** *n.* rowdy behaviour.

rowel ['rəʊəl] *n.* little wheel with spikes, attached to a spur.

rowlock ['rɒlək] *n.* metal support for oars.

royal ['rɔɪəl] **1.** *adj.* referring to a king or queen; **R. Assent** = signing of a Bill by the Queen, by which it becomes an Act of Parliament; **R. Commission** = official group appointed by the government to investigate a problem; **the R. Family** = family of a king or queen; **r. blue** = bright dark blue; **a right r. welcome** = a splendid welcome. **2.** *n. inf.* **the Royals** = members of the Royal Family. **royalist,** *n.* person who is a political supporter of a king. **royally,** *adv.* splendidly/with great pomp. **royalty,** *n.* (*a*) state of being royal; members of a king's family. (*b*) money paid to the author of a book/an actor in a film/the owner of land where oil is found, etc., as a percentage of the receipts of sale.

RSVP [ɑːesviːˈpiː] *abbreviation for* répondez s'il vous plaît *meaning* please reply.

rub [rʌb] *v.* (**rubbed**) to move sth across the surface of sth else. **rubbing,** *n.* action of rubbing; *Am.* **r. alcohol** = pure alcohol used as an antiseptic. **rub down,** *v.* to rub (s.o./a horse) vigorously. **rub in,** *v.* to make (a cream) enter the skin by rubbing; *inf.* **don't rub**

it in = don't go on talking about my mistake. **rub out,** *v.* to remove (a pencil mark) with a rubber. **rub up,** *v. inf.* **to rub s.o. up the wrong way** = to make s.o. irritable.

rubber ['rʌbə] *n.* (*a*) elastic material made from the sap of a tree; **r. plant** = type of indoor plant with thick shiny green leaves. (*b*) *Am.* **rubbers** = rubber/plastic shoes worn over ordinary shoes to protect them. (*c*) number of games of bridge. (*d*) piece of rubber used for removing pencil marks. **rubberize,** *v.* to coat with rubber. **rubberneck. 1.** *n. inf.* tourist. **2.** *v. inf.* to visit a place as a tourist. **rubber stamp. 1.** *n.* stamp made of rubber, with words or figures cut on it, which is used for stamping documents. **2.** *v.* to agree to (sth) automatically without examining it. **rubbery,** *adj.* flexible and strong like rubber.

rubbish ['rʌbɪʃ] *n.* (*no pl.*) (*a*) waste/things which are to be thrown away. (*b*) nonsense. **rubbishy,** *adj.* useless; stupid.

rubble ['rʌbl] *n.* small stones/broken bricks, etc. used in constructing paths, etc.

rubella [ruːˈbelə] *n.* (*formal*) German measles.

rubicund ['ruːbɪkənd] *adj.* (*formal*) red (face).

rubric ['ruːbrɪk] *n.* written instructions; written heading to a piece of writing.

ruby ['ruːbɪ] **1.** *n.* red precious stone. **2.** *adj.* dark red (colour).

ruche [ruːʃ] *n.* cloth gathered into folds. **ruched,** *adj.* gathered in folds.

ruck [rʌk] **1.** *n.* (*a*) crease in cloth. (*b*) (*in Rugby*) group of players who fight for the ball. **2.** *v.* (*also* **ruck up**) to form creases.

rucksack ['rʌksæk] *n.* bag carried on the back of a walker.

ruckus ['rʌkəs] *n. inf.* fight.

ructions ['rʌkʃənz] *n. pl. inf.* argument/angry scene.

rudder ['rʌdə] *n.* flat plate at the stern of a boat/on the tail of an aircraft, used for steering.

ruddy ['rʌdɪ] *adj.* (**-ier, -iest**) (*a*) red/fire-coloured. (*b*) *Sl.* awful.

rude [ruːd] *adj.* (**-er, -est**) (*a*) impolite;

obscene. (*b*) sudden. (*c*) rough/
primitive. **rudely,** *adv.* not politely.
rudeness, *n.* being rude.

rudiments ['ru:dɪmənts] *n.* simple/el-
ementary facts. **rudimentary** [ru:dɪ-
'mentərɪ] *adj.* basic; not fully
developed.

rue [ru:] **1.** *n.* bitter herb. **2.** *v.* to regret.
rueful, *adj.* sorry/regretful. **ruefully,**
adv. in a rueful way.

ruff [rʌf] *n.* (*a*) wide collar of ruffed lace.
(*b*) bird with a ring of coloured feathers
round its neck.

ruffian ['rʌfɪən] *n.* hooligan/violent person.

ruffle ['rʌfl] **1.** *n.* material/lace gathered
into a bunch and used as decoration
on clothes/curtains, etc. **2.** *v.* to disturb
(feathers/water/s.o.'s hair); *inf.* **ruffled**
= flustered.

rug [rʌg] *n.* (*a*) small carpet. (*b*) thick
blanket, esp. one used for travelling.

Rugby ['rʌgbɪ] *n.* type of football played
with an oval ball, which can be passed
from hand to hand as well as being
kicked.

rugged ['rʌgɪd] *adj.* (*a*) rough/uneven.
(*b*) strict; sturdy. **ruggedly,** *adv.* in
a rugged way. **ruggedness,** *n.* being
rugged.

rugger ['rʌgə] *n. inf* Rugby.

ruin ['ru:ɪn] **1.** *n.* (*a*) wreck; complete
loss of all your money. (*b*) **ruins** = remains of collapsed buildings. **2.** *v.* (*a*) to
wreck/to spoil completely. (*b*) to bring
to financial collapse. **ruination** [ruɪ-
'neɪʃn] *n.* act of ruining. **ruined,** *adj.* in
ruins. **ruinous,** *adj.* so expensive as to
cause ruin. **ruinously,** *adv.* extremely
(expensive).

rule [ru:l] **1.** *n.* (*a*) general way of conduct; **as a r.** = generally/usually. (*b*)
strict order of the way to behave; (*in
industry*) **work to r.** = working only
according to the rules laid down in
the union agreement. (*c*) government.
(*d*) wood/metal rod with measurements
on it, used in carpentry. (*e*) straight
line (in printing). **2.** *v.* (*a*) to govern/
to control. (*b*) to give an official/legal
decision. (*c*) to draw a straight line
using a ruler; **ruled paper** = paper with
lines on it. **ruler,** *n.* (*a*) person who
governs. (*b*) strip of wood/plastic with

measurements marked on it, used for
drawing straight lines. **ruling. 1.** *adj.*
(party) which governs; **r. party** = party
which forms the government. **2.** *n.* legal
decision. **rule out,** *v.* to leave (sth) out/
not to consider (sth).

rum [rʌm] **1.** *n.* alcoholic drink made
from the juice of sugar cane. **2.** *adj. inf.*
odd/strange.

rumba ['rʌmbə] *n.* Caribbean dance with
a strong rhythm.

rumble ['rʌmbl] **1.** *n.* (*a*) low rolling
noise. (*b*) *Am. inf.* street fight. **2.** *v.* (*a*)
to make a low rolling noise. (*b*) *inf.* to
realise that (s.o.) is trying to deceive
you.

rumbustious [rʌm'bʌstʃəs] *adj. inf.*
wild/rowdy.

ruminate ['ru:mɪneɪt] *v.* (*a*) to chew
over food which has already been
swallowed once (as a cow does). (*b*)
to think over a problem. **ruminant**
['ru:mɪnənt] *adj.* & *n.* animal (like a
cow) which chews its cud. **rumination**
[ru:mɪ'neɪʃn] *n.* deep thought. **rumi-
native,** *adj.* thoughtful.

rummage ['rʌmɪdʒ] **1.** *n.* (*a*) searching
about for sth. (*b*) old junk; **r. sale** = sale
of unwanted objects for a charity. **2.** *v.*
to search about for sth.

rummy ['rʌmɪ] *n.* card game where each
player tries to collect sets of similar
cards or several cards in sequence.

rumour, *Am.* **rumor** ['ru:mə] *n.* story
passed on from one person to another
without necessarily being true. **rumoured,** *adj.* spread by rumour.

rump [rʌmp] *n.* back part of an animal.

rumple ['rʌmpl] *v.* to crush/to dishevel.

rumpus ['rʌmpəs] *n.* (*pl.* **-es**) noisy
disorder; fuss.

run [rʌn] **1.** *n.* (*a*) act of going quickly
on foot; **prisoner on the r.** = running
away from prison; **the soldiers broke
into a r.** = started to run; **go for a r.**
= (i) to take some exercise by running;
(ii) to go for a short ride in a car. (*b*)
period; **for three days on the r.** = for
three consecutive days; **in the long r.** =
eventually. (*c*) access to; **he has the r.
of the house** = he can go anywhere in
the house. (*d*) track for running, skiiing,
etc. (*e*) caged area where chickens are
kept. (*f*) point made in cricket/baseball.

(g) ladder/long hole in a stocking. (h) excessive demand; **r. on the pound** = sudden selling of the pound on foreign exchanges. (i) carrying out of a task by a computer. **2.** v. **(ran, has run)** (a) to go very quickly on foot; to race. (b) to travel (fast). (c) (of motor, transport) to work. (d) to **r. to** = to amount to. (e) to go in a direction. (f) to direct; **he runs his own business.** (g) to own and drive (a car). (h) to **r. a bath** = to fill a bath with (i) (of liquid) to flow; **this colour won't r.** = will not come out if put in water; **his nose is running** = liquid is coming from his nose (because he has a cold). **run across,** v. (a) to cross quickly on foot. (b) to find/to meet by chance. **run along,** v. to go alongside. **run away,** v. to escape. **runaway. 1.** n. person who has escaped. **2.** adj. **r. success** = great success. **run down,** v. (a) to go down quickly on foot. (b) (of clock, machine) to go slower. (c) to criticize (s.o.). (d) to reduce the quantity of. (e) to knock down (with a vehicle). (f) to **be r. down** = to feel unwell/tired. **rundown. 1.** adj. delapidated/not looked after. **2.** n. summary. **run for,** v. Am. to be a candidate for (an office). **run in,** v. (a) to work (a new engine) slowly until it works properly. (b) inf. to arrest (s.o.). **run into,** v. to meet (s.o.) by chance. **runner,** n. (a) person who is running (in a race). (b) shoot of a plant which makes roots where it touches the soil; **r. bean** = type of climbing bean. (c) sharp blade of a skate/a sledge. (d) narrow carpet. **runner up,** n. (pl. **runners up**) person who comes after the winner in a race. **running. 1.** adj. (a) which runs; **r. commentary** = commentary on an action while the action is taking place; **r. total** = total which is carried from one column of figures to the next. (b) used in running a race. (c) **for three days r.** = one after another. **2.** n. (a) race; **in the r. for** = a candidate for. (b) working. **run off,** v. (a) to escape/to flee. (b) to **run off several photocopies** = to make several photocopies. **run-of-the-mill,** adj. ordinary. **run on,** v. (a) to continue. (b) to use (sth) as a fuel. **run out,** v. (of goods) to go short. **run out of,** v. to be short of. **run over,** v. (a) to look at (sth) quickly. (b) to knock (s.o.)

down with a car. **run up,** v. (a) to go up quickly on foot. (b) to come closer quickly on foot. (c) **to run up against sth** = (i) to find sth by chance; (ii) to find your way blocked by sth. (d) to sew (sth) quickly. **runway,** n. track on which aircraft land.

runes [ru:nz] pl. n. ancient form of writing, used by early Germans. **runic,** adj. referring to runes; magic.

rung [rʌŋ] **1.** n. one of the bars on a ladder. **2.** v. see **ring.**

runnel ['rʌnl] n. gutter.

runny ['rʌni] adj. liquid; **he's got a r. nose** = his nose is running (because he has a cold).

runt [rʌnt] n. small person or animal.

rupee [ru:'pi:] n. money used in India and other countries.

rupture ['rʌptʃə] **1.** n. (a) break (in negotiations); burst/break (of part of the body). (b) hernia. **2.** v. (a) to break off (negotiations). (b) to burst through; **he ruptured himself lifting a heavy box** = the strain caused a hernia.

rural ['ruərəl] adj. referring to the countryside.

ruse ['ru:z] n. clever trick.

rush [rʌʃ] **1.** n. (pl. **-es**) (a) type of wild grass growing in water. (b) fast movement; **r. hour** = time of day when traffic is bad/when trains are full. (c) **rushes** = first prints of a film, before it has been edited. **2.** v. (a) to go forward fast; **don't r. me** = don't keep on hurrying me. (b) to attack suddenly.

rusk [rʌsk] n. hard biscuit given to babies to suck.

russet ['rʌsit] **1.** n. type of sweet brown apple. **2.** adj. & n. reddish-brown (colour).

Russian ['rʌʃn] **1.** adj. referring to Russia. **2.** n. (a) person from Russia. (b) language spoken in Russia.

Russo- ['rʌsəu] prefix meaning between Russia and another country.

rust [rʌst] **1.** n. (a) red substance formed on iron or steel which is left in damp air. (b) red fungus disease of plants. (c) reddish-brown (colour). **2.** v. to get rusty. **rustiness,** n. being rusty. **rustless,** adj. with no rust. **rust proof,** adj. (metal) which will not rust. **rusty,** adj. (-ier, -iest) (a) covered with rust. (b) not in practice; (person) who lacks practice.

rustic ['rʌstɪk] 1. adj. rough/of country style. 2. n. rough peasant. **rusticate,** v. to send (a student) away from university for a period as a punishment.

rustle ['rʌsl] 1. n. noise of dry leaves/silk, etc. rubbing together. 2. v. (a) to make a soft crackling noise. (b) to steal cattle. **rustler,** n. cattle thief. **rustle up,** v. inf. to get (sth) ready quickly. **rustling,** n. stealing (of cattle).

rut [rʌt] n. (a) long deep track made in soft earth by a wheel; **to get into a r.** = to start to lead a dull life with no excitement or career prospects. (b) period when a male deer is sexually excited. **rutted,** adj. (path) full of ruts. **rutting,** adj. (deer) in rut.

rutabaga ['ruːtəbeɪgə] n. Am. swede.

ruthless ['ruːθləs] adj. pitiless/cruel. **ruthlessly,** adv. cruelly. **ruthlessness,** n. cruelty.

rye [raɪ] n. (a) type of dark brown cereal. (b) American whisky made from rye. **ryegrass,** n. type of grass grown in pastures.

Ss

S symbol for sulphur.

Sabbath ['sæbəθ] n. seventh day of the week; religious day of rest; (for Jews) Saturday; (for Christians) Sunday.

sabbatical [sə'bætɪkl] n. & adj. (leave) granted to teachers, etc., for study and travel after a period of work.

sable ['seɪbl] n. small brown-furred arctic animal; fur from this animal.

sabotage ['sæbətɑːʒ] 1. n. malicious/deliberate destruction. 2. v. to destroy/to render useless deliberately. **saboteur** [sæbə'tɜː] n. person who commits sabotage.

sabre, Am. **saber** ['seɪbə] n. sword with curved blade.

sac [sæk] n. bag-like part of an animal/plant.

saccharin ['sækərɪn] n. extremely sweet substance used as a substitute for sugar. **saccharine,** adj. too sweet/sickly.

sacerdotal [sæsə'dəʊtl] adj. referring to priests.

sachet ['sæʃeɪ] n. small bag (of shampoo, etc.).

sack [sæk] 1. n. (a) plundering (of a town). (b) large bag made of strong rough cloth. (c) inf. dismissal; **to get/to be given the s.** = to be dismissed from a job. (d) inf. bed. 2. v. (a) to plunder. (b) inf. to dismiss (s.o.) from a job. **sackcloth,** n. **s. and ashes** = (i) clothes worn at times of penitence; (ii) symbol of repentance. **sackful,** n. amount held in a sack. **sacking,** n. coarse material from which sacks are made; old sacks.

sacrament ['sækrəmənt] n. (a) Christian religious ceremony. (b) the consecrated bread (and wine) taken at Communion. **sacramental** [sækrə'mentl] adj. referring to sacrament.

sacred ['seɪkrəd] adj. (a) associated with religion. (b) holy. (c) respected. **sacred cow,** n. inf. belief/idea which is not to be criticized. **sacredness,** n. being sacred.

sacrifice ['sækrɪfaɪs] 1. n. (a) killing of animal/person as an offering to a god. (b) animal killed as an offering to a god. (c) thing given up at personal cost in order to achieve sth else. 2. v. (a) to offer (sth) as a sacrifice. (b) to give up/to devote. **sacrificial** [sækrɪ'fɪʃl] adj. as a sacrifice.

sacrilege ['sækrɪlɪdʒ] n. using sth sacred in a disrespectful way. **sacrilegious** [sækrɪ'lɪdʒəs] adj. referring to sacrilege.

sacristy ['sækrɪstɪ] n. room in a church where vestments/vessels, etc., are kept. **sacristan,** n. person who looks after a church, esp. the vestments/holy vessels, etc.

sacrosanct ['sækrəʊsæŋkt] adj. very sacred/protected by religious respect.

sacrum ['seɪkrəm] n. triangular bone at the base of the spine.

sad [sæd] adj. (sadder, saddest) unhappy/sorrowful. **sadden,** v. to make unhappy. **sadly,** adv. unhappily. **sadness,** n. being sad.

saddle ['sædl] 1. n. (a) rider's seat on a bicycle/on the back of a horse; **in the s.** = in control. (b) ridge between two mountains. (c) **s. of lamb** = joint of meat from the back of a sheep. 2. v. (a) to put a saddle on (a horse, etc.). (b) to burden (s.o.) **with** a task or responsibility. **saddlebag,** n. bag attached to a bicycle; one of a pair of bags on a horse. **saddler,** n. maker of saddles and other equipment for horses. **saddlery,** *n.* shop making/selling saddles.

sadism ['seidizəm] *n.* pleasure derived from being cruel or watching cruelty. **sadist** ['seidist] *n.* person who delights in sadism. **sadistic** [sə'distik] *adj.* referring to sadism. **sadistically,** *adv.* in a sadistic way.

s.a.e. stamped addressed envelope.

safari [sə'fɑ:rɪ] *n.* hunting expedition in Africa; **s. park** = park where large wild animals run free, and visitors can look at them from their cars.

safe [seif] **1.** *n.* (*a*) fire-proof and burglar-proof box for valuables. (*b*) ventilated cupboard for food. **2.** *adj.* (**-er, -est**) (*a*) uninjured. (*b*) secure/out of danger. (*c*) certain/to be relied upon. **safe-conduct,** *n.* paper which allows s.o. to go through enemy territory. **safe deposit box,** *n.* box (in a bank) in which you can store valuables. **safeguard** ['seifgɑ:d] **1.** *n.* protection. **2.** *v.* to guard/to protect. **safely,** *adv.* without any danger; without being harmed.

safety ['seiftɪ] *n.* freedom from danger or risk; **road s.** = care to be taken by pedestrians and drivers; **s. belt** = belt worn in a car/in an aircraft as protection in case of accident; **s. catch** = lock which stops a gun being fired by accident; **s. curtain** = fireproof barrier between the stage and the auditorium in a theatre; **s. pin** = type of bent pin whose point is protected by a guard; **s. valve** = valve in steam-boiler, which lets out excess pressure automatically.

safflower ['sæflauə] *n.* plant which produces an oil used in cooking.

saffron ['sæfrən] **1.** *n.* orange-coloured powder made from crocus flowers, from which colouring and flavouring are obtained. **2.** *adj.* orange-coloured.

sag [sæg] **1.** *n.* bending under weight or pressure. **2.** *v.* (**sagged**) to sink/to bend (in the middle) under weight or pressure.

saga ['sɑ:gə] *n.* (*a*) story of heroic achievement or adventure. (*b*) series of books telling the history of a family.

sagacious [sə'geiʃəs] *adj.* (*formal*) wise/ shrewd. **sagaciously,** *adv.* wisely. **sagacity** [sə'gæsɪtɪ] *n.* exceptional intelligence/wisdom.

sage [seidʒ] **1.** *n.*: (*a*) aromatic herb used in cookery; **s. green** = greyish green colour. (*b*) very wise man. **2.** *adj.* wise/ discreet. **sagely,** *adv.* in a wise way.

Sagittarius [sædʒɪ'teəriəs] *n.* one of the signs of the zodiac, shaped like an archer.

sago ['seigəu] *n.* white powder used as food; **s. palm** = palm tree whose pith yields sago.

said [sed] *v. see* **say.**

sail [seil] **1.** *n.* (*a*) piece of canvas/nylon, etc., attached to the mast of a boat to catch the wind. (*b*) trip in a boat. (*c*) arm of a windmill which turns with the wind. **2.** *v.* (*a*) to travel on water. (*b*) to travel in a sailing boat; **to s. close to the wind** = (i) to sail nearly against the wind; (ii) to come very near to breaking the law. (*c*) to control (a sailing boat). (*d*) to glide in the air. **sailboat,** *n. Am.* sailing boat. **sailcloth,** *n.* canvas for making sails. **sailing. 1.** *adj.* (ship) which uses sails. **2.** *n.* journey by ship; **plain s.** = straightforward progress with no problems. **sailor** ['seilə] *n.* seaman/ person who sails; **good/bad s.** = person who is liable/not liable to seasickness.

saint [seint] *n.* (*a*) (*abbreviated with names to* **St** [snt]) person recognised by the Christian church as having led an exceptionally holy life, and canonized after death. (*b*) very good/ devoted person. **sainthood,** *n.* being a saint. **saintliness,** *n.* holiness/piety. **saintly,** *adj.* holy. **saintpaulia,** *n.* African violet.

saithe [seiθ] *n.* coley.

sake[1] [seik] *n.* **for the s. of sth/for sth's s.** = out of consideration for/in the interest of.

sake[2] ['sɑ:kɪ] *n.* Japanese rice wine.

salaam [sə'lɑ:m] **1.** *n.* bow made in Eastern countries to greet s.o. **2.** *v.* to make a salaam.

salacious [sə'leiʃəs] *adj.* erotic/obscene. **salaciously,** *adv.* in a salacious way. **salaciousness, salacity** [sə'læsɪtɪ] *n.* being salacious.

salad ['sæləd] *n.* cold dish of various cooked or raw vegetables; cold meat served with a dressing and lettuce; **s. cream** = type of sauce made of eggs/ oil/vinegar, etc., used on salad; **s. dress-**

ing = mixture of oil/vinegar, etc., used on salad; **fruit s.** = mixture of chopped fresh fruit.

salamander ['sæləmændə] *n.* small animal like a lizard.

salami [sə'lɑːmɪ] *n.* salty Italian sausage, eaten cold.

salary ['sælərɪ] *n.* fixed payment made to an employee, usu. every month. **salaried,** *adj.* (person) who is paid a salary.

sale [seɪl] *n.* (*a*) exchange of sth for money; **on/for s.** = ready to be sold. (*b*) goods sold at reduced/special prices for a short period of time. (*c*) organized selling of goods; **jumble s.** = selling of unwanted household goods; **s. of work** = selling of handmade goods. (*d*) **sales** = money received in a business. **saleable,** *adj.* fit for sale. **saleroom,** *n.* room in which an auction is carried out. **sales girl,** *n.* girl in a shop who sells goods to customers. **sales lady,** *n.* woman who sells goods to customers. **salesman,** *n.* (*pl.* **-men**) (*a*) person who sells a producer's goods to a shop. (*b*) man in a shop who sells goods to customers. **salesmanship,** *n.* the art of selling. **salesperson,** *n.* person who sells goods in a shop. **saleswoman,** *n.* (*pl.* **-women**) woman in a shop who sells goods to customers.

salient ['seɪlɪənt] **1.** *n.* projecting part of a fortification/of a line of battle. **2.** *adj.* prominent/conspicuous/most important.

saline ['seɪlaɪn] *adj.* containing salt. **salinity** [sə'lɪnɪtɪ] *n.* amount of salt.

saliva [sə'laɪvə] *n.* liquid formed in the mouth to help digestion. **salivary,** *adj.* **s. gland** = gland which produces saliva. **salivate** ['sæliveit] *v.* to make saliva. **salivation** [sælɪ'veɪʃn] *n.* act of salivating.

sallow ['sæləʊ] **1.** *adj.* (**-er, -est**) sickly yellow (complexion). **2.** *n.* willow tree.

sally ['sælɪ] **1.** *n.* (*a*) sudden rush (of soldiers) out of a defended position. (*b*) witticism. **2.** *v.* (*also* **sally forth**) to go out.

salmon ['sæmən] **1.** *n.* (*pl.* **salmon**) large pink-fleshed fish. **2.** *adj. & n.* orange-pink (colour). **salmon trout,** *n.* large sea trout with pink flesh.

Salmonella [sælmə'nelə] *n.* type of bacteria which grows on meat, eggs, and fish, and causes food poisoning.

salon ['sælɒn] *n.* hairdresser's/dressmaker's business; room/building housing a hairdresser's or dressmaker's.

saloon [sə'luːn] *n.* (*a*) large lounge in a ship. (*b*) comfortable bar in a public house. (*c*) *Am.* public bar. (*d*) **s. (car)** = covered car.

salsify ['sælsɪfɪ] *n.* vegetable with a long white root.

salt [sɔːlt] **1.** *n.* (*a*) white substance (sodium chloride) used to season and preserve food; *inf.* **to take sth with a pinch of s.** = not to believe sth completely. (*b*) (*in chemistry*) combination of a metal with an acid; (*c*) *inf.* **old s.** = experienced sailor. **2.** *adj.* containing salt; cured/preserved/seasoned with salt. **3.** *v.* to add salt to. **salt away,** *v.* to put (sth) aside for the future. **salt cellar,** *n.* small pot containing salt, usu. with a hole in the top so that it can be sprinkled on food. **salt-free,** *adj.* without salt. **saltiness, saltness,** *n.* being salty. **saltlick,** *n.* block of salt put in a field for cattle to lick. **saltpan,** *n.* enclosure where salt is formed as sea water evaporates. **saltpetre,** *Am.* **saltpeter** [sɔːlt'piːtə] *n.* potassium nitrate/powder used to make gunpowder. **salty,** *adj.* (**-ier, -iest**) containing salt.

salubrious [sə'luːbrɪəs] *adj.* (*formal*) healthy. **salubrity,** *n.* healthiness.

saluki [sə'luːkɪ] *n.* breed of hound.

salute [sə'luːt] **1.** *n.* gesture expressing respect/homage/recognition. **2.** *v.* to give a salute to (s.o.).

salutary ['sæljʊtərɪ] *adj.* useful/helpful; which has a good effect. **salutation** [sæljʊ'teɪʃn] *n.* words spoken/written in praise of s.o./to greet s.o.

salvage ['sælvɪdʒ] **1.** *n.* (*a*) payment made for saving a ship/its cargo from loss by wreck. (*b*) objects saved (from a boat/fire, etc.). (*c*) saving rubbish for use. **2.** *v.* to save (from wreck/fire, etc.).

salvation [sæl'veɪʃn] *n.* saving of the soul from sin; saving of a person from evil. **Salvation Army,** *n.* religious organization run on military lines which specializes in missionary and welfare work among poor people.

salve [sælv] **1.** *n.* healing ointment; **lip s.** = ointment which prevents lips cracking in cold weather. **2.** *v.* **to do sth to s. your conscience** = because your conscience tells you to do it.

salver ['sælvə] *n.* large flat plate (usu. made of silver).

salvia ['sælvɪə] *n.* common summer garden plant with red flowers.

salvo ['sælvəʊ] *n.* (*pl.* **-oes**) (*a*) simultaneous firing of several guns in a battle at sea or as a salute. (*b*) round of applause.

sal volatile [sælvə'lætəlɪ] *n.* smelling-salts.

Samaritan [sə'mærɪtən] *n.* person who helps s.o. in trouble.

same [seɪm] **1.** *adj.* identical; monotonous/unchanging; **it's all the s. to me** = I don't mind. **2.** *pron.* the identical thing. **3.** *adv. inf.* **all the s./just the s.** = nevertheless. **sameness,** *n.* (*a*) being the same. (*b*) monotony.

samovar ['sæməʊvɑː] *n.* urn used in Russia for boiling water for tea.

sampan ['sæmpæn] *n.* small Chinese boat.

samphire ['sæmfaɪə] *n.* type of fern which grows near the sea.

sample ['sɑːmpl] **1.** *n.* specimen. **2.** *v.* (*a*) to test/to try (by taking a small amount). (*b*) to ask a group of people questions to find out a general reaction. **sampler,** *n.* decorated tapestry panel (usu. with letters, numbers and simple pictures) made to show skill in sewing stiches.

samurai ['sæmʊraɪ] *n.* medieval Japanese warrior.

sanatorium [sænə'tɔːrɪəm] *n.* hospital for the treatment of invalids, esp. people suffering from tuberculosis.

sanctify ['sæŋktɪfaɪ] *v.* to consecrate/to make holy. **sanctification** [sæŋktɪfɪ'keɪʃn] *n.* making holy. **sanctimonious** [sæŋktɪ'məʊnɪəs] *adj.* pretending to be holy. **sanctimoniously,** *adv.* in a sanctimonious way. **sanctity** ['sæŋktɪtɪ] *n.* holiness of life/saintliness.

sanction ['sæŋkʃn] **1.** *n.* (*a*) law/decree. (*b*) penalty for breaking a rule; **economic sanctions** = restrictions on trade with a country in order to try to influence its political development. **2.** *v.* (*a*) to approve. (*b*) to permit.

sanctuary ['sæŋktjʊərɪ] *n.* (*a*) holy place. (*b*) part of a church where the high altar is placed. (*c*) place for the protection of wild animals or birds. (*d*) refuge.

sanctum ['sæŋktəm] *n.* (*a*) holy place. (*b*) private room; **inner s.** = most private/secret office.

sand [sænd] **1.** *n.* (*a*) mass of tiny fragments of worn-down rock, etc., found on seashores/river beds/deserts, etc. **2.** *v.* (*a*) (*also* **sand down**) to rub smooth with sandpaper. (*b*) to spread sand on (icy roads). **sandbag. 1.** *n.* bag filled with sand and used as a defence/as ballast. **2.** *v.* (**-bagged**) (*a*) to protect (sth) with a wall of sandbags. (*b*) to knock (s.o.) out by hitting him with a sandbag. **sandbank,** *n.* ridge of sand in sea or river. **sand blast,** *v.* to clean (the exterior of a building) by directing a powerful jet of sand on to it. **sander,** *n.* machine/person who sands. **sandpaper. 1.** *n.* paper with a coating of sand for smoothing. **2.** *v.* to rub (sth) smooth with sandpaper. **sandpiper,** *n.* small bird with a long bill which lives on beaches. **sandpit,** *n.* place with sand where children can play. **sands,** *n.pl.* sandy seashore. **sandstone,** *n.* rock made of compressed sand. **sandstorm,** *n.* high wind in a desert blowing clouds of sand. **sandy,** *adj.* like sand; made of sand.

sandal ['sændl] *n.* light open shoe worn in the summer. **sandalled,** *adj.* wearing sandals. **sandalwood,** *n.* (*a*) tropical tree; fragrant wood from this tree. (*b*) scent from this tree.

sandwich ['sændwɪtʃ] **1.** *n.* (*pl.* **-es**) two slices of bread with sweet or savoury filling. **2.** *v.* to insert (sth) between two others. **sandwich board,** *n.* pair of boards worn over the shoulders in the street to advertise sth. **sandwich course,** *n.* course where students spend time working in a factory between periods of study at a college. **sandwich man,** *n.* man who carries a sandwich board.

sane [seɪn] *adj.* (**-er, -est**) reasonable/not mad. **sanely,** *adv.* in a sane way. **sanity** ['sænɪtɪ] *n.* being sane.

sang [sæŋ] *v. see* **sing.**

sangfroid [sɑːŋ'frwɑː] *n.* calmness when in danger.

sanguinary ['sæŋgwɪnərɪ] *adj*. delighting in bloodshed or killing.

sanguine ['sæŋgwɪn] *adj*. confident/optimistic.

sanitation [sænɪ'teɪʃn] *n*. hygiene/conditions affecting health. **sanitary** ['sænɪtərɪ] *adj*. referring to sanitation/hygiene; **s. towel** = pad of material worn by women to absorb blood lost during menstruation.

sank [sæŋk] *v. see* **sink**.

Sanskrit ['sænzkrɪt] *n*. classical language of India.

sans serif [sænz'serɪf] *n*. typeset character with no serifs.

Santa Claus ['sæntə'klɔːz] *n*. Father Christmas.

sap [sæp] **1**. *n*. (*a*) juice circulating in plants and trees. (*b*) (*in warfare*) digging a tunnel to get near to the enemy. (*c*) *inf*. silly person. **2**. *v*. (**sapped**) (*a*) to weaken/to drain away. (*b*) to undermine/to make insecure by removing foundations. **sapper,** *n*. soldier in the Royal Engineers.

sapling ['sæplɪŋ] *n*. young tree.

sapphire ['sæfaɪə] **1**. *n*. blue precious stone. **2**. *adj*. clear blue (colour).

saprophyte ['sæprəʊfaɪt] *n*. fungus which lives on decaying plants. **saprophytic** [sæprəʊ'fɪtɪk] *adj*. living on decaying plants.

saraband ['særəbænd] *n*. slow Spanish dance.

sarcasm ['sɑːkæzəm] *n*. making sharp unpleasant remarks. **sarcastic** [sɑː'kæstɪk] *adj*. scornful, with sarcasm. **sarcastically,** *adv*. in a sarcastic way.

sarcoma [sɑː'kəʊmə] *n*. kind of malignant tumour.

sarcophagus [sɑː'kɒfəgəs] *n*. (*pl*. -**gi** [gaɪ]) stone coffin often decorated with sculpture.

sardine [sɑː'diːn] *n*. small fish of the herring family; **packed like sardines** = very tightly.

sardonic [sɑː'dɒnɪk] *adj*. scornful/cynical. **sardonically,** *adv*. in a sardonic way.

sardonyx ['sɑːdɒnɪks] *n*. semi-precious stone, with red layers.

Sargasso Sea [sɑː'gæsəʊ'siː] *n*. area of the Atlantic Ocean, with few currents, covered with drifting weed.

sari ['sɑːrɪ] *n*. long piece of cloth worn by Indian women.

sarong [sə'rɒŋ] *n*. cloth worn wrapped round the lower part of the body by S.E. Asian men and women.

sarsaparilla [sɑː:spə'rɪlə] *n*. drink made from the root of an American plant.

sarsen ['sɑːsn] *n*. large block of sandstone.

sartorial [sɔː'tɔːrɪəl] *adj*. (*formal*) referring to men's clothes.

sash [sæʃ] *n*. (*pl*. -**es**) (*a*) ornamental scarf. (*b*) wooden frame holding panes of glass. **sash cord,** *n*. rope in a sash window which allows the frames to slide up and down smoothly. **sash window,** *n*. window made of panes of glass set in two frames which slide up and down.

sashay [sə'ʃeɪ] *v. Am*. to walk confidently.

Sassenach ['sæsənæk] *n*. (*in Scotland*) Englishman.

sat [sæt] *v. see* **sit**.

Satan ['seɪtən] *n*. the devil. **satanic** [sə'tænɪk] *adj*. diabolical/like the devil.

satchel ['sætʃəl] *n*. small leather/canvas bag worn on the shoulders.

sate [seɪt] *v*. (*formal*) to satisfy (s.o.) by giving him too much.

sateen [sə'tiːn] *n*. type of fine cotton cloth which looks like satin.

satellite ['sætəlaɪt] *n*. (*a*) heavenly body which goes round a planet. (*b*) artificial body which was launched from and which goes round the earth; **s. broadcast** = radio/TV broadcast which is transmitted via a satellite; **s. dish** = aerial, shaped like a dish, used to capture satellite broadcasts. **satellite state,** *n*. country controlled by a more powerful one. **satellite town,** *n*. small town dependent on a larger town near by.

satiate ['seɪʃɪeɪt] *v*. to satisfy totally/to fill to overflowing. **satiation,** *n*. act of satiating. **satiety** [sə'taɪətɪ] *n*. being satiated.

satin ['sætɪn] **1**. *n*. silk fabric with a glossy surface. **2**. *adj*. made of satin. **satinwood,** *n*. type of hard tropical wood. **satiny,** *adj*. smooth and shiny, like satin.

satire ['sætaɪə] *n*. (*a*) attacking s.o. in speech/writing by making them seem ridiculous. (*b*) humorously critical piece of writing. **satiric, satirical** [sə'tırıkl] *adj.* humorously critical. **satirically,** *adv.* in a satirical way. **satirist** ['sætırıst] *n.* writer of satires. **satirize** ['sætıraız] *v.* to attack (sth) in a more or less amusing way.

satisfaction [sætıs'fækʃn] *n.* (*a*) payment of debt; compensation (for damage). (*b*) good feeling; sense of comfort/happiness. **satisfactory,** *adj.* causing satisfaction; quite good. **satisfactorily,** *adv.* in a satisfactory way. **satisfy** ['sætısfaı] **1.** *v.* (*a*) to comply with/to fulfil. (*b*) to show adequate proof. (*c*) to make (s.o.) content/pleased. (*d*) to make sure/to ascertain. **satisfying,** *adj.* which satisfies.

satsuma [sæt'su:mə] *n.* type of small sweet seedless orange.

saturate ['sætʃʊreıt] **1.** *v.* to make very wet. **saturated fat,** *n.* fat (such as animal fat) which contains the largest amount of hydrogen possible. **saturation** [sætʃʊ'reıʃn] *n.* complete filling; **s. point** = point at which a substance cannot absorb any more liquid.

Saturday ['sætədeı] *n.* sixth day of the week; day between Friday and Sunday.

saturnalia [sætə'neılıə] *n.* wild orgy.

saturnine ['sætənaın] *adj.* gloomy character.

satyr ['sætə] *n.* classical god living in woods, with a human body, but with legs and ears like a goat's.

sauce [sɔ:s] *n.* (*a*) liquid poured over food. (*b*) *inf.* impertinence. **sauceboat,** *n.* vessel in which sauce is served. **saucepan,** *n.* deep metal cooking pot with a long handle. **saucily,** *adv. inf.* cheekily. **sauciness,** *n. inf.* being saucy. **saucy,** *adj.* (-ier, -iest) *inf.* cheeky.

saucer ['sɔ:sə] *n.* shallow dish placed under a cup; **flying s.** = object shaped like a saucer which people say they have seen in the sky.

Saudi (Arabian) ['saʊdı(ə'reıbıən)] *adj. n.* (person) from Saudi Arabia.

sauerkraut ['saʊəkraʊt] *n.* German dish of pickled cabbage.

sauna ['sɔ:nə] *n.* (*a*) very hot steam bath. (*b*) room where you can have a sauna bath.

saunter ['sɔ:ntə] **1.** *n.* stroll/leisurely walk. **2.** *v.* to walk in a leisurely way/ to stroll.

saurian ['sɔ:rıən] *adj. & n.* (animal) like a lizard.

sausage ['sɒsıdʒ] *n.* tube of edible skin full of minced and seasoned pork or other meat. **sausagemeat,** *n.* meat and breadcrumbs minced and seasoned. **sausage roll,** *n.* small piece of sausage cooked in pastry.

sauté ['səʊteı] **1.** *adj.* fried in a little fat. **2.** *v.* (**sautéed**) to fry in a little fat.

savage ['sævıdʒ] **1.** *adj.* (*a*) uncivilized/ primitive. (*b*) fierce/ferocious. **2.** *n.* wild/uncivilized human being. **3.** *v.* to attack with teeth. **savagely,** *adv.* in a savage way. **savageness, savagery,** *n.* being savage.

savanna(h) [sə'vænə] *n.* grassy plain in a tropical country.

savant ['sævɒn] *n.* learned man; **idiot s.** = person of limited intelligence, but with a highly developed skill in a single faculty (such as memorizing numbers).

save [seıv] **1.** *v.* (*a*) to rescue from misfortune. (*b*) to keep for future use/ to reserve; (*computers*) to keep data in storage after it has been keyboarded. (*c*) to make an economy/not to spend. (*d*) (*in sport*) to prevent opponents from scoring. (*e*) to gain (time). (*f*) to avoid (trouble). **2.** *prep. & conj.* except. **Save-As-You-Earn,** *n.* scheme to encourage people to save by placing money into a savings scheme directly out of one's salary. **saver,** *n.* person who saves money. **saving. 1.** *n.* economy. **2.** *adj.* redeeming. **3.** *prep.* (*old*) except. **savings,** *n.* money saved. **savings bank,** *n.* bank which gives interest on small deposits of money.

saveloy ['sævəlɔı] *n.* highly-seasoned dried sausage.

saviour, *Am.* **savior** ['seıvjə] **1.** *n.* person who saves; **our Saviour** = Jesus Christ.

savory ['seıvərı] *n.* herb used in cooking.

savour, *Am.* **savor** ['seıvə] **1.** *n.* (*a*) characteristic taste. (*b*) suspicion/hint. **2.** *v.* (*a*) to appreciate (food and wine). (*b*) **to s. of** = to suggest. **savouriness,** *n.* appetizing taste or smell. **savoury. 1.** *adj.* (*a*) appetizing. (*b*) salty/not sweet.

2. *n.* food (which is not sweet) served at the beginning or end of a meal.

savoy [sə'vɔɪ] *n.* curly winter cabbage.

saw [sɔ:] **1.** *n.* (*a*) steel tool with a blade with a serrated edge, used for cutting wood/metal etc. (*b*) old saying. **2.** *v.* (**sawed**; **sawn**) (*a*) to cut (wood, etc.) with a saw. (*b*) *see also* **see**. **sawdust**, *n.* powder produced from sawing wood. **sawfish**, *n.* large sea fish with a nose shaped like a saw. **sawmill**, *n.* power-driven mill which saws wood mechanically. **sawyer**, *n.* person who saws wood.

sax [sæks] *n. inf.* saxophone.

saxe (blue) ['sæks(blu:)] *n.* pale grey-blue.

saxifrage ['sæksɪfreɪdʒ] *n.* low alpine plant with pink flowers.

saxophone ['sæksəfəʊn] *n.* brass musical instrument with keys. **saxophonist** [sæk'sɒfənɪst] *n.* saxophone player.

say [seɪ] **1.** *n.* right to decide. **2.** *v.* (**said** [sed]) (*a*) to speak. (*b*) to put in writing. (*c*) to give (an opinion); to put an idea into words. (*d*) to suggest. **saying**, *n.* proverb/phrase which is often used.

SAYE *short for* save-as-you-earn.

scab [skæb] *n.* (*a*) dry rough crust formed over a wound when it is healing. (*b*) *inf.* workman who refuses to take part in a strike. **scabby**, *adj.* covered with scabs.

scabbard ['skæbəd] *n.* sheath/holder for a dagger or sword.

scabies ['skeɪbi:z] *n.* (*no pl.*) skin disease which makes you itch.

scabious ['skeɪbɪəs] *n.* perennial plant with pincushion-shaped flowers.

scabrous ['skeɪbrəs] *adj.* (*formal*) with a rough surface.

scaffold ['skæfəld] *n.* platform on which executions take place. **scaffolding**, *n* structure of poles and planks providing workmen with a platform to stand on while working.

scald [skɔ:ld] **1.** *n.* burn caused by boiling liquid. **2.** *v.* to injure with hot liquid or steam. **scalding. 1.** *n.* being burnt by a hot liquid. **2.** *adj.* very hot.

scale [skeɪl] **1.** *n.* (*a*) thin horny plate protecting the skin of fish and snakes; **s. insect** = insect which sucks sap from plants and covers itself with a scale. (*b*) hard deposit stuck to a surface.

(*c*) arrangement of musical notes in order. (*d*) graded system. (*e*) relative measurements of a small object which are exactly similar to those of a larger object. **2.** *v.* (*a*) to remove scales from. (*b*) to remove deposit from (teeth). (*c*) **to s. off** = to drop off in thin layers. (*d*) to climb up/to climb over. (*e*) **to s. up/down** = to increase/to reduce proportionally. **scaleable**, *adj.* which can be scaled. **scales**, *n.pl.* instrument for weighing; (**pair of**) **s.** = weighing machine. **scaly**, *adj.* covered in scales.

scallion ['skælɪən] *n.* young onion eaten raw in salad.

scallop ['skɒləp] *n.* (*a*) type of shellfish with a semi-circular ridged shell. (*b*) ornamental edging of material in small semicircles. **scalloped**, *adj.* with scallops along the edge.

scallywag ['skælɪwæg] *n. inf.* naughty person.

scalp [skælp] **1.** *n.* skin and hair on the top of the head. **2.** *v.* (*a*) to cut off the scalp of (s.o.). (*b*) *inf.* to sell tickets at a very high price. **scalper**, *n. inf.* person who sells tickets at a very high price.

scalpel ['skælpl] *n.* small surgical knife.

scam [skæm] *n. Am.* fraud.

scamp [skæmp] **1.** *n.* rascal. **2.** *v.* to do (sth) in an unsatisfactory way.

scamper ['skæmpə] **1.** *n.* run/gallop. **2.** *v.* to run fast.

scampi ['skæmpɪ] *n. pl.* large prawns.

scan [skæn] **1.** *v.* (**scanned**) (*a*) to test the rhythm of (a line of poetry); (*of poetry*) to fit a regular rhythm. (*b*) to look intently all over. (*c*) to pass a radar beam over (an area); to pass X-rays through part of the body. **2.** *n.* action of passing a radar beam or X-ray over an area; **brain s.** = examining the inside of the brain by passing X-rays through the head. **scanner**, *n.* machine for carrying out scanning.

scandal ['skændl] *n.* (*a*) unkind gossip. (*b*) thing that produces a general feeling of anger. **scandalize**, *v.* to shock. **scandalized**, *adj.* shocked. **scandalmonger**, *n.* person who spreads gossip. **scandalous**, *adj.* shameful. **scandalously**, *adv.* terribly.

Scandinavian [skændɪ'neɪvɪən] *n. & adj.* (person) from Scandinavia.

scansion ['skæn∫n] n. art of scanning poetry.

scant [skænt] adj. hardly enough. **scantily**, adj. **s. dressed** = with very few clothes on. **scantiness**, n. lack; smallness. **scanty**, adj. (-ier, -iest) small/not sufficient.

scapegoat ['skeɪpgəʊt] n. person who carries the blame for s.o. else.

scapula ['skæpjʊlə] n. shoulder blade.

scar [skɑː] 1. n. mark left after a wound has healed. 2. v. (**scarred**) (a) to wound (s.o.) causing a permanent mark. (b) to leave a mark on the mind of.

scarab ['skærəb] n. carved beetle.

scarce [skeəs] adj. (-er, -est) insufficient for the demand/hard to find; inf. **to make oneself s.** = to disappear/to keep out of the way. **scarcely**, adv. hardly/ only just. **scarceness, scarcity,** n. lack/ insufficiency.

scare [skeə] 1. n. fright/terror. 2. v. (a) to frighten. (b) to be alarmed. **scared**, adj. frightened. **scarecrow**, n. figure looking like a man set up in a field to frighten off birds. **scaremonger**, n. person who likes to alarm others. **scaremongering**, n. spreading of alarm. **scary**, adj. (-ier, -iest) frightening.

scarf [skɑːf] n. (pl. **scarves**) long strip or square of material worn round the neck to keep you warm.

scarify ['skærɪfaɪ] v. to make slits in (sth).

scarlet ['skɑːlət] adj. brilliant red colour. **scarlatina, scarlet fever,** n. infectious disease producing a bright red rash.

scarp [skɑːp] n. steep hillside.

scarper ['skɑːpə] v. inf. to run.

scathing ['skeɪðɪŋ] adj. very critical.

scatter ['skætə] 1. v. (a) to throw here and there. (b) to go/to run in all directions. **scatterbrain**, n. forgetful person. **scatterbrained**, adj. forgetful/ careless. **scattered**, adj. spread out. **scatty**, adj. inf. silly/slightly mad.

scaup [skɔːp] n. type of wild duck.

scavenger ['skævɪndʒə] n. (a) animal which feeds on other dead animals. (b) person who looks for useful things among rubbish. **scavenge**, v. to look for useful things among rubbish.

scenario [sɪ'nɑːrɪəʊ] n. (pl. -os) written version of a play with details of characters/scenes, etc.

scene [siːn] n. (a) subdivision of an act in a play; **behind the scenes** = without being obvious/without many people knowing. (b) place in which events actually occur. (c) view/surroundings. (d) display of temper. (e) inf. **it's not my s.** = it doesn't interest me/it is not the sort of thing I usually do. **scenery**, n. (a) painted cloth backgrounds and other props used in a theatre to make the stage resemble the supposed scene of action. (b) view of the countryside. **scenic**, adj. referring to scenery; **s. railway** = miniature railway running through artificial picturesque scenery at a fair; **s. route** = road running through beautiful countryside.

scent [sent] 1. n. (a) pleasant smell. (b) characteristic smell; **on the s. of** = following a trail. (c) perfume. (d) sense of smell. 2. v. (a) to find out by smelling. (b) to begin to suspect. (c) to make fragrant.

sceptic, Am. **skeptic** ['skeptɪk] 1. n. person who doubts the truth of religion. (b) person who always doubts the truth of what he is told. **sceptical**, adj. doubtful/(person) who doubts. **sceptically**, adv. doubtfully/ distrustfully. **scepticism**, n. doubt/ uncertainty.

sceptre, Am. **scepter** ['septə] n. gold stick covered with precious stones carried by a king or queen.

schedule ['∫edjuːl, Am. 'skedʒuːl] 1. n. (a) timetable. (b) programme/list of events. (c) plan. (d) appendix to a document. 2. v. (a) to list officially. (b) to plan (sth) for a particular time; **scheduled service** = regular (bus/train, etc.) service.

scheme [skiːm] 1. n. (a) plan/arrangement. (b) plot. 2. v. to plot. **schematic** [skɪ'mætɪk] adj. laid out like a diagram. **schematically**, adv. in a schematic way. **schemer**, n. person who plots. **scheming**, adj. (person) who plots.

scherzo ['skeətsəʊ] n. (pl. -os) lively section of a longer piece of music.

schism ['skɪzəm] n. division of a religious community into factions. **schismatic** [skɪz'mætɪk] adj. tending to break away.

schist [∫ɪst] n. rock which splits into thin layers.

schizophrenia [skɪtsəʊ'fri:nɪə] *n.* mental illness where thoughts, feelings and actions are all disconnected. **schizoid** ['skɪtsɔɪd] *adj. & n.* (person) suffering from schizophrenia. **schizophrenic** [skɪtsəʊ'frenɪk] *adj.* referring to schizophrenia.

schmaltz [ʃmɒlts] *n.* too much sentimentality (in writing/music, etc.).

schnapps [ʃnæps] *n.* colourless German alcohol.

schnitzel ['ʃnɪtzl] *n.* thin flat piece of veal fried in breadcrumbs.

scholar ['skɒlə] *n.* (a) person who studies. (b) learned person. (c) student at school or university who has a scholarship. **scholarliness,** *n.* being scholarly. **scholarly,** *adj.* learned/seeking to learn. **scholarship,** *n.* (a) profound learning. (b) money given to a student to help pay for the cost of his study. **scholastic** [skə'læstɪk] *adj.* referring to schools or teaching.

school [sku:l] **1.** *n.* (a) place for teaching (usu. children); department of a university. (b) followers of a philosopher/artist, etc. (c) large group of fish or sea animals. **2.** *v.* to teach/to train. **schoolbook,** *n.* book used in school. **schoolboy, schoolgirl,** *n.* child who goes to school. **schoolchildren,** *n.pl.* children who go to school. **schooling,** *n.* education at school level. **schoolmaster, schoolmistress,** *n.* schoolteacher. **schoolmastering,** *n.* profession of teacher. **schoolteacher,** *n.* person who teaches in a school.

schooner ['sku:nə] *n.* (a) sailing ship with two or more masts and sails running lengthwise down the ship. (b) tall glass for sherry.

sciatica [saɪ'ætɪkə] *n.* pain in the back and legs. **sciatic nerve,** *n.* nerve in the hip.

science ['saɪəns] *n.* (a) knowledge obtained from observation and arranged into a system. (b) study based on observation and experiment (such as chemistry/biology, etc.). **science fiction,** *n.* stories on the subject of space travel/life in the future. **scientific** [saɪən'tɪfɪk] *adj.* referring to science. **scientifically,** *adv.* according to scientific experiment. **scientist** ['saɪəntɪst] *n.* person who studies science.

scilla ['sɪlə] *n.* small blue flower, coming from a bulb.

scimitar ['sɪmɪtə] *n.* short sword with a curved blade.

scintillate ['sɪntɪleɪt] *v.* to sparkle. **scintillating,** *adj.* sparkling. **scintillation** [sɪntɪ'leɪʃn] *n.* wit/sparkle.

scion ['saɪən] *n.* piece of a plant which is grafted on to another; young member of a noble family.

scissors ['sɪzəz] *n.pl.* (a pair of) s. = instrument for cutting fabric/paper etc. constructed of two blades with handles for thumb and fingers.

sclerosis [sklə'rəʊsɪs] *n.* hardening of soft tissue; **multiple s.** = gradual disease where hardening of tissue causes general paralysis.

scoff [skɒf] *v.* (a) **to s. at** = to make fun of in a nasty way. (b) *inf.* to eat greedily. **scoffer,** *n.* person who scoffs. **scoffing,** *adj.* mocking. **scoffingly,** *adv.* mockingly.

scold [skəʊld] *v.* to speak to (s.o.) angrily. **scolding,** *n.* rebuke.

sconce ['skɒns] *n.* decorated bracket which holds a light.

scone [skɒn] *n.* small soft cake usu. eaten with cream and jam.

scoop [sku:p] **1.** *n.* (a) short-handled shovel/spoon; round spoon for serving ice cream. (b) portion of ice cream, etc. (c) piece of news which is published in one newspaper before any other. **2.** *v.* (a) to lift, using a scoop; **to s. out the inside of sth** = to remove the inside of sth with a spoon, etc. (b) to obtain against competition. (c) **to s. a newspaper** = to print a news item before another paper does.

scooter ['sku:tə] *n.* (a) child's two-wheeled vehicle with footboard and a long steering handle, pushed along with one foot. (b) **motor s.** = motorized two-wheel bicycle with a curving shield in front and a platform for the feet. **scoot,** *v. inf.* to go quite fast. **scooterist,** *n.* person who rides a scooter.

scope [skəʊp] *n.* (a) reach of observation/action. (b) opportunity.

scorbutus [skɔ:'bu:təs] *n.* scurvy.

scorch [skɔ:tʃ] **1.** *v.* to burn slightly/to brown; **scorched-earth policy** = tactics in war where all the resources are destroyed before retreating and giving up territory to the enemy. **scorcher,** *n. inf.* very hot day. **scorching,** *adj.* very hot/which scorches.

score [skɔː] 1. *n.* (*a*) scratch (in paint, etc.). (*b*) debt; **to settle old scores** = to get your own back on s.o. after a long delay. (*c*) number of points made in a game; *inf.* **he knows the s.** = he knows all the facts of the case. (*d*) piece of music written out showing the parts for each instrument or voice. (*e*) twenty; **scores of** = many. (*f*) question/matter. 2. *v.* (*a*) to scratch. (*b*) to make a point in a game. (*c*) to write down the score in a game. (*d*) to write out (a piece of music) with parts for each instrument or voice. **scoreboard,** *n.* large board showing the score in a tennis match, etc. **scorer,** *n.* person who makes a point in a game; person who writes down the scores in a game. **score off,** *v.* to make points against (s.o.) in a conversation. **score out,** *v.* to cross out.

scorn [skɔːn] 1. *n.* feeling of looking down/disrespect. 2. *v.* to look down on/not to respect. **scornful,** *adj.* disrespectful. **scornfully,** *adv.* in a scornful way.

Scorpio [ˈskɔːpɪəʊ] *n.* one of the signs of the zodiac, shaped like a scorpion.

scorpion [ˈskɔːpɪən] *n.* poisonous tropical insect which stings with a long curved tail.

Scot [skɒt] *n.* person from Scotland. **Scots.** 1. *adj.* referring to Scotland; **S. pine** = common European conifer. 2. *n.* form of English spoken in Scotland. **Scotsman, Scotswoman,** *n.* (*pl.* **-men, -women**) person from Scotland. **Scottish,** *adj.* referring to Scotland.

Scotch [skɒtʃ] 1. *adj.* referring to Scotland; (**Scottish** *is preferred in Scotland, but* **Scotch** *is always used in the following*) **S. broth** = soup made with mutton, barley, etc.; **S. eggs** = hard boiled eggs covered with sausage meat and fried; **S. mist** = thick mist and rain; **S. terrier** = type of black or white terrier; **S. whisky** = whisky made in Scotland. 2. *n.* (*a*) (*pl.* **-es**) Scotch whisky; a glass of this drink. (*b*) trademark for a type of transparent sticky tape 3. *v.* **to s.** = to try to stop (a rumour).

scot-free [skɒtˈfriː] *adj.* **to get off s.** = without being punished.

scoundrel [ˈskaʊndrəl] *n.* wicked person.

scour [ˈskaʊə] *v.* (*a*) to clean by scrubbing with a hard material. (*b*) to search everywhere. **scourer,** *n.* pad of steel wool for cleaning pans.

scourge [skɜːdʒ] 1. *n.* thing which causes suffering. 2. *v.* to cause suffering.

Scouse [ˈskaʊs] *adj. & n. inf.* (person) from Liverpool; dialect spoken in Liverpool.

scout [skaʊt] 1. *n.* (*a*) person sent out to look for information. (*b*) boy who belongs to the Boy Scouts' Association; **the Scouts** = the Boy Scouts' Association. 2. *v.* to reconnoitre; **to s. around for** = to search for. **scoutmaster,** *n.* leader of a group of Boy Scouts.

scowl [skaʊl] 1. *n.* angry look made by wrinkling the forehead. 2. *v.* to make a scowl.

scrabble [ˈskræbl] *v.* **to s. (about)** = to scratch wildly with your hands or feet.

scrag [skræg] *n. s.* (**end**) = sheep's neck used to make soup. **scraggy** [ˈskrægɪ] *adj.* (**-ier, -iest**) thin and bony.

scram [skræm] *inter. meaning* go away!

scramble [ˈskræmbl] 1. *n.* (*a*) act of scrambling (up sth). (*b*) rush. (*c*) cross-country motorcycle race. 2. *v.* (*a*) to hurry along on hands and knees. (*b*) to try to get somewhere by pushing. (*c*) **scrambled eggs** = eggs mixed together and stirred as they are cooked in butter. (*d*) to mix up (a radio signal/telephone link) so that it cannot be understood without an apparatus for unmixing it. **scrambler,** *n.* machine for scrambling radio signals; **s. telephone** = telephone which scrambles the message.

scrap [skræp] 1. *n.* (*a*) small piece. (*b*) waste materials; **scraps** = bits of waste food/waste material; **s. heap** = heap of rubbish; **s. metal/paper** = waste metal/paper. (*c*) *inf.* fight. 2. *v.* (**scrapped**) (*a*) to throw away as waste. (*b*) to give up (plans). (*c*) to fight. **scrapbook,** *n.* large book with blank pages for sticking photographs/newspaper cuttings, etc., into. **scrappy,** *adj.* (**-ier, -iest**) made of bits and pieces.

scrape [skreɪp] **1.** *n.* (*a*) mark made by sth hard being pulled across a surface. (*b*) awkward situation/trouble. (*c*) very thin layer of butter, etc., spread on bread. **2.** *v.* to scratch with a hard object being pulled across a surface. **scraper,** *n.* instrument for scraping. **scrape together,** *v.* to collect with difficulty. **scrape through,** *v.* to get through (an examination) with difficulty. **scrapie,** *n.* disease affecting the brains of sheep, possibly a cause of BSE in cattle. **scrapings,** *n.pl.* pieces which have been scraped off.

scratch [skrætʃ] **1.** *n.* (*pl.* **-es**) (*a*) long slight wound/mark made by a sharp point. (*b*) sound of a sharp point being pulled across a surface. (*c*) act of scratching a part of the body which itches. (*d*) **to start from s.** = to start at the beginning/with no previous preparation; **to come up to s.** = to satisfy. **2.** *adj.* (*a*) **s. team** = team of players brought together at the last minute. (*b*) **s. player** = player who starts with no handicap. **3.** *v.* (*a*) to make a long wound/mark with a sharp pointed instrument; **to s. the surface** = to deal with only the first part of the problem and not to get down to the basic details. (*b*) to make a sound by pulling a sharp point across a surface. (*c*) to rub with your fingernails (a part of the body which itches). (*d*) (*of competitor*) to cross one's name off the list of entrants for a race. **scratchy,** *adj.* which makes a scratching noise.

scrawl [skrɔːl] **1.** *n.* bad/careless handwriting. **2.** *v.* to write badly/carelessly.

scrawny ['skrɔːnɪ] *adj.* (**-ier, -iest**) thin and bony.

scream [skriːm] **1.** *n.* (*a*) loud/piercing cry. (*b*) **screams of laughter** = loud/piercing laughter. (*c*) *inf.* very funny thing/person. **2.** *v.* (*a*) to make loud/piercing cries. (*b*) **s. with laughter** = laugh uproariously. **screamingly,** *adv.* **s. funny** = extremely funny.

scree [skriː] *n.* loose stones on a mountainside.

screech [skriːtʃ] **1.** *n.* (*pl.* **-es**) piercing cry (of an animal). **2.** *v.* to make a piercing cry. **screech owl,** *n.* type of owl which screeches.

screed [skriːd] *n.* very long document.

screen [skriːn] **1.** *n.* (*a*) flat surface which protects/divides. (*b*) thing which acts as protection against draught/fire/noise, etc. (*c*) flat white surface for projecting films/slides; **the small s.** = television. (*d*) device like a large sieve for sifting sand/gravel into varying sizes. **2.** *v.* (*a*) to protect from draught/fire/noise, etc. (*b*) to show on a film/TV screen. (*c*) to question/to examine (people) to find out if they have a disease/if they have committed a crime. (*d*) to sift (sand/gravel) into varying sizes. **screenplay,** *n.* scenario of a film. **screenwriter,** *n.* person who writes screenplays.

screw [skruː] **1.** *n.* (*a*) metal pin with a groove winding up from the point to the head, so that when twisted it goes into a hard surface. (*b*) propeller. (*c*) act of turning a screw with a screwdriver. (*d*) small piece of twisted paper with sth in it. (*e*) twisting motion of a ball. (*f*) *Sl.* pay/wages. (*g*) *Sl.* prison warder. **2.** *v.* (*a*) to attach with screws. (*b*) to attach by twisting; *inf.* **his head's screwed on the right way** = he's very sensible. (*c*) to twist. **screwball,** *n. inf.* odd/crazy person. **screwdriver,** *n.* tool with a long handle and small flat end which is used for turning screws. **screw-top jar,** *n.* jar with a top which screws on and off. **screwy,** *adj.* (**-ier, -iest**) *inf.* mad.

scribble ['skrɪbl] **1.** *n.* (*a*) (child's) meaningless marks. (*b*) bad writing. **2.** *v.* (*a*) to make meaningless marks. (*b*) to write badly/hurriedly. **scribbly,** *adj.* scribbled (writing).

scribe [skraɪb] *n.* (*old*) person who writes copies (of letters/books, etc.) by hand.

scrimmage ['skrɪmɪdʒ] *n.* wild struggle.

scrimp [skrɪmp] *v.* to use as little as possible (of sth).

scrimshank ['skrɪmʃæŋk] *v.* to avoid doing work. **scrimshanker,** *n.* person who avoids doing work.

scrimshaw ['skrɪmʃɔː] *n.* carvings made by sailors on whalebone or ivory.

scrip [skrɪp] *n.* (*no pl.*) new shares issued by a company instead of paying a dividend.

script [skrɪpt] *n.* (*a*) style of handwriting. (*b*) thing written by hand/manuscript;

handwritten answer to an examination. (c) written version of words which are spoken in a film/play.

scripture ['skrɪptʃə] n. holy writing; the Bible. **scriptural**, adj. referring to scripture.

scroll [skrəʊl] 1. n. (a) roll of paper with writing on it. (b) curved shape. 2. v. to move text up or down on a computer screen.

scrotum ['skrəʊtəm] n. bag containing the testicles. **scrotal**, adj. referring to the scrotum.

scrounge [skraʊndʒ] v. to try to get (sth) from s.o. without paying for it. **scrounger**, n. person who scrounges.

scrub [skrʌb] 1. n. (a) (area of land covered by) small bushes. (b) action of cleaning with a stiff brush. 2. v. (scrubbed) (a) to clean by rubbing with a stiff brush. (b) inf. to remove what is recorded on (tape); s. **that** = forget about that. **scrubbing-brush**, n. stiff brush with no handle, for scrubbing floors, etc. **scrubby**, adj. (-ier, -iest) inf. dirty, small and unpleasant.

scruff [skrʌf] n. skin at the back of the neck. **scruffily**, adv. in a scruffy way. **scruffiness**, n. being scruffy. **scruffy**, adj. (-ier, -iest) untidy/dirty.

scrum, scrummage [skrʌm, 'skrʌmɪdʒ] n. (a) (in Rugby football) groups of forwards from both sides pushing against each other to get the ball. (b) struggling crowd.

scrumping ['skrʌmpɪŋ] n. inf. **to go s.** = to steal apples from an orchard. **scrumpy**, n. inf. strong cider.

scrumptious ['skrʌmʃəs] adj. inf. very good to eat.

scrunch [skrʌntʃ] v. inf. to crush.

scruple ['skru:pl] 1. n. doubt about whether sth is right which stops you from doing it. 2. v. **not to s. to do sth** = not to have scruples about doing sth. **scrupulous** ['skru:pjʊləs] adj. very careful. **scrupulously**, adv. in a scrupulous way. **scrupulousness**, n. being scrupulous.

scrutinize ['skru:tɪnaɪz] v. to examine very carefully. **scrutineer** [skru:tɪ'nɪə] n. official observer of an election. **scrutiny**, n. careful examination/very close look.

scuba ['sku:bə] n. underwater breathing apparatus.

scud [skʌd] v. (scudded) (of clouds) to rush past.

scuff [skʌf] v. to scrape the outside surface/the soles of (shoes) when walking.

scuffle ['skʌfl] 1. n. small fight. 2. v. to fight.

scull [skʌl] 1. n. one of two short oars used by a single rower. 2. v. to row a boat with two oars.

scullery ['skʌlərɪ] n. small room at the back of a kitchen, used for washing up.

sculpt [skʌlpt] v. to carve (figures, etc.) out of wood/metal/stone. **sculptor** ['skʌlptə] n. person who makes figures/artistic constructions out of wood/metal/stone. **sculpture** ['skʌlptʃə] 1. n. (a) art of sculpting. (b) figure made by a sculptor. 2. v. to sculpt.

scum [skʌm] n. (a) thick dirty foam layer on the surface of a liquid. (b) people of the worst type; worthless person. **scummy**, adj. covered with scum.

scupper ['skʌpə] 1. n. hole in the side of the ship to let water run off the deck. 2. v. to sink (a ship) intentionally by opening holes in the bottom to let water in. (b) inf. to bring to an end/to ruin.

scurf [skɜːf] n. dandruff/bits of dead skin in the hair.

scurrilous ['skʌrɪləs] adj. very insulting/rude. **scurrilously**, adv. in a scurrilous way. **scurrilousness, scurrility** [skʌ'rɪlɪtɪ] n. being scurrilous.

scurry ['skʌrɪ] 1. n. fast movement. 2. v. to run fast, taking short steps.

scurvy ['skɜːvɪ] n. disease caused by lack of Vitamin C which is found in fruit and vegetables.

scut [skʌt] n. little tail (of a rabbit/deer).

scuttle ['skʌtl] 1. n. type of bucket for keeping coal in the house. 2. v. (a) to sink (a ship) intentionally by opening holes in the bottom to allow water to come in. (b) **to s. off** = to run away fast.

scythe [saɪð] 1. n. tool with a wide blade on the end of a long handle, used for cutting grass. 2. v. to cut (grass) with a scythe.

sea [si:] n. (a) area of salt water; inf. **at s.** = not understanding what is happening. (b) salt water. (c) waves; **a heavy s.**

= very large waves. (*d*) mass (of faces in a crowd). **sea anemone**, *n*. primitive sea animal which looks like a flower. **sea bird**, *n*. bird which lives by the sea. **seaboard**, *n*. land by the edge of the sea. **seaborne**, *adj*. (troops, etc.) brought by sea. **sea breeze**, *n*. light wind blowing inland from the sea. **sea coast**, *n*. land along the edge of the sea. **seafarer**, *n*. person who travels/works on the sea. **seafaring**, *adj*. which works/travels on the sea. **seafood**, *n*. fish and shellfish which can be eaten. **sea front**, *n*. road running along the edge of the sea at a resort town. **seagoing**, *adj*. (boat) which is used on the sea. **seagull**, *n*. white sea bird. **sea horse**, *n*. small black fish which looks like a horse. **sea legs**, *n*. **he's got his s. legs** = he is used to travelling by sea and isn't seasick. **sea level**, *n*. the level of the sea, taken as a point for measuring altitude. **sealion**, *n*. large type of seal. **seaman**, *n*. (*pl*. **-men**) sailor; person who travels/works on the sea. **seamanship**, *n*. art of sailing a ship. **seaplane**, *n*. plane with floats which can land on the sea. **seaport**, *n*. port. **seascape**, *n*. painting of the sea. **seashell**, *n*. shell of a shellfish which lives in the sea. **seashore**, *n*. land along the edge of the sea. **seasick**, *adj*. ill because of the motion of a ship. **seasickness**, *n*. being seasick. **seaside**, *n*. land by the side of the sea. **sea urchin**, *n*. type of small spiny sea animal. **seaward**, *adj*. towards the sea. **seawards**, *adv*. towards the sea. **seaweed**, *n*. plant which grows in the sea. **seaworthy**, *adj*. (boat) which is fit to go to sea.

seal [si:l] **1**. *n*. (*a*) large animal living mainly in the sea, with flippers for swimming. (*b*) piece of hard red wax with a design stamped on it, used for showing that a document has been officially approved or for closing an envelope/parcel so that it cannot be opened secretly. (*c*) metal stamp with a design, used for sealing with wax. (*d*) tight fit (of a bottle, etc.). **2**. *v*. (*a*) to attach and stamp a piece of hard wax to show that a document has been offi- cially approved/to prevent an envelope

being opened. (*b*) to close (sth) tightly so that something cannot be opened. (*c*) to agree on the terms of (an agreement/ bargain). **sealant**, *n*. substance used for sealing. **sealing-wax**, *n*. hard red wax used for making official seals. **seal off**, *v*. to close off so as to prevent anyone getting inside. **sealskin**, *n*. skin of a seal.

seam [si:m] *n*. (*a*) line where two pieces of cloth are sewn together/where two pieces of metal are welded together. (*b*) layer (of coal, etc.). **seamless**, *adj*. (stockings, etc.) with no seam. **seamstress** ['semstrəs] *n*. woman who sews. **seamy**, *adj*. (-ier, -iest) **s. side of life** = the unpleasant parts of life.

séance ['seɪɑːns] *n*. meeting where people try to get in touch with the spirits of dead people.

sear ['sɪə] *v*. to burn severely/to scorch.

search [sɜːtʃ] **1**. *n*. (*pl*. **-es**) trying to find sth; **police s.** = inspection by the police looking for stolen goods/bombs, etc.; **s. warrant** = official permit to carry out a search; **s. party** = group of people sent to look for s.o. **2**. *v*. (*a*) to examine carefully in order to find sth. (*b*) **to s. for** = try to find. **searcher**, *n*. person who searches. **searching**, *adj*. very careful (examination). **searchlight**, *n*. power- ful light used to try to see things, esp. aircraft, at night.

season ['si:zn] **1**. *n*. (*a*) one of four parts into which a year is divided. (*b*) any period of the year when sth usually takes place; **s. ticket** = ticket which is valid for unlimited journeys over a long period. **2**. *v*. (*a*) to add spices to (food). (*b*) to dry (wood) until it is ready to be used. **seasonable**, *adj*. which fits the season. **seasonably**, *adv*. as is usual for the season. **seasonal**, *adj*. which only lasts for a season; (work) for the (summer) season only. **seasoned**, *adj*. (wood) which has been dried; (traveller) who has much ex- perience of travelling. **seasoning**, *n*. spices which are added to food.

seat [si:t] **1**. *n*. (*a*) thing you sit on. (*b*) place (on a committee/town council, etc.); **parliamentary s.** = constituency. (*c*) part of a chair on which you sit. (*d*) part of a pair of trousers which covers the buttocks. (*e*) **s. of government** = place where the government is carried on; **country s.** = large house in the country. (*f*) way of sitting on a horse. **2.** *v.* (*a*) to make (s.o.) sit down. (*b*) to have room for people to sit down. **seat belt,** *n.* belt worn in a car/in an aircraft as protection in case of accident. **seating,** *n.* giving seats to people.

sebaceous [sɪ'beɪʃəs] *adj.* which produces fat.

secant ['si:knt] *n.* line which crosses a curve.

secateurs [sekə'tɜ:z] *n.pl.* **(pair of) s.** = very strong scissors used in gardening.

secede [sɪ'si:d] *v.* (*formal*) to break away from a group. **secession** [sɪ'seʃn] *n.* act of seceding.

secluded [sɪ'klu:dɪd] *adj.* (place) which is quiet/away from crowds. **seclusion** [sɪ'klu:ʒn] *n.* quiet/solitude.

second ['sekənd] (*as a number can be written* **2nd**) **1.** *n.* (*a*) sixtieth part of a minute; a moment; **s. hand** = long fast-moving hand on a watch. (*b*) sixtieth part of a degree. (*c*) person/thing which comes after the first. (*d*) person who helps a boxer/wrestler. (*e*) **seconds** = articles which are not perfect and are sold cheaply. (*f*) second gear. **2.** *adj.* (*a*) coming next after the first; **s. class** = ordinary railway travel, etc., which is not as luxurious or expensive as first class; **s. in command** = person directly under the commanding officer/managing director, etc.; **the s. century** = period from 100 AD to 199. (*b*) **every s. day** = every other day/on alternate days. **3.** *v.* (*a*) to support (a proposal). (*b*) [sɪ'kɒnd] to transfer from one job to another for a period of time. **secondary** ['sekəndrɪ] *adj.* (*a*) second in importance/in position; **s. industry** = industry which takes basic raw materials and processes them into manufactured goods; **s. picketing** = picketing of a factory, etc., by people who do not work there. (*b*) **s. education/s. school** = education/school for children of about 11 years of age and older. (*c*) **s. colours** = colours made by mixing primary colours. **secondarily,** *adv.* in second place in importance. **secondbest,** *adj.* & *adv.* in second place; not as good as

the best. **second childhood,** *n.* period in old age when old people seem to act like children. **seconder,** *n.* person who supports a motion. **second half,** *n.* (*a*) second section (as of a football match). (*b*) second part of a financial year, from July to December. **secondhand,** *adj.* & *adv.* not new/used; **I heard it at s.** = not from the original source of the news. **secondly,** *adv.* in second place. **secondment** [sɪ'kɒndmənt] *n.* being transferred for a period of time to another job. **second nature,** *n.* **it is s. n. to him** = he does it quite naturally. **second-rate,** *adj.* not of good quality. **second sight,** *n.* being able to tell what will happen in the future. **second thoughts,** *n. pl.* **to have s. t. about** = to change one's mind. **second wind,** *n.* **he got his s. w.** = he could breathe again easily after having lost his breath.

secret ['si:krət] **1.** *adj.* hidden from other people; not known. **2.** *n.* thing which is not known/which is kept hidden; **in s.** = without anyone knowing. **secrecy,** ['si:krəsɪ] *n.* keeping sth secret. **secretive,** *adj.* liking to keep things secret. **secretively,** *adv.* in a secretive way. **secretiveness,** *n.* being secretive. **secretly,** *adv.* in secret. **secret service,** *n.* government department which deals in espionage.

secretaire [sekrə'teə] *n.* desk with many little drawers.

secretary ['sekrətərɪ] *n.* (*a*) person who writes letters/files documents, etc., for s.o. (*b*) person who deals with correspondence/arranges meetings, etc., in a club/society. (*c*) minister in a government; **S. of State** = head of a large government department. (*d*) official in a government office/in an embassy; **first s.** = senior official in an embassy; **permanent s.** = main civil servant in a ministry. **Secretary General,** *n.* chief administrative officer of an international organization. **secretarial** [sekrə'teərɪəl] *adj.* referring to a secretary. **secretariat,** *n.* group of officials who administer a large office.

secrete [sɪ'kri:t] *v.* (*a*) to hide. (*b*) to produce (a liquid). **secretion** [sɪ'kri:ʃn] *n.* liquid produced by an organ/a plant.

sect [sekt] *n.* religious group. **sectarian**

[sek'teəriən] *adj.* referring to a religious group.

section ['sekʃn] *n.* (*a*) cutting; cutting tissue in an operation. (*b*) part. (*c*) picture of sth showing what it is like when cut through. (*d*) part of sth which, when joined to other parts, goes to make up a whole. **sectional,** *adj.* (*a*) (diagram) showing a section through sth. (*b*) (built) in sections.

sector ['sektə] *n.* (*a*) section of a circle between two lines drawn from the centre to the circumference; section of the surface of a computer disk. (*b*) **private s.** = part of industry which is privately owned; **public s.** = nationalized industries and the civil service.

secular ['sekjulə] *adj.* not religious/not connected with religion. **secularize,** *v.* to make secular.

secure [sɪ'kju:ə] **1.** *adj.* (*a*) safe. (*b*) firmly fixed; **s. job** = where you can't be sacked. (*c*) confident. **2.** *v.* (*a*) to make firm/to fasten. **securely,** *adv.* in a secure way. **security,** *n.* (*a*) safety. (*b*) protection against criminals/against hardship; **airport s.** = measures to protect aircraft against hijackers. (*c*) thing given to s.o. who has lent you money and which is returned when the loan is repaid. (*d*) **government securities** = papers showing that the government will pay back money which people have lent it. **Security Council,** *n.* ruling body of the United Nations.

sedan [sɪ'dæn] *n.* Am. covered family car. **sedan-chair,** *n.* (*old*) seat in a box carried on long poles by bearers.

sedate [sɪ'deɪt] **1.** *adj.* serious/dignified. **2.** *v.* to give (a patient) sedatives. **sedately,** *adv.* in a calm/serious way. **sedateness,** *n.* being sedate. **sedative** ['sedətɪv] *adj. & n.* (medicine) which makes you calm/which makes you go to sleep. **sedation** [sɪ'deɪʃn] *n.* giving medicine to calm a patient.

sedentary ['sedəntrɪ] *adj.* always sitting down.

sedge [sedʒ] *n.* type of grass which grows in water.

sediment ['sedɪmənt] *n.* solid which forms at the bottom of a liquid. **sedimentary** [sedɪ'mentərɪ] *adj.*

(rocks) which were formed from mud deposited at the bottom of the sea/ rivers, etc. **sedimentation,** *n.* action of depositing solid particles at the bottom of liquid.

sedition [sə'dɪʃn] *n.* encouraging people to rebel against the government. **seditious,** *adj.* which encourages people to rebel.

seduce [sɪ'dju:s] *v.* (*a*) to persuade (s.o.) to do sth which is perhaps wrong. (*b*) to persuade (s.o.) to have sexual intercourse. **seducer,** *n.* person who seduces. **seduction** [sɪ'dʌkʃn] *n.* act of seducing. **seductive** [sɪ'dʌktɪv] *adj.* attractive.

sedulous ['sedjuləs] *adj.* very careful and persistent. **sedulously,** *adv.* in a sedulous way.

sedum ['si:dəm] *n.* succulent rock plant.

see [si:] **1.** *n.* area over which a bishop rules. **2.** *v.* (*saw* [sɔ:], *seen*) (*a*) to sense with your eyes. (*b*) to accompany; **to s. s.o. home.** (*c*) to understand. (*d*) to examine. (*e*) to make sure (**that**). (*f*) to visit/to meet. (*g*) to go to a performance of (a play/film, etc.). **seeing,** *n.* action of sensing with the eyes; **s. that** = since. **see through,** *v.* (*a*) to understand s.o.'s plans to trick you. (*b*) to work on (sth) until it is finished. **see-through,** *adj.* transparent. **see to,** *v.* to busy yourself about sth; **see to it** = make sure (**that**).

seed [si:d] **1.** *n.* (*a*) part of a plant which appears after the flowers and then can produce a new plant; **to go/ to run to s.** = produce flowers and seeds which are not needed; **he's gone to s.** = he's become lazy/he's got worse. (*b*) tennis player selected as one of the best players in a tournament (before the tournament starts). **2.** *v.* (*a*) to produce seeds. (*b*) to select (the best players) in a tennis tournament and arrange them so that they do not play each other until the later rounds. **seedbed,** *n.* special area of fine soil where you can sow seeds. **seedless,** *adj.* (fruit) with no seeds in it. **seedling,** *n.* very young plant. **seedsman,** *n.* (*pl.* **-men**) person who specializes in growing and selling seeds. **seedy,** *adj.* (**-ier, -iest**) worn-out (clothes); sick (person).

seek [si:k] *v.* (**sought** [sɔ:t]) (*a*) to look

for. (b) to ask for. **seeker,** n. person who seeks.

seem [si:m] v. to appear. **seeming,** adj. not real, though appearing to be. **seemingly,** adj. apparently. **seemly,** adj. decent/correct.

seen [si:n] v. see see.

seep [si:p] v. (of a liquid) to pass through a crack. **seepage,** n. act of seeping; liquid which has seeped.

seer ['si:ə] n. (old) person who sees into the future.

seersucker ['siəsʌkə] n. cotton cloth with a wrinkled surface.

seesaw ['si:sɔ:] 1. n. children's toy made of a plank with seats at each end, balanced in the middle, so that when one end goes up the other goes down. 2. v. to go up and down.

seethe [si:ð] v. (a) to be very angry. (b) to move about like boiling water. **seething,** adj. very angry.

segment ['segmənt] n. part of sth (which seems to form a natural division); part of a circle or sphere. **segmentation** [segmən'teɪʃn] n. being segmented. **segmented** [seg'mentɪd] adj. with segments.

segregate ['segrɪgeɪt] v. to divide one group from another. **segregation** [segrɪ'geɪʃn] n. division of one group from another; **racial s.** = splitting of a population into groups according to race or colour.

seine [seɪn] n. type of fishing net.

seismic ['saɪzmɪk] adj. referring to earthquakes. **seismograph,** n. instrument for recording earthquakes. **seismological** [saɪzmə'lɒdʒɪkl] adj. referring to seismology. **seismology** [saɪz'mɒlədʒɪ] n. study of earthquakes.

seize [si:z] v. (a) to grab/to hold tight. (b) to confiscate/to take by force. **seize up,** v. (of an engine) to stop working/to become blocked. **seizure** ['si:ʒə] n. (a) confiscation of goods by the police. (b) stroke/illness caused by lack of blood to the brain.

seldom ['seldəm] adv. rarely/not often.

select [sɪ'lekt] 1. v. to choose. 2. adj. (a) of top quality. (b) **s. club** = club which only lets in certain people; **s. area** = smart area. **Select Committee,** n. special committee of the House

of Commons, which examines the work of a single ministry. **selection** [sɪ'lekʃn] n. (a) choice. (b) things chosen. **selective,** adj. which chooses (carefully); (weedkiller) which only kills certain plants. **selectively,** adv. in a selective way. **selectivity,** n. being able to choose carefully. **selector,** n. person who chooses players to play in a football team/cricket team, etc.

self [self] n. (pl. **selves**) your own person or character; (on cheques) **pay s.** = pay the person who has signed the cheque. **self-addressed,** adj. (envelope) on which you have written your own address. **self-assertive,** adj. (person) who makes others do what he wants. **self-assurance,** n. being self-assured. **self-assured,** adj. sure you are capable of doing sth. **self-catering,** n. doing the cooking for yourself; **s.-c. holiday** = one where you rent accommodation, but cook your own meals. **self-centred,** adj. (person) who only thinks of himself. **self-confidence,** n. being self-confident. **self-confident,** adj. sure you are capable of doing sth. **self-conscious,** adj. embarrassed because you feel you have certain faults. **self-consciously,** adv. with embarrassment. **self-consciousness,** n. being self-conscious. **self-contained,** adj. (flat) which has its own kitchen/bathroom, etc., and does not share these facilities with others. **self-control,** n. keeping your feelings under control. **self-defeating,** adj. (plan) which works in such a way that it defeats its own purpose. **self-defence,** n. protecting yourself. **self-denial,** n. refusing to give yourself sth/going without sth which you would like. **self-determination,** n. choosing your own political future. **self-drive car,** n. car which you can rent and drive yourself. **self-educated,** adj. (person) who has taught himself everything he knows and who has not been to school. **self-effacing,** adj. (person) who tries to be inconspicuous/who does not want people to notice him. **self-employed,** adj. (person) who works for himself, and is not paid a salary by s.o. else. **self-esteem,** n. pride in yourself. **self-evident,** *adj.* obvious. **self-explanatory,** *adj.* obvious/which explains itself. **self-governing,** *adj.* (country) which governs itself. **self-government,** *n.* control of a country by its own people, not by another country. **self-help,** *n.* improving one's condition by one's own efforts. **self-important,** *adj.* (person) who feels he is very important when he really is not. **self-indulgent,** *adj.* (person) who gives himself everything he wants. **self-interest,** *n.* working for one's own benefit. **selfish,** *adj.* only interested in yourself/doing sth only for yourself. **selfishly,** *adv.* (done) only for yourself. **selfishness,** *n.* being selfish. **selfless,** *adj.* not selfish/thinking only of others. **self-made man,** *n.* person who has become rich entirely through his own efforts. **self-pity,** *n.* pity for yourself. **self-portrait,** *n.* painting which an artist has made of himself. **self-possessed,** *adj.* calm/not bothered. **self-raising flour,** *n.* flour which contains baking powder to make cakes rise. **self-reliance,** *n.* being self-reliant. **self-reliant,** *adj.* independent/relying only on yourself. **self-respect,** *n.* pride in yourself/concern that you have a good character and work well. **self-righteous,** *adj.* feeling sure that you are doing what is right. **self-rule,** *n.* self-government. **self-sacrifice,** *n.* giving up sth which you would like, so that others may enjoy it. **self-sacrificing,** *adj.* (person) who gives up pleasures, so that others may enjoy them. **selfsame,** *adj.* exactly the same. **self-satisfaction,** *n.* being self-satisfied. **self-satisfied,** *adj.* contented with what you have done. **self-seeking,** *adj.* (person) who works to his own advantage, at the expense of others. **self-service,** *n. & adj.* (shop) where you take things yourself from the counters and pay at a cash desk. **self-styled,** *adj.* (person) who has given himself a title. **self-sufficiency,** *n.* being self-sufficient. **self-sufficient,** *adj.* producing enough food, etc., for all needs. **self-supporting,** *adj.* providing for one's own needs, with no help from others. **self-taught,** *adj.* (person) who has taught himself a certain skill. **self-**

willed, *adj.* obstinate/always wanting to have your own way.

sell [sel] **1.** *n.* act of selling; **hard s.** = forceful selling of a product. **2.** *v.* (**sold, has sold**) (*a*) to give goods to s.o. in exchange for money. (*b*) *inf.* to betray. **sell-by-date,** *n.* date on a packet of food, which is the last date on which the food is guaranteed to be good. **seller,** *n.* (*a*) person who sells. (*b*) **good s.** = thing that sells well. **sell off,** *v.* to sell (sth) cheaply to get rid of it. **sell out,** *v.* (*a*) to sell so many things that you have none left. (*b*) *inf.* to abandon your principles. **sell-out,** *n.* (*a*) show/play, etc. where all the tickets have been sold. (*b*) *inf.* abandoning of principles. **sell up,** *v.* to sell a business.

sellotape ['seləteɪp] **1.** *n.* trade mark for a type of transparent sticky tape. **2.** *v.* to attack (sth) with sticky tape.

selvage, selvedge ['selvɪdʒ] *n.* edge of a piece of cloth which does not fray.

semantics [sɪ'mæntɪks] *n.* study of the meaning of language. **semantically,** *adv.* in a way which refers to semantics.

semaphore ['seməfɔ:] *n.* way of signalling using two arms (and flags) in different positions for each letter.

semblance ['sembləns] *n.* appearance.

semen ['si:mən] *n.* liquid in which male sperm floats.

semester [sə'mestə] *n. Am.* term in a school or college year which only has two terms.

semi ['semɪ] **1.** *n. inf.* semi-detached house. **2. semi-** *prefix meaning* half. **semi-breve,** *n.* long note in music, lasting two minims. **semicircle,** *n.* half a circle. **semi-circular,** *adj.* like a half circle in shape. **semi-colon,** *n.* punctuation mark (;) showing a pause. **semiconductor,** *n.* material (such as silicon) which is partly able to conduct electricity. **semi-conscious,** *adj.* half conscious. **semi-detached,** *adj.* (house) which is joined to another similar house on one side, but is not joined on the other. **semi-final,** *n.* one of two matches in a competition, the winners of which go into the final game. **semi-finalist,** *n.* team/player in a semi-final. **semi-official,** *adj.* not quite official. **semi-precious,**

n. (stone) which is quite valuable, but not in the same class as diamonds/rubies/sapphires, etc. **semi-quaver,** *n.* note in music lasting half as long as a quaver. **semi-skilled,** *adj.* (worker) who has been trained to a certain level. **semitone,** *n.* (*in music*) half a tone on the scale.

seminal ['seminl] *adj.* which acts as the starting point for sth new.

seminar ['semina:] *n.* class given to a small group of students who meet to discuss a problem with a teacher.

seminary ['seminəri] *n.* college for priests.

Semitic [sə'mitik] *adj.* referring to a group of races including Jews and Arabs.

semolina [semə'li:nə] *n.* hard crushed wheat, used to make spaghetti and milk puddings.

senate ['senət] *n.* (*a*) upper house of parliament in some countries. (*b*) main committee which governs a university. **senator,** *n.* member of the upper house of parliament.

send [send] *v.* (sent) (*a*) to tell (s.o.) to go somewhere; to make (sth) go from one place to another. (*b*) to give (s.o.) a sensation; **it sent him crazy.** (*c*) to put out (roots, etc.). (*d*) *inf.* to make (s.o.) excited. **send away,** *v.* (*a*) to make (s.o./sth) go away. (*b*) **to send away for** = to write asking s.o. to send sth to you. **send back,** *v.* to return (sth). **send down,** *v.* to dismiss (a student) from a university. **sender,** *n.* person who sends. **send for,** *v.* to pass a message to (s.o.) asking them to come. **send off,** *v.* (*a*) to make (s.o./sth) go off. (*b*) to post; **to send off for** = send away for. (*c*) to tell (a player) to leave the football field because of bad conduct. **send-off,** *n.* party to say goodbye to s.o. leaving on a long journey. **send out,** *v.* to make (s.o./sth) go out. **send up,** *v.* (*a*) to make (s.o./sth) go up. (*b*) *inf.* to make fun of (s.o.).

senile ['si:naɪl] *adj.* old and mentally weak. **senility** [sə'nɪlɪtɪ] *n.* being senile.

senior ['si:njə] **1.** *adj.* (*a*) older; **J. Smith S.** = father of J. Smith Junior; **s. school** = school for older children; **s. citizen** = old person living on a pension. (*b*)

more important (rank, etc.); **the Senior Service** = the Royal Navy. **2.** *n.* (*a*) older person; **the seniors** = the older children in a school. (*b*) *Am.* fourth-year student. **seniority** [si:nɪ'ɒrɪtɪ] *n.* being senior.

senna ['senə] *n.* **s. pods** = dried pods used as a laxative.

sensation [sen'seɪʃn] *n.* (*a*) feeling. (*b*) (thing/person that causes) great excitement. **sensational,** *adj.* very exciting. **sensationally,** *adv.* in a sensational way.

sense [sens] **1.** *n.* (*a*) one of the five ways in which you notice sth; **sixth s.** = ability to feel that sth has taken place/will take place, without using any of the five senses. (*b*) feeling. (*c*) **senses** = power of reasoning; **to come to one's senses** = become reasonable. (*d*) meaning; **to make s.** = to have a meaning; **to make s. of** = to understand. (*e*) reasonableness/good judgement. **2.** *v.* to feel. **senseless,** *adj.* (*a*) stupid. (*b*) unconscious. **senselessness,** *n.* stupidity.

sensible ['sensɪbl] *adj.* (*a*) reasonable/well judged. (*b*) (person) who has commonsense. (*c*) **s. walking shoes** = strong, but not fashionable, walking shoes. (*d*) (*formal*) **s. of** = aware of. **sensibility** [sensɪ'bɪlɪtɪ] *n.* being capable of delicate feeling. **sensibly,** *adv.* in a sensible way.

sensitive ['sensɪtɪv] *adj.* (*a*) able to feel keenly/sharply. (*b*) (instrument) which measures very accurately. (*c*) (substance) which reacts to light, etc. **sensitivity** [sensɪ'tɪvɪtɪ], **sensitiveness,** *n.* being sensitive. **sensitively,** *adv.* in a sensitive way. **sensitize** ['sensɪtaɪz] *v.* to make sensitive (to light, etc.).

sensor ['sensə] *n.* apparatus which detects sth by sense of heat/light/smell of smoke, etc. **sensory,** *adj.* referring to the senses.

sensual ['sensjʊəl] *adj.* referring to pleasures of the body, not of the mind. **sensuality,** *n.* experience of sensual pleasure. **sensually,** *adv.* in a sensual way.

sensuous ['sensjʊəs] *adj.* which gives pleasure to the senses. **sensuously,** *adv.* in a sensuous way.

sent [sent] v. see **send**.

sentence ['sentəns] 1. n. (a) words put together to form a complete separate statement, usu. ending with a full stop. (b) decision of a judge which gives the details of punishment. 2. v. to condemn (s.o.) to a certain punishment.

sententious [sen'tenʃəs] adj. too full of moral sense. **sententiously**, adv. in a sententious way.

sentient ['senʃnt] adj. able to feel.

sentiment ['sentɪmənt] n. (a) show of feeling. (b) **sentiments** = opinions. **sentimental** [sentɪ'mentəl] adj. full of emotion/full of feeling. **sentimentality** [sentɪmən'tælɪtɪ] n. playing on the emotions (in literature/music). **sentimentally**, adv. by feeling.

sentinel ['sentɪnl] n. sentry.

sentry ['sentrɪ] n. soldier on duty at a gate, etc. **sentry-box**, n. wooden shelter for a sentry.

sepal ['sepəl] n. green leaf under the petals of a flower.

separate 1. adj. ['seprət] detached/not together. 2. v. ['sepəreɪt] to detach/ to divide. 3. n. **separates** = pieces of women's clothing (skirts/blouse/ jumper, etc.) which can be worn in different combinations. **separable** ['seprəbl] adj. which can be separated. **separately**, adv. in a separate way. **separation** [sepə'reɪʃn] n. dividing/ living apart. **separatism** ['sepərətɪzəm] n. political ideal of separating from a large country. **separatist**, adj. & n. (person) who wants his region to separate from a large country. **separator**, n. person/machine that separates.

sepia ['si:pɪə] n. brown colour.

sepsis ['sepsɪs] n. being septic.

September [sep'tembə] n. 9th month of the year.

septennial [sep'tenɪəl] adj. for seven years.

septet [sep'tet] n. group of seven musicians; piece of music for seven instruments.

septic ['septɪk] adj. (wound) which has gone bad/become poisoned; **s. tank** = underground tank near a house for collecting sewage.

septicaemia [septɪ'si:mɪə] n. poisoning of the blood.

septuagenarian [septjʊədʒə'neərɪən] n. person who is between seventy and seventy-nine years old.

septum ['septəm] n. (pl. **-ta**) wall between two sections of the body/a plant.

sepulchre, Am. **sepulcher** ['sepəlkə] n. tomb. **sepulchral** [se'pʌlkrəl] adj. referring to a sepulchre; very deep gloomy (voice).

sequel ['si:kwəl] n. (a) continuation of a story, play, etc. (b) result.

sequence ['si:kwəns] n. (a) series of things happening; series of numbers which follow each other. (b) scene in a film. **sequential**, adj. in sequence. **sequentially**, adv. in sequence.

sequester [sɪ'kwestə] v. (formal) to seclude. **sequestrate** ['sekwɪstreɪt] v. (formal) to confiscate (property). **sequestrator**, n. person who seizes property on the orders of a court.

sequin ['si:kwɪn] n. small round shiny metal ornament. **sequinned**, adj. covered with sequins.

sequoia [sɪ'kwɔɪə] n. redwood.

seraglio [se'ræljəʊ] n. harem.

seraph ['seræf] n. (pl. **seraphim**) highest angel. **seraphic**, adj. like a seraph.

serenade [serə'neɪd] 1. n. love song. 2. v. to sing a love song to (s.o.).

serendipity [serən'dɪpɪtɪ] n. pleasure which you get from finding things by accident.

serene [sə'ri:n] adj. calm/not worried. **serenely**, adv. in a serene way. **serenity** [sə'renɪtɪ] n. being serene.

serf [sɜ:f] n. peasant/slave working on a farm. **serfdom**, n. state of being a serf.

serge [sɜ:dʒ] n. type of thick cloth.

sergeant ['sɑ:dʒənt] n. senior non-commissioned officer in the army/the police. **sergeant-major**, n. rank in the army above sergeant.

serial ['sɪərɪəl] 1. adj. (number) of a series. 2. n. story/TV play which is told in several instalments. **serialize**, v. to make (a novel, etc.) into a serial.

seriatim [sɪərɪ'ɑ:tɪm] adv. in order.

series ['sɪərɪz] n. (pl. **series**) (a) group of things which come one after the other in a set order. (b) group of things.

serif ['serɪf] n. little line added to the end of a stroke in a typeset character.

serious ['sɪərɪəs] adj. (a) not humorous.

(b) important/bad. **seriously,** *adv.* in a serious way. **seriousness,** *n.* being serious.

serjeant ['sɑ:dʒənt] *n.* **s.-at-arms** = office of a court/of parliament.

sermon ['sɜ:mən] *n.* serious speech made in church. **sermonize,** *v.* to preach to (s.o.).

serpent ['sɜ:pənt] *n.* snake. **serpentine,** *adj.* like a snake; winding.

serrated [sə'reɪtɪd] *adj.* toothed (blade); with a zigzag edge. **serration,** *n.* being serrated; serrated edge.

serried ['serɪd] *adj.* **in s. ranks** = in ranks close together.

serum ['sɪərəm] *n.* yellow liquid in the blood, which can be injected into s.o.'s body to fight disease.

serve [sɜ:v] **1.** *n.* act of serving the ball at tennis. **2.** *v.* (a) to provide/to give (food); to help at table; (of a recipe) to make enough food for. (b) to work for. (c) to be useful (**as**). (d) to deal with (a customer). (e) to undergo punishment. (f) to start a game of tennis by hitting the ball first. (g) **it serves you right** = you deserve the punishment you have got. (h) to assist a priest (at mass). **servant,** *n.* (a) person who is paid to work in the house. (b) **civil s.** = government employee. **server,** *n.* (a) person who serves at table. (b) large flat knife for serving food; spoon/fork for serving fish or salad. (c) person who helps a priest (at mass).

service ['sɜ:vɪs] **1.** *n.* (a) working for s.o.; **military s.** = period which you spend in the army/navy/air force; **s. flat** = flat where cleaning, etc., is provided; **s. charge** = charge added to a bill for the work carried out; **s. road** = road which leads to a house, etc., but nowhere else. (b) group of people working together; **civil s.** = all the government employees; **the foreign s.** = people who represent their country abroad; **the services** = the army, navy and air force. (c) providing basic essentials which people require; **bus s.** = regularly passing bus. (d) regular religious ceremony. (e) act of starting a game of tennis by hitting the ball first. (f) set of china for use at tea/dinner. (g) repairs to a machine, done on a regular basis; **the car needs a s.**

= examination by the garage; **s. area** = place by a motorway where you can stop and buy petrol/get food, etc. **2.** *v.* to do any repairs which need doing to (a car, etc.). **serviceable,** *adj.* practical; which will be useful. **serviceman,** *n.* (*pl.* **-men**) member of the army/navy/air force. **service-station,** *n.* garage which sells petrol/oil, etc. **servicewoman,** *n.* (*pl.* **-women**) woman member of the army/navy/air force.

serviette [sɜ:vɪ'et] *n.* square of cloth or soft paper used to protect your clothes and wipe your mouth at table.

servile ['sɜ:vaɪl] *adj.* like a slave. **servilely,** *adv.* in a servile way. **servility** [sɜ:'vɪlɪtɪ] *n.* acting like a slave. **servitude** ['sɜ:vɪtju:d] *n.* slavery.

servo- ['sɜ:vəʊ] *prefix meaning* power-assisted.

sesame ['sesəmɪ:] *n.* tropical plant whose seeds produce oil or are eaten.

session ['seʃn] *n.* (a) meeting of a committee/parliament, etc.; **in s.** = in the process of meeting. (b) meeting to study/to practise.

set [set] **1.** *n.* (a) group of things which go together; (*in mathematics*) group of numbers, etc., which are linked. (b) apparatus. (c) one of the main parts of a tennis match. (d) group of people. (e) scenery on a stage. (f) position/direction. (g) arranging of hair. (h) **onion s.** = very small onion which is planted and then grows into a large one. (i) burrow of a badger. **2.** *v.* (**set**) (a) to put/to place; **to s. the table** = put the knives and forks, etc. on the table. (b) to arrange/to fix (a machine, etc.). (c) to arrange in place. (d) to give work to. (e) to make (free, etc.). (f) to become solid. (g) (of sun/stars) to go down. (h) to write music to go with (a poem, etc.). (i) to place scenery on a stage; to put (the action of a story) in a certain period. (j) to arrange letters in rows for printing. **3.** *adj.* (a) fixed/which cannot be changed. (b) ready. **set about,** *v.* to start doing (sth). **set aside,** *v.* (a) to put to one side/to reject. (b) to keep to one side (for future use). **set-aside,** *n.* system of using land previously used for farming, for another purpose. **set back,** *v.* (a) to make late. (b) *inf.* **it s. me back £10**

= it cost me £10. **setback**, *n*. holding back progress. **set down**, *v*. (*a*) to write down on paper. (*b*) to let passengers get off. **set forth**, *v*. (*old*) (*a*) to start a journey. (*b*) to write out (a list, etc.). **set in**, *v*. to start; to become fixed. **set off**, *v*. (*a*) to start a journey (*b*) to light (fireworks); to make (a bomb) explode; to start (a reaction). (*c*) to show up. **set out**, *v*. (*a*) to put out. (*b*) to start a journey. **set-square**, *n*. instrument to help you draw lines, shaped like a right angled triangle. **setting**, *n*. (*a*) action of setting. (*b*) background for a story; frame in which a diamond is fixed. (*c*) **place s.** = set of knives/forks/spoons, etc., for one person. **set to**, *v*. to get to work. **set-to**, *n*. *inf*. argument/fight. **set up**, *v*. to build/to establish. **set-up**, *n*. *inf*. arrangement/organization. **set upon**, *v*. to attack.

sett [set] *n*. burrow of a badger.

settee [se'ti:] *n*. sofa.

setter ['setə] *n*. hunting dog trained to point out game by standing still.

settle ['setl] **1.** *n*. long wooden bench with a back. **2.** *v*. (*a*) to arrange/to agree; to end (a dispute); **to s. up** = pay the bill; **to s. on/for** = to decide on/to choose. (*b*) (*also* **settle down**) to place yourself in a comfortable position/to rest. (*c*) to go to live **in** a new country. (*d*) (*of sediment*) to fall to the bottom of a liquid; (*of building*) to sink into the ground. (*e*) **to s. money on s.o.** = to pass money to s.o. by a legal process. **settled**, *adj*. fixed/unchanging. **settlement**, *n*. (*a*) payment (of a bill); agreement in a dispute. (*b*) place where a group of people has settled. (*c*) settling money, etc., on s.o. (*d*) (*of building*) act of sinking into the ground. **settler**, *n*. person who goes to settle in a new country.

seven ['sevn] *n*. number 7. **seventeen**, *n*. number 17. **seventeenth, 17th**, *adj*. & *n*. referring to seventeen; **the s. century** = period from 1600 to 1699. **seventh, 7th**, *adj*. & *n*. referring to seven. **seventieth, 70th**, *adj*. & *n*. referring to seventy. **seventy**, *n*. number 70.

sever ['sevə] *v*. to cut off. **severance**, *n*. cutting off; **s. pay** = money paid as compensation to s.o. who is losing a job.

several ['sevrəl] *adj*. & *pron*. more than a few, but not very many. **severally**, *adv*. separately.

severe [sə'viə] *adj*. (**-er, -est**) (*a*) very strict. (*b*) very bad (illness, weather, etc.). **severely**, *adv*. (*a*) strictly. (*b*) badly. **severity** [sə'veriti] *n*. being severe.

sew [səu] *v*. (**sewn**) to attach/to mend by using a needle and thread; to make (with a needle and thread). **sewing**, *n*. (*a*) action of attaching/mending with needle and thread. (*b*) work which s.o. is in the process of sewing. **sewing machine**, *n*. machine which sews. **sew up**, *v*. (*a*) to close (a hole) by sewing. (*b*) *inf*. to settle (a deal).

sewer ['suə] *n*. large tube in the ground used for taking away waste and dirty water from houses. **sewage** ['su:idʒ] *n*. waste and dirty water; **s. works/s. farm** = place where waste is collected and treated to kill germs. **sewerage**, *n*. system of sewers for removing waste and dirty water.

sex [seks] **1.** *n*. (*pl*. **-es**) (*a*) one of two groups (male and female) into which animals and plants can be divided; **s. appeal** = attractiveness to members of the other sex. (*b*) **to have s. with s.o.** = to have sexual intercourse. **2.** *v*. **to s. chickens** = to tell whether chickens are male or female. **sexism**, *n*. bias against one sex. **sexist**, *adj*. & *n*. (person) who is biased against one of the sexes. **sexless**, *adj*. without sex; not involving sexual feeling. **sexological**, *adj*. referring to sexology. **sexologist**, *n*. person who studies human sex. **sexology** [sek'sɒlədʒi] *n*. study of human sex. **sexual** ['seksjuəl] *adj*. referring to sex; **s. intercourse** = reproductive act between a male and female. **sexuality**, *n*. interest in sexual intercourse. **sexually**, *adv*. in a sexual way. **sexy**, *adj*. sexually attractive.

sexagenarian [seksədʒə'neəriən] *adj*. & *n*. (person) who is between sixty years and sixty-nine years old.

sextant ['sekstənt] *n*. instrument for calculating the position of a ship by referring to the stars.

sextet [seks'tet] *n*. (*a*) group of six musicians playing together. (*b*) piece of music for six musicians.

sexton ['sekstən] *n.* man who works in a church/rings the bells/digs graves, etc.

sh [ʃ] *inter.* used to make silence.

shabby ['ʃæbɪ] *adj.* (**-ier, -iest**) poor/worn out (clothes); mean (trick). **shabbily,** *adv.* in a shabby way. **shabbiness,** *n.* being shabby.

shack [ʃæk] **1.** *n.* rough wooden hut. **2.** *v. Sl.* **to s. up with s.o.** = to go to live with s.o.

shackle ['ʃækl] **1.** *n.* thing which hampers movement; **shackles** = chains (for attaching a prisoner). **2.** *v.* to attach (s.o.) with a chain.

shade [ʃeɪd] **1.** *n.* (*a*) dark place which is not in the sunlight; **to put s.o. in the s.** = to make s.o. seem less important/hardworking, etc. (*b*) dark part of a picture. (*c*) cover put on a lamp; *Am.* blind on a window. (*d*) type of colour; slight difference. (*e*) little bit. (*f*) *Am. inf.* **shades** = sunglasses. (*g*) (*formal*) ghost. **2.** *v.* (*a*) to protect (sth) from sunlight. (*b*) to make (a picture) darker. (*c*) (*also* **shade off**) to change from one colour to another gradually. **shadiness,** *n.* being shady. **shading,** *n.* action of making shade; making part of a picture darker. **shady,** *adj.* (**-ier, -iest**) (*a*) full of shade. (*b*) dishonest/disreputable.

shadow ['ʃædəʊ] **1.** *n.* (*a*) shade made by an object in light; **five o'clock s.** = dark tint on a man's chin as his beard begins to grow. (*b*) small amount. (*c*) person who follows s.o. (*d*) opposition in parliament which parallels the government; **s. cabinet** = senior members of the opposition who parallel the government. **2.** *v.* to follow (s.o.). **shadowy,** *adj.* vague/indistinct.

shaft [ʃɑːft] *n.* (*a*) long stick which is the main part of an arrow/a javelin, etc.; long pole in front of a cart to which a horse is attached. (*b*) ray of light. (*c*) rod which turns in an engine. (*d*) pillar. (*e*) deep hole in the ground; **lift s.** = hole down the centre of a building in which a lift moves up and down.

shag [ʃæg] *n.* (*a*) thick tobacco. (*b*) type of black sea bird. **shaggy** ['ʃægɪ] *adj.* (**-ier, -iest**) with long hair; **s. dog story** = very long story with an unexpectedly silly ending. **shag-pile carpet,** *n.* carpet with thick wool fibres.

shake [ʃeɪk] **1.** *n.* (*a*) act of moving from side to side or up and down. (*b*) drink made by mixing milk and flavouring. **2.** *v.* (**shook** [ʃuːk]; **shaken**) to move from side to side or up and down; **to s. one's head** = to move one's head from side to side to indicate 'no'. **shake down,** *v.* to settle down (after a period of uncertainty). **shakedown,** *n.* rough bed. **shaken,** *adj.* very upset/disturbed. **shake off,** *v.* to get rid of (sth unpleasant). **shaker,** *n.* person/machine which shakes; container for mixing cocktails. **shake-up,** *n. inf.* total change. **shakily,** *adv.* in a shaky way. **shakiness,** *n.* being shaky. **shaky,** *adj.* (**-ier, -iest**) (*a*) wobbly; trembling. (*b*) not very reliable.

shale [ʃeɪl] *n.* type of rock which splits into soft thin slices.

shall [ʃæl] *v.* used with I and we to form future (*negative;* **shan't;** *past* **should**) (*a*) (*suggestion/request*) **s. we sit down?** (*b*) (*emphasis in the future*) **yes I s.!** (*c*) (*negative future*) **I shan't say anything.** (*note: except for* (*a*) **shall** *is gradually being replaced by* **will**); *see also* **should.**

shallot [ʃəˈlɒt] *n.* type of small onion which grows in clusters.

shallow ['ʃæləʊ] **1.** *adj.* (**-er, -est**) (*a*) not deep. (*b*) superficial (mind). **2.** *n.* **shallows** = water which is not deep. **shallowness,** *n.* being shallow.

sham [ʃæm] **1.** *adj.* false. **2.** *n.* thing which is false. **3.** *v.* (**shammed**) to pretend.

shamble ['ʃæmbl] *v.* **to s. along** = to wander along dragging your feet.

shambles ['ʃæmblz] *n.* disorder/mess.

shame [ʃeɪm] **1.** *n.* (*a*) feeling caused by being guilty/being ashamed. (*b*) **what a s.** = what a pity/how sad. **2.** *v.* **to s. s.o. into** = to make s.o. ashamed so that he does sth. **shamefaced,** *adj.* embarrassed/ashamed. **shamefacedly,** *adv.* in embarrassment. **shameful,** *adj.* scandalous/disgraceful. **shamefully,** *adv.* in a shameful way. **shameless,** *adj.* without shame. **shamelessly,** *adv.* in a shamless way.

shampoo [ʃæmˈpuː] **1.** *n.* liquid soap for washing your hair/a carpet, etc. **2.** *v.* to wash (your hair/the carpet, etc.) with a shampoo.

shamrock ['ʃæmrɒk] *n.* small clover-like plant with leaves which are split into three parts.

shandy ['ʃændɪ] *n.* mixture of beer and lemonade.

shanghai [ʃæŋ'haɪ] **1.** *n.* (*in Australia*) catapult. **2.** *v.* (**shanghaied**) to capture (s.o.) and force them to obey your orders.

shank [ʃæŋk] *n.* (*a*) straight shaft. (*b*) leg.

shan't [ʃɑːnt] *v. see* **shall.**

shanty ['ʃæntɪ] *n.* (*a*) rough wooden hut; **s. town** = group of huts belonging to poor people. (*b*) **sea s.** = song sung by sailors.

shape [ʃeɪp] **1.** *n.* (*a*) form; **the picture is taking s.** = is beginning to look like sth. (*b*) mould for making a jelly. (*c*) condition. **2.** *v.* (*a*) to form/ to make into a shape. (*b*) **to s. well** = turn out well. **shapeless,** *adj.* with no definite shape. **shapelessness,** *n.* being shapeless. **shapeliness,** *n.* being shapely. **shapely,** *adj.* with an attractive shape.

shard [ʃɑːd] *n.* piece of broken pottery.

share ['ʃeə] **1.** *n.* (*a*) part which belongs to someone. (*b*) contribution which each person makes. (*c*) one of the parts into which a company's capital is divided. (*d*) ploughshare, the metal blade of a plough. **2.** *v.* (*a*) (*also* **share out**) to divide up among several people. (*b*) **to s. sth with s.o.** = to allow s.o. to use sth which you also use. (*c*) to have/to use (sth) in common. **shareholder,** *n.* person who owns shares in a company. **shareholding,** *n.* group of shares in a company owned by one person. **share-out,** *n.* division of sth among several people.

shark [ʃɑːk] *n.* (*a*) large dangerous fish which can kill a man. (*b*) *inf.* crook/ swindler.

sharp [ʃɑːp] **1.** *adj.* (**-er, -est**) (*a*) with a fine cutting edge. (*b*) very cutting/ harsh. (*c*) with a very acute angle. (*d*) bitter. (*e*) clever/intelligent. (*f*) with a highly-developed sense. (*g*) high-pitched (sound). (*h*) (*in music*) (note) which is slightly higher than the correct pitch. (*i*) clear (image). **2.** *n.* note in music which is a semitone higher. **3.** *adv.* (*a*) acutely. (*b*) exactly. (*c*) (*in*

music) higher than the correct pitch. **sharpen,** *v.* to make sharp. **sharpener,** *n.* **pencil s.** = instrument for sharpening pencils. **sharper,** *n.* person who cheats at cards. **sharply,** *adv.* (*a*) acutely. (*b*) completely. (*c*) harshly. **sharpness,** *n.* being sharp. **sharp practice,** *n.* dishonest activity. **sharpshooter,** *n.* soldier who is trained to shoot very accurately. **sharp-witted,** *adj.* clever.

shatter ['ʃætə] *v.* to break into little pieces; to upset (s.o.) very badly.

shave [ʃeɪv] **1.** *n.* act of cutting off the hair on your face with a razor; **close s.** = near miss. **2.** *v.* (*a*) to cut off the hair on your face. (*b*) to slice very thin pieces off (sth). **shaven,** *adj.* (*old*) shaved. **shaver,** *n.* razor; machine for shaving. **shaving,** *n.* (*a*) act of cutting off hair; **s. cream** = cream which you put on your face before shaving. (*b*) **shavings** = small thin slices of wood cut off by a plane.

shawl [ʃɔːl] *n.* large square of warm material for wrapping round your shoulders/your head.

she [ʃiː] (*a*) *pron. referring to a female person.* (*b*) *prefix meaning* female; **she-wolf.**

sheaf [ʃiːf] *n.* (*pl.* **sheaves** [ʃiːvz]) bundle of corn/of papers.

shear ['ʃɪə] *v.* (**sheared/shorn** [ʃɔːn]) to cut the wool off (sheep, etc.); to cut (**through** sth). **shearer,** *n.* person who cuts the wool off sheep. **shears,** *n.* cutting tool like large scissors. **shearwater,** *n.* type of small dark sea bird.

sheath [ʃiːθ] *n.* (*a*) holder (for a knife, etc.). (*b*) rubber contraceptive. **sheathe** [ʃiːð] *v.* to put a knife back into its sheath. **sheath-knife,** *n.* (*pl.* **-knives**) knife kept in a sheath.

sheaves [ʃiːvz] *n. see* **sheaf.**

shed [ʃed] **1.** *n.* wooden building. **2.** *v.* (**shed**) (*a*) to lose (leaves); to lose/to take off (clothes). (*b*) to let flow (blood, tears, light); **to s. light on** = to make clearer.

sheen [ʃiːn] *n.* brilliant shining surface.

sheep [ʃiːp] *n.* (*pl.* **sheep**) farm animal, reared for wool or for meat; **s. station** = large sheep farm in Australia. **sheep dip,** *n.* bath of disin-

fectant into which sheep are put to kill parasites. **sheepdog**, *n.* type of dog specially trained for herding sheep. **sheepish**, *adj.* ashamed/embarrassed. **sheepishly**, *adv.* with a sheepish air. **sheepishness**, *n.* being sheepish. **sheepmeat**, *n.* meat from a sheep/ lamb. **sheepshank**, *n.* knot tied to make a rope shorter. **sheepskin**, *n.* skin of a sheep with the wool attached.
sheer ['ʃɪə] **1.** *adj.* (*a*) complete/total. (*b*) very steep. (*c*) very fine (stockings, etc.). **2.** *adv.* straight up or down. **3.** *v.* to swerve to avoid sth.
sheet [ʃiːt] *n.* (*a*) large piece of thin cloth which is put on a bed. (*b*) large flat piece (of paper/cardboard/plywood, etc.); **s. feed** = device which allows separate sheets of paper to be fed into a printer. **s. lightning** = lightning which appears as a sheet and not as a single flash. (*c*) rope for attaching a sail. **sheet-anchor**, *n.* large anchor used if a ship is in difficulties.
sheikh [ʃeɪk] *n.* Arab leader. **sheikh-dom** ['ʃeɪkdəm] *n.* country ruled by a sheikh.
sheila ['ʃiːlə] *n.* (*in Australia*) *inf.* girl.
sheldrake, shelduck ['ʃeldreɪk, 'ʃeldʌk] *n.* type of wild duck.
shelf [ʃelf] *n.* (*pl.* **shelves** [ʃelvz] (*a*) plank attached to a wall/in a cupboard on which things can be put; *inf.* **on the s.** = (i) left behind/forgotten about; (ii) not married (when all your friends are married); **s. life** = length of time food can be kept in a shop before it goes bad. (*b*) narrow ledge of rock.
shell [ʃel] **1.** *n.* (*a*) hard outside of some animals. (*b*) hard outside of an egg/a nut. (*c*) exterior of a car/building. (*d*) metal tube full of explosive fired from a gun. **2.** *v.* (*a*) to take (peas) out of their pods/(a hardboiled egg) out of its shell. (*b*) to bombard with shells. **shellfish**, *n.* (*no pl.*) sea animal with a shell (such as a crab/mussel, etc.). **shell out**, *v. inf.* to pay money. **shellshock**, *n.* illness in soldiers caused by being in battle.
shellac ['ʃelæk] *n.* resin used to make varnish.
shelter ['ʃeltə] **1.** *n.* place where you can go for protection. **2.** *v.* to give (s.o.) protection; to take shelter. **sheltered**,

adj. protected from wind/cold/unpleasant happenings; **s. housing** = small flats provided for elderly people, often with a resident warden.
shelve [ʃelv] **1.** *v.* (*a*) to put off discussing a problem. (*b*) to slope down. (*c*) to put (sth) on a shelf. **2.** *n. pl. see* **shelf. shelving**, *n.* set of shelves.
shemozzle [ʃɪ'mɒzl] *n. inf.* fight/row.
shenanigans [ʃɪ'nænɪgənz] *n. pl. inf.* (*a*) wild behaviour. (*b*) dishonest trick.
shepherd ['ʃepəd] **1.** *n.* man who looks after sheep; **s.'s pie** = minced meat cooked with mashed potatoes on top. **2.** *v.* to guide. **shepherdess**, *n.* woman who looks after sheep.
sherbet ['ʃɜːbət] *n.* (*a*) fizzy powder/ fizzy drink. (*b*) *Am.* water ice.
sheriff ['ʃerɪf] *n.* (*a*) *Am.* county police officer. (*b*) (*in England*) ceremonial chief official in a county. (*c*) (*in Scotland*) chief judge of an area.
sherry ['ʃerɪ] *n.* type of strong wine, originally from Spain.
shibboleth ['ʃɪbəleθ] *n.* slogan/policy formerly considered important.
shield [ʃiːld] **1.** *n.* (*a*) large protective plate carried by riot police/knights in armour, etc. (*b*) protection against sth dangerous. **2.** *v.* to protect.
shift [ʃɪft] **1.** *n.* (*a*) change of place/of direction; **s. key** = key on a typewriter/ computer which makes capital letters. (*b*) group of workers who work for a period and whose place is then taken by another group. (*c*) loose dress. **2.** *v.* (*a*) to change position/direction; to move. (*b*) *inf.* **to s. for yourself** = to look after yourself. **shiftiness**, *n.* dishonest look. **shiftless**, *adj.* lazy. **shifty**, *adj.* (**-ier, -iest**) looking dishonest.
shillelagh [ʃɪ'leɪlɪ] *n.* (*in Ireland*) thick stick.
shilling ['ʃɪlɪŋ] *n.* currency used in Kenya and some other countries; old British coin worth 12 pence.
shilly-shally ['ʃɪlɪ'ʃælɪ] *v.* to hesitate.
shimmer ['ʃɪmə] **1.** *n.* soft quivering light. **2.** *v.* to quiver with light.
shin [ʃɪn] **1.** *n.* (*a*) front of the bottom part of your leg. (*b*) **s. of beef** = meat from the bottom part of the front legs of cattle. **2.** *v.* (**shinned**) **to s. up a tree** = to climb up.

shindig, shindy ['ʃɪndɪg, ʃɪndɪ] *n. inf.* row/noisy party.

shine [ʃaɪn] **1.** *n.* (*a*) brightness. (*b*) act of polishing. **2.** *v.* (**shone** [ʃɒn]) (*a*) to glint brightly. (*b*) to be brilliant. (*c*) to polish. **shining**, *adj.* brilliant. **shiny**, *adj.* (**-ier, -iest**) bright/polished.

shingle [ʃɪŋgl] *n.* (*a*) mass of small stones. (*b*) flat piece of wood/asbestos nailed on a wall or roof as a covering. (*c*) **shingles** = infectious disease related to chickenpox causing a painful rash. **shingly**, *adj.* covered with small stones.

ship [ʃɪp] **1.** *n.* large boat for carrying goods/passengers. **2.** *v.* (**shipped**) (*a*) to put/to take on board a ship. (*b*) to send (goods), not necessarily on a ship. **shipbuilder**, *n.* person who builds ships. **shipbuilding**, *n.* building of ships. **shipmate**, *n.* sailor on the same ship as you. **shipment**, *n.* (*a*) sending of goods. (*b*) quantity of goods shipped. **shipowner**, *n.* person who owns a ship. **shipper**, *n.* person who sends goods. **shipping**, *n.* (*a*) sending of goods; **s. company** = which specializes in the sending of goods. (*b*) (group of) ships; **s. lanes** = routes across the sea which are regularly used by ships. **shipshape**, *adj.* neat/tidy. **shipwreck**, *n.* wrecking of a ship. **shipwrecked**, *adj.* (person) involved in a shipwreck. **shipyard**, *n.* works where ships are built.

shire ['ʃaɪə] *n.* county; **s. horse** = large powerful horse used for farm work.

shirk [ʃɜːk] *v.* to try not to do sth/not to work. **shirker**, *n.* person who shirks.

shirr [ʃɜː] *v.* (*a*) to gather (cloth) by running threads through it. (*b*) *Am.* to bake (beaten eggs).

shirt [ʃɜːt] *n.* piece of light clothing worn on the top part of the body; *inf.* **keep your s. on!** = keep calm/don't lose your temper. **shirtsleeves**, *n.* **in one's s.** = not wearing a jacket. **shirtwaister**, *n.* woman's dress where the top part looks like a shirt. **shirty**, *adj. inf.* angry.

shishkebab ['ʃɪʃkɪbæb] *n.* small pieces of meat and vegetables cooked on a skewer.

shit [ʃɪt] **1.** *n.* (*vulgar*) (*a*) excreta/solid waste matter from the body. (*b*) dirt. (*c*) nonsense. **2.** *v.* (*vulgar*) to pass solid waste matter from the body.

shiver ['ʃɪvə] **1.** *n.* tremble (with cold/fear). **2.** *v.* (*a*) to tremble (with cold/fear/fever). (*b*) to break into tiny pieces. **shivery**, *adj.* trembling (esp. with fever).

shoal [ʃəʊl] *n.* (*a*) (*also* **shoals**) bank of sand under the water. (*b*) group of fish swimming about.

shock [ʃɒk] **1.** *n.* (*a*) untidy mass (of hair). (*b*) sudden (unpleasant) surprise. (*c*) mental/physical collapse (after a blow/a sudden surprise). (*d*) **electric s.** = sudden painful passing of electric current through the body; **electric s. treatment** = medical treatment of mental illness using electric shocks. (*e*) great blow; **s. absorbers** = part of a car/aircraft which reduces the effect of bumps. **2.** *v.* to give (s.o.) a sudden (unpleasant) surprise. **shocker**, *n. inf.* shocking person/thing. **shock-headed**, *adj.* with a mass of stiff hair. **shocking**, *adj.* upsetting/unpleasant. **shockingly**, *adv.* in a shocking way. **shock-proof**, *adj.* (watch, etc.) which is not affected by shocks. **shock troops**, *n.* soldiers specially trained to attack violently.

shod [ʃɒd] *adj.* wearing shoes.

shoddy ['ʃɒdɪ] **1.** *n.* poor quality cloth. **2.** *adj.* (**-ier, -iest**) (*a*) badly made. (*b*) low/nasty (trick). **shoddily**, *adv.* in a shoddy way. **shoddiness**, *n.* bad quality.

shoe [ʃuː] **1.** *n.* (*a*) article of clothing which you wear on your feet both inside and outside the house, not covering your ankles; **in his shoes** = in his place/in the situation he is in. (*b*) ring of metal nailed under a horse's hoof. (*c*) **brake shoes** = curved metal blocks which tighten round a wheel. **2.** *v.* (**shod/shoed**) to attach metal horseshoes to the hooves of (a horse). **shoehorn**, *n.* curved piece of plastic/metal which you put into the heel of a shoe to make it easier to put on. **shoelace**, *n.* lace for tying up shoes. **shoemaker**, *n.* person who makes and mends shoes. **shoeshine**, *n.* polishing of shoes. **shoestring**, *n.* shoelace; **on a s.** = with only a little money. **shoetree**, *n.* device which is put in a shoe to help keep its shape.

shone [ʃɒn] *v. see* **shine**.

shoo [ʃuː] **1.** *inter. meaning* go away. **2.** *v.* **to s. away** = to frighten away (birds/ small children, etc.).

shook [ʃʊk] *v. see* **shake.**

shoot [ʃuːt] **1.** *n.* (*a*) new growth on a plant. (*b*) slide for goods/rubbish, etc. (*c*) expedition to kill wild animals with guns. (*d*) land where game can be shot. (*c*) *inf.* **the whole s.** = everything. **2.** *v.* (**shot** [ʃɒt]) (*a*) to fire a bullet from a gun/an arrow from a bow; to kill (s.o./ an animal) with a bullet or an arrow. (*b*) to hunt with a gun. (*c*) to rush/to go fast; **to s. the rapids** = to race through rapids in a light boat. (*d*) to send out new growths. (*e*) to kick a ball hard; to score (a goal). (*f*) to make (a film). **shoot down,** *v.* to make (an aircraft) crash by hitting it with a shell. **shooting. 1.** *n.* action of shooting with a gun; **s. stick** = walking stick with a handle which unfolds to make a seat. **2.** *adj.* which goes very fast; **s. star** = meteor. **shoot up,** *v.* to go up fast.

shop [ʃɒp] **1.** *n.* (*a*) place where you can buy goods; **s. assistant** = person who serves in a shop; *inf.* **all over the s.** = scattered everywhere. (*b*) workshop/ place where goods are made; **closed s.** = works where all the workers have to belong to a single union; **to talk s.** = to talk about your job/about your office. **2.** *v.* (**shopped**) (*a*) to buy things in a shop; **to s. around** = to go to various shops and compare prices before buying what you want. (*b*) *Sl.* to report (s.o.) to the police. **shopfloor,** *n.* working area in a factory. **shopkeeper,** *n.* person who runs a shop. **shoplifter,** *n.* person who steals things from a shop. **shoplifting,** *n.* stealing from a shop. **shopper,** *n.* person who buys goods from a shop. **shopping,** *n.* (*a*) goods which you have bought in a shop. (*b*) action of buying things in a shop. **shop-soiled,** *adj.* made dirty by being on display in a shop. **shop steward,** *n.* elected union representative in a factory/office, etc. **shopwalker,** *n.* person who supervises a department in a shop.

shore [ʃɔː] **1.** *n.* (*a*) land at the edge of the sea or a lake; beach. (*b*) prop. **2.** *v.* to hold **up** (sth) which might fall down.

shorn [ʃɔːn] *adj.* cut off; **s. of sth** = lacking sth; *see also* **shear.**

short [ʃɔːt] **1.** *adj.* (**-er, est**) (*a*) not long. (*b*) not long in time; **in s.** = briefly. (*c*) not tall. (*d*) rude. (*e*) not enough/not as much as is needed (**of**). **s. weight** = not quite as much in weight as supposed. (*f*) light/crumbly (pastry). **2.** *n.* (*a*) short film. (*b*) short-circuit. (*c*) drink of spirits. (*d*) *pl.* **shorts** = trousers not going below the knee. **3.** *adv.* (*a*) abruptly; **to stop s.** (*b*) not far enough; **to fall s. 4.** *v.* to short-circuit. **shortage,** *n.* lack. **shortbread,** *n.* thick sweet crumbly biscuit. **shortcake,** *n.* (*a*) shortbread. (*b*) *Am.* cake with fruit and cream. **shortchange,** *v.* to cheat (s.o.). **short-circuit. 1.** *n.* jump of electric current between two points, missing out part of the normal circuit. **2.** *v.* (*a*) to make a short-circuit. (*b*) to get through difficulties by taking a short cut. **shortcoming,** *n.* fault/defect. **short cut,** *n.* way which is shorter than usual; quicker way of reaching your destination. **shorten,** *v.* to make/to become shorter. **shortening,** *n. Am.* lard/ cooking fat. **shortfall,** *n.* amount which is missing to make up an expected total. **shorthand,** *n.* way of writing fast by using a system of signs; **s. typist** = typist who can take shorthand. **shorthanded,** *adj.* with not enough workers. **shorthold,** *n.* tenancy of a property guaranteed for less than five years. **shorthorn,** *n.* type of cattle with short horns. **short list,** *n.* list of some of the people who have applied for a job, and who have been chosen to come for an interview. **short-list,** *v.* to make a short list of (candidates) for a job; to put (s.o.'s name) on a short list. **shortlived,** *adj.* which does not last long. **shortly,** *adv.* (*a*) soon. (*b*) abruptly/rudely. **shortness,** *n.* (*a*) state of being short. (*b*) rudeness. **short order,** *n. Am.* order given for sth to be cooked on the spot (such as ham and eggs). **short-sighted,** *adj.* (*a*) (person) who can only see near objects. (*b*) not paying attention to what may happen in the future. **short-sightedness,** *n.* being short-sighted. **shortsleeved,** *adj.* (shirt, etc.) with short sleeves. **short-staffed,** *adj.* with not enough workers. **short-tempered,** *adj.*

(person) who easily gets angry. **short-term**, *adj.* not lasting long. **short time**, *n.* shorter working hours than usual. **short wave**, *n.* radio wave about 50 metres long.

shot [ʃɒt] **1.** *adj.* (silk) which changes colour according to the light. **2.** *n.* (*a*) (*no pl.*) small pellets/bullets fired from a gun. (*b*) large heavy ball thrown in a competition; **to put the s.** = throw the weight in a competition. (*c*) act of shooting; the sound of shooting; **like a s.** = very rapidly. (*d*) person who shoots. (*e*) *inf.* attempt. (*f*) *Sl.* injection. (*g*) *Sl.* small drink of alcohol. (*h*) *inf.* photograph. *see also* **shoot. shotgun**, *n.* gun which fires small pellets.

should [ʃʊd] *v.* used to show certain moods. (*a*) ought; **they s. have arrived by now** = they ought to have arrived. (*b*) must; **why s. I be the one to go?** = why must I be the one? (*c*) **who s. we meet but my aunt** = what a surprise we had when we met my aunt. (*d*) (*tentative suggestion*) **s. I try again?** (*e*) (*future after that*) **it is strange that he s. want to go.**

shoulder ['ʃəʊldə] **1.** *n.* (*a*) part of the body at the top of the arm/between the top of the arm and the neck. (*b*) part of a piece of clothing between the top of the arm and the neck. (*c*) top part of the front leg of a sheep. (*d*) **hard s.** = reinforced side part of a road. **2.** *v.* (*a*) to put on your shoulder. (*b*) to push with your shoulder. (*c*) to take on (a burden). **shoulder bag**, *n.* bag which can be carried over the shoulder. **shoulderblade**, *n.* large flat bone in the shoulder.

shout [ʃaʊt] **1.** *n.* loud cry. **2.** *v.* to make a loud cry; **to s. s.o. down** = to shout so loudly that s.o. cannot speak.

shove [ʃʌv] **1.** *n. inf.* sharp push. **2.** *v. inf.* to give a push to. **shove off**, *v. inf.* to go away.

shovel ['ʃʌvl] **1.** *n.* wide spade. **2.** *v.* (**shovelled**) to lift up with a shovel. **shovelful**, *n.* contents of a shovel. **shoveller**, *n.* wild duck with a wide flat beak.

show [ʃəʊ] **1.** *n.* (*a*) exhibition/display; **s. house** = house which is built to show what similar houses can look like.

(*b*) performance; **s. business** = actors/actresses/producers. etc. (considered as a group); the entertainment world. (*c*) pretence. (*d*) *inf.* affair/business. **2.** *v.* (**shown**) (*a*) to make (sth) seen; to allow s.o. to see (sth); to be seen. (*b*) to indicate. (*c*) to point out/to direct. (*d*) to prove/to demonstrate. **showcase**, *n.* cupboard with a glass front/box with a glass top for putting things on show in a shop or museum. **showdown**, *n.* final argument which will solve a crisis. **showily**, *adv.* in a showy way. **showiness**, *n.* being showy. **show-jumper**, *n.* horse specially trained for show-jumping. **show-jumping**, *n.* riding competiton where horses have to jump over different obstacles in a short time. **showman**, *n.* (*pl.* **-men**) person who puts on shows (such as circuses, etc.); person who is good at publicising. **showmanship**, *n.* art of putting on attractive shows. **show off**, *v.* (*a*) to display (sth) to great effect. (*b*) to try to make people look at you by doing sth which will attract their attention. **show-off**, *n. inf.* person who shows off. **showpiece**, *n.* important item in an exhibition. **showroom**, *n.* room where goods are shown to customers. **show up**, *v.* (*a*) to reveal/to show (s.o.'s/sth's faults). (*b*) to stand out. (*c*) *inf.* to arrive. **showy**, *adj.* (**-ier, -iest**) too bright (colours); too ostentatious.

shower ['ʃaʊə] **1.** *n.* (*a*) light fall of rain/small stones, etc. (*b*) spray device in a bathroom for washing your whole body. (*c*) bath taken in a spray of water from above. (*d*) *Am.* party where presents are given to a girl about to get married. **2.** *v.* (*a*) (*also* **shower down**) to pour/to fall in a quantity. (*b*) to wash under a spray. **shower bath**, *n.* (*a*) spray device in a bathroom for washing your whole body. (*b*) bath taken in a spray of water. **showerproof**, *adj.* (coat) which can protect against light rain. **shower room**, *n.* room with a shower bath in it. **showery**, *adj.* with many showers.

shrank [ʃræŋk] *v. see* **shrink.**

shrapnel ['ʃræpnl] *n.* (*no pl.*) pieces of metal from an exploded shell or bomb, etc.

shred [ʃred] **1.** *n.* (*a*) long strip torn off

sth. (b) small piece. **2.** v. (**shredded**) to tear into long strips; to cut into very thin strips. **shredder,** n. machine for tearing waste paper into long strips; device for cutting vegetables into long thin strips.

shrew [ʃruː] n. (a) animal like a mouse with a long nose. (b) unpleasant bad-tempered woman who is always criticizing. **shrewish,** adj. bad-tempered (woman).

shrewd [ʃruːd] adj. (**-er, -est**) clever/wise. **shrewdly,** adv. in a shrewd way. **shrewdness,** n. being shrewd.

shriek [ʃriːk] **1.** n. loud high-pitched cry. **2.** v. to make a shriek.

shrift [ʃrɪft] n. **to get short s.** = to be treated curtly.

shrike [ʃraɪk] n. bird which pins insects to spines before eating them.

shrill [ʃrɪl] adj. (**-er, -est**) high-pitched. **shrilly,** adv. in a shrill way. **shrillness,** n. being shrill.

shrimp [ʃrɪmp] n. (a) small shellfish with a long tail. (b) inf. small person. **shrimping,** n. fishing for shrimps.

shrine [ʃraɪn] n. tomb/chapel where a saint is buried.

shrink [ʃrɪŋk] **1.** n. Sl. psychiatrist. **2.** v. (**shrank; shrunk**) (a) to make smaller; to get smaller. (b) to move back (**from**). **shrinkage,** n. action of shrinking; amount by which sth shrinks.

shrivel [ˈʃrɪvl] v. (**shrivelled**) to make/to become dry and wrinkled.

shroud [ʃraʊd] **1.** n. (a) long cloth covering a dead body. (b) **shrouds** = ropes from a mast to the sides of a ship. **2.** v. to cover up.

Shrove Tuesday [ˈʃrəʊvˈtjuːzdeɪ] n. the Tuesday before Lent.

shrub [ʃrʌb] n. small bush. **shrubbery,** n. part of a garden planted with shrubs.

shrug [ʃrʌg] **1.** n. raising the shoulders to show you are not interested. **2.** v. (**shrugged**) **to s. your shoulders** = to raise your shoulders to show you are not interested. **shrug off,** v. to treat (sth) as if it is not a cause of worry.

shrunk [ʃrʌŋk] v. see **shrink**.

shrunken [ˈʃrʌŋkən] adj. wrinkled; dried up.

shuck [ʃʌk] Am. **1.** n. shell/outer covering. **2.** v. to take the shell off (sth).

shudder [ˈʃʌdə] **1.** n. tremble of horror. **2.** v. to tremble violently with horror.

shuffle [ˈʃʌfl] v. (a) to walk dragging your feet. (b) to mix (playing cards).

shun [ʃʌn] v. (**shunned**) to avoid.

shunt [ʃʌnt] **1.** n. accident where one car bumps into the back of the car in front of it. **2.** v. to move (a train) into a siding; to move (s.o.) backwards and forwards. **shunting yard,** n. area of railway lines where wagons are kept/sorted into trains.

shush [ʃʊʃ] inf. inter. meaning be quiet.

shut [ʃʌt] v. (**shut**) (a) to close. (b) to lock up (sth) so that it cannot escape. (c) to close for business. **shut down,** v. to make (a factory) stop working. **shutdown,** n. closure of a factory. **shuteye,** n. inf. sleep. **shut in,** v. to lock inside; to surround. **shut off,** v. to switch off (an engine/the water supply, etc.). **shut out,** v. (a) to block. (b) to lock (s.o.) outside. **shutter,** n. (a) folding wooden/metal cover which covers a window. (b) (in camera) part which opens and closes very rapidly to allow the light to go on to the film. **shuttered,** adj. with shutters. **shut up,** v. (a) to close. (b) inf. to be quiet; to make (s.o.) be quiet.

shuttle [ˈʃʌtl] **1.** n. part of a loom which carries the thread from side to side; **s. service** = bus/plane which goes backwards and forwards between two places; **s. diplomacy** = action of a diplomat going backwards and forwards between two countries to try to make them reach agreement. **2.** v. to go backwards and forwards; to send (s.o.) backwards and forwards. **shuttlecock,** n. light ball with feathers stuck in it, which is hit in badminton.

shy [ʃaɪ] **1.** adj. timid/afraid to do sth; **to fight s. of doing sth** = to prefer not to. **2.** n. throwing (of a ball); **coconut s.** = game at fairs where you try to knock down a coconut with a hard ball. **3.** v. (a) to throw. (b) (of horse) to jump with fear. **shyly,** adv. timidly. **shyness,** n. being shy. **shyster,** n. Sl. dishonest businessman.

SI abbrev. for Système International, the international system of units for measuring physical properties, such as weight, speed, heat, etc.

Siamese [saɪəˈmiːz] adj. referring to

Siam; **S. twins** = twins born with parts of their bodies joined together; **S. cat** = type of cat with pale fawn fur, dark brown face and blue eyes.

sibilant ['sɪbɪlənt] *adj. & n.* (sound) like a hiss.

sibling ['sɪblɪŋ] *n.* brother or sister.

sic [sɪk] *adv.* thus (used to indicate a mistake).

sick [sɪk] *adj.* (*a*) ill/not well; **s. leave** = time off work because of illness. (*b*) vomiting; feeling ready to vomit. (*c*) (**of**) showing disgust/dislike. **sickbay,** *n.* (*a*) hospital ward (on a ship). (*b*) small hospital attached to a factory/school, etc. **sickbed,** *n.* bed where a sick person is lying. **sicken,** *v.* to become ill. **sickening,** *adj.* which makes you sick; **s. for** = beginning to show signs of (a disease). **sickly,** *adj.* (**-ier, -iest**) not well; weak. **sickness,** *n.* (*a*) illness; **s. benefit** = payment made by the government to s.o. who is ill and cannot work. (*b*) feeling of being about to vomit. **sick pay,** *n.* wages paid to s.o. who is ill and cannot work. **sickroom,** *n.* room where a sick person is in bed.

sickle ['sɪkl] *n.* tool with a semi-circular blade, used for cutting corn.

side [saɪd] **1.** *n.* (*a*) edge; area near the edge; **on the s.** = (i) apart from one's usual job; (ii) dishonestly. (*b*) one of four parts which (with the top and bottom) make a box, etc.; wall (of a house). (*c*) part of the body between the hips and the shoulder; **s. by s.** = close together (in a row). (*d*) surface. (*e*) slope (of a mountain); surface/part. (*f*) team. (*g*) group holding a particular point of view; **to take sides** = to support one party or another in a quarrel. (*h*) family connection. (*i*) *inf.* conceited attitude. **2.** *adj.* (*a*) secondary/less important (road, etc.). (*b*) at the side (not the front or back). **3.** *v.* **to s. with s.o.** = to support s.o. in an argument. **sideboard,** *n.* (*a*) piece of dining room furniture for holding plates, a type of table with a cupboard beneath. (*b*) **sideboards** = sidewhiskers. **sideburns,** *n. Am.* sidewhiskers. **sidecar,** *n.* small compartment for one passenger attached to the side of a motorcycle. **side effects,** *n.* secondary and unex-

pected effects (of a drug). **side issue,** *n.* secondary problem. **sidekick,** *n. inf.* companion/helper. **sidelight,** *n.* (*a*) unusual information. (*b*) small light on the front of a car. **sideline,** *n.* (*a*) business which is extra to your normal work. (*b*) *pl.* **sidelines** = lines at the edge of a football pitch, etc. **sidelong,** *adj.* from one side. **sidesaddle,** *adv.* (*of woman*) (to ride) with both legs on the same side of the horse. **sideshow,** *n.* small show/stall with a game of skill (at a fair, etc.). **sidesman,** *n.* (*pl.* **-men**) assistant in a church. **sidestep,** *v.* (**sidestepped**) to avoid. **sideswipe,** *v. inf.* (*of car*) to hit another vehicle in passing. **sidetrack,** *v.* to attract s.o.'s attention away from the main problem. **sidewalk,** *n. Am.* pavement. **sidewards,** *adv.* to the side. **sideways,** *adv.* to the side; with the side in front. **sidewhiskers,** *n. pl.* whiskers down the side of your face. **siding,** *n.* minor railway line where trains are kept until needed.

sidereal [saɪ'dɪərɪəl] *adj.* referring to the stars.

sidle ['saɪdl] *v.* to walk sideways, not directly forwards.

siege [siːdʒ] *n.* act of surrounding an enemy town with an army to make it surrender.

sienna [sɪ'enə] *n.* **burnt s.** = reddish-brown colour; **raw s.** = yellowish-brown colour.

siesta [sɪ'estə] *n.* afternoon rest.

sieve [sɪv] **1.** *n.* kitchen utensil with very small holes for passing liquid through to hold back lumps/for sorting out large pieces in a powder. **2.** *v.* to pass (a liquid/a powder) through a sieve to sort out large lumps.

sift [sɪft] *v.* (*a*) to sieve. (*b*) to examine carefully. **sifter,** *n.* container with small holes in the lid for sprinkling sugar or flour.

sigh [saɪ] **1.** *n.* deep breath, showing sadness/relief, etc. **2.** *v.* to breathe deeply showing sadness, relief, etc.

sight [saɪt] **1.** *n.* (*a*) one of the five senses, the ability to see. (*b*) glimpse; act of seeing. (*c*) range of vision. (*d*) spectacle; thing which you ought to see. (*e*) funny/odd thing. (*f*) part of a gun through which you look to take aim. (g) *inf.* **a s. more** = a lot more. **2.** *v.* (*a*) to see for the first time. (*b*) to aim a gun. **sightless,** *adj.* blind. **sight-read,** *v.* to play written music without having practised it. **sightscreen,** *n.* large white screen placed behind the bowler in cricket. **sightseeing,** *n.* visiting the sights of a town. **sightseer,** *n.* tourist/person seeing the sights.

sign [saɪn] **1.** *n.* (*a*) movement (of hand/head, etc.) which means sth; **s. language** = signs of the hands used by deaf and dumb people to communicate. (*b*) mark. (*c*) indication/thing which suggests that sth may happen. (*d*) trace. (*e*) advertising board; panel showing the name of a shop; panel showing directions on a road. **2.** *v.* (*a*) to write your signature at the end of (a letter or on a document, etc.). (*b*) to make a movement which has a meaning. **sign away,** *v.* to lose possession of (sth) by signing a document. **signboard,** *n.* panel with a sign. **sign off,** *v.* to end a letter/a radio broadcast. **sign on,** *v.* to join the armed services for a period; to start work. **signpost. 1.** *n.* post with a sign showing directions to a place. **2.** *v.* to indicate a direction with signs. **sign up,** *v.* (*a*) to join the armed services for a period. (*b*) to sign a contract to play only for a particular football club, etc.; to make (a player) sign a contract.

signal ['sɪgnl] **1.** *n.* (*a*) movement of the hand/head, etc., which tells s.o. to do sth. (*b*) lights/mechanical flags, etc., used to tell s.o. to do sth. (*c*) sound heard on a radio receiver. **2.** *adj.* (*formal*) remarkable. **3.** *v.* (**signalled**) to make signs to tell s.o. to do sth. **signal box,** *n.* building by the side of the railway where the signalman controls the signals. **signaller,** *n.* person who signals. **signally,** *adv.* (*formal*) remarkable. **signalman,** *n.* (*pl.* **-men**) person who controls railway signals.

signatory ['sɪgnətrɪ] *n.* person who signs (a treaty, etc.).

signature ['sɪgnətʃə] *n.* (*a*) name which has been signed. (*b*) group of pages of a book (usually 32 or 64) which are folded out of one sheet of paper. (*c*) **s. tune** = tune which is used regularly at the be-

ginning or end of a broadcast to identify the broadcast.

signet ['sɪgnɪt] *n.* seal (for sealing with wax); **s. ring** = ring worn on the little finger with a design carved on to it to use as a seal.

signify ['sɪgnɪfaɪ] *v.* (*a*) to mean. (*b*) to show; **that signifies** = that makes sense. (*c*) to be of importance. **significance,** *n.* (*a*) meaning. (*b*) importance. **significant,** *adj.* which is important/which has a lot of meaning. **significantly,** *adv.* in a significant way. **signification,** *n.* meaning.

silage ['saɪlɪdʒ] *n.* green crops fermented in a silo and used to feed animals.

silence ['saɪləns] **1.** *n.* (*a*) lack of noise. (*b*) not saying anything. **2.** *v.* (*a*) to make (s.o.) stop talking. (*b*) to stop (sth) making a noise. **silencer,** *n.* (*a*) apparatus to stop the noise of the exhaust of a car. (*b*) apparatus attached to a gun to stop the noise of it being fired. **silent,** *adj.* quiet. **silently,** *adv.* in a silent way.

silhouette [sɪluːˈet] **1.** *n.* black outline of s.o.'s head in profile. **2.** *v.* to stand out in profile.

silica ['sɪlɪkə] *n.* mineral compound of silicon. **silica gel,** *n.* hard crystals used to keep things dry in humid conditions. **silicate,** *n.* common silicon compound.

silicon ['sɪlɪkən] *n.* (*element:* Si) common element which is not a metal, and which is usu. found in compounds; **s. chip** = small piece of silicon used in transistors and very small electronic devices.

silicone ['sɪlɪkəʊn] *n.* chemical substance used in making oils.

silicosis [sɪlɪˈkəʊsɪs] *n.* disease of the lungs caused by breathing in dust.

silk [sɪlk] *n.* (*a*) thread which is produced by a caterpillar; cloth woven from this thread. (*b*) **to take s.** = to be accepted as a leading barrister. **silken,** *adj.* soft and shiny. **silkscreen printing,** *n.* printing by forcing colours through a taut piece of cloth. **silkworm,** *n.* caterpillar which produces silk. **silky,** *adj.* soft and shiny.

sill [sɪl] *n.* ledge beneath a window/a door.

silly ['sɪlɪ] *adj.* (**-ier, -iest**) stupid/idiotic. **silliness,** *n.* being silly.

silo ['saɪləʊ] *n.* (*pl.* **-os**) (*a*) large tower for storing grain/for storing green crops (as food for animals). (*b*) deep hole in the ground in which rockets are kept.

silt [sɪlt] 1. *n.* fine mud washed down by a river. 2. *v.* **to s. up** = to fill with silt.

silver ['sɪlvə] *n.* (*a*) (*element:* Ag) precious white metal; **s. jubilee** = 25th anniversary of an important event; **s. wedding** = anniversary of 25 years of marriage. (*b*) **s. foil/paper** = sheet of thin shiny metal which looks like silver, used for wrapping food in. (*c*) coins made of white metal. (*d*) light shining colour like silver. **silver birch**, *n.* common northern tree with white bark. **silverfish**, *n.* small silvery insect found in kitchens, etc. **silverside**, *n.* good quality beef, cut from the back part of the animal. **silversmith**, *n.* craftsman who makes things in silver. **silverware**, *n.* (*no pl.*) articles made of silver. **silvery**, *adj.* (*a*) shiny like silver. (*b*) light ringing (sound).

simian ['sɪmɪən] *adj.* like a monkey.

similar ['sɪmɪlə] *adj.* very alike but not quite the same. **similarly**, *adv.* in a similar way. **similarity**, *n.* sameness/ likeness.

simile ['sɪmɪlɪ] *n.* comparison using 'like' or 'as'.

simmer ['sɪmə] *v.* to boil gently; **to s. down** = to become calmer.

simnel ['sɪmnl] *n.* **s. cake** = fruit cake covered with marzipan.

simper ['sɪmpə] 1. *n.* silly affected smile. 2. *v.* to make a simper.

simple ['sɪmpl] *adj.* (-er, -est) (*a*) not complicated; not difficult. (*b*) *inf.* not very intelligent. (*c*) **s. interest** = interest calculated as a percentage per annum on the original sum without adding each year's interest to the capital. (*d*) plain/ordinary. **simple-minded**, *adj.* not very intelligent. **simpleton**, *n.* person who is not very intelligent. **simplicity** [sɪm'plɪsɪtɪ] *n.* being simple. **simplification** [sɪmplɪfɪ'keɪʃn] *n.* making simple. **simplify** ['sɪmplɪfaɪ] *v.* to make (sth) simple. **simply**, *adv.* (*a*) without complication. (*b*) absolutely. (*c*) purely/only.

simulate ['sɪmjʊleɪt] *v.* to pretend. **simulation** [sɪmjʊ'leɪʃn] *n.* pretence. **simulator** ['sɪmjʊleɪtə] *n.* machine which allows a learner to experience simulated conditions (as in a car/aircraft, etc.).

simultaneous [sɪməl'teɪnɪəs] *adj.* happening at the same time. **simultaneously**, *adv.* at the same time.

sin [sɪn] 1. *n.* wicked deed; action which goes against the rules of religion; **to live in s.** = to live together without being married. 2. *v.* (**sinned**) to do sth wicked/ wrong. **sinful**, *adj.* wicked (person/action). **sinner**, *n.* person who has sinned.

since [sɪns] 1. *adv.* from then onwards. 2. *prep.* from a certain time. 3. *conj.* (*a*) from a certain time. (*b*) because.

sincere [sɪn'sɪə] *adj.* very honest/open. **sincerely**, *adv.* really/truly; **yours s.** = greeting written at the end of a letter. **sincerity** [sɪn'serɪtɪ] *n.* honesty.

sine [saɪn] *n.* (*in mathematics*) ratio between the length of one of the shorter sides opposite an acute angle to that of the hypotenuse in a right-angled triangle.

sinecure ['saɪnɪkjʊə] *n.* job for which you get paid but which does not involve much work.

sine die ['sɪneɪdɪeɪ] *adv.* to a later date, which is unspecified.

sine qua non ['sɪneɪkwɑː'nɒn] *n.* condition without which something cannot function.

sinew ['sɪnjuː] *n.* strong cord which joins a muscle to a bone. **sinewy**, *adj.* very strong.

sing [sɪŋ] *v.* (**sang, sung**) (*a*) to make music with your mouth. (*b*) to make a buzzing noise. **singer**, *n.* person who sings. **singsong**. 1. *adj.* (voice) with a rising and falling tone. 2. *n.* singing party.

singe ['sɪndʒ] *v.* to burn slightly.

single ['sɪŋgl] 1. *adj.* (*a*) alone/one by itself; **s. figures** = numbers from 1 to 9. (*b*) for one person. (*c*) unmarried. (*d*) **s. ticket** = ticket for one journey. (*e*) **s. cream** = light cream. 2. *n.* (*a*) **singles** = tennis game played between two people. (*b*) ticket for one journey. (*c*) (*in cricket*) one run. (*d*) small record of pop music with only one piece of music on each side. 3. *v.* **to s. out** = to select. **singlebreasted**, *adj.* (coat) which does not fold over widely in the front to button. **singledecker,** *n.* bus with only one deck. **singlehanded,** *adj.* all by yourself. **singleminded,** *adj.* thinking only of one aim. **singlemindedness,** *n.* being singleminded. **singleness,** *n.* (a) being single. (b) **s. of purpose** = having only one aim. **singly,** *adv.* one by one.

singlet ['sɪŋglət] *n.* man's (sleeveless) undergarment for the top part of the body.

singular ['sɪŋgjulə] **1.** *adj.* & *n.* referring to one person/thing. **2.** *adj.* (a) odd/peculiar. (b) remarkable. **singularity** [sɪŋgju'lærɪtɪ] *n.* oddness/peculiarity. **singularly,** *adv.* (a) strangely. (b) particularly.

sinister ['sɪnɪstə] *adj.* looking evil; which promises evil.

sink [sɪŋk] **1.** *n.* (a) basin for washing in a kitchen. (b) place where substances pass to be absorbed out of the atmosphere. **2.** *v.* (**sank; sunk**) (a) to (cause to) go to the bottom of water/mud, etc. (b) to go down. (c) to make (a well). (d) **to s. your teeth into** = to bite. (e) to invest. **sinker,** *n.* lead weight used to pull down a fishing-line into the water. **sink in,** *v.* to become fixed in the mind.

Sino- ['saɪnəu] *prefix meaning* Chinese/between China and another country.

sinuous ['sɪnjuəs] *adj.* winding. **sinuosity** [sɪnju'ɒsɪtɪ] *n.* (a) being sinuous. (b) bend (in a pipe or road).

sinus ['saɪnəs] *n.* (*pl.* **-es**) hole in the bones of the head connected with the nose and air passages. **sinusitis** [saɪnə-'saɪtɪs] *n.* infection of the sinuses.

sip [sɪp] **1.** *n.* small quantity of liquid. **2.** *v.* (**sipped**) to drink taking only a small quantity at a time.

siphon ['saɪfn] **1.** *n.* (a) device for making fizzy water. (b) bent tube to allow you to take liquid from one container to another placed at a lower level. **2.** *v.* (a) to remove (liquid) by using a siphon. (b) to remove (money) from a source illegally.

sir [sɜː] *n.* (a) respectful way of addressing a man (usu. an older or more important man). (b) title given to a knight or baronet. (c) way of addressing a man in a formal letter.

sire ['saɪə] **1.** *n.* (a) male horse which is a father. (b) (old) **Sire** = way of

addressing a king. **2.** *v.* (*of a horse*) to be father of.

siren ['saɪrən] *n.* loud warning signal which wails.

sirloin ['sɜːlɔɪn] *n.* best cut of beef from the back of the animal.

sisal ['saɪsl] *n.* rope made from fibres from a tropical plant.

siskin ['sɪskɪn] *n.* small finch.

sissy ['sɪsɪ] *n.* weak girlish man/boy.

sister ['sɪstə] **1.** *n.* (a) female child whose parents are the same as yours. (b) senior nurse. (c) nun; title given to nuns. **2.** *adj.* similar/identical; **s. ship** = ship of the same design. **sisterhood,** *n.* group of nuns/nurses, etc. **sister-in-law,** *n.* (*pl.* **sisters-**) wife of your brother; sister of your husband or wife. **sisterly,** *adj.* like a sister.

sit [sɪt] *v.* (**sat**) (a) to be seated; to make (s.o.) be seated; to rest in a seated position with your behind on a chair/on the ground, etc.; **to s. for your portrait** = to pose (not necessarily in a seated position). (b) to be in session/to meet. (c) to be a member of. (d) (*of bird*) to sit on her eggs. (e) to take (an examination). **sit back,** *v.* to be seated and lean backwards. **sit down,** *v.* to take a seat. **sit-down,** *adj.* (a) **sit-down meal** = meal where you sit at a table. (b) **sit-down strike** = strike where workers do not move from their place of work. **sit-in,** *n.* occupation of the place of work by workers/students, etc. **sit on,** *v.* (a) to be a member of (a committee). (b) *inf.* to delay (a request). **sitter,** *n.* person who sits/poses for a painter; **baby-sitter** = person who looks after a child when its parents are out. **sit tight,** *v.* to stay where you are/to refuse to move. **sitting,** *n.* act of sitting; session. **sitting-room,** *n.* room where you can relax in comfortable chairs. **sit up,** *v.* (a) to straighten yourself on your chair. (b) to stay up/not to go to bed.

site [saɪt] **1.** *n.* (a) place where a building/town is situated. (b) place where an event took place. **2.** *v.* to place (a building/town) on a particular piece of land.

situate ['sɪtjueɪt] *v.* to place. **situation** [sɪtju'eɪʃn] *n.* (a) place where a building is. (b) state of affairs. (c) job; **situations vacant** = list of vacancies in jobs.

sitz bath ['sɪtsbɑːθ] *n.* small low bath in which a person can sit, but not lie down.

six [sɪks] *n.* number 6; *inf.* **they're all at sixes and sevens** = they're very disorganized/they can't agree. **sixteen,** *n.* number 16. **sixteenth, 16th,** *adj.* & *n.* referring to sixteen. **sixth, 6th,** *adj.* & *n.* referring to six; **s. form** = top class in a secondary school. **sixtieth, 60th,** *adj.* & *n.* referring to sixty. **sixty,** *n.* number 60; **she's in her sixties** = she is aged between 60 and 69.

size [saɪz] **1.** *n.* (*a*) largeness of sth. (*b*) measurements. (*c*) type of pastelike glue. **2.** *v.* (*a* **to s. s.o. up** = to judge s.o.'s capabilities. (*b*) to cover with glue. **sizeable,** *adj.* quite large.

sizzle ['sɪzl] *v.* to make a hissing sound when frying; *inf.* to be very hot.

skate [skeɪt] **1.** *n.* (*a*) (*pl.* **skate**) large flat fish with white flesh. (*b*) sharp blade worn under boots for sliding on ice. **2.** *v.* (*a*) to slide on ice wearing skates. (*b*) **to s. over/round sth** = not to mention sth which could be embarrassing. **skateboard,** *n.* board with two pairs of wheels which you stand on to glide about. **skater,** *n.* person who goes skating.

skedaddle [skɪ'dædl] *v. inf.* to go quickly.

skein [skeɪn] *n.* length of wool loosely wound round and round into a loop.

skeleton ['skelɪtn] *n.* (*a*) bones inside a body; **s. in the cupboard** = secret that a family or person is trying to keep hidden. (*b*) **s. staff** = few staff left to carry on essential work while the others are away. (*c*) **s. key** = key which will fit any lock in a building. (*d*) rough outline. **skeletal,** *adj.* like a skeleton.

skep [skep] *n.* straw beehive.

skeptic ['skeptɪk] *n. Am. see* **sceptic.**

skerry ['skerɪ] *n.* low rocky outcrop in the sea.

sketch [sketʃ] **1.** *n.* (*pl.* **-es**) (*a*) rough drawing. (*b*) short amusing play. **2.** *v.* to make a rough drawing/a rough plan of. **sketch-book,** *n.* book of drawing paper for sketching. **sketchily,** *adv.* in a sketchy way. **sketchiness,** *n.* being sketchy. **sketch-map,** *n.* roughly drawn map. **sketchpad,** *n.* pad of paper for sketching. **sketchy,** *adj.* (**-ier, -iest**) rough/incomplete.

skew [skjuː] *adj.* not straight; **on the s.** = askew/not straight.

skewbald ['skjuːbɔːld] *adj.* (horse) with patches of white with another colour, but not black.

skewer ['skjuːə] **1.** *n.* long thin metal rod for putting through pieces of meat when cooking. **2.** *v.* to stick a long metal rod through (sth).

ski [skiː] **1.** *n.* long flat narrow piece of wood, etc., which you attach under your boot for moving over snow; **water skis** = similar pieces of wood for gliding over water. **2.** *v.* to travel on skis; **to go skiing** = to travel on skis as a sport. **skiboots,** *n. pl.* special boots for skiing. **skier,** *n.* person travelling on skis. **ski jump,** *n.* slope with a sudden drop at the bottom to allow a skier to jump high in the air. **ski lift,** *n.* device to take skiers to the top of a slope.

skid [skɪd] **1.** *n.* sliding sideways. (*b*) plank for sliding heavy objects along. **2.** *v.* (**skidded**) to slide sideways in a vehicle with the wheels not gripping the surface. **skidoo** [skɪ'duː], *n. Am. & Canada* small powered sledge for travelling over snow.

skiff [skɪf] *n.* light rowing boat.

skill [skɪl] *n.* cleverness/ability to do something. **skilful,** *adj.* clever/very able. **skilfully,** *adv.* in a skilful way. **skilled,** *adj.* having/requiring a particular skill.

skillet ['skɪlɪt] *n. Am.* frying pan.

skim [skɪm] *v.* (**skimmed**) (*a*) to remove things floating on the surface of (a liquid). (*b*) to dash over the surface of sth; **to s. through a book** = to read a book quickly.

skimp [skɪmp] *v.* (*a*) to do a job badly. (*b*) not to give enough of; **they s. on food** = they don't spend much money on food. **skimpy,** *adj.* (**-ier, -iest**) insufficient (meal); tight/short (clothes).

skin [skɪn] **1.** *n.* (*a*) outer surface of an animal's body; **by the s. of their teeth** = only just. (*b*) outer surface. **2.** *v.* (**skinned**) to remove the skin of. **skin-deep,** *adj.* on the surface/superficial. **skindiver,** *n.* person who goes skindiving. **skindiving,** *n.* sport of swimming underwater with breathing apparatus but without special clothing. **skinflint**, *n.* miser. **skinny**, *adj.* (**-ier, -iest**) *inf.* thin. **skintight**, *adj.* (clothes) which are close-fitting.

skint [skɪnt] *adj. Sl.* having no money.

skip [skɪp] **1.** *n.* (*a*) act of skipping. (*b*) large metal container for builder's rubbish. **2.** *v.* (**skipped**) (*a*) to jump over a rope; to run along half hopping and half jumping. (*b*) to miss out (part of a book). **skipping rope**, *n.* child's rope which you jump over as it turns.

skipper ['skɪpə] **1.** *n.* captain (of a ship/ team). **2.** *v.* to be the captain of (a team).

skirl [skɜːl] *n.* wailing sound made by bagpipes.

skirmish ['skɜːmɪʃ] *n.* (*pl.* **-es**) slight battle between opposite sides.

skirt [skɜːt] **1.** *n.* piece of woman's cloth- ing covering the lower part of the body from the waist to the knees or ankles. **2.** *v.* to go round/to avoid going through. **skirting board**, *n.* decorative board running along the bottom edge of a wall in a room.

skit [skɪt] *n.* play/story which makes fun of s.o./sth.

skittish ['skɪtɪʃ] *adj.* (*of horse, girl, etc.*) liable to jump about unexpectedly.

skittle ['skɪtl] *n.* bottle-shaped wooden object which is to be knocked down with a ball in a game.

skive [skaɪv] *v. inf.* to avoid working. **skiver**, *n. inf.* person who skives.

skivvy ['skɪvɪ] *n. inf.* girl who does the dirty work in a house.

skua ['skjuːə] *n.* type of large sea bird.

skulduggery [skʌl'dʌgərɪ] *n. inf.* some vague unspecified crime.

skulk [skʌlk] *v.* (*a*) to hide away (because you are planning sth wicked). (*b*) to creep about mysteriously.

skull [skʌl] *n.* bony part of the head. **skullcap**, *n.* small round hat which fits tight on the head.

skunk [skʌŋk] *n.* American mammal with black and white fur, which pro- duces a bad smell.

sky [skaɪ] *n.* area above the earth which is blue during the day, and where the moon and stars appear at night. **sky-blue**, *adj. & n.* bright light blue (colour). **sky-diver**, *n.* person who jumps from an aircraft, and falls

freely for some time before opening his parachute. **sky-high**, *adv.* as high as the sky; **to blow sth sky-high** = to blow sth up with a powerful explosive. **skylark**. **1.** *n.* small singing bird which sings as it flies upwards. **2.** *v.* to play wild games. **skylight**, *n.* window in a roof or ceiling. **skyline**, *n.* horizon; shape of buildings silhouetted against the sky. **skyscraper**, *n.* very tall building.

slab [slæb] *n.* thick flat rectangular block.

slack [slæk] **1.** *adj.* (**-er, -est**) (*a*) not taut/not tight. (*b*) not busy. (*c*) lazy/not working well. **2.** *n.* (*a*) looseness; loose part of a rope. (*b*) very small pieces of coal. (*c*) **slacks** = trousers. **3.** *v.* to **s. (off)** = to be lazy/to do less work. **slacken**, *v.* (*a*) to loosen. (*b*) **to s. off** = to work less. **slacker**, *n.* person who doesn't work hard. **slackly**, *adv.* (*a*) loosely. (*b*) lazily. **slackness**, *n.* being slack.

slag [slæg] *n.* waste material left after metal has been extracted from ore; **s. heap** = mountain of slag left near a metal works or coalmine.

slain [sleɪn] *v. see* **slay**.

slake [sleɪk] *v.* (*a*) **to s. your thirst** = to drink to remove your thirst. (*b*) to mix lime with water.

slalom ['slɑːləm] *n.* test in skiing, where you have to ski fast between a series of posts.

slam [slæm] **1.** *n.* (*a*) banging of a door. (*b*) **grand s.** = winning all the card games in a competition. **2.** *v.* (**slammed**) (*a*) to bang. (*b*) *inf.* to criticize very un- favourably.

slander ['slɑːndə] **1.** *n.* untrue thing said about a person which hurts his repu- tation; crime of saying such things. **2.** *v.* to say untrue things about a person. **slanderous**, *adj.* (statement) which is slander.

slang [slæŋ] *n.* words or phrases used by certain groups of people in popular speech which are not used in correct or written language. **slanging match**, *n.* bitter argument where two people call each other rude names. **slangy**, *adj. inf.* using slang.

slant [slɑːnt] **1.** *n.* (*a*) slope; **on the s.** = sloping. (*b*) point of view. **2.** *v.* (*a*) to slope. (*b*) to show (news or infor-

mation) in a biased way. **slanting,** *adj.*
sloping. **slantwise,** *adv.* at an angle; on
a slope.

slap [slæp] **1.** *n.* smack with your hand
flat. **2.** *v.* **slapped)** (*a*) to hit with your
hand flat. (*b*) to bring (sth) down flat
on to a surface; **to s. down** = tell off
sharply. **3.** *adv.* **to run s. into the wall**
= right into the wall. **slapdash,** *adj.*
careless. **slaphappy,** *adj. inf.* happily
careless. **slapstick,** *adj. & n.* rough
(comedy) which depends on physical
jokes. **slap-up,** *adj. inf.* good expensive
(meal).

slash [slæʃ] **1.** *n.* (*pl.* **-es**) long cut. **2.** *v.*
(*a*) to make a long cut. (*b*) to shorten;
to reduce (a price) drastically.

slat [slæt] *n.* thin flat piece of wood.
slatted, *adj.* made of slats.

slate [sleɪt] **1.** *n.* (*a*) dark-grey stone
which splits into thin sheets; piece of
this stone used as a roof covering or
for writing on; **to start a clean s.** =
to start again (without any faults held
against you). (*b*) group of candidates in
an election. **2.** *v. inf.* to criticize (a play/
a book, etc.). **slate grey,** *adj. & n.* very
dark blue-grey (colour).

slattern ['slætən] *n.* dirty woman. **slat-
ternly,** *adj.* (*of a woman*) dirty.

slaughter ['slɔːtə] **1.** *n.* (*a*) killing of
animals for meat. (*b*) killing of people
(in war). **2.** *v.* (*a*) to kill (animals) for
meat. (*b*) to kill (many people) in war.
slaughterhouse, *n.* place where animals are slaughtered.

slave [sleɪv] **1.** *n.* person who belongs to
and works for s.o. **2.** *v.* (*also* **slave away**)
to work hard. **slave driver,** *n. inf.*
employer who makes his workers work
very hard. **slavery,** *n.* being a slave;
buying and selling slaves. **slavish,** *adj.*
exact (imitation) without any imagination. **slavishly,** *adv.* (to obey rules)
exactly without exercising any imagination.

slaver ['sleɪvə] **1.** *n.* liquid which dribbles
out of your mouth. **2.** *v.* to dribble/to let
liquid trickle out of your mouth.

slay [sleɪ] *v.* (*formal*) (**slew** [sluː], **slain**)
to kill.

sleazy ['sliːzɪ] *adj.* (**-ier, -iest**) *inf.* dirty/
disreputable.

sled [sled] *n.* sledge.

sledge [sledʒ] **1.** *n.* small vehicle with
runners for sliding over the snow. **2.** *v.*
to go sledging = to play at sliding on the
snow on a sledge. **sledge-hammer,** *n.*
very large heavy hammer.

sleek [sliːk] **1.** *adj.* (**-er, -est**) smooth/
shiny; well-kept. **2.** *v.* to smooth down
(hair) with oil. **sleekly,** *adv.* in a sleek
way. **sleekness,** *n.* being sleek.

sleep [sliːp] **1.** *n.* state of resting
naturally and unconsciously; **to go/to get
to s.** = to start sleeping; **to send s.o.
to s.** = to make s.o. go to sleep (from
boredom/by hypnosis); **to put to s.** =
to kill; **my foot has gone to s.** = has
become numb. **2.** *v.* (**slept**) (*a*) to be
in a state of natural rest and unconsciousness; **I'll s. on it** = I will make a
decision on the problem in the morning;
to s. sth off = to get rid of the effects
of sth by sleeping; **to s. with s.o.** = to
have sexual intercourse with s.o. (*b*) to
have enough beds for. **sleeper,** *n.* (*a*)
person who is asleep. (*b*) wooden bar
which rails are attached to. (*c*) sleeping
car. (*d*) overnight train with sleeping
cars. **sleepily,** *adv.* in a sleepy way.
sleepiness, *n.* being sleepy. **sleeping.
1.** *adj.* asleep; **s. partner** = partner
who does not take an active interest
in the business. **2.** *n.* being asleep; **s.
pill** = medicine which makes you go to
sleep; **s. car** = carriage on a train with
beds where passengers can sleep; **s. bag**
= quilted bag for sleeping in a tent,
etc.; **s. sickness** = tropical disease which
affects the nervous system. **sleepless,**
adj. with no sleep. **sleeplessness,** *n.*
having no sleep; not able to get to sleep.
sleepwalk, *v.* to walk about when you
are asleep. **sleepwalker,** *n.* person who
sleepwalks. **sleepy,** *adj.* (**-ier, -iest**) half
asleep; ready to go to sleep.

sleet [sliːt] **1.** *n.* mixture of snow and
rain. **2.** *v.* **it is sleeting** = snow and rain
are falling together.

sleeve [sliːv] *n.* (*a*) part of clothing which
covers the arm; **to keep sth up your s.**
= to have a plan which you are keeping secret. (*b*) cover for a piece of machinery. (*c*) square cardboard cover for
a gramophone record. **sleeveless,** *adj.*
with no sleeves.

sleigh [sleɪ] *n.* large sledge pulled by
horses or reindeer, etc.

sleight [slaɪt] *n.* **s. of hand** = quickness of a conjurer's movements when performing a card trick.

slender ['slendə] *adj.* (*a*) very thin/slim. (*b*) not strong; not large. **slenderness**, *n.* being slender.

slept [slept] *v. see* **sleep**.

sleuth [sluːθ] *n. inf.* detective.

slew [sluː] *v.* (*a*) to turn/to twist. (*b*) *see* **slay**.

slice [slaɪs] **1.** *n.* (*a*) thin piece cut off sth. (*b*) **fish s.** = flat broad knife for serving fish. (*c*) (*in games*) stroke which makes the ball spin towards the right. **2.** *v.* (*a*) to cut into slices. (*b*) to cut sharply. (*c*) to hit a ball so that it spins towards the right. **slicer**, *n.* machine for slicing meat/bread, etc.

slick [slɪk] **1.** *adj.* (**-er, -est**) clever (in a way which tricks people). **2.** *n.* **oil s.** = layer of oil which has spilled on the sea from a tanker or oil rig. **3.** *v.* **to s. down** = to make (hair) sleek.

slid [slɪd] *v. see* **slide**.

slide [slaɪd] **1.** *n.* (*a*) action of slipping on a smooth surface. (*b*) slippery surface (on ice); slippery metal slope for children to slide down. (*c*) thin glass plate to put under a microscope. (*d*) plastic transparent photograph which can be projected on a screen. (*d*) clip which slips into the hair to hold it in place. **2.** *v.* (**slid** [slɪd]) (*a*) to move smoothly. (*b*) **to let things s.** = to allow things to become worse/not to care if things get worse. **slide-rule**, *n.* device for calculating, made of a ruler marked with numbers and a central part which slides sideways. **sliding scale**, *n.* system of marks/points/taxes, etc., which vary according to a scale.

slight [slaɪt] **1.** *adj.* (**-er, -est**) (*a*) thin/slender (person). (*b*) not very large; not very important. **2.** *n.* insult. **3.** *v.* to insult/to be rude to (s.o.). **slightingly**, *adv.* rudely/insultingly. **slightly**, *adv.* not very much.

slim [slɪm] **1.** *adj.* (**slimmer, slimmest**) (*a*) thin/slender/not fat. (*b*) small. **2.** *v.* (**slimmed**) to diet in order to become thin. **slimmer**, *n.* person who is trying to lose weight. **slimness**, *n.* being slim.

slime [slaɪm] *n.* thin mud; dirty, sticky liquid. **sliminess**, *n.* being slimy.

slimy, *adj.* (**-ier, -iest**) unpleasantly muddy/slippery/sticky.

sling [slɪŋ] **1.** *n.* (*a*) device for throwing a stone. (*b*) carrying strap; bandage tied round your neck to hold steady your wounded arm. (*c*) apparatus made of ropes and pulleys for hoisting and carrying goods. **2.** *v.* (**slung**) (*a*) to throw. (*b*) to hold up/to hang by a sling. **slingshot**, *n. Am.* catapult/strong elastic band on a forked stick, used for throwing stones.

slink [slɪŋk] *v.* (**slunk**) to creep about furtively. **slinky**, *adj.* (**-ier, -iest**) smooth (shape); tight, smooth (clothes).

slip [slɪp] **1.** *n.* (*a*) action of sliding by mistake. (*b*) mistake; **s. of the tongue** = mistake in speaking. (*c*) **to give s.o. the s.** = to escape from s.o. (*d*) **pillow s.** = cloth bag to cover a pillow. (*e*) small piece of paper. (*f*) petticoat. (*g*) **slips** = long smooth slope on which ships are built. (*h*) mixture of clay and water which is used in pottery. **2.** *v.* (**slipped**) (*a*) to slide by mistake. (*b*) to go quietly. (*c*) (*of machinery*) to miss/not to connect; **slipped disc** = painful state where one of the cushioning discs in the spine has become displaced. **slipper**, *n.* light comfortable shoe worn indoors. **slippery**, *adj.* (*a*) so smooth that one can easily slip on it. (*b*) *inf.* (person) who cannot be trusted. **slippy**, *adj. inf.* slippery. **slip road**, *n.* road which leads on to a motorway. **slipshod**, *adj.* badly carried out (work); careless (dress). **slipstream**, *n.* air blown backwards by an aircraft engine; point just behind a fast-moving vehicle. **slip up**, *v. inf.* to make a mistake. **slip-up**, *n. inf.* mistake. **slipway**, *n.* smooth slope on which ships are built or repaired.

slit [slɪt] **1.** *n.* long cut; narrow opening. **2.** *v.* (**slit**) to make a slit.

slither ['slɪðə] *v.* to slide about in various directions.

sliver ['slɪvə] *n.* thin piece of wood or meat.

slob [slɒb] *n. inf.* sloppy/untidy fat person. **slobber** ['slɒbə] *v.* to dribble saliva from your mouth. **slobbery**, *adj.* covered with saliva.

sloe [sləʊ] *n.* bitter wild fruit like a plum; tree which bears this fruit.

slog [slɒg] **1.** *n.* difficult work; difficult

walk. **2.** *v.* (**slogged**) to work hard at sth difficult. **slogger**, *n.* person who works hard.

slogan ['sləʊgn] *n.* phrase used in publicity for a product/for a political party, etc.

sloop [slu:p] *n.* type of small ship.

slop [slɒp] *v.* (**slopped**) to spill. **sloppily**, *adv.* in a sloppy way. **sloppiness**, *n.* being sloppy. **sloppy**, *adj.* (**-ier, -iest**) (*a*) untidy; badly done (work). (*b*) stupidly sentimental. **slops**, *n. pl.* (*a*) liquid food given to people who are too ill to eat. (*b*) waste food given to pigs. (*c*) liquid refuse.

slope [sləʊp] **1.** *n.* slanting surface; angle of a slanting surface; slanting piece of ground. **2.** *v.* to slant upwards or downwards. **slope off**, *v. inf.* to creep away quietly. **sloping**, *adj.* (roof, etc.) which slopes.

slosh [slɒʃ] *v.* (*a*) to splash. (*b*) *inf.* to hit. **sloshed**, *adj. inf.* drunk.

slot [slɒt] **1.** *n.* narrow opening (for putting a coin into); **s. machine** = machine which (when you put a coin into the slot) will give chocolate/cigarettes, etc., automatically. **2.** *v.* (**slotted**) **to s. into** = to fit into (a slot).

sloth [sləʊθ] *n.* (*a*) (*formal*) laziness. (*b*) slow-moving South American mammal, like a bear. **slothful**, *adj.* (*formal*) lazy.

slouch [slaʊtʃ] *v.* to stand/to sit in a bad position/with bent shoulders; **to s. along** = to walk along bending forwards. **slouch hat**, *n.* hat with a wide brim which can be turned down.

slough 1. *n.* (*a*) [slʌf] old skin of a snake. (*b*) [slaʊ] marshy place. **2.** *v.* [slʌf] (*of a snake*) to lose (its skin).

slovenly ['slʌvənlɪ] *adj.* untidy; careless (work). **slovenliness**, *n.* being slovenly.

slow [sləʊ] **1.** *adj.* (**-er, -est**) (*a*) not fast; **s. train** = train which stops at each station. (*b*) (*of clock, etc.*) **to be s.** = to show a time which is earlier than the correct time. (*c*) not quick to learn; *inf.* **to be s. on the uptake** = not to understand quickly. **2.** *adv.* not fast; **to go s.** = (i) to advance less quickly; (ii) to protest by working slowly. **3.** *v.* **to s. down** = to make (sth) go slowly; to go more slowly. **slowcoach,**

n. inf. person who goes slower than others. **slowdown**, *n.* slowing down (of business activity). **slowly**, *adv.* in a slow way. **slow motion**, *n.* (*in films*) action which appears to take place very slowly because the film speed has been slowed down. **slowness**, *n.* being slow. **slow-worm**, *n.* snake-like lizard.

sludge [slʌdʒ] *n.* wet mud; wet refuse.

slug [slʌg] **1.** *n.* (*a*) common garden animal like a snail with no shell. (*b*) small metal pellet. **2.** *v.* (**slugged**) *inf.* to hit (s.o.) a heavy blow. **sluggard**, *n.* lazy person. **sluggish**, *adj.* lazy/slow-moving. **sluggishly**, *adv.* in a slow way.

sluice [slu:s] **1.** *n.* (*a*) channel for taking water round a dam; gate which allows water to enter this channel. (*b*) washing with buckets of water. **2.** *v.* to wash (sth) with lots of water. **sluice gate**, *n.* gate which allows water to enter the sluice channel.

slum [slʌm] *n.* poor, rundown area of a town. **slumming**, *n.* visiting slums; visiting people who you think are of a lower class or less rich than yourself.

slumber ['slʌmbə] **1.** *n.* gentle sleep. **2.** *v.* to sleep gently. **slumberer**, *n.* person who slumbers. **slumberwear**, *n.* (*no pl.*) clothes worn to go to bed.

slump [slʌmp] **1.** *n.* collapse (of prices); economic collapse (of a country). **2.** *v.* (*a*) to fall suddenly. (*b*) to sit/to lie clumsily/heavily.

slung [slʌŋ] *v. see* **sling**.

slunk [slʌŋk] *v. see* **slink**.

slur [slɜː] **1.** *n.* (*a*) insult. (*b*) slurring of several notes; mark on a musical score to show that notes should be slurred. **2.** *v.* (**slurred**) (*a*) to speak words indistinctly. (*b*) (*in music*) to play several notes without a break between them.

slurp [slɜːp] *v. inf.* to drink noisily.

slurry ['slʌrɪ] *n.* (*no pl.*) watery mud/cement; liquid waste from farm animals.

slush [slʌʃ] *n.* (*a*) half-melted snow. (*b*) sentimentality. **slush fund**, *n. inf.* money kept for the purposes of bribery. **slushy**, *adj.* (*a*) covered with half-melted snow. (*b*) very sentimental.

slut [slʌt] *n. inf.* dirty, untidy woman. **sluttish**, *adj.* like a slut.

sly [slaɪ] *adj.* (**-er, -est**) cunning (person); **on the s.** = without anyone knowing. **slyly,** *adv.* in a sly way. **slyness,** *n.* being sly.

smack [smæk] **1.** *n.* (*a*) blow with the flat of the hand. (*b*) **fishing s.** = small fishing boat. (*c*) loud kiss. (*d*) particular taste. **2.** *v.* (*a*) to hit (s.o.). (*b*) **to s. one's lips** = make a loud noise (as if hungry). (*c*) to smell/to taste; **that smacks of bribery** = it sounds as though bribery is involved. **3.** *adv. inf.* straight/directly. **smacker,** *n.* (*a*) *inf.* loud kiss. (*b*) *inf.* pound note.

small [smɔːl] **1.** *adj.* (**-er, -est**) (*a*) not large; little. (*b*) delicate/soft (voice). (*c*) not imposing. (*d*) petty/thinking only of trivial things. **2.** *n.* (*a*) **the s. of the back** = the lower part of the back. (*b*) *inf.* **smalls** = underwear. **3.** *adv.* into little bits. **smallholder,** *n.* person who owns a smallholding. **smallholding,** *n.* very small farm. **small hours,** *n.* period just after midnight. **small-minded,** *adj.* thinking only of yourself/of trivial things. **smallness,** *n.* being small. **smallpox,** *n.* dangerous infectious disease causing a rash which leaves marks on the skin. **small talk,** *n.* general conversation about sth unimportant. **smalltime,** *n.* unimportant (criminal).

smarmy ['smɑːmɪ] *adj.* (**-ier, -iest**) (person) who is unpleasantly smooth. **smarminess,** *n.* being smarmy.

smart [smɑːt] **1.** *n.* sharp pain (from a wound). **2.** *v.* to hurt/to feel as if burning. **3.** *adj.* (**-er, -est**) (*a*) sharp (blow). (*b*) rapid/efficient. (*c*) clever; **s. card** = plastic card with a microprocessor embedded in it. (*d*) well-dressed/elegant. **smarten,** *v.* **to s. yourself up** = to make yourself look smart. **smartly,** *adv.* in a smart way. **smartness,** *n.* being smart.

smash [smæʃ] **1.** *n.* (*pl.* **-es**) (*a*) crash (of a car). (*b*) financial collapse. (*c*) powerful shot (in tennis). **2.** *v.* (*a*) to break (sth) to pieces. (*b*) to hit sth hard. (*c*) to hit (a ball) hard. **smash-and-grab raid,** *n.* burglary done by breaking a shop window and stealing as much as you can get hold of. **smash hit,** *n. inf.* play/film, etc., which is very successful. **smashing,** *adj. inf.* very good/fantastic.

smattering ['smætrɪŋ] *n.* small knowledge (of a language).

smear ['smɪə] **1.** *n.* (*a*) dirty mark; thing which is smeared (esp. a small amount of sth for examining under a microscope); **s. test** = test for cancer esp. of the cervix. (*b*) insult; **s. campaign** = campaign to discredit s.o. by spreading gossip about his private life. **2.** *v.* (*a*) to make dirty marks. (*b*) to spread (sth greasy).

smell [smel] **1.** *n.* (*a*) one of the five senses, felt through the nose. (*b*) thing which you can sense through the nose. (*c*) unpleasant thing which you can sense through the nose. **2.** *v.* (**smelled/smelt**) (*a*) to notice (sth) by the nose. (*b*) to sniff in order to sense the smell. (*c*) to give off a smell. **smelling salts,** *n. pl.* crystals of a compound of ammonia, which are smelled to cure faintness. **smelly,** *adj.* (**-ier, -iest**) which gives off an unpleasant smell.

smelt [smelt] **1.** *n.* (*pl.* **smelt**) small edible fish. **2.** *v.* (*a*) to produce metal by melting ore. (*b*) *see also* **smell**. **smelter,** *n.* works where metal is extracted from ore. **smelting,** *n.* production of metal by heating ore with coke and limestone.

smidgen ['smɪdʒn] *n. inf.* very small amount.

smile [smaɪl] **1.** *n.* expression of pleasure with the mouth turned up at the corners. **2.** *v.* to make an expression of happiness by turning up the corners of the mouth.

smirk [smɜːk] **1.** *n.* unpleasant superior smile. **2.** *v.* to give a smirk.

smite [smaɪt] *v.* (**smote, has smitten**) (*formal*) to hit; **smitten with** = liking.

smith [smɪθ] *n.* person who works in metal. **smithy** ['smɪðɪ] *n.* workshop where a blacksmith works.

smithereens [smɪðə'riːnz] *n.* very small bits.

smitten ['smɪtn] *v. see* **smite**.

smock [smɒk] *n.* long loose overall worn over clothes to protect them. **smocking,** *n.* embroidery on gathered material.

smog [smɒg] *n.* mixture of fog and exhaust fumes of cars.

smoke [sməʊk] **1.** *n.* (*a*) vapour and

gas given off when sth burns. (b) action of smoking a cigarette. 2. v. (a) to send out clouds of vapour and gas. (b) to cure (bacon/fish, etc.) by hanging in wood smoke. (c) to suck in smoke from a burning cigarette/pipe, etc. **smokeless**, adj. which makes no smoke; s. zone = area where you are not allowed to make any smoke. **smoker**, n. (a) person who smokes cigarettes, etc. (b) railway carriage where you can smoke. **smokescreen**, n. thick smoke made so that the enemy cannot see; anything which is deliberately used to hide what is going on. **smoky**, adj. (-ier, -iest) full of cigarette smoke.

smooth [smu:ð] 1. adj. (-er, -est) (a) (surface) with no bumps/no roughness. (b) with no bumps/jolts. (c) with no hair. (d) too pleasant (person). 2. v. to make smooth; to s. the way for sth = to make it easy; to s. things over = settle an argument. **smoothly**, adv. in a smooth way. **smoothness**, n. being smooth.

smorgasbord ['smɔ:gəsbɔ:d] n. Swedish buffet of many cold dishes.

smote [sməʊt] v. see **smite**.

smother ['smʌðə] v. (a) to stifle and kill (s.o.). (b) to cover.

smoulder, Am. smolder ['sməʊldə] v. to burn slowly.

smudge [smʌdʒ] 1. n. dirty (ink) stain. 2. v. to make a mark, such as by rubbing ink which is not dry. **smudgy**, adj. (paper) with a dirty mark on it.

smug [smʌg] adj. (smugger, smuggest) self-satisfied. **smugly**, adv. in a way which shows you are pleased with yourself. **smugness**, n. being smug.

smuggle ['smʌgl] v. to take (goods) past the customs without declaring them for duty; to take (sth) into or out of a prison without the warders seeing. **smuggler**, n. person who smuggles goods.

smut [smʌt] 1. n. (a) small black mark. (b) indecent stories. **smutty**, adj. (-ier, -iest) indecent.

Sn symbol for tin.

snack [snæk] n. light meal. **snackbar**, n. restaurant where you can have a light meal, usu. sitting at a counter.

snaffle ['snæfl] 1. n. horse's bit. 2. v. inf. to take/to steal.

snag [snæg] 1. n. (a) obstacle; thing

which prevents you from doing sth. (b) sharp point; place where a piece of clothing has been caught on a sharp point. 2. v. (snagged) to catch and tear (your clothes) on a sharp point.

snail [sneɪl] n. common slimy animal with a shell; at a s.'s pace = extremely slowly.

snake [sneɪk] 1. n. long, sometimes poisonous, reptile which wriggles along the ground. 2. v. to wriggle like a snake.

snap [snæp] 1. n. (a) sudden dry noise. (b) cold s. = sudden spell of cold weather. (c) type of brittle biscuit. (d) photograph. (e) card game where you say 'snap' if you play the same card as your opponent. 2. adj. (decision) taken hurriedly. 3. v. (snapped) (a) to try to bite. (b) to speak sharply. (c) to break sharply; to make a dry noise (in breaking). (d) to take a photograph of (s.o.). (e) to s. up = to buy quickly. (f) inf. to s. out of it = to get out of a state of depression. **snapdragon**, n. antirrhinum. **snap fastener**, n. fastening for clothes, made of two small metal studs which fit into each other. **snapper**, n. type of American fish. **snappily**, adv. in a snappy way. **snappy**, adj. (-ier, -iest) (a) irritable/short-tempered. (b) inf. make it s.! = do it quickly. **snapshot**, n. informal photograph taken quickly.

snare ['sneə] 1. n. trap for catching animals made with a noose which is pulled tight. 2. v. to catch with a snare.

snarl [snɑ:l] 1. n. (a) angry growl. (b) tangle. 2. v. (a) to growl angrily. (b) to make tangled. **snarl-up**, n. inf. traffic jam.

snatch [snætʃ] 1. n. (pl. -es) (a) grabbing sth; wages s. = grabbing a company's wages from the pay office. (b) short piece (of a song, etc.). 2. v. to grab (sth) rapidly.

snazzy ['snæzɪ] adj. (-ier, -iest) inf. smart/in fashion.

sneak [sni:k] 1. n. inf. person who tells tales about s.o. 2. v. (a) to creep without being seen. (b) inf. to s. on s.o. = to report that s.o. has done sth wrong. **sneakers**, n. pl. Am. soft sports shoes with rubber soles. **sneaking**, adj. secret. **sneaky**, adj. inf. deceitful/not open.

sneer ['snɪə] **1.** *n.* sarcastic smile; unpleasant smile. **2.** *v.* to give s.o. a sarcastic smile to show contempt; to speak in a contemptuous way.

sneeze [sni:z] **1.** *n.* sudden blowing out of air through your mouth and nose because of irritation in your nose. **2.** *v.* make a sneeze; *inf.* **it's not to be sneezed at** = you should not refuse it/despise it.

snick [snɪk] **1.** *n.* (a) small cut (with a knife). (b) (*in cricket*) sharp stroke. **2.** *v.* to hit (a ball) a sharp glancing blow. **snicker**, *n. & v.* snigger.

snide [snaɪd] *adj. inf.* unpleasant/envious (remark).

sniff [snɪf] **1.** *n.* short intake of air through the nose. **2.** *v.* to take in air rapidly through the nose; *inf.* **it's not to be sniffed at** = you should not refuse it/despise it. **sniffer**, *n.* person who sniffs. **sniffle. 1.** *n.* slight cold in the head. **2.** *v.* to keep on sniffing because of a cold.

snigger ['snɪgə] **1.** *n.* quiet unpleasant laugh. **2.** *v.* to laugh quietly in an unpleasant way. **sniggering**, *n.* hidden laughter.

snip [snɪp] **1.** *n.* (a) piece which has been cut off. (b) *inf.* bargain. **2.** *v.* (**snipped**) to cut with scissors. **snippet**, *n.* little bit (of cloth, etc.).

snipe [snaɪp] **1.** *n.* large marsh bird with a long beak. **2.** *v.* **to s. at s.o.** = to shoot at s.o. from a hiding place/to make continuous criticism of s.o. **sniper**, *n.* hidden soldier who shoots at the enemy.

snitch [snɪtʃ] *v. inf.* to steal.

snivel ['snɪvl] *v.* (**snivelled**) (a) to have a runny nose. (b) to cry and complain.

snob [snɒb] *n.* person who likes people who are of a higher social class than himself; **intellectual s.** = person who looks down on those who are not as well-educated as he feels he is himself. **snobbery, snobbishness**, *n.* being a snob. **snobbish**, *adj.* referring to a snob.

snood [snu:d] *n.* (*old*) ornamental bag-shaped net for holding a woman's hair at the back of the head.

snook [snu:k] *n.* **to cock a s. at** = to make a rude gesture at (s.o.)/to disregard (a rule).

snooker ['snu:kə] *n.* game like billiards played on a table with twenty-two balls of various colours.

snoop [snu:p] *v.* to creep about investigating sth secretly. **snooper**, *n.* person who spies on s.o. secretly.

snooty ['snu:tɪ] *adj.* (**-ier, -iest**) *inf.* superior (air/expression). **snootily**, *adv.* in a snooty way. **snootiness**, *n.* being snooty.

snooze [snu:z] **1.** *n.* short sleep. **2.** *v.* to sleep lightly for a short time.

snore [snɔ:] **1.** *n.* loud noise in the throat made by breathing air when you are asleep. **2.** *v.* to make a snore. **snorer**, *n.* person who snores.

snorkel ['snɔ:kl] *n.* tube which goes from the mouth or mask of an underwater swimmer to the surface to allow him to breathe in air. **snorkelling**, *n.* **to go s.** = to go swimming with a snorkel.

snort [snɔ:t] **1.** *n.* (a) snorting noise. (b) *inf.* small drink. **2.** *v.* to make a loud noise blowing air out through the nose.

snot [snɒt] *n. inf.* mucus in the nose.

snout [snaʊt] *n.* nose of an animal (esp. a pig).

snow [snəʊ] **1.** *n.* water vapour which freezes and falls in light white flakes. **2.** *v.* to fall in flakes of snow; **snowed under** = overwhelmed. **snowball. 1.** *n.* ball of snow. **2.** *v.* (a) to throw snowballs. (b) to get bigger and bigger. **snowblindness**, *n.* painful lack of sight caused by the brightness of snow. **snowdrift**, *n.* heap of snow which has been piled up by the wind. **snowdrop**, *n.* small spring bulb with little white flowers. **snowfall**, *n.* amount of snow which has fallen. **snowflake**, *n.* flake of snow. **snowline**, *n.* point on a high mountain above which there is always snow. **snowman**, *n.* (*pl.* **-men**) figure of a man made out of snow. **snowmobile** ['snəʊməbi:l] *n.* vehicle with caterpillar tracks specially designed for driving on snow. **snow plough**, *Am.* **snow plow**, *n.* heavy vehicle with a plough on the front for clearing snow off roads/railways, etc. **snowshoes**, *n. pl.* frames shaped like tennis rackets, with a light web, which are tied under the feet for walking on snow. **snowstorm**, *n.* storm which brings snow. **snow white**, *adj.* pure white. **snowy**, *adj.* (**-ier, -iest**) covered with snow; white like snow.

snub [snʌb] **1.** *n.* insult; insulting refusal

to speak to s.o. **2.** v. (**snubbed**) to insult (s.o.) by refusing to speak to them/by not paying any attention to them. **3.** adj. **s. nose** = small nose which is turned up at the end.

snuff [snʌf] **1.** n. powdered tobacco which is sniffed into the nose. **2.** v. (a) to put out (a candle). (b) Sl. **to s. it** = to die.

snuffle ['snʌfl] **1.** n. loud sniff. **2.** v. to sniff noisily.

snug [snʌg] adj. (**snugger, snuggest**) warm and comfortable. **snuggle,** v. to curl yourself up to be warm; to curl up close to s.o. for warmth. **snugly,** adv. in a snug way.

so [səʊ] **1.** adv. (a) to such an extent. (b) in this way. (c) true/correct; **I think s.** = I think it is true. (d) in the same way. (e) **or s.** = approximately. (f) **and s. on** = and in a similar way; etcetera. **2.** conj. (a) therefore. (b) **s. that/s. as to** = for the purpose of. **so-and-so,** n. (a) somebody (whom you do not want to name). (b) inf. naughty person. **so-called,** adj. wrongly called. **so-so,** adj. & adv. inf. not very well.

soak [səʊk] **1.** n. being very wet. **2.** v. to put (sth) to lie in a liquid; to get/to make very wet. **soakaway,** n. hole in the ground into which rainwater drains. **soaking. 1.** n. (action of) being soaked. **2.** adj. & adv. wet through. **soak up,** v. to absorb (a liquid).

soap [səʊp] **1.** n. material made of oil and fat used for washing. **2.** v. to wash with soap. **soapbox,** n. box on which a speaker stands to talk to a meeting outdoors. **soap opera,** n. trite serial story on television. **soapstone,** n. type of soft grey stone which can be easily carved. **soapsuds,** n. pl. foam made from soap. **soapy,** adj. full of soap; covered with soap.

soar [sɔː] v. (a) to fly high into the air; (of bird) to glide without beating its wings. (b) to rise rapidly.

sob [sɒb] **1.** n. short breath like a hiccup when crying. **2.** v. (**sobbed**) to weep, taking short breaths like hiccups.

sober ['səʊbə] **1.** adj. (a) not drunk. (b) serious. (c) dark (colour). **2.** v. **to s. up** = to recover from drunkenness. **soberly,** adv. seriously. **soberness, sobriety** [sə'braɪtɪ] n. being sober.

sobriquet ['səʊbrɪkeɪ] n. nickname.

soccer ['sɒkə] n. football/game played between two sides of eleven players who can only kick or head the ball.

sociable ['səʊʃəbl] adj. friendly/liking the company of other people. **sociability** [səʊʃə'bɪlɪtɪ] n. being sociable.

social ['səʊʃl] **1.** adj. (a) referring to society; **s. science** = study of the problems of society; **s. security** = money/help provided by the government to people who need it; **s. services** = state services to help people's problems; **s. worker** = person who works to help families in need; **the s. system** = the way society is organized. (b) living in groups. (c) **s. evening** = evening party for a group of people. **2.** n. party. **socialism,** n. political system where the state owns and runs the wealth of the country; belief that all property should belong to the state and that every citizen is equal. **socialist,** adj. & n. (person) who believes in socialism; (policies) which follow the principles of socialism. **socialite,** n. person who moves in high society. **socialize,** v. (a) to be friendly with other people (at a party). (b) to organize (a country) along the principles of socialism. **socially,** adv. in a social way.

society [sə'saɪtɪ] n. (a) way in which people are organized; group of people who live in the same way. (b) group/club/association of people with the same interests. (c) (also **high society**) top class of people. **sociology** [səʊsɪ'ɒlədʒɪ] n. study of society and how people live in society. **sociological** [səʊsɪə'lɒdʒɪkl] adj. referring to society and the way in which society changes. **sociologist** [səʊsɪ'ɒlədʒɪst] n. person who studies society and how people live in it.

sock [sɒk] **1.** n. woollen covering for the foot and lower part of the leg; inf. **you'll have to pull your socks up** = try to do better. **2.** v. inf. to hit.

socket ['sɒkɪt] n. hole(s) into which sth is fitted; **electric s.** = one which a plug/bulb can be fitted into.

sod [sɒd] n. (a) piece of soil with grass growing on it. (b) Sl. unpleasant/nasty man.

soda ['səʊdə] n. compound of sodium; **s.**

(**water**) = water made fizzy by putting gas into it; **ice cream s.** = sweet fizzy drink mixed with ice cream. **soda fountain**, *n.* bar where sweet drinks and ice cream are served.

sodden ['sɒdn] *adj.* very wet.

sodium ['səʊdɪəm] *n.* (*element:* Na) white soft metal, which can catch fire, and is usu. found in combination with other substances.

sodomy ['sɒdəmɪ] *n.* anal sexual intercourse between men.

sofa ['səʊfə] *n.* long seat with a soft back for several people.

soffit ['sɒfɪt] *n.* underside of an arch.

soft [sɒft] *adj.* (**-er, -est**) (*a*) not hard; (pencil) which makes wide blurred marks. (*b*) quiet (voice). (*c*) not strict. (*d*) *inf.* stupid. (*e*) (water) with little calcium in it; (drink) which is not alcoholic; (drugs) which are not addictive. **soft-boiled**, *adj.* (egg) which has not been boiled very much. **soften** ['sɒfn] *v.* to make/to become soft; **to s. up** = to make weak before attacking or before asking for a favour. **softener**, *n.* water s. = apparatus for making hard water soft. **soft fruit**, *n. pl.* small fruit (like raspberries/strawberries, etc.). **soft-hearted**, *adj.* not strict/too kind. **softly**, *adv.* in a soft way. **softness**, *n.* being soft. **soft soap**, *n. inf.* flattery. **software**, *n.* computer programs (as opposed to the machines). **softwood**, *n.* wood from pine and fir trees.

soggy ['sɒgɪ] *adj.* (**-ier, -iest**) wet and soft. **sogginess**, *n.* being soggy.

soil [sɔɪl] **1.** *n.* earth. **2.** *v.* to make dirty.

sojourn ['sʌdʒən] **1.** *n.* (*formal*) stay. **2.** *v.* (*formal*) to stay.

solace ['sɒləs] *n.* (*formal*) comfort.

solar ['səʊlə] *adj.* referring to the sun; **s. energy/s. power** = electricity produced from the radiation of the sun; **s. heating** = heating system run by light from the sun; **s. system** = series of planets orbiting the sun; **s. plexus** = (i) group of nerves behind the bottom of the lungs and the stomach; (ii) *inf.* the lower part of the body where the stomach is. **solarium** [sə'leərɪəm] *n.* room where you can enjoy real or artificial sunlight.

sold [səʊld] *v. see* **sell**.

solder ['səʊldə] **1.** *n.* soft metal used to join metal surfaces together when it is melted. **2.** *v.* to join (metal surfaces together) with solder. **soldering iron**, *n.* tool which is heated to apply solder.

soldier ['səʊldʒə] **1.** *n.* member of the army. **2.** *v.* (*a*) to be on military service. (*b*) **to s. on** = to continue doing a hard job. **soldiery**, *n.* soldiers.

sole [səʊl] **1.** *n.* (*a*) underside of the foot; bottom part of a shoe. (*b*) flat sea fish. **2.** *v.* to put a new sole on (a shoe). **3.** *adj.* (*a*) only. (*b*) belonging to one person; **he has the s. right to** = he is the only person allowed to. **solely**, *adv.* only.

solecism ['sɒlɪsɪzəm] *n.* embarrassing mistake made in speaking.

solemn ['sɒləm] *adj.* (*a*) special and religious (ceremony). (*b*) very serious. **solemnity** [sə'lemnɪtɪ] *n.* being solemn. **solemnization** [sɒləmnaɪ'zeɪʃn] *n.* celebration (of a marriage/of a religious ceremony). **solemnize** ['sɒləmnaɪz] *v.* to celebrate/to perform (a marriage/a religious ceremony). **solemnly**, *adv.* in a solemn way.

solenoid ['sɒlənɔɪd] *n.* coiled wire which produces a magnetic field when an electric current passes through it.

solfa [sɒl'fɑː] *n.* system of indicating tones in music by syllables (*doh-ray-me*, etc.).

solicit [sə'lɪsɪt] *v.* to ask for. **solicitation** [səlɪsɪ'teɪʃn] *n.* soliciting. **solicitor**, *n.* lawyer who gives advice to people on legal problems. **solicitous**, *adj.* worried/anxious about sth. **solicitously**, *adv.* in a solicitous way. **solicitude**, *n.* anxiety/worry about sth.

solid ['sɒlɪd] **1.** *adj.* (**-er, -est**) (*a*) not liquid. (*b*) not hollow. (*c*) made all of one material; **for eight hours s.** = without stopping. (*d*) trustworthy. **2.** *n.* (*a*) solid sustance. (*b*) three-dimensional shape. **solidarity** [sɒlɪ'dærɪtɪ] *n.* common interest with s.o. **solidification** [sɒlɪdɪfɪ'keɪʃn] *n.* act of solidifying. **solidify** [sə'lɪdɪfaɪ] *v.* to (make sth) become solid. **solidity** [sə'lɪdɪtɪ] *n.* being solid. **solidly**, *adv.* completely. **solid-state**, *adj.* (TV set, etc.) which uses transistors and not valves.

soliloquy [sə'lɪləkwɪ] *n.* speech spoken by a character alone on the stage. **soliloquize**, *v.* to speak all alone.

solitaire [sɒlɪ'teə] n. (a) game for one person, made of balls which have to be jumped from hole to hole removing the intervening balls one at a time. (b) single diamond (in a ring, etc.).

solitary ['sɒlɪtrɪ] adj. (a) single/sole. (b) lonely; **s. confinement** = imprisonment alone in a cell. **solitude,** n. being alone.

solo ['səʊləʊ] 1. n. (pl. -os) piece of music for one person. 2. adj. & adv. carried out by one person. **soloist,** n. musician who plays a solo.

solstice ['sɒlstɪs] n. **summer s.** = period of the longest day (June 21st); **winter s.** = period of the longest night (December 21st).

soluble ['sɒljʊbl] adj. (a) which can be dissolved. (b) (problem) which can be solved. **solubility** [sɒljʊ'bɪlɪtɪ] n. ability to be dissolved/solved. **solution** [sə'lu:ʃn] n. (a) liquid in which sth has been dissolved. (b) act of solving a problem; answer to a problem.

solve [sɒlv] v. to find the answer to (a problem). **solvable,** adj. which can be solved. **solver,** n. person who solves a problem.

solvency ['sɒlvənsɪ] n. state of being solvent. **solvent. 1.** adj. having enough money to pay your debts. **2.** n. liquid which dissolves another substance.

somatotrophin [səmə:təʊ'trɒfɪn] n. growth hormone.

sombre, Am. **somber** ['sɒmbə] adj. dark and gloomy. **sombrely,** adv. in a sombre way.

sombrero [səm'breərəʊ] n. (pl. -os) hat with a wide brim worn in South America.

some [sʌm] **1.** adj. (a) not a particular one. (b) certain; (c) several/a few; a little. (d) inf. wonderful; **that was s. party! 2.** pron. several out of a group; part of a whole. **3.** adv. approximately. **somebody** ['sʌmbədɪ] pron. (a) a particular unknown person. (b) inf. important person. **somehow** ['sʌmhaʊ] adv. (a) in one way or another. (b) for no particular reason. **someone** ['sʌmwʊn] pron. somebody. **some place** ['sʌmpleɪs] adv. Am. somewhere. **something** ['sʌmθɪŋ] pron. (a) a particular unknown thing. (b) thing which is possibly important. (c) (replacing a forgotten detail) **the 4 s. train** = the train which leaves at some time after 4 o'clock. **sometime** ['sʌmtaɪm] adv. (a) at a particular unknown time. (b) (old) formerly. **sometimes** ['sʌmtaɪmz] adv. from time to time/at times. **somewhat** ['sʌmwɒt] adv. rather. **somewhere** ['sʌmweə] adv. at some particular unknown place.

somersault ['sʌməsɔ:lt] **1.** n. rolling over, with your head underneath and feet over your head. **2.** v. to do a somersault/to roll over.

somnambulism [sɒm'næmbjʊlɪzəm] n. walking in your sleep. **somnambulist** [sɒm'næmbjʊlɪst] n. person who walks when asleep.

somnolence ['sɒmnələns] n. (formal) being sleepy/sleepiness. **somnolent,** adj. sleepy.

son [sʌn] n. male child of a parent. **son-in-law** n. (pl. **sons-in-law**) husband of a daughter.

sonar ['səʊna:] n. device for finding underwater objects by using sound waves.

sonata [sə'na:tə] n. piece of music in three or four movements for one or two instruments.

sonde [sɒnd] n. device attached to a balloon, used for taking samples of the atmosphere.

son et lumière [sɒneɪlu:mɪ'ɜ:] n. entertainment consisting of sound and lighting effects, shown in the open air at night.

song [sɒŋ] n. (a) singing. (b) words and music to be sung; **for a s.** = for very little money; inf. **he made a great s. and dance about it** = a great fuss. **songbird,** n. bird which sings particularly well. **songster,** n. person or bird that sings.

sonic ['sɒnɪk] adj. referring to sound waves; **s. boom** = bang made by an aircraft travelling faster than the speed of sound.

sonnet ['sɒnɪt] n. poem with fourteen lines.

sonny ['sʌnɪ] n. inf. way of addressing a boy.

sonorous ['sɒnərəs] adj. which makes a loud ringing noise.

soon [su:n] adv. (-er, -est) (a) in a very short time; **sooner or later** = at some

time to come. (b) **I would as s./sooner
stay than go away** = I would rather stay.

soot [sʊt] n. black carbon dust which
collects in chimneys. **sooty**, adj. (-ier,
-iest) black; covered with soot.

soothe [suːð] v. to calm. **soothing**, adj.
which calms. **soothingly**, adv. in a
soothing way.

soothsayer ['suːθseɪə] n. person who
foretells the future.

sop [sɒp] 1. n. (a) piece of bread dipped
in liquid. (b) sth given as a bribe to
make s.o. keep quiet. 2. v. (sopped) to
soak in liquid; to soak up (a liquid).
sopping, adj. s. wet = soaked. **soppy**,
adj. inf. silly and sentimental.

sophistication [səfɪstɪ'keɪʃn] n. (a)
cultured way of life. (b) advanced ideas
behind the construction of a machine.
sophisticated, adj. (a) cultured. (b)
complicated/advanced (machine).

sophistry ['sɒfɪstrɪ] n. clever argument
which is probably wrong.

sophomore ['sɒfəmɔː] n. Am. second-
year student.

soporific [sɒpə'rɪfɪk] adj. & n. (medicine) which makes you go to sleep.

soprano [sə'prɑːnəʊ] n. (pl. -os) high-
pitched singing voice; woman or boy
with such a voice.

sorbet ['sɔːbeɪ] n. water ice.

sorcery ['sɔːsərɪ] n. witchcraft/magic.
sorcerer, **sorceress**, n. person who
makes magic.

sordid ['sɔːdɪd] adj. unpleasant/dirty.
sordidly, adv. in a sordid way. **sordid-
ness**, n. being sordid.

sore [sɔː] 1. adj. (-er, -est) (a) painful/
which hurts. (b) inf. upset/annoyed. 2.
n. painful spot on the skin. **sorely**, adv.
very much. **soreness**, n. being sore.

sorghum ['sɔːgəm] n. type of grass, used
as a cereal.

sorority [sə'rɒrɪtɪ] n. Am. student society for women.

sorrel ['sɒrəl] n. (a) common sour-tasting
edible plant. (b) (horse which is) a
reddish brown colour.

sorrow ['sɒrəʊ] n. sadness. **sorrowful**,
adj. very sad. **sorrowfully**, adv. in a
sorrowful way. **sorry**, adj. (-ier, -iest)
(a) regretting sth. (b) feeling pity/
sympathy **for** s.o. (c) pitiful.

sort [sɔːt] 1. n. type/variety; **good s.** =

pleasant type of person; inf. **s. of tired**
= rather tired; **a meal of sorts** = not a
very good meal; **out of sorts** = slightly
unwell. 2. v. to arrange in different
groups. **sorter**, n. person who sorts,
esp. letters in a post office; **sorting office**
= department in a post office where
letters are sorted according to their
addresses.

sortie ['sɔːtiː] n. (a) sudden attack;
bombing raid (by aircraft). (b) sudden
excursion into an unpleasant area.

SOS [esəʊ'es] n. international code for
showing that you are in distress.

soufflé ['suːfleɪ] n. light cooked dish,
made from beaten up eggs.

sought [sɔːt] v. see **seek**. **sought after**,
adj. which people want.

soul [səʊl] n. (a) the spirit in a person
(as opposed to the body). (b) **he was
the life and s. of the party** = made
the party go well. (c) **she is the s. of
honour** = a fine example of honour. (d)
person. **soul-destroying**, adj. (work)
which is very dull, or does not allow
you to use your mind. **soulful**, adj.
with a lot of feeling. **soulfully**, adv.
in a soulful way. **soulless**, adj. very
dull/inhuman. **soul music**, n. popular
music played by black musicians, which
conveys deep feelings. **soul-searching**,
n. examination of your own motives/
conscience.

sound [saʊnd] 1. n. (a) noise; **s. wave**
= wave in the air which carries sound;
s. barrier = the speed of sound; **s. bite**
= short sentence spoken by a famous
person when being interviewed, which
is of suitable length for showing on a
TV news broadcast. (b) stretch of sea
water. 2. v. (a) to make a noise. (b) **to
s. like** = to be similar in sound to (sth).
(c) **to s. s.o. out** = to talk to s.o. to test
his opinion. (d) to measure the depth
of water. 3. adj. (-er, -est) (a) healthy/
not rotten. (b) reasonable/trustworthy.
(c) deep (sleep). **sound effects**, n. pl.
noises made in a play/film, etc., which
imitate real sounds (such as thunder/
gunfire, etc.). **sounding**, n. (a) making of noise; **s. board** = (i) board (as
above a pulpit) which reflects sound;
(ii) way of spreading ideas. (b) investigation. (c) measuring the depth

of water. **soundless,** *adj.* which does not make any noise. **soundlessly,** *adv.* not making any noise. **soundly,** *adv.* thoroughly/deeply. **soundness,** *n.* being sound. **sound off,** *v. inf.* to start talking loudly about sth. **soundproof. 1.** *adj.* made so that sound cannot get through. **2.** *v.* to make (a building) soundproof. **soundtrack,** *n.* part of a film where the sound is recorded.

soup [su:p] *n.* liquid dish usu. eaten at the beginning of a meal; *inf.* **in the s.** = in real trouble. **soup-kitchen,** *n.* place where soup and other food is given to the poor/to victims of a disaster. **soup up,** *v. inf.* to increase the power of (an engine).

soupçon ['su:psɒn] *n.* slight taste; very small amount.

sour ['sauə] **1.** *adj.* (**-er, -est**) (*a*) not sweet; sharp-tasting; *inf.* **s. grapes** = saying unpleasant things because of envy. (*b*) (milk) which has gone bad. (*c*) bad-tempered/unpleasant (person). **2.** *v.* to make bad. **sourly,** *adv.* in a bad-tempered way. **sourness,** *n.* being sour. **sourpuss,** *n. inf.* unpleasant bad-tempered person.

source [sɔ:s] *n.* place of origin/place where something starts or comes from.

souse [saus] *v.* (*a*) to soak in water. (*b*) to pickle (herrings) in salt water.

south [sauθ] **1.** *n.* one of the points of the compass; (*in areas north of the equator*) the direction of the sun at midday. **2.** *adj.* of the south. **3.** *adv.* towards the south. **southbound,** *adj.* going towards the south. **southeast,** *adj, adv. & n.* direction between south and east. **south-easterly, south-eastern,** *adj.* referring to the south-east. **southerly** ['sʌðəlɪ] *adj.* (*a*) (wind) from the south. (*b*) **in a s. direction** = towards the south. **southern** ['sʌðən] *adj.* referring to the south. **southerner** ['sʌðənə] *n.* person who lives in the south. **southernmost,** *adj.* furthest south. **southpaw,** *n. inf.* boxer who is left-handed. **southward,** *adj.* towards the south. **southwards,** *adv.* towards the south. **south-west,** *adj., adv. & n.* direction between south and west. **south-westerly, south-western,** *adj.* referring to the south-west.

souvenir [su:və'nɪə] *n.* thing which reminds you of a place/an event.

sou'wester [sau'westə] *n.* waterproof sailor's hat.

sovereign ['sɒvrɪn] **1.** *n.* (*a*) ruler/king or queen. (*b*) British gold coin worth £1. **2.** *adj.* (*a*) powerful (remedy). (*b*) self-governing. **sovereignty,** *n.* total power; self-government.

Soviet ['səʊvɪət] *adj. & n.* (*a*) (person) from the Soviet Union/from Russia. (*b*) council/committee in a Communist country. **Soviet Union,** *n.* USSR/Russia.

sow 1. *n.* [sau] female pig. **2.** *v.* [səu] (**sowed, sown**) to put seed into earth so that it grows. **sower** ['səuə] *n.* person who sows seed.

soy, soya [sɔɪ, 'sɔɪə] *n.* kind of very nutritious tropical bean; **s. sauce** = salty Chinese sauce made from soya beans.

sozzled ['sɒzld] *adj. inf.* drunk.

spa [spɑ:] *n.* place where mineral water comes out of the ground naturally and where people go to drink or bathe in the water because of its medicinal properties.

space [speɪs] **1.** *n.* (*a*) place; empty area between two objects/on a sheet of paper, etc. (*b*) short period of time; **s. bar** = key on a typewriter/computer which makes a space between letters. (*c*) (*also* **outer space**) area beyond the earth's atmosphere. **2.** *v.* **to s. out** = to time (things) at intervals; to place (things) with gaps between them. **spacecraft,** *n.* rocket in which astronauts travel in space. **spaceman,** *n.* (*pl.* **-men**) person who travels in space. **spacesaving,** *adj.* (piece of furniture, etc.) which is compact or which folds, and so saves space. **spaceship,** *n.* rocket in which astronauts travel in space. **spacesuit,** *n.* special clothes worn by spacemen. **spacious** ['speɪʃəs] *adj.* very large/with lots of space. **spaciousness** ['speɪʃəsnəs] *n.* state of being spacious.

spade [speɪd] *n.* (*a*) long-handled tool for digging holes in the ground; **s. work** = the preliminary work; **to call a s. a s.** = to say what you think without trying to hide your opinions. (*b*) **spades** = one of the four suits in a pack of cards.

spaghetti [spə'getɪ] *n.* Italian food formed of long strips of pasta.

span [spæn] **1.** *n.* (*a*) width (of wings/ an arch, etc.). (*b*) arch of a bridge. (*c*) length of time. **2.** *v.* (**spanned**) to stretch across.

spandrel ['spændrəl] *n.* wall between adjoining arches.

spangle ['spæŋgl] *n.* small piece of bright metal which is sewn on a dress as an ornament. **spangled**, *adj.* covered with spangles.

Spaniard ['spænjəd] *n.* person from Spain.

spaniel ['spænjəl] *n.* type of dog with large hanging ears.

Spanish ['spænɪʃ] **1.** *adj.* referring to Spain. **2.** *n.* language spoken in Spain and Latin America.

spank [spæŋk] *v.* to smack on the behind. **spanking. 1.** *adj. inf.* (*a*) fast (pace). (*b*) bright new. **2.** *n.* series of smacks on the behind.

spanner ['spænə] *n.* metal tool with an opening which fits round a nut so that it can be twisted to loosen or tighten; **to throw a s. in the works** = to bring things to a state of confusion.

spar [spɑː] **1.** *n.* (*a*) ship's mast or a wooden beam for holding the sails. (*b*) type of mineral crystal. **2.** *v.* (**sparred**) to practise boxing. **sparring partner,** *n.* person a boxer spars with.

spare ['speə] **1.** *adj.* (*a*) not used/extra; **s. parts** = replacement parts for a machine; **s. wheel** = wheel carried to replace one that has a puncture. *inf.* **s. tyre** = fold of fat round the waist of a plump person. (*b*) thin (person/ body). **2.** *n.* extra thing/replacement. **3.** *v.* (*a*) to do without. (*b*) to give up; not to need. (*c*) **to s. s.o.'s life** = not to kill s.o. whom you have defeated; to have mercy on s.o. (*d*) **he was spared the embarrassment** = it saved him from being embarrassed. **spare ribs,** *n. pl.* cooked pork ribs in a savoury sauce. **sparing,** *adj.* **to be s. with** = to economize. **sparingly,** *adv.* using little.

spark [spɑːk] **1.** *n.* little flash of fire/ of electricity/of life. **2.** *v.* to send out sparks/to make electric sparks. **sparking plug,** *Am.* **spark plug,** *n.*

(*in a car engine*) device which produces a spark which ignites petrol vapour. **sparkle** ['spɑːkl] **1.** *n.* bright shiny light; small spark. **2.** *v.* to glitter/to shine brightly; **sparkling wine** = wine which bubbles. **sparkler,** *n.* type of firework which sends out sparks. **spark off,** *v. inf.* to start.

sparrow ['spærəʊ] *n.* common small brown and grey bird. **sparrowhawk,** *n.* common small hawk.

sparse [spɑːs] *adj.* (**-er, -est**) not thick; thinly spread. **sparsely,** *adv.* with few (things); thinly. **sparseness, sparsity,** *n.* being sparse.

spartan ['spɑːtən] *adj.* harsh/ hard (discipline)/uncomfortable (conditions).

spasm ['spæzəm] *n.* (*a*) sudden uncontrollable pulling of muscles. (*b*) sudden fit (of work). **spasmodic** [spæz'mɒdɪk] *adj.* coming in spasms/from time to time. **spasmodically,** *adv.* from time to time.

spastic ['spæstɪk] *adj. & n.* (person) who has suffered from brain damage which causes partial paralysis.

spat [spæt] **1.** *n.* (*a*) small gaiter which just covers the shoe. (*b*) minor argument. **2.** *v. see* **spit.**

spate [speɪt] *n.* (*a*) **river in s.** = in flood. (*b*) sudden rush (of orders, etc.).

spathe [speɪθ] *n.* leaf which encloses a flower.

spatial ['speɪʃəl] *adj.* referring to space. **spatially,** *adv.* in a spatial way.

spatter ['spætə] *v.* to splash with little spots of liquid.

spatula ['spætjʊlə] *n.* (*a*) wide flat blunt flexible knife. (*b*) doctor's instrument used to hold down your tongue while examining your throat.

spawn [spɔːn] **1.** *n.* eggs (of a fish/ frog, etc.); **mushroom s.** = material like seeds from which mushrooms grow. **2.** *v.* to produce eggs.

spay [speɪ] *v.* to make (a female animal) sterile by removing her ovaries.

speak [spiːk] *v.* (**spoke, spoken**) (*a*) to say words and phrases; **I know him to s. to** = I know him enough to get into conversation with him. (*b*) to talk in public. (*c*) to be able to say things in (a foreign language). **speaker,** *n.* (*a*) person who speaks. (*b*) (*in Parliament*) **the S. of the House of Commons** = the chairman. (*c*) loudspeaker. **speak for,** *v.* to plead on s.o.'s behalf. **speaking,** *n.* action of talking; **we're not on s. terms** = we have quarrelled and don't speak to each other. **speak up,** *v.* (*a*) to speak more loudly. (*b*) **to s. up for** = to support.

spear ['spɪə] **1.** *n.* long pointed throwing weapon. **2.** *v.* to jab (s.o./sth) with a spear. **spearhead. 1.** *n.* front part of a force of attackers. **2.** *v.* to be in the front of an attacking force. **spearmint,** *n.* common type of mint, often used in chewing gum.

spec [spek] *n. inf.* **to buy on s.** = without being sure of the value/condition.

special ['speʃəl] **1.** *adj.* (*a*) particular/referring to one particular thing. (*b*) extraordinary/rare/unusual. **2.** *n.* (*a*) particular edition of a newspaper. (*b*) particular dish on a menu. (*c*) article reduced in price. **specialist,** *n.* person who has studied sth very deeply. **speciality** [speʃɪ'ælɪtɪ] *n.* particular interest; subject which you have studied/thing you are known for. **specialization** [speʃəlaɪ'zeɪʃn] *n.* act of specializing; thing you specialize in. **specialize** ['speʃəlaɪz] *v.* **to s. in sth** = to study/to produce sth in particular. **specially,** *adv.* particularly; unusually.

species ['spiːʃɪz] *n.* (*pl* **species**) (*a*) group of animals/plants which are closely similar, and which can breed together. (*b*) *inf.* sort. **specie,** *n. pl.* (*formal*) coins.

specify ['spesɪfaɪ] *v.* to state clearly what is required. **specific** [spe'sɪfɪk] *adj.* particular/precise (details). **specifically,** *adv.* particularly. **specification** [spesɪfɪ'keɪʃn] *n.* detailed plan/information. **specific gravity,** *n.* density of a substance divided by the density of water.

specimen ['spesɪmən] *n.* (*a*) sample which is selected for study or exhibition. (*b*) sample/example.

specious ['spiːʃəs] *adj.* not really true as it seems. **speciously,** *adv.* in a specious way. **speciousness,** *n.* being specious.

speck [spek] *n.* tiny spot. **speckle,** *n.* small (usu. brown) spot. **speckled,** *adj.* covered with speckles.

specs [speks] *n. pl. inf.* glasses.

spectacle ['spektəkl] *n.* (*a*) show. (*b*) **spectacles** = glasses worn in front of your eyes to correct defects in your sight. **spectacular** [spek'tækjʊlə] *adj.* impressive (show/display). **spectacularly,** *adv.* in a spectacular way. **spectator,** *n.* person who watches a show/a football match, etc.

spectre, *Am.* **specter** ['spektə] *n.* (*a*) ghost. (*b*) fear. **spectral,** *adj.* like a ghost.

spectrum ['spektrəm] *n.* bands of colours varying from red to blue (as seen in a rainbow); range (of ideas, etc.). **spectrography,** *n.* recording of a spectrum, used to analyse the chemical composition of a substance.

speculate ['spekjʊleɪt] *v.* (*a*) **to s. about** = to make guesses about. (*b*) to gamble by buying things whose value you hope will rise. **speculation** [spekjʊ'leɪʃn] *n.* (*a*) guesses made about sth. (*b*) gambling by buying things whose value you hope will rise. **speculative** ['spekjʊlətɪv] *adj.* (*a*) made by guessing. (*b*) gambling; **s. share** = one whose future price is quite uncertain. **speculator** ['spekjʊleɪtə] *n.* person who buys goods in the hope or reselling them again at a profit.

speculum ['spekjʊləm] *n.* (*a*) reflector in a telescope. (*b*) tube for inspecting the interior of the body.

sped [sped] *v. see* **speed.**

speech [spiːtʃ] *n.* (*pl.* **-es**) (*a*) ability to talk. (*b*) spoken language; **the parts of s.** = different groups of words (nouns/verbs, etc.) which are used in a similar way in language. (*c*) talk given in public; **s. day** = day when children are given prizes at school for good work, etc. **speechify,** *v. inf.* to make long speeches. **speechless,** *adj.* incapable of saying anything.

speed [spiːd] **1.** *n.* (*a*) quickness of movement. (*b*) rate of movement. **2.** *v.* (*a*) (**sped**) to go fast. (*b*) (**speeded**) to drive a car faster than the legal speed; to make (progress) go faster. **speedboat,** *n.* racing motor boat. **speedily,** *adv.* very fast. **speediness,** *n.* being speedy. **speedometer** [spiː-'dɒmɪtə] *n.* dial which shows you how fast you are travelling. **speed up,** v. to go faster; to make (sth) go faster. **speedway,** n. racing track for motor cycles. **speedwell,** n. small wild plant with blue flowers. **speedy,** adj. (-ier, -iest) very fast.

speleology [spiːlɪˈɒlədʒɪ] n. pot-holing; climbing down into caves or holes in the ground. **speleological,** adj. referring to speleology. **speleologist,** n. person who climbs in or explores caves and holes in the ground.

spell [spel] **1.** n. (a) magic curse; words which may have a magic effect. (b) period of time. **2.** v. (**spelt**) (a) to say aloud/to write correctly the letters which form a word; **to s. out** = (i) to read with difficulty; (ii) to explain very clearly. (b) to mean. **spellbinder,** n. thing which enchants/attracts and keeps the attention. **spellbound,** adj. bewitched/enchanted. **spell check,** v. to check the spelling of text, using a computer program. **speller,** n. person who spells. **spelling,** n. way in which a word is spelt; writing words correctly. **spelling checker,** n. computer program which checks spelling.

spencer [ˈspensə] n. type of sleeved vest worn by women.

spend [spend] v. (**spent**) (a) to pay (money) in exchange for sth. (b) to pass (time). (c) **to s. oneself** = to tire oneself out. **spender,** n. person who spends. **spending,** n. action of using money to buy sth. **spendthrift,** adj. & n. (person) who spends money fast.

spent [spent] adj. used; **s. fuel** = fuel which has been used in a nuclear reactor; see also **spend.**

sperm [spɜːm] n. (a) male fluid which fertilizes the eggs of a female. (b) **s. whale** = large whale which provides oil. **spermaceti** [spɜːməˈsetɪ] n. (no pl.) white substance taken from a sperm whale, and used as a base for perfumes. **spermatozoa** [spɜːmətəˈzəʊə] n. pl. sperms. **spermicidal,** adj. which kills sperm.

spew [spjuː] v. inf. **to s. (out)** = to vomit; to pour out.

sphagnum [ˈsfægnəm] n. type of moss.

sphere [ˈsfɪə] n. (a) object which is perfectly round. (b) area (of influence);

society. **spherical** [ˈsferɪkl] adj. shaped like a sphere/perfectly round.

sphincter [ˈsfɪŋktə] n. circular muscle which controls an opening.

sphinx [sfɪŋks] n. (pl. -es) legendary animal in Egypt with the head of a woman and the body of a lion; large stone monument of this animal.

spice [spaɪs] **1.** n. (a) flavouring made from seeds/leaves of plants, etc. (b) thing which excites interest. **2.** v. to add spices to (a dish). **spiciness,** n. being spicy. **spicy,** adj. (a) with a lot of spices. (b) rather rude (story).

spick and span [ˈspɪkənˈspæn] adj. very clean/tidy.

spider [ˈspaɪdə] n. eight-legged animal, which makes a web and eats flies; **s. plant** = common house plant, with long yellow and green leaves. **spider's-web,** n. web made by a spider. **spidery,** adj. thin and scrawling (handwriting).

spiel [spiːl] n. inf. long flow of talk (aimed at persuading).

spigot [ˈspɪgət] n. tap (in a barrel).

spike [spaɪk] **1.** n. (a) long sharp point. (b) **spikes** = sharp points in the soles of running shoes. **2.** v. (a) to attach spikes to. (b) to jam (a gun). (c) to cut (another runner) with your spikes. **spiked,** adj. covered with spikes. **spiky,** adj. standing up in sharp points.

spill [spɪl] **1.** (a) fall. (b) long thin piece of wood for lighting cigarettes/candles, etc. **2.** v. (**spilled/spilt**) to pour (liquid) out of a container by mistake. **spillage,** n. action of spilling; amount of liquid spilt.

spin [spɪn] **1.** n. (a) action of turning round and round; inf. **flat s.** = state of confusion. (b) short fast trip. **2.** v. (**spun**) (a) to turn round and round very fast; to throw (a coin) up into the air and catch it, so as to decide which side plays first, etc; to make (a ball) turn as it goes through the air. (b) to twist (raw wool/cotton, etc.) to form a thread. **spin drier,** n. machine for drying washing by turning it round very fast. **spin-dry,** v. to dry (washing) in a spin-drier. **spinner,** n. person who spins thread. **spinneret** [spɪnəˈret] n. part of the spider which spins the threads to make a web. **spinning wheel,** n. apparatus for twisting and winding wool. **spin-off,** *n.* secondary result; useful by-product. **spin out,** *v. inf.* to make (sth) last a long time.

spina bifida [spaɪnə'bɪfɪdə] *n.* condition from birth, where the spine is badly formed allowing the membrane covering the spinal cord to protrude.

spinach ['spɪnɪtʃ] *n.* common green-leaved vegetable.

spindle ['spɪndl] *n.* (a) pin used for twisting thread in a spinning machine. (b) central pin round which sth turns.

spindly ['spɪndlɪ] *adj.* (-ier, -iest) long, thin and weak.

spindrift ['spɪndrɪft] *n.* spray which is blown from breaking waves.

spine [spaɪn] *n.* (a) backbone. (b) back of a book. (c) prickle (on a cactus/hedgehog, etc.). **spinal,** *n.* referring to the spine; **s. column** = backbone; **s. cord** = group of nerves running down the inside of the spine. **spineless,** *adj.* (person) who is weak and indecisive. **spiny,** *adj.* covered with prickles.

spinet [spɪ'net] *n.* old musical instrument, like a small rectangular harpsichord.

spinnaker ['spɪnəkə] *n.* large balloon-like sail on the front of a racing yacht.

spinney ['spɪnɪ] *n.* small wood.

spinster ['spɪnstə] *n.* unmarried woman (usu. middle-aged).

spiral ['spaɪərəl] **1.** *n.* (a) thing which is twisted round and round like a spring. (b) thing which turns round and round getting higher or lower all the time. **2.** *adj.* twisted round and round like a spring. **3.** *v.* (**spiralled**) to go round and round and rise at the same time. **spirally,** *adv.* in a spiral shape.

spire ['spaɪə] *n.* pointed construction on top of a church tower.

spirit ['spɪrɪt] **1.** *n.* (a) soul. (b) ghost; **Holy S.** = the third person of the Christian Trinity. (c) energetic way of doing sth. (d) real meaning (not always expressed in words). (e) alcohol; **surgical s.** = pure alcohol used for rubbing on the skin, etc. (f) **spirits** = strong alcoholic drink (whisky/gin, etc.). **2.** *v.* **to s. away** = to remove as if by magic. **spirited,** *adj.* very vigorous. **spiritedly,** *adv.* in a spirited way. **spirit**

lamp, *n.* lamp which burns spirit. **spirit level,** *n.* tool for testing if a surface is level using a glass tube containing an airbubble. **spiritual. 1.** *adj.* referring to the spirit; dealing with the soul. **2.** *n.* religious song sung by black people in the southern United States. **spiritualism,** *n.* belief that you can communicate with the spirits of dead people. **spiritualist,** *n.* person who tries to communicate with the spirits of dead people. **spirituality,** *n.* love of religion. **spiritually,** *adv.* in a spiritual way. **spirituous,** *adj.* alcoholic.

spit [spɪt] **1.** *n.* (a) long metal rod passed through meat which turns so that the meat is evenly cooked. (b) long thin stretch of land going out into the sea. (c) depth of earth dug by a spade. (d) liquid formed in the mouth; **s. and polish** = excessive cleaning; *inf.* **he is the dead s. and image of his father** = he looks exactly like his father. **2.** *v.* (a) (**spitted**) to put (meat) on a spit to roast. (b) (**spat**) to send liquid out of the mouth; *inf.* **he is the spitting image of his father** = he looks exactly like his father. (c) to send sparks out; to rain slightly. **spittle** ['spɪtl] *n.* saliva. **spittoon** [spɪ'tuːn] *n.* dish for spitting into.

spite [spaɪt] **1.** *n.* (a) bad feeling against s.o./desire to hurt s.o. (b) **in s. of sth** = without bothering about. **2.** *v.* to try to annoy. **spiteful,** *adj.* full of bad feeling/wishing to hurt s.o. **spitefully,** *adv.* in a spiteful way. **spitefulness,** *n.* being spiteful.

splash [splæʃ] **1.** *n.* (pl. **-es**) (a) noisy throwing of liquid; sound of liquid being thrown noisily. (b) mark made by dirty liquid being scattered. (c) bright patch of colour. (d) short spurt (of soda water, etc.). (e) sudden show; sudden spending of money. **2.** *v.* (a) (of liquid) to make a noise while hitting a solid). (b) to send dirty liquid on to. (c) to display. **splash down,** *v.* (of space capsule) to land in the sea. **splashdown,** *n.* landing (of a spacecraft) in the sea. **splash out,** *v. inf.* to spend a lot of money. **splashy,** *adj.* which splashes.

splatter ['splætə] *v.* to splash.

splay [spleɪ] **1.** *adj.* turned outwards. **2.** *v.* to slant outwards.

spleen [spli:n] *n.* organ near the stomach which keeps the blood in good condition.

splendid ['splendɪd] *adj.* magnificent/wonderful. **splendidly,** *adv.* wonderfully/extremely well. **splendour,** *Am.* **splendor,** *n.* magnificence.

splenetic [splə'netɪk] *adj.* violently angry.

splice [splaɪs] **1.** *n.* joint which links two pieces of rope. **2.** *v.* to join (two pieces of rope) by twisting the threads together; to join (two pieces of film) together; *inf.* **to get spliced** = to get married. **splicer,** *n.* device for joining pieces of film together.

splint [splɪnt] *n.* stiff bar tied to a broken leg, etc., to keep it straight.

splinter ['splɪntə] **1.** *n.* small pointed piece (of wood/metal); **s. group** = group of people who have separated from a main group. **2.** *v.* to split into thin pointed pieces.

split [splɪt] **1.** *n.* (*a*) thin crack; sharp break. (*b*) **the splits** = gymnastic exercise where you sit on the floor with one leg stretched out in front, and the other behind you. (*c*) **banana s.** = dessert of bananas, cream, ice cream and nuts. **2.** *v.* (**split**) (*a*) to divide (sth) into parts; to make (sth) divide/crack; *inf.* **my head is splitting** = I have a bad headache. (*b*) *inf.* **to s. on s.o.** = to report s.o. **3.** *adj.* which has been cracked; **s. peas** = dried peas broken in half; **in a s. second** = very fast; **to have a s. personality** = to have two ways of behaving which are quite different in varying circumstances. **split-level,** *adj.* (room, etc.) with part of the floor higher than the rest. **split up,** *v.* to divide.

splodge [splɒdʒ], **splotch** [splɒtʃ] *n.* dirty mark; oddly-shaped spot of colour.

splurge [splɜ:dʒ] **1.** *n. inf.* spending spree. **2.** *v. inf.* to spend money extravagantly.

splutter ['splʌtə] *v.* (*a*) to spit when speaking; to speak rapidly. (*b*) (*of kettle*) to hiss (when boiling).

spoil [spɔɪl] **1.** *v.* (**spoilt/spoiled**) (*a*) to ruin/to make bad. (*b*) to treat (a child) so leniently that it ruins his character.

2. *n. pl.* **spoils** (*a*) booty, goods taken by soldiers from a defeated enemy. (*b*) rubbish from a mine. **spoiler,** *n.* decorative panel at the front or back of a car, which is intended to slow the vehicle down. **spoil for,** *v.* to be eager for (a fight). **spoilsport,** *n.* person who spoils other people's enjoyment. **spoilt,** *adj.* badly brought up (child).

spoke [spəʊk] **1.** *n.* one of the rods running from the axle of a wheel to the rim. **2.** *v. see also* **speak. spokeshave,** *n.* tool with a curved blade for smoothing sth round.

spoken ['spəʊkn] *v. see* **speak.**

spokesman, spokeswoman, spokesperson ['spəʊksmən, -wʊmən, -pɜ:sən] *n.* (*pl.* **-men, -women**) person who speaks on behalf of s.o.

spoliation [spəʊlɪ'eɪʃn] *n.* (*formal*) act of destroying.

spondee ['spɒndeɪ] *n.* measure (two long syllables) used in Latin poetry.

sponge [spʌndʒ] **1.** *n.* (*a*) soft skeleton of a sea animal/block of plastic full of small holes, which soaks up water and is used for washing; **s. bath** = washing a patient in bed, using a sponge; *inf.* **to throw up/in the s.** = to give in/to admit you are beaten. (*b*) act of washing with a sponge. (*c*) **s. cake/pudding** = light soft cake/pudding. **2.** *v.* (*a*) to wash with a sponge. (*b*) *inf.* **to s. on s.o.** = to live by begging for money from s.o. **spongebag,** *n.* small plastic bag for carrying washing things. **sponger,** *n.* person who doesn't work but gets money by begging for it from friends. **spongy,** *adj.* soft and full of holes.

sponsor ['spɒnsə] **1.** *n.* (*a*) person who helps s.o./sth by taking responsibility. (*b*) person or firm who pays for a television show/cricket match, etc., as a form of advertisement. (*c*) person who pays money to a charity if s.o. else walks, swims, runs, a certain distance, etc. **2.** *v.* to be a sponsor; to be responsible for (a bill in parliament); to pay for (a television show/a cricket match, etc.); (*of god-parent*) **to s. a child at baptism** = to promise to help the child to lead a Christian life. **sponsorship,** *n.* action of sponsoring.

spontaneous [spɒn'teɪnɪəs] *adj.* which

happens freely/which is not forced. **spontaneously,** *adv.* in a spontaneous/ natural way. **spontaneity** [spɒntə-'niːɪti] *n.* acting in a natural way.

spoof [spuːf] *n. inf.* hoax/amusing imitation.

spook [spuːk] *n.* ghost. **spooky,** *adj. inf.* frightening; (place) which is likely to be haunted.

spool [spuːl] *n.* cylinder round which sth is wound.

spoon [spuːn] **1.** *n.* eating utensil with a small bowl and a long handle; **wooden s.** = (i) spoon made of wood; (ii) silly prize given to s.o. who is last in a competition. **2.** *v.* **to s. sth up/ into** = to lift sth up/to put sth in with a spoon. **spoonbill,** *n.* large white bird with a spoon-shaped end to its bill. **spoonfeed,** *v.* to give (a baby) food with a spoon; to teach (people) by giving them answers to questions and not allowing them to work by themselves; to provide everything for (s.o.) so that they need do nothing to help themselves. **spoonful,** *n.* amount contained in a spoon.

spoonerism ['spuːnərɪzəm] *n.* exchanging letters of words by mistake (**queer old dean** for *dear old queen*).

spoor ['spʊə] *n.* (*no pl.*) tracks left by an animal.

sporadic [spə'rædɪk] *adj.* which happens at irregular intervals. **sporadically,** *adv.* in a sporadic way.

spore [spɔː] *n.* plant cell which reproduces without requiring to be fertilized.

sporran ['spɒrən] *n.* leather bag worn by Scotsmen in front of the kilt.

sport [spɔːt] **1.** *n.* (*a*) game (such as football/hockey/tennis, etc.); **blood sports** = hunting animals as a sport; **sports car** = light fast open car; **sports jacket/sports coat** = man's tweed jacket. (*b*) *inf.* **good s.** = pleasant person always willing to help. (*c*) animal/plant which is very different from its parents. **2.** *v.* to wear. **sporting,** *adj.* (person) who plays according to the rules/who is pleasant and willing to help; **s. chance** = quite a good chance. **sportive,** *adj.* playful. **sportsman,** *n.* (*pl.* **-men**) (*a*) person who takes part in a sport. (*b*) person

who plays properly. **sportsmanlike,** *adj.* (playing a game) in a proper way/according to the rules; not cheating. **sportsmanship,** *n.* quality of being a good sportsman/of not cheating. **sportswear,** *n.* (*no pl.*) clothes worn to play sports. **sportswoman,** *n.* (*pl.* **-women**) woman who takes part in a sport. **sporty,** *adj.* interested in sport (and in nothing else).

spot [spɒt] **1.** *n.* (*a*) place; **on the s.** = on duty/at your post; **in a s.** = in a difficult position; **to put s.o. on the s.** = in a position where he has to act. (*b*) pimple. (*c*) usu. round coloured mark; *inf.* **to knock spots off** = to defeat easily. (*d*) *inf.* small amount. (*e*) spotlight/ bright light which only shines on one spot. **2.** *v.* (spotted) (*a*) to mark with a spot. (*b*) **it's spotting with rain** = drops are falling here and there. (*c*) to notice. **spot check,** *n.* surprise check (on items at random). **spotless,** *adj.* very clean. **spotlessly,** *adj.* **s. clean** = extremely clean. **spotlight. 1.** *n.* bright light which shines on one small area. **2.** *v.* to highlight/to draw attention to (sth). **spot-on,** *adj. inf.* absolutely correct. **spotter,** *n.* person who notes things. **spotty,** *adj.* (**-ier, -iest**) covered with pimples.

spouse ['spauz] *n.* (*formal*) husband or wife.

spout [spaut] **1.** *n.* tube for pouring liquid out of a kettle, etc.; tube for sending waste water/rainwater away from the wall of a building; *inf.* **up the s.** = lost/ruined/wasted. **2.** *v.* (*a*) to come out in a jet. (*b*) *inf.* to speak continuously.

sprain [spreɪn] **1.** *n.* twist of a joint. **2.** *v.* to twist (a joint).

sprang [spræŋ] *v. see* **spring.**

sprat [spræt] *n.* very small herring-like fish.

sprawl [sprɔːl] **1.** *n.* irregular spread; **urban s.** = unregulated spread of houses built over what formerly was countryside. **2.** *v.* (*a*) to lie with arms and legs spread out. (*b*) to spread out in an irregular way.

spray [spreɪ] **1.** *n.* (*a*) branch with flowers on it. (*b*) liquid in the form of tiny drops/ in a mist. (*c*) sprayer. **2.** *v.* to send out liquid in a fine mist. **sprayer,** *n.* machine for spraying. **spray gun,** *n.* tool shaped like a pistol with a small container attached (used for spraying paint/insecticide, etc.).

spread [spred] **1.** *n.* (*a*) wide expanse; width. (*b*) act of sending out over a wide area. (*c*) *inf.* feast. (*d*) soft paste of meat/cheese. (*e*) **double-page s.** = text which runs over two facing pages in a book or newspaper. **2.** *v.* (**spread**) (*a*) to send out/to go out over a wide area. (*b*) to space out over a period of time. (*c*) to cover with a layer of sth. **spreadeagled,** *adj.* lying flat with arms and legs stretched out. **spreadsheet,** *n.* computer printout of tables of figures.

spree [spri:] *n.* happy time; **to go on a spending s.** = to have a happy time spending money.

sprig [sprig] *n.* (*a*) small branch. (*b*) design of small branches. (*c*) small headless nail.

sprightly ['spraɪtlɪ] *adj.* (**-ier, -iest**) light and vigorous. **sprightliness,** *n.* being sprightly.

spring [sprɪŋ] **1.** *n.* (*a*) small stream of water coming out of the ground. (*b*) season of the year following winter when plants begin to grow and put out leaves; **s. onion** = thin white onion plant eaten raw in salads. (*c*) leap in the air. (*d*) coiled wire which returns to its original shape after being stretched or compressed; strong bent metal plates which allow a vehicle to ride over bumps; **s. clip** = clip which closes with a spring; **s. balance** = device for weighing made of a large spring which stretches when a weight is attached to it. (*e*) bounciness. **2.** *v.* (**sprang, has sprung**) (*a*) to leap/to bounce. (*b*) to set (sth) off/to make (sth) happen suddenly. (*c*) to come **from.** (*d*) **to s. a leak** = to start taking in water through a crack. **springboard,** *n.* long flexible board used to give an impetus to a diver or jumper. **springbok** ['sprɪŋbɒk] *n.* type of African deer. **spring-clean,** *v.* to clean thoroughly after the winter. **spring fever,** *n. Am.* feeling of excitement at the coming of spring. **springiness,** *n.* being springy. **springlike,** *adj.* (weather) which is mild like in spring. **spring tide,** *n.*

tide which rises and falls very sharply, and occurs at the new and full moon. **springtime,** *n.* spring/the season after winter. **springy,** *adj.* (**-ier, -iest**) flexible; (board) which bends; (carpet/grass) which is very soft.

sprinkle ['sprɪŋkl] *v.* to scatter water/sand, etc. **sprinkler,** *n.* device for sprinkling; **s. system** = system of automatic fire control which sprinkles water on a fire and is set off by rising heat. **sprinkling,** *n.* (*a*) action of scattering water/sand, etc. (*b*) small quantities.

sprint [sprɪnt] **1.** *n.* short fast running race. **2.** *v.* to run very fast over a short distance. **sprinter,** *n.* runner who specializes in sprint races.

sprit [sprɪt] *n.* small spar which goes diagonally across a sail. **spritsail,** *n.* sail held by a sprit.

sprite [spraɪt] *n.* fairy.

sprocket ['sprɒkɪt] *n.* small tooth on a wheel. **sprocket-wheel,** *n.* toothed wheel which connects with a chain.

sprout [spraʊt] **1.** *n.* young shoot of a plant; **Brussels sprouts** = edible shoots from a type of cabbage. **2.** *v.* to send out (shoots/horns).

spruce [spru:s] **1.** *n.* type of fir tree. **2.** *adj.* smart. **3.** *v.* **to s. yourself up** = to make yourself neat. **sprucely,** *adv.* in a spruce way. **spruceness,** *n.* being spruce.

sprung [sprʌŋ] *v. see* **spring.**

spry [spraɪ] *adj.* (old person) who is vigorous and active. **spryly,** *adv.* in a spry way. **spryness,** *n.* being spry.

spud [spʌd] *n. inf.* potato.

spume [spju:m] *n.* foam (on the sea).

spun [spʌn] *v. see* **spin.**

spunk [spʌŋk] *n. inf.* courage.

spur [spɜ:] **1.** *n.* (*a*) metal point attached to the heels of a rider's boots which pricks a horse to make it go faster; **to win your spurs** = to show for the first time how good you are. (*b*) low hill running from a higher range of mountains; minor road/railway line leading off a main one. (*c*) impetus/stumulus; **on the s. of the moment** = without planning in advance. **2.** *v.* (**spurred**) to urge (s.o.) **on.**

spurge ['spɜ:dʒ] *n.* common weed with bitter white sap.

spurious ['spjʊərɪəs] *adj.* false. **spuriously,** *adv.* in a spurious way. **spuriousness,** *n.* being spurious.

spurn [spɜːn] *v.* to reject (an offer) scornfully.

spurt [spɜːt] **1.** *n.* (*a*) jet of liquid. (*b*) sudden effort. **2.** *v.* (*a*) **to s. out** = to come out in a jet. (*b*) to run fast suddenly.

sputter ['spʌtə] *v.* to spit/to send out sparks or fat.

sputum ['spjuːtəm] *n.* mucus which is spat out of the mouth.

spy [spaɪ] **1.** *n.* person who is paid to try to find out what the enemy/a criminal gang/a rival firm is planning to do. **2.** *v.* to see; **to s. on s.o.** = to try, in secret, to find out what s.o. is doing. **spying,** *n.* trying to find out information about the enemy. **spy out,** *v.* to examine (the land) secretly.

squab [skwɒb] *n.* small pigeon.

squabble ['skwɒbl] **1.** *n.* quarrel/argument. **2.** *v.* to argue.

squad [skwɒd] *n.* (*a*) small group of soldiers; **firing s.** = group of soldiers who shoot s.o. who has been condemned to death. (*b*) small group of workmen/police; **s. car** = police car on patrol. (*c*) (sports) team.

squadron ['skwɒdrən] *n.* group of soldiers on horseback; group of aircraft; group of naval ships; **s. leader** = rank in the air force above flight lieutenant.

squalid ['skwɒlɪd] *adj.* sordid/unpleasant/dirty. **squalidly,** *adv.* in a squalid way. **squalor,** *n.* dirt; dirty state.

squall [skwɔːl] **1.** *n.* sudden gust of wind. **2.** *v.* to cry loudly. **squally,** *adj.* accompanied by gusts of wind.

squander ['skwɒndə] *v.* to waste (money/energy).

square ['skweə] **1.** *n.* (*a*) shape with four equal sides and four right angles; *inf.* **we're back to s. one** = we'll have to start planning again from the beginning. (*b*) open area in a town, surrounded by buildings. (*c*) instrument for drawing right angles. (*d*) a number multiplied by itself. **2.** *adj.* (*a*) shaped like a square. (*b*) **s. corner** = corner with a right angle. (*c*) fair/straightforward; **s. deal** = honest treatment; **s. meal** = a good filling meal. (*d*) straight. (*e*) multiplied by itself; **s. metre** = area of one metre multiplied by one metre; **s. root** = number which when multiplied by itself produces the number you have. **3.** *adv.* (*a*) in a level/straight way. (*b*) directly. **4.** *v.* (*a*) to make (a round stone, etc.) square; **squared paper** = paper with squares drawn on it (for making graphs, etc.). (*b*) to balance (accounts); to pay (s.o.) what is owed; to pay (s.o.) a bribe. (*c*) to multiply (sth) by itself. (*d*) to straighten (your shoulders); **to s. up to s.o.** = to prepare to fight. **squarely,** *adv.* in a straightforward way.

squash [skwɒʃ] **1.** *n.* (*a*) crowded mass of people. (*b*) concentrated juice of a fruit to which water is added. (*c*) fast game played with rackets in a court with high walls. (*d*) vegetable like a marrow/pumpkin, etc. **2.** *v.* (*a*) to crush. (*b*) to stop (a revolt) by force; to stop (s.o.) speaking by being rude to them. **squash court,** *n.* court for playing squash. **squashy,** *adv.* (**-ier, -iest**) soft and wet.

squat [skwɒt] **1.** *n.* (*a*) action of occupying an empty house without the permission of the owner. (*b*) empty house which is suitable for squatting in. **2.** *v.* (**squatted**) (*a*) to crouch down, sitting on your heels. (*b*) to occupy an empty house without the permission of the owner. **3.** *adj.* (**squatter, squattest**) short and thick. **squatter,** *n.* person who occupies an empty house without the permission of the owner.

squaw [skwɔː] *n.* American Indian woman.

squawk [skwɔːk] **1.** *n.* short harsh cry. **2.** *v.* to make short harsh cries.

squeak [skwiːk] **1.** *n.* little high-pitched cry (like that of a mouse); high-pitched sound (like a rusty hinge); *inf.* **narrow s.** = near miss/narrow escape. **2.** *v.* to make a squeak. **squeaky,** *adj.* (gate) which squeaks.

squeal [skwiːl] **1.** *n.* long loud high-pitched cry. **2.** *v.* to make long loud high-pitched cries.

squeamish ['skwiːmɪʃ] *adj.* easily made sick/easily shocked. **squeamishness,** *n.* being squeamish.

squeegee ['skwiːdʒiː] *n.* implement for cleaning floors, made of a wad of sponge attached to a hinged plate.

squeeze [skwi:z] **1.** *n.* (*a*) pressure; crushing; **tight w.** = crowd of people crushed together. (*b*) **credit s.** = restriction on credit. (*c*) **s. of lemon** = few drops of lemon juice. **2.** *v.* (*a*) to crush/to force/to press. (*b*) to push together; to push to get into/through a small space. **squeezer,** *n.* device for pressing citrus fruit to get the juice out. **squeeze up,** *v.* to crush together to make room for s.o. else.

squelch [skweltʃ] **1.** *n.* noise made by a wet sticky substance. **2.** *v.* to make a wet sucking noise.

squib [skwɪb] *n.* small firework which bangs; **damp s.** = exciting/new thing which doesn't work properly.

squid [skwɪd] *n.* sea animal like a small octopus.

squiggle ['skwɪgl] **1.** *n.* illegible curly marks/handwriting. **2.** *v.* to make squiggles.

squint [skwɪnt] **1.** *n.* (*a*) state where your two eyes look in different directions. (*b*) *inf.* look/glance. **2.** *v.* (*a*) to have eyes which look in different directions. (*b*) to half-close your eyes to look at a bright light.

squire ['skwaɪə] *n.* (*a*) gentleman living in the country, often the owner of a large house. (*b*) *inf.* way of addressing a man.

squirm [skwɜ:m] *v.* to wriggle about; **it makes me s.** = it makes me very embarrassed.

squirrel ['skwɪrəl] *n.* common small mammal with a large bushy tail, living in trees.

squirt [skwɜ:t] **1.** *n.* (*a*) sharp jet of liquid. (*b*) *inf.* **little s.** = small insignificant person. **2.** *v.* to send out a sharp jet of liquid.

squishy ['skwɪʃi] *adj.* soft and squashy.

Sr *symbol for* strontium.

St [snt; stri:t] *short form of* Saint or Street.

stab [stæb] **1.** *n.* would made with a sharp knife; **s. in the back** = attack by s.o. who is thought to be loyal; *inf.* **to have a s. at** = to try to do. **2.** *v.* (**stabbed**) to wound with a sharp knife; **to s. s.o. in the back** = to attack s.o. who thinks you are his friend.

stable ['steɪbl] **1.** *n.* (*a*) building for keep-

ing a horse. (*b*) **stables** = place where horses are kept for breeding/racing, etc. **2.** *v.* to keep (a horse) in a stable. **3.** *adj.* (**-er, -est**) solid; steady/not wobbly. (*b*) (*in chemistry*) (compound) which does not change or decompose easily. **stability** [stə'bɪlɪti] *n.* steadiness. **stabilization** [steɪbɪlaɪ'zeɪʃn] *n.* making stable. **stabilize** ['steɪbɪlaɪz] *v.* to make steady. **stabilizer,** *n.* (*a*) fin attached to the hull of a ship to prevent rolling; small wheels attached to the back wheel of a child's bicycle to allow the child to learn to ride without falling off. (*b*) substance added to processed food to keep it in a stable condition. **stableboy, stablelad,** *n.* man who looks after horses in a stable. **stably,** *adv.* in a stable way.

staccato [stə'ka:təʊ] *adj. & n.* sharp (noise).

stack [stæk] **1.** *n.* (*a*) heap; *inf.* lots (of). (*b*) brick pillar housing a chimney. (*c*) inner part of a library where books are kept without being open to the public. **2.** *v.* (*a*) to pile up. (*b*) (*of aircraft*) to circle round waiting in turn for permission to land at a busy airport.

stadium ['steɪdɪəm] *n.* large building for sport.

staff [sta:f] **1.** *n.* (*a*) long thick stick. (*b*) people working in a school/college/firm; **s. room** = room for teachers in a school. (*c*) officers who help the commander organize a military force; **general s.** = officers who work at headquarters. (*d*) (*pl.* **staves**) set of five lines on which musical notes are written. **2.** *v.* to provide employees for (a firm, etc.). **staffer,** *n. Am.* member of staff.

stag [stæg] **1.** *n.* (*a*) male deer; **s. party** = party for men only. (*b*) person who buys new issues of shares and sells them at a profit. **2.** *v.* to buy shares at a new issue and sell them at a profit. **stag-beetle,** *n.* large black beetle with horns.

stage [steɪdʒ] **1.** *n.* (*a*) platform (on which a play is acted, etc.); **s. directions** = notes in the script of a play showing what the actors have to do; **s. fright** = nervousness before appearing before an audience; **s. whisper** = loud whisper which everyone can hear; **to go on the s.** = to become an actor.

(b) period/phase. (c) each of the parts of a rocket. (d) **landing s.** = wooden platform for boats to tie up to. (e) part of a journey. **2.** v. (a) to put on/to arrange (a performance of a play, etc.). (b) to make/to organize. **stagecoach,** n. (old) horsedrawn passenger coach which ran regularly along certain routes. **stagecraft,** n. art of the theatre. **stagehand,** n. person who moves scenery/prepares the stage (in a theatre). **stage-manage,** v. to arrange/ to organize (a performance); to plan (a trick/a coup). **stage manager,** n. person who organizes a performance of a play/opera, etc. **stager,** n. inf. **old s.** = old experienced person. **staging,** n. (a) putting on (of a play). (b) racks for storing. (c) **s. post** = place where planes/travellers regularly stop on a long journey. **stagy,** adj. unreal; looking too much as if being acted on a stage.

stagflation [stæg'fleɪʃn] n. inflation and stagnation combined.

stagger ['stægə] v. (a) to walk unsteadily. (b) to astonish. (c) to arrange things so that they do not coincide exactly. **staggering,** adj. astonishing. **staggeringly,** adv. astonishingly.

stagnant ['stægnənt] adj. (a) (water) which does not flow/which is not pure enough to drink. (b) (business) which does not make increased sales. **stagflation** [stæg'fleɪʃn] n. period when the economy stagnates but inflation increases. **stagnate** [stæg'neɪt] v. to stay static; not to advance. **stagnation** [stæg'neɪʃn] n. being stagnant.

staid [steɪd] adj. serious/not adventurous.

stain [steɪn] **1.** n. (a) dirty mark which is difficult to remove. (b) liquid used to change the colour of wood. **2.** v. (a) to make a dirty mark on (sth). (b) to change the colour of (wood, etc.); **stained glass** = coloured glass for windows (esp. in church). **stainless,** adj. without any stain; **s. steel** = steel which contains nickel and chromium so that it does not rust in contact with air or water.

stair ['steə] n. (a) step (on a staircase) (b) **(flight of) stairs** = series of steps leading from one floor of a building to the next. **staircarpet,** n. long narrow piece of carpet for covering stairs. **staircase,** n. flight of stairs (usu. with a handrail). **stair rod,** n. metal rod which keeps a staircarpet in place. **stairway,** n. staircase.

stake [steɪk] **1.** n. (a) strong pointed stick. (b) money which is gambled; **he has a s. in the company** = he has invested some money in the company, hoping to make a profit; **at s.** = which may be lost. **2.** v. (a) to put a stick in the ground; **to s. your claim to** = to suggest that you hold the right to own sth. (b) to bet (money, etc.).

stalactite ['stæləktaɪt] n. long point of limestone hanging from the ceiling of a cave, formed by mineral deposits from dripping water.

stalagmite ['stæləgmaɪt] n. long point of limestone rising from the floor of a cave formed by mineral deposits from dripping water.

stale [steɪl] adj. **(-er, -est)** (a) no longer fresh; (joke) that has been repeated many times. (b) **to go s.** = to become bored/tired so that you cannot work well. **stalemate,** n. (a) (in chess) position where a player cannot move without being checkmated. (b) situation where neither side will compromise. **staleness,** n. being stale.

stalk [stɔːk] **1.** n. (a) thin stem of a plant. (b) small part of the stem which attaches a fruit to the plant. **2.** v. (a) to try to get close enough to an animal to shoot it. (b) to march along proudly. **stalker,** n. person who stalks animals. **stalking horse,** n. thing or person used to hide your real plans.

stall [stɔːl] **1.** n. (a) compartment for one animal in a stable, etc. (b) **stalls** = seats in church for the choir and priests; seats on the ground floor (in a theatre/ cinema). (c) table with goods laid out for sale; small moveable shop. **2.** v. (a) (of a car engine) to stop unintentionally. (b) (of an aircraft) to go so slowly that it falls suddenly. (c) to put off making a decision. **stallholder,** n. person who runs a stall in a market.

stallion ['stæljən] n. male horse, esp. one kept for breeding.

stalwart ['stɔlwət] **1.** *adj.* strong/vigorous/brave. **2.** *n.* strong/vigorous/brave person.

stamen ['steimən] *n.* one of the thin spikes in the centre of a flower which carry the pollen.

stamina ['stæmɪnə] *n.* ability to do sth for a long time.

stammer ['stæmə] **1.** *n.* unintentional repetition of sounds when speaking. **2.** *v.* to repeat sounds when speaking. **stammerer,** *n.* person who stammers.

stamp [stæmp] **1.** *n.* (*a*) banging your foot on the ground. (*b*) object for making a mark on sth. (*c*) device for cutting out a design. (*d*) small piece of gummed paper for sticking on an envelope/parcel, etc., to pay for it to be sent by mail; **s. machine** = machine which sells stamps automatically. (*e*) any small piece of gummed paper used to show you have made a payment. (*f*) mark made by a rubber stamp. **2.** *v.* (*a*) to bang your foot hard on the ground. (*b*) to make a mark on sth. (*c*) to stick a stamp on (sth); **stamped addressed envelope** = envelope with your own name, adress and a stamp, which you enclose in a letter so that the person you are writing to can reply. **stamp out,** *v.* to stop/to eradicate.

stampede [stæm'pi:d] **1.** *n.* mad rush (of animals/people). **2.** *v.* to rush madly.

stance [sta:ns] *n.* (*a*) way of standing. (*b*) attitude/position.

stanch [sta:nʃ] *v.* to stop blood flowing.

stanchion ['stænʃn] *n.* vertical post/bar which holds sth up.

stand [stænd] **1.** *n.* (*a*) position; **to make a s. against** = to resist. (*b*) support; thing which holds sth up; flat base. (*c*) arrangement of shelves/posters, etc., at an exhibition. (*d*) **stands** = series of seats for spectators at a football match. (*e*) *Am.* **witness s.** = witness box. (*f*) **taxi s.** = place where taxis wait. (*g*) **one-night s.** = stop for a single performance (of a play/by a pop group) before moving to another location the following night. **2.** *v.* (**stood**) to be/to place in an upright position. (*b*) to be on your feet/not to be sitting down. (*c*) to stay/to remain. (*d*) to bear/to accept. (*e*) to put your name forward in an election.

(*f*) to pay for. **stand aside,** *v.* to step to one side. **stand back,** *v.* to step backwards; to be behind. **stand by,** *v.* (*a*) to be ready. (*b*) to stand at one side without taking part in the action. (*c*) to support/to be faithful. **standby,** *n.* (*a*) thing which is ready to go into action if necessary; **good s.** = thing which is good to have at hand in case of need. (*b*) waiting; **he is on s.** = he is waiting to see if he is needed; (*at an airport*) **s. ticket** = cheap ticket which allows you to wait to see if there are any empty places. **stand down,** *v.* to withdraw from an election, etc. **stand for,** *v.* (*a*) to mean. (*b*) to accept/to allow. (*c*) to be a candidate for (an elected position). **stand in for,** *v.* to take s.o.'s place. **stand-in,** *n.* person who takes s.o.'s place. **standing. 1.** *n.* (*a*) being on your feet; **s. room only** = room for people to stand, not to sit. (*b*) social position. **2.** *adj.* (*a*) upright/not lying or sitting. (*b*) permanent; **s. order** = permanent order to send sth or pay sth regularly; **it is a s. joke** = it is sth we always laugh about. **standoffish,** *adj.* (person) who is cold/who does not make friends. **standoffishness,** *n.* unfriendliness. **stand out,** *v.* to be obvious. **stand over,** *v.* to be just behind (s.o.) and supervise what he is doing. **standpipe,** *n.* upright pipe connected to the water main in the street, with a tap which allows water to be taken off when the supply to houses has been cut. **standpoint,** *n.* point of view/position from which you look at a problem. **standstill,** *n.* state of being stopped. **stand to,** *v.* (*in army, etc.*) to be ready to go into action. **stand up,** *v.* (*a*) to get to your feet. (*b*) **s. up straight!** = hold yourself straight. (*c*) **to s. up for sth** = to defend/to support; **to s. up to s.o.** = to fight s.o. bravely; **to s. s.o. up** = not to meet s.o. at a rendezvous. **stand-up,** *adj.* **stand-up buffet** = buffet where you eat standing up; **stand-up fight** = real fight where people come to blows.

standard ['stændəd] **1.** *n.* (*a*) model with which sth is compared. (*b*) excellent quality which is set as a target. (*c*) large flag. (*d*) **lamp s.** = tall pole with a light on top for lighting a street. (*e*) tree/bush grown with a tall trunk. **2.** *adj.* (*a*) normal/usual; **s. authors** = the classical authors/authors everyone usually reads; **s. pronunciation** = pronunciation which is generally used by educated speakers. (*b*) on a tall pole; **s. lamp** = lamp in a room on a tall pole; **s. rose** = rose grown with a tall trunk. (*c*) which is taken as a measure. **standardization** [stændədaɪ-'zeɪʃn] *n.* setting of a standard; making sure that everything conforms to a standard. **standardize** ['stændədaɪz] *v.* to make everything conform to a standard.

stank [stæŋk] *v. see* **stink**.

stanza ['stænzə] *n.* section of a poem made up of a series of lines.

stapes ['steɪpɪz] *n.* one of the ossicles in the ear.

staphylococcus [stæfɪlə'kɒkəs] *n.* (*pl.* **-cocci** [-kɒkaɪ]) type of bacterium which causes food poisoning and infection in the blood.

staple ['steɪpl] **1.** *n.* piece of strong bent wire used to hold things in place; small wire clip for attaching papers together by being passed through them and then bent over. **2.** *adj.* (*a*) main product of a country/town, etc. (*b*) **s. diet** = main part of what you eat. **3.** *v.* to attach with a staple. **stapler,** *n.* small instrument for stapling.

star [stɑː] **1.** *n.* (*a*) body in the sky like a very distant sun which shines at night. (*b*) the sign of the zodiac which marks your birth; *inf.* **thank your lucky stars** = consider yourself very lucky. (*c*) shape with several regular points. (*d*) asterisk. (*e*) actor/actress who is very well known to the public. **3.** *v.* (**starred**) (*a*) to play an important part (**in** a film). (*b*) to have (a famous actor) playing. (*c*) to mark with a star. **stardom,** *n.* being a film star. **starfish,** *n.* sea animal shaped like a star. **starless,** *adj.* (night) when no stars are visible. **starlet,** *n.* young film actress. **starlight,** *n.* light from the stars. **starlit,** *adj.* (night) lit by the light of the stars. **starry,** *adj.* covered with stars. **starry-eyed,** *adj.* wildly hopeful. **stars and stripes,** *n.* the flag of the USA.

starboard ['stɑːbəd] *n. & adj.* right side of a ship when facing forwards.

starch [stɑːtʃ] **1.** *n.* (*a*) white energy-giving carbohydrate in bread/potatoes/rice, etc. (*b*) white powder mixed with water to make cloth stiff. **2.** *v.* to make (cloth) stiff with starch. **starchy,** *adj.* (*a*) full of starch. (*b*) very formal (manner).

stare ['steə] **1.** *n.* fixed look from the eyes. **2.** *v.* to look at s.o./sth with a fixed gaze; *inf.* **it's staring you in the face** = it is very obvious. **staring,** *adj., adv.* with a fixed look.

stark [stɑːk] **1.** *adj.* (**-er, -est**) (*a*) total/pure (nonsense). (*b*) bare (landscape/details). **2.** *adv.* completely (naked); **s. staring mad** = completely mad. **starkly,** *adv.* in a stark way. **starkness,** *n.* being stark.

starling ['stɑːlɪŋ] *n.* common dark bird with a green sheen to its feathers.

start [stɑːt] **1.** *n.* (*a*) beginning; **for a s.** = in the first place. (*b*) **to give s.o. two metres' s,** = to place them at the beginning of a race two metres in front of you. (*c*) sudden jump/sudden movement; **by fits and starts** = at odd moments. **2.** *v.* (*a*) to begin. (*b*) to (cause to) begin to work. (*c*) to set (sth) going. (*d*) to jump (in surprise). **starter,** *n.* (*a*) person or animal who starts. (*b*) person who gives the signal for the start of a race. (*c*) *inf.* first course in a meal. (*d*) machine which starts a car engine. **starting,** *n.* beginning (of a race, etc.); **starting point** = point from which everything begins. **start off, start out,** *v.* to begin to do/to go. **start up,** *v.* to make (an engine, etc.) begin to work.

startle ['stɑːtl] *v.* to make (s.o.) jump in surprise. **startling,** *adj.* remarkable/surprising.

starve [stɑːv] *v.* not to give enough food to (s.o.); to die from lack of food; *inf.* **I'm starving** = I am very hungry; **starved of** = not having enough of. **starvation** [stɑː'veɪʃn] *n.* lack of food.

stash [stæʃ] *v. inf.* **to s. away** = to store in a safe place.

state [steɪt] **1.** *n.* (*a*) condition; *inf.* **in a s.** = very angry. (*b*) government of a nation; **state-owned** = owned by the country/government (not privately owned). (*c*) independent country. (*d*) one of the semi-independent parts of

a federal country. (*e*) great show.
2. *adj.* belonging to/run by/given by
the government. **3.** *v.* to say clearly/
to claim. **stated**, *adj.* fixed/regulated.
State Department, *n. Am.* section of
the US government dealing with foreign
affairs. **stateless**, *adj.* (person) who is
not a citizen of any state. **stateliness**,
n. being stately. **stately**, *adj.* noble/
dignified; **s. home** = palace/castle belonging to a lord, etc. **statement**, *n.*
declaration clearly written or spoken.
state-of-the-art, *adj.* very advanced
technically. **stateroom**, *n.* large cabin
on a ship. **States**, *n. pl. inf.* the United
States of America. **stateside**, *adj. &*
adv. Am. in/to the United States of
America. **statesman**, *n.* (*pl.* **-men**) person who is or was a member of a government. **statesmanlike**, *adj.* like a
statesman. **statesmanship**, *n.* skill in
government of a country.

static ['stætɪk] **1.** *adj.* not moving; **s. elec-**
tricity = electricity which stays in one
place (in a car/cloth). **2.** *n.* electrical
interference in the air which disturbs
a radio signal. **statics**, *n.pl.* study of
physical forces in equilibrium or of
motionless bodies.

station ['steɪʃn] **1.** *n.* (*a*) place where
trains stop to pick up and put down
passengers; place where coaches/buses
begin or end their journeys. (*b*) central
building for some sort of service.
(*c*) **radio s./TV s.** = broadcasting
headquarters with its own frequency.
(*d*) position in society. (*e*) **sheep s.** =
large sheep farm in Australia. **2.** *v.* to
place (s.o.) at a spot. **stationary**, *adj.*
not moving. **stationmaster**, *n.* man
in charge of a railway station. **station**
wagon, *n.* long car with a part at the
back for carrying goods.

stationer ['steɪʃənə] *n.* person who sells
stationery. **stationery**, *n.* materials for
writing, such as paper/pens/ink.

statistic [stə'tɪstɪk] *n.* fact given in the
form of a figure; **statistics** = study
of facts given in the form of figures.
statistical, *adj.* referring to statistics.
statistically, *adv.* in a statistical way.
statistician [stætɪs'tɪʃn] *n.* person who
studies/analyses statistics.

statue ['stætjuː] *n.* figure of a per-

son carved in stone/made of metal,
etc. **statuary**, *n.* collection of statues.
statuesque [stætju'esk] *adj.* (woman)
who is beautiful but large and dignified.
statuette [stætju'et] *n.* small statue.

stature ['stætʃə] *n.* (*a*) height. (*b*)
importance.

status ['steɪtəs] *n.* (*no pl.*) (*a*) legal position. (*b*) importance/position in the
eyes of other people; **s. symbol** =
object which may make other people
think more highly of you. **status quo**
['steɪtəs'kwəʊ] *n.* state of things as they
are at the moment.

statute ['stætjuːt] *n.* law. **statutory**
['stætjʊtrɪ] *adj.* legal; officially imposed.

staunch [stɔːnʃ] **1.** *adj.* (**-er, -est**) firm
(friend). **2.** *v.* to stop (a flow of blood).
staunchly, *adv.* firmly.

stave [steɪv] **1.** *n.* (*a*) curved piece of
wood which forms part of a barrel. (*b*)
set of five lines on which music is writ-
ten. **2.** *v.* (*a*) (**stove**) **to s. in** = to batter
a hole in a boat/a barrel. (*b*) **to s. off** =
to hold off/to prevent.

stay [steɪ] **1.** *n.* (*a*) time which you spend
in a place. (*b*) **s. of execution** = delay
ordered by a judge in carrying out a sentence. (*c*) strong rope which supports,
e.g. a mast on a ship. (*d*) (*old*) **stays** =
corset. **2.** *v.* to stop in a place. **stay-**
at-home, *n.* person who does not go
out much. **stay away**, *v.* to keep away/
not to come. **stayer**, *n.* person who
can work hard/horse which can run long
distances without tiring. **stay in**, *v.* to
stay at home. **stay out**, *v.* not to come
home. **stay up**, *v.* not to go to bed.

STD *short for* Subscriber Trunk Dialling.

stead [sted] *n.* (*a*) **it stood him in good s.**
= it was very useful to him. (*b*) **in your**
s. = in place of you.

steadfast ['stedfɑːst] *adj.* firm/constant.
steadfastly, *adv.* firmly/constantly.

steady ['stedɪ] **1.** *adj.* (**-ier, -iest**) (*a*)
firm/not wobbling. (*b*) continuing reg-
ularly. (*c*) (person) who is not easily
upset. **2.** *n. inf.* boyfriend/girlfriend
with whom you go out regularly. **3.**
inter. **s. on!** = be careful. **4.** *v.*
to make/to keep firm. **steadily**, *adv.*
(*a*) firmly. (*b*) regularly/continuously.
steadiness, *n.* being steady.

steak [steɪk] *n.* (*a*) thick slice of beef cut

from the best part of the animal. (b) thick slice of fish. **steakhouse,** n. restaurant serving steak and other grilled food.

steal [sti:l] v. (**stole; stolen**) (a) to take (sth which does not belong to you). (b) **to s. a glance at** = to look at quickly and secretly. (c) **to s. a march on s.o.** = to do sth stealthily before s.o. can do it. (d) to creep very quietly (into).

stealth [stelθ] n. **by s.** = in a secret way/ without anyone knowing. **stealthily,** adv. in a stealthy way. **stealthiness,** n. being stealthy. **stealthy** adj. (**-ier, -iest**) without anyone knowing or seeing.

steam [sti:m] **1.** n. (a) vapour which comes off hot water/from warm breath; **s. engine** = engine which runs on steam pressure; inf. **s. radio** = old-fashioned radio (as opposed to television). (b) **in the days of s.** = when railways used steam locomotives. (c) inf. **to let off s.** = (i) to use up your excess energy; (ii) to explode with anger. **2.** v. (a) to cook by steam. (b) to send out steam. (c) to move by steam power. (d) (of window) **to s. up** = to be covered by a mist; inf. **to get steamed up about** = to get very annoyed. **steamboat,** n. boat powered by steam. **steamer,** n. (a) large passenger ship (powered by steam). (b) type of pan with holes in the bottom which is placed over boiling water for steaming vegetables/ puddings. **steamroller,** n. vehicle with a very heavy roller for flattening newly laid road surfaces. **steamship,** n. large passenger ship (powered by steam). **steamy,** adj. full of steam.

steatite ['striətait] n. soft grey stone which can be carved.

steed [sti:d] n. (in literature) horse.

steel [sti:l] **1.** n. (a) hard flexible metal made from iron and carbon; **s. band** = West Indian band which plays music on steel drums of varying sizes. (b) bar of rough steel for sharpening knives. **2.** v. **to s. yourself to do sth** = to get up enough courage to do sth. **steeliness,** n. being steely. **steel wool,** n. very fine steel wire used in wads for cleaning metal. **steelworks,** n. factory which produces steel. **steely,** adj. sharp/hard like steel.

steep [sti:p] **1.** adj. (**-er, -est**) (a) which rises or falls sharply. (b) inf. excessive. **2.** v. to soak in a liquid for a long time. **steepen,** v. to become steeper. **steeply,** adv. (rising) sharply. **steepness,** n. being steep.

steeple ['sti:pl] n. church tower with the top rising to a point. **steeplechase,** n. race run across open country, over fences, hedges, etc.; race on a track over hurdles. **steeplechaser,** n. person/horse that runs in a steeplechase. **steeplejack,** n. person who climbs towers/factory chimneys, etc., to do repairs.

steer ['stiə] **1.** n. young bull raised for meat. **2.** v. to guide/to make (a vehicle) go in a certain direction; **to s. clear of** = to avoid. **steerage,** n. (a) act of steering. (b) cheapest berths in a passenger ship. **steering,** n. mechanism in a car which steers it; **s. wheel** = wheel which is turned by the driver to alter the direction of a car; **s. column** = metal tube to which the steering wheel is attached; **s. committee** = small committee which does detailed work on the agenda for a large committee meeting. **steersman,** n. (pl. **-men**) man who steers a ship.

stele [sti:l] n. carved slab of stone, placed upright.

stellar ['stelə] adj. referring to stars.

stem [stem] **1.** n. (a) long stalk on which flowers and leaves grow. (b) thin part of a wine glass/of a tobacco pipe. (c) basic part of a word to which endings or prefixes are added. (d) **from s. to stern** = from the bows to the stern of a boat. **2.** v. (**stemmed**) (a) to result **from**. (b) to stop/to prevent (a flow, etc.).

stench [stentʃ] n. strong unpleasant smell.

stencil ['stensl] **1.** n. (a) sheet of cardboard or metal with a pattern cut out of it, so that if it is placed on a surface and colour is passed over it, the pattern will appear on the surface; pattern/letters/numbers, etc., which are painted in this way. (b) sheet of waxed paper used for making large numbers of copies. **2.** v. (**stencilled**) (a) to mark with a stencil. (b) to make a copy of (a document) using a stencil.

stengun ['stenɡʌn] *n.* small machine gun.

stenographer [stə'nɒɡrəfə] *n.* person who can write down fast in shorthand. **stenography** [stə'nɒɡrəfi] *n.* shorthand.

stenosis [sten'əʊsɪs] *n.* condition where an artery becomes narrow.

stentorian [sten'tɔ:rɪən] *adj.* (*formal*) very loud (voice).

step [step] **1.** *n.* (*a*) single movement of the foot when walking/running; distance covered by this movement; **s. by s.** = little by little. (*b*) sound made by moving a foot forward. (*c*) regular movement of the feet; **keep in s.** = move at the same pace as everyone else; **out of s.** = not moving at the same pace as everyone else. (*d*) action. (*e*) stair (on a staircase); flat rung (on a ladder); (**a pair of**) **steps** = ladder with two parts hinged at the top, which can stand solidly without leaning against anything. **2.** *v.* (**stepped**) to make a movement with a foot; **to s. on the brakes** = to push the brake pedal hard. **step in,** *v.* to involve yourself/to interfere. **stepladder,** *n.* pair of steps. **stepping-stone,** *n.* one of a series of stones in a stream which allow you to cross it. **step up,** *v.* to increase.

step- [step] *prefix* showing a family relationship which is through a parent who has remarried. **stepbrother,** *n.* male child of your stepfather or stepmother. **stepdaughter,** *n.* daughter of your wife/husband by another marriage. **stepfather,** *n.* husband of your mother who is not your father. **stepmother,** *n.* wife of your father, who is not your mother. **stepsister,** *n.* female child of your stepfather or stepmother. **stepson,** *n.* son of your wife/husband by another marriage.

steppe [step] *n.* wide grass-covered plain in Russia and Asia.

stereo- ['sterɪəʊ] *prefix* referring to sth which has two dimensions.

stereo ['sterɪəʊ] *n. & adj.* (machine) which reproduces sound through two different channels and loudspeakers.

stereophonic [sterɪəʊ'fɒnɪk] *adj.* referring to sound which comes from two places at once.

stereoscope ['sterɪəʊskəʊp] *n.* apparatus which shows a picture which appears to have depth and be three-dimensional. **stereoscopic** [sterɪə'skɒpɪk] *adj.* referring to seeing in three dimensions; **s. vision** = ability to see the same object with both eyes, and so judge distance.

stereotype ['sterɪətaɪp] *n.* pattern for certain types of person. **stereotyped,** *adj.* fitting certain patterns.

sterile ['steraɪl] *adj.* (*a*) not capable of bearing fruit/children. (*b*) so clean that no germs/bacteria can grow. **sterility** [ste'rɪlɪtɪ] *n.* inability to grow fruit/to produce children or ideas. **sterilization** [sterɪlaɪ'zeɪʃn] *n.* action of sterilizing. **sterilize** ['sterɪlaɪz] *v.* (*a*) to make (s.o.) incapable of producing children. (*b*) to make so clean that bacteria/germs cannot grow. **sterilizer,** *n.* apparatus for sterilizing.

sterling ['stɜ:lɪŋ] **1.** *adj.* of a certain standard/of good quality; **s. silver** = silver of a certain high purity. **2.** *n.* standard measure of British currency.

stern [stɜ:n] **1.** *adj.* (**-er, -est**) harsh/strict. **2.** *n.* rear part of a ship. **sternly,** *adv.* in a stern way. **sternness,** *n.* being stern. **sternwheeler,** *n.* large pleasure ship (on American rivers) with a paddle wheel at the stern.

sternum ['stɜ:nəm] *n.* central bone on the chest. **sternal,** *adj.* referring to the sternum.

steroid ['stɪərɔɪd] *n.* one of a group of natural substances in plants and animals, including hormones.

stertorous ['stɜ:tərəs] *adj.* making a snoring sound.

stet [stet] *v.* word showing that a correction should not be made.

stethoscope ['steθəskəʊp] *n.* doctor's instrument for listening to a patient's chest.

stetson ['stetsən] *n.* tall cowboy hat with a wide brim.

stevedore ['sti:vədɔ:] *n.* person who works at a port, unloading or loading ships.

stew [stju:] **1.** *n.* dish of meat and vegetables cooked together for a long time; *inf.* **in a s.** = in an awkward situation. **2.** *v.* to cook for a long time in liquid. **stewed,** *adj. Sl.* drunk.

steward ['stjʊəd] *n.* (*a*) man who serves meals or drinks on a ship/aircraft/ in a club. (*b*) person who organizes a meeting; person who looks after a farm or estate for the owner. (*c*) **shop s.** = elected union representative. **stewardess,** *n.* woman who looks after passengers on a ship or aircraft.

stick [stɪk] **1.** *n.* (*a*) piece of wood; strong piece of wood with a handle used as a support when walking; **hockey s.** = stick with a curved end, used in playing hockey. (*b*) long piece. **2.** *v.* (**stuck**) (*a*) to jab or push (sth sharp) **into** sth. (*b*) to glue; to attach. (*c*) to stay close/ to keep (**to**). (*d*) to be fixed/not to be able to move. (*e*) *inf.* to bear/to accept. **stick at,** *v.* (*a*) **to stick at nothing** = to be ruthless. (*b*) to stay at. **sticker,** *n.* small piece of paper or plastic which you can stick on a surface as a decoration or advertisement. **stickily,** *adv.* in a sticky way. **stickiness,** *n.* state of being sticky. **sticking plaster,** *n.* strip of cloth which can be stuck to the skin to cover a wound. **stick-in-the-mud,** *n. inf.* person who will not accept new ideas. **stick-on,** *adj.* (label) which sticks on to a surface. **stick out** *v.* (*a*) to push out; to be further out than usual. (*b*) to be easily seen. **stick up,** *v.* (*a*) to put up (a notice, etc.); **s. them up!** = put your hands up (to show you surrender). (*b*) *inf.* **to s. up for s.o.** = to defend s.o. **sticky,** *adj.* (**-ier, -iest**) (*a*) covered with glue; which sticks easily. (*b*) *inf.* difficult/awkward; **he came to a s. end** = he died/was put in prison/was ruined, etc.; **s. wicket** = difficult situation.

stickleback ['stɪklbæk] *n.* common small freshwater fish with spines along its back.

stickler ['stɪklə] *n.* (**for**) person who attaches great importance to sth.

stiff [stɪf] *adj.* (**-er, -est**) (*a*) which cannot be bent or moved easily; (brush) with hard bristles; starched (collar); **bored s.** = very bored. (*b*) solid/thick (paste). (*c*) strong (breeze). (*d*) difficult/hard (examination, penalty). (*e*) (whisky, etc.) with not much water added. (*f*) high (price). (*g*) unfriendly/unsociable. **stiffen,** *v.* (*a*) to become/make stiff. (*b*) to become cautious/unfriendly. (*c*)

(*of wind*) become stronger. (*d*) to make (resistance) stronger. **stiffener,** *n.* thing which stiffens. **stiffly,** *adv.* in a stiff way. **stiff-necked,** *adj.* obstinate. **stiffness,** *n.* being stiff.

stifle ['staɪfl] *v.* (*a*) to prevent (s.o.) from breathing. (*b*) to hold back (a yawn, etc.). **stifling,** *adj.* suffocating; extremely hot.

stigma ['stɪgmə] *n.* (*a*) disgrace; feeling of shame. (*b*) top of the centre of a flower which receives pollen to make seeds. **stigmatize** ['stɪgmətaɪz] *v.* to give a bad name to (sth).

stile [staɪl] *n.* steps which allow people, but not animals, to get over a wall or fence.

stiletto [stɪ'letəʊ] *n.* (*pl.* **-os**) (*a*) long thin dagger. (*b*) **s. heels** = high thin heels on women's shoes.

still [stɪl] **1.** *n.* (*a*) apparatus for producing alcohol. (*b*) one picture from a moving film. **2.** *adj.* (**-er, -est**) calm/ motionless; (lemonade, etc.) which is not fizzy; **s. life** = picture of flowers or objects, not people or animals. **3.** *adv.* (*a*) up until this/that moment. (*b*) even. (*c*) however. **stillbirth,** *n.* birth of a dead child. **stillborn,** *adj.* (child) which is born dead; (idea) which is never put into practice. **stillness,** *n.* calm. **stillroom,** *n.* pantry/store in a large house.

stilts [stɪlts] *n. pl.* poles to raise (sth) above the ground; **pair of stilts** = two poles with foot rests to enable you to walk high in the air. **stilted,** *adj.* (style of writing) which is very formal/not natural.

stimulate ['stɪmjʊleɪt] *v.* to excite/ to encourage; to make more active. **stimulant,** *n.* drug which makes you more active. **stimulation** [stɪmjʊ'leɪʃn] *n.* being stimulated. **stimulus,** *n.* (*pl.* **-li** [-laɪ]) thing that encourages further activity.

sting [stɪŋ] **1.** *n.* (*a*) tiny needle in the tail of an insect/leaf of a plant which injects poison. (*b*) wound made by an insect or plant. (*c*) burning feeling. **2.** *v.* (**stung** [stʌŋ]) (*a*) to wound with a sting. (*b*) to have a burning feeling. (*c*) to hurt (s.o.) so that he reacts. (*d*) *inf.* to ask (s.o.) for money. **stinging nettle,** *n.*

common wild plant which causes a rash. **stingray**, *n.* large flat fish with a sting in its tail.

stingy ['stɪndʒɪ] *adj.* (**-ier, -iest**) *inf.* mean; not free with money. **stinginess**, *n.* meanness.

stink [stɪŋk] **1.** *n.* unpleasant smell; *inf.* **to create a s.** = to object vigorously. **2.** *v.* (**stank; stunk**) to make an unpleasant smell.

stint [stɪnt] **1.** *n.* (*a*) amount of work. (*b*) **without s.** = in large quantities/with no restriction. **2.** *v.* to give (s.o.) a very small amount.

stipend ['staɪpend] *n.* salary of a priest or a magistrate. **stipendiary** [staɪ-'pendjərɪ] *adj.* (magistrate) who is paid.

stipple ['stɪpl] *v.* to colour with small dots.

stipulate ['stɪpjʊleɪt] *v.* to insist; to make a condition. **stipulation** [stɪpjʊ'leɪʃn] *n.* condition (in a contract).

stir [stɜ:] **1.** *n.* (*a*) mixing up a liquid. (*b*) fuss/agitation. **2.** *v.* (**stirred**) (*a*) to mix up (a liquid). (*b*) to cause fuss/agitation. (*c*) to move. **stirring**, *adj.* exciting. **stir up**, *v.* to cause (trouble).

stirrup ['stɪrəp] *n.* metal loop hanging from the saddle into which the rider puts his foot; **s. cup** = drink taken on horseback before setting off on a ride.

stitch [stɪtʃ] **1.** *n.* (*pl.* **-es**) (*a*) small loop of cotton or wool made with a needle in sewing or knitting; *inf.* **I haven't got a s. to wear** = I have no suitable clothes. (*b*) small loop of thread used by a surgeon to attach a wound together. (*c*) sharp pain in the side of the body which comes after you have been running; *inf.* **in stitches** = laughing uproariously. **2.** *v.* to attach with a needle and thread.

stoat [stəʊt] *n.* small brown flesh-eating animal whose fur turns white in winter.

stock [stɒk] **1.** *n.* (*a*) plant on which other plants are grafted. (*b*) race/family. (*c*) handle of a rifle. (*d*) **stocks** = yard where ships are built; **on the stocks** = being worked on. (*e*) **stocks** = wooden frame with holes for the feet, in which criminals were placed. (*f*) quantity of things for use; quantities of goods for sale; **to take s.** = (i) to count what you have in stock; (ii) to assess a situation. (*g*) farm animals; **fat s.** = an-

imals reared for meat. (*h*) liquid made from boiling bones, etc., in water, used as a base for soups and sauces. (*i*) common scented garden flower. (*j*) capital invested in a business; **government stocks** = loans made to the state; **s. market** = buying and selling of shares; **s. exchange** = building in which shares are bought and sold. (*k*) reputation (of s.o.). **2.** *v.* (*a*) to keep (goods) for sale. (*b*) to provide with goods/animals/plants, etc. **3.** *adj.* usual; **s. size** = normal size; **s. argument** = one which is frequently used. **stockbreeder**, *n.* farmer who specializes in breeding animals. **stockbreeding**, *n.* breeding animals. **stockbroker**, *n.* agent who buys shares on the stock exchange. **stockcar**, *n.* car adapted for brutal racing. **stockholder**, *n.* owner of government stocks. **stockiness**, *n.* being stocky. **stock-in-trade**, *n.* things needed to carry on a business; habitual way of acting. **stockist**, *n.* person/shop which stocks a certain brand of goods. **stockjobber**, *n.* dealer in shares on the stock exchange. **stockman**, *n.* (*pl.* **-men**) man who looks after farm animals. **stockpile**. **1.** *n.* supplies kept in reserve (in case of an emergency). **2.** *v.* to collect supplies in case of emergency. **stockpot**, *n.* large pot for making soup. **stockroom**, *n.* room where stores are kept. **stock-still**, *adv.* without moving. **stocktaking**, *n.* counting of goods in stock at the end of a period. **stock up with**, *v.* to buy supplies for use in the future. **stocky**, *adj.* (**-ier, -iest**) short and strong (person). **stockyard**, *n.* place where animals are kept before they are slaughtered or shipped.

stockade [stɒ'keɪd] *n.* strong fence made of thick upright poles.

stockinet [stɒkɪ'net] *n.* elastic material.

stocking ['stɒkɪŋ] *n.* long close-fitting piece of clothing to cover your leg and foot; **in his s.** (*also* **stockinged**) **feet** = without his shoes on.

stodge [stɒdʒ] *n.* heavy filling food (such as puddings). **stodgy**, *adj.* (**-ier, -iest**) heavy (food); dull (book).

stoep [stu:p] *n.* (*in South Africa*) verandah.

stoic ['stəʊɪk] *n.* person who accepts

problems or pain without complaining. **stoical**, *adj.* accepting problems or pain without complaining. **stoically**, *adv.* in a stoical way. **stoicism** ['stəʊɪsɪzəm] *n.* being stoical.

stoke [stəʊk] *v.* to put fuel in (a furnace). **stoker**, *n.* person who stokes a furnace; seaman who looks after the engines.

stole [stəʊl] **1.** *n.* wide light scarf worn around the shoulders. **2.** *v. see* **steal.**

stolen ['stəʊlən] *v. see* **steal.**

stolid ['stɒlɪd] *adj.* slow and heavy; not excitable. **stolidity** [stɒ'lɪdɪtɪ] *n.* being stolid. **stolidly**, *adv.* in a stolid way.

stoma ['stəʊmə] *n.* (*pl.* **-ata**) pore in a plant.

stomach ['stʌmək] **1.** *n.* (*a*) bag inside the body in which food is digested; **s. ache** = pain in the stomach. (*b*) part of the body lower than the chest. (*c*) desire/courage. **2.** *v.* to put up with/to tolerate.

stomp [stɒmp] *v.* to stamp/to walk with a heavy tread.

stone [stəʊn] **1.** *n.* (*a*) small piece of rock. (*b*) piece of rock which has been cut for building, etc.; **Stone Age** = prehistoric period when men made tools out of stone; **precious s.** = rare mineral which is very valuable. (*c*) hard seed inside some types of fruit. (*d*) hard piece of mineral which forms inside the body (in the kidneys, etc.) and causes pain. (*e*) measure of weight (= 14 pounds or 6.35 kilograms). **2.** *adv.* completely (deaf); *Am.* **s. broke** = stony broke. **3.** *v.* (*a*) **to s. (s.o.) to death** = to throw stones at (s.o.) and kill him. (*b*) to take the stones out of (fruit). **stonechat**, *n.* small dark bird with a red breast. **stonecrop**, *n.* type of plant which grows among stones. **stoned**, *adj. Sl.* (*a*) drunk. (*b*) drugged. **stonemason**, *n.* person who cuts and builds with stone. **stonewall**, *v.* to speak for a long time without answering the question. **stoneware**, *n.* (*no pl.*) pottery made of rough clay and fired at high temperatures. **stonework**, *n.* walls, etc., made of stone. **stonily**, *adv.* with no feeling. **stony**, *adj.* (**-ier, -iest**) (*a*) covered with stones. (*b*) hard; with no feeling. (*c*) *inf.* **s. broke** = with no money.

stood [stʊd] *v. see* **stand.**

stooge [stu:dʒ] **1.** *n. inf.* (*a*) person who does what he is told to do. (*b*) the stupid one of a pair of comedians. **2.** *v. inf.* **to s. about** = to wander about waiting to be told what to do.

stook [stu:k] *n.* group of sheaves of corn, leaning together.

stool [stu:l] *n.* (*a*) seat with no back; **to fall between two stools** = (i) to miss each of two targets; (ii) not to take up either of two opportunities. (*b*) lump of waste matter passed from the bowels. **stoolpigeon**, *n.* criminal who helps the police to trap another criminal.

stoop [stu:p] **1.** *n.* bending forward. **2.** *v.* (*a*) to bend forward. (*b*) **he stoops** = he has a permanently bent back. (*c*) **to s. to do sth** = to allow yourself to do sth which you feel is beneath you.

stop [stɒp] **1.** *n.* (*a*) act of not moving/not doing sth. (*b*) place where a bus, etc., usually stops to pick up or put down passengers. (*c*) **full s.** = round dot (.) showing the end of a sentence. (*d*) block which prevents a door, etc., closing. (*e*) knob on an organ which switches on a different set of pipes; set of pipes on an organ which produce a particular sound; **to pull out all the stops** = to do everything possible. **2.** *v.* (**stopped**) (*a*) to make (sth which is moving) come to a halt; to come to a halt. (*b*) to make (sth) cease working; to cease working/doing sth. (*c*) to stay in a place. (*d*) to block; to fill (a gap). (*e*) to cut off (supply); to prevent (money) being paid; **to s. a cheque** = to tell the bank not to pay a cheque which you have written; **to s. s.o.'s wages** = not to pay s.o. **stop by**, *v. inf.* to visit s.o. for a short time. **stopcock**, *n.* tap which stops the supply of water. **stop down**, *v.* to make the aperture of a lens smaller. **stopgap**, *n. & adj.* thing which is used temporarily while waiting for sth more suitable to turn up. **stop off**, *v.* to make a stop on a long journey. **stop over**, *v.* to make an overnight stop on a long journey. **stopover**, *n.* overnight stop on a long journey. **stoppage**, *n.* action of stopping/blocking. **stopper**, *n.* piece of glass/cork, etc., which fits the mouth of a jar to close it. **stop press**, *n. & adj.*

last piece of news added to a newspaper before it is printed. **stop watch,** *n.* watch which can be started and stopped by pressing a button, used for timing races.

store [stɔ:] **1.** *n.* (*a*) supply of food, etc., kept for later use; **to set great s. by sth** = think that sth is very important. (*b*) place in which goods are kept; **s. cattle** = cattle bought to be fattened for resale. (*c*) shop. **2.** *v.* (*a*) to keep (sth) for future use. (*b*) to put (sth) in a warehouse. **storage,** *n.* (*a*) act of keeping/putting in store; **night s. heater** = electric heater where the electricity warms bricks which then store the heat and release it gradually. (*b*) memory, the part of a computer where data is stored. **storehouse,** *n.* place where things are stored. **storekeeper, storeman,** *n.* shopkeeper. **storeroom,** *n.* room where things are stored.

storey, *Am.* **story** ['stɔ:rɪ] *n.* whole floor in a building. **storeyed,** *adj.* with several storeys.

stork [stɔ:k] *n.* large, usu. white, bird with long legs and long beak.

storm [stɔ:m] **1.** *n.* (*a*) period of bad weather with wind; **s. in a teacup** = lot of fuss for no good reason. (*b*) **s. of applause** = loud burst of clapping and cheering. (*c*) **to take a town by s.** = (i) to attack a town suddenly and capture it; (ii) to become suddenly very popular in a town; **s. troops** = soldiers who are specially trained to attack and capture. **2.** *v.* (*a*) to be violently angry. (*b*) to attack and capture. **stormy,** *adj.* referring to a storm; like a storm.

story ['stɔ:rɪ] *n.* (*a*) tale of what has happened. (*b*) piece of fiction. (*c*) *inf.* lie. (*d*) *Am.* storey. **storyline,** *n.* plot of a novel/film, etc. **storyteller,** *n.* (*a*) person who tells a story. (*b*) *inf.* person who tells lies.

stoup [stu:p] *n.* bowl for holy water in a church.

stout [staʊt] **1.** *adj.* (**-er, -est**) (*a*) fat. (*b*) strong/thick (material). (*c*) brave. **2.** *n.* strong dark beer. **stout-hearted,** *adj.* brave. **stoutly,** *adv.* (*a*) vigorously. (*b*) solidly/strongly. **stoutness,** *n.* being stout.

stove [staʊv] *n.* machine for heating or

cooking. **stovepipe,** *n.* metal chimney which carries the smoke from a stove.

stow [staʊ] *v.* to put away; to pack. **stow away,** *v.* (*a*) to pack. (*b*) to travel secretly on a ship/aircraft without paying the fare. **stowaway,** *n.* person who stows away.

strabismus [strə'bɪzməs] *n.* squint.

straddle ['strædl] *v.* to stand with legs apart, and your feet on either side of (sth).

strafe [stra:f] *v.* to attack (sth) by shooting at it from a low-flying plane.

straggle ['strægl] *v.* to hang/to walk in an untidy way. **straggler,** *n.* person who walks well behind the main group of people. **straggling, straggly,** *adj.* which grows untidily.

straight [streɪt] **1.** *adj.* (**-er, -est**) (*a*) not curved; **s. hair** = not curly. (*b*) honest/frank. (*c*) simple/not complicated; (whisky, etc.) with nothing added; **s. fight** = election where there are only two candidates. (*d*) tidy; not crooked. (*e*) serious (actor/ play); **to keep a s. face** = to stop yourself smiling. (*f*) *Sl.* not homosexual. **2.** *n.* **the s.** = part of a racecourse (usu. near the finish) which is not curved. **3.** *adv.* (*a*) in a straight line. (*b*) immediately. (*c*) directly. (*d*) honestly; *inf.* **to go s.** = to lead an honest life after having been a criminal. **straight away,** *adv.* immediately/ at once. **straighten,** *v.* to make/to become straight. **straightforward,** *adj.* frank/honest. **straightforwardly,** *adv.* in an honest way. **straightness,** *n.* being straight. **straight off,** *adv.* at once. **straight out,** *adv.* directly.

strain [streɪn] **1.** *n.* (*a*) act of pulling tight; tension. (*b*) hurt caused by pulling a muscle too hard. (*c*) stress; mental/ physical tension. (*d*) way of speaking. (*e*) breed. (*f*) quality or defect which is inherited. (*g*) tune. **2.** *v.* (*a*) to pull/ to work too hard. (*b*) to make a great effort (**to**). (*c*) to put too much stress on (credulity/patience). (*d*) to pass (a liquid) through a sieve to separate it from solids. **strained,** *adj.* (*a*) which has been pulled/worked too hard. (*b*) tense/unfriendly. **strainer,** *n.* sieve for separating liquids from solids.

straits [streɪts] *n. pl.* (*a*) narrow piece of

sea water between two masses of land. (b) money difficulties. **straitened,** adj. **in s. circumstances** = not having enough money to live on. **straitjacket,** n. (a) strong coat whose sleeves are tied behind the back to prevent a mad person from attacking people. (b) thing which prevents you from acting freely. **straitlaced,** adj. with very strict ideas about correct moral behaviour.

strake [streɪk] n. plank which runs along a ship lengthwise.

strand [strænd] 1. n. (a) long piece of hair/thread, etc. (b) (formal) shore. 2. v. to leave (your ship) on the shore. **stranded,** adj. alone and helpless.

strange [streɪnʒ] adj. (-er, -est) (a) odd/bizarre. (b) which you have never seen/heard before. **strangely,** adv. oddly/curiously. **strangeness,** n. being strange. **stranger,** n. person whom you do not know; **you're quite a s.** = I haven't seen you for a long time; **he is a s. to the town** = he does not know it well.

strangle ['stræŋgl] v. to kill (s.o.) by pressing on his throat so that he cannot breath; to crush (initiative/a plan). **stranglehold,** n. control which prevents you doing what you want to do. **strangler,** n. person who strangles. **strangulation** [stræŋgjʊ'leɪʃn] n. being strangled.

strap [stræp] 1. n. long flat piece of leather or material for attaching sth. 2. v. (strapped) (a) to attach with a strap. (b) to wrap a bandage tightly round a wound. (c) to hit (s.o.) with a strap. **strap-hanging,** n. travelling standing in a crowded bus/train, holding on to a strap attached to the roof. **strapless,** adj. with no straps. **strapping,** adj. big/strong (young man/girl).

strata ['strɑːtə] n. see **stratum.**

stratagem ['strætədʒəm] n. clever plan to trick an enemy.

strategic, strategical [strə'tiːdʒɪk(l)] adj. referring to strategy; (position) which gives an advantage over the enemy. **strategically,** adv. according to strategy. **strategist** ['strætədʒɪst] n. officer who plans military attacks. **strategy** ['strætədʒɪ] n. planning of war/of an action.

stratify ['strætɪfaɪ] v. to form layers; to be arranged in layers. **stratification** [strætɪfɪ'keɪʃn] n. forming layers; arranging in layers.

stratosphere ['strætəsfɪə] n. upper layer of the earth's atmosphere.

stratum ['strɑːtəm] n. (pl. **-ta** [-tə]) layer (esp. of rock); **social strata** = levels of society.

stratus ['strɑːtəs] n. **s. clouds** = low flat clouds.

straw [strɔː] n. (a) dry stalks of plants like corn. (b) one single dry stalk of a plant; thin plastic tube for sucking liquid; inf. **that's the last s.** = that is all I can stand/as much as I can take; **s. poll** = random questioning to test the general opinion of the public/of a group. **strawberry,** n. common red summer fruit growing on low plants; **s. mark** = red mark on the skin, which is present from birth.

stray [streɪ] 1. adj. & n. (animal, etc.) which is wandering away from home. 2. adj. (bullet, etc.) wandering off course. 3. v. to wander.

streak [striːk] 1. n. (a) band/line (of colour); flash (of light). (b) quality of character. 2. v. (a) to rush. (b) inf. to run about naked in public. **streaker,** n. inf. person who runs about naked in public. **streaky,** adj. (a) with smudges of colour or dirt. (b) (bacon) with fat and lean streaks.

stream [striːm] 1. n. (a) small flow of water; small river. (b) continuous flow. (c) current. (d) **to come on s.** = to start to be produced/to function. (e) (in school) group of children selected for a certain class. 2. v. (a) to flow. (b) (in school) to put (children) into a stream. **streamer,** n. long thin flag; long paper or ribbon used as a decoration. **streaming,** adj. dripping (wet). **streamline,** v. (a) to design (a car/plane/boat, etc.) so that it can move easily through water or air. (b) to make more efficient; to modernize.

street [striːt] n. road in a town, with houses or shops on each side; **the man in the s.** = the ordinary citizen; **at s. level** = on the same level as the street; inf. **streets ahead** = much more advanced; inf. **right up my s.** = I am very interested in/sth I know a lot about. **streetcar,** *n. Am.* tram.

strength [streŋθ] *n.* (*a*) being strong. (*b*) numbers; **in full s.** = all together. (*c*) number of people employed. (*d*) **on the s. of** = because of. **strengthen,** *v.* to make stronger.

strenuous ['strenjʊəs] *adj.* energetic. **strenuously,** *adv.* vigorously. **strenuousness,** *n.* being strenuous.

streptococcus [streptə'kɒkəs] *n.* (*pl.* **-cocci** [-kɒkaɪ]) bacterium which causes infections, such as a sore throat. **streptomycin** [streptə'maɪsɪn] *n.* type of antibiotic.

stress [stres] **1.** *n.* (*pl.* **-es**) (*a*) force; pressure. (*b*) nervous strain. (*c*) emphasis. **2.** *v.* to emphasize; to put stress on (sth).

stretch [stretʃ] **1.** *n.* (*pl.* **-es**) (*a*) act of being pulled out. (*b*) act of putting out your arms and legs as far as they will go. (*c*) long piece (of road); long period (of time); *Sl.* time spent in prison. **2.** *v.* (*a*) to pull out (sth elastic). (*b*) to pull (sth) out too far. (*c*) to be able to be pulled out. (*d*) to put out your arms or legs as far as they will go. (*e*) **to s. to** = to be enough for. (*f*) to lie for a great distance. (*g*) to relax (a rule). **stretcher,** *n.* (*a*) portable bed with handles at each end for carrying sick people; **s. bearer** = person who lifts one end of a stretcher. (*b*) thing which stretches.

strew [stru:] *v.* (**strewn**) to scatter.

striated ['straɪeɪtɪd] *adj.* marked with parallel furrows. **striation,** *n.* furrow/ridge parallel to several others.

stricken ['strɪkn] *adj.* hit/struck by disease/emotion, etc.

strict [strɪkt] *adj.* (**-er, -est**) (*a*) exact (meaning). (*b*) (orders) which must be obeyed. (*c*) severe/harsh; (person) who insists that rules are obeyed. **strictly,** *adv.* in a strict way. **strictness,** *n.* being strict. **stricture** ['strɪktʃə] *n.* criticism/words of blame.

stride [straɪd] **1.** *n.* long step with your legs. **2.** *v.* (**strode** [strəʊd]) to take long steps.

strident ['straɪdənt] *adj.* unpleasantly loud harsh high (sound). **stridency,** *n.* being strident. **stridently,** *adv.* in a strident way.

strife [straɪf] *n.* fighting; trouble between people.

strike [straɪk] **1.** *n.* (*a*) stopping of work by workers (because of disagreement with management). (*b*) **air s.** = rapid attack from the air. (*c*) **oil s.** = discovery of oil. **2.** *v.* (**struck** [strʌk]) (*a*) to hit. (*b*) to light (a match); to make (a coin/a medal); to make/to agree (a bargain). (*c*) **to be struck down with flu** = to have a sudden attack of flu. (*d*) to make an impression on (s.o.). (*e*) to discover (oil, etc.). (*f*) to lower (a flag); to pack up (a tent). (*g*) to make (a note) sound in music; (of clock) to ring (the hour). (*h*) to go in a certain direction. (*i*) to stop working because of disagreement or in protest. **strikebound,** *adj.* not able to move because of a strike. **strikebreaker,** *n.* worker who continues to work when his colleagues are on strike. **strike off,** *v.* to cross off (a list). **strike out,** *v.* (*a*) (**for**) to swim hard towards. (*b*) to cross off (a list). **strike pay,** *n.* wages paid to striking workers by their union. **striker,** *n.* (*a*) person who goes on strike. (*b*) football player whose job is to score goals. **strike up,** *v.* (*a*) to start playing a piece of music. (*b*) **to s. up an acquaintance with s.o.** = to start getting to know s.o. **striking,** *adj.* remarkable. **strikingly,** *adv.* remarkably.

string [strɪŋ] **1.** *n.* (*a*) thin rope for tying things together; *inf.* **strings** = hidden conditions; *inf.* **to pull strings** = to try to obtain sth through influential friends. (*b*) series of things tied together. (*c*) thin wire in a musical instrument; **the strings** = part of an orchestra playing stringed instruments. (*d*) tough thread (in meat/vegetables). **2.** *v.* (**strung** [strʌŋ]) (*a*) to tie together in a series. (*b*) to put a string in (a musical instrument). (*c*) **highly strung** = excitable; very nervous. **string along,** *v.* (*a*) to go along in a line behind s.o. (*b*) to make (s.o.) promises to get him to co-operate. **string bag,** *n.* shopping bag made of a net of knotted string. **string bean,** *n. Am.* runner bean. **string course,** *n.* horizontal line of projecting bricks. **stringed,** *adj.* (musical instrument) with strings. **string out,** *v.* to put

(things) in a long line. **string up,** *v.* to hang up with a string; *inf.* to hang (s.o.).
string vest, *n.* vest made of cotton woven like a net. **stringy,** *adj.* (meat/vegetables) with tough threads.

stringent ['strɪndʒənt] *adj.* strict/severe. **stringency,** *n.* being stringent. **stringently,** *adv.* in a stringent way.

strip [strɪp] 1. *n.* long narrow piece; **s. cartoon/comic s.** = cartoon story made of a series of small drawings side by side. 2. *v.* (**stripped**) (*a*) to make naked; to take off your clothes. (*b*) to remove (sth). **strip down,** *v.* to take (an engine) to pieces. **strip lighting,** *n.* lighting using long round tubes. **stripper,** *n.* (*a*) liquid for removing old paint; sharp tool for stripping off old paint or old wallpaper. (*b*) woman who performs a striptease. **striptease,** *n.* entertainment where s.o. takes their clothes off piece by piece.

stripe [straɪp] *n.* (*a*) long strip of colour. (*b*) strip of coloured cloth sewn to a uniform to show a certain rank in the army. **striped,** *adj.* with stripes. **stripy,** *adj.* covered with many stripes.

stripling ['strɪplɪŋ] *n.* very young man.

strive [straɪv] *v.* (**strove** [strəʊv]; **has striven**) to try very hard (**to**).

strobe [strəʊb] *n.* light which flashes on and off very rapidly. **stroboscope,** *n.* illuminated figures on a turntable, which enable you to tell if it is turning at the correct speed; device which makes lights flash on and off (on a dance floor).

strode [strəʊd] *v. see* **stride.**

stroke [strəʊk] 1. *n.* (*a*) gentle touch. (*b*) line made by a pen/brush, etc.; **oblique s.** = printing sign (*/*) used to show an alternative. (*c*) blow. (*d*) illness/paralysis caused by damage to part of the brain. (*e*) one movement; **s. of luck** = piece of luck. (*f*) particular style of swimming. (*g*) one ring of a bell. (*h*) rower seated in the stern who gives the time for all the others in a boat. 2. *v.* (*a*) to run your hands gently over. (*b*) to set the time for the other rowers in a boat.

stroll [strəʊl] 1. *n.* short leisurely walk. 2. *v.* to walk slowly along. **stroller,** *n.* (*a*) person who strolls. (*b*) light pram for babies.

strong [strɒŋ] 1. *adj.* (**-er, -est**) (*a*) powerful. (*b*) large (in numbers). (*c*) with a powerful smell/noise, etc.; **s. drink** = alcohol. 2. *adv. inf.* **still going s.** = still working well after a long time. **strong box,** *n.* small safe for keeping jewels. **stronghold,** *n.* fortress; place which is difficult to capture. **strongly,** *adv.* powerfully. **strong man,** *n.* powerful man. **strong-minded** *adj.* with clear fixed ideas. **strong point,** *n.* quality/good characteristic. **strongroom,** *n.* room with thick walls and door where a bank keeps money/jewels, etc. **strong-willed,** *adj.* with a strong character.

strontium ['strɒntɪəm] *n.* (*element:* Sr) white radioactive metal.

strop [strɒp] 1. *n.* leather strap for sharpening razors. 2. *v.* (**stropped**) to sharpen (a razor) on a strop. **stroppy,** *adj. inf.* angry/obstinate.

strove [strəʊv] *v. see* **strive.**

struck [strʌk] *v. see* **strike.**

structure ['strʌktʃə] 1. *n.* (*a*) way in which things are put together. (*b*) building. 2. *v.* to arrange in a certain way. **structural,** *adj.* referring to a structure. **structurally,** *adv.* referring to a structure.

struggle ['strʌgl] 1. *n.* bitter/violent fight. 2. *v.* to fight violently.

strum [strʌm] *v.* (**strummed**) to play a piano/guitar) in an informal way.

strung [strʌŋ] *v. see* **string.**

strut [strʌt] 1. *n.* (*a*) bar of wood, metal, etc., which supports sth. (*b*) strutting way of walking. 2. *v.* (**strutted**) to walk in a proud and important way.

strychnine ['strɪkniːn] *n.* bitter poison.

stub [stʌb] 1. *n.* (*a*) small piece left after sth has been used. (*b*) piece of paper left after a cheque or a ticket has been torn out of a book. 2. *v.* (**stubbed**) (*a*) to hurt (your toe) by hitting it against a rock. (*b*) to put out (a cigarette) by pressing the stub against sth. **stubby,** *adj.* short and fat (fingers).

stubble ['stʌbl] *n.* (*a*) short stems left after corn has been cut. (*b*) short hairs which grow if a man does not shave for several days. **stubbly,** *adj.* covered with short bristles.

stubborn ['stʌbən] *adj.* obstinate; (person) who will only do what he wants to do; (thing) which will not do what you want it to do. **stubbornly,** adv. obstinately. **stubbornness,** n. being stubborn.

stucco ['stʌkəʊ] n. plaster put on walls and painted; plaster used to make moulded decorations in buildings. **stuccoed,** adj. covered with stucco.

stuck [stʌk] v. see **stick. stuck-up,** adj. inf. supercilious/proud.

stud [stʌd] n. (a) nail with a large head; metal marker on a road to show a pedestrian crossing, etc. (b) type of button with two heads for passing through two holes to fasten a shirt. (c) horses which are kept for breeding; (also **stud farm**) farm where horses are kept for breeding; **s. book** = register of pedigree horses, etc. 2. v. (**studded**) to cover with nails. **studded,** adj. covered (**with** nails/stars, etc.).

student ['stjuːdənt] n. person who is studying at college/university; Am. person studying at high school.

studio ['stjuːdɪəʊ] n. (pl. -os) (a) place where artists paint/where photographers take photographs. (b) place where films/broadcasts/recordings are made. (c) very small flat.

studious ['stjuːdɪəs] adj. (a) showing careful study. (b) careful. **studiously,** adv. carefully. **studiousness,** n. being studious.

study ['stʌdɪ] 1. n. (a) act of examining sth carefully to learn more about it; course at university, etc. (b) room in which s.o. works/studies. (c) piece of music which aims to improve the players' technique; work of art in which new ideas are practised; **her face was a s.** = it was instructive/amusing to watch her expression. 2. v. (a) to examine (sth) in detail to learn more about it. (b) to follow a course at college or university. **studied,** adj. done very carefully; done on purpose.

stuff [stʌf] 1. n. (a) material of which sth is made. (b) inf. equipment/belongings; **do your s.** = do what you have to do; **that's the s.** = that's it! **s. and nonsense!** = rubbish! (c) cloth. 2. v. (a) to fill (sth) very full. (b) to block (a hole). (c) to fill the skin of (a dead animal) with material to make it look lifelike.

(d) to put stuffing into (a chicken, etc.); Sl. **you can s. it** = I don't want to have anything to do with your plan; Sl. **get stuffed!** stop bothering me! **stuffing,** n. (a) savoury mixture put inside a chicken, etc., before cooking. (b) material used to fill cushions/chair seats, etc.

stuffy ['stʌfɪ] adj. (-ier, -iest) (a) (room) full of bad air from lack of ventilation. (b) prudish; old-fashioned. **stuffily,** adv. in a stuffy way. **stuffiness,** n. being stuffy.

stultify ['stʌltɪfaɪ] v. (formal) to make (s.o.) stupid. **stultification** [stʌltɪfɪ'keɪʃn] n. act of stultifying.

stumble ['stʌmbl] 1. n. tripping over; awkward step. 2. v. (a) to trip over sth; to walk awkwardly. (b) **to s. across** = to find by chance. **stumbling block,** n. thing which prevents you doing sth.

stump [stʌmp] 1. n. (a) short piece left after sth has been finished or cut down. (b) one of the three sticks placed in the ground as a target in cricket; **stumps were drawn** = the game of cricket came to an end (temporarily). 2. v. (a) **to s. along** = to walk along heavily. (b) inf. to puzzle. (c) (in cricket) to put (a batsman) out by touching the stumps with the ball when he is not in the hitting area. **stump up,** v. inf. to pay up. **stumpy,** adj. (-ier, -iest) inf. short and squat.

stun [stʌn] v. (**stunned**) to knock out; to shock completely. **stunning,** adj. extraordinary/marvellous.

stung [stʌŋ] v. see **sting.**

stunk [stʌŋk] v. see **stink.**

stunt [stʌnt] 1. n. trick; dangerous action done to attract attention. 2. v. to shorten/to prevent (sth) from growing. **stunt man,** n. person who carries out dangerous actions in films in place of a film star.

stupefy ['stjuːpɪfaɪ] v. (a) to make stupid. (b) to astonish. **stupefaction** [stjuːpɪ'fækʃn] n. astonishment.

stupendous [stjuː'pendəs] adj. extraordinary/magnificent.

stupid ['stjuːpɪd] adj. (a) not very intelligent; with no sense. (b) dull; with a dull mind. **stupidity** [stjuː'pɪdɪtɪ] n. being stupid. **stupidly,** adv. in a stupid way. **stupor** ['stju:pə] *n.* being in a daze; being half senseless.

sturdy ['stɜ:dɪ] *adj.* (**-ier, -iest**) strong and vigorous. **sturdily,** *adv.* in a sturdy way. **sturdiness,** *n.* being sturdy.

sturgeon ['stɜ:dʒən] *n.* (*pl.* **sturgeon**) large edible fish whose eggs are caviare.

stutter ['stʌtə] **1.** *n.* speech defect where you stutter. **2.** *v.* to repeat the same sounds when speaking.

sty [staɪ] *n.* shed in which a pig lives; *see also* **stye.**

stye, sty [staɪ] *n.* infected pimple near the eye.

style [staɪl] **1.** *n.* (*a*) way/manner of doing sth; **in s.** = very grandly. (*b*) fashion. (*c*) elegance. **2.** *v.* (*a*) to name. (*b*) to give a certain style to (hair, etc.). **stylish,** *adj.* elegant/fashionable. **stylishly,** *adv.* in a stylish way. **stylishness,** *n.* fashion/ elegance. **stylist,** *n.* person who gives (*a*) style to sth; **hair s.** = hairdresser. **stylistic** [staɪ'lɪstɪk] *adj.* referring to style in art. **stylistically,** *adv.* referring to style in art. **stylistics,** *n.* study of style of writing. **stylization** [staɪlaɪ-'zeɪʃn] *n.* showing sth in a stylized way. **stylize,** *v.* to show (sth) according to a fixed pattern/not in a natural way.

stylus ['staɪləs] *n.* needle of a record player.

stymie ['staɪmɪ] *v.* to block (a plan).

styptic ['stɪptɪk] *adj.* which stops bleeding; **s. pencil** = small stick of white substance (alum) which stops bleeding from cuts.

suave [swɑ:v] *adj.* (**-er, -est**) extremely polite with very smooth manners (but often with an unpleasant character). **suavely,** *adv.* in a suave way. **suavity,** *n.* being suave.

sub [sʌb] **1.** *n. inf.* (*a*) subsidy; money lent to s.o. until he gets his wages. (*b*) subscription. (*c*) subeditor. (*d*) submarine. **2.** *v.* (**subbed**) *inf.* (*a*) to subedit. (*b*) to act as a substitute. **3.** *prefix* **sub-** = below/under.

subaltern ['sʌbəltən] *n.* junior army officer.

subaqua [sʌb'ækwə] *adj.* referring to underwater sports.

subcommittee ['sʌbkəmɪtɪ] *n.* small committee which is part of a large committee.

subconscious [sʌb'kɒnʃəs] **1.** *adj.* (idea/feeling) which you have in your mind without being aware of it. **2.** *n.* part of your mind which has subconscious ideas or feelings. **subconsciously,** *adv.* in a subconscious way.

subcontinent [sʌb'kɒntɪnənt] *n.* mass of land which is part of a continent.

subcontract 1. *n.* [sʌb'kɒntrækt] agreement between a main contractor and another firm who will do part of the work which the contractor has agreed to do. **2.** *v.* [sʌbkən'trækt] to agree with a firm that they will do part of the work which you have agreed to do. **subcontractor,** *n.* person/company who does work for a contractor.

subcutaneous [sʌbkju'teɪnɪəs] *adj.* (*formal*) under the skin.

subdivide [sʌbdɪ'vaɪd] *v.* to divide (sth) which has already been divided. **subdivision,** *n.* (*a*) division of sth into smaller units. (*b*) *Am.* land which has been divided up into plots for houses.

subdue [sʌb'dju:] *v.* (*a*) to overcome/to conquer. (*b*) to make quiet; to make less bright. **subdued,** *adj.* (*a*) overcome/beaten. (*b*) low (light); **s. colours** = (i) dull colours; (ii) pastel shades.

subedit [sʌb'edɪt] *v.* to correct (what s.o. has written) before it is printed. **subeditor,** *n.* person who subedits.

subheading ['sʌbhedɪŋ] *n.* secondary heading.

subhuman [sʌb'hju:mən] *adj.* less advanced than a human.

subject 1. *n.* ['sʌbdʒɪkt] (*a*) person who belongs to a country. (*b*) word which shows the person or thing which does an action. (*c*) thing which is being discussed. (*d*) thing which is being studied. **2.** *adj.* ['sʌbdʒɪkt] (*a*) belonging to; under the power of (a king). (*b*) **s. to** = (i) likely to be ruled by/to suffer from; (ii) depending on. **3.** *v.* [sʌb'dʒekt] (**to**) to make (sth/s.o.) undergo sth unpleasant. **subjection** [sʌb'dʒekʃn] *n.* being subjected. **subjective** [sʌb'dʒektɪv] *adj.* seen from your own point of view. **subjectively,** *adv.* in a subjective way. **subjectivity,** *n.* being subjective. **subject-matter,** *n.* subject dealt with in a book/TV programme.

subjoin [sʌb'dʒɔɪn] v. to add (sth) at the end.

sub judice [sʌb'dʒuːdɪsɪ] adv. being considered in a court of law (and therefore not to be mentioned in the press).

subjugate ['sʌbdʒugeɪt] v. (formal) to bring (a country) under your control. **subjugation** [sʌbdʒu'geɪʃn] n. act of subjugating.

subjunctive [sʌb'dʒʌŋktɪv] adj. & n. (referring to) a form of a verb used to show doubt/desire, etc.

sublease [sʌb'liːs] 1. n. lease of a building which is already leased. 2. v. to sublet.

sublet [sʌb'let] v. (sublet) to lease (a building/room) which you yourself rent.

sublieutenant [sʌblef'tenənt] n. junior officer in the navy below the rank of lieutenant.

sublimate. 1. n. ['sʌblɪmət] substance formed when a substance is changed from solid to vapour. 2. v. ['sʌblɪmeɪt] (a) to change a substance from solid to vapour. (b) (formal) to channel (crude energy/emotion) into an activity which is accepted in society. **sublimation**, n. act of sublimating.

sublime [sə'blaɪm] adj. grand/wonderful; noble; very great. **sublimely**, adv. wonderfully.

subliminal [sʌb'lɪmɪnl] adj. below the consciousness of the senses.

submachine gun [sʌbmə'ʃiːngʌn] n. light machine gun.

submarine [sʌbmə'riːn] 1. adj. which lives/takes place under the water. 2. n. ship which can travel under the water. **submariner** [sʌb'mærɪnə] n. member of the crew of a submarine.

submerge [sʌb'mɜːdʒ] v. (a) to (make sth) go under the surface of the water. **submergence, submersion** [sʌb'mɜːʃn] n. being submerged.

submission [sʌb'mɪʃn] n. (a) state of giving in/giving way. (b) evidence/document/opinion submitted to s.o. **submissive** [sʌb'mɪsɪv] adj. meek (person) who gives in easily. **submissively**, adv. in a submissive way. **submissiveness**, n. meekness. **submit**, v. (a) to give way; to yield. (b) to give (evidence/documents/opinion) for s.o. to examine.

subnormal [sʌb'nɔːml] adj. less than normal; below normal standard.

subordinate 1. adj. & n. [sə'bɔːdnət] (person) who is under the control of s.o. else; **s. clause** = phrase in a sentence which cannot stand alone, and which is dependent on another clause. 2. v. [sə'bɔːdɪneɪt] to put (sth) in a less important position; to consider (sth) is less important. **subordination** [sʌbɔːdɪ'neɪʃn] n. act of subordinating.

suborn [sə'bɔːn] v. (formal) to bribe (s.o.) to commit perjury.

subpoena [sə'piːnə] 1. n. order to come to a court. 2. v. to order (s.o.) to come to a court.

subscribe [sʌb'skraɪb] v. (a) to give money (to a charity). (b) to pay for a series of issues of a magazine/for a series of tickets to concerts, etc. (c) to **s. to an opinion** = to agree with it. **subscriber**, n. person who subscribes to a charity/to a magazine; person who has a telephone; **s. trunk dialling** = telephone system where you can dial long distance or international numbers without asking the operator to do so for you. **subscription** [sʌb'skrɪpʃn] n. (a) money paid to a charity. (b) money paid to a magazine/to a club for a a series of issues/a year's membership.

subsection ['sʌbsekʃn] n. part of a section.

subsequent ['sʌbsɪkwənt] adj. which follows later. **subsequently**, adv. later.

subservient [səb'sɜːvɪənt] adj. weak/always giving in to s.o. **subserviently**, adv. in a subservient way. **subservience**, n. being subservient.

subside [sʌb'saɪd] v. (a) to sink down. (b) to become less violent. **subsidence** [sʌb'saɪdəns] n. sinking down (of the ground).

subsidiary [sʌb'sɪdjərɪ] adj. & n. (thing) which is less important; **s. (company)** = company which is controlled by another.

subsidy ['sʌbsɪdɪ] n. money given to help pay for sth unprofitable. **subsidize** ['sʌbsɪdaɪz] v. to help by giving money.

subsist [sʌb'sɪst] v. to exist (with difficulty). **subsistence** [sʌb'sɪstəns] n. existence; survival with very little money or food; **s. level** = having only just enough to live on.

subsoil ['sʌbsɔɪl] *n.* layer of soil under the topsoil.

subsonic ['sʌbsɒnɪk] *adj.* (plane) which flies at a speed less than the speed of sound.

substance ['sʌbstəns] *n.* (*a*) matter/material of which things are made. (*b*) basis (of an argument/report). (*c*) **a man of s.** = a wealthy man. **substantial** [sʌb'stænʃl] *adj.* (*a*) large/important. (*b*) large/solid. **substantially**, *adv.* mostly/mainly. **substantiate** [sʌb'stænʃɪeɪt] *v.* to justify; to prove that (sth) is true. **substantiation** [sʌbstænʃɪ'eɪʃn] *n.* act of substantiating.

substandard [sʌb'stændəd] *adj.* second-rate; below the normal standard.

substantive ['sʌbstəntɪv] 1. *adj.* (*a*) real; existing. (*b*) [sʌb'stæntɪv] permanent (military rank). 2. *n.* noun.

substation ['sʌbsteɪʃn] *n.* small local electricity station.

substitute ['sʌbstɪtjuːt] 1. *n.* person/thing taking the place of s.o./sth else. 2. *v.* to put (sth/s.o.) in the place of (s.o./sth). **substitution** [sʌbstɪ'tjuːʃn] *n.* act of substituting.

substratum [sʌb'strɑːtəm] *n.* (*pl.* **-ta**) lower layer of rock/soil.

subsume [səb'sjuːm] *v.* (*formal*) to include in a certain category.

subtenant [sʌb'tenənt] *n.* person to whom a flat/house has been sublet. **subtenancy**, *n.* act of subletting.

subterfuge ['sʌbtəfjuːdʒ] *n.* trick; clever plot.

subterranean [sʌbtə'reɪnɪən] *adj.* under the ground.

subtitle ['sʌbtaɪtl] 1. *n.* (*a*) secondary title on a book. (*b*) **subtitles** = translation of the dialogue of a foreign film which is shown on the bottom of the screen. 2. *v.* to give a subtitle or subtitles to (sth).

subtle ['sʌtl] *adj.* (*a*) difficult to explain; very delicate (scent). (*b*) cunning. **subtlety** ['sʌtltɪ] *n.* thing which is difficult to explain/to describe. **subtly**, *adv.* in a subtle way.

subtopia [sʌb'təʊpɪə] *n. inf.* supposedly ideal suburbs.

subtotal ['sʌbtəʊtl] *n.* total of one section of a set of figures.

subtract [sʌb'trækt] *v.* to take away

(sth from a group). **subtraction** [sʌb'trækʃn] *n.* act of subtracting.

subtropical [sʌb'trɒpɪkl] *adj.* referring to the subtropics. **subtropics**, *n.* areas of the world between the tropics and the temperate zones.

suburb ['sʌbɜːb] *n.* residential area on the outskirts of a town; **the suburbs** = area all round a town where most people live. **suburban** [sə'bɜːbən] *adj.* referring to the suburbs; **s. trains** = trains which go from the town centre to the suburbs. **suburbia** [sə'bɜːbɪə] *n. inf.* the suburbs.

subvention [sʌb'venʃn] *n.* subsidy.

subversion [sʌb'vɜːʃn] *n.* act of subverting. **subversive** [sʌb'vɜːsɪv] *adj.* which tries to subvert. **subvert** [sʌb'vɜːt] *v.* to try to destroy the authority of (the government).

subway ['sʌbweɪ] *n.* (*a*) underground passage. (*b*) *Am.* underground railway system.

subzero [sʌb'zɪərəʊ] *adj.* (temperature) below zero degrees.

succeed [sək'siːd] *v.* (*a*) to follow on; to take the place of. (*b*) to do well; to do what you have been trying to do. **success** [sək'ses] *n.* (*pl.* **-es**) (*a*) doing what you have been trying to do. (*b*) thing/person who does well. **successful**, *adj.* which succeeds. **successfully**, *adv.* in a successful way. **succession** [sək'seʃn] *n.* (*a*) series. (*b*) right to take s.o.'s place; act of taking s.o.'s place. **successive** [sək'sesɪv] *adj.* one after the other. **successively**, *adv.* one after the other. **successor**, *n.* person who takes someone's place.

succinct [sək'sɪŋkt] *adj.* concise/not using many words. **succinctly**, *adv.* in a succinct way.

succour, *Am.* **succor** ['sʌkə] 1. *n.* (*formal*) help. 2. *v.* (*formal*) to help.

succulent ['sʌkjʊlənt] 1. *adj.* juicy/full of juice. 2. *n.* type of plant with thick fleshy leaves and stems (like a cactus).

succumb [sə'kʌm] *v.* (**to**) to give in/to yield; to die (from).

such [sʌtʃ] 1. *adj.* (*a*) like/similar. (*b*) so large/so great. (*c*) of this type. 2. *pron.* thing/person of a certain kind; **s. as it is** = although it is not very good. **such-and-such**, *pron.* a particular/a certain.

suchlike, *adj. pron.* similar (people/things).

suck [sʌk] **1.** *n.* action of drawing in liquid through the mouth. **2.** *v.* (*a*) to pull (liquid) into your mouth. (*b*) to pull in (sth) by suction. **sucker,** *n.* (*a*) shoot which sprouts from a stock, not from the grafted plant. (*b*) thing which sticks on to a surface by suction. (*c*) *inf.* person who is easily tricked. **suckle,** *v.* to give (a child) milk from the breast. **suckling,** *n.* young animal/child still taking milk from its mother. **suck up to,** *v. inf.* to try to make (s.o.) like you (by giving presents/making compliments, etc.). **suction** ['sʌkʃən] *n.* action of sucking in air/liquid, so that sth will be pulled in/will stick to a surface because of the vacuum created; **s. pad** = small concave pad which will stick to a surface if pressed hard; **s. pump** = pump which sucks up liquid when air is pulled out of it.

sucrose ['su:krəuz] *n.* sugar found in plants.

sudden ['sʌdn] *adj.* which happens rapidly/unexpectedly; **all of a s.** = suddenly. **suddenly,** *adv.* rapidly/unexpectedly. **suddenness,** *n.* being rapid/unexpected.

suds [sʌdz] *n. pl.* foam made with soap.

sue [su:] *v.* to take (s.o.) to court/to start a lawsuit against (s.o.).

suede [sweɪd] *n.* soft leather with a rough/furry surface.

suet ['suɪt] *n.* hard fat from an animal, used in cooking. **suety,** *adj.* made of suet; like suet.

suffer ['sʌfə] *v.* (*a*) to feel pain; to be in a difficult situation. (*b*) to put up with. (*c*) to undergo. **sufferance,** *n.* **he is only here on s.** = we allow him to be here but we don't really want him. **sufferer,** *n.* person who suffers. **suffering,** *n.* feeling pain.

suffice [sə'faɪs] *v.* (*formal*) to be enough. **sufficiency** [sə'fɪʃənsɪ] *n.* enough supplies. **sufficient** [sə'fɪʃənt] *adj.* enough. **sufficiently,** *adv.* enough.

suffix ['sʌfɪks] *n.* (*pl.* -es) part added after a word to make another word.

suffocate ['sʌfəkeɪt] *v.* not to be able to breathe; to kill/to die by stopping breathing. **suffocation** [sʌfə'keɪʃn] *n.* not being able to breathe.

suffragan ['sʌfrəgən] *n.* bishop who helps another bishop run a large diocese.

suffrage ['sʌfrɪdʒ] *n.* right to vote in elections. **suffragette,** *n.* (*old*) woman who campaigned for the right to vote.

suffuse [sə'fju:z] *v.* to cover with (colour). **suffusion,** *n.* act of suffusing.

sugar ['ʃʊgə] **1.** *n.* sweet substance made from the juice of a sugar cane or from sugar beet. **2.** *v.* to put sugar into; **to s. the pill** = to make some unpleasant news more acceptable. **sugar beet,** *n.* plant with a large root which when crushed gives sugar. **sugar cane,** *n.* tropical plant whose stalks when crushed give sugar and rum. **sugarcoated,** *adj.* covered with a coating of hard sugar. **sugar daddy,** *n.* old man who entertains young girls, and gives them presents. **sugar soap,** *n.* soft material for cleaning paintwork. **sugary,** *adj.* with too much sugar.

suggest [sə'dʒest] *v.* (*a*) to propose (an idea). (*b*) to hint/to insinuate. **suggestible,** *adj.* (person) who can easily be influenced. **suggestion,** *n.* proposal. **suggestive,** *adj.* (*a*) which suggests. (*b*) which gives an impression of indecency. **suggestively,** *adv.* in a suggestive way.

suicide ['suɪsaɪd] *n.* (*a*) killing yourself; **to commit s.** = to kill yourself. (*b*) person who has killed himself. **suicidal** [suɪ'saɪdl] *adj.* referring to suicide.

suit [su:t] **1.** *n.* (*a*) two or three pieces of clothing made of the same cloth (jacket/waistcoat and trousers or skirt). (*b*) lawsuit/court case. (*c*) one of the four groups with the same symbol in a pack of cards; **to follow s.** = to do what s.o. else has done. **2.** *v.* (*a*) to fit together. (*b*) to be completely acceptable/convenient; **s. yourself** = do what you want. (*c*) to fit s.o.'s appearance. **suitability** [su:tə'bɪlɪtɪ] *n.* being suitable. **suitable** ['su:təbl] *adj.* convenient; (thing) which fits. **suitably,** *adv.* in a convenient/fitting way. **suitcase,** *n.* box with a handle for carrying clothes in when you are travelling. **suitor,** *n.* person who wants to marry a certain girl.

suite [swi:t] *n.* (*a*) series of rooms/pieces

of furniture which make a set. (*b*) group of people accompanying a king, queen or other important person. (*c*) several short pieces of music which are played together as a group. (*d*) **en s.** ['ɒn'swi:t] = attached.

sulfa ['sʌlfə] *n. Am. see* **sulpha.**

sulfur ['sʌlfə] *n. Am. see* **sulphur.**

sulk [sʌlk] **1.** *n.* **sulks** = being grumpy/ annoyed in silence. **2.** *v.* to show you are annoyed by not saying anything. **sulkily**, *adv.* in a sulky way. **sulkiness**, *n.* being sulky. **sulky**, *adj.* bad-tempered/grumpy.

sullen ['sʌln] *adj.* silently angry; unpleasant. **sullenly**, *adv.* in a sullen way.

sully ['sʌlɪ] *v.* (*formal*) to dirty (a reputation).

sulpha, *Am.* **sulfa** ['sʌlfə] *n.* **s. drug** = sulphonamide.

sulphur, *Am.* **sulfur** ['sʌlfə] *n.* (*element:* S) solid substance, usu. found as a yellow powder. **sulphate**, *n.* salt formed from sulphuric acid. **sulphide**, *n.* combination of sulphur with another substance. **sulphonamide**, *n.* drug used against bacteria. **sulphuric acid** [sʌl'fjʊərɪk'æsɪd] *n.* very strong acid containing sulphur. **sulphurous** ['sʌlfərəs] *adj.* like sulphur.

sultan ['sʌltən] *n.* Muslim prince. **sultana** [sʌl'tɑːnə] *n.* (*a*) wife of a sultan. (*b*) type of seedless raisin. **sultanate**, *n.* country ruled by a sultan.

sultry ['sʌltrɪ] *adj.* (**-ier, -iest**) (*a*) hot/ heavy (weather). (*b*) attractive in a dark way; passionate. **sultriness**, *n.* being sultry.

sum [sʌm] **1.** *n.* (*a*) total of numbers added together; **the s. total** = the total of several sums added together. (*b*) quantity of money. (*c*) arithmetic problem. **2.** *v.* (**summed**) **to s. up** = to make a summary/to tell briefly what has happened. **summarize** ['sʌmərɑɪz] *v.* to make a brief account of (sth). **summary. 1.** *n.* short account of what has happened; short version of sth longer. **2.** *adj.* (*a*) brief. (*b*) done quickly without wasting too much time. **summarily**, *adv.* quickly. **summing-up**, *n.* summary of evidence made by a judge at the end of a trial.

summer ['sʌmə] *n.* season of the year following spring, when plants begin to make fruit; the warmest season; **s. holidays** = main/longest holidays during a school year; **s. school** = classes held at a school/university during the summer holiday. **summerhouse**, *n.* small house in a garden where you can sit in the summer. **summertime**, *n.* summer season. **summer time**, *n.* system of altering the clocks during the summer to take advantage of the longer period of daylight. **summery**, *adj.* like the summer.

summit ['sʌmɪt] *n.* (*a*) top (of a mountain). (*b*) **s. (meeting)** = meeting of heads of government to discuss international problems. **summitry**, *n. inf.* diplomacy carried on at summit meetings.

summon ['sʌmən] *v.* (*a*) to call. (*b*) **to s. up courage** = to get together courage to do sth. **summons. 1.** *n.* (*a*) official demand to go to see s.o. (*b*) official legal order to appear in court. **2.** *v.* to order (s.o.) to appear in court.

sump [sʌmp] *n.* (*a*) part of a car engine containing the oil. (*b*) pit in which water collects.

sumptuous ['sʌmtʃʊəs] *adj.* very luxurious/splendid. **sumptuously**, *adv.* in a sumptuous way.

sun [sʌn] **1.** *n.* (*a*) very hot body around which the earth revolves and which provides heat and daylight. (*b*) light from the sun. **2.** *v.* (**sunned**) **s. yourself** = to sit in the sun. **sunbathe**, *v.* to lie in the sun to get your body brown. **sunbeam**, *n.* ray of sunlight. **sunburn**, *n.* painful inflammation of the skin caused by being in the sun for too long. **sunburnt**, *adj.* made brown or red by the sun. **sundeck**, *n.* top deck of a passenger ship where people can sit in the sun. **sundial**, *n.* round clock face with a central pointer whose shadow points to the time when the sun shines on it. **sundown**, *n.* moment when the sun goes down. **sundrenched**, *adj.* (always) very sunny. **sunflower**, *n.* very large yellow flower on a tall stem; **s. oil** = oil made from its seeds. **sunglasses**, *n.* dark glasses to protect your eyes from the sun. **sunlamp**, *n.* lamp which gives off ultraviolet rays like the sun, used to give a suntan indoors. **sunless**, *adj.* with no sun. **sunlight**, *n.* light from the sun. **sunlit**, *adj.* lit by the sun. **sunnily**, *adv.* in a happy way. **sunny**, adj. (**-ier**, **-iest**) full of sunlight; happy (character); *Am. inf.* **s. side up** = (egg) fried without being turned over. **sunrise**, *n.* time at which the sun rises. **sunroof**, *n.* part of a roof of a car which slides open. **sunset**, *n.* time when the sun goes down behind the horizon; colourful sky as the sun goes down. **sunshade**, *n.* light bright-coloured umbrella to protect from the sun. **sunshine**, *n.* light from the sun. **sunshine roof**, *n.* sunroof. **sunspot**, *n.* dark spot which appears on the surface of the sun. **sunstroke**, *n.* illness caused by being too much in the sunlight. **suntan**, *n.* brown colour of the skin caused by the sun. **suntanned**, *adj.* with a tan made brown by the sun. **suntrap**, *n.* very sunny place. **sun-up**, *n.* sunrise.

sundae ['sʌndɪ] *n.* dessert of ice cream, cream and fruit.

Sunday ['sʌndɪ] *n.* last day of the week; day between Saturday and Monday; **S. best** = best clothes; **S. school** = school for teaching religion to children, usu. held on a Sunday.

sunder ['sʌndə] *v.* (*formal*) to split into parts.

sundew ['sʌndjuː] *n.* wild plant which catches insects for food.

sundry ['sʌndrɪ] **1.** *adj.* various. **2.** *n.* (*a*) **all and s.** = everyone. (*b*) **sundries** = various small articles/small items on a list.

sung [sʌŋ] *v. see* **sing**.

sunk [sʌŋk] *adj.* ruined/lost; *see also* **sink**. **sunken**, *adj.* (*a*) which is beneath the surface. (*b*) lower than the surrounding area.

sup [sʌp] **1.** *n.* mouthful of liquid. **2.** *v.* (**supped**) to drink in small mouthfuls.

super ['suːpə] **1.** *adj. inf.* wonderful. **2.** *n. inf.* (*a*) police superintendent. (*b*) extra actor. **3.** **super-** *prefix meaning* more/greater/of better quality.

superabundance [suːpərə'bʌndəns] *n.* great abundance; very large quantity. **superabundant**, *adj.* very abundant/in very large quantities.

superannuated [suːpə'rænjʊeɪtɪd] *adj.* too old to work properly; old-fashioned. **superannuation** [suːpərænjʊ-'eɪʃn] *n.* (*a*) retirement of workers when they reach a certain age. (*b*) pension paid to s.o. who has retired.

superb [suː'pɜːb] *adj.* marvellous/wonderful. **superbly**, *adv.* wonderfully.

supercharged ['suːpətʃɑːdʒd] *adj.* (motor/person) with much increased energy. **supercharger**, *n.* apparatus on a car engine for increasing the power.

supercilious [suːpə'sɪlɪəs] *adj.* looking down on others; considering others as inferior. **superciliously**, *adv.* in a supercilious way. **superciliousness**, *n.* being supercilious.

superficial [suːpə'fɪʃl] *adj.* touching only the top surface; not going deeply beneath the surface. **superficiality** [suːpəfɪʃɪ'ælɪtɪ] *n.* being superficial. **superficially**, *adv.* in a superficial way.

superfine [suːpə'faɪn] *adj.* very fine.

superfluous [suː'pɜːflʊəs] *adj.* which is more than is needed. **superfluity** [suːpə'fluːɪtɪ] *n.* being superfluous/more than is needed; excess. **superfluously**, *adv.* in a superfluous way.

superhighway [suːpə'haɪweɪ] *n. Am.* important motorway.

superhuman [suːpə'hjuːmən] *adj.* more than is normal in human beings.

superimpose [suːpərɪm'pəʊz] *v.* to place on top of sth.

superintend [suːpərɪn'tend] *v.* to be in charge. **superintendent**, *n.* (*a*) person in charge. (*b*) senior police officer.

superior [suː'pɪərɪə] **1.** *adj.* (*a*) of better quality; of a larger quality. (*b*) higher in rank. (*c*) thinking yourself to be better than others. **2.** *n.* (*a*) person of higher rank. (*b*) leader of a religious community. **superiority** [suːpɪərɪ'ɒrɪtɪ] *n.* being superior.

superlative [suː'pɜːlətɪv] **1.** *adj.* of the best quality. **2.** *n.* form of an adjective or adverb showing the highest level of comparison. **superlatively**, *adv.* extremely well.

superman ['suːpəmæn] *n.* (*pl.* **-men**) man who has superhuman strength/power/ability.

supermarket ['suːpəmɑːkɪt] *n.* large store selling mainly food, where you serve yourself.

supernatural [su:pə'nætʃərəl] *adj.* & *n.* (things) which happen not in accordance with the laws of nature. **supernaturally,** *adv.* in a supernatural way.

supernova ['su:pənəuvə] *n.* large star which explodes and suddenly appears in the sky.

supernumerary ['su:pə'nju:mərəri] *adj.* & *n.* (person) who is in addition to the usual number of people.

superphosphate [su:pə'fosfeit] *n.* fertilizer based on phosphates.

superpower ['su:pəpauə] *n.* extremely powerful country.

superscription [su:pə'skripʃn] *n.* words written above sth.

supersede [su:pə'si:d] *v.* to take the place of (sth which is older or less efficient).

supersonic [su:pə'sonik] *adj.* faster than the speed of sound.

superstition [su:pə'stiʃn] *n.* belief in magic and the supernatural. **superstitious** [su:pə'stiʃəs] *adj.* believing in magic and the supernatural.

superstore ['su:pəstɔ:] *n.* large supermarket.

superstructure ['su:pəstrʌktʃə] *n.* top structure of a ship; structure built on top of sth else.

supertanker ['su:pətæŋkə] *n.* very large oil tanker.

supertax ['su:pətæks] *n.* tax on very high incomes.

supervene [su:pə'vi:n] *v.* to happen so that things are changed.

supervise ['su:pəvaiz] *v.* to watch over work, etc., to see that it is well done. **supervision** [su:pə'viʒn] *n.* act of supervising. **supervisor** ['su:pəvaizə] *n.* person who supervises. **supervisory** [su:pə'vaizəri] *adj.* as a supervisor.

superwoman ['su:pəwumən] *n.* (*pl.* **-women**) woman who has superhuman strength/power/ability.

supine ['su:pain] *adj.* (*formal*) (*a*) lying flat on your back. (*b*) uninterested/lazy.

supper ['sʌpə] *n.* evening meal.

supplant [sə'plɑ:nt] *v.* to take (s.o.'s) place by cunning manœuvres.

supple ['sʌpl] *adj.* flexible/which bends easily. **suppleness,** *n.* being supple. **supplely, supply** ['sʌpli] *adv.* in a supple way.

supplement 1. *n.* ['sʌplimənt] (*a*) thing which is in addition. (*b*) addition to a book; magazine which is part of a newspaper. **2.** *v.* ['sʌpliment] to add to. **supplementary** [sʌpli'mentri] *adj.* in addition; **s. benefits** = payments from the Government to people who have very low incomes.

suppliant ['sʌpliənt] *n.* person who begs for help.

supplicate ['sʌplikeit] *v.* (*formal*) to beg for sth. **supplicant,** *n.* person who begs for help. **supplication** [sʌpli'keiʃn] *n.* (*formal*) begging for help.

supply [sə'plai] **1.** *n.* (*a*) providing sth which is needed; **Supply Bill** = bill which provides money which the government needs. (*b*) stock of sth which has been provided. (*c*) **supplies** = food, etc., which has been stocked/which is going to be provided. **2.** *adj.* **s. teacher** = teacher who replaces a permanent teacher who is away. **3.** *v.* (*a*) to provide (sth which is necessary). (*b*) **to s. s.o. with sth** = to provide sth to s.o. (*c*) to satisfy. **4.** *adv.* ['sʌpli] *see* **supple. supplier** [sə'plaiə] *n.* person/ shop/country which supplies.

support [sə'pɔ:t] **1.** *n.* (*a*) thing which supports. (*b*) moral/financial encouragement. **2.** *v.* (*a*) to hold up. (*b*) to provide/to earn money so that s.o. can live. (*c*) to encourage/to agree with. **supporter,** *n.* person who encourages a plan/a football team, etc. **supporting cast,** *n.* group of actors who play the minor parts in a play.

suppose [sə'pəuz] *v.* (*a*) to assume sth to be correct (even if it is not). (*b*) to think. (*c*) what happens if? **supposedly** [sə'pəuzidli] *adv.* as it is assumed. **supposing,** *conj.* what happens if? **supposition** [sʌpə'ziʃn] *n.* thing which is assumed; guess.

suppository [sə'pozitəri] *n.* tablet of medicinal material which is put into the rectum or vagina where it melts.

suppress [sə'pres] *v.* (*a*) to crush; to stop (a revolution). (*b*) to forbid the publication of (sth). (*c*) to hide (feelings). **suppression** [sə'preʃn] *n.* act of suppressing. **suppressor,** *n.* machine which prevents an electric appliance from interfering with radio/ TV signals.

suppurate ['sʌpjʊreɪt] v. (formal) to produce pus.

supra- ['suːprə] prefix. beyond.

supranational [suːprə'næʃnl] adj. over/beyond the interests of a single nation or several nations.

supreme [sʊ'priːm] adj. highest; total (indifference). **supremely,** adv. totally/completely. **supremacy** [sʊ'preməsɪ] n. highest power. **supremo** [sʊ'priːməʊ] n. inf. person in charge of many organizations; officer in charge of several armies.

surcharge 1. n. ['sɜːtʃɑːdʒ] extra charge. 2. v. [sɜː'tʃɑːdʒ] to charge an extra amount.

surd [sɜːd] n. (in mathematics) quantity (like a root) which cannot be expressed as a whole number.

sure [ʃɔː, 'ʃuːə] 1. adj. (-er, -est) (a) without any doubt; certain; **for s.** = for certain. (b) reliable. (c) **s. of yourself** = confident. 2. adv. certainly. **sure-fire,** adj. Am. inf. absolutely certain. **sure-footed,** adj. able to walk on slippery rocks/narrow ledges without slipping. **surely,** adv. (a) carefully. (b) naturally/of course. **sureness,** n. being sure. **surety,** n. (a) person who takes the responsibility that s.o. will do sth. (b) money paid as a guarantee that s.o. will appear in court.

surf [sɜːf] 1. n. line of breaking waves along a shore; foam from breaking waves. 2. v. to ride on breaking waves on a board. **surfboard,** n. board which you stand on to ride on breaking waves. **surfboat,** n. light boat for riding on surf. **surfer,** n. person who surfs. **surfing, surf-riding,** n. riding on breaking waves as a sport.

surface ['sɜːfəs] 1. n. top layer; outside of sth. 2. v. (a) to come up from under/to appear on the top of water, etc. (b) to cover (a road, etc.) with a hard substance. **surface mail,** n. post which travels by van/train/ship, etc., and not by air.

surfeit ['sɜːfɪt] 1. n. (formal) too much. 2. v. to feed (s.o.) too much.

surge [sɜːdʒ] 1. n. (a) rising up of water into waves. (b) sudden increase. 2. v. (a) to rise up. (b) move (forward) in a mass.

surgeon ['sɜːdʒən] n. doctor who carries out operations; **house s.** = young surgeon in a hospital; **dental s.** = dentist. **surgery,** n. (a) treatment of disease or wounds by cutting open part of the body. (b) doctor's/dentist's consulting room. (c) consultation given by a member of parliament to any of his constituents. **surgical** ['sɜːdʒɪkl] adj. referring to surgery; **s. gloves** = gloves worn by a surgeon; **s. spirit** = pure alcohol used to rub on the skin. **surgically,** adv. in a surgical way.

surly ['sɜːlɪ] adj. (-ier, -iest) grumpy/sullen. **surliness,** n. being surly.

surmise [sə'maɪz] 1. n. guess/supposition. 2. v. to guess.

surmount [sɜː'maʊnt] v. (a) to overcome (an obstacle). (b) to be on top of (sth). **surmountable,** adj. which can be surmounted.

surname ['sɜːneɪm] n. family name.

surpass [sə'pɑːs] v. to do better than.

surplice ['sɜːpləs] n. long white robe worn by priests/choirboys.

surplus ['sɜːpləs] n. & n. (pl. -es) extra (stock); (material) left over.

surprise [sə'praɪz] 1. n. shock caused by sth unexpected. 2. v. (a) to give (s.o.) a surprise/an unexpected shock. (b) to catch (s.o.) unexpectedly. **surprising,** adj. astonishing/unusual. **surprisingly,** adv. in an unusual way.

surrealism [sə'rɪəlɪzm] n. 20th century art movement in which an artist depicts realistic objects in an unreal environment, emphasizing the meaning he sees beyond reality. **surrealist,** adj. & n. (artist) following the principles of surrealism. **surrealistic,** adj. very strange/totally unreal.

surrender [sə'rendə] 1. n. (a) giving in (to an enemy). (b) giving up (of goods); giving up (of an insurance policy); **s. value** = amount of money you will receive if you end an insurance before the normal completion date. 2. v. (a) to give in (**to** an enemy). (b) to give up (a ticket/insurance policy, etc.).

surreptitious [sʌrəp'tɪʃəs] adj. done in secret. **surreptitiously,** adv. in secret.

surrogate ['sʌrəgɪt] n. deputy/person who acts in place of s.o.

surround [sə'raʊnd] 1. n. border; edge; bare floor space round a carpet. 2. v. to

be/to come all round (sth). surrounding, *adj.* which surrounds. **surroundings,** *n.pl.* area around a place/person.

surtax ['sɜːtæks] *n.* extra tax on high incomes.

surveillance [sɜː'veɪləns] *n.* strict watch.

survey 1. *n.* ['sɜːveɪ] (*a*) general account. (*b*) careful examination of a building to see if it is in good condition. (*c*) taking measurements of land heights/distances/roads/buildings, etc., to produce accurate plans or maps. **2.** *v.* [sə'veɪ] (*a*) to look at/to talk about (sth) in a general way. (*b*) to make a survey of (a building). (*c*) to measure (land) in order to produce an accurate plan or map. **surveyor,** *n.* person who surveys buildings or measures land.

survive [sə'vaɪv] *v.* (*a*) to continue to live (after an accident, etc.). (*b*) to live longer than (s.o.). **survival,** *n.* continuing to live. **survivor,** *n.* person who survives.

susceptible [sə'septɪbl] *adj.* (*a*) **s. of proof** = which can be proved; **s. to** = likely to catch (a disease). (*b*) easily upset. **susceptibility** [səseptə'bɪlɪtɪ] *n.* being susceptible.

suspect 1. *adj. & n.* ['sʌspekt] (person) who is thought to have committed a crime; (food) which might be poisonous. **2.** *v.* [sə'spekt] (*a*) **to s. s.o. of** = to think that (s.o.) may have committed a crime. (*b*) to guess/to think.

suspend [sə'spend] *v.* (*a*) to hang; to make (sth) hang in a liquid, (*b*) to stop (sth) for a time. (*c*) to take (sth) away as a punishment; to stop (s.o.) from doing sth. **suspenders,** *n.pl.* (*a*) elastic straps to hold up stockings or socks. (*b*) *Am.* braces. **suspense,** *n.* impatient wait for sth to happen or for a decision to be reached. **suspension,** *n.* (*a*) act of suspending; being suspended; **s. bridge** = one which hangs by ropes/chains, etc., from tall towers. (*b*) system of springs, etc., in a car which attaches the chassis to the axles.

suspicion [sə'spɪʃn] *n.* (*a*) feeling that sth is wrong or that s.o. has committed a crime. (*b*) guess; general feeling. (*c*) slight hint. **suspicious,** *adj.* which can be suspected. **suspiciously,** *adv.* (*a*) in

a suspicious way. (*b*) as if suspecting sth.

suss [sʌs] **1.** *n. Sl.* suspicion. **2.** *v. Sl.* to suspect; **to s. s.o. out** = to find out.

sustain [sə'steɪn] *v.* (*a*) to keep (sth) going. (*b*) to suffer. (*c*) to support. **sustained,** *adj.* which continues for a long time. **sustaining,** *adj.* which will support or nourish.

sustenance ['sʌstənəns] *n.* (*a*) food. (*b*) **means of s.** = way of keeping alive/of keeping strong.

suture ['suːtʃə] *n.* thread used for stitching wounds together; stitching (of a wound); stitch made to hold a wound together.

suzerain ['suːzəreɪn] *n.* (*formal*) overlord. **suzerainty,** *n.* rule over (a state).

svelte [svelt] *adj.* slim and graceful.

swab [swɒb] **1.** *n.* (*a*) cloth for wiping floors clear of water. (*b*) piece of material (like cottonwool) used for cleaning a wound or for taking samples of infection for analysis. (*c*) sample of infection taken for analysis. **2.** *v.* (**swabbed**) to clean (a floor) with a swab.

swaddle ['swɒdl] *v.* (*old*) to wrap (a baby) in pieces of cloth.

swag [swæg] *n. inf.* (*a*) stolen goods (esp. jewellery/silver, etc.). (*b*) (in Australia) bundle of belongings. **swagman,** *n.* (in Australia) tramp.

swagger ['swægə] **1.** *n.* proud way of walking. **2.** *v.* to walk in a proud way, swinging your body.

swallow ['swɒləʊ] **1.** *n.* (*a*) mouthful of liquid which you drink in one movement; act of swallowing. (*b*) common fast-flying bird with long wings and tail. **2.** *v.* (*a*) to make (food/liquid) pass down your throat from your mouth to the stomach. (*b*) to accept (a story) as true. **swallow dive,** *n.* dive where the arms are stretched out sideways at the start. **swallow hole,** *n.* cave formed in limestone rock. **swallow up,** *v.* to make (sth) disappear inside.

swam [swæm] *v. see* **swim.**

swamp [swɒmp] **1.** *n.* area of wet soft land. **2.** *v.* to fill (a boat) with water; **swamped with** = having so much (work, etc.) that it is impossible to deal with. **swampy,** *adj.* (**-ier, -iest**) wet (land) like a marsh.

swan [swɒn] 1. *n*. large white water bird with a long curved neck. 2. *v*. (**swanned**) *inf*. to travel about in a leisurely way. **swan song**, *n*. last performance by an artist (esp. a singer); last work by a writer.

swank [swæŋk] 1. *n. inf.* (*a*) showing off. (*b*) person who shows off. 2. *v. inf.* to show off; to show that you think a lot of yourself. **swanky**, *adj. inf.* pretentious; (acting) in a swanking way.

swap, swop [swɒp] 1. *n. inf.* (*a*) exchange. (*b*) **swaps** = stamps/coins, etc., which a collector has ready to exchange for others. 2. *v.* (**swapped/swopped**) *inf.* to exchange (sth **for** sth).

sward [swɑːd] *n.* soft grassy surface.

swarm [swɔːm] 1. *n.* large group of insects, etc., flying about together. 2. *v.* (*a*) to move about in a large group. (*b*) (**up**) to climb using your hands and feet like a monkey.

swarthy ['swɔːðɪ] *adj.* (**-ier, -iest**) with a dark complexion.

swashbuckling ['swɒʃbʌklɪŋ] *adj.* daring; living dangerously.

swastika ['swɒstɪkə] *n.* ancient sign, shaped like a cross with each arm bent at right angles.

swat [swɒt] 1. *n.* flat disc on a handle for killing flies, etc. 2. *v.* (**swatted**) to hit and kill (a fly, etc.). **swatter,** *n.* swat.

swatch [swɒtʃ] *n.* (*pl.* **-es**) small sample of fabric.

swath [swɒθ] *n.* strip cut by a scythe/harvester/mower.

swathe [sweɪð] *v.* to wrap up.

sway [sweɪ] 1. *n.* (*a*) power. (*b*) act of swaying. 2. *v.* (*a*) to (cause to) move from side to side. (*b*) to influence.

swear [sweə] *v.* (**swore** [swɔː]; **sworn** [swɔːn]) (*a*) to promise solemnly. (*b*) to (make s.o.) take an oath. (*c*) to curse. (*d*) to s. **by** = to believe completely or enthusiastically in. **swear word,** *n.* word used as a curse or to show annoyance.

sweat [swet] 1. *n.* drops of liquid which come through your skin when you are hot. 2. *v.* to produce sweat; **we'll have to s. it out** = keep on with it, even if it is unpleasant/difficult. **sweat band,** *n.* band of towelling worn round your head or wrist to stop sweat trickling down. **sweated,** *adj.* s. **labour** = (i)

people who work hard for little money; (ii) hard work which is very badly paid. **sweater,** *n.* pullover. **sweatshirt,** *n.* light long-sleeved cotton shirt with no collar or buttons. **sweat shop,** *n.* factory using sweated labour. **sweaty,** *adj.* damp with sweat.

Swede [swiːd] *n.* (*a*) person from Sweden. (*b*) **swede** = type of root vegetable like a yellow turnip. **Swedish.** 1. *adj.* referring to Sweden. 2. *n.* language spoken in Sweden.

sweep [swiːp] 1. *n.* (*a*) act of sweeping (with a brush); act of swinging (a sword or your hand); **to make a clean s.** = to clear sth away completely/to win completely. (*b*) wide stretch (of water, etc.). (*c*) person who cleans chimneys. (*d*) sweepstake. 2. *v.* (**swept** [swept]) (*a*) to clean with a brush; **to s. the board** = to win completely. (*b*) to clear up (dust/snow, etc.) with a brush. (*c*) to make a wide movement. (*d*) to move rapidly; to carry (sth) along rapidly. **sweeper,** *n.* person/machine that sweeps. **sweeping,** *adj.* wide-ranging/far-reaching; s. **statement** = statement which is partly true but too general. **sweepstake,** *n.* form of gambling on a horserace where the holders of the winning tickets take all the money which has been bet.

sweet [swiːt] 1. *adj.* (**-er, -est**) (*a*) tasting like sugar; not sour; s. **tooth** = liking for sweet things. (*b*) pleasant; s. **pea** = pea with scented flowers. (*c*) fresh (air). 2. *n.* (*a*) small piece of sweet food, made with sugar or chocolate. (*b*) sweet course at the end of a meal. **sweetbread,** *n.* pancreas of an animal eaten as food. **sweet corn,** *n.* maize, eaten as food. **sweeten,** *v.* (*a*) to make sweet. (*b*) *inf.* to give (s.o.) a bribe to make sure he is favourable to you. **sweetener,** *n.* (*a*) thing/material which sweetens. (*b*) *inf.* bribe. **sweetening,** *n.* act of making sweet; substance which makes sweet. **sweetheart,** *n.* darling; boy/girl friend. **sweetie,** *n. inf.* (*a*) sweet. (*b*) darling. **sweetly,** *adv.* in a sweet way. **sweetmeat,** *n.* (*old*) sweet. **sweetness,** *n.* being sweet. **sweet potato,** *n.* yam. **sweetshop,** *n.* shop which sells sweets and chocolates.

sweet william, *n.* type of common scented garden flower.

swell [swel] **1.** *n.* (*a*) rising movement of the sea. (*b*) increasing loudness. **2.** *adj. Am.* fine. **3.** *v.* (**swollen/swelled**) (*a*) to increase. (*b*) **to s.** (**up**) = to become larger/to increase in size. (*c*) **to s.** (**out**) = to become/to make (sails) fully rounded. **swelling,** *n.* part of the body which has swollen up.

swelter ['sweltə] *v.* to be very hot. **sweltering,** *adj.* very hot.

swept [swept] *v. see* **sweep.**

swerve [swɜ:v] **1.** *n.* movement to the side. **2.** *v.* to move to one side.

swidden ['swɪdən] *n.* type of farming, where forest is cut down to create space for growing crops.

swift [swɪft] **1.** *adj.* (**-er, -est**) fast. **2.** *n.* fast-flying bird like a swallow but with shorter wings and tail. **swiftly,** *adv.* fast. **swiftness,** *n.* rapidity.

swig [swɪg] **1.** *n. inf.* large mouthful of liquid. **2.** *v.* (**swigged**) *inf.* to drink in large mouthfuls.

swill [swɪl] **1.** *n.* (*a*) washing a floor with a lot of water. (*b*) food for pigs. **2.** *v.* (*a*) to wash a floor with a lot of water. (*b*) *inf.* to drink a lot of alcohol.

swim [swɪm] **1.** *n.* act of moving in the water using arms/legs/flippers, etc.; **in the s.** = up to date/knowing what's going on. **2.** *v.* (**swam; swum**) (*a*) to move in water using arms, legs, flippers, etc. (*b*) to cross (a river, etc.) by swimming. (*c*) to be covered with liquid. (*d*) (*of head, room*) to seem to turn. **swimmer,** *n.* person who swims. **swimming,** *n.* action of swimming; **s. trunks** = shorts worn for swimming. **swimming bath,** *n.* large public pool for swimming. **swimmingly,** *adv. inf.* very well. **swimming pool,** *n.* pool for swimming. **swimsuit,** *n.* bathing costume.

swindle ['swɪndl] **1.** *n.* trick to get money from s.o. **2.** *v.* to get money from (s.o.) by a trick. **swindler,** *n.* person who swindles s.o.

swine [swaɪn] *n.* (*no pl.*) (*a*) pig. (*b*) *inf.* unpleasant person. **swine fever,** *n.* infectious disease of pigs. **swineherd,** *n.* (*old*) person who looks after pigs.

swing [swɪŋ] **1.** *n.* (*a*) movement from side to side or forwards and backwards; movement of voters to vote for a certain party. (*b*) **to go with a s.** = (i) to have a regular beat; (ii) to go very well; **in full s.** = going very well. (*c*) seat on the end of two ropes which you can sit on and swing backwards and forwards. **2.** *v.* (**swung** [swʌŋ]) (*a*) to move from side to side or forwards and backwards. (*b*) to make (sth) turn round; to turn round. (*c*) to move in a rhythmic way with a regular motion. **swing bridge,** *n.* bridge which can be made to turn to allow ships to pass underneath. **swing door,** *n.* door which is not attached with a catch, and which opens when you push it. **swinger,** *n.* person who is fashionably modern. **swinging,** **1.** *n.* action of moving backwards and forwards. **2.** *adj.* (*a*) moving backwards and forwards. (*b*) *inf.* lively; fashionably modern. **swing-wing,** *adj.* (aircraft) with adjustable wings.

swingeing ['swɪndʒɪŋ] *adj.* harsh (tax); severe (blow, measure).

swipe [swaɪp] **1.** *n. inf.* sweeping hit/blow. **2.** *v.* (*a*) *inf.* to hit (s.o.) with a sweeping blow. (*b*) *Sl.* to steal.

swirl [swɜ:l] **1.** *n.* whirling/twisting movement. **2.** *v.* to move with a whirling/twisting motion.

swish [swɪʃ] **1.** *adj. inf.* smart. **2.** *n.* soft rustle (of a dress/of dead leaves); whistle (of a stick). **3.** *v.* to make a whistling noise with a whip/stick.

Swiss [swɪs] **1.** *adj.* (*a*) referring to Switzerland. (*b*) **swiss roll** = type of thin sponge cake rolled up with cream or jam as a filling. **2.** *n.* (*pl.* **Swiss**) person from Switzerland.

switch [swɪtʃ] **1.** *n.* (*pl.* **-es**) (*a*) apparatus for starting or stopping an electric current. (*b*) sudden change. (*c*) whip made of a thin stick. (*d*) lock of hair tied at one end. **2.** *v.* (*a*) to send (a train, etc.) in a different direction; to do sth quite different. (*b*) to hit with a switch. **switchback,** *n.* (*a*) fairground railway which goes up and down steep slopes. (*b*) road or railway which goes up and down hills. **switchboard,** *n.* central telephone panel where calls can be transferred to different rooms. **switch off,** *v.* to stop an electric current; *inf.* to stop listening to what s.o. is saying. **switch on,** *v.* to start an electric current flowing; *inf.* **switched on** = up to date/ knowing all that is happening. **switch over to,** *v.* to change to sth quite different.

swivel ['swɪvl] **1.** *n.* joint between two parts which enables either part to turn without the other. **2.** *v.* **(swivelled)** to turn around; to pivot. **swivel chair,** *n.* chair which pivots, so that the seat can turn while the legs stay stationary.

swizzle ['swɪzl] *n. inf.* swindle/trick. **swizzlestick,** *n.* small stick put into a glass of fizzy drink to make it less fizzy.

swollen ['swəʊlən] *adj.* blown up; increased in size; **swollen-headed** = (person) who has a high opinion of himself; *see also* **swell.**

swoon [swu:n] *v.* to faint.

swoop [swu:p] **1.** *n.* coming rapidly down from a height to attack; sudden attack; **at one fell s.** = in a sudden move/ all at once. **2.** *v.* to come down rapidly to attack; to attack suddenly.

swop [swɒp] *n. & v. see* **swap.**

sword [sɔːd] *n.* weapon with a long sharp blade held by a handle; **to cross swords with** = to get into an argument with. **swordfish,** *n.* fish with a long pointed upper jaw like a sword. **swordsman,** *n.* (*pl.* **-men**) person who fights well with a sword. **swordstick,** *n.* hollow walking stick containing a long sharp blade.

swore [swɔː] *v. see* **swear.**

sworn [swɔːn] *adj.* **s. enemies** = total enemies; *see also* **swear.**

swot [swɒt] **1.** *n. Sl.* (*a*) hard school work. (*b*) person who studies hard. **2.** *v.* **(swotted)** *Sl.* to study hard.

swum [swʌm] *v. see* **swim.**

swung [swʌŋ] *v. see* **swing.**

sybarite ['sɪbəraɪt] *n.* person who enjoys luxury. **sybaritic** [sɪbə'rɪtɪk] *adj.* very comfortable and luxurious.

sycamore ['sɪkəmɔː] *n.* common deciduous tree with very large leaves.

sycophant ['sɪkəfænt] *n.* person who flatters s.o. in power. **sycophantic** [sɪkə'fæntɪk] *adj.* which flatters excessively.

syllable ['sɪləbl] *n.* unit of sound which forms a whole word or part of a word. **syllabic** [sɪ'læbɪk] *adj.* referring to a syllable.

syllabub ['sɪləbʌb] *n.* sweet food made of cream whipped with wine.

syllabus ['sɪləbəs] *n.* (*pl.* **-es**) list of subjects to be studied.

syllogism ['sɪlədʒɪzəm] *n.* logical reasoning where a conclusion is reached from two statements.

sylph [sɪlf] *n.* thin girl. **sylphlike,** *adj.* very slim.

sylvan ['sɪlvən] *adj.* (*formal*) referring to woods.

symbiosis [sɪmbɪ'əʊsɪs] *n.* state where two living organisms live close together and depend on each other to a certain extent. **symbiotic** [sɪmbaɪ'ɒtɪk] *adj.* referring to symbiosis.

symbol ['sɪmbl] *n.* sign/letter/picture/ object which represents sth/which is a short way of indicating sth. **symbolic(al)** [sɪm'bɒlɪk(l)] *adj.* which acts as a symbol. **symbolically,** *adv.* used as a symbol. **symbolism,** *n.* (*a*) movement in literature and art which used symbols to express emotion, etc. (*b*) using symbols to express emotion, etc. **symbolist,** *adj. & n.* (follower) of symbolism. **symbolize** ['sɪmbəlaɪz] *v.* to represent (sth) by a symbol; to be a symbol for (sth).

symmetry ['sɪmətrɪ] *n.* state where two sides of sth are exactly similar. **symmetrical** [sɪ'metrɪkl] *adj.* referring to symmetry.

sympathy ['sɪmpəθɪ] *n.* (*a*) feeling of pity or sorrow because s.o. else has problems. (*b*) common feeling; sharing ideas. **sympathetic** [sɪmpə'θetɪk] *adj.* showing sympathy. **sympathetically,** *adv.* in a sympathetic way. **sympathize,** *v.* (**with**) (*a*) to show sympathy to (s.o. in trouble). (*b*) to approve; to agree. **sympathizer,** *n.* person who sympathizes with s.o.'s political views.

symphony ['sɪmfənɪ] *n.* piece of music in several parts for a full orchestra. **symphonic** [sɪm'fɒnɪk] *adj.* referring to a symphony.

symposium [sɪm'pəʊzɪəm] *n.* (*pl.* **-ia**) organized meeting to discuss a specific subject; collection of articles written on a specific subject.

symptom ['sɪmptəm] *n.* thing which shows visibly that feelings exist/that changes are taking place. **symptomatic** [sɪmptə'mætɪk] *adj.* (**of**) which shows visibly that changes are taking place or that feelings exist.

synagogue ['smagng] *n.* building where Jews worship.

synapse ['smæps] *n.* point in the nervous system where neurones join.

sync [sɪŋk] *n. inf.* synchronization; **out of s.** = not synchronized.

synchromesh ['sɪŋkrəmeʃ] *n.* type of gear system where the gears revolve at the same speeds before being engaged.

synchronize ['sɪŋkrənaɪz] *v.* to adjust (watches) to the same time; to arrange (things) so that they happen at the same time. **synchronization** [sɪŋkrənaɪ'zeɪʃn] *n.* act of synchronizing.

syncopate ['sɪŋkəpeɪt] *v. (in music)* to stress (a beat) which would not normally be stressed and so change the rhythm. **syncopation** [sɪŋkə'peɪʃn] *n.* act of syncopating.

syncope ['sɪŋkəpɪ] *n.* fainting attack.

syndicalism ['sɪndɪkəlɪzm] *n.* form of socialism, where control is in the hands of the trade unions.

syndicate 1. *n.* ['sɪndɪkət] group of people or companies working together to make money. **2.** *v.* ['sɪndɪkeɪt] to produce (an article/a cartoon) which is then sold to a series of newspapers. **syndication** [sɪndi'keɪʃn] *n.* act of syndicating.

syndrome ['sɪndrəʊm] *n. (a)* series of symptoms which show an illness. *(b)* symptoms which show a general feeling/way of approaching a problem, etc.

synergy ['sɪnədʒɪ] *n. (of two organizations)* working together better than working separately.

synod ['sɪnəd] *n.* meeting of religious leaders.

synonym ['sɪnənɪm] *n.* word which means the same thing as another word. **synonymous** [sɪ'nɒnɪməs] *adj.* which has the same meaning.

synopsis [sɪ'nɒpsɪs] *n. (pl.* **-ses**) summary (of main points made in a book or article).

synovitis ['saɪnəʊ'vaɪtɪs] *n.* inflammation of the membrane covering a joint.

syntax ['sɪntæks] *n.* grammatical rules for putting words together into sentences. **syntactic** [sɪn'tæktɪk] *adj.* referring to syntax.

synthesis ['sɪnθəsɪs] *n. (pl.* **-ses**) bringing several parts together to form a whole. **synthesize** ['sɪnθəsaɪz] *v.* to combine (several things) together to make a whole. **synthesizer,** *n.* electronic device which can make musical sounds similar to those of different instruments.

synthetic [sɪn'θetɪk] **1.** *n.* artificial/man-made material. **2.** *adj.* artificial; made in such a way that it looks natural. **synthetically,** *adv.* in a synthetic way.

syphilis ['sɪfɪlɪs] *n.* serious disease transmitted by sexual intercourse or inherited. **syphilitic,** *adj. & n.* (person) suffering from syphilis.

Syrian ['sɪrɪən] *adj. & n.* (person) from Syria;

syringa [sɪ'rɪŋgə] *n.* tall shrub with scented white flowers.

syringe [sɪ'rɪndʒ] **1.** *n.* tube with a piston or rubber bulb so that liquids can be sucked into it then squeezed out, as in giving injections; **garden s.** = instrument for spraying trees with insecticide, etc. **2.** *v.* to clean by blowing liquid with a syringe.

syrup ['sɪrəp] *n.* thick sweet liquid; thick golden juice from sugar. **syrupy,** *adj.* like syrup; very sweet.

system ['sɪstəm] *n. (a)* arrangement of things which work together. *(b)* way of organizing things to work together. *(c)* method. *(d)* body. **systematic** [sɪstə'mætɪk] *adj.* orderly/methodical. **systematically,** *adv.* in a methodical way. **systematize** ['sɪstəmətaɪz] *v.* to organize into a system. **systemic** [sɪs'temɪk] *adj.* which affects the whole system. **systems analysis,** *n.* use of a computer to forecast needs, etc., by analysing the way in which a system is actually operating. **systems analyst,** *n.* person who specializes in systems analysis.

systole [sɪs'təʊlɪ] *n.* phase in the heartbeat, when the heart contracts and pumps blood out.

Tt

T, t [tiː] *inf.* **it suits him to a T** = it suits him perfectly; **to dot one's i's and cross one's t's** = to settle the final details (of an agreement)/to be very careful about sth; **T-bone steak** = type of beef

steak with a bone shaped like a T in it;
T-junction = junction where one road
joins another at right angles; **T shirt** =
light short-sleeved shirt with no buttons
or collar; **T square** = device shaped like
a T for drawing right angles.

ta [tɑ:] *inter. inf.* thank you.

tab [tæb] *n.* (*a*) small loop of cloth for
hanging up a coat/for pulling open a
box. (*b*) little coloured marker attached
to cards in an index so that they can be
found easily; *inf.* **to pick up the t.** = to
pay the bill; **to keep tabs on s.o.** = to
keep watch on s.o.

tabard ['tæbɑ:d] *n.* short sleeveless coat
worn by heralds.

tabasco [tə'bæskəʊ] *n.* trademark for a
hot red sauce.

tabby (cat) ['tæbi(kæt)] *n.* striped black,
brown, and grey cat.

tabernacle ['tæbənækl] *n.* (*a*) place of
worship. (*b*) ornamental box for consecrated bread and wine.

table ['teɪbl] **1.** *n.* (*a*) piece of furniture
with a flat top and legs, used for eating
at/for working at, .etc.; **to set the t.** =
to get the table ready for a meal; **to
clear the t.** = to remove dirty plates/
knives, etc. after a meal; **to turn the
tables on s.o.** = to put yourself in a
superior position, where before you
were in an inferior one. (*b*) printed list
of figures/facts; **multiplication tables** =
lists of figures to learn by heart how
each number is multiplied. **t. of contents**
= list of contents of a book. **2.** *v.* to
suggest (items for discussion); to put
(additional information) on the table
at a committee meeting. **tablecloth**,
n. cloth for covering a table during
a meal. **tableland**, *n.* high flat land.
table linen, *n.* tablecloths/serviettes,
etc. **table manners**, *n. pl.* polite way
of eating according to the rules of society. **table mat**, *n.* mat for protecting the surface of a table. **tablespoon**,
n. large spoon for serving food at
table. **tablespoonful**, *n.* quantity held
in a tablespoon. **table tennis**, *n.* game
played on a large table with a net across
the centre, using small round bats and
a very light white ball. **tableware**, *n.*
knives, forks, spoons, plates, etc.

tableau ['tæbləʊ] *n.* (*pl.* **-eaux** [-əʊz])
scene where actors represent a historic
occasion, etc., without moving.

table d'hôte ['tɑ:blədəʊt] *n.* menu
which has a restricted number of dishes
at a reduced price.

tablet ['tæblət] *n.* (*a*) small round pill
of medicine. (*b*) flat stone with an
inscription on it. (*c*) bar (of soap/
chocolate).

tabloid ['tæblɔɪd] *n.* popular newspaper
with a small page size, usu. with a large
number of pictures.

taboo [tə'bu:] **1.** *adj.* forbidden (by
religion/by custom). **2.** *n* (religious)
custom which forbids sth.

tabor ['teɪbɔ:] *n.* small drum beaten with
the hand.

tabular ['tæbjʊlə] *adj.* arranged in a
table. **tabulate** ['tæbjʊleɪt] *v.* to arrange
(figures) in a table. **tabulation** [tæbjʊ-
'leɪʃn] *n.* arrangement (of figures)
in a table. **tabulator**, *n.* device on
a typewriter/in a computer program
which allows the typist to make columns
automatically.

tachograph ['tækəgrɑ:f] *n.* machine
placed in the cab of a lorry which
records details of the mileage and time
spent on a journey.

tachycardia [tækɪ'kɑ:dɪə] *n.* rapid
heartbeat.

tacit ['tæsɪt] *adj.* (agreement, etc.) which
is understood, but not actually given.
tacitly, *adv.* (agreement given) without
speaking, but nevertheless understood.
taciturn, *adj.* (person) who does not
say much; **taciturnity** [tæsɪ'tɜ:nɪtɪ] *n.*
silence/not saying much.

tack [tæk] **1.** *n.* (*a*) small nail (with a large
head); *inf.* **to get down to brass tacks** =
to talk real business/to start discussing
the real problem. (*b*) (*in sewing*) light
stitch to hold cloth in place and which
can be taken out later. (*c*) diagonal
movement of a ship so that it is sailing
against the wind; **on the right t.** = doing
the right thing. *n.* (*d*) saddle and equipment for horse-riding. (*e*) (*Scotland*)
lease. **2.** *v.* (*a*) to nail (sth) using tacks;
(*b*) to make a light temporary stitch.
(*c*) to change direction so that you are
sailing against the wind; **they were tacking
up the river** = they sailed in a zigzag
way up the river against the wind. **tack
on**, *v.* to add (sth) at the end.

tackle ['tækl] **1.** *n.* (*a*) equipment. (*b*) **block and t.** = arrangement of ropes, pulleys and hooks for lifting heavy weights. (*c*) (*in football, etc.*) trying to get possession of the ball from an opposing player; (*in Rugby*) grabbing an opposing player so that he falls to the ground and releases the ball. **2.** *v.* (*a*) to grab (s.o./sth); to try to deal with (a problem). (*b*) (*in football etc.*) to try to get possession of the ball from an opposing player; (*in Rugby*) to grab (an opposing player) so that he falls to the ground. **tackler,** *n.* person who tackles.

tacky ['tæki] *adj.* (**-ier, -iest**) sticky. **tackiness,** *n.* being tacky.

tact [tækt] *n.* care in your relationships with people so that you do not offend them. **tactful,** *adj.* using tact. **tactfully,** *adv.* in a tactful way. **tactless,** *adj.* lacking tact/unintentionally offensive. **tactlessly,** *adv.* in a tactless way. **tactlessness,** *n.* lack of tact.

tactic ['tæktɪk] *n.* (*often pl.*) way of doing sth so as to be at an advantage; way of placing troops/guns, etc., so as to be in a better position than the enemy. **tactical,** *adj.* (*a*) referring to tactics; **tactical error** = mistake in planning. (*b*) (nuclear weapon) which is used in a limited area. **tactically,** *adv.* in a tactical way. **tactician** [tæk'tɪʃn] *n.* person who is expert at tactics.

tactile ['tæktail] *adj.* sensitive to touch; referring to the sense of touch.

tadpole ['tædpəʊl] *n* baby frog/toad in its first stage after hatching.

taffeta ['tæfitə] *n.* thin shiny stiff cloth.

taffrail ['tæfreil] *n.* guard rail round the stern of a ship.

tag [tæg] **1.** *n.* (*a*) small loop of cloth; metal piece at the end of a shoelace. (*b*) label. (*c*) common old saying. (*d*) children's game where you have to try to touch another child who chases the others in his turn. **2.** *v.* (**tagged**) *inf.* **to t. on to s.o.** = to stay close to s.o.; **to t. along behind** = to follow closely.

taiga ['taigə] *n.* forest in north Siberia.

tail [teil] **1.** *n.* (*a*) part of an animal at the rear of its body, usu. sticking out at the back; **to turn t.** = run away. (*b*) back part of a long coat/of a shirt, etc.; **wearing tails** = wearing evening-dress.

(*c*) back part (of a line); back (of a car). (*d*) **tails** = reverse side of a coin/ the side of a coin without the head of a king, etc., on it. (*e*) *inf.* detective who is following s.o. closely. **2.** *v.* (*a*) to take the stems off (gooseberries, etc.). (*b*) to follow (s.o.) closely. **tail away,** *v.* to die away/to fade away. **tailback,** *n.* long line of cars held up by an accident, etc. **tailboard, tailgate,** *n.* hinged board at the back of a lorry which can be let down to load or unload the contents. **tail coat,** *n.* man's black evening jacket with a long tail at the back. **tail end,** *n.* back part (of a queue); last part (of a film, etc.). **tailless,** *adj.* (animal) with no tail. **taillight,** *n.* rear light (of a car, etc.). **tail off,** *v.* to die away/to fade away. **tailpipe,** *n. Am.* exhaust pipe. **tailplane,** *n.* flat wings on the tail of an aircraft. **tailspin,** *n.* dive by an aircraft, where the machine turns round and round. **tail wind,** *n.* wind blowing behind an aircraft, making it go faster.

tailor ['teilə] **1.** *n.* person who makes outer clothes (suits/coats, etc.) usu. for men. **2.** *v.* (*a*) to make clothes which fit. (*b*) to make (sth) fit particular circumstances. **tailor-made,** *adj.* made to fit.

taint [teint] **1.** *n.* slight trace of evil/of corruption. **2.** *v.* to infect/to corrupt; **tainted food** = food which has become rotten (by touching other rotten food).

take [teik] **1.** *n.* (*a*) one scene of a film which has been filmed. (*b*) money taken in a shop/in a business. **2.** *v.* (**took; has taken**) (*a*) to hold/to grasp/to carry. (*b*) to remove/to steal. (*c*) to buy/to rent/to occupy; to have a (newspaper) delivered to your house regularly; **to t. a seat** = sit down; **to t. the chair** = to act as chairman (at a meeting). (*d*) to win (a prize). (*c*) to be a candidate for (an examination). (*f*) to eat/to drink (usually); **do you t. sugar in your tea?** (*g*) to make (a photograph). (*h*) to accept; **t. it from me** = believe what I say; **she's taking legal advice** = she is consulting a lawyer; **t. my advice** = do as I suggest. (*i*) to need; **it took three men to lift the piano; we took two days/it took us two days to get to London.** (*j*) to lead; to go (in a direction); **can you t. me to the station?** = can you drive me to the station? (*k*) to hold; (*of machine*) to accept/to be able to work with. (*l*) to do (a certain action); **to t. a walk/ a bath/a holiday; to t. a decision** = to decide. (*m*) to stand/to put up with. (*n*) to be successful/to have effect; **the kidney transplant has taken** = has been successful; **the cuttings have taken** = have sprouted roots. **take after,** *v.* to be like (a parent). **take away,** *v.* (*a*) to remove. (*b*) to subtract. **takeaway,** *n. & adj. inf.* (shop where you can buy) hot food to eat elsewhere. **take back,** *v.* (*a*) to return. (*b*) **I take it all back** = I withdraw what I said and apologise for having said it. **take down,** *v.* (*a*) to lower (sth which is hanging). (*b*) to write down (what s.o. says). (*c*) to demolish. **take-home pay,** *n.* amount of money you actually receive out of your wages, after tax, etc., has been deducted. **take in,** *v.* (*a*) to accept/ to bring inside. (*b*) to include. (*c*) to trick (s.o.). (*d*) to understand. (*e*) to make (a skirt, etc.) smaller. **taken with,** *adj. inf.* attracted by. **take off,** *v.* (*a*) to remove (clothes). (*b*) to fly into the air. (*c*) *inf.* to imitate. **takeoff,** *n.* (*a*) departure (of an aircraft). (*b*) *inf.* imitation. **take on,** *v.* (*a*) to agree to do (some work). (*b*) to agree to employ (s.o.). (*c*) to fight; to play against. (*d*) to make a scene. **take out,** *v.* (*a*) to pull (sth) out. (*b*) to invite (s.o.) to go out. (*c*) **to take out an insurance policy on** = to start to insure. (*d*) **to take it out on s.o.** = to make s.o. suffer to help relieve your own feelings. (*c*) **the heat takes it out of me** = makes me very tired. **takeout,** *n. Am.* takeaway. **take over,** *v.* (*a*) to buy (a business). (*b*) **to take over from s.o.** = to start to do sth in place of s.o. else. **takeover,** *n.* buying of a business; **t. bid** = offer to buy a business. **taker,** *n.* person who wants to buy. **take to,** *v.* (*a*) to start to do sth to help you out of a bad situation; **he took to the woods** = went into the woods to hide; **she took to drink** = started to drink alcohol regularly. (*b*) to start to like (s.o.). **take up,** *v.* (*a*) to pick up; **they've taken up the road** = removed the road surface. (*b*) to occupy (space). (*c*) to start to do (a sport/a craft). (*d*) to start to work on (an idea);

to start to discuss (a case). (*e*) to make (a skirt, etc.) shorter. (*f*) *inf.* **to take s.o. up on sth** = to accept a suggestion which s.o. has made. **take up with,** *v.* to become friendly with (s.o.). **takings,** *n. pl.* money received in a shop/in a business.

talaq ['tælæk] *n.* Islamic form of divorce.

talc [tælk] *n.* smooth soft mineral used to make powder to put on the body; powder made from this mineral. **talcum powder,** *n.* powder made from talc.

tale [teɪl] *n.* story; **old wives' t.** = superstitious belief.

talent ['tælənt] *n.* (*a*) natural gift/ability. (*b*) people with natural ability. **t. contest** = contest to find new singers/ comedians, etc. **talented,** *adj.* very gifted.

talisman ['tælɪzmən] *n.* object kept because it supposedly brings good luck.

talk [tɔːk] **1.** *n.* (*a*) spoken words; **idle t.** = gossip; **double t.** = saying one thing and thinking the opposite. (*b*) conversation. (*c*) lecture/informal speech. **2.** *v.* (*a*) to speak (a language). *inf.* **now you're talking** = that's a good idea. (*b*) to gossip. (*c*) to give information (usu. unwillingly). **talkative,** *adj.* (person) who likes to chat/to gossip. **talk down,** *v.* (*a*) to speak in a condescending way/in an exaggeratedly simple way (**to** s.o.). (*b*) to give instructions over the radio to a pilot for landing his aircraft when visibility is bad. **talker,** *n.* person who talks. **talking,** *n.* speech, conversation; **he did all the t.** = the others said nothing. **talking-point,** *n.* thing people argue about. **talking-shop,** *n.* place where things are discussed but no action is ever taken. **talking-to,** *n. inf.* scolding. **talk into,** *v.* **to talk s.o. into doing sth** = to persuade. **talk over,** *v.* **I talked him over** = I persuaded him to change his mind; **come and talk it over** = come and discuss it. **talk round,** *v.* **I talked him round** = I persuaded him to change his mind; **we just talked round the subject** = we never discussed the main problem.

tall [tɔːl] *adj.* (**-er, -est**) (*a*) high. (*b*) *inf.* unbelievable (story); **t. order** = command which is extremely difficult to carry out. **tallboy,** *n.* type of tall chest of drawers.

tallow ['tæləʊ] *n.* fat from animals, used to make candles.

tally ['tælɪ] **1.** *n.* note/account. **2.** *v.* to agree (**with**).

talon ['tælən] *n.* claw (of a bird).

tamarisk ['tæmərɪsk] *n.* shrub with feathery evergreen leaves, which is often grown near the sea.

tambourine [tæmbə'ri:n] *n.* small drum with metal pieces loosely attached to the rim, so that they jangle when it is beaten.

tame [teɪm] **1.** *adj.* (**-er, -est**) (*a*) (animal) which is not wild/which can be approached by human beings; *inf.* **our t. tax expert** = the tax expert whom we call on regularly for advice. (*b*) not very exciting. **2.** *v.* to make (an animal) tame; to make safe. **tamely,** *adv.* humbly. **tameness,** *n.* being tame. **tamer,** *n.* person who tames wild animals.

tam-o'-shanter [tæmə'ʃæntə] *n.* flat Scottish cap, like a beret.

tamp [tæmp] *v.* to press down.

tamper ['tæmpə] *v.* **to t. with** = to meddle with.

tampon ['tæmpɒn] *n.* pad of cotton wool used to soak up blood.

tan [tæn] **1.** *n. & adj.* brownish yellow (colour). **2.** *n.* brown colour of the skin after being in the sun. **3.** *v.* (**tanned**) to treat (animal skin) to make leather. (*b*) to get brown by sitting in the sun. **tanner,** *n.* person who makes animal skins into leather. **tannery,** *n.* factory where skins are made into leather.

tandem ['tændəm] *n.* bicycle for two people; **in t.** = in pairs/together.

tang [tæŋ] *n.* sharp smell/taste. **tangy,** *adj.* with a sharp taste/smell.

tangent ['tændʒənt] *n.* line which touches a curve without cutting through it; **to go off at a t.** = to change direction/ to follow another line of thought. **tangential** [tæn'dʒənʃl] *adj.* referring to a tangent.

tangerine [tændʒə'ri:n] *n.* small orange with soft skin which peels easily.

tangible ['tændʒəbl] *adj.* which can be touched; real. **tangibility** [tændʒɪ'bɪlɪtɪ] *n.* being tangible. **tangibly,** *adv.* in a real/definite way.

tangle ['tæŋgl] **1.** *n.* mix of threads/ string/hair; **in a t.** = all mixed up. **2.** *v.* to mix (things) together in knots; **to t. with s.o.** = to get into an argument.

tango ['tæŋgəʊ] *n.* (*pl.* **-os**) dance where you glide sideways.

tank [tæŋk] *n.* (*a*) large (metal) container for liquids. (*b*) **t. wagon** = railway wagon for carrying liquids. (*c*) armoured vehicle with caterpillar tracks and a powerful gun. **tanker,** *n.* (*a*) special ship for carrying liquids (esp. oil). (*b*) special lorry for carrying liquids. **tank up,** *v. inf.* to drink a lot.

tankard ['tæŋkəd] *n.* large metal mug for drinking beer.

tannin ['tænɪn] *n.* red-brown liquid (found in the bark of trees/in tea) which is used to make leather. **tannic,** *adj.* **t. acid** = tannin.

tannoy ['tænɔɪ] *n.* trademark for a public loudspeaker system.

tansy ['tænzɪ] *n.* herb with yellow flowers.

tantalize ['tæntəlaɪz] *v.* to tease (s.o.) by offering him sth which he can't have. **tantalizing,** *adj.* which tantalizes. **tantalizingly,** *adv.* in a tantalizing way.

tantamount ['tæntəmaʊnt] *adj.* equivalent/equal (**to**).

tantrum ['tæntrəm] *n.* attack of uncontrollable bad temper.

Taoiseach ['ti:ʃək] *n.* (*in Republic of Ireland*) Prime Minister.

tap [tæp] **1.** *n.* (*a*) apparatus with a twisting knob and a valve which, when you turn it, allows liquid to come out of a pipe/container; **t. water** = water which comes from the mains and not from a well; **on t.** = readily available. (*b*) slight blow; light knock. **2.** *v.* (**tapped**) (*a*) to run liquid out of (a barrel) by fixing a tap; to cut a ring round the stem of (a rubber tree) so that the sap flows down and drips from a small spout. (*b*) to attach a secret listening device to (a telephone). (*c*) to start to exploit (sth new). (*d*) to hit lightly. **tap dance,** *n.* dance done by beating time to the music with metal-soled shoes. **tap dancer,** *n.* dancer who specializes in tap dancing. **tap dancing,** *n.* dancing with special shoes with metal soles, so that the dancer beats time to the music. **tap root,** *n.* main root (of a tree) which goes straight down into the soil.

tape [teɪp] **1.** *n.* (*a*) long thin flat strip (of cloth/plastic, etc.); **sticky t.** = glued plastic strip for sticking things together, etc.; **insulating t.** = sticky tape for wrapping round electrical connections; **measuring tape** = long strip marked in centimetres/inches, etc. for measuring; **magnetic t.** = sensitive plastic tape for recording. (*b*) long string held across the finishing line of a race. **2.** *v.* (*a*) to attach with a tape. (*b*) to record (sth) on magnetic tape. (*c*) *inf.* **I've got him taped** = I know exactly what he's like/I understand him completely; **we've got it all taped** = everything is under control/we know how to do it perfectly. **tape deck,** *n.* apparatus which plays tape and records on tape, but does not have its own amplifier or loudspeakers. **tape measure,** *n.* long strip of cloth/metal marked in centimetres/inches, etc., used for measuring. **tape-record,** *v.* to record (sth) on tape. **tape-recorder,** *n* apparatus which records on tape and plays back these tapes. **tape-recording,** *n.* recording done on tape. **tapeworm,** *n.* long flatworm which lives in the intestines of man and other animals.

taper [ˈteɪpə] **1.** *n.* long slender candle, made of a wick covered with a thin layer of wax. **2.** *v.* to make (sth) become thinner at the end; (*also* **taper off**) to become thinner at the end.

tapestry [ˈtæpɪstrɪ] *n.* thick woven cloth with a picture or design, usu. hung on walls or used to cover chairs.

tapioca [tæpɪˈəʊkə] *n.* white starchy powder which comes from a tropical plant and is used to make puddings.

tapir [ˈteɪpə] *n.* South American animal like a pig with a short trunk.

tappet [ˈtæpɪt] *n.* small projecting piece which opens or closes a valve by tapping on it.

tar [tɑː] **1.** *n.* (*a*) black oily substance which comes from coal and is used for covering roads. (*b*) *inf.* sailor. **2.** *v.* (**tarred**) to cover with tar; **tarred paper** = thick brown waterproof paper with an inner layer of tar; **to t. and feather s.o.** = to cover s.o. with hot tar and

feathers as a punishment; **to be tarred with the same brush** = to have the same weaknesses/to make the same mistakes (as s.o.).

tarantula [tæˈræntjʊlə] *n.* large mildly poisonous tropical spider.

tardy [ˈtɑːdɪ] *adj.* (**-ier, -iest**) (*formal*) late. **tardily,** *adv.* late. **tardiness,** *n.* being tardy.

tare [teə] *n.* (*a*) allowance made for the weight of the lorry, etc., in calculating transport costs. (*b*) (*old*) weed.

target [ˈtɑːgɪt] *n.* thing which you aim at; **t. practice** = practising at shooting at a target; **t. language** = language which you are learning/into which you are translating.

tariff [ˈtærɪf] *n.* (*a*) tax to be paid for importing goods; **to lift t. barriers** = to reduce import taxes. (*b*) list of prices (in a restaurant/hotel/bar, etc.).

tarmac [ˈtɑːmæk] *n.* (*a*) trademark for a hard surface of a road made of tar mixed with small stones. (*b*) runway of an airport. **tarmacked,** *adj.* covered with tarmac.

tarn [tɑːn] *n.* small mountain lake in the Lake District.

tarnish [ˈtɑːnɪʃ] *v.* (*of metal*) to become discoloured; to ruin (a reputation).

tarot [ˈtærəʊ] *n.* set of cards designed for use in telling fortunes.

tarpaulin [tɑːˈpɔːlɪn] *n.* large waterproof cloth.

tarragon [ˈtærəgən] *n.* common herb used in cooking.

tarry [ˈtærɪ] *v.* (*old*) to stay behind.

tarsus [ˈtɑːsəs] *n.* set of bones in the ankle.

tart [tɑːt] **1.** *n.* (*a*) small pastry dish filled with sweet food. (*b*) *Sl.* prostitute. **2.** *adj.* (**-er, -est**) (*a*) bitter (taste). (*b*) sharp (answer). **3.** *v. inf.* **to t. yourself up** = to make yourself look smart. **tartly,** *adv.* sharply. **tartness,** *n.* sourness (of taste).

tartan [ˈtɑːtən] *n. & adj.* (cloth) woven into a special pattern for one of the Scottish clans; distinctive pattern in such a cloth.

tartar [ˈtɑːtə] *n.* (*a*) hard substance which forms on teeth. (*b*) **cream of t.** = white powder used in cooking and in medicine. (*c*) *inf.* fierce person. **tartaric**

[tɑː'tærɪk] *adj.* **t. acid** = acid used in cooking.

tartare sauce [tɑː:tɑː'sɔːs] *n.* mayonnaise containing finely chopped pieces of vegetables.

task [tɑːsk] *n.* (*a*) work which has to be done. (*b*) **to take s.o. to t. for** = to criticize. **task force,** *n.* special group (esp. of soldiers) chosen to carry out a hard task. **taskmaster,** *n.* person who sets a hard task.

tassel ['tæsl] *n.* group of threads tied together at one end to form a ball, with the other ends hanging free. **tasselled,** *adj.* with tassels.

taste [teɪst] **1.** *n.* (*a*) sense by which you can tell differences of flavour between things you eat; **t. buds** = cells on the tongue which enable you to tell differences in flavour. (*b*) flavour of food or drink. (*c*) very small quantity (of food/drink); **he's had a t. of prison** = he has been in prison once. (*d*) liking (for sth); **expensive tastes** = liking for expensive things. (*c*) **good/ bad t.** = ability/inability to judge what is fine/beautiful/refined. **2.** *v.* (*a*) to sense the flavour of (sth). (*b*) to have a flavour (**of**). (*c*) to try (sth); to experience (freedom). **tasteful,** *adj.* showing good taste. **tastefully,** *adv.* in good taste. **tasteless,** *adj.* (*a*) with no particular flavour. (*b*) showing bad taste. **tastelessly,** *adv.* in a tasteless way. **taster,** *n.* person whose job is to taste food to test its quality. **tasty,** *adj.* (**-ier, -iest**) with a particular pleasant flavour.

tat [tæt] *n.* (*no pl.*) *inf.* shabby/cheap things; *see also* **tit.**

ta-ta [tə'tɑː] *int. inf.* goodbye.

tatters ['tætəz] *n.* **in t.** = (i) torn (clothes); (ii) (person) wearing old torn clothes. **tattered** ['tætəd] *adj.* torn and old.

tatting ['tætɪŋ] *n.* type of lace made by hand.

tattle ['tætl] *v.* (*formal*) to gossip.

tattoo [tə'tuː] **1.** *n.* (*a*) military parade in the evening. (*b*) rapid beating (of drums). (*c*) decoration on skin made by pricking with a needle and putting colour into the wound. **2.** *v.* to make decorations on s.o.'s skin by pricking it and putting colour into the wound.

tatty ['tætɪ] *adj.* (**-ier, -iest**) untidy/ shabby.

taught [tɔːt] *v. see* **teach.**

taunt [tɔːnt] **1.** *n.* sarcastic jeering. **2.** *v.* to jeer at (s.o.) sarcastically.

Taurus ['tɔːrəs] *n.* one of the signs of the zodiac, shaped like a bull.

taut [tɔːt] *adj.* stretched tight. **tauten,** *v.* to make tight; to become tight. **tautly,** *adv.* tightly. **tautness,** *n.* being taut.

tautology [tɔː'tɒlədʒɪ] *n.* unnecessary use in a phrase of different words which mean the same thing. **tautological,** *adj.* using tautology.

tavern ['tævən] *n.* inn/public house.

taw [tɔː] *n.* big marble.

tawdry ['tɔːdrɪ] *adj.* (**-ier, -iest**) cheap and in bad taste.

tawny ['tɔːnɪ] *adj.* (**-ier, -iest**) orange brown.

tawse [tɔːz] *n.* (*in Scotland*) strap for beating schoolchildren.

tax [tæks] **1.** *n.* (*pl.* **-es**) (*a*) money taken by the state from incomes/sales, etc., which pays for government services; **t. free** = without having to pay any tax. (*b*) burden; **it's a severe t. on our resources** = it strains our resources. **2.** *v.* (*a*) to put a tax on (sth/s.o.). (*b*) to strain. (*c*) (*formal*) **to t. s.o. with** = to accuse s.o. of. **taxable,** *adj.* which can be taxed. **taxation** [tæk'seɪʃn] *n.* (*a*) (system of) imposing taxes. (*b*) money raised from taxes. **taxman,** *n.* (*pl.* **-men**) *inf.* civil servant who deals with tax (usu. income tax). **taxpayer,** *n.* person who pays taxes. **tax point,** *n.* date on which goods are supplied and VAT becomes chargeable. **tax return,** *n.* form to be filled in to report your earnings and allowances to the tax office.

taxi ['tæksɪ] **1.** *n.* car which can be hired; **t. rank** = place in the street where taxis can wait. **2.** *v.* (*of an aircraft*) to go along the ground before take-off or after landing. **taxicab,** *n.* taxi. **taximeter,** *n.* machine fitted inside a taxi which shows the price for the journey.

taxidermy ['tæksɪdɜːmɪ] *n.* art of stuffing the skins of dead animals so that they look lifelike. **taxidermist,** *n.* person who stuffs the skins of dead animals so that they look lifelike.

taxonomy [tæk'sɒnəmɪ] *n.* scientific classification (esp. of plants and animals). **taxonomist,** *n.* person who specializes in taxonomy.

TB ['tiː'biː] *abbreviation for* tuberculosis.

TD [tiː'diː] *abbrev. for* Teachta Dala, a Member of the Irish Parliament.

tea [tiː] *n.* (a) dried leaves of a tropical plant which are used to make a common drink. (b) drink made by pouring boiling water on to dried leaves of the tea plant. (c) any hot drink made in a similar way; **lime t.** = tea made with the dried flowers of the lime tree. (d) afternoon meal; **t. service/t. set** = plates/cups/saucers, etc., used at tea; **high tea** = large meal eaten in the early evening in the North of England and Scotland. **teabag,** *n.* small paper bag full of tea which is put into the pot instead of loose tea. **tea break,** *n.* rest period at work, when you can drink tea. **teacake,** *n.* type of bun with raisins in it, usu. eaten hot with butter. **teachest,** *n.* light wooden packing case in which tea is shipped. **teacloth,** *n.* cloth for drying dishes. **tea cosy,** *n.* cover for putting over a teapot to keep it warm. **teacup,** *n.* large cup for tea. **tealeaf,** *n.* (pl. **-leaves**) small piece of tea left in the cup after you have drunk the tea. **tea party,** *n.* party (held in the afternoon or early evening) when you drink tea, eat cakes, etc. **teapot,** *n.* special pot with a handle and spout for making tea in. **tearoom, teashop,** *n.* small restaurant which serves mainly tea and light meals. **teaspoon,** *n.* small spoon for stirring tea. **teaspoonful,** *n.* quantity contained in a teaspoon. **teatime,** *n.* time when you have tea (about 4 o'clock in the afternoon). **tea towel,** *n.* cloth for drying dishes. **tea trolley,** *n.* small table on wheels from which you can serve food.

teach [tiːtʃ] *v.* (**taught** [tɔːt]) to give (s.o.) information; to give lessons (in a school); to show (s.o.) how to do sth; *inf.* **that'll t. him to be so rude** = will punish him for being rude. **teachable,** *adj.* which can be taught. **teacher,** *n.* person who teaches. **teach-in,** *n. inf.* informal discussion on a topic. **teaching,** *n.* (a) action of giving knowledge/giving lessons; **the t. profession** = teachers as a group. (b) political or moral ideas/philosophy.

teak [tiːk] *n.* large tropical tree; hard wood of this tree, which does not warp, and is used for making furniture, etc.

teal [tiːl] *n.* (pl. **teal**) small type of wild duck.

team [tiːm] **1.** *n.* (a) group of people playing together/working together. **t. spirit** = good feeling of those who play or work well together as a team. (b) group of animals working together. **2.** *v.* **to t. up with s.o.** = to join s.o. to work together. **teamster,** *n. Am.* lorry driver. **teamwork,** *n.* ability to work together as a group; working together as a group.

tear¹ ['tɪə] *n.* drop of water formed in the eyes when you cry; **he burst into tears** = suddenly started to cry; **in tears** = crying. **teardrop,** *n.* one tear. **tearful,** *adj.* sad/crying. **tearfully,** *adv.* in a tearful way. **tear-gas,** *n.* gas which makes you cry, used to control crowds of rioters. **tear-jerker,** *n. inf.* film/novel which makes you cry. **tear-stained,** *adj.* (face) with the marks of tears.

tear² ['teə] **1.** *n.* (a) hole torn in a piece of cloth; (b) **wear and t.** = normal usage (of a house/car, etc.) which wears sth away. **2.** *v.* (**tore** [tɔː]; **has torn** [tɔːn]) (a) to make a hole in (sth) by pulling; **torn between** = unable to decide between; *inf.* **that's torn it** = that has ruined what we were planning/that has spoilt everything. (b) to pull to pieces; **to t. into s.o.** = to attack s.o.; **they tore up the road** = dug up the road surface; **to t. oneself away from** = to leave reluctantly. (c) *inf.* to go fast; **in a tearing hurry** = very fast. **tearaway,** *n. inf.* wild young hooligan.

tease [tiːz] **1.** *n.* person who annoys/irritates people on purpose. **2.** *v.* (a) to annoy (s.o.)/to irritate (s.o.) on purpose. (b) to disentangle threads (with a comb); to brush (cloth) to make it soft. **teaser,** *n. inf.* problem which is difficult to solve/question which is difficult to answer.

teasel ['tiːzl] *n.* tall plant with prickly flower heads.

teat [tiːt] *n.* (a) projection on a cow's

udder through which milk passes. (b) rubber cap put on a baby's feeding bottle through which the baby sucks milk.

technical ['teknɪkl] adj. (a) referring to a particular industry/practical work, etc.; **t. term** = term used by specialists; **t. college** = college where technical skills are taught; **t. subjects** = subjects which teach practical skills (such as woodwork, engineering, etc.); **t. training** = training in a practical skill. (b) referring to a fixed interpretation of the rules; **t. knockout** = where the referee stops the fight because a boxer is too hurt to continue. **tech** [tek] n. inf. technical college. **technically**, adv. (a) in a technical way; (b) strictly speaking. **technicality** [teknɪ'kælɪtɪ] n. (a) technical detail. (b) strict interpretation of rules/of laws. **technician** [tek'nɪʃn] n. person who is specialized in industrial or scientific work. **technique** [tek'niːk] n. skilled way of doing sth. **technocrat** ['teknəkræt] n. person with particular technical/organizational skills, brought in to run a country/an organization. **technological** [teknə'lɒdʒɪkl] adj. referring to technology. **technologically**, adv. in a technological way. **technologist**, n. specialist in technology. **technology** [tek'nɒlədʒɪ] n. knowledge/study of new industrial or scientific skills.

tectonics [tek'tɒnɪks] n. study of the earth's crust and its movements.

teddy (bear) ['tedɪ('beə)] n. child's toy bear.

tedious ['tiːdɪəs] adj. boring. **tediously**, adv. in a boring way. **tediousness**, **tedium** ['tiːdɪəm] n. boredom/being boring.

tee [tiː] **1.** n. (a) spot on a golf course where the ball is placed before you hit it. (b) little peg, on which the golf ball is placed. **2.** v. **to t. off** = to hit the ball from a tee.

teem [tiːm] v. (a) to be full of/covered with sth; (b) inf. **it's teeming** = it's pouring (with rain).

teens [tiːnz] n. pl. age between 13 and 19. **teenage** ['tiːneɪdʒ] adj. adolescent; referring to s.o. aged between 13 and 19. **teenager**, n. person aged between 13 and 19.

teeny(-weeny) ['tiːnɪ('wiːnɪ)] adj. inf. very small.

tee-shirt ['tiːʃɜːt] n. light short-sleeved shirt with no buttons or collar.

teeter ['tiːtə] v. to wobble. **teeter-totter**, n. Am. seesaw.

teeth [tiːθ] n. see **tooth**. **teethe** [tiːð] v. to grow your first teeth. **teething troubles**, n. problems which develop when a baby grows its first teeth/when anything is in its first stages.

teetotal [tiː'təʊtl] adj. (person) who never drinks any alcohol. **teetotaller**, n. person who never drinks any alcohol.

Teflon ['teflɒn] n. trademark for a non-stick surface, used on frying pans, etc.

tele- ['telɪ] prefix meaning over a distance.

telecast ['telɪkɑːst] n. TV broadcast.

telecommunications [telɪkəmjuːnɪ'keɪʃnz] n. pl. system of passing messages over a great distance (such as telephone/radio, etc.).

telegram ['telɪgræm] n. message sent by telegraph.

telegraph ['telɪgrɑːf] **1.** n. system of sending messages along wires; **t. line** = wire along which telegraph messages are sent; **t. pole** = pole which holds up a telegraph line; inf. **bush t.** = passing information by gossip. **2.** v. to send (a message) along wires. **telegrapher** [tə'legrəfə] n. person who sends messages by telegraph. **telegraphese**, n. abbreviated language used when writing telegrams. **telegraphic** [telɪ'græfɪk] adj. referring to telegraph; **t. address** = short form of an address used on telegrams. **telegraphist** [tə'legrəfɪst] n. person who sends messages by telegraph. **telegraphy** [tə'legrəfɪ] n. sending messages by telegraph.

telepathy [tə'lepəθɪ] n. sending feelings/sympathy/mental images from one person to another without the use of the senses. **telepathic** [telɪ'pæθɪk] adj. referring to telepathy.

telephone ['telɪfəʊn] **1.** n. device/system for speaking to s.o. over a distance using electric current running along wires, or by radio; **on the t.** = (i) speaking into the telephone; (ii) (house) with a telephone; **t. box** =

outdoor booth with a public telephone in it. **2.** to speak to (s.o.) by telephone. **telephonic** [telɪˈfɒnɪk] *adj.* referring to the telephone. **telephonist** [təˈlefənɪst] *n.* person who connects telephone calls in a central exchange. **telephony,** *n.* science of telephones.

telephoto lens [telɪˈfəʊtəʊˈlenz] *n.* lens for a camera which gives a large picture of sth which is at a distance.

teleprinter [ˈtelɪprɪntə] *n.* apparatus like a typewriter which sends out and receives messages by telegraph, and which prints them when they are received.

telesales [telɪˈseɪlz] *n.* sales made by telephone.

telescope [ˈtelɪskəup] **1.** *n.* tube with a series of lenses for looking at very distant objects; **radio t.** = apparatus which detects radio signals from stars and follows their movements. **2.** *v.* to push together, so that one piece slides into another; to crush together. **telescopic** [telɪˈskɒpɪk] *adj.* (*a*) referring to a telescope. (*b*) (parts) which slide together like a telescope.

teletypewriter [telɪˈtaɪpraɪtə] *n. Am.* teleprinter.

television [telɪˈvɪʒn] *n.* system for sending pictures by radio waves; **t. (set)** = apparatus for showing pictures sent by radio waves. **televise** [ˈtelɪvaɪz] *v.* to broadcast (sth) by television. **televised live** = shown direct/not recorded and broadcast later.

telex [ˈteleks] **1.** *n.* (*pl.* **-es**) system of sending messages by teleprinter; message sent by teleprinter. **2.** *v.* to send a message to (s.o.), using the teleprinter.

tell [tel] *v.* (**told**) (*a*) to say. (*b*) to pass on information. (*c*) to give instructions (**how** to do sth). (*d*) to make out (the difference) **between** two things); to notice a quality. (*e*) to have an effect; **his age told in the end** = finally he lost because he was older than the other competitors. (*g*) to count (money/votes); **all told** = altogether. **teller** [ˈtelə] *n.* person who counts votes; clerk in a bank who counts money and pays it out to customers. **telling,** *adj.* which has an effect. **tellingly,** *adv.* in a telling way. **tell off,** *v. inf.* to reprimand/to

criticize (s.o.). **tell on,** *v. inf.* **to tell on s.o.** = to let out a secret about someone. **telltale. 1.** *n.* person who gives away a secret. **2.** *adj.* (thing) which gives away a secret.

telly [ˈtelɪ] *n. inf.* television.

temerity [təˈmerɪtɪ] *n.* audacity; daring to do sth.

temp [temp] **1.** *n. inf. short for* temporary secretary. **2.** *v. inf.* to work as a temp.

temper [ˈtempə] **1.** *n.* (*a*) usually calm state of mind; **he lost his t.** = he became very angry; **she kept her t.** = she stayed calm and did not get angry. (*b*) (good/bad) state of mind. (*c*) fit of anger. (*d*) hardness of a metal due to beating. **2.** *v.* (*a*) to harden (steel). (*b*) to moderate/to make less strong.

tempera [ˈtempərə] *n.* type of thick paint which can be diluted with water.

temperament [ˈtemprəmənt] *n.* state of mind; nature of a person. **temperamental** [temprəˈmentl] *adj.* (person) likely to change his state of mind frequently; likely to get easily excited or depressed. **temperamentally,** *adv.* according to a state of mind.

temperance [ˈtemprəns] *n.* (*a*) being moderate/controlled. (*b*) not drinking alcohol; **t. movement** = group of people who try to persuade others not to drink alcohol.

temperate [ˈtemprət] *adj.* (*a*) moderate/sober (language/habits). (*b*) (climate) which is neither extremely hot nor cold. **temperature** [ˈtemprətʃə] *n.* (*a*) amount of heat measured in degrees. (*b*) state where the temperature of the body is higher than it should be.

tempest [ˈtempɪst] *n.* storm. **tempestuous** [temˈpestjuəs] *adj.* violently stormy/very wild; very enthusiastic (applause).

template [ˈtemplɪt] *n.* thin sheet used as a pattern for cutting pieces of wood/metal, etc., to an exact shape.

temple [ˈtempl] *n.* (*a*) flat part of the front of the head on each side of the forehead. (*b*) building for worship (not usu. Christian or Muslim).

tempo [ˈtempəʊ] *n.* (*pl.* **-os/tempi** [ˈtempiː]) rhythm; beat (of music, etc.).

temporal ['temprəl] *adj.* (*a*) referring to the temple/the flat part of the side of the head near the forehead. (*b*) referring to this world/not eternal/not spiritual. (*c*) referring to time.

temporary ['temprəri] *adj.* which only lasts a short time/which is meant to last a short time. **temporarily** ['temprərəli] *adv.* for a short time. **temporize**, *v.* to try to gain time.

tempt [temt] *v.* (*a*) to attract (s.o.); to try to persuade (s.o.) to do sth. (*b*) **I am tempted to accept** = I think I will accept. (*c*) **to t. providence** = to take a great risk. **temptation** [tem'teɪʃn] *n.* state of being tempted; thing which attracts you. **tempter, temptress,** *n.* person who tempts. **tempting,** *adj.* attractive.

ten [ten] *n.* number 10; *inf.* **t. to one he finds out** = he's very likely to find out.

tenable ['tenəbl] *adj.* (theory) which can be held/supported.

tenacious [tɪ'neɪʃəs] *adj.* which holds on to sth tightly; obstinate; determined. **tenaciously,** *adv.* in a tenacious way. **tenacity** [tə'næsɪtɪ] *n.* holding to sth too tightly.

tenant ['tenənt] *n.* person who rents a room/flat/house/land; **to buy a house with a sitting t.** = with s.o. living in it and paying rent. **tenancy,** *n.* period during which a tenant rents a property.

tench [tentʃ] *n.* (*pl.* **tench**) type of small fish.

tend [tend] *v.* (*a*) to look after. (*b*) to be likely (to do sth). (*c*) to lean (in a certain direction). **tendency,** *n.* being likely to do sth. **tendentious** [ten'denʃəs] *adj.* (book/article/speech) which puts over a strong point of view which is not generally approved.

tender ['tendə] **1.** *n.* (*a*) boat which brings supplies to a large ship; wagon carrying coal behind a coal-burning locomotive. (*b*) offer to do work at a certain price. (*c*) **legal t.** = coins/notes which are legally acceptable when offered in payment. **2.** *adj.* (*a*) soft/delicate; **t. meat** = which can be chewed/cut easily. (*b*) **t. plants** = which cannot stand frost; **child of t. years** = very young child. (*c*) **with a t. heart** = very affectionate/very loving. (*d*) painful; *inf.* **you've touched him on a t.**

spot = you have mentioned sth which he is very touchy about. **3.** *v.* (*a*) (*formal*) to offer. (*b*) (**for**) to offer to do work at a certain price. **tenderfoot,** *n.* inexperienced person. **tenderhearted,** *adj.* kind. **tenderize,** *v.* to make (meat) tender. **tenderloin** ['tendəlɔɪn] *n.* piece of tender beef or pork from the side of the backbone. **tenderly,** *adv.* gently; with kindness. **tenderness,** *n.* being tender.

tendon ['tendən] *n.* strong cord of tissue attaching a muscle to a bone.

tendril ['tendrəl] *n.* thin curling part with which a plant clings to a support.

tenement ['tenəmənt] *n.* (*a*) large (often dilapidated) building which is divided into flats. (*b*) (*in Scotland*) building which is rented as flats.

tenet ['tenet] *n.* basic principle/belief.

tenfold ['tenfəuld] *adv.* ten times as much.

tenner ['tenə] *n. inf.* ten pound note.

tennis ['tenɪs] *n.* game for two players or two pairs of players who use rackets to hit a ball backwards and forwards over a net; **t. court** = specially marked ground for playing tennis; **t. elbow** = painful condition of the elbow joint caused by strain.

tenon ['tenən] *n.* small projection from the end of a piece of wood which fits into a corresponding mortise in another piece to form a joint.

tenor ['tenə] *n.* (*a*) man who sings with the highest normal male voice. (*b*) highest male voice; musical instrument with a high pitch. (*c*) (*formal*) general meaning. (*d*) (*formal*) general way (of living).

tense [tens] **1.** *n.* form of a verb which shows when the action takes place. **2.** *adj.* (**-er, -est**) (*a*) stretched tight. (*b*) nervous and anxious. (*c*) warlike (state between countries). **3.** *v.* to make/to become tense. **tensely,** *adv.* in a tense way. **tenseness,** *n.* being tense. **tensile** ['tensail] *adj.* referring to tension; **t. strength** = force needed to stretch sth until it breaks. **tension** ['tenʃn] *n.* (*a*) tightness; being stretched; (*in knitting*) tightness of the stitches calculated as the number of stitches or rows per centimetre. (*b*) nervous anxiety. (*c*) state of aggravation (between countries). (*d*) electric power; **high-tension cables.**

tent [tent] *n.* small canvas shelter held up by poles and attached to the ground with pegs and ropes; **to pitch a t.** = to put up a tent; **oxygen t.** = cover put up over a sick person's bed to allow oxygen to be pumped in.

tentacle ['tentəkl] *n.* long arm with suckers (such as that of an octopus).

tentative ['tentətɪv] *adj.* uncertain; done as a trial; **t. proposal** = made to find out what the response is. **tentatively,** *adv.* in a tentative way.

tenterhooks ['tentəhu:ks] *n. pl.* **on t.** = impatiently waiting/anxious and uncertain.

tenth [tenθ], **10th,** *adj. & n.* referring to ten; **the t. century** = period from 900 to 999.

tenuous ['tenjʊəs] *adj.* thin; not strong. **tenuously,** *adv.* in a tenuous way. **tenuousness,** *n.* being tenuous.

tenure ['tenjə] *n.* (*a*) right to hold property/to have employment; holding of a property or employment. (*b*) right to hold a job permanently.

tepee ['ti:pi:] *n.* cone-shaped tent of North American Indians.

tepid ['tepɪd] *adj.* slightly warm.

tequila [te'ki:lə] *n.* Mexican alcoholic drink.

tercentenary [tɜ:sen'ti:nərɪ] *n* anniversary of 300 years.

term [tɜ:m] **1.** *n.* (*a*) length of time; **in the long t./in the short t.** = for a long period from now/for a short period from now. (*b*) end of a period of time; **she was approaching her t.** = nearly at the end of her pregnancy. (*c*) part of a school/university year. (*d*) conditions; **terms of reference** = areas which a committee/an inspector has to examine or discuss; **to come to terms with** = to accept as inevitable; **they came to terms** = they reached agreement; **terms of payment** = way in which a payment shall be made; **our terms are ninety days** = we allow 90 days' credit. (*e*) relationship; **on good/bad terms** = having a friendly/unfriendly relationship. (*f*) particular word. (*g*) expressing; **in terms of health/in health terms** = regarding health; **I'm**

thinking **in terms of weekly payments** = my idea is that the payments should be made each week. **2.** *v.* to call.

termagant ['tɜ:məgənt] *n.* noisy woman who bullies people.

terminal ['tɜ:mɪnl] **1.** *adj.* (*a*) at the end; **t. shoot** = shoot at the end of a branch. (*b*) referring to a school term. (*c*) in the last period of life; **t. case** = patient who is soon going to die. **2.** *n.* (*a*) building at an airport where passengers arrive or leave. (*b*) terminus; **air t.** = building in the centre of a town where coaches arrive from an airport. (*c*) **electric t.** = one of the connecting points in an electric circuit. (*d*) apparatus which can be used for putting information into and getting information from a distant computer (to which it is linked by cable). **terminable,** *adj.* which can be terminated. **terminally,** *adv.* in a terminal way; **t. ill** = in the last stages of an illness before death. **terminate** ['tɜ:mɪneɪt] *v.* to finish/to bring (sth) to an end. **termination** [tɜ:mɪ'neɪʃn] *n.* bringing to an end.

terminology [tɜ:mɪ'nɒlədʒɪ] *n.* special words or phrases used in a particular science. **terminological** [tɜ:mɪnə'lɒdʒɪkl] *adj.* referring to terminology.

terminus ['tɜ:mɪnəs] *n.* (*pl.* **-ni** [-naɪ]) station at the end of a railway line; station at the end of a journey for a bus or a coach.

termite ['tɜ:maɪt] *n.* destructive white insect, rather like an ant, which lives in tropical countries.

tern [tɜ:n] *n.* white sea bird similar to a gull.

terrace ['terəs] **1.** *n.* (*a*) flat area which is raised above another area. (*b*) row of houses connected together and built in a similar style. (*c*) **terraces** = rows of wide steps on which the spectators stand (at a football stadium). **2.** *v.* (*a*) to make a flat raised area. (*b*) **terraced houses** = connected houses built all in a similar style.

terracotta [terə'kɒtə] *n.* red clay used to make small statues; statue made of red clay.

terra firma ['terə'fɜ:mə] *n.* dry land.

terrain [tə'reɪn] *n.* area of country.

terrapin ['terəpɪn] n. type of small American turtle.

terrarium [te'reərɪəm] n. glass box in which flowers are grown.

terrazzo [te'rætsəʊ] n. polished surface, made of little chips of stone embedded in mortar.

terrestrial [tə'restrɪəl] adj. referring to the earth.

terrible ['terɪbl] adj. (a) awful/which makes you very frightened. (b) inf. very bad. **terribly**, adv. (a) frighteningly. (b) inf. very.

terrier ['terɪə] n. small dog (originally used in hunting).

terrific [tə'rɪfɪk] adj. inf. awful/wonderful. **terrifically**, adv. inf. wonderfully/awfully. **terrify** ['terɪfaɪ] v. to frighten completely. **terrifying**, adj. frightening.

terrine [teə'ri:n] n. type of pâté.

territory ['terɪtrɪ] n. (a) land which belongs to a country; large stretch of land. (b) area which an animal/bird, etc. considers as its own. (c) area visited by a travelling salesman. **territorial** [terɪ'tɔ:rɪəl] adj. referring to territory; **t. waters** = area of sea round a country which that country controls. **Territorial Army,** n. volunteer reserve army. **Territorials,** n. pl. inf. the Territorial Army.

terror ['terə] n. (a) extreme fear. (b) thing which causes fear. (c) inf. naughty/uncontrollable person. **terrorism,** n. policy of using violence in a political cause. **terrorist,** adj. & n. (person) who practises terrorism. **terrorize,** v. to frighten (s.o.) very much. **terror-stricken, terror-struck,** adj. extremely frightened.

terry ['terɪ] n. type of cloth where uncut loops stand above the surface.

terse [tɜ:s] adj. concise/short; using few words. **tersely,** adv. briefly/concisely. **terseness,** n. being terse.

tertiary ['tɜ:ʃərɪ] adj. referring to a third stage, esp. to the level of education after the secondary; **t. sector/t. industry** = industries which provide services.

Terylene ['terɪli:n] n. trademark for a type of man-made thread; cloth made of this thread.

tessellated ['tesəleɪtɪd] adj. covered with mosaic.

test [test] **1.** n. (a) examination to see if sth works well/is reliable/if s.o. is healthy. **t. pilot** = pilot who flies a new aircraft to see if it works well. (b) short written or practical examination to see if s.o. knows information/knows how to do sth; **intelligence t./aptitude t.** = test to show how intelligent/how capable you are; **driving t.** = to see if you can drive a car. (c) **to put sth/s.o. to the t.** = to try sth/s.o. out to see if they can stand up to certain conditions. (d) international cricket match. **2.** v. (a) to examine (sth) to see if it is working well; to examine (s.o.) to see if he is healthy. (b) to give (s.o.) a short examination. **test case,** n. court case where the decision sets a precedent for other similar cases to follow. **test-drive,** v. to drive (a new car) before you buy it to see if it works well. **test match,** n. international cricket match. **test tube,** n. small round-bottomed glass tube used in a laboratory for making chemical tests; **t.-t. baby** = baby born through artificial insemination.

testament ['testəmənt] n. (a) **last will and t.** = document written by a person before death to indicate what should happen to his property after he dies. (b) **Old T./New T.** = the two main sections of the Bible. **testamentary,** [testə'mentərɪ] adj. referring to a will.

testate ['testeɪt] adj. (person who has died) leaving a will. **testator, testatrix** [tes'teɪtə, -'teɪtrɪks] n. (pl. **-trices** [-'trɪsi:z]) man/woman who makes a will.

testicle ['testɪkl] n. one of two male glands which produce sperm.

testify ['testɪfaɪ] v. to give evidence that sth is true. **testimonial** [testɪ'məʊnɪəl] n. (a) statement showing what you know of a person's qualities. (b) thing done for a person/given to a person to show appreciation; **t. dinner** = dinner organized to give a present to s.o. **testimony** ['testɪmənɪ] n. evidence that sth is true.

testis ['testɪs] n. (pl. **testes** ['testi:z]) (formal) testicle.

testosterone [tes'tɒstərəʊn] n. male sex hormone.

testy ['testɪ] adj. irritable; easily made angry. **testily,** adv. irritably/angrily.

tetanus ['tetənəs] *n.* serious disease caused by infection in a wound, which can make esp. the jaw muscles stiffen.

tetchy ['tetʃɪ] *adj.* (**-ier, -iest**) bad-tempered. **tetchily,** *adv.* in a tetchy way.

tête-à-tête [teɪtɑːˈteɪt] *n.* private conversation between two people.

tether ['teðə] **1.** *n.* rope which attaches an animal to a post; **he's at the end of his t.** = he can't stand any more/he has lost all patience. **2.** *v.* to attach (an animal) to a post with a rope.

tetrahedron [tetrəˈhiːdrən] *n.* solid shape with four sides, each of which is a triangle.

Teutonic [tjuːˈtɒnɪk] *adj.* German.

text [tekst] *n.* (*a*) main written part of a book (not the notes or pictures, etc.). (*b*) original words of a speech. (*c*) quotation from the Bible used as a moral guide. **textbook,** *n.* book which students read for information about the subject they are studying. **textual,** *adj.* referring to a text.

textile ['tekstaɪl] *adj. & n.* (referring to) cloth.

texture ['tekstʃə] *n.* quality which can be felt; degree of fineness. **textured,** *adj.* with a certain feel.

than [ðæn, ðən] *conj. & prep. used to introduce the second part of comparisons and clauses;* **I have less t. you; there are more t. twenty people in the room; no sooner had we arrived t. the music started.**

thank [θæŋk] *v.* **to t. s.o. for** = to show gratitude to (s.o.). **thankful,** *adj.* showing gratitude; glad because an anxiety has gone. **thankfully,** *adv.* showing relief that an anxiety has gone. **thankfulness,** *n.* being thankful. **thankless,** *adj.* (work) for which no one will thank you; difficult/hopeless (task). **thanklessly,** *adv.* in a thankless way. **thanklessness,** *n.* being thankless. **thanks,** *n.pl.* (*a*) word which shows you are grateful; **to pass a vote of t. to s.o.** = to thank s.o. officially in the minutes of a meeting. (*b*) thank you; **no, t.** = no, thank you. (*c*) **t. to** = as a result of. **thanksgiving,** *n.* (religious) festival where thanks are shown to God; **Thanksgiving** = American and Canadian festival when thanks are given for a safe harvest. **thank you,** *inter.* showing gratitude (**for**); **thank-you letter** = letter in which you thank s.o. for sth.

that [ðæt] **1.** *adj. & pron.* (*pl.* **those** [ðəuz]) *used to indicate* something further away (*as opposed to* **this**) **2.** *pron. linking a subject or object to a verb* **where is the letter t. he sent you? 3.** *adv. inf.* to such an extent; so much; **I knew they were going to be early, but not t. early. 4.** *conj. introducing a clause* **he knew t. we were late.**

thatch [θætʃ] **1.** *n.* reeds/straw, etc., used to make a roof. **2.** *v.* to cover (a house) with a roof of reeds/straw, etc. **thatcher,** *n.* a person who thatches houses.

thaw [θɔː] **1.** *n.* warm weather (which results in the melting of snow/ice). **2.** *v.* (*a*) to melt; to unfreeze (sth which is frozen). (*b*) to get less unfriendly/less shy.

the [ðə] (*before a vowel or when stressed* [ðiː]). **1.** *definite article.* (*a*) (*referring to a particular person or thing*) **the man with the red nose.** (*b*) (*referring to something in general*) **the Russians are lively people.** (*c*) (*stressed*) **it is the shop for furniture. 2.** *adv.* (*in comparisons*) **it will be all the easier** = that much easier; **the sooner the better.**

theatre, *Am.* **theater** ['θɪətə] *n.* (*a*) building in which plays are performed. (*b*) *Am.* cinema. (*c*) art of acting/of producing plays; business of putting on plays. (*d*) collection of plays. (*e*) place where important events happen. (*f*) **operating t.** = room in a hospital where operations take place. **theatregoer,** *n.* person who goes to the theatre. **theatrical** [θɪˈætrɪkl] *adj.* (*a*) referring to the theatre. (*b*) very dramatic/not acting naturally. **theatrically,** *adv.* in a theatrical way. **theatricals,** *n.pl.* **amateur t.** = performances of a play by amateurs.

thee [ðiː] *pron.* (*old*) you.

theft [θeft] *n.* stealing.

their ['ðeə] *adj.* belonging to them.

theirs ['ðeəz] *pron.* belonging to them; **she's a friend of t.**

theism ['θiːɪzm] *n.* belief that a god exists. **theist,** *n.* person who believes that a god exists.

them [ðem] *pron. referring to persons/ things which are objects of a verb.*

themselves [ðem'selvz] *pron. referring to a plural subject;* **all by t.** = without any help from anyone else.

theme [θi:m] *n.* (*a*) subject (of book/ article). (*b*) main tune in a piece of music; **t. tune/t. song** = catchy tune/ song played several times in a film or TV serial which makes the audience recognize it. **thematic** [θɪ'mætɪk] *adj.* referring to a theme.

then [ðen] **1.** *adv.* (*a*) at that time; **t. and there** = immediately; **now and t.** = from time to time. (*b*) afterwards. (*c*) also/in any case. (*d*) therefore; the result is. **2.** *n.* that time. **3.** *adj.* existing at that time; **the t. Prime Minister.**

thence [ðens] *adv.* (*formal*) (*a*) from that place; from there. (*b*) so/therefore. **thenceforth,** *adv.* (*formal*) from that time onwards.

theodolite [θɪ'ɒdəlaɪt] *n.* device for measuring angles when surveying land.

theology [θɪ'ɒlədʒɪ] *n.* study of belief in God; study of God and God's relations with man. **theologian** [θɪə'ləʊdʒɪə n] *n.* person who specializes in the study of God/in the interpretation of religion. **theological** [θɪə'lɒdʒɪkl] *adj.* referring to theology; **t. college** = college where people study to become priests. **theologically,** *adv.* in a theological way.

theorem [θi:ərəm] *n.* thing which has to be proved in mathematics.

theory [θɪərɪ] *n.* (*a*) explanation of sth which has not been proved but which you believe is true. (*b*) statement of general principles (which may not apply in practice); **in t. it should work** = if you follow general principles. **theoretical** [θɪə'retɪkl] *adj.* referring to a theory; not proved in practice. **theoretically,** *adv.* in theory, but not in practice. **theoretician, theorist** [θɪərə-'tɪʃn, 'θɪərɪst] *n.* person who forms (political) theories. **theorize** ['θɪəraɪz] *v.* to make up a theory about sth.

theosophy [θɪ'ɒsəfɪ] *n.* religion which states that certain people can understand the working of God.

therapy ['θerəpɪ] *n.* treatment of illness (esp. without using medicine); **speech t.** = treatment of difficulty in speak-

ing; **occupational t.** = treatment by getting patients to do things; **group t.** = treatment by getting patients together in groups to discuss their problems. **therapeutic** [θerə'pju:tɪk] *adj.* which may cure. **therapeutically,** *adv.* in a therapeutic way. **therapeutics,** *n. pl.* study of curing diseases. **therapist,** *n.* person who applies therapy.

there ['ðeə] **1.** *adv.* in that place/to that place; *inf.* **t. she goes again** = that is her doing it again. **2.** *inter. showing various feelings* **t., t., don't cry. 3.** *pron. used as subject of a clause usually with the verb* to be, *when the real subject follows the verb* **there's a big car coming up the hill; t. weren't very many people at the meeting; t. appears to be a mistake. thereabouts** [ðeərə'baʊts] *adv.* approximately. **thereafter** [ðeər-'ɑːftə] *adv.* (*formal*) after that. **thereby** [ðeə'baɪ] *adv.* (*formal*) by doing this. **therefore** ['ðeəfɔː] *adv.* consequently; for this reason. **thereupon** [ðeərə'pɒn] *adv.* (*formal*) immediately after that.

therm [θɜ:m] *n.* measure of heat, used for measuring gas in Britain. **thermal 1.** *adj.* referring to heat; **t. baths** = baths of natural hot water; **t. underwear** = which keeps you warm; **t. current** = current of warm air/water. **2.** *n.* current of warm air.

thermionic [θɜ:mɪ'ɒnɪk] *adj.* (radio valve) made of a vacuum tube containing heated electrodes.

thermo- ['θɜ:məʊ] *adj.* referring to heat.

thermodynamics [θɜ:məʊdaɪ-'næmɪks] *n.* study of heat and its relationship to power.

thermometer [θɜ:'mɒmɪtə] *n.* instrument for measuring the temperature.

thermonuclear [θɜ:məʊ'nju:klɪə] *adj.* referring to the high temperature caused by atomic fusion.

thermoplastic [θɜ:mə'plæstɪk] *adj. & n.* (material) which becomes soft when heated and hard when cold.

Thermos (flask) ['θɜ:məs'flɑ:sk] *n.* trademark for a type of vacuum flask.

thermostat ['θɜ:məstæt] *n.* instrument which controls the temperature by setting off heating or cooling devices. **thermostatic** [θɜ:mə'stætɪk] *adj.* referring to a thermostat. **thermostatically,** *adv.* (controlled) by a thermostat.

thesaurus [θəˈsɔːrəs] *n.* (*pl.* **-es**) book with words collected according to their similar meanings, and not in alphabetical order.

these [ðiːz] *adj. & pron. see* **this.**

thesis [ˈθiːsɪs] *n.* (*pl.* **-ses** [-siːz]) (*a*) long piece of written research done for a higher university degree. (*b*) particular point of view.

Thespian [ˈθespɪən] *n.* actor, actress.

thews [θjuːz] *n.pl.* strength.

they [ðeɪ] *pron. subject* (*a*) *referring to several persons or things* (*b*) (*referring to people in general*) **t. say it's going to rain.**

thiamine [ˈθaɪəmiːn] *n.* Vitamin B, found in cereals, liver and pork.

thick [θɪk] **1.** *adj.* (**-er, -est**) (*a*) fat/not thin/with a large distance between the two surfaces. (*b*) with a large diameter. (*c*) dense/packed close together. (*d*) (liquid) which does not flow easily. (*e*) (voice) which is not clear. (*f*) *inf.* **that's a bit t.** = that's very unreasonable. (*g*) *inf.* stupid; **she's a bit t.** (*h*) *inf.* very friendly. **2.** *n.* (*a*) centre (of a battle). (*b*) **through t. and thin** = through times of difficulty as well as through easy times. **3.** *adv.* in a thick layer; *inf.* **to lay it on t.** = to praise s.o. excessively; **t. and fast** = rapidly and heavily. **thicken,** *v.* to make thick/to become thick. **thicket** [ˈθɪkɪt] *n.* small wood of trees and bushes growing close together. **thickly,** *adv.* in a thick way. **thickness,** *n.* being thick; distance between sides. **thickset,** *adj.* (*a*) (hedge) planted with bushes close together. (*b*) short stocky (person). **thick-skinned,** *adj.* (*a*) (fruit) with a thick skin. (*b*) (of person) insensitive/not easily hurt.

thief [θiːf] *n.* (*pl.* **thieves** [θiːvz]) person who steals. **thieve,** *v.* to steal. **thievery,** *n.* stealing. **thieving,** *n.* act of stealing. **thievish,** *adj.* like a thief.

thigh [θaɪ] *n.* thick top part of the leg between the knee and the hip.

thimble [ˈθɪmbl] *n.* small cover worn to protect the end of your finger when sewing. **thimbleful,** *n. inf.* very small quantity (of liquid).

thin [θɪn] **1.** *adj.* (**thinner, thinnest**) not thick/with only a small distance between the two surfaces. (*b*) not fat.

(*c*) with a small diameter. (*d*) not very dense/not close together. (*e*) very watery (liquid). **2.** *adv.* in a thin way. **3.** *v.* (**thinned**) (*a*) to become thin. (*b*) to make liquid thin. (*c*) to make less dense; to become less dense. **thin down,** *v.* to reduce; to make (sth) thinner. **thinly,** *adv.* in a thin way. **thinner,** *n.* substance used to thin paint. **thinness,** *n.* being thin. **thinnings,** *n.* small plants which are removed to allow others more space. **thin out,** *v.* to remove (seedlings) to give more room to those which are left. **thin-skinned,** *adj.* (*a*) (fruit) with a thin skin. (*b*) (of person) sensitive/easily hurt.

thine [ðaɪn] *pron.* (*old*) your.

thing [θɪŋ] *n.* (*a*) object. (*b*) *inf.* person/animal. (*c*) **things** = clothes/equipment. (*d*) item; unspecified subject; object referred to; **it's just one t. after another** = one problem after another; **it's a good t. you came with us** = it's lucky. (*e*) **first t. in the morning/last t. at night** = as soon as you get up/just before you go to bed. (*f*) *inf.* **to have a t. about sth** = to like/dislike sth irrationally. (*g*) *inf.* **he wants to do his own t.** = to do what he really feels like doing. **thingamajig, thingummy** [ˈθɪŋəmədʒɪg, ˈθɪŋəmɪ] *n. inf.* some object/person whose name you have forgotten.

think [θɪŋk] **1.** *n.* time when you have thoughts/when you consider plans in your mind; *inf.* **you've got another t. coming** = you'll have to change your ideas, as this idea won't work. **2.** *v.* (**thought** [θɔːt]) (*a*) to use your mind; **to t. aloud** = to speak your thoughts as they come into your mind. (*b*) to believe; to have as your opinion. (*c*) to expect. (*d*) to plan; **to t. again** = to change your mind; *inf.* **t. big!** = consider only large-scale projects. **thinkable,** *adj.* which can be thought. **think about,** *v.* (*a*) to consider (sth) in your mind. (*b*) to plan (sth). (*c*) to have an opinion. **think back,** *v.* to remember. **thinker,** *n.* person who thinks; **great t.** = philosopher. **thinking,** *n.* reasoning; **to my way of t.** = my opinion is. **think of,** *v.* (*a*) to consider (sth) in your mind. (*b*) to plan (sth). (*c*) to remember. (*d*) to have an opinion;

I told him what I thought of him = I criticized him; **he thinks highly of his teacher** = has a high opinion of him; **she thinks nothing of working 12 hours a day** = she finds it easy; **think nothing of it** = don't bother to thank me for it; **he thought better of it** = changed his mind. **think out**, v. to consider carefully all the details. **think over**, v. to consider (sth) seriously. **think tank**, n. group of experts who advise the government on matters of general policy. **think through**, v. to consider carefully all the details. **think up**, v. to invent.

third, 3rd [θɜːd] n. & adj. referring to three; **t. person** = pronoun or part of a verb referring to a person or thing who is being referred to. **the car went up the hill in t.** = in third gear; **the Third World** = countries with no strong connections to the superpowers. **third degree**, n. hard questioning (by the police). **third party**, n. any person who is not one of the two parties involved in a contract; person (usu. s.o. injured in an accident) who is not the driver of the car or the insurance company which insured it. **t. party insurance** = insurance which covers s.o. not named in it; **third-rate**, adj. very bad.

thirst [θɜːst] **1.** n. (a) wanting to drink. (b) desire (for). **2.** v. (formal) to desire (after/for sth). **thirsty**, adj. (-ier, -iest) wanting to drink; **t. work** = hard/hot work which makes you thirsty. **thirstily**, adv. in a thirsty way.

thirteen [θɜːˈtiːn] n. number 13; **the t. hundreds** = years between 1300 and 1399. **thirteenth, 13th**, adj. & n. referring to thirteen; **the t. century** = period from 1200 to 1299.

thirty [ˈθɜːtɪ] n. number 30; **she's in her thirties** = she is more than thirty years old but less than forty. **thirtieth, 30th**, adj. & n. referring to thirty.

this [ðɪs] **1.** adj. & pron. (pl. **these** [ðiːz]) used to indicate something near (as opposed to that). (a) **t. is the book I meant, not that one.** (b) **t. morning/t. evening** = today in the morning/evening. **2.** adv. inf. to such an extent; **I didn't expect you to be t. late** = so late.

thistle [ˈθɪsl] n. large prickly weed with purple flowers. **thistledown**, n. soft white feathery substance attached to thistle seeds.

thither [ˈðɪðə] adv. (formal) to that place.

thole [θəʊl] n. peg used as a rowlock.

thong [θɒŋ] n. (a) thin leather strap used for tying. (b) light sandal, held by a strap between the toes.

thorax [ˈθɔːræks] n. part of the body between the neck and the abdomen; chest (of an animal/a person); part of an insect's body to which the wings and legs are attached. **thoracic** [θɔːˈræsɪk] adj. referring to a thorax.

thorn [θɔːn] n. spike (of a prickly plant); **a t. in the flesh** = a constant annoyance. **thorny**, adj. (-ier, -iest) covered with thorns; (problem) which is difficult to solve.

thorough [ˈθʌrə] adj. (a) very careful/detailed. (b) complete. **thoroughbred**, adj. & n. pure-bred (horse). **thoroughfare**, n. way through which the public can go. **thoroughgoing**, adj. complete. **thoroughly**, adv. completely/totally. **thoroughness**, n. completeness.

those [ðəʊz] adj. & pron. see **that**.

thou [ðaʊ] pron. (old) you.

though [ðəʊ] **1.** conj. although; in spite of the fact that; **strange it may seem** = although it may seem strange; **as t.** = as if. **2.** adv. in spite of this.

thought [θɔːt] **1.** n. (a) action of thinking; **he was lost in t.** = thinking so hard that you could not attract his attention. (b) considering in your mind; **after much t.** = after considering (the plan) for a long time; **on second thoughts** = having considered everything a second time. (c) plan. (d) regard. **2.** v. see **think**. **thoughtful**, adj. (a) thinking hard. (b) considerate to other people. (c) showing deep thought. **thoughtfully**, adv. in a thoughtful way. **thoughtfulness**, n. being thoughtful. **thoughtless**, adj. without thinking; not thinking about. **thoughtlessly**, adv. in a thoughtless way. **thoughtlessness**, n. being thoughtless. **thought reader**, n. person who claims to be able to say what s.o. else is thinking.

thousand [ˈθaʊzənd] n. number 1000. **thousandth, 1000th. 1.** adj. referring to thousand. **2.** *n.* one of a thousand parts.

thrall [θrɔ:l] *n.* (*formal*) **in t.** = in slavery.

thrash [θræʃ] *v.* (*a*) to beat (with a stick). (*b*) to beat (another team) decisively. **thrash about,** *v.* to move/to wave your arms and legs violently. **thrashing,** *n.* beating. **thrash out,** *v.* to discuss in detail.

thread [θred] **1.** *n.* (*a*) long thin piece of cotton/silk, etc.; **his life hangs by a t.** = he is very likely to die. (*b*) **to lose the t. of a conversation** = to miss what the conversation is about. (*c*) spiral ridge going round a screw/a bolt or inside a nut; **a screw with a left-handed t.** = which you have to turn to the left to tighten. **2.** *v.* (*a*) to put a piece of cotton, etc., through the eye of a needle; to pass (a magnetic tape) through a slit. (*b*) to put (beads, etc.) on a string. (*c*) **to t. your way through a crowd** = to squeeze through a crowd carefully. **threadbare,** *adj.* worn out (clothes). **threadlike,** *adj.* long and thin like a thread. **threadworm,** *n.* long thin worm which lives in human intestines.

threat [θret] *n.* (*a*) warning that sth unpleasant will happen or will be done. (*b*) person/thing which may harm. **threaten,** *v.* to warn that sth unpleasant will be done/that some action will be taken. **threateningly,** *adv.* menacingly.

three [θri:] *n.* number 3. **three-act,** *adj.* (play) with three acts. **three-cornered,** *adj.* with three corners; (election) where there are three candidates. **three-dimensional,** *adj.* (picture) which has depth as well as length and breadth. **threefold,** *adv.* three times as much. **three-piece,** *adj.* with three parts; (suit) with jacket, trousers and waistcoat; (suite of living room furniture) consisting of a sofa and two armchairs. **three-ply,** *adj.* (wool) with three threads twisted together; (plywood) made of three layers stuck together. **three-point turn,** *n.* turning a car in a narrow street in three movements. **three-quarter. 1.** *adj.* referring to three fourths of a whole. **2.** *n.* (*a*) **three-quarters** = three fourths of a whole; **three-quarters of an hour** = 45

minutes. (*b*) (*in Rugby*) one of the fast attacking players behind the forwards. **3.** *adv.* **three-quarters** = three fourths. **threescore,** *n.* (*old*) sixty. **threesome,** *n.* group of three people, esp. three players playing a game.

threnody ['θrenədɪ] *n.* (*formal*) funeral song.

thresh [θreʃ] *v.* to beat (corn) so that the grain falls out; **threshing machine** = machine which threshes corn automatically. **thresher,** *n.* person/machine that threshes.

threshold ['θreʃəʊld] *n.* (*a*) bar across the floor of a doorway. (*b*) edge/beginning; **tax t.** = point at which a higher level of tax is charged. (*c*) limit; **t. of pain** = point at which pain becomes felt.

threw [θru:] *v. see* **throw.**

thrice [θraɪs] *adv.* three times.

thrift [θrɪft] *n.* (*a*) saving (money) by wise use and restricting spending. (*b*) type of seashore plant with small tufts of pink flowers. **thriftily,** *adv.* in a thrifty way. **thriftiness,** *n.* being thrifty. **thrifty,** *adj.* (**-ier, -iest**) careful with money.

thrill [θrɪl] **1.** *n.* (shudder of) excitement. **2.** *v.* to give (s.o.) a shudder of excitement; to be excited. **thriller,** *n.* exciting novel/film, etc. (usu. about crime). **thrilling,** *adj.* very exciting.

thrips [θrɪps] *n.pl.* small insects which live on plants.

thrive [θraɪv] *v.* (**thrived/throve** [θrəʊv]) to grow well/to be strong.

throat [θrəʊt] *n.* (*a*) front part of your neck below the chin. (*b*) pipe running from the back of your mouth down the inside of your neck; **to clear your t.** = to give a short cough; *inf.* **he's always ramming figures down my t.** = telling me figures. **throatily,** *adv.* in a throaty voice. **throaty,** *adj.* **t. voice** = low, rough-sounding voice.

throb [θrɒb] **1.** *n.* beating (of heart/machine). **2.** *v.* (**throbbed**) to beat regularly; to have a regular pain.

throes [θrəʊz] *n.pl.* **death t.** = great suffering just before death; **in the t. of** = in the middle.

thrombosis [θrɒm'bəʊsɪs] *n.* clot in a blood vessel, esp. in the heart.

throne [θrəʊn] *n.* ceremonial chair for a king/queen, etc.; **the t.** = the position of king.

throng [θrɒŋ] **1.** *n.* great crowd of people. **2.** *v.* to crowd together.

throttle ['θrɒtl] **1.** *n.* valve on a pipe which allows variable quantities of steam/petrol, etc., to pass into an engine; **to open up the t.** = to make the engine go faster. **2.** *v.* to strangle (s.o.) by squeezing the neck, and preventing them breathing. **throttle back, throttle down,** *v.* to reduce the supply of petrol to an engine, making it go more slowly.

through [θruː] **1.** *prep.* (*a*) crossing sth on the inside/going in at one side and coming out at the other. (*b*) during. (*c*) *Am.* up to and including; **Monday t. Friday** = from Monday to Friday inclusively. (*d*) by means of. (*e*) because of. **2.** *adv.* (*a*) from one side to another. (*b*) completely/to the finish; **we must see the plan t.** = see that it is completed. (*c*) in contact by telephone. **3.** *adj.* (*a*) which goes from one side to the other without stopping; **t. ticket** = ticket for a whole journey, with possibly changes of transport; **t. traffic** = traffic going through a town without stopping. (*b*) finished/completed; *inf.* **I'm t. with her** = I've broken off our friendship. **through and through,** *adv.* completely. **throughout** [θruː'aʊt] **1.** *prep.* in every part; at all times; from beginning to end. **2.** *adv.* everywhere; at all times. **throughput** ['θruːpʊt] *n.* amount of work done/of goods produced in a certain time. **throughway,** *n. Am.* motorway.

throve [θrəʊv] *v. see* **thrive.**

throw [θrəʊ] **1.** *n.* (*a*) sending sth through the air. (*b*) distance sth is sent through the air; **they live a stone's t. away** = quite close. **2.** *v.* (**threw; has thrown**) (*a*) to send (sth) through the air. (*b*) to shine (a light) **on; can you t. any light on the problem?** = make the problem clearer. (*c*) to make (a pot) with clay on a wheel. (*d*) *inf.* to hold (a party). (*e*) *inf.* to surprise/to confuse (s.o.). **throw away,** *v.* (*a*) to get rid of (sth) which you no longer need. (*b*) to waste. **throwaway,** *adj.* which can be got rid of. **throwback,** *n.* person/animal showing characteristics of distant ancestors; thing which shows

a connection with the past. **thrower,** *n.* person who throws. **throw in,** *v.* (*a*) to add. (*b*) (*in football*) to throw the ball back into play. **throw-in,** *n.* (*in football*) throwing the ball back into play from the touch line. **throw off,** *v.* to get rid of (sth). **throw out,** *v.* (*a*) to put (sth/s.o.) outside using force. (*b*) to send out (heat). (*c*) to reject. **throw over,** *v.* to reject (a lover). **throw up,** *v.* (*a*) to send up into the air. (*b*) to vomit. (*c*) to give up/to abandon.

thru [θruː] *prep., adv. & adj. Am. inf.* = **through. thruway,** *n. Am.* = **throughway.**

thrum [θrʌm] *v.* (**thrummed**) to make a continuous low-pitched sound.

thrush [θrʌʃ] *n.* (*a*) (*pl.* **-es**) common brown bird with a speckled breast. (*b*) infectious throat disease caused by the bacterium *Candida.*

thrust [θrʌst] **1.** *n.* (*a*) push; force which pushes. (*b*) stab with a sword or dagger. **2.** *v.* (**thrust**) (*a*) to push energetically. (*b*) **to t. yourself on s.o.** = to force s.o. to accept you as a guest/companion, etc.

thud [θʌd] **1.** *n.* dull, heavy noise. **2.** *v.* (**thudded**) to make a dull noise.

thug [θʌg] *n.* ruffian/violent person.

thumb [θʌm] **1.** *n.* (*a*) short thick finger which is placed apart from the other four fingers on each hand; **his fingers are all thumbs** = he is awkward with his hands; **it's a useful rule of t.** = (i) a useful way of calculating approximately; (ii) a practical way of approaching a problem; **to be under s.o.'s t.** = to be dominated by s.o.; *inf.* **thumbs up (sign)** = gesture to show that everything is all right; *inf.* **thumbs down (sign)** = gesture to show disapproval. (*b*) part of a glove into which the thumb goes. **2.** *v.* (*a*) **to t. through** = to flick through (a book) using your thumb; **well-thumbed book** = one which has been used often. (*b*) **to t. a lift** = to get a lift from a passing car by making a sign with your thumb. **thumbnail,** *n.* nail on a thumb; **t. sketch** = rapid, very small sketch/description. **thumb-index. 1.** *n.* series of notches cut in the edges of the pages of a book so that you can easily see where a new letter starts. **2.** *v.* to give a book a thumb-index. **thumbscrew**, *n*. machine for torturing, which squeezes the victim's thumb. **thumbtack**, *n*. *Am*. drawing pin.

thump [θʌmp] **1.** *n*. (*a*) dull noise. (*b*) punch; heavy blow with the fist. **2.** *v*. (*a*) to hit with the fist. (*b*) to make a dull noise. **thumping**, *adj*. *inf*. very large.

thunder ['θʌndə] **1.** *n*. (*a*) rumbling noise in the air caused by lightning; **to steal s.o.'s t.** = to take the credit for sth done by s.o. else/to do sth remarkable so that no one notices what another person has done. (*b*) loud rumbling noise. **2.** *v*. (*a*) to make a rumbling noise. (*b*) to speak loudly. **thunderbolt**, *n*. (*a*) flash of lightning and thunder. (*b*) sudden (unpleasant) surprise. **thunderclap**, *n*. sudden noise of thunder. **thundercloud**, *n*. large black cloud which will bring thunder and lightning. **thundering**, *adj*. *inf*. very big/terrible. **thunderous**, *adj*. very loud (applause). **thunderstorm**, *n*. rainstorm with thunder and lightning. **thunderstruck**, *adj*. astonished. **thundery**, *adj*. (weather) when thunder is likely.

Thursday ['θɜːzdeɪ] *n*. fourth day of the week/day between Wednesday and Friday.

thus [ðʌs] *adv*. (*formal*) (*a*) in this way. (*b*) and so.

thwack [θwæk] **1.** *n*. sound made when hitting sth hard. **2.** *v*. to hit (sth) hard.

thwart [θwɔːt] **1.** *n*. seat for a rower in a boat. **2.** *v*. to prevent (s.o.) doing sth.

thy [ðaɪ] *adj*. (old) your. **thyself**, *pron*. (old) yourself.

thyme [taɪm] *n*. common herb used as flavouring.

thymus ['θaɪməs] *n*. lymph gland at the base of the neck.

thyroid (gland) ['θaɪrɔɪd('glænd)] *n*. gland in the neck which influences the growth, etc., of the body. **thyroidectomy**, *n*. operation to remove the thyroid.

Ti *symbol for* titanium.

tiara [tɪ'ɑːrə] *n*. headpiece with jewels, like a small crown.

tibia ['tɪbɪə] *n*. one of the two large bones between the knee and the ankle.

tic [tɪk] *n*. twitch of the muscles which cannot be controlled.

tick [tɪk] **1.** *n*. (*a*) *inf*. very short moment. (*b*) mark on paper to indicate that sth is correct. (*c*) small insect or similar creature which lives on the skin of birds and animals. (*d*) *inf*. **on t.** = on credit. (*e*) small click made by a clock/watch, etc. **2.** *v*. (*a*) to mark with a tick. (*b*) to make a small clicking noise; *inf*. **what makes s.o. t.** = what is the reason for his behaviour. **tick away**, *v*. (*of time*) to pass. **ticker**, *n*. *inf*. (*a*) watch. (*b*) heart. **tickertape**, *n*. long paper tape which carries information printed automatically by telegraph. **tick off**, *v*. (*a*) to mark with a tick. (*b*) *inf*. to reprimand (s.o.). **tick over**, *v*. (*of car engine*) to run gently while the car is stationary. **tick-tack**, *n*. system of hand signals used by bookmakers to pass information at racecourses.

ticket ['tɪkɪt] **1.** *n*. (*a*) piece of paper/card allowing you to travel, to go into a theatre/cinema, etc.; piece of paper showing a price/information; receipt for a coat in a cloakroom; **parking t.** = piece of paper showing that you have parked illegally and must pay a fine. (*b*) **master's t.** = licence held by the captain of a ship which shows he is qualified. (*c*) *Am*. list of candidates sponsored by a political party. **2.** *v*. to stick a ticket on (sth for sale).

ticking ['tɪkɪŋ] *n*. thick cloth for covering mattresses, etc.

tickle ['tɪkl] **1.** *n*. irritation which makes you laugh/cough. **2.** *v*. (*a*) to irritate mildly (a part of s.o.'s body) in order to make him laugh; *inf*. **tickled pink** = very pleased and amused. (*b*) to itch/to be irritated. **ticklish**, *adj*. (*a*) (person) who is easily made to laugh by tickling. (*b*) *inf*. difficult (problem). **tickly**, *adj*. irritated so as to make you want to scratch.

tic-tac-toe [tɪktæk'təʊ] *n*. *Am*. noughts and crosses.

tidbit ['tɪdbɪt] *n*. *Am*. see **titbit**.

tiddler ['tɪdlə] *n*. *inf*. very small fish.

tiddly ['tɪdlɪ] *adj*. (**-ier, -iest**) *inf*. rather drunk. **tiddly-winks**, *n*. game where small discs have to be flicked into a little cup.

tide [taɪd] **1.** *n*. (*a*) regular rising and falling movement of the sea. (*b*) movement (of public opinion, etc.); **to swim against the t.** = to go against what most people think. **2.** *v.* **to t. s.o. over** = to help him get past a difficult period. **tidal**, *adj.* referring to the tide; **t. wave** = huge wave in the sea; **t. stretch of the river** = part of the river near its mouth where the movement of the tides is noticeable. **tidemark**, *n.* (*a*) mark showing the top limit of a tide. (*b*) *inf.* dirty line round a bath showing where the water reached to; line (as on your neck) showing which part of the body has been washed and which has not. **tideway**, *n.* current caused by the tide running in a tidal stretch of a river.

tidings ['taɪdɪŋz] *n. pl.* (*formal*) news.

tidy ['taɪdɪ] **1.** *adj.* (-ier, -iest) (*a*) neat/in good order. (*b*) *inf.* quite large (sum). **2.** *n.* small container for putting things in to keep them tidy. **3.** *v.* to make (sth) neat. **tidily**, *adv.* in a tidy way. **tidiness**, *n.* being tidy. **tidy up**, *v.* to make (sth) completely tidy; to remove (a mess).

tie [taɪ] **1.** *n.* (*a*) thing which attaches/ which restricts; **the ties of friendship.** (*b*) band of cloth which is worn knotted round the neck under the shirt collar; **old school t.** = particular tie which shows which school you went to. (*c*) linking mark in music to show that several notes are to be played as one long note. (*d*) equal score in a competition/election; **there was a t. for second place** = two people were equal second. (*e*) **cup t.** = football match as a result of which one team is eliminated from a championship. **2.** *v.* (*a*) to attach/to fasten; **she's tied to her work** = can never get away from it. (*b*) to make (a knot). (*c*) to come equal in a competition. **tie-breaker**, *n.* (*in tennis*) game to decide the winner of a set, played when the score is 6-6. **tied**, *adj.* attached; **t. house** = public house which belongs to a brewery; **t. cottage** = cottage belonging to a farmer who rents it to his farmworkers. **tie down**, *v.* to attach (to the floor/ground); **to tie s.o. down** = to make s.o. accept certain conditions. **tie-dyed**, *adj.* (shirt, etc.) which has been tied and then dyed to give a mottled effect. **tie-on**, *adj.* **tie-on label** = label with a string attached

so that it can be tied. **tiepin**, *n.* pin for attaching a tie. **tie up**, *v.* (*a*) to attach/ to fasten. (*b*) to keep motionless; **rather tied up** = rather busy. (*c*) to use (money) to purchase sth, so that it is not available for other purposes. **tie-up**, *n.* link/connection.

tier ['tɪə] *n.* one of a series of steps, usu. a row of seats in a theatre; **wedding cake with four tiers** = made of four separate cakes balanced one on top of the other. **tiered**, *adj.* with tiers.

tiff [tɪf] *n.* small argument/quarrel.

tiffin ['tɪfɪn] *n.* (*in India, etc.*) lunch.

tiger ['taɪgə] *n.* large striped cat-like wild animal; **t. lily** = lily with spotted orange flowers; **paper t.** = thing which seems fierce but is really harmless. **tigress**, *n.* female tiger.

tight [taɪt] **1.** *adj.* (-er, -est) (*a*) which fits (too) closely; (*b*) closely packed together; (schedule) which allows no spare time. (*c*) stretched taut. (*d*) *inf.* (money) which is difficult to get. (*e*) *inf.* drunk. **2.** *adv.* (*a*) closely/firmly (shut). (*b*) closely packed. (*c*) *inf.* **to sit t.** = to stay where you are. **tighten**, *v.* to make/to become tight; **we must t. our belts** = be prepared to eat less/ to spend less. **tightfisted**, *adj. & n.* mean/not generous. **tightfitting**, *adj.* which fits tightly. **tightlipped**, *adj.* with the mouth firmly closed; (person) who refuses to speak. **tightly**, *adv.* in a tight way. **tightness**, *n.* being tight. **tightrope**, *n.* rope stretched between two poles on which s.o. can walk/ can perform tricks. **tights**, *n.pl.* close-fitting piece of clothing worn by girls, women, dancers, etc., on the legs and lower part of the body.

tile [taɪl] **1.** *n.* flat piece of baked clay used to cover floors/walls/roofs; **carpet tiles** = square pieces of carpet which can be laid on a floor like tiles. **2.** *v.* to cover (a roof/a floor/a wall) with tiles. **tiler**, *n.* person who tiles (a roof, etc.).

till [tɪl] **1.** *n.* drawer for keeping cash in a shop. **2.** *v.* to cultivate (land). **3.** *prep.* until/up to (a time). **4.** *conj.* up to/until.

tiller ['tɪlə] *n.* handle which is attached to a rudder and so steers a boat.

tilt [tɪlt] **1.** *n.* (*a*) slope/slant. (*b*) **at full t.** = at full speed. **2.** *v.* to slope; to place at a slope.

tilth [tɪlθ] *n.* good crumbly soil.

timber ['tɪmbə] *n.* (*a*) cut wood ready for building; **t. merchant** = person who sells timber. (*b*) growing trees which could be cut down and used for building. (*c*) large beam/plank used in building. **timbered**, *adj.* (house) made of wooden beams. **timberyard**, *n.* place where cut wood is sold.

timbre ['tæmbə] *n.* quality of sound (of voice/musical instrument).

time [taɪm] **1.** *n.* (*a*) existence for a period (such as years/centuries, etc.); **t. alone will tell** = the result will only become apparent later; **to have t. on your hands** = to have a period with nothing to do; **there's no t. to be lost** = we must hurry; **to make up for lost t.** = to do things rapidly because time has been wasted. (*b*) period between two happenings; **in three weeks' t.** = three weeks from now; **all the t.** = continuously. (*c*) particular period; *inf.* **to do t.** = to serve a prison sentence. (*d*) **times** = age/period; **behind the times** = out of date. (*e*) particular point at which sth took place; **I was away at the t.** = when it happened; **at the present t.** = now; **by the t. I got there** = when I got there; **from t. to t./at times** = occasionally; **for the t. being** = temporarily. (*f*) point expressed in hours and minutes; **Greenwich Mean Time** = internationally accepted correct time system. (*g*) hour at which sth usually happens; **the train arrived on t.** = at the right time; **we were in t.** = we were early enough. (*h*) (pleasant/bad) period. (*i*) one of several occasions. (*j*) **times** = multiplied by. (*k*) rhythm. **2.** *v.* (*a*) to choose the right moment. (*b*) to calculate the time sth takes. **time bomb**, *n.* bomb with a clock attached, which sets off the bomb at a particular moment. **time-honoured**, *adj.* (custom) observed for a long time, and therefore respected. **timekeeper**, *n.* (*a*) person who times a race. (*b*) **good t.** = (i) person who is always on time; (ii) watch which always shows the correct time. **timekeeping**, *n.* being on time. **timelag**, *n.* delay. **timeless**, *adj.* permanent; untouched by time. **timelessness**, *n.* being timeless. **time**

limit, *n.* period during which sth should be done. **timeliness**, *n.* being timely. **timely**, *adj.* which happens at the right moment. **timepiece**, *n.* old-fashioned watch or clock. **timer**, *n,* (*a*) person/device which times; **egg t.** = device which times how long an egg boils. (*b*) time switch. **timesaving**, *adj.* (device) which saves time. **timeserver**, *n.* person who changes his opinions to match those of people in power. **timesharing**, *n.* system where several people buy shares in a property, each one being allowed to use it for a limited period each year. **time-signal**, *n.* accurate radio signal showing the exact time. **time-switch**, *n.* switch which can be set to start a machine/to stop a light, etc., at a particular time. **timetable. 1.** *n.* list which shows the times of trains/aircraft/classes in school/appointments. **2.** *v.* to draw up a list of times; to appear on a list of times. **time-work**, *n.* work which is paid for at a rate of money for a particular time. **time zone**, *n.* zone on the earth in which a uniform time is kept. **timing**, *n.* (*a*) action of recording the time (of a race). (*b*) controlling the time at which sth happens. (*c*) (*in a car engine*) rate at which the spark coincides with the flow of petrol.

timid ['tɪmɪd] *adj.* afraid/frightened. **timidity** [tɪmɪdɪtɪ] *n.* being timid. **timidly** ['tɪmɪdlɪ] *adv.* in a timid way. **timorous** ['tɪmərəs] *adj.* very frightened.

timpani ['tɪmpənɪ] *n.pl.* group of kettledrums in an orchestra. **timpanist**, *n.* person who plays the timpani.

tin [tɪn] **1.** *n.* (*a*) (*element: Sn*) silvery metal. (*b*) metal covered with a thin layer of tin. (*c*) (usu. round) metal box for keeping food in; **cake t.** = tin for baking or keeping cakes in. **2.** *v.* (**tinned**) to preserve (food) by packing it in a tin. **tinfoil**, *n.* thin metal sheet used esp. to wrap food up. **tinny** ['tɪnɪ] *adj.* (**-ier, -iest**) weak, metallic (sound); (car) which rattles. **tin opener**, *n.* device for opening tins. **tin pan alley**, *n. inf.* area where publishers of popular music have offices. **tin plate** ['tɪnpleɪt] *n.* thin sheet of iron covered with tin. **tinpot**, *adj. inf.* not of good quality. **tin tack**, *n.* nail with a large head used to fasten down carpets, etc.

tincture ['tɪŋktʃə] *n.* medicine dissolved in alcohol.

tinder ['tɪndə] *n.* very dry material for starting a fire.

tine [taɪn] *n.* prong of a fork.

tinge [tɪndʒ] 1. *n.* slight colour/taste, etc., of sth. 2. *v.* to give a slight colour/taste to (sth).

tingle ['tɪŋgl] 1. *n.* sharp prickling feeling. 2. *v.* to have a sharp prickling feeling; **tingling with excitement** = very excited.

tinker ['tɪŋkə] 1. *n.* mender of saucepans who travels from place to place. 2. *v.* **to t. with sth** = to try (often in a clumsy way) to make sth work better.

tinkle ['tɪŋkl] 1. *n.* ringing (like a little bell). 2. *v.* to make a little ringing noise.

tinnitus [tɪ'naɪtəs] *n.* ringing noise in the ears.

tinsel ['tɪnsl] *n.* thin strips of glittering metal used for decorating Christmas trees, etc.

tint [tɪnt] 1. *n.* slight shade of colour. 2. *v.* to give a slight shade of colour; **tinted glass** = glass which has a slight shade of brown/blue, etc.

tiny ['taɪnɪ] *adj.* (-ier, -iest) very small.

tip [tɪp] 1. *n.* (a) pointed end; **the t. of the iceberg** = small part of sth (usu. unpleasant) which makes you eventually discover the rest. (b) money given to a waiter, etc., to show thanks for his services. (c) piece of helpful information; **racing tips** = suggestions as to which horses are likely to win; **take my t.** = take my advice. (d) **rubbish t.** = public place where rubbish can be dumped. 2. *v.* (**tipped**) (a) to put a tip on (sth); (b) to make (sth) slope/lean. (c) to pour out/to empty (sth). (d) to throw away (rubbish). (e) to give (a waiter, etc.) a small gift of money. (f) to give (s.o.) a piece of helpful information; **to t. s.o. off**/*inf.* **to t. s.o. the wink** = to warn s.o. (g) to forecast confidently that s.o. with do sth. **tip-off,** *n. inf.* piece of useful information; warning. **tip over,** *v.* to lean and fall over; to make (sth) lean and fall over. **tipper,** *n.* truck, etc., which tips. **tipster,** *n.* person who gives advice on which horse is likely to win a

race. **tiptoe.** 1. *n.* **on t.** = quietly on the tips of your toes. 2. *v.* to walk quietly on the tips of your toes. **tiptop,** *adj. inf.* excellent. **tip up,** *v.* (a) to turn (sth) over so that the contents fall out. (b) to swing on a hinge. **tip-up,** *adj.* (chair/lorry) which tips up.

tipple ['tɪpl] 1. *n. inf.* drink. 2. *v. inf.* to drink alcohol regularly.

tipstaff ['tɪpstɑːf] *n.* official of a law court.

tipsy [tɪpsɪ] *adj.* (-ier, -iest) *inf.* rather drunk; **t. cake** = cake soaked in sherry, etc. **tipsily,** *adv.* in a tipsy way. **tipsiness,** *n.* being tipsy.

tirade [taɪ'reɪd] *n.* long angry speech.

tire [taɪə] 1. *n. Am. see* **tyre.** 2. *v.* (a) to become/to make weary; to need a rest after physical exercise. (b) (of) to lose interest in doing sth. **tired,** *adj.* (a) feeling sleepy/in need of rest. (b) **t. of sth** = bored with sth/having no patience with sth. **tiredness,** *n.* feeling in need of rest. **tireless,** *adj.* full of energy/never needing to rest. **tirelessly,** *adv.* in a tireless way. **tiresome,** *adj.* annoying/bothering. **tiring,** *adj.* which makes you tired.

tiro ['taɪrəʊ] *n.* (*pl.* -os) complete beginner/person with no experience.

tissue ['tɪʃuː] *n.* (a) group of cells which make up a part of an animal or plant. (b) thin cloth. (c) soft paper handkerchief. (d) **t. of lies** = mass of lies. **tissue paper,** *n.* thin soft paper used for wrapping delicate objects.

tit [tɪt] *n.* (a) type of common small bird. (b) *Sl.* teat; breast. (c) **t. for tat** = paying back a blow with another blow.

titan ['taɪtn] *n.* very large/strong person. **titanic** [taɪ'tænɪk] *adj.* very large.

titanium [tɪ'teɪnɪəm] *n.* (*element:* Ti) light grey metal.

titbit, *Am.* **tidbit** ['tɪtbɪt] *n.* special little piece (of food/of information).

tithe [taɪð] *n.* (*old*) produce paid to the church. **tithebarn,** *n.* barn in which tithes were kept.

titillate ['tɪtɪleɪt] *v.* to excite. **titillation,** *n.* act of titillating.

titivate ['tɪtɪveɪt] *v. inf.* **to t. (yourself)** = to make yourself look smart.

title ['taɪtl] *n.* (a) name of a book/play/film, etc.; **t. page** = page at the beginning of a book, where the title is written in large letters; **t. role** = part in a play/film which gives the name to the play/film; **credit titles** = words at the beginning of a film showing who is the director, etc. (*b*) word (usu. put in front of a name) to indicate an honour/ a qualification. (*c*) (*in sport*) position of champion. (*d*) right to own (property); **t. deed** = paper showing that you are the owner of a property. **titled,** *adj.* with a title (such as Lord, Sir, etc.) to show that you are a nobleman.

titmouse ['tɪtmaʊs] *n.* (*pl.* **-mice**) type of small bird.

titrate [taɪ'treɪt] *v.* to analyse the concentration of a chemical solution. **titration** [taɪ'treɪʃn] *n.* act of titrating.

titter ['tɪtə] **1.** *n.* little laugh. **2.** *v.* to give a little laugh.

tittle-tattle ['tɪtl'tætl] *n. inf.* gossip.

titular ['tɪtjʊlə] *adj.* holding a title but without direct power.

tiz, tizwaz, tizzy [tɪz, 'tɪzwɒz, 'tɪzɪ] *n. inf.* bother/nervous state.

TNT ['ti:en'ti:] *abbreviation for* trinitrotoluene, common high explosive.

to [tu:] **1.** *prep.* (*a*) (*showing direction or position*) **he went to France; move to the right.** (*b*) (*showing time*) **from day to day; it's ten to six** = ten minutes before six o'clock. (*c*) (*showing person who receives something*) **give it to me.** (*d*) (*showing relationship*) **is this the key to the box? secretary to the managing director.** (*e*) concerning; **there's nothing to it** = there's no difficulty in doing it. (*f*) (*showing ratio*) **they lost by six goals to four; the rate is two dollars to the pound.** (*g*) (*showing comparison*) **I prefer butter to margarine. 2.** *adv.* (*a*) **he came to** = he regained consciousness. (*b*) **pull the door to** = pull it until it is almost shut. **3.** (*forming infinitive*) (*a*) *after verbs* **they came to help us.** (*b*) *after adjectives* **good to eat.** (*c*) *after nouns* **he made no attempt to run away.** (*d*) *when the verb is a subject* **to refuse the invitation would have been rude. to and fro,** *adv.* backwards and forwards. **-to-be** *suffix showing something in the near future* a **mother-to-be.**

toad [təʊd] *n.* amphibian like a large

frog, which lives mostly on land; **t. in the hole** = sausages cooked in a dish of batter. **toadstool,** *n.* fungus shaped like a mushroom, but usu. not edible, and sometimes poisonous. **toady. 1.** *n.* person who flatters s.o. (in the hope of getting sth in return). **2.** *v.* to flatter (s.o.).

toast [təʊst] **1.** *n.* (*a*) slices of bread which have been grilled brown. (*b*) taking a drink and wishing s.o. success. **2.** *v.* (*a*) to grill (bread, etc.) until it is brown; to warm. (*b*) to drink and wish s.o. success. **toaster,** *n.* electric device for toasting bread. **toastmaster,** *n.* person (at a banquet) who calls on people to speak and announces the toasts. **toastrack,** *n.* device for holding slices of toast.

tobacco [tə'bækəʊ] *n.* (dried leaves of a) plant used for smoking in cigarettes/ cigars and in pipes. **tobacconist,** *n.* person who sells tobacco/cigarettes, etc.

toboggan [tə'bɒgən] **1.** *n.* long sledge curved upwards at the front. **2.** *v.* to slide on a toboggan. **tobogganing,** *n.* sport of sliding on a toboggan.

toby jug ['təʊbɪ 'dʒʌg] *n.* small mug made in the shape of a head.

toccata [tɒ'kɑːtə] *n.* piece of music for the organ or piano.

tocsin ['tɒksɪn] *n.* warning bell.

today [tə'deɪ] *adv. & n.* (*a*) this present day; **t. week/a week t.** = in exactly seven days' time. (*b*) this present time.

toddle ['tɒdl] *v.* to walk unsteadily. **toddler,** *n.* child who is just learning to walk.

toddy ['tɒdɪ] *n.* alcohol and hot water and sugar.

to-do [tə'duː] *n. inf.* excitement/confusion/bother.

toe [təʊ] **1.** *n.* (*a*) one of the five parts like fingers at the end of your foot; **big t./ little t.** = the largest/smallest of the five toes; **to be on your toes** = to be ready/ prepared. (*b*) end part of a shoe/a sock; **t. cap** = hard end to a shoe. **2.** *v.* to touch with the toe; **to t. the line** = to do what you are told to do. **toehold,** *n.* grip with the toes; small foothold. **toenail,** *n.* nail at the end of a toe.

toff [tɒf] *n. inf.* aristocrat.

toffee ['tɒfɪ] *n.* sticky sweet made with

sugar and butter; **t. apple** = apple covered with toffee; *inf.* **he can't do it for t.** = he can't do it at all. **toffee-nosed,** *adj. inf.* supercilious.

toga ['təʊgə] *n.* robe worn by men in Ancient Rome.

together [tə'geðə] *adv.* (*a*) in a group/all at the same time; **get t.** = meet. (*b*) into contact one with another; **stick the pieces t. togetherness,** *n.* being together with other people.

togged [tɒgd] *adj. inf.* **t. out/up in** = wearing. **togs** [tɒgz] *n. pl. inf.* clothes.

toggle ['tɒgl] *n.* short piece of wood attached to a coat with string, used in place of a button; small clasp used for attaching a scarf.

toil [tɔɪl] **1.** *n.* hard work. **2.** *v.* to work hard.

toilet ['tɔɪlət] *n.* (*a*) washing and dressing. (*b*) bowl with a seat on which you sit to pass waste matter from the body; room with this bowl in it; **t. paper** = soft paper for wiping your anus after getting rid of waste matter; **t. roll** = roll of toilet paper; **t. water** = scented water. **toiletries,** *n. pl.* facecloths/soap/perfume, etc., used in washing.

token ['təʊkən] *n.* (*a*) visible thing which is a mark/sign (of respect, etc.); **by the same t.** = in a similar way; **t. strike** = short strike which stands as a symbol of grievances; **t. payment** = a small symbolic payment; **t. woman/black** = woman/black person appointed to a position (on a committee, etc.) to placate rights movements. (*b*) piece of paper/card/plastic which is used to replace money; **book/flower/record t.** = card which can only be exchanged for books/flowers/records.

told [təʊld] *v. see* **tell**.

tolerate ['tɒləreɪt] *v.* (*a*) to suffer (noise, etc.) without complaining. (*b*) to allow (sth which you do not agree with) to exist. **tolerable** ['tɒlərəbl] *adj.* (*a*) bearable. (*b*) fairly good. **tolerably,** *adv.* in a fairly good way; **a t. good film** = quite a good film. **tolerance,** *n.* (*a*) putting up with (unpleasantness, etc.); allowing (sth which you do not agree with) to exist. (*b*) amount by which a measurement can vary from what is specified on a plan. (*c*) ability to stand the effect of a drug/a poison. **tolerant,** *adj.* (person) who tolerates. **tolerantly,** *adv.* in a tolerant way. **toleration** [tɒlə-'reɪʃn] *n.* allowing (sth which you do not agree with) to exist.

toll [təʊl] **1.** *n.* (*a*) payment for using a road/a bridge/a ferry; **t. bridge** = one where a toll is paid. (*b*) loss/damage; **death t.** = number of deaths. (*c*) solemn ringing of a bell. **2.** *v.* to ring (a bell) solemnly as for a funeral. **toll call,** *n. Am.* long-distance telephone call. **toll free,** *adv. Am.* without having to pay the charge for a long-distance call. **tollgate,** *n.* gate across a road where a toll has to be paid. **tollhouse,** *n.* house where the tollkeeper lives. **tollkeeper,** *n.* person who takes the toll on a road/bridge, etc.

tom(cat) ['tom(kæt)] *n.* male cat.

tomahawk ['tɒməhɔːk] *n.* light North American Indian axe.

tomato [tə'mɑːtəʊ; *Am.* tə'meɪtəʊ] *n.* (*pl.* **-oes**) red fruit growing on annual plants and used in salads; plant which bears tomatoes; **t. sauce** = sauce made with tomatoes.

tomb [tuːm] *n.* large grave (usu. with an underground vault in which to put a dead person). **tombstone,** *n.* large stone placed on a grave with the name of the dead person written on it.

tombola [tɒm'bəʊlə] *n.* game where people buy numbered tickets and one or more tickets win prizes.

tomboy ['tɒmbɔɪ] *n.* girl who plays rough games like a boy.

tome [təʊm] *n.* (*formal*) large book.

tomfool ['tɒmfuːl] *adj. inf.* idiotic. **tomfoolery,** *n.* stupid behaviour.

tommy gun ['tɒmɪgʌn] *n.* small machine gun.

tomorrow [tə'mɒrəʊ] *adv. & n.* (*a*) the day which follows today. (*b*) the future.

tomtom ['tɒmtɒm] *n.* small drum beaten with your hands.

ton [tʌn] *n.* (*a*) weight equal to 2240 pounds; **metric t.** = 1000 kilograms. (*b*) space in a ship equivalent to 100 cubic feet. (*c*) *inf* **tons of** = lots. (*d*) *Sl.* **to do a t.** = to go at 100 miles per hour. **tonnage,** *n.* (*a*) space in a ship measured in tons. (*b*) total number of ships in a navy/belonging to a company, calculated by adding together their individual sizes. **tonne** [tʌn] *n.* metric ton.

tone [təʊn] **1.** *n.* (*a*) quality of sound of music/voice. (*b*) (*in music*) difference between two notes which have one note between them on the piano. (*c*) way of speaking/writing which shows a particular emotion. (*d*) shade of colour. (*e*) strength of the body and muscles. (*f*) general quality or appearance. **2.** *v.* **to t. in with** = to fit in well/to harmonize. **tonal** ['təʊnl] *adj.* referring to tone. **tonality** [tə'nælɪtɪ] *n.* quality of tone (in the colours of a painting/in a piece of music). **tone-deaf**, *adj.* not able to recognize differences in musical pitch. **tone down**, *v.* to reduce (sth) excessive. **toneless**, *adj.* with no variation in tone. **tone up**, *v.* to make fitter.

tongs [tɒŋz] *n. pl.* (**pair of**) **t.** = instrument for picking things up, with small claws on the end of two arms; **sugar t.** = tongs for picking up lumps of sugar.

tongue [tʌŋ] *n.* (*a*) long, movable piece of muscular flesh in the mouth, which is used for tasting and speaking; **to say sth with one's t. in one's cheek** = not really to mean it seriously; **to hold one's t.** = not to speak; **it's on the tip of my t.** = I will remember it in a moment. (*b*) piece of movable flesh in an animal's mouth, used as food. (*c*) language; **mother t.** = first language. (*d*) loose piece of leather under the laces in a shoe. (*e*) long, thin flame/piece of land. **tongue-and-groove**, *n.* type of interlocking board, with a projecting tongue along one edge which fits into a corresponding groove along the edge of the next board. **tongue-tied**, *adj.* so shy as to be unable to say anything. **tonguetwister**, *n.* phrase (like **red lorry, yellow lorry**) which is difficult to say quickly.

tonic ['tɒnɪk] **1.** *adj.* (*a*) referring to a musical tone; **t. solfa** = system of writing the tones in music using syllables (*doh-ray-me*, etc.). (*b*) referring to physical strength/wellbeing. **2.** *n.* (*a*) note which sets the key to a scale of music. (*b*) anything (such as medicine) which strengthens the body; **to act as a t. on s.o.** = make s.o. more energetic.

(*c*) **t.** (**water**) = fizzy drink containing quinine.

tonight [tə'naɪt] *adv. & n.* the night of the present day.

tonnage ['tʌnɪdʒ] *n. see* **ton.**

tonne [tʌn] *n. see* **ton.**

tonsil ['tɒnsl] *n.* one of two soft lumps of flesh at the back of your throat. **tonsillectomy**, *n.* operation to remove the tonsils. **tonsillitis** [tɒnsɪ'laɪtɪs] *n.* painful infection of the tonsils.

tonsure ['tɒnʃə] *n.* shaving off all or part of the hair of people becoming monks; part of the head which has been shaved. **tonsured**, *adj.* with a tonsure.

tontine ['tɒntiːn] *n.* type of investment where the survivors each receive more as investors die.

too [tuː] *adv.* (*a*) more than necessary. (*b*) as well/also. (*c*) *inf.* very; **t. bad!** = it's a shame!

took [tʊk] *v. see* **take.**

tool [tuːl] **1.** *n.* hard instrument for doing work (such as hammer/spade, etc.); person used by s.o. else. **2.** *v.* to decorate using a tool. **tool up**, *v.* to equip (a factory) with machinery.

toot [tuːt] **1.** *n.* short sound made by a horn. **2.** *v.* to blow a horn sharply.

tooth [tuːθ] *n.* (*pl.* **teeth** [tiːθ]) (*a*) one of a set of bony structures in the mouth, used by animals for chewing and biting; **milk teeth** = first set of teeth grown by a baby, and replaced by permanent teeth as a child; **false teeth** = set of plastic teeth to replace teeth which have been taken out; **in the teeth of** = running against/into; **long in the t.** = old; **armed to the teeth** = fully armed. (*b*) part of a saw/of a comb/of a cogwheel shaped like a tooth. **toothache** ['tuːθeɪk] *n.* pain in a tooth. **toothbrush**, *n.* small brush with a long handle used for cleaning your teeth. **toothcomb**, *n.* comb with teeth set close together; **to go through sth with a (fine) t.** = to inspect sth very carefully. **toothed** *adj.* with teeth; **t. wheel** = cogwheel. **toothless**, *adj.* with no teeth. **toothpaste**, *n.* paste used with a toothbrush for cleaning your teeth. **toothpick**, *n.* small pointed piece of wood/metal, etc., for pushing between the teeth to remove pieces of food. **toothsome**, *adj.* good to eat. **toothy**, *adj.* showing a lot of teeth.

tootle ['tu:tl] **1.** *n. inf.* little toot. **2.** *v. inf.* (*a*) to make a tootle. (*b*) to go (**along/off**).

top [top] **1.** *n.* (*a*) highest point; **on t. of everything else** = in addition to everything else. (*b*) flat upper surface; lid. (*c*) *Am.* roof (of a car). (*d*) highest/most important place. (*e*) **big t.** = large circus tent. (*f*) **at the t. of his voice** = as loud as possible. (*g*) (*in vehicle*) highest gear. (*h*) child's toy which spins when twisted sharply. (*i*) piece of clothing covering the upper part of the body. **2.** *adj.* (*a*) highest. (*b*) most important. **3.** *v.* (**topped**) (*a*) to cut the top off. (*b*) to put sth on top. (*c*) to go higher than; *inf.* **to t. it all** = in addition to everything else. (*d*) *Sl.* to execute (s.o.). **topcoat**, *n.* overcoat. **top dog**, *n. Sl.* winner. **top dressing**, *n.* scattering fertilizer on the surface of the soil; fertilizer to be scattered in this way. **top flight**, *adj. inf.* excellent/of very high quality. **top hat**, *n.* man's tall black hat. **top-heavy**, *adj.* unstable because the top part is heavier than the bottom. **topknot**, *n.* small bunch of hair tied on the top of the head. **topless**, *adj.* (*of woman*) wearing nothing on the top part of the body. **top-level**, *adj.* (talks) involving important people. **topmost**, *adj.* highest. **top notch**, *adj.* top flight. **topper**, *n. inf.* top hat. **topping. 1.** *n.* cream, etc., put on the top of a cake. **2.** *adj. inf.* very good. **topping out**, *n.* ceremony to mark the completion of the main work on a new building. **top secret**, *adj.* very secret. **topside**, *n.* best quality beef for roasting. **topsoil**, *n.* layer of good light soil on the surface (of a field, etc.). **top up**, *v.* to fill completely (sth which is half empty).

topaz ['təʊpæz] *n.* yellow semi-precious stone.

topee, topi ['təʊpɪ] *n.* helmet worn in hot countries to protect your head from the sun.

topiary ['təʊpjərɪ] *n.* art of cutting bushes into odd shapes for ornament.

topic ['tɒpɪk] *n.* subject (for discussion/of a conversation). **topical**, *adj.* which is of interest at the present time. **topicality**, *n.* being topical. **topically**, *adv.* in a topical way.

topography [tə'pɒgrəfɪ] *n.* description of land mentioning rivers, mountains, roads, buildings, etc. **topographer**, *n.* person who studies topography. **topographical** [tɒpə'græfɪkl] *adj.* which describes land.

topology [tə'pɒlədʒɪ] *n.* study of the properties of geometrical shapes which remain the same even when the shapes change.

topple [tɒpl] *v.* to make a government/dictator lose power. **topple over** ['tɒpl'əʊvə] *v.* to make (sth) fall down; to fall down.

topsy-turvy ['tɒpsɪ'tɜ:vɪ] *adj. & adv.* upside down/in confusion.

toque [təʊk] *n.* round hat (for a woman) with no brim.

tor [tɔ:] *n.* rocky hill.

torch [tɔ:tʃ] *n.* (*pl.* **-es**) (*a*) portable electric light which you can hold in your hand. (*b*) flaming piece of wood. **torchlight**, *n.* light from a flaming torch; **t. procession** = procession of people carrying flaming torches.

tore [tɔ:] *v. see* **tear.**

toreador ['tɒrɪədɔ:] *n.* Spanish bullfighter.

torment 1. *n.* ['tɔ:mənt] extreme pain; **in t.** = in great pain. **2.** *v.* [tɔ:'ment] to make (s.o.) suffer. **tormentor**, *n.* person who torments.

torn [tɔ:n] *v. see* **tear.**

tornado [tɔ:'neɪdəʊ] *n.* (*pl.* **-oes**) violent whirlwind.

torpedo [tɔ:'pi:dəʊ] **1.** *n.* (*pl.* **-oes**) self-propelled missile which travels through the water. **2.** *v.* to sink (a ship) using a torpedo; to ruin (s.o.'s plans). **torpedo boat**, *n.* small fast naval ship which carries torpedoes.

torpid ['tɔ:pɪd] *adj.* half asleep with heat; dull; sluggish. **torpor**, *n.* being half asleep/sluggish.

torque [tɔ:k] *n.* (*a*) mechanical force to make sth rotate. (*b*) prehistoric necklace made of twisted gold or silver.

torrent ['tɒrənt] *n.* (*a*) fast rushing stream. (*b*) fast flow. **torrential** [tə'renʃəl] *adj.* like a torrent.

torrid ['tɒrɪd] *adj.* (*a*) very hot. (*b*) intense (passion).

torsion ['tɔ:ʃn] *n.* being twisted; strain caused by twisting.

torso ['tɔːsəʊ] n. (pl. **-os**) body (excluding the head, arms and legs).

tort [tɔːt] n. act which is the subject of a civil action in court.

tortilla [tɔːˈtiːjə] n. type of Spanish omelette, with vegetables.

tortoise ['tɔːtəs] n. reptile covered with a hard domed shell, which moves very slowly and can live to a great age. **tortoiseshell**, adj. & n. speckled brown material (from the shell of a tortoise) used for making combs/frames for glasses, etc.; **t. cat** = brown, yellow and black cat; **t. butterfly** = common brown and red butterfly.

tortuous ['tɔːtjʊəs] adj. which twists and turns. **tortuously**, adv. in a tortuous way.

torture ['tɔːtʃə] 1. n. pain inflicted on s.o. as a punishment or to make them reveal a secret. 2. v. to inflict torture on s.o. **torturer**, n. person who tortures.

Tory ['tɔːrɪ] adj. & n. (member) of the Conservative party.

toss [tɒs] 1. n. (pl. **-es**) (a) action of throwing sth into the air; **t. of a coin** = throwing a coin up to see which side is on top when it comes down; **to argue the t.** = to argue about s.o.'s final decision; (in sport) **to win the t.** = guess correctly which side of the coin comes down on top and so play first. (b) sharp disdainful movement of the head. 2. v. (a) to throw (sth) into the air; **to t. a coin** = to throw a coin to see which side is on top when it comes down; **let's t. for it** = the person who guesses right, starts to play first/has first choice. (b) to move (sth) about; to mix (a salad); **she tossed her head** = made a sharp disdainful movement of her head. **toss up**, v. to toss a coin. **toss-up**, n. inf. it's **a toss-up which one will win** = you can't tell which one will win.

tot [tɒt] 1. n. (a) little child. (b) inf. small glass of alcohol. 2. v. (**totted**) **to t. up** = to add up.

total ['təʊtl] 1. adj. & n. complete/whole (amount). 2. v. (**totalled**) to add up (to). **totality** [təʊˈtælɪtɪ] n. whole amount. **totalize**, v. to add up (figures). **totally**, adv. completely.

totalitarian [təʊtælɪˈteərɪən] adj. (state) governed by a single party/group which refuses to allow the existence of any opposition.

totalizator ['təʊtəlaɪzeɪtə] n. machine which calculates the amount to be paid to people who bet on a winning horse.

tote [təʊt] 1. n. inf. the t. = totalizator. 2. v. Am. to carry. **tote-bag**, n. large carrying bag.

totem pole ['təʊtəmpəʊl] n. tall carved pole on which North American Indians carve figures of gods.

totter ['tɒtə] n. to walk unsteadily/to wobble. **tottery**, adj. wobbly/likely to fall.

toucan ['tuːkæn] n. American tropical bird with huge coloured beak.

touch [tʌtʃ] 1. n. (pl. **-es**) (a) sense by which you feel sth. (b) way of bringing your fingers into contact with sth; **she's lost her t.** = she isn't as successful as she was. (c) slight tap. (d) slight stroke (of a paintbrush); **to put the finishing touches to sth** = to finish sth off. (e) contact; **to get into t. with/to lose t. with** = to contact/to lose contact with. (f) slight taste/trace. (g) (in football) part of the field outside the playing area. 2. v. (a) to feel (with the fingers); to come into contact; **I wouldn't t. it** = I wouldn't have anything to do with it; **don't t. my things** = don't interfere with them/don't move them. (b) **to t. on** = to refer to (a subject). (c) to eat or drink. (d) to affect the emotions of (s.o.). (e) to reach the same level as (s.o.). (f) inf. to ask (s.o.) **for** a loan. **touch and go**, n. it was touch and go = it was doubtful. **touch down**, v. (a) (of plane) to land. (b) (in Rugby) to score a try. **touchdown**, n. (a) landing (of a plane). (b) (in Rugby) scoring a try. **touché** ['tuːʃeɪ] inter. meaning you have scored a point against me. **touched**, adj. (a) grateful/pleased with (b) slightly mad. **touchiness**, n. being susceptible/easily offended. **touching**. 1. adj. which affects the emotions. 2. prep. concerning/about. **touch line**, n. white line along one side of a football pitch. **touch off**, v. to set off (an explosion, etc.). **touch on**, v. to refer to (a question) briefly. **touchpaper**, n. chemically treated paper used as a fuse to light a firework. **touch screen**, *n.* computer screen which is sensitive to touch, and where a cursor can be positioned by touching the screen. **touchstone,** *n.* thing used as a standard to test other things against. **touch type,** *v.* to type without looking at the keys on the typewriter. **touch up,** *v.* to add little strokes of paint to improve the appearance of sth. **touchy,** *adj. inf.* highly susceptible/easily offended.

tough [tʌf] **1.** *adj.* **(-er, -est)** (*a*) hard; difficult to chew/to cut/to break; *inf.* **it's as t. as old boots** = extremely tough. (*b*) strong/hardy. (*c*) difficult; **to get t. with s.o.** = to deal roughly/harshly with s.o. (*d*) *inf.* **t. luck!** = hard luck! **2.** *n. inf.* rough criminal. **toughen,** *v.* to make tough; **toughened glass** = specially strengthened glass. **toughness,** *n.* being tough.

toupee ['tuːpeɪ] *n.* small wig.

tour ['tʊə] **1.** *n.* journey which goes round various places and returns to its starting point; **package t.** = one which has been totally organized in advance. **2.** *v.* to visit; to go on a tour; **touring company** = theatre company which goes from one town to another in the provinces. **tourism,** *n.* business of providing lodging and entertainment for tourists. **tourist,** *adj. & n.* person who goes on holiday to visit places; **t. class** = type of seating in an aircraft which is cheaper than first class; **t. trap** = place whch overcharges tourists.

tour de force [tuːədə'fɔːs] *n.* act showing remarkable skill.

tourmaline ['tʊəməliːn] *n.* type of semi-precious stone.

tournament ['tʊənəmənt] *n.* (*a*) (*old*) contest between groups of knights. (*b*) sporting competition with many games which eliminate competitors.

tournedos ['tʊənədəʊ] *n.* piece of fillet steak.

tourniquet ['tʊəniˌkeɪ] *n.* tight bandage put round an arm or leg to stop bleeding from a wound.

tousle ['taʊzl] *v.* to make (hair) untidy.

tout [taʊt] **1.** *n.* (*a*) person who tries to sell something to people he meets; **ticket t.** = person who sells tickets at high prices to people in the street. (*b*) person who touts. **2.** *v.* (*also* **tout for**)

to try to persuade people to vote/to buy things/to stay in a hotel.

tow [təʊ] **1.** *n.* (*a*) pulling a car/a ship behind you; **he had his family in t.** = coming behind him. (*b*) short, coarse pieces of flax. **2.** *v.* to pull (a car/a ship) which cannot move by itself. **towbar,** *n.* bar fitted to a car, to attach a caravan/trailer. **tow-headed,** *adj.* with yellow hair. **tow-line, tow-rope,** *n.* rope which attaches a car/a ship to sth being towed. **towpath,** *n.* path along the bank of a river/canal (along which horses used to walk to tow barges).

towards [tə'wɔːdz] *prep.* (*also* **toward**) (*a*) in the direction of. (*b*) to (a person/a country, etc.). (*c*) as part payment for. (*d*) near (a time).

towel ['taʊəl] **1.** *n.* piece of soft absorbent cloth for drying; **to throw in the t.** = to give up/not to continue a contest. **2.** *v.* (**towelled**) to rub dry with a towel. **towelling,** *n.* rough soft cloth used for making towels.

tower ['taʊə] **1.** *n.* tall building; **control t.** = tall airport building containing the control room; **t. of strength** = very strong and sympathetic person. **2.** *v.* to rise very high (**above**). **towering,** *adj.* (*a*) very tall. (*b*) very great (rage).

town [taʊn] *n.* place where people live and work, with houses, shops, offices and factories (as opposed to the country); **t. clerk** = formerly, senior adminstrative and legal officer in a town (now called Chief Executive); **t. council** = elected committee which runs a town; **t. hall** = offices of the town council; public building used for meetings; **t. planning** = science of planning the development of a town; *inf.* **to go to t. over sth** = to spend a lot of money/time on sth; *inf.* **to paint the t. red** = to have a wild party in the town. **townee,** *n. inf.* person who lives in a town. **town house,** *n.* (*a*) house in a town. (*b*) expensive modern terraced house. **townsfolk,** *n. pl.* people who live in a town. **township,** *n.* (*a*) (*in US and Canada*) small town and the administrative area round it. (*b*) (*in South Africa*) area where black people live near a large town. **townsman, townswoman,** *n.*

(*pl.* **-men, -women**) person who lives in a town. **townspeople**, *n. pl.* people who live in a town.

toxaemia, *Am.* **toxemia** [tɒkˈsiːmɪə] blood poisoning. **toxic** [ˈtɒksɪk] *adj.* poisonous. **toxicity**, *n.* being toxic. **toxicologist** [tɒksɪˈkɒlədʒɪst] *n.* scientist who studies poisons. **toxicology**, *n.* scientific study of poisons. **toxin**, *n.* poisonous substance.

toxophily [tɒkˈsɒfɪlɪ] *n.* (*formal*) archery.

toy [tɔɪ] **1.** *adj. & n.* thing which children play with. **2.** *v.* **to t. with** = (i) to eat (food) reluctantly; (ii) to turn over (an idea) in your mind. **toyshop**, *n.* shop which sells toys.

trace [treɪs] **1.** *n.* (*a*) **traces** = set of tracks/footprints left by an animal. (*b*) small amount; **he's vanished without a t.** = leaving nothing behind to show where he has gone. (*c*) **traces** = straps by which a horse is attached to a carriage; **to kick over the traces** = to rebel (against authority). **2.** *v.* (*a*) to follow the tracks left by (sth); to try to find where (s.o./sth) is. (*b*) to copy (a picture/a map) by placing a piece of thin transparent paper over it and drawing on it. **traceable**, *adj.* which can be traced. **trace element**, *n.* chemical element of which a tiny amount is needed by a plant or animal to grow properly. **tracer**, *n.* type of bullet/shell which leaves a visible stream of sparks/smoke as it flies. **tracery**, *n.* delicate stone patterns holding the glass in a church window. **tracing**, *n.* drawing done by tracing; **t. paper** = thin transparent paper for tracing drawings.

trachea [trəˈkiːə] *n.* windpipe. **tracheotomy** [trækɪˈɒtəmɪ] *n.* operation to make a hole in the windpipe from the outside of the neck.

trachoma [trəˈkəʊmə] *n.* eye disease caused by a virus.

track [træk] **1.** *n.* (*a*) footprints of animal/marks of wheels, etc.; **the police are on his t.** = they are following him; **to keep t. of** = to keep an account/to keep oneself informed of; **to lose t. of sth** = not to know where it is any longer; **to make tracks for home** = to set off for home. (*b*) path; **on the wrong**

t. = working wrongly/making a wrong assumption. (*c*) course for racing; **t. events** = running competitions in an athletics tournament; **t. suit** = type of warm two-piece suit worn by sportsmen when practising; **t. shoes** = running shoes with spikes in the soles; **he has a good t. record** = he has been very successful in the past. (*d*) line of rails; **single-track railway** = on which trains go up and down the same rails when passing places at intervals; *inf.* **to have a one-track mind** = to think on only one thing/have only one interest. (*e*) endless belt on which a caterpillar tractor/tank, etc., runs. (*f*) part of a magnetic tape on which sth can be recorded. (*g*) one song on a record containing several popular songs. **2.** *v.* to follow (an animal); to follow (a moving subject) with a camera. **track down**, *v.* to follow and catch (an animal/a criminal). **tracker**, *n.* animal/person who follows tracks. **trackless**, *adj.* with no paths.

tract [trækt] *n.* (*a*) wide stretch of countryside. (*b*) short (religious) pamphlet. (*c*) system of organs in the body which are linked together.

tractable [ˈtræktəbl] *adj.* which can be tamed/made to do what is necessary. **tractability** [træktəˈbɪlɪtɪ] *n.* being tractable.

traction [ˈtrækʃn] *n.* (*a*) pulling force; **t. engine** = large steam-driven engine which used to be used for pulling heavy loads. (*b*) pulling (a broken leg, etc.) up with pulleys.

tractor [ˈtræktə] *n.* farm vehicle with large back wheels for pulling a plough, etc.; **t. feed** = paper feed in a printer, where the paper is pulled by sprocket wheels.

trad [træd] *adj. inf.* traditional.

trade [treɪd] **1.** *n.* (*a*) business; buying and selling. (*b*) people who buy and sell a particular type of goods/who work in a particular industry; **t. price** = special price to another dealer in the same business. (*c*) job. **2.** *v.* (*a*) to carry on a business. (*b*) to exchange (sth for sth). **trade in**, *v.* to exchange an old car, etc., as part payment for a new one. **trade-in**, *n.* exchange of an old car, etc., for a newer one. **trademark, trade name,** *n.* particular name, sign, etc., which has been registered by a producer and which cannot be copied by other manufacturers. **trade on,** *v.* to exploit/to profit from. **trader,** *n.* person who does business. **tradesman,** *n.* (*pl.* **-men**) person who runs a shop. **tradespeople,** *n. pl.* shopkeepers. **trade union, trades union,** *n.* organization which groups together workers from similar industries to represent them in wage bargaining with employers. **trade unionist,** *n.* member of a trade union. **tradewind,** *n.* tropical wind blowing towards the equator. **trading,** *n.* business. **trading estate,** *n.* group of factories built together.

tradition [trə'dɪʃn] *n.* customs/habits/ stories which are passed from generation to generation. **traditional,** *adj.* referring to tradition. **traditionalist,** *n.* person who does things in a traditional way. **traditionally,** *adv.* according to tradition.

traduce [trə'djuːs] *v.* (*formal*) to slander (s.o.).

traffic ['træfɪk] **1.** *n.* (*a*) movement of vehicles, esp. cars/lorries/buses, etc., on the roads; **t. jam** = blockage of traffic on a road; *Am.* **t. circle** = roundabout; **air t.** = aircraft flying. (*b*) illegal international business. **2.** *v.* (**trafficked**) to deal **in** (drugs) illegally. **trafficator,** *n.* light on a car which flashes to show that the car is about to turn. **traffic lights,** *n.* red, green and amber lights which regulate the movement of traffic. **traffic warden,** *n.* person who controls traffic, esp. the parking of cars. **trafficker,** *n.* person who traffics (in drugs).

tragedy ['trædʒədɪ] *n.* play/film/story with a sad story; unhappy event. **tragedian** [trə'dʒiːdɪən] *n.* person who acts in tragedies. **tragic,** *adj.* referring to tragedy; very sad. **tragically,** *adv.* very sadly.

trail [treɪl] **1.** *n.* (*a*) tracks left by an animal. (*b*) path. (*c*) thing which stretches a long way behind. **2.** *v.* (*a*) to let (sth) drag behind you. (*b*) to follow the tracks of (an animal/a person). (*c*) **trailing plant** = one which hangs or creeps along the ground. **trailer,** *n.* (*a*) goods vehicle

pulled behind a car. (*b*) caravan. (*c*) short film showing parts of a full-length film as an advertisement.

train [treɪn] **1.** *n.* (*a*) series of coaches or wagons pulled by a railway engine; **t. ferry** = boat which carries a train across water. (*b*) series of events; line of animal carrying goods; retinue (of an important person); **t. of thought** = series of thoughts following one another. (*c*) long fuse (to light an explosive). (*d*) part of a dress which hangs down on to the ground at the back. **2.** *v.* (*a*) to teach (s.o./an animal) to do sth; to learn how to do sth; **to t. a plant up a stick** = to attach a plant so that it will climb upwards. (*b*) to practise (for a sport). (*c*) to point (a rifle/a telescope) at sth. **trainable,** *adj.* which can be trained. **trainee** [treɪ'niː] *n.* person who is being taught. **trainer,** *n.* (*a*) person who trains animals/sportsmen. (*b*) small aircraft in which you learn to fly. **training,** *n.* action of being taught/of practising; in t. = (i) practising (for a sport); (ii) fit/ in good physical condition; **t. college** = college where teachers are trained.

traipse [treɪps] *v. inf.* to walk about in a heavy/tired way.

trait [treɪ(t)] *n.* particular point of s.o.'s character.

traitor ['treɪtə] *n.* person who sides with the enemy/who gives away secrets to the enemy. **traitorous,** *adj.* like a traitor.

trajectory [trə'dʒektrɪ] *n.* curved course taken by sth which has been thrown through the air.

tram [træm] *n.* form of public transport, consisting of carriages running on rails laid in the street. **tramcar,** *n.* single carriage of a tram. **tramlines,** *n. pl.* (*a*) rails along which a tram runs. (*b*) two parallel side lines on a tennis court. **tramway,** *n.* rails, etc., on which trams run.

trammel ['træml] **1.** *n.* (*a*) type of fishing net. (*b*) thing which prevents you from doing sth. **2.** *v.* (**trammelled**) (*formal*) to stop (s.o.) doing sth.

tramp [træmp] **1.** *n.* (*a*) noise of feet hitting the ground heavily. (*b*) long energetic walk. (*c*) person who has nowhere to live and walks from place to place begging for food or money. **2.**

v. (*a*) to walk heavily. (*b*) to trample on (sth); to crush (grapes) by stepping on them to extract the juice. **tramp steamer,** *n.* cargo boat which goes from port to port, but not on a regular route.

trample ['træmpl] *v.* (**on**) to crush (by walking).

trampoline ['træmpəli:n] *n.* frame with a large sheet of elastic material on which you can bounce/perform exercises, etc.

trance [trɑ:ns] *n.* state when you are not fully conscious, and do not notice what is going on.

tranny ['trænɪ] *n. inf.* transistor radio.

tranquil ['træŋkwɪl] *adj.* calm/peaceful. **tranquillity** [træŋ'kwɪlɪtɪ] *n.* calm. **tranquillize** ['træŋkwɪlaɪz] *v.* to make (s.o.) calm (by giving drugs). **tranquillizer,** *n.* drug which makes a person calm. **tranquilly,** *adv.* in a tranquil way.

trans- [trænz] *prefix meaning* through/across.

transact [træn'zækt] *v.* to carry out (a piece of business). **transaction,** *n.* piece of business; **cash t.** = piece of business paid for in cash; **transactions** = report of what takes place at a meeting of a learned/scientific society.

transatlantic [trænzət'læntɪk] *adj.* across the Atlantic; from the other side of the Atlantic; involving countries on both sides of the Atlantic.

transceiver ['trænzsi:və] *n.* transmitter and receiver.

transcend [træn'send] *v.* to go better/further than sth. **transcendent,** *adj.* which transcends. **transcendental** [trænsən'dentəl] *adj.* which rises above the level of ordinary thought or reasoning.

transcontinental [trænzkɒntɪ'nentl] *adj.* across a continent.

transcribe [træn'skraɪb] *v.* to write out the text (of sth which is heard); to write out in full (what has been written down in shorthand); to rewrite (a piece of music) for another instrument than the one for which it was originally written. **transcript** ['trænskrɪpt] *n.* written text of what was said (on the radio/at a trial, etc.). **transcription,** *n.* act of transcribing.

transept ['trænsept] *n.* one of the two branches at right angles to the nave and choir in a cross-shaped church.

transfer 1. *n.* ['trænsfə] (*a*) movement of sth/s.o. to a new place; **t. list** = list of footballers whom a club would agree to see move to another team. (*b*) design which can be stuck on to a surface. **2.** *v.* [træns'fɜ:] (**transferred**) to move (sth/s.o.) to another place. **transferable** [trænz'fɜ:rəbl] *adj.* which can be transferred; **not t.** = (ticket) which can only be used by the person to whom it was issued. **transference,** *n.* act of transferring.

transfigure [trænz'fɪgə] *v.* to change for the better (the appearance of sth/s.o.). **transfiguration,** *n.* act of transfiguring.

transfix [trænz'fɪks] *v.* to prevent (s.o.) from moving (by giving a shock).

transform [trænz'fɔ:m] *v.* to change completely. **transformation** [trænzfə-'meɪʃn] *n.* complete change of appearance. **transformer** [trænz'fɔ:mə] *n.* apparatus for changing the voltage of an alternating electric current.

transfuse [trænz'fju:z] *v.* to move liquid from one container to another. **transfusion** [trænz'fju:ʒn] *n.* moving of liquid from one container to another; **blood t.** = giving blood to a sick patient.

transgress [trænz'gres] *v.* (*formal*) to go against (a rule). **transgression,** *n.* act of transgressing. **transgressor,** *n.* person who transgresses.

tranship [træns'ʃɪp] *v.* (**transhipped**) to move (goods) from one ship or lorry to another.

transience ['trænzɪəns] *n.* state of not being permanent. **transient** ['trænzɪənt] *adj. & n.* which will not last; *Am.* **transients** = people who stay in a hotel for a short time.

transistor [træn'zɪstə] *n.* (*a*) device made of semi-conductors which can increase an electric current. (*b*) **t.** (**radio**) = small pocket radio which uses transistors. **transistorize,** *v.* to put transistors into (sth).

transit ['trænzɪt] **1.** *n.* (*a*) movement of passengers/goods (on the way to another destination); **t. lounge** = waiting room in an airport where you wait for a connecting flight. (*b*) moving of a planet across the face of the sun or other planet. **2.** *v.* (*formal*) to go across. **transition** [træn-

'zɪʃn] *n.* movement between one state and another. **transitional,** *adj.* referring to transition; **t. government** = temporary government between two different constitutions.

transitive ['trænzɪtɪv] *adj.* (verb) which has an object.

transitory ['trænzɪtrɪ] *adj.* which does not last for long.

translate [trænz'leɪt] *v.* (*a*) to put (words) into another language. (*b*) to move (a bishop) to another see. **translatable,** *adj.* which can be translated. **translation** [trænz'leɪʃn] *n.* text which has been translated; action of translating; **simultaneous t.** = translating directly into another language what a speaker is saying. **translator,** *n.* person who translates.

transliterate [trænz'lɪtəreɪt] *v.* to put (words) into the letters of a different alphabet. **transliteration,** *n.* act of transliterating.

translucent [trænz'lu:snt] *adj.* which light can pass through, but which you cannot see through. **translucence,** *n.* being translucent.

transmigration [trænzmaɪ'greɪʃn] *n.* moving of a soul from a dead body to a living one.

transmit [trænz'mɪt] *v.* (**transmitted**) (*a*) to pass (from one person to another). (*b*) to send out by rado/TV. **transmission** [trænz'mɪʃn] *n.* (*a*) passing (of disease) from one person to another. (*b*) sending out by radio/TV; a radio/TV broadcast. (*c*) (*in a car*) series of moving parts which pass the power from the engine to the wheels. **transmitter,** *n.* apparatus for sending out radio/TV signals.

transmogrify [trænz'mɒgrɪfaɪ] *v.* to change (sth) totally.

transmute [trænz'mju:t] *v.* to make (sth) change its shape or substance. **transmutation,** *n.* act of transmuting.

transom ['trænsəm] *n.* (*a*) cross beam in a window; beam across the top of a door. (*b*) stern piece of a boat.

transparency [træns'pærənsɪ] *n.* (*a*) being transparent. (*b*) photograph which is printed on transparent film so that it can be projected on to a screen. **transparent,** *adj.* (*a*) which

you can see through. (*b*) obvious (lie). **transparently,** *adv.* obviously.

transpire [træn'spaɪə] *v.* (*a*) to happen. (*b*) to pass moisture through the surface of the skin/of a leaf, etc. **transpiration** [trænspɪ'reɪʃn] *n.* act of transpiring.

transplant 1. *n.* ['trɑ:nsplɑ:nt] (*a*) act of taking an organ from one person and grafting it into another's body. (*b*) small plant which is moved to another place to grow. **2.** *v.* [træns'plɑ:nt] (*a*) to graft (an organ) into s.o.'s body. (*b*) to plant (small plants) in another place where they will grow permanently.

transport 1. *n.* ['trænspɔ:t] (*a*) movement of goods/people; means of moving goods/people; **public t. system** = system of buses/trams/underground trains for moving the public; **t. café** = restaurant where lorry-drivers eat. (*b*) ship/aircraft which carries goods or soldiers. (*c*) great emotion. **2.** *v.* [træn'spɔ:t] (*a*) to move (goods/people) from one place to another. (*b*) **transported with joy** = very happy. (*c*) (*old*) to send (a criminal) to a prison in a colony. **transportable,** *adj.* which can be transported. **transportation** [trænspɔ:'teɪʃn] *n.* (*a*) movement of goods/people; means of moving goods/people. (*b*) (*old*) sending of a criminal to a prison in a colony. **transporter** [træn'spɔ:tə] *n.* large lorry for carrying several cars; **t. bridge** = platform which is suspended from a bridge and moves across a river on cables, carrying cars, etc.

transpose [træn'spəʊz] *v.* to make (two things) change places. **transposition** [trænspə'zɪʃn] *n.* act of transposing.

transship [træns'ʃɪp] *v.* (**transshipped**) to move (goods) from one ship or lorry to another.

transubstantiation [trænsʌbstænʃɪ'eɪʃn] *n.* belief that the wine and bread become the blood and body of Christ at the Communion service.

transuranic [trænzjʊ'rænɪk] *adj.* (element) which has atoms heavier than those of uranium.

transverse ['trænzvɜ:s] *adj.* which lies across.

transvestite [trænz'vestaɪt] *n.* person who wants to wear the clothes of the opposite sex. **transvestism** [trænz-'vestɪzəm] *n*. desire to wear the clothes of the opposite sex.

trap [træp] **1.** *n*. (*a*) device to catch an animal; plan to catch (s.o.)/to take (s.o.) by surprise; **police radar t.** = device to catch a motorist who is driving too fast. (*b*) gate which allows a greyhound to start to run in a race. (*c*) **t. door** = door in a floor/in a ceiling. (*d*) bend in a waste pipe which is filled with water, and so stops unpleasant smells coming back up the pipe from a sewer. (*e*) *Sl.* mouth. (*f*) small light horse-drawn carriage. **2.** *v.* (**trapped**) to catch. **trapper,** *n.* person who catches wild animals for their fur.

trapeze [træ'piːz] *n.* bar which hangs from ropes, and which acrobats use in a circus.

trapezium [træ'piːzɪəm] *n.* (*a*) four-sided shape, where two of the sides are parallel. (*b*) *Am.* trapezoid. (*c*) little bone in the wrist. **trapezoid** ['træpɪzɔɪd] *n.* (*a*) four-sided shape, where none of the sides is parellel. (*b*) *Am.* trapezium.

trappings ['træpɪŋz] *n. pl.* ornaments/clothes/decorations which are suitable for a particular occasion.

trash [træʃ] *n.* rubbish. **trash-can,** *n. Am.* dustbin. **trashy,** *adj.* (**-ier, -iest**) very bad/completely worthless.

trauma ['trɔːmə] *n.* (*a*) sharp shock/unpleasant experience which affects your mental outlook. (*b*) injury. **traumatic** [trɔː'mætɪk] *adj.* which gives a sharp and unpleasant shock. **traumatically,** *adv.* in a traumatic way.

travel ['trævl] **1.** *n.* moving from one country to another/from one place to another. **2.** *v.* (**travelled**) (*a*) to move from one country to another/from one place to another. (*b*) to be a sales representative (in an area). **travel agency,** *n.* office which arranges tickets/hotel reservations, etc., for you when you are making a journey. **travel agent,** *n.* person who runs a travel agency. **travelator,** *n.* moving belt which you stand on to move from one point to another (such as in an airport). **traveller,** *n.* (*a*) person who is travelling from one place to another; **traveller's cheques** = cheques which you can buy at your bank and which can then be cashed

in a foreign country. (*b*) (**commercial**) t. = sales representative. **travelogue,** *n.* film describing travel.

traverse 1. *n.* ['trævɜːs] (*a*) crossing. (*b*) thing which crosses another. (*c*) (*in mountaineering*) crossing of a dangerous flat rock face. **2.** *v.* [trə'vɜːs] to cross.

travesty ['trævəstɪ] **1.** *n.* parody; ridiculous copy/poor imitation. **2.** *v.* to imitate (sth) in a ridiculous way.

trawl [trɔːl] **1.** *n.* long net shaped like a bag, pulled at sea by a trawler. **2.** *v.* to fish with a trawl. **trawler,** *n.* fishing boat which uses a trawl.

tray [treɪ] *n.* (*a*) flat board for carrying glasses/cups and saucers, etc. (*b*) flat open box/basket for papers.

treachery ['tretʃərɪ] *n.* act of betraying/being a traitor to your friends, etc. **treacherous,** *adv.* (*a*) likely to betray. (*b*) dangerous. **treacherously,** *adv.* in a treacherous way.

treacle ['triːkl] *n.* thick dark-brown syrup produced when sugar is refined. **treacly,** *adj.* thick and sticky like treacle.

tread [tred] **1.** *n.* (*a*) way of walking. (*b*) sound of a footstep. (*c*) part of a step (on stairs/an escalator) on which you put your foot. (*d*) surface of a tyre marked with a pattern of lines. **2.** *v.* (**trod** [trod]; **has trodden**) (*a*) to walk. (*b*) to trample on/to crush with your feet; **to t. water** = to keep afloat in water by moving your legs up and down. **treadle** ['tredl] **1.** *n.* foot pedal which makes a machine turn. **2.** *v.* to push a treadle with the foot. **treadmill,** *n.* (*a*) device turned by people/animals as they walk around a circular path or inside a large wheel. (*b*) dull routine work.

treason ['triːzn] *n.* betraying your country/giving your country's secrets to the enemy. **treasonable,** *adj.* which can be considered as treason.

treasure ['treʒə] **1.** *n.* (*a*) store of money/jewels/gold, etc.; **t. trove** = buried treasure found by accident which then becomes the property of the state; **t. hunt** = game where you follow clues from place to place until you find a prize. (*b*) thing which is highly valued. **2.** *v.* to value (sth) very highly.

treasurer, *n.* person who looks after the finances of a club, etc. **treasury,** *n.* (*a*) place where treasure is kept. (*b*) government department which deals with the nation's money.

treat [tri:t] **1.** *n.* special meal/outing, etc., which should give pleasure; **a t. in store** = a special future surprise; **this is my t.** = I am paying the bill. **2.** *v.* (*a*) to deal with; to write about (a subject). (*b*) **to t. s.o. to** = to give (s.o.) a special meal/outing as a surprise gift. (*c*) to look after (a sick person). (*d*) to pass (a substance) through a certain process. (*e*) (*formal*) to negotiate (**with** an enemy). **treatment,** *n.* (*a*) way of dealing with sth. (*b*) way of looking after a sick person.

treatise ['tri:tɪz] *n.* long learned piece of writing on a subject.

treaty ['tri:tɪ] *n.* (*a*) agreement between two or more countries. (*b*) agreement between private people; **to sell a house by private t.** = in private, after having offered it for auction.

treble ['trebl] **1.** *n.* (*a*) voice which sings high-pitched notes; high-pitched musical instrument. (*b*) thing which is three times as large; three points. **2.** *adj.* (*a*) three times as large; **t. chance** = possible way of winning the football pools, where you try to forecast the matches which will be drawn. (*b*) high (voice/note); **t. clef** = sign in music showing that the notes are in a high pitch. **3.** *adv.* three times as much. **4.** *v.* to increase by three times. **trebly,** *adv.* three times as much.

tree [tri:] *n.* (*a*) large plant with a wooden stem and branches. (*b*) **family t.** = diagram showing the development of a family over a long period of time. **treecreeper,** *n.* small bird which creeps up the trunk of trees, looking for insects. **treeless,** *adj.* with no trees. **treeline,** *n.* line at a certain altitude above which trees do not grow. **treen,** *n.* (*no pl.*) small spoons/rings, etc., made of wood. **treetop,** *n.* top of a tree.

trefoil ['tri:fɔɪl] *n.* design/leaf shaped in three equal parts like that of a clover.

trek [trek] **1.** *n.* long and difficult journey. **2.** *v.* (**trekked**) to make a long and difficult journey.

trellis ['trelɪs] *n.* (*pl.* **-es**) openwork fence made of thin pieces of wood in a crisscross pattern.

tremble ['trembl] **1.** *n.* shaking/shuddering. **2.** *v.* (*a*) to shake/to quiver. (*b*) to be very worried. **trembly,** *adj.* shaky/doddery.

tremendous [trɪ'mendəs] *adj.* (*a*) enormous/very large. (*b*) wonderful. **tremendously,** *adv.* greatly.

tremolo ['tremələʊ] *n.* (*pl.* **-os**) trembling note in music.

tremor ['tremə] *n.* shaking; **earth t.** = slight earthquake.

tremulous ['tremjʊləs] *adj.* shaking/quivering.

trench [trentʃ] **1.** *n.* (*pl.* **-es**) long narrow ditch in the ground. **2.** *v.* to dig a long narrow ditch. **trench coat,** *n.* belted waterproof coat.

trenchant ['trentʃənt] *adj.* sharp/biting (remark); vigorous (style).

trencher ['trentʃə] *n.* (*old*) wooden plate for food. **trencherman,** *n.* **good t.** = person who eats a lot.

trend [trend] *n.* general tendency. **trendiness,** *n.* being trendy. **trendsetter,** *n.* person who sets the fashion. **trendy. 1.** *adj.* (**-ier, -iest**) *inf.* following fashion; fashionable. **2.** *n. inf.* person who follows fashion.

trepan, trephine [trɪ'pæn, trɪ'fi:n] **1.** *n.* saw for cutting out round pieces of bone. **2.** *v.* (**trepanned**) to cut a round piece of bone out of (esp. the skull).

trepidation [trepɪ'deɪʃn] *n.* anxiety.

trespass ['trespəs] *v.* (**on**) to go into s.o.'s property without permission. **trespasser,** *n.* person who trespasses.

tresses ['tresɪz] *n. pl.* long hair.

trestle ['tresl] *n.* pair of folding legs which can be used to hold up a table; **t. table** = table made of planks resting on folding legs.

trews [tru:z] *n. pl.* close-fitting trousers made of tartan cloth.

tri- [traɪ] *prefix meaning* three.

triad ['traɪæd] *n.* Chinese secret society.

trial ['traɪəl] *n.* (*a*) court case to judge a criminal; **to stand t.** = to appear in court. (*b*) test; **sheepdog trials** = competition to select the best sheepdogs; **on t.** = being tested to see if it is acceptable; **t. and error** = testing and rejecting various things until you find the one which works. (c) game played to test the skills of players before they are selected for a team. (d) motorcycle competition held on rough ground.

triangle ['traɪæŋgl] n. (a) geometrical shape with three sides and three angles; **eternal t.** = situation where s.o. is in love with s.o. who is in love with a third person. (b) musical instrument made of a piece of metal bent into the shape of a triangle. **triangular** [traɪ'æŋgjʊlə] adj. shaped like a triangle. **triangulation** [traɪæŋgjʊ'leɪʃn] n. method of measuring land to produce maps.

tribe [traɪb] n. (a) group of people ruled by a chief. (b) inf. large family/group. **tribal**, adj. referring to a tribe. **tribalism**, n. organization of tribes. **tribesman**, n. (pl. -men) member of a tribe.

tribulation [trɪbjʊ'leɪʃn] n. (formal) great misery.

tribunal [traɪ'bjuːnl] n. court/official committee which judges special problems or writes a report on a special problem; **industrial t.** = court which decides in disputes between employers and workers; **rent t.** = court which decides if a rent is fair or excessive. **tribune** ['trɪbjuːn] n. leader who upholds the rights of the people.

tribute ['trɪbjuːt] n. (a) money paid to a conqueror by people who have been conquered. (b) words/gifts, etc., to show thanks/praise; **to pay t. to** = to praise; **floral tributes** = flowers sent to a funeral. **tributary. 1.** adj. (person) who pays tribute. **2.** n. river which flows into a larger river.

trice [traɪs] n. **in a t.** = very rapidly.

trichology [trɪk'ɒlədʒɪ] n. study of the diseases of the hair. **trichologist**, n. person who studies the diseases of the hair.

trick [trɪk] **1.** n. (a) clever action which can deceive/confuse s.o.; **to play a t. on s.o.** = to deceive/confuse s.o.; inf. **tricks of the trade** = clever dealings which are associated with a certain trade; **card tricks/conjuring tricks** = clever games with cards/with hats, handkerchiefs, etc., to amuse an audience; inf. **that should do the t.** = should do what is wanted/should make

it work; inf. **he doesn't miss a t.** = he is very alert. (b) (in card games) points won at the end of a round. (c) odd way of doing sth. **2.** adj. which deceives; **t. question** = one which is intended to catch people out. **3.** v. to deceive/to confuse; **to t. s.o. into doing sth** = to deceive s.o. so that he does sth which he did not intend to do. **trickery**, n. act of deceiving. **trickiness**, n. being tricky. **trickster**, n. person who tricks; **confidence t.** = person who cheats s.o. out of his money by some fraudulent scheme which seems to be honest. **tricky**, adj. (-ier, -iest) (a) difficult/awkward. (b) inf. sly/deceitful/untrustworthy.

trickle ['trɪkl] **1.** n. small flow of water; **t. charger** = device which charges a car battery slowly. **2.** v. to flow/move in a small quantity.

tricolour ['trɪkələ] n. flag with three bands of colour, esp. the national flag of France.

tricycle ['traɪsɪkl] n. three-wheeled pedal vehicle like a bicycle with two back wheels.

trident ['traɪdənt] n. spear with three prongs.

tried [traɪd] v. see **try**.

triennial [traɪ'enɪəl] adj. happening every three years.

trier ['traɪə] n. person who tries.

trifle ['traɪfl] **1.** n. (a) small insignificant thing. (b) small amount. (c) pudding made of cake/biscuits/jelly/jam/sherry and cream. **2.** v. (with) to play with/not to treat (sth) seriously. **trifler**, n. person who trifles with s.o./sth. **trifling**, adj. slight/very small.

trigger ['trɪgə] **1.** n. small metal lever on a gun which you pull to fire it. **2.** v. **to t. off** = to start (a series of things) happening. **trigger-happy**, adj. ready to shoot/ready to act quickly without thinking.

trigonometry [trɪgə'nɒmɪtrɪ] n. science which deals with the relationships between the sides and angles of triangles.

trike [traɪk] n. inf. tricycle.

trilateral [traɪ'lætrəl] adj. with three people/groups taking part.

trilby ['trɪlbɪ] n. type of man's hat.

trilingual [traɪ'lɪŋgwəl] adj. (person) who can speak three languages.

trill [trɪl] **1.** *n.* (*a*) warbling song (like a bird). (*b*) (*in music*) two notes rapidly repeated. **2.** *v.* to warble/to sing like a bird.

trillion ['trɪljən] *n.* (*a*) one million million millions. (*b*) *esp. Am.* one million millions.

trilobite ['traɪləbaɪt] *n.* ancient shellfish found in fossils.

trilogy ['trɪlədʒɪ] *n.* novel/play in three separate related parts.

trim [trɪm] **1.** *n.* (*a*) neatness. (*b*) cutting (of hair/bush, etc.). (*c*) decoration (on a car). **2.** *adj.* (**trimmer, trimmest**) neat. **3.** *v.* (**trimmed**) (*a*) to cut (sth) so that it is tidy. (*b*) to cut back; to reduce. (*c*) to ornament/to decorate. (*d*) (*on a sailing boat*) to put sails into the best position. (*e*) to change your political opinions to fit the current popular trend. **trimly,** *adv.* in a trim way. **trimmer,** *n.* person/device which trims; **hedge t.** = electric cutter for hedges. **trimming,** *n.* (*a*) ornament added to decorate sth; **roast pork with all the trimmings** = with the usual sauces and vegetables. (*b*) **trimmings** = pieces cut off (a hedge, etc.) when it is being trimmed. **trimness,** *n.* being trim.

trimaran ['traɪməræn] *n.* yacht with three parallel hulls.

trinitrotoluene [traɪnaɪtrəʊ'tɒljuːiːn] *n.* high explosive/TNT.

trinity ['trɪnɪtɪ] *n.* (*a*) group of three. (*b*) **the T.** = the three persons in the Christian God—the Father, Son and Holy Ghost. **Trinity House,** *n.* body which runs lighthouses and pilots.

trinket ['trɪŋkɪt] *n.* cheap ornament.

trio ['triːəʊ] *n.* (*pl.* **-os**) (*a*) piece of music for three instruments. (*b*) three musicians; group of three people.

trip [trɪp] **1.** *n.* (*a*) journey; **day t.** = journey lasting one day. (*b*) switch which activates a motor/light, etc. (*c*) *Sl.* trance caused by drugs. **2.** *v.* (**tripped**) (*a*) **to t. along** = to go along with light footsteps. (*b*) to catch your foot so that you stagger and fall. (*c*) to set off (a switch). (*d*) *Sl.* to go into a trance induced by drugs. **tripmeter,** *n.* dial on a car dashboard which shows how far you go on one particular journey. **tripper,** *n.* person on a short

(usu. one day) trip. **trip up,** *v.* **to t. s.o. up** = (i) to make s.o. fall down; (ii) to force s.o. to make a mistake. **trip wire,** *n.* wire stretched low above the ground, which, when you touch it, sets off a gun/camera, etc.

tripartite [traɪ'pɑːtaɪt] *adj.* with three parts; (agreement) between three countries.

tripe [traɪp] *n.* (*a*) part of a cow's/sheep's stomach used as food. (*b*) *inf.* rubbish/nonsense.

triple ['trɪpl] **1.** *adj.* made of three parts; three times as big. **2.** *v.* to become three times as large; to make (sth) three times as large. **triplet,** *n.* (*a*) (*in music*) three notes played quickly together. (*b*) one of three children born at the same birth. **triplex,** *adj.* with three layers. **triplicate,** *n.* **in t.** = in three copies.

tripod ['traɪpɒd] *n.* stand with three legs.

tripos ['traɪpɒs] *n.* final examination at Cambridge University.

triptych ['trɪptɪk] *n.* religious picture formed of three parts, often placed on or above an altar.

trite [traɪt] *adj.* very ordinary/unexciting (remark). **tritely,** *adv.* in a trite way. **triteness,** *n.* being trite.

triumph ['traɪəmf] **1.** *n.* (*a*) great victory. (*b*) celebration of a victory. **2.** *v.* **to t. over s.o.** = to win a victory over s.o.; to show that you are very glad that you won a victory. **triumphal** [traɪ'ʌmfl] *adj.* referring to triumph; **t. arch** = archway set up to celebrate a victory. **triumphant,** *adj.* victorious. **triumphantly,** *adv.* in victory.

triumvirate [traɪ'ʌmvɪrət] *n.* group of three people who rule/manage.

trivet ['trɪvət] *n.* (*a*) small three-legged stand for a kettle, etc. (*b*) metal stand for putting inside a pan to stop food sticking to the bottom.

trivial ['trɪvɪəl] *adj.* not important; ordinary. **trivia,** *n. pl.* unimportant details. **triviality** [trɪvɪ'ælɪtɪ] *n.* being unimportant; unimportant detail. **trivialize,** *v.* to make (sth) trivial. **trivially,** *adv.* in a trivial way.

trochee ['trəʊkiː] *n.* poetic measure made of one strong beat followed by a weak one. **trochaic** [trəʊ'keɪɪk] *adj.* referring to trochee.

trod [trɒd, 'trɒdn] v. see **tread**.

troglodyte ['trɒglədaɪt] n. person who lives in a cave.

troika ['trɔɪkə] n. (a) Russian carriage pulled by three horses. (b) three people holding power together (usu.) in Communist countries).

Trojan ['trəʊdʒn] adj. & n. **to work like a T.** = to work very hard; **T. horse** = trick carried out to infiltrate an enemy and ruin his plans.

troll [trəʊl] n. (in Scandinavia) bad-tempered dwarf.

trolley ['trɒlɪ] n. (a) wheeled cart for carrying luggage (such as at an airport); wheeled cart for pushing round a supermarket; small wheeled table for putting food on; **sweet t.** = trolley with a selection of desserts in a restaurant. (b) Am. tram. **trolley-bus,** n. bus which works on electricity taken from overhead wires by contact poles.

trollop ['trɒləp] n. dirty woman.

trombone [trɒm'bəʊn] n. brass wind instrument with a sliding tube. **trombonist,** n. person who plays the trombone.

troop [tru:p] 1. n. (a) group of people. (b) group of boy scouts. (c) **troops** = soldiers; **t. ship/t. train** which carries soldiers. 2. v. to move in a large group. **trooper,** n. (a) cavalry soldier. (b) Am. policeman from a state police force. **trooping,** n. **t. the colour** = military parade with the regimental flag.

trophy ['trəʊfɪ] n. (a) prize given for winning a competition. (b) thing taken from the enemy and kept as a prize.

tropic ['trɒpɪk] n. (a) **T. of Cancer/of Capricorn** = two imaginary lines running round the earth, parallel to the equator, and about 23° north/south of it. (b) **the tropics** = the hot areas of the world lying between these two imaginary lines. **tropical,** adj. very hot; (plant, etc.) growing in the tropics.

tropism ['trɒpɪzəm] n. growth of a plant towards or away from sth.

troposphere ['trɒpəsfɪə] n. layer of atmosphere between the surface of he earth and the stratosphere.

trot ['trɒt] 1. n. running with short regular steps; **they broke into a t.** = started to run; inf. **to keep s.o. on the t.** = to make s.o. work continuously. inf. **four games on the t.** = one after the other. 2. v. (**trotted**) to run with short regular steps; inf. **to t. out** = to produce (the same excuse, etc.) again. **trotter,** n. pig's foot cooked for food.

troth [trəʊθ] n. (old) promise.

Trotskyite ['trɒtskɪaɪt] n. person opposed to the central authority of a communist party, but who advocates continual revolution giving power to small groups of activists.

troubadour ['tru:bədʊə] n. wandering medieval singer.

trouble ['trʌbl] 1. n. (a) misfortune. (b) problem/difficult situation; **it's just asking for t.** = that type of behaviour will simply cause problems for you; **he's in t. with the police** = has been accused by the police of a crime; **to get s.o. into t.** = (i) to make s.o. be accused of doing sth wrong; (ii) to make s.o. pregnant. (c) care which is put into an action. (d) illness; mechanical defect. (e) **troubles** = riots/disturbances. 2. v. (a) to worry (s.o.). (b) to create problems for (s.o.); to bother (s.o.). (c) to bother (**to do** sth). **troublemaker,** n. person who creates problems/who stirs up unrest. **trouble-shooter,** n. person whose job is to sort out problems. **troublesome,** adj. causing trouble. **troublespot,** n. area where trouble is likely to occur.

trough [trɒf] n. (a) large container for animal food or drink; **horse t./water t.** = container for water for horses to drink. (b) low place; low point between two peaks (on a graph); low-pressure area in the atmosphere; low part of the sea between two waves.

trounce [traʊns] v. to beat (s.o.) soundly.

troupe [tru:p] n. company (of actors/circus clowns, etc.). **trouper,** n. member of a troupe.

trousers ['traʊzəz] n. pl. (**pair of**) **t.** = outer clothes which cover the legs and the lower part of the body.

trousseau ['tru:səʊ] n. clothes and linen collected by the bride before her wedding.

trout [traʊt] n. (pl. **trout**) type of edible freshwater fish; **salmon t.** = large sea trout with pink flesh like that of a salmon.

trove [trəʊv] *adj. see* **treasure**.

trowel ['traʊəl] *n.* (*a*) small hand spade used in gardening. (*b*) tool with a flat blade used for spreading mortar between bricks.

troy [trɔɪ] *n.* **t. weight** = system for weighing gold/silver.

truant ['truːənt] *adj. & n.* (child) who is absent from school without permission; **to play t.** = not to go to school. **truancy** ['truːənsɪ] *n.* being away from school without permission.

truce [truːs] *n.* period when two armies/enemies, etc., agree to stop fighting temporarily.

truck [trʌk] *n.* (*a*) open railway wagon for carrying goods. (*b*) heavy lorry. (*c*) small hand cart. (*d*) **to have no t. with** = not to have anything to do with. (*e*) *Am.* fruit and vegetables grown for sale in a town market. **truck driver, trucker,** *n.* lorry driver. **trucking,** *n. Am.* transport of goods by lorry. **truckload,** *n.* amount carried in a truck.

truckle ['trʌkl] *v.* to give in (**to** s.o.) weakly. **truckle bed,** *n.* low bed which can be pushed under another bed in daytime.

truculence ['trʌkjʊləns] *n.* being truculent. **truculent,** *adj.* threatening/fierce; eager to quarrel. **truculently,** *adv.* in a truculent way.

trudge [trʌdʒ] **1.** *n.* tiring walk. **2.** *v.* to walk heavily.

true [truː] **1.** *adj.* (**-er, -est**) (*a*) correct. (*b*) real. (*c*) correctly adjusted; **t. north** = north towards the north pole, and not the magnetic north. (*d*) faithful. **2.** *adv.* correctly; **to come t.** = to happen as forecast; **the wheel wasn't running t.** = wasn't turning straight. **3.** *n.* **out of t.** = not quite straight/not correctly adjusted. **true-blue,** *adj.* completely typical; totally loyal. **trueness,** *n.* being true. **truly,** *adv.* really; **yours t.** = ending of a slightly formal letter.

truffle ['trʌfl] *n.* (*a*) type of round black edible fungus found under the earth. (*b*) soft chocolate-covered sweet (usu. flavoured with rum).

trug [trʌg] *n.* long shallow basket for picking flowers.

truism ['truːɪzəm] *n.* saying which is quite obviously true and therefore need not be said.

trump [trʌmp] **1.** *n.* (*in card games*) suit which is chosen as being of higher value than the other suits; *inf.* **to turn up trumps** = very generous/helpful; **t. card** = advantage which is kept ready for use to win an argument. **2.** *v.* (*a*) **to t. a card** = to play a card of the suit which is trumps, and so win. (*b*) **to t. up** = to invent; **trumped-up charge** = false charge.

trumpery ['trʌmpərɪ] *adj.* (*formal*) useless and showy.

trumpet ['trʌmpɪt] **1.** *n.* brass musical instrument with three keys; *inf.* **to blow your own t.** = to praise what you yourself have done. **2.** *v.* (*a*) to play the trumpet. (*b*) to make a loud noise. (*c*) (*of elephant*) to call. **trumpeter,** *n.* person who plays the trumpet.

truncated [trʌn'keɪtɪd] *adj.* cut off; shortened.

truncheon ['trʌnʃn] *n.* short, heavy stick used by policemen.

trundle ['trʌndl] *v.* to roll/to push along (sth heavy).

trunk [trʌŋk] *n.* (*a*) main stem (of a tree); body (of a person). (*b*) long nose (of an elephant). (*c*) large box for sending clothes, etc., in. (*d*) *Am.* boot of a car. (*e*) **trunks** = men's shorts for swimming. **trunk call,** *n.* long-distance telephone call. **trunk road,** *n.* main road.

truss [trʌs] **1.** *n.* (*pl.* **-es**) (*a*) bundle of straw. (*b*) beam holding up a bridge/a roof. (*c*) belt to support a hernia. **2.** *v.* (*a*) to tie up (straw) into bundles. (*b*) to tie up (a chicken) ready for the oven; to tie up (a prisoner).

trust [trʌst] **1.** *n.* (*a*) confidence that sth is correct/is good/will work well, etc.; **to take on t.** = without examining to see if it is all right. (*b*) hope. (*c*) responsibility. (*d*) passing of goods/money to s.o. who will look after it; **family t.** = family money put in the hands of a group of people who will administer it. (*e*) group of business companies which combine to avoid competing with each other. **2.** *v.* (*a*) to be sure of (s.o.); to have confidence in (s.o.); *inf.* **t. him to be late** = as usual, he is late. (*b*) to hope. **trustee** [trʌs'tiː] *n.* person who has charge of money on trust for s.o.; person who administers a family trust/who directs a charity, etc. **trusteeship**, *n.* position of trustee. **trustful, trusting**, *adj.* full of confidence (in s.o.). **trustfully, trustingly**, *adv.* in a trustful/trusting way. **trustworthiness**, *n.* being trustworthy. **trustworthy**. *adj.* which can be depended upon. **trusty** ['trʌstɪ] 1. *n.* prisoner who is given certain responsibilities because he can be trusted. 2. *adj.* (**-ier, -iest**) which can be depended upon.

truth [truːθ] *n.* thing which is true; true story; **to tell s.o. a few home truths** = to tell s.o. what you think of them/ to criticize s.o.'s behaviour/character. **truthful**, *adj.* (person) who always tells the truth. **truthfully**, *adv.* in a truthful way. **truthfulness**, *n.* being truthful.

try [traɪ] 1. *n.* (*a*) attempt (to do sth). (*b*) goal scored in Rugby by touching the ball down behind the opposing goal line. 2. *v.* (*a*) to test. (*b*) to attempt. (*c*) to make (sth) suffer. (*d*) to judge (a case/a person) in court. **trying**, *adj.* difficult to put up with. **try on**, *v.* to put (clothes) on to see if they fit; *inf.* **to try it on with s.o.** = to act boldly to see if s.o. will accept your behaviour. **try out**, *v.* to test (sth).

trypanosome ['trɪ'pænəsəʊm] *n.* parasite, carried by the tsetse fly, causing sleeping sickness.

tryst [trɪst] *n.* (*old*) lovers' meeting.

tsar [zɑː] *n.* former title of the emperor of Russia.

tsetse ['tsetsɪ] *n.* type of African fly which transmits disease by biting.

tub [tʌb] *n.* (*a*) round (wooden) container; small, round cardboard box for ice cream. (*b*) bath. (*c*) *inf.* old ship. **tubbiness**, *n.* being tubby. **tubby**, *adj.* (**-ier, -iest**) *inf.* fat.

tuba ['tjuːbə] *n.* large bass brass instrument.

tube [tjuːb] *n.* (*a*) long pipe for carrying liquids or gas; **inner t.** = rubber pipe for air inside a tyre. (*b*) long pipe (in the body); **bronchial tubes** = tubes leading to the lungs. (*c*) soft pipe with a screw top which contains paste, etc. (*d*) (*esp. in London*) the underground railway system. (*e*) glass bulb in a television set which projects the picture on the screen. **tubeless**, *adj.* (tyre) with no inner tube. **tubing**, *n.* tubes made of metal/plastic, etc. **tubular** ['tjuːbjʊlə] *adj.* like a tube; **t. bells** = pieces of metal tubing of varying lengths which when hung up and hit with a hammer give different notes.

tuber ['tjuːbə] *n.* thick piece of root which can be planted to make a new plant grow. **tuberous**, *adj.* (root) which produces tubers.

tubercle ['tjuːbəkl] *n.* rounded bump on the skin; scar caused by tuberculosis. **tuberculosis** [tjʊbɜːkjuˈləʊsɪs] *n.* disease of the lungs. **tubercular** [tjuːˈbɜːkjʊlə] *adj.* suffering from tuberculosis. **tuberculin-tested**, *adj.* (milk/ cow) which has been tested to show that it is free from tuberculosis.

TUC [tiːjuːˈsiː] *abbrev. for* Trades Union Congress.

tuck [tʌk] 1. *n.* (*a*) little fold/pleat in a piece of cloth. (*b*) *inf.* cakes/sweets, etc., eaten by schoolchildren; **t. shop** = shop in a school selling sweets/cakes, etc. 2. *v.* (*a*) to fold (a blanket) around s.o. and push the ends underneath. (*b*) to fold cloth into little pleats. **tucker**, *n.* (*in Australia*) *inf.* food. **tuck in**, *v.* (*a*) to push the edge of a piece of cloth underneath s.o. to keep them warm. (*b*) *inf.* to eat a large quantity of food. **tuck-in**, *n.* *Sl.* big meal. **tuck up**, *v.* to **tuck s.o. up (in bed)** = to push the edge of the bedclothes around (s.o.) to keep them warm.

Tuesday ['tjuːzdeɪ] *n.* second day of the week/day between Monday and Wednesday.

tufa ['tjuːfə] *n.* type of porous volcanic rock.

tuft [tʌft] *n.* small bunch of grass/hair, etc. **tufted**, *adj.* with tufts.

tug [tʌg] 1. *n.* (*a*) sudden pull. (*b*) tugboat. 2. *v.* (**tugged**) to pull hard. **tugboat**, *n.* powerful boat used for towing barges/ships. **tug-of-war**, *n.* (*a*) competition where two teams pull against each other on a strong rope. (*b*) bitter struggle where two sides win alternately.

tuition [tjʊˈɪʃn] *n.* teaching (esp. of one student).

tulip ['tjuːlɪp] *n.* common spring bulb

with brilliant flowers shaped like cups.

tulip tree, *n.* large evergreen tree, with big shiny leaves and large white flowers.

tulle [tjuːl] *n.* thin silk/artificial material like a veil.

tumble ['tʌmbl] **1.** *n.* fall. **2.** *v.* (*a*) to fall (**down**). (*b*) to come down in confusion. **tumbledown,** *adj.* (house) which is falling down/coming to pieces. **tumbler,** *n.* round, straight glass for drinking. **tumbler dryer,** *n.* machine which dries washing. **tumble to,** *v. inf.* to understand.

tumescent [tjuːˈmesənt] *adj.* swollen.

tummy ['tʌmɪ] *n. inf.* stomach. **tummyache,** *n. inf.* pain in the stomach.

tumour, *Am.* **tumor** ['tjuːmə] *n.* abnormal growth in or on the body.

tumult ['tjuːmʌlt] *n.* loud, excited noise (of a crowd). **tumultuous** [tjʊˈmʌltjʊəs] *adj.* noisy/excited.

tumulus ['tjuːmjʊləs] *n.* (*pl.* **-li**) mound of earth covering an ancient tomb.

tun [tʌn] *n.* large barrel (for wine/beer).

tuna ['tjuːnə] *n.* (*pl.* **tuna**) large sea fish (used for food).

tundra ['tʌndrə] *n.* Arctic plain with no trees.

tune [tjuːn] **1.** *n.* (*a*) series of musical notes which make a recognizable melody; **he's changed his t.** = he has changed his way of thinking; *inf.* **to the t. of £100** = at least £100. (*b*) **in t.** = with the correct musical tone; **in t. with** = harmonizing with/similar to. **2.** *v.* (*a*) to adjust (a musical instrument) so that it has the correct tone. (*b*) to adjust (an engine) so that it works more efficiently. **tuneful,** *adj.* full of catchy tunes. **tune in,** *v.* to adjust a radio to a particular station. **tuner,** *n.* **piano t.** = person who tunes pianos. **tune up,** *v.* (*a*) to adjust instruments before playing. (*b*) to adjust (an engine) so that it works more efficiently. **tuning fork,** *n.* metal fork which gives a correct note when it is hit.

tungsten ['tʌŋstən] *n.* (*element:* W) hard grey metal used to make steel and electric light filaments.

tunic ['tjuːnɪk] *n.* (*a*) loose top garment. (*b*) short jacket worn by soldiers/policemen, etc.

tunnel ['tʌnl] **1.** *n.* long hole in the ground. **2.** *v.* (**tunnelled**) to make a long passage under the ground.

tunny ['tʌnɪ] *n.* (*pl.* **tunny**) tuna.

tup [tʌp] *n.* male sheep.

turban ['tɜːbən] *n.* long piece of cloth wrapped round the head to cover the hair.

turbid ['tɜːbɪd] *adj.* muddy (water). **turbidity** [tɜːˈbɪdɪtɪ] *n.* being turbid.

turbine ['tɜːbaɪn] *n.* engine driven by the force of water/steam which turns a wheel with blades.

turbo-jet [tɜːbəʊˈdʒet] *n.* jet engine driven by a turbine; aircraft powered by this engine. **turbo-prop** ['tɜːbəʊˈprɒp] *n.* jet and propeller engine driven by a turbine; aircraft powered by this engine.

turbot ['tɜːbət] *n.* (*pl.* **turbot**) large flat edible sea fish.

turbulent ['tɜːbjʊlənt] *adj.* (*a*) disturbed/violently moving (water/air). (*b*) likely to riot. **turbulence,** *n.* disturbance in the air causing an aircraft to rock suddenly; disturbance in water.

turd [tɜːd] *n.* lump of human excreta.

tureen [tjʊˈriːn] *n.* large bowl for serving soup.

turf [tɜːf] **1.** *n.* (*a*) stretch of grassy lawn. (*b*) (*pl.* **turves** [tɜːvz]) piece of grass and soil which can be planted to form a lawn; (*in Ireland*) block of peat for burning. (*c*) **the t.** = the world of horse racing; **t. accountant** = bookmaker. **2.** *v.* (*a*) to make a lawn by putting turves on the ground. (*b*) *inf.* **to t. s.o. out** = to throw s.o. out.

turgid ['tɜːdʒɪd] *adj.* swollen; grand-sounding, meaningless (words). **turgidly,** *adv.* in a turgid way.

Turk [tɜːk] *n.* person from Turkey.

turkey ['tɜːkɪ] *n.* large domestic bird, often eaten at Christmas.

Turkish ['tɜːkɪʃ] **1.** *adj.* referring to Turkey; **T. bath** = steam bath after which you plunge into cold water. **T. delight** = scented sweet jelly eaten in lumps. **2.** *n.* language spoken in Turkey.

turmeric ['tɜːmərɪk] *n.* yellow spice, used esp. in curries.

turmoil ['tɜːmɔɪl] *n.* wild disorder.

turn [tɜːn] **1.** *n.* (*a*) circular movement (of a wheel, etc.); **the meat is done to a t.** = properly cooked all through. (*b*) change of direction; **to take a t. for the**

better/for the worse = suddenly to start to get better/worse; **the tide is on the t.** = is about to start rising/falling; **at the t. of the century** = about 1900. (c) sudden attack (of illness). (d) chance to do sth in order; (of several people) **to take (it in) turns to do sth** = to do sth, each person dong it in order. (e) way of speaking/thinking/acting. (f) **to do s.o. a good t.** = to do sth to help them. (g) performance (in a variety show). **2.** v. (a) to go round; to make (sth) go round in a circle. (b) to change direction; (of tide) to start to rise/fall; **his luck turned** = changed. (c) to change (**into** sth else); (of milk) to go sour. (d) to aim (a gun). (e) **to t. s.o.'s head** = to make s.o. very proud/vain; **to t. s.o.'s stomach** = to make s.o. feel sick. (f) to shape (a round piece of wood) by carving it on a lathe. (g) to pass a particular point in time; **it's turned seven** = it is past seven o'clock; **he's turned fifty** = he's more than fifty years old. **turnabout,** n. act of turning to face in another direction. **turn aside,** v. to move to one side. **turn away,** v. (a) to move away. (b) to send (s.o.) away. **turn back,** v. (a) to turn and go back in the opposite direction. (b) to send (s.o.) back. **turncoat,** n. person who switches from one opinion to another. **turncock,** n. stopcock. **turn down,** v. (a) to refuse. (b) to reduce. (c) to fold back (a sheet on a bed), so that the pillow is uncovered. **turner,** n. person who makes chair legs, etc., on a lathe. **turnery,** n. (a) trade of a turner. (b) articles which are turned on a lathe. **turn in,** v. (a) to hand back (equipment) to s.o. in authority. (b) inf. to go to bed. (c) **to t. oneself in** = to give oneself up to the police. **turning,** n. (a) action of moving in a circle/ of changing direction. (b) point where a road leaves another road. **turning point,** n. important/decisive moment. **turn off,** v. (a) to switch off. (b) to change direction away from a straight line. **turn on,** v. (a) to switch on. (b) to attack. **turn out,** v. (a) to throw (s.o.) out. (b) to clear out. (c) to produce. (d) to switch off. (e) to happen. (f) to come out in a crowd. (g) **well turned-out** = well dressed. **turnout,** n. crowd of people who turn out. **turn over,** v.

(a) to move (the page of a book) so that you can read the next one. **to turn over a new leaf** = to be better behaved. (b) to think about. (c) to roll over. (d) (of engine) to run gently. (e) to have sales of (a certain amount). (f) to hand (a criminal) to the police. **turnover,** n. (a) type of pie made with pastry turned over a filling. (b) change (in staff). (c) amount of sales. **turnpike,** n. Am. motorway with tolls. **turnstile,** n. gate which turns round on a pivot, allowing only one person to go through at a time. **turntable,** n. (a) flat part of a record player which turns with the record on it. (b) flat turning platform with rails on it, to enable railway locomotives to go off in a different direction. **turn up,** v. (a) to arrive; to be found. (b) to increase. (c) to roll up. (d) to unfold/unroll (a collar). **turnup,** n. folded part at the bottom of each leg of a pair of trousers.

turnip ['tɜ:nɪp] n. common vegetable, with a round white root.

turpentine ['tɜ:pəntaɪn] n. oil which comes from fir trees, used for removing or thinning paint. **turps** [tɜ:ps] n. inf. turpentine.

turpitude ['tɜ:pɪtju:d] n. (formal) wickedness.

turquoise ['tɜ:kwɔɪz] **1.** n. green-blue precious stone. **2.** adj. green-blue (colour).

turret ['tʌrɪt] n. small tower; small armoured construction housing a gun (on a ship/tank,etc.). **turreted,** n. with turrets.

turtle ['tɜ:tl] n. sea reptile with a hard shell like a tortoise; **to turn t.** = to capsize. **turtledove,** n. type of wild pigeon with a soft, cooing call. **turtleneck pullover,** n. pullover with a high rolled neck.

turves [tɜ:vz] n. see turf.

tusk [tʌsk] n. long tooth coming far out from the mouth of some animals (such as elephants/walruses, etc.). **tusker,** n. inf. elephant.

tussle ['tʌsl] **1.** n. fight/argument. **2.** v. to fight/to struggle.

tussock ['tʌsək] n. large tuft of grass.

tussore ['tʌsɔ] n. type of coarse silk.

tutelage ['tju:təlɪdʒ] n. being responsible for s.o.; training given to pupil.

tutor ['tju:tə] **1.** n. teacher (esp. one who

teaches one student or small group of students). **2.** *v.* to teach (a small group of students). **tutorial** [tjʊ'tɔ:rɪəl] *n.* discussion meeting between a tutor and students.

tutti frutti ['tʊtɪ'frʊtɪ] *n.* icecream with pieces of preserved fruit in it.

tut-tut [tʌt'tʌt] **1.** *n.* sound made to show you disapprove. **2.** *v.* (**tut-tutted**) to make disapproving sounds.

tutu ['tu:tu:] *n.* girl ballet dancer's short stiff skirt.

tuxedo [tʌk'si:dəʊ] *n.* (*pl.* **-os**) *Am.* dinner jacket.

TV [ti:'vi:] *n.* (*a*) television. (*b*) television set.

twaddle ['twɒdl] *n. inf.* rubbish/ nonsense.

twain [tweɪn] *n.* (*formal*) two things.

twang [twæŋ] **1.** *n.* (*a*) sound made, such as when a guitar string is pulled and released. (*b*) **nasal t.** = accent made by speaking through the nose. **2.** *v.* to make a twang.

tweak [twi:k] **1.** *n.* sharp pull. **2.** *v.* to pull suddenly.

twee [twi:] *adj. inf.* small, delicate and sentimental.

tweed [twi:d] *n.* rough woollen cloth made of strands of different colours. **tweeds,** *n. pl.* suit made of tweed.

tweet [twi:t] **1.** *n.* little sound made by a small bird. **2.** *v.* to make a little sound like a bird. **tweeter,** *n.* loudspeaker which reproduces high sounds.

tweezers ['twi:zəz] *n. pl.* (**pair of**) **t.** = small pincers.

twelve [twelv] *n.* number 12. **twelfth** [twelfθ] **12th,** *adj. & n.* referring to twelve; **the t. century** = period from 1100 to 1199.

twenty ['twentɪ] *n.* number 20; **she's in her twenties** = she is over twenty but under thirty years old. **twentieth, 20th,** *adj. & n.* referring to twenty; **the t. century** = period from 1900 to 1999.

twerp [twɜ:p] *n. Sl.* stupid person.

twice [twaɪs] *adv.* two times; double; **he's t. my age** = two times as old as I am.

twiddle ['twɪdl] *v.* to turn/to twist with no particular aim; **to t. your thumbs** = holding your hands together, to turn your thumbs round and round as a sign of not having anything to do. **twiddly,** *adj. inf.* awkward and curly.

twig [twɪg] **1.** *n.* little branch. **2.** *v.* (**twigged**) *inf.* to understand.

twilight ['twaɪlaɪt] *n.* (period of) weak light between night and sunrise or between sunset and night.

twill [twɪl] *n.* thick cloth woven in diagonal lines.

twin [twɪn] **1.** *adj. & n.* (child) born at the same birth as another; **identical twins** = two children born at the same time who look very similar. **2.** *adj.* made of two similar parts. **3.** *v.* (**twinned**) (**with**) to join (a town) to a similar town in another country for exchange visits and to encourage international understanding. **twinset,** *n.* matching jumper and cardigan.

twine [twaɪn] **1.** *n.* thick, rough string. **2.** *v.* to twist round and round.

twinge [twɪnʒ] *n.* short sharp pain; short worry.

twinkle ['twɪŋkl] **1.** *n.* little flicker of light; **with a t. in his eye** = with his eyes shining with amusement. **2.** *v.* (*a*) to glitter. (*b*) (*of eyes*) to shine (with amusement/wickedness, etc.). **twinkling,** *n.* little flicker; **in the t. of an eye** = very fast.

twirl [twɜ:l] **1.** *n.* (*a*) spinning movement. (*b*) spiral shape. **2.** *v.* (*a*) to spin round. (*b*) to twist in your fingers. **twirly,** *adj. inf.* twisting.

twirp [twɜ:p] *n.* twerp.

twist [twɪst] **1.** *n.* (*a*) thing which has been twisted; **t. of paper** = small container made of a piece of paper with its end twisted. (*b*) piece which twists. (*c*) act of twisting; **a new to to the story** = an unexpected change. **2.** *v.* (*a*) to turn round and round. (*b*) to wind (sth) round sth. (*c*) to bend in the wrong way; to sprain (an ankle); *inf.* **to t. s.o.'s arm** = to persuade s.o. to do what you want. (*d*) to change the meaning of (words). **twister,** *n. Sl.* (*a*) dishonest person. (*b*) *Am.* whirlwind. **twisty,** *adj.* which twists.

twit [twɪt] **1.** *n. Sl.* silly idiot. **2.** *v.* (**twitted**) to make fun of (s.o.).

twitch [twɪtʃ] **1.** *n.* (*pl.* **-es**) sudden jerk/sudden movement. **2.** *v.* to jerk suddenly/to make a sudden movement. **twitcher,** *n. inf.* birdwatcher who travels long distances to see a rare bird.

twitter ['twɪtə] **1.** *n.* little calls made by birds; **she was all of a t.** = very excited. **2.** *v.* to make little sounds (like birds).

twixt [twɪkst] *prep.* (*old*) between.

two [tuː] *n.* number 2. (*a*) **one or t.** = a few; **to put t. and t. together** = to come to a conclusion by comparing various facts; **to be in t. minds about sth** = not to be able to decide. **two-bit**, *adj. Am. inf.* cheap/second-rate. **two-edged**, *adj.* (*a*) (knife) with two sharp edges. (*b*) (remark/action) which has two results (one good, one bad). **two-faced**, *adj.* deceitful. **twofold**, *adv.* twice as much. **two-legged** [tuː'legɪd] *adj.* with two legs. **twopenny** ['tʌpnɪ] *adj.* costing two pence. **two-piece**, *adj.* made of two pieces; **two-piece suit** = suit made of a jacket and skirt/trousers. **two-ply**, *adj.* made of two threads/two pieces. **two-seater**, *n.* car/aircraft with only two seats. **twosome**, *n.* two people (playing a game); game for two people. **twostep**, *n.* dance with smooth steps. **two-stroke**, *adj.* (engine) with two pistons; **two-stroke fuel** = fuel for small engines. **two-time**, *v. inf.* to be unfaithful (to a girlfriend/boyfriend). **two-timer**, *n. inf.* unfaithful person. **two-tone**, *adj.* coloured with two tones of the same colour. **two-way**, *adj.* going in two directions.

tycoon [taɪ'kuːn] *n.* wealthy businessman.

tying ['taɪɪŋ] *v. see* **tie**.

tyke [taɪk] *n.* (*in N. of England*) naughty child; small dog.

tympanum [tɪm'pɑːnəm] *n.* (*formal*) eardrum.

type [taɪp] **1.** *n.* (*a*) sort/kind. (*b*) example; **a real northern t.** = a good example of a northerner. (*c*) small pieces of metal with letters moulded on them, used for printing; collection of pieces of metal for printing. **2.** *v.* to write with a typewriter. **typecast**, *v.* (**typecast**) to give (an actor) the same type of part all the time. **typescript**, *n.* document typed on a typewriter. **typesetter**, *n.* person who sets manuscripts in type ready for printing. **typesetting**, *n.* action of setting type; type which has been set. **typewriter**, *n.* machine which prints letters on a piece of paper when you press the keys. **typewritten**, *adj.* (document) which has been written with a typewriter. **typing**, *n.* (*a*) action of writing letters with a typewriter; **t. pool** = group of typists who work for several departments in a company; **t. paper** = special paper for typewriters. (*b*) action of classifying into types; **blood t.** = classification of blood into a certain group. **typist**, *n.* person whose job is to type letters on a typewriter. **typographer**, *n.* specialist in typography. **typographic(al)** [taɪpə'græfɪk(l)] *adj.* referring to typography. **typography** [taɪ'pɒɡrəfɪ] *n.* (*a*) art of arranging material for printing/of designing a printed page. (*b*) study of the appearance of printed characters.

typhoid ['taɪfɔɪd] *adj. & n.* **t.** (**fever**) = serious disease caused by infected food or drink.

typhoon [taɪ'fuːn] *n.* tropical storm (in the Far East).

typhus ['taɪfəs] *n.* serious fever, where the virus is carried by lice.

typical ['tɪpɪkl] *adj.* obviously belonging to a particular group; characteristic; **that's t. of him** = that's exactly what he always does. **typically**, *adv.* in a typical way. **typify**, *v.* to be an excellent example of.

typo ['taɪpəʊ] *n. Am.* typesetting mistake.

tyranny ['tɪrənɪ] *n.* cruel rule by undemocratic government/ruler. **tyrannical, tyrannous** [tɪ'rænɪkl, 'tɪrənəs] *adj.* cruel. **tyrannize**, *v.* to rule (s.o.) in a cruel way. **tyrant** ['taɪrənt] *n.* cruel, undemocratic ruler.

tyre, *Am.* **tire** ['taɪə] *n.* thick rubber cover round a wheel; **flat t.** = the tyre has a hole in it so that the air has come out.

tyro ['taɪrəʊ] *n.* (*pl.* **-os**) complete beginner/person with no experience.

Uu

U, u [juː]; **U-turn** = turn made by a car in a road so that it faces in the opposite direction; **to do a U-turn** = change policy completely; *inf.* **non U** = not polite in upper class style. **U-boat**, *n.* German submarine.

U *symbol for* uranium.

ubiquitous [ju:'bɪkwɪtəs] *adj.* (thing) which is/which seems to be everywhere. **ubiquity,** *n.* being everywhere.

udder ['ʌdə] *n.* bag producing milk which hangs under the body of a cow or goat.

UDI [ju:di:'aɪ] *abbrev. for* unilateral declaration of independence.

UFO [ju:ef'əʊ] *n. abbrev. for* unidentified flying object.

ugh [ɜ:] *inter. showing a feeling that something is unpleasant.*

ugly ['ʌglɪ] *adj.* (-ier, -iest) (a) not pleasant to look at. (b) dangerous (mood). **ugliness,** *n.* being ugly.

UHF [ju:eɪtʃ'ef] *abbrev. for* ultra high frequency.

UHT [ju:eɪtʃ'ti:] *adj. abbrev. for* ultra heat treated.

UK [ju:'keɪ] *abbrev. for* United Kingdom.

ukulele [ju:kə'leɪlɪ] *n.* very small guitar.

ulcer ['ʌlsə] *n.* sore on the body. **ulcerate,** *v.* to cover with ulcers; to become covered with ulcers. **ulceration,** *n.* being covered with ulcers; place where an ulcer is. **ulcerous,** *adj.* covered with ulcers.

ullage ['ʌlɪdʒ] *n.* amount of missing liquid which would make a container full.

ulna ['ʌlnə] *n.* one of the two bones of the lower arm.

ulterior [ʌl'tɪərɪə] *adj.* hidden/secret; **u. motive** = reason for doing sth. which anticipates the result of the action.

ultimate ['ʌltɪmət] *adj.* final. **ultimately,** *adv.* finally.

ultimatum [ʌltɪ'meɪtəm] *n.* message sent to an opponent stating that unless demands are met by a certain time, violent action (usu. war or a strike) will start.

ultra- ['ʌltrə] *prefix meaning* extremely/very. **ultramarine** [ʌltrəmə'ri:n] *adj. & n.* (colour) of deep sea blue. **ultramodern,** *adj.* extremely modern. **ultrasonic,** *adj.* (sound waves) which cannot be heard by humans. **ultrasound,** *n.* very high frequency sound wave, used to detect objects in the body or under water. **ultraviolet** [ʌltrə'vaɪələt] *adj.* (light rays) which are beyond the violet of the spectrum and which tan the skin. **ultra vires,** *adv.* (acting) beyond one's powers.

umbel ['ʌmbl] *n.* flower head · made of many single flowers on long stalks. **umbelliferous** [ʌmbə'lɪfərəs] *adj.* (plant) with umbels.

umber ['ʌmbə] *adj. & n.* brown (colour) like earth; **burnt u.** = reddish-brown (colour).

umbilical [ʌm'bɪlɪkl] *adj.* **u. cord** = tube joining the mother to her baby before birth, and through which nourishment passes.

umbra ['ʌmbrə] *n.* (*formal*) shadow.

umbrage ['ʌmbrɪdʒ] *n.* **to take u. at** = to feel insulted by.

umbrella [ʌm'brelə] *n.* round shade of folded cloth which opens on a frame and is held over your head to keep off the rain; **u. organization** = large organization which includes small ones.

umpire ['ʌmpaɪə] **1.** *n.* person who acts as a judge in cricket/tennis/baseball, etc., to see if the game is played according to the rules. **2.** *v.* to act as umpire.

umpteen [ʌm'ti:n] *adj. & n. inf.* very large number. **umpteenth,** *adj. inf.* referring to umpteen.

un- [ʌn] *prefix meaning* not; the opposite.

'un [ʌn] *pron. inf.* one.

UN ['ju:'en] *abbrev. for* United Nations.

unabashed [ʌnə'bæʃt] *adj.* not ashamed/not timid.

unabated [ʌnə'beɪtɪd] *adj.* with no loss of vigour.

unable [ʌn'eɪbl] *adj.* not able.

unabridged [ʌnə'brɪdʒd] *adj.* (text) which has not been shortened.

unacceptable [ʌnək'septəbl] *adj.* which cannot be accepted.

unaccompanied [ʌnə'kʌmpnɪd] *adj.* alone; (singer/instrument) without any accompaniment.

unaccountable [ʌnə'kaʊntəbl] *adj.* which cannot be explained. **unaccountably,** *adv.* without explanation. **unaccounted for,** *adj.* lost, with no explanation for the loss.

unaccustomed [ʌnə'kʌstəmd] *adj.* not accustomed.

unacquainted [ʌnə'kweɪntɪd] *adj.* **to be u. with** = not to know.

unadopted [ʌnə'dɒptɪd] *adj.* (road) which it is not the duty of the local council to keep in good repair.

unadulterated [ʌnə'dʌltəreɪtɪd] *adj.* pure; with nothing added.

unaffected [ʌnə'fektɪd] *adj.* sincere/ natural.

unaided [ʌn'eɪdɪd] *adj.* without help.

unalloyed [ʌnə'lɔɪd] *adj.* pure.

unalterable [ʌn'ɒltrəbl] *adj.* which cannot be altered. **unaltered,** *adj.* which has not changed.

unambiguous [ʌnæm'bɪgjʊəs] *adj.* clear/not ambiguous.

unanimous [jʊ'nænɪməs] *adj.* where everyone agrees. **unanimously,** *adv.* all agreeing together. **unanimity** [jʊnə-'nɪmɪtɪ] *n.* being unanimous.

unannounced [ʌnə'naʊnst] *adj.* which has not been announced.

unappetizing [ʌn'æpɪtaɪzɪŋ] *adj.* which does not make you want to eat/which takes away your appetite.

unapproachable [ʌnə'prəʊtʃəbl] *adj.* (person) who is very formal; (place) which cannot be approached easily.

unarmed [ʌn'ɑːmd] *adj.* with no weapons.

unashamed [ʌnə'ʃeɪmd] *adj.* not ashamed.

unasked [ʌn'ɑːskt] *adj.* without being asked.

unassuming [ʌnə'sjuːmɪŋ] *adj.* quiet/ modest.

unattached [ʌnə'tætʃt] *adj.* not attached; not married.

unattainable [ʌnə'teɪnəbl] *adj.* which cannot be reached.

unattended [ʌnə'tendɪd] *adj.* alone; not looked after.

unattractive [ʌnə'træktɪv] *adj.* not attractive.

unauthorised [ʌn'ɔːθəraɪzd] *adj.* which is not permitted.

unavoidable [ʌnə'vɔɪdəbl] *adj.* which cannot be avoided. **unavoidably,** *adv.* in an unavoidable way.

unaware [ʌnə'weə] *adj.* (of) not knowing/not aware. **unawares,** *adv.* without noticing; **to catch s.o. u.** = by surprise.

unbalanced [ʌn'bælənst] *adj.* erratic/ slightly mad.

unbearable [ʌn'beərəbl] *adj.* which cannot be borne. **unbearably,** *adv.* so much that you cannot bear it.

unbeatable [ʌn'biːtəbl] *adj.* which cannot be beaten. **unbeaten,** *adj.* which has not been beaten.

unbecoming [ʌnbɪ'kʌmɪŋ] *adj.* which is not decent.

unbeknown [ʌnbɪ'nəʊn] *adj. inf.* **u. to anyone** = without anyone knowing.

unbelievable [ʌnbɪ'liːvəbl] *adj.* incredible/which you cannot believe. **unbelievably,** *adv.* incredibly/amazingly. **unbeliver,** *n.* person who does not believe in god.

unbend [ʌn'bend] *v.* (**unbent**) to stop being stiff and start behaving naturally. **unbending,** *adj.* inflexible/ harsh (rule).

unbiased [ʌn'baɪəst] *adj.* impartial/not biased.

unbidden [ʌn'bɪdn] *adj.* (*formal*) without having been asked.

unbleached [ʌn'bliːtʃt] *adj.* (cloth, etc.) which has not been bleached.

unblock [ʌn'blɒk] *v.* to take a blockage away from (sth).

unblushing [ʌn'blʌʃɪŋ] *adj.* showing no shame.

unbolt [ʌn'bəʊlt] *v.* to pull back the bolt on (a door).

unborn [ʌn'bɔːn] *adj.* not yet born.

unbosom [ʌn'bʊzəm] *v.* **to u. oneself to s.o.** = tell all one's private thoughts and troubles.

unbounded [ʌn'baʊndɪd] *adj.* with no limits.

unbreakable [ʌn'breɪkəbl] *adj.* which cannot be broken.

unbridled [ʌn'braɪdld] *adj.* (passion) which is not controlled.

unbroken [ʌn'brəʊkn] *adj.* which has not been broken; (case of wine) which has not been opened.

unburden [ʌn'bɜːdn] *v.* **to u. yourself to s.o.** = to tell (s.o.) all your troubles/ secrets.

unbutton [ʌn'bʌtn] *v.* to undo the buttons on.

uncalled for [ʌn'kɔːldfɔː] *adj.* not necessary; not deserved.

uncanny [ʌn'kænɪ] *adj.* mysterious/ which seems unnatural.

uncared for [ʌn'keədfɔː] *adj.* not looked after.

unceasing [ʌn'siːsɪŋ] *adj.* ceaseless; without any stopping.

unceremonious [ʌnserɪ'məʊnɪəs] *adj.* not dignified; not polite. **unceremoniously,** *adv.* in an undignified way.

uncertain [ʌn'sɜːtən] *adj.* (*a*) not certain/not sure. (*b*) which cannot be forecast. **uncertainty**, *n.* being uncertain; lack of certainty.

unchallenged [ʌn't∫æləŋʒd] *adj.* without a challenge; **to let sth pass u.** = to let sth be said or written without questioning it.

uncharacteristic [ʌnkærəkte'rɪstɪk] *adj.* not in character.

uncharitable [ʌn't∫ærɪtəbl] *adj.* unkind. **uncharitably**, *adv.* in an uncharitable way.

unchecked [ʌn't∫ekt] *adj.* with no check.

unchristian [ʌn'krɪst∫n] *adj.* not kind/generous, etc.

uncial ['ʌnsɪəl] *adj. & n.* (rounded) letters used in early medieval manuscripts.

uncivilized [ʌn'sɪvɪlaɪzd] *adj.* not civilized; barbarous.

unclaimed [ʌn'kleɪmd] *adj.* which has not been claimed; **u. baggage** = cases, etc., which have been left in a left-luggage office and not been taken back by their owners.

unclassified [ʌn'klæsɪfaɪd] *adj.* not classified/not secret.

uncle ['ʌŋkl] *n.* brother of your father or mother; husband of your aunt. **Uncle Sam**, *n. inf.* person symbolizing the USA.

unclean [ʌn'kliːn] *adj.* dirty.

unclouded [ʌn'klaʊdɪd] *adj.* not troubled/clear (liquid).

uncluttered [ʌn'klʌtəd] *adj.* tidy.

uncoil [ʌn'kɔɪl] *v.* to unwind.

uncomfortable [ʌn'kʌmftəbl] *adj.* (*a*) not comfortable. (*b*) embarrassed; ill at ease. **uncomfortably**, *adv.* in an uncomfortable way.

uncommitted [ʌnkə'mɪtɪd] *adj.* with no strong beliefs; (country) which has not decided which group to support; (voter) who has not decided which way to vote.

uncommon [ʌn'kɒmən] *adj.* (**-er, -est**) strange/odd; rare. **uncommonly**, *adv.* in an uncommon way; *inf.* very.

uncommunicative [ʌnkə'mjuːnɪkətɪv] *adj.* silent/not talkative.

uncomplimentary [ʌnkɒmplɪ'mentərɪ] *adj.* rude/not complimentary.

uncompromising [ʌn'kɒmprəmaɪzɪŋ] *adj.* unwilling to give in or to change ideas.

unconcealed [ʌnkən'siːld] *adj.* open; not hidden.

unconcerned [ʌnkən'sɜːnd] *adj.* not worried/not bothered.

unconditional [ʌnkən'dɪ∫nl] *adj.* without any conditions. **unconditionally**, *adv.* without insisting on conditions.

unconnected [ʌnkə'nektɪd] *adj.* with no connection.

unconscious [ʌn'kɒn∫əs] **1.** *adj.* (*a*) not conscious. (*b*) not aware. **2.** *n.* **the u.** = deep level of the mind, with thoughts or feelings of which you are not conscious. **unconscionable** [ʌn'kɒn∫nəbl] *adj. inf.* unreasonable/excessive. **unconsciously**, *adv.* in an unconscious way. **unconsciousness**, *n.* being unconscious.

unconstitutional [ʌnkɒnstɪ'tjuː∫ənl] *adj.* going against the constitution.

uncontested [ʌnkən'testɪd] *adj.* (divorce) which is not disputed.

uncontrollable [ʌnkən'trəʊləbl] *adj.* which cannot be controlled.

unconventional [ʌnkən'ven∫nl] *adj.* not usual.

uncooked [ʌn'kʊkt] *adj.* not cooked.

uncooperative [ʌnkəʊ'ɒpərətɪv] *adj.* unhelpful/not cooperative.

uncork [ʌn'kɔːk] *v.* to take the cork out of (a bottle).

uncorroborated [ʌnkə'rɒbəreɪtɪd] *adj.* (evidence) which has not been confirmed.

uncouple [ʌn'kʌpl] *v.* to detach (things) which are coupled.

uncouth [ʌn'kuːθ] *adj.* rude/badly brought up.

uncover [ʌn'kʌvə] *v.* (*a*) to take the cover off. (*b*) to find (sth hidden).

uncritical [ʌn'krɪtɪkl] *adj.* (person) who does not think critically.

uncrossed [ʌn'krɒst] *adj.* (cheque) which has not been crossed.

uncrowned [ʌn'kraʊnd] *adj.* (king) who has not been crowned; (leader) who is like a king.

uncrushable [ʌn'krʌ∫əbl] *adj.* (material) which does not make creases if it is crushed.

unction ['ʌŋk∫n] *n.* putting oil on a person in a religious ceremony. **unctuous**

['ʌŋkʃʊəs] *adj.* extremely and unpleasantly polite. **unctuously,** *adv.* in an unctuous way.

uncultivated [ʌn'kʌltɪveɪtɪd] *adj.* (land) which has not been cultivated.

uncut [ʌn'kʌt] *adj.* which has not been cut; (film) which has not been censored; (book) with pages still joined together at the edges.

undaunted [ʌn'dɔːntɪd] *adj.* bold/with no fear.

undecided [ʌndɪ'saɪdɪd] *adj.* (person) who has not made up his mind.

undeclared [ʌndɪ'kleəd] *adj.* which has not been declared.

undefended [ʌndɪ'fendɪd] *adj.* not defended; (divorce case) which the defendant does not defend.

undemanding [ʌndɪ'mɑːndɪŋ] *adj.* not difficult.

undemocratic [ʌndemə'krætɪk] *adj.* not democratic.

undeniable [ʌndɪ'naɪəbl] *adj.* which cannot be denied/which is quite clearly true.

under ['ʌndə] **1.** *prep.* (*a*) in a place which is directly below; **u. water** = below the surface of the water. (*b*) less than; **u. age** = younger than the legal age. (*c*) being ruled/managed/commanded by s.o. (*d*) because of/according to (terms). (*e*) in a state of; **u. repair** = being repaired; **u. lock and key** = locked up; **u. treatment** = being treated; **u. control** = controlled. **2.** *adv.* in a lower place; **to go u.** = to fail/to go bankrupt; *inf.* **down u.** = in Australia and New Zealand. **3.** *adj.* lower/bottom. **4. under-** *prefix meaning* less important; not enough.

underachieve [ʌndərə'tʃiːv] *v.* to do less well than expected. **underachiever,** *n.* student who does not do as well as expected.

underarm ['ʌndərɑːm] *adv. & adj.* (thrown) with the hand kept lower than the shoulder.

undercarriage ['ʌndəkærɪdʒ] *n.* aircraft's wheels and supports.

undercharge [ʌndə'tʃɑːdʒ] *v.* to charge less than you should.

underclothes ['ʌndəkləʊðz] *n. pl.* clothes worn next to the skin, under other clothes.

undercoat ['ʌndəkəʊt] *n.* first coat of paint.

undercover ['ʌndəkʌvə] *adj.* secret; **u. agent** = spy.

undercurrent ['ʌndəkʌrənt] *n.* (*a*) current of water under the surface. (*b*) hidden feelings.

undercut ['ʌndəkʌt] *v.* (**undercut**) to sell more cheaply than (s.o.).

underdeveloped [ʌndədɪ'veləpt] *adj.* not developed; not industrially advanced.

underdog ['ʌndədɒg] *n.* person who is weaker/who always loses.

underdone [ʌndə'dʌn] *adj.* not cooked enough; not too cooked.

underestimate 1. *n.* [ʌndər'estɪmət] estimate which is less than the real quantity. **2.** *v.* [ʌndər'estɪmeɪt] to estimate at less than the real quantity.

underexposed [ʌndərɪk'spəʊzd] *adj.* (film) which has not been exposed sufficiently.

underfed [ʌndə'fed] *adj.* with not enough to eat.

underfelt ['ʌndəfelt] *n.* soft material put beneath a carpet.

underfloor [ʌndə'flɔː] *adj.* (heating system) which is under the floor.

underfoot [ʌndə'fʊt] *adv.* under the feet.

undergarment ['ʌndəgɑːmənt] *n.* piece of clothing worn next to the skin, under other clothes.

undergo [ʌndə'gəʊ] *v.* (**underwent, undergone**) to suffer/to experience.

undergraduate [ʌndə'grædjʊət] *n.* student at university who has not yet passed the final examination.

underground 1. *adv.* [ʌndə'graʊnd] (*a*) under the ground. (*b*) in hiding. **2.** *adj.* ['ʌndəgraʊnd] (*a*) under the ground. (*b*) secret; against the ruling authorities. **3.** *n.* ['ʌndəgraʊnd] (*a*) city railway which runs beneath the ground. (*b*) secret organization.

undergrowth ['ʌndəgrəʊθ] *n.* bushes which grow thickly together under trees.

underhand(ed) [ʌndə'hænd(ɪd)] *adj.* cunning; deceitful.

underlay ['ʌndəleɪ] *n.* material for putting under a carpet; *see also* **underlie.**

underlie [ʌndə'laɪ] v. (**underlay, underlain**) to be underneath; to be the basic cause (of sth). **underlying,** adj. basic (cause).

underline ['ʌndəlaɪn] v. to write a line under (a word); to emphasize.

underling ['ʌndəlɪŋ] n. person who works for s.o. else.

undermanned [ʌndə'mænd] adj. with not enough staff.

undermentioned [ʌndə'menʃənd] adj. mentioned lower down on the page.

undermine [ʌndə'maɪn] v. to weaken.

underneath [ʌndə'niːθ] 1. prep. under/beneath. 2. adv. under. 3. n. the bottom part.

undernourished [ʌndə'nʌrɪʃt] adj. not having enough to eat.

underpaid [ʌndə'peɪd] adj. not paid enough.

underpants ['ʌndəpænts] n. pl. men's undergarment for the lower part of the body.

underpass ['ʌndəpɑːs] n. (pl. **-es**) place where one road goes under another.

underpin [ʌndə'pɪn] v. (**underpinned**) to support. **underpinning,** n. support.

underprivileged [ʌndə'prɪvɪlɪdʒd] adj. not having the same opportunities as other people.

underrate [ʌndə'reɪt] v. to value (sth) less than you ought.

underscore [ʌndə'skɔː] v. to underline.

undersea ['ʌndəsiː] adj. & adv. under the sea.

underseal ['ʌndəsiːl] 1. n. protective paint to stop the underneath of a car rusting. 2. v. to paint the underneath of (a car) with underseal.

undersecretary [ʌndə'sekrətrɪ] n. person in charge of a government department under a minister.

undersell [ʌndə'sel] v. (**undersold**) to sell more cheaply than (s.o.).

undershirt ['ʌndəʃɜːt] n. Am. vest.

underside ['ʌndəsaɪd] n. side which is underneath.

undersigned ['ʌndəsaɪnd] n. person who has signed a letter.

undersize(d) ['ʌndəsaɪz(d)] adj. smaller than normal.

underslung ['ʌndəslʌŋ] adj. (car chassis) which hangs below the axles.

understaffed [ʌndə'stɑːft] adj. with not enough staff.

understand [ʌndə'stænd] v. (**understood**) (a) to know; to see the meaning of (sth). (b) to be an expert in (sth). (c) to think/to have an impression. (d) to take sth for granted, even if it is not written or spoken. (e) to know why (sth is done) and accept it. **understandable,** adj. which can be understood. **understandably,** adv. in a way which can be understood. **understanding. 1.** n. (a) ability to understand. (b) sympathy for another person's problems. (c) private agreement. **2.** adj. sympathetic.

understate [ʌndə'steɪt] v. to make (sth) seem less important than it really is. **understatement,** n. statement which does not tell the facts forcefully enough.

understeer [ʌndə'stɪə] v. (of car) to turn a corner less sharply than it should.

understood [ʌndə'stʊd] v. see **understand**.

understudy ['ʌndəstʌdɪ] 1. n. actor who learns a part in the play so as to be able to act it if the main actor is ill. 2. v. to be the understudy of (an actor).

undertake [ʌndə'teɪk] v. (**undertook, has undertaken**) to promise to do (sth); to accept to do (sth). **undertaker,** n. person who organizes funerals. **undertaking,** n. (a) business. (b) promise. (c) job; **quite an u.** = very difficult job.

undertone ['ʌndətəʊn] n. (a) quiet voice. (b) hidden feeling.

undertow ['ʌndətəʊ] n. strong current under the surface of water, which flows in a different direction to that on the surface.

undervalue [ʌndə'vælju:] v. to value at less than the true rate.

underwater [ʌndə'wɔːtə] adj. below the surface of the water.

underwear ['ʌndəweə] n. (no pl.) clothes worn next to your skin under other clothes.

underweight [ʌndə'weɪt] adj. which weighs less than usual.

underwent [ʌndə'went] v. see **undergo**.

underworld ['ʌndəwɜːld] n. (a) (in mythology) place inhabited by the dead. (b) criminal world; **u. killing** = murder of a criminal by other criminals.

underwrite [ˌʌndəˈraɪt] v. (**underwrote, has underwritten**) to insure (esp. ships); to accept responsibility for (sth). **underwriter** [ˈʌndəraɪtə] n. person who insures (esp. ships).

undeserved [ˌʌndɪˈzɜːvd] adj. not deserved. **undeservedly** [ˌʌndɪˈzɜːvɪdlɪ] adv. in an undeserved way.

undesirable [ˌʌndɪˈzaɪərəbl] 1. adj. not wanted; not pleasant. 2. n. person who is not wanted/ who is considered a bad influence. **undesirability** [ˌʌndɪzaɪərə-ˈbɪlɪtɪ] n. being undesirable.

undetected [ˌʌndɪˈtektɪd] adj. not noticed. **undetectable**, adj. which cannot be detected.

undeterred [ˌʌndɪˈtɜːd] adj. not put off.

undeveloped [ˌʌndɪˈveləpt] adj. which has not been developed.

undid [ʌnˈdɪd] v. see undo.

undies [ˈʌndɪz] n. pl. inf. (women's) underwear.

undignified [ʌnˈdɪgnɪfaɪd] adj. not dignified.

undiluted [ˌʌndaɪˈljuːtɪd] adj. without any water added.

undischarged [ˌʌndɪsˈtʃɑːʒd] adj. (debt) which has not been paid; **u. bankrupt** = person who is still legally a bankrupt.

undistinguished [ˌʌndɪsˈtɪŋgwɪʃt] adj. ordinary.

undivided [ˌʌndɪˈvaɪdɪd] adj. complete/ not split.

undo [ʌnˈduː] v. (**undid, has undone**) (a) to untie (a knot); to unbutton. (b) to ruin. **undoing**, n. ruin. **undone**, adj. (a) unfastened. (b) not complete.

undoubted [ʌnˈdautɪd] adj. certain. **undoubtedly**, adv. certainly.

undreamt of [ʌnˈdremtɒv] adj. which no one can imagine.

undress [ʌnˈdres] v. to take off (usu. all your) clothes. **undressed**, adj. not wearing clothes.

undrinkable [ʌnˈdrɪŋkəbl] adj. (liquid) which is so unpleasant/so polluted that you cannot drink it.

undue [ˈʌndjuː] adj. excessive/too much. **unduly** [ʌnˈdjuːlɪ] adv. excessively/too much.

undulant [ˈʌndjʊlənt] adj. **u. fever** = brucellosis.

undulate [ˈʌndjʊleɪt] v. to rise and fall like waves. **undulation** [ˌʌndjʊˈleɪʃn] n. rise and fall (of land, etc.).

undying [ʌnˈdaɪɪŋ] adj. (emotion) which lasts for ever.

unearned [ˈʌnɜːnd] adj. (income) from investments/rents, etc.

unearth [ʌnˈɜːθ] v. to dig up; to discover. **unearthly**, adj. supernatural; inf. very early/late (hour).

uneasy [ʌnˈiːzɪ] adj. (-ier, -iest) worried. **uneasily**, adv. in an uneasy way. **uneasiness**, n. worry/anxiety.

uneatable [ʌnˈiːtəbl] adj. (food) which is so unpleasant that you cannot eat it.

uneconomic(al) [ʌniːkəˈnɒmɪk(l)] adj. which is not economic/which does not make a profit.

uneducated [ʌnˈedjʊkeɪtɪd] adj. not educated; (person) who has not been well brought up; (way of speaking) which is not refined.

unemployed [ˌʌnɪmˈplɔɪd] adj. without any permanent work; **the u.** = people with no jobs. **unemployment** [ˌʌnɪm-ˈplɔɪmənt] n. lack of jobs; **mass u.** = situation where large numbers of people are out of work.

unending [ʌnˈendɪŋ] adj. ceaseless/with no end.

unenlightened [ˌʌnɪnˈlaɪtənd] adj. lacking knowledge.

unenviable [ʌnˈenvɪəbl] adj. which no one would envy.

unequal [ʌnˈiːkwəl] adj. (a) not equal. (b) **u. to** = not good/strong enough for. **unequalled**, adj. which has no equal.

unequivocal [ˌʌnɪˈkwɪvəkl] adj. clear; easily understood; which cannot be misunderstood.

unerring [ʌnˈɜːrɪŋ] adj. faultless/making no mistake.

unethical [ʌnˈeθɪkl] adj. (conduct) which does not follow the usual rules of a profession.

uneven [ʌnˈiːvn] adj. (a) bumpy/not flat. (b) not always very good. **unevenness**, n. being uneven.

uneventful [ˌʌnɪˈventfl] adj. without any particularly exciting incidents.

unexampled [ˌʌnɪgˈzɑːmpld] adj. extraordinary; of which there is no other example.

unexceptionable [ˌʌnɪkˈsepʃənəbl] adj. very satisfactory.

unexceptional [ʌnɪk'sepʃnəl] *adj.* ordinary.

unexpected [ʌnɪk'spektɪd] *adj.* which was not expected. **unexpectedly,** *adv.* in an unexpected way.

unexplored [ʌnɪk'splɔːd] *adj.* which has never been explored.

unexposed [ʌnɪk'spəʊzd] *adj.* (film) which has not been used.

unexpurgated [ʌn'ekspɜːgeɪtɪd] *adj.* (book, etc.) which has not had offensive parts removed.

unfailing [ʌn'feɪlɪŋ] *adj.* which never fails. **unfailingly,** *adv.* without fail.

unfair [ʌn'feə] *adj.* not fair; **u. dismissal** = removing of a person from his job for reasons which are not fair.

unfaithful [ʌn'feɪθfəl] *adj.* not faithful (to your husband or wife).

unfamiliar [ʌnfə'mɪlɪə] *adj.* not familiar.

unfasten [ʌn'fɑːsn] *v.* to undo (sth which is fastened).

unfathomable [ʌn'fæðəməbl] *adj.* (mystery) which cannot be solved.

unfavourable [ʌn'feɪvrəbl] *adj.* not favourable.

unfeeling [ʌn'fiːlɪŋ] *adj.* insensitive; not sympathetic to s.o.

unfettered [ʌn'fetəd] *adj.* free.

unfit [ʌn'fɪt] *adj.* (a) (person) who is not fit/not in good physical condition. (b) not suitable.

unflagging [ʌn'flægɪŋ] *adj.* tireless.

unflappable [ʌn'flæpəbl] *adj.* (person) who is always calm.

unflinching [ʌn'flɪntʃɪŋ] *adj.* brave. **unflinchingly,** *adv.* bravely.

unfold [ʌn'fəʊld] *v.* (a) to spread out (a newspaper). (b) (*of story*) to become clear/be told.

unforeseen [ʌnfɔː'siːn] *adj.* not foreseen/not anticipated.

unforgettable [ʌnfə'getəbl] *adj.* which cannot be forgotten.

unfortunate [ʌn'fɔːtʃənət] *adj.* (a) unlucky. (b) sad; to be regretted. **unfortunately,** *adv.* sadly.

unfounded [ʌn'faʊndɪd] *adj.* without any basis in truth.

unfreeze [ʌn'friːz] *v.* (**unfroze, unfrozen**) to warm (sth) so that it stops being frozen.

unfrequented [ʌnfrɪ'kwentɪd] *adj.* (place) where few people go.

unfriendly [ʌn'frendlɪ] *adj.* (**-ier, -iest**) not like a friend.

unfrock [ʌn'frɒk] *v.* to remove (a priest) from holy orders.

unfurl [ʌn'fɜːl] *v.* to unroll (like a flag).

unfurnished [ʌn'fɜːnɪʃt] *adj.* (house) with no furniture in it.

ungainly [ʌn'geɪnlɪ] *adj.* awkward/clumsy (way of walking).

ungentlemanly [ʌn'dʒentəlmənlɪ] *adj.* (behaviour) not like that of a true gentleman.

ungetatable [ʌnget'ætəbl] *adj.* which you cannot reach easily.

ungodly [ʌn'gɒdlɪ] *adj.* wicked; unpleasant/inconvenient; *inf.* very early/late (hour).

ungracious [ʌn'greɪʃəs] *adj.* not gracious/not polite.

ungrammatical [ʌngrə'mætɪkl] *adj.* which goes against the rules of grammar.

ungrateful [ʌn'greɪtfəl] *adj.* not grateful.

unguarded [ʌn'gɑːdɪd] *adj.* careless; **in an u. moment** = without thinking about the consequences.

unguent ['ʌngwənt] *n.* (*formal*) ointment.

ungulate ['ʌngjʊleɪt] *n.* animal with hooves.

unhappy [ʌn'hæpɪ] *adj.* (**-ier, -iest**) sad. **unhappily,** *adv.* sadly/unfortunately. **unhappiness,** *n.* being unhappy.

unharmed [ʌn'hɑːmd] *adj.* safe.

unhealthy [ʌn'helθɪ] *adj.* (**-ier, -iest**) (a) not healthy. (b) unnatural.

unheard of [ʌn'hɜːdɒv] *adj.* strange/odd.

unheated [ʌn'hiːtɪd] *adj.* which has no heating.

unhelpful [ʌn'helpfəl] *adj.* not helpful.

unheralded [ʌn'herəldɪd] *adj.* not announced/publicized beforehand.

unhinged [ʌn'hɪndʒd] *adj.* mad.

unholy [ʌn'həʊlɪ] *adj. inf.* unpleasant.

unhook [ʌn'hʊk] *v.* to take (sth) off a hook; to unfasten (sth) which is attached with hooks.

unhoped for [ʌn'həʊptfɔː] *adj.* unexpected.

unhorse [ʌn'hɔːs] *v.* to make (s.o.) fall off his horse.

unhurt [ʌn'hɜːt] *adj.* not hurt; safe and sound.

unhygienic [ʌnhaɪˈdʒiːnɪk] *adj.* dirty/ not hygienic.

unicameral [juːnɪˈkæmərəl] *adj.* system of government where the parliament has only one chamber.

unicorn [ˈjuːnɪkɔːn] *n.* mythical animal like a horse, with one long, straight horn.

unidentified [ʌnaɪˈdentɪfaɪd] *adj.* which has not been identified; **u. flying object** = mysterious object in the sky which cannot be identified.

unification [juːnɪfɪˈkeɪʃn] *n.* act of unifying; joining together into one.

uniform [ˈjuːnɪfɔːm] **1.** *n.* specially designed clothing worn by all members of a group. **2.** *adj.* all the same; never changing. **uniformity** [juːnɪˈfɔːmɪtɪ] *n.* being uniform. **uniformly,** *adv.* in a uniform way.

unify [ˈjuːnɪfaɪ] *v.* to join together into one.

unilateral [juːnɪˈlætərəl] *adj.* on one side only; done by one side only. **unilaterally,** *adv.* (done) by one side only.

unimaginative [ʌnɪˈmædʒɪnətɪv] *adj.* lacking flair.

unimpaired [ʌnɪmˈpeəd] *adj.* not damaged.

unimpeachable [ʌnɪmˈpiːtʃəbl] *adj.* which can be trusted completely.

unimportant [ʌnɪmˈpɔːtənt] *adj.* not important.

uninformed [ʌnɪnˈfɔːmd] *adj.* without full knowledge.

uninhabitable [ʌnɪnˈhæbɪtəbl] *adj.* which cannot be lived in. **uninhabited,** *adj.* not lived in.

uninhibited [ʌnɪnˈhɪbɪtɪd] *adj.* free; not bound by the customs of society.

uninitiated [ʌnɪˈnɪʃɪeɪtɪd] *n.* **the u.** = people who are not experts.

unintelligible [ʌnɪnˈtelɪdʒəbl] *adj.* which cannot be understood.

uninterrupted [ʌnɪntəˈrʌptɪd] *adj.* with no breaks; continuous.

uninvited [ʌnɪnˈvaɪtɪd] *adj.* without an invitation. **uninviting,** *adj.* not very attractive.

union [ˈjuːnɪən] *n.* (*a*) being joined together; countries or states which are joined together. (*b*) (*formal*) marriage. (*c*) group of people working in the same type of industry joined together for mutual protection. **unionist,** *n.* member of a trade union. **unionize,** *v.* to form a trade union in (a factory/a group of workers). **Union Jack,** *n.* national flag of the United Kingdom.

unique [juːˈniːk] *adj.* so special that there is nothing similar to it. **uniquely,** *adv.* in a special or unique way.

unisex [ˈjuːnɪseks] *adj.* which can be used by both men and women.

unison [ˈjuːnɪsn] *n.* **in u.** = (i) singing the same note all together; (ii) in total agreement.

unit [ˈjuːnɪt] *n.* (*a*) one part (of a larger whole); one cupboard/one set of shelves, etc., which can be matched with others to form a whole kitchen. (*b*) one part (of an army). (*c*) standard measurement by which sth is counted. (*d*) one single part of a group investment; **u. trust** = company which invests its members' money in a varied range of investments, each member buying one or more units. (*e*) number one; single number. **unitary,** *adj.* referring to a unit.

unite [juːˈnaɪt] *v.* to join together as a whole. **unity** [ˈjuːnɪtɪ] *n.* being one whole.

univalve [ˈjuːnɪvælv] *n.* animal (such as a snail) with a single shell.

universe [ˈjuːnɪvɜːs] *n.* all that exists, including the earth, the planets and the stars. **universal** [juːnɪˈvɜːsəl] *adj.* which is everywhere; which affects everyone; **u. joint** = mechanical joint made so that each of two connected rods can move in any direction; **u. suffrage** = situation where all adults have the right to vote. **universally,** *adv.* everywhere; by everyone.

university [juːnɪˈvɜːsɪtɪ] *n.* place of high learning, where degrees are given to successful students, and a wide range of specialized subjects are taught.

unjust [ʌnˈdʒʌst] *adj.* not fair. **unjustly,** *adv.* in an unjust way.

unjustified [ʌnˈdʒʌstɪfaɪd] *adj.* which is not justified.

unkempt [ʌnˈkempt] *adj.* dishevelled/ untidy.

unkind [ʌnˈkaɪnd] *adj.* (**-er, -est**) harsh/ cruel. **unkindly,** *adv.* in a cruel way.

unknown [ʌnˈnəʊn] *adj.* not known.

unladen [ʌnˈleɪdn] *adj.* without a load.

unladylike [ʌnˈleɪdɪlaɪk] *adj.* (behaviour) which is not like that of a lady.

unlawful [ʌnˈlɔːfəl] *adj.* against the law.

unleaded [ʌnˈledɪd] *adj.* (petrol) without lead additives.

unleash [ʌnˈliːʃ] *v.* to unfasten the leash (of a dog); to set free/to set loose.

unleavened [ʌnˈlevnd] *adj.* (bread) made without yeast.

unless [ʌnˈles] *conj.* (a) if. . .not. (b) except if.

unlike [ˈʌnlaɪk] *adj. & prep.* not similar to; different from; **it is u. him to be rude** = he is not usually rude.

unlikely [ʌnˈlaɪklɪ] *adj.* improbable; (story) which is probably not true.

unlimited [ʌnˈlɪmɪtɪd] *adj.* with no limits.

unlined [ʌnˈlaɪnd] *adj.* (a) without lines. (b) without a lining.

unlisted [ʌnˈlɪstɪd] *adj.* not included in a list; (shares) which are not dealt with on the Stock Exchange.

unload [ʌnˈləʊd] *v.* to remove a load from (a vehicle). **unloaded,** *adj.* (gun) with no bullets in it.

unlock [ʌnˈlɒk] *v.* to open (sth) which was locked.

unlooked for [ʌnˈlʊktfɔː] *adj.* not expected.

unlucky [ʌnˈlʌkɪ] *adj.* (-ier, -iest) not lucky; bringing bad luck. **unluckily,** *adv.* unfortunately.

unmanageable [ʌnˈmænɪdʒəbl] *adj.* difficult to control.

unmanned [ʌnˈmænd] *adj.* without a crew/without any staff.

unmannerly [ʌnˈmænəlɪ] *adj.* with no manners.

unmarried [ˈʌnmærɪd] *adj.* not married; **u. mother** = woman who has a child but is not married.

unmask [ʌnˈmɑːsk] *v.* to remove a mask; to show (s.o.) as they really are.

unmatched [ʌnˈmætʃt] *adj.* which has no equal.

unmentionable [ʌnˈmenʃnəbl] *adj.* which you must not talk about because it is so indecent/unpleasant, etc.

unmistakable [ʌnmɪsˈteɪkəbl] *adj.* which is easily recognized/which cannot be mistaken.

unmitigated [ʌnˈmɪtɪgeɪtɪd] *adj.* total/complete.

unmoved [ʌnˈmuːvd] *adj.* not touched/not affected.

unmusical [ʌnˈmjuːzɪkl] *adj.* not interested in music; not able to play a musical instrument.

unnamed [ʌnˈneɪmd] *adj.* (person) who has not been named.

unnatural [ʌnˈnætʃərəl] *adj.* which is not natural; which does not follow the usual pattern.

unnecessary [ʌnˈnesəsərɪ] *adj.* which is not necessary. **unnecessarily,** *adv.* uselessly; for no good reason.

unnerve [ʌnˈnɜːv] *v.* to make (s.o.) lose his nerve/his courage.

unnoticed [ʌnˈnəʊtɪst] *adj.* not noticed; without anyone noticing.

unnumbered [ʌnˈnʌmbəd] *adj.* with no numbers; which cannot be counted.

unobservant [ʌnəbˈzɜːvənt] *adj.* not observant; (person) who does not notice things.

unobstructed [ʌnəbˈstrʌktɪd] *adj.* with nothing in the way.

unobtainable [ʌnəbˈteɪnəbl] *adj.* which cannot be obtained.

unobtrusive [ʌnəbˈtruːsɪv] *adj.* not obvious; not easily noticed.

unoccupied [ʌnˈɒkjʊpaɪd] *adj.* not occupied; empty.

unofficial [ʌnəˈfɪʃl] *adj.* not official; (strike) which has not been officially approved by a union. **unofficially,** *adv.* in an unofficial way.

unopposed [ʌnəˈpəʊzd] *adj.* with no opposition; (elected) because there is no other candidate.

unorthodox [ʌnˈɔːθədɒks] *adj.* not usual.

unpack [ʌnˈpæk] *v.* to take (things) out of containers in which they were transported.

unpaid [ʌnˈpeɪd] *adj.* (person) who is not paid a salary; (bill) which has not been settled.

unpalatable [ʌnˈpælətəbl] *adj.* not pleasant to the taste; unpleasant (fact).

unparalleled [ʌnˈpærəleld] *adj.* with no parallel or no equal.

unpardonable [ʌnˈpɑːdnəbl] *adj.* which cannot be excused.

unparliamentary [ʌnpɑːlɪˈmentərɪ]

adj. (*in Parliament*) offensive (language/behaviour).

unpatriotic [ˌʌnpætrɪˈɒtɪk] *adj.* not patriotic.

unperson [ˈʌnpɜːsən] *n.* person who is treated as if he did not exist (because of opposition to the government).

unpick [ʌnˈpɪk] *v.* to remove (stitches).

unplaced [ʌnˈpleɪst] *adj.* (horse) which is not one of the first three in a race.

unpleasant [ʌnˈplezənt] *adj.* not pleasing. **unpleasantness,** *n.* argument/disagreement.

unpopular [ʌnˈpɒpjʊlə] *adj.* not popular. **unpopularity** [ʌnpɒpjʊˈlærɪtɪ] *n.* being unpopular.

unprecedented [ʌnˈpresɪdentɪd] *adj.* which has never happened before.

unprejudiced [ʌnˈpredʒʊdɪst] *adj.* fair; not prejudiced.

unpremeditated [ʌnprɪˈmedɪteɪtɪd] *adj.* which has not been planned.

unprepared [ʌnprɪˈpeəd] *adj.* not ready.

unprepossessing [ʌnpriːpəˈzesɪŋ] *adj.* not very attractive.

unpretentious [ʌnprɪˈtenʃəs] *adj.* modest/not showing off.

unprincipled [ʌnˈprɪnsɪpld] *adj.* without any moral standards.

unprintable [ʌnˈprɪntəbl] *adj.* (words) so rude that you cannot print them.

unproductive [ʌnprəˈdʌktɪv] *adj.* (discussion) which does not produce any result; (land) which does not produce any crops.

unprofessional [ʌnprəˈfeʃnəl] *adj.* (conduct) which is not of the sort you would expect from a member of the profession.

unprofitable [ʌnˈprɒfɪtəbl] *adj.* which does not make a profit; which is useless.

unprompted [ʌnˈprɒmptɪd] *adj.* without anyone suggesting it.

unpronounceable [ʌnprəˈnaʊnsəbl] *adj.* (name) which is difficult to say.

unprovoked [ʌnprəˈvəʊkt] *adj.* (action) which was not provoked.

unqualified [ʌnˈkwɒlɪfaɪd] *adj.* (*a*) (person) who has not passed the examinations to qualify for a profession. (*b*) total/complete (success).

unquestionable [ʌnˈkwestʃənəbl] *adj.* which is certain/not doubtful. **unques-**

tionably, *adv.* certainly. **unquestioning,** *adj.* without doubting.

unquote [ˈʌnkwəʊt] *v.* to indicate the end of a quotation (when speaking).

unravel [ʌnˈrævl] *v.* (**unravelled**) to disentangle (sth knotted); to solve (a mystery).

unreadable [ʌnˈriːdəbl] *adj.* (book) which is so boring that you cannot read it.

unreal [ʌnˈriːl] *adj.* not like the real world. **unrealistic** [ʌnriːəˈlɪstɪk] *adj.* impractical/not facing facts.

unreasonable [ʌnˈriːznəbl] *adj.* not reasonable/too large.

unrecognizable [ʌnrekəgˈnaɪzəbl] *adj.* which cannot be recognized.

unreel [ʌnˈriːl] *v.* to undo (sth wound round a reel).

unrefined [ʌnrɪˈfaɪnd] *adj.* (sugar/oil) which has not been refined.

unrelated [ʌnrɪˈleɪtɪd] *adj.* not related/with no connection.

unrelenting [ʌnrɪˈlentɪŋ] *adj.* which never stops/weakens.

unreliable [ʌnrɪˈlaɪəbl] *adj.* which cannot be relied on.

unrelieved [ʌnrɪˈliːvd] *adj.* not lessened.

unremitting [ʌnrɪˈmɪtɪŋ] *adj.* never ceasing.

unrequited [ʌnrɪˈkwaɪtɪd] *adj.* (love) which is not returned.

unreserved [ʌnrɪˈzɜːvd] *adj.* not reserved. **unreservedly** [ʌnrɪˈzɜːvɪdlɪ] *adv.* definitely.

unrest [ʌnˈrest] *n.* being restless/dissatisfied; agitation to get political/industrial change.

unrivalled [ʌnˈraɪvəld] *adj.* with no equal.

unroll [ʌnˈrəʊl] *v.* to undo (sth which is rolled up).

unruffled [ʌnˈrʌfld] *adj.* calm/not anxious.

unruly [ʌnˈruːlɪ] *adj.* wild/with no discipline. **unruliness,** *n.* rowdy behaviour.

unsafe [ʌnˈseɪf] *adj.* (**-er, -est**) dangerous.

unsaid [ʌnˈsed] *adj.* **better leave it u.** = better not to say it.

unsalted [ʌnˈsɒltɪd] *adj.* (butter, etc.) with no salt.

unsatisfactory [ʌnsætɪs'fæktrɪ] *adj.* not satisfactory.

unsatisfied [ʌn'sætɪsfaɪd] *adj.* not satisfied.

unsaturated [ʌn'sætjuːreɪtɪd] *adj.* (fat) which contains little hydrogen, and so can be broken down easily in the body.

unsavoury, *Am.* **unsavory** [ʌn'seɪvərɪ] *adj.* unpleasant/disgusting.

unscathed [ʌn'skeɪðd] *adj.* not harmed.

unscheduled [ʌn'ʃedjuːld] *adj.* not on a schedule.

unschooled [ʌn'skuːld] *adj.* not taught; without any experience (in).

unscientific [ʌnsaɪən'tɪfɪk] *adj.* not scientific.

unscramble [ʌn'skræmbl] *v.* to put back in order; to put (a coded message) back into plain language.

unscrew [ʌn'skruː] *v.* to open by twisting a screw or a screw lid anticlockwise.

unscripted [ʌn'skrɪptɪd] *adj.* (broadcast) made without a script.

unscrupulous [ʌn'skruːpjuləs] *adj.* not worrying too much about honesty.

unsealed [ʌn'siːld] *adj.* (envelope, etc.) which has not been sealed.

unseasonable [ʌn'siːzənəbl] *adj.* not usual for the season.

unseat [ʌn'siːt] *v.* to make (s.o.) fall off a horse; to remove (a Member of Parliament) at an election.

unseemly [ʌn'siːmlɪ] *adj.* offensive/rude (behaviour).

unseen [ʌn'siːn] *adj. & n.* not seen/invisible; (piece of writing) which you have not seen before, and which you have to translate in an examination.

unselfish [ʌn'selfɪʃ] *adj.* not selfish/ thinking of others before yourself.

unserviceable [ʌn'sɜː'vɪsəbl] *adj.* not in a good enough state to be used.

unsettle [ʌn'setl] *v.* to upset. **unsettled**, *adj.* (weather) which changes often.

unshakeable [ʌn'ʃeɪkəbl] *adj.* solid/ firm (belief/faith).

unsightly [ʌn'saɪtlɪ] *adj.* ugly.

unsigned [ʌn'saɪnd] *adj.* not signed.

unskilled [ʌn'skɪld] *adj.* (worker) who has no particular skill.

unsociable [ʌn'səʊʃəbl] *adj.* not friendly; not wishing to make friends.

unsocial [ʌn'səʊʃəl] *adj.* (hours of work) where the worker is rarely free at the same time as his family.

unsolicited [ʌnsə'lɪsɪtɪd] *adj.* which has not been asked for.

unsolved ['ʌnsɒlvd] *adj.* (problem) which has not been solved.

unsophisticated [ʌnsə'fɪstɪkeɪtɪd] *adj.* simple; not sophisticated.

unsound ['ʌnsaʊnd] *adj.* (*a*) **of u. mind** = mad. (*b*) (reasoning) not based on fact or logic.

unsparing [ʌn'speərɪŋ] *adj.* generous; not reluctant.

unspeakable [ʌn'spiːkəbl] *adj.* extremely unpleasant.

unspoilt ['ʌnspɔɪlt] *adj.* (countryside) which has not been spoilt.

unstable [ʌn'steɪbl] *adj.* (*a*) not stable; changeable; (government) which is likely to fall at any moment. (*b*) dangerously mad.

unsteady [ʌn'stedɪ] *adj.* not steady; wobbly.

unstick [ʌn'stɪk] *v.* (**unstuck**) to remove sth which is stuck on; **to come unstuck** = to go badly wrong.

unstoppable [ʌn'stɒpəbl] *adj.* which cannot be stopped.

unsuccessful [ʌnsək'sesfəl] *adj.* not successful.

unsuitable [ʌn'suːtəbl] *adj.* not suitable.

unsullied [ʌn'sʌlɪd] *adj.* pure.

unsung [ʌn'sʌŋ] *adj.* (hero) who is not famous.

unsure [ʌn'ʃʊə] *adj.* not sure; **u. of oneself** = lacking self-confidence.

unsuspected [ʌnsəs'pektɪd] *adj.* which is not suspected to exist. **unsuspecting**, *adj.* (person) who does not realize sth/that a danger is imminent.

unsweetened [ʌn'swiːtənd] *adj.* (food) with no sugar added.

unswerving [ʌn'swɜːvɪŋ] *adj.* (loyalty) which does not change.

unsympathetic [ʌnsɪmpə'θetɪk] *adj.* not sympathetic.

untangle [ʌn'tæŋgl] *v.* to disentangle.

untapped [ʌn'tæpt] *adj.* not previously used.

untenable [ʌn'tenəbl] *adj.* (position/ theory) which cannot be defended.

unthinkable [ʌn'θɪŋkəbl] *adj.* which cannot be considered or thought of.

unthinking [ʌn'θɪŋkɪŋ] *adj.* done without thinking. **unthought-of,** *adj.* which no one has thought possible.

untidy [ʌn'taɪdɪ] *adj.* (**-ier, -iest**) not tidy/in disorder. **untidily,** *adv.* in an untidy way. **untidiness,** *n.* being untidy.

untie [ʌn'taɪ] *v.* to unfasten (sth which is tied with a knot).

until [ʌn'tɪl] *prep. & conj.* (*a*) up to (a certain time). (*b*) up to (a certain place).

untimely [ʌn'taɪmlɪ] *adj.* (*a*) happening too soon. (*b*) not suitable.

unto ['ʌntʊ] *prep.* (*old*) to.

untold [ʌn'təʊld] *adj.* very large; so large that it cannot be counted.

untouchable [ʌn'tʌtʃəbl] **1.** *adj.* which cannot be touched. **2.** *n.* person from the lowest caste in India.

untoward [ʌntə'wɔːd] *adj.* unlucky/inconvenient; **nothing u. took place** = everything went off well.

untrained [ʌn'treɪnd] *adj.* (person) who has had no training.

untried [ʌn'traɪd] *adj.* which has not been tested.

untrue [ʌn'truː] *adj.* wrong/not true.

untrustworthy [ʌn'trʌstwɜːðɪ] *adj.* (person) who cannot be trusted.

untruth [ʌn'truːθ] *n.* lie. **untruthful,** *adj.* (person) who does not tell the truth; (statement) which is wrong.

unusable [ʌn'juːzəbl] *adj.* which cannot be used.

unused *adj.* (*a*) [ʌn'juːzd] new/clean; which has not been used. (*b*) [ʌn'juːsd] not accustomed (**to**).

unusual [ʌn'juːʒʊəl] *adj.* strange/extraordinary. **unusually,** *adv.* strangely/extraordinarily.

unutterable [ʌnʌ'tərəbl] *adj.* so terrible that it cannot be expressed.

unvarnished [ʌn'vɑːnɪʃt] *adj.* with no varnish; plain/simple (truth).

unveil [ʌn'veɪl] *v.* to uncover (a new statue/a new plan, etc.).

unversed [ʌn'vɜːst] *adj.* with no experience (**in**).

unwanted [ʌn'wɒntɪd] *adj.* which is not wanted.

unwarranted [ʌn'wɒrəntɪd] *adj.* which is not justified.

unwary [ʌn'weərɪ] *adj.* (person) who does not take care.

unwell [ʌn'wel] *adj.* sick/ill.

unwholesome [ʌn'həʊlsəm] *adj.* not healthy/which might harm.

unwieldy [ʌn'wiːldɪ] *adj.* large and awkward.

unwilling [ʌn'wɪlɪŋ] *adj.* reluctant; not willing.

unwind [ʌn'waɪnd] *v.* (**unwound** [ʌn'waʊnd]) (*a*) to undo (sth which has been wound). (*b*) *inf.* to relax.

unwise [ʌn'waɪz] *adj.* rash/imprudent; not wise.

unwitting [ʌn'wɪtɪŋ] *adj.* not knowing/intending. **unwittingly,** *adv.* without intending to; not intentionally.

unwonted [ʌn'wɒntɪd] *adj.* not usual.

unworkable [ʌn'wɜːkəbl] *adj.* (plan) which will not work in practice.

unworthy [ʌn'wɜːðɪ] *adj.* (**of**) (*a*) which does not deserve (sth). (*b*) not as good as one might expect from (a person).

unwound [ʌn'waʊnd] *v. see* **unwind.**

unwrap [ʌn'ræp] *v.* (**unwrapped**) to take the wrapping off (sth).

unwritten [ʌn'rɪtən] *adj.* **u. law** = custom which has grown up over a period of time but which is not written down.

unzip [ʌn'zɪp] *v.* (**unzipped**) to undo a zip fastener.

up [ʌp] **1.** *adv.* (*a*) towards a higher place; **hands u.!** = lift your hands into the air to show you surrender. (*b*) in a higher place; **this side u.** = this side must be on top. (*c*) to an important town; towards the north. (*d*) to a higher level. (*e*) to the end; completely. (*f*) not in bed. (*g*) close to. **2.** *prep.* (*a*) towards a higher part of (sth). (*b*) along; towards the source of (a river); **to walk up and down** = backwards and forwards. **3.** *adj.* (*a*) which is going up. (*b*) which is in a higher position; completely built; **the road is all up** = being dug up for repairs. (*c*) not in bed. (*d*) finished; **your time is up** = you have to stop now; **his leave is up** = he has to go back to the army. (*e*) *inf.* **what's up** = what is the matter **4.** *n.* **the ups and downs of business** = the good and bad periods. **5.** *v.* (**upped**) (*a*) to raise (prices, etc.). (*b*) *inf.* to get up suddenly. **up-and-coming** [ʌpən'kʌmɪŋ] *adj.* (person) who looks as though he might succeed. **up-and-up** ['ʌpənʌp] *n.* **to be on the up-**

and-up = to be doing well. **upcoming,** *adj.* imminent/likely to happen soon. **up for,** *prep.* ready for; **up for sale** = on sale. **up-market,** *adj.* aiming at the expensive end of the market. **up to,** *prep.* (*a*) as many as. (*b*) capable enough to do (sth). (*c*) **it's up to you** = it is your responsibility. (*d*) doing (sth bad). **up to date,** *adj. & adv.* modern/ using the most recent information, etc.

upbraid [ʌp'breɪd] *v.* (*formal*) to scold.

upbringing ['ʌpbrɪŋɪŋ] *n.* education; training of a child.

update [ʌp'deɪt] *v.* to revise (sth) so that is is more up to date.

upend [ʌp'end] *v.* to stand (sth) on its end.

upgrade [ʌp'greɪd] *v.* to put (s.o.) into a more important job; to improve the quality of (sth).

upheaval [ʌp'hiːvəl] *n.* great change/ disturbance.

uphill [ʌp'hɪl] **1.** *adj.* going upwards; difficult. **2.** *adv.* upwards.

uphold [ʌp'həʊld] *v.* (**upheld**) to support; to say that (a decision) is right.

upholster [ʌp'həʊlstə] *v.* to cover (chairs, etc.) with padded seats and covers. **upholsterer,** *n.* person who upholsters. **upholstery,** *n.* (*a*) covering chairs, etc. with padded seats and covers. (*b*) covers for chairs; padded seats and cushions.

upkeep [ʌp'kiːp] *n.* (cost of) keeping a house/a car, etc., in good order.

upland [ʌp'lənd] *n.* mountainous area (of a country).

uplift 1. *n.* ['ʌplɪft] (*a*) thing which gives a feeling of happiness or goodness. (*b*) increase/raising. **2.** *v.* [ʌp'lɪft] to lift up/ to raise.

upon [ʌ'pɒn] *prep.* (*formal*) on; **battle u. battle** = one battle after another.

upper ['ʌpə] **1.** *adj.* (*a*) higher. (*b*) further up. (*c*) more important; of higher rank; **the u. classes** = the nobility; (*in a school*) **the u. forms** = forms with older pupils; **u. case** = capital (letters); **u. chamber/house** = (*in UK*) House of Lords; (*in other countries*) senate; **to get the u. hand** = begin to win. **2.** *n.* top part of a shoe. **uppercut,** *n.* blow with the fist upwards on the chin. **uppermost. 1.**

adj. (*a*) highest. (*b*) furthest up. (*c*) most important. **2.** *adv.* **what is u. in their minds** = the subject they think about most. **uppish, uppity,** *adj. inf.* feeling superior to other people.

upright ['ʌpraɪt] **1.** *adj.* (*a*) vertical. (*b*) very honest. **2.** *n.* (*a*) vertical post. (*b*) piano with the strings and body vertical.

uprising ['ʌpraɪzɪŋ] *n.* revolt (against authority).

uproar ['ʌprɔː] *n.* loud noise/disturbance. **uproarious** [ʌp'rɔːrɪəs] *adj.* noisy.

uproot [ʌp'ruːt] *v.* (*a*) to dig up (a plant) with its roots. (*b*) to make (a family) move to a totally new area.

upset 1. *n.* ['ʌpset] (*a*) complete change for the worse. (*b*) great worry/cause of unhappiness. (*c*) slight illness. (*d*) (*at an auction*) **u. price** = price which an item has to reach before the owner allows it to be sold. **2.** *v.* [ʌp'set] (**upset**) (*a*) to knock over; to fall over. (*b*) to change completely (for the worse). (*c*) to make (s.o.) worried/unhappy. (*d*) to make (s.o.) slightly ill. **3.** *adj.* [ʌp'set] (*a*) very worried/unhappy/anxious. (*b*) made ill.

upshot ['ʌpʃɒt] *n.* result.

upside down ['ʌpsaɪd'daʊn] *adv.* with the top turned to the bottom.

upstage [ʌp'steɪdʒ] **1.** *adv.* at the back of the stage. **2.** *v.* (*a*) to move nearer the front of the stage than (s.o.). (*b*) to take attention away from (s.o. who feels he ought to have it).

upstairs [ʌp'steəz] **1.** *adv.* towards the upper part of a house. **2.** *adj.* on the upper floors of a house. **3.** *n.* the upper floors of a house.

upstanding [ʌp'stændɪŋ] *adj.* strong/ honest.

upstart [ʌp'stɑːt] *n.* inexperienced person who has become unexpectedly important.

upstream [ʌp'striːm] *adv. & adj.* (moving) towards the source or a river, against the flow of the current.

upsurge ['ʌpsɜːdʒ] *n.* sudden increase (of emotion).

uptake ['ʌpteɪk] *n.* **slow/quick on the u.** = slow/quick to understand.

uptight ['ʌptaɪt] *adj. inf.* nervous and annoyed.

upturn ['ʌptɜːn] *n.* movement upwards

(in sales, etc.). **upturned,** *adj.* (boat, etc.) turned upside down.

upward ['ʌpwəd] *adj.* moving towards a higher level. **upwards,** *adv.* (*a*) towards a higher level. (*b*) on the top. (*c*) more. **upwards of,** *prep.* more than.

uranium [jʊ'reɪnɪəm] *n.* (*element:* U) radioactive metal used in producing atomic energy.

urban ['ɜːbən] *adj.* (*a*) referring to towns. (*b*) living in towns. **urbanization,** *n.* act of urbanizing. **urbanize,** *v.* to make (an area) into a town; to make (sth/s.o. from the country) become accustomed to the town.

urbane [ɜː'beɪn] *adj.* very polite. **urbanity** [ə'bænɪtɪ] *n.* being urbane.

urchin ['ɜːtʃɪn] *n.* dirty little boy; **sea u.** = small sea creature with a round shell covered with spikes.

urea [ju:'ri:ə] *n.* substance produced by the liver and excreted into the urine.

ureter [ju:'ri:tə] *n.* tube taking urine from the kidneys to the bladder.

urethra [ju:'ri:θrə] *n.* tube taking urine from the bladder out of the body.

urge [ɜːdʒ] **1.** *n.* strong desire. **2.** *v.* (*a*) to encourage; to push (s.o.) to do sth. (*b*) to suggest strongly. **urgency** ['ɜːdʒənsɪ] *n.* being urgent; need for sth to be done quickly; **what's the u.?** = why are you all hurrying? **urgent,** *adj.* which needs to be done quickly. **urgently,** *adv.* quickly/immediately.

urine ['jʊərɪn] *n.* liquid waste matter from the body. **urinal** [jʊə'raɪnəl] *n.* place where men can pass waste liquid from the body; bowl to catch waste liquid passed from the body. **urinary** ['jʊərɪnərɪ] *adj.* referring to urine; (tube) one uses to pass urine; **u. system** = organs which create and excrete urine. **urinate,** *v.* to pass waste liquid from the body.

urn [ɜːn] *n.* very large vase; **tea u.** = large metal container with a tap, in which large quantities of tea can be made.

us [ʌs] *pron.* (*a*) *referring to* we. (*b*) *inf. referring to* I; **let us/let's have a go** = let me have a go.

US, USA ['jʊ'es, jʊes'eɪ] *abbreviations for* United States (of America).

use 1. *n.* [ju:s] (*a*) being used; way in which sth is used. (*b*) ability to be used. (*c*) usefulness. **2.** *v.* [ju:z] (*a*) to put to a purpose. (*b*) to take advantage of (s.o.). (*c*) *inf.* **I could use a beer** = I would like a beer. (*d*) [ju:s] to do sth regularly in the past; **she used not to smoke/she did not u. to smoke. usable** ['ju:zəbl] *adj.* which can be used. **usage** ['ju:sɪdʒ] *n.* (*a*) custom; way of doing things. (*b*) way of using a word. **used,** *adj.* (*a*) [ju:zd] not new; which has been put to a purpose. (*b*) [ju:sd] accustomed (**to**). **useful** ['ju:sfəl] *adj.* which helps; **to make oneself u.** = to do helpful things. **usefully,** *adv.* in a helpful way. **usefulness,** *n.* being useful. **useless** ['ju:sləs] *adj.* which does not help; *inf.* **she is quite u.** = of no help at all. **uselessness,** *n.* being useless. **user** ['ju:zə] *n.* person who uses; **road u.** = person who drives on the road. **user-friendly,** *adj.* (program/machine) which a user finds easy to use. **use up,** *v.* to finish.

usher ['ʌʃə] **1.** *n.* person who shows people to their seats (in a theatre/in a church). **2.** *v.* **to u. in** = (i) to bring (s.o.) in; (ii) to be the beginning of. **usherette** [ʌʃə'ret] *n.* girl who shows people to their seats in a cinema.

USSR [jʊ:es:es'a:] *abbreviation for* Union of Soviet Socialist Republics.

usual ['ju:ʒʊəl] *adj.* ordinary; which happens often. **usually,** *adv.* mostly/ordinarily.

usurer ['ju:zjʊrə] *n.* person who lends money for high interest. **usurious** [ju:'zjʊərɪəs] *adj.* excessively high (interest rate). **usury,** *n.* lending money for high interest.

usurp [ju:'zɜːp] *v.* to take the place of (s.o.). **usurpation** [ju:zɜː'peɪʃn] *n.* act of usurping. **usurper,** *n.* person who usurps (a throne).

utensil [ju:'tensl] *n.* tool/pan/knife, etc., used for work in the kitchen.

uterus ['ju:tərəs] *n.* part of a female body where an unborn baby is carried. **uterine** ['ju:təraɪn] *adj.* referring to the uterus.

utility [ju:'tɪlɪtɪ] *n.* (*a*) usefulness; **u. van** = small van for carrying goods; **u. room** = room in a house where you put the washing machine/freezer, etc. (*b*) **utilities** = essential public services

(such as electricity/gas/water, etc.).
utilitarian [ju:tɪlɪ'teərɪən] *adj.* used for a practical purpose, not decoration.
utilizable [ju:tɪ'laɪzəbl] *adj.* which can be used. **utilization** [ju:tɪlaɪ'zeɪʃn] *n.* making use of sth. **utilize** ['ju:tɪlaɪz] *v.* to use; to make use of (sth) for profit.
utmost ['ʌtməʊst] *adj.* (*a*) greatest that can be. (*b*) furthest.
utopia [jʊ'təʊpɪə] *n.* imaginary perfect world. **utopian**, *adj.* very perfect (ideas).
utter ['ʌtə] 1. *adj.* complete/total. 2. *v.* to speak; to make (a sound). **utterance**, *n.* thing spoken. **utterly**, *adv.* completely. **uttermost**, *adj.* (*a*) greatest that can be. (*b*) furthest.
UV ['ju:'vi:] *abbrev. for* ultraviolet.
uvula ['ju:vjʊlə] *n.* small lump of flesh hanging down at the back of the mouth.
uxorious [ʌk'sɔ:rɪəs] *adj.* (man) who is very fond of his wife.

Vv

V,v [vi:]. **V-neck pullover** = one with a neckline shaped like a V; **V sign** = sign made with two fingers raised in the air (either meaning victory or showing extreme rudeness).
v. ['vɜ:səs] *prep.* against; *see* **versus**.
vac [væk] *n. inf.* vacation.
vacancy ['veɪkənsɪ] *n.* (*a*) being vacant. (*b*) empty place/room/job. **vacant**, *adj.* (*a*) empty/not occupied; **to sell a house with v. possession** = with no one living in it; **situations v.** = jobs which need to be filled. (*b*) (expression) showing no interest/liveliness. **vacantly**, *adv.* with a vacant expression. **vacate** [və'keɪt] *v.* to leave/to make (sth) empty. **vacation** [və'keɪʃn] 1. *n.* (*a*) holiday (esp. in universities and law courts). (*b*) act of vacating (an office, etc.). 2. *v. Am.* to go on holiday.
vaccinate ['væksɪneɪt] *v.* **to v. s.o. against a disease** = to put a vaccine into s.o.. so that his body will react against it and thus protect him from catching the disease. **vaccination** [væksɪ'neɪʃn] *n.* act of vaccinating. **vaccine** ['væksi:n] *n.* substance which contains the virus of a disease which when injected, gives protection against the disease.

vacillate ['væsɪleɪt] *v.* to waver/to hesitate. **vacillation** ['væsɪ'leɪʃn] *n.* hesitation/wavering.
vacuous ['vækjʊəs] *adj.* with no meaning/sense; silly/vacant (expression). **vacuity** [və'kjʊɪtɪ], **vacuousness**, *n.* emptiness of meaning/silliness.
vacuum ['vækjʊəm] 1. *n.* space from which all matter, including air, has been removed; **vacuum-packed** = (food) packed in a vacuum, so that no air can enter the package. 2. *v. inf.* to clean with a vacuum cleaner. **vacuum cleaner**, *n.* cleaning machine which sucks up dust. **vacuum flask**, *n.* bottle with double walls to keep liquids warm or cold.
vagabond ['vægəbɒnd] *adj. & n.* (person) who wanders about/who has no home.
vagary ['veɪgərɪ] *n.* oddity/strange behaviour.
vagina [və'dʒaɪnə] *n.* tube in a female mammal connecting the uterus to the vulva and through which a baby is born. **vaginal**, *adj.* referring to the vagina.
vagrant ['veɪgrənt] *adj. & n.* (tramp/person) who wanders from place to place with no home or work. **vagrancy**, *n.* being a vagrant.
vague [veɪg] *adj.* (**-er, -est**) not clear/not precise; **I haven't the vaguest idea** = I have no idea at all. **vaguely**, *adv.* more or less; in a vague way. **vagueness**, *n.* being vague.
vain [veɪn] *adj.* (**-er, -est**) (*a*) useless; meaningless; (*b*) very proud of one's appearance; (*c*) **in v.** = without any success/result. **vainly**, *adv.* with no success/with no result.
valance ['væləns] *n.* short frilled curtain.
vale [veɪl] *n.* (*used in names of places*) valley.
valediction [vælɪ'dɪkʃn] *n.* (*formal*) farewell. **valedictory**, *adj.* which says farewell.
valence, valency ['veɪləns, 'veɪlənsɪ] *n.* (*in chemistry*) power of an atom to combine.
valentine ['væləntaɪn] *n.* (*a*) person chosen as a loved one on February 14th (St Valentine's Day). (*b*) (usu. unsigned) card sent to someone you love on February 14th.

valerian [vəˈlɪərɪən] n. type of wild plant with pink flowers.

valet [ˈvæleɪ, ˈvælɪt] n. male servant who looks after his master's clothes; **v. service** = cleaning service in a hotel.

valetudinarian [vælɪtjuːdɪˈneərɪən] n. person who likes to feel he is an invalid.

valiant [ˈvælɪənt] adj. brave. **valiantly,** adv. bravely.

valid [ˈvælɪd] adj. (a) which is acceptable because it is true. (b) which can be lawfully used for a time. **validate,** v. to make valid. **validation** [vælɪˈdeɪʃn] n. act of validating. **validity** [vəˈlɪdɪtɪ] n. (a) legal force. (b) truth.

valley [ˈvælɪ] n. long stretch of low land through which a river runs.

valour, Am. **valor** [ˈvælə] n. bravery.

value [ˈvæljuː] 1. n. (a) worth (in money or esteem); **to get v. for money** = to get a good bargain. (b) usefulness. (c) **values** = principles/important things in life. 2. v. (a) to put a price in money on (an object). (b) to set a high value on (sth). **valuable.** 1. adj. worth a lot of money; very useful. 2. n. **valuables** = objects of great value. **valuation** [væljuˈeɪʃn] n. estimate of the worth of sth; act of estimating the worth of sth. **value added tax,** n. tax imposed on the value of goods or services. **valueless,** adj. worthless/with no value which is more than their cost. **valuer,** n. person who estimates the value of property.

valve [vælv] n. (a) mechanical device which allows air/liquid to pass through in one direction only; **safety v.** = valve which allows gas/steam, etc. to escape if the pressure is too great. (b) flap in a tube in the body which allows air/blood, etc. to circulate in one direction only. (c) part of a radio/TV set which controls the flow of electricity. (d) part of a brass musical instrument which lengthens the tube. (e) single shell (of a shellfish). **valvular** [ˈvælvjʊlə] adj. referring to a valve in the heart.

vamp [væmp] n. (a) front part of the upper of a shoe or boot. (b) (old) flirtatious woman.

vampire [ˈvæmpaɪə] n. person who supposedly sucks blood from his victims. **vampire bat,** n. type of small bat which sucks blood from animals.

van [væn] n. (a) small vehicle for carrying goods by road or rail; **guard's v.** = wagon at the end of a train where the guard rides. (b) **in the v.** = in the front (of a movement/of an attack).

vandal [ˈvændl] n. person who destroys property for the pleasure of destruction. **vandalism,** n. meaningless destruction of property. **vandalize,** v. to smash (sth) for no reason at all.

vane [veɪn] n. one of the blades on a water wheel/pump, etc.

vanguard [ˈvæŋgɑːd] n. front part of an army; **in the v.** = in the front (of a movement).

vanilla [vəˈnɪlə] n. flavouring made from the seed pods of a tropical plant.

vanish [ˈvænɪʃ] v. to disappear/to go out of sight; **to v. into thin air** = disappear completely. **vanishing cream,** n. scented cream rubbed into the skin to make it soft. **vanishing point,** n. point in a drawing where the horizontal lines seem to meet at eye level.

vanity [ˈvænɪtɪ] n. (a) pride/feeling that you are more handsome that you really are. (b) uselessness. **vanity case,** n. small bag for carrying makeup/powder, etc.

vanquish [ˈvæŋkwɪʃ] v. to defeat.

vantage point [ˈvɑːntɪdʒpɔɪnt] n. place from which you can see well.

vapid [ˈvæpɪd] adj. dull (conversation). **vapidity** [vəˈpɪdɪtɪ] n. dullness.

vaporize [ˈveɪpəraɪz] v. to turn into vapour. **vaporization** [veɪpəraɪˈzeɪʃn] n. changing into vapour. **vaporizer,** n. machine which turns liquids (esp. water) into vapour. **vapour,** Am. **vapor,** n. gas form of a liquid, usu. caused by heating; **v. trail** = line of white vapour left in the sky by an aircraft.

variability [veərɪəˈbɪlɪtɪ] n. being variable. **variable** [ˈveərɪəbl] 1. adj. which varies/changes all the time. 2. n. thing which varies. **variance** [ˈveərɪəns] n. **to be at v. with** = to disagree. **variant,** adj. & n. (version/spelling, etc.) which is slightly different. **variation** [veərɪˈeɪʃn] n. (a) act of varying. (b) amount by which sth varies. (c) **variations** = pieces of music which repeat the same theme but written in a different fashion.

varicella [værɪ'selə] *n.* chicken pox.
varicoloured ['vɛərɪkʌləd] *adj.*
variegated.
varicose vein ['værɪkəus'veɪn] *n.* swollen vein, esp. in the leg.
variegated ['vɛərɪgeɪtɪd] *adj.* (plant which is) striped/marked in contrasting colours. **variegation** [vɛərɪ'geɪʃn] *n.* irregular marking in contrasting colours.
variety [və'raɪətɪ] *n.* (*a*) being of different sorts; **for a v. of reasons** = for several different reasons. (*b*) different type (of plant). (*c*) **v. show** = entertainment which includes several different types of performer (such as singers/conjurors/ventriloquists, etc.). **varietal,** *adj.* referring to a variety of plant. **various** ['vɛərɪəs] *adj.* different/ several. **variously,** *adv.* in different ways.
varnish ['vɑːnɪʃ] **1.** *n.* (*a*) liquid which when painted on sth gives it a shiny surface. (*b*) shiny surface made by painting with varnish. **2.** *v.* (*a*) to paint with a liquid varnish; to give a shiny surface to sth. (*b*) to cover up (a mistake/disagreement).
vary ['vɛərɪ] *v.* (*a*) to make different; to become different; **you ought to v. your diet** = eat different sorts of food. (*b*) to have different views. **varied,** *adj.* of various kinds/different.
vas [væs] *n.* tube in the body.
vascular ['væskjulə] *adj.* referring to veins, etc., which carry blood or sap.
vase [vɑːz] *n.* container for cut flowers.
vasectomy [və'sektəmɪ] *n.* operation on a man to cut the tubes through which sperm flows and so to make him sterile.
vassal ['væsl] *n.* (*a*) servant. (*b*) **v. state** = country which is under the rule of another.
vast [vɑːst] *adj.* very large. **vastly,** *adv.* very much. **vastness,** *n.* large size.
vat [væt] *n.* large container for liquids (esp. wine).
VAT [væt, viːeɪ'tiː] *abbrev. for* Value Added Tax, government tax on goods or services. **vatman,** *n.* (*pl.* **-men**) *inf.* government inspector dealing with VAT.
vaudeville ['vɔːdəvɪl] *n.* variety show.
vault [vɔːlt] **1.** *n.* (*a*) arched stone ceiling.

(*b*) underground room (for keeping things safe). (*c*) underground room for burying people. (*d*) high jump; **pole v.** = leap over a high bar, using a pole to swing you up. **2.** *v.* to jump over (sth) by putting one hand on it to steady yourself. **vaulted,** *adj.* with a stone arch.
vaunt [vɔːnt] *v.* to boast about (sth).
VD ['viː'diː] *abbrev. for* venereal disease.
VDU [viːdiː'juː] *abbrev. for* visual display unit.
veal [viːl] *n.* meat from a calf.
vector ['vektə] *n.* (*in mathematics*) (*a*) thing which has both direction and size. (*b*) insect, etc., which carries disease.
veer ['vɪə] *v.* to turn.
veg [vedʒ] *n.* (*no pl.*) *inf.* (cooked) vegetable(s).
vegan ['viːgən] *adj. & n.* (person) who only eats vegetables and fruit.
vegetable ['vedʒɪtəbl] *adj. & n.* (*a*) (referring to) plants; **the v. kingdom** = all plant life. (*b*) plant grown for food, not usu. sweet. (*c*) person who is more or less incapable of movement or thought. **vegetarian** [vedʒɪ'tɛərɪən] *adj. & n.* (person) who does not eat meat; (restaurant) which does not serve meat. **vegetarianism,** *n.* belief that not eating meat is good for you. **vegetate,** *v.* to live like a vegetable, not moving or doing anything. **vegetation** [vedʒɪ'teɪʃn] *n.* (*a*) act of vegetating. (*b*) plants.
vehemence ['vɪəməns] *n.* forceful way (of saying what you think). **vehement** ['vɪəmənt] *adj.* forceful. **vehemently,** *adv.* in a forceful way.
vehicle ['vɪəkl] *n.* (*a*) machine on wheels which travels along the road; rocket which travels in space; **commercial v.** = one which carries goods. (*b*) **v. for** = means of expressing (sth). **vehicular** [vɪ'ɪkjulə] *adj.* referring to vehicles.
veil [veɪl] **1.** *n.* light cloth which can cover a woman's head or face; **to draw a v. over sth** = not to mention sth which is wrong/unpleasant; **to take the v.** = to become a nun. **2.** *v.* to cover with a veil; **veiled** = half-hidden.
vein [veɪn] *n.* (*a*) small tube in the body along which blood runs to the heart. (*b*) thin line on the leaf of a plant. (*c*) thin

layer of a mineral in a rock. (*d*) mood; **in poetic v.** = feeling poetic. **veined**, *adj.* covered with veins.

veldt [velt] *n.* grass-covered plain in South Africa.

vellum ['veləm] *n.* (*a*) good quality writing paper. (*b*) skin of an animal made very thin and used for binding books or writing on.

velocity [və'lɒsɪtɪ] *n.* speed.

velour [və'luə] *n.* thick, soft cloth with a soft surface like velvet.

velum ['viːləm] *n.* soft membrane. **velar**, *adj.* referring to a soft membrane.

velvet ['velvət] *adj. & n.* (*a*) cloth (made from silk, etc.) with a soft surface of cut threads; **v. lawn** = soft and smoothly cut like velvet. (*b*) soft skin covering a deer's antlers. **velveteen**, *n.* velvet made of cotton. **velvety**, *adj.* with soft surface like velvet.

venal ['viːnəl] *adj.* (person) who will take a bribe; (act) which is dishonest/which is done for a bribe. **venality** [vɪ'nælɪtɪ] *n.* being venal.

vendetta [ven'detə] *n.* private quarrel between families/persons.

vending ['vendɪŋ] *n.* selling; **v. machine** = machine which provides cigarettes/ chocolate, etc., when money is put into a slot. **vendor** ['vendə] *n.* person who sells.

veneer [və'nɪə] **1.** *n.* (*a*) thin layer of expensive wood glued to the surface of ordinary wood. (*b*) thin layer of politeness/knowledge which covers a person's bad qualities. **2.** *v.* to cover (wood) with a veneer.

venerate ['venəreɪt] *v.* to respect greatly. **venerable**, *adj.* very old and likely to be respected. **veneration** [venə'reɪʃn] *n.* respect; **to hold s.o. in v.** = to respect s.o. greatly.

venereal [və'nɪərɪəl] *adj.* (disease) transmitted during sexual intercourse.

venetian blind [və'niːʃn'blaɪnd] *n.* blind to shut out light, made of horizontal strips of plastic/wood, etc., which can be opened or shut or raised and lowered by pulling a string.

vengeance ['vendʒəns] *n.* harm caused to s.o. in return for harm they have caused you; *inf.* **with a v.** = very strongly.

venial ['viːnɪəl] *adj.* slight (mistake); (sin) which can be excused. **veniality** [viːnɪ'ælɪtɪ] *n.* being venial.

venison ['venɪzn] *n.* meat from a deer.

venom ['venəm] *n.* (*a*) poison (from a snake, etc.). (*b*) bitter hatred. **venomous**, *adj.* (*a*) poisonous. (*b*) bitterly spiteful.

venous ['viːnəs] *adj.* referring to veins (in the body).

vent [vent] **1.** *n.* (*a*) hole through which air/gas can escape. (*b*) slit in the back of a coat. (*c*) **to give v. to** = to let (an emotion) come out. **2.** *v.* **he vented his anger on her** = he made her the target of his anger.

ventilate ['ventɪleɪt] *v.* (*a*) to allow fresh air to come into. (*b*) to discuss (a question) in the open. **ventilation** [ventɪ-'leɪʃn] *n.* (*a*) bringing in fresh air; **v. shaft** = tube which allows fresh air to go down into a coal mine. (*b*) public discussion (of sth). **ventilator** ['ventɪleɪtə] *n.* opening which allows fresh air to come in; machine which pumps in fresh air.

ventral ['ventrəl] *adj.* (*formal*) referring to the abdomen.

ventricle ['ventrɪkl] *n.* space in the heart which fills up with blood and then pumps it out into the arteries.

ventriloquist [ven'trɪləkwɪst] *n.* person who can make his voice appear to come from a puppet. **ventriloquism**, *n.* act of being a ventriloquist.

venture ['ventʃə] **1.** *n.* commercial deal which involves risk. **2.** *v.* to dare/to be bold enough to do sth dangerous. **venturesome**, *adj.* (person) who dares to take a risk.

venue ['venjʊ] *n.* agreed place where sth will take place.

veracious [və'reɪʃəs] *adj.* truthful. **veracity** [və'ræsɪtɪ] *n.* truth.

veranda(h) [və'rændə] *n.* covered terrace along the side of a house with no outside wall.

verb [vɜːb] *n.* part of speech which shows how s.o./sth acts or feels. **verbal**, *adj.* (*a*) referring to a verb. (*b*) spoken; not written down. **verbalize**, *v.* to express in words. **verbally**, *adv.* in spoken words.

verbatim [vɜː'beɪtɪm] *adj. & adv.* word for word; in exactly the same words.

verbena [vɜːˈbiːnə] *n.* type of scented herb, used to make soap or in hot drinks.

verbiage [ˈvɜːbɪdʒ] *n.* lot of useless words.

verbose [vəˈbəʊs] *adj.* using more words than necessary. **verbosity** [vəˈbɒsɪtɪ] *n.* being verbose.

verdant [ˈvɜːdənt] *adj.* (*formal*) green (grass).

verdict [ˈvɜːdɪkt] *n.* (*a*) judgement/decision by a judge or jury. (*b*) opinion.

verdigris [ˈvɜːdɪɡrɪs] *n.* green discolouring of copper, etc., through contact with damp.

verdure [ˈvɜːdjʊə] *n.* (*formal*) green vegetation.

verge [vɜːdʒ] **1.** *n.* edge; grass strip along the side of a road; **on the v. of** = near to. **2.** *v.* **to v. on** = to be near to.

verger [ˈvɜːdʒə] *n.* man who looks after a church.

verify [ˈverɪfaɪ] *v.* to check/to see if (a statement) is correct. **verifiable** [verɪˈfaɪəbl] *adj.* which can be verified. **verification** [verɪfɪˈkeɪʃn] *n.* checking that sth is correct.

verily [ˈverɪlɪ] *adv.* (*old*) truly.

verisimilitude [verɪsɪˈmɪlɪtjuːd] *n.* appearance of being true.

veritable [ˈverɪtəbl] *adj.* true/real.

vermicelli [vɜːmɪˈselɪ] *n.* type of very thin spaghetti.

vermiculite [vɜːˈmɪkjuːlaɪt] *n.* grains of silica, used as a growing medium for some types of pot plants.

vermiform [vəˈmɪfɔːm] *adj.* shaped like a worm.

vermilion [vəˈmɪlɪən] *adj. & n.* bright red (colour).

vermin [ˈvɜːmɪn] *n.* (*a*) insects which live on other animals. (*b*) unwanted animals or birds which are pests. **verminous,** *adj.* covered with fleas.

vermouth [ˈvɜːməθ] *n.* type of strong wine flavoured with herbs.

vernacular [vəˈnækjʊlə] *adj. & n.* (referring to) the ordinary spoken language of a country or region.

vernal [ˈvɜːnl] *adj.* (*formal*) referring to the spring.

veronica [vəˈrɒnɪkə] *n.* low creeping plant with blue flowers.

verruca [vəˈruːkə] *n.* wart.

versatile [ˈvɜːsətaɪl] *adj.* (person/machine) able to do various things equally well; (musician) who can play many different instruments. **versatility** [vɜːsəˈtɪlɪtɪ] *n.* ability to do various things with equal skill.

verse [vɜːs] *n.* (*a*) group of lines of poetry which form a part of a poem. (*b*) poetry; lines of writing with a rhythm and sometimes rhyme. (*c*) one line of a poem. (*d*) short (numbered) sentence from the Bible; **to give chapter and v. for sth** = to quote exactly the origin of a statement. **versed,** *adj.* **well v. in** = knowing a lot about/being well skilled in. **versification** [vɜːsɪfɪˈkeɪʃn] *n.* making of poetry; way in which a poem is written. **versify** [ˈvɜːsɪfaɪ] *v.* to write (usu. bad) poetry.

version [ˈvɜːʃn] *n.* (*a*) story of what happened as seen from a particular point of view. (*b*) translation. (*c*) model (of car, etc.).

verso [ˈvɜːsəʊ] *n.* left side/back (of a piece of paper/a page of a book, etc.).

versus [ˈvɜːsəs] *prep.* (*usu. written* v.) (*in a civil court case/in sport*) against.

vertebra [ˈvɜːtɪbrə] *n.* (*pl.* **-brae** [-briː]) one of the bones which form the spine. **vertebrate** [ˈvɜːtɪbrət] *adj. & n.* (animal) which has a backbone.

vertex [ˈvɜːteks] *n.* (*pl.* **-tices** [-tɪsiːz]) top; angle at the top of a triangle.

vertical [ˈvɜːtɪkl] **1.** *adj.* upright. **2.** *n.* upright line (in geometry); **out of the v.** = leaning at an angle. **vertically,** *adv.* straight up/down.

vertigo [ˈvɜːtɪɡəʊ] *n.* dizziness caused by heights. **vertiginous** [vɜːˈtɪdʒɪnəs], *adj.* which makes one dizzy.

verve [vɜːv] *n.* enthusiasm/feeling of liveliness.

very [ˈverɪ] **1.** *adv.* (*a*) to a high degree. **v. much the same** = almost the same. (*b*) exactly; **the v. same** = exactly the same. **2.** *adj.* (**-ier, -iest**) exactly the same/exactly the right (person). **at the v. beginning** = right at the beginning.

vesicle [ˈvesɪkl] *n.* small hollow in the body (usu. filled wih liquid). **vesicular** [veˈsɪkjʊlə] *adj.* referring to a vesicle.

vespers [ˈvespəz] *n.* church service in the evening.

vessel [ˈvesl] *n.* (*a*) container (for

liquid); **blood v.** = tube which carries blood round the body. (b) ship.

vest [vest] n. (a) light undergarment for the top half of the body. (b) Am. waistcoat. **vested,** adj. **v. interest** = sth which is to s.o.'s advantage, and makes him want to avoid changes, because it is in his interest to keep the present system.

vestibule ['vestɪbjuːl] n. entrance hall.

vestige ['vestɪdʒ] n. trace/remains. **vestigial** [ves'tɪdʒəl] adj. which exists as a vestige; **v. tail** = very small tail.

vestments ['vestmənts] n. pl. clergyman's robes.

vestry ['vestrɪ] n. clergyman's room in a church.

vet [vet] 1. n. inf. veterinary surgeon. 2. v. (**vetted**) to examine carefully.

vetch [vetʃ] n. (pl. **-es**) type of wild pea.

veteran ['vetrən] 1. n. (a) person who has given long service. (b) old/retired soldier. (c) Am. person (not necessarily old) who has served in the armed services. 2. adj. old; experienced; **v. car** = car made before 1916.

veterinary ['vetrɪnrɪ] adj. referring to the treatment of sick animals; **v. surgeon** = doctor who specializes in treating sick animals. **veterinarian** [vetərɪ'neərɪən] n. Am. veterinary surgeon.

veto ['viːtəʊ] 1. n. (pl. **-os**) power to forbid sth. 2. v. to forbid.

vex [veks] v. to annoy. **vexation** [vek'seɪʃn] n. annoyance. **vexatious** [vek'seɪʃəs] adj. annoying; **v. litigant** = person who starts legal actions very often, for no solid reason. **vexed,** adj. (a) annoyed. (b) (question) which is often discussed but which has not been solved.

VHF [viːeɪtʃ'ef] abbreviation for very high frequency.

via ['vaɪə] prep. (travelling) through.

viable ['vaɪəbl] adj. (a) able to work in practice. (b) (of new-born young) sufficiently developed to survive. **viability** [vaɪə'bɪlɪtɪ] n. being viable.

viaduct ['vaɪədʌkt] n. long bridge carrying a road/railway over a wide valley.

vial ['vaɪəl] n. small glass bottle.

viands ['vaɪəndz] n. pl. (formal) food.

vibes [vaɪbz] n. pl. inf. (a) vibraphone. (b) sensations.

vibrate [vaɪ'breɪt] v. to shudder/to shake. **vibrancy,** n. being vibrant. **vibrant** ['vaɪbrənt] adj. full (of energy). **vibraphone,** n. instrument like a xylophone with an amplifier. **vibration** [vaɪ'breɪʃn] n. act of vibrating; rapid movement. **vibrato** [vɪ'brɑːtəʊ] n. (in music) trembling effect. **vibrator,** n. machine which vibrates. **vibratory,** adj. which vibrates.

viburnum [vaɪ'bɜːnəm] n. common shrub with pink or white flowers.

vicar ['vɪkə] n. clergyman in charge of a parish. **vicarage** ['vɪkrɪdʒ] n. vicar's house.

vicarious [vɪ'keərɪəs] adj. felt through imagining what another person feels; (pleasure) felt because you imagine how s.o. is enjoying sth. **vicariously,** adv. in a vicarious way.

vice [vaɪs] n. (a) sexual wickedness/immorality; **v. squad** = police department dealing with prostitution, etc. (b) great wickedness. (c) bad habit. (d) tool with jaws that screw tight to hold sth. **vice-like,** adj. tight like a vice.

vice- [vaɪs] prefix meaning deputy; second in rank.

vice-chancellor [vaɪs'tʃɑːnsələ] n. executive head of a university.

vice-president [vaɪs'prezɪdənt] n. deputy to a president.

viceroy ['vaɪsrɔɪ] n. person who represents a king or queen. **viceregal** [vaɪs'riːgl] adj. referring to a viceroy.

vice versa [vaɪsə'vɜːsə] adv. the other way round.

vicinity [vɪ'sɪnɪtɪ] n. area around sth; **in the v. (of)** = near (by).

vicious ['vɪʃəs] adj. (a) wicked. (b) **v. circle** = interlocking chain of bad circumstances from which it is impossible to escape. **viciously,** adv. in a wicked/spiteful way.

vicissitude [vɪ'sɪsɪtjuːd] n. (formal) variation in luck.

victim ['vɪktɪm] n. person who suffers an attack/an accident. **victimization** [vɪktɪmaɪ'zeɪʃn] n. act of victimizing. **victimize** ['vɪktɪmaɪz] v. to choose (s.o.) as a victim; to treat s.o. more harshly than others.

victor ['vɪktə] n. person who wins (a game/a battle). **Victorian** [vɪk'tɔːrɪən] *adj.* referring to the reign of Queen Victoria (1837–1901). **victorious** [vɪk'tɔːrɪəs] *adj.* (person/general) who has won a game/a battle. **victory** ['vɪktrɪ] *n.* win; winning of a battle.

victual ['vɪtl] (*formal*) **1.** *n.* **victuals** = food. **2.** *v.* to supply (a ship/an army) with food. **victualler** ['vɪtlə] *n.* licensed **v.** = innkeeper.

vicuna [vɪ'kjuːnə] *n.* soft wool from a South American animal.

vide ['vɪdeɪ] *Latin word meaning* see.

video ['vɪdɪəʊ] *adj. & n.* (system) which shows pictures on a television screen. **videocassette**, *n.* small cassette containing a videotape. **videodisc**, *n.* disc which contains recorded sound and pictures. **video-recorder**, *n.* machine which records television pictures on tape, so that they can be played back later. **videotape**. **1.** *n.* magnetic tape which can record pictures and sound for playing back through a television set. **2.** *v.* to record (pictures/film, etc.) on magnetic tape.

vie [vaɪ] *v.* **to v. with s.o.** = to rival/to try to beat s.o.

view [vjuː] **1.** *n.* (*a*) scene (which you can see from a certain place). (*b*) sight/action of looking at sth; **on v.** = on show for people to look at. (*c*) opinion. **I share your v.** = I agree with your opinion; **to take a dim v. of** = to disapprove of. (*d*) **in v. of** = when you consider. (*e*) intention/what you hope to do; **with a v. to** = planning to. **2.** *v.* (*a*) to look at (sth)/to consider (a problem). (*b*) to watch television; **the viewing public** = people who watch television. **viewer**, *n.* (*a*) person who watches television. (*b*) small device for looking at colour slides. **viewfinder**, *n.* small window in a camera which you look through when taking a picture, and which shows the exact picture you are about to take. **viewpoint**, *n.* way of looking at things/of considering things.

vigil ['vɪdʒɪl] *n.* keeping awake/on guard all night. **vigilance**, *n.* being watchful/on guard. **vigilant**, *adj.* watchful/on guard. **vigilante** [vɪdʒɪ'læntɪ] *n.* person who tries to enforce law and order, esp. when the police find it impossible to do so.

vignette [vɪ'njet] *n.* small sketch.

vigour, *Am.* **vigor** ['vɪgə] *n.* energy. **vigorous**, *adj.* energetic/very active; strong. **vigorously**, *adv.* in a vigorous way.

vile [vaɪl] *adj.* extremely unpleasant/bad. **vilely**, *adv.* in a vile way. **vileness**, *n.* being vile.

vilify ['vɪlɪfaɪ] *v.* to say extremely bad things about (s.o.). **vilification** [vɪlɪfɪ'keɪʃn] *n.* act of vilifying.

villa ['vɪlə] *n.* (*a*) large country (or seaside) house (usu. in a warm country). (*b*) suburban house.

village ['vɪlɪdʒ] *n.* small group of houses (usu. with a church) in the country. **villager**, *n.* person who lives in a village.

villain ['vɪlən] *n.* wicked person. **villainous**, *adj.* wicked. **villainy**, *n.* wickedness.

villein ['vɪleɪn] *n.* medieval agricultural labourer.

vim [vɪm] *n. inf.* energy.

vinaigrette [vɪneɪ'gret] *n.* (*a*) small bottle of smelling salts. (*b*) sauce made of oil and vinegar.

vindicate ['vɪndɪkeɪt] *v.* to justify; to show that (s.o.) was right. **vindication** [vɪndɪ'keɪʃn] *n.* (**of**) proving that sth was right.

vindictive [vɪn'dɪktɪv] *adj.* wanting to take revenge; spiteful. **vindictively**, *adv.* spitefully. **vindictiveness**, *n.* spite; desire to take revenge.

vine [vaɪn] *n.* (*a*) climbing plant which bears grapes. (*b*) climbing plant.

vinegar ['vɪnɪgə] *n.* liquid made from sour wine/cider, used in cooking and for preserving food. **vinegary**, *adj.* (wine, etc.) tasting like vinegar; bad-tempered (person).

vineyard ['vɪnjəd] *n.* field of vines for producing wine.

vino ['viːnəʊ] *n. Sl.* cheap wine.

vinous ['vaɪnəs] *adj.* referring to wine.

vintage ['vɪntɪdʒ] *n.* (*a*) collecting of grapes to make wine; grapes which are collected. (*b*) fine wine made in a particular year; **v. wine/v. port** = fine/expensive old wine/port. (*c*) year of make; **v. car** = one made between 1917 and 1930. (*d*) of typical high quality.

vintner ['vɪntnə] *n.* person who sells wine.

vinyl ['vaɪnl] *n.* type of plastic sheet which looks like leather/tiles, etc.

viol ['vaɪəl] *n.* early stringed instrument.

viola [vaɪ'əʊlə] *n.* (*a*) small pansy-like garden flower. (*b*) stringed instrument slightly larger than a violin.

violate ['vaɪəleɪt] *v.* (*a*) to break/to go against (the law/a treaty). (*b*) (*formal*) to rape. **violation** [vaɪə'leɪʃn] *n.* act of violating; **in v. of an agreement** = against the terms of the agreement. **violator**, *n.* person who violates.

violence ['vaɪələns] *n.* (*a*) force/strength. (*b*) rough action. **violent**, *adj.* (*a*) strong. (*b*) rough. **violently**, *adv.* strongly; roughly.

violet ['vaɪələt] *n. & adj.* (*a*) small wild plant with bluish purple flowers. (*b*) bluish purple (colour).

violin [vaɪə'lɪn] *n.* stringed musical instrument played with a bow. **violinist**, *n.* person who plays the violin. **violoncello** [vaɪələn'tʃeləʊ] *n.* (*pl.* -os) (*formal*) cello.

VIP [viː'aɪ'piː] *abbreviation for* very important person; **VIP treatment** = being treated like a very important person.

viper ['vaɪpə] *n.* adder/poisonous snake.

virago [vɪ'rɑːgəʊ] *n.* (*pl.* -os) fierce loud-mouthed woman.

viral ['vaɪrəl] *adj.* referring to a virus.

virement ['vaɪəmənt] *n.* moving money from one area of a budget to another.

virgin ['vɜːdʒɪn] **1.** *n.* (*a*) person who has never had sexual intercourse. (*b*) **the V. (Mary)** = the mother of Jesus Christ. **2.** *adj.* pure/untouched. **virginal**, *adj.* pure like a virgin. **virginals**, *n. pl.* type of 16th century harpsichord. **virginity** [vɜː'dʒɪnɪtɪ] *n.* being a virgin; **to lose your v.** = to have sexual intercourse for the first time.

virginia creeper [vɜː'dʒɪnɪə'kriːpə] *n.* common climbing plant which grows on walls, with leaves which turn bright red in autumn.

Virgo ['vɜːgəʊ] *n.* one of the signs of the zodiac, shaped like a girl.

virile ['vɪraɪl] *adj.* manly; masculine. **virility** [vɪ'rɪlɪtɪ] *n.* being virile; strength; manliness.

virology [vaɪ'rɒlədʒɪ] *n.* study of viruses. **virologist**, *n.* scientist who studies viruses.

virtual ['vɜːtjʊəl] *adj.* almost, if not in fact. **virtually**, *adv.* almost.

virtue ['vɜːtjuː] *n.* (*a*) particular goodness (of character); good quality. (*b*) special quality. (*c*) **by v. of** = because of. **virtuous**, *adj.* very good/very honest. **virtuously**, *adv.* in a virtuous way.

virtuoso [vɜːtjʊ'əʊzəʊ] *n.* (*pl.* -os/-si [-siː]) person who is skilled in an art, esp. who can play a musical instrument extremely well. **virtuosity** [vɜːtjʊ'ɒsɪtɪ] *n.* ability to play a musical instrument/sing, etc., extremely well.

virulence ['vɪrjʊləns] *n.* (*of a disease*) great strength. **virulent**, *adj.* very bad (attack of disease); very harsh (attack). **virulently**, *adv.* in a virulent way.

virus ['vaɪrəs] *n.* (*pl.* -es) (*a*) germ which is smaller than bacteria and which causes colds/pneumonia, etc. (*b*) hidden routine placed in a computer program, which corrupts or destroys files.

visa ['viːzə] *n.* special mark on a passport/special paper allowing you to enter a country; **30-day v.** = visa which allows you to stay in a country for 30 days.

vis-à-vis [viːzɑː'viː] *prep.* (*a*) in relation to. (*b*) compared with.

viscera ['vɪsərə] *n. pl.* organs inside the body, esp. the intestines. **visceral**, *adj.* referring to the viscera.

viscosity [vɪs'kɒsɪtɪ] *n.* state of being viscous. **viscose** ['vɪskəʊz] *n.* man-made silk material, made from viscous cellulose. **viscid, viscous** ['vɪsɪd, 'vɪskəs] *adj.* thick/sticky (liquid).

viscount ['vaɪkaʊnt] *n.* title of a nobleman below an earl. **viscountess**, *n.* (*pl.* -es) wife of a viscount.

vise [vaɪs] *n. Am.* tool with jaws that screw tight to hold sth. **viselike**, *adj. Am.* tight, as in a vise.

visible ['vɪzɪbl] *adj.* which can be seen. **visibility** [vɪzɪ'bɪlɪtɪ] *n.* ability to be seen clearly; **good v.** = ability for things to be seen at long distances because the air is clear. **visibly**, *adv.* obviously; in a way which can be seen.

vision ['vɪʒn] *n.* (*a*) ability to see; **field of v.** = range from one side to another over which you can see clearly; **tunnel v.** = seeing only the area immediately in front of the eye. (*b*) ability to look and plan ahead. (*c*) thing which you imagine; **he has visions of himself as Prime Minister** = he imagines he will be Prime Minister one day. (*d*) ghost; strange sight. **visionary. 1.** *adj.* idealistic/impracticable (plan). **2.** *n.* person whose plans are idealistic and impracticable.

visit ['vɪzɪt] **1.** *n.* short stay; **to pay a v. to** = to go to see (s.o.)/to stay a short time in (a place). **2.** *v.* to stay a short time (in a place/with s.o.); **visiting hours** = times when you can visit patients in hospital; **visiting team** = opposing team who has come to play on the home ground. **visitant,** *n.* ghost. **visitation** [vɪzɪ'teɪʃn] *n.* (*a*) trouble which is thought to be sent as a divine punishment. (*b*) official visit. **visitor** ['vɪzɪtə] *n.* person who visits; **summer v.** = person/bird which only comes to this country in the summer; **prison v.** = private person who regularly spends time visiting prisoners and talking to them.

visor ['vaɪzə] *n.* moveable part of a helmet, which drops down to protect the face; folding shield above the windscreen which protects the driver of a car from bright sunshine.

vista ['vɪstə] *n.* wide view.

visual ['vɪzjuəl] *adj.* referring to what can be seen; **v. arts** = painting/sculpture, etc. (as opposed to music); **v. aids** = slides/films used for teaching purposes. **visualize** ['vɪzjuəlaɪz] *v.* to picture/to see (sth) in your mind. **visually,** *adv.* in a visual way.

vital ['vaɪtl] *adj.* (*a*) very important. (*b*) vigorous/energetic (person). (*c*) (organs in the body) which are essential to life. **vitally,** *adv.* in a very important way. **vitality** [vaɪ'tælɪtɪ] *n.* great energy. **vitalize,** *v.* to make (sth) more energetic. **vitals,** *n. pl.* important organs in a body. **vital statistics,** *n.* (*a*) official statistics concerning populations, births, deaths, etc. (*b*) *inf.* measurements of bust, waist and hips of a woman.

vitamin ['vɪtəmɪn] *n.* chemical substance occurring in food which is important for the development or health of the human body. **vitaminized** ['vɪtəmɪnaɪzd] *adj.* with vitamins added.

vitiate ['vɪʃɪeɪt] *v.* to make bad/to make weak. **vitiation** [vɪʃɪ'eɪʃn] *n.* act of vitiating.

vitreous ['vɪtrɪəs] *adj.* like glass. **vitrification** [vɪtrɪfɪ'keɪʃn] *n.* act of vitrifying. **vitrify** ['vɪtrɪfaɪ] *v.* to make into glass; to become like glass.

vitriol ['vɪtrɪəl] *n.* sulphuric acid. **vitriolic** [vɪtrɪ'ɒlɪk] *adj.* very violent/very rude (attack).

vituperation [vɪtjʊpə'reɪʃn] *n.* (*formal*) abuse; insulting words. **vituperative,** *adj.* (*formal*) insulting/abusive.

viva (voce) ['vaɪvə ('vəʊsɪ)] *n.* oral examination.

vivacious [vɪ'veɪʃəs] *adj.* full of life/ full of excitement. **vivaciously,** *adv.* in a vivacious way. **vivaciousness, vivacity** [vɪ'væsɪtɪ] *n.* being vivacious.

vivid ['vɪvɪd] *adj.* (*a*) very bright (light/ colour). (*b*) very lifelike (description); very lively (imagination). **vividly,** *adj.* in a vivid way. **vividness,** *n.* being vivid.

viviparous [vɪ'vɪpərəs] *adj.* (animal) which produces live young (that is, which does not lay eggs).

vivisection [vɪvɪ'sekʃən] *n.* operating on a live animal for the purpose of scientific research.

vixen ['vɪksn] *n.* female fox.

viz. [vɪz *or* 'neɪmlɪ] *adv.* namely.

vocabulary [və'kæbjʊlərɪ] *n.* (*a*) words used by a person or group of persons. (*b*) printed list of words.

vocal ['vəʊkl] **1.** *adj.* (*a*) referring to the voice; **v. cords** = muscles in the throat which produce sounds. (*b*) very loud/ insistent (opposition). **2.** *n. pl.* **vocals** = popular songs performed with a group. **vocalic** [vəʊ'kælɪk] *adj.* referring to vowels. **vocalist,** *n.* singer. **vocalize,** *v.* to make a sound with your voice. **vocally,** *adv.* in a loud way.

vocation [və'keɪʃn] *n.* job which you feel you have been called to do/for which you have a special talent; **she missed her v.** = she should be in another job for which she is better suited. **vocational,** *adj.* referring to a vocation; **v. training** = training for a particular job.

vociferate [və'sɪfəreɪt] *v.* (*formal*) to shout protests against sth. **vociferous,** *adj.* loud/shouting. **vociferously,** *adv.* loudly.

vodka ['vɒdkə] *n.* colourless alcohol made originally in Russia or Poland.

vogue [vəʊg] *n.* fashion; popularity; **in v.** = fashionable.

voice [vɔɪs] **1.** *n.* (*a*) sounds made by a person speaking or singing; **she's lost her v.** = she can't speak (because of a cold); **in a low v.** = quietly; **don't raise your v.** = don't talk so loudly. (*b*) right to express an opinion. (*c*) **active v./passive v.** = forms of a verb which show whether the subject is doing sth or having sth done to it. **2.** *v.* to express (an opinion). **voiceless,** *adj.* silent; with no voice.

void [vɔɪd] **1.** *adj.* (*a*) empty. (*b*) **null and v.** = not valid. **2.** *n.* emptiness. **3.** *v.* to empty.

voile [vɔɪl] *n.* very thin cotton or silk material.

volatile ['vɒlətaɪl] *adj.* (*a*) (liquid) which can easily change into vapour. (*b*) (person) who changes his mind/his mood frequently. **volatility** [vɒlə'tɪlɪtɪ] *n.* being volatile. **volatize,** *v.* to make sth. evaporate.

vol-au-vent [vɒləʊ'vɒn] *n.* small pastry case with savoury mixture inside.

volcano [vɒl'keɪnəʊ] *n.* (*pl.* **-oes**) mountain with a hole on the top through which lava, ash and gas can come. **volcanic** [vɒl'kænɪk] *adj.* referring to volcanoes. **volcanology** [vɒlkə'nɒlədʒɪ] *n.* vulcanology.

vole [vəʊl] *n.* small animal, resembling a mouse.

volition [və'lɪʃn] *n.* (*formal*) wish/will. **of one's own v.** = because one wants to and not because one is told to.

volley ['vɒlɪ] **1.** *n.* (*a*) series of shots/missiles which are fired/thrown at the same time. (*b*) (*in sport*) hitting the ball before it touches the ground. **2.** *v.* (*a*) to fire several shots/throw several missiles at the same time. (*b*) (*in sport*) to hit the ball before it touches the ground. **volleyball,** *n.* team game in which a large ball is thrown across a high net, and must not touch the ground.

volt [vɒlt] *n.* standard unit of electric potential. **voltage,** *n.* amount of electric force. **voltmeter,** *n.* instrument for measuring voltage.

volte face ['vɒlt'fæs] *n.* sudden unexpected change of opinion.

voluble ['vɒljʊbl] *n.* (person) who speaks easily with a lot of words. **volubility** [vɒljʊ'bɪlɪtɪ] *n.* use of a lot of words. **volubly,** *adj.* with a lot of words.

volume ['vɒljuːm] *n.* (*a*) book (esp. one book of a series). (*b*) space taken up by sth. (*c*) amount. (*d*) loudness. **voluminous** [və'ljuːmɪnəs] *adj.* large; taking up a lot of space.

volunteer [vɒlən'tɪə] **1.** *n.* (*a*) person who offers to do sth without being told to do it. (*b*) soldier who has joined the army of his own free will. **2.** *v.* (*a*) to offer to do sth; to join the armed services of your own free will. (*b*) to give (information) without being forced to do so. **voluntarily,** *adv.* freely. **voluntary** ['vɒləntrɪ] **1.** *adj.* (*a*) done of your own free will. (*b*) done for no payment; **v. organization** = charity/organization which is organized by voluntary help and not subsidized by the government. **2.** *n.* **organ v.** = solo piece of music played on the organ during or at the beginning or end of a church service.

voluptuous [və'lʌptjʊəs] *adj.* absorbed in/evoking sensual pleasure. **voluptuary,** *n.* person who enjoys sensual pleasure. **voluptuously,** *adv.* in a voluptuous way.

vomit ['vɒmɪt] **1.** *n.* food vomited. **2.** *v.* to bring up food through your mouth when you are sick.

voodoo ['vuːduː] *n.* witchcraft practised in the West Indies. **voodooism,** *n.* belief in voodoo.

voracious [və'reɪʃəs] *adj.* greedy; wanting to eat a lot; **v. reader** = person who reads a lot. **voraciously,** *adv.* greedily. **voraciousness, voracity** [vɒ'ræsɪtɪ] *n.* being voracious.

vortex ['vɔːteks] *n.* (*pl.* **-tices** [-tɪsiːz]) matter which is turning round and round very fast.

votary ['vəʊtrɪ] *n.* (*formal*) person who worships/who admires sth fervently.

vote [vəʊt] **1.** *n.* (*a*) expressing your opinion by marking a paper/by holding up your hand/by speaking. (*b*) action of voting; **to put sth to the v.** = to ask people to vote on sth; **v. of censure** = vote criticizing (the government, etc.). (*c*) **to v.** = the right to vote in an

election/to vote on a proposal. **2.** *v.*
(*a*) to express an opinion by marking
a paper/by holding up your hand/by
speaking. (*b*) **he was voted on to/off the
committee** = he was elected/was not reelected a member of the committee.
voter, *n.* person who votes/who has the
right to vote; **floating v.** = person who
has not decided which party to vote for
in an election.
votive ['vəʊtɪv] *adj.* (offering) given to
fulfil a promise made to a god or to a
saint.
vouch [vaʊtʃ] *v.* **to v. for sth** = to
guarantee sth. **voucher,** *n.* paper which
guarantees payment; **gift v.** = ticket
bought from a shop, which you give as
a present, and which can be used to
buy articles in the shop; **luncheon v.** =
ticket (given by an employer) which can
be exchanged for food in a restaurant.
vouchsafe [vaʊtʃ'seɪf] *v.* (*formal*) to
ensure/to guarantee (that s.o. has the
right to do sth).
vow [vaʊ] **1.** *n.* solemn promise (esp. one
sworn to God). **2.** *v.* to make a solemn
promise.
vowel ['vaʊəl] *n.* sound made without
using the teeth, tongue or lips; one of
the five letters (a, e, i. o, u) which
represent these sounds.
voyage ['vɔɪdʒ] **1.** *n.* long journey (esp.
by sea). **2.** *v.* to make a long journey (by
sea). **voyager,** *n.* person who voyages.
voyeur [vwɑː'jɜː] *n.* person who watches
people making love.
vulcanize ['vʌlkənaɪz] *v.* to treat rubber
with sulphur so that it is made stronger,
harder and more elastic. **vulcanite,** *n.*
vulcanized rubber. **vulcanization,** *n.*
process of vulcanizing.
vulcanology [vʌlkə'nɒlədʒɪ] *n.* study of
volcanoes.
vulgar ['vʌlgə] *adj.* (*a*) rude/indecent.
(*b*) not in good taste. (*c*) **v. fraction**
= fraction written as one number
above and another below a line.
vulgarian [vʌl'geərɪən] *n.* vulgar person. **vulgarism,** *n.* rude expression.
vulgarity [vʌl'gærɪtɪ] *n.* rudeness; lack
of good taste. **vulgarization,** *n.* making common/popular. **vulgarly,** *adv.* in
a rude/indecent way.
vulnerable ['vʌlnərəbl] *adj.* which can
be easily attacked/easily hurt. **vul-**

nerability [vʌlnərə'bɪlɪtɪ] *n.* being
vulnerable.
vulpine ['vʌlpaɪn] *adj.* referring to foxes.
vulture ['vʌltʃə] *n.* large tropical bird
that eats mainly dead flesh.
vulva ['vʌlvə] *n.* part of female body
around the opening of the vagina.

Ww

wacky ['wækɪ] *adj.* (**-ier, -iest**) *inf.* crazy/
silly.
wad [wɒd] **1.** *n.* (*a*) thick piece of soft
material. (*b*) thick pile of banknotes/
papers. (*c*) *inf.* thick sandwich. **2.** *v.*
(**wadded**) to stuff/to press into a wad.
wadding, *n.* thick, soft material used
for lining a coat/quilting/stuffing.
waddle ['wɒdl] **1.** *n.* walk swaying from
side to side like a duck. **2.** *v.* to walk
with a waddle.
wade [weɪd] *v.* to walk through deep
water or mud; **to w. through** = to
find (a book) difficult to read; **to w.
into a pile of work** = to start dealing with a pile of work vigorously.
wader, *n.* (*a*) bird which spends most
of its time in shallow water or mud. (*b*)
waders = long waterproof boots worn
by fishermen.
wafer ['weɪfə] *n.* (*a*) thin sweet biscuit
eaten with ice cream. (*b*) thin disc of
bread eaten at communion or mass.
waffle ['wɒfl] **1.** *n.* (*a*) type of crisp cake
cooked in an iron mould and eaten
with syrup. (*b*) unnecessary or muddled
speaking/writing. **2.** *v.* to talk too much
without saying anything clearly. **waffle-
iron,** *n.* iron mould used for making
waffles.
waft [wɒft] **1.** *n.* gentle smell. **2.** *v.* to
carry (sth) gently through the air.
wag [wæg] **1.** *n.* (*a*) movement from side
to side or up and down. (*b*) *inf.* person who likes making jokes/facetious
remarks. **2.** *v.* (**wagged**) to move from
side to side or up and down. **waggish,**
adj. joking (remark).
wage [weɪdʒ] **1.** *n.* (*also* **wages**) weekly
payment given for work done; **w. freeze**
= period of standstill in wages. **2.** *v.* to
fight (a war); **to w. war (on sth)** = to
fight against sth. **wage-earner,** *n.* person who works for wages.

wager ['weɪdʒə] **1.** *n.* bet/money which you promise to pay if sth you expect to happen does not take place. **2.** *v.* to bet.

waggle ['wægl] *v.* to move from side to side.

wagon, waggon ['wægn] *n.* (*a*) four-wheeled vehicle pulled by horses and used for carrying heavy loads. (*b*) railway truck. (*c*) *inf.* **to be on the w.** = to drink only non-alcoholic drinks. **wag(g)oner**, *n.* person who drives a wagon.

wagtail ['wægteɪl] *n.* small bird which wags its tail up and down as it walks.

waif [weɪf] *n.* homeless child or animal; **waifs and strays** = homeless abandoned children or animals.

wail [weɪl] **1.** *n.* high-pitched sad cry. **2.** *v.* to make a high-pitched mournful cry.

wainscot(ing) ['weɪnzkət(ɪŋ)] *n.* wood panelling covering the lower part of a wall in a house. **wainscoted**, *adj.* with a wainscot.

waist [weɪst] *n.* (*a*) narrow part of the body between the chest and the hips. (*b*) narrow part (of a bottle, etc.). **waistband**, *n.* band of cloth round the waist of a pair of trousers/skirt. **waistcoat** ['weɪskəut] *n.* short close-fitting sleeveless garment which goes over a shirt and under a jacket. **waistline**, *n.* measurement around the waist.

wait [weɪt] **1.** *n.* act of staying until sth happens or s.o. arrives; **to lie in w. for s.o.** = to hide waiting for s.o. to pass by in order to attack him. **2.** *v.* (*a*) (**for**) to stay somewhere until sth happens or s.o./sth arrives. (*b*) **to w. on s.o.** = to serve food to s.o. at table. **waiter**, *n.* man who serves food to people in a restaurant; **head w.** = person in charge of other waiters; **dumb w.** = (i) small table (usu. with wheels) for keeping food on; (ii) lift for carrying food from one floor to another. **waiting-room**, *n.* room where travellers wait for their trains/buses, etc./where patients wait to see a doctor, etc. **waiting list**, *n.* list of people waiting to see s.o. or do sth. **waitress**, *n.* (*pl.* **-es**) woman who serves food to people in a restaurant. **waits**, *n. pl.* (*old*) carol singers. **wait up**, *v.* to stay up/not to go to bed.

waive [weɪv] *v.* to give up (a right/a claim). **waiver**, *n.* giving up (of a right/claim).

wake [weɪk] **1.** *n.* (*a*) waves left by a boat, etc., moving through water; **in the w. of** = immediately behind. (*b*) staying up all night with a dead body before a funeral. **2.** *v.* (**woke** [wəuk]; **has woken**) to stop (s.o.) sleeping; to stop sleeping. **wakeful**, *adj.* not at all sleepy/not able to go to sleep. **waken**, *v.* to stop (s.o.) sleeping. **wakes**, *n. pl.* holiday for industrial workers in the North of England. **wake up**, *v.* (*a*) to stop sleeping. (*b*) **to wake up to** = to realize. **wakey-wakey**, *inter.* used to wake s.o. **waking**, *adj.* not asleep.

walk [wɔːk] **1.** *n.* (*a*) journey on foot. (*b*) way of walking. (*c*) wide path in a park or garden. (*d*) **w. of life** = social position or occupation. **2.** *v.* (*a*) to move along on the feet at a normal speed. (*b*) to accompany (s.o./an animal) on foot. **walkabout**, *n.* walk among a crowd by an important person. **walker**, *n.* person who walks, or who is fond of walking. **walkie-talkie**, *n.* portable two-way radio-telephone. **walk in**, *v.* to enter. **walk-in**, *adj.* (cupboard) which you can walk into. **walking stick**, *n.* stick used to rest on when walking. **walk into**, *v.* (*a*) to enter. (*b*) to hit by accident. **walk off**, *v.* (*a*) to go away; **to walk off with** = (i) to win (a prize) easily; (ii) to steal. (*b*) **to walk off your dinner** = to go for a walk after a big dinner to help you digest it. **walk on**, *v.* (*a*) to continue walking. (*b*) to have a non-speaking part in a play. **walk-on**, *adj.* (part) in a play where the actor doesn't have to speak. **walk out**, *v.* (*a*) to go out. (*b*) to leave angrily. (*c*) to go on strike. (*d*) **to walk out on s.o.** = to leave s.o. suddenly. **walkout**, *n.* strike of workers. **walk over**, *v.* to walk across; to cross (a room) **to see** s.o./to go up to s.o. **walkover**, *n. inf.* easy victory. **walk up**, *v.* (*a*) to climb (on foot). (*b*) **to walk up (to s.o.)** = to approach/to go to speak (to s.o.). **walkway**, *n.* passage/path where you can walk.

wall [wɔːl] *n.* structure of brick/stone, etc., forming the side of a room/building, or the boundary of a piece of land;

w. painting = mural; to go to the w. = to be defeated; inf. he sends me up the w. = he makes me furious. walled, adj. with walls. wall-eyed, adj. (person) who squints badly. wallflower, n. (a) garden flower with a sweet scent. (b) (at a dance) inf. woman who is not asked to dance and is left sitting alone. wall in, v. to surround with walls. wallpaper. 1. n. decorative paper stuck on the walls of a room. 2. v. to stick paper on the walls of (a room). Wall Street, n. American finance centre. wall-to-wall, adj. (carpet) which covers all the floor space of a room. wall up, v. to close/to block with a wall.

wallaby ['wɒləbɪ] n. Australian animal like a small kangaroo.

wallet ['wɒlɪt] n. small leather case used for holding banknotes in a pocket.

wallop ['wɒləp] 1. n. inf. (a) hard blow. (b) beer. 2. v. inf. to hit hard. walloping, adj. inf. huge.

wallow ['wɒləʊ] 1. n. mud hollow where animals can roll. 2. v. (a) (of animals) to roll delightedly around in mud. (b) (of person) to take too much pleasure in.

walnut ['wɒlnʌt] n. (a) hard round nut with a wrinkled shell. (b) tree on which walnuts grow. (c) wood from a walnut tree.

walrus ['wɒlrʌs] n. (pl. -es) Arctic animal like a large seal with two long tusks pointing downwards; w. moustache = moustache whose long ends point downwards.

waltz [wɒls] 1. n. (pl. -es) (a) dance in which a man and woman turn around together as they move forwards. (b) music suitable for such a dance. 2. v. (a) to dance together. (b) inf. to walk smoothly/happily.

wan [wɒn] adj. pale/looking ill. wanly, adv. in a wan way. wanness, n. being wan.

wand [wɒnd] n. slim magic stick.

wander ['wɒndə] v. (a) to walk about with no special purpose or direction. (b) to w. off = to walk away from the correct path. (c) to go away from the subject when talking. (d) to be confused because of illness or old age. wanderer, n. person who wanders. wanderings, n. long random journeys. wanderlust,

n. passion for going off on journeys and adventures.

wane [weɪn] 1. n. the moon is on the w. = appears to be getting smaller; his influence is on the w. = is diminishing. 2. v. to appear smaller; to decrease.

wangle ['wæŋgl] 1. n. inf. trick/thing dishonestly obtained. 2. v. inf. to get (sth) by a trick. wangler, n. inf. person who gets things by a trick.

want [wɒnt] 1. n. (a) state of being without; for w. of sth better = as sth better is not available. (b) desire/wish. (c) wants = things needed. 2. v. (a) to wish/to desire/to long for. (b) to need/to require. (c) to look for (s.o.) to ask him questions. wanted, adj. (a) desired/needed. (b) searched for by the police, usu. because of a crime. wanting, adj. (a) needing. (b) having very little of sth.

wanton ['wɒntn] adj. wild/undisciplined.

war [wɔː] n. (a) fighting carried on between two or more nations; civil w. = war between two parties in one country; inf. he's been in the wars = he looks as though he has had a fight. (b) fight/battle; w. of words = bitter argument. warcry, n. loud shout given when going into battle; slogan used in a political campaign. war-dance, n. dance before the start of a battle. warfare, n. fighting a war; type of war. warhead, n. explosive top of a missile. warhorse, n. (a) heavy, strong horse formerly used for carrying soldiers into battle. (b) old soldier/politician who has seen many battles. warlike, adj. for war; like war. warlord, n. military leader who rules part of country. warmonger, n. person who wants to start a war. warpaint, n. bright colour put on the face and body before battle to make the enemy afraid. warpath, n. inf. to be on the w. = to be angry and looking for a fight. warring, adj. at war. warship, n. armed fighting ship. wartime, n. time of war.

warble ['wɔːbl] 1. n. trembling song (of a bird). 2. v. to sing with a trembling note. warbler, n. type of bird which sings with a trembling note.

ward [wɔːd] 1. n. (a) young person in the care of s.o. other than his parents; w. of court = child who is under the protection of the court. (*b*) large room in a hospital; section of a hospital. (*c*) part of a town for election purposes. **2.** *v.* **to w.** (sth) **off** = to keep away. **warden**, *n.* (*a*) person in charge of an institution/old people's home/students' hostel, etc. (*b*) person who looks after a park or forest; **traffic w.** = person who controls the parking of cars, etc., in a town. **warder, wardress,** *n.* prison officer/person who guards prisoners.

wardrobe ['wɔ:drəub] *n.* (*a*) large cupboard in which clothes may be hung. (*b*) a person's clothes. (*c*) costumes in a theatre; **w. mistress** = woman in charge of the costumes in a theatre.

wardroom [wɔ:drum] *n.* general living-room of officers on a warship.

ware ['weə] *n.* (*a*) *suffix meaning* goods made of a certain material/for a special purpose. (*b*) *pl.* **wares** = things that have been made and are for sale. **warehouse** ['weəhaus] **1.** *n.* large building for storing goods. **2.** *v.* to store (goods) in a large building. **warehouseman**, *n.* (*pl.* **-men**) person who works in a warehouse.

warm [wɔ:m] **1.** *adj.* (**-er, -est**) (*a*) quite hot/pleasantly hot; (*in a game*) **you're getting w.** = you're near the right answer. (*b*) kind and friendly (welcome). **2.** *n.* (*a*) being/keeping warm; warm place. (*b*) **British w.** = man's military-style beige overcoat. **3.** *v.* to make hot or hotter; **to w. to s.o.** = to feel more and more friendly towards s.o. **warm-blooded**, *adj.* having warm blood. **warm-hearted**, *adj.* friendly and welcoming. **warming pan**, *n.* metal container in which hot coals were put and which was used to warm beds. **warmly**, *adv.* in a warm way. **warmth**, *n.* (*a*) heat/state of being warm. (*b*) enthusiasm. **warm up**, *v.* (*a*) to heat/to make warm again; to become warm again. (*b*) to exercise before a game/a contest.

warn [wɔ:n] *v.* to tell of possible danger; to inform (s.o.) in advance; **to w. s.o. off sth** = to advise s.o. not to eat/drink/touch sth. **warning. 1.** *n.* (*a*) notice of danger. (*b*) **without w.** = suddenly. **2.** *adj.* which tells of danger.

warp [wɔ:p] **1.** *n.* (*a*) twisting out of

shape of a piece of wood. (*b*) threads running lengthwise in a piece of material. (*c*) heavy rope used for moving boats along. **2.** *v.* (*a*) to twist out of shape. (*b*) to make (mind/character) evil. (*c*) (*of boats*) to move by pulling on a rope. **warped**, *adj.* twisted (wood/character).

warrant ['wɒrənt] **1.** *n.* (*a*) written official paper permitting s.o. to sth. (*b*) **w. officer** = highest non-commissioned officer in the army. **2.** *v.* (*a*) to guarantee/to promise. (*b*) to justify/to deserve. **warranty**, *n.* guarantee/legal document promising that a machine will work, etc.

warren ['wɒrən] *n.* land with rabbit burrows.

warrior ['wɒrɪə] *n.* person who fights in a war.

wart [wɔ:t] *n.* small, hard, dark lump on the skin; **warts and all** = with all faults shown. **warthog**, *n.* type of wild African pig.

wary ['weərɪ] *adj.* (**-ier, -iest**) careful/cautious. **warily**, *adv.* cautiously/looking around all the time. **wariness** ['weərɪnəs] *n.* being wary.

was [wɒz] *v. see* **be.**

wash [wɒʃ] **1.** *n.* (*pl.* **-es**) (*a*) act of cleaning with water or another liquid; *inf.* **it will all come out in the w.** = it will all be made clear in due course. (*b*) clothes which are being washed. (*c*) movement of the sea or water. (*d*) waves left behind a boat. (*e*) thin mixture of liquid; **colour w.** = thin pale mixture of paint and water. **2.** *v.* (*a*) to clean with water or another liquid. (*b*) to be able to be washed; *inf.* to be believable. (*c*) (*of water*) to flow past/to touch. (*d*) **to be washed overboard** = to be swept off the deck of a ship by a wave. **wash away**, *v.* to remove by water. **washable**, *adj.* able to be washed. **washbasin**, *n.* fixed container, with taps, for holding water for washing the hands and face. **washbowl**, *n.* bowl for holding water, but not fixed and with no taps. **washcloth**, *n. Am.* flannel. **washday**, *n.* day when the clothes are washed. **wash down**, *v.* (*a*) to clean with a lot of water. (*b*) **to w. down the medicine with a drink of**

water = to drink water to help swallow the medicine. **washdown,** n. quick wash all over. **washer,** n. (a) person who washes. (b) steel or rubber ring under a bolt or nut; rubber ring inside a tap which prevents water escaping when the tap is turned off. (c) machine for washing. (d) **windscreen w.** = attachment on a car which squirts water on to the windscreen to clean the glass. **washerwoman,** n. (pl. -women) woman who washes clothes. **washing,** n. (a) act of cleaning with water. (b) clothes which are to be washed/which have just been washed. **washing day,** n. day when clothes are washed. **washing machine,** n. machine for washing clothes. **washing-up,** n. washing of cups/plates/knives and forks, etc., after a meal. **washing-up bowl,** n. bowl or container in which the plates/cups/knives and forks, etc., are washed after a meal. **washleather,** n. piece of soft leather used for cleaning windows. **wash off,** v. to clean away with water. **wash out,** v. (a) to clean/to be cleaned with water. (b) **washed out** = tired and without energy. (c) **the game was washed out** = could not be played because of rain. **washout,** n. inf. (a) useless person. (b) thing that has failed. (c) removal of pollutants by the rain. **washroom,** n. room where you can wash your hands and use the toilet. **washstand,** n. (a) (old) table on which a washbowl and jug of water stood in a bedroom. (b) Am. fixed bowl, with taps, for holding water for washing the hands and face. **wash up,** v. (a) to clean with water the cups/plates/knives and forks, etc., used during a meal. (b) Am. to wash yourself. (c) (of the sea) to throw (wreckage) on to the shore.

wasp [wɒsp] n. striped insect, like a bee, which can sting but which does not make honey; **w. waist** = (woman's) very slim waist. **WASP,** n. Am. White Anglo-Saxon Protestant. **waspish,** adj. irritable/quick-tempered. **waspishly,** adv. in a waspish way.

wassailing ['wɒseɪlɪŋ] n. (old) going from house to house singing Christmas carols.

waste [weɪst] 1. n. (a) wild/uncultivated land. (b) unnecessary use (of time/ money). (c) rubbish; **w. pipe** = pipe which takes dirty water from a sink to the drains; **w. disposal unit** = machine attached to a kitchen sink which grinds up and washes away kitchen rubbish. 2. v. (a) to use more than necessary/to use badly. **w. not, want not** = don't throw anything away, you may need it later. (b) **to w. away** = to become thin/to lose weight. 3. adj. (a) (of land) uncultivated/not used for any particular purpose; **to lay w.** = to destroy the crops and houses in an area, esp. in time of war. (b) old and useless; **w. paper basket** = small container where useless papers can be put. **wastage,** n. (a) loss; **natural w.** = reducing numbers of workers by not replacing those who leave. (b) amount lost by waste. **wasteful,** adj. extravagant/which wastes a lot. **wastefully,** adv. in an extravagant way. **waster,** n. (a) person/thing which wastes a lot. (b) wastrel. **wastrel,** n. person who is useless and idle.

watch [wɒtʃ] 1. n. (pl. -es) (a) act of looking at s.o./sth; observation. (b) (old) group of people who patrolled a town or village at night. (c) period of duty for sailors on a ship. (d) small clock worn on the arm or carried in a pocket; **digital w.** = watch which shows the time in numbers (10.27) rather than on a circular dial. 2. v. (a) to look at/to observe. (b) to be careful. **watch committee, neighbourhood watch,** n. group of people in a town or village who make sure that people and houses are safe at night. **watchdog,** n. (a) dog which guards a house or other buildings. (b) person/committee which examines public spending/public morals, etc. **watcher,** n. person who watches/observes. **watchful,** adj. very careful. **watchfully,** adv. very carefully. **watching,** n. act of looking/observing. **watchmaker,** n. person who makes and mends clocks and watches. **watchman,** n. (pl. -men) person who guards a building, usu. when it is empty. **watch out,** v. to be careful; **to watch out for** = to be careful to avoid. **watch tower,** n. tower from the top of which you can see if the enemy is coming. **watchword,** *n.* slogan/password.

water ['wɔːtə] **1.** *n.* (*a*) compound of hydrogen and oxygen; liquid that is in rain/rivers/lakes and the sea; **drinking w.** = water that is safe to drink; **hot w. bottle** = rubber or stone bottle filled with hot water and used to warm a bed; **by w.** = on a boat; **to be under w.** = to be covered by water; **to have w. laid on to a house** = to have pipes put from the main water supply to the house; **high w./low w.** = high/low tide; **to keep your head above w.** = (i) to swim with your head out of the water; (ii) to be able to keep out of difficulties; **to pass w.** = to urinate. (*b*) **waters** = large amount of water in a lake/sea; **to take the waters** = to drink mineral water at a spa. (*c*) *inf.* **w. on the brain** = illness where liquid forms on the brain, causing mental deficiency. (*d*) mixture of water with other substances. (*e*) (*of diamonds/precious stones*) brilliance; **of the first w.** = of the finest quality. **2.** *v.* (*a*) to give water to. (*b*) (**down**) to add water to (wine or spirits); to make (a statement) less forceful. (*c*) (*of eyes/mouth*) to fill with water. (*d*) (*of boats*) to take in supplies of drinking water. **water bed,** *n.* mattress made of a plastic bag filled with water. **water biscuit,** *n.* thin hard biscuit eaten with cheese. **water-boatman,** *n.* insect which skims across the surface of lakes/rivers, etc. **waterborne,** *adj.* (troops) carried in boats; (disease) carried in water. **waterbrash,** *n.* bitter liquid which comes up from the stomach into the mouth. **water buffalo,** *n.* large Asian animal, with a hump, which is used for farm work. **waterbutt,** *n.* barrel for collecting rainwater. **water cannon,** *n.* machine for sending strong jets of water (for dispersing rioters, etc.). **water closet,** *n.* (*formal*) lavatory. **watercolour,** *n.* (*a*) paint used by artists which is mixed with water, not oil. (*b*) picture painted in watercolours. **watercourse,** *n.* path of a stream/river. **watercress,** *n.* creeping plant grown in water and eaten in salads. **watered,** *adj.* (silk) with wavy markings in it. **waterfall,** *n.* fall of a river, etc., from a high level over the edge of a cliff. **waterfowl,** *n.pl.* birds which like to live around ponds and lakes (such as ducks/geese, etc.). **waterfront,** *n.* bank of a river/shore of the sea and the buildings along it. **waterhole,** *n.* pond in the desert, where wild animals come to drink. **water ice,** *n.* type of light ice cream made of water and flavouring. **watering,** *n.* (*a*) act of giving water. (*b*) **w. down** = dilution (of wine or spirits) by adding water. (*c*) filling of the eyes with water. **watering-can,** *n.* container with a long spout used for giving water to plants, etc. **watering hole,** *n.* *inf.* bar where a group of people often get together. **waterless,** *adj.* without water. **waterlevel,** *n.* level of water. **waterlily,** *n.* plant with round leaves and big flowers, growing in water. **waterline,** *n.* line where the water reaches on the hull of a ship. **waterlogged,** *adj.* very wet/full of water. **Waterloo,** *n.* *inf.* **to meet one's W.** = to have a disaster. **water-main,** *n.* principal pipe carrying water underground along a road, and into buildings. **waterman,** *n.* (*pl.* **-men**) man who ferries people in a rowing boat. **watermark,** *n.* (*a*) faint design put in paper to show who made it. (*b*) mark showing where the tide reaches. **watermeadow,** *n.* meadow often flooded by a river. **water-melon,** *n.* large juicy fruit with red flesh. **water-mill,** *n.* mill driven by the power of water running over a large wheel. **water pistol,** *n.* toy gun which squirts water when the trigger is pressed. **water-polo,** *n.* ball game played in water between two teams. **water-power,** *n.* power/energy of running water, used to drive machines. **waterproof. 1.** *adj.* which will not let water through. **2.** *n.* coat which will not let water through. **3.** *v.* to make (sth) waterproof. **water rat,** *n.* small mammal living in holes in a river bank. **watershed,** *n.* (*a*) high ground separating different rivers and the streams that run into them. (*b*) point where the situation changes permanently. **waterside,** *n.* bank of a river/lake/sea; houses which front a river/

lake/sea. **waterskier,** n. person who goes in for waterskiing. **water-skiing,** n. sport of gliding along the surface of water standing on a pair of skis pulled by a fast boat. **water softener,** n. chemical/device for removing the hardness in water. **watersplash,** n. place where a shallow stream flows over a road. **waterspout,** n. (a) pipe carrying rainwater away from a roof. (b) tornado at sea when the water rises in a high column. **water supply,** n. system of pipes/tanks, etc., bringing water to people's homes; amount of water in the system. **water table,** n. natural level of water below ground. **watertight,** adj. (a) fitting so tightly that water cannot get in or out. (b) (argument) so strong that it cannot be disproved. **water tower,** n. tower holding a large tank of water. **waterway,** n. canal or deep river along which boats can easily travel. **waterweed,** n. weed which grows in water. **waterwheel,** n. wheel which is turned by water and so makes a machine work. **waterwings,** n. inflatable rings attached to the arms of children learning to swim. **waterworks,** n. (a) buildings from which water is piped to houses and factories. (b) inf. urinary system; **to turn on the w.** = to cry. **watery,** adj. which has a lot of water.

watt [wɒt] n. standard unit of electrical power. **wattage** ['wɒtɪdʒ] n. amount of electricity in watts.

wattle ['wɒtl] n. (a) woven twigs/laths used to make light walls; **w. and daub** = type of medieval construction consisting of woven strips of wood covered with mud. (b) type of Australian tree. (c) fold of red skin hanging under the throat of some birds (such as turkeys).

wave [weɪv] **1.** n. (a) ridge on the surface of the sea. (b) up-and-down movement; **she gave me a w.** = she waved to me. (c) ridge on the surface; **permanent w.** = treatment which makes hair wave and curl. (d) sudden feeling (usu. affecting many people); sudden spell (of hot/cold weather). **2.** v. (a) to move up and down; **to w. to s.o.** = to signal to s.o. with the hand; **to w. s.o. aside** = to dismiss s.o. with a

movement of the hand; **to w. s.o. on** = to tell s.o. to go on by a movement of the hand. (b) to have/to make ridges on the surface. **waveband,** n. group of wavelengths which are close together. **waved,** adj. (of hair) treated to look wavy. **wavelength,** n. distance between similar points on radio waves; inf. **they're not on the same w.** = they do not understand each other at all. **wavy,** adj. (-ier, -iest) which goes up and down.

waver ['weɪvə] v. (a) to tremble/to move from side to side. (b) to hesitate. **waverer,** n. person who hesitates. **wavering,** adj. trembling/hesitant.

wax [wæks] **1.** n. (a) solid substance made by bees to build the cells of their honeycomb. (b) solid substance similar to this. **2.** v. (a) to put polish on (furniture, etc.). (b) (of the moon) to grow bigger. **waxen,** adj. pale (like wax). **waxwing,** n. small bird with bright marks on its wings. **waxworks,** n. exhibition of wax models of famous people. **waxy,** adj. (a) like wax. (b) yellowish (potatoes).

way [weɪ] **1.** n. (a) road/path; **to make your w. through a crowd** = to push through a crowd; **w. in** = entrance; **w. out** = exit; **by the w.** = incidentally/in passing; **by w. of** = (i) via;.(ii) as a sort of. (b) right direction/right road; **to go out of your w. to help s.o.** = to make a special effort to help s.o. (c) particular direction; **one-way street** = street where the traffic can only move in one direction. (d) method/means/manner; **she always gets her own w.** = she gets what she wants; **to have a w. with** = know how to amuse and please; **I know all his little ways** = I know all the odd little things he does; **w. out of a difficulty** = solution to a problem. (e) distance (from one place to another); **he'll go a long w.** = he will be very successful. (f) space in which s.o. wants to move. (g) state/condition; **in the ordinary w.** = usually; **out of the w.** = unusual; **in many ways** = in lots of aspects/points; **(in) no w.** = not at all. (h) progress/movement forwards; **under w.** = moving forwards; **to make your w. in the world** = to be successful; **to pay your w.** = to pay for yourself. **2.** adv. inf. away/far. **waybill,** n. list of goods/passengers carried. **wayfarer,** *n.* (*formal*) traveller. **waylay** [weɪˈleɪ] *v.* (**waylaid**) to wait for (s.o.) in order to attack/to ambush. **waymark,** *v.* to show a public path, using special signs. **way-out,** *adj. Sl.* strange/unusual. **wayside,** *adj. & n.* (referring to the) side of the road. **wayward,** *adj.* (child) who wants to do what he wants. **waywardness,** *n.* being difficult/uncontrollable.

WC [ˈdʌbljuːsiː] *n. short for* water closet.

we [wiː] *pron.* (*a*) referring to people who are speaking/to the person speaking and others. (*b*) *inf.* you.

weak [wiːk] *adj.* (**-er, -est**) (*a*) not strong in body or in character. (*b*) (*of a liquid*) watery/not strong. (*c*) not good at (a subject). (*d*) (*in grammar*) (verb) which forms its past tense using a suffix. **weaken,** *v.* to make/to become weak. **weak-kneed,** *adj.* soft/timid/cowardly. **weakling,** *n.* weak person. **weakly. 1.** *adj.* not strong. **2.** *adv.* not strongly/feebly. **weak-minded,** *adj.* not strong in character. **weakness,** *n.* (*a*) being weak. (*b*) *inf.* liking (**for**).

weal [wiːl] *n.* raised mark left on the skin by a blow from a whip or a stick.

wealth [welθ] *n.* (*a*) riches. (*b*) large amount. **wealthy,** *adj. & n.* (**-ier, -iest**) very rich (person).

wean [wiːn] *v.* to make (a baby) start to eat solid food after only drinking milk; **to w. s.o. off/away from sth** = to get s.o. to drop a (bad) habit.

weapon [ˈwepən] *n.* object with which you fight. **weaponry,** *n.* (*no pl.*) weapons.

wear [ˈweə] **1.** *n.* (*a*) act of carrying on your body as a piece of clothing; **normal w. and tear** = normal use. (*b*) clothes. (*c*) damage through much use. (*d*) ability to stand much use. **2.** *v.* (**wore** [wɔː]; **has worn** [wɔːn]) (*a*) to carry on your body as a piece of clothing. (*b*) to become damaged through much use. (*c*) to stand up to much use/to last a long time. (*d*) to have (an expression) or your face. (*f*) *inf.* to accept/to put up with (sth); **the boss won't wear it** = will never accept this suggestion. **wearable,** *adj.* able to be worn. **wear away, wear down,** *v.* to disappear/to make (sth) disappear by rubbing or

much use. **wearer,** *n.* person who wears clothes. **wearing,** *adj.* tiring. **wear off,** *v.* to disappear gradually; to make (sth) disappear. **wear on,** *v.* (*of time*) to pass. **wear out,** *v.* (*a*) to become useless through much use; to make (sth) become useless through much use. (*b*) **to wear yourself out/to be worn out** = to become tired through doing a lot.

weary [ˈwɪərɪ] **1.** *adj.* (**-ier, -iest**) very tired/tiring. **2.** *v.* to become tired/to make tired. **wearily,** *adv.* in a tired way. **weariness,** *n.* tiredness. **wearisome,** *adj.* tiring/boring.

weasel [ˈwiːzl] *n.* small animal with a long thin body and short legs, which kills and eats rabbits, etc.

weather [ˈweðə] **1.** *n.* state of the air and atmosphere at a certain time; **in all weathers** = in every sort of weather; **to make heavy w. of a job** = to have unnecessary difficulty in doing the job; **under the w.** = miserable/unwell. **2.** *v.* (*a*) (*of sea/frost/wind, etc.*) to wear down (rocks, etc.). (*b*) to season (planks of wood); to make (wood) suitable for use by leaving it outside for several years. (*c*) to survive (a storm/crisis). **weather-beaten,** *adj.* (*a*) marked by the weather. (*b*) (*of face*) tanned/made brown by the wind, rain and sun. **weather boarding,** *n.* overlapping boards of wood used for covering the sides of a building to protect them against bad weather. **weather bureau, weather centre,** *n.* office where the weather is forecast. **weathercock,** *n.* weather vane in the shape of a cock. **weather forecast, weather report,** *n.* description of the weather about to come in the next few hours or days. **weatherman,** *n.* (*pl.* **-men**) *inf.* expert who describes the coming weather, usu. on TV or radio. **weatherproof,** *adj.* able to keep out the wind and the rain. **weather station,** *n.* place where weather conditions are recorded. **weather strip(ping),** *n.* strip of plastic foam/of metal which is attached to the inside of a window frame to prevent draughts. **weather vane,** *n.* metal pointer on a high building which turns round to show the direction of the wind.

weave [wiːv] **1.** *n.* pattern of cloth;

way in which cloth has been woven.
2. *v.* (**wove** [wəʊv], **has woven**) (*a*) to
make cloth by winding threads in and
out. (*b*) to make (sth) by a similar
method, using straw, etc. (*c*) to twist
and turn. **weaver,** *n.* person who
weaves. **weaving,** *n.* action of making
cloth by winding threads in and out; *inf.*
to get weaving = to start work.

web [web] *n.* (*a*) thing that is woven.
(*b*) net spun by spiders. (*c*) skin between the toes of a water bird, etc.
webbed, *adj.* with skin between the
toes. **webbing,** *n.* strong tape used
in upholstery. **webfooted,** *adj.* with
webbed feet.

wed [wed] *v.* (**wedded**) (*a*) (*formal*) to
marry (s.o.); to become husband and
wife. (*b*) **to be wedded to an idea** = to
be firmly attached to an idea. **wedding,**
n. marriage ceremony; **silver/golden w.**
= anniversary of 25/50 years of marriage; **w. breakfast** = meal eaten after
the wedding ceremony. **w. ring** = ring
which is put on the finger during the
wedding ceremony. **wedlock,** *n.* being
married.

wedge [wedʒ] **1.** *n.* (*a*) V-shaped piece
of wood/metal, used for splitting wood;
thin end of the w. = small beginning
which will bring greater changes later.
(*b*) V-shaped piece. **2.** *v.* (*a*) to split with
a wedge. (*b*) to fix firmly with a wedge.
(*c*) to become tightly fixed.

Wednesday ['wenzdı, 'wedənzdeı] *n.*
third day of the week/day between
Tuesday and Thursday.

wee [wiː] **1.** *adj.* (*in Scotland*) very small.
2. *n.* (*child's word*) (*also* **wee-wee**)
urine. **3.** *v.* (*child's word*) (*also* **wee-
wee**) to urinate.

weed [wiːd] **1.** *n.* (*a*) plant that you
do not want in a garden. (*b*) (*old*)
weeds = black clothes worn by a widow.
(*c*) *inf.* weak person. (*d*) *inf.* tobacco;
Sl. marijuana. **2.** *v.* (*a*) to pull out
unwanted plants from. (*b*) **to w. out** = to
remove. **weedkiller,** *n.* chemical which
kills unwanted plants. **weedy,** *adj.*
(**-ier, -iest**) (*a*) covered with weeds. (*b*)
thin and weak (person).

week [wiːk] *n.* (*a*) period of seven
days. **a w. from now/a w. today** =
this day next week; **yesterday w.** =

a week ago yesterday. (*b*) part of
a seven day period; **he works a 35-
hour w.** = he works 35 hours every
week. **weekday,** *n.* any day of the
week except Sunday (and sometimes
Saturday). **weekend,** *n.* period from
Friday evening or Saturday morning
until Sunday evening. **weekly. 1.** *adv.*
& *adj.* once a week. **2.** *n.* magazine
published once a week.

weeny ['wiːnı] *adj. inf.* very small.

weep [wiːp] *v.* (**wept** [wept]) to cry.
weeping, *adj.* (*a*) crying. (*b*) (*of tree*)
with branches hanging down.

weevil ['wiːvl] *n.* type of beetle which
eats plants, grain, etc.

weft [weft] *n.* threads going across a
length of material.

weigh [weı] *v.* (*a*) to measure how
heavy sth is. (*b*) to have a certain
heaviness; **time weighs heavily on his
hands** = he has nothing to do. (*c*) **to
w. anchor** = to lift the anchor of a ship
in order to sail away. **weighbridge,**
n. large machine for weighing heavy
lorries and their goods. **weigh down,**
v. (*a*) to press down. (*b*) to make
(s.o.) gloomy. **weigh in,** *v.* (*of boxers/
jockeys*) to be weighed before a fight
or race. **weighing machine,** *n.* device
for weighing. **weigh up,** *v. inf.* to guess
rightly what s.o./sth is like; **to weigh up
the pros and cons** = to examine all the
arguments for and against.

weight [weıt] **1.** *n.* (*a*) heaviness (of
sth); **to lose/put on w.** = to get thinner/
fatter; **to pull your w.** = to do your best.
(*b*) piece of metal used to measure the
exact heaviness of sth else. (*c*) heavy
object; **that's a w. off my mind!** = I
no longer need to worry about that.
(*d*) importance; *inf.* **to throw your w.
about** = to use your authority in an
arrogant way. **2.** *v.* (*a*) to attach a
weight to (sth). (*b*) to add (a quantity)
to a sum to produce a certain result.
weighting, *n.* additional salary paid to
compensate for living in an expensive
area. **weightless,** *adj.* with no weight.
weightlessness, *n.* having no weight.
weightlifter, *n.* person who lifts heavy
weights as a sport. **weightlifting,** *n.*
sport of lifting heavy weights. **weighty,**
adj. (**-ier, -iest**) (*a*) heavy. (*b*) important
(problem, etc.).

weir ['wɪə] n. (a) small dam built across a river to control the flow of water. (b) fence across a lake or river to trap fish.

weird ['wɪəd] adj. (-er, -est) strange/odd. **weirdly,** adv. in a strange way. **weirdness,** n. being weird. **weirdo** ['wɪədəʊ] n. (pl. -os) inf. strange/odd person; person who behaves in a strange way.

welcome ['welkəm] 1. n. greeting/reception. 2. v. (a) to greet (s.o.) as he arrives. (b) to hear (news) with pleasure. 3. adj. (a) pleasing/received with pleasure. (b) (to) willingly permitted. (c) Am. inf. (as a reply to thank you) **you're w.** = it was a pleasure to do it.

weld [weld] 1. n. joint made by joining two pieces of metal together by first heating, then pressing. 2. v. to join (two pieces of metal) together by first heating, then pressing. **welder,** n. person/machine that welds metal. **welding,** n. process of joining two pieces of metal together; place where two pieces are welded.

welfare ['welfeə] n. happiness/comfort/freedom from want; **Welfare State** = state which looks after the health and wellbeing of its citizens; **child w.** = health and wellbeing of children.

welkin ['welkɪn] n. (old) sky.

well [wel] 1. n. (a) deep hole at the bottom of which is water or oil. (b) deep hole; space in the centre of a building where the staircase or lift is. (c) low part of a courtroom where clerks, etc., sit. 2. v. to w. up = to start to flow. 3. adv. (better, best) (a) in a good way/properly; to do w. = to prosper; to go w. = (i) to be successful/to have good results. (ii) to fit/to suit; to speak w. of = to praise/to say nice things about. (b) to a large degree; w. after 7 o'clock = a long time after 7 o'clock; pretty w. all the family = almost all the family; to be w. up in = to know a lot about (a subject). (c) lucky/desirable; you may w. be right = you probably are right; all's w. that ends w. = if the result is fine then everything is fine; to wish s.o. w. = to wish them good luck. (d) as well = also/too. 4. adj. healthy and in good condition. 5. inter. starting a sentence and meaning nothing in particular or showing surprise. **well-advised,** adj. wise. **well-appointed,** adj. luxuriously furnished. **well-balanced,** adj. steady/sensible. **well-behaved,** adj. good/having good manners. **wellbeing,** n. health and happiness. **well-born,** adj. of an aristocratic family. **well-bred,** adj. polite/well educated. **well-connected,** adj. with influential friends or family. **well-disposed,** adj. kindly. **well done,** adj. (meat) which has been cooked a long time. **well-earned,** adj. which has been deserved. **wellfounded,** adj. (fears) which are justified. **well-groomed,** adj. clean and tidy (person). **well-grounded,** adj. (fears) which are justified. **well-heeled,** adj. inf. rich. **well-informed,** adj. knowing a lot about a subject. **well-intentioned,** adj. (person) with good intentions. **well-knit,** adj. strong (body). **well-known,** adj. famous/known by many people. **well-mannered,** adj. polite/with good manners. **well-meaning,** adj. (person) who does sth with good intentions. **well-meant,** adj. (action) done with good intentions. **wellnigh,** adv. (formal) almost. **well-off,** adj. inf. rich. **well-oiled,** adj. Sl. drunk. **well-read,** adj. having read many books and therefore knowing a lot. **well-spoken,** adj. (person) who speaks politely and correctly. **well-timed,** adj. which happens at the right time. **well-to-do,** adj. inf. wealthy. **well-wisher,** n. person who is friendly towards another. **well-worn,** adj. used a lot.

wellington boots, wellingtons, inf. **wellies** ['welɪŋtən'buːts, 'welɪŋtənz, 'welɪz] n. pl. rubber waterproof boots.

Welsh [welʃ] 1. adj. referring to Wales; **W. rarebit** = toasted cheese on bread. 2. n. (a) pl. the **W.** = the people of Wales. (b) language spoken in Wales. 3. v. to w. = to leave without paying your debts; to w. on s.o. = to break a promise made to s.o. **Welshman, Welshwoman,** n. person from Wales.

welt [welt] n. (a) leather edging for attaching the upper part of a shoe to the sole. (b) strong edge to a piece of knitting. (c) weal.

welter ['weltə] n. confused mass. **welterweight,** n. medium weight in boxing between middleweight and lightweight.

wen [wen] n. tumour.

wench [wenʃ] n. (pl. **-es**) (old) young woman.

wend [wend] v. **to w. one's way** = to go.

went [went] v. see **go.**

wept [wept] v. see **weep.**

were [wɜː] v. see **be.**

werewolf ['wɪəwʊlf] n. (pl. **-wolves**) person who changes into a wolf.

west [west] 1. n. (a) one of the points of the compass, the direction in which the sun sets; **w. wind** = wind coming from the west. (b) **the W.** = the non-communist world. 2. adv. towards the west; inf. **gone w.** = broken; disappeared. **westbound,** adj. going towards the west. **West End,** n. the fashionable part of London, where the main shopping area is found. **westerly,** adj. (a) (wind) from the west. (b) towards the west. **western.** 1. adj. of the west. 2. n. novel/film about cowboys and Indians in the USA. **westerner,** n. person who lives in the west. **westernization,** n. act of westernizing. **westernize,** v. to make more European or American. **westernmost,** adj. furthest west. **West Indian,** n. & adj. (person) from the West Indies. **Westminster,** n. borough in London where the Houses of Parliament are situated; Parliament itself. **westward,** adj. towards the west. **westwards,** adv. towards the west.

wet [wet] 1. adj. (**wetter, wettest**) (a) covered or soaked with water or other liquid; **I'm w. through/soaking w.** = all my clothes are very wet; inf. **w. blanket** = person who spoils any fun. (b) rainy. (c) inf. dull/uninteresting/weak (person). 2. n. (a) rain. (b) inf. weak/moderate person. 3. v. (**wetted**) to dampen with water. **wetlands,** n. marshy areas which are often covered by water. **wetness,** n. being wet. **wetsuit,** n. suit worn by divers which keeps the body warm with a layer of warm water. **wetting,** n. soaking/getting wet.

wether ['weðə] n. castrated ram.

whack [wæk] 1. n. (a) hard, noisy blow. (b) inf. **let's have a w. at it!** = let's try to do it. 2. v. (a) to hit hard, making a loud noise. (b) to defeat (in a match). **whacked,** adj. (a) beaten. (b) inf. worn out/tired. **whacker,** n. inf. huge thing. **whacking.** 1. adj. inf. huge. 2. n. beating.

whale [weɪl] n. (a) huge sea mammal. (b) inf. **we had a w. of a time** = we enjoyed ourselves very much. **whaleboat,** n. boat used when hunting whales. **whalebone,** n. thin bone taken from the jaws of whales and formerly used in corsets. **whaler,** n. (a) boat used when hunting whales. (b) person who hunts whales. **whaling,** n. hunting of whales.

wharf [wɔːf] n. (pl. **wharfs/wharves** [wɔːvz]) place in a dock where a ship can tie up and load or unload. **wharfinger,** n. person who is in charge of a wharf.

what [wɒt] 1. adj. (a) that which. (b) (asking a question) which? **w. good is this to us?** = what is the use of this? (c) (showing surprise) how much/how great/how strange. 2. pron. (a) that which; **come w. may** = whatever happens. (b) (asking a question) which thing or things; **w. is the German for table?** = which is the German word meaning table? **what's the use of learning Latin?** = why learn Latin? **w. about stopping for lunch now?** = do you think we should stop for lunch now?; **w. did you say?/**(not polite) **w.?** = I didn't hear what you said, please say it again; **w. if?** = what will happen if; **he knows what's w.** = he knows what the situation is and what to do. 3. inter. showing surprise. **what's-it, what-d'you-call-it,** n. inf. thing of which you have forgotten the name for the moment. **whatever** [wɒt'evə] 1. pron. anything at all. 2. adj. (a) (strong form of **what**) (b) **none w.** = none at all. **what for,** pron. (a) why. (b) what is the purpose of. (c) inf. **to give s.o. what for** = to be angry with s.o. **whatnot,** n. (a) vague object/idea. (b) wooden stand with shelves for small books and ornaments. **whatsoever** [wɒtsəʊ'evə] adj. & pron. (strong form of **whatever**) **none w.** = none at all.

wheat [wiːt] n. cereal plant. **wheatear,** n. brown bird living in fields. **wheaten,**

adj. made of wheat. **wheatgerm**, *n.* central part of a grain of wheat. **wheatmeal**, *n.* brown flour containing most of the grain. **wheatsheaf**, *n.* large bundle of stalks of wheat bound together.

wheedle ['wi:dl] *v.* to ask s.o. for sth in a flattering way.

wheel [wi:l] **1.** *n.* (*a*) circular frame which turns around a central axis (as a support for cars/trains/bicycles, etc.). (*b*) any similar circular object; **steering w.** = wheel which the driver of a car holds and turns to follow the road; **to take the w.** = to drive; **potter's w.** = horizontal disc on which a potter throws the clay to make pottery. **2.** *v.* (*a*) to push along (sth) that has wheels. (*b*) **to w. round** = to turn around suddenly. (*c*) (*in army*) to change direction; **left w.!** = turn left! (*d*) to fly in circles. **gulls wheeling above the boats.** (*e*) **to w. and deal** = to negotiate to obtain concessions in business. **wheelbarrow**, *n.* small handcart used by builders and gardeners, which has one wheel in front, and two handles behind. **wheelbase**, *n.* distance between the front and rear axles of a car/lorry, etc. **wheelchair**, *n.* chair on wheels used by people who cannot walk. **wheeler-dealer**, *n.* businessman who lives by making deals. **wheelwright**, *n.* man who makes wheels.

wheeze [wi:z] **1.** *n.* (*a*) noisy breathing. (*b*) *inf.* clever trick. **2.** *v.* to breathe noisily and with difficulty. **wheezily**, *adv.* in a wheezy way. **wheeziness**, *n.* being wheezy. **wheezy**, *adj.* (person) who wheezes.

whelk [welk] *n.* type of edible sea snail.

whelp [welp] **1.** *n.* young of a dog. **2.** *v.* to give birth to a young dog.

when [wen] **1.** *adv.* (*asking a question*) at what time. **2.** *conj.* (*a*) at the time that. (*b*) if. **whenever** [we'nevə] *adv.* at any time than.

whence [wens] *adv.* (*formal*) from where.

where ['weə] **1.** *adv.* (*asking a question*) in/at/to what place? **whereabouts. 1.** *n. pl.* ['weərəbauts] place where s.o./sth is. **2.** *adv.* [weərə'bauts] in what place?

whereas [weər'æz] *conj.* on the other hand/while/in contrast with the fact that. **whereby** [weə'bai] *adv.* (*formal*) by which; according to which. **wherefore,** *conj. & adv.* (*old*) why. **wherein** [weər'in] *adv.* (*formal*) in which. **whereupon** [weərə'pɒn] *conj.* at that point/after that. **wherever** [weər'evə] *adv.* in every place. **wherewithal,** *n.* (*formal*) necessary money.

wherry ['weri] *n.* small rowing boat.

whet [wet] *v.* (**whetted**) (*a*) to sharpen (a knife). (*b*) **to w. your appetite** = to make you more interested in sth by giving you a little taste of it. **whetstone,** *n.* stone used to sharpen knives, etc.

whether ['weðə] *conj.* (*a*) if. (*b*) either.

whey [wei] *n.* liquid left when milk is made into cheese.

which [witʃ] **1.** *adj.* what (person/thing). **2.** *pron.* (*a*) (*asking a question*) what person/what thing. (*b*) (*only used with things not persons*) that/the thing that. **whichever,** *pron. & adj.* (*a*) anything that. (*b*) no matter which.

whiff [wif] *n.* slight smell.

while [wail] **1.** *n.* (*a*) length of time; **quite a w./a good w.** = a fairly long time; **once in a w.** = from time to time. (*b*) **to be worth w.** = to be worth doing. **2.** *v.* **to w. away the time** = to make the time pass while you are waiting for something. **3.** *conj.* (*a*) during/as long as. (*b*) although. (*c*) whereas/in contrast with. **whilst** [wailst] *conj.* while.

whim [wim] *n.* sudden wish or desire. **whimsical** ['wimzikl] *adj.* odd/fanciful. **whimsicality,** *n.* being whimsical. **whimsy,** *n.* strange/fanciful idea.

whimper ['wimpə] **1.** *n.* sad/weak cry. **2.** *v.* (*of small dogs*) to cry weakly.

whine [wain] **1.** *n.* complaint/moan. **2.** *v.* to moan/to complain in a long high voice.

whinge [windʒ] *v. inf.* to complain in a whining voice.

whinny ['wini] **1.** *n.* sound which a horse makes when pleased. **2.** *v.* (*of a horse*) to make a happy neigh.

whip [wip] **1.** *n.* (*a*) long, thin piece of leather fixed to a handle and used for hitting animals. (*b*) **party w.** = member of parliament whose job it is to keep order among members of his party. (c) instructions given by a party whip; **three-line w.** = the strictest instructions. (d) **instant w.** = sweet milk pudding made quickly by adding milk to a packet of powder. **2.** v. (**whipped**) (a) to hit with a whip. (b) to beat sharply. (c) to beat (cream) until it is firm. (d) to wind string round (the end of a piece of rope). (e) inf. to move quickly; **to w. out a gun** = to pull a gun out quickly. **whipcord,** n. type of corduroy. **whiphand,** n. advantage. **whiplash,** n. (a) piece of thin leather which is part of a whip. (b) neck injury, caused by the head moving back suddenly. **whip off,** v. to move quickly; to remove quickly. **whippersnapper,** n. boy/young man who is too sure of himself. **whipping,** n. beating. **whip round,** v. to turn round quickly. **whip-round,** n. inf. **to have a whip-round** = to ask everyone to give some money. **whip up,** v. to encourage/to make (sth) increase.

whippet ['wɪpɪt] n. breed of small thin dog trained for racing.

whirl [wɜ:l] **1.** n. (a) rapid turning movement. (b) giddy/dizzy feeling. **2.** v. (a) to turn round quickly/to spin. (b) to move quickly. **whirligig,** n. something which turns round rapidly (like a top). **whirlpool,** n. water which turns rapidly round and round. **whirlwind,** n. (a) wind blowing round and round in a circle. (b) confused rush; **w. engagement** = very rapid engagement before marriage.

whirr, Am. **whir** [wɜ:] n. noise of sth spinning round quickly. **2.** v. to make a spinning noise.

whisk [wɪsk] **1.** n. (a) swift movement. (b) light brush for removing dust. (c) kitchen utensil used for beating eggs/cream, etc. **2.** v. (a) to move quickly. (b) to beat (eggs/cream) very quickly.

whisker ['wɪskə] n. (a) long stiff hair at the side of an animal's mouth. (b) **whiskers** = moustache and beard on the side of a man's face. **whiskery,** adj. covered with whiskers.

whisky ['wɪskɪ] n. alcoholic drink (usu. made in Scotland), distilled from grain; glass of this drink. **whiskey** ['wɪskɪ]

n. whisky (made in Ireland and North America).

whisper ['wɪspə] **1.** n. (a) quiet sound/words quietly spoken. (b) rumour. **2.** v. (a) to speak very quietly. (b) to make a very quiet sound.

whist [wɪst] n. card game for four people; **w. drive** = competition of several games of whist played at the same time in a large room.

whistle ['wɪsl] **1.** n. (a) simple instrument played by blowing; **penny w./tin w.** = cheap metal flute. (b) small pipe which gives a loud shrill noise when blown. (c) musical sound made by almost closing the lips and blowing air through the small hole; **to wet one's w.** = to have a drink. **2.** v. (a) to blow through the lips and make a musical or shrill sound; inf. **you can w. for it** = you will never get it. (b) to make a shrill sound. **whistlestop tour.** n. Am. election tour where a candidate stops for a brief period in many different towns. **whistle up,** v. to create (sth) out of nothing.

whit [wɪt] n. very small amount; **not a w. more** = nothing more.

Whit [wɪt] adj. referring to Whitsun.

white [waɪt] **1.** adj. (-er, -est) colour of snow; **w. coffee** = coffee with milk; **white Christmas** = Christmas with snow on the ground. **2.** n. (a) colour of snow. (b) person whose skin is not black, brown, yellow or red. (c) light-coloured meat (on a chicken); **w. of an egg** = part of the egg which is not yellow. **white ant,** n. termite. **whitebait,** n. (pl. **whitebait**) small young fish eaten fried. **whitecollar worker,** n. office worker. **white elephant,** n. thing which is big and expensive but useless to its owner. **white ensign,** n. flag of the Royal Navy. **white flag,** n. symbol of surrender. **white goods,** n. household linen (sheets, pillowcases, etc.); household machines, such as refrigerators and washing machines, which are usually white. **white-haired,** adj. with white hair. **Whitehall,** n. inf. British Civil Service; **W. mandarins** = top civil servants. **white heat,** n. very high temperature, when white light is produced by heated metal. **white hot,**

adj. extremely hot. **White House,** *n.* house of the President of the USA; *inf.* the US government. **white knight,** *n.* person/company which rescues another threatened with a takeover. **white lie,** *n.* innocent lie. **whiten,** *v.* to make white. **whitener, whitening,** *n.* white liquid for making shoes, etc., white. **whiteness,** *n.* being white. **white out,** *n.* blinding conditions caused by wind and snow. **White Paper,** *n.* government report on a problem. **white sale,** *n.* sale of sheets/pillowcases, etc. **white slave,** *n.* white girl captured and sent abroad as a prostitute. **white slavery,** *n.* trade in white slaves. **white spirit,** *n.* turpentine substitute used for cleaning paint-brushes, etc. **whitewash. 1.** *n.* (*a*) mixture of water and lime used for painting the walls of houses. (*b*) attempt to cover up mistakes. **2.** *v.* (*a*) to paint with a mixture of water and lime. (*b*) to attempt to cover up (mistakes). **whitewood,** *n.* unpainted soft wood, such as pine. **whitish,** *adj.* quite white.

whither ['wɪðə] *adv.* (*formal*) to which place.

whiting ['waɪtɪŋ] *n.* (*pl.* **whiting**) type of small sea fish.

whitlow ['wɪtləʊ] *n.* infected spot near a nail.

Whitsun ['wɪtsən] *n.* Christian festival on the seventh Sunday after Easter.

whittle ['wɪtl] *v.* (*a*) to shape (a piece of wood) by cutting off small pieces with a knife. (*b*) **to w. sth away/down** = to make sth gradually smaller.

whiz [wɪz] *v.* (**whizzed**) to move very fast. **whiz-kid,** *n. inf.* brilliant young businessman.

who [hu:] *pron.* (*asking a question*) which person/which people? (*b*) the person/people that. **whodunit** [hu:'dʌnɪt] *n. inf.* detective story. **whoever,** *pron.* (*a*) anyone who/no matter who.

WHO *abbrev.* for World Health Organization.

whoa [wəʊ] *inter.* used to tell a horse to stand still.

whole [həʊl] **1.** *adj.* complete; not broken/not damaged; **he ate the w. cake** = he ate all the cake; **he ate the cake**

w. = he put it all in his mouth at once and ate it, without cutting it up. **2.** *n.* all; **as a w.** = altogether; **on the w.** = for the most part. **wholefood,** *n.* food, grown naturally, which has not been given artificial fertilizers, and has not been processed. **wholehearted,** *adj.* complete/total. **wholeheartedly,** *adv.* completely/totally. **whole life insurance,** *n.* insurance where a sum of money is paid when the insured person dies. **wholemeal,** *n.* brown flour containing all parts of the grain. **whole number,** *n.* number which is not a fraction. **wholesale. 1.** *n.* & *adj.* sale of goods in large quantities to shops which then sell them to people in small quantities. **2.** *adj.* in large quantities/on a large scale. **wholesaler,** *n.* person who buys and sells goods in large quantities. **wholesome,** ['həʊlsəm] *adj.* healthy/good; **w. food** = food that is good for your health. **wholesomeness,** *n.* being wholesome. **wholewheat,** *n.* brown flour containing all the grain. **wholly,** *adv.* completely/altogether.

whom [hu:m] *pron.* (*a*) (*formal*) (*object in questions*) which person/which persons. (*b*) (*object in statements*) the person/persons that.

whoop [wu:p] *n.* loud cry. **whoopee** [wʊ'pi:] *inter. showing excitement;* **to make w.** = to enjoy yourself noisily. **whooping cough** ['hu:pɪŋkɒf] *n.* children's illness which causes coughing and loud noises when the child tries to breathe. **whoops,** *inter. showing surprise.*

whoosh [wu:ʃ] *n.* sound of air blowing past.

whopper ['wɒpə] *n. inf.* (*a*) very large thing. (*b*) very big lie. **whopping,** *adj. inf.* very large.

whore ['hɔ:] *n.* (*formal*) prostitute.

whorl [wɜ:l] *n.* coiled/spiral shape.

whose [hu:z] *pron.* (*a*) (*asking a question*) of who. (*b*) belonging to who. **whosoever** [hu:səʊ'evə] *pron.* whoever.

why [waɪ] **1.** *adv.* (*asking a question*) for what reason. **2.** *n.* the reason. **3.** *inter. showing surprise.*

wick [wɪk] *n.* length of string in the middle of a candle/piece of material in an oil lamp which is lit and burns slowly.

wicked ['wɪkɪd] *adj.* very bad/very nasty. **wickedly,** *adv.* in a wicked way. **wickedness,** *n.* evil; being wicked.

wicker ['wɪkə] *n.* thin twigs used to make chairs or baskets. **wickerwork,** *n.* (*no pl.*) objects made of thin twigs woven together.

wicket ['wɪkɪt] *n.* (*a*) small door set in or next to a larger one (as in a castle gate or city wall). (*b*) *Am.* position on the counter in a post office/bank, etc. (*c*) (*in cricket*) set of three sticks put in the ground and used as the target; main playing area between two sets of these sticks; **slow/fast w.** = where the ball moves slowly/fast off the ground; *inf.* **a sticky w.** = an awkward/difficult situation. **wicket-keeper,** *n.* (*in cricket*) player standing behind the wicket to stop the balls that the batsman does not hit.

wide [waɪd] **1.** *adj.* (**-er, -est**) (*a*) stretching far from side to side. (*b*) measurement from side to side. (*c*) enormous (range). **2.** *adv.* (*a*) greatly/a long way apart/far. (*b*) **to fall w. of the target** = miss the target. **3.** *n.* (*in cricket*) ball which passes too far to the side of the wicket. **wide-angle,** *adj.* (lens) which takes in a wider area than an ordinary lens. **wide awake,** *adj.* very much awake/not at all sleepy. **widely,** *adv.* (*a*) greatly; **w. read** = (i) (book) which many people have read; (ii) (person) who has read many books. **widen,** *v.* to make larger/to become wide. **wideranging,** *adj.* (discussion) which covers a wide field of subjects. **widespread,** *adj.* far/over a large area.

widgeon ['wɪdʒn] *n.* (*pl.* **widgeon**) type of small wild duck.

widow ['wɪdəʊ] *n.* woman whose husband has died; **grass w.** = woman whose husband is away from home on business. **widowed,** *adj.* (woman) who has become a widow; (man) who has become a widower. **widower,** *n.* man whose wife has died; **grass w.** = man whose wife is away from home on business. **widowhood,** *n.* being a widow.

width [wɪdθ] *n.* (*a*) measurement from side to side. (*b*) piece of material (cut right across a roll).

wield ['wiːld] *v.* (*a*) to hold (sth), usu. by the handle, and use it. (*b*) to use/to control (power).

wiener ['wiːnə] *n. Am.* frankfurter. **wiener schnitzel,** *n.* veal escalope, fried in breadcrumbs.

wife [waɪf] *n.* (*pl.* **wives**) woman to whom a man is married. **wifely,** *adj.* like a wife.

wig [wɪg] *n.* false hair worn on the head. **wigging,** *n.* (*old*) *inf.* sharp rebuke.

wiggle ['wɪgl] *v. inf.* to move slightly up and down or from side to side. **wiggly,** *adj. inf.* wavy; (line) which goes up and down.

wigwam ['wɪgwæm] *n.* cone-shaped tent of the North American Indians.

wild [waɪld] **1.** *adj.* (**-er, -est**) (*a*) not tame/free to live naturally. (*b*) (plant) which is not a garden plant. (*c*) stormy/rough (sea/wind). (*d*) savage/angry/fierce (animal); *inf.* **to be w. with s.o.** = to be angry with s.o.; **to be w. with excitement** = to be over-excited; *inf.* **w. about** = very enthusiastic about. (*e*) rough/uncivilized (country). (*f*) rash/reckless (plan); badly aimed (shot). **2.** *n.* **in the w.** = in country which is uninhabited and where animals can live freely. **wildcat. 1.** *n.* small wild animal of the cat family. **2.** *adj.* risky/reckless; **w. strike** = unofficial strike/strike of workers without the union's permission. **wilderness** ['wɪldənəs] *n.* uncultivated/uninhabited country; desert. **wildfire,** *n.* **like w.** = very quickly. **wildfowl,** *n. pl.* wild birds shot for sport (such as ducks and geese). **wildfowler,** *n.* person who shoots wildfowl. **wild goose chase,** *n.* hopeless search. **wildlife,** *n.* (*no pl.*) birds/plants/animals living free, untouched by man; **w. park** = park where wild animals are allowed to run wild. **wildly,** *adv.* in a wild way; **w. inaccurate** = completely wrong. **wildness,** *n.* being wild.

wildebeest ['wɪldɪbiːst] *n.* large African antelope.

wiles [waɪlz] *n. pl.* clever tricks.

wilful ['wɪlfəl] *adj.* (*a*) (person) determined to do what he wants. (*b*) done on purpose; **w. murder** = murder which was planned. **wilfully,** *adv.* intentionally/on purpose.

will [wɪl] **1.** *n.* (*a*) strength of mind and character; **to work with a w.** = to work very hard and earnestly. (*b*) wish; **of one's own free w.** = not forced; **at w.** = as you wish. (*c*) written instructions made by s.o. as to what should happen to his belongings when he dies. **2.** *v.* (*a*) **to w. s.o. to do sth** = to suggest strongly to s.o. else by power of mind. (*b*) to leave (your belongings) after death to others by writing down your wishes. **3.** *v.* (*used with an infinitive*) (*a*) to wish; **I won't have it!** = I will not allow it. (*b*) (*polite form of asking someone to do something*) **would you please sit down?/ won't you sit down?** (*c*) (*stressed*) to be certain to happen. **4.** *used with verbs forming future tense.* **willing. 1.** *adj.* wanting (**to** do sth); eager (**to** help). **2.** *n.* eagerness to help; **to show w.** = to show you are ready to help. **willingly,** *adv.* eagerly. **willingness,** *n.* eagerness. **willpower,** *n.* strength of will.

willies ['wɪlɪz] *n. pl. inf.* **it gives me the w.** = it makes me scared.

will-o'-the-wisp ['wɪləðəwɪsp] *n.* bluish light caused in marshes by burning methane gas.

willow ['wɪləʊ] *n.* tree with thin supple branches often found along river banks. **willowherb,** *n.* common weed with tall spikes of pink flowers. **willow pattern,** *n.* china with a blue and white Chinese design on it. **willowy,** *adj.* tall and slender.

willy-nilly [wɪlɪ'nɪlɪ] *adv.* whether you want to or not.

wilt [wɪlt] **1.** *n.* disease of plants which makes them droop. **2.** *v.* to become weak and droop.

wily ['waɪlɪ] *adj.* (**-ier,-iest**) crafty/full of tricks. **wiliness,** *n.* being wily.

wimp [wɪmp] *n.* weak individual.

wimple ['wɪmpl] *n.* linen covering worn by nuns over their heads.

win [wɪn] **1.** *n.* action of beating s.o. in a competition/game. **2.** *v.* (**won** [wʌn]) (*a*) to defeat s.o. in a contest/race, etc.; to be first in a race/competition. (*b*) to gain/to get (a prize). **win back,** *v.* to get back/to regain. **winner,** *n.* (*a*) person who has won a race/a prize, etc. (*b*) *inf.* thing which is (certain to be) successful. **winning. 1.** *adj.* (*a*) which wins. (*b*) attractive (smile). **2.** *n.* (*a*) victory; **w. post** = post which marks the end of the race. (*b*) **winnings** = money, etc., which has been won at a game of chance. **win over,** *v.* to persuade. **win through,** *v.* to succeed in the end after many difficulties.

wince [wɪns] **1.** *n.* movement which shows you feel pain. **2.** *v.* to show signs of pain, esp. by moving the face.

winceyette [wɪnsɪ'et] *n.* soft cotton material, often used for night clothes.

winch [wɪntʃ] **1.** *n.* (*pl.* **-es**) device which pulls things up by winding a rope around a drum. **2.** *v.* to pull up/to lift by using a winch.

wind¹ [wɪnd] **1.** *n.* (*a*) moving air; **in high winds** = in very strong winds; **head w.** = wind blowing straight towards the face; **in the teeth of the w.** = against the wind; *inf.* **to go like the w.** = to run quickly; *inf.* **to get/to have the w. up** = to be frightened; *inf.* **to put the w. up s.o.** = to frighten s.o.; **to sail close to the w.** = (i) to sail a boat almost directly into the wind; (ii) to be very near to being dishonest or rude; **to take the w. out of s.o.'s sails** = to spoil s.o.'s plans, usually by doing what he was going to do. (*b*) breath; **to get your second w.** = to get enough breath again after being tired; to be able to make a second effort. (*c*) smell/scent, when hunting; **to get w. of** = to hear a rumour about. (*d*) gas in the stomach. (*e*) (*also* **wind instruments, wind section**) woodwind instruments in an orchestra. **2.** *v.* (*a*) to make (s.o.) breathless, esp. by hitting him in the chest. (*b*) to smell/scent when hunting. **windbag,** *n. inf.* person who talks too much. **windbreak,** *n.* fence/hedge which protects sth against the wind. **windburn,** *n.* inflammation of the skin caused by cold wind. **windcheater,** *Am.* **windbreaker,** *n.* short jacket, often with a hood, to keep out the wind. **windchill factor,** *n.* air temperature including the effect of the wind. **windfall,** *n.* (*a*) fruit which has been blown to the ground from a fruit tree. (*b*) unexpected good fortune. **wind gauge,** *n.* instrument for measuring the force of the wind. **windjammer,**

n. (*old*) large sailing ship. **windless,** *adj.* with no wind. **windmill,** *n.* mill driven by sails pushed around by the wind. **windpipe,** *n.* pipe leading from the nose and mouth to the lungs. **windscreen,** *n.* glass window in the front of a car/lorry, etc. **windshield,** *n.* (*a*) screen on a motorcycle. (*b*) *Am.* windscreen. **windsock,** *n.* tube of material at the end of a tall pole, which shows the direction of the wind at an airfield. **windsurfer,** *n.* person who does windsurfing. **windsurfing,** *n.* sport of riding on the sea on a surfboard with a sail attached. **windswept,** *adj.* blown by strong winds. **windward,** *adj., adv. & n.* (side of a ship) from which the wind blows. **windy,** *adj.* (**-ier, -iest**) (*a*) having much wind. (*b*) *inf.* cowardly.

wind² [waɪnd] **1.** *n.* bend/twist/turn. **2.** *v.* (**wound** [waʊnd]) (*a*) to turn. (*b*) to roll up/to roll round. (*c*) to turn a key of (a watch/clock) until the spring is tight. **winding. 1.** *adj.* turning/twisting. **2.** *n.* action of turning/rolling. **wind up,** *v.* (*a*) to roll up. (*b*) to tighten a spring on a watch/clockwork toy, etc. (*c*) to finish; to put (a company) into liquidation. (*d*) *inf.* **to be wound up** = to be nervous/tense.

windlass ['wɪndləs] *n.* (*pl.* **-es**) hand winch for pulling sth up by winding a rope round a drum.

window ['wɪndəʊ] *n.* (*a*) opening in a wall/door, etc., filled with glass; **stained-glass w.** = window made of small pieces of coloured glass, found esp. in churches; **w. of opportunity** = short moment when the conditions for something are especially favourable. (*b*) section of a computer screen reserved for a special purpose. **window box,** *n.* long box for plants kept on an outside windowsill. **window dressing,** *n.* (*a*) displaying goods in an artistic way in a shop window. (*b*) putting on a display to hide the real state of affairs. **windowledge, windowsill,** *n.* ledge/flat piece of wood, etc., inside and outside a window. **window-pane,** *n.* single piece of glass, used as part of a whole window. **window shopping,** *n.* looking at goods in shop windows without buying them.

wine [waɪn] **1.** *n.* (*a*) alcoholic drink made from the juice of grapes; **w. list** = list of wines which are available at a restaurant. (*b*) alcoholic drink made from the juice of fruit or flowers. **2.** *v.* **to w. and dine s.o.** = to take s.o. out for an expensive dinner and drinks. **wine cellar,** *n.* cool room underground where wine is kept. **wineglass,** *n.* glass used for drinking wine. **wine-growing,** *adj.* (district) where vines are grown to produce wine. **wine merchant,** *n.* person who sells wines and spirits in a shop. **wine waiter,** *n.* person in charge of serving the wines in a restaurant.

wing [wɪŋ] **1.** *n.* (*a*) one of the two limbs which a bird/butterfly, etc., used to fly; to take s.o. under your w. = to protect/look after. (*b*) one of the two flat projecting parts on an aircraft. (*c*) side part of a large building which leads off the main part. (*d*) part of a car body which covers the wheel. (*e*) part of an army which stretches to one side; part of a political party which has a certain tendency. (*f*) group of squadrons in the air force; **w. commander** = rank in the air force below group captain. (*g*) **wings** = side of the stage in a theatre where actors wait before going on stage. (*h*) **wings** = pilot's badge. (*i*) side of a football/hockey pitch. (*j*) (*in football/hockey*) forward player on the side of the pitch. **2.** *v.* (*a*) to fly. (*b*) to shoot (in the wing/arm). **winged,** *adj.* with wings. **winger,** *n.* (*a*) forward player on the side of the pitch in football/hockey. (*b*) *suffix showing* person on the right/left of a political party. **wingless,** *adj.* having no wings. **wing nut,** *n.* nut with two projecting parts for screwing easily. **wingspan,** *n.* distance from the tip of one wing to the tip of another (of a bird/aircraft, etc.).

wink [wɪŋk] **1.** *n.* act of quickly shutting and opening one eye; *inf.* **to have forty winks** = to have a short sleep; *inf.* **to tip s.o. the w.** = to warn s.o. of sth. **2.** *v.* (*a*) to shut one eye and then quickly open it again. (*b*) (*of lights/stars*) to shine on and off. **winker,** *n.* flashing light (on a car).

winkle ['wɪŋkl] **1.** *n.* edible snail which lives in salt water. **2.** *v.* **to w. sth out** = to get sth out with difficulty.

winnow ['wɪnəʊ] v. to separate the grain from chaff, by allowing the wind to blow the chaff away.

winsome ['wɪnsəm] adj. pleasant/charming.

winter ['wɪntə] 1. n. coldest season of the year; w. **sports** = sports which are played on snow or ice. 2. v. to spend the cold months of the year. **wintry**, adj. like winter; unfriendly/cold (smile).

wipe [waɪp] 1. n. act of cleaning or drying with a cloth. 2. v. to clean/to dry with a cloth. **wipe away**, v. to clean away. **wipe out**, v. (a) to clean and dry the inside of (sth). (b) to kill/to destroy. **wiper**, n. thing that wipes; device on a car which wipes rain away from the windscreen; **rear w.** = device for wiping the rain from the rear window of a car.

wire ['waɪə] 1. n. (a) thin metal line or thread; w. **netting** = pieces of wire twisted together to make a net, used as a fence; **barbed w.** = wire with sharp pieces of metal twisted in at intervals, used to stop animals or people from getting in or out; **live w.** = (i) wire which carries an electrical current; (ii) person who is full of energy; **telegraph/telephone w.** = wire along which telegraph/telephone messages are sent; inf. **we must have got our wires crossed** = we must have misunderstood each other; **w. service** = news agency sending news to subscribers by teleprinter; **w. tapping** = listening to other people's telephone conversations with special equipment. (b) inf. telegram. 2. v. (a) to fasten with wires. (b) to put in wires to carry electricity to (a house). (c) to send a telegram. **wireless**. 1. n. radio. 2. adj. without wires. **wireworm**, n. type of small insect which attacks plants. **wiring**, n. system of wires used to carry electricity. **wiry**, adj. (-ier, -iest) (a) (of person) thin but strong. (b) (of hair) stiff and strong, not easily combed.

wisdom ['wɪzdəm] n. intelligence/knowledge/common sense; **w. tooth** = one of four back teeth which grow when you are an adult.

wise [waɪz] adj. (-er, -est) having intelligence and common sense/knowing a great deal/prudent; **no one will be any the wiser** = no one will know anything about it; **I'm none the wiser** = I know no more than I did before. **wisecrack**. 1. n. clever remark. 2. v. to make a joke/a wisecrack. **wise guy**, n. person who pretends to know more than anyone else. **wisely**, adv. (a) in a wise way. (b) prudently.

wish [wɪʃ] 1. n. (pl. -es) want/desire. (b) **good wishes** = kind feelings/greetings. 2. v. (a) to want/to desire sth which is unlikely to happen. (b) to express a desire or a hope. **wishbone**, n. V-shaped bone in a chicken's breast, which you are supposed to pull with your partner, the person who holds the larger piece being in luck. **wishful**, adj. **w. thinking** = believing sth because you would like it to happen.

wishy-washy ['wɪʃiwɒʃi] adj. watery; not strong (colour/character, etc.).

wisp [wɪsp] n. small strand; little piece. **wispy**, adj. thin/slight.

wistaria, **wisteria** [wɪ'steərɪə, wɪ-'stɪərɪə] n. climbing plant with sweet-smelling blue flowers.

wistful ['wɪstfəl] adj. longing for sth, but sad as there is no hope of getting it. **wistfully**, adv. in a wistful way. **wistfulness**, n. being wistful.

wit [wɪt] 1. n. (a) (usu. wits) intelligence; **at your wit's ends** = not knowing what to do next; **to keep your wits about you** = to keep calm in a difficult situation and think hard what to do next. (b) ability to say clever/funny things. (c) person who says clever and funny things. 2. v. (old) **to w.** = namely/that is.

witch [wɪtʃ] n. (pl. -es) woman believed to have evil magic powers. **witchcraft**, n. art of magic. **witch doctor**, n. man in a primitive tribe who appears to cure illnesses by magic. **witchery**, n. witchcraft. **witch hazel**, n. shrub with tiny yellow flowers blooming in early spring. **witch hunt**, n. cruel investigation of people who are supposed to be politically unreliable.

with [wɪð, wɪθ] prep. (a) accompanied by/together/beside. (b) having/possessing. (c) in spite of (faults). (d) using; **pouring w. rain** = raining hard. (e) from/because of. (f) showing (an emotion). (g) (used after many verbs to show a connection) **to part w. sth** = to give

sth away; **to meet w.** = to have/to experience unexpectedly; **I can do nothing w. him** = I can't change him; **to
have nothing to do w.** = to have no
connection with; **I'm w. you there!** =
(i) I agree with you! (ii) I understand
you; *inf.* **to be w. it** = to be fashionable/
modern.

withdraw [wɪθ'drɔ:] *v.* (**withdrew; withdrawn**) to move back/to take back/
to pull back; to take (money) out of
a bank account; to retract (sth which
has been said). **withdrawal,** *n.* taking
back; removing of money (from a bank
account); **w. symptoms** = symptoms
shown by s.o. who is trying to stop taking a drug/smoking, etc. **withdrawn,**
adj. shy; (person) who does not like
meeting other people.

wither ['wɪðə] *v.* (a) (*of plants*) to
grow weaker and dry up. (b) to make
(sth) grow weaker and dry up; to
make (s.o.) feel embarrassed by looking disapprovingly. **withering,** *adj.*
scornful/disapproving (look).

withers ['wɪðəz] *n. pl.* part of a horse's
back just below the neck.

withhold [wɪθ'həʊld] *v.* (**withheld**) to
keep back/to refuse to give.

within [wɪ'ðɪn] *prep.* inside.

without [wɪ'ðaʊt] *prep.* not having/not
with; **to go w.** = not to have (sth); **it
goes w. saying that** = it hardly needs to
be said that.

withstand [wɪθ'stænd] *v.* (**withstood**) to
resist/to endure.

withy ['wɪðɪ] *n.* thin willow twig used to
tie things together.

witness ['wɪtnəs] **1.** *n.* (*pl.* **-es**) (a) person who sees sth happening. (b) **to
bear w. to** = to be evidence of. (c)
person who witnesses s.o.'s signature.
2. *v.* (a) to see (sth) happen. (b) to
sign your name on a legal paper to say
that s.o.'s signature is genuine. (c) to
give evidence in court. **witness-box,**
Am. **witness stand,** *n.* place where a
witness stands in a law court.

wittingly ['wɪtɪŋlɪ] *adv.* on purpose/in-
tentionally.

witty ['wɪtɪ] *adj.* (**-ier, -iest**) clever and
funny. **witticism** ['wɪtɪsɪzəm] *n.* clever/
funny remark.

wives [waɪvz] *n. see* **wife.**

wizard ['wɪzəd] *n.* (a) man who is
believed to have magic powers. (b)
clever person/expert. **wizardry,** *n.* being a wizard; cleverness.

wizened ['wɪzənd] *adj.* dried up and
wrinkled (face).

woad [wəʊd] *n.* wild plant with blue
flowers, used to make a blue dye.

wobble ['wɒbl] **1.** *n.* shaking movement. **2.** *v.* to shake/to move unsteadily.
wobbly, *adj.* unsteady/shaking.

wodge [wɒdʒ] *n. inf.* thick piece.

woe [wəʊ] *n.* sadness/trouble. **woe-
begone,** *adj.* very sad (look). **woeful,**
adj. full of sadness. **woefully,** *adv.*
sadly; *inf.* totally.

wog [wɒg] *n. Sl.* foreigner.

woke, woken [wəʊk, wəʊkn] *v. see*
wake.

wold [wəʊld] *n.* (*used in place names*)
area of gently rounded hills.

wolf [wʊlf] **1.** *n.* (*pl.* **wolves**) (a) wild animal like a dog, usu. living in a large
group in cold northern regions; **pack
of wolves** = group of wolves living together; **lone w.** = person who prefers
to be alone/who does not associate
with other people; **she-wolf** = female
wolf; **w. cub** = young wolf; **w. in
sheep's clothing** = person who seems
inoffensive but really is wicked; **to
keep the w. from the door** = to have
enough food to live on; **to cry w.**
= to raise a false alarm. (b) *inf.*
man who chases women; **w. whistle** =
whistle of admiration given by men as
a pretty woman passes. **2.** *v.* to eat
quickly. **wolfhound,** *n.* large hunting
dog. **wolfish,** *adj.* like a wolf.

wolverine ['wʊlvəri:n] *n.* dark-furred
North American carnivorous mammal.

woman ['wʊmən] *n.* (*pl.* **women**
['wɪmɪn]) (a) female adult human being; *inf.* fussy old man; **Women's Lib**
= movement to free women so that
they can have equal status in society. (b) female. **womanhood,** *n.*
state of being a woman. **womanish,**
adj. (man) who behaves like a
woman. **womanize,** *v.* to try to
seduce women often. **womanizer,** *n.*
man who womanizes. **womankind,** *n.*
all women. **womanliness,** *n.* being
womanly. **womanly,** *adj.* feminine,

like a woman. **womenfolk,** *n. pl.* all women (in a family, etc.).

womb [wu:m] *n.* uterus.

wombat ['wɒmbæt] *n.* small Australian animal.

won [wʌn] *v. see* **win.**

wonder ['wʌndə] **1.** *n.* (*a*) amazing thing; **no w.** = it isn't surprising. (*b*) astonishment/surprise. **2.** *v.* (*a*) to be surprised/to marvel (**at**). (*b*) to want to know/to ask someone (why). (*c*) (*used when asking someone politely to do something*) **I w. if you could open the door. wonderful,** *adj.* marvellous/very good/exciting. **wonderfully,** *adv.* in a wonderful way. **wonderland,** *n.* marvellous place. **wonderment,** *n.* astonishment/wonder. **wondrous,** *adj.* (*old*) wonderful.

wonky ['wɒŋkɪ] *adj.* (**-ier, -iest**) *inf.* unsteady/wobbly.

wont [wəʊnt] *n.* (*formal*) habit; **as is his w.** = as he usually does. **wonted,** *adj.* (*formal*) habitual.

won't [wəʊnt] *v. see* **will.**

woo [wu:] *v.* to try to attract (a woman) to marry you; to try to get (s.o.) to support you/to vote for you, etc. **wooer,** *n.* person who woos.

wood [wʊd] *n.* (*a*) large group of trees/small forest; **not to see the w. for the trees** = concentrate on the details, and not appreciate the main problem; **we're not out of the w. yet** = our problems are not over. (*b*) material that a tree is made of. **woodbine,** *n.* wild climbing plant. **woodburning stove,** *n.* stove which is designed to use wood as a fuel. **woodcarving,** *n.* (i) art of sculpture in wood; (ii) wooden sculpture. **woodchuck,** *n.* North American rodent. **woodcock,** *n.* small brown bird shot for sport or food. **woodcraft,** *n.* skill at finding your way about woods and forests and living in them. **woodcut,** *n.* print made from a carved wooden plate. **wooded,** *adj.* covered in trees. **wooden,** *adj.* (*a*) made of wood. (*b*) stiff/showing no feeling. **woodenly,** *adv.* stiffly. **woodland,** *n.* country covered in woods. **woodlouse,** *n.* (*pl.* **-lice**) very small animal with a hard shell, which curls up when attacked, and lives in

rotten wood, etc. **woodpecker,** *n.* bird with a long sharp beak which finds insects under the bark of trees. **woodpigeon,** *n.* common wild pigeon. **wood pulp,** *n.* fragments of wood made into a pulp, used for making paper. **woodshed,** *n.* small shed/hut used for storing wood. **wood(s)man,** *n.* (*pl.* **-men**) man who works in woods and forests. **woodwind,** *n.* wind instruments in an orchestra which are usu. made of wood. **woodwork,** *n.* (*a*) carpentry. (*b*) wooden parts of a building. **woodworm,** *n.* small grub which bores holes in wood. **woody,** *adj.* (**-ier, -iest**) like wood; made of wood.

woof [wʊf] **1.** *n.* (*a*) weft. (*b*) sound of a dog's bark. **2.** *v.* (*of dog*) to bark. **woofer,** *n.* loudspeaker which reproduces low sounds.

wool [wʊl] *n.* (*a*) short, thick hair of a sheep/goat, etc. (*b*) long threads of twisted hair, used to make clothes/carpets, etc.; cloth woven from hair; **to pull the w. over s.o.'e eyes** = to deceive s.o. (*c*) material which looks like sheep's wool; **cotton w.; steel w. wool-gathering,** *n.* daydreaming/not thinking of what you are doing. **woollen,** *adj.* made of wool. **woollens,** *n. pl.* clothing made of knitted wool. **wooliness,** *n.* being woolly. **woolly, 1.** *adj.* (**-ier, -iest**) (*a*) made of wool/like wool. (*b*) vague/not clear. **2** *n. inf.* cardigan/jumper. **woolsack,** *n.* large cushion on which the Lord Chancellor sits.

woozy ['wu:zɪ] *adj. inf.* dizzy/in a daze.

word [wɜːd] **1.** *n.* (*a*) unit of speech either spoken or written; **to have words with s.o.** = to quarrel with s.o.; **to have a w. with s.o.** = to have a short talk with s.o.; **in other words** = explaining sth in a different way; **you've taken the words out of my mouth** = you've said what I was going to say; **without a w.** = without speaking; **for w.** = exactly as is said or written. (*b*) message/news; **by w. of mouth** = by spoken message. (*c*) promise; **to give one's w.** = to promise; **he kept his w.** = he did what he promised to do; **I'll take your w. for it** = I'll believe what you say. (*d*) **my w.!** *inter. expressing* sur-

prise. (e) **w. of command** = order. **2.**
v. to put in words, either written or
spoken. **wordily**, *adv.* in a wordy way.
wordiness *n.* being wordy. **wording**,
n. choice of words. **word-perfect**, *adj.*
able to repeat exactly what has been
learnt. **word processor**, *n.* typewriter
with a computer memory and a screen
on which the text can be displayed.
wordy, *adj.* (**-ier, -iest**) *adj.* using too
many words.
wore ['wɔː] *v. see* wear.
work [wɜːk] **1.** *n.* (a) mental or physical
activity; **to have one's w. cut out** = find
it difficult (to do sth). (b) job; **out of
w.** = with no job. (c) thing that has
been made by s.o. (d) **works** = factory.
(e) **road works** = repairs to a road. (f)
works = moving parts of a machine;
inf. **to give s.o. the works** = to give
s.o. everything/the full treatment. **2.**
v. (a) to use energy/to make s.o. use
energy in carrying out an activity. (b)
(*of machine*) to operate/to move. (c)
to make (a machine) function. (d) to
have a job. (e) to be successful. (f)
to embroider/to sew. (g) **to w. one's
way** = to move gradually; **he was working himself into a rage** = he was becoming more and more angry. (h) to
take coal/copper, etc., from (a mine);
worked out = (mine) where all the ore
has been extracted. **workable**, *adj.* able
to be worked. **workaday**, *adj.* plain/
ordinary. **workaholic**, *n. inf.* person
who cannot stop working. **workbook**,
n. book of excercises to help teach
a subject. **worked up**, *adj.* excited/
annoyed (**about**). **worker**, *n.* (a) person who works. (b) member of the
working class. (c) type of female bee
which works to provide the queen with
honey, but which is sterile. **workforce**,
n. all the workers (in a factory).
workhorse, *n.* person who can work
hard. **workhouse**, *n.* (old) place where
poor people were made to live and
work. **working. 1.** *adj.* which works;
referring to work; **w. party** = group
of experts who investigate a certain
problem and report on it; **w. class** =
people who work with their hands/who
earn wages not salaries. **2.** *n.* (*usu.
pl.* **workings**) (a) place where min-

eral has been dug. (b) way sth works.
workman, *n.* (*pl.* **-men**) man who
works with his hands. **workmanlike**,
adj. skilful/expert. **workmanship**, *n.*
skill of a good workman. **work off**, *v.*
to get rid of (sth) by working. **work
on**, *v.* (a) to continue to work. (b)
to be busy doing sth. (c) to try to
influence/to persuade. **work out**, *v.*
(a) to succeed/to do well. (b) to plan
(sth) in detail/to find an answer to
(sth). (c) (**at**) to amount to (a price).
workout, *n.* exercise/practice before
a sports contest. **workroom**, *n.* room
where work is done. **work-sharing**, *n.*
arrangement where two people work
part-time to do one job. **workshop**,
n. place where things are made in
a small factory or house. **workshy**,
adj. reluctant to work. **workspace**,
n. memory available on a computer
for current use. **workstation**, *n.* desk
with terminal, monitor, keyboard, etc.,
where a computer operator works.
work to rule, *v.* to protest by working
strictly according to the rules laid down,
in such a way that the work is done
excessively slowly. **worktop**, *n.* top of a
kitchen cupboard, etc., for working on.
work up, *v.* to develop/to reach slowly.
world [wɜːld] *n.* (a) the earth; particular part of the earth; **the Old W.**
= Europe, Asia and Africa; **the New
W.** = North and South America; **the
Third W.** = countries with no strong
connections to the superpowers; **W.
War** = war in which many countries
all over the world take part. (b) people
on Earth; everything; **to come into the
w.** = to be born; **to be all alone in
the w.** = to have no family; **out of
this w.** = magnificent; **to think the w.
of s.o.** = to think very highly of s.o.;
it will do you the w. of good = it
will help you greatly. (c) people with
a particular interest/things which form
a particular group. **world-famous**,
adj. known everywhere. **worldliness**,
n. being worldly/not being idealistic.
worldly, *adj.* (a) of the material world.
(b) not idealistic. **worldly-wise**, *adj.*
wise about worldly things. **worldwide**,
adj. & adv. throughout the whole
world.

worm [wɜːm] **1.** n. (a) small, spineless burrowing creature which looks like a very small snake and lives in earth. (b) similar animal which lives in the intestines of animals. (c) woodworm. (d) spiral thread of a screw. **2.** v. to move slowly like a worm; **to w. yourself into s.o.'s favour** = to make s.o. like you by being especially nice to them; **to w. information out of s.o.** = to get information by asking many persistent questions. **wormcast,** n. small pile of earth thrown up by a worm. **wormeaten,** adj. which has been eaten by woodworms. **wormwood,** n. bitter plant.

worn [wɔːn] adj. much used; see also **wear. worn out,** adj. (a) used so much that it is now useless. (b) tired.

worry ['wʌrɪ] **1.** n. (a) thing which makes you anxious. (b) being anxious. **2.** v. (a) to be upset/anxious; to make (s.o.) upset/anxious. (b) (of dogs) to shake and tear with the teeth; **to w. sheep** = to chase and attack sheep. **worried,** adj. anxious/troubled. **worrier,** n. person who worries. **worrisome,** adj. which makes you worried/anxious.

worse [wɜːs] **1.** adj. (a) more bad. (b) more ill. **2.** n. more awful thing. **3.** adv. more badly. **worsen,** v. to become or make worse. **worse off,** adj. with less money.

worship ['wɜːʃɪp] **1.** n. (a) praise and honour shown to God. (b) praise and honour shown to s.o./sth. (c) **Your W.** = title of respect used when speaking to a mayor or a magistrate in a law court. **2.** v. (worshipped) (a) to praise and love (God). (b) to take part in a church service. (c) to praise and love (s.o./sth). **worshipper,** n. person who worships; **sun w.** = person who loves sunbathing.

worst [wɜːst] **1.** adj. very bad/worse than anyone/anything else. **2.** n. most awful thing. **3.** adv. very badly/worse than anyone/anything else.

worsted ['wʊstɪd] n. fine woollen cloth.

worth [wɜːθ] **1.** adj. (a) having a value/price. (b) useful; giving satisfaction; **it is w. (your) while** = it is worth the effort. (c) having riches/money, etc; **for all you are w.** = as much as possible.

2. n. value. **worthily,** adv. in a worthy way. **worthiness,** n. being worthy. **worthless,** adj. having no worth/no use. **worthwhile** [wɜːθ'waɪl] adj. which is worth doing. **worthy** ['wɜːðɪ] **1.** adj. (-ier, -iest) deserving. **2.** n. notable person (in a town).

would [wʊd] v. see **will.**

wound [wuːnd] **1.** n. (a) cut/damage to the skin, usu. received in a fight. (b) hurt to the feelings. **2.** v. (a) to hurt. (b) to hurt the fellings of (s.o.). (c) [waʊnd] see also **wind².**

wove, woven [wəʊv, 'wəʊvn] v. see **weave.**

wow [waʊ] **1.** n. inf. (a) great success. (b) fluctuation of sound in a record-player. **2.** v. inf. (of a singer, etc.) to excite (the audience).

WPC ['dʌblju:pi:'si:] n. woman police constable.

wrack [ræk] n. seaweed.

wraith [raɪθ] n. ghost.

wrangle ['ræŋgl] **1.** n. argument/dispute. **2.** v. to argue.

wrap [ræp] **1.** n. shawl; inf. **to keep sth under wraps** = to keep sth a secret. **2.** v. (wrapped) to cover (sth) all round with paper/cloth, etc. **wrap up,** v. (a) to cover up completely. (b) to wear warm clothes. (c) **to be wrapped up in your work** = to think only of the work and take no notice of other things. **wrapper,** n. piece of paper used to cover sth. **wrapping,** n. paper/ cardboard/plastic, etc., used to wrap things; **w. paper** = paper used to wrap presents.

wrasse [ræs] n. type of sea fish.

wrath [rɒθ] n. great anger. **wrathful,** adj. angry.

wreak [riːk] v. to carry out/to do (sth violent).

wreath [riːθ] n. (a) circle of flowers or leaves esp. given at a funeral in memory of the dead person. (b) winding clouds (of smoke/mist). **wreathe** [riːð] v. (a) to put a circle of flowers on (s.o./sth). (b) to cover with twisting clouds of smoke/mist.

wreck [rek] **1.** n. (a) ship which has been sunk/badly damaged on rocks, etc. (b) action of being wrecked. (c) anything which has been damaged and is useless.

(d) person who, because of illness, can do very little. **2.** v. to cause severe damage to (sth); to ruin (sth). **wreckage,** n. broken remains of a building/ship, etc., after a disaster. **wrecker,** n. (a) person who destroys a building/plan, etc., on purpose, or tries to make a ship crash on to rocks. (b) person who is employed to destroy old buildings/break up old cars, etc. (c) Am. truck which goes to help cars which have broken down on the road; engine which goes to help a train which has broken down on the track.

wren [ren] n. (a) very small brown songbird. (b) **Wren** = woman member of the Royal Navy.

wrench [renʃ] **1.** n. (pl. -es) (a) violent twisting movement. (b) large spanner for turning nuts. (c) sadness at leaving. **2.** v. to turn and pull (sth) violently.

wrest [rest] v. (formal) to twist/to wrench away.

wrestle [ˈresl] v. (a) to fight with s.o. in a contest by trying to throw him to the ground. (b) to fight struggle with (a problem). **wrestler,** n. person who wrestles in contests. **wrestling,** n. **w. match** = contest of wrestlers watched by crowds of people.

wretch [retʃ] n. (pl. -es) (a) person who looks poor and miserable. (b) naughty/annoying person. **wretched** [ˈretʃɪd] adj. (a) miserable and poor; **to feel w.** = to feel ill. (b) terrible/ annoying. **wretchedly,** adv. miserably. **wretchedness,** n. being wretched.

wriggle [ˈrɪgl] v. to twist and turn; **to w. out of** = to get out of (a difficult situation) by trickery.

wring [rɪŋ] v. (wrung) to twist (sth), esp. to get water out of it; **to w. information from** = to manage to get information with difficulty; **to w. one's hands** = to twist and turn one's hands, showing sadness and emotion. **wringer,** n. machine for squeezing the water out of wet washing. **wringing,** adj. very (wet).

wrinkle [ˈrɪŋkl] **1.** n. (a) line/fold of the skin. (b) line or crease in cloth. **2.** v. to make lines/creases in.

wrist [rɪst] n. joint between the arm and the hand; **w. watch** = small watch worn on a strap around the wrist. **wristlet,** n. band worn round the wrist.

writ [rɪt] n. legal paper ordering s.o. to do/not to do wth. **Holy Writ,** n. the Bible.

write [raɪt] v. (wrote [rəʊt], has written) (a) to put down words on paper. (b) to be the author of books/music, etc.. (c) to put a letter in writing and send it to s.o. inf. **that's nothing to w. home about** = it's nothing special. **write in,** v. (a) to write to (a radio station, etc.). (b) Am. to vote for a candidate whose name does not appear on the ballot paper, by writing the name there. **write off,** v. to remove (sth) from a written list; to cancel (a debt); to see that (sth) is a failure; **the car was written off** = the insurance company considered it a total loss. **write-off,** n. inf. total loss. **writer,** n. person who writes, esp. to earn money. **write up,** v. to describe fully in writing. **write-up,** n. inf. article in a newspaper. **writing,** n. (a) thing that is written; **w. paper** = paper used for writing letters. (b) handwriting. **writings,** n. pl. books, etc., written by an author.

writhe [raɪð] v. to twist and turn (in agony).

wrong [rɒŋ] **1.** adj. (a) bad/not right. (b) not right/incorrect. (c) **what's w.?** = what is the matter? **I hope nothing's w.** = I hope nothing bad has happened. **2.** n. bad/incorrect thing; **to be in he w.** = to have made a mistake. **3.** adv. badly/ incorrectly; **to go w.** = to break down/ not to work properly. **4.** v. to treat (s.o.) unfairly. **wrongdoer,** n. person who has committed a crime. **wrongdoing,** n. crime/unlawful act. **wrongful,** adj. unjust/unlawful. **wrongfully,** adv. in a wrongful way. **wrongheaded,** adj. mistaken but refusing to admit it. **wrongly,** adv. incorrectly/badly.

wrote [rəʊt] v. see **write.**

wrought [rɔːt] adj. **w. iron** = hammered, twisted and bent iron used for making decorative gates/balconies, etc.

wrung [rʌŋ] v. see **wring.**

wry [raɪ] adj. showing dislike by twisting the mouth.

wych elm [ˈwɪtʃelm] n. elm with wide spreading branches.

WYSIWYG [ˈwɪzɪwɪg] what-you-see-is-what-you-get (when the text on a computer screen is exactly the same as the printed output).

Xx

X, x [eks]. **X-ray. 1.** *n.* (*a*) ray which will pass through solids and is used esp. in hospitals for photographing the inside of the body. (*b*) photograph taken with X-rays. **2.** *v.* to take an X-ray photograph of.

xenophobe ['zenəfəʊb] *n.* person who dislikes foreigners. **xenophobia** [zenə-'fəʊbɪə] *n.* hatred of foreigners. **xenophobic,** *adj.* hating foreigners.

xerox ['zɪərɒks] **1.** *n.* (*pl* **-es**) trademark for a type of photocopier. (*b*) photocopy made with this machine. **2.** *v.* to make a photocopy with a Xerox machine.

Xmas ['krɪsməs, 'eksməs] *n. short for* Christmas.

xylophone ['zaɪləfəʊn] *n.* musical instrument consisting of wooden bars of different lengths which make different notes when they are tapped with a hammer.

Yy

yacht [jɒt] *n.* sailing boat; boat used for pleasure and sport; **y. club** = sailing club. **yachting,** *n.* art of sailing a boat. **yachtsman,** *n.* (*pl.* **-men**) person who sails a yacht.

yahoo ['jɑːhuː] *n. inf.* crude boorish person.

yak [jæk] *n.* long-haired ox from Asia. **2.** *v. inf.* to talk incessantly.

yam [jæm] *n.* tropical plant with an edible root.

yank [jæŋk] **1.** *n. inf.* short sharp pull. **2.** *v. inf.* to pull hard and sharply. **Yank, Yankee,** *n. inf.* American (esp. from the northern states).

yap [jæp] **1.** *n.* short sharp bark of a dog. **2.** *v.* (**yapped**) to make short sharp barks.

yard [jɑːd] *n.* (*a*) measure of length (= 0.91 metre). (*b*) piece of wood attached to the mast holding a sail. (*c*) enclosed space (often paved) behind a house or other building. (*d*) *Am.* small garden round a house. (*e*) enclosed space used for a certain purpose; **builder's y.** = place where a builder keeps stocks of wood/bricks, etc.; **goods' y.** = space where trains are loaded with goods; **Scotland Y./***inf.* **the Y.** = headquarters of the London Metropolitan Police. **yardage,** *n.* length in yards or area in square yards. **yardarm,** *n.* end of the yard holding a sail. **yardstick,** *n.* standard for measurement.

yarn [jɑːn] **1.** *n.* (*a*) long thread of wool/ fibre used in knitting or weaving. (*b*) *inf.* long story. **2.** *v. inf.* to tell stories.

yarrow ['jærəʊ] *n.* wild plant with clusters of small white flowers.

yashmak ['jæʃmæk] *n.* veil worn by Muslim women.

yaw [jɔː] *v.* (*of ship/aircraft*) to go away from the course.

yawl [jɔːl] *n.* type of two-masted fishing boat.

yawn [jɔːn] **1.** *n.* movement of opening the mouth when tired; **to stifle a y.** = to try to stop yawning. **2.** to open the mouth wide when feeling sleepy, and to breathe in and out; **to y. your head off** = to yawn again and again. **yawning,** *adj.* open wide; **y. hole** = deep wide hole.

yaws [jɔːz] *n. pl.* tropical skin disease.

yd *short for* yard.

ye [jiː] **1.** *pron.* (*old*) you. **2.** *article used in false old names* the.

yea [jeɪ] *adv.* (*old*) yes.

year ['jɜː] *n.* (*a*) period of twelve months starting on 1st January and ending on 31st December; **the New Y.** = the first few days of the year; **to see the New Y. in** = to stay up until midnight on 31st December and celebrate with a party the beginning of the next year; **calendar y.** = year beginning on 1st January and ending on 31st December; **leap y.** = year with 366 days in it, one more than the normal year. (*b*) any period of twelve months; **school y.** = year starting in September and ending in July of the following year; **financial y.** = (i) twelve month period for a firm's accounts; (ii) (*in UK*) period beginning on April 6th and ending on the following April 5th considered for tax purposes; **all (the) y. round** = through the whole year; **y. in, y. out** = happening regularly over a long period of time. (*c*) **his early years** = his childhood; **getting on in years** = quite old; **I haven't seen him for (donkey's) years** = I haven't seen him for a long time. **yearbook**, *n.* reference book which comes out each year with up to date information. **yearling**, *n.* one year old animal. **yearly**, *adj. & adv.* every year; once a year.

yearn [jɜːn] *v.* to long for sth/to want sth. **yearning**, *n.* desire/longing.

yeast [jiːst] *n.* living fungus used to make bread and beer. **yeasty**, *adj.* like yeast; referring to yeast.

yell [jel] **1.** *n.* loud shout. **2.** *v.* to shout loudly.

yellow ['jeləʊ] **1.** *n. & adj.* (*a*) colour of the sun/of gold; **y. fever** = type of tropical fever; **y. pages** = section of a telephone directory giving a classified list of businesses. (*b*) cowardly. **2.** *v.* to turn yellow. **yellowhammer**, *n.* small bird with a yellow breast. **yellowish**, *adj.* rather yellow.

yelp [jelp] **1.** *n.* cry of pain. **2.** *v.* (*usu. of animals*) to cry out in pain.

yen [jen] *n.* (*a*) currency of Japan. (*b*) *inf.* strong desire.

yeoman ['jəʊmən] *n.* (*pl.* **-men**) (*old*) farmer with his own land; **to do y. service** = work long and hard. **yeomanry**, *n.* (*old*) all yeomen.

yes [jes] *adv. & inter.* expression of agreement. **yes man**, *n.* person who always agrees with a person in authority.

yesterday ['jestədeɪ] *adv. & n.* (*a*) the day before today; **the day before y.** = two days before today. (*b*) recent times. **yesteryear**, *adv. & n.* (*formal*) times past.

yet [jet] **1.** *adv.* (*a*) up till now/up till this time. (*b*) in spite of everything. (*c*) even. **2.** *conj.* still/but.

yeti ['jetɪ] *n.* large animal, like an ape or bear, which is said to exist in the snows of the Himalayas.

yew [juː] *n.* evergreen tree with small cones and poisonous red berries.

Yiddish ['jɪdɪʃ] *n.* language spoken by European Jews.

yield [jiːld] **1.** *n.* crop/product; return on your investment. **2.** *v.* (*a*) to give/ to produce. (*b*) to produce money. (*c*) (**to**) to give up/to surrender. (*d*) to give way when pressed. (*e*) (**to**) (*of traffic*) to allow other vehicles to pass first.

yob(bo) ['jɒb(əʊ)] *n. Sl.* (*pl.* **-os**) rude/ violent young man.

yodel ['jəʊdl] *v.* to sing with quick changes from low to high notes. **yodeller**, *n.* person who yodels

yoga ['jəʊgə] *n.* system of exercises and meditation practised by Hindu thinkers, and now popular in western countries.

yoghurt, yogurt ['jɒgət] *n.* fermented milk usu. eaten as a dessert.

yogi ['jəʊgɪ] *n.* Hindu thinker who practises yoga.

yoke [jəʊk] **1.** *n.* (*a*) piece of wood placed over the neck of a pair of animals when they are used for ploughing, etc.; **y. of oxen** = two oxen attached together. (*b*) part of a dress which covers the shoulders and upper chest. **2.** *v.* to join together (with a yoke).

yokel ['jəʊkl] *n.* stupid man from the country.

yolk [jəʊk] *n.* yellow part of an egg.

yon, yonder [jɒn, 'jɒndə] *adj. & adv.* (which is) over there.

yore [jɔː] *n.* (*formal*) **in days of y.** = in the past.

yorker ['jɔːkə] *n.* (*in cricket*) ball which pitches just under the bat. **york**, *v.* to bowl (*s.o.*) out with a yorker.

Yorkshire pudding ['jɔːkʃə'pʊdɪŋ] *n.* batter pudding eaten with roast beef.

you [juː] *pron.* (*a*) (*referring to the person/persons to whom we are speaking*) (*b*) (*referring to anybody/people in general*)

young [jʌŋ] **1.** *adj.* (**-er**, **-est**) not old/ recently born. **2.** *n.* (*a*) young animals or birds. (*b*) young people. **youngster**, *n.* young person.

your ['jɔː] *adj.* belonging to you. **yours** ['jɔːz] *pron.* belonging to you. **yourself, yourselves** [jɔː'self, jɔː'selvz] *pron.* referring to the subject you.

youth [juːθ] *n.* (*a*) time when you are young. (*b*) young man. (*c*) young people; **y. club** = club where young people meet; **y. hostel** = building where young walkers, etc., can stay the night cheaply. **youthful**, *adj.* young. **youthfulness**, *n.* being youthful.

yowl [jaʊl] *v.* (*esp. of animals*) to howl/ to cry out loudly.

yo-yo ['jəʊjəʊ] *n.* toy made of a circular piece of wood/metal with a groove round the edge, which can be made to run up and down a string.

yucca ['jʌkə] *n.* type of large succulent plant.

Yugoslav ['ju:gəʊslɑ:v] *adj. & n.* (person) from Yugoslavia.

yukky ['jʌkɪ] *adj. inf.* which has a nasty taste.

yule [ju:l] *n.* Christmas; **y. log** = log burnt at Christmas. **Yuletide**, *n.* the Christmas period.

yumyum ['jʌmjʌm] *inter. showing* liking for food. **yummy**, *adj. inf.* nice to eat.

Zz

zany ['zeɪnɪ] *adj.* (**-ier, -iest**) *inf.* wildly mad.

zap [zæp] *v.* (**zapped**) *inf.* to hit/kill.

zeal [zi:l] *n.* keenness/eagerness. **zealous** ['zeləs] *adj.* eager. **zealot** ['zelət] *n.* person who is too enthusiastic about religion or politics.

zebra ['zebrə] *n.* African animal similar to a horse, but with a striped coat; **z. crossing** = pedestrian crossing painted with white stripes.

zenith ['zenɪθ] *n.* (*a*) point of the sky directly overhead. (*b*) highest point.

zephyr ['zefə] *n.* (*formal*) gentle (often westerly) breeze.

zero ['zɪərəʊ] *n.* (*a*) number 0/nothing/nil. (*b*) freezing point of water when measured on a Celsius thermometer. **zero hour,** *n.* time fixed to start sth important. **zero in on,** *v.* to aim at (sth)/to go straight to (sth). **zero-rated,** *adj.* (item) which has a 0% VAT applied to it.

zest [zest] *n.* (*a*) enthusiasm/enjoyment. (*b*) added pleasure/spice. (*c*) thin piece of orange or lemon peel. **zestful,** *adj.* enthusiastic.

zigzag ['zɪgzæg] **1.** *adj. & n.* (line) which turns sharply one way, then the opposite way. **2.** *v.* (**zigzagged**) to move in a zigzag.

zilch [zɪltʃ] *n. Am. Sl.* nothing/zero.

zinc [zɪŋk] *n.* (*element:* Zn) hard bright light-coloured metal.

zinnia ['zɪnjə] *n.* annual garden plant with bright flowers.

zip [zɪp] **1.** *n.* (*a*) whistling sound made by a bullet as it goes through the air. (*b*) *inf.* energy. (*c*) (*also* **zip fastener**) device for closing openings on trousers/

dresses, etc., consisting of two rows of teeth which lock together. (*d*) *Am.* **z. code** = post code. **2.** *v.* (**zipped**) (*a*) to go fast; to whistle by. (*b*) **to z. up** = to close a zip (fastener). **zipper,** *n. inf.* zip (fastener). **zippy,** *adj. inf.* quick and lively.

zirconium [zɜ:'kəʊnɪəm] *n.* (*element:* Zr) rare metal used in alloys.

zither ['zɪðə] *n.* flat musical instrument played by plucking strings.

Zn *symbol for* zinc.

zodiac ['zəʊdɪæk] *n.* part of the sky (divided into twelve imaginary sections) through which the sun and planets are supposed to travel during the year; **signs of the z.** = twelve signs named after groups of stars. **zodiacal** [zəʊ'daɪəkəl] *adj.* referring to the zodiac.

zombie ['zɒmbɪ] *n.* (*a*) (West Indian) dead body which is revived and controlled by witchcraft. (*b*) *inf.* person who is half-asleep/moving slowly.

zone [zəʊn] **1.** *n.* (*a*) region/area/part (of a country/town). (*b*) region of the Earth showing a particular type of climate. **2.** *v.* to divide (a town) into parts for planning purposes. **zonal,** *adj.* of a zone. **zoning,** *n.* the splitting up (of a town or area) into zones.

zoo [zu:] *n.* place where wild animals are kept in enclosures and which the public can visit.

zoology [zu:'ɒlədʒɪ] *n.* study of animals. **zoological** [zu:ə'lɒdʒɪkl] *adj.* referring to the study of animals; **z. gardens** = zoo. **zoologist** [zu:'ɒlədʒɪst] *n.* person who studies animals.

zoom [zu:m] **1.** *n.* deep buzzing noise made by sth travelling fast. **2.** *v.* (*a*) to make a deep buzzing noise when moving fast. (*b*) (*of prices, etc.*) to rise suddenly and steeply. (*c*) **to z. in on sth** = to focus a camera lens so that it makes a distant object appear to come closer. **zoom lens,** *n.* camera lens which allows you to change quickly from distant to close-up shots while still keeping in focus.

zoonosis [zəʊə'nəʊsɪs] *n.* disease which can be caught from animals.

zucchini [zʊ'ki:nɪ] *n.* courgette.

zwieback ['zwi:bæk] *n. Am.* type of hard crumbly biscuit.

Information Section

Units of Money used in Various Countries

Argentina	austral	Lebanon	pound
Australia	dollar	Libya	dinar
Austria	schilling	Malaysia	dollar
Belgium	franc	Malta	lira (pound)
Brazil	cruzado	Mexico	peso
Canada	dollar	Netherlands	gulden
Chile	escudo	New Zealand	dollar
China	yuan	Nigeria	naira
Cuba	peso	Norway	krone
Cyprus	pound	Pakistan	rupee
Czechoslovakia	koruna	Peru	inti
Denmark	krone	Philippines	peso
Egypt	pound	Poland	zloty
Finland	markka	Portugal	escudo
France	franc	Romania	leu
Germany	mark	Saudi Arabia	riyal
Ghana	cedi	South Africa	rand
Greece	drachma	Spain	peseta
Hungary	forint	Sri Lanka	rupee
India	rupee	Sweden	krona
Iran	rial	Switzerland	franc
Iraq	dinar	Syria	pound
Ireland	punt (pound)	Thailand	baht
Israel	pound	Tunisia	dinar
Italy	lira	Turkey	lira
Jamaica	dollar	United Kingdom	pound
Japan	yen	United States	dollar
Kenya	shilling	USSR	rouble
North Korea	won	Yugoslavia	dinar
South Korea	won	Zaire	zaire
Kuwait	dinar	Zambia	kwacha

The Solar System

	distance from Sun (millions of km)	diameter (km)	rotation period on its axis (days hours minutes)	revolution round the Sun
Sun	0	1,392,000	25 09 00	
Mercury	58	4,880	59 00 00	87.97 days
Venus	108	12,100	243 00 00	224.70 days
Earth	150	12,756	00 23 56	365.25 days
Mars	228	6,790	00 24 37	1.88 years
Jupiter	778	142,800	00 09 50	11.86 years
Saturn	1,427	120,000	00 10 14	29.45 years
Uranus	2,870	52,000	00 16 00	84.00 years
Neptune	4,497	48,000	00 10 00	164.79 years
Pluto	5,950	?3,000	6 09 14	247.7 years

The World's Largest Cities

The following list is of those urban areas in the world which have a population of more than six million. City limits often fall short of, or exceed, the built-up or urban area.

Mexico City	18,748,000	Los Angeles	8,505,000
Cairo	14,000,000	São Paulo	8,490,763
Shanghai	12,620,000	Bombay	8,202,000
Tokyo	11,680,282	London	6,696,000
Seoul	9,991,089	Manila	6,720,050
Buenos Aires	9,968,000	Jakarta	6,503,449
Beijing	9,957,000	Karachi	6,500,000
Calcutta	9,166,000	Delhi	6,220,000
Moscow	8,815,000	Chicago	6,199,000
Paris	8,706,963	Tehran	6,000,000
New York	8,529,000		

The Highest Mountain in each of the Continents

Continent		Height	Country
Asia	Everest	8,848 m	Nepal-China
South America	Aconcagua	6,960 m	Argentina
North America	McKinley	6,194 m	Alaska
Africa	Kilimanjaro	5,895 m	Tanzania
Europe	El'bruz	5,633 m	USSR
Australia	Kosciusko	2,228 m	N.S.W.

The World's Ten Longest Rivers: their length and outflow

	Length	*Outflow*
Nile	6,690 km	Mediterranean
Amazon	6,280 km	Atlantic Ocean
Mississippi-Missouri	6,270 km	Gulf of Mexico
Ob-Irtysh	5,570 km	Gulf of Ob
Zaire (Congo)	4,670 km	Atlantic Ocean
Amur	4,410 km	Tatar Strait
Huang Ho (Yellow River)	4,350 km	Yellow Sea
Lena	4,260 km	Laptev Sea
Yangtze	4,090 km	East China Sea
Mackenzie	4,040 km	Arctic Ocean

The Largest Lakes in the World

	Continent	*Area in 1,000 km^2*
Caspian Sea	Asia	424
Lake Superior	N. America	82
Lake Victoria	Africa	69
Aral Sea	Asia	63
Lake Huron	N. America	59
Lake Michigan	N. America	58
Lake Tanganyika	Africa	32
Lake Baikal	Asia	31
Great Bear Lake	N. America	31
Great Slave Lake	N. America	28

The Largest Oceans and Seas

	Area in 1,000 km^2
Pacific Ocean	165,721
Atlantic Ocean	81,660
Indian Ocean	73,442
Arctic Ocean	14,351
Mediterranean Sea	2,966
Bering Sea	2,274
Caribbean Sea	1,942

Time Zones

Standard time is reckoned from Greenwich, England, which is recognized as being on the Prime Meridian of Longitude. The world is divided into twenty-four zones, each fifteen degrees of arc, or one hour in time apart. Greenwich meridian (0) extends through the centre of the first zone. The zones to the east are numbered from minus one to minus twelve, the minus indicating the number of hours which must be subtracted to obtain Greenwich Time. The zones to the west are numbered plus one to plus twelve, the plus indicating the number of hours which must be added to obtain Greenwich Time. These zones are generally used in sea areas, but in many countries Standard Time does not coincide with zone time.

The International Date Line is a zig-zag line that approximately follows the 180° meridian. The time must be advanced by twenty-four hours when it is crossed in a westerly direction and must be set back by twenty-four hours when it is crossed in an easterly direction.

The following list gives the Standard Time in various cities of the world when it is 12.00 (midday) in Greenwich, England.

City	Time	City	Time
Adelaide	2100	Dubai	1600
Algiers	1300	Dublin	1200
Amsterdam	1300	Gibraltar	1300
Ankara	1500	Helsinki	1400
Athens	1400	Hobart	2200
Beijing	2000	Hong Kong	2000
Beirut	1400	Istanbul	1500
Belgrade	1400	Jerusalem	1400
Berlin	1300	Kuwait City	1500
Berne	1300	Lagos	1300
Bonn	1300	Leningrad	1500
Bombay	1730	Lima	0700
Brasilia	0900	Lisbon	1300
Brisbane	2200	London	1200
Brussels	1300	Luxemburg	1300
Bucharest	1400	Madeira	1200
Budapest	1300	Madrid	1300
Buenos Aires	0900	Malta	1300
Cairo	1400	Mexico City	0600
Calcutta	1730	Montevideo	0830
Cape Town	1400	Montreal	0700
Caracas	0800	Moscow	1500
Chicago	0600	Nairobi	1500
Colombo	1730	New Orleans	0600
Copenhagen	1300	New York	0700
Delhi	1730	Oslo	1300

Ottawa	0700	Singapore	2000
Panama	0700	Stockholm	1300
Paris	1300	Suez	1400
Perth (Austr)	2000	Sydney	2200
Prague	1300	Tehran	1500
Pretoria	1400	Tokyo	2100
Quebec	0700	Toronto	0700
Rangoon	1830	Tunis	1300
Rio de Janeiro	0900	Valetta	1300
Riyadh	1500	Vancouver	0400
St Louis (USA)	0600	Vienna	1300
San Francisco	0400	Warsaw	1300
Santiago	0800	Wellington (NZ)	2400

The United Kingdom: counties (with abbreviations) and county towns

England

County	Abbreviation	County town
Avon		Bristol
Bedfordshire	(Beds.)	Bedford
Berkshire	(Berks.)	Reading
Buckinghamshire	(Bucks.)	Aylesbury
Cambridgeshire	(Cambs.)	Cambridge
Cheshire		Chester
Cleveland		Middlesbrough
Cornwall		Truro
Cumbria		Carlisle
Derbyshire	(Derbys.)	Matlock
Devon		Exeter
Dorset		Dorchester
Durham		Durham
East Sussex	(E. Sussex)	Lewes
Essex		Chelmsford
Gloucestershire	(Glos.)	Gloucester
Greater London		
Greater Manchester		Manchester
Hampshire	(Hants.)	Winchester
Hereford & Worcester	(Hereford & Worc.)	Worcester
Hertfordshire	(Herts.)	Hertford
Humberside		Beverley
Isle of Wight	(I. of Wight)	Newport
Kent		Maidstone
Lancashire	(Lancs.)	Preston
Leicestershire	(Leics.)	Leicester
Lincolnshire	(Lincs.)	Lincoln
Merseyside		Liverpool
Norfolk		Norwich
Northamptonshire	(Northants.)	Northampton
Northumberland	(Northd.)	Morpeth
North Yorkshire	(N. Yorkshire)	Northallerton
Nottinghamshire	(Notts.)	Nottingham
Oxfordshire	(Oxon.)	Oxford
Shropshire	(Salop)	Shrewsbury
Somerset		Taunton
South Yorkshire	(S. Yorkshire)	Barnsley
Staffordshire	(Staffs.)	Stafford
Suffolk		Ipswich
Surrey		Kingston-upon-Thames
Tyne & Wear		Newcastle upon Tyne

Warwickshire	(Warwicks.)	Warwick
West Midlands	(W. Midlands)	Birmingham
West Sussex	(W. Sussex)	Chichester
West Yorkshire	(W. Yorkshire)	Wakefield
Wiltshire	(Wilts.)	Trowbridge

Wales

Clwyd		Mold
Dyfed		Carmarthen
Gwent		Cwmbran
Gwynedd		Caernarfon
Mid Glamorgan	(M. Glamorgan)	Cardiff
Powys		Llandrindod Wells
South Glamorgan	(S. Glamorgan)	Cardiff
West Glamorgan	(W. Glamorgan)	Swansea

Scotland (Regions)

Borders	Newtown St Boswells
Central	Stirling
Dumfries & Galloway	Dumfries
Fife	Glenrothes
Grampian	Aberdeen
Highland	Inverness
Lothian	Edinburgh
Strathclyde	Glasgow
Tayside	Dundee
Orkney	Kirkwall
Shetland	Lerwick
Western Isles	Stornoway

Northern Ireland

Since 1973 local government in Northern Ireland has not been based on the counties, but on 23 district councils and 9 area boards.

The United States of America: the states (with zip codes) and their capitals

Alabama	(AL)	Montgomery
Alaska	(AK)	Juneau
Arizona	(AZ)	Phoenix
Arkansas	(AR)	Little Rock
California	(CA)	Sacramento
Colorado	(CO)	Denver
Connecticut	(CT)	Hartford
Delaware	(DE)	Dover
Florida	(FL)	Tallahassee
Georgia	(GA)	Atlanta
Hawaii	(HI)	Honolulu
Idaho	(ID)	Boise
Illinois	(IL)	Springfield
Indiana	(IN)	Indianapolis
Iowa	(IA)	Des Moines
Kansas	(KS)	Topeka
Kentucky	(KY)	Frankfort
Louisiana	(LA)	Baton Rouge
Maine	(ME)	Augusta
Maryland	(MD)	Annapolis
Massachusetts	(MA)	Boston
Michigan	(MI)	Lansing
Minnesota	(MN)	St Paul
Mississippi	(MS)	Jackson
Missouri	(MO)	Jefferson City
Montana	(MT)	Helena
Nebraska	(NE)	Lincoln
Nevada	(NV)	Carson City
New Hampshire	(NH)	Concord
New Jersey	(NJ)	Trenton
New Mexico	(NM)	Santa Fe
New York	(NY)	Albany
North Carolina	(NC)	Raleigh
North Dakota	(ND)	Bismarck
Ohio	(OH)	Columbus
Oklahoma	(OK)	Oklahoma City
Oregon	(OR)	Salem
Pennsylvania	(PA)	Harrisburg
Rhode Island	(RI)	Providence
South Carolina	(SC)	Columbia
South Dakota	(SD)	Pierre
Tennessee	(TN)	Nashville

Texas	(TX)	Austin
Utah	(UT)	Salt Lake City
Vermont	(VT)	Montpelier
Virginia	(VA)	Richmond
Washington	(WA)	Olympia
West Virginia	(WV)	Charleston
Wisconsin	(WI)	Madison
Wyoming	(WY)	Cheyenne
District of Columbia	(DC)	Washington

Australia: the states (with abbreviations) and their capitals

New South Wales	(N.S.W.)	Sydney
Queensland	(Qld.)	Brisbane
South Australia	(S.A.)	Adelaide
Tasmania	(Tas.)	Hobart
Victoria	(Vic.)	Melbourne
Western Australia	(W.A.)	Perth

The Territories

Northern Territory	(N.T.)	Darwin
Australian Capital Territory	(A.C.T.)	Canberra

Canada: the provinces (with abbreviations) and their capitals

Alberta	(Alta.)	Edmonton
British Columbia	(B.C.)	Victoria
Manitoba	(Man.)	Winnipeg
New Brunswick	(N.B.)	Fredericton
Newfoundland	(Nfld.)	St John's
Nova Scotia	(N.S.)	Halifax
Ontario	(Ont.)	Toronto
Prince Edward Island	(P.E.I.)	Charlottetown
Quebec	(Que.)	Quebec
Saskatchewan	(Sask.)	Regina

The Territories

Yukon Territory	(Y.T.)	Whitehorse
Northwest Territories	(N.W.T.)	Yellowknife

Kings and Queens of England from 1066

The House of Normandy
William I	1066–1087
William II	1087–1100
Henry I	1100–1135
Stephen	1135–1154

The House of Anjou or Plantagenet
Henry II	1154–1189
Richard I	1189–1199
John	1199–1216
Henry III	1216–1272
Edward I	1272–1307
Edward II	1307–1327
Edward III	1327–1377
Richard II	1377–1399

The House of Lancaster (sub-division of Plantagenet)
Henry IV	1399–1413
Henry V	1413–1422
Henry VI	1422–1461

The House of York (sub-division of Plantagenet)
Edward IV	1461–1483
Edward V	1483
Richard III	1483–1485

The House of Tudor
Henry VII	1485–1509
Henry VIII	1509–1547
Edward VI	1547–1553
Mary I	1553–1558
Elizabeth I	1558–1603

The House of Stuart

James I	1603–1625
Charles I	1625–1649
The Commonwealth	1649–1659
Charles II	1660–1685
James II	1685–1688
Mary II	1689–1694
&	
William III	1689–1702
Anne	1702–1714

The House of Hanover

George I	1714–1727
George II	1727–1760
George III	1760–1820
George IV	1820–1830
William IV	1830–1837
Victoria	1837–1901

The House of Saxe-Coburg

Edward VII	1901–1910

The House of Windsor

George V	1910–1936
Edward VIII	1936
George VI	1936–1952
Elizabeth II	1952–

The Prime Ministers of Great Britain
(with their political party and dates in office)

Sir R Walpole	(Whig)	1721–1742
Earl of Wilmington	(Whig)	1742–1743
H Pelham	(Whig)	1743–1754
Duke of Newcastle	(Whig)	1754–1756
Duke of Devonshire	(Whig)	1756–1757
Duke of Newcastle	(Whig)	1757–1762
Earl of Bute	(Tory)	1762–1763
G Grenville	(Whig)	1763–1765
Marquess of Rockingham	(Whig)	1765–1766
Earl of Chatham	(Whig)	1766–1768
Duke of Grafton	(Whig)	1768–1770
Lord North	(Tory)	1770–1782
Marquess of Rockingham	(Whig)	1782
Earl of Shelburne	(Whig)	1782–1783
Duke of Portland	(Coalition)	1783
W Pitt	(Tory)	1783–1801
H Addington	(Tory)	1801–1804
W Pitt	(Tory)	1804–1806
Lord Grenville	(Whig)	1806–1807
Duke of Portland	(Tory)	1807–1809
S Perceval	(Tory)	1809–1812
Earl of Liverpool	(Tory)	1812–1827
G Canning	(Tory)	1827
Viscount Goderich	(Tory)	1827–1828
Duke of Wellington	(Tory)	1828–1830
Earl Grey	(Whig)	1830–1834
Viscount Melbourne	(Whig)	1834
Sir Robert Peel	(Tory)	1834–1835
Viscount Melbourne	(Whig)	1835–1841
Sir Robert Peel	(Tory)	1841–1846
Lord Russell	(Whig)	1846–1852
Earl of Derby	(Tory)	1852
Earl of Aberdeen	(Peelite)	1852–1855
Viscount Palmerston	(Liberal)	1855–1858
Earl of Derby	(Conservative)	1858–1859
Viscount Palmerston	(Liberal)	1859–1865
Earl Russell	(Liberal)	1865–1866
Earl of Derby	(Conservative)	1866–1868
Benjamin Disraeli	(Conservative)	1868
W E Gladstone	(Liberal)	1868–1874
Benjamin Disraeli	(Conservative)	1874–1880
W E Gladstone	(Liberal)	1880–1885
Marquess of Salisbury	(Conservative)	1885–1886

W E Gladstone	(Liberal)	1886
Marquess of Salisbury	(Conservative)	1886–1892
W E Gladstone	(Liberal)	1892–1894
Earl of Rosebery	(Liberal)	1894–1895
Marquess of Salisbury	(Conservative)	1895–1902
A J Balfour	(Conservative)	1902–1905
Sir H Campbell-Bannerman	(Liberal)	1905–1908
H H Asquith	(Liberal)	1908–1915
H H Asquith	(Coalition)	1915–1916
D Lloyd George	(Coalition)	1916–1922
A Bonar Law	(Conservative)	1922–1923
S Baldwin	(Conservative)	1923–1924
J R MacDonald	(Labour)	1924
S Baldwin	(Conservative)	1924–1929
J R MacDonald	(Labour)	1929–1931
J R MacDonald	(Coalition)	1931–1935
S Baldwin	(Conservative)	1935–1937
N Chamberlain	(Conservative)	1937–1940
W S Churchill	(Coalition)	1940–1945
W S Churchill	(Conservative)	1945
C R Attlee	(Labour)	1945–1951
Sir W S Churchill	(Conservative)	1951–1955
Sir A Eden	(Conservative)	1955–1957
H Macmillan	(Conservative)	1957–1963
Sir A Douglas-Home	(Conservative)	1963–1964
J H Wilson	(Labour)	1964–1970
E R G Heath	(Conservative)	1970–1974
J H Wilson	(Labour)	1974–1976
L J Callaghan	(Labour)	1976–1979
Mrs M H Thatcher	(Conservative)	1979–1990
J Major	(Conservative)	1990–

The Presidents of the United States
(and their political affiliation)

George Washington	(Federalist)	1789–1797
John Adams	(Federalist)	1797–1801
Thomas Jefferson	(Republican)	1801–1809
James Madison	(Republican)	1809–1817
James Monroe	(Republican)	1817–1825
John Quincy Adams	(Republican)	1825–1829
Andrew Jackson	(Democrat)	1829–1837
Martin Van Buren	(Democrat)	1837–1841
William Harrison	(Whig)	1841
John Tyler	(Whig)	1841–1845
James Polk	(Democrat)	1845–1849
Zachary Taylor	(Whig)	1849–1850
Millard Fillmore	(Whig)	1850–1853
Franklin Pierce	(Democrat)	1853–1857
James Buchanan	(Democrat)	1857–1861
Abraham Lincoln	(Republican)	1861–1865
Andrew Johnson	(Republican)	1865–1869
Ulysses Grant	(Republican)	1869–1877
Rutherford Hayes	(Republican)	1877–1881
James Garfield	(Republican)	1881
Chester Arthur	(Republican)	1881–1885
Grover Cleveland	(Democrat)	1885–1889
Benjamin Harrison	(Republican)	1889–1893
Grover Cleveland	(Democrat)	1893–1897
William McKinley	(Republican)	1897–1901
Theodore Roosevelt	(Republican)	1901–1909
William Taft	(Republican)	1909–1913
Woodrow Wilson	(Democrat)	1913–1921
Warren Harding	(Republican)	1921–1923
Calvin Coolidge	(Republican)	1923–1929
Herbert Hoover	(Republican)	1929–1933
Franklin Roosevelt	(Democrat)	1933–1945
Harry Truman	(Democrat)	1945–1953
Dwight Eisenhower	(Republican)	1953–1961
John Kennedy	(Democrat)	1961–1963
Lyndon Johnson	(Democrat)	1963–1969
Richard Nixon	(Republican)	1969–1974
Gerald Ford	(Republican)	1974–1977
Jimmy Carter	(Democrat)	1977–1981
Ronald Reagan	(Republican)	1981–1989
George Bush	(Republican)	1989–

Modern Olympic Games

The Olympic Games were revived in 1896, having been held every four years from 776 B.C. to 393 A.D. The modern Olympic Games have moved from site to site:

1896 Athens	1932 Los Angeles	1972 Munich
1900 Paris	1936 Berlin	1976 Montreal
1904 St Louis	1948 London	1980 Moscow
1908 London	1952 Helsinki	1984 Los Angeles
1912 Stockholm	1956 Melbourne	1988 Seoul
1920 Antwerp	1960 Rome	1992 Barcelona
1924 Paris	1964 Tokyo	1996 Atlanta
1928 Amsterdam	1968 Mexico City	

Table of Chemical Elements

The commonest elements are also given as headwords in the main dictionary.

Name & Symbol	Atomic Number	Name & Symbol	Atomic Number
Actinium (Ac)	89	Indium (In)	49
Aluminium (Al)	13	Iodine (I)	53
Americium (Am)	95	Iridium (Ir)	77
Antimony (Sb)	51	Iron (Fe)	26
Argon (Ar)	18	Krypton (Kr)	36
Arsenic (As)	33	Lanthanum (La)	57
Astatine (At)	85	Lawrencium (Lr)	103
Barium (Ba)	56	Lead (Pb)	82
Berkelium (Bk)	97	Lithium (Li)	3
Beryllium (Be)	4	Lutetium (Lu)	71
Bismuth (Bi)	83	Magnesium (Mg)	12
Boron (B)	5	Manganese (Mn)	25
Bromine (Br)	35	Mendeleevium (Md)	101
Cadmium (Cd)	48	Mercury (Hg)	80
Caesium (Cs)	20	Molybdenum (Mo)	42
Californium (Cf)	98	Neodymium (Nd)	60
Carbon (C)	6	Neon (Ne)	10
Cerium (Ce)	58	Neptunium (Np)	93
Chlorine (Cl)	17	Nickel (Ni)	28
Chromium (Cr)	24	Niobium (Nb)	41
Cobalt (Co)	27	Nitrogen (N)	7
Copper (Cu)	29	Nobelium (No)	102
Curium (Cm)	96	Osmium (Os)	76
Dysprosium (Dy)	66	Oxygen (O)	8
Einsteinium (Es)	99	Palladium (Pd)	46
Erbium (Er)	68	Phosphorus (P)	15
Europium (Eu)	63	Platinum (Pt)	78
Fermium (Fm)	100	Plutonium (Pu)	94
Fluorine (F)	9	Polonium (Po)	84
Francium (Fr)	87	Potassium (K)	19
Gadolinium (Gd)	64	Praseodymium (Pr)	59
Gallium (Ga)	31	Promethium (Pm)	61
Germanium (Ge)	32	Protactinium (Pa)	91
Gold (Au)	79	Radium (Ra)	88
Hafnium (Hf)	72	Radon (Rn)	86
Hahnium (Ha)	105	Rhenium (Re)	75
Helium (He)	2	Rhodium (Rh)	45
Holmium (Ho)	67	Rubidium (Rb)	37
Hydrogen (H)	1	Ruthenium (Ru)	44

Name & Symbol	Atomic Number	Name & Symbol	Atomic Number
Rutherfordium (Rf)	104	Thorium (Th)	90
Samarium (Sm)	62	Thulium (Tm)	69
Scandium (Sc)	21	Tin (Sn)	50
Selenium (Se)	34	Titanium (Ti)	22
Silicon (Si)	14	Tungsten (W)	74
Silver (Ag)	47	Uranium (U)	92
Sodium (Na)	11	Vanadium (V)	23
Strontium (Sr)	38	Xenon (Xe)	54
Sulphur (S)	16	Ytterbium (Yb)	70
Tantalum (Ta)	73	Yttrium (Y)	39
Technetium (Tc)	43	Zinc (Zn)	30
Tellurium (Te)	52	Zirconium (Zr)	40
Terbium (Tb)	65		

Conversion Tables

LENGTH			WEIGHT		
centimetres	cm or inches	inches	kilogrammes	kg or pounds	pounds
2.54	1	0.39	0.45	1	2.20
5.08	2	0.79	0.91	2	4.41
7.62	3	1.18	1.36	3	6.61
10.16	4	1/58	1.81	4	8.82
12.70	5	1.97	2.27	5	11.02
15.24	6	2.36	2.72	6	13.23
17.78	7	2.76	3.18	7	15.43
20.32	8	3.15	3.63	8	17.64
22.86	9	3.54	4.08	9	19.84
25.40	10	3.94	4.54	10	22.05
50.80	20	7.87	9.07	20	44.09
76.20	40	15.75	18.14	40	88.19
127.00	50	19.69	22.68	50	110.23
162.40	60	23.62	27.22	60	132.28
177.80	70	27.56	31.75	70	154.32
203.20	80	31.50	36.29	80	176.37
228.60	90	35.43	40.82	90	198.41
254.00	100	39.37	45.36	100	220.46

kilometres	km or miles	miles	tonnes	tonnes or tons	tons
1.61	1	0.62	1.02	1	0.98
3.22	2	1.24	2.03	2	1.97
4.83	3	1.86	3.05	3	2.95
6.44	4	2.49	4.06	4	3.94
8.05	5	3.11	5.08	5	4.92
9.66	6	3.73	6.10	6	5.91
11.27	7	4.35	7.11	7	6.89
12.88	8	4.97	8.13	8	7.87
14.48	9	5.59	9.14	9	8.86
16.09	10	6.21	10.16	10	9.84
32.19	20	12.43	20.32	20	19.68
48.28	30	18.64	30.48	30	29.53
64.37	40	24.86	40.64	40	39.37
80.47	50	31.07	50.80	50	49.21
96.56	60	37.28	60.96	60	59.05
112.65	70	43.50	71.12	70	68.89
128.75	80	49.71	81.28	80	78.74
144.84	90	55.92	91.44	90	88.58
160.93	100	62.14	101.60	100	98.42

661

AREA			**CAPACITY**		
hectares	hectares or acres	acres	litres	litres or gallons	gallons
0.41	1	2.47	4.55	1	0.22
0.81	2	4.94	9.09	2	0.44
1.21	3	7.41	13.64	3	0.66
1.62	4	9.88	18.18	4	0.88
2.02	5	12.36	22.73	5	1.10
2.43	6	14.83	27.28	6	1.32
2.83	7	17.30	31.82	7	1.54
3.24	8	19.77	36.37	8	1.76
3.64	9	22.24	40.91	9	1.98
4.05	10	24.71	45.46	10	2.20
8.09	20	49.42	90.92	20	4.40
12.14	30	74.13	136.38	30	6.60
16.19	40	98.84	181.84	40	8.80
20.23	50	123.56	227.31	50	11.00
24.28	60	148.27	272.77	60	13.20
28.33	70	172.98	318.23	70	15.40
32.38	80	197.69	363.69	80	17.60
36.42	90	222.40	409.15	90	19.80
40.47	100	247.11	454.61	100	22.00

Speed

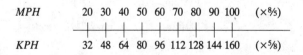

MPH	20 30 40 50 60 70 80 90 100	(×8/5)
KPH	32 48 64 80 96 112 128 144 160	(×5/8)

Temperature

Centigrade	−18° −10 0 10 20 30 40°
Fahrenheit	0° 10 20 32 40 50 60 70 80 90 100 110°

$$C = \frac{5}{9}(F - 32) \qquad F = \frac{9C}{5} + 32$$

Weights and Measures

Metric Measures

Length
1 millimetre (mm)		= 0.0394 in
1 centimetre (cm)	= 10 mm	= 0.3937 in
1 metre (m)	= 100 cm	= 1.0936 yds
1 kilometre (km)	= 1000 m	= 0.6214 mile

Weight
1 milligramme (mg)		= 0.0154 grain
1 gramme (g)	= 1000 mg	= 0.0353 oz
1 kilogramme (kg)	= 1000 g	= 2.2046 lb
1 tonne (t)	= 1000 kg	= 0.9842 ton

Area
1 cm^2	= 100 mm^2	= 0.1550 sq. in
1 m^2	= 10 000 cm^2	= 1.1960 sq. yds
1 are (a)	= 100 m^2	= 119.60 sq. yds
1 hectare (ha)	= 100 ares	= 2.4711 acres
1 km^2	= 100 hectares	= 0.3861 sq. mile

Capacity
1 cm^3		= 0.0610 cu. in
1 dm^3	= 1000 cm^3	= 0.0351 cu. ft
1 m^3	= 1000 dm^3	= 1.3080 cu. yds
1 litre	= 1 dm^3	= 0.2200 gallon
1 hectolitre	= 100 litres	= 2.7497 bushels

Imperial Measures

Length
1 inch		= 2.54 cm
1 foot	= 12 inches	= 0.3048 m
1 yard	= 3 feet	= 0.9144 m
1 rod	= 5.5 yards	= 4.0292 m
1 chain	= 22 yards	= 20.117 m
1 furlong	= 220 yards	= 201.17 m
1 mile	= 1760 yards	= 1.6093 km
1 nautical mile	= 6080 feet	= 1.8532 km

Weight

1 ounce	= 437.6 grains	= 28.350 g
1 pound	= 16 ounces	= 0.4536 kg
1 stone	= 14 pounds	= 6.3503 kg
1 hundredweight	= 112 pounds	= 50.802 kg
1 ton	= 20 cwt	= 1.0161 tonnes

Area

1 sq. inch		= 6.4516 cm^2
1 sq. foot	= 144 sq. ins	= 0.0929 m^2
1 sq. yard	= 9 sq. ft	= 0.8361 m^2
1 acre	= 4840 sq. yds	= 4046.9 m^2
1 sq. mile	= 640 acres	= 259.0 hectares

Capacity

1 cu. inch		= 16.387 cm^3
1 cu. foot	= 1728 cu. ins	= 0.0283 m^3
1 cu. yard	= 27 cu. ft	= 0.7646 m^3
1 pint	= 4 gills	= 0.5683 litre
1 quart	= 2 pints	= 1.1365 litres
1 gallon	= 8 pints	= 4.5461 litres
1 bushel	= 8 gallons	= 36.369 litres
1 fluid ounce	= 8 fl. drachms	= 28.413 cm^3
1 pint	= 20 fl. oz	= 568.26 cm^3

US Measures

Dry Measures

1 pint	= 0.9689 UK pt	= 0.5506 litre
1 bushel	= 0.9689 UK bu	= 35.238 litres

Liquid Measures

1 fluid ounce	= 1.0408 UK fl. oz	= 0.0296 litre
1 pint (16 oz)	= 0.8327 UK pt	= 0.4732 litre
1 gallon	= 0.8327 UK gal	= 3.7853 litres